# EDUCAT

# PSYCHOLOGY

in the Canadian Classroom

# EDUCATIONAL PSYCHOLOGY

## in the Canadian Classroom

**MARGRET WINZER**
*University of Lethbridge*

**NANCY GRIGG**
*University of Lethbridge*

Prentice-Hall Canada Inc., Scarborough, Ontario

**Canadian Cataloguing in Publication Data**

Winzer, Margret, 1940-
  Educational psychology in the Canadian classroom
  Includes index.
ISBN 0-13-236316-X

1. Educational psychology.  I. Grigg, Nancy Carol, 1956-  . II. Title.

LB1051.W5 1991      370.15     C91-094317-6

Prentice Hall, Inc., Englewood Cliffs, New Jersey
Prentice-Hall International, Inc., London
Prentice-Hall of Australia, Pty., Ltd., Sydney
Prentice-Hall of India Pvt., Ltd., New Delhi
Prentice-Hall of Japan, Inc., Tokyo
Prentice-Hall of Southeast Asia (Pte.) Ltd., Singapore
Editora Prentice-Hall do Brasil Ltda., Rio de Janeiro
Prentice-Hall Hispanoamericana, S.A., Mexico

ISBN 0-13-236316-X

Acquisitions Editor: Michael Bickerstaff
Copy Editor: Jean Ferrier
Production Editor: Valerie Adams
Production Coordinator: Florence Rousseau
Cover Design: Brian Bean
Page Layout: Brian Bean
Cover Photo: Vine/Focus/TSW
Illustrator: Greg Dorosh
Formatting: Hermia Chung

1 2 3 4 5  JD   96 95 94 93 92

Printed and bound in Canada by John Deyell Company.

# TABLE OF CONTENTS

**Chapter 3**

## Cognitive development **77**

**Chapter 7**

## Atypical children 250

**Chapter 13**

## Principles of instruction **497**

**Chapter 14**

## Testing and assessment **537**

**Chapter 15**

## Classroom management **574**

# PREFACE

Educational psychology is an exciting and fascinating topic. The major principles of educational psychology underlie, illuminate, and direct teaching practice and student learning. This text is designed to serve as an introduction to the field of educational psychology as it is currently practiced in Canada. We intend to provide readers with an introduction to educational psychology in Canada, and how this field influences classroom practice.

It is our intent that the book be useful, readable, and readily understood by a variety of professionals. The major objective is to lay out in a concise, systematic, and interesting manner the major aspects of educational psychology as it exists in Canada today. However, while students must be apprised of the facts and statistics of the science of educational psychology, we approach the topic in the most informal, "reader-friendly" manner possible.

The book is intended for use in courses offered by departments of education, educational foundations, nursing, social work, and psychology, which enroll students whose interests include regular education, special education, early childhood education, psychology, social work, and allied child-care disciplines. The text would be suitable at both the college and university levels.

Teaching is intimately interwoven with children's development and how children learn. Because of this, the opening chapters in the text focus on child development across a number of domains—physical, cognitive, moral, socio-emotional, and language. Certainly, no single model of child development exists. We present the most commonly used models of development and those that are most relevant to classroom teachers.

Not only must teachers have a deep acquaintance with child development, but they must be acutely aware of how children learn. Two major models of learning—behavioural and cognitive/information processing are fully detailed in the next section. The principles of humanistic education are also presented.

The final section of the text focuses on teaching and learning, classroom management and discipline, and testing and assessment. When teaching and learning are discussed, they are related to behavioural, cognitive, and humanistic models and modes.

Each section begins with an outline to help students organize their reading. Sections also include student learning objectives and a section map illustrating how the chapters and topics are related. Chapters end with lists of key terms and concepts. Whenever possible, jargon and technical language are avoided. However, when it is necessary to introduce new terms, they are presented in boldface, and a definition is provided in the margin. This allows the students ready access to definitions without having to flop to the back of the book for a definition. For further convenience, an alphabetical glossary is included at the end of the book. Throughout the chapters, boxed items contain discussions of historical precedents, contemporary issues and trends, and classic studies in the field of educational psychology.

There is nothing particularly nationalistic about educational psychology; however, our Canadian school systems, school law and legislation, and the characteristics of our school population, are unique. Therefore, where relevant, we provide a Canadian focus on educational psychology; Canadian research and examples are cited and practice in Canadian schools discussed. This point of view will be most obvious in the chapters on special education, the role of the educational psychologist, and assessment. As well, issues important to Canadian educators, such as multiculturalism, bilingualism, second language issues, and native education are covered. However, while this text covers a great deal of the excellent research conducted in Canada, students are exposed to the best and most relevant research, whether it originates in Canada, the United States, Europe, or elsewhere.

## ACKNOWLEDGMENTS

Many people contributed to this book. The authors are grateful to our students at the University of Lethbridge who were sounding boards for our topics and provided such good suggestions and feedback.

We would also like to thank Kas Mazurek for his shoulder and his suggestions. Patti Merrick and Helen Ford, both with endless patience and enduring good humour, contributed significantly to this text.

# 1

**INTRODUCTION TO EDUCATIONAL PSYCHOLOGY**

Teaching is an art. Therefore there is no science of education .... If the teacher wants aid from the scientific spirit, and counsel from scientific education, there stands ... above all, psychology (Royce, 1891).

I say moreover that you make a great, a very great, mistake if you think that psychology, being the science of men's lives, is something from which you can deduce definite programs and schemes and methods of instruction for immediate school use. Psychology is a science, and teaching is an art; and sciences never generate arts directly out of themselves. An intermediarary inventive mind must must make the approach, using its originality (James, 1899, p. 23).

[E]ducational psychology is that special branch of psychology concerned with the nature, conditions, outcomes, and evaluation of school learning and retention. As such, the subject matter of educational psychology consists primarily of the theory of meaningful learning and retention, and the influence of all significant variables—cognitive, developmental, affective, motivational, personality, and social—on school learning outcomes, particularly the influence of those variables that are manipulable by the teacher, by the curriculum developer, by the programme instruction specialist, by the educational technologist, by the school psychologist or guidance counselor, by the educational administrator, or by society at large (Ausubel, 1969, p. 232).

**MAJOR OBJECTIVES**

This section is designed to

- introduce the discipline of educational psychology;

- illustrate the relationship between educational psychology and classroom practice;

- introduce the major themes of the text;

- present an overview of the methods used in educational psychology and the contributions of school psychologists;

- discuss the roles of educational psychologists, school psychologists, and teachers as researchers; and

- outline some of the research methods used in educational psychology.

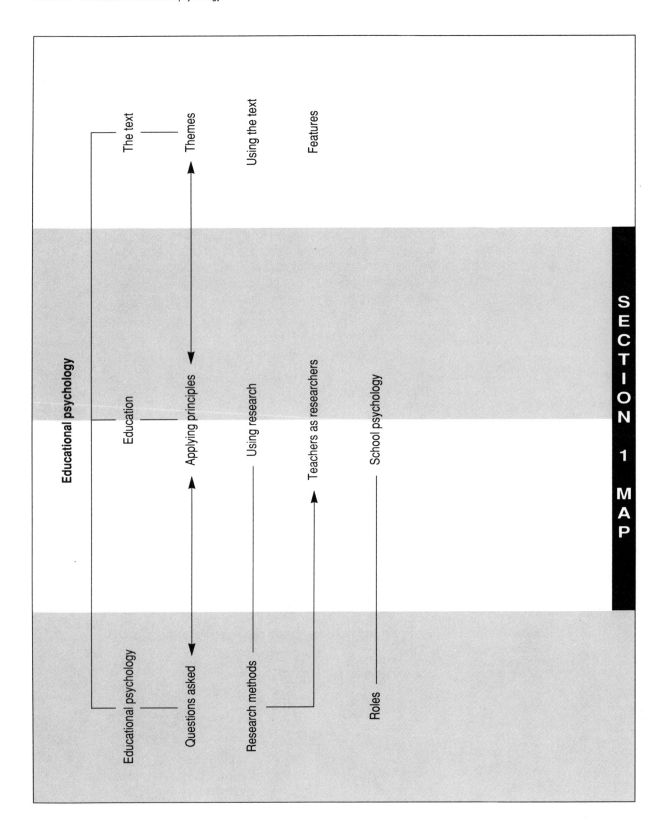

On the bookshelf of time, more than three quarters of a century separates the three quotes that open this section. In the last decade of the nineteenth century, when Royce and James were writing, modern psychology was still a very young science; educational psychology as a sub-discipline would not emerge for another decade. By the time Ausubel (1969) wrote his exposition of educational psychology, the field was firmly ensconced as a potent discipline within psychology and as an integral part of educational practice.

Only by implication did Royce (1891) and James (1899) stress the crucial nature of psychology to the classroom teacher. William James, one of the first and best commentators on the problems of teaching and learning, agreed with Royce in viewing teaching as an art, different from music or painting, but nevertheless an enterprise more informed by intuition than by science. Both writers felt that education and psychology, while not mutually incompatible, still required a mediator to translate psychological principles into classroom practice. In contrast, Ausubel, writing more than sixty years later, viewed educational psychology as a broad and comprehensive discipline that provides direction as it underlies and illuminates teaching and learning, classrooms, and school systems. Ausubel (1969) stressed that educational psychology is not general psychology applied to educational problems; rather educational psychology is a foundational discipline of education, just as physics is a foundation for engineering. For Ausubel, the educational psychologist does not simply marry psychology to education. Instead, he sees educational psychology as so inherently a part of education that each reflects, influences, and interacts with the other.

Throughout this text, we adopt Ausubel's (1969) view. We do not see educational psychology as simply "psychology applied to teaching" (Biehler and Snowman, 1990) or even as "a bridge stepped on at both ends" (Sprinthall and Sprinthall, 1987). Rather, educational psychology is crucial to the teaching and learning enterprise and a discipline upon which teachers draw constantly.

Educational psychologists ask themselves many questions in each of the following areas:

**Growth and development**   The process and progression through which children grow into adults is of central importance to developmental and educational psychologists. Educational psychologists study the growth and developmental processes so as to isolate the principles involved in, and responsible for, both the differences and similarities in students.

**The effects of development on learning and socialization**   For teachers to instruct effectively in the classroom, they must understand their students. As students change in chronological age, the processes by which they learn also change. As they grow older, their abilities to understand more complex and abstract material expands. So as individual groups of students develop in their ability to think, speak, write, conceptualize, and abstact information, the teaching methods must alter to parallel these changes.

**Individual differences**   Even children of approximately the same age vary enormously in appearance, abilities, temperament, interests, attitudes, motivation, adjustment, family background, and the language of the home, to mention just a sampling of the myriad individual differences we see. Educational psychologists study these individual differences and their effects on the ways that students learn.

**Models of learning**   Educational psychologists study different models of learning in order to determine which are most suitable in different situations.

**Instructional goals and teaching methods**   Educational psychologists attempt to identify effective instructional approaches; they then work to develop a range of teaching approaches and strategies applicable to diverse situations and to diverse students. Not only do they look at the effect of general principles such as the use of behavioral techniques in a classroom, but they also focus on curriculum areas, such as the advances that may be created by a whole-language philosophy.

**Evaluation of teaching and learning**   As well as studying development and learning, educational psychologists are interested in methods to evaluate teaching and learning in order to determine which students learn successfully and those who do not, the teaching methods that prompt efficient learning, and the classroom environments and systems of reinforcement that best promote learning.

### The effects of teacher expectations

Educational psychologists attempt to determine how teachers' attitudes toward students influence motivation, instruction, learning, and evaluation in the classroom.

### Technology
Educational pychologists study the way in which our rapidly changing technologically oriented society affects students and their families.

### Research
Educational pychologists have questions about how to answer their questions; about the research that allows the best answers. The goals of research in educational psychology are to carefully examine questions that impinge on classroom practice and student learning as well as to test ideas about the factors that contribute to learning. To accomplish this, psychologists collect data to refute or confirm assumptions. However, educational research should not be thought of as providing the key to all the problems encountered in a classroom. Rather, it should be seen as providing guidelines and broad principles that can underlie efficient practice.

We can recognize that the answers to the questions that arise in each of the foregoing areas are important for teachers, parents, those who formulate educational policy, and others either directly or peripherally involved with children and youth. While educational psychology is most intimately connected with classroom practices and students' learning, it is of deep consequence to a greater audience than teachers alone. Anyone who attempts to interact with children or instruct others, from parents to teachers to teacher educators, can benefit from the principles of educational psychology. The parents of a stubborn, tantrum-throwing two year old, for example, may feel less

frustrated if they are familiar with some of the principles of "ages and stages" and recognize that temper tantrums, while worrying, are fairly common behaviours as small children begin to assert their independence.

Many of the questions asked by educational psychology are addressed in this text. Certainly, in a book of this size and nature, we cannot present the entire story. To do so would take many, many volumes and even then it would be difficult to capture all the complexities of child development, teaching and learning, and evaluation. We present broad overviews of child development and the most common models or those that are particularly relevant to the classroom.

## OUTLINE OF THE TEXT

This book was written for two major reasons. First, it is imperative that those aspiring to teach understand the psychology of learners at different ages and the psychological principles of learning and motivation. As well, teachers require specific procedures to increase their effectiveness in the classroom. Teachers must certainly understand students but they must also know how to prepare and present a lesson, how to motivate students and how to effectively manage a classroom. Some ways in which educational psychology can assist classroom teachers and prospective teachers are found in Box S1-1.

In the text, we first talk about children, about the major determinants of behaviour, and about how behaviour changes with age. The focus is on the theories and models that are used to explain development. Development across the physical, cognitive, socio-emotional, moral, and language domains is discussed. Following the section on child development, we discuss differences in behaviour such as in motivation and learning and differences that occur because of individual differences or exceptional conditions.

Once we have developed an acquaintance with children, their development, and the differences

## Box S1-1 **Educational psychology in the classsroom**

**1.** *Why study educational psychology?*

Educational psychology presents theories bolstered by practical suggestions that all teachers can use in their classrooms and can alter to match their own unique teaching styles and philosophies.

**2.** *Are the principles of educational psychology really relevant to my classroom?*

In the final analysis, the best way to understand educational psychology is to apply some of the principles. Teachers who actively and systematically attempt to apply educational psychology in their daily teaching will have a better basis for understanding students, and for designing appropriate instructional experiences and learning situations.

**3.** *Will an understanding of educational psychology make me a better teacher?*

People have different views about what makes a good teacher. There is no single, easily measured or even measurable criterion for good teaching. However, the theoretical principles and research findings of educational psychology provide a basis for planning and implementing instruction.

**4.** *Will educational psychology help me to understand the children in my class?*

To effectively instruct children and youth, teachers must be aware of their developmental levels—their capacities at certain age ranges. Knowledge of how children and youth develop is basic to educational psychology.

**5.** *How will the principles of educational psychology assist me in dealing with individual children?*

In any classroom, teachers have children from different social and experiential backgrounds, from different cultures, and with different first languages. There are also children who learn differently and those who respond and behave differently. Educational psychology underlines what teachers may expect as some type of norm and uses this as a reference for different functioning in a range of behavioural and learning areas.

**6.** *Will educational psychology provide me with specific teaching approaches?*

One of the goals of educational psychologists is to assess the value of various instructional approaches. General principles about teaching and learning are foundations of the discipline.

**7.** *Can the principles of educational psychology help me to maintain discipline in my clasroom?*

Classroom management and student discipline are ongoing concerns for teachers, whether beginning or experienced. No one method of control works with all students all the time and what worked with one group one day may not work with a different group or even with the same group on a different day. Many different methods have been proven successful for classroom management and these are examined by educational psychologists.

that occur in development, we look at theories of learning. Behavioural, cognitive, and humanistic theories of learning are stressed.

The final section of the text applies the ideas about development and the theories of learning to classroom learning and instruction. From a discussion of motivation in the classroom we move to the principles of instruction and learning, assessment and evaluation, and classroom organization and management.

We also offer selections from scientific research and delve into current topics that of necessity are of intense interest to teachers. Apart from the practical applications, we present current research into such social issues as teenage pregnancies and drug use. Teachers will confront these issues and must be acutely aware of their impact on all students.

## Special features of the book

A few comments on the design of the book are important at this point. Each section begins with an introduction of the major points of the section as well as a map showing where items are to be found. The major terms to be met are found at the beginning of each chapter and are defined in marginal notes.

# EDUCATIONAL PSYCHOLOGY AND CLASSROOM TEACHERS

**Educational psychology:** discipline which combines the paradigms, methods, and skills of psychology with the functioning of teachers, students, and schools.

## INTRODUCTION

An enormous and complex host of variables underlie effective teaching. Some of the most potent of these factors revolve around the teacher's knowledge. In this sense, knowledge implies far more than a deep acquaintance with the subject matter to be taught. It includes knowledge about how children develop, their current levels, and where they are going. Knowledge also means an awareness of how children and youth learn at different developmental levels, how to employ various models of instruction and learning, how to find approaches and strategies for effective teaching, and how to adapt and modify instruction for children functioning above or below the norm. Classroom organization, classroom management and student discipline are crucial factors, for efficient learning requires an orderly and disciplined atmosphere. Further, teachers must know about evaluation and assessment, and about curricula and the way they change in response to pressures from within and without the school system. They should possess knowledge about how school systems function, about how to deal with parents and about the manner in which parental influences affect children's learning.

Many of the general principles that underlie this knowledge arise from the discipline of **educational psychology**. Throughout this text, we adhere to the views articulated by Ausubel (1969) and others. We believe that educational psychology forms a crucial component of education; that it is not a separate discipline that simply seeks to apply the concepts of psychology to education but rather a fundamental discipline of education. Essentially, educational psychology combines the paradigms, the methods, and the skills of psychology with the functioning of schools, classrooms, and the individuals within those classrooms. It provides a framework for looking at students, the learning process, and the learning situation. No teacher can afford not to know educational psychology; it touches every aspect of teachers' professional lives.

Knowingly or unwittingly, teachers employ the principles of educational psychology in many of their classroom actions and procedures. The vignettes of classroom interactions in Box 1-1 illustrate the nature of educational psychology as underlying practice in a variety of classroom situations.

## Box 1-1 **In the classroom**

- Mrs. Gomez is preparing her timetable for a grade two class, relating it to provincial mandates regarding time spent on specific subject areas. As she works, Mrs. Gomez decides that reading and arithmetic should be in the morning, art and music in the afternoon. From what her experience tells her about children's attention spans and their prime time for concentration, Mrs. Gomez realizes that very young pupils concentrate best in the early part of the school day.

- In the grade three classroom, Mr. Abu provides many rewards to his students for work accomplished well. Sometimes he uses tokens such as gold stars; often he charts the pupils' progress. He also uses many social reinforcers such as a smile, a pat on the back, or a special word of praise. However, Mr. Abu realizes that not all children can accomplish the same amount in the same time and structures his reward system to individual children.

- For many years, Mrs. O'Brien was a very successful grade six teacher. However, when her family moved, the only class available in her new location was a grade one. Mrs. O'Brien approached her new teaching task with some trepidation but, holding the opinion that "children are children" and "teaching is teaching," did not attempt many changes in what she believed were tried and true teaching strategies.

On the first day of class, Mrs. O'Brien sits her twenty-five children in straight rows of desks and begins the day by asking them to list rules for the classroom. Not surprisingly, the children present very few rules. She discourages "baby talk" and instead stresses the three Rs. The lesson ends with most of the class squirming on hard chairs and a frustrated teacher at the head of the class.

- The school principal, the teachers, and most of the students are dismayed with the disruptive and abusive behaviour of 12 year old James. So unruly is this child in the classroom that he has been spending a great deal of his time sitting outside the principal's office. Even though the teacher calls for stern punishment, the principal recognizes that James has been punished so often at home and at school that additional aggression on the part of adults probably won't work. Instead, the teacher, the principal, and James devise a contract. If James works in class and controls his behaviour, he will earn a reward; bonuses are added for especially positive behaviour, penalties for poor behaviour. All three people—the teacher, the principal and James—sign the contract and review it weekly. The principal is also trying to have the parents become part of the contract procedure.

- The grade 12 teacher is lecturing to her history class about the Fathers of Confederation. Although she tends to rely on a lecture format, the teacher also uses the chalkboard often to sketch time lines, note important elements and list names of historical figures. She repeats and stresses important points and uses visual aids—pictures in this case—to add relevance to the lesson.

- John Cowan serves in his school as part-time teacher, part-time counselor. At the moment, he is assisting grade nine students in choosing their courses for senior high school. This is how John explained one interview to his wife. "Marcia," he started, "is one of the prettiest and most popular girls in the school. When I checked her record, I was surprised to see that she maintained straight A's. But when she said she hoped to be a dentist and wanted to take courses in chemistry, mathematics and biology, I was really surprised." John's wife winced a little, but he plowed on. "I had to talk her out of taking such hard subjects," he explained. "After all, girls aren't much good at high level math and as soon as school is finished she'll find herself a husband anyway."

Even without any formal background in educational psychology, it is fairly easy to identify the teachers employing acceptable principles and those who are not, and to pick out the principles used or ignored. Mrs. O'Brien seems to have forgotten that young children are not yet ready for formal instruction but require lots of activity and many concrete objects to manipulate. She also overlooks the fact that young children see rules as inviolable and that they need keener direction than older children who can more readily understand the changing nature of rules.

Mrs. Gomez is quite different from Mrs. O'Brien in her understanding of the needs and learning attributes of young children. She is acutely aware that young children require lots of activity, but also periods of quiet time, and plans her timetable accordingly. The grade twelve teacher, while recognizing that many students of this age are capable of abstract thought, still uses visual aids to reinforce her instruction. Both Mr. Abu and the school principal realize that concrete and social reinforcers stimulate learning and acceptable behaviour and prompt their reccurrance. The principal also realizes that punishment may, in this case, be more self-defeating than helpful.

And what of poor John Cowan and his unfortunate female students? "Poor John," because he holds a naive and totally assailable view that females are cognitively and socially different from males; "unfortunate students," because such attitudes may propel them first into classes and later into careers and roles that they are now socialized to believe are more appropriate for women.

## MAJOR THEMES IN THE TEXT

In this text we focus on the major determinants of child behaviour and how behaviour changes with age. We present theories and models that seek to explain how growth, development, and learning occur across different age levels and in different domains, most specifically in the physical, cognitive, moral, socio-emotional, and language areas. We stress how growth and development affect children in classrooms and the influence of innate and environmental factors on learning. Much emphasis is placed on the way in which teachers can employ the principles of educational psychology to enhance and improve classroom instruction, student learning, and classroom management.

A number of themes run through the entire text. Our central theme is that educational psychology is far more than just psychology applied to education; rather it underlies, illuminates, and directs educational practice. Classroom teachers make dozens, if not hundreds, of decisions every day about global issues such as the most appropriate instructional techniques, classroom organization and management, scheduling and timetabling, evaluation and grading. They make decisions concerning lesson presentation—the amount of information to present at any one time, the sequence in which to present it, the pace of presentation, the best way in which to present material, and the amount of practice needed to ensure understanding. Students who do not seem to learn in the same way as everyone else or those who lag in certain areas require decisions about individualization and modified curricula. Each of these decisions has a theory behind it, although the teacher may not always be aware of this, and these theories arise from educational psychology.

The other themes carried through this text are chiefly related to fundamental questions that underlie the methodology, the practice, and the application of the principles of educational psychology in classroom situations. The following discussions introduce the most important themes.

## The nature/nurture controversy

In both historical and contemporary terms, the study of child development has been deeply concerned with a fundamental issue that revolves around the relative impact of heredity (nature) or environment (nurture) on development. The familiar phrase, "nature versus nurture," was coined in Victorian England by Francis Galton, a British scientist and researcher.

Yet, since the time of Classical Greece, philosophers and psychologists have debated whether development is guided by heredity—which we now conceive as an unfolding of the genetic blueprint held in the DNA—or whether developmental changes are mediated primarily by environmental influences. While this contentious issue is unlikely ever to be conclusively resolved, it is critical in all of psychology, and especially so in developmental psychology.

The "nature" point of view holds biological maturation to be the most important determinant of development. At the opposite end of the spectrum, the "nurture" argument promotes the environment as having the primary impact on development. Throughout history, the pendulum has swung back and forth between nature and nurture, called by different names and promoted as much in relation to the social, political, and economic stances of an era as to psychological principles (Winzer, 1990b).

Early Greek philosophers wrestled with the problem of innate or external influences on the development of humans. Aristotle promoted nature; Plato leaned more to a nurture point of view. In the span of the centuries between Classical Greece and the eighteenth century, nature views largely held sway. Then, prodded by John Locke, George Berkeley, and the philosophers of the French Enlightenment, the nurture view resurfaced and remained prominent until the second third of the nineteenth century. A matrix of social, economic and political factors melded with psychological principles to once more elevate the nature argument as the dominant ideology (see Winzer, 1990b).

Hereditarian principles dominated at the opening of the twentieth century. One of the strongest proponents of the application of evolutionary theory to the study of development was G. Stanley Hall, an early and prominent architect of the developing field of child study. Hall wielded profound influence and holds a prime position in the history of North American psychology. His contributions are detailed in Box 1-2.

## Box 1-2 Biographical note: G. Stanley Hall (1844–1924)

G. Stanley Hall was one of America's earliest and most prominent psychologists. He is universally recognized as one of the pioneers of both North American psychology in its more general aspects and developmental psychology. Hall's "genetic" psychology (which meant development at that time) deserves its place as the first developmental psychology in America (Grinder, 1967). Essentially a synthetic rather than an original thinker, Hall had an influence on educational thought that reached practically all school systems in North America (McCullers, 1969). His work stimulated educators to tailor instruction to children's individual needs; to what they could learn and do during various stages of development.

Hall taught at Johns Hopkins University, and was the first president of Clarke University, a guiding force in the American Psychological Association, the editor of four prestigious journals, and the mentor for a number of important psychologists. Arnold Gesell, Lewis Terman, James McKeen Cattell, John Dewey, and William Burnham worked with Hall at Johns Hopkins and at Clarke University. As well, Hall brought Sigmund Freud to the United States for a series of lectures at Clarke University in 1909. While Freud's psychoanalytic theory had been highly influential in Europe in the late 1800s, it was not until this visit that his views began to profoundly influence the field of psychology in North America.

Hall is best remembered, however, for his contributions to the emerging field of child development and especially for his delineation of the period of adolescence. Hall was the first person to conduct empirical research in the area of child development, and child psychology in North America developed largely as a result of his empirical work and his efforts to link human and animal psychology (Kessen, 1965).

In 1879 Hall went to Germany and became the first American to participate in Wundt's newly established psychological laboratory. Hall was appointed to Johns Hopkins University in 1882 and opened a small laboratory there a year later. In 1883 he began his most important research which involved the administration of questionnaires to children designed to explore "the content of the mind" (Hall, 1891). With the questionnaire responses, Hall attempted to empirically establish a picture of how children viewed the world.

For example, a group of Boston kindergarten children were asked about their concepts of nature, numbers, religion, their own bodies, mortality, and so on. In this study, Hall found that 80 percent of the children did not know what a beehive was, while 50 percent could not describe a frog (Hothersall, 1984). However, through this research, Hall contributed greatly to the understanding of individual differences by recording the range of information children possessed about the social and physical world (Bell 1980).

Hall moved the study of child development from the philosophical approaches of Locke and Rousseau to the level of actual scientific study (Bell and Harper, 1977). Hall was strongly influenced by evolutionary theory, particularly the notion that "ontogeny recapituates phylogeny" (McCullers, 1969).

Hall viewed child development as a process that unfolded in a regular, orderly fashion, with the emergence of each stage prompted largely through internal cues.

In 1889 Hall became the first president of Clarke University which opened that year with an exclusive emphasis on graduate education, primarily in psychology. Clarke University became the chief source of early Ph.D.s in American psychology. The year 1905 saw the publication of Hall's volume on adolescence. This book, often referred to as the formal beginning of developmental psychology (Hothersall, 1984), was the first to discuss adolescence as a separate stage of development in the human life cycle. Hall's reference to the Sturm und Drang (storm and stress) of adolescence was to be repeatedly echoed by later authors.

It was not until the 1930s that the strong emphasis on nature as the prime factor in development faded. After that time, the notions of nature and nurture both remained on the stage of psychology. Today, despite an expanded knowledge base, an increased repertoire of methods, and the availability of populations for studying the problem, the controversy still flourishes and has produced some of the most emotional debates of the day. For example, a massive controversy among both professionals and the public was refueled by Arthur Jensen in the late 1960s when he proposed that differences in intellectual ability could be traced to racial heritage (Jensen, 1968, 1969).

Of course, an even cursory examination of the nature/nurture debate would lead to the realization that neither extreme position can adequately explain human development. A child's genetic potential does not unfold in a vacuum, nor does a child emerge from a vacuum, devoid of ancestors, to be shaped by the environment. Psychologists certainly agree that some part of what we call intelligence is inherited, yet the importance of nurturing has been clearly evidenced by the many deprivational studies that demonstrate the negative effects of malnutrition and lack of stimulation on infant functioning. The high proportion of first-borns among the gifted population also suggests the importance of environment to the full development of intellectual potential (Laycock, 1979). Unlike younger siblings, first-borns receive full attention and much stimulation from their parents, even if only for a short time. Thus, the question is not really whether nature or nurture is the determinant of development, but rather how each influences the process (Salkind, 1990).

## Teaching: art or science?

Of all the fundamental questions raised in educational psychology, one of the most crucial is also one of the most simple: "What is teaching?" Royce (1891) and William James (1899) conceived teaching to be an art. James (1899) also said that the key to effective teaching was to arouse in the student a devouring curiosity. When one considers the countless volumes of theory and research that have been published on good teaching since the days of James, one may find the question itself preposterous. Still, the answer is elusive. Is teaching an art? Is it a technology? Is it a science? If it is a melding of all three of these constituents, then what are the proportions that make for success?

As we commented earlier, the art of teaching is not an instrumental or practical art like music or painting. As an art, teaching includes many virtually unteachable intangibles. Teaching incorporates emotions, values, flexibility, improvisation, ingenuity, spontaneity, humour, style, and pace. Teaching can also, at some level, be seen as a performing art. Good teachers excite students with learning and instinctively respond to their students' instructional needs. These components cannot stand on their own; they are mixed with subject matter, structural components, and managerial strategies in exceedingly complex ways.

As well as being partly an art, teaching is also a science because there exists a measurable relationship between what teachers do and what children learn. Moreover, teaching uses practices confirmed by research that rest on the theories of the science of educational psychology. There are also a variety of technical skills that underlie successful instructional practice. These range from writing lesson plans and units, to using programmed instruction, to employing computers in the classroom. The question then is not whether teaching is an art or a science but how all the components can meld comfortably with teachers' individual styles to provide the most effective classroom practice.

As an art, teaching includes many virtually unteachable intangibles.

**Pedagogy:**

the link between what a
teacher wants students to
learn and students' actual
learning.

This text holds the view that teaching is an activity that mixes components of skill, theory, art, technology, and organization. And, while teaching is an intellectual activity with intellectual ends, it is also a profoundly personal and deeply moral activity. It is personal because a teacher's interactions with students form a major factor in the success of any instruction; a poor teacher can confuse children, make them miserable, and induce a dislike of learning. In addition, teaching is a moral activity because teachers impart to children principles of socialization as well as systems of values.

## Teaching defies formulation

In presenting a paradigm of teaching, Alter and Goldstein (1985) observed that someone (the manager of the learning) teaches something (the content of the curriculum) to somebody (the learner) somehow (according to a schedule, at a particular pace, and with attention to learning variables). How this is done depends on a matrix of factors and variables, many of which form the basis of this book.

The link between what a teacher wants students to learn and students' actual learning is instruction or pedagogy (Slavin, 1988). Pedagogy consists of three components. First, teacher performances common to instruction in all disciplines form the generic component. Second, performances unique to particular subjects of instruction form the content-specific component. Third, concepts which sort and explain teacher performances and the processes of learning and development form the theoretical component. Together, they constitute the primary content of pedagogical education (Smith, 1985).

Effective instruction, or good pedagogy, does not rely on any one method or approach but rather on the use of diverse alternate strategies as well as all the tasks involved in effective instruction. There are simply too many decisions, too many diverse personalities and needs among students, and too many appropriate instructional stategies for any cookbook approach to teaching to be sufficient. What teachers need are general principles to consider as an aid in analyzing situations and making decisions.

## Classroom management

Although perhaps less philosophical than our other themes, the issue of classroom management and behaviour control comes up again and again in this text. Study after study has shown that teachers consider classroom management to be their major problem, a perception echoed by parents and the public in general.

Good classroom organization and management are essential to job success. It must therefore be among teachers' first considerations, for without a positive and efficient classroom environment, very little teaching and learning will occur. Discipline is one component of classroom management that ensures the effectiveness of the teaching.

Effective teachers direct the behaviour of their students as well as organizing their learning activities (McShane and Cox, 1989; Nowacek and Saunders, 1989). Four components are necessary for efficient classroom management—establishing classroom discipline and control; writing lesson plans; dealing with individual students; and maintaining variety and flexibility (Gage and Berliner, 1986).

Effective teachers direct the behaviour of their students as well as organizing their learning activities.

Nevertheless, as teaching cannot be reduced to a formula, neither can classroom management, especially when it applies to student discipline. The causes of misbehaviour lie within a complex pattern of relationships. Therefore, student misbehaviour cannot be handled through a mechanical approach of predetermined techniques. All discipline problems are, to some extent, unique and the problem of discipline is a personal one for teachers.

## Applying research to practice

To be applicable, educational psychology must take into account the interactive, contextual and temporal features of schools; research must be relevant to classrooms. Sometimes the principles of educational psychology lead directly to the solution of a problem; just as often they form the basis for a solution. For example, teachers' efforts to control discipline problems are influenced by a range of variables such as classroom standards, role expectations, classroom dynamics, personality characteristics, and management skills. Given the high incidence of students exhibiting problem behaviour who are referred to special education (Pugash, 1985; Ritter, 1989), as well as the managerial difficulties that many teachers experience (Brophy and Rohrkemper, 1981), it is important to identify the characteristics of students, teachers, and school environments that must be addressed or modified to enhance classroom organization and management.

Among the many things that research has revealed about classroom management are the following findings: teachers should have a system of rules that allows pupils to attend to their personal and procedural needs without having to check with the teacher. Teachers should also move around the classroom a lot, monitoring pupil's seat work and communicating to the students an awareness of their behaviour, while attending to their academic needs (Gage, 1978).

**Assessment:**

any process of gathering data on a student's skills and behaviour.

## Use of psychological and educational assessment

Within the school system, the assessment and evaluation of pupil performance has become accepted practice; the use of assessment data to prescribe, implement, evaluate, and revise instructional programs forms an integral part of modern education. In an educational context, **assessment** is any process of gathering intrapersonal or interpersonal data on a pupil's current behaviour, language, motor skills and other areas of functioning in any environment that involves a part of the pupil's current or planned educational program (Berdine and Meyer, 1987, p. 4).

Accurate evaluation of students' progress through school is basic to responsible education. Without reliable assessment of children's performance in critical areas such as reading and mathematics, the provision of appropriate teaching and learning procedures becomes haphazard, with both high- and low-achieving extremes being ignored as teachers focus upon the large middle-of-the-range group that they often presume makes up the major part of their class. Teachers therefore need to be aware of a range of formal and informal instruments for classroom use. They require some knowledge of the material contained in psycho-educational reports and should understand how measuring instruments are used (and misused).

## Individual differences

The study of psychological development is the study of generalities, rather than individual differences. In its early years, modern psychology concentrated on aspects of human behaviour as they affected the group, not the individual. Only grudgingly did psychologists turn to the study of individual differences. But how individual students develop, learn, and interact is a lynch pin of teaching.

Teachers are faced with the task of educating heterogeneous groups of children with skills and weaknesses as diverse as their individual personalities. A teacher will readily observe a range of individual differences: some students learn easily and quickly; others learn more slowly, or seem to require different methods; others seem little interested in learning at all. Not only do children have different intellectual levels, different levels of motivation, and different learning styles, but there are a range of other factors which affect children's learning in gross or subtle ways and may affect teachers' expectations about children.

Urie Bronfenbrenner (1979) has pointed out that we know much more about children than we do about the environments in which they live. What we do know is that each child comes to school with a different experiential background and that many differences in behaviour and the way students learn in school are the result of environmental conditions. A student from a socially disadvantaged home, for example, may respond quite differently from the student from the middle class environment.

The home background of pupils, their socioeconomic status, their race, their gender—even their physical attractiveness—have all been shown to affect learning and teacher expectations. As well, there are children who, because of some mental, physical, or social disability, suffer hindrances to learning and may be categorized within the compass of children with exceptionalities.

The range of individual differences among students is enormous. Throughout this text, many of these individual differences are discussed. An appreciation of the manner in which the variety of individual differences occur and manifest themselves is vital for teachers to understand if they are to program effectively for each member of the class.

**Figure 1-1**
Individual differences

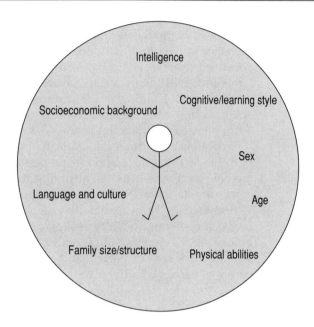

## Gender

Historically, the way psychologists have thought about the psychology of gender has grown out of thinking about individual differences. Of course, as Maccoby (1990) points out, almost every individual is clearly male or female so it was only natural for psychologists to ask how much variance among individuals was accounted for by this beautifully binary factor.

This is a truism of psychological research; it is also true that historically men and women have received different and unequal opportunities in nearly every aspect of life. A misogynous ethic, emerging from Classical times, viewed females as mentally and physically fragile. Women were accredited with a generous portion of emotion, passion, and intitution but were held to be less capable of rational thought than men.

Although such attitudes are generally obsolete, many barriers to females remain and greater limitations are placed on women than on men. Educators have been aware of the way in which unquestioned cultural assumptions about sex-linked aptitudes and abilities have damaging effects on the career choices made by females.

**Theory:**

a set of assumptions or a system of beliefs that tries to explain events that have happened in the past as well as predict events that will happen in the future.

Certainly, some characteristics are seen as peculiar, by and large, to one sex or the other. But which differences are determined by biology and which by culture? Do males and females really differ in terms of cognitive and affective variables? And why? Are men really more rational and women more emotional?

Men are more often agents of aggression than are women (Eagly, 1987). It is fairly well documented that males tend to be more aggressive than females across all ages, from the preschool to the adult range (Maccoby and Jacklin, 1974, 1980). Some earlier studies have indicated that males tend to be better than females at higher level mathematics and spatial analysis, while females tend to be better in the use of oral language. Both language and spatial abilities are represented more bilaterally in females than males (Stellern, Marlowe and Croissard, 1984). However, there are probably intervening factors other than sex at work here. Nothing in these differences, well documented as they may be, suggests that either sex possesses a generally heightened intellectual capacity. Also, personality traits in general, as measured as characteristics of individuals, do not appear to differ systematically by sex (Huston, 1985). This may reflect, in part, the fact that male and female persons really are much alike and their lives are governed mainly by the attributes that all persons in a given culture have in common (Maccoby, 1990).

Because we do not hold that significant cognitive and social differences between males and females exist, we largely abandon the traditional terminology of "sex differences" in favour of "gender issues." The studies in the former area are, of course, important and pervasive, but we stress the social and cultural nature of perceived differences reported.

## Theories and models

Often, the word "theory" has a bad reputation among educational practitioners. Teachers often see a dichotomy between educational psychology and teaching practice and reject the notion of theories. Yet good theory is at the heart of what professionals do. Without theory to guide us, we will act, at best, on intuition, folk wisdom, conventional "truths," or flat-out whim (Wassermann, 1987).

A theory may be seen as a hypothesis arising from theoretical deductions that is converted into a prediction that can be tested and confirmed or discounted by the obtained data. A good theory guides research, focuses attention on different aspects of the total problem, and suggests new solutions or relationships. We need theories because without them there would be no cohesive thread and every researcher would be discovering the same theories over and over again. Models are similar to theories; they are used to present ideas about how certain things develop in discrete stages (Slavin, 1988). From theories we derive principles and laws. Principles explain relationships between factors, such as the effects of alternate grading systems on student motivation (Slavin, 1988). Laws are simply principles that have been thoroughly tested and found to apply to a wide variety of situations.

According to Wassermann (1987), educators should cry out for theory to guide their decisions. They should insist on knowing what theory lies behind some of the practices now being advocated. Theory, stresses Wassermann (1987), should point to hypotheses to be tested and should anchor classroom practices in thoughtfully examined frameworks of clear and well-researched ideas.

### Models of child development

Because educational psychology is so closely identified with what happens in classrooms, it must necessarily be concerned with child development. Therefore, many of the concepts, models and theories of developmental psychology become important. Certain models and theories of development are detailed in this text. The stress is on the models that underlie the development of children and youth across developmental domains and the theories that are important for classroom practice. By no means are they the only theories and models in the field; rather they are the most prominent or the ones most relevant to classroom teachers.

### Theories of learning

Closely aligned to models of development are theories that attempt to explain how students learn. Three major theories of learning organize the text—behavioural, cognitive, and humanistic. In some ways, these theories are contradictory; in others, they may be seen as complementary. Teachers should be fully cognizant of the major theories that apply to learning and select the principles and applications most apt for their own unique styles and situations.

## Current issues

Few activities of significance are free from controversy. Lively and heated debate on fundamental issues is to be found in politics, economics, and the social and physical sciences (Mazurek, 1991). Education is no exception. Educational change, a multilevel social process, entails the integrated efforts of a large number of stake holders who are responsible for the business of education. Teachers or future teachers cannot remain neutral from the controversies found in contemporary Canadian education. Simply by choosing the profession, teachers are placed at the centre of the debates about schooling. In their ideas and in their pedagogical and professional activities—whether they are conscious of it or not—teachers will be taking a stand on many controversial issues. An essential part of training as a future teacher should be the development of a sophisticated professional grasp on what the issues are and the ability to intelligently and critically analyze educational controversies (Mazurek, 1991).

The issues in today's education are both general and specific. Massive social changes have spilled over to affect the schools, the curriculum, and the composition of classrooms. In the interests of social equity, the school system is increasingly asked to provide special services for those who traditionally have not been served or well served by the system. Special programs for pregnant teenagers, Native students, or children with specific disabilities are often demanded by the public and by parents. The school system is also busy reconceptualizing existing programs, such as early childhood services, and multicultural and bilingual programs.

## Canadian content

There are many values and attitudes that Canadians share with other countries. There are also certain priorities and values that are specific to the notion of Canada and being a Canadian.

A myriad of cross-cultural studies have shown that children tend to learn in many domains in much the same way and at much the same time. Toddlers in Montreal, Melbourne, and Milwaukee, for example, are all likely to develop language in the same stages and at about the same ages. By the time they reach school, these same children will have developed sophisticated language use and a lexicon of words that will grow throughout their lifetimes. Even though they may all speak English, their accents will be different and their speech will be sprinkled with local idioms and slang; however, they may easily communicate with each other.

Just as a unique Canadian way of acquiring language does not exist, neither does a unique Canadian educational psychology. What does exist is a unique Canadian school system, distinct Canadian curricula, and Canadian teachers immersed in the prevailing culture. In this text, therefore, it is the application of the principles of development, instruction and learning to Canadian classrooms that we stress. Where possible, we use examples and relevant research from the Canadian situation and apply them to our expanding and changing educational system. Stress is placed on areas that are uniquely Canadian or that are handled uniquely within our system. The concept of multiculturalism, now entrenched in the Charter of Rights and Freedoms, is an area of particular interest to Canadian teachers. Similarly, bilingualism and its practice is an increasingly prominent aspect of instruction.

Bilingualism is an increasingly prominent aspect of instruction.

22

As the study of the human mind and human behaviour, psychology was a matter of concern to even our earliest ancestors. At first it was considered within the broad category of philosophy. In fact, of the four main branches of philosophy—logic, ethics, epistemology, and metaphysics—the first three revolved largely around what could be described as psychological principles. Metaphysics was more deeply concerned with the relations of humans with a creator.

The birth of the modern scientific method that directs contemporary psychology is usually dated from 1879, the year when Wilhelm Wundt (1832-1920) opened a psychological laboratory in Leipzig. Wundt's psychology was a mixture of physiology and philosophy; his goal was to model the new field of psychology after the field of chemistry. Wundt wanted to break down conscious experience into its basic elements and analyze how they related. Therefore, he took a cognitive perspective that focused on mental experiences through introspection—an individual's observation and recording of the nature of his or her own perceptions, thoughts and feelings. Some of North America's pioneer psychologists studied with Wundt and imported his ideas and methods (see Hilgard, 1987; Winzer, 1990b).

Behind Wundt's modern psychology lay the fundamental idea that the mind and behaviour, like plants, animals, and human organs, could be the subject of scientific analysis. Therefore, as a science, psychology may be defined as the study of the integrated behaviour of an organism as a whole; this includes everything from simple instinctive actions to those higher forms of intellectual, emotional and social behaviours of animals and humans that have traditionally been attributed to the mind and to consciousness (Salkind, 1990).

The scientific study of behaviour and mental processes covers an astonishing variety of topics; major branches of psychology include biological psychology, experimental psychology, developmental psychology, social psychology, the psychology of personality, clinical and counseling psychology, school and educational psychology, industrial and engineering psychology, and forensic psychology. As a basic science, psychology aims to understand the fundamental psychological or behavioural processes that are involved in complex forms of integrated behaviour: animal and human, intellectual and social, and normal and abnormal.

One way of defining psychology by sub-type is through the setting in which it is practised. Taking this view, educational psychology is intimately related to schools, students, teachers, and educational systems. Since both psychology and educational psychology deal with the problem of learning, it is important to distinguish between the theoretical and research interests of each discipline in this area. It can be said that psychologists' interests in learning are more general and that many aspects of learning concern them. Educational psychology is not as concerned with the general laws of learning, per se, but chiefly with those properties of learning that can be related to "efficient ways of deliberately effecting stable cognitive changes which have social value" (Ausubel, 1953). Problems that are unique to educational environments such as classroom management, instructional practices, grouping of pupils, and alternate methods for grading and reporting, fall under the scrutiny of educational psychology. Substantial improvements in the practice of instruction and in student learning form the ultimate objectives of courses on educational psychology.

As a discrete discipline, subsumed within general psychology, educational psychology emerged in North America in the first decade of the twentieth century, accompanying the first American translations of IQ tests, the strict enactment of compulsory school laws, and the formation of special education classes within urban school systems (Winzer, 1990b). School psychology, the branch of educational psychology with practitioners working directly in school systems, emerged in name later; it was first mentioned in the literature in 1923 (Hutt, 1923). Since its debut in about 1910, the discipline of educational psychology has demonstrated rapid growth and taken on its own particular colours and roles as researchers have increasingly turned their attention to the realities of classroom instruction. A brief outline of the development of educational psychology is presented in Box 1-3.

---

## Box 1-3 Historical note: Development of educational psychology

In 1900 psychology was a young science, determined to conquer the complexities of the human mind through the astute application of experimental science. Wundt's introspective psychology expanded as workers in the emerging field directed their interests toward a range of topics. The outlines of the field of educational psychology were sketched by the opening decades of the twentieth century and then clarified by two specific happenings—the rapid expansion of the public school system and the importation of the first IQ tests from France in 1910.

The quest for universal schooling accelerated in the second half of the nineteenth century as reformers promoted universal education as the panacea for many of society's ills. Free and compulsory schooling became a reality in 1870 with the passage of Ryerson's school law in Ontario. Children were compelled to attend school for four hours a day for four months a year. But the laws on the statute

books did not translate into universal school attendance. It was not until the opening decades of the twentieth century that mandatory school attendance was rigorously enforced.

When this happened, the schools were faced with hordes of youngsters, many of whom came from backgrounds that militated against their success in the traditional structured classrooms of the time. The bureaucratic solution was the formation of special segregated classes for children variously described as unruly, feeble-minded, truant, incorrigible, immigrant, and so on. So quickly did these ungraded special classes spread that by 1910 they had become a feature of most urban school systems in Canada.

This was exactly the time when Henry Goddard, an American psychologist, imported the IQ test devised by Alfred Binet and Theophile Simon in France and translated it into English. Goddard's 1910 revision was followed by a revision by Lewis Terman of Stanford Univerisity in 1916 which further popularized the measures.

North Americans were immediately enamored of the new IQ measures; they viewed them as an infallible key to unlocking the mysteries of those differences in intelligence that were so clearly seen in human beings. With the assiduous use of "modern psychometric tests," educators were confident that the intelligence of a child could be "accurately measured and a very close estimate made as to what his mental development will be when he [reached] adult life" (Fernald, 1924, p. 966). Educational usage could become universal. The 1916 revision of the Binet scale by Terman made possible the use of the test by any school teacher who could afford to buy the book.

The IQ tests were used with a variety of populations—immigrants, prisoners, persons in state institutions, juvenile delinquents, and regular and special students. With school children, the IQ tests were specifically employed as the tool to measure intelligence and thereby assign students to different streams within the school system. Once objective methods for testing intelligence were in place, the discipline of psychology grew rapidly, the public role of psychologists came to the fore, and institutions of higher learning embraced psychology. As new professions, educational and clinical psychology became part of graduate training programs and distinct departments within normal schools, or teachers' colleges, with different degrees and their own professional journals.

Clinics that focused on counseling children and parents as well as providing psychological assessment sprang up. School districts began to constructively employ the skills of the new discipline; in 1915 the Connecticut Board of Education was the first to appoint a psychologist to help plan education for "backward" and "defective" children. Within the schools, however, the chief occupation of school psychologists was testing children for special placements, correlating the results of IQ tests with certain human traits, and using the tests to warn the Canadian public of the "threat of the feeble-minded." It was not until the 1930s that North American faith in the infallibility of IQ tests wavered and educational psychologists turned more of their attention to other educational concerns.

**SOURCE:** Winzer, 1990b, 1990c

## The role of the school psychologist

Sometimes the titles "educational psychologist" and "school psychologist" are used interchangeably. Just as often, educational psychologist refers to a researcher, chiefly working from a university, and school psychologist refers to an individual interacting directly with teachers and students within a school system. Although we see the roles as complementary and becoming increasingly more interchangeable, we adhere to the traditional distinction in this text.

The term "school psychologist" first appeared in print more than sixty years ago (Hutt, 1923), but it took almost three decades after that for the American Psychological Association Council to recognize school psychology as a speciality within psychology. Today, however, school psychologists are integral components of the school system and important members of school-based educational teams.

These are challenging times for school psychologists. Partly because of the newness of the discipline, the outlines of educational and school psychology remain a little murky. Lack of a crystal clear delineation of the field is also related to changing notions of the entire educational system and altered views of the role of the school psychologist within the system. As well, because of the school-based nature of school psychology, there is often overlap with social workers and counselors that leads to role confusion. Moreover, because there are divergent standards of training and accreditation prevailing in different provinces, titles and job descriptions may change in different parts of the country (Dumont, 1987).

Because school psychology does not yet possess a readily distinctive trademark, it may mean different things to different people. There exist different expectations from different clientele that leave the discipline open to criticism. Teacher-psychologist relationships have too often been marred by poor relations; many teachers rate psychologists negatively and see them as far removed from the child and the everyday activity of the classroom. Educational psychologists may join teachers' meetings to discuss classroom management and discipline, and provide some general guidelines. This may frustrate the teacher who wants specific directions regarding particular students. The teacher may view educational psychology as a discipline that embraces broad principles that are of little use to her in the classroom yet she must realize that, lacking theory, practice has nothing to guide it.

Other related personnel may also have different views. The school principal, for example, may see the role of the educational psychologist only in terms of his or her ability to psycho-educationally assess numbers of children. Parents may see the psychologist as another of "those people" related to the school, although they are unsure of what psychologists actually do. To the public, educational psychology may be another of those bandwagons that educators seem to so dearly love, such as new math.

Essentially, school psychology grew from the need to examine children for placement in special classes and for the diagnosis of learning, behavioural, and emotional difficulties. The traditional beginnings of educational psychology still impinge on today's conception of the role of the school psychologist so that the role remains closely identified with assessment and diagnosis. When Dumont (1987) obtained job descriptions of school psychologists from the various ministries of education in Canada, assessment and diagnosis were always included. In fact, school psychologists spend as much as 70 percent of their time in traditional test-related activities (Graden et al., 1984).

To remain a viable force within the school system, the role of the school psychologist needs to expand and change beyond the traditional emphasis on assessment. Psychologists themselves have expressed a desire to move away from "stereotypic psychometric roles" in hopes of providing more consultation and counseling services (Abel and Burke, 1985). The impetus for increased consultation comes from both psychologists and from consumers. Many see consultation as the most important professional function of the school psychologist. This is based on the premise that positive changes in student behaviour can be produced indirectly when a consultant engages with teachers and other school personnel in collaborative problem solving (Kratchowill and Van Someren, 1985).

Roberts (1985) sees the school psychologist as a psychometrist, diagnostician, consultant, mental hygienist, researcher, therapist, and educational programmer. Similarly, Granowsky and Davis (1974) feel that the roles played by school psychologists include: psycho-educational specialist, school specialist in community-based psychological services, and psycholoist focusing on the social structure of schools. Other roles may encompass intervention with students with behaviour disorders and their families, preparation of Individual Education Plans for students with exceptionalities in cooperation with teachers, working on educational teams to assist children with learning difficulties, and dealing with parents and community agencies. Finally, psychologists can assume important roles in cases of child maltreatment (see Melton and Limber, 1989).

## SUMMARY

1. This chapter outlines some of the fundamental issues and problems in today's educational psychology and stresses the role that educational psychology plays in the daily activities of every classroom teacher.

2. Educational psychology underlies and illuminates classroom instruction. It provides a framework for looking at the learner, the learning process, the learning situation, the teacher and the educational system. It includes an understanding of educational objectives, student development in all domains, classroom management, and evaluation procedures.

3. School psychologists forge the critical link between education and psychology. They are highly trained to perform a variety of sophisticated functions that range from assessment and instructional planning for students experiencing academic and behavioural problems to individual therapy and behavioural treatment consultation. Educational psychologists work with teachers, function as members of school teams and consult with students and families.

4. Educational psychology is a science; knowledge within the field develops as there is an examination of evidence following certain rules. Some see educational psychology as the knowledge gained from psychology applied to the classroom. Others believe it involves applying the methods of psychology to the study of classrooms and school life. Most researchers today, however, see educational psychology as a distinct discipline with its own set of theories and research techniques that provide principles that underlie teaching and learning.

## Key Terms

assessment
pedagogy

educational pschology
theory

# APPENDIX:

# RESEARCH METHODS IN EDUCATIONAL PSYCHOLOGY

Since the establishment of the first psychological laboratories at the end of the nineteenth century, much of the development of psychology has consisted of the development of research methods that permit deeper analysis into questions of age-old interest. Educational research was launched by Edward L. Thorndike in the first decades of this century and since that time a scientific method of enquiry has been employed in psychology. Researchers carefully observe what happens as people learn and make accurate recordings of these observations in a meaningful way.

Like any science, educational psychology sets out to understand, predict, and control the phenonomen with which it is concerned. In this context, to understand means to account for relationships between variables in ways that obey the laws of logic. A variable is anything that can take on one or more values, such as sex, age, or academic level. To predict is to foretell, given a value for one variable. To control is to manipulate one variable in such a way as to bring about desired values in another variable (Gage and Berliner, 1984).

Educational research is based on the belief that the process of how people learn (education) can be studied in a scientific manner. We can carefully and systematically observe what takes place in learning, and intervene, manipulate variables, and record any changes that occur. Educational psychologists adopt a scientific method in their research. The methods used to collect data are therefore rigorous. They must be unbiased in that they do not favour one hypothesis over another. As well, the data collection methods must be objective: qualified people must be able to repeat the procedures and obtain similar results.

The scientific method consists of four distinct steps:

1. Formulating a research question. The nature of the question to be asked must be defined.

2. Formulating a hypothesis. "If...then" questions give direction to a study.

3. Collecting and analyzing data. Data is the term used for the information collected during a scientific study.

4. Drawing conclusions and finding implications.

In order to study the various strands that constitute the discipline of educational psychology—essentially, child development, principles of learning, learning models, and evaluation—educational psychologists have developed a set of research tools. They use particular research tools for studying growth and development as well as statistical analysis for evaluating the data obtained in the research. Statistical analysis is a powerful research tool that helps make sense out of data; it is rare to see empirical research in educational psychology that does not have some recourse to statistical analysis.

## RESEARCH DESIGN

The design of a study—how it will proceed and how data will be collected—depends on what researchers want to know and how much control they have over the conditions of the study. There exist two distinct groups of research designs. The first is whether a study is normative-descriptive, experimental, or correlational. The second is whether the study is cross-sectional or longitudinal. Cross-sectional designs examine age differences between children such as the play behaviour of children at different ages. Jean Piaget, for example, used cross-sectional methods to observe the behaviour of children as they solved problems requiring the ability to think and to understand. Longitudinal studies examine age changes in the same children across time.

Studies may also be categorized as qualitative or quantitative. At the simplest level, quantitative studies, as the name suggests, depend largely on measuring some aspect of behaviour and presenting results in some numerical form such as percentages, frequencies, correlations, or probabilities. Qualitative studies, on the other hand, place more stress on observation, interviews and working with subjects in classroom situations. One of the most unfortunate aspects of educational research is that a schism has opened between the two types of research. Yet both hold great value for devising and testing hypotheses and principles upon which to base instruction.

Many of the classic studies in educational psychology—those that became prototypes for a body of replicated or similar research—have been of a longitudinal nature. Box A-1 presents a classic longitudinal study undertaken by Lewis Terman on the lives of gifted children. Terman's study began in about 1923 and he followed his subjects from school to retirement in 1959.

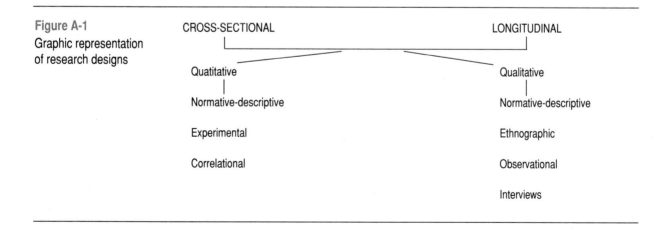

**Figure A-1**
Graphic representation of research designs

CROSS-SECTIONAL

Quatitative

Normative-descriptive

Experimental

Correlational

LONGITUDINAL

Qualitative

Normative-descriptive

Ethnographic

Observational

Interviews

## Box A-1 **Classic study: Gifted children**

Lewis Terman (1877-1956) is one of the most prominent pioneers in the history of mental testing and of special education. Like Henry Goddard, Terman imported Binet's IQ tests and in 1916 adapted them for American conditions. Because Terman was on the faculty of Stanford University at the time, the revised test became known as the Stanford-Binet Individual Test of Intelligence.

Terman coined the slogan, "A mental test for every child" (Chapman, 1981). He stressed the use of IQ tests for precise tracking in the schools and suggested a system of vocational and educational guidance based on the results to steer students into different educational streams. An IQ below 70, observed Terman, "rarely permits anything better than skilled labour," while scores above 115 "permit one to enter the professions or the larger fields of business" (Terman, 1920).

Terman used his test with a wide clientele—school children, mentally retarded persons, and institutionalized Californians, including prisoners at Alcatraz. However, he also believed that the IQ test could be used legitimately with students functioning at the higher end of the educational spectrum.

In 1919 Terman began a longitudinal study that continued until 1959. This study, which included 1 528 children "was designed to discover what physical, mental, and personality traits are characteristic of gifted children as a class, and what sort of adult the typical gifted child becomes" (Terman and Oden, 1951, p. 21). Terman's massive study of giftedness among California school children represented the first full-scale longitudinal study of the nature of giftedness. It defined the general characteristics of the gifted population and wielded profound influence. In fact, the serious inception of a gifted movement began with Terman.

Terman believed that intelligence was manifested essentially in the ability to acquire and manipulate concepts. He defined the gifted as those who scored in the top one percent level of general intellectual ability as measured by the Stanford-Binet Scale or a comparable instrument (Terman, 1926). Terman carefully distinguished giftedness from talent and creativity; he viewed talent as the potential for unusual achievement, but only when combined with high IQ scores. Creativity, he believed, was a personality factor, and thus differed from both giftedneses and talent (Wolf and Stephens, 1982).

Many of Terman's findings remain remarkably relevant; so far, his study is unsurpassed in the field of giftedness. From his gifted sample, Terman found that most came from a middle or higher socioeconomic group, with a low incidence of broken homes. Nearly half of the children could read before entering kindergarten, one in five children skipped part or all of the first grade, and on average the children finished school 14 percent faster than normal students. The children averaged 40 percent higher than their age mates on achievement tests. In school, they preferred abstract subjects, such as literary debate and ancient history, and were less interested in such practical concerns as penmanship and manual training. They read more and better books, made numerous collections, had many hobbies, and were also far superior to their age mates in general health, physique, mental health, and emotional adjustment. When retested as adults, Terman's people were found to have retained their intellectual superiority; they were ahead in terms of occupational status, earned incomes, publications, and patents (Callahan, 1981; Passow, 1981).

**SOURCE:** Winzer, 1990a, 1990b

# Experiments

An experiment is a deliberate test of a hunch or hypothesis. In real life, we experiment and test hypotheses every day. We may experiment with a new hairstyle, a new backhand or a different route to work on the hypothesis that we may look better, win a tennis match, or miss heavy traffic.

Within educational research, experiments provide some of the most convincing evidence upon which to judge alternatives. An experiment takes place when researchers create (a) special condition(s) and then study the effects. It is necessary to study both an experimental group that experiences the condition as well as a control group that does not. Experiments are done to investigate the cause and effect relationships between an independent variable and a dependent variable. Independent variables are those that are manipulated or changed by the researcher and are the hypothetical "cause" of the relationship being studied. Dependent variables are those that are hypothesized to demonstrate the "effect" of manipulating the independent variable.

The experimenter sets up the study so that only the difference between the groups is the hypothesized cause of changes (independent variable[s]). This is accomplished by two means. First, the experimenter makes sure that all other conditions are constant; for example, the ages at which the children are tested, the kind of test they are given, even their socioeconomic status, and so on. Second, the experimenter assigns subjects to groups randomly; this is, subjects are put in a particular group on the basis of pure chance. Because of the impossibility of testing every child, researchers use samples, a portion of the population that accurately represents the entire group.

Some experiments fit under the rubric of laboratory experiments—they take place in a specific artificial setting created for a brief period of time. The advantage of laboratory experiments is that they permit researchers to exert a high degree of control over all the factors involved in the study. Such studies are high in internal validity, which is to say that any differences they find can be attributed, with a good deal of confidence, to the treatment itself rather than to other factors. The primary limitation of laboratory experiments is that they are typically so artificial and so brief that

their results may have little relevance to real life situations.

Randomized field experiments are often used in educational research. In this method, educational programs or other practical treatments are evaluated over relatively long periods of time in real classes and schools under realistic conditions. Laboratory experiments are important in building and testing theories, while randomized field experiments are the acid test for evaluating practical programs or improvements in instruction. Field experiments have a higher external validity—they have a far greater relevance to the actual classroom.

Researchers also talk about generability—whether the data can be replicated. Replication can be direct or systematic. Direct replication involves a precise repetition of an experiment; systematic replication means that the procedures of the earlier research can be modified. For instance, a researcher may change the setting, vary the target behaviours (the behaviours to be studied), or change the type of subjects used in the study.

## Case studies

Often educational psychologists use a single case experiment in which they study a single event or a single student. For example, a researcher may study a student with severe behavioural problems and record the instances of poor behaviour over a certain period, no shorter than five days. An intervention is then used and the student's behaviour is further recorded. If the behaviour returns to a poor level after the intervention is withdrawn, then it is clear that the intervention was successful in eliminating some poor behaviour.

When conducting research with a single subject, the researcher must obtain repeated, frequent measures of the subject's behaviour before and after treatment. Data is collected during the baseline or pretreatment phase to establish the subject's current level of performance and this becomes the standard against which the effects of any treatment are measured. That is, it would be assumed that in the absence of treatment, no change in the behaviour would occur. By comparing data from the baseline and treatment phase, it is possible to determine whether the treatment produced a change in behaviour.

Take the case of Natalie who refuses to participate in discussions during class, especially during social studies. Natalie seems to know and enjoy the material, but rarely if ever comments or questions. To begin with, the researcher collects data that reflects Natalie's current or typical level of performance and shows this in graphic form. For treatment, the teacher is directed to reinforce Natalie's voluntary contributions with verbal and non-verbal messages of approval. This appears to alter Natalie's behaviour positively. To assure that the change in Natalie came about because of the treatment and not because of some other intervening variable, the treatment can be withdrawn to see whether there is a drop in the positive behaviour. Natalie's behaviour does revert, but when the treatment is reintroduced, improves again. The graphic representation is shown in Figure A-2.

## Correlational studies

Perhaps the most frequently used research method in educational psychology is the correlational study, the major alternative to experiments. In contrast to an experiment where the researcher deliberately changes one variable to see how this will affect other variables, in correlational research the investigator studies the variables as they are to see whether they are related.

In the correlation method, the purpose is to establish the degree of relationship between two variables. The values of the two variables are studied to discover whether they have so much in common that when one changes the other will also. For example, the researcher may obtain intelligence scores and grades on provincial departmental examinations. Through statistical analysis, it is possible to see whether the scores are related and whether students with high intelligence scores receive higher grades on the examinations. If they are related, the correlation value will indicate how strong the association is.

Correlation coefficients provide the keys to treating and interpreting correlational studies. The degree of relationship between variables (all of which are dependent in a correlational study) is expressed as a numerical index called the correlation coefficient which ranges from -1.00 (a perfect negative correlation) to +1.00 (a perfect positive correlation). The symbol $r$ stands for the correlation coefficient. When r is positive, there is a high correlation betwen the two sets of scores, so that individuals high on one measure are likely to be high on the other. When $r$ is negative, there is an inverse relation (negative correlation) between the two sets of scores so that individuals high on one measure are likely to be low on the other. When $r$ is zero, there is no correlation at all between the two sets of scores, so individuals' scores on the first measure provide no information about their probable scores on the second measure.

For example, there exists a positive correlation between teachers' ratings and students' scores on

**Figure A-2**
Single case experiment

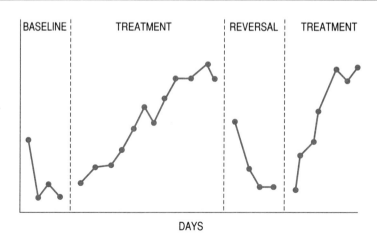

IQ tests. When elementary teachers are asked to rate the children in their classrooms in terms of brightness, correlations between the teacher ratings and the scores on IQ tests range from .6 to .8 (Atkinson et al., 1990). Similarly, positive correlations exist between reading achievement and spelling performance. Poor readers almost invariably tend to be poor spellers so there is a high positive correlation between deficits in reading and problems in spelling. As well, children with behaviour disorders often display reading difficulties and there is, in fact, a correlation between reading achievement and behaviour disorders.

Correlational studies are useful where children are studied in natural settings such as the home or the classroom. Correlations are also useful in exploring the stability of individual differences. For example, researchers may wish to know whether newborn height and weight is related to adult height and weight. They are also interested in whether complex traits such as intelligence are stable from infancy to later childhood. To find out, they determine the correlation between the given characteristics at the two ages. If the relationship is strong (high positive correlation) then the adult characteristic can be predicted from the infant characteristic (Rosenblith and Sims-Knight, 1985).

Prediction is a prime use of correlational studies, but how well can one variable predict another? When we have a strong positive or negative correlation, we are able to predict one value when we know the other. For example, there is a strong positive correlation between height and weight. As height increases so weight will also gradually increase.

The limitations of correlational research become apparent when attempts are made to interpret the findings. Because the correlations are not perfect, the predictions will not always be correct. Moreover, although correlational studies can show that variables are indeed related, they cannot demonstrate the way in which they are related.

One familiar use of the correlation method involves tests that measure some aptitude, achievement, or other psychological trait. Of particular importance to psychologists and teachers are correlational studies that investigate how well certain instruments correlate with each other. This is important to know. If a psychologist presents a child with a battery of measures, the scores and recommendations are more efficient if interpreted in light of each other. Moreover, a psychologist wants to know whether tests reported to measure similar domains, such as mental ability, correlate well with each other.

In North America the most widely used test of mental ability (IQ test) is the Wechsler Intelligence Scale for Children-Revised (WISC-R) (Wechsler, 1974). Because of its enduring popularity and use with a wide range of normal and exceptional students, a plethora of studies, including correlational investigations, have been undertaken on the WISC-R. Table A-1 presents some of the findings on correlations of the WISC-R with other tests.

**Normative-descriptive research**
Academics interested in public education and educational practice have increasingly called for educational research based in the naturalistic paradigm and reflective of the practical world (Seller, 1989). Qualitative methodology is associated with case studies, ethnographic descriptions, interviews, long-term observations, and the discovery of the meaning of social phenonema.

Descriptive research is often (though not always) unlike experimental or correlational research in that the former looks for a relationship between variables and the latter usually seeks to describe something of interest. Normative-descriptive studies chart developmental sequences and are designed to determine when something develops and how it develops in the sense of what aspects develop early and what aspects develop late. Normative studies often rely on observation; researchers carefully observe children and chart changes along some domain. These studies cannot by themselves determine what causes behaviour. By their nature, they can only describe observed behaviour at certain points.

Mounting in popularity today are forms of descriptive research known as ethnographic and ecological. These essentially involve observation in a certain setting, such as a classroom or a playground, over an extended period. They include the study of naturally occurring behaviour and the effects that the environment has on that behaviour.

33

**Table A-1** Correlational studies using the WISC-R

| MEASURE | CORRELATION | POPULATION | RESEARCHERS |
| --- | --- | --- | --- |
| Culture Fair Intelligence Test | .76 | Juvenile delinquents | Smith, Hays, and Solway (1977) |
| McCarthy Scales of Development | .89 | Normal | Reilly et al., (1985) |
| Otis-Lennon Mental Ability Test | .72 | Suspected mentally retarded | Covin (1976) |
| Peabody Individual Achievement Test | .80 | Normal | White (1979) |
| Peabody Picture Vocabulary Test (PPVT) | .66 | Normal | Hodapp and Hodapp (1986) |
| PPVT | .71 | Emotionally disturbed | Hodapp and Hodapp (1986) |
| PPVT | .407 | Learning disabled | Hodapp and Hodapp (1986) |
| PPVT | .496 | Mentally retarded | Hodapp and Hodapp (1986) |
| PPVT | .50 | Reading disabled | Sattler, Bonohan and Moore (1980) |
| Slosson Intelligence Test | .65 | Gifted | Karnes and Brown (1979) |
| Woodcock Johnson | .90 | Normal | Reilly et al., (1985) |
| Stanford Binet | .83 | Mentally retarded | Kaufman and Hagen (1977) |

# TEACHERS AS RESEARCHERS

One step toward a better understanding of educational psychology is knowing how information in the field is created and how to judge that information. Teachers need new knowledge to cope with the complex issues they face and they are continually seeking such information. It may be highly effective for teachers to participate at some level in the actual research.

In the past, teachers were at best peripheral to the conduct of educational research. They were often studied but were seldom encouraged to undertake systematic studies of educational problems themselves. Although there exist many constraints to the process, teachers are more often being drawn into research. Collaboration between educational researchers and teachers is on the increase but it does not yet take full advantage of the teachers' knowledge and expertise.

## Teacher autobiographies

A promising step in the direction of building a core of teacher-generated knowledge is the growing body of case studies written by teachers themselves to highlight their perceptions of their own practice. Teachers are encouraged to reflect on their own work in writing. The case studies that teachers write are then considered collabaratively by groups of teachers interested in the events described.

An example of a teacher autobiography comes from a teacher in Western Canada. After a poor teaching experience, the teacher moved to another school and described his new experiences:

> I became a "closet teacher" in that I would listen to suggestions, not offering any suggestions, and then "do my own thing." I found great success with this mode of operation and up to a few years ago, I hesitated to share any of my strate-

*gies/worksheets/lessons I developed on my own. Becoming an administrator forced me into sharing, for I wanted to provide teachers with access to as many resources as possible—the better the programs they had, the better it was for the school. It also started to make me feel worthwhile and proud when teachers tried some of my ideas and they actually worked for them as well (Butt, Raymond, and Yamagashi, 1988).*

## Action research

There are several varieties of action research, which places the practitioner squarely in the middle. Action research is a process designed to help teachers to test and revise their own theories. It is essentially a study by the teacher as part of classroom practice (see Milburn, Goodson, and Clark, 1989). Gibson (1986) defines action research in this way:

> *Action research is research into their schools and classrooms by teachers who are committed to improving their practice through the process of self-reflection and collaborative action. Therefore, they work out their own solutions to their own (not other's) problems, and they employ their own language and concepts rather than those of "experts." Action research thus offers to participants the opportunity to gain greater control over their lives (p. 162).*

## TEACHERS AS USERS OF RESEARCH

Literally thousands of educational journals and magazines are published annually and find their way into staffrooms or the mailboxes of individual teachers. It has been estimated that 100 000 articles on educational research are published each year (Gibboney, 1989). Professional publications serve as a means of recording the progress of the field and of sharing the latest developments. They present the results of recent research on aspects of educational psychology as it relates to some area of classroom practice such as why some programs work and why others fail.

For many people, reading the research, especially quantitative research, leads to confusion rather than comprehension. Some are convinced that they will never make sense of it at all. Certain things should be considered when reading a research article. Consumers of research should be reflective and skeptical but still open-minded. To read the article and assess the major points, a reader needs to understand what the researcher has written and be able to evaluate what the research has accomplished (Erickson, 1982). The reader should take into account:

**Research problem**   What is the researcher trying to accomplish? What type of probem is it and what is the significance of the problem?

**Concepts and assumptions**   There are probably concepts or notions that underlie the author's assumptions. A researcher, for example, studying the use of token economy systems in elementary classrooms, probably assumes that behavioural principles are efficient in modifying behavior.

**Survey of the literature**   Most papers present a survey of findings in the area that is under study. These show what other people studying the same or similar phenomena have discovered.

**Methodology**   The rules or principles used to test theoretical propositions include the design of the study—the way the researcher laid out the investigation and collected the data—as well as instruments used, if any, and the methods the researcher employed to analyze the data.

**Instrument**   In some studies the researcher uses a particular instrument for assessment or other purposes. This may be a standardized test or, quite often, a measure devised specifically for the study. In a study of nomination procedures with gifted students, for example, the researchers (Winzer, Harper, and Clarke, 1990) devised special nomination forms to use with parents, teachers, peers, and the students themselves.

**Results**   Very often, these are presented in statistical terms. In fact, most empirical research uses data analysis as a powerful research tool. Many times the statistics present the results as differences among groups found in an experiment. To be significant, these results are usually said to have occurred by chance only five times out of a hundred. In research this is reported as $p = .05$, which means that the probability of the result occurring simply by luck or chance is very low. If the probability is presented as $p = .01$, it is even more stringent and means that the likelihood of the result happening by chance is less than one in one hundred.

**Conclusions**    Here the researcher draws together the major threads of the study and makes broad statements about findings. For example, in the gifted study mentioned above, the authors

concluded that their preliminary work found parent and peer nominations to be advantageous in nominating gifted students.

**Implications for practice**    This explains how the author sees the study as valuable for classroom use. Many authors also add recommendations for future or further research.

**Bibliographical information**    The bibliography at the end of the paper tells the reader the sources from which the author obtained background information. In the field of educational psychology, authors typically employ the referencing system set forth by the American Psychological Association, the APA referencing system.

2

**HUMAN GROWTH AND DEVELOPMENT**

Heredity is herein proven law, as inexorable in the descending as it is beneficial in the ascending scale; heredity—whether it be direct from parent to child, collateral as from other relatives, or reversational, appearing ever and anon through generations—none can escape (Barr, 1913, p. 123).

Give me a baby and I'll make it climb and use its hands in construction of buildings of stone or wood. I'll make it a thief, a gunman or a dope fiend. The possibilities of shaping it in any direction are almost endless. Even gross anatomical differences limit us far less than you may think .... Make him a deaf mute, and I'll build you a Helen Keller. Men are built, not born (Watson, 1927, p. 233).

**M** **This section is designed to**
**A**
**J** • Explain the differences between growth, development, maturation, and learning;
**O**
**R** • Describe the major developmental stages through which children pass and explain the major principles governing this development;

**O** • Discuss the stage-dependent explanation of development and contrast this with continuous theories;
**B**
**J** • Describe how children and youth develop across the various domains—physical, cognitive, socio-emotional, moral, and language;
**E**
**C** • Outline how classroom instruction and learning is matched to children's development across the various domains; and
**T**
**I** • Introduce current issues that are necessarily of concern to teachers.
**V**
**E**
**S**

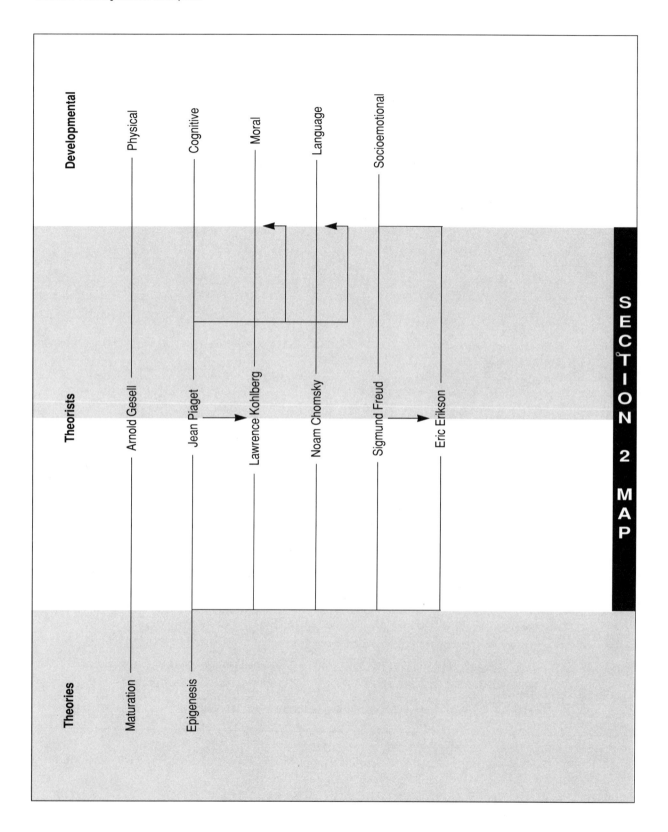

Much of the nature/nurture controversy has centred on how humans develop intelligence, but it has spilled over to encompass all other developmental domains—language, socio-emotional functioning, physical development, and the development of social conventions, values, and morality.

Early proponents of either a nature or nurture position tended to adopt definite stances. Martin Barr (1913), an early psychologist interested in the problems of mental retardation, or feeble-mindedness as it was called in his day, leaves no doubt as to his strong adherence to the dominance of nature and hereditarian principles. Barr and other hereditarians claimed that all psychological traits were transmitted directly through the genes from generation to generation. In striking contrast, those who leaned toward nurture principles believed that the environment was the chief force that shaped an individual's development. John B. Watson, whose theory of behaviourism first appeared in 1913, saw environmental reinforcement as the central force in moulding a child into just about any adult image from, as he said, a thief to a person of Helen Keller's stature.

Barr (1913) and Watson (1927) spoke from quite different ends of the nature/nurture continuum. Even in the early decades of the twentieth century, however, only the most radical exponents of heredity or environmental thinking were so adamant (Winzer, 1990b). Most of those involved in the broad field of human development assumed more moderate stances. Contemporary thinking likewise stresses the complex interplay between nature and nurture—heredity and environment—in the make-up of a human being.

Nonetheless, theories of child development generally can be differentiated in terms of where they fall along the nature/nurture continuum. Some theorists base their theoretical positions on the assumption that development is primarily a function of the natural, predetermined unfolding of one's genetic heritage, while others contend that the environment is the primary determinant of development. As well, it is possible to distinguish between theories according to their beliefs about the manner in which development unfolds. Some see the process of development as occurring in a series of distinct stages tied to broad chronological ages; others contend that growth is continuous and that transitions from each tiny step to the next cannot be readily and reliably distinguished.

It is no secret, then, educational psychology regarding the whole area of child development is rife with dispute. The best that can be said is that there exists no generally accepted theory of child development. Rather, there are several theories that differ from one another in what they hold to be important. Some overlap occurs, as in age and stage models; others, such as behaviourist theories, are in direct contrast to these.

If so many models exist, and none can satisfactorily explain human development and behaviour on its own, then why bother with models at all? They exist because theories and models can be seen as frameworks that facilitate the organization of observations about children and the establishment of relationships between otherwise disconnected pieces of information. For example, developmental psychologists are engaged in gathering lots of information about how children change over time. This great volume of information must be organized in some fashion in order to produce some type of coherent picture of how children grow and change.

We have many models that look at different aspects of development such as physical, cognitive, language, and socio-emotional development. Certainly, these are interrelated but the complexity of human behaviour generally means that they are examined separately. Also, diversity simply indicates that our knowledge is imperfect and that human development is too complex to be captured easily in a single theory. The conflicting, competing, contradictory or sometimes complementary models of child development reflect the state of knowledge in the area.

Child development research has expanded vigorously during the past few decades. Knowledge about children has increased, new kinds of questions are being asked, and new areas of study are developing. The five chapters that comprise this section focus on children's development across the physical, cognitive, language, and socio-emotional domains. The material is organized around specific topics or skills of the developing child; this organization reflects a belief that the full swing of developmental changes in any one domain can be understood only after looking at the pattern across ages.

We stress the models of child development that are particularly relevant to the classroom for, if teachers are to deal with students effectively, it is helpful for them to know where the students have been and where they are likely to be going, not just where they are currently. This requires a developmental perspective—a concern with changes that occur over time. The chapters outline human development and focus on important models that assist in understanding the process. We present the theories that are most widely accepted and those that contain principles most directly applicable to the classroom.

Physical models of development use concepts and principles largely drawn from physiology and other branches of biology; the other models rely on concepts that are more psychological in nature. Cognitive development implies orderly changes that occur in the way children understand and cope with their worlds. Beyond physical growth and internal development of the central nervous system, cognitive development also involves the methods a child uses to organize, store, and retrieve information for problem solving. The modern study of cognition is concerned with mental processes such as perceiving, remembering, reasoning, deciding, and problem solving. Several different approaches to understanding cognition have emerged. The predominant method for studying cognitive development focuses on changes that occur with increasing age. Jean Piaget demonstrated that children's mental abilities undergo changes analogous to physical growth and development. Piaget's theories are basic to understanding how the human mind develops by gradually constructing knowledge about the world from feedback received through interactions with it.

Jean Piaget is one of the most widely cited child development authors of this century and, although he did not write specifically for the area of education or even educational psychology, his insights into children's cognitive development are crucial for teachers' understanding of children's developmental levels. Piaget called himself a genetic epistimologist and was most interested in how children construct knowledge rather than how they are taught or how they learn in the classroom. However, his principles have been translated into instructional principles. These are most often applied in preschool and kindergarten programs that operate under the assumption that children learn through discovery with a variety of materials. The teacher's role is not to instruct directly but to act as a director, setting up an environment in which children can have a wide variety of experiences (Slavin, 1988).

There are currently two dominant theories about moral development. One is the cognitive-developmental approach that originated with Piaget in 1932 and has been advanced by Lawrence Kohlberg of Harvard since the 1950s. The other is Albert Bandura's social learning theory. Kohlberg's elaboration of Piaget's work is important because it has laid some of the roots for today's teaching of moral and values education in the school system. The whole issue of values, both in the sense of moral education and in the context of the changing aspects of Canadian society must be addressed by teachers.

Socialization is the learning process that guides the growth of our social personalities. It is by means of socialization that we become reasonably acceptable and competent members of our society. Through socialization, we acquire the discipline, the skills, the knowledge, the ambitions, and the empathy for those around us that allow us to participate in the life of the family and later the school and the community. Socialization and personality development are part of the wider sphere of socio-emotional development.

Any theory of the development of interpersonal relationships should account for at least two kinds of things. First, it ought to deal with any developmental progressions that are observed, such as the development of the sequence of early attachments. Second, a theory in this area should also take into account individual differences in character such as aggression and dependency. Only psychoanalytic theorists—Freud and Erikson—have dealt with both of these in any detail (Bee, 1978).

While few would dispute Freud's premier position in the development of the field of psychology and psychoanalytic thought in particular, today's developmental psychologists do not place a great deal of stress on the psychosexual stages as Freud described them. We briefly overview Freud's theory because Erikson's alternate psychosocial theory owes its roots to Freud. A progression can be seen from Freud to Erikson just as an expansion of one aspect of Piaget's work can be seen in Lawrence Kohlberg's model of moral development.

Language development represents part of a larger concern for child development. Every theory advanced to explain language development has been criticized. The question is fiercely debated today and there are champions of every conceivable position. Occasionally one theory predominates, but generally portions of each are used to explain different aspects. Part of the problem in designing an overall theory is the complexity of both language and communication behaviour (Owens, 1988). We emphasize the acquisition and development of language in children and delve into bilingualism as it influences Canadian schools today.

<sup>C</sup><br>
<sup>H</sup><br>
<sup>A</sup><br>
<sup>P</sup><br>
<sup>T</sup><br>
<sup>E</sup><br>
<sup>R</sup><br>
<sup>2</sup><br>

# PHYSICAL DEVELOPMENT

**Child development:**
the scientific study of the way
children change over time.

## INTRODUCTION

During infancy and childhood, children undergo tremendous increases in
physical and motor ability. From helpless, totally dependent neonates, infants
in one short year begin to walk, to talk, and to revel in increased motor control. By the time children reach their fifth birthdays and are ready to enter
school, they have developed enormous capability. They can control motor
responses in extremely complex ways and with a great deal of grace; they can
move around with ease; they can think and solve highly complex problems;
and they can communicate their ideas to others so they can be understood.
Once they reach adolescence, young people are at the stage of full sexual
maturity. They are planning their lives, moving away from their protective
home environments, interacting with peers, dating, and forming their own
unique identities.

How and why development occurs are the chief foci of the field of child
development, the scientific study of the way children change over time. **Child
development** might be seen as a series of patterned and predictable changes
that foster a child's ability to cope with and master the external environment.
It is a process influenced by a complex of interwoven factors. The psychological, social, and educational elements cannot easily be separated from biomedi-
cal factors. Walking, for example, requires not only learning but also
maturation of the skeletal and muscular systems and the neuromuscular
mechanism. Well-developed sight and hearing are also needed to help children keep their balance and steer their course. Then, too, children need to
have developed the confidence to explore their environment, the motivation
to do so, the cognitive structures to learn from earlier experiences, and the
language to be able to communicate at some level about the event.

The fields of child development, child study, and parent education came
together in the early decades of this century, although the early stress lay in

44

immediate practical applications (Schlossman, 1981). From the turn of the century through the 1940s, many major research programs, devoted primarily to the study of the long-term physical and mental growth of children, were undertaken. Early research took the form of baby biographies or daily diaries recording physical, mental, and emotional development. Charles Darwin (1877), for example, used a descriptive diary to produce evidence for his theory of evolution. Darwin's baby biography is of particular interest because of the impressiveness of its detail, the many hypotheses regarding the nature of development (Gibson, 1978), and the fact that it formed a prototype for later studies. Many institutes and research stations were opened to undertake "growth" studies, like the Institute of Child Studies at the University of Toronto, created in the 1920s.

The field of child development remained somewhat barren until the opening of the twentieth century partly because children historically were considered to be just small adults and not to be much different from one another in the ways they grew, thought, felt, and lived their young lives. Box 2-1 presents a brief overview of the development of a discrete concept of childhood.

### Box 2-1 Historical note: The development of a concept of childhood

Today childhood is a special time, a period of little responsibility evidenced by special dress, food, games, toys, stories, and the like. Yet the concern for the child as a separate and important part of society is a relatively new phenomenon, a European invention of the past 400 years (Plumb, 1974). Until a society developed a social philosophy that recognized the child as an active, feeling, inherently valuable person, and saw childhood as a discrete state of development, special facilities for the care and training of children were not made available.

In the past, there were no special nurseries, no playgrounds, and certainly no special toys. Things such as nursery rhymes were unknown four hundred years ago; special books for children only began to appear in the nineteenth century. Few children went to school. Although today the education of children is basically linked with the calendar age of the child, "school age" people in earlier times were not necessarily children. It was

not until the seventeenth century that children were even thought worthy of a teacher's attention.

Until the end of the thirteenth century, childhood as a distinct stage of development was virtually unacknowledged. Children were not considered legally to be persons: they had no rights and were usually seen as the property of their parents until they were grown. Children were viewed as miniature adults; pictorial representations of children are unknown before the fourteenth century and, when they were depicted, they were always shown as part of the world of adults, not as separate beings (Ariès, 1962).

Many children were mistreated in early societies. Infanticide was widely practised: it was not until the fourth century that the Church completely halted the custom. After that, many children were abandoned to wander, beg, or die by the wayside (see De Mause, 1974; Winzer, 1990b). By the thirteenth century childhood as a discrete period of development was conceptualized. However, during the Middle Ages, it was understood that individuals were granted wealth, not according to their intellectual gifts, but according to the values by which God's grace enabled them to persevere (Byrd, 1974). Hence, the celebrated notion of childhood innocence was often manifested in the Church where children were acolytes.

The fourteenth to seventeenth centuries are more clearly recognized as the period when a growing awareness of children's needs occurred; nevertheless, this awareness did not expurgate the simultaneous belief that the child's "nature" entailed adult hostilities and sexual desires and, as such, had to be treated with strict and harsh discipline.

Ideas about children slowly changed so that by the seventeenth century the principle of infant innocence led to two different sorts of behaviour toward the child: an attempt to protect it against "pollution by life" and an effort to strengthen it by "the development of reason and character" (Ariès, 1962, p.119). Still, intrusive parenting, characterized by draconian authoritarianism, tended to be the eighteenth century mode. Infant mortality was high; even in the mid-eighteenth century, less than half the children born were expected to reach adulthood.

Ideas about childhood and about schooling for all children crystallized in the nineteenth century. Urbanization and industrialization saw a new consistency in child rearing; nineteenth century social and educational reformers conceptualized childhood differently from their forebears, so they interpreted children's needs differently. Faith in the potential of education is most intimately associated with North America. In the flurry of early nineteenth century industrialization and urbanization, American reforming elements grew increasingly fretful about the exposure of young children to the demands of adult society. Young children, unable to withstand the buffetings of reality, required the ministering of a facility designed to accommodate their needs: the school. Also, a rapidly growing population and a swiftly developing economy created the need for an educated citizenry that was essential to the survival of the Canadian nation. By the middle decades of the nineteenth century, the acquisition of literacy skills began to constitute a principal developmental task for children between the ages of six and twelve.

As far as the evolution of child psychology and the notion that children as learners need carefully constructed tutorial environments, the latter half of the nineteenth century represents something of a watershed (Finklestein, 1985). During this time, nurture writers and educational reformers began to consciously conceptualize children as learners and helped to instruct them in ever increasing numbers in special environments.

By the late 1800s, Canadians recognized children as sensitive individuals, rather than chattels. A number of child welfare reforms were passed concerning orphans, child labour, truancy, apprenticeships, and so on (Spettigue, 1955). In 1893 new legislation led to the formation of the first Children's Aid Societies. These reforms, together with the advent of free and compulsory education, offered all children a greater chance to develop to their full potential. However, the ethic of universal educational provision arrived later. Even though Ontario passed Canada's first compulsory attendance law in 1870, average school attendance remained below 50 percent (Ray, 1989). However, the period from 1875 to 1914 established the public school as an integral part of the new, mass-industrialized society and by the early 1900s schooling was a social norm for the great majority of children.

**Growth:**
changes in height, weight, and other aspects of physical size.

**Development:**
changes in the mind and body that occur in humans between conception and death.

The impetus for today's research in child development comes from a variety of sources, including academic concerns about the nature of children and pragmatic concerns for the welfare of children (Gibson, 1978). Many current researchers see child development as best examined as development through stages. These stages are not like stepping stones in the sense that children forget one stage when they move onto the next more complex stage. They are more like building blocks in which each forms the crucial foundation for the next.

## MODELS OF CHILD DEVELOPMENT

Theories are sets of related principles and laws that explain broad aspects of learning, behaviour, or other areas of interest. Models are similar to theories; they are used to present ideas about how certain things develop in discrete stages (Slavin, 1988). Once a theoretical framework has been adequately developed, it should not only allow us to explain events that have already happened, it should also enable us to predict events that will happen in the future. While many practitioners despair of the "jargon" of theories, it should be remembered that every profession, quite properly, uses a technical language and that technical terms are indispensible because they communicate precisely certain concepts that are not readily translated into lay terms. While the excessive use of jargon should be avoided, the precise and accurate use of terminology can facilitate communication and understanding among those conversant with a particular theory.

Theoretical models of behaviour have been developed by psychologists to allow the prediction of behaviour on the basis of chronological age as well as on the basis of environmental factors. Some of these theories complement each other; others differ rather dramatically. However, the theories that stress ages and stages use some general underlying principles that include such ideas as development, maturation, and critical periods.

### Growth and development

It is useful to distinguish growth from development when dicussing physical changes. Growth usually refers to changes in height, weight, and other aspects of physical size. Development is a broader term than growth and refers both to the mind and the emotions as well as the body. In the most general sense, it refers to certain changes that occur in humans between conception and death, rather than from conception to the attainment of physical maturity. Bodily changes occur throughout life so development is a continuous process from birth through adulthood to old age.

Development can also be seen as an orderly progression to increasingly higher levels of differentiation or organization. Development can occur when no growth is taking place. This is most obvious in early childhood when, for example, children of similar age and size can differ considerably in their ability to ride a tricycle, use a pencil, or use language.

Although developmental changes occur continually throughout life, the rate, with some exceptions, tends to slow with age. The younger the child, the more rapid the rate of development. The most rapid growth occurs prenatally; during this 267 day period, from conception to birth, the developing individual grows from a one-celled organism into a complex human being of approximately 200 billion cells. The second phase of rapid physical growth is during puberty, from age 10 to 12 to about age 15 or 16.

## Ages and stages

Many of you have probably heard about the "terrible twos." If you are a parent, you remember that this is the time when children are walking and exploring and into everything. They are talking, and although their language may be simple and their articulation deficient, they can readily make themselves understood. This is also the stage of toilet training and temper tantrums, the time when young children begin to really assert their independence. "No" becomes a favourite word of the child and "Don't do that" a favourite phrase of the parents. By the time those same children reach adolescence, parents are talking about stages again. The adolescent who is sulky, uncommunicative, messy, and rebellious is commonly described as "going through a stage"—one which parents hope sincerely will pass quickly.

What parents recognize through their own experiences, psychologists and child development researchers attempt to explain in terms of models of development. These models often focus on ages and stages. Universal sequences of development have been proposed which are said to proceed across all domains, usually in an unvarying sequence. The motor and physical development of two year olds, for example, allows them greater movement and mobility and therefore increased independence in the environment. Rapid language acquisition

During infancy and childhood, children undergo tremendous increases in physical and motor ability.

**Developmental psychology:**

the study of the changes that take place in people as they age; views the process of growing up as a sequence of stages characterized by specific types of behaviour that increase in complexity.

**Developmental stage:**

a description of age-related behaviour and changes that are predictable with increasing age.

and use provide a vehicle to communicate wants and needs and to understand the utterances of others. Cognitive skills expand as children begin to develop representational thought and the ability to think about things and to plan ahead. At the same time, children are being socialized to parental expectations and are, in turn, socializing their parents as they develop a sense of autonomy, a desire to do things for themselves.

Some theorists see development as discontinuous, as a series of distinct stages that are qualitatively different and quite separate from one another. Others see it as proceeding gradually and continuously through small increments. Changes, they would argue, are quantitative in nature—more of the same—rather than reflective of qualitative differences. For example, although there have been models of language development based on behavioural principles, most current researchers see language development as an unending acquisition of new vocabulary and grammatical skills. These are added to an existing fund of knowledge, rather than signifying changes in the underlying mental structures. These differing views are shown in Figure 2-1.

**Figure 2-1**
Continuous and discontinuous views of development

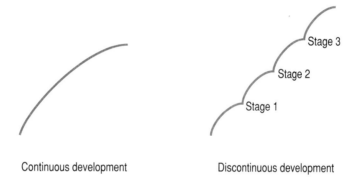

Continuous development          Discontinuous development

Developmental psychology is the study of the changes that take place in people as they age. Many developmental psychologists view the process of growing up as a sequence of stages characterized by specific types of behaviour that increase in complexity. In this sense, a developmental stage is a description of age-related behaviour and changes that are predictable with increasing age. Hence, developmental stages are more than simply descriptions of age-related behaviour; they also describe certain sequences of behaviour that gradually and predictably change in some specific order.

Although there is some disagreement among researchers about exactly what characterizes each stage, about the average ages at which particular stages occur, and just what role learning plays in affecting stages, it has nonetheless been shown that all individuals complete stages characterized by simple behaviour before they advance to more complex ones. This holds true for both physical and mental development. Many of the sequences involving physical growth and development are under the control of genetics and maturation; however, universal sequences have been proposed for aspects of psychological development as well.

**Developmental milestones:**
the various critical behaviours, such as sitting, walking, and using the first words, that children learn to perform at roughly the same age.

**Developmental delay or maturational lag:**
failure to develop according to normal patterns.

**Physical development:**
physical growth and motor control.

Most stage theorists correlate various stages of development with particular chronological ages. Such information is often sought by parents and teachers who are interested in the types of behaviours that are typically demonstrated by children at a particular age—in other words, what behaviour is "normal." Parents are concerned with developmental milestones, the various critical behaviours, such as sitting, walking, and using the first words, that children learn to perform at roughly the same age. Although there is individual variation, most children reach milestones such as walking and talking at about the same age. Children who fail to develop according to normal patterns are considered to be experiencing developmental delays or maturational lags.

A belief in chronological stages of development does not mean that stage theorists believe that a six year old will wake up on his or her birthday with an entirely new set of behaviours, or that a teenager will be rebellious one week, then compliant and cooperative the next. Changes are not abrupt leaps to the next developmental steps. Changes, especially in the cognitive and social domains, occur gradually over time in increments too small to be readily recognized. However, stage theorists are able to separate the flow of the unfolding developmental process into unique and distinct stages; they view each stage as qualitatively different from the others, with specific identifying traits or behaviours.

Stages are also generally believed to be universal and invariant. Referring to stages as universal implies that the same stages would be seen in all children, regardless of the social or cultural environment in which they are raised. Referring to stages as invariant means that all children will go through the stages in the same order, rather than skipping randomly forward and back. It does not mean that children will progress at the same rate but that, regardless of the speed of development, the same sequence of development will be followed.

## MODELS OF PHYSICAL DEVELOPMENT

Physical development implies physical growth and motor control. In physical development, there is an orderly sequence of development that unfolds as children interact with the environment. Many developmental changes occur simply as a result of biological aging. These changes cause the similarities we often see in groups of students of the same age in terms of general height and weight.

Models are far less prominent in the area of physical development than in the cognitive, language, and socio-emotional domains. This is chiefly because physical development is largely the product of maturation which is, in turn, determined by the genes with which each individual is endowed at conception. Hence, medical correlates tend to be more important than psychological ones here.

There is no question, however, that physical development can affect the manner in which children interact and learn in the school situation. In classrooms, teachers see students who vary greatly in size and maturity. Students may be of the same chronological ages but be quite different in their physiological (developmental) ages. Physical changes expand the range of experiences open to children and change their interactions with the environment and people in that environment. Teachers should understand the manner in which physical development interacts with other developmental areas and the way in which it can affect children's learning, social interactions, and self-images. Teachers should be aware of, for example, the motor skills of children in physical education and sports; of their fine motor capacities for areas such as cutting and pasting and hand writing; and of the differences between early and late maturers in the adolescent years.

## Arnold Gesell

To early researchers in the field of child development, physical maturation was an area of intense interest. Large numbers of normative-descriptive studies were undertaken to determine the ways in which physical development progressed. One of the most prominent early contributors to the study of children was Arnold Gesell (1880-1961) who established the Yale University Child Guidance Clinic in 1930. Details of Gesell's contributions are found in Box 2-2.

### Box 2-2 **Biographical note: Arnold Gesell (1880—1961)**

Gesell taught high school and later earned a Ph.D. at Clarke University under G. Stanley Hall in 1906 with a dissertation on jealousy in children and animals. In 1911, Gesell entered Yale Medical School, set up the Yale Psychological Clinic in the same year, and completed his M.D. in 1915.

Gesell's work set a standard for the scientific study of human development that lasted fifty years; much of today's knowledge of the development of early motor skills comes from research spurred by Gesellian theory. With Myrtle MaGraw, Gesell made elegant and painstaking catalogues of the acquisition of motor skills in infants.

After a 1919 study charting behaviour from birth to age six, Gesell (1925) codified his developmental schedule and in 1926 began a normative study using movies. Gesell was a pioneer in the use of the moving picture camera to study infant development. He used motion pictures, which had only recently been developed, because, he said, "The wealth and complexity of infant behavior are beyond

human description" (Gesell, 1934, p. 20). He constructed a dome, similar to a small observatory, so that the camera could be placed at any angle for viewing the infant lying on a table or seated at the centre of the dome (Hilgard, 1987). He then analyzed the pictures frame by frame.

Gesell had a considerable impact on the lay public; his work was widely popularized through a nationally syndicated newspaper column. After his initial scientific books, he and his colleagues wrote books specifically designed for parents and child-care workers. Many generations of North American children were raised by parents who compared their babies to Gesell's norms and to their friends' babies (Rosenblith and Sims-Knight, 1985).

Gesell's work was criticized for lack of rigour and control. However, he wielded considerable influence in the emerging field of child development. He called on those involved in medicine, sociology, embryology, neuro-psychology, biochemistry, genetics, and anthropology to carry out fruitful research into the development of young children in order to understand the interplay of organism and environment. Moreover, the data that he and his colleagues produced on children's developmental sequences have withstood the test of time.

Gesell is regarded as a pioneer in longitudinal research methods. At the outset, Gesell was particularly concerned with the first five years of life. These years, said Gesell, include changes "so swift and varied that they cannot be taken in at a single glance" (Gesell et al., 1974, p. 19). Gesell was most interested in the development of motor behaviour, language, personal and social relationships, and what was termed adaptive behaviour—learning to use present and past experiences to adapt to the environment (Gibson, 1978).

In 1929 Gesell published *The mental growth of the preschool child*. Then in 1946 he and his colleague, Ilg, published another descriptive record of child development, *The child from five to ten*. In this, they examined motor characteristics, personal hygiene, emotional expression, fears and dreams, interpersonal relations, play and patterning, school life, ethical sense, and philosophical outlook.

Gesell was a student of G. Stanley Hall and echoes of Hall's work can be seen in Gesell's beliefs. He was struck by the enormous similarities among children in their physical development. We are the same, he observed, because our genetic codes make us the same. His belief in the primacy of genetic determination in the development of motor and cognitive skills was supported by his observations of thousands of children at the clinic.

Gesell believed that each child has a unique pattern of physical and mental growth that constitutes the core of his or her individuality. He also held that biological maturation was the central force in child development and that training, practice, and other environmental factors had little effect on physical development. "Environmental factors support, inflect,

and modify but they do not generate the progression of development," observed Gesell. "The glove goes on the hand; the hand determines the glove" (Gesell, 1954, p. 13). To Gesell, a child's behaviour is a function of growth and that same growth is structured, orderly, predictable, and measurable by a simple screening test. Gesell, however, suggested many inter-relationships between different aspects of development. He saw the physical, social, emotional, and intellectual aspects of a child as interdependent and stressed the importance of each and every aspect.

Gesell placed special emphasis on the development of the nervous system since he understood the growth of the mind to be bound up with the growth of this system (Gesell et al., 1974). Also, the development of the motor system was seen as autonomous, and Gesell believed that the process of development would be unaffected by training or experiences. For example, Gesell believed that children, regardless of their home environment, would begin walking around the age of twelve months and no amount of early training could teach them the skills until they were ready. This concept of readiness to learn new skills is probably one of the most useful implications of Gesell's studies. He insisted on the importance of children being ready before they are asked to learn a new skill. For example, he would point out that it would not be reasonable to expect an twelve month old baby to ride a bicycle because the child's muscles and balance are not sufficiently matured. On the other hand, four year olds who are physically ready to ride bicycles need to be given opportunities that take advantage of their level of physical maturity.

There is no question that Gesell believed that children develop in "ages and stages" and that keeping these criteria in mind was the best strategy in rearing and teaching them. Of all stage theorists, Gesell's levels of development are perhaps most closely tied to particular ages: he provided tables for the expected behaviour at certain ages and these scales are quite specific about the behaviours that should be demonstrated by one year olds, two year olds, and so on. The developmental scales emerging from Gesell's studies (Gesell and Amatruda, 1947) have been widely used by medical and other child-care personnel working with young children.

Gesell further saw the stages of development as universal, as they were seen in all children observed, and invariant, as each set the stage for the next. In other words, children crawl before they walk, not the reverse.

**Maturation:**
biologically controlled development that is independent of outside learning experiences.

**Cephalocaudal principle:**
the tendency for development to reach from the head downward.

## Maturation

As children grow, many of the changes they undergo depend primarily on maturation. Arnold Gesell coined the term "maturation" and introduced it to the field of child development to describe the sequential unfolding that he thought was based on genetic instructions. Maturation refers to those internally determined patterns of change in such things as body size, shape and skill that begin at conception and continue until death. It is development that is biologically controlled and independent of outside learning experiences. In its pure form, maturationally determined development proceeds regardless of practice or training.

"Maturation" and "growth" are often used synonymously although the meanings are somewhat different. Growth refers to a step-by-step change in quantity, such as changes in size. A child's body size may increase tremendously because the child overeats junk food or it may decrease because the child is malnourished. This is what is meant by growth. On the other hand, maturation and biological inheritance control a great deal of physical development such as height and weight. For example, tall parents whose children are adequately nourished can expect their children to be tall.

## General principles of physical development

One of the first general principles of physical development is patently obvious: children develop at different rates. This is most noticeable in infancy and adolescence; development in middle childhood tends to be much more even and gradual. Even though it is genetically programmed and proceeds at different rates in different children, development is nevertheless gradual and even and follows an orderly progression. In infancy and adolescence, when body growth is so rapid, the pattern is still orderly and predictable. Arnold Gesell was one of the first to convince psychologists that development occurs in an unvarying sequence. He identified the major patterns as follows:

**1.** The tendency for development to reach from the head downward is known as the cephalocaudal principle. In the fetus, the head forms first and arm buds form before leg buds. Infants can hold their heads up before they can sit unsupported.

**Proximodistal principle:**
the tendency for development to occur from the torso out.

**Differentiation:**
pattern of general development in which physical responses move from global reactions to more controlled, specific reactions.

2. The tendency for development to occur from the torso out is known as the **proximodistal principle**. Hence the baby has greater control of the whole arm before gaining control of the wrists and fingers.

3. The third pattern of general development is for physical responses to move from global reactions to more controlled specific reaction, a process known as **differentiation**. This process of differentiation also occurs in other patterns of growth, particularly in cell division and brain growth.

## Developmental predictability

Developmental patterns are predictable in character but the physical growth pattern is asynchronous. The inner ear and the eye, for example, reach maturity very early; limbs only reach their mature stage at the close of puberty. Asynchronous growth is also reflected in body sizes; the head increases to twice its size from birth to maturity; the torso increases to three times its birth size; and the limbs to four or five times their size. Weight distribution changes: the brain, which accounts for one eighth of total body weight at birth equals only one fortieth at maturity. During adolescence, asynchrony of all aspects of growth is one important characteristic of physical development. Variations occur in the developmental sequence for various parts of the body: feet, for example, suddenly grow more rapidly than other parts of the body. So do ears.

Human growth patterns exhibit rapid growth in the first two years of life, slower but noticeable growth over the next eight to twelve years, followed by a second period of rapid growth during adolescence, and a fairly rapid tapering off thereafter. Within these larger sequences, growth typically occurs in spurts. There may be noticeable growth occurring over a period of a few months, followed by no noticeable growth for the next six months to a year (Tanner, 1970).

The timing of growth spurts and the course of physical development in general is controlled by secretions of growth hormones from the pituatary gland, which in turn are ultimately controlled by the genes inherited at conception. Assuming adequate nutrition and exercise, these inherited growth patterns determine the timing and duration of increases in body size. Of course health, sex, and socioeconomic status all contribute to children's growth patterns. On the other hand, an individual's size and rate of growth are not influenced significantly by consuming health foods or large quantities of vitamins, or by doing calisthenics or stretching exercises. Some of these may affect physical appearance or muscle tone, but they do not stimulate actual growth (Salkind, 1990).

## Body types

Increases in height and general body size follow cycles or growth curves (Tanner, 1970) that are genetically programmed for each individual. Some individuals will be very close to average for their sex and ethnic group throughout development; others will be taller than average for much of childhood but end up shorter than average as adults. Some will show relatively even growth throughout childhood and others will shoot up every couple of years with little observable growth in between.

Children's body types and rates of development can affect the way they see themselves and are seen by others.

There are a number of aspects of body type and these can affect children's development as well as their self-image and self-satisfaction. Early psychologists differentiated among ectomorphs (lean, elongated bodies), mesomorphs (muscular, athletic bodies), and endomorphs (heavy set, fleshy bodies). This is further discussed in Box 2-3.

### Box 2-3 **Classic study: Body types**

Body physique and cranial and facial structures have long been a popular basis for personality typologies. In the 1800s Franz Gall popularized the pseudo-science of phrenology that purported to determine intellect and talents through an examination of a person's skull. Later Arthur MacDonald moved to anthrometrics; he proposed that certain physical stigmata, or particular facial and bodily features, determined criminal personalities (Winzer, 1990b). The idea that body build and personality are related still comes through in such stereotypes as "fat people are jolly" or "skinny people are intellectuals" (Atkinson et al., 1990).

One of this century's proponents of the view that there existed relationships between body types and personality was an American physician, William Sheldon. After studying men and boys, Sheldon reported that there were actually three major body types, which he called somototypes, and identified certain personality or temperament traits that accompanied each type.

According to Sheldon, each man's physical build could be described in terms of its degree of endomorphy, mesomorphy, or ectomorphy. Generally, he assessed endomorphs by the amount of body fat; mesomorphs by the amount of muscle; and ectomorphs by the amount of bone (Bee, 1978). He described endomorphs as relaxed and sociable while mesomorphs were athletic, assertive, and courageous. Ectomorphs he saw as more sensitive, restrained, artistic, fearful, introverted, and aesthetic (Sheldon, 1954).

Some early studies supported Sheldon's view. Walker (1962) studied endomorphic preschool children and found that they were rated by their teachers as aggressive. Endomorphs were seen as thoughtful and considerate but lacking energy and assertiveness, and mesomorphs were leaders in play with lots of self-confidence, although they were difficult to handle. Other research (e.g., Cortes and Gatti, 1965) suggested that these patterns persisted through adolescence and perhaps into adulthood. In adolescence, ectomorphic boys were followers, while the mesomorphs were the leaders.

Sheldon's evidence was not very strong and his methods left open the possibility that his temperament and body type ratings simply reflected popular stereotypes. Most recent information has found no strong correlations between body type and personality. When individuals are rated on specific behaviours rather than on global traits, there are no strong associations between body type and personality (Mischel, 1968).

While linking body types with peculiar personality traits has not been upheld by scientific research, children's body types and rates of development and maturity can affect the way that children see themselves and feel that they are seen by others. This is especially true during adolescence, as we see in the two students appearing in Box 2-4.

Box 2-4 **In the classroom**

Fourteen-year-old Randy has just begun grade eight in a large urban junior high school. Randy's previous school records describe a high achieving student with a marked flair for writing and literature. If the grade eight teacher had not seen Randy's dossier, however, he would have easily believed that the boy has a long history of mild behaviour disorders, low motivation, poor attitudes, and depressed achievement.

In an interview with the parents, the teacher finds that school is not the only problem; at home, Randy has become more and more depressed and moody. "I thought it was just adolescence," explains Randy's mother, "but he does not seem to be growing much at all lately."

Apparently, this is the source of the trouble. After many casual chats with Randy, the teacher discovers that the boy is suffering deep qualms about his lack of physical maturity. He always excelled in academics and, while not the best at games, was able to keep up. Now many of his classmates have left him lagging behind physically and socially. Most of the boys in the class are taller and heavier, stronger, and more athletic. Some are casually dating.

Randy now feels different from the boys with whom he has grown up. His frustration manifests itself in sloppy dressing, moodiness at home, and a sharply decreased interest in school work.

Brett is the same age as Randy but his experience has been quite different. Brett's adolescent growth spurt began early and he gained height and weight rapidly. At fourteen, he is one of the tallest in the class, well coordinated and athletic.

Brett is on most of the school's sports teams. In class, the other students seem to look up to him. He was even elected class president—quite a surprise for a boy who is only a mediocre student. Nevertheless, the homeroom teacher seems to feel that he can handle the job and Brett's own new found confidence in himself leads him to believe that he can do the job efficiently.

**Critical period:** time at which a body part or organ system is growing most rapidly in both cell number and size.

## Differentiation

Most physical development involving differention of new parts occurs in the early weeks following conception as the fertilized egg, starting with a single cell, continually reproducing itself as the separate organs and systems differentiate.

## Critical periods

When a body part or organ system is growing most rapidly in both cell number and size, this is known as a critical period. For example, six to seven weeks after conception is a critical period for the normal development of the fetus's sex organs. If an environmental factor, such as a chemical or virus, interferes with growth during this period, development of that organ system will be permanently affected. We discuss this aspect in terms of infections and intoxications in Box 2-5.

### Box 2-5 Infections at critical periods

Because the timing is so important, rubella provides an example of the devastating effects of an infection during a critical period in embryonic development. Rubella is the culprit in many childhood handicapping conditions. The virus can cross the placenta and damage the developing fetus, especially during the first trimester of pregnancy. If the mother contracts rubella during that first trimester, it is estimated that 50 percent of fetuses are damaged from a first month contraction of the disease, while 20 percent of embryos affected in the second month are born with defects (Rosenblith and Sims-Knight, 1985).

The fetal organs likely to be affected by rubella are those whose development is underway when the mother contracts the virus. The eyes, ears, nervous system, and heart are especially vulnerable at early periods of fetal development. While severe sensorineural hearing loss is the major effect of maternal rubella (Hardy and Bordley, 1973), other major permanent effects include cataracts, glaucoma, mental retardation, congenital heart disease, and cerebral palsy. At its most devastating, rubella causes deaf-blindness and severe multiple disabilities. Most children who have combined sight and hearing problems due to rubella are neither totally blind nor profoundly deaf. However, the combination of sensory impairments creates severe learning difficulties for these children (Van Dijk, 1982).

As well, a number of reports (e.g., Hanid, 1976; Menser, Forrest, and Bransky, 1978; Preece, Kearney and Marshall, 1977) have documented a significant occurrence of late onset defects of rubella, including vascular disease, growth hormone deficiency, thyroid dysfunction, and diabetes mellitus.

Syphilis in the mother is another disease that can cross the placental barrier and damage the fetus. One of the venereal diseases, syphilis is produced by the bacterium Treponema pallidum (also called Spirocheta pallida). It does not affect the developing organs as does rubella but produces destructive lesions (abnormal changes in structure) of already developed organs. Twenty-five percent of affected babies die before birth; 33 percent of those who survive die in early childhood. Other affected infants are handicapped with blindness, liver problems, peritonitis, central nervous system disorders, and pegged teeth (Rosenblith and Sims-Knight, 1985).

While rubella is most critical during the first trimester of pregnancy, syphilis affects the fetus after the sixteenth or eighteenth week of gestation. If the disease is controlled by penicillin before the fifth month, only about two percent of fetuses will contract it. After the fifth month, uncontrolled syphilis will affect about 40 percent of fetuses (see Winzer, 1990a).

## Developmental opportunity

While much development is the result of maturation, learning is also important. The opportunity to learn must be present if the child is to develop. Walking, for example, cannot occur on schedule unless the child is given an opportunity to practise the prerequisite skills. For most young children, practice is not a serious undertaking because it occurs in the context of play.

## Readiness

Ideas about readiness consistently occur in stage theories of development. Maturation and learning have been described as being "in a circular relationship, each feeding into the other" (Stone and Church, 1973, p. 162). In other words, maturation brings with it readiness for the appearance of new and more complex behaviour.

Gesell and his co-worker, Thompson, looked at the development of readiness through studying twins. One member of each pair of twins was provided with special training and practice in acquiring skills such as climbing stairs, while the other twin was left to develop naturally. The purpose of the study was to assess whether special instruction and opportunities for practice could speed up development. In most cases, it could not. The special intervention did not seem to have any effect until the time that the skill being taught could develop naturally. Once this point was reached, the twin lacking special help rapidly caught up with the other.

More recent studies indicate that early motor practice or stimulation can accelerate the appearance of motor behaviour, at least to some extent. The stepping reflex of newborns is one example. If you hold an infant in an upright position so that the feet touch a solid surface, the baby reacts with an automatic toe walking response, placing the foot down in a heel toe sequence. A group of infants who were given stepping practice for a few minutes several times a day during the first two months of life began walking five to seven weeks earlier than babies who had not had this practice (Zelazo, Zelazo, and Kolb, 1972).

The influence of the concept of readiness is apparent in our public schools. Children are assigned to grade levels according to chronological age on the assumption that children in the same age group possess the same level of skill. In addition, many assessment devices have been developed for the purpose of allowing teachers to assess a child's readiness to learn various skills.

## STAGES OF PHYSICAL DEVELOPMENT

Children's physical development interacts with all the other developmental domains. In physical development, the two major periods of growth and development occur prenatally and during puberty. The brain is crucial for the development of that intelligent behaviour that marks humans and the central nervous system (CNS) as a whole governs all bodily functions.

Physical development can be examined within fairly broad chronological ranges. These are shown in Table 2-1. Our discussion is cursory; we can highlight only the major points of development and stress those that are important in classrooom functioning.

Table 2-1  Major stages of physical development

| AGE | STAGE OF DEVELOPMENT |
| --- | --- |
| Prenatal | |
| 0-2 weeks | zygote |
| 2-8 weeks | embryo |
| 2-9 months | fetus |
| 0-1 month | neonate |
| 1-12 months | infant |
| 12-30 months | toddler |
| 30-60 months | preschooler |
| 5-11 years | school-age child |
| 11+ | adolescent |

Autosomal:
identical; refers to the first 22
pairs of chromosomes.

# Pre-natal development

Except to the parents, an infant doesn't have much reality before he or she is born. Yet life begins not at birth but at conception and those months are the most crucial in an individual's entire existence. Here the die is cast; the groundwork is laid for everything that follows.

The prenatal period encompasses three stages. The first two weeks are known as the period of the ovum or the zygote. Next, the period of the embryo lasts until the beginning of the third prenatal month. The remaining gestation time is known as the period of the fetus. The change of labels charts the organism's growth from a simple cell to a recognizable human creature.

The human body is made up of billions of cells. Almost every cell contains a complete package of hereditary instructions for the characteristics that comprise the individual. These instructions are located in 46 chromosomes, arranged in 23 pairs. The first twenty-two chromosomal pairs are **autosomal** (identical) and determine the thousands of traits that make up a human being, whether male or female. The twenty-third pair determines the sex of the individual.

When an egg is penetrated by a sperm (fertilization), the single fertilized cell, some time during the first 24 to 36 hours after conception, splits into two (mitosis). Mitosis continues so that within a few days there are several dozen cells, while the whole is still about the size of a pinhead. Within two weeks, the fertilized ovum, now called the zygote, still continuing to divide, has travelled down the Fallopian tube and nestled itself into the wall of the uterus. This is a critical period in gestation because if the fertilized egg (blastocyst) does not implant itself properly—at the right time and in the right place—the cell mass will die before it can reach the following stage of the embryo.

At this point, the blastocyst is still a hollow ball of cells. In the first clear differentiation of cells, one group of cells forms into a sphere and the other into tiny tendrils, the villi, that attach themselves to the wall of the uterus. Five months into gestation these will have developed into the placenta. When the tiny cell, or blastocyst, is implanted in the wall of the uterus, the period of the embryo begins. The time of the embryo is from this two week implantation mark until about eight weeks into gestation.

A series of membranes develop around the embryo. Growth is extremely swift with rapid cell divisions and much differentiation occurring among the developing cells. During the 46 day embryo stage, the embryo grows to a length of more than 2.5 cm. By the end of this stage, many body systems will be in operation and the embryo will begin to appear human.

The remaining seven months, the period of the fetus, involve primarily a proces of refining and improving what has already been developed. The fetus can open and close its mouth, swallow, and make certain head movements. It may even suck its thumb. The fastest growth period of the fetus is in the fourth month when it almost doubles in length, reaching about 15 cm from crown to rump. Limbs become sensitive to touch and a heartbeat can be heard with a stethoscope.

The main exception to this developmental pattern is the nervous system which is present in only a very rudimentary form at eight weeks. At that point only a very small part of the brain and only the suggestion of the spinal cord have developed. The major development of the brain and the nervous system

**Apgar score:**
score assigned to every newborn which provides general information about whether the infant's life-sustaining systems appear normal and what kinds of potential problems may be present.

does not occur until the last three months or so of pregnancy and continues after the child is born. Specifically, the brain grows most rapidly between twenty weeks after conception and two years after birth.

One of the most important aspects of prenatal development is the predictable and orderly patterns that occur. Growth during this period is controlled by the developmental code contained in the genes and the various changes take place in a fixed order and on a fixed schedule.

## The birth process

Birth takes place in three stages; labour, delivery, and afterbirth, also known as the dilation (opening), expulsion, and placental stages. Birth is a long process; an average first labour takes 14 hours; the average for later labours is eight hours. Too long or too short a labour produces a greater likelihood of problems for the infant.

In a normal birth, the head appears first. Once babies were held up by their feet and slapped to stimulate breathing. It is now more common practice to aspirate the mucus from the baby's mouth and nose by suction as soon as the head is delivered in order to give the baby a slight head-start on breathing. As soon as delivery is complete, the umbilical cord is clamped and cut and the baby is wrapped in a blanket. Every newborn is assigned an Apgar score, based an infant screening device developed by Dr. Virginia Apgar in 1953, which provides very general information about whether the infant's life-sustaining functions appear normal and what kinds of potential problems may be present. The baby is evaluated one, three, and five minutes after delivery in five areas of functioning—heart rate; respiratory effect; muscle tone; reflex irritability; and skin colour. Its responses are graded zero for absent, and one or two for normal, for an optimal score of ten. The majority of children score between five and ten and 90 percent have a score of seven or better (See Apgar and Beck, 1974).

## Infant development

Until quite recently, psychologists almost universally assumed that infants were rather uninteresting. The infant was seen as a reactor, rather than an actor, and a confused reactor at that. William James (1890) put the feeling in perspective when he suggested that, "The baby, assailed by eyes, ears, nose, skin, and entrails at once, feels that all is one blooming, buzzing confusion" (p. 488). The suspicion that infants might be able to learn from their early experiences hardly ever arose. Many doctors and nurses believed that newborns were blind at birth, could not discriminate sounds, and did not feel pain (Lipsitt, 1990). Parents tended to agree.

However, it is now clear that the newborn is a perceptually and socially competent organism. The most basic ideas about the human infant, and particularly the human neonate, have changed drastically in the past half century. Newborn babies are far more able to sense significant features in their environment and to learn from their experiential inputs than was realized a mere two or three decades ago (Werner and Lipsitt, 1981). It appears that newborns differ not only in their sensitivity to auditory, visual, and tactile stimulation, but in how easily

**Habituate:**

to become familiar with a stimulus and show a decreasing reaction to it.

**Motor skill:**

a smoothly integrated series of movements undertaken for a specific purpose.

**Prehension:**

the ability to reach for and grasp objects.

they are upset, in how readily they are calmed, and in their capacity to buffer stress (Birns, Blank, and Bridges, 1966).

### Neonatal development: birth to one month

Even though parents may not agree, their new baby is often not beautiful. In babies born by natural childbirth, the skin is often red and wrinkled. The head, which may be bluish and puffy from the passage of childbirth, is one-third to one-quarter of the total body length, as opposed to one-eighth for adults, and makes the neonate appear top heavy and awkward. The torso is small in comparison to the head, and the limbs even more so.

Recent investigations show that babies are capable of tasting and responding differently to fluids made available to them; they can detect their own mother's odour by five or six days of age (Lipsitt, 1990). Tiny babies also begin to habituate. This occurs when the baby becomes familiar with a stimulus and shows a decreasing reaction to it. Habituation is felt to be one of the best signs of learning in the neonate.

Over the first few months of life, the child's visual acuity improves greatly. Totally adult visual acuity isn't reached until about eight years of age, but the infant possesses vision that is perfectly adequate for any normal needs. Auditory acuity appears to improve steadily until adolescence.

### Infant development: three to 12 months

By the third month of life, the infant becomes less incessantly demanding and also more reliably rewarding. Smiling is a central feature of the changes in an infant's social behaviour (Gibson, 1978). (See Chapter 4).

The bones are soft in the neonate. Skull bones, for example, are soft and connected only by fibrous tissues. The skull contains six soft spots or openings called fontanelles where the bones have not yet grown together (Gibson, 1978). As bones harden, the flexible skeleton is transformed into a sturdy frame. Bones harden at different rates; those of the hand and wrist harden first, which then increases the baby's ability to reach and grasp. Infants are probably born with all the muscle fibres they will ever have. Muscle growth results from increases in the length and thickness of those fibres. As the baby grows, muscles increase not only in size but also in the precision and control with which they can be used.

Motor learning involves using the body in such ways as to make the best use of what is perceived (Gibson, 1978). A motor skill is a smoothly integrated series of movements undertaken for a specific purpose. During the first six months of life, the infant gains voluntary muscle control rapidly and begins to examine objects, people and events that occur close at hand. Prehension—the ability to reach for and grasp objects—improves. Infants are able to grasp voluntarily at two months but cannot accurately control their reach. Increasing arm control enables infants to hit, then reach for, and finally grasp objects. Most objects are brought to the mouth, a very sensitive and highly developed area, for tactile examination and identification.

Increased motor abilities enable the infant to sit, thus freeing the hands for object appraisal. Vision has been a strong modality since the earliest days, for

Smiling is a central feature of the changes in an infant's behaviour.

the baby is born with greater control over the eyes than over other parts of the body (Bee, 1978). Now, however, vision and reach become coordinated and the infant is able to reach and grasp. Social behaviours also increase as the infant gains the ability to recognize and respond to familiar faces and situations.

The second six months of life are filled with new methods of locomotion and new abilities. The downward progression of motor skills continues and the infant learns to sit unaided, to creep back and forward, to crawl, and finally to walk. During the seventh month, the infant sits, creeps, and begins to experiment with standing. Within a month, standing has improved greatly but descent to the floor still needs additional practice. By ten months the infant is able to push to a stand from a crawl and return to sitting on the floor. In the meantime, crawling speed and style improve. Two months later, the infant may walk unsupported for a few steps but still crawl when in a hurry. While walking, the infant extends the arms for balance and stops by falling or grabbing nearby furniture or people (Bee, 1978; Salkind, 1990). However, these milestones offer children increased opportunities to make better use of sensory experience, to gain greater perceptual awareness, and to learn to manipulate objects and self.

## Toddlers: 12 to 30 months

Most children take their first steps alone at about twelve months and walk soon after that. Infants, then, begin the second year of life with a new, albeit shaky, method of locomotion. Much of the second year is spent practising and perfecting walking skills. The new mobility and increasing motor control over fine motor abilities give toddlers new freedom to explore. They get into everything (Owens, 1988).

The child changes from a dependent infant to a more independent toddler. There is a deceleration in bodily growth rate, both in height and weight. Brain growth also decelerates and head size increases only slightly. The processes of bone ossification and calcification are well underway during the toddler stage. The spine is slowly beginning to harden and to take on the S shape that is characteristic of adult humans. The number of bones in the body actually changes. Several smaller bones fuse together to form larger units while elsewhere new bones are being formed from what was originally cartilage, as in the wrists and ankles. The open spaces of the cranium, the fontanelles, are closing as bone growth catches up with the rapid enlargement of the brain that occurred during infancy.

The second of many milestones in motor development is lifting the chin and chest.

Table 2-2 Milestones in motor development

| MONTH | ACCOMPLISHMENTS |
|---|---|
| 1 | Lifts chin while lying on stomach |
| 2 | Lifts chin and chest |
| 4 | Rolls with difficulty<br>Can sit with pillows propped on three sides |
| 6 | Rolls over easily |
| 7 | Picks up objects (no finger-thumb opposition) |
| 8 | Crawls<br>Tries to stand holding on to furniture |
| 9 | Stands independently |
| 12 | Takes a few steps alone |
| 14 | Grasps with finger-thumb opposition |
| 18 | Grasp, prehension and release fully developed<br>Gait still stiff<br>Creeps downstairs backwards |
| 21 | Clumsily throws a ball |
| 24 | Better coordination<br>Runs well<br>Walks up and down stairs |
| 30 | Walks on tiptoe<br>Moves digits independently<br>Can build a tower of six cubes |
| 36 | Rides tricycle<br>Can jump twelve inches |
| 48 | Walks down stairs one foot at a time<br>Throws ball overhand |
| 60 | Hops on one foot |

## Preschoolers: 30 to 60 months

Although the rapid growth spurt of infancy is complete and growth is more steady and even, children's body proportions change dramatically in the pre-school years. The trunk and legs grow rapidly but cranial growth is not as fast as before. At age three the average boy is a little over 90 cm tall and weighs over 13 1/2 kg. By age five he has grown to about 110 cm and weighs about 19.3 kg. Girls tend to be slightly shorter and lighter than boys (Salkind, 1990).

Muscular development accounts for most of the weight gained during the preschool years by both boys and girls. Other physiological changes occur: breathing becomes slower and deeper; the heart beats more slowly and steadily and, especially in boys, blood pressure increases.

Preschool children are very mobile and curious about the world. The motor behaviour of three year olds shows an increased control over their bodies. At age four most children can jump forward as well as straight up and down. They probably cannot yet throw a ball with much strength but they can swing their arms freely without exaggerated movements of the torso. By the time they five or six, children are capable of increasingly complex feats such as skipping, climbing, balancing, and throwing. Their skills are recognized by other children and games begin to involve rivalry and competition (Salkind, 1990).

As children discover they can lift and manipulate objects that defeated them earlier, their new muscular ability contributes to a growing sense of self-confidence. There seems to be little difference in the strength of boys and girls until around six years and the lead that boys take from then on does not become pronounced until adolescence (Salkind, 1990).

Fine motor abilities continue to develop slowly. Three year olds can generally dress themselves, except for shoe tying. They can use a knife for spreading but not cutting. They continue to be interested in fine motor manipulation and explore by dismantling or dismembering household objects or favourite toys (Owens, 1988). However, the small muscles do not reach maturity until adolescence.

## School-age children: 5 to 11 years

Over the past fifty to one hundred years, the rates of growth and health during childhod have increased in all developed countries. This results from a variety of factors—better nutrition, more protein in the diet, better prenatal care, greater parental knowledge about rearing and nutrition, childhood innoculations, and the elimination of many childhood diseases such as scarlet fever.

Wide size differences are not particularly prevalent in school-age children; the rate of growth in the elementary years is not as spectacular as that seen in infancy or adolescence. Children grow fairly evenly during middle childhood, although some children do experience a growth spurt between the ages of six and eight years. As children grow, they assume more adult-like proportions. Their trunks tend to be slimmer, their chests broader, and their arms and legs longer. They attain an adult look—the pot belly of the younger child disappears and the head is in better proportion.

Girls' physical growth is steadier and more predictable than boys'. However, girls and boys do not differ markedly in physical strength and endurance until adolescence. Throughout elementary school, many of the girls are likely to be as large or larger than the boys in their classes. Between the ages of eleven and fourteen girls are, on the average, taller and heavier than boys of the same age (Tanner, 1970). After that, boys experience a sharp increase in physical strength as a result of major changes in musculature.

During the school years, physical and motor development continue to play major roles, both in academic learning and social activities. After the age of six or seven, children gain few completely new basic skills; rather the quality and complexity of their movement improves (Malina, 1982). School-age children gain greater coordination of fine and gross muscle movements. Children's physical coordination also allows them to perform more motor acts at one time and therefore to enjoy sports and coordinated games. As children develop a general sense of physical mastery, they hone skills in such activities as swimming, riding, skating, basketball, soccer, and so on. At the same time, better fine motor abilities and eye-to-hand coordination enable children to engage in hobbies and crafts.

Even though growth is more even and steady, all children will be different—tall, short, thin, plump, dark, fair, and so on. Genes determine these characteristics and they are relatively unamenable to change. Some children will also undountedly be more physically attractive than others. Physical attractiveness is a potent force in children's social lives and in the way that others, including teachers, perceive them. This aspect is detailed in Box 2-6.

## Box 2-6 **In the classroom: Physical attractiveness**

A body of research data demonstrates that physical attractiveness can be a potent force in the development of children and adolescents. For children themselves, a perception of attractiveness is important. In our society, physical appearance seems to be particularly important in adolescence, no doubt partly because of the changes that occur in the body are signs of physical maturity and of reaching adult status (Bee, 1978).

Just as importantly, perceptions and expectations about children are often founded on physical attributes. In fact, the data on stereotypes and behavioural expectations associated with facial attractiveness provide one of the most consistent and pervasive findings in social-developmental psychology (Langlois et al., 1987).

Both adults and children prefer attractive over unattractive individuals. They attribute positive qualities and abilities to attractive individuals and negative qualities and abilities to unattractive ones. Among school children, for example, attractive children are more often chosen for activities reflecting acceptance (Gronlund, 1959; Salvia, Sheare and Algozzine, 1975).

There is also growing research evidence to suggest that the way children look influences teachers' attitudes toward them. Teachers make more favourable judgments about attractive students (Clifford and Walster, 1973). Berscheid and Walster (1972) concluded that teachers are prone to regard attractive students as brighter, more interesting, more responsive, more poised, and more honest than their unattractive peers.

Clifford and Walster (1973) sent comprehensive report cards of high-achieving fifth-grade students to more than 400 fifth-grade teachers. Each report card was accompanied either by a photograph of an attractive boy, an attractive girl, an unattractive boy, or an unattractive girl. Teachers were asked to judge the children's IQs and peer relationships. They were also asked to speculate on the parents' attitude toward school, and to predict how far the students would go in school. The attractive students received the most favourable responses to all four questions.

In another study (Algozzine, 1977b), teachers of grades four and five in one school were observed with eighty boys and girls and their interactions classified as positive, negative or neutral. After the observations were made, the teachers classified the students in several ways, including most and least attractive. Attractive boys and girls were involved in more positive interactions than the unattractive children. Unattractive girls received more negative interactions, but this was not true for boys.

## Adolescence

Adolescence may be a biological state, but the idea of an adolescent society or youth culture was late to emerge. The period of adolescence was not recognized as a stage of human development until quite recently. G. Stanley Hall, the chief architect of the concept of adolescence, published an extensive work on the topic in 1905. Hall described the period of adolescence as a time of storm and stress. Sigmund Freud assumed a similar stance when he observed that, "To be normal during the adolescent period is by itself abnormal" (1958, p. 275). Youth were perceived as troubled and potentially troublesome. Their nature required their separation from the stable, orderly, responsible world of adults. In fact, Hall (1905) and Key (1909) saw removal of adolescents from the adult world as the "crowning achievement of an enlightened civilization."

Hall and other researchers viewed the study of adolescence as essentially a study of change. Adolescents were seen to exhibit impulsive and unpredictable behaviour. It was understood that for some, sudden emotional energy led them into socially unacceptable areas; others fantasized and daydreamed to excess; and still others demonstrated increased interest in sexual activity, erotic fantasy, and experimentation.

There is no question that adolescence is a time of vast physical and physiological changes; with their physical transformations, adolescent youth often experience dramatic shifts in school environment, their peer group, and family orientation. However, recent research somewhat discredits the notion that social and emotional difficulties are a universal characteristic of adolescents. In fact, serious family conflicts are not characteristic for most adolescents in North America (Hill, 1987). Nonetheless, conflicts certainly do occur over such mundane issues as family chores, curfews, eating practices, dating, and personal appearance (Powers, Hauser, and Kilmer, 1989).

Recent research somewhat discredits the notion that social and emotional difficulties are a universal characteristic of adolescents.

**Adolescence:**

period from the onset of puberty to the beginning of adulthood.

**Puberty:**

period when an individual reaches sexual maturity.

**Puberty**

Some people confuse the terms adolescence and puberty. Adolescence can be roughly defined as the period from the onset of puberty to the beginning of adulthood. Puberty is the shorter period confined within adolescence during which an individual reaches sexual maturity. Puberty takes from two to four years and is marked by great physical and psychological changes. Children's bodies become capable of functioning sexually and attitudes and behaviours become more mature (Salkind, 1990).

Puberty is not a single event but a series of changes involving almost evert part of the body. The final outcome of all these changes is the ability to reproduce. Puberty can be divided into three stages:

1. Prepubescent state: the secondary sex characteristics begin to develop but the reproductive organs do not yet function.

2. Pubescent stage: the secondary sex characteristics continue to develop and the reproductive organs become capable of producing ova and sperm.

3. Postpubescent stage: the secondary sex characteristics are well developed and the sex organs are capable of adult functioning.

During prepubescence (the year or two prior to maturation of the sex organs) there is increased secretion of hormones by the endocrine glands. The pituitary gland begins increasing its production of growth hormones, producing a period of rapid growth that is quite noticeable for a year or two and continues at a reduced pace therafter for several more years (Tanner, 1970; Faust, 1977; Stolz and Stolz, 1951). The thyroid gland aids in the process by releasing large amounts of the hormones that permit the conversion of foods into tissue and energy. The gonads (the ovaries in the female and the testes in the male) are stimulated by hormonal secretions from the adrenal and pituitary glands.

While the pituitary gland is secreting increased amounts of growth hormones, the gonads are beginning to secrete hormones that stimulate the development of the sex organs. The result is growth of the primary sex characteristics and the development of the secondary characteristics.

This hormonal activity may influence not only growth but also, either directly or indirectly, behaviour. With few exceptions (sexual and aggressive behaviour) hormones are thought to influence behaviour indirectly, via excitability, arousal, or emotionality, which in turn may influence how individuals behave (Brooks-Gunn and Warren, 1989). It is not surprising then, that hormonal factors have been long thought to account for the rise in negative emotions of adolescence (Beach, 1975; Tieger, 1980).

Growth of the primary sex characteristics occurs externally, and thus visibly, in males, but internally in females. At birth the male testes are only about ten percent of their mature size. They grow rapidly during the first year or two of puberty, then grow more slowly, not reaching mature size until the age of twenty or twenty-one. The penis also grows during puberty, first in length and then in circumference (Ford and Beach, 1951).

Puberty in boys can occur from ten to 18 years, with an average age of 14. The onset of puberty in males is usually measured by the first appearance of sperm in the urine. At this time pubic hair begins to develop at the base of the penis and the larynx enlarges. Most boys reach a stage at about age 14 when the prostate glands produce fluid ejaculate during orgasm. Mature sperm are present about a year later. The development of primary sex characteristics is soon accompanied by secondary sex characteristics which include growth of facial and body hair, change to a lower voice pitch, and general changes in body contour that occur as the child gradually takes on the adult male form.

Perhaps the most noticeable change in boys is the deepening of the voice. Usually by the time a boy is 13, his voice has become husky. Only later, when he is about 16 or 17, does his voice begin to "crack." This may last for a year or two, until the voice change is complete. The voice change occurs because the male hormones cause the larnyx to enlarge and the vocal cords to lengthen. Later in adolescence, the male voice drops an octave or more in pitch, increases in volume, and develops a more even tonal quality (Salkind, 1990).

For the typical girl, the adolescent growth spurt begins with breast development between the ages of ten and 11 and continues for about three years (Dusek, 1987). While this is the average time frame for girls, the actual range of onset is from nine to 16 years. There is a growth spurt of the ovaries followed shortly by menarche, or the onset of menses, which is often considered to be the beginning of puberty in girls. Young female adolescents, in the first few months after menarche, are not capable of complex functions of reproduction. They cannot yet conceive or nurture a child. Within a short period of time, however, more complex functions occur. Once menarche accurs, the growth rate slows. About 12 to 18 months after the first menstrual period begins, ovulation takes place (Hafez, 1973). However, following menarche, menstruation may come at irregular intervals. For six months to one year, ovulation may not always occur.

Healthy, well-nourished children mature earlier than less advantaged children, urban children earlier than rural children, and children living in temperate climates earlier than those living in tropic or arctic zones (Tanner, 1970). For some time, researchers have noted that youngsters in countries with high standards of living, such as Canada and the United States, have been reaching puberty at progressively younger ages. Biological changes in humans in the past two centuries, made possible by the control of infectious diseases, better nutrition (Hamburg and Takanishi, 1989), and increased protein in the diet, particularly in developed countries, has lowered the average age of menarche. In recent years, however, the trend toward earlier puberty has tended to slow (Winter, Faiman, and Reyes, 1978). The average age at which females experienced menarche was 17 a century ago. Today in America it is 12.5 years with a range from 9.8 to 15.8 years (Eveleth, 1986). However, in Czechoslovakia the median age is 14.2 years (Whiting, Burbank, and Ratner, 1986). It is 15.9 years among the Kikuyu of Kenya (Worthman, 1986) and 18 years among the Bindi of New Guinea (Eveleth, 1986).

Adolescents grow in both height and weight, with increases in height occurring first. As they gain weight, the amount and distribution of fat in their bodies changes and the proportion of bone and muscle tissue increases as well. By the age of 11, boys have attained most of their mature height. During puberty, the final 20 to 25 percent of increase in height is achieved, as is the final 50 percent increase in weight (Barnes, 1975).

Generally, girls begin puberty about two years ahead of boys and reach their final height by age 16; most boys continue growing until about age 18. Typically, boys are more variable than girls when it comes to the physical changes of adolescence. The length of time that is required for all the changes of puberty to occur varies more with boys, and the range of differences in height and weight at the end of puberty is greater for boys than for girls (Rogers, 1985).

At about age 14, males tend to develop greater muscular strength than females, with particularly strong increases in their hands and forearms. This increase is due to major physical changes. Males develop larger hearts and lungs than females relative to body size, higher systolic blood pressure, lower resting heart rate, a greater capacity for carrying oxygen in the blood, and a greater capacity for neutralizing chemical products of muscular exercise (Malmquist, 1978).

The age at which an individual reaches puberty (full sexual maturity) provides another example illustrating the complex relationship between physical and psychosocial development. Pubertal age varies from individual to individual. Its timing appears to be related to the personality of the adolescent (Jones and Mussen, 1958; Mussen and Jones, 1957); indeed, some of the personality correlates of the timing of puberty are still evident in adult samples (Newcombe, Dubos, and Baenninger, 1989).

A sizable literature exists on the personality correlates of early and late maturers. (Some of the possible problems were illustrated in the vignettes of Brett and Randy that appeared earlier in this chapter.) Peskin (1967) demonstrated that early maturers experience more anxiety, more temper tantrums, more conflict with their parents, and lower self-esteem at puberty than do late maturers. This passes rapidly. Early maturing males seem to develop confidence earlier than late maturers, who are far more likely to feel inadequate. Among males, early maturers are more popular and better socialized. They are more likely to be class leaders and leaders in student government and extra-curricular activities. They are looked up to by other teenagers, and appear to develop generally positive images about themselves. Early maturing boys are heavier, taller and more muscular than their age mates and they tend to excel at sports. Earlier maturing boys also tend to be more interested in girls and gain the advantages of acquiring social graces early. As adults, early maturers are likely to be more sociable and less neurotic, more likely to be successful socially and vocationally, and more conventional in career and life-style choices (Salkind, 1990).

On the other hand, later maturers are often more anxious about their bodies, their slow development, and their acceptance by the group. They may find it difficult to get attention because of their underdeveloped physical prowess so they try to attract attention in other ways—they may be talkative, bossy, and physically restless (Bee, 1978). There may be some compensations for late maturity, however. Late maturers may turn out to be more personally flexible (Jones, 1957; Mussen and Jones, 1957). Some studies show that in adulthood those males who matured early are less flexible and less creative in their thinking, whereas those who matured later tend to be more creative, tolerant and perceptive (Woolfolk, 1990).

The problems of late maturing seem to be greater for boys than for girls. In fact, among girls very early maturity is not highly valued. In sixth grade, for example, social status is determined by other means. Early maturing girls find that few other girls and almost no boys are as tall and well developed as they are. Friends may avoid them simply because they are bigger. Early maturing girls seem to elicit more freedom from parents, are likely to have older friends (Brooks-Gunn and Furstenberg, 1989), and tend to date older boys until their peers catch up with them (Salkind, 1990).

Among females, late maturers have greater interest in achievement and may date later (Jones and Mussen, 1958; Presser, 1978). Thus, in several respects, late maturers of both sexes can be considered less traditionally sex-typed than early maturers.

There have also been suggestions that puberty and pubertal timing are related to cognitive ability. Tanner (1962) believed that early maturers performed better than late maturers on IQ tests. A recent meta-analysis confirmed the existence of a reliable, although small, IQ advantage for early maturers. It was less clear whether this difference is an enduring one, or whether it is due to a spurt in cognitive ability, analogous to the spurt of physical growth at puberty (Newcombe, Dubos, and Baenninger, 1989).

As we have stressed, the physical changes of adolescence can have significant changes on an individual's identity, particularly in the case of early and late maturers. Sexually mature adolescents are physically and hormonally equipped for sexual relationships. The problem is that physiological and psychological development occur at different paces. What may result is a psychologically immature but sexually mature adolescent or a psychologically mature but sexually immature young person. One manifestation of this is illustrated in Box 2-7.

## Box 2-7 **Teenage pregnancies**

Teenage pregnancy becomes an important social issue for several reasons. Rates are on the rise in Canada and many teens who opt to keep and rear their babies almost inevitably become part of the poverty cycle with little education, no job, and few prospects. Another very important reason is that babies of teenage mothers have twice the normal chance of being born prematurely or with low birth weight, neurological defects, or birth injuries (Harris, 1986).

Mothers between the ages of 23 and 29 have the largest proportion of healthy, normal children (Montagu, 1977). While the precise causal links between early childbearing and the well-being of the child have not been clearly delin-

eated, younger mothers, between 17 and 23, run a greater risk of bearing premature or still-born children, or children who have not developed properly (Montagu, 1977).

Generally speaking, the younger a girl is when she conceives, the greater is the risk to herself and the infant (Petersen and Boxer, 1982). Fourteen percent of pregnant adolescents miscarry as compared to two percent of the general population (Conger, 1975).

Children who are born to teenage mothers are generally at a disadvantage compared to children born to older mothers. Small but consistent differences in cognitive functioning between the offspring of early and late childbearers appear in pre-school and continue into elementary school (Maracek, 1979, 1985). In one study (Thompson, Cappleman, and Zeitschel, 1979) the Brazelton Neonatal Assessment Scale was given to 30 infants of adolescent mothers and 30 infants of older mothers when the infants were two to five days old. The children of adolescent mothers were found to be less alert and less likely to respond to normal stimuli.

There is also an increased likelihood of complications for the mother. Apart from prematurity and miscarriage, these include eclampsia, prolonged labour, and a higher rate of Cesearean sections.

Most teens do not deliberately plan to become pregnant. For most young women it is an accident, a result of poor planning, early experimentation, or even rebellion against some parental rules. When Jessor and Jessor (1977) surveyed young people about premarital sex, they found that 60 percent of their female respondents mentioned fear of pregnancy as a reason for abstention. Sixty percent also mentioned fear of parental disapproval and 55 percent mentioned fear of damaging their reputation. It does seem, however, that teens who rate perceived communication with their parents as poor are more likely to begin smoking and drinking earlier and more likely to initiate sex early (Jessor and Jessor, 1977), thus placing themselves at greater risk for an unwanted or unplanned pregnancy.

Few teenagers use proper contraception. Less than half of all adolescents use any form of contraception during their first intercourse,

although the older the adolescent becomes, the more likely they are to use some method of birth control (Kanter and Zelnik, 1972, 1973; Zelnik and Kanter, 1977, 1978).

Teenage girls who become pregnant are not usually promiscious; their sexual activity is usually limited to one partner (Chilman, 1980). A teen's response to an unplanned pregnancy is influenced by a myriad of conditions, such as her scholastic ambitions, relationship with the father of the baby, perceived family support for keeping the child, and how many of her peers have become parents (see Furstenberg, Brooks-Gunn, and Chase-Lansdale, 1989).

While some girls decide to keep and rear the child, abortion is the option of others. Furstenberg, Brooks-Gunn, and Chase-Lansdale (1989) report that teens who decide to abort are more educationally ambitious and more likely to be good students. They are more likely to be from higher socioeconomic backgrounds, more likely to be from less religious families, more likely to have mothers or peers who hold more positive attitudes to abortion, and are less likely to have friends who are teenaged single parents.

For the girl who decides to keep the child, a host of present and future problems ensue. The girl must face the difficulties of pregnancy along with the challenges of adolescence and try to meet two sets of needs—her own and the child's. She may become alientated from the family and may enter into an unsatisfactory marriage. Financial strain is a common accompaniment.

## THE QUESTION OF GENDER

Theorists who take an essentially environmental position in explaining observed sex differences stress that males and females have different experiences and different reinforcement patterns, and that these differences account for the variation in behaviour between the sexes. Others have argued that there may be hormonal or other biological differences as well and that these initial differences form the base on which later experiences are built.

There is little question that males and females have different social experiences and expectations, even in an era when the equality of the sexes is heralded as public policy. It is much less clear whether any perceived differences in intelligence and learning are a result of biological or environmental attributes. However, when physical development is examined, there are, of course, large and obvious anatomical and physiological differences between males and females. Some of the most important of these are:

1. At birth girls are physically more mature than boys. Girl babies are, on average, smaller and lighter than are newborn boys, but they are a month or six weeks ahead in overall bodily development. Myelinization of the nerve sheaths is further advanced in girls than boys at birth (Bee, 1978). Then, as Tanner (1970) points out, "Girls grow up faster than boys: that is, they reach 50% of their adult height at an earlier age (on average 1.75 years as compared to 2 years in boys), enter puberty earlier and cease to grow earlier" (p. 58). This last growth spurt may be another example of the faster maturational process in girls.

2. From birth on, a large proportion of a boy's body weight is devoted to muscle tissue. In a girl's body, the muscle tissue is more fully developed, but it represents a smaller amount of total weight. Male muscle tissue also develops more rapidly. Also from birth, girls have a thicker layer of fat directly below the skin.

3. Girls show greater sensitivity to some kinds of stimulation, particularly touch and pain stimuli; this difference is observable as early as the first day of life (Bee, 1978).

4. Unlike many of the elusive differences said to exist between the sexes, male vulnerability is particularly well established. Males tend to be physically more vulnerable than females and this differential vulnerability is particularly pronounced at the beginning and at the end of the life span.

Girls are less vulnerable to virtually all varieties of physical stress both pre- and post-natally. While many more males than females are conceived (approximatelty 105:100), many more males than females die before birth (McMilen, 1979). More males than females suffer difficulties during the birth process, resulting in more males with birth defects. Even the birth of males takes longer—on average an hour longer than the births of females (Jacklin and Maccoby, 1982). Among children, handicapping conditions are almost always more prevalent in boys than girls. This has been true ever since records were kept (Winzer, 1990b). There is a higher proportion of boys who suffer from, for example, deafness, blindness, mental retardation, cleft palates, stuttering, and learning disabilities (Winzer, 1990a).

The reasons for this are not well established. The apparent greater incidence of all types of learning problems in males suggests that cerebral specialization in males is associated with some hazard, whereas there may be some advantage to the more symmetrical organization of female brain function (Kolb and Whishaw, 1980).

One controversial rationale was forwarded by Gualtieri and Hicks (1985). They hypothesize an immunoreactive theory of selective male affliction and suggested that there is "something about the male fetus that evokes an inhospitable intrauterine environment" (p. 427). They believe that the mother's body is stimulated to produce a kind of antibody against a male fetus but not against the female who is genetically more compatible with her.

## SUMMARY

1. Much of what we know about children we learn through the study of child development which might be seen as a series of patterned and predictable changes that foster the child's ability to cope with and master the external environment.

2. Developmental psychologists believe that the best way to understand why students are the way they are, why they behave the way they do, and why they learn in certain ways, is to examine their actions in the context of the developmental stages through which they are passing at a particular time.

3. Many models and theories exist in the area of child development and educational psychology. Psychological theorists are committed to a careful and comprehensive analysis of what it means to be human. But the theories and models of development can differ both superficially and substantively, as may be witnessed in the nature/nurture controversy. Similarly, some theorists may stress continuity of development while others look at development across ages and stages.

4. No one model holds the key to child development. They differ from one another according to what they determine the most important aspects of development to be. In the area of physical development, models are not as prominent as they tend to be in other areas of development, such as language and cognition.

5. Interest in the behaviour of young infants and in the study of their development began to flourish at the turn of the twentieth century. Arnold Gesell provoked a great deal of descriptive-normative research from the 1920s on, and much of today's knowledge of the development of early motor skills comes from research spurred by Gesellian theory. As well, the development stages proposed by Gesell in the 1930s remain a touchstone for any citation of physical, motor, and perceptual milestones.

6. In the past, human development was assumed to follow a smooth progression from infancy to adulthood. Recent explorations of behaviour have led psychologists to make generalizations about the sorts of behaviour that can be expected from children at various ages. Gesell and others proposed stage theories that emphasized development as a series of building blocks. Discontinuous or stage theories of development usually include the concepts of maturation and readiness.

7. Psychologists interested in development usually look at three aspects—the order in which changes occur, the speed of the changes, and the shape or

appearance of the child at any one time. In physical development, children progress through certain steps in a sequence that is patterned, orderly and invariant. Several hierarchies appear—cephalocaudal, proximodistal, and gross to fine motor development.

**8.** Life begins not at birth, but at conception. During the prenatal period, major organs and basic tissues take shape and develop into their finished forms; after this stage, it is difficult to affect their growth in any fundamental way.

**9.** Human beings grow most rapidly at two times during their lives: before they are six months old and then again during adolescence. Tremendous growth in the early years tapers off to more gradual development during the preschool period. Physical development during the school years consists of simple growth and progress toward higher levels of organization and coordination of existing body parts. The next period of rapid growth, the adolescent growth spurt, takes from two to three years. In this period, the changes in physiology, glands, and psychological systems are some of the most profound that a human undergoes. Not since infancy has growth been so rapid and not since prenatal development have so many biological changes occurred. In adolescence, a restless transition is common, marked by temporary increases in conflict. Although many adolescents pass through this period in relative calm, others are dominated by social and emotional difficulties.

**10.** There may be different expectations in school and at home in fast and slow developing children. This seems to be most true in adolescence when early developers attain sexual maturity earlier.

## Key Terms

| | | |
|---|---|---|
| adolescence | Apgar score | autosomal |
| cephalocaudal principle | child development | critical period |
| development | developmental delays | developmental milestone |
| developmental psychology | developmental stage | differentiation |
| growth | habituate | maturation |
| maturational lags | motor skills | physical development |
| prehension | proximodistal principle | puberty |

# COGNITIVE DEVELOPMENT

**Cognitive development:**
the thinking processes and how
children understand and learn
about the world in which they
live.

## INTRODUCTION

The ability to entertain complex thoughts, communicate them to others, and reformulate them in light of new information is one of the greatest human accomplishments. The process, called cognition, essentially involves learning and knowing. **Cognitive development** refers to the thinking processes and how children understand and learn about the world in which they live. Cognition includes perception, reasoning, reflection, problem solving, and all verbal behaviour (Kagan and Kagan, 1970), as well as memory, creativity, and the capacity for both logical and abstract thought.

The study of cognitive development in children is fairly new, at least in the orientation that children interact with the environment as they develop cognitively and pass through specific and identifiable stages as they do so. Looking at cognitive development in this way began in North America only during the 1960s. Before that time, the view that behaviour was learned from the environment—from stimuli and reinforcement—generally held sway. This behaviourist stance is fully discussed in Chapter 8.

The notion that cognition develops in an invariant sequence of stages came along as part of what is sometimes called the cognitive revolution. To a large extent, this so-called revolution was a reaction against the strict view of behaviourism that saw humans merely as pawns of the environment. Much of the change in ideas about how children learn was stimulated by the work of the Swiss theorist, Jean Piaget. Kagan (1980) observed that Piaget's theory "relieved the child from the chains of reward and punishment, made the child active rather than passive in dealing with experience, and assumed that intellectual growth consisted of a connected series of structures from birth to adulthood" (p. 245).

Within the context of modern psychology, studies on the development of children's thinking have traditionally encompassed three quite separate bodies of research and theoretical tradition, which do not mix very comfortably (Bee, 1978). First, there is the whole testing movement. During the past hundred years extensive efforts have been made to devise and perfect measures to assess individual differences in intellectual skills (see Chapter 6). Second, the learning theorists, their students, and their followers who worked with children emphasized that the processes of learning were the same regardless of the age of the child or the particular task learned. Intellectual development in children was considered to be essentially a growth process; children's minds were thought to be the same as those of adults, albeit smaller, and they were thought to expand gradually as knowledge and experience accumulated.

Child psychologists trained in this school of thought have studied the whole gamut of developmental problems (personality, socialization, language, perception, and so on) to try to demonstrate a fundamental set of laws of learning that could account for the child's acquisition of skills and traits in all areas of development. The heaviest emphasis in learning research, however, has been on a set of problems that would ordinarily be considered to be related to the problem of the development of thinking (Bee, 1978).

The third tradition in the study of children's cognitive development is Jean Piaget's work that has focused most precisely on the question of children's changing strategies and logic. Piaget's cognitive development stages were the major intellectual force that generated the cognitive revolution (Sigel, 1981).

To study cognition we need to look at how it is measured, how it develops, and the underlying processes—attention, memory, elaboration, rehearsal, forgetting, and retrieval. Since about 1960 Piaget's theories have exerted a major theoretical influence on developmental psychology in North America (Bee, 1978). His views have been blended with other theories and have been extended, elaborated upon, and modified. What has evolved is a series of basic theoretical understandings about the development of thinking in which most (though certainly not all) current researchers agree. We do the same in this chapter as we examine the development of cognition in children. Although we use Piagetian principles as the base, a number of other ideas and stances on cognitive development are included.

Understanding the values of society and regulating behaviour accordingly are important aspects of development. Children's ability to make moral judgments is related to their levels of cognitive development. Piaget was one of the first to examine how children develop morally. His work was expanded and elaborated on by Lawrence Kohlberg who proposed discrete stages of moral development analogous to the development of cognition.

In this sense, Kohlberg is the natural successor of Piaget. Keep in mind, however, that the whole issue of morality and values education is of acute interest to psychologists, especially those who are part of the humanist school (see Chapter 11). Abraham Maslow, Carl Rogers, and many others who we will encounter later in this text also wrote explicitly on values and values education.

## JEAN PIAGET

Piaget devoted a sixty-year research career to observing changes in the ways that children solve different kinds of problems. In his lifetime, Piaget produced a staggering number of books and articles in his field. Some details about Piaget and his work are presented in Box 3-1.

## Box 3-1 **Biographical note: Jean Piaget (1896–1981)**

Jean Piaget was born in the small university town of Neuchâtel in Switzerland. His father was a professor of history who specialized in medieval literature and no doubt fostered this alert and curious child's rare intellectual precocity.

Young Piaget developed an early interest in nature and, at the age of ten, wrote an article describing an albino sparrow he had observed, which was published in a natural history magazine. His early interest in nature led to work in the natural history museum in his home town. He began to study mollusks and published a series of articles on shellfish. This led to the offer of a post as curator of the mollusk collection of the natural history musuem in Geneva which Piaget, then 15, declined in order to complete his education.

In 1916, Piaget completed his undergraduate degree in natural science; two years later, at the age of twenty-one, he completed his doctorate with a dissertation on mollusks. He then decided to study psychology and worked for a short time in several clinics in Zurich. In 1919 he entered the Sorbonne in Paris to study psychology and philosophy. Pursuing this interest, he accepted a position, in 1920, at the Binet laboratory in Paris working with Theophile Simon, one of the developers of the Binet-Simon intelligence test. Piaget was assigned the task of developing a standardized reasoning test for children. To accomplish this, he had to administer hundreds of IQ tests to children of different ages in order to establish age norms at which children could be expected to pass or fail each item.

The test instructions allowed children credit only if their answers were correct. But while studying the children's responses, Piaget became more interested in certain patterns in their incorrect answers; he discovered that children at certain ages missed the same questions and that there were similarities in the responses of children of the same age.

Piaget drew a number of conclusions from these early observations. The first and crucial point was that children reach different conclusions than adults do because they think differently. Piaget saw the study of cognitive development as essentially the discovery of the different modes of thinking used at different developmental levels and the transitions between stages. His study of cognitive development focused not on the quantity of children's knowledge, but on the quality of their thinking—their manner of solving problems, the logic they bring to bear, the way they use information, and so on. Piaget further concluded that standardized testing was too rigid and that modified psychiatric interviews were more appropriate. By employing this technique, he reasoned, he could best discover the actual thought processes of children.

Piaget returned to Switzerland in 1921 to work at the Rousseau Institute in Geneva where he continued his research. He published five books between 1923 and 1932. In the first one, *Language and thought of the child* (1926), Piaget noted the egocentric nature of the young child's speech and the gradual decrease of this quality as the child becomes older. Given the stature gained from the publication of his books and his innovative work, Piaget was appointed a professor first at

Geneva and then at Lausanne University. In 1940 he became director of Geneva's Psychological Laboratory. He also became co-director of the Rousseau Institute.

His ongoing research served to further convince him of the qualitative differences between adult and child thought. He reasoned that an understanding of human intelligence could be attained only through study of its development in the child. In addition, he concluded that the child's intellectual development was not greatly influenced by the environment but instead by the child's interaction with the environment.

He continued to write and in the period 1940 to 1970 Piaget published a number of books on childrens' concepts of time, quantity, movement, speed, space and geometry, and perception. In 1947 he gave a series of lectures, later published as *The psychology of intelligence* (1950), which provided an overview of his theory of cognitive development. Piaget's work was expanded in further studies of pre-school children (1952, 1954), school-age children and adolescents (Piaget and Inhelder, 1958) and early school-age children (Piaget and Inhelder, 1964). In 1969 Piaget and Barbel Inhelder published an introduction to Piaget's general theory of intellectual development, *The psychology of the child* (Piaget and Inhelder, 1969).

In his lifetime, Piaget published over thirty volumes and hundreds of articles on child development. Even when he was well into his seventies, he was still active in research and writing. Upon his death in 1981 he had become a world figure and a recognized leader in the field of child psychology.

Piaget systematically observed his own and other children in order to describe how children developed the ability to think (Piaget, 1932, 1970). Essentially, Piaget presented children with varieties of problems to solve and then asked detailed questions about why they gave the answers they did. He carefully and sytematically collected the data and used it to formulate a theory based on a sequence of stages of development. The theory attempted to explain how and why mental development proceeds as it does.

Piaget received early recognition in North America and was highly regarded in the 1920s and 1930s. As the years passed, however, he came under increasing criticism for his somewhat open-ended anecdotal methods of collecting data. Much of his initial work on infant behaviour was based on observations of his own three children in their natural surroundings. He did not work in a laboratory setting with established, scientific instruments (Voyat, 1982), but rather used homemade methods. He also did not always report his procedures fully enough for others to replicate them. These methods and the results made further studies by other researchers difficult. For a long time, Piaget's work was disparaged by American psychologists because it seemed unscientific.

In the decade of the 1950s, when Piaget's work was first translated into English, North American psychologists had entered a process of intense experimentation with children of various ages and had begun to discover that differences did indeed exist in the ways children of different ages approached problems. Piaget's ideas were then supported by the investigations of others, many of whom had initially set out to disprove him.

Piaget and other stage theorists reject the notion of intellectual development as a smooth, gradual process in which each new concept or item of knowledge is just added to the cognitive structure. Instead, they believe that children develop through a series of qualitatively different stages which each represent a level of organization of knowledge. Thus, each stage signifies a different kind of knowledge for the child, not just more of the same.

Piaget considered himself to be a philosopher interested in epistimology, the philosophy of knowledge. In fact, he defined his theory as genetic epistimology. His concern was with the development of knowledge throughout the lifespan. Piaget viewed his experimental work as a means of gaining information about how knowledge is acquired, not as a goal in itself. He was aware of the psychological and educational implications of his work but he persisted for more than fifty years in focusing primarily on epistemological questions (Piaget, 1973).

Thus, although Piaget had much to say about how children learn, he had little to say about what to actually teach them in the classroom. Certainly, given the intense interest that educators had in his findings, Piaget made general observations about the educational implications of his work, but he did not delve into real specifics. In one of the two books that he wrote that touched on education, Piaget (1948) stated that a school based on his theory would be radically different from those that existed because its very aim would be different. For Piaget, the aim of education was intellectual and moral autonomy (Kamii, 1984). Since he made few specific statements about the implications of his work for educational theory or practice, discussions of Piagetian psychology as it applies to education are mostly interpretations by others. Any curriculum or idea labelled as Piagetian is an interpretation of Piaget's work and not a direct statement from Piaget himself (Ginsburg and Opper, 1979). The greatest impact of Piagetian principles applied to classroom instruction and organization has been for young children, those at the pre-school and early elementary grades.

## PIAGET'S THEORY OF COGNITIVE DEVELOPMENT

In order to understand the sort of theory Piaget suggested, it is important to remember his background and early training in biology since he uses some of the principles of biology to explain the development of cognition in humans. Obviously, cognitive and biological functioning are not exactly the same, nor does cognitive development depend solely upon biological development. However, Piaget repeatedly refers to intelligence as "a particular instance of biological adaptation" (1952, pp. 3-4) and "a system of living and acting operations" (1950, p. 7).

Through his early biological research, Piaget realized that all living organisms adapt to changes in the environment. He theorized that such adaptations, especially in humans, were intellectual or cognitive as well as physical. He declared the basic principles of cognition and biological development to be the same and believed cognition to be inseparable from the organism's total functioning (Piaget, 1952). The organism organizes and stores material in differing ways as a result of its maturation. Then, as it develops, its conceptual system changes. These changes occur through the organism's active involvement with the environment. The motivation for change or learning is internal as the organism attempts to reach a balance between new and previously known information.

Piaget believed that the motivation for change or learning is internal as an organism attempts to reach a balance between new and previously known information.

As a stage theorist, Piaget believed cognitive development changed qualitatively at discrete stages. He divided all of development into four major stages, which he called periods. These periods are not fixed as securely to chronological age spans as Gesell's stages of physical development, but their approximate relationship to specific ages is shown in Table 3-1.

**Table 3-1** Piaget's periods of cognitive development

| Approximate Ages | Piaget's periods | Substages |
|---|---|---|
| 0-2 years | Sensorimotor | |
| 0-1 month | | I Reflex structures |
| 1-4 months | | II Primary circular reactions (self repetitions) |
| 4-8 months | | III Secondary circular reactions |
| 8-12 months | | IV Coordination of secondary schemata |
| 12-18 months | | V Tertiary secondary schemata |
| 18-24 months | | VI Mental combinations |
| 2-7 years | Preoperational | |
| 2-4 years | | I Preoperational |
| 4-7 years | | II Intuitive |
| 7-12 years | Concrete operational | |
| 12 years + | Formal operational | |

# PIAGET'S CONCEPTS AND TERMINOLOGY

**Organization:**
the way humans arrange, develop, and use their cognitive structures.

**Schema:**
a set of ideas that helps an individual organize information; mental representations of classes of people, objects, events, and so on.

Before entering fully into a discussion of Piaget's stages, we shall first address those concepts upon which the theory rests, as well as the specialized terminology used to describe development within and between periods.

To Piaget, cognitive development is characterized by specifable, progressive changes which endow children with the readiness skills necessary to learn increasingly complex material, solve increasingly complex problems, and use increasingly complex strategies. Cognitive readiness depends both on biological maturation (as does physical development), but also on the quality of the environment and the child's interaction with it. "Biological maturation," Piaget claims, "does nothing more than open the way to possible constructions (or explain transient impossibilities). It remains for the subject to actualize them" (Piaget, 1970, p. 712).

Individuals proceed from one stage to the next in the same sequence, but the ages at which each stage is entered into will vary between individuals, as well as between cultures. Piaget notes that

> in considering the problem of duartion or rate of succession of the stages, we can readily observe that acceleration or delays in the average chronological age of performance depend on specific environments (e.g., abundance or scarcity of possible activities and spontaneous experiences, educational or cultural environment), but the order of succession will remain constant (1970, p. 713).

Finally, a thorough understanding of Piaget's stage theory depends on familiarity with the following terminology: organization, schemata (plural of scheme or schema—he uses both spellings at different times), organization, adaptation, assimiliation, accommodation, and equilibration.

## Organization of schemata

We inherit the tendency toward organization, the ongoing process of arranging information and experience into mental systems or categories that Piaget calls schemata (Woolfolk, 1990). These schemata, or "mental blueprints of experience" (Kagan, 1971), enable the swift and economical processing of incoming stimuli. Imagine, for example, that a small boy has not developed a schema for "dog." Without such a schema, every time he sees a new size, shape, or species of dog he will have to create a separate schema anew.

Perception, comprehension, language, and memory all involve the interaction of new information with existing schemata. An event is perceived in a certain way and organized or categorized according to the characteristics it has in common with the individual's existing schemata. This is an active process involving interpretation and classification. With each new experience, schemata change and become more refined. The individual's response stimuli at any given time reflects the level and functioning of his or her current schemata. In addition, new information may force the reorganization of schemata. This cognitive evolution is a result of organization and adaptation working toward equilibrium. According to Piaget, intelligence "is the form of equilibrium toward which the

Without a schema for "dog," these boys would have to create new and separate schemata for every dog they encounter.

successive adaptations and changes between the [individual] and his environment are directed" (Piaget, 1950, p. 6). Thus, intelligence is not fixed: children may be said to experience a succession of intelligences.

Although he tends to regard children as sole explorers, single-handedly building their own cognitive structures in interaction with the environment, Piaget allows that maturation, the unfolding of genetically programmed biological changes, is also an important influence on the development of schemata. With increasing activity, children are better able to interact with the environment and learn from it.

Piaget uses the term "schema" loosely and the resulting flexibility is an asset (Bee, 1978). In the cognitive development of infants, *sensorimotor* or *behavioural schemata* refer to specific behavioural knowledge and skills such as the coordination of the sensorimotor abilities required to reach out and grasp an object, walk, or open bottles. *Verbal schemata* refer to word meanings and communication skills such as associating names with their physical referents or mastering basic grammar and syntax. *Cognitive schemata* refer to concepts, such as understanding the differences between plants and animals, thinking about images, such as being able to envision a triangle, and reasoning ability, such as being able to reason from causes to effects.

Under the heading of cognitive schemata, Piaget also speaks of schemata of events and objects as well as schemata of operations. Schemata for events and objects are internal representations of information from our environment, or "whatever is out there." Schemata for operations are essentially internal representations of the means of manipulating data. Piaget also uses the term to refer to a complex body of knowledge and skills, such as the ability to reason deductively.

# Adaptation

Piaget sees **adaptation** as the tendency of all organisms to change in response to the environment. It is a continuous process of interacting with the environment and learning to predict and control it to some degree. Knowledge about self, the immediate physical and social environment, and the world generally, is literally constructed as the child gains experience, resolves some apparent contradictions, and coordinates isolated schemata first into clusters and ultimately into a stable, internally consistent cognitive structure.

Cognitive readiness is contributed to both by maturation and fruitful interaction with an appropriately stimulating environment, and children assimilate or learn new information when it fits with what they already know. When it does not, they will do one of two things. They will ignore it if it is simply too far from anything they understand, as a baby would ignore, say, a tennis racket, or they will accommodate (modify their understanding) so that they can act upon the stimulus. Presumably, the latter will happen when some aspect of the environmental event or object is similar enough to their current schema that they can stretch or modify their understanding to fit the new stimulus.

Once the child has accommodated the schema to the external stimulus, the new information is assimilated, or incorporated into the new or modified schema. The new schema does not replace the old one; they are both retained. Thus, the processes of assimilation and accommodation are complementary and mutually dependent. New or modified structures are created continually and then used to aid the child's comprehension of the environment.

### Assimilation

Assimilation is the use of existing schemata or cognitive structures to incorporate external stimuli. However, assimilation means more than simply taking in new information. Rather, it is the "filtering and modification of input" (Piaget and Inhelder, 1973). In other words, assimilation is an attempt to deal with stimuli in terms of present cognitive structures. During assimilation, individuals learn to use objects in their environment which they have not had to deal with previously to do things they already know how to do. An example would be a child picking up a new toy and winding it up, just as the child has done with other wind-up toys.

Through assimilation, an individual continually integrates new perceptual matter into existing patterns. Without such categorization, children could make little sense of the environment. Thus assimilation is the goal of all adaptation. But not all stimuli fit into available existing schemata and mental structures must be adapted to these novel stimuli.

### Accommodation

Accommodation is the transformation of cognitive structures in response to external stimuli that do not fit into any available schema and therefore cannot be assimilated. As such, an individual has the option of modifying an existing schema or developing a new schema. In accommodation, individuals use objects with which they are already familiar but they use them in brand new ways. One

**Equilibration:**
maintaining a balance between present understanding and new experiences.

example is a child picking up a spoon and using it for the first time to get food into his or her mouth without help (Gibson, 1978).

Assimilation results in the immediate and automatic handling of a situation. Familiar everyday activities mostly involve assimilation, although some accommodation may be demanded—although we walk automatically we must make accommodations when we encounter obstacles, staircases, corners, and so on. Theoretically, all behaviour includes both assimilation and accommodation.

The process of accommodation is circular and continuous. By increasing the number of objects to which one responds (assimilation), one simultaneously increases the probability that one can make new responses to these stimuli (accommodation). Situations that are entirely foreign to previous experience presumably would produce panic or behavioural paralysis, since we would have no adaptative mechanisms to call upon. Such situations rarely exist in practice because virtually any situation is partially assumable to existing schemata (Woolfolk, 1990).

## Equilibration

The quest for equilibrium is the driving force of cognitive and other biological changes because each organism is more effective in interacting with the environment if it is in equilibrium with the environment. Obviously, equilibrium is only momentary for any given stimulus but nonetheless is a state toward which all organisms strive.

According to Piaget, disequilibrium is created when a child cannot handle new information since he or she cannot fit it into an existing scheme. (Other researchers refer to this as cognitive dissidence). If you think about it, the concept of equilibration underlies many of the situation comedies on television. Characters meet situations that are bizarre or outside their experience and the laugh tracks come in as they try to accommodate to this strangeness in half an hour. Sometimes this may be funny, but in real life a continual state of disequilibrium would lead to confusion and withdrawal.

Hence, the object of adaptation is equilibration—maintaining a balance between present understanding and new experiences. The entire process as outlined by Piaget is illustrated in Figure 3-1.

**Figure 3-1**
Organization and adaptation

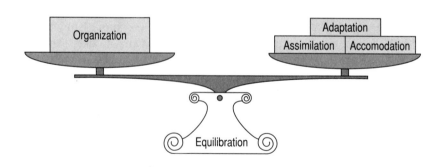

# PIAGET'S PERIODS OF COGNITIVE DEVELOPMENT

## Sensorimotor period

Piaget's first period is infancy, or the period of sensorimotor development, which lasts for the first two years of life. The sensorimotor period can be divided into six substages and the infant progresses through each in an invariant sequence. In each stage the infant's cognitive understanding is distinctly different from that of other stages. Through adaptation, the infant's behavioural schemes (the structures of the sensorimotor period) become more complex and gradually change into the next, more sophisticated form. As Piaget observed, each substage is

> *defined by the fact that the child becomes capable of certain behaviour patterns of which he was up to then incapable; it is not the fact that he renounces the behaviour patterns of the preceding stages, even if they are contrary to the new ones (Piaget, 1964, p. 299).*

Of course, the transition from one substage to another during infancy (and at other periods) is gradual, involving a consolidation of earlier skills so that they become automatic. A child doesn't suddenly wake up one morning possessing a whole new range of skills. But although the changes are gradual, major new accomplishments are acquired in sequence and at a fairly standard rate. This continuous progress is broken down into substages for the sensorimotor period for ease of description and because the child in the middle of one stage really is qualitatively different from a child in the middle of another substage (Bee, 1978).

Piaget did not believe that reinforcement by the environment was necessary to motivate infants to act (Rosenblith and Sims-Knight, 1985). Rather, central to his theory is the belief that infants are active and will use their cognitive structures, beginning with reflex structures, to interact with the environment. Infants understand and organize their world through physical acts such as looking, grasping, and sucking. The motor act itself is the means by which the infant learns about the world. Repetition of these motor acts forms the infant's cognitive structures, the framework by which they organize their understanding.

The cognitive structures of infancy are called behavioural schemes and are individually labeled by the respective acts, such as the sucking scheme or the grasping scheme. (Remember that the scehme is not the act itself but is the residue left from the repetition of actions; it is the means by which the meaning of environmental events become codified and remembered.) A familiar pattern such as sucking is modfied and expanded by means of the two processes that are invariant and occur at all stages of development—assimilation and accommodation.

Children in the sensorimotor stage may be said to think to the extent that they interact with familiar people and objects in predictable ways that demonstrate recognition. Thus, the child's cognitive structures, or schemata, represent an action-oriented functioning. They possess a "hands-on," trial and error type of thinking by which they know objects only in terms of their own direct physical interactions with those objects. For example, rather than labeling or classifying an object, sensorimotor children will behave toward the object in a way that

**Object permanence:**

ability to mentally represent an object or person when that object or person is no longer in sight.

**Symbol:**

an image, word or activity that represents something else.

indicates they know its function; their schemata are organized according to sensory input and motor responses. Sensiromotor intelligence may be seen as similar to the level of cognition used by adults for routine motor tasks such as pulling off socks.

Piaget devoted much attention to the six substages of infant cognitive development. The following is a brief explanation.

**Substage I** Reflex structures (birth to one month) At birth, infants have no cognitive structures. However, newborns are equipped with reflex structures that Piaget considers to be the first building blocks of cognitive development. These reflex structures (by the process of adaptation) undergo significant changes as a result of interaction with the environment. They begin to develop into cognitive structures which, in turn, form the basis both of knowledge of the physical world and of understanding of general principles (Rosenblith and Sims-Knight, 1985). By the end of Substage 1, infants have already begun to differentiate their sucking responses to accommodate to the environment (e.g., by sucking differently with different stimuli). This small, yet significant experience-based change indicates cognitive growth.

**Substage II** Primary circular reactions (one to four months) Gradually, through repeated use, reflex structures are transferred into sensorimotor cognitive structures called behavioural schemata. The behaviour itself is circular in that the infants are reacting to the pleasure they have derived from chance actions or unplanned behaviour by seeking to repeat this behaviour in a trial and error fashion.

**Substage III** Secondary circular reactions (four to eight months). During this stage infants begin to turn their attention toward objects and occurrences in the external environment; they show the beginnings of what may be called intention and learn to willfully repeat acts. Infants at this stage will throw all their toys out of the crib, cry until they get them back, and then throw them out again.

The beginning of the development of the concept of permanent objects also appears within this substage. **Object permanence** implies an elementary memory for children—they can now hold an image in their minds. Previously, infants were not capable of mentally constructing symbols to represent an object that was no longer visible. Without a system of symbols—a **symbol** being an image, word, or activity that represents something else—infants were limited to their immediate experiences. In this third stage of infancy, however, infants now search for missing objects and will anticipate, to some degree at least, the position of objects momentarily hidden from view. Children now realize that mother is still close even if they can't see her. Or, if a toy is placed behind a screen on one side of little Tony's visual field, he will move his eyes to look for the toy's reappearance on the other side.

**Substage IV** Coordination of secondary schemes (eight to 12 months) By now, behaviour is much more intentional, and much more "intelligent." Babies can now figure out how to use old and familiar strategies in new situations; they no longer simply respond to accidental events but set out to create happenings themselves.

**Substage V** Tertiary secondary schemata (12 to 18 months) By this time babies are walking and beginning to use the rudiments of language although they understand far more than they can say. During this period, Piaget observed what may reasonably be called the beginning of experimentation (Bee, 1978). Children seem to explore objects in new ways, using new methods of trial and error, experimenting, for example, with new ways of dropping them or holding them. Object permanence becomes fully developed during this period. Children, too, become more proficient at imitating the simple behaviours of adults such as pointing a finger to the forehead (Salkind, 1990).

**Substage VI** Mental combinations (18 to 24 months). Children are about 18 months old before they can begin to think about the effects of their behaviour and to think before they act. In this final stage of sensorimotor development, toddlers begin combining skills.

By the end of this stage, the transition to deliberate symbolic thought takes place. This amounts to a change to a higher plane of reality and one on which individuals will spend the rest of their lives (Salkind, 1990). Children are now capable of thought that transcends the immediate situation. When now the child meets a problem, trial and error methods no longer limit experimentation. Children need not immediately charge into action but can, on a very basic level at first, do what an adult does in solving problems. They can envision a solution to the difficulty first and then act to bring about the proposed result. Children also learn, though gradually, to use the objects around them to represent other things, such as a doll for a baby.

In the sensorimotor stage, the development of object permanence, linked as it is to memory and cognitive development, represents a major milestone. The same can be said of representational thought. Children are now capable of reflection and of re-examining what they already know; they can contemplate as well as act. Children can think ahead during a sequential task like block building or copying letters, whereas previously they had to try everything behaviorally and made many errors. As well, representational thought enables children to deal with numbers and such quantities as size. By thinking with symbols they can extend their scope beyond themselves and the concrete objects they encounter every day (Salkind, 1990).

## Preoperational period

Piaget calls this the instructive stage of mental development. The really important feature of this stage is children's attainment of a rudimentary ability to represent objects and events to themselves, although such internal representations remain limited and are still tied to specific events and not yet organized into a complex system. Small children can only represent states of being and cannot conceive of the transformation that takes place from one state to another. In solving problems, they still focus on attributes they can see, taste, or touch, and then only on one attribute at a time.

Schemata are unstable during this stage because children have not yet learned to distinguish invariant and universal aspects of the environment from aspects that are specific to particular situations and relatively unimportant. They are easily confused by conservation problems, problems that require them to conserve invariant aspects of objects in their minds and avoid becoming confused by manipulations of unimportant characteristics.

Preoperational thought tends to be irreversible; children cannot retrace their steps to re-examine a conclusion they have already formed. For example, in an

**Centration:**
the tendency to centre attention on a single feature of an object or situation.

**Conservation:**
the ability to understand that the same amount remains, regardless of shape or the way an object or substance looks.

**Egocentrism:**
seeing only one's own point of view.

**Deduction:**
reasoning from general rules to particular instances.

**Induction:**
reasoning in which we start with particular facts and use them to formulate general rules.

**Transduction:**
reasoning that two events are connected because they occur together.

early study (Stevenson and Bitterman, 1955) the researchers presented children at this stage with three different sized objects and rewarded them each time they selected the middle-sized object. They then presented three new objects, each different in size from the originals. The children in this study had not grasped the concept of intermediate size independent of the specific sizes of the originals, and they tended not to choose the middle-sized objects. Instead they chose those most closely matching the exact size of the objects for which they were originally rewarded.

**Centration** is the child's tendency to centre attention on a single feature of an object or situation. As part of his classic studies on children's grasp of **conservation**—the fact that the same amount remains regardless of shape or the way it looks—Piaget asked many children of different ages the question, "Which of the two jars in front of you holds the larger amount of beans?" When young children were shown two same sized jars, each half full of beans, they reported correctly that both contained the same amount. But when the same beans were emptied into a tall, thin jar right in front of the children they reported that the tall jar held more beans. Children at the preoperational stage are still dominated by visual impressions. Somewhere between the ages of five and seven, children in Piaget's studies began to report correct answers to the question. At this age the children began to understand the concept of conservation.

However, some researchers point out that many of the difficulties in conserving at this early stage of cognitive development may be due to the inability to organize information, and to use various strategies to assist memory. Younger children may be unable to acquire certain concepts simply because they cannot hold enough items of information in their minds simultaneously. Piaget feels that the ability to remember is linked to a child's level of cognitive development (Piaget and Inhelder, 1973), and that it is in the middle years of childhood that children become more adept at retrieving information from long term memory. Also, as language develops children are provided with richer associations between objects, which in itself makes it easier to learn and to remember (Ornstein and Naus, 1985).

By adult standards the reasoning of preschool youngsters is unsystematic and heavily influenced by their own wants and desires. It is as if they see the world only through their own needs. In fact, Piaget suggests that one of the overriding characteristics of children's thought during the preoperational period is the quality he terms **egocentrism** which refers to the self-centred quality of the preschool child's thoughts and behaviour. No moral judgment is assigned here; it simply means that children cannot yet see another's point of view.

Since children of this age have not yet developed the ability to see things from other people's perspectives, they act as if everyone else thinks exactly the same way they do, knows exactly what they mean, and so on. Further, they often seem not to notice or be bothered by indications that their assumptions are incorrect (Miller, Bronwell, and Zukier, 1977; Vygotsky, 1962).

In our society, adult reasoning is based on two logical processes. First, we reason from general rules to particular instances, a process of **deduction**. In contrast, **induction** means that we start with particular facts and use them to formulate general rules. Preschoolers resort to a process called **transduction**—two events are connected because they occur together. Salkind (1990) uses the example of a young boy who comes to believe that, because daddy comes home

**Operation:**
a mental routine for transposing information; an action in which an experience can be mentally transformed back to its original shape.

**Concept:**
a mental structure or representation that defines how a set or class of entities, events, or abstractions are related.

**Category:**
an extension of a concept which implies a class or partition of objects, sets of objects, events, people, etc.

**Categorization:**
treating two or more distinct entities as if, in some way, they are equivalent.

**Seriation:**
the ability to place a group of objects in order from least to most in length, width, weight, or some other common property.

each evening at twilight, one event causes the other. He might even turn on the lights to make daddy appear.

## Concrete operational period

As children enter the concrete operational period, a whole series of more complex schemata, which Piaget calls operations, are developed. An operation is an mental roadmap, a way of organizing information. Every operation is reversible; it has a logical opposite. Therefore, an operation may be defined as an action in which an experience can be mentally transformed back to its original shape. For example, 3 + 6 = 9 is an operation because it can be reversed (i.e., 9 - 6 = 3). So is the child's ability to recognize that a ball of clay retains the same amount of clay even when rolled into a snake or flattened into a pancake.

Although they have been developing concepts and categories all along, children now become more sophisticated in this area as well. Concepts and categories serve as the building blocks of human behaviour. Roughly, a concept is an idea that includes all that is characteristically associated with it. It is a mental structure of representation that defines how a set or class of entities, events, or abstractions are related. Concepts, or types of schemata, help us organize a vast amount of information into meaningful units.

A category is an extension of a concept. It implies a class, or partition, of objects, or sets of objects, or events, or people, and the like. Categorization, then, implies the processes that are involved in defining categorical membership; the means by which knowledge directs our interactions with the environment (Quinn and Eines, 1986). That is, categorization means treating two or more distinct entities as if, in some way, they were equivalent.

Children show the capacity for operational thinking at five or six years, but they usually don't become functionally operational, with the ability to use operational thinking most of the time, until they are at least two years older. By about seven years of age, children reach the stage of true concrete operations. In the next few years they will gradually develop the ability to apply logic to their reasoning. However, until they are about 11 years old they are still bound by their perceptions.

Piaget stresses three stages in the process of becoming operational:

- developing the ability to discriminate between variant and invariant aspects of the environment;

- coordinating separate schemata into larger ones and ultimately into concrete operations and a unified cognitive structure; and

- achieving the ability to reason forward from causes to effects and backwards from effects to causes (reversability) (Good and Brophy, 1986).

Throughout this stage the motivation for equilibration causes children to become more active in seeking information, particularly by asking questions and, when they are able, by reading. It is during this operational stage as well that children attain conservation and develop seriation, the ability to place a group of objects in order from least to greatest in length, width, weight, or some other property. They gradually increase their classification skills as well as the ability to reverse classification.

An enormous body of research has investigated children's cognitive development in the stage of concrete operations. There has been, in particular, intense research into children's attainment of conservation, not only to determine the age at which children typically acquire conservation, but also to discover just what kinds of experiences lead children from nonconservation to conservation.

According to Piaget, children's ability to solve conservation problems depends on understanding three basic aspects of reasoning: identity, compensation, and reversability. Identity comes when a child realizes that if nothing is added or taken away, the material remains the same. Compensation is attained when a child becomes aware that an apparent change in one direction can be compensated for by a change in the other direction (Woolfolk, 1990). Reversability comes when children understand that an action can be undone or something returned to its original state. Children must also attain decentration—the ability to consider several aspects of a physical problem at once, instead of focusing on only one attribute.

Conservation comes about when responses are internalized and brought together to form a stable consistent system. The fundamental principle is that certain properties of objects—their quantity, number, weight, and so on—stay the same, even when the shape or spatial arrangement is altered. The classic experimental situation begins with two balls of clay that children agree have the same amount of clay in each ball. When the shape of one ball is changed—rolled into a snake or flattened into a pancake—children in the preoperational period will assert that the amount of clay has changed, and will probably think there is more in the pancake or snake. On the other hand, children who have attained the stage of concrete operations readily recognize that the amount remains the same even if the shapes are different.

A child's ability to solve conservation problems depends on understanding identity, compensation, and reversibility.

The ability to conserve actually begins before the period of concrete operations but, as children progress, the principle becomes more and more general in their thinking and children can apply it to increasingly more complex problems. By the age of five or six, the ability to conserve has begun to develop and is well established in seven year olds. However, conservation of different properties occurs at different ages. Generally, findings on age indicate that children around ages six or seven attain conservation of substance (relating to the amount of a substance that does not change if it is divided into parts) and length (realizing that the length of a wire or piece of string does not change if it is cut into parts or bound into a curved shape) and continuous quantity (realizing that pouring liquid from one container into another does not change the amount of liquid). At about seven years of age children attain conservation of number (realizing that the number of objects does not change if they are placed close together or spread far apart) and area (realizing that the total area covered by a piece of paper will not change if the paper is cut into pieces or if the pieces are rearranged into new shapes). Somewhere between ages nine and 12 children attain conservation of weight (realizing that a piece of clay weighs the same regardless of the shape). Finally, at around age 11 or 12, children attain conservation of volume (realizing that a single piece of clay that has been reformed into various shapes will occupy the same volume when immersed in liquid) (see Atkinson et al., 1990; Good and Brophy, 1986; Salkind, 1990).

Examples of conservation problems are shown in Figure 3-2.

**Figure 3-2**
Conservation problems.

Mass

Quantity

Number

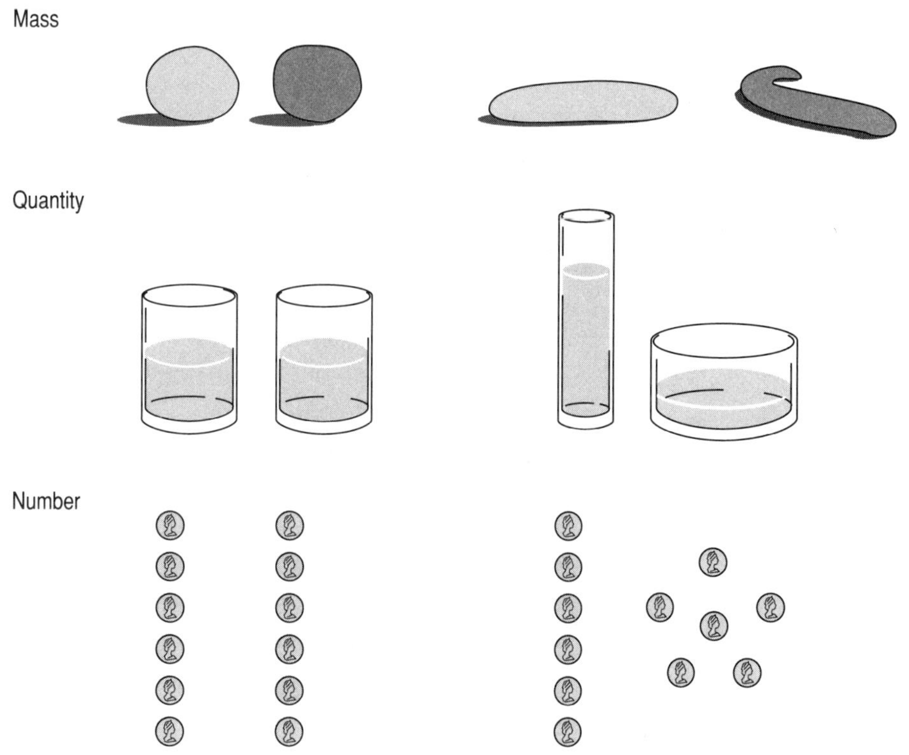

In addition, as they gain conservation, operational children attain the concept of negation. They recognize that an action can be negated or reversed so that events will return to the state they were before the original action. In a liquid conservation exercise, for example, children immediately recognize that amounts are the same even if poured from pitcher to pitcher and back again.

Children come to solve class inclusion problems. For example, when presented with twelve flowers—consisting of two subclasses such as ten daisies and two roses—and asked whether the collection contains more flowers or more daisies, young children say "daisies" because there are only two roses (McCabe and Siegel, 1987). By age seven or eight (Piaget, 1971), or perhaps nine or ten in North America (Winer, 1980), children are usually capable of reasoning about this hierarchy of classes.

A Canadian study (McCabe and Siegel, 1987) trained children in the concept of class inclusion and found that training is effective in improving performance on such problems, even in children as young as five years. However, not all children retained the concept, as revealed by a delayed post-test. Some children attained the concept and performed on an immediate post-test (perhaps the result of positive feedback) but then reverted back to former levels.

## Formal operational period

Formal operation implies the ability to deal with potential or hypothetical situations. The period of formal operations begins at about age 12 and gradually consolidates over the next several years. Of course, like the other stages, formal operations does not arrive suddenly: adolescents gradually develop the capacity to reason through the use of abstractions. They master the ability to think about thoughts; they are able to reason not only about things they actually experience but also about things that have no concrete existence, such as abstract ideas.

Adolescents can now imagine several alternative explanations of the new phenomenon and are no longer bound by one solution to a problem. When given information, students begin gradually to make logical deductions without first turning to concrete examples because they have learned to evaluate objects without needing the concrete forms in front of them. They can operate with symbols that have abstract definitions and so are ready to study more abstract subjects such as algebra and those that rest on more hypothetical principles, such as civics. They can understand similes, metaphors, sarcasm, and satire. The better thinkers take logical and systematic approaches to problem solving.

The stage of formal operational thought may be attained as early as eleven or twelve years of age, although some people attain it much later in adolescence and some people not at all (Vikan, 1983). The development of well-functioning formal operations apparently occurs only among individuals whose cognitive structures have been well-developed and integrated at the level of concrete operational thought. Many young adolescents moving into this stage go through only part of the transition. In fact, Bee (1978) points out that formal operations are only achieved by about one half to two-thirds of the people in our culture and by far fewer in less complex cultures. Evidence of formal operations is lacking altogether in certain societies, especially those without formal educational systems (Luria, 1976; Riegel, 1973) when measured with the usual Piagetian

**Social cognition:**

the knowledge of social relationships which includes an awareness and understanding of how people think, feel, and see things from a different point of view and what they mean or intend.

tasks. In our society, some students never develop formal operations to the point that they can be used efficiently in thinking and problem solving. They may memorize the formulae in algebra or the dates in history, for example, but never really understand their implications or uses.

It is more accurate to assume that college students can handle purely abstract material (Lawson, 1975), particularly in courses such as advanced mathematics or philosophy. Piaget (1974) suggested that many adults may be able to use formal operational thought in only a few areas, particularly those where they have the greatest experience or interest. This seems to apply to college students whose formal operations are more developed with reference to the content related to a student's major than to other content (DeLisi and Staudt, 1980).

Together with their ability to function with abstract thought, adolescents advance in social cognition, the knowledge of social relationships which includes an awareness and understanding of how people think, feel, and see things from a different point of view and what they mean or intend. Social cognition seems to affect peer acceptance, self-definition, and learning through interaction (Salkind, 1990).

## CRITICISMS OF PIAGETIAN PRINCIPLES

Not everyone agrees with all the points Piaget makes. In fact, as Kagan (1980) noted, it would be impossible for a scholar to create a theoretical edifice as ambitious as Piaget's that was totally invulnerable. So although Piaget's theories are easily the most influential in the area of cognitive development, they are not without their problems and their critics. Extensive and often abstruse argument continues to prevail about some of Piaget's basic premises as well as about his descriptions of specific sequences. Some of the major controversies centre around the points below.

1. Piaget does not postulate reasons for the differences in rates of development. Piaget's stages have been the most widely used theoretical context for cross-cultural research (Nyiti, 1982) and such investigations have indeed shown that the order of stages through which children pass is the same, regardless of the culture in which the child is growing up. But even though the stages seem to be invariant, there are differences in children's rates of development. Piaget has little to say about the possible reasons for these differences and, because this is a critical question for many researchers, some dissatisfaction with this aspect of the theory exists.

    These differences may be related to the Piagetian in tasks and the manner in which they are presented. Nyiti (1982) discussed a fascinating study of children from two Canadian cultural groups, European (white, English-speaking Canadians) and Native Micmac Indians from the Eskasani Reserve in Cape Breton. A total of 48 Native and 39 European children, aged 10 and 11, were selected. While European children were interviewed in English, the Native children were divided into two groups. Children in Group One were interviewed first in English by an English-speaking European and then in Micmac by a Micmac Indian. Group two children were first interviewed in Micmac and then in English. Each subject was interviewed individually and presented with Piaget's tasks on the conservation of substance, weight, and displacement of volume. There were no significant differences in development between the two groups of children when the language of testing matched that of the child. When it did not, the English-speaking examiner found that Native children seemed to lag in development on Piagetian tasks. The answers they gave in English, to the European examiner, did in fact differ from the answers they gave in their own language.

2. Piaget seems to suggest that children should be at least somewhat consistent in their approaches to different tasks or problems at given ages. Yet children don't in fact seem to be at a given stage on every task or in every situation so, in this sense, consistency does not seem to be a hallmark of cognitive development at all.

3. Piaget was uninterested in determining environmental features that influence development. Many researchers, teachers, and parents are interested in the effects of the environment on children's development and whether or not development can be hastened. Piaget called this the "American question" and showed little interest in it himself. Certainly, he acknowledged the significance of social and cultural factors affecting the course of cognitive development (Piaget and Inhelder, 1969), but he did not detail the characteristics of the environment that influence the course of development. And, faced with a host of environmentally induced instances of developmental unevenness in performance (called horizontal decalage), Piaget said he simply could not explain them (Piaget, 1971, p. 11).

   In trying to accelerate cognitive growth, however, the main conclusion drawn from many studies is that it really cannot be done. In truth, teachers can only provide children with opportunities by presenting materials at "stage + 1," which is slightly higher than the children's developmental level. ("Stage + 2" materials would be ineffective.)

4. Some of the ages proposed by Piaget seem to be incorrect. Even though he set broad age ranges, there is research to indicate that the ages assigned Piaget's first three periods may be inaccurate. Piaget's conception of a series of qualitatively changing cognitive stages or levels in the first two years of life has, with a few modifications, received increasing theoretical and empirical support from various independent sources during the past decades (e.g., Fischer, 1980; McCall, Eichorn, and Haggarty, 1977). However, infants are capable of many complex cognitive behaviours and it may be that Piaget underestimated these behaviours. As well, preoperational children seem to be more capable than Piaget thought (see Gelman and Baillargeon, 1983).

   Carefully designed studies show that the stages of cognitive development may be are reached earlier than Piaget thought (Case, 1978b; Scandura and Scandura, 1980). Further, success on Piagetian tasks may not be the clearest indicator of children's abilities in some areas, partly because traditional Piagetian tasks may use language that is confusing and abstract or tasks that are too difficult. Young children, for example, may not be able to conserve numbers but they do have a sense of numeracy (Winzer, 1989). Counting and related number concepts and operations may be more basic to children's development of knowledge about numbers than is the ability to succeed on Piagetian tasks (Clements, 1984; Fuson, Secada, and Hall, 1983).

As well, there is some question about the strength of egocentricity in pre-operational children. In some situations at least, children dispense with some egocentric behaviour. When showing a toy, they will turn the toy to face the other person (Gelman, 1979); when speaking with younger children they change the pitch and intonation of their voices (Winzer, 1990a).

In the case of formal operations, Piaget may have erred in the other dire-cection—he may have assigned too young an age to it (Bee, 1978). A proportion of the population never fully attains formal operations, and many students at the age of eleven or twelve are far from possessing the cognitive abilities that characterize this stage. In a group of ninth graders, for example, one study  found that 32 percent were just beginning concrete operations, 43 percent were into the concrete operational stage, 15 percent were entering formal operations, and only 9 percent were at the stage of mature formal operations. In a similar study, Kamii (1984) reported that only 20 to 25 percent of college freshmen consistently used formal operational reasoning.

It may be that the period of formal operations needs to be extended upwardrds and that the concept of formal operations be elaborated to take into account cognitive development that occurs beyond the adolescent years (Commons, Richards, and Kuhn, 1982). Riegel (1973) and Arlin (1975) argue that there is a fifth stage of cognitive development that occurs in adulthood. Arlin sees this as a problem-solving stage that builds on the problem-solving abilities associated with the attainment of formal operations. People who attain this stage not only solve problems but infer implications and think creatively and divergently about the objects of their thought.

5. Another recurring source of controversy, if not especially criticism, is the question of whether or not there is a correlation between intellectual abilities and cognitive development as measured by Piagetian tasks given that different domains may be being assessed (see Lempers et al., 1987).

Evidence has been provided for the hypothesis that psychometric brightness (as indicated by IQ scores) implies precocity (early development or achievement) in cognitive development. In two studies, Toronto researcher Dan Keating and his colleague (Keating, 1975; Keating and Schaefer, 1975) showed that psychometrically bright (98th percentile or higher on the Iowa Test of Basic Skills) fifth, sixth, seventh, and eighth graders evidenced formal operational reasoning ability much earlier than did those students of average ability (48th to 52nd percentile).

6. Piaget laid great stress on thought, or cognitive schemes, and relatively little on language, or verbal schemes. He viewed language as little more than a means for communicating thought. Although Piaget (1967) maintained that the development of language is dependent on the prior development of thought, many researchers place great stress on the importance of language to thought (see Chapter 5).

## INDIVIDUAL DIFFERENCES

Piaget's theory looks at broad ranges of children as they develop cognitively across certain ages and stages. The focus is on the general population, not on individuals or particular groups within that population. A number of researchers, however, are interested in how certain traits and characteristics affect children's cognitive development and have set out to investigate various aspects of Piagetian task development in relationship to individual differences. Much of this work has been carried out in relation to children at the opening two stages on Piaget's model. For example, in investigating the play behaviour of children at these levels, investigators have found a range of individual differences.

Jennings and her colleagues (1979) studied a variety of qualitative and quantitative aspects of play in a sample of one year olds. One of their findings concerned the relationship between individual differences in exploratory play and other aspects of early development. Significantly, the researchers found a number of relationships between quality of play and scores on infant IQ tests; however,

The range of different behaviours that infants use during play is important for cognitive development.

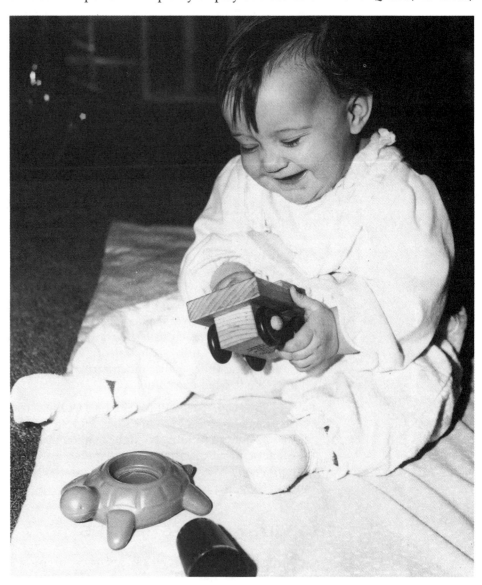

they discovered no relationship between the quantity of play engaged in and IQ test scores. In other words, whether or not infants engage in play that is mature for their age and has continuity from one play episode to another seems to be a much more important factor for early mental development than the amount of play in which they engage.

Caruso (1986) also examined the relationship between individual differences in play and specific cognitive abilities. He found that the variety of behaviours one year olds use to explore was related to their success and sophistication in problem solving at one year and later when they were two years of age. This finding suggests that it is the range of different behaviours that infants use during play that is important for cognitive functioning, rather than the amount of any given behaviour, regardless of its degree of maturity and sophistication.

Collard (1971) was a pioneer in examining the influence of the environment on exploratory quality. She found that infants reared in institutions, which provided less opportunity to explore and a simpler environment, had lower quality and quantity of exploratory play than had home-reared infants. High quality and quantity of exploratory play was linked to maternal positive affect and mothers responsive to their infant's behaviour (Yarrow et al., 1972), to more responsive and less restrictive parenting, and to the responsiveness of the physical environment (Watson and Ramey, 1972). Caruso (1986) found that maternal responsiveness and less restrictive home environments were associated with the use of more sophisticated exploratory play.

In general what all these findings suggest is that play is vital for the cognitive development of young children. The type and range of play is important so therefore parents or caregivers should provide a variety of toys and stimulating activities. Children trapped in cribs for hours on end will not have the same opportunities to explore and play, and therefore develop, as their peers who are allowed more freedom. As well, an environment where the caregiver is sensitive to infants' behaviour can influence their exploratory play.

## The question of gender

Boys and girls in Canada pass through Piaget's stages of cognitive development in the same sequence and at about the same ages. The question is whether they each develop similar capacities for certain skills and whether these capacities are environmentally or genetically controlled.

Several sex differences have been identified with regard to the cognitive play categories. Boys have been found to engage in more functional play whereas girls are more likely to exhibit constructive play (Johnson and Roopnarine, 1983). Gender differences also appear to be connected to the social quality of constructive play, with girls engaged in more solitary constructive and parallel constructive play than boys (Pellegrini, 1982; Rubin, Maioni, and Hornung, 1976; Rubin, Watson, and Jambon, 1978).

Moreover, girls' play activities are more closely directed and structured by adults than are boys' activities (Caldera, Huston, and O'Brien, 1989). While children's behaviour varies with the structure of the play activities, within activites there are very few differences between boys and girls (Carpenter, 1983; Huston et al., 1986).

**Spatial visualization:**
the ability to see, manipulate, and compute the position of an abstract or real figure in the mind's eye.

At a much later stage of development, researchers have found small but statistically significant differences favouring males over females in formal operations (Meehan, 1984) possibly due to sex differences in course enrolments in science and mathematics. However, the debate as to whether males are better at higher level mathematics functioning and spatial abilities and females in verbal functioning is relatively long standing. It is of particular interest because significant differences found even 20 years ago have tended to disappear which indicates clearly the cultural and social aspects of the manifestations of cognitive development.

Male verbal proficiency has been increasing over the years to match that of females, while female ability on tests of mathematical reasoning has been increasing to match that of males (Hyde and Linn, 1988a,b; Linn and Hyde, 1989). The one area of cognitive ability that continues to show a consistent sex difference is visual spatial relations, or spatial visualization—the ability to see, manipulate, and compute the position of an abstract or real figure in the mind's eye (Phillips, 1990). Tests of spatial visualization still show superior performance for males, particularly when these tests are timed and require mental rotation of objects (Burnett, 1986).

## MORAL DEVELOPMENT

Moral development, values, social conventions, ethics, and conscience are all terms used to describe efforts to deal fairly with one another. More specifically, ethics refers to the science of the systematic reasoning about and study of morals. Morals are concerned with right and wrong behaviour.

Three themes emerge in writings about morality. First, there is the theme that moral values are social values positive for society as a whole. Next there is the theme that the fully moral person behaves in accordance with a system of values that is self-enforced and self-accepted. Third, moral persons see themselves as part of a social network in which all have mutual responsibilities (Maccoby, 1980).

How humans come to learn a sense of morality, to make moral judgments, and then to act on those judgments, has recently become an area of intense debate and research. In the school system, the inculcation of morals and the virtues required to live in society has traditionally been a motivating force. In fact, to our educational predecessors, morality and schooling were virtually synonymous, as can be seen in Box 3-2.

### Piaget's theory of moral development

Because it appears to be linked to cognitive development, similar invariant sequential stages have been proposed for moral development. Piaget (1932) was one of the first to study the changes in levels of moral reasoning that accompany changes in cognitive development. When Piaget was motivated to explain the moral nature of human beings, he sided with those who felt that moral propositions were to be based on biological fact (Kagan, 1980). His classic work, *The moral judgment of the child* (1932) was a study of five to 13 year old children of the Genevan working class.

Box 3-2 **Historical note**

Nineteenth century school promoters and reformers in North America insisted, like their European forebears and counterparts, that all children would be moral. Morality and a work ethic were raised to the dominant ideologies and these were to form the cornerstones of the emerging common (public) school systems.

Egerton Ryerson is often considered the architect of the Canadian public school system. He transformed a scattered and sparse group of common schools into a strong consolidated public school system, supported by taxes, with the passage of Ontario's 1870 school law. Like his counterpart, Horace Mann, in the United States, Ryerson maintained that veracity, probity, and rectitude (truth, honesty, and uprightness in principles and conduct) were the chief goals of education. Ryerson saw the schools as the mechanisms to cleanse society of its evils and to build character and strong citizenship within and among its pupils (Winzer, 1990b).

Mid-nineteenth century Ontario was moving toward cultural and material transformation and was trying to cope with an influx of immigrants. Ryerson and other public school promoters were faced with the challenge of transmitting Anglo-American virtues to children often raised according to different customs and mores. The implicit mandates of the public schools became the provision to an increasingly diverse school-age population of the skills needed to contribute to a complex, rapidly changing society, while simultaneously inculcating the newcomers with the religious and moral values that were held dear by the dominant society. The schools would make all children socially acceptable—they were to have refined manners and taste, respectable religious knowledge and practice, proper speech, and literacy. Schooling was fashioned largely on three objectives: to educate, to evangelize and to elevate industrially.

In the industrializing society, the public schools also became places designed to complete a transition from agrarian to industrial modes of production. Educators were expected to ready people for contractual relationships, for impersonal rather than personal modes of association, and for labour in factory and line, rather than field and craft (Finkelstein, 1988). In order to accomplish these goals the five Rs—reading, 'riting, 'rithmetic, religion, and rules of conduct were stressed (Lee and Stevens, 1981). Teachers rained on children a torrent of moral and religious prescriptions. Moral education included instruction about traditional values such as honesty, thrift, and toleration as well as a more specifically religious, though non-denominational, orientation.

Piaget began with the assumption that a sense of justice and respect for the social order are the two central elements in mature morality. He studied how children conceptualize rules and their validity; honesty (in terms of telling lies versus telling the truth); and authority (including what they perceive to constutite a legitimate basis for assumption of authority) (Maccoby, 1980). In doing this, Maccoby (1980) points out that Piaget not only provided the first systematic account of the development of moral concepts, but he also evolved a method of questioning children that has been used (with modifications) by most of the researchers on moral judgment who followed him.

Piaget (1932, 1977) claimed that there are two childhood moralities: one of adult restraint and one of mutual respect. These he termed heteronomous morality (subject to the rules imposed by others) and autonomous morality (subject to the rules imposed by self).

Younger children, those in Piaget's heteronomous stage, seem to be rule-oriented and need a rule for every contingency. In the classroom, for example, young children will propose such rules as "Be early," "Don't be late," "Walk," "Don't run." Moreover, they are often very strict with rule breakers. Piaget (1948) explained that

> in these children's eyes, punishment consists, as a matter of course, in inflicting on the guilty party a pain that will smart enough to make them realize the gravity of their misdeed. Narturally, the fairest punishment will be the most severe (p. 211).

Heteronomous morality is in general the morality of children under nine; these children regard moral rules as sacred and inviolable. But as children overcome egocentrism and develop the cognitive abilites necessary to put themselves in the place of others, they begin to understand concepts such as fairness and reciprocity that underlie "golden rule" morality. Children do not become truly moral individuals capable of guiding their own behaviour by a set of stable ethical principles until they enter the concrete operational period, sometime during the elementary grades. For older children, rules signify adult restraint less and seem more like the products of lawful conventions and mutual respect among peers.

Piaget believed that moral knowledge changes as children mature but did not see the changes clearly related to specific ages nor to be sequential. However, the current developmental model for understanding moral judgments rests primarily on a complex scheme of universal, invariant, and sequential stages that were described and elaborated by Lawrence Kohlberg. Table 3-2 shows the relationship between Piaget's and Kohlberg's perspectives.

**Table 3-2** Moral development stages according to Piaget and Kohlberg

| AGE | COGNITIVE STAGE | MORAL STAGE | |
|-----|-----------------|-------------|---|
| | | *Piaget* | *Kohlberg* |
| 0-2 | Sensorimotor | Heteronomous | Premoral |
| 2-7 | Preoperational | | Conventional conformity |
| 7-12 | Concerete operational | Autonomous | |
| 12+ | Formal operational | | Post conventional moral thinking |

## Kohlberg's theory of moral development

For over two decades, Kohlberg elaborated on Piaget's ideas. He developed a stage theory of the development of moral judgment which he refined over the years, using different terminology and even varying numbers of stages (Kohlberg, 1978, 1981; Kohlberg, Levine, and Hewer, 1983). Typically, however, Kohlberg discusses three levels of moral thinking with two stages at each level. Table 3-3 outlines Kohlberg's stages.

**Table 3-3:** Kohlberg's levels and stages of moral development

| LEVEL | BEHAVIOURAL INTERPRETATION |
|---|---|
| I Premoral | |
| 1. Punishment and obedience orientation | Most swayed by personal results of an action; obeys rules to avoid punishment |
| 2. Naive instrumental hedonism | Looks beyond the immediate consequences and considers the views and approval of others. Conforms to obtain rewards. Unquestioning deference to power. |
| II Conventional conformity | |
| 3. Good boy/good girl morality | Considers the underlying, individual values that might be involved in rule making. Conforms to rules get approval and to avoid disapproval. Behaviour, for the first time, is judged by intentions. |
| 4. Authority-maintaining morality | Conforms to avoid censure by authority. Actions are governed by duty, respect for authority, fixed rules, and maintaining the social order. |
| III Post conventional moral thinking | |
| 5. Morality of contract orientation | Conforms to gain respect of impartial spectators. Actions are defined in terms of general individual rights. |
| 6. Morality of individual principles of conscience | Principles are abstract, ethical, universal, and consistent. Conforms to avoid self-condemnation. Actions are defined by decisions of conscience. |

Kohlberg postulated that the term "moral" referred to a judgment or way in which an individual engages in a decision-making process. He viewed children as "moral philosophers" who develop moral standards on their own that emerge from cognitive interactions with the environment.

Kohlberg claimed that one attains higher forms of morality by attaining higher levels of reasoning (Kohlberg, 1981) and through the benefit of direct instruction in virtue (Stott, 1985). Children proceed through an invariant sequence, analogous to Piaget's stages of cognitive development. Movement from one stage of moral development to the next involves an internal cognitive reorganization rather than the simple acquisition of more moral concepts prevalent in the culture (Kohlberg, 1973).

Early on, Kohlberg suggested that there are 32 moral issues such as the value of human life and the reasons for moral action. Kohlberg's Moral Dilemma Interview used open-ended, free responses that were designed to explore one or more of these 32 issues. Kohlberg arrived at his theory by using Piaget's method of presenting a group of subjects with little stories that revolved around moral issues or dilemmas.

Then, to discover children's stage orientation—the particular moral stage they were likely to attain at certain ages—Kohlberg analyzed his subjects' responses to the moral dilemmas contained in the stories. He scored these responses with respect to issues such as "considering the value of life in judging actions" or "considering the risk of punishment in judging actions" (Kohlberg, 1976, p. 45). Finally, he classified his subjects' reasoning about moral dilemmas into his six stages of development.

In his initial research, Kohlberg interviewed boys aged ten to sixteen, and asked them to solve problems containing hypothetical moral dilemmas involving conflicts. Once the boys had decided on a solution to the problem, Kohlberg asked them to explain themselves. Kohlberg's problems actually held no exact answers. The boys' responses could be based on anything, ranging from conformity to social expectations, to adherence to law and order, to concerns for social welfare.

The best known of Kohlberg's stories involves a European man, a dying wife, and an unattainable drug:

> Heinz's wife lay dying of cancer and her doctors believed that the only treatment that might save her life involved a form of radium newly discovered by a druggist who lived in the same town as Heinz. The radium cost the druggist $200 but he charged $2 000 a dose. By borrowing from friends Heinz could obtain $1 000. He therefore asked the druggist to either lower the price or let Heinz pay the other $1 000 later. When the druggist refused, Heinz broke into the drugstore to steal the radium. Should he have done that? (Kohlberg, 1964).

On this problem, as on all of Kohlberg's dilemmas, a yes or no answer does not suffice to allow a determination of a person's moral stage. To determine the stage, Kohlberg followed up the story with some probing questions such as "Did the druggist have the right to charge so much?" and "Should the punishment be greater if Heinz's wife is an important person?"

### Level I: Premoral

Individuals at the premoral level of conventional morality do not possess an organized system of moral concepts from which to operate. At Stage 1, which Kohlberg defined as the level of punishment and obedience orientation, individuals (chiefly young children) are highly egocentric. They are concerned with their own interests but not the interests of others. Moral dilemmas are solved solely on the basis of specific rewards or punishments individuals might receive.

At Stage 2 (naive instrumental hedonism), individuals also lack generalized moral notions. Such people are concerned primarily with themselves although they will enter into limited reciprocity agreements. In other words, children at this stage are interested in exchanging favours and use people to get what they want.

Another of Kohlberg's stories illustrates this point. This story presents children with a dilemma concerning punishment and reward. It tells of a boy whose mother told him to watch the baby while she went to the store. However, as soon as the mother left, the boy went outside and played. When the mother returned, she gave the boy some candy. Four-year-old children are likely to disregard the boy's disobedience because he got a reward anyway. On the other hand, seven year olds expressed a sense of injustice because disobedience was rewarded. Most seven year olds felt that disobedience necessarily led to punishment and therefore the story was unrealistic.

## Level II: Conventional conformity

By the end of their elementary school years, children are at least beginning to apply the Golden Rule. They can understand why trust and mutual helpfulness are essential to human relationships and they want to be nice persons by living up to the expectations of significant others and following the nudge of conscience (Kohlberg, 1981). From about the age of ten, the responses of many children to moral dilemmas showing Level II thinking increase. By the age of 13 or so most children resolve moral judgments at Level II.

Persons who reveal conventional levels of moral thinking accept and internalize the moral socialization they receive from their families and from society generally. Their thinking depends on distinct stereotypes and sharp differences and they tend to conform strictly to the conventions of the society in which they live. Children at Stage 3, the stage of good boy/good girl morality, identify strongly with their parents and other adult authority figures and strive to please them by doing what they ask. Students at this stage seek approval from parents and teachers as well as from peers, and make their decisions on the basis of what they think others will think of them.

Older persons who are still characterized by Stage 3 thinking display more adult forms of these same moral notions. Stage 3 perspectives presume that society is a sort of homogeneous, harmonious "we" composed of people who share moral values (Selman, 1976b). People at this stage use more general and abstract moral concepts; these people think in terms of doing their duty, living up to expectations, and displaying virtues (Good and Brophy, 1986).

Stage 4 morality is more abstract than Stage 3 in its underlying assumptions about the nature of society. It is what Kohlberg called a "systems perspective" because it assumes that the solutions to social conflicts reside in the context of political and legal institutions. Individuals who develop from Stage 3 to Stage 4, the authority-maintaining morality stage, look to rules, laws, or codes for guidance in difficult situations. They change from a moral orientation based on pleasing others to a more generalized orientation that considers law and social expectations as means toward the end of maintaining the social system as a whole.

However, they hold a rather rigid law and order orientation and tend to be more concerned with what is right rather than with consequences. Stage 4 persons are impressed with the need for order and for all persons to fulfill their duties and obligations. They often, however, carry their emphasis on the need to uphold the law to extremes. This issue is examined in Box 3-3 which illustrates a dilemma in the classroom.

## Box 3-3  **In the classroom**

This is the case of a school principal and a teacher assigned a particularly difficult class of grade eight boys. These boys brought to the classroom a long history of behaviour disorders, aggressive outbursts and occasional physical violence toward teachers.

After trying various modes of behaviour control and discipline, the teacher implemented a token economy system. For accomplishing certain amounts of assigned work, the pupils could earn small tokens that could then be traded in on a Friday afternoon for a larger reward. She allowed the boys to choose the Friday reward and they opted for such activities as a trip to the library, half an hour of free reading, and a special art period. The token economy system worked extremely well with these pupils and, when the boys asked whether the Friday reward could be a baseball game, the teacher acquiesced.

All that week, the boys worked well to earn their tokens. However, just as they were leaving the classroom for their game the school principal walked in and announced that the game was cancelled since playing baseball during what should have been an English period was against the rules of the school.

The boys were extremely disappointed and argued that they had worked hard, that they had earned the game, and that they had a promise from the teacher. The school principal argued that there were rules, and that rules could not be broken under any circumstances. The teacher argued that she and the boys had made a contract and the boys had fulfilled their end. She argued that in this case the end result of continually improving behaviour and increased acacemic standards justified breaking the rules. Who presented the best argument? With whom would you agree?

### Postconventional moral thinking

Persons who attain the postconventional level of moral thinking develop more abstract and better integrated moral concepts; they move beyond the emphasis on social conventions and law and order of Stage 4. Within Stage 5, termed the morality of contract orientation, individuals make choices on the basis of people's rights and obligations in a democratically established order. They begin to view laws more flexibly and realize that laws can be changed if they are not meeting the needs of a society. Stage 5 individuals appreciate that certain basic values such as liberty and equality might take precedence over the law itself. However, Stage 5 individuals confine their attempts to change laws to orderly, democratic activities.

At the highest stage of moral thinking—Stage 6, the morality of individual principles of conscience—moral thinking and judgments are complex and comprehensive; diverse points of view are considered. Judgments are based on consistency and universality together with concern for human life, equality, and dignity. Individuals hold clear conceptions of abstract universal principles such as fairness, justice, and individual human dignity that transcend the law.

Kohlberg has difficulty defining this stage in ways that differentiate it clearly from Stage 5 and feels that few persons ever reach this stage. He reported that fewer than ten percent of his adult subjects showed the kind of "clear-principled" thinking needed for Level 6 (Kohlberg, 1969a).

## Problems with Kohlberg's theory

Kohlberg has claimed that his theory is superior to Piaget's on a number of points—it accounts for moral development following childhood, meets the criteria that define a stage sequence, and carefully considers the underlying structure of an individual's moral reasoning (Siegel, 1980). Although some certainly see Kohlberg's work as an innovative and major extension of that of Piaget, other researchers have suggested that Kohlberg's theory is but a modest improvement on Piaget's and that both have much to contribute to the study of moral development (Siegel, 1980). Kohlberg's work, in fact, has been the object of important criticisms by a significant number of social scientists and philosophers. Some of the major areas of debate and criticism follow below.

1. Kohlberg defined six stages of moral reasoning that were assumed to be universal across cultures. Since he originated his original set of studies in the 1960s, there has been a substantial increase in the amount of research evidence in support of Kohlberg's stage and sequence framework. Moreover, moral development research has found that there are generally no reversals; major regressions in moral growth do not occur (Rest, 1973).

2. Further, Kohlberg's model assumes that the moral life is primarily the result of the development of specific, often abstract, moral principles that are capable of being expressed in verbal form. Everyone begins at Stage 1 and, if given an adequately stimulating cognitive environment, will develop from Stage 1 to Stage 5 or 6.

   Like other developmental stage theorists, Kohlberg found a positive relationship between age and stage. Older children tended to solve problems at higher levels on his scales than did younger children. Kohlberg did note, however, that people do not automatically increase the level at which they respond with age. In addition, most adults—perhaps 95 percent—never reach the highest level, that of morality based on universal ethical principles (Sanborn, 1971).

3. Although the stage and sequence orientation is well accepted, the types of dilemmas Kohlberg studied have not been as easily embraced. Kohlberg's stages of moral development were originally thought to apply to nearly all types of moral conflicts. However, the moral dilemmas used by Kohlberg to assess moral judgment centre on issues related to prohibitions or conflicts between explicit standards of justice; for example, conflicts related to laws, formal obligations, and punishment. These kinds of issues, important as they may be, may not be representative of the type of moral dilemmas that children and adolescents routinely face (Yussen, 1977). Kohlberg (1969b) found that middle-class children are more advanced in moral judgment than lower-class children. It may be simply that the type of dilemmas these children and youth encounter do not match the dilemmas of Kohlberg's orientation. That is to say, there may be a socioeconomic bias to the dilemmas chosen for study.

4. Kohlberg may not have been entirely correct in believing that moral reasoning develops in much the same way as cognition does. He reported that individuals can reach higher levels of moral reasoning if they are given experiences in interacting with others and in solving moral problems. Other psychologists disagree. Morality, they argue, is more than just cognitive organization. It also includes an internal value system as well as the ability to perceive long-range consequences of an action, and the ability to empathize with others. The development of a sense of right and wrong is part of the general process of socialization and is largely the result of models provided by parents, peers, and other significant persons. Psychologists have shown that parents and teachers are very important role models in this process, but many other people such as friends and relatives are also very important (Windmiller, 1980). Specifically, a child can learn many moral behaviours through modeling of adults, rather than merely through solving hypothetical moral problems.

5. Even though moral development is linked to cognitive development, it may be wrong to suppose that gifted children move more swiftly through the moral development stages than average children. It is logical to expect that those who can function intellectually (academically and creatively) on a very high level could function on a more or less similar level morally (at least from the viewpoint of reasoning). Piaget (1973) also claimed that bright children are capable at an earlier age than their peers of thinking on the level of formal operational thought which is characterized by abstract reasoning and logical, rational thought. In addition, Gowan and Bruch (1971), Drews (1972), and Malone (1975) noted that gifted children differ from their peers in their early concern with questions about values and morals.

   However, in a study of gifted students in Toronto, Tan-Willman and Gutteridge (1981) found that the moral development of gifted students could be viewed as being undeveloped when their superior academic competencies and high socio-cultural backgrounds were taken into account. Although their test results were somewhat better, they were in fact functioning predominantly on the conventional level of moral reasoning, just like their age group in the general population.

6. In reality, the stages Kohlberg describes do not seem to be separate, sequenced, and consistent. It now appears that the reasoning of children and adolescents about positive justice (e.g., Damon, 1977) and prosocial issues (Eisenberg, Lennon, and Roth, 1983; Gilligan, 1982) may differ somewhat from the stages proposed by Kohlberg (Fuchs et al., 1986). Also, people often give reasons for moral choices that reflect several different stages simultaneously. In addition, a person's choices in one instance might fit one stage and in a different situation reflect another stage.

7. Kohlberg was not fundamentally interested in children's moral behaviour but rather with their moral judgments, the basis on which they decide that something is right or wrong. But critics of his theory have emphasized the importance of distinguishing between moral reasoning and moral behaviour, since moral judgments focus on intentions, rather than consequences (Siegel, 1980), and moral reasoning may not correspond to moral behaviour. In fact,

there is some question about whether the ability to reason at a particular level of a moral development has much to do with actual reasoning in real situations or with actual behaviour.

What people believe is right and wrong and what they do is often contradictory. Some studies have revealed no correlation at all between moral judgment and moral behaviour. Others have shown correlations at the extreme levels. For example, individuals who score particularly low in moral judgments are especially likely to be involved in disruptive behaviour in school (Bear and Richards, 1981; Geiger and Turiel, 1983) or to become involved in juvenile delinquency (Hains and Miller, 1980). In contrast, individuals who score at Stage 5 tend to be especially likely to engage in principled moral behaviour (Good and Brophy, 1986).

In general, however, the research relating to the moral levels of behaviour in specific situations—whether a student will cheat, for example—have found low correlations (Mischel and Mischel, 1976; Rest, 1973). In one study, 15 percent of students judged to be at postconventional reasoning actually cheated on a task. Fifty-five percent of students at the conventional level and 70 percent of students at the preconventional level also cheated (Kohlberg, 1975). The fact that some students cheated in spite of their ability to reason at a principled, postconventional level suggests that a full understanding of moral (and immoral) actions requires more than knowledge about moral reasoning abilities.

Clearly, the ability to reason on a higher level does not mean that people will always act in a manner consistent with their principles. We discuss cheating further in the classic study outlined in Box 3-4. As these studies illustrate, moral reasoning does not necessarily predict moral behaviour.

8. The correlation Kohlberg envisions between cognitive development and the shift from egocentrisim to seeing things from others' points of view may not exist. Selman (1971, 1976a, 1976b, 1980), who developed a hierarchy of children's ability in perspective taking, studied how the growing abilty to take the perspective of others affects morality.

   In a group of children of about the same age and level of general intelligence, Selman found that the children who had reached the higher levels of perspective taking on his scale were also the ones who were most likely to have reached the higher levels of moral reasoning on Kohlberg's dilemma discussions. However, the relationships seemed to be one-sided. In other words, while individuals at the postconventional level of morality are alomost all skilful at taking other perspectives, individuals with excellent perspective taking abilities are not necessarily highly moral (Maccoby, 1980).

9. There have also been significant criticisms of Kohlberg's approach because his dilemmas emphasize rational thought at the expense of religion (Salkind, 1990).

10. Another criticism is that Stage 6 reasoning is biased in favour of Western, libertarian values that emphasize individualism. In cultures that are more family-centred or group-oriented, the highest moral value might involve placing the opinions of the group before decisions based on individual conscience. This may, however, have more to do with the wording and context of the dilemmas than the culture, per se. When Snarey (1985) adapted the

### Box 3-4 **Classic study**

In the 1920s, two researchers, Hugh Hartshorne (1885-1967) and Mark May (1891-1977) of the University of Chicago conducted a long series of studies that they replicated over and over again as part of their Character Education Enquiry. Their investigation centred on the notion of stable character traits such as honesty or dishonesty but also encompassed aspects of moral behaviour and the effect of instruction in morals and values.

Hartshorne and May (1928-1930) presented children of various ages with opportunities to cheat or steal when the children thought they would not be caught. Very few children behaved honestly in every case, and a very few behaved badly or dishonestly in every case. As well, the researchers found no relationship between what the children said about morality and the way they acted. People who expressed great disapproval about cheating and stealing actually stole and cheated as much as anyone else. The risk of detection seemed to be the single most important factor in deterring cheating. Therefore, Hartshorne and May decided that it was meaningless to divide people into simple categories and label them as either honest or dishonest. Like so many other aspects of human nature, cheating is normally distributed around a moderate level of cheating (Sprinthall and Sprinthall, 1987). The researchers found that this was true not only for traits such as honesty and dishonesty but also for such human traits as altruism and selfishness, and self-control and impulsiveness.

A second major finding was that virtues are relatively unamenable to teaching. Hartshorne and May studied classes in character education, such as Sunday school classes and Boy Scout classes. After studying 10 000 children and adolescents, Hartshorne and May found no consistent moral behaviour in the same person from one situation to another based on character education. They concluded that there was no correlation between character education and virtue training and actual behaviour, such as cheating. Formal character training had no positive effect. In general, they observed that moral and ethical traits seemed mythical and moral behaviour unpredictable.

dilemmas for different cultures, he found, in both cross-sectional and longitudinal studies from different cultures, that all stages of moral development were represented and that development proceeded in the same sequence.

11. There has been much disagreement about the highest moral stage. In later years, Kohlberg himself had questioned the inclusion of Stage 6. Very few people other than trained philosophers reason naturally or easily at this level.

12. Kohlberg's cognitive approach to values education, with its attention to stages of reasoning was, for a long time, the cornerstone approach to moral education. However, its effectiveness is now in question. The premise of cognitive

development in values education is that the sequence of changes in one's social concepts and the underlying mechanisms of stage changes form the basis for the sequencing and design of social values curricula. The nature of moral education is a process in which morals teaching (classroom discussions aimed at stimulating students' movement to the next stage of moral development) is practised (Kohlberg, 1964, 1967; Kohlberg and Turiel, 1971a, b). The ultimate goal of moral education is the development of principled moral judgments.

If Kohlberg is correct, then it might be possible for teachers to stimulate their students' moral development. The procedure would involve:

- presenting moral dilemmas;

- encouraging students to think such problems through and to discover flaws in their reasoning; and

- exposing them to attitudes that would be expressed at the stage immediately above their own.

But problems exist with the concept of moral education, at least as elucidated by Kohlberg. Certainly, when Kohlberg's ideas have been applied to educational programs designed to increase children's moral judgment levels, they have been generally successful (e.g., Damon and Killen, 1982; Mosher, 1980). Typically, programs involve presenting students with moral dilemmas such as those used by Piaget and Kohlberg and employing the "stage plus one" matching principle, which is usually effective (Enright et al., 1983; Mosher, 1980; Walker, 1983).

Even though plus one matching has been widely used in moral education with apparent success, critics of the method have questioned whether the procedure is essential for development or simply catalytic (Kuhn, 1979; Rest, 1974). Even those sympathetic to values education have questioned the emphasis this approach places on cognition over feeling, on structure of reasoning over content of values, and on hypothetical over real life dilemmas (e.g., Fraenkel, 1978). And nearly everyone, including Kohlberg himself, has wondered whether student gains in moral judgment would translate into observable changes in student moral behaviour (Reimer, 1981).

Researchers have pointed out difficulties that can occur. For one thing, Kohlberg postulated that only about ten percent of the adult population develops to Stage 5 or 6 of moral reasoning (Kohlberg and Turiel, 1971a, b). If this is so, then how can a teacher at Stage 3 present a higher level of argument if the teacher cannot even comprehend such an argument? (Fraenkel, 1976) In other words, how can teachers raise the moral levels of students when they are themselves reasoning at conventional levels?

Apart from this, there is the question of whether moral development can actually be accelerated by direct instruction. Lockwood (1978) summarized the findings of almost a dozen studies on the acceleration of moral reasoning and concluded that the strongest effects (about one-half a stage increase in reasoning) occurred among individuals whose reasoning reflected Kohlberg's Stages 2 and 3. However, treatment effect varied considerably; some students showed substantive changes in moral reasoning while others showed none. Other researchers (Schaefli, Rest, and Thomas, 1985) have reached similar conclusions. They found that moral education programs produce modest positive effects. They also found that the strongest effects are found in adult subjects.

Current approaches to moral education include those based on values clarification (Raths, 1972; Simon, Howe, and Kirschenbaum, 1972), on the Reflective Ethics Approach (Beck, 1971), on Kohlberg's claim that one attains higher forms of morality by attaining higher levels of reasoning (Kohlberg, 1981), and on direct instruction in virtue (Stott, 1985).

**13.** Kohlberg's ordering of the stages of moral development indicates certain biases, specifically in relation to sex differences. No females were included in Kohlberg's original data; the sample population was restricted to small numbers of white, middle-class males.

## The question of gender

When Kohlberg's study was first validated, there were two studies, one in Canada (Sullivan, McCullough, and Stager, 1970) and one in the United States (Turiel, 1976) that specifically examined the relationship between gender and stage of moral development. Both studies indicated that gender differences did not exist.

However, Carol Gilligan (1977, 1982), one of Kohlberg's colleagues, formulated ideas that encouraged a serious enquiry about sex bias in his theory and research findings. Gilligan believes that the study of moral development has, up to now, been concerned more with the "justice and autonomy" orientation that is characteristic of the way men think than with the "care and responsibility" concerns that women bring to moral issues (Cordes, 1984). For example, more women than men are identified as being at Stage 3 as opposed to Stage 4, partly because women tend to value the approval of others and to favour merciful behaviour. The fact that Kohlberg sees these qualities as representing a lower stage of moral development, suggests that his ordering of stages may reflect a bias in favour of males (Gilligan, 1977).

Gilligan and her coworkers hold that a conception of the self as independent or separate from others is associated with a conception of morality and justice, whereas a conception of the self as connected to others is related to a conception of morality as responsibility (Gilligan et al., 1982; Lyons, 1983). These differences tend to be associated with gender, with women more likely to express concerns about responsibility and men more likely to orient toward considerations of justice. Gilligan also argues that when women are faced with real-life moral dilemmas such as abortion or civil rights they, are more likely to maintain a caring-helping, cooperative orientation than a justice-individual rights orientation (Biehler and Snowman, 1990).

The charge of sex bias has not been proven. Recent data on this issue seem to support Kohlberg's contention that when samples are controlled for education, socioeconomic status, and occupation, there are no differences between males and females in average stage level attainment (Brabeck, 1983; Kohlberg, 1982; Vasdudev and Hummel, 1987). Lawrence Walker of the University of British

Men are thought more likely than women to orient themselves toward considerations of justice.

Columbia (Walker, 1984, 1986) was one who critically reviewed studies of sex differences. He essentially found few differences in the studies he reviewed (Bracey, 1984). Some researchers, however, continue to find and explain sex differences in Kohlberg's theory (Baumrind, 1986).

## SUMMARY

1. The major stage theory of cognitive development is that evolved by Jean Piaget. To Piaget, the mind of the child is a structure that evolves through successively higher levels of organization and integration. As children grow, they are able to solve increasingly complex problems because new learning and experiences allow cognitive structures of increasing complexity.

2. The essence of Piaget's theory lies in the notion that it is the nature of human functioning to organize and adapt, whether physically or mentally, biologically

or intellectually. To explain his theory, Piaget used the related concepts of schemata, organization, adaptation, assimilation, accommodation, and equilibration.

3. Within the first two years of life, children pass through a series of substages of mental development carefully described by Piaget. Most of the schemata of the newborn infant are simple reflexes but new schemata begin to appear quickly and existing schemata become coordinated into larger cognitive structures. Children in the sensorimotor period gradually progress from reflexive to goal-directed and intentional behaviour.

4. The functioning of preschool children is not as reflective in nature as that of adults but is shown in organized patterns of actions that Piaget characterized as preoperational. Two to four year olds at the beginning of the preoperational period are starting to construct their knowledge on a conceptual plane, but they have not yet developed the ability to think logically or abstractly and still tend to rely on perceptual analyses of situations rather than on conceptual references. It is at about age four that children begin to be able to construct more complex images and more elaborate concepts. In the next three years or so, they add more information and learn increasing numbers of symbols. At this stage of development children are ready to assimilate much new information.

5. As children become operational, their cognitive schemata, especially their thinking and problem-solving skills, become organized into concrete operations, mental representations of potential actions. New experiences are assimilated through more complex methods of analysis. In turn, children's methods of anaylsis become more and more refined because of encounters with new experiences. In the period of concrete operational thought, children learn to develop concepts based on many dimensions, rather than just one. They are ready to understand conservation.

6. When students reach the formal operational period they enter a new world of ideas and conceptions and begin to hypothesize about relationships.

7. Piaget was the first to attempt a systematic tracing of the transformations in children's moral reasoning. Developmental change in moral thought is not merely an intensification of belief in the values advocated by adults. The changes take place in children's ideas about the basis for avoiding wrongdoing.

8. Lawrence Kohlberg hypothesized a complex sequence of stages of moral reasoning, thinking, and problem solving. Kohlberg stressed that reason is a necessary springboard to morality. Kohlberg used an invariant sequence of stages tied roughly to chronological ages. He expanded on Piaget's levels which defined children up to about the age of ten as within the morality of constraint and those older as within the morality of cooperation. Like Piaget, Kohlberg believed that small children are ruled by adult constraint and the shift from blind acceptance of authority and rules to reciprocal understanding becomes evident as they develop. By the age of 10 or 11, children enter a more mature stage of moral development.

9. What people believe is right and wrong and what they do is often contradictory. Psychologists argue over whether to judge a person's moral development

by beliefs or actions. Kohlberg focused on beliefs and moral judgments; other psychologists focus on actions.

## Key Terms

| | | |
|---|---|---|
| adaptation | category | categorization |
| centration | cognitive development | concept |
| conservation | deduction | egocentrism |
| equilibration | induction | object permanence |
| operation | organization | schemata |
| seriation | social cognition | social transmission |
| spatial visualization | symbol | transduction |

# SOCIAL AND EMOTIONAL DEVELOPMENT

C
H
A
P
T
E
R

4

**Socio-emotional development:**

the development of personality, the ability to interact socially, the ability to make value judgements, and the ability to understand cultural mores.

## INTRODUCTION

**Socio-emotional development** refers to the development of an individual's personality, ability to interact socially, the ability to make value judgments, and ability to understand cultural mores. Socio-emotional development depends upon a huge matrix of factors that are difficult to really separate from each other. These factors are illustrated in Figure 4-1.

**Figure 4-1**
Factors affecting socio-emotional development

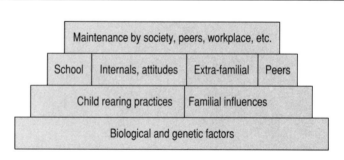

To understand where children are currently in the socio-emotional context, where they have come from, and where they are going, a number of models of socio-emotional development have evolved. Most are discontinuous theories that view children's socio-emotional development as progressing through distinct and identifiable stages that are roughly tied to chronological ages. In this chapter, we stress the theories of Eric Erikson; these are most relevant to the classroom teacher because they help alert teachers and parents to students' varying levels of development. First, however, we briefly overview Freudian constructs as Erikson's roots lie in the theory of personality proposed by Freud at

**Affective variables:**
feelings that, along with cognition, govern all behaviour.

**Affectivity:**
mental state pertaining to emotion–how one feels, how one manifests those feelings–and all other motivating conditions such as drive states and intentions.

**Temperament:**
the behavioural style of an individual.

the opening of this century. Erikson modernized Freudian theory and although his terms are different from those of Freud, his assumptions are the same. Erikson, as a stage theorist, subscribes to the epigenetic principle that individuals are born with the potential for growth and that, through interaction with the environment and those in it, their socio-emotional development proceeds in accordance with the biological plan.

## TEMPERAMENT

Individuals are the sum of what they know and feel. What they know and feel is reflected in their behaviour. Technically, behaviour is influenced by, and reflective of, cognitive and affective variables. Affectivity pertains to emotion—how one feels and how one manifests those feelings—and to all other motivating conditions such as drive states and intentions (Zivin, 1986). All emotions, then, are affects but only some affects are emotions.

States of emotions (i.e., affects) may be temporary and amenable to change; they include such things as anxiety and depression. Traits, however, are enduring aspects of personality such as locus of control, creativity and self-concept. These are all components of temperament which may be defined as the behavioural style of an individual. It is claimed that temperament is a potent factor in determining psychosocial functioning (e.g., Barron and Earls, 1984).

Psychologists are less certain about the relationship between biological inheritance and socio-emotional development than they are about the relationships between biological inheritance and physical development. There seem to be very few biological predispositions for personal and social traits, even though there are family resemblances for everything from food preferences (Rozin, Fallon and Mandell, 1974) to political philosophies (Boshier and Thom, 1973). Plomin (1989) believes that 40 percent of the personality differences between children can be accounted for by genetic factors. In particular, he identifies three areas that might be particularly susceptible to genetic influences: environmental adjustment, or how well children get along with others; activity level, or the general amount of movement; and sociabilitiy, or how much children like to be with other people. However, along with genetic potential, maturation interacts with learning experiences in complex ways and researchers are still learning how biologically controlled development affects and is, in turn, affected by behaviour.

From birth, certain individual differences in temperament exist. In fact, it is clear that infants and children differ strikingly in their behavioural characteristics; that there are temperamental characteristics that can be measured reliably by various techniques; and that temperament plays a functionally significant role in the course of normal and deviant  psychological development (Rutter, 1982). Early temperamental attributes may be seen as the early building blocks for an individual's later personality (Thomas and Chess, 1977).

As early as the first weeks of life, infants show individual differences in activity level, responsiveness to change, and irritability. Some infants are alert and physically active much of the time, exploring the environment and reacting to stimulation; others sleep much of the time, and even when awake are mostly quiet and relatively unresponsive.

Certain individual differences in temperament exist from birth.

Thomas and Chess and their colleagues (1968, 1977) classified temperamental responses along nine dimensions—activity, rhythmicity, adaptability, approach-withdrawal, threshold, intensity, mood, distractability, and persistance. Particular groupings for infants within these classifications were "difficult," "easy" or "slow to warm up."

Difficult children are viewed as intense, irregular, withdrawing, nonadaptable, and predominantly negative in mood. The easy children possess exactly the opposite set of characteristics. They are seen to be regular in biological functioning—they have good sleep cycles, eat at regular intervals, approach new events positively, are usually happy, adaptable to change, and in general moderately responsive to stimulation. Children seen as slow to warm up are low in activity and intensity and show a pattern of slow adaptation characterized by initial withdrawal, but eventual adjustment.

Temperamental differences observed in infants tend to persist to some degree through childhood and correlate with differences in arousal level and behaviour observed later (Thomas and Chess, 1977). Numerous researchers have reported that temperament is related to developmental problems or gains in later life. The consistent direction of this assessment is that children with difficult temperamental styles are more likely than easy children to meet problems later on (Riese, 1987; Thomas and Chess, 1977). They tend to exhibit such behaviours as excessive crying in infancy (Carey, 1983); temper tantrums and accident proneness in early and later childhood (Thomas and Chess, 1977); and less psychological adjustment in childhood, adolescence, and early adult life (Barron and Earls, 1984; Chess and Thomas, 1984). On the other hand, an easy temperament has been identified as a protective factor for children at risk for maladjustment (Garmezy, 1974; Rutter, 1981). Once in school, reflective children persist longer with difficult tasks and show higher standards of intellectual performance than do impulsive children (Kagan, 1965) (see Chapter 6).

As well as the differentiation between easy, difficult, and slow to warm up, certain sex differences in temperament are observable in many children from birth. Boys tend to be relatively more active, initiatory, aggressive, and oriented toward physical manipulation of objects in the environment. Although girls tend to be more physically mature, especially in their neurophysiological control mechanisms, they are more apt to observe environmental events than to manipulate objects. They also do more watching, listening, and verbalizing.

Even where biological predispositions toward personal and social traits exist, environmental influences play a crucial role, for they interact with these innate predispositions to affect behaviour. An active and initiatory child, for example, who has siblings or peers available, may spend much time in rough and ready play, but one who does not have playmates readily available may spend a lot of time actively exploring the physical environment. Physically active children raised in an atmosphere of hostility and violence are likely to become predisposed to fighting and bullying (Huessman et al., 1984; Patterson and Stouthamer-Loeber, 1984), but the same type of children raised in a warmer and more humanistic environment tend to become active and asssertive but nonaggressive peer leaders (Maccoby and Martin, 1983; Rohner and Nielson, 1978; Staub, 1979).

Psychologists have not always recognized the interplay of heredity and environment in personality development, however, as can be seen in the historical notes in Box 4-1.

---

## Box 4-1 Historical note: Moral imbeciles

In the late nineteenth century, North American morality was far more absolutist than it is today. The present orthodoxy is to look for environmental causes of crime and delinquency; a hundred years ago it was assumed that adults chose a life of crime or, at least, did nothing to halt their inevitable degeneration. It was thought that criminals were born to be criminals, and that they could be identified by the "stigmata of degeneracy." The narrowing bounds of conduct acceptable to society in the nineteenth century wrought a moral revolution that conditioned attitudes toward a construct of moral insanity, later moral imbecility.

The term "moral insanity" was first used in England during the 1850s (see Walton, 1979) just at the time when physicians and educators were beginning to make more precise diagnostic distinctions among the population of people seen to be mentally retarded, or feeble-minded as the condition was then called (Winzer, 1990b). Isaac Kerlin, the superintendent of a large institution for mentally retarded persons, used the term "moral imbecile" in the 1880s to describe those youth displaying a perverted moral nature that frequently manifested itself in juvenile crime (Kerlin, 1879). He then identified four classes of moral

imbecile—alcoholic inebriates, tramps, prostitutes, and habitual criminals.

Moral imbeciles were not necessarily
thought to be mentally retarded (although
high numbers were deemed to be so), but
were considered to be afflicted with minor
mental defects—"fertile ground that allowed
ineradicably evil mental attitudes to take
ready root" (Vineland, 1894, p. 37). Moral
imbeciles suffered an irreparable defect of the
moral faculties comparable with the intellectual damage suffered by the truly retarded.
Moral perversions were difficult to separate
from merely evil and vicious tendencies (see
Carlson and Dain, 1962). The moral imbecile
was viewed as bad and practically incurable:
"an instinctive liar and thief, cunning and
skillful in mischief making" (Vineland, 1894,
p. 41). This was the youngster who

> lights a bon-fire on the carpet of the liv-
> ing-room of his home and accuses his
> younger brother or, perhaps, the cat for
> overturning a lamp. He has only two
> interests—one, to see a good big blaze
> with the resulting confusion and terror
> on the part of the family, and the other,

> to escape the personal consequences of
> discovery (Pratt, 1920, p. 363).

Moreover, moral imbecility was viewed as
being solely due to heredity. Charles
Davenport (1866-1944), an American geneti-
cist, focused his studies primarily on those
regarded as moral imbeciles—the tramps, the
prostitutes, and the criminals. Davenport
found a common association between
nomadism and "well-known aberrant errors
and mental state" (1915a, p. 24). Davenport
discovered that nomadism occurred more
often males, and suspected it to be a sex-
linked recessive monohybrid trait, a fundamental human instinct that was typically
inhibited in intelligent adults of civilized peoples (Davenport, 1915b). "All the evidence,"
said Davenport, "supports the hypothesis
that the nomadic impulse depends upon the
absence of a simple sex-linked gene that
'determines' domesticity" (Davenport, 1915b,
p. 23). As those nomadic men who tended to
marry chose women with similar impulses,
all of their offspring tended to be nomadic.

**SOURCE:** Winzer 1990b.

---

The temperament of each child may influence not only how parents treat the
child but also how this treatment may affect the child. Parents of passive children, for example, may become very protective, particularly with young boys
who appear more vulnerable in the rough world of other preschool boys.
Passive temperament, a largely biologically determined characteristic, helps create a particular environment (protective parenting) that can have lasting effects
(Kagan, 1979). The profundity of the effects may even be increased given the
original temperament of the child.

Social behaviour is the function of interactions between two or more persons.
The manner in which parents and children respond to one another form
behaviours. Different parenting styles have been identified that drastically influence children's social and emotional development in all areas, and especially in
aggression, conformity, immaturity, and passivity.

Diana Baumrind (1971, 1973) identified three major parenting styles—authoritative, authoritarian, and permissive. Of course, most parents don't consistently

**Personality:**

pattern of behaviours and thoughts that characterize individuals and distinguish them from others.

fit precisely into one style or another. One primary style may be modified or give way to another as the circumstances or the particular subculture dictate (Lamb and Baumrind, 1978).

Some parents are authoritarian—they are controlling, uninvolved, and cold. They demand compliance and enforce rules harshly. Authoritarian parents make demands and wield power but their lack of warmth and failure to take the child's point of view into account lead to resentment and insecurity on the part of the child (Baumrind, 1971). Children of authoritarian parents may do what they are told but they are likely to do it out of compliance or fear, not out of a desire to earn love or approval. These children tend to become withdrawn and unhappy; they have trouble trusting others and may be low achievers in school.

Because their parents tend toward aggression, these children do the same. Once learned, aggression tends to be a stable personality feature over time. Eron and Huessman (1987) tested 632 males and females at eight and again at 30 years of age. They found that the most aggressive eight year olds at the beginning of the study were also the most aggressive adults at the end (see Chapter 6). Longitudinal research also shows that aggression perpetuates itself within the family and even across generations; this effect has been observed across three generations (Huessman, Eron, and Yarmel, 1987).

Authoritative parents are firm and demanding but also consistent, loving, and communicative (Baumrind, 1971). They have confidence in their abilities as parents and provide competent models for their children to imitate. When they establish limits they explain the reasons for the restrictions. They encourage their children to set standards for themselves and to think about why certain procedures should be followed. Their children tend to be competent, content, self-reliant, and assertive. They also display high self-esteem.

Finally, permissive parents are warm and undemanding. They set few rules and avoid punishing their children. Permissive parents can be disorganized, inconsistent, and lacking in confidence. Their children are likely to imitate such behaviour. They do not demand much from their children and do not discourage immature behaviour (Biehler and Snowman, 1990). Their children don't seem to learn self-reliance and tend to be unhappy. Boys in particular may be low achievers (Baumrind, 1973).

When parents are generally permissive yet occasionally resort to physical punishment, the inconsistency will produce aggression in children. Attempts to reduce aggression through socialization do not succeed when parents are arbitrary in their own actions and attitudes regarding physical aggression. The families with the least aggressive children seem to be those where the parents practice a combination of nonpermissiveness, nonpunishment, and nonrejection. They try to avoid letting potentially explosive situations develop and they head off quarrels and arguments by separating the children before they begin. When aggression does occur, they don't punish it severely (Bee, 1978).

## Personality

**Personality** is the pattern of behaviour and thoughts that characterizes individuals, distinguishes them from others, and remains relatively stable throughout their lives. It is a unique complex of emotional responses that differentiates one

**Self-concept:**
the composite of ideas, feelings, and attitudes people have about themselves.

**Self-esteem:**
the degree of satisfaction with the self.

**Self-awareness:**
an attempt to explain ourselves to ourselves and to organize our impressions, feelings, and attitudes about ourselves in some way. Self-awareness leads children to compare themselves with others.

person from another and makes up an important part of an individual's identity (Salkind, 1990).

Although physical appearance, growth rate, and temperament have biological correlates, most personality traits are almost entirely the products of environmental rather than genetic influences. The personality traits we see developing in children result from conditioning by social experiences and reinforcement, and from modeling by significant others in their lives, especially their parents. These traits include cooperativeness, competitiveness, motivation, optimism, pessimism, and sociability, and are reflected in activity preferences, personal interests, social status (as peer leaders, followers, or isolates) problem-solving styles, and ways of coping with frustrations.

Two affective variables that are particularly important for school performance and social success are self-concept and locus of control. The importance of their behavioural manifestations for learning (such as independence, self-confidence, flexibility, experimentation, internal locus of evaluation, and a preference for the complex) have been shown in a variety of studies (e.g., Tetenbaum and Houtz, 1978).

**Self-concept** is "the composite of ideas, feelings, and attitudes people have about themselves" (Hilgard, Atkinson, and Atkinson, 1979, p. 605). The beliefs that form self-concept help to make a child what she or he is, does, can do, and wants to do. This self-concept serves three purposes—it maintains inner consistency, determines the interpretation of experiences, and provides expectations (Felker, 1974).

It is important to distinguish between self-concept and self-esteem. While the self-concept is descriptive and non-judgmental, **self-esteem** is evaluative, and reflects the degree of satisfaction with the self. Self-awareness, which also rides tandem with self-concept and self-esteem, is more concerned with information about the self. **Self-awareness** is the attempt to explain ourselves to ourselves and to organize our impressions, feelings, and attitudes about ourselves in some way. Self-awareness leads children to compare themselves with others.

Self-concept includes the social, environmental, and physical domains. A child's early self-concept is formed by parents, siblings, peers, and then the neighbourhood and the school. Once established, it is thought that the self-concept does not change greatly in response to interpersonal or achievement situations. That is, self-concept is resistant to change through short-term or artificial intervention.

As children grow, enter school, and meet the complexities of reading, writing, and mathematics, their self-concept seems to become increasingly organized along both academic and non-academic lines so that there seem to be two self-concepts (Marsh and Shavelson, 1985; Shavelson and Bolus, 1982). The academic self-concept is based on ability in the various academic areas. The non-academic self-concept is founded on relationships with peers and significant others, on emotional states, and on physical status.

Self-concept and self-esteem are centrally involved in the learning process. Feldhusen and Hoover (1986) observe that they are probably major influences that impel an individual to work, to investigate, to learn, to solve problems, to compete, and to achieve. Teachers, therefore, must ask themselves how

**Motivation:**
the energy or force that directs human behaviour; the affect, or emotional response to a problem situation which then influences how the problem will be viewed and solved.

**Locus of control:**
the source to which an individual attributes responsibility for the outcome of events or behaviours. The tendency of individuals to perceive reinforcements as deriving either from within themselves or from forces beyond their immediate control indicates an internal or external locus of control.

**Socialization:**
a process by which children learn the behaviours, ideas, attitudes, and values accepted by their culture.

self-concept affects a student's behaviour in school as well as how school life affects a developing self-esteem.

Children's self-concepts, for example, will affect their behaviour by limiting or extending the range of things they will attempt in school and the environment. Low self-esteem tends to make children less original and more imitative whereas high self-esteem brings out initiative and independent judgment (Salkind, 1990). As well, positive self-esteem seems to be related to more favourable attitudes toward school (Metcalfe, 1981) and more positive characteristics in the classroom (Reynolds, 1980).

In general, there appears to be a moderate relationship between self-esteem and measures of achievement, with the correlations increasing when specific school-related self-concepts are examined (see Chapman, 1988). Children who hold positive perceptions of themselves are more highly motivated; they usually try harder and persist longer when faced with difficult or challenging tasks. On the other hand, students who feel relatively worthless and have low self-esteem tend not to try as hard, to reduce their efforts, or to give up altogether (Chapman, 1988).

Self-esteem develops through different evaluations in different situations (Shavelson and Bolus, 1982) so a student's sense of self-esteem may vary from situation to situation and from one interaction to another. The athletic student who is full of self-confidence on the football field, for example, may not feel as worthy when confronted with high-level algebra.

One of the most widely used and perhaps abused concepts in educational psychology is that of motivation. It has served to explain why children do or do not work, learn, or succeed in school (Chan, 1978). The term "motivation" generally incorporates concepts such as drive, intention, desires, incentives, inducements, and other psychological constructs. It is a component of personality and closely tied to another aspect that particularly affects learning in individuals: the degree to which they feel responsible for their own success. Locus of control refers to the source to which an individual attributes responsibility for the outcome of events or behaviours. Individuals who consider the locus of control to be internal believe that the reinforcements they receive are contingent on their own behaviour, capacities, or attributes. Those who consider the locus of control to be external believe reinforcements are not under their personal control but are rather controlled by powerful others, chance, luck, or fate.

The difference between students who feel internally controlled and those who feel externally controlled are significant. People value what they want to do more highly than what they have to do. They are more likely to assume responsibility for voluntary behaviour than for compulsory behaviour and will work harder if they believe their own efforts will bring reward. In many situations, shifting of the locus of control helps both teachers and students. (See Chapter 12.)

## Socialization

Socialization is the learning process by which children learn the behaviours, attitudes, ideas, and values accepted by their culture. It is by means of socialization that we become reasonably acceptable and competent members of our society.

Socialization enables us to participate in the life of the family and later the school and the community. The object of socialization is not merely to elicit obedience from children. It is to teach cultural values, attitudes, beliefs, and rules, in the hope that they will be internalized.

In the previous chapter, we pointed out how researchers such as Jean Piaget and Lawrence Kohlberg see children as moral entrepreneurs, developing their own senses of morality as they pass through the sequence of cognitive development. Both Piaget and Kohlberg stress the role of the child's interaction with the environment in the development of cognition and morality, although they see this development and interaction as initiated by the child. Other learning theorists, most specifically Alfred Bandura (see Chapter 8), stress the role of modeling and imitation in the formation of personality, the development of appropriate moral values, and the socialization of children. In the whole area of socio-emotional development, these theories are not mutually exclusive; cognitive development, a growing innate sense of right and wrong, imitation and modeling, and interaction with parents, significant others, and the environment, probably all blend in the social and emotional development of a child.

There are five identifiable stages of child rearing, and the process of socialization is different in each. The stages are: care of the newborn, nurturance of the infant, enculturation of the young child, emancipation of offspring, and termination of child rearing (Harris and Ammerman, 1986).

Parents and other caregivers are the earliest socializers and are a determining factor on an individual's development. The personality, social class, education, and religious and political beliefs of each parent influence the version of the culture that is presented to the child (Salkind, 1990). Parental contributions to children's socialization also specifically include the provision of:

- sex-role models;
- attitudes that are a primary source of a child's self-concept;
- expectations regarding aggressiveness achievement, and independence;
- ways to express caring behaviour toward others;
- responsibility in the home and later the schools and the neighbourhood;
- directions and rules to follow;
- feelings about the family and home;
- support and guidance in school achievement;
- assistance in helping older children to attain personal and social repsonsibility.

Undoubtedly, parenting styles affect socialization but, as we stressed earlier, socialization is not a one-way process; children are active in socializing their parents. From the baby's first smile to the adolescent's bid for independence, children are countering the parents with their own values and attitudes. Moreover, each child responds in a unique way to the socialization of adults in his or her environment. Children may condition their parents to treat them in certain ways. Some girls, for example, seem to relish protection; others defeat all efforts to make them conform.

Children respond in unique ways to the socialization of adults in their environment.

In the socialization of their children, parents may unconsciously emphasize sex differences. The majority of parent research that focuses on sex differences in socialization have looked at the parent as disciplinarian—that is, how the parent manages and controls children's behaviour. The evidence suggests that sons are treated differently from daughters, and the effect is usually one of increased strictness and demands for independence with males (Snow, Jacklin, and Maccoby, 1983). The issue of how children develop sex roles and sex-typing is discussed in detail later on in this chapter.

## MODELS OF SOCIO-EMOTIONAL DEVELOPMENT

Several distinct stages can be proposed in socio-emotional development. Children develop from relatively undifferentiated infants without much "personality" to well-defined individuals with many stable traits and predictable personal qualities and behaviour. It must be cautioned at the ourset that few theories of personality and socio-emotional development are supported by a firm body of qualitative and quantitative empirical data. This is true even of Erikson's eight stages of socio-emotional development, which we shall describe, although his theory does provide a strong basis for teachers and parents to begin to understand children's levels of socio-emotional development (see Bee, 1978).

### Freud's theory of psychosexual development

Sigmund Freud (1856-1939) was the first to present what was then a revolutionary theory of personality development. In some respects, Freud's work was a

**Fixation:**

a Freudian term for the arresting of development and progress caused by frustration of basic needs.

blend of nineteenth century versions of cognition and physiology. Freud compared the human mind to an iceberg, likening the small part above the water to conscious experience and the much larger part below the water to the unconscious, a storehouse of impulses, passions, and inaccessible memories affecting thoughts and behaviour (Atkinson et al., 1990). Hence, the basic assumption of Freud's theory is that much of human behaviour stems from processes that are unconscious. According to Freud, there are two drives: primary and secondary. The former are physiological and genetic in origin, such as the sex drive. The essential operation of a primary drive is expressed in devotion toward pleasure. Secondary drives are regulative; they are social in nature and, unlike primary drives, they are conscious. However, secondary drives are necessarily determined by the primitive, subconscious primal drives.

When Freud began his work late in the nineteenth century, he was not concerned with children's development. His patients were mostly adults, and most of his clinical writing was concerned with the causes of adult disturbances, both emotional and physical. But Freud found that he could neither understand nor treat his patient's emotional problems until he could trace their origins into early childhood experiences. This led him to stress the importance of early childhood experiences in psychosexual development.

Freud developed a stage theory of personality development that stressed the role of experience. He proposed five stages, each characterized by a particular socialization issue. Table 4-1 presents an outline of Freud's stages of psychosexual development.

Table 4-1  Freud's stages of psychosexual development

| STAGE | APPROXIMATE AGE | FOCUS |
|---|---|---|
| Oral | birth-1 year | oral pleasure |
| Anal | 1- $2\frac{1}{2}$ years | control of bodily functions |
| Phallic | $2\frac{1}{2}$- 5 years | sex role identity |
| Latency | 6 - 12 years | dormant sexuality; same sex identification |
| Genital | 12 + years | mature sexuality |

Freudian theory maintains that, for normal development to proceed, an individual's basic needs must be satisfied at each stage of development. If they are not met, personality development will be arrested. Freud believed that this arresting of development and progress, which he termed fixation, was caused by frustration of basic needs. According to Freud, fixation retards personality development at all later stages. An individual who is frustrated in meeting needs at an early stage will behave in certain ways associated with this need as he or she gets older and at times when such behaviour is no longer appropriate.

The Freudian view also holds that babies come into the world equipped with several sets of instincts, including self-preservation (breathing, hunger, and the like) and the drive for sexual gratification (the word sexual is used very broadly in this context). The sexual instinct, as a whole, is directed toward various objects in a fixed sequence throughout the individual's life. At each of Freud's five stages, sexual energy (libido) is invested in a single part of the body, a single erogenous zone. These stages also have a distinct maturational basis: the shift from one stage to another is triggered by changes in sensitivity of various regions of the body. The specific experiences each child encounters will affect the resolution of the conflicts that accompany each stage. The stages may be described as follows:

**The oral stage**     (birth to one year) is characterized by passive and dependent bahaviour. The major source of gratification is sucking: the first contacts that a baby makes with the world are through the mouth, tongue, and lips. The oral region becomes the centre for pleasure for the baby. Fixation at this stage, caused by parents or other caretakers who wean the child too early or, conversely, who provide too much gratification of the child's oral needs, can lead to continuation of the need for sucking in later life.

**The anal stage**     ($1$-$2\frac{1}{2}$ years) is associated with concerns for the bladder and bowels. Children at this stage are learning to control themselves and their environments. Fixation at this stage—caused by nervous parents or caretakers who provide rigid or highly punitive toilet training—may be the cause, according to psychoanalytic theory, of behaviour disorders of excessive orderliness or sloppiness.

**The phallic stage**     ($2\frac{1}{2}$-5 years) is when children first become aware that they can derive pleasure from their genitals.

**The latency stage**     (6-12 years) delineates the time at which children begin to divert attention to friends outside the home. Elementary school children become intensely interested in sex-role identification and teachers notice increased play with peers of the same sex. As well, children of this age develop increased affection for the parent of the opposite sex. Personality, according to Freud, now begins to take shape as the child explores the world and begins to internalize a value system.

**The genital stage**     (12+ years) is associated with the development of an upsurge of instinctual sexual drives accompanying a physical growth spurt. From the beginning of this period, the young person's sexual objects are those of the opposite sex. Adolescence brings with it the need to dissolve parental attachments. In order to avoid fixation, basic adolescent needs such as increased autonomy must be met.

## Erikson's theory of psychosocial development

Freudian theory is sequential and focuses attention on the importance of the child/caregiver relationships. Another important aspect of Freud's theory of personality is that it is a holistic model that encompasses social, physiological, and psychological factors. Eric Erikson derived his essential tenets from Freud but developed a sequence of development that carried through the entire life cycle. He expanded on Freud's theory to describe eight stages of psychosocial development, the "eight ages of man," each with its particular goals, concerns, accomplishments, and dangers. In this, Erikson emphasized the emergence of self, the search for identity, and the relation of an individual to others throughout life.

## Box 4-2 **Biographical note: Eric Erikson (b. 1902)**

Eric Honberger Erikson, born in Germany of Danish parents, was left fatherless at an early age when his parents divorced. His mother soon remarried and his stepfather, a pediatrician, adopted the boy and gave Eric his own surname of Honberger.

Like Piaget, Eric Erikson did not start out to become a psycholgist. In fact, Erikson had no formal academic training beyond the gymnasium. He spent his early adult years traveling around Europe as an itinerant artist. He painted portraits and soon gained a reputation, especially for his paintings of young children. Erikson described his youthful travels as a moratorium, a term he later used to describe part of development during adolescence.

From 1927 until 1933 Erikson was in Vienna where he taught art at a school designed along psychoanalytic lines (Hilgard, 1987). While in Vienna he underwent psychoanalysis with Anna Freud for an hour a day at the Vienna Psychoanalytic Institute. He apparently also received an invitation from Sigmund Freud to study psychoanalysis, which he accepted.

In Vienna, Erikson met and married an American woman. With the first rumblings of Hitler, the couple went first to Denmark and then, in 1931, when Erikson was 29, they emigrated to the United States. Shortly thereafter, Erikson abandoned his stepfather's name and adopted his original surname.

Erikson first went to Boston and became one of the first child analysts in the Boston area. He taught at Harvard, spent a brief time at the Yale Institute of Human Relations, and was for a brief time a psychiatrist at Arnold Gesell's clinic. While there, he was recommended as a psychoanalyst to participate in the Berkeley Growth Studies. He was thus brought into direct contact with the American child development movement (Hilgard, 1987). From 1939 through 1959 Erikson was at the Univeristy of California. He returned to Harvard in 1960.

At the same time, Erikson did private counseling and he became interested in studying Native Americans. His study of the Native people and his observations of patients under treatment helped him in devising his eight stages of human development. Erikson also wrote in the area of psychohistory with works on Martin Luther (1958) and Ghandi (1969).

Erikson's theory was based in large part on Freud's work. But as he expanded on Freud's notions, Erikson interwove artistic and literary sensitivity with psychoanalytic insights. He formulated a comprehensive theory of emotional and social development involving a series of eight critical stages, each leading to a positive or negative outcome, the successful resolution of each stage contributing to the ability to meet future stages. In his influential *Childhood and society* (1950/1963) Erikson offered a basic framework for understanding the needs of young people in relation to the society in which they grow, learn and later make contributions.

Erikson was particularly interested in the relationship between the culture in which a child is raised and the kind of adult the child becomes. After studying child-rearing practices in several societies, he hypothesized that all humans have the same basic needs and that each society must provide in some way for these needs. Erikson concluded that, despite the cultural differences, there were recurring patterns of similar emotional and social development. Recognition of the relationship between culture and the individual led Erikson to propose a psychosocial theory of development. As he uses the term, psychosocial describes the relation of an individual's social needs to the social environment.

Like Freud, Erikson sees development as a passage through a series of stages and believes in sensitive points of development. Erikson calls these crisis points and sees them appearing in each of the eight developmental stages. Each crisis involves a conflict between a positive alternative and a potentially unhealthy alternative. The manner in which an individual resolves each crisis has a lasting effect on that person's self-image and view of society. Erikson's stages of psychosocial development are shown in Table 4-2.

**Table 4-2** Erikson's stages of psychosocial development

| STAGE | APPROXIMATE AGE |
| --- | --- |
| 1. Basic trust vs. mistrust | First year of life |
| 2. Autonomy vs. shame and doubt | Second and third years |
| 3. Initiative vs. guilt | Third to fifth years |
| 4. Industry vs. inferiority | Sixth to twelfth years |
| 5. Identity vs. role confusion | Puberty and adolescence |
| 6. Intimacy vs. isolation | Young adulthood |
| 7. Generativity vs. stagnation | Adulthood |
| 8. Ego integrity vs. despair | Maturity |

The transition from one stage to the next comes about not exclusively because of maturational changes, but because of changes in children's cognitive abilities and changes in the social structure around them. Erikson sees the crises as outgrowths of many forces operating at the same time—psychosexual development, mental development, physical abilities, and the new demands made by society.

Successful resolution of each crisis as it is encountered provides a reasonably solid foundation for identity and for dealing with the next crisis. An unhealthy nonresolution of problems in the early stages can have potentially negative repercussions throughout life. However, Erikson is more optimistic than Freud about what happens when a particular crisis is left unresolved. Erikson suggests that failure to solve one problem does not necessarily keep an individual from resolving different issues later. Partly because none of the developmental crises are ever completely resolved, damage sometimes can be repaired in later stages.

### Stage 1: Trust vs. mistrust

Erikson identified trust versus mistrust as the basic conflict or crisis of infancy. In the first year of life, human infants are helpless and completely dependent on their caretakers. Babies derive their sense of self as their parents hold them and as they interact with others. Infants under six months of age probably do not

**Attachment:**
the bonding between the infant and the caretaker that is necessary for survival and successful growth.

recognize their caretakers on a really individual basis. Almost anyone who provides the desired stimulation will be accepted as a substitute. As they grow, they develop preferences for their primary caretakers, who are fixtures in their environments.

While almost everything that an infant does is of interest to new parents, Kagan (1989) stresses the importance of the temperamental qualities of smiling, degree of motor activity, and adaptability to new situations. Many parents view the first smile as a milestone, the first step in the baby's trek to social behaviour.

Erikson believed that the way in which the primary caregiver (usually the mother, in his work) interacts with the infant is critical to the child's successful or unsuccessful resolution of this first crisis. To Erikson, trust implies

> *not only that one has learned to rely on the sameness and continuity of the outer providers, but also that one may trust oneself and the capacity of one's own organs to cope with urges; and that one is able to consider oneself trustworthy enough so that the providers will not need to be on guard lest they be nipped (1963, p. 248).*

The quality of the maternal relationship largely determines whether trust or mistrust wins out. Closeness and responsiveness on the part of the parents contribute to a sense of trust as does the meeting of needs for food and care with comforting regularity. Infants discover whether they can rely on the world around them, whether they can trust in the predictability of their world, and whether they can trust in their own ability to affect the happenings around them.

Individuals who develop normally in this stage will have characteristics that reflect trustfulness. Basic trust leads to a sense of confidence and control: in general, people who trust others are happier, better adjusted, and better liked than those who lack trust in others (Rotter, 1980). One whose early care has been erratic or harsh may develop mistrust and in later life will show characteristics that reflect a lack of trust, or mistrustfulness. Basic mistrust leads to self-defeating behaviour patterns and an inability to deal positively with others. Once children develop an orientation of mistrust, their environment may work to reinforce it. Their parents may conclude that they are difficult and hard to handle and then use more directive parenting that only intensifies the problem.

Research on infant development of attachment supports Erikson's ideas about a baby's need to develop trust. Infants tend to seek closeness to particular people and to feel more secure in their presence. This is known as attachment, the bonding between the infant and the caretaker that is necessary for survival and successful growth. In a study of the differences between babies who are "securely attached" to their mothers and those who are "anxiously attached," Ainsworth (1979) used what she called the Strange Situation measure. Securely attached children, those who have developed trust, use their caretaker as secure bases for exploration, knowing that their mothers will respond when needed. This leads children to explore their environments with greater enthusiasm and persistance than anxiously attached babies (Campos et al., 1983).

Moreover, small children who are securely attached seem to cry less often, to be more responsive to their mother's verbal commands, and to be less upset by their mother's coming and going (Ainsworth, 1979). Such children seem to be more cooperative and less aggressive in their interactions with their mothers and, as they grow older, more competent and sympathetic with their peers. One study of 48 infants found that those who were securely attached at 18 months were more enthuistatic, persistent, cooperative, and in general, more effective by the age of two than were infants who were insecurely attached (Matas, Arend, and Sroufe, 1978).

Early relationships set the stage for later social and emotional development. By the preschool years, children who were securely attached as infants were rated by teachers as more self-reliant and less dependent (Sroufe, Fox, and Pancake, 1983). Children with secure relationships often turn out to be more popular in nursery school than insecurely attached ones; they tend to engage more frequently in social contact; and tend to be more effective in offering guidance and suggestions to others (Hartup, 1979). In addition, teacher-child relationships are different. Insecurely attached preschoolers are more dependent on their teachers for emotional support than their securely attached classmates (Sroufe and Fleeson, 1986). Evidence also links the quality of attachments between child and mother among six year olds to the child's self-esteem (Cassidy, 1988).

This trust versus mistrust period, as outlined by Erikson, matches the early stages of Piaget's sensorimotor stage. Infants are learning that they are separate from the world around them and that objects and people exist outside their range of vision or hearing. The realization of separateness is what makes trust so important; infants must trust the aspects of their world that are beyond their control (Bretherton, 1985).

## Stage 2: Autonomy vs. shame and doubt

This stage occurs during the second and third years of life, and marks the beginning of a child's self-control. One year olds are still highly dependent on adults, but increased mobility constitutes a major change. Two and three year olds can move easily and quickly around their worlds. They can now find the cookie jar, or their sister's toys, or the front gate for themselves. They can use language to express their wants, needs—and frustrations. They begin to assume important responsibilities for self-care such as feeding, dressing, and going to the bathroom as they are strive toward autonomy. Two year olds can easily distinguish between parents and other people and are discovering that not all these people treat them in the same way. Some are warm and supportive, but others are little impressed by the toddler's endless questions and restless energy (Owens, 1988).

Part of the early task of socialization for young children is to learn a degree of independence from their caretakers. Young children at this stage are capable of and interested in doing more and more on their own. They want to explore their own choices of options, forming the basis for autonomy. Automony represents the will of children to be themselves. It is understanding and using the words and the concepts "I," "me," and "mine."

As young children become capable of some self-control, parents expect them to conform to certain rules. In the second year, child rearing becomes more complex as parents take on the trickier tasks of discipline, control and character building. Parents differ greatly in their expectations of children's behaviour, but at some point they expect children to stop wetting and soiling, to keep their clothes on, to go to bed on time, and so on. The child leaves the high chair and joins the family at the table and is expected to begin to eat with utensils, learn basic manners, and stop throwing and playing with food.

If such socialization is carried out with proper timing and appropriate methods, children are likely to adjust to it smoothly and without losing their sense of personal autonomy. Parents must tread a fine line: they must be protective but not overprotective, strict but not rigid in their guidance. Options and choices must be realistic. If children gain too much autonomy—have too many choices—they may be subject to the "meaningless and arbitrary experiences of shame and doubt" (Erikson, 1963, p. 254).

Whether or not the parents achieve this balance exerts a strong influence on the child's ability to achieve autonomy. If parents make too many demands (and especially if they make them too early), if they use inadvisable socialization methods (such as threats and punishment) to enforce these demands, if they do not maintain a reassuring, confident attitude, and do not reinforce the child's efforts to master basic motor and cognitive skills, children may begin to feel shame and doubt instead of a basic sense of self-control and self-worth. Children who encounter difficulties at this stage because they experience repeated failure or earn ridicule may begin to doubt their own value and their own abilities to master the external environment on their own terms. They may lose their sense of personal autonomy and begin to feel completely dependent on and under the control of adults. Children who experience too much doubt at this stage, Erikson believes, will lack confidence of their own powers throughout life and are likely in later life to be strict and rigid.

Toilet training, which occurs in this period, is especially important since it is an area in which there are more taboos and more occasions when the child may

When socialization occurs smoothly, children can usually develop a strong sense of autonomy through newly acquired skills.

experience failure or ridicule (Bee, 1978). Postponing toilet training until the age of two greatly reduces bed wetting, soiling, and constipation in later childhood (Brazelton, 1962; B. White, 1975), since these problems are sometimes associated with training that was too early or too coercive.

Although the toilet training experience is important in the early struggle for autonomy, many other kinds of experiences are also crucial. Toilet training is just one example of the more general crisis that results from the child's increasing wish for autonomy and adjusting to the fact that adults are, for the time being, and for the first time, imposing rules and expectations for self-control and self-denial.

One manifestation of these conflicts is the temper tantrum which, as many parents assert, is a characteristic of the "terrible twos." Temper tantrums are alarming to parents and onlookers. Children scream, kick, writhe, and throw themselves about; they may even indulge in self-injurious behaviours such as holding their breath, pulling their hair, or biting themselves.

To compare Erikson's second stage with Piaget and Freud reveals that children are beginning to carry out the goal-directed activities of the later part of Piaget's sensorimotor stage. They are developing the mental and physical abilities that allow them to take some control of their lives. Freud termed this the anal stage because conflict often appears when parents attempt to toilet train their children.

**Stage 3: Initiative vs. guilt**
According to Erikson, a child faces the conflict of initiative versus guilt, sometime between the ages of three and five. Children at this age are not only able to move around successfully but they possess many new skills and abilities—they are able to plan, to take initiative in reaching particular goals, and to use language to express these goals. As children at this age develop an interest in themselves and their own capabilities, they also develop an interest in showing off to parents and interested others.

For Erikson "initiative adds to autonomy the quality of undertaking, planning, and attacking a task for the sake of being active and on the move" (Erikson, 1963, p. 233). But as children try out their new skills in conquering new goals, they face environmental restrictions and the realization that some activities are forbidden. At times children may feel torn between what they want to do and what they are allowed to do. Take, for example, four-year-old Harry and his new tricycle. The neighbourhood beckons, just waiting to be explored, but mother has forbidden Harry to pedal past the end of the driveway. His initiative is to go, but if he does, he may later be overwhelmed by guilt.

The challenge is for children to maintain a zest for activity and at the same time understand that they cannot act upon every impulse. The challenge for parents is to provide supervision without undue interference and to help children focus on what is permissible. Successful growth during this period depends on children feeling they are accepted for themselves. Children at this stage require confirmation from adults that their initiative is accepted and that their contributions, no matter how small, are highly valued. These children are eager for responsibility. They can imagine themselves in various adult roles and begin to test their powers at grown-up tasks. Three and four-year-olds want to play house, fill the car with gas, and talk for hours on play telephones. If children are not allowed to do things on their own, a sense of guilt may develop; they may come to believe that what they want to do is always wrong.

### Stage 4: Industry vs. inferiority

Adults define much of their social experience in terms of success and failure. According to Erikson, children too encounter the crisis of success versus failure, or in his terms, industry versus inferiority, throughout the elementary school years, from ages six to twelve years. In the early school years, children develop what Erikson calls a sense of industry; they are beginning to see the relationship between perseverance and the pleasure of a job completed. Children now learn the basic skills of literacy and numeracy. They learn to manipulate their society and they have a greater sense of the options available.

In this period Erikson also stresses the experience of broadening horizons: children must conquer the world outside the home and learn to move freely in three overlapping worlds—home, school, and neighbourhood. Interaction with peers becomes increasingly important.

These changes stimulate children by presenting new roles and related work expectations that youngsters usually are motivated to try to fulfill successfully (Havinghurst, 1972). Within the peer group, this means learning to cooperate and share as well as to master the various skills involved in childhood play. In school, it means assuming the role of pupil and mastering school tasks.

Achievement in school is more closely related to self-perceptions of ability than to general self-concept (Burns, 1982; Byrne, 1984, 1986). Young children

When children learn to manipulate their surroundings, they gain a greater sense of the options available.

initially equate effort and ability and it is not until early adolescence that an understanding of ability as capacity is mastered completely (see Nicholls and Miller, 1984).

Perceptions of reduced ability occur for most children around the ages of seven or eight (Eshel and Klein, 1981; Nicholls, 1979) but are more marked for children experiencing frequent academic failure during the early school years (Dweck and Bempechat, 1983). Typically, perceptions of diminished ability occur after initial overestimates of abilities and achievement expectations (Entwhistle and Hayduk, 1978; Stipek, 1984) and in response to information about performance provided by teachers and peers (Rosenholtz and Simpson, 1984).

Motivation refers to a student's affective or emotional response to a problem situation which influences how the problem will be viewed and solved. Motivation, an essential ingredient of efficient learning, arises from a number of intrinsic and extrinsic forces. In the classroom, motivation is reasonably specific to a given task and is dependent on the consequences known to follow performance. Children are motivated when they perform in certain ways. High motivation results in a task properly completed (as instructed) and the production of a reasonable amount of good quality work. In turn, children feel highly motivated by success. Low motivation, on the other hand, will probably result in the opposite—poor quality work demonstrating lack of interest and commitment (Winzer, 1989).

When children meet success in school-related tasks, a chain of positive self-fulfilling prophecy effects is set off that paves the route for later life. For example, Valliant and Valliant (1981) followed 450 males for 35 years, beginning in early childhood. Their conclusion was that the men who had been the most industrious and willing to work as children were the best adjusted and best paid as adults. These men also had the most satisfying personal relationships. The ability and the willingness to work hard as a child seemed to be more important for success in later life than intelligence or family background.

A child's ability to adapt to the demands of home and neighbourhood and to cope with academics, group activities, and friends will lead to a growing sense of competence. On the other hand, difficulty with these challenges can result in feelings of inferiority. As children picture themselves as underachieving or nonachieving, they become passive and lose their initiative. They grow overly dependent on others to tell them what to do, surrendering to an external locus of control.

In terms of Piagetian stages, this is the period when children are beginning to conquer the physical environment as they move into the stage of concrete operations. Play satisfied them until this time but now they want to do productive work on their own and are physically and mentally ready for it. Social relations become more complex. Piaget observed that social interaction is the principal factor in decentration, the decline of egocentricity. In their contacts with others, especially their age peers, children must now increasingly defend their own opinions and views of the world.

## Box 4-3  **In the classroom: Grade retention**

The concept of the standard grade was first introduced in Massachusetts in 1847 in response to the organizational needs of the evolving school system. Children of the same ages were expected to master pretty much the same curriculum in the same time. As Kozens (1990) says, the standard grade theory implied an eleventh commandment: Thou shalt progress at the same rate as thy neighbour.

Today's educators still live with the myth that all children will fit the standard grade concept. Schools assign children to the same grade levels based on their ages, assuming that children of the same age possess the same level of ability. When children do not succeed, educators believe that grade retention is an effective solution to problems of academic failure and social immaturity (Byrnes and Yamamato, 1984; Nikelson, 1984). The public seems to agree (Gallup, 1984).

The research evidence does not in the least support the widespread belief in the benefits of retention. For one thing, given the tremendous differences we see in the developmental levels of perfectly normal children, admission to public school according to a strict chronological age requirement is faulty as an ideal. For another, Jackson (1975) summarized available studies and concluded that "there is no reliable body of evidence to indicate that grade retention is more beneficial than grade promotion for students with serious academic and adjustment difficulties" (p. 627). Jackson (1975) and others have deplored retaining students merely to recycle them through a program that was unsuccessful the first time round, advocating instead a special remedial program.

Teachers and parents are generally of the opinion that if a retention is indicated, it should take place early in the child's schooling. Many years ago, Goodland (1954) found less damage to the child's social relations with

peers among first grade retainees than for those retained in the later grades. Retention practices reflect this belief, for the highest incidence of non-promotions has been found in the first grade (Rose et al., 1983).

The fact that most children who are held back a grade do not benefit academically, but actually experience less growth than similarly functioning children who are promoted, has been well established in retention studies. After examining a number of studies on kindergarten retention, Shepard and Smith (1987) concluded that retention did not improve children's subsequent academic performance although it did impose a significant social stigma on the retained students. Low achieving children who are promoted learn more the following year, have a stronger self-concept and are better adjusted than similar children who are retained (Bracey, 1988; Bruce, 1988; Smith and Shepard, 1987). Further, research has shown that when a student repeats a grade, the probability of that student dropping out prior to graduation increases by 20 to 40 percent (Shepard and Smith, 1987). A recent meta-analysis of retention studies (Holmes and Matthews, 1984) reinforced this conclusion across achievement, adjustment, attitude, behaviour, and attendance variables.

Nevertheless, the practice appears to be growing (Rose et al., 1983). Many authors have recently stated the opinion that retention may be beneficial under certain conditions and for children with certain characteristics. In retaining grade one children, for example, Lieberman (1980) looks at youngsters of small stature; temporary slow learners; socially immature or neurologically immature children; children with low self-concept; children immature in assuming responsibility for their own learning; and young children.

## Stage 5: Indentity vs. role confusion

Identity may be understood as the organization of the individual's drives, abilities, beliefs, and history into a consistent image of self. It involves deliberate choices and decisions, particularly about vocation, sexual orientation, and a "philosophy of life" (Marcia, 1980). Erikson wrote more about the identity crisis than about any other stage. He specifically postulated that this search was the central crisis of the developing human, and that adolescence was the time for the process to take place (1963, 1968).

Adolescence has been described as a period of "storm and stress" (Hall, 1905) and as a vortex of change (Jackson and Hombeck, 1989). Erikson sees adolescents as caught between two major systems, both of which are in flux. They have to cope with internal, glandular, and cognitive changes and they must also confront a series of changing, sometimes inconsistent, external regulations. For example, young adolescents change from the relatively warm and very personal local elementary school to the larger junior high school that draws its clientele from a larger area. Their contacts become more diverse and they are less informed by parental standards. Peers influence attitudes and behaviour—they offer information, reward conformity, and punish nonconformity. For adolescents, expressing ideas and beliefs that the group considers to be correct is just as important as wearing clothes the group considers to be appropriate.

Early understandings of adolescent mental health stressed the storm and stress; explosive conflicts with family, friends, and authority were thought to be commonplace. However, recent research refutes this view (Powers, Hauser, and Kilmer, 1989). Although there are certainly tremendous biological, sociological, and psychological changes, adolescence is not ordinarily a time of great emotional turmoil. Some adolescents may be expected to be moody and depressed one day, excitable and high the next; others will pass through this period in relative calm.

Moreover, as Ianni (1989) observed, we tend to talk about adolescence as if it were a single unified period of life. But teenagers more often experience adolescence as a number of more or less coterminous periods, each structured by such socializing influences as the family, the peer group, the work place, or the criminal justice system (Ianni, 1989). The opening years of adolescence are highlighted by the conflicting desires for independence, especially in relation to parents and teachers, and for the security of more childish activities. It is in the early adolescent life phase that emotional expression may become more intense, unstable, and negative as compared to late childhood (Brooks-Gunn and Warren, 1989). Early adolescence is a time of particular vulnerability due to huge biological, cognitive, and physical changes. These are accompanied by experimentation that is developmentally appropriate and socially adaptive for most, but some behaviours are aversive—expecially with alcohol, other drugs and sexual activity. Some aspects of the mounting problems of drug use are detailed in Box 4-4.

Behaviourally, late adolescence is more of a stage of equilibrium and relative stability. Students are capable of accepting constructive criticism with more grace. They have developed more adult social skills, and more stable and reciprocal friendships. They are also more able to control their feelings, and outwardly exhibit less emotional extremes (Winzer, 1989).

## Box 4-4 **Drug use among adolescents**

Adolescence is a period of experimentation, exploration, and curiousity. Drug use has become one aspect of this natural process. It has also become one of the greatest challenges of our times; many, in fact, see the drug problem as epidemic.

However, it seems that drug use among young people is not on the increase, but rather may be declining. For example, a longitudinal study of drug use in Ontario from 1977 to 1985, showed a decrease in use by 1985. However, the decline in use was not accompanied by a reduction in the frequency of use among users. Drug use in adolescents encompasses a variety of substances ranging from tobacco and alcohol to illicit drugs such as marijuana, narcotics (primarily heroin), stimulants such as cocaine and amphetimines, and hallucinogens such as PCP (Harris, 1986).

Any regular use of a psychoactive drug by a child can be considered abuse (Newcomb and Bentler, 1989). For adolescents, the distinction is more complicated. Occasional use of beer or wine may not be abuse; too much occasionally is at least temporary abuse; chronic use is abuse (Newcomb and Bentler, 1989). A heightened risk for alcohol abuse is seen among adolescents who have parents drinking at home (Lawson, Peterson, and Lawson, 1983). Some estimates show that up to 50 percent of the youth in the criminal justice system come from families in which chemical dependence is a prominent factor (O'Gorman and Ross, 1984).

Increased identification with peers in early adolescence serves to fulfill needs for autonomy from parents, but also provides increased pressure to engage in adult behaviours such as having sex, smoking, and drinking. Most initial experiences with cigarettes, alcohol, and illegal drugs take place during the middle grades. The prevalence of delinquent behaviour rises dur-

ing the early and middle adolescent years and falls in young adulthood. Truancy, and running away also show substantial increases in prevalence as youth enter early adolescence (Achenbach and Edelbrook, 1981). Occasional drug and alcohol abuse is only slightly more common among boys than girls. However, heavy drinking or daily marijuana use is twice as common among boys and they are also more likely to use cocaine and heroin (Slavin, 1988).

The precursors of and the influences on drug abuse are complex and intertwined. More than just the natural, adolescent inclination to experiment seems to be involved in chronic drug use. Peer pressures, past behaviours, and temperamental characteristics have all been identified as precursors of drug use.

A large number of studies point to the peer group as the major training ground for delinquent acts and substance abuse (Elliott, Huizinga, and Ageton, 1985). Peer influence (modeling use, encouraging use, and provision of substances) are the most consistent and strongest of all factors (Newcomb and Bentler, 1989) in the wide range of influences of initial involvement in substance use.

In drug use, past behaviour is often a very strong predictor of future behaviour. Earlier use may be of a similar but less serious form of drug. A typical progression may be from tea or coffee, beer or wine, or cigarettes, to hard liquor and marijuana, and subsequently moving to other illicit drugs such as ampthetamines, cocaine, or heroin (Kandel, Kessler and Margulies, 1978). While involvement at one stage is unlikely without prior involvement at an earlier stage, involvement in one stage does not necessarily mean movement to the next.

Only two truly long-term investigations into the childhhood antecedents of drug use have appeared. The Woodlawn study by Kellam and his asociates (Kellam et al., 1975; Kellam et al., 1983) traced the development of a group of poor, black, urban children beginning at age six or seven. In the Woodlawn study, Kellam found that psychological characteristics assessed at age six or seven foretold use of drugs at age 16 or 17, a decade later.

Similarly, Block and colleagues followed a group of San Francisco Bay area children from nursery school on and found numerous theoretically coherent relations between psychological characteristics assesssed in nursery school and subsequent drug use in adolescence (Block and Block, 1980; Block, Block, and Keyes, 1988). When researchers (Block and Shedler, 1988) followed this group to age 18, they found users to be alienated, deficient in impulse control, and manifestly distressed, as compared to those who only experimented with drugs. These characteristics mirrored those found when the children were assessed at seven and eleven years of age.

The central issue for adolescents is the development of an identity that provides a firm basis for adulthood. The individual has, of course, been developing a sense of self, or identity, since infancy. But adolescence marks the first time that a conscious effort is made to answer the now pressing question—"Who am I?" The conflict defining this stage is identity versus role confusion. Erikson observes that the healthy resolution of earlier conflicts can now serve as a foundation for the search for identity. A basic sense of trust, if established, has prepared the young person to find people and ideas in which to have faith. A firm sense of autonomy gives the adolescent courage to insist upon the chance to decide freely upon his or her career or life style. The initiative that prompted the young child to play lawyer or painter can prompt the student to take steps toward assuming an adult role in reality. And, out of a strong sense of industry can grow a feeling of competence, a belief in one's ability to make meaningful contributions to society (Bee, 1978).

At first, as these feelings of role identity evolve, they are diffuse and fluctuating. Erikson suggests that not one, but two identities are involved here—a "sexual" identity and an "occupational" identity. As a sexual identity develops, friendships, conflict with peers, dating, and sexual relationships all take a tremendous amount of the adolescent's time and energy. In terms of the occupational identity, Erikson feels that occupational choice has a great impact on an adolescent's sense of identity. This is true since, perhaps more than any other single factor, the occupations we choose influence other aspects of our lives. Our job determines, among other things, our income, our life style, our ambitions, our friends, and what we can provide for our children.

James Marcia and his colleagues (Marcia, 1980; Orlofsky, Marcia, and Lesser, 1973; Schiedel and Marcia, 1985) have carefully examined the identity crisis, chiefly though interviews with young men. The researchers asked about careers, personal value systems, sexual attitudes, and religious beliefs. Although Marcia was more concerned with college students, his findings are relevant for high school teachers.

Marcia proposes that the criteria for the attainment of a mature individual rests on two critical variables—crisis and commitment. A crisis occurs when adolescents are actively sorting through alternatives; commitment occurs when the student actively and personally invests in an occupation or belief. He suggests that there are four alternatives for adolescents as they confront themselves, their lives, and their occupational choices.

Status one is *identity achievement*, which is reached when, after considering the realistic options available, an individual has made choices and is pursuing them. But it appears that few students achieve this status by the end of high school; most are not firm in their choices for several more years (Archer, 1982). Marcia's second status, *identity foreclosure*, describes the situation of adolescents who do not experiment with different identities or consider a range of options. They simply commit themselves to the goals, values, and life styles of their parents and of other significant authority figures. *Identity diffusion*, the third of Marcia's statuses is, in some respects, the opposite of identity foreclosure. A core of personality has not been established and individuals reach no conclusions about what they are or what they want to do with their lives; they have no firm direction and probably feel a sense of alienation. Adolescents experiencing identity diffusion may have struggled unsuccessfully to make choices, or they may have avoided thinking seriously about these issues at all.

Finally, adolescents in the midst of struggling with choices are experiencing a *moratorium*. Erikson described his early travels around Europe as a moratorium. Later (1968), he pointed out that our society, unlike many others, provides what he called a psychosocial moratorium. This implies the creation of some breathing space in order to explore one's own psychological self and one's own reality. During this mortorium period, youngsters can avoid answering questions about their futures, can experiment with different roles, and can explore different dimensions of life without choosing any one of them.

For Erikson, the term "moratorium" refers to a delay in the adolescent's commitment to personal and occupational choices. Marcia uses the term in a way that differs slightly from Erikson's original meaning. For Marcia, a moratorium involves actively dealing with the crisis of shaping an identity. If adolescents fail to integrate all of the aspects of choices, or if they feel unable to choose at all, role confusion becomes a threatening possibility. It should be noted that, for bright students, upper grade boys are more aware of career choices than girls of comparative superior ability (Kirschenbaum, 1980).

The four identity status categories are not always related to other variables in ways that would be predicted by Erikson's theory (Cote and Levine, 1983) but they have proven useful in conceptualizing and measuring progress toward achieving identity. In one sense, adolescence officially ends at the age of eighteen or so with graduation from high school. However, identity formation will almost certainly continue. Waterman (1982) sees the process as continuing until much later. In a sample of college students, he found that less than 50 percent had actually reached identity resolution by their senior year.

When Archer (1982) studied sixth, eighth, tenth, and twelfth grade students, he found that identity status increased significantly with each increase in grade level, although the diffusion and foreclosure statuses were evident in all grade

## Box 4-5 **Eating disorders**

Anorexia nervosa and bulimia are disorders of eating. The conditions are often related in their physical manifestations, their psychological correlates, and the course of the condition. Between 40 and 50 percent of all anorexics develop bulimia (Casper et al., 1980). Anorexia nervosa is a condition characterized by excessive dieting and excessive weight loss. Sufferers of bulimia crave the weight loss, but gorge and then use purges or other means to rid themselves of the excess calories. Both conditions are fairly common and overwhelmingly affect females. Ninety-five percent of all anorexics are women (Bruch, 1973). Bulimia is twenty times more likely to appear in women, particularly in young women in high school and early college.

It is estimated that anorexia affects one out of every 250 women in their adolescent and young adult years. Bulimia may affect 15 to 20 percent of young women in North America (Atkinson et al., 1990). The peak ages of onset appear to be between 12 and 13 years and around 19 to 23 (Harris, 1986). The dieting and weight loss are usually triggered by a crisis such as the onset of menstruation or an exaggerated misperception of the fatty weight gain normal in adolescence.

Anorexia nervosa combines disturbed eating habits with other psychological conflicts. An anorexic person may lose 25 percent or more of normal body weight, resulting in emaciation, susceptibility to infection, and other symptoms of malnourishment. The cycle of bulimia can be just as destructive as anorexia, if not more so. The bulimic can consume almost 30 000 calories (the equivalent of 45 hot fudge sundaes) at one meal and then purge herself by vomiting or using laxatives or enemas. Unlike the anorexic, the bulimic seems to fluctuate between weight loss and weight gain and also experiences bouts of serious depression and anxiety (Schlesier-Stropp, 1984). The medical consequences of bulimia include metabolic changes due to rapid ingestion of carbohydrates, as well as hernias, ulcers, bowel problems, and increased tooth decay (Johnson, 1982).

Anorexia may be in response to society's dictates about physical beauty. anorexics suffer a disturbance in body image (Bruch, 1973). One of the most consistent findings is that anorexic women have difficulty in establishing a sense of identity that is independent of their parents and of others who wish to control their lives. Instead of feeling that they are pursuing their life goals, anorexics are likely to feel unloved, exploited, and stifled (Bruch, 1973). Parents of anorexic females tend to be controlling, to depend on the girl for nurturance, and to encourage perfectionist overachievment (Goldstein, 1981).

Anorexics have often been model girls with high grades in school and from unpwardly mobile families that stress achievement (Garfinkel and Gardner, 1982). This demanding background may contribute to the development of stress. Incessant dieting may be a form of seeking autonomy (Atkinson et al., 1990).

Behaviour modification through using rewards and punishments may not prevent the recurrence of the disorder but appears to hold real value when used in conjunction with individual and family therapy (Garfinkel, Gardner and Moldofsky, 1977). The prognosis is good in about half the cases of anorexia (Hsu, Crusp, and Harding, 1979).

levels. Even by grade twelve, only a minority of students had reached the identity achievement level. The status generally achieved varied with the particular aspect of identity being studied. When identity achievement status was attained, it was most likely to be in the area of vocational choice or religious belief (Good and Brophy, 1986). Moratorium status was also seen most frequently with respect to vocational choice, whereas foreclosure status was most frequent with sex roles preferences. Identity diffusion status was most frequent with political philosophy. In general, the most extensive advances in identity formation occur during the college rather than the high school years (Waterman, 1982).

Along with their occupational identity, adolescents encounter their awakening sexual identities. As we explained in Chapter 2, puberty is marked by a profound biological change involving rapid physical growth, large increases in levels of hormones, and the appearance of secondary sexual characteristics. The psychological experiences of puberty can also be profound, involving changes in body image, self-concept, and social relationships with peers and parents (Steinberg, 1981).

This is a period when adolescents are particularly conscious of their own bodies and whether or not their bodies measure up to the standards of physical maturity held by our society. Girls worry about their developing figures, their height, their skin, their looks, and their image. Boys worry about when they'll have to shave, whether they will have chest hair, whether they are developed sexually, and when their voices will break.

Sex differences in emotional expression and clinical disorders often emerge in early to middle adolescence. In the early school years, boys are more likely to have problems but by late adolescence girls display more disorders of certain types. In their mild or severe forms, problems such as depression and eating disorders are more characteristic of young women than of young men (Rutter et al., 1976)

Adolescents have new notions about their developing sexual identities which bring new ways of interacting and new groups into prominence in their lives. They have changing perceptions of their parents, a decreased dependence on parental control, and they set out to balance peer, parental and individual expectations. Schooling may not be as important as deep concerns with peer approval and group identity.

### Stage 6: Intimacy vs. isolation

Young adults who emerged successfully from the previous stage with identity conflict resolved now seek intimacy—merging one's identity with that of another. They are ready psychologically and socially to establish relationships with others that go beyond acquaintanceship and to make commitments "to concrete affiliations and partnerships and to develop the ethical strength to abide by such commitments, even though they may call for significant sacrifices" (Erikson, 1963, p. 263).

Such intimacy is really only possible for someone who has dealt successfully with the earlier stages, since only a person with a well developed identity can now enter into this type of merger. But if young adults have weathered previous stages successfully, they will enter this crisis with the ability to trust, with a sense of autonomy, with the ability to take initiative, with high self-esteem and confidence in their abilities, and with reasonable certainty about who they are and what they want (Bee, 1978). These factors will facilitate their initiation and maintenance of truly intimate relationships, sharing everything about themselves with their partners.

The young adult who does not seek out intimacy or whose repeated tries fail may retreat into isolation. As well, young adults may be on guard against anyone who might encroach on their territory, and thus risk isolating themselves.

Marcia and his colleagues (Orlofsky, Marcia, and Lesser, 1973), have elaborated and operationalized Erikson's intimacy stage as they did with the stage of identity crisis. They assigned individuals to one of five intimacy stages based on three general criteria: presence or absence of close relationships with male or female friends; presence or absence of an enduring, committed, sexual relationship, and depth or superficiality of peer relationships. The five intimacy stages based on these criteria are:

- isolate—living in an interpersonal void with only casual relationships;

- stereotyped—being pleasant and friendly, but shallow and conventional in personal relationships;

- pseudo-intimate—similar to the stereotyped but involved in a relatively permanent sexual relationship defined more by conventional roles than by sharing of deep feelings and self disclosure;

- pre-intimate—having a close, open relationships with others based on mutuality and understanding, yet being ambivalent about sexual commitment in an enduring relationship;

- intimate—similar to the pre-intimate, but also having a committed, long-term sexual relationship.

Studies indicate that an intimate relationship with a supportive partner contributes significantly to a person's emotional and physical health. People who have someone with whom to share their ideas, feelings, and problems are happier and healthier than those who do not (Traupman and Hatfield, 1981). Other researchers (Orlofsky, 1976; Orlofsky and Ginsburg, 1981) have indicated that people whose interview responses place them in higher intimacy categories know their friends better and can predict their partner's responses to a personality or attitude inventory better. They are more self-disclosing in their interactions with other people and are better able to conceptualize and anticipate their emotional experiences.

Research also supports Erikson's hierarchical stage notions concerning the relationship betweeen identity and intimacy. Persons typically do achieve high status on identity measures before they attain high status on intimacy (Kacerguis and Adams, 1980; Schiedel and Marcia, 1985). These findings are clearer for males than for females, however, and it is not uncommon to find that some women deal successfully with intimacy issues before they resolve identity issues. It may be that sex differences are due to differences in gender role socialization; more often, females are directed toward interpersonal relationships and thus toward dealing with both identity and intimacy issues throughout their adolescent and early adult years. Males, on the other hand, are oriented more toward a preoccupation with identity issues and their resolution during the adolescent years. For them, intimacy issues come to the fore in the young adult years (Good and Brophy, 1986).

### Stage 7: Generativity vs. stagnation

Much has been written in the popular literature about the so-called midlife crisis. Several longitudinal studies have reported that men in their forties experience a period of emotional turmoil centred around conflicts about sexual relationships, family roles, and work values (Levinson et al., 1978; Vaillant, 1977). A similar midlife crisis has been proposed for women (Sheehy, 1976). The transition to middle adulthood is, according to one view, like the emotional turmoil of adolescence during which goals and values are re-evaluated. Some researchers question this view, however. They find little evidence that people in their forties report more symptoms of emotional distress than younger or older people (Shaie and Willis, 1986).

To Erikson, this stage of generativity versus stagnation constitutes the major crisis of adulthood. The focus shifts to the pleasure inherent in conceiving and raising children. Generativity indicates the ability to care for another person and involves caring and guidance for the next and future generations. Yet, while generativity frequently refers to bearing and rearing children, it encompasses the broader meanings of productivity and creativity. Achieving generativity may not only affect individuals' views of themselves but the way that they treat other people. If the status of generativity is not achieved, a sense of stagnation or purposelessness may arise.

### Stage 8: Ego integrity vs. despair

Erikson admits lacking a clear definition of ego integrity, but it seems to include such things as dignity, practical wisdom, and acceptance of one's own life pattern (Bee, 1978). Achieving integrity means consolidating one's sense of self and fully accepting that self with its unique and unalterable history. Having achieved ego integrity, a person in the later years can look back on his or her life and recognize with satisfaction that it was the right life to have lived. One who fails to attain ego integrity despairs that life has been wasted and that it is too late to salvage it. Such individuals fear death, thereby increasing the despair that they feel.

## General comments on Erikson's theory

Because he offers one of the few real syntheses between cognitive development and personality development, Erikson's theory has been widely influential (Bee, 1978). This is not because everyone agrees that his descriptions of individual crises are absolutely accurate. However, most agree that it is the most comprehensive theory of psychosocial development across the entire life span.

Research using Erikson's work has drawn close relationships with other aspects of development. For example, a positive relationship between emotional development and moral development scores has been found. Children who exhibit higher levels of emotional development tend to exhibit higher levels of moral development, while children who manifest lower levels of emotional development similarly tended to manifest lower levels of moral development (see Aronfreed, 1971; Callen, 1978).

**Gender identity:**
perception of oneself as male or female and the acceptance of one's identity as male or female.

**Sex role:**
the way in which individuals internalize the roles considered appropriate for their own sex.

**Sex typing:**
the acquisition of characteristics and behaviour that a culture considers appropriate for each of the sexes.

**Sex-role preferences:**
the desire or preference for sex-typed activities.

**Sex-role adoption:**
the actual performance of sex-typed behaviour.

**Sex-role stereotype:**
the belief that an individual should act in certain ways because of sex.

A major criticism of Erikson's theories lies in the fact that familiarity with the theory does not necessarily translate into a thorough understanding of why students actually behave the way they do in and out of school. Modeling the behaviour of those in the environment is a powerful way through which children are socialized. The ideas of Alfred Bandura and other social learning theorists are discussed in Chapter 8.

## INDIVIDUAL DIFFERENCES

Because socialization is unique to particular families, the individual differences that can occur are almost limitless. But although many socializing influences are unique to certain families and to the children within those families, there are also broad influences that can be expected to more or less effect all children in a given society. Prominent among these are the norms for personal qualities and behaviour that tell children what is expected of boys or girls at a particular age level.

### The question of gender

Erikson's emphasis is on the psychology of males. He also apparently views heterosexual orientation as normal. He felt that sex roles were particularly important in the development of identity because they established a pattern for many types of behaviour (Biehler and Snowman, 1990). Parents clearly play a major part in the development of sex roles and in sex-typing because they serve as the child's first models for masculine or feminine behaviour.

**Gender identity** is the degree to which one perceives and accepts oneself as male or female. **Sex role** refers to the way in which individuals internalize the roles considered appropriate for their own sex. **Sex typing** is the acquisition of characteristics and behaviour that a culture considers appropriate for females and males. There are also **sex role preferences** which refer to the desire or preference for sex-typed activities. **Sex-role adoption** relates to the actual performance of sex-typed or nonsex behaviour.

Finally, a **sex-role stereotype** is the belief that an individual should act in certain ways because of his or her sex. For example, in one study (Condry and Condry, 1976) college students viewed a videotape of a nine month old's response to a Jack in the Box. Some students were led to believe that the child was a girl, others believed it to be a boy. When the infant showed a strong reaction to the toy, the reaction was more often labeled as anger if the child was thought to be a boy and fear when the infant was thought to be a girl.

There are three explanations of how sex differences tend to originate—biology, parental influence, and children's imitation of adults of their own sex. Nearly every individual is born clearly male or female. But being male or female is a social as well as a biological role. Parental influences and children's imitative behaviour play major roles in the development of sex differences as do cultural mores and societal expectations.

To some extent, the behaviour of children is circumscribed by their sex from the moment they are born and wrapped in the first pink or blue blanket. Once children understand that they are either boys or girls, usually at about two or three years of age, they begin to stress both age and sex in defining themselves and their peers. By age four or five, children understand the differences in body structure and capacity of males and females. By age five they understand the concept of permanent sexual identity as well (Hartup and Zook, 1960) and they have developed an awareness of sex differences and of masculine and feminine roles (Wynn and Fletcher, 1987).

Most young children seem highly motivated to learn about and fulfill role expectations (Bradbard and Endsley, 1983). That is, once a little girl understands that she is a girl, she is likely to search for the meaning of being a girl and the implications for clothing and grooming, toy and game preferences, and personal mannerisms and interests (Good and Brophy, 1986).

Parents clearly play a major part in the development of sex roles and in sex typing because they serve as a child's first model for masculine or feminine behaviour. Young parents actually respond differently to boy and girl infants. In one study, young mothers were permitted to play with a six month old baby (Wills, Self, and Dalan, 1976). Sometimes this baby was dressed in girl's clothes, sometimes in boy's. The mothers treated the baby differently depending on what the infant was wearing. They provided dolls for the baby in the dress; cars and trucks for the baby in the pants.

In their early interactions, parents seem to treat infants in different ways. Fathers are more likely to play in physical or novel ways; mothers play more traditional games such as "Peek-a-boo" and provide most of the routine care (Lamb, 1978). Different treatment of the sexes seems to continue in early childhood.

Since there exist predictable differences in the ways mothers and fathers interact with their babies, Lamb (1979) believes that this is a major factor influencing the development of a child's gender identity. That is, parents' attitudes toward their own gender roles and the ways they interact with each other will influence the child's views. Parents shape sex-typed behaviour by the toys they provide, the activities they encourage, and their responses to behaviour considered appropriate or inappropriate for the child's sex (Atkinson et al., 1990).

The different treatment of the sexes seen in infancy seems to continue in early childhood. Boys are encouraged to be more physically active; girls are encouraged to be affectionate and tender. Boys seem to be given more freedom to roam the neighbourhood and are not protected as long as girls from potentially dangerous activities. By one year of age, girls play differently from boys, are more attached to their mothers, and ask for help more consistently than boys (Goldberg and Lewis, 1972). Parents are quick to come to the aid of their daughters but are more likely to insist that their sons handle problems themselves (Block, 1983). Independence and initiative seem to be more encouraged in boys although it may be that girls are not so much trained in dependency as they are deprived of the independent training offered to boys (Hoffman, 1977).

Parents expect and condone more aggressive behaviour from boys (Gibson, 1978). In the early years, boys are subject to more physical punishment and girls to more psychological punishment, such as the threat of the withdrawal of love (Deaux, 1984).

Furthermore, the pressures to conform to sex-appropriate expectations seem to be more intense for boys. Independence and initiative also seem to be encouraged more in boys than in girls. Fathers appear to be more concerned with sex-typed behaviour than mothers, particularly with their sons. They tend to react negatively (interfering with the child's play or expressing disapproval) when their sons play with feminine toys whereas mothers do not. On the other hand, there is more latitude for girls during childhood. The tomboy image may be acceptable for a girl but the sissy is not for a boy. Fathers are less concerned when their daughters engage in masculine play, but they still show disapproval more than mothers do (Langlois and Downs, 1980).

Not only do parents behave differently toward boys and girls, but they provide them with entirely different environments. Rheingold and Cook (1975) studied the bedrooms of boys and girls under the age of six. They found striking differences both in the furniture and the toys selected by the parents. Boys' rooms tended to be decorated in masculine colours and designs, girls' in feminine decor.

These trends toward differential treatment also exist in parents' teaching behaviour. For example, Block (1984) summarized findings obtained during a study of parents who taught their nursery school children to construct squares to match a standard. Parents pressed more for achievement when teaching sons than when instructing girls in this cognitive task.

Children soon learn to imitate the same sex parent. Even if both parents interact with them equally, the youngsters tend to display differences in imitative behaviour. Two-year-old boys, for example, learn to imitate their father's behaviour rather than their mother's (Lamb, 1974, 1975). According to Kagan (1971) the greater the number of similar features, the firmer the belief of the child that the model is similar. For this reason, children tend to imitate the behaviour of the same-sex, similar-appearing parent. The three-year-old boy who washes the car is exhibiting sex-typed behaviour (Gibson, 1978). Interestingly, children's sex-typed behavior does not always duplicate that of adults. For example, elementary school boys tend to cluster in all-boy groups and they do not see their fathers do this on a regular basis. Finally, Maccoby and Jacklin (1974) suggest that parents' socialization practices reflect a cross-sex indulgence, same-sex severity rule. Specifically, these researchers concluded that a review of the literature suggests a trend in which fathers are more indulgent to daughters than to sons and mothers are more demanding of daughters than sons.

When we look at the effects of the types of toys provided for youngsters, it can be seen that play becomes sex stereotyped by the types of toys provided (Karpoe and Olney, 1983). Even very young children tend to play with sex-typed toys; in a daycare setting with a range of toys, it was found that boys play with trucks, trains and tools, girls with dolls and tea sets, or with neutral toys such as blocks (Atkinson et al., 1990). Other research confirms this; boys favour toy vehicles, construction toys, and action games. Girls prefer art activities, doll play, and dancing (Carter, 1987).

It appears that boys develop sex-typed preferences for toys earlier and more consistently than do females (Gibson and Chandler, 1988). As they grow older, boys make increasingly sex-typed choices. Beginning at about age seven, girls often decline in their preference for feminine play activities and become increasingly interested in masculine ones (Huston-Stein and Higgins-Trenk, 1978). Girls then fluctuate between male and female choices until about age ten when they show a rapid shift in preference for feminine toys.

Aggressive behaviour is more likely to be condoned in boys than in girls.

The firm development of gender identity by the age of three or so leads to a preoccupation with sex differences, development of a preference for playmates of the same sex, and temporary separation and occasionally even alientation from the opposite sex. This builds to a peak during middle childhood, typically around eight years of age in brighter and more mature children. In one study (Jacklin and Maccoby, 1978) of pairs of previously unacquainted children (average age 33 months), some pairs had same-sex play partners while others were mixed pairs. Observers recorded the behaviour on a time sampling basis and scored each child for the total social behaviour directed toward the partner (for example, negative and positive behaviour such as offering or grabbing a toy, tugging or pushing, vocally greeting, and inviting or protesting). They found that children of each sex had much higher levels of social behaviour when playing with a same-sex partner than when playing with one of the opposite sex (Maccoby, 1990).

By the age of four and a half, children were spending nearly three times as much time with the same-sex partner. By six and a half the preference had grown much stronger. At this time, children were spending eleven times as much time with the same-sex playmate (Maccoby, 1990).

In their play, striking differences are seen between boys and girls. Porat (1989) observes that girls are more interested in turn-taking than competing. They will sacrifice winning for the sake of maintaining a relationship. But to boys, the game is all. They learn to play with their enemies and compete with their friends (Porat, 1989).

## SUMMARY

1. Contemporary personality theory began with the publications of Sigmund Freud. Freud argued that children pass through a series of psychosexual stages, just as Piaget found that cognition developed in stages. To Freud, the

sequence of emotional transformations leaves an indelible imprint on adult personality. Erikson expanded on Freud's work and proposed that psychosocial development may be broken into eight stages, each marked by conflict.

2. The theory of socio-emotional development forwarded by Erikson is widely accepted. It sees the individual interacting with the environment and passing through a series of stages throughout the lifespan. Although Erikson stresses the roles of maturation and environmental interaction, his theory does not really encompass such aspects as imitation and modeling.

3. Personality is shaped by environmental factors. Failure to secure attachments in the early years has been related to an inability to develop close personal relationships in adulthood.

4. Self-concept—the perception of self—underlies, illuminates, and directs personality. Every child has a self-concept, before reaching the first grade, shaped by experience with parents, peers, and others in his or her world.

5. Self-concept and its development underlies Erikson's theory. Successful resolution of one conflict not only builds self-concept but allows successful transition to the next stage of development. To Erikson, the period of adolescence, when both sexual and occupational identities are formed, is the most crucial in all of development.

6. Parents play an important role in developing notions of gender identity and sex-role typing in their children while social learning situations may reinforce sex roles.

## Key Terms

| | | |
|---|---|---|
| affective variables | affectivity | attachment |
| fixation | gender identity | locus of control |
| motivation | personality | self-awareness |
| self-concept | self-esteem | sex role |
| sex-role adoption | sex-role preference | sex-role stereotypes |
| sex-typing | socialization | socio-emotional development |
| temperament | | |

**5**

# LANGUAGE DEVELOPMENT

## INTRODUCTION

Of all the achievements of early childhood, the acquisition and development of speech and language is one of the most remarkable. From their earliest days, infants process language, preparing to become competent communicators. By about two months of age, infants are producing speech-like sounds; the first meaningful words emerge at about one year. By the age of two or so, most children know the relationship between words and are mastering the fundamentals of grammar; soon they are able to produce an infinite variety of intelligible utterances. As children grow, they acquire communicative competence, the ability to understand and use communication commensurate with developmental levels. By the age of five, most children have acquired such mastery over language that they have a firm linguistic base on which teachers can formally build reading and writing (Winzer, 1990a).

Although small children accomplish the monumental task of language acquisition with ease, linguists, psychologists, anthropologists, and many others either directly or peripherally involved in language research, remain unsure of how the process actually occurs. Because language emerges when children are very young and because children of this cannot discuss language acquistion, the major source of information about their language learning comes from recording their speech. Investigators carefully transcribe what they say and what other people say to children.

People study language development for a number of reasons and from a number of perspectives. In fact, as Rice (1989) observes, the study of child language sits at an interface among linguistics, developmental psychology, sociology, anthropology, and education. It links basic questions about the nature of human intellectual competencies to applied questions of how to teach young children. Early interest in language was studied under the disciple of philology rather than psychology. Serious psychological study of language acquisition and development is of relatively recent origin. It was not until the early 1950s that psychologists began to turn their attention to language; in 1953 the term "psycholinguistics," meaning the cognitive as well as the linguistic side of language use, was popularized (Hilgard, 1987). After that, the study of psycholinguistics proliferated so rapidly that it was as though something totally new had been discovered (Hilgard, 1987).

Although language acquisition has only recently become a topic of major interest to developmental and cognitive psychologists, in the past authors from a variety of disciplines directed their attention toward children's language acquisition. In fact, the study of language and how it develops in humans has interested enquiring minds for thousands of years. Some early findings are shown in Box 5-1.

## Box 5-1 **Historical note: Early studies in language**

The development of language and speech in humans has intrigued philosophers, educators and physicians for centuries. As an essentially human trait, speech was revered as "the breath of God" and the "voice of the soul" (Amman, 1700).

For many centuries, it was believed that if children were raised in an environment in which no language was spoken, they would naturally speak the most ancient of tongues. Herodotus, in the fifth century B.C. reported that various monarchs tried the experiment. Psamtik, a pharaoh of Egypt in the seventh century B.C., isolated two infants under the care of a shepherd, who was ordered to remain silent in order to see whether they would speak Phrygian or Egyptian. Two years later, the children muttered *becos* which was determined to be the Phrygian word for bread. Thus the Egyptians admitted that Phrygian was the more ancient language.

Later, in the thirteenth century, the Holy Roman Emperor, Frederick II of Hohenstaufen, tried the same experiment to settle a controversy as to whether children would speak Hebrew, Latin, Arabic, or the language of their parents. Unfortunately, the children died. James IV, King of the Scots in the fifteenth century,

repeated the experiment with more successful results. He claimed that his children "spak verey guid Ebrew" (Fromkin et al., 1974, p. 82).

Virtually all the major philosophers since Plato and Aristotle have considered the problems of the origin and role of human language. Debates centred on the role of language in the progressive differentiation of humans from other creatures and the way in which reason manifested itself in language (see Winzer, 1990b).

In the Christian era, for example, St. Augustine discussed language development in *The confessions*. The birth of the British Royal Society in London in the mid-1600s also stimulated much philosophical interest and speculation about how language develops in humans. However, it was during the mid-eighteenth century, as part of the broad intellectual movement known as the French Enlightenment, that some of the most interesting studies were attempted.

A rigorous analysis of the structures and functions of language formed an important tenet of Enlightenment thought. The origin of speech and language was seen as the key to the history of thought (Knowlson, 1965), while the use of language was viewed as the mode through which people would be taught to think rationally, clearly and, above all, scientifically (Seigel, 1969). The focus was on language as a system of communication somehow able to explain reflective thought, rather than language as a system of syntactic and semantic structures.

Much of the speculation of the French philosophers drew on the empirical philosophy of John Locke. When Locke speculated on language and its place in human development he pointed to the arbitrary nature of language. He asserted that words derive their meaning from a culture that accepts certain relationships and certain designations. In his view, "words in their primary or immediate signification stand for nothing but the ideas in the mind of him that uses them" (Locke, 1690).

With Locke as a touchstone, the French philosophers used accounts of feral children (those that had been abandoned in the wilderness) and the commmunication of deaf persons as basic data for their debate. This concern for language led first to a systematic study of communication, language, and symbol and ultimately to imaginative experiments with deaf persons and their sign language. Contemporary arguments concerning language centred on whether or not gesture preceded speech as a natural antecedent or whether they were completely unrelated in evolution (Knowlson, 1965; Rudowski, 1974).

One of the most prominent of the French philosophers, the Abbé Condillac, viewed humans as intelligent beings, capable of reflection because of the gift of language. To Condillac, the progress of the human intellect was basically a study of the growth and development of language (Seigel, 1969). As a strong gestural theorist, Condillac suggested that sounds were initially added to a natural gesture language; he believed that the recall of ideas could be aided by the use of signs (Kyle, 1980). Condillac placed great stress on the part played by language and saw ideas as becoming fixed by association with a sign or a word. Although primary learning was through the senses, Condillac theorized that it was shaped by language, as was the acquisition of theoretical knowledge.

Another prominent philosopher, Denis Diderot, held that gesture preceded language, and was in fact more sublime than verbal utterances. In his 1751 *Lettre sur sourds et muets*, he suggested that the natural order of the development of language would be best examined by studying the sign language of the deaf (Kyle, 1980). Julien La Mettrie wrote on language in *L'historie naturalle de l'ame* (1745) and *L'homme machine* (1748). He suggested trying to educate orangutans in the same way as the deaf are taught (Lane and Pillard, 1978). Language was also discussed by Rousseau, Helvetius, Bonnet, and Condorcet (Seigel, 1969).

**SOURCE:** Winzer 1990b

Enormously complex and comprehensive research into the nature and acquisition of language continues apace and builds on early studies which, although lacking a strong theoretical base, laid the foundations for later investigations. In the study of language acquisition and development, a number of shifts in emphasis have been witnessed. Some of the first researchers embarked on diary studies. For example, Charles Darwin, father of modern evolutionary theory, published a narrative of his son's development, noting language learning (1877). Diary studies, however, were soon abandoned because they were unavoidably biased. Then examinations of children's vocabulary became one of the most common approaches to the study of language acquisition. Edward Thorndike (1913) used word counts as a simple empirical method in the study of children's language. But these early studies of language tended to create a static picture for, in focusing on semantics, researchers overlooked such elements as the development of syntax and the transition from two- to three-word sentences. In the 1930s and 1940s, evaluation and intervention strategies targeted phonology, which led to the age of articulation proficiency tests (Hasenstab, 1983). Psychologists later began to study patterns of language development across a wide range of children, focusing on the frequency of certain words, parts of speech, and average sentence length at various ages. Studies on the form of language ceded in the 1950s to research on what children seem to know about language at various ages. In the 1960s, Chomsky's generative and transformational grammar made a number of converts and rapidly became influential in psycholinguistics. Chomsky (1957) brought teachers, researchers, speech pathologists, and other professionals into the world of syntax with sentence trees and basic sentence patterns.

As the '60s drew to a close, the primacy of syntax in research gave way to a broadening interest that included the context in which children's language emerges and an emphasis on the kinds of semantic relations children attempt to express in their early utterances. Then semantics enjoyed a brief period of dominance before pragmatics rose to the fore (Hasenstab, 1983). Studies throughout the 1980s have included all the traditional topics: phonology, morphology, syntax, and semantics. Stress has been placed on the acquisition of pragmatics, the ability to use language appropriately in social situations. There has also been an increasing interest in the importance of language development as a predictor of normal and abnormal development. This new research is confirming the earlier suspected notion that a child's level of language skills is one of the best indicators and predictors of the child's cognitive capabilities (Salkind, 1990).

Language is based on a very complex system of symbols and rules for using these symbols; it is a dynamic interplay of sound, syntax, semantics, and other elements, formed and developed by interaction among people. Communicative development is related to other developmental areas. The development and use of linguistic symbols depends upon attaining certain cognitive, social, and motor skills. Speech requires the physical growth of certain neuromuscular structures and the motor control of these functions. Competence with language also has a direct influence on a child's ability to learn and later to read and to write (Polloway and Smith, 1982).

As children acquire speech and language they typically pass through certain stages. These should not be viewed as a set of discrete milestones through which children pass on the way to mastering adult communication. The growth of communication is cumulative rather than linear, so language development should be seen as a process that is generative, systematic, and rule governed. In language, as in most models of mental growth, past learning is never shed—it becomes assimilated and transformed into more advanced skills and knowledge. Language learning begins in infancy and continues throughout life. Formal language use, then, is one point on a continuum of communication

**Language maturity:**
the ability to use the phonological, morphological, syntactical, and semantic
elements of language.

behaviour that begins in non-verbal social exchanges during infancy and extends through the use of written language.

Most children come to school in possession of an intuitive knowledge of language, although they will differ in their language maturity, their ability with the phonological, morphological, syntactical, and semantic elements of language. The differences correspond to mental age, sensory status, environmental background, dialect characteristics, and previous instruction. In the classroom, it is the teacher's task to help each child to learn the words, grammar, meaning, and correct speech sounds appropriate for each developmental level. Students must be provided with opportunities and practice in using the skills for communication and thinking, and in reading and writing (Winzer, 1989).

It is crucial that teachers and parents understand the nature of language acquisition in children—both the developmental sequence and the processes that children employ—in order to move with the wave rather than interfere with it. Moreover, language and speech are basic components of instruction, for teaching is essentially a linguistic activity that depends on transmitting and receiving messages. Not only should teachers understand child language and its development, but they should also be aware of the effects of their own communication in the classroom.

No chapter on the development of language in Canadian schools today would be complete without a discussion of bilingualism, the ability to think and speak in two languages. The number of students in Canadian schools whose native language is not English and who have to learn English as a second language is surprisingly high.

As well, the two official languages of Canada mean that bilingualism in those two languages is on the rise. According to the 1981 census, 60 percent of Canadians had English as their mother tongue while 25 percent had French. Of those whose mother tongue was French, 33 percent were bilingual while only eight percent of people whose mother tongue was English were bilingual. In 1986 French was reported as the mother tongue of 83 percent of Quebec residents and 34 percent of residents of New Brunswick (Lachapelle, 1990). In Quebec, 50 percent of native English speakers are bilingual as compared to 7 percent in Ontario (see Alcock, Carment, and Sadava, 1988). In Canada, bilingualism is increasing. While the population grew only 12 percent between 1971 and 1981, the extent of bilingualism increased 27 percent.

French immersion programs have been the most common mode for assisting children whose mother tongue is not French in acquiring that language. Numbers involved in French immersion programs have risen dramatically in the past 15 years. In British Columbia, for example, enrolment in French immersion programs at the elementary level has risen from under 1 000 in 1976 to nearly 20 000 students (Day and Shapson, 1988). In Ottawa, 40 percent of English speaking parents are sending their children to French immersion kindergarten (Reich, 1986).

## COMMUNICATION

Communication with others is one of the most complex activities that humans undertake. Effective communication is vital to our daily existence and social

**Communication:**
the process of exchanging information and ideas between participants.

**Language:**
a system of symbols organized into conventional patterns to communicate meaning.

progress. In a general sense, we know what communication, language, and speech mean, but when we try to define them completely and definitively we meet difficulties. There are problems in attempting to encompass all the complex and diverse aspects of human communication and language in tidy definitions. However, the essential obscurity of the nature of language may be related to its loose relationship to that elusive and inapprehensible process which we call thought (Macnamara, 1977).

Both speech and language are parts of a larger process of communication, the process of exchanging information and ideas between participants. Probably all living things have some form of communication, however simple. Therefore the concept of communication includes the entire spectrum of acts performed by living creatures by which to pass on and respond to messages. Our chief interest here, however, is with human communication and that uniquely human characteristic—the ability to acquire and use language.

Communication may be viewed as any process where meaning is stimulated (Hurt, Scott, and McCrokey, 1978). Communication is the essence of human socialization—it is the essential means through which people initiate and maintain social relationships (Hazen and Black, 1989) and the link that provides reciprocal interaction between the individual and the milieu (Levine, 1981). In this sense, communication is an active process that involves encoding, transmitting, and decoding the intended message. It requires a sender and a receiver and each communication partner must be alert to the communicative needs of the other to ensure that messages are communicated effectively and that intended meanings are preserved.

As an integral part of communication, language is a typically human activity. Essentially, language is a system of symbols organized into conventional patterns used by humans to communicate meaning. Language and speech are not the same thing. Certainly, of all the language forms we use, spoken language, or speech, is the most common and useful coin of communicative exchange. It is, however, only one medium. While language can exist without speech, as in the sign language used by deaf persons, speech cannot exist without the language that lends it meaning. This is diagrammed in Figure 5-1.

**Figure 5-1**
**Communication**

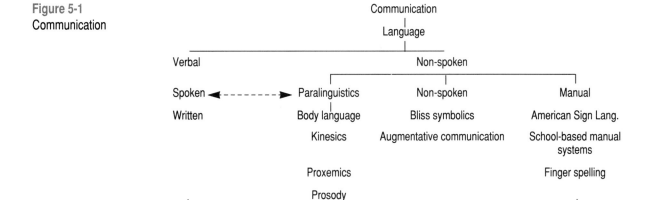

Human language is incredibly complex, bound by structured rules and characteristic patterns of usage that change in different settings—intrapersonal, interpersonal, group, and societal (Levine, 1981). Language also consists of interrelated and intertwined components, all of which must be present or developing for appropriate usage. Meaning is the essence of language and is encoded in vocabulary, syntax, and phonology. Language users need to know *phonology*, or the sound structure of the language *syntax* and *grammar*, the rules that govern the ordering of words within sentences, *semantics*, the meaning of words, phrases, and sentences, and *morphology*, the system of word building. It is equally important to employ *pragmatics*—the use of language in its social context—to attain and convey appropriate meaning.

Language is inextricably intertwined with our mental life—our perceiving, remembering, attending, comprehending and thinking—in short, all of our attempts to make sense of our experiences with the world. Language acquisition, therefore, overlaps and relies upon social and cognitive growth. These aspects of development are closely intertwined, and really cannot be considered separately. A linguistic environment, an intact cognitive/perceptual system, and normal social interaction all underlie the normal development of language. If the child does not hear language or has some impairment of the cognitive/perceptual mechanism, or has a troubled family background, the child's development of language will reflect these problems (Winzer, 1990a).

Small children learn language long before school age and do so with vivacity and playfulness. For most children, the ready acquisition of their culture's language and speech is a natural part of early maturation. The first two years are critical, for this is when children typically make enormous progress in speech and language development. Initially infants are able to produce only vegetative sounds and reflexive cries, but most children, by the age of two, develop a lexicon of spoken words and learn to form simple multilevel utterances. They develop communicative competence rapidly—they know how to interact, how to communicate appropriately in various situations, and how to make sense of what others say and do in communicative interactions (Winzer, 1990a).

An important aspect of language is the creativity involved. Children are not passive organisms into which language is poured but rather catalytic agents. In other words, language does not merely develop but it is also actively acquired. The process is clearly marked by open-endedness and productivity. It is clear quite early that children do not put words together only if they have heard those words together in combination before; rather, they produce utterances they have never before heard. As children develop vocabulary and internalize a knowledge of the rules of their native language, they can potentially create an infinite number of unique utterances.

In acquiring language, the rate and development appears to be the same whether the child is monolingual or bilingual (Doyle, Champagne, and Segalowitz, 1978; Padilla and Lindholm, 1976). In spite of the linguistic load inherent in bilingualism, children acquire both languages at a comparable rate to that of monolingual children (Padilla and Liebman, 1975). The degree of dissimilarity between the two languages does not appear to affect the rate of acquisition. The key to development is the consistent use of the two languages within their primary use environments.

**Communicative competence:**

the degree to which someone is successful in communicating, as measured by the appropriateness and effectiveness of the message.

# ELEMENTS OF LANGUAGE

Language proficiency consists of different kinds of proficiencies (Snow, 1987). The kind of language used to do one's shopping is different from that used to prepare an essay on an abstract topic. The former is relatively undemanding; the latter is relatively demanding, requiring language use that is complex, literate, and creative (Cummins, 1981).

The degree to which a speaker is successful in communicating, measured by the appropriateness and effectiveness of the message, is called **communicative competence** (Dore, 1986; Hymes, 1972). Communicative competence entails all of the language skills—semantics, syntax, phonology, morphology, and pragmatics. The competent communicator "has the capacity not only to conceive, formulate, modulate and issue messages but also to perceive the degree to which intended meanings are appropriately coded in a matrix of referential codes and conveyed" (Muma, 1978, p. 119).

Each of the language skills must be present and increase at an appropriate rate for normal language acquisition and development to occur. Language development can also be separated into structural and functional aspects. The former involves learning how the elements of sentences are combined to form meaningful phrases that conform to the structural requirements of the language, or syntax. The latter concerns the ability to use language to communicate, think, and solve problems. We speak also of two other descriptive aspects of language—production (expressive language) and comprehension (receptive language).

**Figure 5-2**
Views of the elements of language

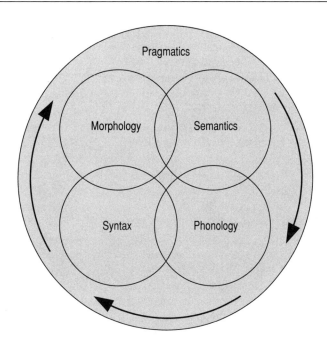

## Box 5-2 **The development of a language of signs**

During the French Enlightenment, that spanned from about 1740 to 1780, philosphers studying language development often used the communication systems of deaf people as basic data for their debates. This philosophical speculation soon translated into imaginative teaching interventions for deaf persons (Winzer, 1990b) and the development of special schools and a special language of signs.

It was the French priest, Michel Charles de l'Epee (1712-1789), who astutely applied the theories regarding the psychology of deafness and the evolution of language to the education of the deaf. In 1760, when he was almost 50 years old, de l'Epee opened a class for six poor, deaf children in his home on rue de Moulins in Paris (Rae, 1848).

As his fundamental assumption, the Abbé took John Locke's notion that language was artificial and arbitrary. The Abbé speculated that "it would be possible to instruct the Deaf and Dumb with written characters, always accompanied by sensible signs" (de l'Epee, 1784/1860, p. 26). De l'Epee also became convinced that the natural signs his students made with their hands when trying to communicate with each other were the basis of a mother tongue for them, in much the same way that one's native language is for a hearing person. "The natural language of the deaf and dumb," concluded the Abbé, "is the language of signs" (de l'Epee, 1784/1860, p. 127).

De l'Epee decided to devise a sign language for his deaf students, the first formal system of signs for the first deaf persons ever to have been formally educated. To do this, he observed his students closely and recorded the natural signs they used in their communication with each other. To *le language des signes naturelles*, the core group of signs which he observed his students using spontaneously, de l'Epee added many of his own, sometimes based on those employed by his pupils, sometimes entirely original. While his pupils' signs largely designated objects, qualities, and events, the Abbé's *signes methodiques* corresponded to grammatical functions in French, such as tense and person, and also signs to relay abstract relationships and metaphysical and religious concepts (de l'Epee, 1784/1860). Under the Abbé's tutelage, there evolved a fully articulated language of signs. Finger spelling was also incorporated (Winzer, 1990b).

When de l'Epee developed a formalized sign language for his deaf students, he drew on an already existing body of gestures, signs and finger alphabets. He did not build the house from the foundations up but rather systemized and standardized the design and layout (Winzer, 1990b). The manual components of the systems were not original. Dactylology, or finger spelling, was a borrowed art, formulated neither by the deaf nor by their teachers. While the origins of dactylology are unknown, there is evidence of the use of manual alphabets dating from pre-classical times, which probably owe their origin to the development of manual signs for numbers. That manual alphabets served a useful if limited purpose is suggested by the fact that through the centuries they continued to be used and improved (Hodgson, 1973).

Sign language is ancient; early literature contains scattered references to sign language systems employed by deaf persons as well as methods in general use. Plato, for example, mentioned that meaning could be signified by the hands and head and other parts of the body. The Roman writer, Quintilian, observed that sign language originated in heroic times and met with the approval of the Greeks. "Amidst the great diversity of tongues pervading all nations and people," noted Quintilian, "the language of the hands appears to be common to all men" (in Pettergill, 1872, p.10).

Sign systems were widely used by the Egyptians, the Greeks and Romans, Moslems, Tahitians, Arabs, and Mexicans (Tyler, 1879). In Rome the pantomimes, who maintained their reputation from the time of Augustus until the sixth century, expressed through stylized sign and mime fables about the gods and ancient heroes. Elizabethan theatre used stylized gestures to communicate different emotions such as doubt and repulsion, which remained conventional until the talkies of the early twentieth century (Winzer, 1990b). Sign language systems also served more nefarious purposes and a variety of hand signals and gestures were used by people who needed to communicate covertly–spies and members of secret societies. The Thugs, for example, who specialized in ritual murder had a series of formal signs for "all clear" (touching the ear lobe) and the obviously very useful "kill" (placing a hand on the chest with the second and third fingers crossed) (Daraul, 1961).

De l'Epee did not intend his sign system to be local and idiosyncratic but a universal medium of communication for deaf people. Indeed, when the French system was brought to the United States in 1817, it was very similar to the system that de l'Epee had devised and was structured by a dictionary based on de l'Epee's system (Winzer, 1990b). But, like any language, sign language grew and changed. Today each country has its own system of signs and, just in spoken language, universality is not a characteristic of the sign languages used by deaf persons.

**SOURCE:** Winzer 1990b.

**Paralanguage:**
aspects of communication that may enhance or change the linguistic code.

# Other aspects of communication

Language and speech are only a portion of communication. Other aspects of communication that may enhance or change the linguistic code may be classified as paralinguistic, nonlinguistic, and metalinguistic. These aspects are sometimes grouped together as paralanguage, meaning "beside language."

### Paralinguistic elements

Another level to the sound system consists of the paralinguistic codes that are superimposed on speech to signal intentions or emotions. Paralinguistic mechanisms are called suprasegmental devices because they can change the form and meaning of a sentence by cutting across elements or segments of a sentence. They include intonation, stress and emphasis, speed or rate of delivery, and pauses or hesitations.

Intonation patterns are changes in pitch that signal the mood of an utterance. Some of intonation results from the way we breathe: we only have limited breath and so tend to drop our voices at the end of a sentence as we run out. Stress is employed for emphasis while rate varies with the speaker's state of excitement, familiarity with the content, and perceived comprehension of the listener. Pauses may be used to emphasize a portion of the message or to replace the message. Even young children recognize that a short maternal pause after a request usually signals a negative response.

**Nonlinguistic clues:**
gestures, body language, facial expressions, hand and body movements, and physical distance which complement and supplement language and account for a great deal of communicative competence.

**Kinesics:**
the study of communica-tion codes that use body movements to construct meanings.

## Nonlinguistic elements

**Nonlinguistic clues,** which include gestures, body language, facial expressions, hand and body movements, and physical distance, complement and supplement language and account for a great deal of communicative competence. It is generally agreed that nonverbal behaviour is partly taught, partly imitative, and partly instinctive (Hammermeister and Timms, 1989). Nonverbal behaviour serves a number of functions (M. L. Patterson, 1982, 1983). It provides information about feelings and intentions, regulates interactions, expresses intimacy, promotes social control, and facilitates goal attainment (such as in pointing to something).

Moreover, nonverbal communication is more powerful and more subtle than verbal communication in expressing emotions. A raise of the eyebrows, a pucker of the lips, or a clenching of the fist can often communicate more about our feelings than a string of words. Women are somewhat better at both sending and picking up nonverbal clues according to a wide range of studies (Brown, 1986). As well, women show more facial displays of emotion and spend more time smiling than do males (Mayo and Henley, 1981).

**Kinesics** is the study of communication codes that use body movements to construct meanings. Some of the most obvious and strong kinesic signals are sent through facial expressions. Certain facial expressions seem to have a universal meaning, regardless of the culture; others are learned from a particular culture. While nonverbal signals are usually involuntarily sent and subconsciously received, the affective state of an individual can be communicated by nonverbal facial expressions (Daly, Abromovitch, and Pliner, 1980). In fact, facial expressions may be the best indicator of one's emotions at a certain time.

It seems that there are universal patterns of facial displays, with a smile being a positive response in all cultures. Two kinds of facial displays seem particularly important in the communication development of children—smiles and eye contact.

Nonlinguistic forms of communication, such as eye contact and facial expressions, provide information about feelings and intentions.

**Proxemics:**
the study of how people use spaces between them and the characteristics of the territory used for communication.

**Metalinguistic skills:**
the abilities to talk about language, analyze it, think about it as an entity separate from its content, and judge it.

In some cultures, direct gaze is considered disrespectful. However, in many Canadian cultural groups, eye contact is used in face to face communication to indicate willingness to communicate. Avoiding another's glance is usually taken as an evasive manoeuver.

Body language also includes the clothes we wear, the gestures and body movements we make, and actual body contact. Body movements and hand gestures are important in communicating feelings and in regulating language; hand gestures can control the synchronization of language (Hammermeister and Timms, 1989). **Proxemics** is the study of how people use spaces between them and the characteristics of the territory used for communication. The closer one feels to another, the closer one will move to that person. Hall (1959) devided personal space into four zones:

1. Intimate zone (0-18 inches)—very close communication (e.g., holding a baby;

2. Personal zone (2-4 feet)—close speech with family or close friends;

3. Social zone (4-7 feet)—the general conversational zone with friends and acquaintances; and

4. Public zone (8+ feet)—teaching or public speech.

### Metalinguistic abilities

Metacognitive skills are monitoring skills that are activated during learning and instruction. In the area of language, metalinguistic skills refer to the ability to talk about language, analyze it, think about it as an entity separate from its content, and judge it. Metalinguistic abilities enable the language user to think about language independently of comprehension or production abilities; an individual can focus on and reflect upon language as a decontextualized object (Van Kleek, 1982).

These linguistic intuitions or metalinguistic skills allow us to make decisions about the grammatical acceptability of a sentence and judge the correctness or appropriateness of the language we produce and receive. Hence, metalinguistic clues signal the status of the transmission or the success of communication. Moreover, once children have begun to develop metalinguistic skills at around five or six years of age, they can use language as an object of analysis and observation; they are able to use language to describe language (Cazden, 1974). Although explanations for the correlations have not been very convincing, metalinguistic ability has repeatedly been shown to correlate with cognitive development, literacy skills and, to some extent, with oral language skills (Gleitman and Gleitman, 1979; Menyuk, 1984).

## THE NATURE OF LANGUAGE DEVELOPMENT

As we pointed out, language abilities increase both qualitatively and quantitatively with age. Language development may be seen to begin immediately after the infant's birth cry and continue throughout life. It used to be assumed that language development, with the exception of semantics, was pretty well complete by the time a child entered school. Although the first two years of life are still considered the critical stage for language acquisition and the five year old is

**Motherese:**
child-adult communicative interaction characterized by unique alterations in speech, meaning, form, and even language usage.

still considered to have made spectacular progress in only a few short years, many aspects of speech, language, and communication are mastered later in life. The school ages and, to a lesser degree the adult years, are characterized by growth in all aspects of language, and especially in semantics and pragmatics.

There are three major components of language acquisition: the language to be acquired; the child and the abilities the child brings to the task; and the language learning environment, including adult-child interactions.

All children in all cultures seem to learn language in the same way and at about the same time. That is, they acquire and use the elements of language in the same way and reach language learning milestones at much the same time.

In order to learn a language, children need the ability to remember the sounds they hear and to identify them at a later time (Elliott, 1981). In other words, they need working auditory, perceptual, cognitive, and neurological systems. The study of the anatomy, physiology, and biochemistry responsible for language processing and formulation is called neurolinguistics. Most neurolinguists agree that language development is highly correlated with brain maturation and specialization. But whether the relationship is based upon maturation of specific structures or upon the development of particular cognitive abilities is unknown (Owens, 1988).

In almost all humans, the left hemisphere of the brain is specialized for language in all forms (oral, visual and written), temporal or linear order perception, arithmetic calculations, and logical reasoning. The left hemisphere is best at step by step processing as opposed to the holistic processing characteristic of the right hemisphere. Only about two percent of the human population, including left-handers, is right dominant for language. A miniscule proportion of humans display bilateral linguistic performance with no apparent dominant hemisphere (Owens, 1988). However, lateralization in this domain may be a matter of degree rather than the all or nothing pattern suggested. (See Corballis, 1983).

Language is first a social behaviour based on social interaction that arises from a child's early nonverbal communicative exchanges with caregivers. In fact, the quality of adult-child interactions is the single most important influence on the child's language development. To gain control over linguistic structures, children require a high degree of participatory activity. The adult role in the child's learning is one of encouragment and provision of resources for skills and information (Wells, 1981).

Infants acquire early language through social interaction. They express and experience early communication through a wide variety of vocal interchanges with their mothers (Stern, 1977). Comprehensive studies of early language development clearly demonstrate the importance of mother's talk to infants (Stern, 1977). Overall, researchers have demonstrated, in both concurrent and longitudinal studies of 12 to 30 six-month-old children, that high levels of responsive maternal verbal and play stimulation are associated with relatively advanced cognitive and language skills. (e.g., Carew, 1980; Olson, Bates, and Bayles, 1984).

Child-adult communicative interaction is sometimes called motherese and is characterized by rather unique alterations in speech, meaning, form, and even language usage. Adult to child and child to child communication show register changes and differences in language usage.

Parent communication is neither random nor haphazard. Parents interact with their infants in regular and systematic ways. When interacting with infants, both adults and children tend to use a different register, or form of speech, with a higher pitch, exaggerated intonation, clear enunciation, slower rate (with more pauses between utterances), simplified speech sounds, repeated syllables, and simplified syntax. As children grow, caregivers use modeling, imitation, and expansion of the child's utterances to encourage their language development.

## Language acquisition

From the beginning of life, infants produce their own sounds and cries; by about six months of age they begin to also imitate the voiced sounds made by those around them. In another half year, they move to using single words and then on to syntactically correct sentences. How does this come about? How does a baby learn to understand and respond? How does a small child accomplish the acquisition of conventional communication competence?

Language is probably the most important single learning that children experience in their entire  lives. It is also an intensely human experience. All animals communicate but whether they can actually learn language has been an area of intense research, as outlined in Box 5-3.

## Box 5-3  Language learning in apes

A number of researchers have undertaken studies aimed at teaching apes to use some form of communication. Early endeavours demonstrated that apes can learn symbolic communication by using sign language and, in some studies, computer language (Fouts, 1972). Psychologists also taught gorillas and chimpanzees American Sign Language (ASL). In fact, one chimp, using a series of hand signs to communicate, was able to answer correctly a sufficient number of questions on an intelligence test designed for nonverbal children to receive an IQ score equivalent to the score of a five-year-old child.

One of the earliest studies on animal communication was undertaken by Gardner and Gardner (1969, 1975) who raised a baby chimp named Washoe in their home and used ASL to communicate. Washoe picked up signs rapidly; after four years she had a vocabulary of 150 signs and used combinations of two to three words quite often. Washoe also learned to create new words such as "water bird" for duck (Owens, 1988). However, she did not seem capable of learning word order. Washoe performed at a level equal to the expressive linguistic abilities of a 12 to 24 month old child (Brown, 1973).

Recent studies with Koko, a mountain gorilla, and other primates seem to give indications that, although primates appear capable of creating sentences, they have failed to do so and therefore have failed to master the more difficult task of true language usage: the chimpanzee Koko memorized an extensive naming vocabulary but she could not solve problems that involved more than memorizing and labeling (Limber, 1977).

While chimps can learn to use signs, there are many nonhuman patterns to their discourse (Terrance et al., 1979). Apes, even highly intelligent ones, do not seem to be able to learn the rules of language. Rumbaugh

(1980) showed that chimpanzees are able to learn stock sentences with fixed and variable elements. But the data suggests that the chimpanzees' learning of language apparently bails down to really simple associations of pairs of words and simple conditioned learning—a type of learning far less complex than that hypothesized by Chomsky for human language.

It is extremely difficult to separate speech and language development in the early years because language usage is expressed so cogently in speech forms in most children. The following brief discussion encompasses both expressive and receptive language acquisition and development.

### Crying and cooing

In infancy two crucial interwoven facets of language emerge—pragmatic or communicative behaviour and the rudiments of phonology. Infants begin to experiment with sound in the early months of life and increase their sound making capacity in conjunction with other aspects of development, specifically neural, motor, and social. The development of expressive language parallels the development of motor abilities; in the very early stages, speech and motor development are seen as occurring in a synchronous fashion so that acquisition follows an orderly progression with advances in speech and motor skills intertwined to a considerable extent.

Infants attend to speech from a very early age and quickly learn to produce their own sounds, such as gurgles and cries. Mothers learn to discriminate happy from unhappy sounds and respond accordingly.

Cooing—using modulated vowel sounds—babbling—repeating and playing with sounds—and crying are early signs of receptive and expressive language. Table 5-1 shows early development. The uttering of first words is a major milestone that demonstrates cognitive, neurological, motor, social, as well as language development.

### First words

The age for first words ranges from nine to nineteen months for normal children but it usually around the first birthday that children produce their first word. Although they have responded to and produced words previously, children now produce them in the presence of the referent.

Several weeks after the first word, vocabulary begins to grow quite rapidly as new words are learned daily. After this spurt, vocabulary growth is slow and children may appear to plateau for short periods. Some words are lost as the

**Holophrasic speech:**

the use of single utterances to express a more complex idea.

child's interest changes and production abilities improve (McLaughlin, 1978). Children also continue to use a large number of vocalizations that are jargon, not real words.

The advent of single word utterances represents a giant stride on the road to language acquisition. Most experts interpret the first words to mean that the child associates the word with meaning in some limited manner. Thus, first words mark a progression from using sounds as simple markers or indicators to more precise encoding of persons, objects or events.

Children's first single word utterances are remarkably efficient and maximally communicative. They are described as **holophrasic speech** because the child uses single utterances to express meaning; a single word is used to express a more complex idea (McNeill, 1970). Young children use their words in a variety of contexts, most frequently to label objects or to interact socially, but always limit their messages to speaking one word at a time (Gleason, 1985). In this context, Lois Bloom (1973) believes that even though children can easily produce more than one word at a time, they are completely unfamilar with how these words might go together.

Infants quickly learn to produce their own sounds such as gurgles and cries.

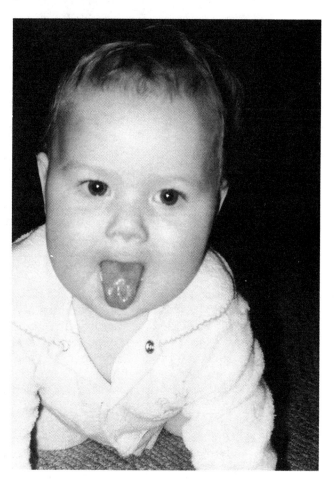

By 18 months of age, toddlers possess a lexicon of approximately 50 words. Each toddler has his or her own individual lexicon of words that reflect, in part, the child's environment. In general, the toddler's definitions are not the same as those of adults in the same environment. The word "horse," for example, might apply to all four-legged animals, regardless of size (Owens, 1988). Nouns or object words predominate; collective nouns or abstractions do not appear (Gentner, 1982). In fact, nouns account for 60 to 65 percent of the first fifty words. (Benedict, 1979) and action words for less than 20 percent of the total (Owens, 1988).

**Table 5-1** Speech and language development, birth to 20 months

| | |
|---|---|
| Birth-8 weeks | Reflexive crying, swallowing, sneezing. Brief cooing sounds that may be associated with smiling. |
| 10-13 weeks | More frequent cooing. Human face elicits cooing response. During cooing, some articulatory organs are moving. |
| 13-20 weeks | Vowel-like cooing, laughter, chuckles. |
| 20 weeks-6 months | Vocal play. Sounds become more differented into vocalic and consonantal components. New articulatory modulations appear. |
| 6-9 months | Babbles, resembling one word utterances. Reduplicated babbling (series of repeated consonant-vowel syllables). The child responds to intonational qualities of what is said. |
| 9 months | The appearance of specific actions in response to specific words such as "Wave bye bye." |
| 12 months | The first utterance of meaningful words. |
| 15 months | Non-reduplicated babbling, expressive jargon (stress and intonation patterns imposed on babbling). Uses jargon in words and conversation. Points to clothes, persons, toys and animals named. Has four to six word vocabulary. |
| 18 to 20 months | Begins to use two word utterances. Has a vocabulary of approximately twenty words. Identifies some body parts. Refers to self by name. Sings and hums spontaneously. |

**Telegraphic speech**

Gentner (1983) suggests that nouns are favoured over verbs in acquisition because they are less linguistically arbitrary. In other words, the noun can be forced to serve a variety of purposes. For instance, a child who does not know or remember the word "drive" may use "car" instead, as in "Let's car to the store" (Gleason, 1985).

Tiny children have a spurt in vocabulary and then go on to simple word combinations (NP + NP) and move rapidly to syntax acquisition (NP + VP). The early word combinations appear to follow predictable patterns (Bloom, 1970) and the toddler produces phrases such as "More cookie" or "Daddy hat." Children's early phrases are the precursors of sentences. Their first utterances may be incomplete or incorrect, but their listeners know what they mean. Children show a wide range of variation in the number of pre-sentences they

**Telegraphic speech:**
a stripped-down form of language containing only the elements that are essential to the meaning of the message.

use. Some children use only a few, and others as many as a thousand (Byrne and Shervanian, 1977).

As children move to use true sentences (NP + VP) they use a stripped down form of language referred to as telegraphic speech. This is called telegraphic because the reduced speech resembles a telegram in that only the essential aspects of the message, those possessing meaning, are included. In telegraphic speech, articles, modifiers, and prepositions are ignored. Yet despite their brevity, the utterances of telegraphic speech express most of the basic intentions of the speakers, such as locating objects and describing events and actions.

When young children first begin to combine words, they are concerned with word order. In English, word order rules seem to be the first rules acquired (de Villiers and de Villiers, 1978). For example, the child may group the following words: "Me fall," "Bump table," "Cup in box," or "No more milk" (Winzer, 1990a).

Expansions of the verb phoneme appear to be the first complex syntactic constructions that occur. These are followed by the use of conjunctions and then the use of grammatical morphemes. Children's initial words are free morphemes. As they progress to longer sentences, they also learn to make use of bound morphemes to give their speech more precision. Children at this stage also use function words such as "in" and "on," and the articles, "a," "an," and "the." They also use inflections to signify plurality, possession, verb tense, subject-verb agreement, and comparative and superlative forms of adjectives (Rogow, 1987a).

The transition from two to three word utterances is characterized by more than mere sentence length. There are significant changes in the child's understanding of syntax and grammatical rules. Accompanying the increases in utterance lengths and vocabulary is a decrease in jargon and babbling (Owens, 1988).

In first using language, children tend to use known or mastered forms to express new ideas while known ideas are often expressed in new forms. As well, young child tend to regularize the language because they have not yet learned the exceptions. A small child is likely to say, "He runned," or "He hurt hisself." After they learn regular plurals (as in "horses") and past tenses (as in "skated") they create some forms of their own, like "mouses" and "eated" (Gleason, 1985).

Vocabularly growth begins slowly but increases rapidly. At age two, toddlers have an expressive vocabulary of about 150 to 300 words (Lipsitt, 1966). There is also a great spurt in word learning between 24 and 30 months (Reich, 1986). By the time they are using simple sentences at about two years of age, children are about 70 to 80 percent intelligible in their speech. However, the full development of all of the sounds of English is a slow process. It is not until they are about eight years of age that children are able to produce all the speech sounds: vowels, consonants, dipthongs, and blends.

At this time children seem to be absorbed in speech and language play. They like rhymes, songs, and stories and much of their activity is accompanied by speech. Young children, regardless of where they grow up or what language they use to communicate, all speak egocentrically—"Me want," "Me go," "Me see." Some researchers believe that egocentric children often use language to communicate with themselves. Egocentric speech, says Piaget, is that uttered when the child is alone or in the presence of others but has no communication aim (Piaget, 1926). As they grow older, youngsters begin to use more sociocentric speech that is directed toward others and used to talk about issues other than themselves.

### Preschoolers

Between the third and fourth year, language is established in all its main forms. By three years of age, most children demonstrate the construction of simple affirmative-declarative sentences. They put together a noun phrase for a subject and a verb phrase for a predicate (Elliott, 1981).

The language of the three year old consists of simple sentences that frequently omit small, unstressed words. Most sentences follow a subject-verb-object format, though the child has begun to employ variations of adult negatives, interrogatives, and imperative forms. As syntax develops, the child learns how to change word order and add and replace words to express more complex grammatic relationships. These changes are called transformations; as syntax becomes more complex, many transformations are used within the same utterances. However, small children still sometimes reach beyond the borders of word meaning and overextend their word usage. An example of overextension is the little boy who calls every animal a "doggie" (Rogow, 1987). There is also a tremendous growth in vocabulary: the three year old uses an expressive vocabulary of 900 to 1 000 words and employs about 12 000 individual words a day (Lipsitt, 1966).

Speech and language are used in many other ways. Two aspects of the linguistic environment most readily reflected in the speech of this age group are adult intonation and swearing. By this time children can also speak about things and events that are distant in time or space. The three or four year old child is able to describe the events of the past and expectations of the future as well as present experiences. In addition, children become increasingly aware of their listener's needs for information and are soon able to communicate with people outside of their immediate families.

The ability to carry a role through story play is reflected in the language of four year olds. They can tell simple stories of their own or other's authorship. Their increased language skills enable them to form more complex sentences while their vocabulary has increased to 1 500 to 1 600 words with approximately 15 000 used each day (Lipsitt, 1966). Most sentences average four or five words. The four year old demonstrates good usage of the declarative, negative, interrogative, and imperative forms and joins sentences together to form longer units using simple conjunctions. Language becomes a real tool for exploration; four year olds are full of questions and may ask several hundred in a single day, causing parents to wonder why they ever longed to hear their child speak (Owens, 1988).

By the age of five, children have acquired about 80 percent of the syntactic structures they will use as adults. Recall and increased language skills mean that children of five are able to use language to converse and to entertain. They can tell stories, have a budding sense of humour, can tease, and can discuss emotions (Owens, 1988).

**Table 5-2** Speech and language development, 21 months and older

| | |
|---|---|
| 21 months | Likes rhyming games. Pulls person to show something. Tries to tell about happenings. Understands some personal pronouns. Uses "I" and "mine." |
| 2 years | Uses two word noun phrases and two word verb phrases. Has 200 to 300 word vocabulary. Names most common everyday opbjects. Uses some prepositions such as "in" and "on" and some pronouns, but not always correctly. Uses some regular verb endings such as "s," "ed," and "ing." Words have good initial consonants. Uses stress and intonational patterns. |
| 30 months | Spurt in vocabulary growth. Average sentence length of three words. Regularizes language: "I runned." Experiments with many sentences. |
| 3 years | Has 900 to 1 000 word vocabulary. Uses simple sentences with subject and verb. Follows two-step commands. Talks about the present. Asks for much information. Swears. Plays with words and sounds. Uses initial and most common medial and final consonants; 80 percent intelligible. Inflection patterns not yet stable. |
| 40 months | Has 1 500 to 1 600 word vocabulary. Asks many questions. Uses increasingly complex sentence forms. Recounts stories of the recent past. Understands most questions about the immediate environment. |
| 48 months | Vocabulary of 2 100 to 2 200 words. Relies on word order for interpretation. Some difficulty in answering how and why questions. Uses modals, singulars, and plurals, irregular tenses, contractions, possessives, and complex sentences. Uses slang. Uses good initial, medial, and final consonants. 85 percent of sounds are produced correctly and speech is 98 percent intelligible. |
| 5 years | Understands before and after. Follows three-step commands. Has 90 percent of grammar acquired. Vocabulary of at least 5 000 words. Sentence length of four to six words. Sentence structure expanding rapidly in accuracy and complexity; essentially adult syntax. Articulation almost fully intelligible although may miss f, v, and l which may not be stable in all positions and contexts. Vocal patterns firm, with adult intonation. |
| 6 years | Expressive vocabulary of 2 600 words and receptive vocabulary of 20 000 to 24 000 words. Many well-formed complex sentences; uses all parts of speech to some degree. Talks a lot; verbalizes ideas and problems readily. |
| 8 years | Communicates thoughts. Uses comparatives. All speech sounds well developed. |
| 10 years | Spends a lot of time talking. Good comprehension. |
| 12 years | Receptive vocabulary of 50 000 words. Adult-like definitions. |

### School-age children

In the past it was assumed that children's language development was complete by the time they entered school (McNeill, 1970). School and adult development was seen to be chiefly an expansion of vocabulary and fine tuning of earlier acquired syntactic structures. However, it now seems that the school years are crucial to language development. Throughout this period, there is an increase in the size and complexity of children's linguistic repertoires and in the use of these repertoires within communicative contexts (Owens, 1988).

By the time they are six, children are sophisticated language users. They have become aware of how language is used (de Villiers and de Villiers, 1978). The early school-age period is one of tremendous linguistic creativity filled with rhymes, songs, word games and those special rhymes and incantations passed along on the network from child to child (Owens, 1988).

The vocabulary growth of school age children reflects the systematic development of word formation rules. First grade is a period of stabilization of rules previously learned and the addition of new rules (Meynuk, 1964). Kozoil (1973) has reported that the major learning period for the rules of pluralization of nouns is kindergarten through first grade. By second grade, children use regular plurals correctly, irregular plurals, and plurals of nouns ending in "s". Blends, such as "sk" and "str" are accurately produced by third grade. In the second and third grade, the child also attains accurate use of the rules for noun and adverb derivation (Berko, 1958; Carrow, 1973). The first grader has an expressive vocabulary of approximately 2 600 words but may understand as many as 20 000 to 24 000 words. Aided by schooling, this receptive vocabulary expands to approximately 50 000 words by sixth grade and 80 000 words by high school (Palermo and Molfese, 1973).

School-age children begin to comprehend the sentence and as a whole and do not depend on word order for interpretation. Their own sentence structure becomes more elaborate—of older children can use embed subordinate clauses. There are also significant increases in the child's ability to comprehend comparative, passive, temporal, and spatial, and familial relationships (Wiig and Semmel, 1984).

Children at this age learn to pun and to find humour in word play. Six-year-old children can recognize the nuances of language, and begin to take delight in jokes and riddles that rely on ambiguity (de Villiers and de Villiers, 1978). School-age children also learn to understand (albeit slowly) and to use figurative language that consists of idioms, metaphors, similes, and proverbs that represent abstract concepts not always stated in a literal interpretation.

Metalinguistic ability the awareness that enables a language user to think and reflect on language, also becomes well developed during the school-age period. Metalinguistic abilities appear in the preschool years, but full awareness is found only in seven or eight year olds who can repeatedly demonstrate awareness of many linguistic activities (Saywitz and Cherry-Wilkinson, 1982). Younger children view language primarily as a means of communication rather than focusing on the manner by which it is conveyed (Van Kleek, 1982). By kindergarten, the child is just beginning to separate what is said from how it is said. The ability to detect syntactic errors comes first. Then the school-age child demonstrates an increased ability to judge grammatical acceptability and to correct unacceptable sentences (Bowey, 1986, deVilliers and deVilliers, n.d.).

The ability to think about language is reflected in the development of reading and writing skills. Since these skills are formally taught, acquisition patterns are quite different from that of language learning via the speech and auditory mode. Reading and writing training removes language from the conversational context and this requires the child to consider language in the abstract. It is not surprising, therefore, that reading, writing, and metalinguistic skills seem to be related (Kemper, 1985).

# MODELS OF LANGUAGE DEVELOPMENT

Human language is incredibly complex, both in its acquisition and usage, so many researchers have concentrated on specific elements, such as semantic use or syntax development. Simplishically speaking, the two major schools of thought, cognitive and behavioural, are represented by Jean Piaget and B.F. Skinner, respectively. Other theorists of note in this area are Martin Braine and Noam Chomsky.

## Jean Piaget

Although his later work examined more general cognitive processing, Piaget's interest was initially piqued by the way in which children develop speech and language. In fact, his earliest research in the 1920s concentrated on speech. His work was fueled by questions like, "Does there exist a significant relationship between language and thought or do they proceed independently of each other?" and, "Does language shape thought or does thought shape language?"

Piaget did not specify verbal behaviour as a stage in the development of intelligent behaviour, but identified it as a particular and unique type of intelligence. He assumed that children's thought to be the dominant influence on how they talk. Piaget believed the early sounds infants and young children make to be linked to the ways they think and solve problems. He stressed however that the utterances are reflections rather than causes of children's thinking. He interpreted the early words as an indication of the stage of development at which a child was operating (Gibson, 1978).

Piaget called language "the essential instrument of social adaptation" (Piaget and Inhelder, 1969). Before the age of three—the period that Piaget described as the egocentric stage of development—all children talk primarily about themselves and use language to satisfy their own needs. Piaget and Erikson both suggested that egocentric speech parallels children's thinking and reflects their inability at this age to separate themselves from other people (Erikson, 1963; Piaget and Inhelder, 1969). At about three years of age, all children first begin to understand themselves as entities separate from the rest of the world. At the same time they begin to develop sociocentric speech that communicates to others what they are doing as well as what other people are doing (Owens, 1988).

Not everyone agrees with Piaget. Vygotsky (1962) observed that "Thought is not merely expressed words, it comes into evidence through them." Vygotsky also added another interpretation to egocentric and sociocentric speech. He argued that very young children use speech as a way to guide their behaviour and are telling themselves out loud what they are doing. Later this overt speech cedes to internalized speech.

Others have argued that language is not merely a means of expression, but is also a kind of mould that shapes the mind of the speaker. Words and sentence structures used by people affect the way they see their world (e.g., Whorf, 1956). In 1984, for example, George Orwell emphasized that Big Brother's Newspeak shaped the thought of the citizens. In today's society, we have new words about, say, women's role in society or handicapped persons. Does the use of the term,

**Reinforcer:**

an event or stimulus that
strengthens behaviour.

"person with mental retardation," instead of the traditional terms "feeble-minded person," shape people's ideas about mental retardation? Or has thinking already changed ideas so that they are expressed in gentle, nonpejorative terms? The debate continues although many psycholinguists today suggest that language is neither a cause nor an effect of thinking but is actually one of many extremely complex manifestations of cognitive, social, and neurological development.

## B.F. Skinner

B.F. Skinner and other behaviourists assumed stances entirely different from that of the cognitive psychologists. The rationale, genesis, development, and implications of behavioural theories of learning are fully discussed in Chapter 8. Suffice it to say here that Skinner believed that all behaviour is learned as a consequence of reinforcement from the environment. Skinner's view of operant conditioning largely dominated North American psychology for about three decades, beginning in the 1930s.

Skinner made an early attempt to specify a reinforcement theory of language acquisition—he presented a thoughtful analysis of how his operant conditioning could account for an array of facts of language behaviour through the reinforcement and shaping of this behaviour (Hilgard, 1987).

In Skinner's lexicon, a **reinforcer** is an event or stimulus that strengthens behaviour. Shaping means that an approximation of a behaviour is reinforced until the correct behaviour is emitted. According to Skinner, a child acquires language, or verbal behaviour, "when relatively unpatterned vocalizations, selectively reinforced, gradually assume forms which produce appropriate consequences in a given verbal community" (1957, p. 31). Parents reinforce vocalizations, and especially the sounds of the child's native language. For example, take the nine month old lying in her crib playing with strings of sounds (vocal play). The child babbles "da-da" and daddy picks her up and hugs her thus reinforcing her behaviour. "She said my name," he cries, thus helping the child to have a referent for the word. The likelihood that the child will emit the behaviour again—that is, say "da-da" when she sees daddy—is increased.

Skinner began his controversial *Verbal behavior* (1957) as early as 1932 (Hilgard, 1987). In this publication, he defined language as a verbal behaviour, a learned behaviour subject to all the rules of operant conditioning. Verbal behaviour, said Skinner, is modified by the environment or "reinforced through the mediation of other persons" (Skinner, 1957, p. 14). Through classical conditioning, a child learns the names of objects by hearing the sounds and seeing or feeling the object at the same time. Later, behaviour is produced and then reinforced through operant conditioning. In *Verbal behavior* the "how" of language took precedence over the 'what' of language form. Skinner minimized language form and described language as a set of functional units (Owens, 1988). Traditional language units, such as syntactic factors, were irrelevant. Instead, language was viewed as something we do (Lee, 1981).

There are a number of criticisms directed at Skinner's theory, including the following:

1. Skinner argued that language behaviour is acquired through the same mechanism of reinforcement as other behaviour. He stressed that a child is shaped into forming more and more gramatically correct sentences through systematic changes and the rewards given by parents. But parents reinforce only a small number of utterances. Indeed, parents are more concerned with the truthfulness of an utterance than with the grammar. A child, seeing a sheep, may say, "Mommy, me see cow-cow." The parent is more likely to respond to the truth value of the sentence (that it is a sheep) than to the grammatical complexity (deVilliers and deVilliers, n.d.).

2. Children do more than respond to reinforcement or imitate sentences that they have heard. If a child's task is to discover the rules that make it possible to speak and understand sentences never heard or spoken before, then imitating a sample of utterances would not be very helpful. In fact, imitation accounts for little syntactic learning (Bee, 1978).

3. Reinforcement cannot account for either the creativity or the regularization of children's early utterances. Not only do young children produce an infinite variety of utterances that they have never heard before but, as they learn morphemic and tense rules, they tend to regularize the language. Children say "He runned," before "He ran," They are unlikely to have heard adults use this form (de Villiers and de Villiers, 1978).

4. Skinner seems to assume that all parents reinforce similar behaviours—this would be the only way to account for the fact that all children pass through similar stages of language learning. Even with poor models and minimal reinforcement, children develop language at about the same rate and at about the same time (Bee, 1978).

5. Skinner's account of verbal behaviour was mostly based on generalizations from his experimental findings on other kinds of behaviour. He provided no experimental data although others (Braine, 1963; Staats, 1968) gave moderate support to his theory with appropriate data (Hilgard, 1987).

## Martin Braine

The rules of grammar and syntax govern the ways in which the parts of language are put together to create meaningful utterances. The concept of grammar is the very cornerstone of language learning. Without it, we might know the meanings of any number of words but could not put them together to form meaningful sentences beyond the simplest level. Experts are sharply divided as to what accounts for children's ability to form complete and grammatical sentences, and the question of when syntax is present is difficult to answer. Martin Braine was one of the first to attempt to write a kind of grammar for the sentences of young children. He listened to his own three children when each was in the beginning stages of two-word usage. Braine collected as many different sentences as he could from each child and then tried to see rules were built into their utterances. Braine (1963) was able to divide the embryonic grammar of children into two classes of words—pivot words and open words. Pivots are words that are used in constant repetition in any number of combinations.

Braine (1963) called this system of language learning contextual generalization. What this means is that children learning a word in a particular linguistic context will tend to use that word in the same position in another context. From this definite preference for some words over others in early speech, Braine (1963) identified what he called pivot grammar. A child, for example, may learn the word "car" and use it as a pivot as in "Go car," "Me car" or "Mommy car." After a time, a particular pivot word seems to have been practised enough to be replaced by a new one. As more pivot words are learned and employed, language usage increases.

But although a pivot grammar seems a good approximation of what young children are doing, it is clear that early sentences are more complex than this. Pivot grammar also seems to gloss over some interesting semantic distinctions that occur (Bee, 1978).

## Noam Chomsky

Skinner's contention that verbal behaviour is learned strictly through conditioning did not go unchallenged. A sharp attack came from Noam Chomsky (1959), a linguist at the Massachusetts Institute of Technology. Chomsky contended that Skinner was overly simplistic and totally rejected behavioural explanations (Chomsky, 1965). Chomsky (1959) stated that human language was characterized by a generativity and creativity unmatched by any other form of communication between animals and was therefore not amenable to behavioral analysis, with its dependence on associative principles. Reinforcement, argued Chomsky, cannot explain why and how children regularly use sentences that they have never spoken or heard before.

Chomsky reasoned that there must be some universality or commonality to the rules followed in the diverse languages of humans. He presented convincing

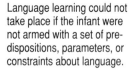

Language learning could not take place if the infant were not armed with a set of predispositions, parameters, or constraints about language.

**Language Acquisition Device (LAD):**
term used by Chomsky to denote the innate genetic factor in humans that gives them the unique ability to acquire language.

data and arguments showing that structural aspects of language are learned spontaneously. In other words, language learning could not take place if the infant were not armed with a set of predispositions, parameters, or constraints about language (Hyams, 1986).

Reich (1986) explains that Chomsky also believed that the linguistic rules and the principles to modify them are species specific; they exist only in humans which is why human beings have language. They are also task specific. The rules and principles have as their sole purpose the learning of language; they are not related to other cognitive abilities.

Chomsky imagined an innate genetic factor in humans that gives them the unique ability to acquire language. He called this the **Language Acquisition Device** (LAD). According to Chomsky, the uniqueness of the human brian lies in this capacity to handle large numbers of imitative patterns simultaneously and the ability to extend its intellectual system indefinitely by adding more and more patterns in an infinite variety of combinations.

### Transformational grammar

Chomsky's theory of language, known as transformational grammar, proposes two levels of linguistic processing. The initial level operates using phrase structure rules; the second level employs transformational rules. Phrase structure rules define sentence elements, describe their relationships and explain the formation of different sentence types. Transformational rules delineate the basic relationships underlying all sentence organization regardless of the language being used.

One universal thing about sentences is that they have subjects and predicates. The subject is what the sentence is about and the predicate is what happens to the subject. Phrase structure rules divide sentences or phrases into these two parts and then into constituent elements, as shown in Figure 5-3.

**Figure 5-3**
Example of phrase structure

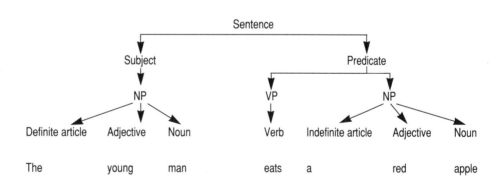

In any language, a sentence can be assigned a deep structure, the idea of kernel of the sentence, and a surface structure, the grammatical string of words. The deep structure of the sentence is translated or transfered into a surface structure by the application of sets of rules. The relationship between the deep structure and the surface structure is expressed in the transformational rules which govern the rearrangement of phrase structure elements. Syntactic processing with transforms is shown in Figure 5-4.

**Figure 5-4**
Syntactic processing

Deep structure ⟶ Transform ⟶ Surface structure

The boy eats an apple.   Declarative to interrogative   Did the quiet little boy eat the big red apple?

As children acquire language, they actually learn a linguistic code—a deciphering of the morphological and syntactic rules of language. The LAD allows all children to understand the code, so that even those with a limited vocabulary can find meaning in what they hear and make an infinite number of sentences themselves. This is true regardless of the language spoken, and for all children.

Knowing the linguistic code also allows a child to understand the kernel of a sentence despite ambiguities in the surface structure of a sentence. Only a knowledge of the deeper structure, which may be implied by the context, can permit the listener to understand the intent of the speaker. Take, for example, the following sentences:

**a)** The little boy eats ice cream.

**b)** Ice cream is eaten by the little boy.

**c)** Ice cream eats the little boy.

We know about the structure of these sentences implicitly because the ability to learn deep structures is inborn. Therefore, we can interpret the kernel of the sentences (a) and (b) even without a knowledge of passive and active voice. Sentence (c), however, presents more difficulties to the theory of transformational grammar. Semantics tells us that this sentence is incorrect. However, transformational grammar is unable to explain a syntactically correct but semantically incorrect sentence.

To Chomsky, a complete grammar must have syntax, phonology and semantics. Of these, he sees syntax as the most important element (Chomsky, 1965) because it enables language users to generate sentences. But transformational grammar largely ignores the contributions of phonetics and semantics. Moreover, while Chomsky may have explained acquisition of the structural elements of language, language development is also affected by environmental input (Nelson, 1977; Whitehurst, 1977).

## INDIVIDUAL DIFFERENCES

Many individual differences are apparent in the development of language. Psychologists believe that there are many sources of differences among children's language development such as birth order or the educational status of the parents (Nelson, 1977). Birth order, for example, is an important component of the children's environment and affects both personality and behaviour. In general, younger siblings speak later than do older siblings (Gibson, 1978). Other factors that affect language development include the child's socioeconomic status, early experiences, gender, and even geography.

## The question of gender

One of the standard psychological generalizations over the decades from the 1940s to the 1960s was that girls were more verbal. There were fragments of early data that suggested that girls talked sooner, had larger vocabularies and were generally more skilled in all linguistic tasks. Certainly, girls tend to speak earlier than do boys. The mean age for speaking 50 words for girls is 18 months; while it is 22 months for boys (Gibson, 1978). However, as they grow, significant verbal differences among boys and girls tend to disappear although the way they use and manipulate language may differ.

## Native children

Native people in Canada are not homegeneous in cultural and linguistic background. There are 11 different language families spoken, including many different languages and dialects. Not only are there several different Native languages but for many of these children English is also a second language. In the Canadian North, the language spoken before the coming of the Europeans is still the first language of the people (Winzer, 1990a). Many Native students come to school speaking a non-standard English dialect, made up of elements of standard English, with some pronunciations, grammar, and idioms transferred from the Native language (Barth, 1979).

Native children's achievement is one or more years below expected grade level standards and the gap increases as the pupils proceed through the grades (Report, 1981). One study found that Native students in grade eight were about two grade levels behind in almost all core skill areas (Report, 1981). The average Native student fails about half of all school courses (More, 1984). Among Native students, the high school completion rate is about a third of the rate for non-Native students.

Recent improvements are attributed to more appropriate curricula, more Native run schools, and the use of Native people as teachers and teacher's aides (More, 1984). But although the educational attainments of Native students have improved considerably over the past decade, results are still below the goals and needs of the Indian communities (More, 1984).

The causes of underachievement among Native students are complex. Factors include lack of home support for education, poor home-school relations, lack of motivation, and insufficient school financing. Dialect differences and the cultural usage of language form additional important factors.

Some children come to school with different rules for the social use of language; these may contrast sharply with the behaviours expected of them in the classroom and can lead to serious misunderstandings between child and teacher. Many culturally different children are taught to restrain their expressive behaviour in the presence of adults and strangers (Alleyne, 1976). In Canadian schools, however, children are continually required to express themselves in front of adults and strangers despite cultural norms to the contrary.

We think using language. If you try to keep your mind blank, words simply pop in. So we must ask what happens to children who do not use language so adeptly. Alcock, Carment, and Sadava (1988) report on a study that compared eight year old Indian children to middle-class white children in Alberta in terms of their ability to learn a task which involved choosing one of a stimulus pair in order to earn candies (Knowles and Boersma, 1971). For each pair of different stimuli presented, some common rule such as "the smaller of the two" or "the darker of the two" governed which stimulus, if chosen, would be followed by reinforcement. Subsequently, the rule was simply reversed.

The Indian children were less successful than the white children in learning the reversal shift. Yet in another condition in which some Indian children were required to verbalize (for example the researcher would say, "I want you to tell me what picture you are going to choose before you push the stick,"), they learned the initial discrimination and made the reversal shift more often than did the other Indian children in the non-verbal situation. The authors suggest that, barring the development of an educational system based on traditional Native skills and experience, Native students may be handicapped to the extent that they are slow to use verbal mediation in problem solving. This characteristic affects their ability even within the scope of problem solving that does not involve linear comprehension and expression.

In an attempt to differentiate linguistic and cultural factors from learning problems, many researchers have recommended a more comprehensive focus on both first and second language proficiency, more Native language achievement and intelligence testing, and increased attention to pragmatic language use in natural contexts (Holtzman and Polyzoi, 1987; Mattes and Omark, 1984; Ortiz and Yates, 1987).

## Children from diverse cultural backgrounds

Canada is a country of ethnic and linguistic differences. The number of immigrants who have come to Canada since Confederation have dramatically changed the composition of the country. Whereas at the time of Confederation Canada was basically a bicultural society—British and French—it is now a multicultural society. Today a great many cultures are represented in Canadian classrooms. Culturally different children come from subgroups within our society that differ on a variety of factors, including racial, geographic, economic, educational, and ethnic backgrounds (Winzer, 1990a).

Language is the most important aspect of culture and is the chief vehicle in learning other aspects of culture (Yu, 1988). Speaking a language other than English reinforces the loneliness of a child from a different culture. At the same time, linguistic distinctness is a basic component of personal identity for many of Canada's ethnic minorities (McLeod, 1975).

For many children from different cultures, language acquisition and use will present problems. To the educational system, these language minority children also present a dilemma. Those with limited English proficiency need to gain English skills as rapidly as possible. But, while doing this, should they be taught math, science, and so on in the first or second language?

In discussing language acquisition and usage for minority language students, it is first necessary to distinguish between the acquisition of conversational English skills and those skills required for academic success in school. Very different time

**Dialect:**

a language variation that is systematic and associated with a specific geographic, cultural, or socioeconomic group.

periods are required for minority students to achieve peer appropriate levels in these two aspects of second language proficiency (Winzer, 1990a).

Most culturally different children acquire fairly fluent peer-appropriate face to face communication skills within the first two years of their arrival in Canada (Cummins, 1984). However, these face to face communication skills develop more quickly than academic language skills. Cummins (1984), in a longitudinal study of the achievement of immigrant children in a large Canadian city, found that while most students had superficial language competence after three years of English as a Second Language (ESL) training, it was not until they had been functioning in English for at least five years that they demonstrated comprehension of concepts at the level that is normally required for academic work. This means that teachers may see the students as functioning normally in English when, in fact, they do not possess enough language competence to grasp complex verbal and semantic relationships (see Winzer, 1990a).

Even when children acquire English as a second language, they may still remain different from the students in the dominant culture. They may speak with an accent caused by the nonequivalence of sounds between languages. As well, different languages and cultures have many rules which govern language behaviour and these differ from language to language and culture to culture (Winzer, 1990a).

Considerable research data suggests that for minority groups who experience disproportionate levels of academic failure, the extent to which a student's language and culture are incorporated into the school program constitutes a significant prediction of academic success (e.g., Campos and Keating, 1988; Cummins, 1985). In programs in which minority students' first language skills are strongly reinforced, their school success appears to reflect both the more solid cognitive and academic foundation derived through first language instruction and also the reinforcement of their cultural identity (Cummins, 1989).

## Dialects

Language variations, if systematic and associated with a specific geographic, cultural, or socioeconomic group, are called dialects. A dialect is usually associated with a particular group of people who have something in common about the way they talk. Conditioned as they are by linguistic, social, educational, and geographic experiences, dialects are variations on the standard language content and form. Dialects are often associated with geographical areas; they are not associated with second language learning. Some dialect differences are noticeable in the pronunciation of words, the word combinations used, and the words themselves (see Winzer, 1990a).

Dialects should not be considered ungrammatical or substandard, only different and less valuable in some situations. Children who speak a dialect usually communicate effectively with others in their culture. The problem therefore is not one of communication but rather of social acceptance (Otta and Smith, 1980). Our perceptions of cultural differences are enhanced by linguistic differences and we tend to hold preconceived attitudes toward regional dialects and the people who use them (Lindfors, 1987) which in turn may influence our conceptions of that person's competence.

## BILINGUALISM

Canadian education, with the student population it serves, is increasingly multi-cultural and multi-racial in nature. The responsibility for preparing all children to live in Canada's multicultural society has significant implications in terms of general approaches for education, as well as in the provisions for special populations. Therefore, no discussion of language and language development as it applies to Canadian children today would be complete without reference to bilingualism and the efforts of schools to promote it. When we speak of bilingualism in an educational context, we include two broad groupings—students from diverse cultural backgrounds learning English and students of English heritage learning our other official language, French.

Bilingualism is a term that has been used to describe an attribute of individual children as well as social institutions (Hakuta and Garcia, 1989). The combination of languages is not the important facet, the number of languages spoken is. Many Canadians are bilingual in French and English and others have English or French and their mother tongue such as Ukranian, Cantonese, or Italian. A number of people are bilingual in English and ASL (American Sign Language) which linguists view as a language in its own right.

The prevalence of bilingualism reflects the cultural mix of a nation. In the United States, approximately 17 percent of the population is bilingual, chiefly in English and Spanish (Kloss and McConnell, 1978). Canada, where bilingualism is official policy and where two official languages exist, boasts a higher bilingual rate of 24 percent (de Vries and Vallee, 1980) and rising (see Walker, 1990).

Canada is one of the few countries where bilingualism is official policy. Safty (1988) explains that from its very beginnings, Canada gave English and French equal official recognition (the Royal Proclamation Act of 1763) and, when the Constitution Act of 1791 divided the Canadian territories into Upper Canada and Lower Canada, both languages were granted equal status in the Legislative Assembly of Canada. The BNA Act of 1867 that created the Canadian confederation recognized the  official character of both languages in the various territories (Yalden, 1981). Following the recommendations of the Royal Commission on Bilingualism and Multiculturalism (1965), the Federal Government of Canada gave bilingualism a statuatory basis with the passage of the Official Languages Act in 1969. This Act dictates that English and French are "equal in status, rights, and privileges" (Yalden, 1981). The Canadian Charter of Rights recognizes the rights of Canadian citizens to receive education on either of the two official languages (Safty, 1988).

With the recognition of two official languages in Canada, there is an increasing interest across the country in fostering bilingualism among children. Moreover, the controversy surrounding bilingualism is magnified by the sense of urgency created by the changing demographic picture of Canada.

### Learning a second language

A second language can be acquired either in a natural or a formal way. Krashen (1981) refers to the types of second language learning as subconscious language acquisition and conscious language learning. Owens (1988) calls the processes simultaneous and successive language acquisition.

**Bilingual education:**
schooling provided fully or partly in the second language with the object of making students proficient in the second language, while at the same time maintaining and developing their proficiency in the first language and fully guaranteeing their educational development.

Natural bilingualism occurs when the two parents speak different languages in the home or when the family has emigrated to an area that speaks a different language. Formal learning is what goes on in the schools (Reich, 1986). When a family moves to a region that speaks a different language before the child's first language is established, the child will usually learn both languages, and will do so without difficulty. Arbitrarily, it can be said that if acquisition begins before the third birthday then the process is simultaneous; after that time, it is successive language learning (McLaughlin, 1978; Owens, 1988; Reich, 1986).

Simultaneous acquisition is the development of two or more languages prior to age three (McLaughlin, 1978). There seem to be specific stages in the simultaneous acquisition of two languages in young children (Volterra and Taeschner, 1978). During the first stage, the child has two separate lexical systems; vocabulary words rarely overlap as the child learns one word from each language for each referent (Owens, 1988). Once children realize they are speaking two languages, they begin to learn the words from both languages simultaneously. When the two languages are related, children may attempt to convert a word they know in one language by pronouncing it according to the phonology of the other language (Reich, 1986).

Grosjean (1982) has characterized the stages of simultaneous acquisition as:

- initial language mixing followed by a slow separation and increasing awareness of the differences;

- influence of one language on the other when one is favoured in the environment;

- avoidance of difficult words and constructions in the weaker language;

- rapid shifts in the dominance of each language with environmental shifts;

- final separation of the phonological and grammatical systems but enduring influence of the dominant system in vocabulary and idioms.

For nonsimultaneous or successive acquisition, success seems to be closely related to the learner's attitude and identification with the uses of the language being acquired (Owens, 1988). Many factors affect an individual's ability to learn a new language. These include motivation, the difficulty of the second language itself, an individual's learning style, the perceptions of the broader society of the child's identity group, and the child's desire or need to understand and/or identify with speakers of the new language (see Ovanso and Collier, 1985).

Most children acquire a second language rapidly, though the strategies differ with age, the child's linguistic knowledge, and the nature of the two languages. Learning seems to mirror first language acquisition and use determines which language will eventually become dominant.

### Bilingual education

Stern (1972) defines **bilingual education** as "schooling provided fully or partly in the second language with the object of making students proficient in the second language while at the same time maintaining and developing their proficiency in the first language and fully guaranteeing their educational development" (in Swain and Barik, 1978, p. 22). However, bicultural, bilingual and immersion are related educational terms. The philosophy of bilingual education

**Immersion program:** program in which students learn a second language not as a subject but through being exposed to it as the language of instruction and interaction.

has been to offer the student the benefit of learning and reinforcing a first language while acquiring a second (Langdon, 1983).

Bilingual programs vary enormously in content and quality. In Canada, bilingual education was propelled into national prominence in the mid-1960s when a group of Anglophone parents in the community of Lambert, a suburb of Montreal, convinced school administrators to start an experimental bilingual program for their children. The program began in September, 1965, with two classes of children, all of whom came from English speaking families (Safty, 1988). The experimental project proved successful and was quickly emulated across the country, even before formal evaluation of the bilingual experiment was completed. It quickly became a landmark in bilingual teaching methodology, not only in Canada but around the world (Safty, 1988).

### Immersion programs

The most widely used approach to the involvement of children in bilingualism is some form of immersion program in which the child learns the second language not as a subject but through being exposed to it as the language of instruction and interaction.

Immersion requires the exclusive use of the target language as the medium of instruction at the early grade levels (McEachern, 1982). Within immersion programs, the major thrust is the recreation in school of an environment that approximates as far as possible the natural environment in which the first language was acquired (Safty, 1988). Attempts to reduplicate the natural language learning environment in the school reflect the firm conviction, shared by psychologists and linguists, that the psycholinguistic and sociolinguistic principles of naturalistic and imitative methods of first language acquisition can aid in the acquisition of the second language (Safty, 1988).

There are various modes of immersion: some involve immersion from nursery school on, others involve only partial immersion in which the student spends only a part of the day or the week in immersion.

In Canada, we may tend to think of immersion programs only in terms of English speaking children learning French but there exist similar immersion programs involving other languages. New people arriving in Canada, for example, may be placed in English immersion programs. Use of the immersion approach potentially provides an effective approach for providing children from different cultural backgrounds with the kind of language skills they need for academic activities. By its very nature, immersion promotes acquisition of language skills appropriate to school related tasks while at the same time incorporating the linguistic adjustments that are needed by students limited in English proficiency. Children learn English but receive basic academic instruction in their first language so that they do not fall behind academically.

There are also programs designed to maintain the language of French-speaking children. Carey and Cummins (1983) point out that for Francophone children outside Quebec, French must be strongly promoted in school and home in order to maintain and improve students' French skills.

**French immersion**     Right across the country, the number of French immersion programs has grown phenomenally. In 1986 pupils in French immersion

Introduced in the 1960s, French immersion programs in English-speaking Canada have continued to grow in popularity.

classes and those attending French schools or classes accounted for nine percent of children attending school outside Quebec (Lachapelle, 1990).

In French immersion methodology, a child is plunged into a French speaking environment from the first day of school, immersed in linguistic waters and expected to sink or swim (Safty, 1988). There is no attempt to teach children to read in English and parents are "specifically warned not to do so at home" (Lambert, 1974, p. 104). In the beginning, children speak only French; as they progress, they are permitted to speak English although the use of French is highly encouraged. Slowly, some English is introduced into the curriculum.

However, although early immersion is common, the question of the age at which students should start programs remains a matter of debate since partial and late immersion programs also exist. One study (Swain, 1978) compared the achievement over a six year period of students in three different French immersion programs—early, late, or partial—to those of comparable groups of students from the regular English program. Swain reported that students enrolled in the early French immersion program performed better than at least 50 percent of native French students who served as a norming population for the standardized tests employed.

Bruck, Lambert, and Tucker (1976) compared students in early and late French immersion. The subjects were early French immersion students who had taken French from kindergarten to grade seven and late French immersion students who had taken a one year French immersion program in grade seven. They found that the early students were more proficient with a broader range of intellectual and scholastic abilities.

When first initiated in the 1960s, the premise of immersion programs raised apprehension among opponents and enthuisism among proponents. Many expressed concern about the social impact while others debated the possible negative consequences of bilingualism on the cognitive and psychological development of children (Safty, 1988).

The educational value of French immersion programs is no longer a matter of sharp debate. Nevertheless, the education of bilingual citizens through French immersion schooling is increasingly controversial (Nagy and Klaiman, 1988). The rhetoric of French immersion supporters and detractors marks a number of underlying worries about sociological and political effects of the programs (Safty, 1988).

Nagy and Klaiman (1988) found, among other things, apprehension about the effects that French immersion would have on the flexibility of English programs and worries about supervision and staffing among school personnel. Our interest here, however, is on how programs function and their effects on participants. For children, concerns have centred on the suitability of French immersion programs for working class children and whether children with learning difficulties should be in these programs.

## ESL programs

Within the English school system, rapid acquisition of English for non-English speaking students, and a successful language shift is the major aim, since inadequate English results in poor academic achievement and denial of social mobility (Paulston, 1980). The combination of unfamiliarity with language and the problems of learning to read produce lack of success in both areas.

In many urban areas, schools offer special classes to provide English instruction. These ESL classes often act as reception classes for new arrivals. ESL is an integral component of transitional, maintenance and two-way bilingual education; however, it is not by itself a form of bilingual instruction.

ESL methodology is very different from remedial English. The assumption underlying ESL methods is not that students need correcting in the language they already have, but that they are learning a language they do not yet have (Goldberg and Bordman, 1975). ESL instruction includes English taught from a second language point of view aimed at the students' level of English proficiency (Ovanso and Collier, 1985). Students who can not yet adequately express themselves in English spend no time studying grammar but are instead "bathed" in communication. By providing enough opportunities for practice and review, the teacher helps the child acquire and internalize the language.

Many Native Canadian children learn English as their second language.

Teachers may encourage students to use regular dialect in school but to retain their own patterns outside (Risko, 1981).

ESL methodology is based on the fact that any person who wants to acquire use of a language he or she did not grow up hearing must have a reliable model to follow in expressing his or her own ideas. They must also practise a great deal (Goldberg and Bordman 1975).

Ramirez and Stromquist (1978) identified teacher behaviours that had significant positive associations with second language achievement. These include requiring the students to manipulate objects or aids so the teacher can check comprehension; asking students questions based on previously presented information in order to reduce ambiguity; and clarifying the meaning of new words using antonyms and synonyms. The researchers also identified behaviours that had negative impacts on second language learning, such as inappropriate or ambigious use of visual aids; use of repetition or imitation as a means of teaching language structures; and a concern for linguistic errors in the students' spoken messages irrespective of the communication's effectiveness.

**Effects of bilingualism**
The acceptance of bilingual education generally, and immersion programs in particular, has revolved around the question of the extent to which students can master academic content in a second language (Cummins, 1984; Swain and Lapkin, 1982) as well as the extent to which bilingual education exacerbates learning disabilities or learning problems in students (Bruck, 1978, 1982; Trites and Price, 1978; Wiss, 1987).

For many years, educators in Canada viewed early bilingualism as a hazard to school learning. They feared that two languages could lead to confusion and language handicaps. Some believed  that bilingualism could impair intelligence and cripple its creativity (see McLaughlin, 1978). Parents were advised not to teach more than one language at home and educators did not introduce a second language until the late elementary grades.

Early studies of second language learning  demonstrated the limitations inherent in later language acquisition. It was reasoned that the brain becomes less flexible with age and that the ability to learn language changed with age. Learning a new language was seen to be more difficult for older than for younger people.

Since the revolution in linguistics generated by Chomsky's ideas, much has been learned about the processes of first and second language acquisition. Recent research looks askance at the notion that efficient new language acquisition is restricted to young children. Indeed, there do seem to be critical periods for learning phonemes; the first months of life seem to be critical for learning the phonemes of one's own language. After a few years of second language learning, young children are more likely than adults to speak the language without an accent and to be better able to understand the language when it is spoken in noisy conditions (Snow, 1987). By the late teens, it is difficult for a speaker to acquire native language pronunciation characteristics in a second language (Snow and Hoefnagel-Holle, 1978).

However, except for the late teenage disclaimer, the notion of the importance of the age of acquisition is not supported in actual practice (Genesee, 1978; Seliger, 1978). Persons who learn a language after adolescence usually sound a little different, but phonological differences do not mean that persons cannot communicate in the new language very effectively. Older children and adults, who are more cognitively mature and whose first language proficiency is more fully developed, acquire cognitively demanding aspects of the second language faster than younger children (Ovanso and Collier, 1985). Reich (1986) points out that one estimate of the amount of exposure for a child to acquire competence for a language at the six year old level is 9 000 hours. Compare this with the estimate of 1 300 hours by the United States Military deemed appropriate for an adult to attain near native competence in Vietnamese.

Bilingualism itself has not been found to interfere with performance in either language and has been found in Canadian studies to increase achievement in areas other than language studies (Perl and Lambert, 1986). Research has compared immersion students with regular program students to determine whether it is possible for immersion students to master the academic content of their courses (Carey, 1987). Most have found that the progress of children on language and cognitive measures challenge long held perceptions about the detrimental effects of bilingualism (Lambert and Tucker, 1977). The concensus has been that little or no academic mastery is lost by being instructed in second language immersion programs (Cummins, 1987; Swain, 1978; Swain and Lapkin, 1982). It has been consistently demonstrated that students in early and late immersion programs suffer no harm to their cognitive or native language development through being schooled in a second language and they can master content subjects such as mathematics and science as well as their unilingually educated peers (Day and Shapson, 1988).

Bain and Yu (1980), for example, studied a cross-cultural sample of monolingual and bilingual children from Alsace, Alberta, and Hong Kong who spoke

German, French, Chinese or combinations of these languages. They found there was a significant cognitive acceleration in bilingual children, particularly in those who had learned to be bilingual at a very early age.

Lambert (1977) embarked on a series of studies of bilingual and monolingual French-English speaking Canadian children. The researchers used two groups of children who took their schooling exclusively in French during kindergarten and grade one. From grades two to four they were taught mainly in French except for two 35 minute periods of English language arts, and in grade five arithmetic was taught in English (Lambert and Tucker, 1977). The research demonstrated that, far from hurting children, bilingualism helps thinking. Children who learn to be bilingual at early ages actually score significantly higher on nonverbal tests of intelligence than do monolingual children. Bilingual children also scored better on verbal intelligence measures. Scott (in Saunders, 1982) reported that his Canadian bilingual students demonstrated "greater adeptness at divergent thinking" (p. 19) in which cognitive flexibility was seen as an index of creativity and rich imagination.

Other studies have attempted to determine whether learning disbilities are language specific (Carey, 1978). The long held assumption that bilingual children are at a disadvantage when learning language and that their progress in both languages is delayed has not been supported by recent research. However, the effects of bilingualism differ with age and the manner of acquisition and there exist differences between simultaneous and sequential acquisition.

Too, there is the issue of whether working class children can benefit from French immersion programs. Research (see Swain and Barik, 1978) has shown that these programs are just as appropriate for working class children as they are for those from the middle class.

The use of minority language in the home is not a handicap to children's academic progress (Cummins and Mulcahy, 1978). In fact, children may perform better academically because bilingualism positively influences their intellectual and academic development. Minority group children who are comfortable in their emotional adjustment to both the majority culture and the culture of the home perform better academically than do those who are ambivalent. The quality of parent-child communication in the home greatly influences school performance and if parents are not comfortable in English, the quality of their interaction with their children in English is likely to be inferior to that in the mother tongue (Cummins 1981). What matters for minority students' academic success then is not the language being used in the home, but rather the quality of communication between adults and children (Cummins, 1984).

Winzer (1990a) points out that if parents want their children to reap the potential personal and academic benefits of full bilingualism, they should use the minority language as much as possible. Educators should advise parents on ways to expose their children through the mother tongue, to a rich linguistic environment in the home. Children who come to school with a solid conceptual foundation in Chinese, Italian, Portugese, or any other language, will have little difficulty transferring this foundation to the school language. On the other hand, the child who comes to school fluent in surface aspects of English but with little conceptual foundation of any language will likely experience considerable academic difficulty (Cummins 1987).

## SUMMARY

1. Communication is the foundation of social interaction. Language is the essentially human facet of communication. Stripped to its bare essentials, language is a system of symbols organized into conventional patterns to communicate meaning. Both language and speech are learned by exposure and experience.

2. Language includes written language and speech as well as a variety of non-speech forms and many non-verbal forms such as gesture and body language. Speech is essentially a mechanical production of language. Other methods than speech may be appropriately employed to express language—sign language and writing, for example. However, while it is possible to possess language and lack the ability to speak, it is not possible to have speech without language.

3. Without formal instruction, most children typically acquire a substantial lexicon of spoken words and begin to combine words to express more complex ideas. At one year of age, children are ready to make their first linguistic utterances, sounds used to tell the world what they are thinking. Between 18 and 24 months of age, children begin to combine words and, as they develop two and three word utterances, begin to express their knowledge of syntax and morphology. As children expand their vocabulary and increase their need for productive communication, they begin to use words in sequence; the sentence is the key landmark in language acquisition. Language skills develop rapidly during the preschool years. By kindergarten the child has acquired much of the structure of the mature language user. Language development in the school age period consists of simultaneous expansion of existing syntactic forms and the acquisition of new forms. Development continues as the child adds new forms and gains new skills in transmitting messages. The process continues throughout life, especially in regard to semantic aspects of language.

4. Significant differences in children's language development exist. Such differences are often reflective of variations in environmental and social contexts.

5. Speech development begins with the first sound following the birth cry and ends with full articulatory control. The first three years are the crucial period. In speech, humans produce a great variety of sounds and the human body is capable of modifying or resonating the vibrations produced.

6. Early studies on language lacked a linguistic theory and therefore a foundation for learning language. As models of language development emerged, there were seen major contradictions between the behavioural view and the innate view of language development.

7. French immersion programs have been a major factor in the increase of bilingualism among young people whose mother tongue is not French. Numerous recent studies report that bilingualism contributes to cognitive and intellectual development.

# Key Terms

bilingual education
dialects
kinesics
language maturity
nonlinquistic clues
reinforcer

communication
holophrasic speech
language
metalinguistic skills
paralanguage
telegraphic speech

communicative competence
immersion programs
language acquistion device
motherese
proxemics

# 3 INDIVIDUAL DIFFERENCES

I admit it. I hate the impudence of the claim that in fifty minutes you can judge and classify a human being's predestined fitness for life. I hate the pretentiousness of the claim. I hate the abuse of the scientfic method which it involves. I hate the sense of superiority which it creates, and the sense of inferiority which it imposes (Lippmann, 1923, p. 146).

When an IQ test like Binet's is given to school children, we ignore these variations and assume that all children have an interest in all fields or disciplines and that they have had the same opportunity of acquiring that knowledge. Therefore, if children do poorly on the test, it is not regarded as an absence of knowledge; rather it is proof of poor ability! This ability is "general." We can already see why doing well in school is predicted by IQ (Das, 1988).

**MAJOR OBJECTIVES**

This section is designed to

- assist readers to appreciate the many differences—social, emotional, intellectual, and physical—that occur among students;

- show how the study of intelligence relates to the nature-nurture controversy, hereditability and measurement;

- acquaint readers with IQ tests, their history, types, and uses;

- illustrate the differences in cognitive and learning styles found among students;

- help to develop an understanding of children with exceptional conditions and their education in today's Canadian schools;

- introduce a range of familial and extra-familial influences that can affect children's development and functioning; and

- describe the manner in which children with exceptionalities are integrated into today's schools.

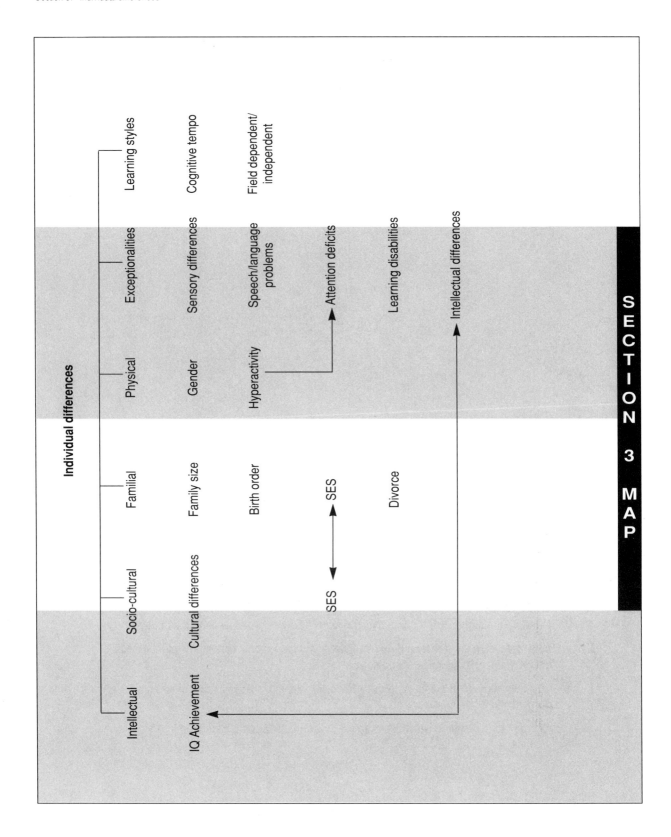

SECTION 3 MAP

Individual differences

- Intellectual
  - IQ
  - Achievement
- Socio-cultural
  - Cultural differences
  - SES ⟷ SES
- Familial
  - Family size
  - Birth order
  - Divorce
- Physical
  - Gender
  - Hyperactivity → Attention deficits
- Exceptionalities
  - Sensory differences
  - Speech/language problems
  - Learning disabilities
  - Intellectual differences
- Learning styles
  - Cognitive tempo
  - Field dependent/independent

Teachers cannot help but be aware of the differences that exist among the pupils they instruct. Every day, faced with a group of shining faces, teachers can readily observe the physical differences among students. Children are tall, short, heavy, light, pretty, or not so attractive. The list is virtually endless. More importantly, some students are well nourished, dressed, and cared for. Others are not so lucky; the results of poverty or discouraging home environments are manifested by such things as coming to school without breakfast, ill-clothed, and unready for learning.

Further individual differences show up in social interactions and on the playground. Some students emerge as leaders, others as followers, and a few as isolates. Physical skills differ—while some children can wield a mean baseball bat, others cannot come close to hitting or catching a ball.

As they present instruction and evaluate students' responses and achievement, teachers will recognize further differences. Some children fly through the curriculum, always eager, motivated and interested. Others need more practice and repetition but still learn and achieve adequately. Then, in every classroom, teachers will encounter students for whom learning seems a great trial and who need large amounts of practice to attain mastery of basic skills and concepts.

Not only will students differ in the pace and amount of their learning, but teachers can also observe differences in how children learn—in their cognitive and learning styles. School learning involves making sense out of information, sorting it out until it fits into a neat and orderly way and using old information to help assimilate the new learning. Students approach problems in different ways. Some work better in groups, others alone; some are impulsive, some reflective; and some bring new and innovative approaches to solving problems, some demonstrate poor problem solving strategies. As well, some children show a greater capacity for independent work than others.

Obviously, a class of students is not homogeneous. In fact, the diversity of children found in Canadian classrooms has increased dramatically. Today, we find children from low income backgrounds, students from diverse cultural backgrounds, and students with limited English proficiency. During the past 15 years the number of students in Canadian urban schools systems whose home language is different from that in the schools has increased dramatically. In Metropolitan Toronto, for example, close to half the students in the major school boards have learned English as a second language (Cummins, 1987). Some children come to school with different rules for the social use of language which may contrast sharply with the behaviours expected of them in the classroom. Serious misunderstandings between child and teacher may ensue.

In addition, with the educational philosophy of mainstreaming, or educational integration as it is more commonly called in Canada, scores of exceptional children have moved within the orbit of the public schools. Many of these children suffer from mildly handicapping conditions and can be successfully integrated into regular classrooms. Accompanying these mildly handicapped students are children with more severe impairments to learning. These children, too, are moving into regular school settings. They are riding school buses, attending assembly programs, eating lunch, and participating in art, music and recess with their non-handicapped peers (Cypher et al., 1984).

Special education is no longer a sanctuary for a few children, separate from the mainstream of education; it is now everybody's concern, from the specialist to the regular education teacher (Winzer, 1990a). Approximately 77 percent of Canadian exceptional students now receive instruction in integrated settings (Council of Ministers, 1982-83). In 1983 there were 251 448 full-time teachers in Canadian schools, of whom 28 884 were providing some special education programming. This meant that approximately one in nine teachers spent some time working with exceptional children or in special programs (Council of Ministers, 1982-83).

Because each human being is unique, the differences that occur among people encompass every aspect of physical, cognitive, and personality functioning. Some of the factors that influence each child's development are friends, the media, culture, nutrition, parents, family status, family stability, and socioeconomic status. One variable that will have a profound impact on a child's development and functioning is that elusive and virtually indefinable trait known as intelligence. How much intelligence a child has, how to measure it, how it is shaped and molded, what a child does with it, and how it effects a child in school and later life, are questions of great concern to psychologists, geneticists, educators, and those in allied disciplines.

As a seemingly crucial factor in human development, the whole area of intelligence has been one of the most deeply researched and one of the most controversial subjects in psychology. There have evolved a number of ways of examining the concept of intelligence. P.E. Vernon (1969) suggested three manners of investigation:

1. Intelligence as genetic capacity. Looking at intelligence this way assumes that it is a trait that is part of an individual's genetic makeup.

2. Intelligence as observed behaviour. This examines intelligence on the basis of what an individual does and sees intelligence as a result of interactions between heredity and the environment.

3. Intelligence as a test score. This means that intelligence is what a test of mental ability (IQ test) measures.

Research into intelligence—how it develops, how we use it, the influences that determine it, and why some people seem to be better endowed than others—is inextricably enmeshed with the nature/nurture controversy. It is also closely tied to the measurement of intelligence, the tools that are used for assessment, and the uses to which the data are put. And obviously, notions about intelligence are tied to teaching and learning. Teachers may not be aware of the IQ scores of children in their classes, but they do know which children learn quickly and which ones flounder. To explain these individual differences in learning, teachers are apt to use words such as "intelligence" or "motivation." Children, too, are characterized on the basis of intelligence. A label of mental retardation, for example, brings to mind a child functioning below what is considered normal while gifted implies ability above the norm.

Since their inception, IQ tests have been controversial. Lewis Terman, one of the leaders of the early American testing movement, coined the slogan, "A mental test for every child" (see Winzer,

1990b). Even at this early stage, criticisms were virulent. Walter Lippman, who was then more clearly identified as a left-wing socialist, attacked the mental testing movement in a series of articles that appeared in the *New Republic*. One of Lippman's cries is seen in the quotes that open this section. Lewis Terman (1922) responded to Lippman with a sarcastic piece that spoke to Lippman's lack of rationality. Terman supported his arguments with the research and academic credentials of the leaders of the testing movement. Lippman's essential questions concerned the early training opportunities available to children of different abilities and whether people could attain similar abilities if they were provided with similar training. More than half a century later, researchers such as Das, who is shown in the second opening quote, are mulling over the same questions. How much of the IQ, they ask, is due to heredity and how much determined by the environment and the opportunity to learn?

Among students, many categories of variation exist. The enormous range of differences cannot be covered in this section; rather, the focus is on areas that are particularly significant in the classroom. We will examine the still controversial and unresolved issue of the roles of heredity and environment in creating individual differences, look briefly at the concept of hereditability and examine the development and use of measures of mental ability (IQ tests). We will also focus on aspects of individual difference such as birth order, gender and cognitive and learning styles.

Particularly important in the study of inter- and intra-individual differences is an understanding of children considered to be *exceptional*—those whose physical, social, emotional, or intellectual functioning falls above or below the norm. The importance of individual differences in learning characteristics and in developing appropriate programs is reflected in the mounting movement toward the educational mainstreaming of exceptional students. Helping such children to fit into the mainstream of school, society and community life has become a major goal of special education during the past decade. Chapter 7 examines a range of exceptional conditions and stresses the manner in which teachers can accommodate these students in regular classrooms.

# INDIVIDUAL DIFFERENCES

## INTRODUCTION

All students differ from one another to varying degrees. Every child possesses a unique combination of likes and dislikes, abilities and problems, interests and fears, successes and failures. Some children are bright and quick, others are slower. Some children learn easily and do so with joy and vivacity; for others, learning is a painful trek into the unknown. These individual differences in learning, behaviour, and personality that we observe among students fall along a continuum and are characteristic of all humans.

The differences between one person and another that comprise each one's individuality were slow to be accepted as part of scientific psychology when the primary interest was discovering the laws of the human mind in common to all persons (Hilgard, 1987). Early psychology was essentially the study of groups from which generalizations about human behaviour could be drawn. Uniformities rather than differences in behaviour became the focus of Wundt and the pioneer North American psychologists. Edward Thorndike, for example, tended to measure, "statistize" and generalize about groups. Jean Piaget was not particularly concerned with individual differences in intelligence. He was not interested in investigating why one child was more clever than another but focused on the intellectual processes that, he believed, would prove to be common to all children.

Attention to the individual and to the variability that existed among humans across domains was more within the scope of anatomists, physicians, and special educators. It was not until the opening of the twentieth century that researchers developed the tools, the measures and the statistical analyses to enable them to systematically study the ways that thinking develops (Winzer, 1990b). Only then, and only grudgingly, did psychologists turn to the study of individual differences. When they did, the major area of concern became the elusive and controversial concept of intelligence. Of course, it was the individual differences and not the intelligence per se that constituted a new area of research.

IQ tests were crucial to the early modern study of intelligence. For decades, psychologists, educators, and the general public adhered to the notion that intelligence was what the tests tested. Even so, a number of researchers questioned the infallibility of the IQ measures and, indeed, IQ testing has been controversial since its inception.

The way humans think and process knowledge has been of perennial interest to philosophers and educators. Intelligence seems to be more complicated than any other variable characteristic and, because it underlies so much of human functioning, has generated interest since the time of Plato and Aristotle.

Current conceptions about intelligence have expanded and we no longer place uncritical faith in intelligence tests. Nevertheless, the precise nature of intelligence remains mysterious and its definition a major source of debate. Simply because human beings are so complicated, methods for studying differences in intelligence have been and remain problematic. Because the environment, the opportunity to learn, and how we shape our environments are so crucial to the development of what we call intelligence, it is nearly impossible to determine the relative contributions of heredity and environment.

## NATURE AND NURTURE

As philosophical and psychological concepts, nature and nurture have been debated for centuries and the pendulum has swung sharply between both schools of thought. Eighteenth century philosophers, influenced by the views of John Locke and other empiricists, held firmly to a nurture orientation (Winzer, 1990b). In the mid-nineteenth century, a series of prompts—urbanization, industrialization, and a more class-structured society—militated toward attitude change. Darwin's disturbing and controversial 1859 publication of *The origin of the species* sent the pendulum swinging rapidly toward the nature side of the debate. Darwin's publication coincided with geological and archeological discoveries that unsettled accepted explanations of the origin and development of humans (Winzer, 1990b). Social Darwinism emerged—a theory that ranked people, cultures, and societies in a hierarchy narrowly constructed along ethnocentric perspectives and one that sought to view human society through Darwin's vision of the animal world (Rogers, 1972).

Darwinian thinking, with its hierarchy that established differences between lower animals and humans, was well accepted and, together with advances in the field of genetics, stimulated wide public interest in human heredity (Winzer, 1990b). Evolutionary theories and the new biological doctrines inevitably drew attention to differences within the species and to the selective significance of inborn differences in human beings.

The central dogma of scientific racism revolved around the heredibility of intelligence and nearly all other human characteristics. Not only were the qualities of the mind said to be subject to the laws of heredity, but so were deformities said to be acquired and transmitted. Social Darwinists saw every aspect of human life, from socioeconomic status to the condition of health and educational achievement, as immutably predetermined by the genes received at the moment of conception (Chase, 1977). Scientists increasingly disputed the contention that the environment was important in human development. The evolutionary mechanism was seen to be natural selection—and its mechanism was, of course, heredity. After years of neglect, great attention was directed toward the importance of inborn instincts which were seen as unfolding at certain predetermined points of development. Psychologists held to the notion of fixed intelligence and predetermined development; individual differences were dismissed as mere inconsequential variations of instinctual patterns (Bell, 1980).

By the beginning of World War I, the heredity-environment debate was well underway; biologists, sociologists, and psychologists entered the arena and all brought the tools of their separate disciplines to the debate (Winzer, 1990b). Nature reigned supreme until the period following World War I. However, the late 1920s seemed to usher in a period of tempered conflict and reliance on research findings to settle issues relating to intelligence (Hilgard, 1987). One reason for this was the critical questioning of the power of IQ tests used to measure intelligence. Also, innate concepts had tied intelligence to race and class, but at the same time sensitivity to issues of racial bias was mounting rapidly as many

Debate continues on whether intelligence results more from hereditary or environmental factors.

North Americans and other people around the world grew increasingly aghast at the implications of Hitler's *Rasenhygiene* and heinous policies and perceptions.

Heredity principles further wavered under the impact of the new behaviourist theories in psychology. Behaviourism was the work of several psychologists, although it was John Watson who defined it, shaped it, promoted it, coined the terminology, and gave American psychology its behavioural footing after he announced his platform in 1913 (Winzer, 1990b). Although American psychology was not immediately converted to Watson's approach, with its emphasis on habits and conditioned reflexes rather than instincts, by the 1920s behaviourism was spreading on a wave of revolutionary fervour in education. Progressive schools, adopting the tenets of John Dewey and other exponents of American progressivism in education, embraced the concepts. The three Rs became less important as emotional training became an integral part of the new education (Winzer, 1990b).

Under a barrage of criticism, and in light of new findings about human heredity, psychologists, medical personnel, and educators revamped their previous imperious stances. But extremism was not easily vanquished and the controversy surfaced again in 1940. This time, however, the ensuing debate ushered in a significant breakthrough for psychologists concerned with the development of intelligence. There was a radical movement away from the previously held notion of fixed intelligence and predetermined development (Hilgard, 1987).

In 1940 a *Year Book of the National Society for the Study of Education* appeared in two parts (Stoddard, 1940). In this, researchers from Stanford University, following the lead of Lewis Terman, tended to promote heredity. Other researchers came to the opposite conclusion, claiming that environment was the primary determinant of intellectual ability.

Researchers working at the Iowa Child Welfare Research Station attempted to produce evidence that intelligence, especially that measured by intelligence tests, was a product of the environment. They tried to show that manipulations in the environment produced variations in intelligence and that intelligence tests were not really measuring native intelligence. This work, which has become grouped together and known as the Iowa studies, came out strongly for nurture principles.

Even though the California and Iowa researchers held different views about whether intelligence was determined more by genetics or more by environmental influences, stances were not as irreconcilable as they had tended to be earlier. By this time, researchers were beginning to agree that both genes and the environment contributed to the intelligence of a human being. In 1949, Canadian psychologist Donald Hebb proposed that environment and heredity interact with each other to produce individual differences—or the range of various outcomes that we see among children. He discarded the idea that it was possible to obtain precise ratios for the discrete contributions of heredity and environment but rather proposed that both nature and nurture operate 100 percent of the time. In other words, each plays a role at all times, and while one or the other may predominate at a particular time, both are always influencing the process of development (Hilgard, 1987). Hebb contributed significantly to the study of intelligence, especially from the standpoint of neurology. Some details of his work are found in Box 6-1.

## Box 6-1 **Biographical note: Donald Olding Hebb (1904–1985)**

Donald Hebb was born in Nova Scotia, the son of two family doctors who practised jointly. He received his first degree from Dalhousie and then was for a year the principal and teacher in his hometown high school. It was a disappointing year and Hebb turned to odd jobs and finally entered graduate school at McGill University in Montreal in 1929. He attended part-time because he was still working as a teacher and also worked part-time under the supervision of the Russian workers trained by Pavlov himself (Hilgard, 1987). At the age of 30, Hebb began a Ph.D. in physiological psychology in Chicago. He soon went to Harvard and received a Harvard degree in 1936 with a dissertation that had to do with the size and brightness discrimination in rats raised in darkness.

From 1937 to 1939 Hebb became a Fellow of the Neurological Institute in Montreal, working with Wilder Penfield (1891-1976) the distinguished brain surgeon. From 1939 to 1942 Hebb was a lecturer at Queens University in Kingston. His work there in IQ tests led him to the conviction that intelligence, like perception, must be a product of experience. Through his studies on intelligence, Hebb came to believe that a child slowly develops the concepts, models of thought, and perception that constitute intelligence. He also felt that it takes more brain power (or more brain tissue) to establish intelligence than to retain it. Therefore, he argued that an adult can lose a great deal of brain tissue and still suffer little loss of intelligence (Hebb, 1942).

In 1949 Hebb published *Organization of behaviour* which, according to Hilgard (1987), combined great originality with both breadth and specificity. With this work, Hebb revitalized interst in physiological psychology and in the nervous system. He introduced the concepts of cell assemblies, phase sequence, and central facilitation with evidence from and appropriate to a great variety of psychological problems (Hilgard, 1987). This book "had an enormous impact and continues to be influenctial throughout a wide span of experimental and physiological psychology" (Estes, 1979, p. 650).

Hebb became chair of the department of psychology at McGill and later chancellor of McGill. He served as president of the American Psychological Association (APA) and held membership in numerous groups. He received the gold medal of the APA for his contributions.

For further information on Hebb see Hilgard (1987), Rabinowitz, (1987), Rouland and McGuire (1969), and Salkind (1990).

In a similar vein, Anna Anastasi (1958) felt that the nature/nurture controversy had run its course and was no longer an issue to be resolved in general terms. Instead, appropriate enquiries would have to be directed to the interactive functioning of heredity and environment in specific situations.

However, disagreement over matters as complex as the nature/nurture issue are never altogether inactive, although they are more lively at certain periods.

The issue flared again in 1969, primarily over racial differences. In the United States, President Johnson's War on Poverty donated funds to programs such as Head Start for underprivileged children. In this context, the nature/nurture controversy again reached the public forum when Arthur R. Jensen (1968) of the University of California at Berkeley reopened a series of social and political arguments regarding the inheritability of intelligence. Jensen came out strongly on the heritability of racial differences. He fueled massive controversy among both professionals and the public when he proposed that differences in intellectual ability could be traced to racial heritage (Jensen, 1968, 1969).

Jensen interpreted the difference between the tested IQs of blacks and whites as implying that white children are genetically superior to black children. His argument claimed that IQ had an extremely high genetic factor (about 80 percent) and that there must therefore exist racial differences in intelligence (Jensen, 1969). According to Jensen (1968), "Biological and social environmental factors associated with social class, race, and family background account for most of the variance in intellectual ability and school performance" (p. 2). He therefore argued "that individual differences in mental abilities are largely heredity in origin is well established" (p. 5).

Pursuing this argument concerning the innate nature of intelligence, Jensen believed that compensatory education, such as the Head Start programs for young disadvantaged children, had been tried and had failed. Although programs such as Head Start might have generated some short term IQ gains, he argued, these were not sustained over the years. Moreover, he felt that since blacks inherited lower IQs, early education programs were unlikely to affect the genes and were therefore too time-consuming and financially burdensome.

Jensen's hypothesis has not been proved—nor is it likely to be. Apart from the public and professional furor surrounding his contentions, many thoughtful analyses emerged. The concensus was that the economic and social disadvantages suffered by American Blacks were the crucial elements in lower IQ scores, not that some hereditary disability or disadvantage was passed through the genes.

Today, the debate continues although it can be said that we have moved from a rigid adherence to either environmental or genetic explanations for behaviour to a more balanced perspective that recognizes genetic as well as environmental sources of intellectual differences. Current debates tend to focus on heritability ratios—just how much of intelligence is contributed by the genes and how much by the environment.

## IDEAS ABOUT INTELLIGENCE

"Intelligence" and "IQ" are terms which have entered the common lexicon. In fact, among laypersons the term "intelligence" is probably the most widely used psychological concept of all.

More assessments of other people's intelligence take place in the real world than in the testing room (Weinberg, 1989). We can all imagine a prototype of an intelligent person against which we compare examples in our own daily lives (Neisser, 1979). When commuters waiting for a train, shoppers in a supermarket, and university students were asked, "What is intelligence?" there was agreement that intelligence had three facets:

1. Practical problem solving ability (reasoning logically, seeing all sides of a problem, keeping an open mind);

2. Verbal ability (being a good conversationalist, reading often and well);

3. Social intelligence (being sensitive to social cues, admitting mistakes, displaying interest in the world at large) (Weinberg, 1989).

Academics who work in the area of intelligence are in strong agreement with the laypersons' conceptions of intelligence (Sternberg et al., 1981). Nearly all theories of intelligence include ideas about:

• the capacity to learn;

• the total knowledge that a person has acquired; and

• the ability to adapt successfully to new situations and to the environment generally.

Nevertheless, no psychological concept has engendered more controversy than intelligence. This is because intelligence is not a thing—it is a hypothetical construct, an abstraction inferred from assorted behaviours that a given culture happens to value. Because cultural values are diverse, intelligence is related to whatever values are demanded at a particular time and place. An individual considered to be intelligent in a great Canadian or European city could seem a little lost in, say, a jungle village in Africa.

Alfred Binet, who devised the first viable tool for the assessment of mental ability, decided that he was measuring a construct that could be viewed as "the tendency to take and maintain a definite direction; the capacity to make adaptations for the purpose of attaining a desired end; and the power of autocriticism" (Binet and Simon, 1916, p. 45). Floyd Allport, another prominent researcher, called intelligence "the capacity for solving the problems of life" (1924, p. 104), while E.G. Boring somewhat cynically observed that "Intelligence is what the tests test" (1923, p. 35). In the view of Jean Piaget, intelligence is a process of cognitive development that involves many operations and intellectual growth that progresses through distinct and identifiable developmental periods. Piaget saw intelligence as an extension of biological adaptation and defined it in terms of the processes that help humans adapt to their environment. Flavell (1963), a leading Piagetian scholar, says that intelligence is "an interesting and highly developed extension of more primitive [biological] activities whose most general characteristics—the functional invariants—it shares" (p. 44). David Wechsler (1958), who was responsible for three of the most frequently used individual measures of intelligence, maintained that intelligence is the aggregate of the global capacity of an individual to act purposefully, to think rationally, and to deal effectively with the environment.

## THE STUDY OF INTELLIGENCE

In the study of intelligence, researchers are assigned to one of two camps which Mayr (1982) calls the lumpers and the splitters. Lumpers define intelligence as a general unified capacity for acquiring knowledge, reasoning, and problem solving. These theorists believe that intelligence is a basic ability that affects performance on all cognitively oriented tasks. An intelligent person will do well across a range of activities from math problems to analyzing poetry. Evidence for this position comes from correlational studies of IQ tests where testees who do well on subtests are likely to do well across the entire test. In contrast to Mayr's lumpers, the splitters hold that intelligence is not a unified capacity but is composed of many separate abilities.

One of the pioneers in the modern study of intelligence was the British psychologist, Charles Spearman (1863-1945), who had become interested in the theory and practice of IQ testing even before the first report of the Binet tests (Spearman, 1904). Spearman viewed intelligence as a mental capacity that underlies all cognitive performance and saw levels of intelligence as related to levels of cognitive performance.

When presenting children with batteries of tests, Spearman noticed two trends. Some children showed a strong tendency to rank consistently from test to test; children who scored high on one test, such as memory, tended to score high on the other tests. Other children scored well on some tests, poorly on others.

Spearman ascribed the tendency to do well over all the measures as a general or "g" factor. He ascribed the differential rankings for individuals to specific or "s" factors which referred to particular abilities. Spearman (1904) proposed that all individuals possess the general intelligence factor, "g," in varying amounts so a person could be described as bright or dull depending on the amount of "g" he or she possessed. Further, the "g" factor was the driving force that would power the set of special skills unique to specific situations. The "g" factor, therefore, was seen to be a form of dynamic brain energy. Spearman also determined that any test of mental performance would reflect greater or lesser amounts of the "g" factor.

Spearman wanted to define intelligence objectively; to him this necessitated a quantitative description. Spearman's two tier view of intelligence with its general "g" factor and its specific ability "s" factor is intuitively understandable—two persons might be of equal intellectual competence if judged on the basis of a variety of intellectual tasks while at the same time one might differ from the other in some special aptitude such as musical ability or skill in acquiring a foreign language (Hilgard, 1987). However, critics of Spearman's position refused to accept the existence of a general intelligence, a "g" factor. Instead, they suggested that intelligence is composed of several "primary mental abilities."

Lewis L. Thurstone (1887-1935) worked diligently from the 1920s through the 1940s to refine Spearman's factors but could find no substantive evidence to support the "g" concept. Thurstone was led to contradict Spearman and deny a general factor for intelligence (Thurstone, 1938). Instead, Thurstone suggested that intelligence was always a composite of special factors, each peculiar to a particular task. He established a profile, using the statistical device of factor analysis, of seven scores reflecting each of what he called the primary abilities or the "vectors of the mind" that were the major components of intelligence. Thurstone felt that intelligence could be broken down into a number of primary abilities: verbal comprehension, word fluency, number, space, memory, perceptual speed, and reasoning.

R.B. Cattell (1963) conceived intelligence as having two forms, fluid and crystallized. Fluid intelligence comprises an individual's brightness or adaptability while crystallized intelligence results from experience and education. When an individual of high fluid intelligence is restricted in experience or education, he or she will show less crystallized intelligence.

Fluid intelligence involves many basic processes such as reasoning, forming concepts, drawing inferences, and dealing with abstractions. It is not dependent on formal education and is sometimes considered the basic ability to solve new and unpractised problems. On the other hand, crystallized intelligence depends on education. It is made up of the abilities that are valued by a culture such as reading comprehension, vocabulary, and general knowledge (Horn, 1978; Horn and Donaldson, 1980).

## The structure of intellect

For many years psychologists were satisfied with a largely operational definition of intelligence; that is, intelligence is what IQ tests measure. This complete reliance on IQ tests continued into the 1960s, even though it was not clear which mental abilities and cognitive processes the tests actually measured. Only in recent decades have researchers determined that intelligence comprises a variety of distinct abilities and capabilities (Winzer, 1990a).

The psychologist, J.P. Guilford was one of the key contributors to the multidimensional theory of intelligence. Guilford argued against Spearman's "g" factor. He used factor analysis, as did Thurstone, to broaden the concept of intelligence to include psychological faculties not covered by most intelligence tests. He also made a distinction between convergent and divergent operations and hypothesized 120 separable abilities. Guilford's distinctive approach prompted researchers to reconsider intelligence as a diverse range of intellectual and creative abilities. Guilford also inspired interest in the characteristics of creative thought processes and creativity tests. His contributions have been of major importance to the study of intelligence and in the education of gifted, talented, and creative children.

Guilford developed a model, called the Structure of Intellect, that outlined many different types of intellectual ability (Guilford, 1967). Figure 6-1 presents a representation of Guilford's model.

Figure 6-1
Guilford's Structure
of Intellect

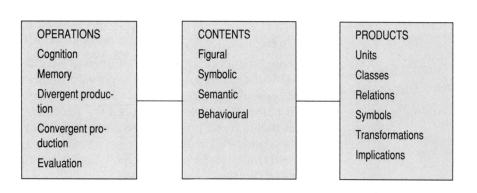

| OPERATIONS | CONTENTS | PRODUCTS |
|---|---|---|
| Cognition | Figural | Units |
| Memory | Symbolic | Classes |
| Divergent production | Semantic | Relations |
| Convergent production | Behavioural | Symbols |
| Evaluation | | Transformations |
| | | Implications |

Guilford determined his Structure of Intellect by analyzing intelligence in terms of its specific skills; his "periodic table" is one of different kinds of intellectual functioning. He divided intellectual performance into three dimensions: operations, contents, and products, each of which encomapasses several abilities.

**Operations**    These are the methods people use to process information. The five operations are:

- Cognition, or the ability to recognize and comprehend data.

- Memory, or the ability to retain newly gained information.

- Divergent production, or the ability to generate logical alternatives and new ideas.

- Convergent production, or the ability to use information for problem solving.

- Evaluation, or the ability to make appropriate judgments.

**Contents**    These have to do with how the learner classifies processed information. The four content areas are:

- Figural contents, or information about tangible objects derived through our senses.

- Symbolic contents, or information derived from symbols such as numbers, letters, musical notes, or formulae.

- Semantic contents, or information derived from language.

- Behavioural contents, or information involving human interaction.

**Products**    These refer to the forms and structures that people use to organize information. The six forms of product are:

- Units, individual pieces of information.

- Classes, or objects that share some common attribute.

- Relations, or meaningful connections between items of information.

- Systems, or organized aggregates of information.

- Transformations, or modifications of existing information.

- Implications, or predictions, deductions, and conclusions about information.

Although Guilford's Structure of Intellect may be too complex to serve as a guide in real situations, it broadens our view of intelligence by adding such factors as those related to social judgment and creativity (Gleitman, 1986). One area of particular influence has been the education of gifted students. In this field, curriculum and program designs have an array of models to draw upon to provide a basis and structure. Bloom's taxonomy (which will be discussed in Chapter 11) is popular although the greatest amount of curriculum effort has centred on Guilford's work (Winzer, 1990a).

## Theory of Multiple Intelligence

Howard Gardner (1983) is another prominent proponent of the theory of multiple cognitive abilities. Gardner (1983) believes that intelligence governs more than cognitive functioning and that it is composed of separate abilities. He has based his notions of separate abilities in part on evidence that brain damage from a stroke, for example, often interferes with functioning in one area such as language but does not affect functioning in other areas (Woolfolk, 1990).

Gardner's conception of intelligence, referred to as the Theory of Multiple Intelligence, is broad and describes six separate types of intelligence. The types of intelligence that Gardner recognizes include:

- linguistic intelligence;
- musical intelligence;
- logical/mathematical intelligence;
- spatial intelligence;
- bodily-kinesthetic intelligence; and
- personal/social intelligence.

These categories of intelligence are presumed to be independent, so each individual may show different levels across domains. It should be noted that while Gardner (1983) contends that there are many types of intelligence, he feels that too often we pay attention to only one type of intelligence—verbal proficiency.

## Information processing

Some researchers argue that intelligence has to do with how we process information, rather than with how much information we have. Thinking is the main function of the mind—how we think when we have obtained information through our sense organs is the basic concern of intelligence (Das, 1988). In recent years, psychologists have turned to the work of cognitive psychology and information processing for guidance in the understanding of intelligence. Information processing theories are fully discussed in Chapter 9.

A number of psychologists have studied the mental processes that individuals use to solve problems both on intelligence tests and in real life. Robert J. Sternberg, a Yale psychologist, hypothesizes that there are three distinct types of intellectual abilities which he called intelligence, wisdom and creativity. Sternberg argues that an individual can be strong in any of these areas without necessarily being strong in all areas (Sternberg, 1985).

Sternberg views intelligence from an information processing perspective. He uses a componential analysis of intelligence, a component being "an elementary information process that operates upon internal representations of objects or symbols" (Sternberg, 1985, p. 97). Components are classified by the functions they serve and by how general they are. There are at least three different functions served (Good and Brophy, 1986).

Sternberg decided that intelligence was made up of three components: meta-components, performance components, and knowledge components.

**Metacomponents**    These are the higher order executive processes used in planning, monitoring, and decision making. In a sense, these metacomponents match Spearman's "g" factor.

**Performance components**    These components are the processes used in the execution of a task.

**Knowledge components**    These are acquisition components—the process-es used in learning new information. Knowledge is further broken down into sub-components of selective encoding, selective combination, and selective com-parison (Sternberg, 1985).

Some components are specific; they are necessary for one kind of task but not for another. In contrast, other components are very general and may be neces-sary in almost every cognitive task. Metacomponents, for example, are very gen-eral as we are constantly monitoring our progress and selecting strategies.

## MEASURING INTELLIGENCE

Early researchers were concerned about the nature of intelligence; however, they were equally involved in the measurement of human intelligence. The foundations to finding a method to measure mental ability were laid in the rise of experimental psychology in Germany. Wilhelm Wundt, working in his labo-ratories at Leipzig in 1875, formulated generalized descriptions of human behaviour. Wundt conceived psychology as the science of the human mind, to be studied through introspection; he studied areas such as sensory phenomena by measurement of reaction time and made qualitative checks of introspection. Wundt did not devise a mental test, per se; his contribution to the testing move-ment was the methodology he utilized in his experimental studies. Wundt's emphasis on standardized conditions and procedures became a legacy for mod-ern psychology and measurement (Goodenough, 1949; Linden and Linden, 1968).

In England, Francis Galton, a scion of a leading British family, the Wedgewoods, and a second cousin of Charles Darwin, became interested in the study of human differences. Galton undertook intense psychological research that contributed to and potently influenced the study of individual differences and the mathematical formulae to quantify them (Winzer, 1990b). He studied hereditary character and talent and, while it was Galton who coined the expres-sion "nature versus nurture," he allowed barely a nod to nurture himself. In his studies on hereditary genius, Galton found that eminence followed a few family lines (one of which was his own). He stressed biological and hereditary factors and overlooked the wealth, leisure, medical aid, nutrition, and other factors underlying the rise to eminence of so many of England's prominent families (Winzer, 1990b).

Galton attempted to define intelligence in terms of its behavioural correlates. To accomplish this and to measure individual ability and achievement, he created a test method that was characterized by its brevity and its ability to sample large numbers of people. Galton's measures did not distinguish between potential capacity and actual academic or social success, however. He considered repetition to be an accurate measure of ability and especially stressed a test that had the subject cancel all the As on a page as rapidly as possible. Other measures included discrimination between weights, colours, and sounds, and word association (Winzer, 1990b). Galton's work did not translate into specific measures for the measurement of intelligence; he introduced the idea of intelligence tests but left their actual development as a major research problem for the future (Fancher, 1985).

Other researchers also delved into devising tests of mental ability. However, most of the early tools were single tests that relied on quite specific functions and were not organized into scales. They therefore had limited application. Tests were not standardized and no methods for ascertaining reliability or validity existed (Freeman, 1926). The prime test was the cancellation of As, as used by Galton. Content dealt with sensory and motor processes and, even if a battery of tests was used, results were not combined. The early measures failed to make much impression, and were even viewed negatively (Freeman, 1926). Educators at the time saw little value in using mental tests in the schools (Linden and Linden, 1968).

It is generally conceded that Alfred Binet, aided by his young assistant, Theophile Simon, devised the first commercially acceptable test of mental ability. Binet's initial psychological work was with hypnosis and parapathology and, by the time he began publishing his work on mental tests in 1895, he was considered a leader in experimental psychology and experimental pedagogy, and had substantial experience in the measurement of individual differences (Winzer, 1990b).

It was in 1904 that the French government asked Binet to produce a measure that would identify those children who did not possess the potential to achieve in regular classrooms under regular school instruction. To avoid injustice, the selection was to be made on objective, diagnostic procedures. With these goals in mind, Binet devised thirty sub-tests that could be objectively scored and used to differentiate mentally retarded from normal children. The tests required children to carry out simple verbal commands, coordinate actions, recognize and use common objects, define words, and complete sentences (Luftig, 1989). After presenting the items to 50 normal children ranging in age from three to 11 and a number of subnormal and retarded children, each item was placed at the age level at which 60 to 90 percent of children in that age group passed the item. Children who passed were considered normal or above average; conversely, failures were seen as below average. The result was Binet and Simon's Measuring Scale of Intelligence, first aired in 1905 (Winzer, 1990b).

Binet quickly recognized the weaknesses of the 1905 scale, produced as it was under time constraints. Binet and Simon's 1908 revision was more statistically representative; they generated its standardization norm from a sample of 203 children. On the 1908 scale Binet and Simon added some items, eliminated others, and made a significant advance: items were grouped according to age and the concept of mental age was introduced. Binet and Simon revised their scale again in 1911 (Winzer, 1990b).

**Intelligence quotient (IQ):** the relationship between the child's mental age (MA) and chronological age (CA); it reflects the difference between a child's performance on the tests and the normative performance for that child's age level.

**Inter-individual differences:** variations among members of an age group or grade level.

# Early advances in North America

Much of the impetus for the promotion and direction of the early testing movement in America arose from initiatives taken at the New Jersey Institution for Feeble-Minded Boys and Girls at Vineland, most specifically by Henry Goddard, Director of the Psychological Laboratory at Vineland. Henry Goddard had earned his Ph.D. in 1899 under G. Stanley Hall at Clarke University and became director of the research department at Vineland that opened in September, 1906, with the primary purpose of finding the causes of mental retardation and eradicating the condition (Winzer, 1990b). Goddard's early psychological studies and experiments with psychomotor tests stimulated his interest in the 1905 Binet scale which was translated by Elizabeth Kite, his assistant and field worker. In 1908, Goddard introduced the 1905 Scale to North America and in 1910 adapted the 1908 revision. In 1911 he standardized this revision on 2 000 school age children in Vineland public schools; he discovered at least two percent of the sample to be mentally retarded, unable to achieve in traditional classrooms (Goddard, 1911).

The Goddard revision of 1910 became one of the most commonly used versions of the Binet Scale in the United States (Sattler, 1982) although it was not the only one. In 1911, Lewis Terman, who had also studied under Hall, became interested in the intelligence testing of school-aged children. With his coworker, H.G. Childs, Terman published the Terman and Childs Revision of the Binet-Simon Scale in 1912 (Terman and Childs, 1912). In 1916 Terman linked Stanford's name with the Binet test to provide the most widely known English title for the test, the Stanford-Binet Individual Test of Intelligence. The Stanford-Binet provided the model for future IQ tests and later achievement measures.

Binet did not use the term "intelligence quotient" to describe the results of his measure—it was first used in 1911 by William Stern, a German psychologist interested in the characteristics of prominent men (Stern, 1914). Terman used the term "intelligence quotient" to express the numerical relationship of an individual's mental age to chronological age. Psychologists adopted the simple formula, and the term has entered the language of everyday life, although not always with precision (Laycock, 1979).

The **intelligence quotient** (IQ) is the relationship between the child's mental age (MA) and chronological age (CA); it reflects the difference between the child's performance on the tests and the normative performance for the child's age level. Thus, if eight-year-old Tom takes an IQ test and is assigned a mental age of eight, his IQ would be 100. The IQ is obtained by dividing the child's mental age by his chronological age, and multiplying the answer by 100:

$$\frac{MA}{CA} \times 100 = IQ \text{ or, in this case, } \frac{8}{8} \times 100 = 100.$$

If five-year-old Mary then takes the test and obtains the same score, she can be said to have a MA of 8. Her IQ would be

$$\frac{8}{5} \times 100 = 160$$

# Modern IQ tests

IQ tests are designed to assess global aspects of intelligence. They are used primarily to determine **inter-individual differences**—those that exist between members

**Intra-individual differences:**
the variations of performance that are observed as an individual performs several tasks.

**Normal distribution:**
a continuum of scores that vary from the average score by predictable amounts.

**Age scale tests:**
tests arranged into age levels according to their difficulty and without regard for content.

**Content scales:**
tests organized in a hierarchical fashion that contain a number of subtests, each of which deals with the assessment of a single type of content or ability.

of an age group or grade level—and **intra-individual differences**—the variations of performance that are observed as an individual performs several tasks.

As general intellectual functioning is measured by means of intelligence tests, certain assumptions underlie the procedure. The most crucial is the notion that intelligence, as measured on standardized tests of mental ability, is normally distributed. Tests of mental ability are based on a **normal distribution**—a continuum of scores that vary from the average score by predictable amounts.

Binet arranged his test according to an age scale. **Age scale tests** are arranged into age levels according to their difficulty and without regard for content. An item is regarded as suitable for use at that age level when 50 percent of children of that age pass it. The age scale is created by placing several tests of age-specific groups of items together in a series.

However, many of today's tests of mental ability are content scaled. Content scales are arranged differently, but in a manner which greatly facilitates the intepretation of results. **Content scales** contain a number of subtests, each of which deals with the assessment of a single type of content or ability. The items in each of these subtests are organized in an hierarchical fashion according to their difficulty.

There are literally dozens of intelligence tests available today. Some are for use with normal students; others are more specialized, such as measures designed for deaf children, blind children, or those with delayed or deviant language. A listing of some of the more widely used tests of mental ability is presented in Table 6-1.

Tests assume mental ability to be normally distributed.

Table 6-1 Examples of tests of mental ability

| INSTRUMENT | AGE RANGE | SPECIAL FEATURES |
|---|---|---|
| Columbia Mental Maturity Scale (3rd. ed.) (Burgemeister, Bluma and Lorge, 1972) | 31/2 to 9 years | |
| Detroit Tests of Learning Aptitude (Baker and Leland, 1967; Hammill, 1984) | 3 years to adult | Specific sub-areas may be selected. |
| Hiskey Nebraska Test of Learning Aptitude (Hiskey, 1966) | 3 1/2 to 18 1/2 | Normed for hearing-impaired students; Non-verbal instrument. |
| Kaufman Assessment Battery for Children (Kaufman and Kaufman, 1983) | 2 1/2 to 12 1/2 years | Measures intellectual functioning and acquired knowledge. 16 subtests. Non-verbal scale for use with language delayed children. |
| Leiter International Performance Scale (Leiter, 1948) | 2 to 12+ years and up | Can be used nonverbally. |
| McCarthy Scales of Children's Abilities (McCarthy, 1972) | 2 1/2 to 8 1/2 years | Provides a general estimate of intellectual functioning and a profile of abilities. |
| Raven's Coloured Progressive Matrices Revised order (Raven, 1962) | 5 to 11 years | Also used for the elderly and handicapped. |
| Raven's Progressive Matrices (Raven, 1948) | 5 years to adult | A nonverbal test of reasoning ability based on figured material. |
| Slosson Intelligence Test (2nd. ed) (Slosson, 1981) | Infant to adult | Brief individual screening test. An adaptation of items from the Stanford-Binet |
| Stanford-Binet Individual Intelligence Test (Terman and Merrill, 1973) | 2 years to adult | Seldom used for individuals over 10 or 12 years of age. |
| System of Multi-Cultural Pluralistic Assessment (SOMPA) (Mercer and Lewis, 1977) | 5 to 11 years | 3 assessment models— medical, defecit and social system. Tests cognitive functioning, sensory motor, and adaptive behaviour. |
| Test of Nonverbal Intelligence (Brown, Sherbenou and Dollar, 1982) | | A language-free method of cognitive ability. |

**Deviation IQ score:**
a number that tells exactly
how much above or below
the average an individual
scored on the test.

| Wechsler Adult Intelligence Scale- Revised (WAIS-R) (Wechsler,1981) | 15 years and up | Performance and verbal scales with 5 subtests and a supplementary subtest for each scale. |
| --- | --- | --- |
| Wechsler Intelligence Scale for Children- Revised (WISC-R) (Wechsler, 1974) | 5 to 15 years | |
| Wechsler Pre-School and Primary Scale of Intelligence (WPPSI) (Wechsler, 1967) | 4 1/2 to 6 1/2 years | |
| Woodcock Johnson Psychoeducational Battery (Woodcock and Johnson, 1977) | School age children | Cognitive and achievement batteries. |

Compared to most psychological tests, the Stanford-Binet Individual Intelligence Test and the Wechsler Intelligence Scale for Children-Revised (WISC-R) are among the most reliable and best validated. They are therefore the most popularly used measures of mental ability. However, surveys of clinical and school psychologists over the past 25 years have indicated a shift within these groups from the primary use of the Stanford-Binet toward use of the WISC-R (Wade and Baker, 1977).

### The Stanford-Binet intelligence scale
The Stanford-Binet has been revised four times, in 1937, 1960, and 1972, most recently in 1986 (Thorndike, Hagan, and Sattler, 1986). The 1937 revision expanded the norming sample to 3 184 children. The 1960 revision used a different method for computing IQ, a method used by David Wechsler called the "deviation IQ." The problem with the original method of calculating IQ was that by about age 13, the ratio between mental age and chronological age began to break down. The ratio could only be used with young children; adolescents and adults do not continue to increase their mental ages as they did when they were younger.

The **deviation IQ score** is a number that tells exactly how much above or below the average an individual scored on the test. The different rates of growth at different ages, the changes in the variabilities of mental age and individual differences in development are taken into account by basing the score on the standard deviation for each age group. When the Stanford-Binet was restandardized in 1972, the new norms produced a mean of 100 and a standard deviation of 16. The revised scale measures verbal reasoning, qualitative reasoning, abstract-visual reasoning, and short-term memory.

### The Wechsler scales
A series of intelligence tests were developed by David Wechsler who began by devising a test to compete with the Stanford-Binet Individual Intelligence Scale.

In 1939, Wechsler developed the Wechsler-Bellevue Adult Intelligence Scale, an adult test standardized on an adult sample. This scale and its scoring marked a rather significant departure from the tradition of the Binet tests. Wechsler believed that the Binet tests were too heavily loaded with verbal items, so he added a performance scale. As far as the scoring went, Wechsler preserved the IQ concept through devising a scale of similar units without employing the concept of mental age. Rather, he used a deviation IQ score. That is, the numerical scores at each chronological age were converted to standard scores derived statistically with a mean of 100 and a standard deviation of 15.

Wechsler's original adult scale became the Wechsler Adult Inteligence Scale, now revised (WAIS-R). He also devised the Wechsler Intelligence Scale for Children, also revised (WISC-R) for use with children between the ages of about six and 16. The Wechsler Preschool and Primary Scale of Intelligence- Revised (WPPSI-R) is for use with four to six year olds.

The three tests, all designed for individual administration, are similar in that they contain two scales with a number of subtests. The WISC-R yields three summary scores: Performance scale, Verbal scale, and Full scale. The Wechsler scales do not contain as many tasks as the Stanford-Binet; items on the WISC-R range from easy to more difficult. The Verbal and Performance scales of the WISC-R each contain five subtests, with an extra subtest to be used if the examiner requires more information. Within each subtest, certain domains are explored. For example, short term memory is tested by the digit span test but it is also involved in coding; long-term memory is tested with the subtests for arithmetic, comprehension, vocabulary, and similarities.

Responses on each subtest are first given a raw score which is then converted to a scaled score by using a table in the *Manual* which converts scores according to the child's chronological age. Scales' scores range from one to 19, with an average score of ten and three standard deviations in each direction. If a student receives a scaled subtest score or 14 or above, the score is therefore regarded as above average. Conversely, a score of six or below would be below average for that age group.

For each subtest, a precise set of directions tells the examiner where to begin, how to present the items, what to say, what type of help, correction or reinforcement to offer, when to stop, and how to score the responses. Spontaneous comments and the child's presenting behaviour—the attitudes of the child to the testing session and the examiner are carefully recorded.

The size of a child's IQ score depends on more than just the number of correct answers. It also depends on how those answers compare with those of the standardized population of children who have taken the same test. High scores on both scales also depend, at least to some extent, on the individual's ability to work quickly because some of the tests are timed.

On the Wechsler tests, the mean is 100, with a standard deviation of 15. Of all scores on the WISC-R, 99.73 percent fall within 55 and 145; half the scores fall between 90 and 110. Figure 6-2 shows the normal curve of intelligence, based on the scores of the Wechsler Intelligence Scale for Children-Revised (WISC-R) (Wechsler, 1974). Each standard deviation, or 1 $\sigma$, represents 15 points on this scale. Most people score around the middle of the curve, with an IQ between 85 and 115, or one standard deviation below or above the norm.

Figure 6-2
Normal curve of
intelligence

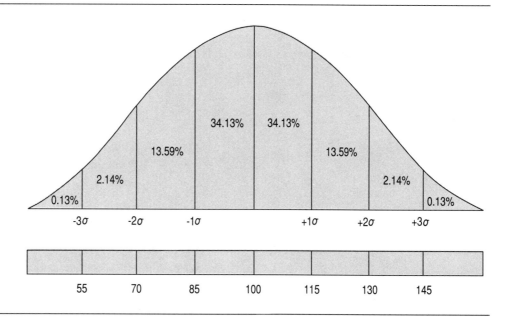

For the WISC-R and most IQ tests, the standard error of measurement is about five points. If, then, a student obtains a score of 105, we can be reasonably confident that the true IQ is somewhere between 100 and 110. The score may not be said to be exactly 105 as IQ tests are simply not that precise.

Teachers may be presented with psychological reports on exceptional students that contain WISC-R results. The psychologist's report to the teacher should contain scores for both scales, as well as the *Full scale score*. This final score is not an average of the Performance and Verbal scales but is computed on a formula. Box 6-2 presents an extract from a psycho-educational report. Complete reports would contain additional information about results of other types of assessment, school and family history and the child's presenting behaviour.

The WISC-R has been normed on normal children. However, for children with special needs the WISC-R is often inappropriate in its usual form. Adaptations for special populations have been devised. IQ testing with special populations is discussed in Box 6-3. For children with very special needs, such as those suffering from childhood psychoses, infantile autism, or multiple handicaps, IQ testing is often entirely inappropriate and other ways to assess potential must be found.

### Group intelligence tests
There are two broad categories of intelligence tests—those administered to groups, and those administered individually, such as the Wechsler scales. Because the administration, scoring, and interpretation of individual IQ tests are very complex, they should only be given by qualified personnel. Group tests are often used to screen children who require further testing (Winzer, 1990a).

Box 6-2 **In the classroom: Extract from a psycho-educational report**

Name: Harry
D.O.B.: 23 January, 1982
C.A.: 9.00
School: Canada Elementary
Grade: 4

Reason for referral:

Harry was referred for psycho-educational assessment by the classroom teacher because of his severe defecits in most academic activities. Although Harry has just completed the first term of grade four, his reading, language arts and math are below grade level. This spills over to affect other areas such as social studies and science. Harry's oral language is good but he does not seem to be able to handle written forms. Handwriting and other manual activites show particular gaps.

The school psychologist presented Harry with a battery of measures, beginning with the WISC-R. Results of the WISC-R are as follows:

| Verbal scale | | Performance scale | |
|---|---|---|---|
| Information | 13 | Picture completion | 9 |
| Similarities | 12 | Picture arrangement | 5 |
| Arithmetic | 5 | Block design | 8 |
| Vocabulary | 14 | Object assembly | 8 |
| Comprehension | 12 | Coding | 4 |

Verbal scale: 106; Performance scale: 90; Full scale: 92.

With a Full scale score of 92 (+/- 5) on the WISC-R, Harry is in a slightly low category of functioning. However, it is important to look at the scatter of scores and the discrepancy between the Verbal and the Performance scales. With the exception of the arithmetic subtest which depends on attention and past learning, Harry scored well on the Verbal scale. In the Performance areas he did more poorly, consistent with the teacher's observations that visual memory and manipulation present problems to this child.

## Box 6-3 **IQ testing with special populations**

In individual psychological assessments, three major concerns arise. These are the instruments to use for appropriate assessments, the best way to present unbiased testing to students from minority groups and those with less than efficient English, and the assessment of the abilities of students with handicapping conditions.

Assessment of children with handicaps is particularly difficult; often the greater the intensity and degree of handicap, the more difficult the assessment and tenuous the results. When assessing handicapped children, a number of adaptations to standard routines may need to be considered. Sometimes a child will need a support adaptation; for example, the child may need to be placed in a certain position, or provided with some general form of support. Then there are prosthetic adaptations which means that the child needs a specific piece of equipment such as braces or a hearing aid. A general adaptation is one that does not require support or a piece of equipment but still represents a change in the basic requirements of the task or changes in the utility of the skill. For example, a hearing impaired child may need to perform communication tasks using sign language (White et al., 1981).

Children with severe visual impairments and severe hearing losses are particularly difficult to assess using standard measures and procedures. Hearing impaired children are paralyzed by identification instruments whose content and idiom are not designed for that group. Any measures employed must circumvent the language defects imposed by hearing impairment.

Nonverbal tests are the most appropriate for deaf children. The most widely used IQ test is the Wechsler Intelligence Scale for Children-Revised (WISC-R) (Wechsler, 1974). This is believed to yield fairly valid IQ scores for deaf children aged nine to 16. The Verbal Scale is usually omitted from the battery, and an IQ score is calculated on the basis of the Performance Scale alone.

The Performance scale of the WISC-R was standardized using a hearing impaired sample (Anderson and Sisco, 1977). Its now widely used in conjunction with the Hiskey Nebraska Test of Learning Aptitude (Hiskey, 1966) to evaluate the cognitive abilities of the hearing impaired population between six and 17 (Sullivan and Vernon, 1979). Test instruction may be given orally, in pantomime, through total communication, or with the use of visual aids. Other popular nonverbal scales include the Goodenough Harris Drawing Test (Harris, 1963) and Raven's Progressive Matrices (Raven, 1948) for children nine years and older. The Leiter International Performance Scale (Leiter, 1948) has remained popular for young children because it is administered by pantomime and needs no verbal cues or responses. As well, the Nonverbal Test of Cognitive Skills is coming into use (Johnson and Boyd, 1981) as is the Test of Nonverbal Intelligence (Brown, Sherbenou and Dollar, 1982).

Few measures have been designed exclusively for children with visual impairments and their assessment in any domain requires considerable judgment on the part of the examiner. To circumvent the visual disabilities, much IQ testing for blind children has been conducted using only the verbal scales of IQ tests. Some modifications of the Stanford-Binet have been made, specifically the Interim Hayes Stanford-Binet and the Perkins-Binet (Warren, 1984).

Group IQ tests are widely employed because of their seeming objectivity, low expense and ease of administration. However, group tests are notably less reliable than the individually administered batteries (Hopkins and Bracht, 1975). They are generally inappropriate due to their low ceilings, low predictive validity, and low reliability, especially in the higher ranges of IQ; a limited number of abilities can be assessed by paper and pencil and many items are ambiguous (Berdine and Meyer, 1987). Hence, all currently available group intelligence tests have a high prevalence of under-identification and over-identification of children, particularly with reference to creative divergent thinkers and very young children (Borthwick et al., 1980; Lichtenstein, 1982; Roedell, Jackson, and Robinson, 1980).

It is not unusual for scores on group intelligence tests and individual IQ tests to vary as much as thirty points (Martinson, 1975). In addition, group intelligence tests may identify proficient test takers at the expense of those who may score somewhat lower, but who are highly creative and original thinkers (Renzulli, 1979). Group intelligence tests also appear to penalize children from lower socioeconomic and minority groups (Elkin, 1982).

## Controversy about IQ tests

In the past, the mystique of IQ tests—the illusion that they measured what was most significant about a student's cognitive abilities—led psychologists and educators to believe that they possessed supreme and irrefutable validity. Intelligence tests were used as the sole criterion in the assessment and placement of children.

Starting as far back as the 1920s and accelerating rapidly by the early 1960s, critics from diverse backgrounds began to point out some of the disadvantages of IQ testing and school grouping. They argued that human behaviour resists compartmentalization and defies quantification. They pointed out that since a single measure of a single aspect of functioning provides only the most limited information, it is a flagrant misuse of standardized tests to use the results as the sole criteria for determining educational placements. Other measures must complement and supplement the data.

The difficulties and contradictions inherent in placing uncritical faith in IQ tests were brought forcefully to public attention in a number of court cases in the United States in the early 1970s. Remember that this was the period of an enormous swell in civil rights promotion but also the time when Arthur Jensen and others were arguing for the genetic differences in IQ scores among Blacks and whites. It was also a period when special education classes in both Canada and the United States were filled with children from minority and disadvantaged groups.

In fact, a disproportionate representation of minority group students in certain programs for exceptional children is a recurring concern in special education (Chinn and Hughes, 1987; Reschly, 1988). Immigrant and minority group children have been overrepresented in such classifications as slow learners, educable mentally retarded, and learning disabled (Cummins, 1984; Gelb and Miskokawa, 1986; Sleeter, 1986). Disproportionate numbers of these students are referred for psychological services. They are more likely to be referred for special education (Tomlinson, Acker, and Chan, 1977) and are at greater risk of being inappropriately placed in special classes.

For a variety of reasons, widely used assessment measures and procedures are inappropriate with minority group children (Winzer, 1990a). For one thing, school psychologists may not be fully conversant with this area. One study of 402 psychologists (Klausmieir, Shitala, and Maker, 1987) found that a significant number of respondents considered their training in the assessment of minority children and those from low socioeconomic groups to be below average or completely lacking.

As well, clinicians charged with the psychological assessment of ethnic and minority group children are frequently faced with the problem of employing IQ tests which have been standardized on a representative sample of the general population. Good and Brophy (1986) point out that a method called stratified random sampling is used in norming these tests. In this method, the key to accuracy is the identification of a representative sample. Samples are stratified by ensuring that certain percentages of identifiable groups in the population are included. Socioeconomic status, sex, and geogrpahical area are typical variables used for stratification. Within these limits, sampling is supposed to be random. According to Good and Brophy, (1986), appropriate stratified random sampling procedures can produce remarkably accurate results even though the sample includes only a tiny segment of the population. The weakness is that the behaviour of one member in the sample is taken as representative of thousands of others in the same category (Good and Brophy, 1986).

Moreover, most of the IQ tests in popular use in this country have been normed on American, not Canadian, samples. No national norms exist for the WISC-R in Canada although some provincial norms are in place (e.g., Holmes, 1981). Few norms have been taken for Canadian minority groups. For example, none of the tests commonly used in Canada have been normed on Natives (Bachor and Crealock, 1986). One of the results of using non-normed measures is that proportionatcly three times as many Native as non-Native students are labeled as learning disabled (Darou, 1982) or delinquent (Csapo, 1981).

Under most circumstances, typical IQ tests are biased against many minority children (Cummins, 1987). Many tests lend much credence to verbal responses which place children at a disadvantage both because of culture and because of language. On the reserve, for example, orientation toward speech and verbal fluency play a minor role in the culture.

Any form of measurement and evaluation must place priority on the child's language. A major problem lies in the determination that a student has acquired full language competence when actually the student has only conversational English. The disparity between superficial and substantial competency leads psychologists and teachers to administer English language tests of intelligence and achievement and to interpret the findings as they would for children whose first language is English (Winzer, 1990a). When, for example, Cummins (1984) analyzed more than 400 psychological assessments of children from non-English-speaking backgrounds in a western Canadian city, he found that minority students performed very much below norms on the WISC-R which is the most commonly used IQ test in Canadian schools. Performance was significantly more depressed on the verbal parts of the test compared with the non-verbal parts (Cummins, 1987).

Another problem in using standardized tests is that many children from other cultures have never had the opportunity to develop test-taking skills. Some have never seen the puzzles and games that the tests use and so often children must be first trained in how to take the test (Omark and Watson, 1983). As well, they must understand the purpose of the procedure if they are to be motivated to perform their best.

One of the most prominent and telling legal cases concerning IQ testing and educational placement in the United States was *Larry P. v. Riles* which began in 1971 and, with appeals, lasted more than 15 years (Taylor, 1990). When the suit was filed in San Francisco, black children comprised only 28.5 percent of San Francisco's total school population, but made up 66 percent of classes for the mentally retarded. Statewide, Blacks were 9 percent of the total school population but 27 percent of the classes for the mentally retarded (News Notes, 1979). In 1979 a California court ruled that IQ test scores could not be used as the primary criterion for recommending children for special class placement (classes for the retarded) unless the tests met certain criteria. The test scores had to be known to predict academic achievement and classroom performance fairly well and all groups of students had to have the same patterns of scores on the tests as the mean scores (Bersoff, 1981). In making this ruling, the judge assumed that any test yielding different mean scores for different groups of students was automatically biased.

In 1984, the Ninth Circuit Court of Appeals upheld the 1979 ruling (Presse and Reschly, 1986). However, other legal challenges about testing, such as *Pace v. Hammon*, reached opposite conclusions (Slavin, 1988).

Policies regarding test procedures have not emerged strongly from Canadian school boards although they may do so under the Charter of Rights (Winzer, 1990a). Only a handful of boards seem to have any policies for the assessment and placement of children from non-English-speaking backgrounds (Samuda and Crawford, 1980). Even among those that do have policies, Cummins (1987) notes that they are not being observed by those charged with their implementation.

## Predictive value of IQ tests

The notion of IQ implied that the early mastery of skills would predict a future capacity to master more advanced skills. For many psychologists, the crucial question about any test is still, "What does it predict?" A test based on theory that does not predict anything is not of much use. Although we no longer place uncritical faith in intelligence tests, they have, on the whole, been fine predictors of school success. IQ scores predict achievement in school quite well, at least for larger groups, and are used with considerable success to predict academic achievement. Students who score well on IQ tests tend to do better in school and to stay in school longer. The correlation between performance on the WISC-R and on children's performance in school is about .60 (Bee, 1978); the correlation of the WISC-R and school achievement tests is .65 (Sattler, 1982).

**Behavioural genetics:**
the study of the genetic factors involved in characteristics such as intelligence, musical ability, or temperament.

For children under the age of two, IQ scores have been shown to have low or negligible predictive power. It is also interesting to note that as students move up the educational ladder—from kindergarten to high school, to university, to graduate school—the correlations between IQ and measures of academic performance become progressively lower, as can be seen in Table 6-2. Only a select group go to college and this narrow sample gives lower correlations.

**Table 6-2** Correlations with IQ scores

|  | TYPICAL |
|---|---|
| Elementary | .6-.7 |
| High school | .5-.6 |
| College | .4-.5 |
| Graduate school | .3-.4 |

**SOURCE:** Atkinson et al. (1990).

While good IQ scores correlate with school success, it is less clear whether good IQ scores on standardized tests translate into success in after school life. If you complete university, your chances of doing well in your careers in comparison to your classmates cannot be predicted accurately from your scores on an IQ tests (McClelland, 1973). Factors such as motivation, social skills, and luck make the difference. However, high IQ scores are more often found among top civil servants, professors, research scientists and the like; they are found less often among unskilled labourors (Woolfolk, 1990). Similarly, Duncan, Featherman and Duncan (1972) found that IQ had a significant correlation with income. In this study, IQ predicted a person's income better than other measures such as the parents' education or the parents' income.

When Lewis Terman followed the lives of his gifted subjects in order to find out whether adult achievement correlated with the high IQs seen in childhood, he found that the group continued to be successful. As adults, they earned more money, had more managerial jobs, and made more literary and scientific contributions than the average adult (Terman and Oden, 1959). When checked in 1959, Terman's group had published over 2 000 scientific papers and 33 novels and taken out 230 patents (Sprinthall and Sprinthall, 1988).

## INDIVIDUAL DIFFERENCES IN INTELLIGENCE

Until fairly recently, it was difficult to even consider the nature versus nurture question scientifically; answers lay in the realm of philosophical speculation, metaphysical argument, and personal opinion. Little was known about behavioural genetics—the study of the genetic factors involved in characteristics such as intelligence, musical ability, or temperament. Even with modern scientific techniques, definite answers are not readily forthcoming.

In the study of cognition and intelligence, the field of genetics has been crucial. Plomin (1989) points out that genetics plays a role in all of the following: IQ;

**Hereditability:**

a statistic that describes the proportion of observed variance for the behaviours that can be ascribed to genetic differences among individuals in a particular population.

**Hereditability ratio:**

the proportion of a characteristic's variability attributable to genetic causes.

specific cognitive abilities; academic achievement; reading disability and mental retardation; personality factors, including extroversion and neuroticism; temperament in childhood; as well as attitudes and beliefs. There also appears to be a genetic factor involved in psychopathology, schizophrenia, affective disorders, delinquent and criminal behavior, and alcoholism (Plomin, 1989).

Scientists and psychologists use the term "hereditability" when discussing how much of a certain characteristic is due simply to the action of the genes. **Hereditability** is a statistic that describes the proportion of observed variance for the behaviours that can be ascribed to genetic differences among individuals in a particular population (Plomin, 1989, p. 105). A **hereditability ratio**, then, is the proportion of a characteristic's variability attributable to genetic causes. The ratio expresses the relationship of heredity. Hereditability can vary from 0.0 where none of the variance is due to heredity to 1.0 where all of the variance is due to heredity. Thus, if all the variation in IQ scores in a given population is due to genetic factors, the hereditability of IQ would be 1.0. If all the variability is due to environment, then the hereditability would be zero.

Rarely is there agreement among researchers on hereditability. To be sure, determining such physical traits as red hair or tallness is a relatively easy task. But mental abilities, to the extent that they are determined by heredity, are polygenic, or influenced by many sorts of genes. There is no single relationship like eye colour or blood type. Therefore, the size and meaning of hereditability factors for traits such as intelligence form major questions in psychology, genetics, and allied fields.

Several factors should be borne in mind when figures about hereditability are encountered:

• It is now fairly certain that intelligence has a genetic component. A genetic component sets the limits as to how any given trait will respond to environmental stimulation. In other words, heredity limits the extent to which intelligence can be influenced by the environment.

• Even traits that are 100 percent hereditable may be modified by changes in the environment. However, there are limits to the degree of modification that can occur. This genetically constrained range is the reaction range (Gottesman, 1974).

• Hereditability is a numerical estimate taken from measurements made in a single generation. It is based on the likelihood that a given, genetically encoded trait will be modified by the environment. In this sense, it does not measure hereditability at all but rather what is left after environmental influences have been accounted for.

• The figures themselves refer to the relative contribution of heredity to differences among individuals in a given population and not to the specific contribution of heredity to a particular individual (Woolfolk, 1990). Hirsh (1971) has said that hereditability only explains variation in some particular population at a single generation under one set of conditions. Therefore, hereditability is a relative concept. The ratio determined applies only to a particular population and the conditions under study. Comparisons across different races of very different environmental conditions may not be appropriate.

More behavioural genetic data has been obtained for IQ than for any other trait. A recent survey of over 1 000 scientists and educators indicates that most now believe that individual differences in IQ scores are at least partially inherited (Snyderman and Rothman, 1987). Most experts would agree that the hereditability of human intelligence in modern industrialized countries is somewhere between .4 and .8 (Gleitman, 1986).

In behavioural genetics, researchers study the differential effects of heredity and environment on human development. As long ago as 1937 it was demonstrated that the closer two people are genetically related, the more similar their IQs will be (Newman, Freeman, and Holtzinger, 1937). Since then, one of the major methods of behavioural genetics has been twin design, in which the resemblance of fraternal twins and identical twins is compared. Twin data naturally falls into the correlation form of data analysis because investigators are interested in the resemblance between members of twin pairs such as monozygotic (identical) twins and dizygotic (fraternal) twins raised together or apart.

A second important area of research, closely related to twin studies, is adoption data, in which genetically related individuals reared apart and genetically unrelated individuals reared together are studied (Plomin, 1989). Adoptions are not all that common and multiple births relatively rare (about one in every 80 live births for twins and about one in every 700 live births for triplets) so researchers naturally turn to other genetically related individuals for study, such as parents and offspring.

Eighty percent of all twins are dizygotic and such twins are no more genetically alike than other siblings born to the same parents. Monozygotic twins, on the other hand, not only look like mirror images of each other, but they often share behaviours and habits that are strikingly similar (Harris, 1986).

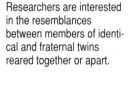

Researchers are interested in the resemblances between members of identical and fraternal twins reared together or apart.

Since monozygotic twins share the same genotype, any differences between them must be due to environmental factors. The degree of similarity between twin pairs with respect to a particular trait is called concordance and is usually expressed in percentages. A high concordance between monozygotic twins would indicate a strong hereditary influence. In height, weight, physical appearance and other biological measurements such as heart rate, respiration rate and blood pressure, monozygotic twins are more similar than dizygotic twins. The rate of physical maturation is similar among monozygotic twins as measured by the age of the first menarche, the pattern of bone ossification, and age-related changes such as graying and wrinkling (see Harris, 1986).

Intelligence as measured by IQ tests is more similar among those with strong genetic bonds (Bouchard, 1981). A study (Erlenmeyer-Kimling and Jarvik, 1963) surveyed 52 separate investigations and found that the IQ scores of monozygotic twins differed by only a few points. Another summary of dozens of studies prior to 1980 included nearly 100 000 twins and biological and adopted relatives and made it difficult to escape the conclusion that heredity is important in influencing individual differences in IQ scores (Bouchard and McGue, 1981). In this summary of 111 studies that have appeared in the world literature, the usual finding was that the highest correlation was found for identical twins reared together; the next highest for identical twins reared apart—commonly higher than for fraternal twins reared together (Bouchard and McGue, 1981). When there were triplets with two monozygotic twins and a third singleton, the monozygotic twins shared many similarities while the third sibling was different from the other two (Keith and Hughey, 1979). Correlations are shown in Table 6-3.

**Table 6-3** Twin studies

| | |
|---|---|
| Identical twins reared together | .87–.88 |
| Identical twins reared apart | .70–.75 |
| Fraternal twins of the same sex | .53 |
| Fraternal twins of different sexes | .49 |
| Ordinary siblings reared together | .52–.55 |
| Ordinary siblings reared apart | .23–.47 |
| Unrelated children reared together | .23–.24 |
| Unrelated children reared apart | .0–.01 |
| Parent and child | .50 |
| Foster parent and child | .20 |
| Grandparent and child | .27 |

**SOURCE:** Gage and Berliner (1984), Sprinthall and Sprinthall (1988).

As well as showing how closely monozygotic twins correlate, the chart also demonstrates the effects of environmental influences. When, for example, identical twins are reared together their IQs are more similar than when they are reared apart. Also, when unrelated children are reared together their IQs tend to be correlated.

One thing to keep in mind is that there may be problems with the validity of all separated twin studies (Lewontin, Rose, and Kamin, 1984) because the research design inevitably yields biased results. Twins who have been truly raised apart, that is, separated from birth, may not even know of each other's existence. These twins therefore cannot respond to the appeals from scientists for volunteers.

As well as studies on twins, researchers are interested in the environment and its effects on adopted children. Even if they were adopted in the first year of life, children's IQ by school age more closely resembles the IQs of the biological parents than those of the adoptive parents (Bouchard, 1981; Scarr and Weinberg, 1976). Adoption studies have also shown higher relationships between the intelligence of adolescents and their natural parents than between adolescents and their adoptive parents (Scarr and Weinberg, 1983). Of course, environment plays a part. Schiff and colleagues (1982) report that children of unskilled workers adopted as infants into families that enjoyed a high socioeconomic status had IQs averaging 14 points higher than those of their other siblings who were reared by their natural parents.

Correlations in IQ are, naturally, found among parents and offspring. Reed and Rich (1982), in studies of resemblance among parents and offspring for measured intelligence, reported a "substantial" hereditability. Simonton (1983), in a study of individual differences in ability among members of European royal families, came to the same conclusion. Simonton showed that at least some parts of what we think of as intelligence appears to be best explained as inherited.

Clearly, both heredity and environment influence intelligence. However there is no firm evidence that one or the other is dominant. As with any other issue of hereditability, it is almost impossible to separate intelligence in the genes from intelligence due to environment and experience. The interactions between intelligence, motivation, and affect cannot be ignored when the whole personality is under consideration. Psychologists generally assume that heredity sets the upper limits on intelligence but that environment determines whether or not those limits will be attained.

Sandra Scarr (1981) has presented observations that follow on those of Hebb and Anastasi that we discussed earlier. Scarr noted that, from the point of view of biology, intelligence has evolved as a primary adaptive mechanism and as such shows typical patterns of individual variability. Scarr argues that this is precisely how the nature/nurture interaction works. When the environment is good," she says, "heredity exerts a strong influence on IQ" (Scarr and Weinberg, 1978, p. 33). Scarr-Salapatek (1975) has defined what she calls the "myth of hereditability." This is, if intelligence is largely determined by genetic factors, it must not be very malleable or changeable. Scarr-Salapatek contends that what we inherit is not a fixed ability or level of competence but a range of reaction or a genetic potential for development which is expressed in complex ways as a result of combined transactions between a person's genetic code and the environment. In other words, genes do not fix behaviour; rather they establish a range of possible reactions to the range of possible experiences presented by the environment. To the extent that the individual is raised in a more favourable or stimulating environment, there exists a greater chance of that person reaching his or her full potential.

## Environmental influences

No discussion of hereditability is complete without a glance at environmental influences. As we have stressed, genetics map out the limits on IQ and other traits, but it is the environment that brings IQ to its full blossoming or, conversely, depresses potential IQ.

An important environmental factor in intelligence is stimulus variety, especially in early childhood. Psychologists such as Jerome Bruner (1969) and Benjamin Bloom (1964) feel that stimulus variety is perhaps the most important ingredient in intellectual development. Bruner believes that infants must be exposed to a wide variety of stimulus input and a shifting environment if normal intellectual growth is to be maintained. Bloom feels that an abundant early environment is the key to the full development of intelligence. Bloom outlined three environmental variables that he sees as important in developing the intellectual abilities of a child:

- the amount of stimulation children receive for verbal development;

- the amount of affection and reward that children receive for verbal reasoning accomplishments;

- the amount of encouragement children receive for what he describes as "active interaction with problems, exploration of the environment and the learning of new skills" (Bloom, 1964).

The importance of environmental stimulation may be clearly seen in the case of children suffering from mild mental retardation. Known organic causes account for only a small percentage of retardation. As few as 20 to 25 percent of the total retarded population suffer from medical abnormalities caused by clearcut organic conditions (Garrard and Richmond, 1975). Organic causes are far more common among moderately to severely/profoundedly retarded individuals. Yet most children with mental retardation are categorized as mildly retarded with an etiology of "causes unknown." Because these children often come from deprived backgrounds, they are described as suffering from cultural-familial retardation. Many of their problems spring from psycho-social disadvantage, poverty, inadequate nutrition, family instability, lack of educational opportunity, or an unstimulating infant environment (Winzer, 1990a).

The positive or negative effects of environment can also be seen in studies concerning children labeled as gifted. Certainly, no race, ethnic group or culture holds a monopoly on giftedness. However, the statistical probability of giftedness increases when a child's parents have higher than average intelligence, and provide a better than average home environment. Gifted children are also more likely to have parents of above average income (Winzer, 1990a).

Numerous studies have attempted to identify family characteristics associated with gifted level abilities in children. But although many positive papers on the socioeconomic development of gifts and talents have emerged, contrary evidence exists (e.g., Atkins, 1980; Braken, 1980), raising questions about the generality of such a tendency.

Some studies have emphasized the many favourable qualities of these families, particularly the importance of parental interest in child rearing and strong commitment to the development of the child's talents and abilities (Bloom, 1982, 1985).

Parental attitudes that are encouraging and supportive, but relatively less authoritarian and controlling have been identified as especially desirable (Domino, 1979).

Studies have also found that parents' superior social and educational background was the best correlate of superior intelligence (Fisch et al., 1976; Willerman and Fiedler, 1974). In a Canadian study of gifted kindergarten children, Perks (1984) found that 59.5 percent of the fathers and 50 percent of their mothers had post secondary education. This compared to 30.9 percent of fathers and 27 percent of mothers for non-gifted children. Perks compared the reading material available in the children's homes. She found that 61.9 percent of the families of gifted children had more than 300 books, as compared to 18.4 percent of families of non-gifted children. A similar study in the United States, although not specifically concerned with children identified as gifted, made similar findings. Garber and Ware (1970) studied the homes of 133 children who were mostly from white, lower socioeconomic status homes. A correlation of .43 was found between the quality of the home environment and the IQ of the child. Important home factors were the number of books and other learning materials in the home; the amount of reward and recognition received from the parents for academic achievement; and the parents' expectations regarding their children's academic achievement.

More highly educated parents at higher socioeconomic levels appear more likely to produce gifted children and to provide them with enriching environments. However, it must also be taken into account that, in a home, it is relevant knowledge and experience, not financial resources, that seem to be the key to the quality of the environment provided (e.g., Freeberg and Payne, 1976; Gottfried, 1984; Hess, 1970; Hess and McDevitt, 1984). Parents can provide a stimulating environment and interact with their children frequently and for extended periods in ways that are likely to stimulate thinking (Brophy, 1970; Hess, 1970; Hess and McDevitt, 1984). Children's cognitive development depends more on the stimulation, especially the modeling the parents provide, than on the mere presence of material possessions.

## THE QUESTION OF GENDER

Male/female differences did not become a widely used variable in psychological research until the mid-1960s (Jacklin, 1989). As far as intelligence goes, the question of whether differences truly exist between males and females is confounded by such things as cultural values, social roles, sex roles and sex typing, teacher attitudes, and teacher expectations.

Nearly twenty years ago, Maccoby and Jacklin (1974) reported well-documented sex differences in school-aged children. These studies and others found the following:

• Girls surpassed boys in verbal ability. Girls learn to talk and to use sentences earlier than do boys. They also use a greater variety of words, speak more clearly, read earlier, and do consistently better in tests of spelling and grammar (Maccoby, 1966; Sherman, 1978). However, results were not as consistent in demonstrating female superiority in the areas of verbal reasoning and comprehension (Tyler, 1965).

- Boys showed better performance on visual and spatial tasks.

- Boys were superior in mathematics performance. No important gender differences in this area are evident during the preschool years; by the end of elementary school, however, males began to excel in mathematical reasoning. The gap between female and male performance continued to increase throughout high school and college and into adulthood (Fennema, 1973; Maccoby, 1966).

Even so, Jacklin and Maccoby (1974) felt that, on all the studies of sex differences, "the yield was thin" (p. 513). There were very few attributes on which the average values for the two sexes differed consistently (Maccoby, 1990). Hyde (1981) found the differences on verbal, spatial and mathematical ability to be statistically significant but rather small in size.

From infancy through the preschool years, most current studies find few differences between boys and girls in mental and motor development generally or in specific ability. When any differences are noted, they usually favor girls but are quite small. During the school years and beyond, psychologists find no differences in general intelligence on the standard measures although these tests have been designed to eliminate sex differences (Good and Brophy, 1986).

Some differences are found, howevever, in school performance. Girls tend to outperform boys academically during the first four years of elementary school (Gibson, 1978). Later, although their behaviour tends to be rated as better, the achievement of girls relative to boys generally drops.

## Verbal ability

Young girls, on the average, consistently outperform boys on a variety of verbal performance and reading measures (Johnson, 1976; Maccoby and Jacklin, 1974). The sex differences on verbal skills have been statistically significant, but somewhat small, leading some critics to suggest that the sex differences found in the verbal domains have cultural rather than biological causes. Hyde (1981) estimated that only about one percent of the variation in verbal ability could be accounted for by genetic differences in gender. Boocock (1980) reported no gender differences on verbal measures.

Further, earlier studies that showed differences in verbal ability (Maccoby and Jacklin, 1974) are contradicted by current research (see Hyde and Lynn, 1988 a, b) that does not find these differences. In their comparison of verbal ability scores in girls and boys, Hyde and Lynn (1988a) found that the differences between the sexes had been reduced across the last decades. Similar decreases in gender differences over the last two decades have been shown in a variety of other intellectual abilities.

## Reading ability

Another difference that had been encountered was that girls were better readers than boys. In addition, boys are more likely to suffer severe reading problems than girls. Boys with learning disabilities outnumber girls by about four to one (MacGregor, Rosenbaum, and Skoutajan, 1982) and reading disabilities are endemic in the learning disabled population, affecting at least 85 percent of students (Winzer, 1989).

A number of theories have been forwarded that attempt to explain the reading differences observed in boys and girls. These include such arguments as:

- girls mature earlier than boys and therefore are better prepared to learn to read;

- the content of textbooks for beginning readers is of more interest to girls than to boys;

- girls relate better to female teachers and are, in return, treated better, so boys develop an aversion to school;

- boys, in building their schemata for sex-typed behaviours, categorize reading as an activity for girls (Gibson and Chandler, 1978).

Carol Dwyer (1974) examined these four theories and concluded that the first three did not stand up. But she found evidence, consistent with the Jackson and Maccoby position, to support the fourth explanation. She concluded that there was little doubt that reading is generally seen as a feminine activity and that such a classification has the effect of lessening the motivation of boys to excel in reading, probably since there are very strong taboos against males participating in any part of the feminine role (Gibson and Chandler, 1978).

Some authors (Pavlidis and Miles, 1981) view boys as more disposed than girls to reading problems. They see four predisposing factors—less developed right hemisphere functions; greater specialization of right hemisphere spatial skills; a lesser degree of left hemisphere dominance; and slower maturation, despite earlier lateralization of functions.

Other data contradict the argument that boys cannot read as well as girls. Research shows that boys in some cultures do show superior reading ability. Comparing fourth and sixth grade students in Germany and the United States, Preston (1962) found that German boys outperformed girls in both reading comprehension and speed. Johnson's (1972, 1976) study of second, fourth, and sixth grader's reading performance in four countries supports Preston's findings. In England and Nigeria, boys significantly outscored girls, with the reverse occurring in Canada and the United States. Johnson (1976) was lead to conclude that "sex differences in reading must be attributed primarily to cultural rather than to physiological determinants" (p. 13).

Asher and Markell (1974) found that when fifth grade boys read a story drawn from a high interest area, they read as well as fifth grade girls (who also read high interest material). In contrast, boys were significantly poorer readers of low interest material than were girls. Whether reading content was of high or low interest, girls read well. Stanchfield (1973) also reported that a reading series with content of high interest for first grade boys eliminated reading differences between boys and girls.

## Math ability

In the early 1980s, Benbow and Stanley (1980, 1982, 1983) published a series of articles that described scores on standardized tests of mathematics ability of bright boys and girls. In every study, the boys scored higher than the girls, which led Benbow and Stanley (1980) to conclude that the differences are biological in nature.

More recent studies have suggested that sex role standards and career orientations are salient factors (Fennema, 1981). Other variables unrelated to innate intelligence also seem to intervene. Math differences are influenced by subtle pressures such as:

- degree of math anxiety;

- lower self-estimates of ability in math among females than males (Brush, 1980; Fennema and Sherman, 1978; Sherman, 1980); (Even among the math precocious, female adolescents report less interest in math than do males [Fox and Denham, 1974]).

- parental beliefs about sexual stereotypes;

- the preconceieved value of math to the student;

- the mother's belief concerning the difficulty of math (Eccles and Jacobs, 1986);

- as soon as math courses become optional, many girls avoid them.

When researchers (Eccles, Adler, and Kaczala, 1982; Eccles et al., 1983; Eccles and Jacobs, 1986; Eccles, Kaczala, and Meece, 1982) collected a large data base on math course taking and achievement in seventh and ninth graders they found math anxiety and the perceived value of math to account for the major portion of sex differences in achievement. As with verbal ability, Hyde (1981) again estimated that gender differences in math aptitude could account for only one percent of the variation seen in the population. Further, there is mounting evidence that the differences between boys and girls in math achievement decrease substantially or disappear altogether when the actual number of courses taken by each student is considered (Fennema and Sherman, 1978; Pallas and Alexander, 1983).

## Spatial ability

Another area identified by Maccoby and Jacklin (1974) was spatial ability. Some researchers feel that in this area males have a clear superiority. Of all gender differences found in the cognitive domain, the disparity in spatial task performance appears to have the most likelihood for a genetic component (Fennema, 1981). Boocock (1980) writes that, "Biological research indicates that spatial ability is highly heritable, transmitted via chromosomal combinations that are more common in males than females." However, the magnitude of the gender differences is small and accounts for no more than five percent of the variation (Hyde, 1981).

Other researchers have examined the relationship between math, science, and spatial ability (Linn and Petersen, 1985). They examined the nature and magnitude of age and gender differences in these three domains. After an extensive analysis, they concluded that there is no consistent pattern of gender differences either between or within these ability areas (Jacklin, 1989).

Signorella and Jamison (1986) found that people who described themselves as being more masculine and/or less feminine tended to do better on a set of spatial and math tasks. Other researchers have found girls better on computational and logical abstract problems, boys better on story problems and spatial relation problems (Pattison and Grieve, 1984).

## School performance

In elementary school, girls tend to outstrip boys academically. However, as Brophy and Good (1986) point out, the achievement of girls progressively falls behind that of boys. They surmise that the main reason for this is the gradual change in the relationship between gender role and student role. As boys get older and move into high school, the conflict that once existed between the student role and the male sex role disappears,  and achievement in school becomes perceived as a stepping stone toward later achievement. An occupation becomes a basic part of the sex role expectation. Do, however, remember the work of Marcia and his colleagues (1980) here. Leanings toward an occupation are part of the development of identity and not all high school students have reached this stage.

For girls, Brophy and Good (1986) argue that the harmony between the student role and the sex role that exists when young girls are in the first few grades of elementary school gradually lessens. The smaller proportion of girls who achieve highly in school may arise from many bases. Winzer (1990a) points out that barriers may come from protection of feminine self-image (Meece et al., 1982), non-assertiveness (Hollinger and Fleming, 1984), fear of success (Lavach and Lanier, 1975), conflicts arising from achievement versus self-concept (Fox, 1977) or fear of loss of social acceptance (Casserly, 1979). Conflicts may also stem from achievement, sex role identity and social acceptance. Girls may find it difficult to reconcile their academic interests with the areas of excellence traditionally seen by society as sex role appropriate for women (Schwartz, 1980). As high achievers, girls are expected to be active, assertive, and exploratory; as females, they are encouraged to be nurturant, passive and dependent (Handel, 1983).

Much of the research in this area has centred on gifted girls. In school, more males than females are considered gifted and talented. During early adolescence, the age when sex roles are heavily reinforced by parents and peers (Handel, 1983), girls generally begin to encounter problems that obscure their achievement or giftedness (Dishart, 1981). In our society, it is considered neither proper nor advantageous for girls to be too superior. Girls are encouraged to become musicians or artists, rather than physicists or engineers. Many adolescent girls have little opportunity to explore their true interests. They are placed under more pressure to conform, and are less likely than males to find learning opportunities with a supportive teacher (Dishart, 1981).

## Sex typing in the schools

When we discussed personality development in Chapter 4, we briefly looked at the development of sex roles, gender identity, and sex typing. We stressed that, as a learning process, socialization starts well before an infant is a year old and, in many ways, continues throughout the course of a lifetime. One of the important facets of socialization for a child, initially gained from the parents, is the notion of what it is to be a boy or a girl.

All cultures define ways in which men and women are expected to behave. Definitions of sex appropriate behaviour change from culture to culture and from era to era. Ours have changed radically in the past 50 years. While overt female discrimination in Canada has declined, it has not necessarily been accompanied by a decline in underlying prejudice (Bechtold, Naccarato and Zanna, 1986) or in the options available to women.

There still remain clear patterns of occupational segregation in Canada. Once in careers, men achieve high status and recognition more frequently than women of the same age by an overwhelming margin. The 1970 Royal Commission on the Status of Women found in Alberta that "a man was 7.5 times more likely to become a principal, although he was only 2.5 times as likely to have higher qualifications than a woman" (Nixon, 1989). Twenty years later, few women hold positions of power and influence in education. Ways of thinking are still stuck in old grooves. Visualize an educational leader, says Porat (1989) and chances are that your vision is a male. In another field, Alcock, Carment, and Sadava (1988) report that 73 percent of Canadian bank employees are women. However, the number of executives with the rank of vice-president or higher at Canada's "big five" banks is 750—of which fewer than 12, or less than two percent, are women.

Until quite recently in Canada, females were more likely than males to finish high school and males predominated post-secondary institutions (Marsden and Harvey, 1971). There was a drastic increase in the overall number of female

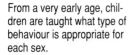

From a very early age, children are taught what type of behaviour is appropriate for each sex.

**Sex-role stereotype:** the belief that an individual should act in certain ways because of sex.

degree holders between 1971 and 1981, particularly during the period 1976 to 1981. By 1981, 50 percent of all university undergraduates and 50 percent of all those earning degrees were female (Looker and McNutt, 1989).

Today, more women are entering such non-traditional professions as chemistry, engineering, dentistry, and physics, but the numbers are still very small. Even when female students are encouraged to enter the fields of their choice, they are often rewarded inappropriately for their performance (Winzer, 1990a). They are assessed by irrelevant criteria, and rewarded with affection rather than promotion (Hallahan and Kauffman, 1986). A woman's success is generally measured as wife and mother, not as a professional. If she succeeds in all three roles, critics often insist that she is doing a poor job in one of them. She may be accused of using sexual favours to raise her professional status, or described as an exception to the rule (Schwartz, 1980).

There is no conclusive evidence that the disparity in school achievement and occupational status is the result of biological differences. Available research points far more clearly to social and cultural expectations as an explanation for the disproportionate number of males who achieve highly in and out of school (Callahan, 1981).

Beliefs in what it means to be male or female are strongly influenced by the culture, especially parents and the schools. We all learn very early what it means to be male or female through the actions of our parents in the first years of our lives. Teachers and parents are known to reinforce quiet, gentle, nonaggressive, noncompetitive, feminine behaviour among girls. They criticize boys for the same behaviour as early as the preschool years (Fagot, 1977).

Elementary school teachers have long been known to anticipate and to perceive girls as more obedient, cooperative and better socialized than boys (Wickman, 1928). Female teachers often tend to see the bahaviour of girls as closer to that of the ideal student. Male teachers, on the other hand, do not. Research by Grant (1984) on the quality of interactions that young girls share with their teachers suggests that teachers socialize girls to be responsible and conforming rather than competent or creative.

Girls are usually less assertive than boys. In seeking approval, girls are much more likely than boys to use withdrawal and other avoidance-oriented strategies rather than more direct techniques (Lahaderne and Jackson, 1970). All teachers tend to discipline boys more harshly but to give more attention to boys than to girls (Gibson, 1978) so that boys have most of the interaction with the teacher and make most of the contributions to discussions. At the fifth grade level, for example, Torrance (1961) found that girls initiated as many ideas as boys, but chose to explain fewer principles.

**Sex-role stereotypes** are the belief that an individual should act in certain ways because of sex. Sex-role stereotyping inhibits cognitive and emotional growth in boys and girls by establishing artificial boundaries. Stereotypes set unnecessary limits and cast stones at the concept of equal educational opportunity (Kirschenbaum, 1980). The goal of nonsexist education should be to help each child to develop an overall identity as a person with an integrated value system, unrestricted in his or her thinking by stereotyped sex roles (Kirschenbaum, 1980). Teachers need to be more sensitive to subtle but important differences in socialization that can affect the extent to which a student is

**Cognitive styles:**
tendencies to respond to a variety of intellectual tasks and problems in a particular fashion.

**Learning style:**
the way individuals respond to the world around them.

interested in science or mathematics as a career (Brophy and Good, 1986). Teachers and school systems need to pay attention to the ways the schools and the workplace approve, develop and channel the skills and abilities of men and women instead of assuming a meritocratic process.

# COGNITIVE AND LEARNING STYLES

As we saw in Chapter 4, children come into the world equipped with certain temperamental characteristics. While these characteristics are prone to modification by the environment, they do seem to persist, to a greater or lesser extent, in children. These may translate into cognitive styles—essentially, the way children process, retain, and retrieve information.

Children differ in the speed at which they process and respond to information. Individual differences in the way children organize what they learn, categorize concepts, and employ strategies to deal with problem solving are called cognitive styles (Gibson, 1978). Because cognitive styles are indicative of different learning approaches, they are sometimes referred to as learning styles. However, there are differences. Cognitive style has to do with preferred ways for organizing and processing information; it refers to the way the brain processes information. More specifically, cognitive styles are tendencies to respond to a variety of intellectual tasks and problems in a particular fashion. The term has been used most frequently to denote consistencies in individual modes of functioning in various situations.

Learning style refers to the way individuals respond to the world around them (Dunn, 1981). The term learning style is used in different ways. It may refer to:

• the educational conditions under which a student learns most effectively;

• the instructional approaches that a student prefers; or

• environmental elements such as heat and lighting.

The notion of cognitive style is fairly new. It grew out of research on how individuals perceive and organize information from the world around them (Woolfolk, 1990). Research suggests that individuals differ in the way they approach experimental tasks but that these variations do not reflect levels of intelligence, or patterns of special abilities (Tyler, 1974), or overall achievement differences (Good and Brophy, 1986). Instead, they have to do with preferred ways that different individuals have for processing and organizing information and for responding to environmental stimuli (Shuell, 1981 a, b) for achievement in various subjects.

However, it is very difficult to separate intelligence and cognitive style—the way an individual handles problems—from emotions, temperament, and personality. In fact, cognitive styles are often described as falling on the borderline between mental abilities and personality traits (Schuell, 1981a) because they are styles of thinking and these are probably influenced by and in turn influence cognitive abilities. These preferred ways of dealing with the world also affect social relationships and personal qualities (Woolfolk, 1990).

It is not clear what influences the early development of cognitive styles. Genetic factors may play a role, but the role of heredity in producing differences in cognitive functioning and social behaviour is still debated (Brooks-Gunn and Matthews, 1979; Wittig and Peterson, 1979). After an exhaustive review, Maccoby and Jacklin (1974) concluded that all behavioural differences other than those involving aggression, probably result from socialization factors rather than heredity.

Psychologists agree that cognitive styles are shaped by early life experiences. One study (Swan and Stavros, 1973) examined the relationship between cognitive stlyes and the child-rearing practices used by parents. The researchers found that parents who tended to be more helpful and encouraging and who provided a great deal of pleasant and mutually satisfying verbal interactions during the preschool years were those most likely to have children who entered school with cognitive stlyes most conducive to academic success.

School achievement can be viewed as a function of the interaction between cognitive style and learning environment (McCall, 1983). Various temperaments are differentially associated with achievement patterns (Lerner and Lerner, 1983).

A match between a child's temperament and the demands of the educational setting appear to be critical for school success. Lerner et al. (1982) examined the relationship between the temperaments of eighth graders and the teachers' perceptions of their abilities and school adjustment. The researchers found that the better a student's temperament fitted the teacher's pedagogical style, the greater was the likelihood of receiving a positive teacher rating.

Cognitive styles most conducive to learning seem to be those problem solving methods that allow children to listen carefully before making use of information presented to them, to try new approaches to problems when old ones do not work, and to take risks leading to greater intellectual performance and classroom success (Swan and Stavros, 1973).

## Impulsive and reflective learners

One dimension of cognitive style is cognitive tempo or degree of reflectivity or impulsivity. As far as school learning goes, there appear to be differences in the way impulsive and reflective children process, store, and use information. When cognitive tempo was first described (Kagan et al., 1964) the emphasis was on the speed of response and rather than other qualitative characteristics that might affect accuracy. Today, it has become clear that other aspects besides speed must also be considered.

Very generally, impulsive children may be seen as quick and inaccurate and reflective children slow and accurate (Zelniker and Jeffrey, 1976). Impulsive children may have poorly developed memories and greater difficulty transferring strategies from one situation to another (Borkowski, Peck, and Reid, 1983). Kagan (1971) indicates that impulsive children get bored easily although the loss of interest does not result from rapid processing of all available information but from superficial processing and the failure to impose a plan of action.

Reflective children take in information more systematically (Wright and Vliestra, 1977). Reflective children make fewer errors, take longer to solve problems, persist at tasks for relatively long periods, and hold high standards for individual performance. Reflective children perform better on tasks requiring anaylsis of details while impulsive children are more likely to do better on tasks requiring global interpretation, although this does not necessarily mean that either group will do better in school (Zelniker and Jeffrey, 1976). Reflective children seem more afraid of making mistakes and less likely to try. They seem to be analytical and more likely to note details when exposed to a complex stimulus. On the other hand, impulsive children are more thematic or holistic and tend to respond to a pattern as a whole.

One study (Borkowski, Peck, and Reid, 1983) classified a group of second and third graders as having either impulsive or reflective cognitive styles. They found that both groups of children learned problem solving strategies equally well. However, reflective children tended to show better transfer of skills and also showed better metamemory skills (i.e., they used memorization processes, such as rehearsal and subvocalization, more effectively). In a similar study, Zelniker and Jeffrey (1976) examined problem solving stlyes in fourth grade children. Students were classified as either impulsive or reflective as measured by the Matching Familiar Figures Test (Kagan, 1965). The reflective group performed better on tasks requiring attention to detail, whereas impulsive children did better on tasks demanding a holistic analysis. This tends to confirm Kagan's (1964) findings that reflective children are more likely to be analytical and impulsive children more thematic or holistic.

The most common measure for assessing impulsivity-reflectivlity styles is the Matching Familiar Figures Test (Kagan, 1965). Items on this test have children, for example, find the identical match to one picture from among a group of similar pictures. Impulsive children tend to select the first match that looks right without scanning all the examples and comparing each with the given figure.

Buss and Plomin (1975) point out that very active persons are more likely to be impulsive. However, not everyone who works quickly is impulsive. Some people are simply bright and quick to understand. These individuals are called fast-accurate. Those who are slow and make many errors are called slow-inaccurate.

Impulsive and reflective cognitive styles are not related to intelligence within the normal range (Woolfolk, 1990). Nevertheless, conceptual tempo is important to education because it is related to early reading progress (Kagan and Kagan, 1970) and to performance on other tasks commonly encountered in school (Good and Brophy, 1986).

Reflective children are more careful in analyzing solutions to problems (Mitchell and Ault, 1979), show better school performance (Loper and Hallahan, 1980), and are less likely to fail in the early grades (Messer, 1970). In contrast, teachers rate impulsive students as less attentive and more hyperactive than reflective children (Ault, Crawford, and Jeffrey, 1972). They are also seen as less task-oriented and less considerate. Teachers rate boys as more impulsive and distractible (McKinney, 1975).

As children grow, they generally become more reflective. For school-age children, being reflective does seem to improve performance on school tasks such as reading (Messer, 1976). Students can learn to be more reflective if they are taught specific strategies. Self-instruction has proven successful where students learn to remind themselves to proceed slowly and carefully.

**Figure 6-3**
Example of Matching
Figures Test

## Field dependence and field independence

**Field dependence:**
a global perceptual style; field dependent people tend to perceive a pattern as a whole and have difficulty focussing on one aspect of a situation or analyzing a pattern with different parts.

**Field independence:**
an analytic perceptual style; field independent people are more likely to perceive separate parts as a total pattern and be able to analyze a pattern according to its components.

Another type of cognitive style is marked by **field dependence** or **field independence** according to the manner in which individuals perceive things. This is also known as global versus analytic perceptual style.

Field-independent individuals are able to make finer discriminations than others in what they see; they can isolate important elements from the surroundings or background. These people have good figure-ground perception. Field-dependent people tend to perceive a pattern as a whole. They have difficulty in focusing on one aspect of a situation or analyzing a pattern with different parts. Field-independent people are more likely to perceive separate parts as a total pattern and be able to analyze a pattern according to its components (Wittrock, 1978).

Field dependence or independence is shown in a remarkable variety of situations. It is not related to IQ but is a true difference in perceptual style. It affects

235

**Creativity:**
capacity to restructure the world in unusual or useful conceptual terms; results in new, ususual, original, independent or innovative ways of thinking about and dealing with problems and leads in directions not predicted prior to the thinking.

**Divergent thinking:**
a type of thinking in which many possible answers for a given problem are imagined.

students' preferences for and responses to different kinds of learning content and different types of teaching methods.

Individuals who are field independent are better at analyzing complex material and organizing it to solve problems. Science and mathematics may be their stronger subjects and they often work well alone (Shuell, 1981a, 1981b).

People who are field dependent tend to be more oriented toward people and social relationships, whereas field independent individuals are more likely to be task-oriented.

Field independent learners are more impersonal in their orientation; they tend to be more individualistic, competitive, sensitive to intrinsic motivational factors, and more attentive to significant details (Dixon, 1977).  In contrast, field dependent people are superior in remembering social information such as conversations or interpersonal interactions. Dixon (1977) reported that field dependent learners are more attentive to such cues as body language, facial expressions, and eye contact. In school, field dependent children are often better at subjects such as history, literature, and the social sciences and they may work better in groups.

Field independent children tend to achieve better in school (Vaidya and Chansky, 1980). This was confirmed in a study (Blackman and Goldstein, 1982) that found that field independent and reflective cognitive stlyes were associated with better school performance. Some studies show that boys tend to be more field independent than girls (Woolfolk, 1990).

As children grow older, they generally become more field independent, at least until the middle teenage years. Then development levels off until later adult life when there is a tendency to become more field dependent (Woolfolk, 1990).

Teachers have their own cognitive and learning styles which affect their approaches to teaching. Field-dependent teachers often have a more interpersonal style of teaching and they may be less critical of wrong answers. Field-independent teachers may prefer to organize the classroom and materials themselves with less input from the students. They may also focus more on wrong answers (Woolfolk, 1990). A relative emphasis on field independence is likely among math, science, and industrial arts teachers as compared to social studies, humanities, or general elementary school teachers (Good and Brophy, 1986).

## Creativity

Since creativity is a complex phenonmen, it is not surprising that its definitions are many and varied. Almost all definitions, however, include the elements of the quality of novelty or unusualness. Cole and Sarnoff (1980) refer to creativity as "activities and products invented in the interest of solving a problem" (p. 6). Hence, creativity refers to the process of bringing unusual and unexpected responses to bear on given situations. It is a capacity to restructure the world in unusual or useful conceptual terms and results in new, unusual, original, independent, or innovative ways of thinking about and dealing with problems.

Other qualities related to creativity include originality, divergent thinking, and fluency and flexibility. Divergent thinking is a type of thinking in which many possible answers for a given problem are imagined. It opens up novel ways of conceiving the world, identifies new problems, and leads in directions not predicted prior to the thinking. Divergent thinking is the basis of creative

**Convergent thinking:**
a type of thinking that focuses on one right answer, or toward a uniquely determined answer.

problem solving and is in some ways the opposite of convergent thinking, which is focusing on coming up with one right answer. Fluency is the ability to express meaning through multiple ideas and concepts. Flexibility implies shifts in thinking from one category to another; it is the ability to change one's mind set, to look for alternate solutions when the obvious answers are wrong.

Some psychologists see creativity as a personal quality or trait. When Lewis Terman, for example, identified his gifted population for his longitudinal study, he was uninterested in measures of creativity, believing that IQ alone determined giftedness (Winzer, 1990b). In contrast to Terman, many of today's psychologists suggest that creativity is not simply a personality trait but is a skill or process that produces a "creative product" such as an invention or work of art. Nevertheless, creativity is not an either/or proposition. Like intelligence and other human characteristics, it is best viewed along a continuum.

Creativity may very well be an innate trait that can be stimulated or quashed. Creativity seems generally to decrease as children get older, a tendency that may be accounted for by both age and culture. The drop in creativity experienced by most children at about fourth grade level is well documented by Torrance (1962) and others. Torrance (1961) observed that by third grade, girls are conditioned to accept the status quo better than boys and score lower on measures of creativity. Prince (1967) found that only ten percent of seven year olds were as creative as five year olds and only two percent of 45 year olds were highly creative.

As well, creativity tends to occur in spurts. During the first three years of school, most children's creativity increases, perhaps because teachers in these grades allow much freedom of expression. After grade three, a sharp drop in creativity occurs, followed by a gradual decrease during the remaining elementary and middle school years (Bernard, 1973). Declining creativity, then, may be linked to the educational system. It may occur when teachers discourage creativity because it disrupts lesson plans. Also, school tests tend to measure rote learning rather than new and innovative types of responses, while social stereotypes are fostered by our society and may lead to rigid non-creativity (Bernard, 1973). Gowan (1980) suggests that the drop in creativity is due to the extinction of right hemisphere imagery caused by overteaching of the left hemisphere functions of reading, writing and arithmetic and the lessening or lack of right hemisphere stimulation procedures.

It appears that at least average intelligence is required to be creative but, beyond this, creativity and IQ are not related (Woolfolk, 1990). Keep in mind though that children who are extremely competent convergent thinkers are likely to be nominated by teachers as gifted; these children are likely to do well in school although they are typically not very innovative (Terman and Oden, 1959). The child who is a creative, divergent thinker is more likely to be overlooked by teachers in nomination procedures (Winzer, 1990a).

## BIRTH ORDER

The number, sex, spacing, and birth order of children can influence children's interactions with each other and affect each child's development. While findings on birth order tend to be equivocal, birth order and family size have been shown to be associated with children's intellectual achievement, psychosocial adjustment, and physical growth (Mednick, Baker, and Hocevan, 1985).

The first-born child enjoys a special position in the family. Even though it may be only for a very short time, eldest children bask in the complete and undivided attention of their parents without pressure to share the parents or their possessions with anyone else.

Children who were born early in the birth order tend to have higher IQs than children born later (Hilgard, Atkinson, and Atkinson, 1979) and first-borns seem to be have a greater need to achieve (Sampson, 1962). Studies have shown that first-borns score higher on general achievement tests than later borns and are more likely to score higher on IQ tests. They receive good grades in college, and are more likely to be cited in Who's Who (Hilgard, Atkinson, and Atkinson, 1979). Poole and Kuhn (1973) found that first borns were overrepresented among the graduates of British universities.

Lest it be thought that first borns have all the advantages, there are negative notes. Although some first borns are overprotected and indulged by their parents, many report harsher treatment than their siblings who seem to receive more consideration and leniency as the parents mellow with age and experience (Harris, 1986). Parents often have higher expectations for their first-borns than for later children; among these is often the expectation that they will be more responsible for their siblings (Falbo, 1981).

First-borns tend to be more adult-oriented, more self-controlling, more conforming, more anxious, more fearful of failure, more studious, and more passive than later borns (Hetherington and Parke, 1979). They seem to be more apprehensive about pain and may be less able to cope with some anxiety-producing situations than later borns. There is also some evidence that first-borns are more often referred for treatment for psychiatric problems than are individuals of other birth order positions (Lahey et al., 1980; Schrader and Leventhal, 1979). First-born males are more likely than later borns to exhibit behaviour disorders and to be rated by their teachers as anxious and aggressive toward their peers (Lahey et al., 1980).

The circumstances of an only child are similar to those of a first-born except that the only child never has to adapt to other siblings and never suffers from sibling rivalry. The stereotype of the lonely only child is not confirmed by the research (Falbo, 1977). There is little evidence that only children are selfish, egotistical, self-centred, and spoiled. Only children seem to have all the advantages of first-borns. In fact, as a group they tend to be more secure, better adjusted socially, and are higher achievers than children with siblings, including first-borns (Polit, Nuttall, and Nuttall, 1980) even though the IQ scores of only children tend to fall slightly below those of first-borns. This may be because only children do not have the opportunity to consolidate their knowledge by teaching younger siblings (Harris, 1986).

The last born is often the indulged baby of the family and seems to have all the advantages of first-borns and few of the problems (Woolfolk, 1990). There are siblings to influence the last born child and the parents probably now feel very secure in their child-rearing skills. Last borns tend to be high achievers, popular, and more optimistic, secure and confident than first borns (Hetherington and Parke, 1979).

Research is not as clear for middle children. These children seem to be extroverted and pleasure-seeking but they are not terribly effective or successful in their social encounters (Harris, 1986). Studies also indicate that middle children are less achievement-oriented and have shorter attention spans than do firstborns.

Later borns are more likely to be diagnosed as aggressive or hyperactive (Harris, 1986). Research has consistently reported children in middle positions, especially next-to-last children, to manifest a higher incidence of antisocial or acting out behaviour as compared with first-borns or last born children.

Aggression is of particular concern to teachers, parents and the community. some aspects of aggression are discussed in Box 6-4.

---

### Box 6-4 **Aggression**

Aggressive behaviour is behaviour that is intended to hurt another, either physically or verbally, or intended to injure property. Among all human emotions, aggression is probably the most studied. For one thing, it brings the conflict between psychoanalytic and social learning theories to head. Freud held that aggression was a drive; in contrast, social learning theorists see aggression as particularly sensitive to reinforcement and hold that it is learned through modeling.

Although aggressive behaviour in moderation is a useful survival tool, it becomes a problem when it is prolonged, frequent, and severe. Psychologists have distinguished two major types of aggression, hostile and instrumental (Feshbach, 1970). Hostile aggression seems to occur for its own sake and is its own goal. The bully who steals from a smaller child or calls the child names is exhibiting hostile aggression. Rewards for hostile aggression often come from other children or it may come through vicarious means, such as identification with a bullying parent. Instrumental aggression is directed toward achievement of a nonagressive goal. A child or adolescent may want something another student has and

first try a series of nonagressive tactics—such as asking or offering to trade—to attain the object. Finally, he or she resorts to aggression—grabbing, punching, and using verbal abuse or other antisocial behaviours. If the child obtains the object then the reward increases the probability that instrumental aggression will occur again.

The knowledge that other people can serve as obstacles that block one's own intended course of action probably comes very early, and between the ages of one and two years this knowledge seems to be extended (Maccoby, 1980). The process of converting at least some anger into aggression also seems to involve several cognitive achievements—specifically, the knowledge that others can feel distress and that one's own actions can cause distress (Maccoby, 1980).

As the child matures, there seems to be a gradual shift from undirected anger to true aggression: that is, aggression focused on a specific person (Maccoby, 1980). As well, the circumstances that provoke anger change with age. In the second and third year, as children find that their parents expect more of them, anger occurs most commonly over parental efforts to establish physical routines such as toilet training and going to bed (Maccoby, 1980). Before the age of three, children usually express their anger through undirected temper tantrums, hitting and angry cries.

After age three, when many children have their first social encounters, disputes with playmates rather than their parents are the primary cause of angry outbursts (Harris, 1986). Techniques for controlling others by aggressive means are rapidly acquired (Maccoby, 1980).

Children who are four years old and older know a variety of means to hurt others. Between the ages of three and five, children become more retaliatory and begin to express their anger verbally by scolding, insulting or threatening others (Harris, 1986).

Children are more likely to be aggressive if they have opportunities to practise aggression, especially if no unpleasant consequences follow. Children learn aggression in many ways—by observing parents, siblings, friends, and characters from television and films. The early part of life is a particularly critical time for learning about aggression (Olweus, 1972). Highly aggressive three year olds are likely to become aggressive five year olds (Emmerich, 1966). Children's levels of verbal and physical aggression at ages six through 12 are fairly good predictors of their tendency to threaten, insult, tease, and compete with peers at ages ten to 14 (Kagan and Moss, 1962; Olweus, 1979).

Parents often provide abundant opportunities for children to develop conflicting feelings about the expression of aggression. There is a long history of empirical research that has identified family variables as consistent factors for the early forms of antisocial behaviour and for later forms of delinquency. There is a high degree of intergenerational similarity for antisocial behaviour (Farrington, 1987) and, as a predictor of an antisocial adult personality, having an antiso-

cial parent places the child at significant risk for antisocial behaviour; having two antisocial parents puts the child at even greater risk (Robins and Earls, 1985). In other words, children in aggressive families are more likely to be aggressive and, in turn, their children are likely to be more aggressive (Huessman and Eron, 1983). Families of antisocial children are characterized by harsh discipline, little parental involvement with the child, and poor monitoring and supervision of the child's activities (Patterson, De Baryshe and Ramsey, 1989).

There are a number of variables related to aggression. One of the most clear is the relationship between aggression and physical punishment. Here a number of factors seem to be implicated:

- physical punishment is frustrating and leads to hostility and aggression;

- parental use of physical punishment provides both a model and a partial sanctioning of aggressive responses;

- hostile and punitive parents may reinforce a child's aggressive behaviour toward others (Alcock, Carment, and Sadava, 1988).

The problems created by the behaviour of aggressive children, for themselves and for those in their environments, should not be underestimated. Children with excessive feelings of aggression and defiance develop intense and far-ranging interpersonal problems (see Chapter 7). In school, aggressive students are perceived to be low achievers. Teachers complain that aggressive students do not cooperate with classroom routines or pay attention to instruction, and they usually do poorly in their academic work (Patterson, 1976). Low-achieving students are at risk in school. In one study (Phipps, 1982), 82 percent of the boys referred for special education were referred primarily because of their behaviour.

**Socio-economic status:** a statistic compiled from indices such as type of occupation, years of education, size of income, quality of housing, and desirability of neighbourhood.

**Social class:** class distinction defined in a personal way that expresses local prestige and respectability.

# FAMILY SIZE

As family size increases, children have to share parental attention and family and financial resources with a larger number of people. While the literature on psychosocial functioning and family size also tends to be inconsistent, Terhune (1974) noted that overall the data suggest that only children, first-borns and in general all children from small sibling families reflect a high degree of vitality, extroversion, and independence. But the influence of increasing family size is seen as having a decreasingly depressing effect on the IQ score range, with an attendant progressive disadvantage for the youngest in comparison with the oldest in large families (Belmont, Stein, and Wittes, 1976; Eysenck and Cookson, 1970).

# SOCIOECONOMIC STATUS

The term "at risk" has been used to describe a number of different categories of children. It refers to children who are physically, medically, and psychologically in danger of failing to thrive. It also refers to those who are affected by adverse economic, environmental, and geographic factors. Where a child comes from and where a child goes at the end of the school day is a crucial variable in that child's development and academic and social progress. Conditions of dire poverty may breed lack of interest in education, lowered motivation, poor grades, and early dropping out of school. Worse, a severe lack of financial resources may translate to malnutrition, neglect, and hopelessness. The only common denominator for childen of poverty is that they are brought up under desperate conditions beyond their control—and equal opportunity seems a cruel hoax (Reed and Saulter, 1990).

The terms "socioeconomic status" (SES) and "social class" are often used interchangeably although they are defined and measured differently. SES is a statistic compiled from indices such as type of occupation, years of education, size of income, quality of housing and desirability of neighbourhood. Social class is defined in a more personal way that expresses local prestige and repectability (Good and Brophy, 1986).

When we talk about socioeconomic status as related to students and their schooling, the term, says Brophy (1986) is a "proxy" for a complex of correlated cognitive and affective differences between subgroups of students. The cognitive differences involve IQ, ability, or achievement levels. This is because what occurs in schools reflects and strengthens the process of social ranking. Although children may start out in school with similar levels of ability, economically and socially privileged children acquire increasingly higher grades, achievement test scores, and even IQ scores (Oakes, 1985). The ranking continues after school. Given an average IQ, the child from a middle class family is 25 times more likely to end up with a well-paying high-status job than is the child from a working class family (Bowles and McGintis, 1976).

People at the lowest SES levels are often referred to as disadvantaged or culturally disadvantaged. This means that a child, compared to average children, is lacking in many things that would allow him or her to live in today's increasingly industrialized society. Many of these students come from environments that have a restricted use of language and that ultimately hinder growth. Coupled with poor family attitudes, poor motivation, and poor facilities, it is easy to see the formidable problems presented.

Individuals who are disadvantaged are often stereotyped as holding values and attitudes contrary to middle class values. However, the major difference between advantaged and disadvantaged parents is that disadvantaged parents lack the knowledge that would enable them to obtain the things they want (Hess, 1970). Any inhibiting attitudes that are held, however, often result from poor socioeconomic circumstances.

As Good and Brophy (1986) observe, all the variables that make up SES, along with race, ethnicity, political, and social customs, tend to correlate together into clusters (Yando, Seitz, and Zigler, 1979). No single SES variable covers all the others in a simple way. However, the educational level of the parents is probably the most basic in the sense that the other variables lose their power for predicting such things as student achievement once the educational level of the parents is statistically controlled  (Hess, 1970; Stevenson et al., 1978). Parental education level is important to teachers because it is linked to parental interests and attitudes toward education (Laosa, 1982). For children, a high level of parental education correlates with positive attitudes toward education (Laosa, 1982) because parents who are well-educated value education and expect their children to be well-educated. From the educational system, middle class parents demand that children learn responsibility, self-direction and creativity. Lower class parents are more likely to want a "no frills" curriculum stressing the three Rs (Slavin, 1988).

Parents from lower socioeconomic groups may be less involved in their children's education. As well, ethnically diverse parents tend to be less knowledgeable about and involved in their children's educational problems than other parents (Lynch and Stein, 1987). However, a growing body of literature has affirmed that parental participation is an indispensible ingredient in academic excellence (Epstein, 1987). An active parent-school partnership can contribute to the enhancement of educational performance of students as well as the improvement of parenting skills and family life (Cone, Delawyer, and Wolfe, 1985). Research confirms that parents who attend parent-teacher conferences, who set aside time to help their children with homework, who give encouragement, and provide help with particular problems, have children who enjoy school and who score higher on achievement tests than those parents who are uninvolved (Greenberg and Davidson, 1972).

Social class and intelligence have a moderate correlation, about .50 (Howley, 1982). Bornstein (1985) found a correlation between the child's IQ and the quality of the interactions between mother and child, assessed when the child was one year old. Studies (e.g., Hess and Shipman, 1970) have shown that middle-class mothers talk more, give more verbal guidance, help their children understand the course of events, make plans and anticipate consequences, direct their children's attention to the relevant details of a problem, and encourage children to problem solve for themselves (Woolfolk, 1990). Mothers from lower socioeconomic brackets tend to be more strict and to demand more conformity from their children in the preschool years than do middle class mothers (Gibson, 1978), although they provide older children with more freedom.

Disadvantaged children are more likely to underachieve at school. Some educational sociologists see similarities between the problems of deprived children from poor homes and the problems of immigrant children in Canadian cities. De Blassie and Franco (1983) maintain that the academic success of ethnic minority children is heavily influenced by their family's socioeconomic status. Poverty, alienation, and family breakdown create conditions that cause anger, hopelessness, and, finally, crime. Dropouts tend to be more frequent among those groups who are economically disadvantaged.

Students from lower socioeconomic homes are less likely to enter school knowing how to count, to make letters, to cut with scissors, or to name colours. They are less likely to perform as well in school as children who are from middle-class homes (Boocock, 1980; Duncan, Featherman, and Duncan, 1972). Higher SES students show higher average levels on achievement test scores, receive better grades, and stay in school longer than lower SES students (Alwin and Thornton, 1984). Children from lower socioeconomic levels are more likely to be regarded as problems. There is a higher prevalence of aggressive behaviour among lower class children as opposed to those from middle and upper classes (Hallahan and Kauffman, 1986) and a higher proportion of those identified as behaviourally disordered are from minority groups (Rich, 1982).

The effects of SES may be cumulative. Durkin (1966) found that SES was not as influential in early reading achievement as in later achievement. Early reading seemed as much related to the mother's wilingness and ability to involve children with books as it related to SES. Bloom (1964) found no correlation between reading achievement and the father's occupation in grade two; however, by grade eight, the correlation was .50.

Another study (Heyns, 1978) found that students from families of different social backgrounds achieved in similar fashions during the school year. However, over the summer students from poor families lost much of the achievement they had gained while those in wealthier families gained in achievement levels.

In a classroom, teachers may react and interact differently with children from lower socioeconomic groups and hold different expectations for these students than they do for other classes of children. Darley and Gross (1983) examined the contention that social class stereotypes could serve to bias teacher perceptions. The study began by providing teachers with a detailed description of a child as well as a photograph of a child, either taken in front of an obviously middle-class house or an obviously lower-class house. Teachers were then shown a videotape of the child taking an achievement test, in which the child appeared either attentive or interested, or bored and distracted. They were then asked to predict future academic performance and to support their predictions with observations from the tape. Those who saw the middle-class child predicted better performance in school than those who viewed the lower class child. They recalled instances of the middle class child acting like a good student, even on the bored and distracted tape, and instances of the lower class student acting like a poor student even when they had been shown the video of an attentive, interested child.

**Culture:**

denotes works of art, philosophy, music and literature as well as the ways that different groups of people organize their daily lives within national and ethnic groups, urban neighbourhoods, companies and professions, and other settings. It includes the rules, expectations, attitudes, beliefs and values that guide behaviour in a particular group of people.

# CHILDREN FROM DIVERSE CULTURAL BACKGROUNDS

A great many cultures are represented in Canadian classrooms. Culturally different children come from subgroups within our society that differ on a variety of factors, including racial, geographic, economic, educational, and ethnic background. Children and groups may be described in a number of ways—the terms minority group, ethnic group, culturally different, new Canadian, and immigrant are widely used.

McLaren (1988) points out that in the past decade more than 100 000 school children—most of them who do not speak English—have flooded into Ontario, Quebec, British Columbia, and Alberta under a federal government policy of increased immigration. Ethnic diversity brings language diversity, although the latter tends to be an urban phenonomen. The 1986 census data showed that 13.4 percent of the nearly three million residents of Montreal reported a non-official mother tongue compared to a figure of only 1.5 percent for the province of Quebec as a whole. For Vancouver, the percentage was 21.3 compared to 11.8 for British Columbia. For Toronto, the figure was 26.3 percent compared to Ontario's 10.9 percent (Walker, 1990). It is not surprising then that in Toronto and Vancouver, roughly a quarter  of the student population does not speak English (McLaren, 1988). Apart from their academic studies, these children may also be suffering emotionally and psychologically. This is especially true for immigrants from the war-torn countries of Central America and South East Asia (McLaren, 1988).

There are many definitions of culture. Sometimes culture is used to denote works of art, philosophy, music, literature, and so on. Culture also refers to the way that different groups of people organize their daily lives within national and ethnic groups, urban neighbourhoods, companies and professions, and other settings (Trachtenberg, 1990). Culture includes the rules, expectations, attitudes, beliefs and values that define regional, ethnic, religious, or other groups of people (Woolfolk, 1990).

Every aspect of human life is profoundly related to cultural expectations and norms. Although individuals may transfer into another society, they do not leave behind the influence of their culture—the social value systems, traditions and symbolic communication patterns of their native environments.

Cultural factors vary widely from group to group. Cultures differ in:

• the rules for conducting interpersonal relationships;

• the orientation toward the past, present and future;

• the beliefs about how best to use time;

• the images of the ideal personality;

• the ideas about the relationship betweeen humans and nature;

• the most cherished values (Kagan, 1983; Maehr, 1974).

Within cultures, the similarity among members tends to be encouraged, which then reinforces the differences among cultural groups and the cultural diversity of the overall population. Each culture has a set of beliefs and values

A great many cultural backgrounds are represented in most Canadian schools.

that guide members of that culture in social interactions. What is accepted as desirable conduct in one culture may be considered inappropriate in another. For example, there exist many discrepencies between the values of the Native culture in Canada and that of the dominant culture.

Membership in an ethnic group has a marked influence upon scholastic achievement. For example, in Canada ethnic affiliation affects the aspiration to attend university (Dennis, 1976). As it relates to ethnic differences in children, culture can affect various aspects of learning (Coop and Seigel, 1974). There are many students whose daily living experiences are influenced by cultural beliefs that differ from the majority thought patterns. These students must learn to live and negotiate in at least two different social and linguistic systems that often dictate conflicting expectations for normal behaviour and appropriate development (Luce and Smith, 1986). Often, they are suspended between getting along in the home environment, which has its own expectations, and negotiating the school system, which also has its own cultural codes for thought and conduct (Winzer, 1990a).

Culture influences behaviour. Because of basic cultural differences, the behaviours and values a student learns at home and in the community may not fit the expectations of the school and its teachers. In general, schools expect and reward the behaviours, attitudes, and abilities fostered by white, middle-class society—the culture of most teachers (Woolfolk, 1990). Culturally different students may have distinctive work styles, views, values, and language. They may bring standards and expectations to the classroom and their backgrounds may affect their reactions to the classroom climate, the classroom structure, and classroom discipline. The regimented school day typical of an urban industrial society, for example, is often alien to Native children (Winzer, 1990a). Children from some minority groups are less willing to compete and more willing to cooperate with their peers than middle-class children (e.g., Kagan, 1983; Richmond and Weiner, 1973). Because of the mismatch between the cooperative orientation of some children and the competitive orientation of some classrooms, Kagan (1983) has argued that there is a "structural bias" in that classrooms may actually work against these children.

Students from different cultural backgrounds may meet a host of learning problems. Ashworth (1975) circulated a questionnaire to teachers of immigrant children to Canada. The groups that were perceived as having the greatest social adjustment difficulties were those whose language and culture differed most from the English language and Canadian culture. Teachers also reported that lack of prior education contributed to school adjustment problems, especially for children from developing countries.

Children who come from different cultural backgrounds may also encounter difficulties in acquiring the rules of English in a sufficiently sophisticated form to enable them to function in academic settings. Many children acquire fairly fluent peer-appropriate face-to-face communication skills within the first two years of their arrival in Canada (Cummins, 1984) although these skills develop more quickly than the skills needed for academics. It seems that students need about five years before they can demonstrate comprehension of concepts at the level that is normally required for academic work (Cummins, 1984).

Children who do not speak English will encounter the greatest difficulties in the content subjects. Language arts, especially reading, presents the greatest difficulties; math is less of a problem. An estimated 50 percent of West Indian children in Toronto, for example, have severe difficulties in the language arts (D'Oyley, 1976). A study of 106 North York schools in Ontario listed the main reasons for reading problems: in 69 percent of the schools, the main reason given was that there was another language spoken in the home (Wancyzki, 1983).

## Box 6-5 **Multiculturalism in Canada**

Multiculturalism was first introduced as policy during the Trudeau years. The Canadian Multiculturalism Act (December, 1987) provides a legislative basis and firm foundation for governmental initiatives for multicultural purposes. Its passage is concrete proof that Canada is officially and politically committed to the preservation and enhancement of the multicultural character of the country, to equality of both majority and minority ethnocultural groups, and to the promotion of cultural interaction and sharing (President's, 1988).

Multiculturalism depends upon the desire of ethnic groups to maintain their own distinctive culture and the commitment of the majority group to provide support (Young, 1979). Yet while multiculturalism is now official Canadian policy it has many faces and there are varied perceptions of the concept. So far only broad typologies have been established (Mazurek, 1987). This may be said for multicultural edcuation as well. The type of multicultural education that may be legitimately implimented in Canadian schools has been a matter of contention because it remains unclear how we can find a conception that consistently and fully corresponds to Canadian multiculturalism.

Since "multiculturalism within a bilingual framework" became official policy in 1971, the social and political idea of a Canadian mosaic has become one of our most cherished goals, says Mazurek (1981). The only way to create a climate of tolerance and respect for all ethnic groups is through education (Canadian Consultative Council, 1978). Therefore multiculturalism must find expression in the schools if we hope to ensure its ultimate survival (Mazurek, 1981).

The concept of multicultural education rejects assimilation and values cultural pluralism. Multicultural education does not attempt to eliminate differences; rather, the idea is to build on cultural diversity as a strength of our society. School districts, mostly in Winnipeg, Saskatoon, Vancouver, and Metropolitan Toronto, have adopted multiculturalism and race relations policies (Wood, 1986).

Gibson (1976) identified five approaches to the conceptualization of multicultural education. She sees it as variously education of culturally different students; education about cultural differences; education for cultural pluralism; bicultural education; and as a normal human experience.

The multicultural curriculum should provide and promote values, attitudes, and behaviours that support ethnic pluralism. A multicultural curriculum generally includes aspects such as multicultural perspectives, demonstration of the racial and cultural diversity of Canada, and the study and sharing of cultures. In a multicultural program, all students should have access to materials that provide accurate information about cultural groups (Banks, 1981). Students need many opportunities to develop an appreciation of varied cultures. It is necessary to provide culturally relevant materials and resources, such as readers with pictures of culturally different children and kits designed to teach about specific cultures. Children should be encouraged in the sharing of esthetic traditions from various ethnic groups.

## SUMMARY

1. At the outset, the goal of scientific psychology revolved around discovering the laws of the human mind common to all normal persons. Only grudgingly did psychologists turn to the study of individual differences.

2. The classic nature/nurture question has been posed for centuries. It asks whether as child's development is the result of biologically based hereditary information transmitted from the parents or the result of environmental influences. The debate continues and has produced some of the most emotional debates of our day.

3. Intelligence is one of the most deeply researched areas in psychology and remains controversial in all its spheres. In the early years, most psychologists assumed that intelligence was a unitary trait or an absolute like height or eye

colour. Today, we have adopted a less cavalier stance as we come to the realization that intelligence is a multifaceted and virtually indefinable construct. We now present children with a battery of measures of which IQ tests are only one component.

4. Tests of mental ability, or IQ tests as they are more commonly called, first surfaced in 1904, arising from the seminal work of Alfred Binet and Theophile Simon in France. Binet derived the mental age of a child by corresponding the tasks the child could perform to the age scale he had carefully developed. In 1912, William Stern, a German pioneer in differential psychology, first used the term intelligence quotient (IQ) to match the developmental levels of Binet's tests to the child's chronological age.

5. IQ cannot be measured directly. Tests provide an estimate at a particular time. IQ tests relate better to classroom achievement than they do to anything else.

6. Although the WISC-R is one of the best and most widely used instruments available, it is not perfect and problems do exist. No score on any test should be regarded as immutable or infallible.

7. Intelligence testing has been controversial since its inception. It has been under attack by those that believe there are inherent cultural biases, that tests favour white middle class students, and by those who believe that tests simply label students without doing them any good.

8. Much research, time, and attention has been devoted to determine the precise contribution of heredity and environment to the development of a human being. Not surprisingly, there is seldom agreement on hereditability ratios for humans; a ratio often depends on the rater so the size and meaning of hereditability factors for things such as intelligence have formed major controversies in psychology and education.

9. Because there is evidence that intellectual abilities are determined in part by heredity, some psychologists have suggested that these differences among groups on average test scores indicate genetic differences. Certainly, abilities as measured by standardized IQ tests seem to be highly affected by heredity, but what people do with their abilities and their level of achievement seems very much influenced by the environment.

10. Other individual differences concern learning styles and cognitive styles. Impulsivity and reflectivity refer to the tempo or speed with which individuals process information. Students may also be more field independent or field dependent, which may affect their perception of wholes or parts.

11. Within the family structure, birth order and family size may affect development.

12. The home environment of a student is important for school success. The term used by sociologists for variations in wealth, power, and prestige is socioeconomic status or SES. Mostly, this is divided into three levels—high, middle, and low.

**13.** Cultural diversity is a reality in Canadian education. However, immigrant and minority group children have been over-represented in such classifications as slow learner, educably mentally retarded, and learning disabled.

## Key Terms

| | | |
|---|---|---|
| age scale tests | behavioural genetics | cognitive styles |
| content scales | convergent thinking | creativity |
| culture | deviation IQ score | divergent thinking |
| field dependence | field independence | heredity |
| heredity ratio | intelligence quotient | inter-individual differences |
| intra-individual differences | learning styles | normal distribution |
| sex-role stereotypes | social class | socioeconomic status (SES) |

# ATYPICAL CHILDREN

**Students with exceptionalities:**
those whose intellectual, emotional, physical, or social performance falls below or rises above that of other children, and thus, have difficulty in realizing their full human potential.

**Special education:**
instruction specially designed to meet the needs of exceptional children.

## INTRODUCTION

An enormous range of individual differences can be seen in any class of students. The previous chapter described differences that can be accounted for by such variables as intelligence, cognitive tempo, gender, and socioeconomic status. Teachers will also find in their classrooms students whose learning potential falls above or below the norm. They will also meet students who fail to reach adequate levels of performance despite consistent instruction, and children who tend to be less task-oriented, more distractible, and those with more overt behaviours than regular students. Virtually every teacher will have at least one student who might be described as a behaviour problem. These inattentive, hyperactive, acting out, or disruptive children and youths who fail to comply with simple requests pose special problems to educators. As well, teachers may encounter students suffering from sensory handicaps of visual impairment or hearing disability. There may also be students with such medical problems as epilepsy, orthopedic and urologic difficulties, allergies, or asthma.

Many of these students will be described within the broad category of exceptional or special needs. **Students with exceptionalities** are those who have difficulty in realizing their full human potential. Their intellectual, emotional, physical, or social performance falls below or rises above that of other children. The differences may be related to physical, psychological, cognitive, emotional, or social factors, or a combination of these. Exceptional students require skilled intervention and special care from trained professionals. This is one reason why we recognize gifted and talented children as exceptional. They too need specialized help from professionals to fully develop their gifts and talents (Winzer, 1990a).

**Special education** is instruction that is specially designed to meet the

**SOURCE:** Much of the information in this chapter has been taken from Margret Winzer, *Children with exceptionalities*, Scarborough, Ontario: Prentice-Hall Canada, 1990.

**Related services:**
services such as transportation, physical and occupational therapy, and diagnostic medical services that permit an exceptional student to benefit from special education.

unique needs of exceptional children. The onus for direct instruction is placed on teachers, whether regular classroom teachers or special education personnel, but they are not alone in their efforts. Psychologists, speech therapists, counselors, and other professionals work with teachers to help them to plan the best possible education for each exceptional student. These people form part of an interdisciplinary team to offer related services, those services that permit an exceptional student to benefit from special education. Related services include transportation, physical and occupational therapy, and diagnostic medical services.

A handicapping condition can alter children's physical, intellectual, and social development and progress in a number of ways. Intellectual differences directly relate to classroom learning; some students will be slower to obtain and retain information and may require different skill emphasis, slower pacing, and sustained and extended drill and practice of skills. Students with physical handicaps such as cerebral palsy may have restricted ambulation or be confined to wheelchairs, and have difficulty in movement and in speech. Students with severe visual or auditory dysfunctions must learn to make complete use of their remaining intact senses. Those with health problems such as muscular dystrophy or asthma may be restricted in some physical activities.

Social development may be affected in a variety of ways, for a handicapping condition can explicitly or implicitly limit specific behavioural interactions. Youngsters with physical handicaps, for example, may lack the motor movements for waving and smiling. Blind children may not look toward other people and rather typically may not smile. Deaf children experience a delay in communication that often inhibits social relationships and interactions. Children with mild mental handicaps may be deficient in social skills; they may not recognize greetings or respond appropriately to requests. The disorders in the verbal and social skills of learning disabled students have also been well documented (Bryan, 1978) and, typically, the behaviour of children with conduct disorders is intimidating and socially unacceptable (Winzer, 1989).

In the past few decades, the prospects for exceptional students have altered dramatically. We have made major gains in our ability to provide sophisticated services for exceptional individuals. In medicine, great strides have been made in the prevention, intervention, and care of handicapping conditions. Closely linked to medicine, technological advances have provided a variety of devices and aids to help exceptional children. In education, significant philosophical changes are occurring in the areas of school responsibility, program delivery, and program implementation for special education. The concept of equal educational opportunities for exceptional children has become a dominant ideology which means that vastly increased numbers of students with exceptional conditions have moved within the orbit of the public schools.

With the advent of mainstreaming, or educational integration as the process is more commonly called in Canada, a larger range of children with more varied learning styles and learning difficulties will appear in regular classrooms. These students may vary in their ability to learn, to socialize, and to achieve independence; they may learn at a different tempo and may learn in different ways, but they do learn (Winzer, 1989).

The question of who should be integrated and where these students should be placed has garnered more attention in special education than has the question of what these students should be taught. Certainly, no perfect relationship exists between severity of handicap and regular classroom success. Few studies demonstrate success in the regular classroom for trainable mentally retarded or multiply handicapped students (Birch, 1976). There are more reports of successful integration of mildly disabled students into regular classrooms, including those labeled as learning disabled (Ritter, 1978), educable mentally retarded (Gottlieb, Campbell, and Budoff, 1975), hearing impaired (Reich, Hambleton, and Houldin, 1977), and mildly emotionally disturbed (Macy and Carter, 1978).

In this chapter we introduce some exceptional learners. No notion of completeness is present here: in a chapter, we could not possibly discuss the enormous range of possible handicapping conditions, their etiology, their developmental consequences, or the special types of intervention, whether medical, technical, or educational, that are necessary. Rather, we present brief overviews of a number of exceptional conditions and discuss their impact on children. Selections are based on the fact that these are the students that teachers are most likely to meet in regular classrooms. What we do explore in greater depth are the philosophical and legal bases underlying today's commitment to educational integration and some aspects of integration, such as team approaches and resource rooms, that should be considered. We also briefly present ideas about how teachers can assist students with mild handicapping conditions in their classrooms.

## STUDENTS WITH EXCEPTIONALITIES

The history of special education is replete with controversy over descriptive and functional definitions of acknowledged disabilities. Even today, the search for universal or specific features of various conditions is ongoing, futile, and frustrating. Relatively little standardization exists in the study of exceptional children and there is not a single consistent and universally accepted method of describing different kinds of children. Some researchers assess differences according to how development deviates from the norm. Others classify differences in terms of some underlying organic or functional cause while others describe them in terms of educational functioning and achievement. In general, the special traits of students with exceptional conditions fall into the following categories:

- Intellectual differences, which include children who are intellectually superior (gifted, creative and talented) and those who are mentally handicapped.

- Sensory handicaps, which include children with auditory impairments and those with visual problems.

- Communication disorders, which include children with speech difficulties and language problems. Because of the high number of learning disabled children

Labeling:

categorizing children on the basis of their primary disability.

suffering communication deficits, we group them in this category although they could be placed in other areas.

- Behaviour disorders, which include social maladjustment, emotional disturbance, and childhood psychoses.

- Physical handicaps and impaired health, which include children with neurological defects, orthopedic conditions, birth defects, and conditions that are a result of infection and disease.

- Developmental disabilities, which include children with pervasive disorders such as infantile autism and those with multiple handicaps, such as cerebral palsy combined with mental retardation, or deaf-blindness.

While these labels are commonly used to describe and identify students with exceptional conditions, the use of labels is fraught with problems. Labeling refers to the categorizing of children on the basis of their primary disability. But although labels broadly define categories of exceptionality, no one classification can adequately describe the social, psychological, and physical qualities of an exceptional individual.

The benefits of labeling are of a general administrative nature. Labels can serve to simplify information for administrators, placement counselors, educators, legislators, and parents. Within the school system, the label may be a necessary administrative lever to obtain funding for special services. Labels can also promote effective communication among agencies, services, and professionals that deal with exceptional children. Parents may find labels helpful, especially when a condition is initially diagnosed. For parents, the name of a handicap may seem to give them some control over it (Akerly, 1975).

However, the practice offers few benefits to the labeled individual. There are many reasons for this:

- The labeling of exceptional children has one prominent objective: labels differentiate between normal and abnormal, or what a certain society calls normal and abnormal. Too often, a label describes only the lacks, problems, and deficiencies of a person. It picks out a single quality, calls attention to it, and stresses how this quality differs from the norm.

- A label suggests a permanent disorder requiring long-term professional treatment. Children must wear their labels everywhere and all the time, although they may not apply in all situations.

- Sometimes the labels are incorrect, as in using "dyslexia" synonymously with learning disabilities.

- Labels may exaggerate the severity of a disability, as in the labeling of a hard-of-hearing child as deaf or a visually impaired youngster as blind.

- The use of discrete categories for exceptional children tends to oversimplify the facts. Although individual children may share a common exceptionality, they do not form a homogeneous group because each disability ranges from mild to severe. A subgroup of children suffering mild mental retardation, for example, is extremely heterogeneous: children exhibit different behaviours and are affected by the disability in various ways. Moreover, a mildly mentally retarded child functions quite differently than a child with severe mental retardation. To further confuse the issue, children who have been traditionally classified and grouped as mildly handicapped—those described as learning disabled, mildly mentally retarded, and mildly emotionally disturbed—often exhibit similar behaviour.

- According to researchers, many people tend to view a labeled person differently from a non-labeled one (Langer and Abelson, 1974; Salvia, Clark, and Ysseldyke, 1973).

- Labels accentuate stereotyping (Foster, Ysseldyke, and Reese, 1975) and may affect children's self-images, parents' images of their children, and teachers' expectations of what a child is capable of accomplishing (Hiebert, Wong, and Hunter, 1982).

- Labels may affect a teacher's interactions with students, induce lower teacher expectations (Reynolds and Birch, 1982), and may tend to absolve teachers of their responsibilities. For example, a teacher may not even try to help little Jimmy with arithmetic because Jimmy has been labeled as mildly mentally retarded and the teacher does not believe that mentally retarded children can learn to add and subtract.

There is currently a move away from labeling, especially for students with mild handicapping conditions. Educators are abandoning traditional medical orientations and focusing on the social and academic behaviours displayed by children as they follow the strong trend toward non-categorical or generic approaches, especially for mildly handicapped students.

A non-categorical approach implies that the functional behaviour of a child is the most important factor in the child's educational program, not a diagnostic category. Non-categorical approaches are most prevalent in the area of mild disabling conditions and encompass disorders traditionally labeled as learning disabilities, educable mental retardation, and mild emotional disturbance (behaviour disorders). Given special help, these students can function quite adequately in regular classrooms.

A matrix of factors underlie the current movement toward generic approaches including labeling, similarities among categories, difficulties in categorization, and similarities in academic performance.

**Labeling**     Labels are often inappropriate in their application and use. Especially for students with mild handicapping conditions, the use of labels may attach a stigma and still not result in improved treatment for the child.

**Similarities among categories**     Disabilities are not mutually exclusive, but overlap. Children with special needs, whether mental, physical, or emotional, usually have learning and developmental disabilities that extend across several categories of behaviour—physical, intellectual, linguistic, perceptual, social, or emotional.

**Difficulties in categorization**     Children with mild problems are difficult to categorize through diagnostic methods. Their treatments often overlap, suggesting that diagnostic and intervention methods cut across the existing categories.

**Similarities in academic performance**    Traditionally, mildly handicapped students have been thought not to share common etiological factors and behavioural characteristics and to differ in performance levels in certain areas. Among learning disabled, mildly mentally retarded and behaviourally disordered students, differences were said to exist in the level of cognitive ability, in academic achievement, in patterns of cognitive performance, in degree of under-achievement, and in adaptiveness of social and emotional development. But when the children's actual performance in school is examined, there is seen to be considerable overlap.

A number of studies demonstrate the similarities in functioning of mildly handicapped children. For example, Beare's (1985) data based study of 90 categorically labeled and served junior high students found that significant differences in all or even most instructionally relevant characteristics did not exist between mildly emotionally disturbed and learning disabled students. They were virtually the same in IQ, patterns of cognitive ability, and number of behaviours rated as significantly deviant by their teachers. Reading achievement—lower for the learning disabled group—was the only major significant difference. The mildly retarded group was less proficient than the other two groups on measures directly related to cognitive ability but not on other measures. There were very large overlaps of range, even on the ability measures, and standardized testing could not distinguish students as belonging to separate groups.

**Similarities in teaching methods**    Marston (1987) studied the types of teacher certification in relation to the types of pupils instructed. He found that a significant relationship did not exist between teacher certification and student type. Over the course of an academic year, learning disabled students taught by teachers trained in learning disabilities did not improve more than learning disabled students taught by teachers trained for educable mentally retarded students. Similarly, Algozzine, Morsink, and Algozzine (1988) found that instruction in 40 classrooms serving groups of students designated as educationally handicapped, educable mentally retarded, and learning disabled did not differ to any significant degree.

# PREVALENCE

About three percent of newborn infants have a handicap that can be considered a developmental delay or developmental disability. Another three percent are born with significant conditions capable of causing medical or social handicaps (Berlin, 1983). For other children, problems appear later as a result of disease or accident. During the school years, approximately 15.5 percent of the Canadian school-age population will be considered exceptional. These children will require special education services for at least some part of their school careers (Council of Ministers, 1983). Table 7-1 presents some provincial figures on the numbers of children and youth with exceptional conditions (as of January, 1988).

A huge variety of factors account for handicapping or potentially handicapping conditions in children. There are, for example, more than 200 known causes

Table 7-1  Number of Canadian students with exceptionalities, January, 1988

| | TOTAL NUMBER OF CHILDREN SERVED | NUMBER OF EXCEPTIONAL CHILDREN SERVED | COMMUNICATION DISORDERS | LEARNING DISABILITIES | BEHAVIOUR DISORDERS | EDUCABLE MENTALLY RETARDED | TRAINABLE MENTALLY RETARDED | HEARING IMPAIRED | VISUALLY IMPAIRED | OTHER | NON-CATEGORICAL | GIFTED |
|---|---|---|---|---|---|---|---|---|---|---|---|---|
| Newfoundland | 136,228 | 10,165 | — | — | — | — | 800 | 200 | 200 | 200 | 8,700 | |
| Nova Scotia | 169,581 | 18,822 | — | 12,106 | 747 | 1,599 | 452 | 173 | 147 | 323 | — | |
| PEI | 24,000 | 400 | No categories | | | | | | | | | |
| NB | 138,002 | 14,300 | No categories | | | | | | | | | |
| Quebec | 943,652 | 126,417 | — | 96,585 | 13,722 | 4,955 | 2,404 | 472 | — | 8,269 | | |
| Ontario | 1,796,244 | 136,356 | 6,520 | 55,768 | 8,104 | 23,559 | 7,600 | 1,581 | 512 | 101,949 | — | 23,756 |
| Manitoba | 209,352 | 2,000 | Unavailable | | | | | | | | | |
| Saskatchewan | 204,097 | 6,016 | | 3,665 | 548 | — | 728 | 252 | 80 | 747 | | |
| Alberta | 426,476 | NA | Unavailable | | | | | | | | | |
| B.C. | 514,464 | 60,623 | | 6,637 | 2,579 | 4,108 | 1,254 | 797 | 402 | 34,691 | | 9,161 |
| NWT | 13,000 | 2,000 | — | | | | | | | | | |
| Yukon | 4,922 | Varies | — | | | | | | | | | |

SOURCE: Keeping in Touch, 1989 pp. 2, 3.

**Mental retardation:**
significantly sub-average intellectual functioning resulting in, or associated with, impairments in adaptive behaviour, and manifested during the developmental period.

**Sub-average intellectual functioning:**
a tested potential of 70 IQ or below, two standard deviations below the mean.

**Developmental period:**
the time between conception and the eighteenth birthday.

of mental retardation and perhaps nearly 2000 inborn errors of metabolism (Berlin, 1983). However, despite all that is known, nearly half of all childhood exceptionalities are attributable to unknown causes.

## INTELLECTUAL DIFFERENCES

Intellectual differences comprise a category that includes two very different groups of children. Yet, both children with intellectual handicaps and those who are gifted are considered exceptional and require special education and related services to develop their full human potential.

Mentally retarded children are markedly slower than their age mates in many areas. They demonstrate impaired or incomplete mental development; their problems are specifically retardations in the development of intellectual and adaptive behaviour. Their ability to learn and their capacity for putting learning to use is limited but certainly not nonexistent. Mentally retarded persons should not be viewed as part of a homogeneous population; there will probably be as much variability within the groups labeled as retarded as there is between this group and the non-retarded.

Gifted children tend to be superior in many ways. Gifted children learn more, faster, and more thoroughly than their peers. They demonstrate a wide range of interests and special aptitudes. They also tend to be better adjusted socially and enjoy more stable mental health. They are more popular, more socially responsible and have a wider range of social interests and commitments. They are more also flexible, mature, tactful, realistic, and independent (see Winzer, 1990a).

### Mental retardation

Today's primary definition of mental retardation is that proposed by the interdisciplinary American Association on Mental Deficiency (AAMD, today known as the American Association on Mental Retardation). Under this widely accepted definition, mental retardation refers to significantly sub-average intellectual functioning resulting in, or associated with, impairments in adaptive behaviour, and manifested during the developmental period (Grossman, 1977, 1983). Therefore, for a student to be considered within the category of mental retardation three factors must be present:

1. sub-average general intellectual functioning,

2. deficits in adaptive behaviour, and

3. manifestation during the developmental period.

Sub-average intellectual functioning within the AAMD definition of mental retardation means a tested potential of 70 IQ or below, two standard deviations below the mean. The developmental period refers to the time between conception and the eighteenth birthday.

Adaptive behaviour is crucial to today's definition of mental retardation. In the past, children were identified as retarded solely on the basis of an intelligence test. With the adaptive behaviour criterion added in 1961, the conception

**Adaptive behaviour:**

the degree and efficiency with which an individual meets the standards of personal independence and social responsibility of his or her age or cultural group.

of mental retardation broadened. **Adaptive behaviour** refers to how well a person is able to adapt to environmental demands. Grossman (1977) defines it as the degree and efficiency with which an individual meets "the standards of personal independence and social responsibility of his age or cultural group" (p. 11).

As a construct, adaptive behaviour refers to how well an individual performs those behaviours necessary for success in his or her environment. It is composed of personal independence (from basic self-care to money and money management), social competence (interacting effectively with others), and attitudinal dimensions (such as willingness to cooperate, motivation to succeed, and perseverance) (Terrasi and Airosian, 1989). Adaptive behaviour differs according to the child's age group and particular situation. The preschooler needs sensory-motor skills, communication, self-help skills, and socialization to adapt to the environment. We do not expect the preschooler to be interested in vocational prospects and an expanded peer group; these are the adaptive concerns of the adolescent.

Most professionals classify mentally retarded persons according to the severity of their problems. The most generally accepted approach is to consider retardation along a continuum of scale of severity as proposed by the American Association on Mental Retardation (AAMR)—mild, moderate, severe, and profound retardation.

**Table 7-2**  Degrees of mental retardation and expected developmental and academic characteristics

| SCHOOL TERMINOLOGY | AAMR TERMINOLOGY | IQ LEVEL | EXPECTATIONS |
|---|---|---|---|
| Dull normal (not retarded) | | 75-90 | Capable of competing in school in nearly all areas. |
| Educable | Mild | 50-75 | Capable of basic academic subjects up to advanced elementary levels. General achievement ranges from second to fifth grade. |
| Trainable | Moderate | 25-49 | Capable of attaining self-help skills, communication skills, and social adjustment. Limited academic achievement. Can achieve economic usefulness later in sheltered workshops or in routine jobs under supervision. |
| Severe and profound | Severe and Profound | below 25 | With intensive training, may learn basic self-help and communication skills. |

While many educators prefer the AAMR classification system, others still employ the terms "educable" and "trainable." Educators have used these categories over the years to try to describe the educational needs of retarded children. The terminology reflects the ability of educable mentally retarded (EMR) children to benefit from academic instruction as opposed to moderately mentally retarded or trainable mentally retarded (TMR) children who are generally, but

Individuals who are diagnosed as mentally retarded vary widely in almost every aspect of behaviour, personality, and temperament.

certainly not always, placed in special nonacademic programs where they are trained in skills to take care of their basic needs.

There is a higher incidence of retardation during the school years, with lower incidence figures during the preschool years and adulthood. More males and more individuals from ethnic and minority groups and from lower socioeconomic groups are labeled as retarded.

### Consequences of mental retardation

The term mental retardation covers a variety of physical, intellectual, academic, and behavioural characteristics. Individuals who are described as mentally retarded vary widely in almost every aspect of behaviour, personality, and temperament. The amount and degree of the retardation is of prime importance; within the various levels of retardation there are found a wide range of behaviours and abilities. Viewing mental retardation on a continuum, we can place mildly retarded children who are having trouble with academic subjects at one end and profoundly retarded youngsters who may be non-ambulatory and non-responsive to their surroundings at the other.

The most specific consequences of mental retardation involve its effects on an individual's ability to learn and to progress academically. Mildly mentally retarded children present few if any divergent types of physical symptoms that differentiate them from their peers. Their major problems are in academic learning and socialization. They are less efficient, for example, in using memory effectively, associating and classifying information, reasoning, and making judgments.

In school, mildly retarded students can progress in the elementary school

**259**

grades but, as they continue, the lags between them and their non-handicapped peers widen. They achieve about two-thirds of what other children will accomplish in an academic year. Most mildly mentally retarded students will be above the 2.5 level in reading, language arts, and math and will possess the oral language and listening skills sufficient to give and follow instructions. Depending on the degree of retardation, the maximum level of achievement for mildly mentally retarded youngsters is generally believed to fall somewhere between third and seventh grades in most academic areas.

Mildly mentally retarded pupils are the largest group of retarded learners and possess probably the widest range of skills and needs. With the current emphasis on educational integration, these students are very likely to be accommodated in regular classrooms. Moderately retarded individuals have limited intellectual ability, difficulties in working with abstract ideas, and problems in generalizing learning to new situations. They are not ready for much academic work until their early teens.

Moderately retarded students also have rather clear-cut deficits in adaptive behaviour; they have problems with interpersonal relationships, social concepts, emotional instability, and communication. As moderately retarded children grow older, the progressive widening of their developmental lag tends to make their retardation more obvious. This is in contrast to mildly retarded persons whose condition becomes less obvious in adulthood as they merge into occupations and communities.

Down syndrome accounts for approximately ten percent of all cases of moderate and severe mental retardation (Hallahan and Kauffman, 1986). Intellectually, the Down child can fall anywhere in the spectrum from mild to profound retardation; most tend to be classed as moderately retarded. Down individuals with normal intellectual development are almost exclusively those with the mosaic form of the condition.

Severely retarded children and young adults experience major challenges to successful adaptation. They present intensive instructional and technological needs in order to meet the intellectual and adaptive demands of their homes, schools, and communities. Many individuals suffer such serious problems that they will likely require life care and supervision. However, learning is both possible and common for these children (Haywood, Meyers and Switzky, 1982). Using classical and operant conditioning procedures (see Chapter 11), educators have taught many skills in the domains of adaptive behaviour, simple academics, and vocational skill formation to severely retarded, and some profoundly retarded, individuals.

Profoundly retarded individuals are some of the most seriously impaired of all disabled people. The nature and degree of their handicap is so great that, without various forms of intensive training and therapy, they exhibit virtually no adaptive behaviour. Profoundly retarded persons have the highest incidence of devastating motor, sensory, and physical handicaps. A British Columbia study of non-specific retardation (Herbst and Baird, 1983) found that 27 percent of mildly retarded people had additional handicapping conditions. Contrastingly, 73.1 percent of the profoundly retarded suffered additional handicaps. Expressive speech and language skills are extremely limited, with blindness, deafness, cerebral palsy, epilepsy, and other physical anomolies the rule rather than the exception.

Box 7-1 **Down syndrome**

Down syndrome is by far the most common and widely known form of chromosomal aberration. The condition occurs in one in 640 live births and can occur in any family, regardless of race, socio-economic class, or education. It usually happens only once in a family, and strikes most often when the mother is approaching the end of her childbearing days.

The condition is characterized by mental and physical anomolies and was first described by John Langton Down (1866). Down syndrome was one of the first conditions to be linked to a genetic abnormality. The major breakthrough came in 1959 when scientists discovered the extra twenty-third chromosome and associated it with the syndrome (Carr, 1975).

There are three major types of Down syndrome—Trisomy 21, translocation, and mosaicism. In each type, the mental and physical problems of the afflicted child are caused by extra chromosomal material which somehow disturbs the orderly development of the body and brain. Trisomy 21 accounts for about 95 percent of children afflicted with Down syndrome. There are actually 14 different types of Trisomy 21, but they are all basically problems of dysfunction. In all of them, the twenty-first pair of chromosomes contains three chromosomes instead of two. This may result from a mistake in chromosomal distribution in the egg or sperm, or because the chromosomes were distributed unequally when the fertilized egg began to divide (Winzer, 1990a).

The tiny fragment of extra chromosome that characterizes the condition has devastating effects on the physical and intellectual development of affected children. Many of these are apparent almost from birth. For example, Down infants and other children with neurological abnormalities have cries that differ from those of normal infants in pitch, rhythm, accentual character, volume, and latency of cry following the onset of stimulation (Michelsson and WaszHockert, 1980). Down babies as young as two and four months of age also use vision less effectively than normally developing infants, perhaps due to delayed assimilation of information from the environment (Miranda and Franz, 1973).

Disruptions in early social interactions may contribute to the particular difficulties experienced by Down syndrome infants in the development of language and higher level exploratory skills (Coggins and Morrison, 1981). In social interactions with their mothers, Down syndrome infants show atypical interactive behaviours when compared with normal infants matched for mental age (Coggins and Morrison, 1981). To overcome difficulties in parent-child interaction, and in the child's physical, mental and language development, early intervention is both crucial and beneficial. Down syndrome children have been shown to benefit from early and consistent stimulation (Sharav and Schomo, 1986).

Mentally retarded children may be placed in regular classes, self-contained classrooms, or special day schools. In each case, the child's degree of retardation and adaptive behaviour are the determining factors. The current trend is to mainstream mildly retarded students to whatever extent is appropriate and yields success. Educational options depend on a child's unique set of strengths and weaknesses. A child's success in the regular classroom depends on such factors as support services, resource-room assistance, curriculum modifications, acceptance by the other students, the classroom teacher's experience with and exposure to exceptional children, and the availability of community resources.

Although mildly mentally retarded youngsters are prime candidates for integration into regular classrooms, the measure of success would appear to vary with age level. Younger children acclimatize more rapidly to mainstream settings than do older students. Integration at the secondary levels is harder to implement: not only does the mental gap between non-handicapped and retarded students continually widen with age but the instructional emphasis at the secondary levels is different from that of the elementary school. Generally, traditional secondary school subjects are not related to the future needs of mildly handicapped students and the overall curriculum is not congruent with their present wants. Preparation for independent living requires much more than academic goals for mentally retarded adolescents. Their hope is to work—not to continue schooling.

Moderately retarded children may learn in the regular class or in special self-contained classrooms; they would still be able to integrate with their non-handicapped peers for such non-academic subjects as physical education and art in the self-contained classrooms. Severely and profoundly retarded children may learn in special classes, special schools, or in group homes. Integration into regular classrooms for social skills and social interaction is both possible and ongoing in Canadian schools.

## Giftedness

The category of giftedness encompasses students who are gifted as well as those who are creative or talented. Talent refers to a specific area, as in the visual arts or athletics. Creativity, as we discussed in Chapter 6, implies bringing new and unusual responses and solutions to problems.

Gifted, creative, and talented people do not form a homegeneous population. Passow (1981) observes that gifted and talented individuals come in a tremendous variety of shapes, forms and sizes. Some gifted students are only slightly above average while others are so unusual as to be extremely rare. Some individuals are gifted or talented in a single area while others seem to be unusually able in practically any area. Some individuals who seem to have outstanding ability have relatively little motivation or interest in developing that potential while others are highly motivated. In some, gifts show early; others are "late bloomers."

Many definitions of giftedness exist. In the past, definitions stressed IQ, as we saw in Terman's study. Today's conceptions of giftedness are far broader. Joseph Renzulli (1978) analyzed current definitions of giftedness and reviewed the characteristics of gifted individuals. From this, Renzulli proposed a definition of giftedness that he believed was useful to practitioners and defensible in terms of research findings. Renzulli's conception of giftedness contains three elements:

- above average ability;

- task commitment, which represents the energy brought to bear on a particular task or specific performance area;

- creativity.

All three characteristics are required for remarkable achievement. The interaction is shown in Figure 7-1.

**Figure 7-1**
Renzulli's conception of giftedness

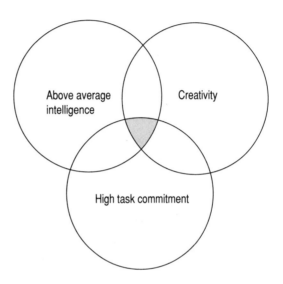

Nevertheless, there is no diagnosis so fraught with political, emotional, and educational issues as giftedness. Hoge (1988) has argued that giftedness is usually defined by school boards in terms of one or more of the following characteristics: superior performance on a standardized intelligence test; superior performance on a standardized achievement test of specific aptitudes; evidence of creativity; or a high level of motivation. Most identification, however, relies on teacher nominations and IQ tests.

### Consequences of giftedness

The one thing that gifted children have in common "is the ability to absorb abstract concepts, to organize them more effectively, and to apply them more appropriately than the average youngster" (Gallagher, 1975, p. 19). Gifted students learn more, faster, and more easily than do their age mates. They learn to read sooner and continue to read at a consistently more advanced level. Gifted students can master the curriculum content of a grade two or three times faster than the average child. They like learning, enjoy difficult subjects, and are willing to spend extra time on projects that stimulate their interest. Gifted children are also more adept at critically evaluating facts and arguments. Because they more readily recognize relationships and comprehend meanings, they can reason out problems more effectively.

Giftedness in children needs to be fostered and nurtured.

All these factors place gifted children far ahead in academic achievement. They tend to be more advanced in reading than in areas that require manual dexterity, such as writing and art. They also tend to be more advanced in reading than in mathematics, which depends more on the sequential development of concepts and skills (Gallagher, 1966). Many gifted children are younger than their classmates because they have been accelerated due to superior academic performance. Nevertheless, gifted children tend to receive more As and Bs, even when they are competing for grades with older classmates (Barnette, 1957; Shannon, 1957).

There is no magic in giftedness that will allow children to overcome all the obstacles to development without special assistance. An increasing number of educators, administrators, legislators, parents, and researchers support the idea that giftedness needs to be fostered and nurtured. They argue that gifted children have the same right as other children to develop to their full potential and therefore require special education and appropriate related services. Without educational opportunities and challenges, gifted children may hide their abilities or bury them in underachievement. Some become dropouts or deviants in a society that has ignored or even abused them.

Whitmore (1980) has attributed these failures primarily to the social and academic environment of the classroom. The gifted child is "turned off" by conformity to precise directions, excessive repetition, memorization and drill,

**Problem behaviour:**
behaviour that makes it difficult for children to interact with peers, parents, teachers, and others.

uniformity of assignments, and the lack of opportunity to pursue interests and work independently. Chalk and talk, endless drill and practice, and repetition, along with a concomitant lack of stimulation and challenge, can bore and frustrate gifted learners. Some gifted children may be bored and daydream in school while others may pace themselves so as to finish with the rest of the class. By the age of 13 or 14, some of these youngsters have a motivation to avoid failure at any costs rather than a motivation to succeed. These children are often too critical of others and of themselves and need help in accepting failure. However, even though gifted youngsters have often been depicted as bored with and antagonistic to school, studies have shown that most gifted children like school (Gallagher, 1966).

Nobody is sure of the best way to educate gifted students and numerous programs have been attempted, all of which are intended to come to grips with three major problems: the wide range of abilities amomng the gifted population, teachers' limited knowledge in content areas, and teachers' lack of special instructional methods (Gallagher, 1985). Programs in Canada for gifted students are of long standing. However, the basic educational goals for gifted students are the same as for all other pupils: to develop their abilities in ways that are consistent with their personal needs and the best interests of society.

## BEHAVIOUR AND PERSONALITY DISORDERS

Psychologically speaking, normal children are those whose behaviour is in harmony with their environment and with themselves. Abnormal behaviour has, as an obvious referent, normal behaviour. Any deviation in behaviour should, however, be viewed along a continuum from normal to markedly abnormal.

Behaviour disorders have been defined in many ways from many different perspectives. Behaviours that make it difficult for children to interact with others is **problem behaviour**. Simply, children encounter difficulties interacting with peers, parents, teachers, and others.

Problematic behaviour is fairly common in childhood. Problems fluctuate, however, and decline as children get older and are not necessarily signs of clinical deviance. Lying, for example, is reported to be a problem for the majority (53 percent) of six-year-old, normal boys; by the age of ten, lying decreases to ten percent of boys. In girls, the pattern is more dramatic with a high rate (about 48 percent) at age six and no lying reported as a problem at age 11 (see Kazdin, 1989).

Mild behavioural problems are faced by most teachers every day. At the same time, teachers may meet students who demonstrate persistent and chronic classroom behaviour problems that extend far beyond the norm. These are exhibited by children who move the process of behaviour management from a task to a preoccupation. Students with serious behaviour disorders seem intent on satisfying impulses that are incompatible with the kinds of classroom control and academic activities that a teacher has in mind (Winzer, 1989).

Behaviourally disordered children are not rare and most of us have come into contact or observed such young people. In fact, in one survey of teachers, chronic student misbehaviour was noted as the main source of job stress by 50 percent of the respondents (Feitler and Tokar, 1982). Classroom behaviour problems constitute the most common reason that children are referred to special education (Ysseldyke and Algozzine, 1984). Too much activity, too little activity, not paying attention, excessive talking, not completing assignments, not doing homework, and other such problems are often listed on special education referral forms.

Some behaviourally disordered children withdraw; the great majority strike out. The behaviour disorders of these students include aggression, hostility, bizarre statements or actions, disruptive rule violations, and the like. These children are troubled, and they cause trouble for those with whom they interact. They exhibit, to a marked extent and over a long period of time, behaviour that is clearly undesirable, inappropriate, and maladaptive in the social context. Their behaviour affects their own learning and the equilibrium of those in their environments.

There is no symptom which is common to all behaviourally disordered pupils, or even to a sub-group of these children because there is no such thing as a typical behaviourally disordered student. Many of these youngsters actually show the same behaviours as other children but they show them far more often or far more intensely, or not often enough, or intensely enough. Non-handicapped children may, for example, hit, spit, swear, and throw tantrums occasionally, but behaviourally disordered students do it far more often, for more prolonged periods, and with far greater intensity. Other students, of course, exhibit different repertoires of behaviour in school.

Children in ever increasing numbers are currently being identified as behaviourally disordered. However, estimates of the prevalence of behavioural disorders vary tremendously, chiefly because of the lack of a clear and precise definitional construct. The best available research data indicates that six to ten percent of the school-aged population exhibit serious and persistent behavioral problems (Kauffman, 1985).

A major problem when evaluating behaviour centres on what is normal behaviour as opposed to what is abnormal in the classroom. Disruptive behaviour is often "in the eye of the beholder." Parents and teachers tend to describe 20 to 30 percent of children at any given age as "having problems" (e.g., Rich, 1982). They see 10 to 15 percent of children as in need of professional assistance for behavioural problems (Wood, 1982). Other surveys have indicated that anywhere from 10 to 40 percent of children may be considered behaviourally disordered, depending on the age of the children, the criteria used (e.g., Balow, 1979; Morse, 1975), and the level of severity focused upon.

Students regarded as disruptive by one teacher may be ignored by another; rules might be enforced by one teacher but not by another. An individual's interpretation of a situation is precariously subjective and more objective standards are desirable. Regular classroom teachers, for example, appear to be more upset, or less tolerant, of the behaviour problems of students than are special education teachers (Algozzine, 1980). Algozzine (1977a) found two types of disturbing behaviour—social immaturity, where children were shy, withdrawn, and anxious, and social defiance, where children were destructive, disobedient, and aggressive. The type of behaviour that most upset teachers was social defiance (Algozzine, 1977a). As well, the behavioural characteristics of boys are more upsetting to teachers than the behavioural characteristics of girls (Schlosser and Algozzine, 1979).

The vast majority of children identified as behaviourally disordered fall into the mild and moderate categories. Boys outnumber girls by at least two to one in every classification from mild through profound (Reinert, 1976); boys with the more serious forms of these disorders may outnumber girls by ratios estimated from seven- to twelve-to-one (Cummings and Finger, 1980; Reinert, 1980; Rich, 1982). As well, boys are eight or nine times more likely to be in a special education class than girls (Reinert, 1976).

Children from lower socioeconomic levels are also more likely to be regarded as problems. There is a higher prevalence of aggressive behaviours among lower class children as opposed to those from middle and upper classes (Hallahan and Kauffman, 1986) and a higher proportion of those identified as behaviourally disordered are from minority groups (Rich, 1982).

Many behaviourally disordered children come to the attention of professionals in the middle childhood and early teen years. The prevalence of behaviour disorders is low in the beginning grades, reaches a peak in the middle grades, and begins to fall off in junior high until the last years of high school (Morse, Cutler, and Fink, 1964).

There are a number of ways to differentiate and describe the general population of students who exhibit disordered behaviour. We look only at conduct disorders which are of such grave consequence to educators, socialized aggression (juvenile delinquency), anxiety, and withdrawal.

## Conduct disorders

Students with conduct disorders exhibit problem behaviours that are acute, chronic, and characterized by various forms of aggression, antisocial behaviour, and a concomitant paucity of social skills. Such youngsters exhibit behaviour that:

- deviates in an extreme way from the norm;
- recurs chronically;
- violates social or cultural expectations;
- affects a child's self esteem, interpersonal relationships and probably school achievement;
- requires special education intervention.

Conduct disordered children display a spectrum of aggressive behaviours—hitting, biting, and kicking—as well as numerous other behaviours such as dependency, crying, whining, and non-compliance. In Chapter 6, we outlined some of the characteristics associated with aggression and pointed out that males are more physically aggressive than females. In fact, the sex differences in the incidence of aggressive behaviour has been found in a number of different cultures ranging from tribal villages to highly industrialized societies (Whiting and Whiting, 1975). We also noted the inter-generational characteristics associated with aggression and indicated that aggressive children are severely at risk for a range of social and academic problems.

**Aggression:**
any form of behaviour designed to harm or injure another living being who is motivated to avoid such treatment.

**Antisocial behaviour:**
repeated infractions of socially prescribed patterns that violate social norms and the rights of others.

Aggression can be defined as any form of behaviour designed to harm or injure another living being who is motivated to avoid such treatment (Baron and Byrne, 1981). In instrumental aggression, the aggressor produces distress in another person in order to obtain something the aggressor wants, while in hostile aggression hurting becomes an end in itself (Maccoby, 1980).

Aggression is intimately related to a conception of rights and justice and the legitimacy of defending one's own interests and the interests of those in one's social group (Maccoby, 1980). Maccoby (1980) notes that children, as they mature, develop a concept of fairness and, as they learn that they have certain territory to defend, may become more angry and aggressive.

The ability to inhibit aggression or to behave in nonaggressive ways is not merely the ability to possess alternative social skills but also a matter of feeling positive affection for others and having the concomitant desire not to hurt them (Maccoby, 1980). As children grow, their frustrations may not diminish but their ability to cope with them may. They are better able to inhibit and control emotional reactions (Maccoby, 1980).

Aggression is of more concern to teachers than any other behavioural disorder (Bullock and Brown, 1972). Teachers worry that the aggressive child may injure himself or herself or harm others. As the child acts out, the optimum learning situation is not occurring. Moreover, the child, without help, may develop even more deviant or antisocial behaviour patterns.

Conduct disordered children are unwilling to submit to teacher authority; they refuse to comply with requests, school rules, and the conventional limits of behaviour. They create problems in classroom management, often alienating teachers and other students in the process. They soon learn to dislike the learning process and resent the school experience, and often resort to truancy. Students with conduct disorders are often said to exhibit antisocial behaviour— repeated infractions of socially prescribed behaviour patterns that violate social norms and the rights of others (Loeber, 1985).

Prosocial behaviour may be defined as "actions that are intended to benefit another person or group of people without the actor's anticipation of external rewards" (Mussen and Eisenberg-Berg, 1977, p. 3). For school children, skills such as cooperation, positive peer interaction, sharing, greeting, asking for and giving information, and making conversation, are all predictive of social acceptance (Asher and Hymel, 1981).

For the majority of children, adequate training in social skills takes place in the home by the family, and later in the community. However, children with conduct disorders do not seem to acquire social skills without formal instruction. Children who lack social skills may experience:

• poor academic success (Cartledge and Milburn, 1978; Walker et al., 1987; Wilson and Hernstein, 1985);

• school maladjustment;

• few or no friends (Gronlund, 1959);

• tendencies to drop out of school;

• juvenile delinquency;

• mental health problems later in life.

## Consequences of conduct disorders

Children with conduct disorders have failed to develop reliable internal inner controls; their behaviour is impulsive, distractible, hyperactive, and disruptive. They have short attention spans and sometimes seem not to know right from wrong. They often lack social skills and possess unfortunate personality traits that elicit dislike and rejection from others. Frequently, they suffer low self-esteem and poor self-concept. The behaviour of conduct disordered children is not age-appropriate. Among normal children, for example, unfocused temper tantrums diminish during the preschool period and are uncommon after age four (Hartup, 1974). In behaviourally disordered children tantrums are more likely to continue; a 12 year old throwing a temper tantrum is demonstrating clearly inappropriate behaviour.

Most students identified as behaviourally disordered display problems early in their school careers. They are lower in IQ and achievement than the means for their normal classmates (Kauffman, 1985). Compared to the normal distribution of intelligence, many behaviourally disordered children children fall into the slow learner or mildly retarded category; most have IQs in the dull-normal range—around ninety—and very few score above the bright-normal range (Hallahan and Kauffman, 1986).

Behaviour problems are often the cause of academic failure. Many of these children are underachievers at school, as measured by standardized tests (Kauffman, 1985). Seldom are behaviourally disordered children academically advanced: children who are busy being aggressive and disruptive are not participating in the instructional process. They enter a pattern of severe academic failure that quickly becomes cyclical. The correlation between achievement and aggression is .39 for boys and .36 for girls (Feldhusen, 1979). Because these children do not learn the skills to cope with academic pressures, they react by withdrawing or lashing out in angry frustration. Behaviourally disordered children are usually behind in reading, arithmetic, and spelling.

Children with excessive feelings of aggression and defiance develop intense and far-reaching interpersonal problems. First of all, they meet trouble in the classroom not only with academics but with interactions with teachers and other students. Studies of regular classroom teachers' perceptions and tolerance for behaviour problems have suggested that accommodation for problem behaviour may be less feasible than accommodation for instructional needs (Ritter, 1989). When Walker and Rankin (1983) studied the behaviour standards and expectations of regular classroom teachers they found them to be narrow, intense, and very demanding. These teachers seem to be less tolerant than special educators (Safran and Safran, 1985).

Teachers favour students with behaviour disorders less than they do learning disabled students (Gottlieb, Leyser and Michaels, 1990). If teachers are predisposed to expect behaviour consonant with a child's classification, it may negatively affect interactions with the child. However, it should be noted that Curci and Gottlieb (1990) found that teachers interact with children differently according to their classroom behaviour and not according to their handicap classification. Regular classroom teachers tend to instruct children with behaviour disorders with fewer academic questions, less extended feedback, and less one-on-one work interactions. Thus, the children's academic achievements fall still more and problems may become even more pronounced.

In addition to failing to interact appropriately with their teachers, behaviourally disordered children are disliked by most of their peers (Drabman and Patterson, 1981; Newman and Simpson, 1983). Highly aggressive children are more likely to make fewer friends and be attacked by peers. Studies of children with behaviour disorders at elementary and secondary levels indicate that they are seldom socially accepted; in fact, they are often actively rejected, not merely neglected by their peers. Aggressive children provoke a large number of fights and are more likely to become the targets of aggression. In fact, nonaggressive children who are harmed under ambiguous circumstances are much more likely to retaliate if the harm doer has a reputation as an aggressive child (Dodge and Frame, 1982).

Children do not grow out of conduct disorders. Aggression at age two or three will predict aggression at age five (Cummings, Ionotti and Zahn-Waxler, 1989; Emmerich, 1966) while children's level of physical and verbal aggression at ages six through twelve are fairly good predictors of their tendency to threaten, insult, tease, and compete with peers at ages ten to fourteen (Kagan and Moss, 1962; Olweus, 1979).

Antisocial behaviour in childhood generally leads to poor mental health and adjustment in later years, especially for boys. Truancy and delinquency are strongly related (Gold, 1970) and conduct disordered children are at a high risk for both (Gold, 1970; Robins, 1979). However, the majority of aggressive, antisocial children do not become delinquent (Quay and Werry, 1986); about half of antisocial children become adolescent delinquents and roughly one-half to three-quarters of delinquents become adult offenders (Blumstein, Cohen and Farrington, 1988; Farrington, 1987). However, the behaviour patterns of children with conduct disorders are often one of the most salient and frequently observed precursors of delinquency (Quay and Werry, 1986). The progression is shown in Figure 7-2.

**Figure 7-2**
Developmental progression of antisocial behaviour

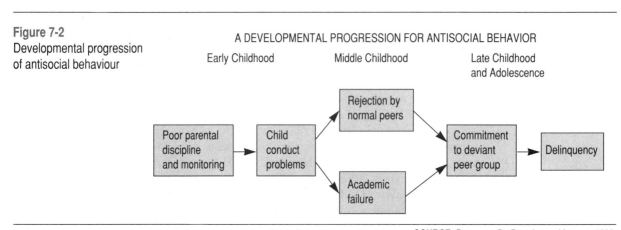

A DEVELOPMENTAL PROGRESSION FOR ANTISOCIAL BEHAVIOR

Early Childhood    Middle Childhood    Late Childhood and Adolescence

**SOURCE:** Patterson, De Baryshe, and Lancey, 1989.

Students who are socially maladjusted take part in behaviours that include gang vandalism, stealing, fighting, truancy, sexual precocity, and substance abuse. These behaviours can lead rapidly to trouble with the law. Children and youth who come to the attention of the courts are then labeled as juvenile delinquents or young offenders. Those who do not come into court are not formally designated as delinquent but they may very well be acting in ways that are indicative of problems in socialization and ethic development that fall within the scope of behaviour disorders.

### Anxiety

Fear is characterized by the anticipation of pain or great distress and is asociated with a specific object or event (Harris, 1986). The majority of fears are learned, usually linked to a specific cause, and are common to a culture. They can be learned by the same identification and imitation processes that teach socialization; students who are exposed continually to adult's fears in certain situations are likely to be fearful in the same situations. Violent episodes on television can produce similar results. Fears can also develop from real and unpleasant experiences children have, regardless of the amount of protection afforded them.

Almost all children are afraid of something: sometimes the fears are unrealistic, sometimes they are well-grounded. Most of the fears expressed by three to six year olds, for example, are unrealistic and involve nearly impossible events such as attacks by exotic animals or imaginary creatures (Harris, 1986). Children in this age group mention snakes more than any other animals as an object of fear but also identify lions, tigers, bears, ghosts, witches, and monsters as scary (Schwartz, 1979).

Anxious children sometimes develop a defeatist attitude, along with feelings of worthlessness and excessive self-criticism.

271

**Anxiety:**
a strong feeling of uneasiness or apprehension that occurs in anticipation of something unpleasant.

**Phobia:**
a severe and excessive fear aroused by a particular object or situation and characterized by an extreme desire to avoid that object.

**Obsession:**
a persistent preoccupation or idea someone can't get out of his or her head.

**Psychoses:**
serious mental disorders in which behavioural and thought processes become so disturbed that the person is out of touch with reality.

**Depression:**
characterized in children as a disorder of mood.

Occasionally a fear that gets out of control becomes anxiety or a phobia, an irrational fear of something. Generalized fear or anxiety is a strong feeling of uneasiness or apprehension that occurs in anticipation of something unpleasant. Anxiety, a fear with a future reference, is quite common in children. Many are apprehensive of new situations but perform satisfactorily after their initial anxiety. Anxiety is considered abnormal when it happens in situations that most people can handle with little difficulty.

Anxious children develop a defeatist attitude, along with feelings of worthlessness and excessive self-criticism. These children are also seriously hampered in social relationships. There is evidence that these and other behaviourally disordered children view themselves as alientated from the social mainstream (Weinstein, 1965).

A phobia is an anxiety reaction that is specific to one stimulus, a severe and excessive fear aroused by a particular object or situation and characterized by an extreme desire to avoid that object (Salkind, 1990). Some of the most common phobias are fear of the dark, of animals, of vehicles, and of school. However, any object or event can become the occasion for a phobic reaction. Rachman and Seligman (1976) have reported cases in which people developed powerful fears of chocolates and vegetables.

School phobia refers to an extreme reluctance to go to school as a result of severe anxiety and a morbid dread of some aspect of the school situation. It is accompanied by somatic symptoms that are used as a device to remain at home and that often disappear once the child is assured that he or she does not have to attend school.

Clinical deviations are far more serious. An obsession is a persistent preoccupation, an idea a child can't get out of his or her head. Many obsessions begin as phobias. Neuroses are groups of disorders characterized by anxiety, personal unhappiness and maladaptive behaviour. Psychoses are serious mental disorders: behavioural and thought processes become so disturbed that the person is out of touch with reality.

Depression in children is characterized as a disorder of mood. Several different theories of why children become depressed have surfaced. Psychoanalytic theory sees a major loss such as the death of a parent as a primary factor. The learning theory view stresses the loss of reinforcement; the activity level of the depressed child decreases because behaviour is no longer being reinforced. There may also be biological and genetic bases for depression.

### Consequences of personality disorders

Anxiety, at first glance, may not seem as serious as aggression. It can, however, lead to serious consequences. Timid, passive behaviour, dependency, isolation, and withdrawal interfere with children's development of their potential (Conger and Keane, 1981).

Anxious and withdrawn children internalize their behaviour. They may suffer from nausea, pains, headaches, phobias, fears, obsessions, shyness, nightmares, crying, depression, self-consciousness, and withdrawal. Withdrawn children are fearful, secretive, and apathetic. They tend to spend large amounts of time fantasizing and daydreaming instead of interacting with those around them. Extremely withdrawn children appear to dislike interacting with others so much that it becomes painful for them to go to school. Younger children may show regressive behaviours such as thumb sucking, clinging, and toilet accidents.

Children whose anxiety disorders diminish in adolescence are not particularly likely to show serious maladjustment in adulthood. Children who are neurotic and withdrawn are apparently more likely to later find and hold jobs, overcome their emotional problems, and stay out of jails and mental hospitals than children with conduct problems (Hallahan and Kauffman, 1986). However, anxiety disorders in later adolescence do appear to predict adult maladjustment (Gersten et al., 1976).

Suicide is the most serious consequence of depression. While the suicide rate in children under the age of 15 has remained stable and relatively low, for 15 to 19 year olds it has increased steadily and rapidly during the past 25 years (Harris and Ammerman, 1986).

---

### Box 7-2 **Teenage suicide**

Pfeffer (1986) defines suicidal behaviour as "any self-destructive behaviour that has an intent to seriously damage oneself or cause death" (p. 14). Suicide is any "self-destructive action that caused the death of the child" (p. 21).

Suicide is only one part of a variety of social problems that affect young people such as pregnancy, drug and alcohol abuse, crime and delinquency, and dropping out of school. However, although the rates are tending to stabilize, they are still very high and suicide among young people has become a major concern of parents, educators, mental health professionals, and public officials in both the United States and Canada.

In contrast to mortality among children and adults, causes of adolescent mortality are not diseases, but are primarily related to preventable social, environmental, and behavioural factors (Irwin and Millstein, 1986). Among American adolescents, there are three major causes of mortality—accident, homicide and suicide (Millstein, 1989).

Suicide is among the ten leading causes of death in most Western countries (Den Houler,

1981). There was a greater than 200 percent increase in suicide rates for adolescent males and females from 1960 through 1977 (Sheras, 1983). Suicide is the second leading cause of death in American teenagers, ranking after accidents. Furthermore, it has been estimated that there are at least ten nonfatal, serious suicide attempts for each one that results in a death (Maris, 1985). Another study estimated that, for every completed suicide among high school students, there are 350 suicide attempts (Edward, 1988). Another (PDK Task Force, 1988) places the proportion of high school students who will attempt suicide in any given month at three percent.

Girls commit suicide less often than boys— at a rate between one third to one quarter of boys. It is more common in urban than in rural youth (Frymmer, 1989). Most young people do not attempt suicide by overdosing on medication or using firearms, as adults do. Instead, methods of childhood suicide include stabbing, cutting, scalding, burning, stepping in front of a moving car, or jumping from high buildings (Paulson, Stone, and Sposto, 1978).

Even young children, once thought to be incapable of understanding the irreversability of death and therefore of fully self-intentioned death, are increasingly at risk (Hayes and Sloat, 1988). However, childhood suicides are not common and there is no consistent information on the relationship among sex, race, and ethnicity and the incidence of childhood suicide (Joffe and Offord, 1983). On the other hand, adolescent suicide seems to be associated with a variety of demographic and family variables.

A significantly higher incidence of suicide exists among children whose parents are abusive, depressed, alcoholic, psychopathic, and suicidal themselves (Pettifor et al., 1983). Frymmer (1989) sees three strong correlates of suicidal behaviour: family breakdown, a youth's unemployment, and decreasing religious observance among the young.

Adolescents who attempt suicide are usually experiencing considerable stress within the family. Conflict with the mother is often the focal point of the difficulties (Farebow and Reynolds, 1981). Also, studies of youth who have committed suicide have often revealed disproportionate numbers of exceptional children among the victims (Peck, 1985). Children with learning probems may be at high risk for depression and suicidal behaviour. Researchers have noted relationships between depression and cognitive deficits (Brumbeck, Staton, and Wilson, 1980) and between suicidal behaviour and diminished problem solving abilities (Levenson and Neuringer, 1971). Pfeffer (1986) has cited depression and suicidal behaviour as special problems of learning disabled children who are excessively stressed by the demands of the school. According to Pfeffer (1981), the most important issue seems to be the degree of the child's worry about academic achievement, rather than school performance. Feelings of low self-esteem are a contributing factor. Other authorities have noted suicidal behaviour in gifted and talented students (Delisle, 1986; Leroux, 1986; Willings and Arseneault, 1986).

But despite the efforts of a great number of researchers, the exact cause of suicide remains a mystery (Guetzloe, 1988). Authorities generally agree that suicidal behaviour results from a complex interaction of a number of factors and that there is no single cause (Hawton, 1986; Pfeffer, 1986). Any problem that contributes to feelings of depression, worthlessness, helplessness, or hopelessness has the potential to trigger suicidal behaviour in a vulnerable individual. Among the many factors that have been cited as contributing to youth suicide are isolation, alienation, loss, physical or psychologial abuse, disturbances in peer relationships, substance abuse, rejection, incarceration, family disorganization, availability of weapons, fear of punishment, fear of failure, knowledge of suicide, and humiliation (Pfeffer, 1986; Strother, 1986).

Severe behavioural disorders are by far the most prevalent conditions associated with suicidal behaviour. Many studies have confirmed the link between suicidal behaviour and emotional instability (Cosand, Bourque, and Kraus, 1982; Garfinkel and Golumbek, 1974; Pfeffer, 1986; Toolan, 1962). According to Garfinkel (in Strother, 1986) young people rarely kill themselves without having some kind of psychiatric disorder.

The relationship between depression and suicide is multidimensional and complex. For one thing, there is a strong relationship between the mother's depression and the occurrence of psychiatric problems, including depression, in children (e.g., Cytryn et al., 1984; Orvaschel, Weissman and Kidd, 1980). Children of depressed parents have shown greater impairments in social and cognitive functioning and are more likely to engage in destructive behaviour, tantrums, and fighting than children of nondepressed control parents (Beisser, Glasser and Grant, 1967; Harris and Ammerman, 1986). As well, teacher ratings indicate greater disruptiveness, impatience, disrespect, defiance, inattention, and social withdrawal, and poorer comprehension, creativity, and relations with teachers (Weintraub, Neale and Liebert, 1975) among these children.

Depression in children and youth has been found to be associated with a variety of other long lasting problems such as impaired peer relationships, poor communication, high irritability, lack of warmth, and parent-child hostility. A significant relationship between depression and suicidal behaviour in children and adolescents has been confirmed by recent studies (Kazdin et al., 1983; Robins and Alessi, 1985). Children who are suffering from depression are therefore considered to be at high risk for suicidal behaviour (Pfeffer, 1986).

Teachers should be aware of symptoms of depression in students. For one thing, self-deprecation and crying spells are common symptoms of depression. As far as suicidal behaviour goes, psychiatrist Barry Garfinkel points to three clusters of symptoms:

- signs of academic deterioration and falling grades, tardiness, and incomplete assignments;

- students at risk seem to slow down physically. They may have trouble staying awake and may suddenly drop out of athletic activities;

- they may withdraw from involvement with peers (Frymmer, 1989).

According to Frederick (1985), suicidal individuals suffer from the three Hs—haplessness, helplessness, and hopelessness. For example, suicidal youngsters may often have suffered a series of misfortunes over which they had little or no control. Following these events, they do not have the internal or external resources to deal with the problems and finally feelings of hopelessness ensue and suicide seems the only answer. The immediate task of a potential rescuer is to provide relief from feelings of helplessness or hopelessness, explore alternatives to suicidal behaviour and instill in the student some feeling of being in control. Others stress that the focus of intervention should not be on why suicide is a choice but rather on solving problems. With appropriate intevention, depressed and/or suicidal youngsters often show considerable improvement, often within a few weeks (Peck, 1985). But depressive symptoms can recur. Plans must be made for long-term intervention and follow up because a suicidal child may be at risk for several years after the initial threat or attempt.

## COMMUNICATION DISORDERS

Any degree of disturbance in our communication with others in the environment has an impact on social adjustment. Therefore, all types of speech and language disorders affect the ease with which children can communicate with their world. Children who communicate poorly, whether due to speech problems or to language disorders, are usually painfully aware of the fact. They may react by withdrawing from social contact or by using physical means to gain others' attention. Many children find it so difficult to communicate that they become frustrated, withdrawn, and depressed. Others learn to rely on gesture and body language.

Table 7-3 Signs and effects of communication disorders

| DISORDER | SIGNS | EFFECTS |
|---|---|---|
| Language disorders | May show impaired comprehension and poor verbal expression | Fail to understand instructions; withdraw from group situations |
| Articulation disorders | Abnormal production of speech sounds; speech not typical of chronological age | May be ridiculed by peers; may have decoding and comprehension problems with respect to specific words |
| Fluency | Impaired fluency and rhythm | Peer ridicule, oral difficulties |
| Voice disorders | Abnormal vocal quality, pitch, loudness, or duration | Self confidence may suffer; withdrawal |

## Speech and language disorders

In some children, speech and language difficulties are the sole or primary area of dysfunction. However, problems in speech and language not only constitute a field of exceptionality by themselves but they cut across other areas. Many, if not most, children with other handicapping conditions also manifest speech and language problems that further hinder their optimal development.

Speech and language disabilities are manifested in a staggering array of distinct forms. Speech problems include delayed onset of speech, speech usage below age level expectations, oddities in articulation, peculiar usage of grammar, stuttering, unusual intonations or voice quality, paucity of speech, inability to recall familiar words, poor self-expression, or total absence of speech (Chess and Rosenberg, 1974). However, all speech disorders have in common an impairment of verbal communication so that the intelligibility of spoken language is reduced. No such commonality is found among language disorders which may include children with delayed language, different language, deviant language, or even no language. Typically, language disorders are more complex in identification, diagnosis, and remediation than are speech problems.

Reliable figures on the prevalence of speech disorders among children are difficult to obtain because criteria and definitions of communication disorders vary. Speech problems are more common among boys than girls, especially in the early grades and this is particularly true in the case of stuttering. Problems decrease as grade level increases. Milisen (1971) estimates that between 12 to 15 percent of children in kindergarten to grade four suffer speech problems. In grades five to eight, the proportion drops to four to five percent and this remains constant after grade eight unless treatment intervenes.

Because researchers disagree on the definition of language disorders, they often cite different prevalence figures. To further confuse the issue, children in other categories of exceptionality often have language problems. For example, learning disabled students more often than not demonstrate deviations or delays in language; mentally retarded children do not develop language commensurate

**Speech disorders:**
speech patterns which interfere with communication.

**Language disorders:**
problems in the recognition and understanding of spoken language or in the ability to formulate well-organized grammatical sentences.

**Receptive language disorders:**
problems which interfere with the comprehension of spoken language

**Expressive language disorders:**
problems which affect the formulation of grammatic utterances.

**Articulation problems:**
communication disorders characterized by omissions, substitutions, distortions, and additions of speech sounds.

**Voice disorders:**
vocal problems including voices that are too high, too low, too loud, too soft, or too nasal. In children, most voice disorders are functional, and are related to poor learning of voice control.

**Fluency:**
the smoothness with which sounds, syllables, words, and phrases flow together.

with their intellectual ability; and language problems are the chief difficulty of hearing impaired children. One thing that does seem clear is that, of all language disabled children, about two-thirds are boys (Silva, 1980).

Children with **speech disorders** are those whose speech interferes with communication (Van Riper, 1978). Young children make many speech errors when learning to talk. Mispronunciations and dysfluencies are common, but these errors are part of the developmental process. Children are, in fact, about eight years of age before they are stable in all the sounds of the English language. Mispronunciations and dysfluencies only become disorders when they persist as characteristics in the speech of children who should have acquired certain sounds. We would worry more, for example, about the seven year old who talked about his "Wittle wellow wabbit" than the child of the same age who could not get her tongue around the "zh" in leisure and measure.

**Language disorders** are problems in the recognition and understanding of spoken language or in the ability to formulate well-organized, grammatical sentences. Language disorders may be classified as receptive or expressive. **Receptive language disorders** are those which interfere with the comprehension of spoken language; **expressive language disorders** are those which affect the formulation of grammatic utterances (Byrne and Shervanian, 1977). Language disorders in children frequently combine both receptive and expressive problems. They range in severity from mild language learning difficulties to profoundly debilitating disorders.

Children are also characterized as having delayed or disordered language, a distinction that depends on the type, intensity, and duration of the difficulties. A child with delayed language development learns language in an orderly progression but more slowly and with less proficiency than normal age peers. Minor delays in language development may be caused by generalized immaturity rather than a pervasive language problem. Many young children who show minor delays catch up with their peers by the time they are five or six.

On the other hand, some children with deviant or disordered language show such difficulties in developing language in a normal progression that they may never attain adult levels. Some language disordered children may demonstrate bizarre language behaviour. The great majority meet such difficulties with acquisition that they require structured and systematic intervention. Many children with disordered or deviant language suffer additional handicapping conditions.

As we observed, minor speech disorders are rather common in young children. **Articulation problems**, which are characterized by omissions, substitutions, distortions, and additions of speech sounds, are the most usual type of communication disorder. It is particularly difficult to estimate numbers because many articulation problems simply disappear as children mature.

**Voice disorders** include voices that are too high, too low, too loud, too soft, or too nasal. In children, most voice disorders are functional, and are related to poor learning of voice control. Children who scream or talk loudly are in danger of abusing their vocal cords (Perkins, 1978). Vocal abuse can lead to vocal nodules or polyps that may have to be removed surgically. Children in the lower grades of school are likely to present more voice disorders (Moore, 1986).

**Fluency** is the smoothness with which sounds, syllables, words, and phrases flow together (Perkins, 1978). Stuttering is the major subcategory of dysfluency

**Dysfluency:**
a speaking disorder (also known as stuttering) characterized by blocking, repetitions, or prolongations of sounds, words, phrases, or syllables.

disorder, and affects approximately one percent of the population (Shames and Florance, 1982). Two to ten times more males than females stutter.

**Dysfluency**, or stuttering, is characterized by blocking, repetitions or prolongations of sounds, words, phrases, or syllables. The rate and rhythm of speech is affected, and facial tension or other types of body distortions may also appear. Stutterers often present a wide variety of secondary symptoms such as eye blinking, head jerking, and facial grimaces. Many demonstrate muscular tension and forcing when they try to speak.

Structural inadequacies are another major cause of speech disorders in children. These may be structural inadequacies in the vocal folds (larynx), tongue, teeth, lips, palate, and resonating cavities. Most defects of this type are of a developmental nature, although they can result from physical injury or disease.

Clefts are known as midline defects. They are only one of the wide variety of craniofacial anomolies, but they are also one of the most common and generally least severe. Many children with clefts are born with a gap in the roof of the mouth which opens into the nasal cavity. Children with clefts may encounter problems with swallowing, chewing, and correct respiration. In addition, slow language development and delayed articulation are not uncommon in children with clefts.

## Consequences of speech and language disorders

Speech disorders do not impinge on intellectual functioning or learning capacity and nearly all children with speech problems can be successfully integrated into regular classrooms. In fact, any other placement for students with speech problems only would be detrimental to their educational and social progress. Even students with additional handicapping conditions, such as cerebral palsy, that necessitate the use of communication boards or other augmentative speech devices, can be effectively instructed in regular classrooms (Winzer, 1989).

Children with language disorders often perform within normal limits on nonverbal intelligence tests (Leonard, 1981). However, many cognitive abilities are clearly language-dependent. As one would expect, children with language disorders perform poorly in those aspects of learning that rely on language.

The vocabulary used by language impaired children tends to be small, superficial, and reflective of reductions in the development of underlying concepts. Language impaired children have a tendency to deal with objects or events in wholes rather than parts. Children with language problems tend to be more rigid and literal in their thinking: they lack the flexibility required for pretending, for playing word games, for laughing at riddles and jokes and for effective social interaction. Deficits in expressive language, for example, limit the development of higher forms of group play. In turn, disabled children have fewer opportunities to learn the social, play, and communication skills that are unique to and emerge from child-child social interchange (Guralnick, 1986).

Children with problems in language acquisition invariably have difficulties learning to read. During grades three and four, the demands of language proficiency increase. New content areas are introduced, such as social studies and science. Abstract and symbolic material make it increasingly difficult for children with language disorders to cope with academic subjects. Severe language delay will probably affect every aspect of functioning and can have devastating effects on educational, emotional, and interpersonal development. There is a fairly large body of literature that suggests that when communicatively disordered children are considered as a group, they have an increased prevalence of psychiatric disorders (Cantwell and Baker, 1977). With respect to the more typical speech and language delayed children seen in school, some researchers (Baker, Cantwell and Mattison, 1980) found immaturity, short attention span, excitability, tantrums, and solitary behaviour to be characteristic of children with both speech and language disorders. Children with articulation problems and those with language problems tend to demonstrate a higher prevalence of behaviour problems (Baker and Cantwell, 1982).

## Learning disabilities

In almost every classroom across the country there are one or two pupils who fail to achieve adequate levels of performance despite conventional and consistent instruction. These students often bother and frustrate teachers with their unpredictable behaviour, their impulsiveness, their emotional instability (mood swings), their hyperactivity, their lack of attention, and their widely varied achievement in academic subjects (Winzer, 1989). Some of these students may suffer from learning disabilities. These students make up the largest single group of children with disabilities.

Learning disabilities is the newest area of special education and the fastest growing.

But in special education, no term is more controversial and no diagnosis more fraught with difficulties than learning disabilities. Many definitions of learning disabilities exist. For our purposes, we can examine some of the commonalities that occur in the plethora of definitions. The components generally found in definitions of learning disabilities include neurological dysfunction, uneven growth patterns, difficulty in learning tasks, discrepancy between potential and performance, exclusion of other causes, and average or above average intelligence.

**Neurological dysfunction**    Some students with learning disabilities are said to suffer from minimal brain dysfunction which impinges on their learning.

**Uneven growth patterns**    Commonly, students with learning disabilities show peaks and valleys in their functioning. They are strong in some areas, and very weak in others. An example would be the student who can tell a wonderful story but cannot write it down.

**Difficulty in learning tasks**    The hallmark of the learning disabled population is academic underachievement. Learning disabilities should be viewed as a syndrome, a group of behaviours that adversely affect a child's academic and/or social and emotional functioning. The common thread is the inability of these students to learn adequately in regular classrooms under traditional teaching approaches and methods.

**Discrepancy between potential and performance**    Students with learning disabilities are perhaps best described as those who manifest educationally significant discrepancies between their tested potential for academic tasks and their performance in academic and social domains. The discrepancy between a child's potential and performance refers to the gap between what a child is capable of learning and what the child actually achieves. The child's potential is judged by the mental age obtained on standardized tests of mental ability which is then compared to the child's performance on achievement tests. A difference of two years between the estimated potential and the performance is frequently used as an indicator of academic retardation.

**Exclusion of other causes**    Most definitions of learning disabilities exclude children whose learning deficits can be accounted for by such handicaps as mental retardation or hearing impairment.

**Average or above average intelligence**    Inherent in the whole concept of learning disabilities and closely associated with the exclusionary cluase, is the notion that students with learning disabilities are of average or above average intelligence.

### Consequences of learning disabilities

Many people mistakenly associate learning disabilities with limited intelligence. By definition, however, learning disabled students are of average or above average intelligence. But they lag in some or all academic areas: they are unable to acquire skills at a normal rate.

Academic underachievement is the major characteristic of the learning disabled population. Some children suffer deficits in all areas; for others, only a few specific academic skills may be affected. Reading, writing and mathematics are three of the main areas in which difficulties occur.

Approximately 10 to 15 percent of the general school age population have reading difficulties (Harris and Sipay, 1980); however, among learning disabled students, the figure could be as high as 85 percent (Kaluger and Kolson, 1978). At the secondary level, the primary reading disability of learning disabled students is in the area of reading comprehension (Lindsey and Kerlin, 1979).

Children with learning disabilities manifest a range of learning problems, varied behaviours, and disparate characteristics. Their difficulties in dealing with various types of information may cause them to be less verbally facile and less responsible than non-learning disabled students. Learning disabled children are likely to have attention problems, be less task-oriented and more distractible, and face difficulties in social interactions (Bryan, 1978). They are often disorganized, uncooperative, socially awkward, slow to adapt to change, and overly active. They may demonstrate behavioural problems which may mask the learning disability (Winzer, 1989).

Perhaps as many as half of all learning disabled children have speech and language problems (Marge, 1972). Although they have problems with both expressive and receptive language, they seem to have greater difficulty using expressive language (Hessler and Kitchen, 1980). These may be the students who sit at the back of the class and hope that the teacher won't call on them. They rarely volunteer answers and when they are asked to speak they may be hesitant, stumble over words, and use a sparse vocabulary.

Visual perception problems are most commonly associated with learning disabilities. Children with visual perceptual problems are prone to difficulties with oculomotor coordination, spatial relations, figure ground perception, discrimination of differences, and recognition of likenesses. Many studies (e.g., Calfee, 1977; Coleman, 1968; Whipple and Kodman, 1969) indicate that visual perception problems are common among reading disabled children. Although some of these studies can be criticized on methodological grounds, the evidence strongly suggests that learning disabled children, as a group, perform poorly on tasks designed to assess visual perceptual abilities (Hallahan, 1975).

Several studies (e.g., Flynn and Byrne, 1970; Golden and Steiner, 1969; Harber, 1980; Lingren, 1969) have shown that auditory disorders occur with greater than normal frequency among learning disabled children. In the classroom, the child with an auditory dysfunction may have difficulty synthesizing sounds into words, analyzing words into word parts, and associating sounds with symbols. These children are often first recognized when they attempt to spell words. Their poor spelling results from their inability to discriminate sounds, to blend sounds, and to encode (spell) or decode (read) words.

Children with motor problems may show a range of specific behaviours. They may be uncoordinated in physical activities. They may have balance problems or spatial disorganization manifested by poorly developed concepts of space and a distorted body image. They may show overflow movements that occur when they want to perform a movement with one hand and the other hand involuntarily follows in a shadow movement. General uncoordination refers to a lack of muscular control. A student with gross motor control problems may walk with an awkward gait, have difficulty throwing or catching a ball, or trouble skipping or hopping.

Children with perceptual-motor impairments have problems identifying or reproducing information they receive through their senses. These children have difficulty discriminating symbols and may reverse letters and shapes in their printing and drawing. They do poorly in accurately reproducing or copying information received visually or auditorily. Examples of perceptual-motor problems include difficulties in identifying the letters of the alphabet, reading the printed page from left to right, drawing basic shapes, and staying on the line when printing or writing.

Keogh and Margolis (1976) outlined three categories of attention difficulties: coming to attention, decision making, and maintaining attention. Students with learning disabilities are generally slow to get actively involved in tasks placed before them and they meet problems in selecting the important information to which they should be attending (Keogh and Margolis, 1976). In relation to decision making, they are impulsive; for example, when confronted with several possibilities, learning disabled students tend to choose the first alternative before considering any of the rest (Hallahan and Kauffman, 1986). Children with learning disabilities also meet problems in maintaining attention once they have begun a task, a problem accentuated when the task is of relatively long duration (Pelham, 1981).

Students who have trouble learning often develop social and emotional problems: their academic inabilities can provoke frustration, anxiety, and anger. If these difficulties are neglected, students may eventually become caught in a spiral of failure and dissatisfaction, become frustrated, and lose their self-esteem and motivation. As well, academic problems can cause disappointment to parents and bring ridicule from peers (Winzer, 1989).

**Hyperactive children:**
children who display rates of
motor behaviour that are too
high for their age groups and
engage in excessive, non-
purposeful movement.

Learning disabled children tend to be rejected by their peers (Bryan, 1974); they receive more criticism from their peers, as well as from their teachers. The reasons why learning disabled children inspire negative responses are not clear. Perhaps they speak in a less pleasant manner and tend to ignore interpersonal signals from their peers (Bryan and Bryan, 1978). Or perhaps it is because they are less accurate than non-disabled children in interpreting the nonverbal behaviour of others.

## Attention deficit/hyperactivity

While children with diagnosed learning disabilities exhibit a wide range of academic and behavioural problems, one of the most often mentioned characteristics is that of attention deficits (Hallahan and Reeve, 1980). Hyperactivity has been identified as the most common childhood behaviour disorder presented to doctors, psychiatrists, teachers, and other related professionals, not to mention parents. Estimates of the prevalence of hyperactivity range from one to 20 percent for all school age children (Gadow, 1979). Hyperactive boys outnumber girls four or five to one (Rutter, 1975).

Attention deficits, hyperactivity, and learning disabilities are not the same although much confusion exists between the various designations. This happens because attention deficits and hyperactivity are closely related and the conditions are often seen in students with learning disabilities. Most researchers, however, believe that attentional problems are the key factor.

Hyperactive children display rates of motor behaviour that are too high for their age groups. They indulge in excessive, non-purposeful movement. Their accelerated rates of activity disturb others, worry teachers, and cause their families discomfort and even despair. Hyperactive children often cannot run as fast as other children, but they cannot slow down their rates of movement on demand (Maccoby, 1980). Their activity is disorganized and not modulated or regulated to meet the demands of a given situation (Maccoby, 1980).

However, children who are referred to as hyperactive generally have more problems in regulating their attention and maintaining concentration than they do with their restlessness or excessive motor activity (Henker and Whalen, 1989). This is reflected in the new combination of terms used in the *Diagnostic and Statistical Manual of Mental Disorders* (DSM-R 111) where the condition is now called attention-deficit hyperactivity disorder (APA, 1987).

Attention disorders are characterized by distractibility, difficulty in concentrating and failure to complete assignments. Students with attention disorders are often impulsive; they do things without thinking and do not learn from experience. They are easily distractible; they are unable to concentrate on a task because they have not learned to screen out irrelevant stimuli. Students may also perseverate—they purposelessly and sometimes disadvantageously repeat an activity. For example, a child may finish addition problems on page one and continue them on page two, even though the instructions clearly indicate a switch to subtraction.

### Consequences of attention deficit/hyperactivity

The hallmark of childhood hyperactivity is trouble—trouble getting things done, both at home and at school, and trouble getting along with adults and with other children (Henker and Whalen, 1989). Young hyperactive children are constantly on the move, pushing, poking, asking questions, but never waiting for answers. In the classroom, they are unable to sit still. When confined to a seat, they translate their need to be active into finger and foot tapping, as well as other disruptive activities. Hyperactive teenagers may manifest their condition differently. These students drum their fingers, shuffle their feet, open and close their desks, and continually visit the pencil sharpener, other desks, and other areas of distraction. Time of day may be a potent factor. In their classroom behaviour, hyperactive children exhibit more interference, off-task behaviour, noncompliance, and minor motor movements in the afternoon (Zagan and Bowers, 1983). Hyperactive children suffer from short attention spans that elicit negative teacher responses. One study (Peter, Allen, and Horvath, 1983) found that hyperactive boys see greater teacher disapproval directed toward them.

Children with attention disorders tend to be distractible and to spend more time in off-task behaviour than do their peers. These youngsters find it hard to focus and hold their attention for appropriate lengths of time. They cannot sit still long enough to initiate and sustain the thought processes needed for school work and are repeatedly unable to concentrate on specific tasks long enough to complete them.

Attention disorders cause or compound academic problems. Children with intrinsic attention problems are difficult to handle in groups and teachers may consider reducing the amount of time these students spend in group settings. Proximity control—seating the student near the teacher—may also help to sustain his or her attention (Winzer, 1989). It is possible for teachers to hold attention for longer periods by facing the student in order to establish eye contact. Concrete aids such as flow charts, flip charts and overhead projectors are important. Students may exhibit closer attention if they are provided with a lesson outline or a glossary of key terms prior to the lesson (Winzer, 1989).

## SENSORY HANDICAPS

Hearing and vision are known as the distant senses because they connect us so closely with the environment. The loss of hearing or vision isolates an individual from family, friends, community, and the physical environment. Hearing and visual handicaps can damage a person psychologically, socially, emotionally, and educationally.

Few children of school age are completely blind or completely deaf. Far more common are children who see poorly or who are hard-of-hearing. Many visual and auditory problems go unidentified until school age. Some children are never identified and are mislabeled as learning disabled or slow learners or dismissed as dull or lazy.

Visual handicaps include a wide range of degree and type of disability. At one end of the spectrum are the totally blind, those who have no sight at all. At the other end are those with near normal vision. Most visually handicapped persons, however, have low vision—their corrected vision is lower than normal (Colenbrander, 1976). Similarly, the broad category of hearing impairment stretches from those who have marginal hearing losses that may only be a real concern in noisy situations, to profound deafness where individuals cannot hear voiced sounds, even with amplification (hearing aids) and must resort to speech reading and, often, sign language.

Hearing impairment poses a serious threat to children's learning. The greatest single handicap of defective hearing is its effect on the development of communication skills because hearing loss interferes with both the reception and the production of language. Providing the most appropriate medical, educational, and social resources for hearing-impaired students is a challenge.

## Hearing impairment

Hearing loss is classified according to the amount of hearing in a person's better ear. Decibels and hertz are used to measure the loudness and the frequency. Individuals are classed as deaf or hard-of-hearing, depending on whether they hear sounds at certain intensities of loudness across a range of frequencies. This classification is further structured by designation as mild, moderate, severe, or profound hearing loss.

**Table 7-7** Degrees of hearing impairment

| RANGE | SEVERITY | IMPLICATIONS |
|---|---|---|
| 0-25 dB | Insignifiicant | |
| 25-40 dB | Mild hearing loss; hard of hearing | May have difficulty with faint or distant sounds. May have problem in conversations, groups, or settings with much ambient noise. |
| 40-60 dB | Moderate hearing loss; hard-of-hearing | Frequent difficulty with normal speech, especially in conversations, groups, and class discussions. |
| 60-90 dB | Severe hearing loss; hard-of-hearing | Great difficulty with even loud or amplified speech which seems faint and distorted. Requires amplification and intense speech and lan guage training. |
| 90 dB+ | Profound hearing loss deaf | May be aware of loud sounds and vibrations, but generally cannot understand even amplified speech. |

A number of definition and classification systems are used for the hearing impaired. The Conference of Executives of American Schools for the Deaf (1974) has developed a widely accepted definition with an educational orientation. According to this definition:

• Hearing impairment is a generic term indicating a hearing disability that may range in severity from mild to profound. It includes the subsets of deaf and hard-of-hearing.

• A hard-of-hearing person is one who, generally with the use of a hearing aid,

**Otitis media:**
a condition in which the mucosal lining of the middle ear becomes inflamed and the cavity filled with fluid, hindering the air conduction of sound.

has residual hearing sufficient to enable successful processing of linguistic information through audition.

- A deaf person is one whose hearing disability precludes successful processing of linguistic information through audition, with or without a hearing aid.

Teachers should be especially aware of otitis media, the most common form of ear infection that can cause mild hearing loss in children. **Otitis media** is a condition in which the mucosal lining of the middle ear becomes inflamed and the cavity filled with fluid. When this happens, air conduction of sound is hindered. The prevalence of otitis media is higher among lower socioeconomic groups, Native populations, children with cleft palates and other craniofacial anomolies, and more common in males than in females. There is a higher incidence in summer than in winter (Canada, Health and Welfare, 1984). The peak prevalence for otitis media is between six and 36 months. After six years of age, the incidence of otitis media steadily decreases. However, in the normal school environment, 20 to 30 percent of children between the ages of five and 12 will have at least one bout of middle ear effusion. Of these, 10 to 20 percent will probably develop chronic middle ear problems (Liden and Renvall, 1977).

Otitis media causes temporary to chronic mild conductive hearing losses. Because of the nature of otitis media, the degree of hearing loss may fluctuate. Under certain conditions, such as when the child has a heavy cold, the loss may be much greater. As well, certain environments, such as a noisy classroom, can compound the effects of a mild conductive hearing loss (Winzer and Lafleur, 1991).

The most devastating hearing impairments are caused by sensori-neural problems of the inner ear. A great many childhood sensori-neural impairments are attributed to "causes unknown." However, Moores (1982) has documented five major causes of sensori-neural deafness: heredity, maternal rubella, meningitis, mother-child blood incompatibility (Rh factor), and prematurity. The most profound losses stem from meningitis, maternal rubella, and hereditary factors.

### Consequences of hearing impairment

Speech and language are the areas of development most severely affected by a hearing impairment. However, speech and language problems vary considerably within the hearing impaired population.

For children with mild or moderate hearing losses, the effect on speech and language may be minimal. As long as the voiced sounds of conversational speech remain audible, effective communication skills are possible. Hard-of-hearing children can use spoken language adequately to transmit and receive information. They can use their residual hearing to develop speech and language skills although they may use speech reading to supplement auditory skills. However, even with adequate speech and language skills, hard-of-hearing children may be at risk educationally. Mild losses can be educationally devastating; children may be left with permanent effects, such as inefficient listening strategies that persist into later life. To prevent language delays, impairments must be diagnosed and treated early.

For deaf children, most loud speech is inaudible, even with the most sophisticated hearing aids. These children have significant problems in learning language.

**Visual acuity:**
the measure of the smallest image distinguishable by the eye.

**Visual functioning:**
what the impaired person is doing with his or her residual vision.

Because deaf children cannot hear the words of people around them, they have no language models. Speech is another area of serious difficulty. In one study (Jensema, Karchmer and Trybus, 1978) where teachers rated the intelligibility of the speech of their hearing impaired students, more than 42 percent of the children were rated as unintelligible or barely intelligible. According to the survey, approximately 13 percent of the children would not even try to use their voices for speech.

When communication is blocked in the oral modality, the manual modality frequently assumes the functional burdens of speech. In other words, deaf students will rely on speech reading to access information and may use sign language for communication.

The current emphasis on appropriate integration for students with disabilities means that more and more students with hearing impairments are being educated in regular classrooms. Students with severe and profound hearing losses require a great deal of special help; those with moderate losses can be successfully integrated with periodic help in a resource room or from an itinerant teacher; students with marginal and mild hearing losses need little special help when integrated in regular classrooms although teachers will need to monitor their progress carefully.

## Visual impairments

The visual system consists of the eye, which receives the light image; the nerve pathways, which transmit the image to the optical centres of the brain; and the brain itself, which interprets the image. Visual impairments can result from any interference of the passage of light as it travels from the outer surface of the eye along the nerve pathways to the brain (Harley and Lawrence, 1977).

The category of visually impaired includes both blind persons and those with low vision. Two different types of definitions are used—legal definitions and educational definitions. In Canada, legal blindness is defined as an acuity measure of 20/200 (6/60 [metric]) or less in the better eye with the best correction; or visual acuity of more than 20/200 if the widest diameter of the field of vision subtends an angle of no greater than 20 degrees (CNIB, 1980 ). The legal definition of partial sight includes those who have a visual acuity greater than 20/200 but not greater than 20/70 in the better eye after correction (CNIB, 1980). These legal definitions are founded on visual acuity, the measure of the smallest image distinguishable by the eye. Visual acuity of 20/200 means, for example, that a normally sighted person can see at 200 feet what the visually impaired person can see at 20 feet.

Visual functioning or visual efficiency is what the impaired person is doing with his or her residual vision. For educational purposes, functional definitions have been found more useful than legal ones. Educators look at whether the student will need alternate methods, such as braille, or whether the student can function with large print materials and optical aids.

### Consequences of visual impairment
Because visual impairment follows a continuum from mild loss to total blindness, it is best to consider the consequences as becoming greater as vision

decreases. The developmental consequences of total blindness differ obviously from those related to low vision. Blindness sharply reduces the range and variety of a child's experiences and restricts the child's ability to move freely within an environment.

Hearing is the only distance sense available to blind idividuals and it must function in an entirely different way, uniformed by vision. Verbal language serves many important social and information-gathering functions for blind children. Even before they develop speech, blind children use vocalizations to achieve and maintain social contact. They also learn a great deal about people in their environment from voices. They learn to measure personal attention by the nearness of the speaker and the touch gestures that accompany speech. They become adept at interpreting meaning from nuance or variations in voice tone (Rogow, 1987b). Visually impaired children tend to ask more questions than other children as part of their information gathering. As sight increases, so questions decrease (Erin, 1986).

There is no magical sensory compensation of the remaining senses. Learning to compensate for lack of sight does not happen automatically; the touch and auditory senses do not become more accurate without effort and concentration (Rogow, 1987b). Locating objects by sound is something that we all do, but we are rarely conscious of it when we do it. Blind persons must learn to pay more attention to those auditory and tactual clues that sighted people can afford to ignore. By using alternate sensory stimuli, blind children form meaningful notions of the objects around them. Visual impairment does not affect intelligence or langauge development. The main challenge for educators is to provide an adequate alternate method for gathering information or an adequate method of developing the student's visual ability to the fullest. Braille reading and writing, large print, reading devices, audio aids, concrete materials, and embossed maps, graphs, and geometric designs all allow visually impaired students to receive information (Winzer, 1989).

## Box 7-3 **Braille**

Braille is the medium of literacy for blind persons. The Braille alphabet uses six dots arranged in two vertical rows of three dots each; each dot is numbered. Numbers and punctuation signs are also represented in Braille. Numbers use dots 3 to 6 and the use of dot 6 just before a letter indicates a capital. Braille has been adapted to many written languages, including those that do not use Roman letters. As well, a scientific and mathematical code has been developed.

As a system of reading and writing for blind persons, Braille has a relatively short history, especially in American educational circles. Although Louis Braille developed the idea of a raised alphabet for the blind in 1829, North American educators were markedly reluctant to accept the system. In the last century, schools for the blind used a variety of systems such as Moon print, New York print, and raised print. Braille became the accepted mode only by the closing decade of the nineteenth century (Winzer, 1990b).

Braille originally arose from the work of Charles Barbiere, engineer, inventor, philanthropist, and officer in Napoleon's army, who devised a code which he called *ecriture nocturne*—night writing. These were not tracings of the ordinary alphabet but a secret code based on a twelve dot unit or cell two dots wide and six high. Each dot or combination of dots stood for a letter or a phonetic sound. In 1808, when Barbiere's system was presented to the French Academy of Sciences, it was hailed as a brillant invention. Various adaptations of the system were undertaken by Barbiere and duly submitted to the Academy. One report found its way to the school for the blind in Paris where the twelve dot system was tried but rejected as impractical in 1820: the cells were simply too large to be read by a single finger tip. At the time when blind people rejected Barbiere's system, Louis Braille (1809-1852) was only eleven years of age (Winzer, 1990b).

Louis Braille was the son of a harness maker. He slit an eye at the age of three while playing with a sharp knife and the resulting infection destroyed the vision in his other eye. In 1819 Braille went to the Paris school and later became an instructor there. Disconcerted with the raised print method of teaching reading to blind pupils, Braille embarked on a search for a more efficient means. When he discovered Barbiere's military code, he set out to adapt it to the specific needs of blind individuals (Winzer, 1990b).

When Braille undertook the adaptation of the Barbiere system, he first determined that the cell of twelve dots, two vertical rows of

six dots in height, was too tall to be comprehended by a finger tip. After cutting the number of dots in half, Braille then devised a new code, alphabetic rather than phonetic, employing combinations of six dots. Because the new code was arbitrary, the symbols could stand for anything the users wanted to code. Braille's alphabetic code was published in 1834; his music notations in 1839. The Braille system for reading and writing was officially adopted at the Paris School for the Blind in 1854 (Winzer, 1990b). Dr. Simon Pollak, one of the founders of the Missouri School for the Blind, brought Braille from Europe in the 1950s, but the Braille code failed for many decades to find a niche in North America. Once accepted as a system to assit blind persons with reading and writing, however, Braille evolved into a well-established system that employs many abbreviated signs and symbols (Winzer, 1990b).

The complex rules underlying Braille structure, together with the many accepted abbreviations, make the teaching of Braille reading more complex and time-consuming than teaching print reading. For the reader, the process is slower than reading print because the reading range of the fingers is much narrower than the eye. Reading efficiency is more difficult, and readers must develop tactile tracking skills, a light touch, good reading posture, and smooth coordination of both hands (Mangold, 1982).

A skilled two-handed reader begins by placing both hands at the beginning of a line. When the middle of the line is reached, the right hand continues across the line while the left hand locates the begining of the next line. The left begins to read the first several words of the new line while the right hand moves to its new reading position (Mangold, 1982).

# NORMALIZATION

The catchwords of today's special education are normalization and mainstreaming. These widespread movements entail many different strategies, including deinstitutionalization, integration, non-categorical approaches to teaching, and a rejection of traditional labeling. All these strategies aim to provide exceptional individuals with an education and a lifestyle as close to normal as possible.

Normalization is the philosophical belief that all exceptional individuals, no matter what their level and type of handicap, should be provided with an education and living environment as close to normal as possible. The principle of normalization, in its simplest form, calls for the use of "culturally valued means, in order to enable people to live culturally valued lives" (Wolfensberger, 1981, p. 8).

Normalization principles assert that handicapped persons learn appropriate skills most efficiently in settings which demand a knowledge of those skills—such as public schools.

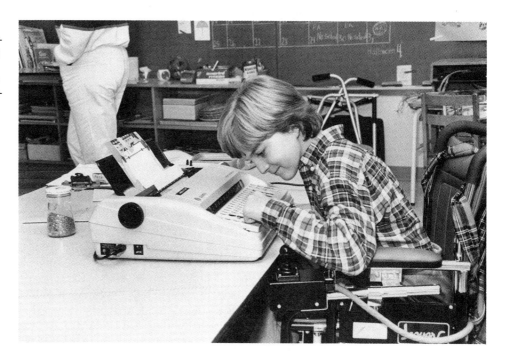

The normalization movement provides guidelines for the treatment of handicapped people, as well as concrete suggestions for action. Its adherents want society to regard disabled persons as individuals and to treat them fairly and humanely. The major goal is a normal family and community life for all individuals. Normalization principles assert that handicapped persons learn appropriate skills most efficiently in settings which demand a knowledge of those skills, such as the public schools, industry, or the local neighbourhood. In addition, non-handicapped persons are most likely to alter their perceptions of deviance through positive interactions with handicapped persons who display competencies in ordinary community settings (Voeltz, 1982).

**Mainstreaming:**
the physical, intellectual, social, and emotional integration of exceptional children and youth into the regular educational milieu.

## Mainstreaming

The principle of normalization has been extended to preschool and school-age children, resulting in a parallel educational process known as mainstreaming, or educational integration as it is more commonly referred to in Canada. Mainstreaming represents both an ideal and an ongoing process. The basic goal is the provision of free, appropriate education in the most suitable setting for all exceptional youngsters. Mainstreaming has been defined in many ways (Blacher-Dixon and Turnbull, 1979; Meyen and Lehar, 1980), which only reflects the difficulty of the construct. Winzer sees it as both a philosophy and a process:

> *Mainstreaming is the physical, intellectual, social, and emotional integration of exceptional children and youth into the regular educational milieu. It demands individual programming, cooperative planning, and a range of educational options and support services (Winzer, 1989).*

According to Winzer (1989) mainstreaming is the educational parallel of normalization. It is the integration of children with learning, behaviourial, physical, or other problems in order to provide them with the opportunities for as normal an education as is consistent with their needs. As well, it is a learning experience that is ongoing—a process through which exceptional children will be prepared for work and for life.

Under mainstreaming principles, the focus is on the integration of exceptional children with their non-handicapped peers within the context of the regular neighbourhood school. A range of available services allows exceptional pupils to be integrated into the regular milieu in the manner best suited to their individual needs. Students may be physically integrated in the sense that the special education services are offered within the same school plant as is the education of other youngsters. Some youngsters may partake of non-academic integration; their core and content subjects will be provided in a special class, but they will join the regular stream for areas such as art, music, and physical education. Other students may be partially integrated; they may move between the regular class and the special class as their unique learning needs dictate. Most mildly handicapped children will be fully integrated into regular classrooms, receiving additional help in the resource room, from itinerant teachers, or from other specialists.

## Legislation and litigation

Notions of normalization and mainstreaming rest on a strong philosophical belief that every person, regardless of handicaping condition, has the right to a lifestyle as normal as possible. Bolstering philosophical commitment is legislation and litigation that ensures the rights of handciapped persons in the community and exceptional pupils in the schools.

Court decisions and legislative actions can have a dramatic impact on education. In the United States, the passage of PL94-142, the Education of All Handicapped Children Act, made special education a national concern. Across Canada, legislation and policies are in place that compel respect for the unique needs of every exceptional child.

Special education has emerged as a key priority; policies related to the rights of exceptional individuals are formulated at the federal, provincial, and local district levels of government. However, in Canada, except for the Declaration of Human Rights, there is no federal law to outline or guarantee the rights of exceptional children. Each of the ten provinces has its own school system based upon provincial education legislation. Legislation governing the rights of Canadian exceptional children to education and the responsibility of school boards to provide suitable programs has been enacted in some provinces and contemplated in others.

## MAKING MAINSTREAMING WORK

Mainstreaming is probably best conceptualized as a social experiment in which, in many ways, the philosophical commitment is ahead of research and practice. While educators, legislators, parents, and others advance the notion, the manner in which the process will work most successfully has not yet been clearly delineated. There is not yet a quantitative measure of how great a handicap must be for special services to be offered, nor is there established an absolute number or combinations of characteristics that must be identified before a pupil is diagnosed as exceptional.

Reports in the literature about the results of mainstreaming have been termed "inconclusive" (Salend, 1984, p. 409). For one thing, mainstreaming solves several important problems. It gives mildly handicapped students an opportunity to interact with their non-handicapped peers and to learn normal behaviour. But it also creates other problems such as teacher modifications of programs and instruction and non-acceptance of exceptional students by their peers. Another reason is that mainstreaming is not an entity but a set of proedures, as Peck and Cooke (1983) have noted. Different procedures are implemented by different mainstream programs. In addition, many classroom teachers are minimally equipped to deal with the needs of those not responding to group instruction. Teachers also face time restraints, limited resources, and finite energy and patience. These can each undermine efforts. Further investigations of the success of the integration of mildly handicapped students still present results that are mixed and inconclusive (Caparulo and Zigler, 1983; Polloway, 1984).

To compound the difficulties, even though mainstreaming seems the best way to normalize exceptional children, major barriers continue to exist. Some of these are simply physical, such as lack of school ramps or elevators for wheelchair-bound children. More problematic, however, are the barriers created by people's attitudes and actions. Sometimes parents resist the notion of mainstreaming. The parents of non-handicapped children may believe their offspring are being denied teacher time and instruction. Some may hold traditional prejudices about exceptional children.

A few parents of exceptional children also oppose the idea of mainstreaming. They believe their children's needs can be better met in a segregated setting with a structured curriculum and a lower pupil-teacher ratio. Sometimes, they fear for the social consequences of integration, and anticiapte stigmatization and rejection for their children. Mylnek, Hannah, and Hamloin (1983) surveyed parent members of an advocacy organization for children with behaviour disorders, learning disabilities, and mental retardation regarding their attitudes toward mainstreaming. Results revealed that parents of learning disabled students were significantly more positive than were parents of behaviourally disordered or mentally retarded childern. Parents of children with learning disabilities believed that regular classroom integration would facilitate their children's over-all adjustment and development including the development of better coping abilities, reduction of negative peer interactions, and more involvement in school activities. The parents of behaviourally disordered and mentally retarded children voiced concern that regular classroom teachers lacked the time to work adequately with handicapped pupils. At the same time, they did not perceive segregated instruction as effective. Simpson and Myles (1989) also assessed the attitudes of parents of learning disabled, mentally retarded, and behaviourally disordered pupils on mainstreaming. They found the parents willing to support mainstreaming, but only if adequate support was available. About 24 percent of the parents rejected mainstreaming outright regardless of professional efforts to make it a viable option. Parents who supported mainstreaming seemed to do so based on the benefits of social integration and improved academic performance perceived to result from such an educational organization (Simpson and Myles, 1989). Parents preferring segregated programs seemed to do so to avoid ridicule of their children by non-handicapped peers and to minimize unfair grading based in comparison with other children in the mainstream.

One potent factor that will militate toward the success or failure of educational integration is the attitude of regular classrom teachers. Classroom teachers carry the primary responsibility for the integration of the exceptional child and, for most, the role of mainstreaming implementor is new. Teachers are expected to take on additional work loads and anxieties, and to devote extra time to assessment and referral. They must also find time to work with a team to develop, implement, and evaluate mainstreaming programs. Teacher attitudes also influence those held by non-handicapped children in the classroom as well as the extent to which exceptional children are truly integrated with their class and can reap the concomitant academic, social, and emotional benefits (Baker and Gottlieb, 1980).

Mainstreaming is based on the assumption that, when exceptional children are placed in regular classrooms, constructive relationships will form between these children and their non-handicapped peers. For mainstreaming to be effective, children must be integrated physically, intellectually, socially, and emotionally. The process involves peer relationships, the opportunity to gain status and acceptance, and feeling comfortable with members of the classroom group. This allows children the corresponding rights and responsibilities of group membership.

Winzer (1989) stresses that mainstreaming implies more than physical proxomity—the spatial distance between handicapped and non-handicapped children. There is considerable evidence that physical integration does not ensure social integration (e.g., Meyer and Kishi, 1985); efforts are not likely to be successful if they consist of the mere exposure to non-handicapped peers. In addition, mainstreaming implies more than intellectual integration—the modification of curricula directed to children's unique sets of learning and behavioural characteristics. The brightest classroom and the most thorough Individual Education

For mainstreaming to be effective, children must be integrated physically, intellectually, socially, and emotionally.

Program (IEP) will not promote successful integration unless exceptional children are also socially accpeted.

Social integration refers to the child's physical proximity to, interactive behaviour with, and acceptance by non-handicapped classmates. It is the active inclusion of exceptional children into the social activities of the classroom. In the classroom, exceptional students must be provided with the opportunities to make friends, to win the approval of peers, to assume diverse roles, and to become helpers and leaders. Only when the social intent is met will the anticipated human benefits of mainstreaming become possible. Stereotypes will be destroyed, differences valued rather than rejected, and the classroom environment enriched for all students and teachers. It is when handicapped children are liked, accepted, and chosen as friends that mainstreaming becomes a positive influence on the lives of both exceptional and regular students (Winzer, 1989).

But studies of the acceptance of handicapped children in regular classrooms do not present encouraging findings. Research has shown that interaction patterns between non-handicapped and handicapped children occur at extremely low rates and are often negaitve in nature (see Winzer, 1990a).

## SUMMARY

**1.** Only recently has society come to the realization that exceptional individuals have the right to as normal a living environment as possible. As a new evolving social philosophy has stressed the rights of individuals, the prospects for exceptional adults and students have altered dramtically.

2. Children with all types and degrees of disability benefit from ongoing opportunities to interact with, observe, model, and develop friendships with other less disabled and non-disabled children. Throughout the country, more and more intensive services designed to meet children's individualized instructional needs are being delivered within the mainstream of school and society. Children with even the most severe disabilities are receiving their education alongside their non-disabled peers within regular schools, classrooms, and community environments.

3. Mental retardation is related to delayed intellectual development while giftedness implies development above the norm. Behaviourial disorders are easier to identify than to define or classify: children with conduct disorders attract attention with their overtly disruptive behaviours. Immature and withdrawn children are a little harder to identify but are still fairly recognizable. Children with language problems or speech disorders may not only be hindered in their academic performance but in almost every aspect of functioning. The conditions covered by the term visually impaired cover a range of conditions. In school, students with visual impairments have the same needs as other children and teachers need not change the content and aims of their education significantly. Deaf children are some of the most difficult to integrate because of their language difficulties. Hard-of-hearing children can work in regular classrooms, perhaps with some instructional modifications.

4. Clearly the traditional system of labeling children by their primary disability is not always useful. Administrators and professionals will likely continue to use categories of exceptionality. However, in the classroom alternate approaches may serve exceptional children better.

5. It is extremely difficult to distinguish between or within the categories describing students with mild disabilities. When students' actual performance in school is examined, there is seen to be considerable overlap. With this in mind, special educators are developing non-categorical, or generic approaches.

6. Successful integration implies alterations in the traditional conception of two separate eduational systems. It will not work unless staff, regular students, and exceptional pupils are committed to the idea and cooperate in finding ways to overcome the obstacles that inevitably and continually arise. The regular classroom teacher will require many support services, and will need to rely heavily on the special education or the resource room teacher. The classroom teacher can also look to support from the other educators and allied child-care personnel.

7. Because of the wide range of symptoms and disabling conditions, there is no one instructional approach or remedial procedure.

## Key Terms

adaptive behaviour
anxiety
developmental period
fluency
language disorders
normalization
phobia
receptive language disorders
speech disorders
visual acuity
voice disorders

aggression
articulation problems
dysfluency
hyperactive children
mainstreaming
obsession
problem behaviour
related services
students with exceptionalities
visual functioning

antisocial behaviour
depression
expressive language disorders
labeling
mental retardation
otitis media
psychoses
special education
sub-average intellectual
    functioning

# 4 LEARNING THEORIES

On December 15, 1911, at exactly 1:55 in the afternoon a dog secreted nine drops of saliva (Pavlov, cited in Skinner, 1983, p. 287).

With teaching machines and programmed instruction one could teach what is now taught in American schools in half the time with half the effort (Skinner, 1986, p. 116).

We teach a subject not to produce little living libraries on the subject, but rather to get a student to think mathematically for himself, to consider matters as an historian does, to take part in the process of knowledge-getting. Knowing is a process, not a product (Bruner, 1966, p. 72).

Many students perceive school as a place where one is forced to do things which have little pertinence to life as he experiences it. Education must be concerned with values, beliefs, convictions and doubts of students. These realities as perceived by an individual are just as important, if not more so, as the so-called objective facts. (Combs, 1962, pp.68-69).

**M**
**A**
**J**    This section is designed to:
**O**
**R**    •    define the process of learning;

         •    distinguish between the views of learning set forth by behavioural, cognitive, and
              humanistic psychologists;

**O**    •    compare and contrast the major views of learning in terms of their utility in the class-
**B**         room; and
**J**
**E**    •    trace the development of major models of learning.
**C**
**T**
**I**
**V**
**E**
**S**

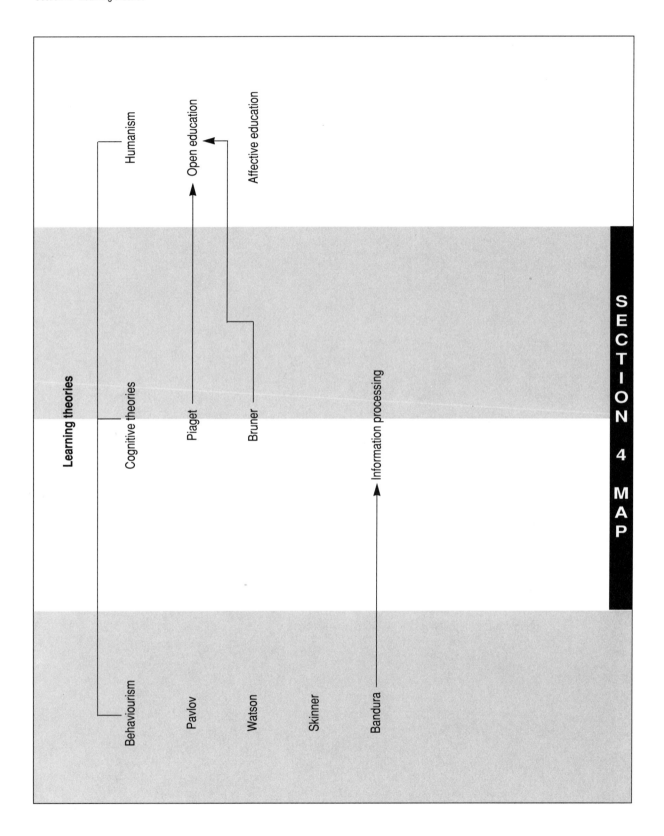

Children are sent to school to learn the skills, competencies, and attitudes they will need to successfully move into adult society. The main job of the teacher is to motivate children to learn, to stimulate their learning, and to assess how much and how well learning has taken place.

But learning is not a unitary thing or concept; nor do all children learn in the same way, at the same rate, or under the same conditions. How then can a teacher, faced with 30 or so children who all have different learning styles and needs, accommodate each of them so they accomplish what the schools are charged to do? A good way is to develop ideas about learning; to become acquainted with the different theories of learning and their applicability in different situations and with different students.

When teachers understand how learning occurs, this knowledge will guide their classroom practice. Theories of learning attempt to describe the process of learning—as it is currently believed to occur. Theories are therefore directly applicable to classrooms, for they guide teacher behaviour, use of materials, structure of lessons, evaluative processes, and even classroom climate and management.

Psychologists have studied the process of learning for generations but, given its complexity and diversity, it is not surprising that a single or encompassing explanation of how we learn has failed to emerge from this extensive body of research. For one thing, it is difficult to differentiate learning from development. For another, learning is not the same as thinking, although the processes are closely linked and mutually supportive.

Although the study of learning has been at the core of psychology, the pursuit of the subject has been anything but serene. Two main schools of theoretical thought about learning have emerged although, of course, there exist many variations in each basic structure. The two major schools may be divided under the encompassing terms "behaviourism" and "cognitive learning" and stress, respectively, overt, observable behaviours and unobservable mental processes.

How different these ideas are can be seen in the opening quotes. B.F. Skinner, doyen of the behavioural school, promotes structure and learning from environmental consequences. In contrast, Jerome Bruner stresses the inner or unobservable workings of the mind. Bruner's position is more consistent with the cognitive view. He insists, for example, that the goal of teaching is to promote a "general understanding of the structure of a subject matter" (Bruner, 1962, p. 6).

While a number of theorists fall within the broad grouping of behaviourists, they differ from one another in many significant ways. All behaviourists, however, focus on observable, measurable behaviours that are demonstrated by humans and animals. Many behaviourists have studied the behaviour of lower organisms, particularly rats and pigeons, in order to examine how these creatures are influenced by different types of environmental stimuli and behavioural consequences. The ideas gained from animal studies are seen as applicable to humans. Behavioural theorists are particularly interested in the way that pleasurable or painful consequences that follow a behaviour can change an individual's behaviour over time. In this sense, the psychological theories of behaviourism provide the foundation for the principles of behaviour modification that are widely employed in classrooms.

Most behaviourists are not concerned with internal events, such as thinking, intentions, moods, or emotions. Their basic premise is that every human and animal action constitutes a response to a stimuli. The exception to this rule is Albert Bandura, a social learning theorist, who incorporated cognitive mediation into his theory of learning. Bandura's ideas are important for classroom learning and instruction as well as for classroom motivation and management.

From perhaps 1930 to 1960 behaviourism in general, and the findings of B.F. Skinner in particular held an elevated position in North American psychology. However, the 1960s witnessed the beginning of what has been described as the cognitive revolution. The assumptions of the behaviourists were challenged from ethological and cognitive perspectives. Essentially, ethologists study animals not in closed laboratories but rather in their natural settings. The ethological approach disputed the claim made by the behaviourists that animal and human development are continuous and that the laws of learning are the same for all organisms and for all situations.

In the opinion of psychologists from the cognitive school, something important was missing from the behavioural conception of how learning occurs. The cognitive theorists disputed the behaviourists' assumptions that associations between stimuli and responses are the only building blocks of learning. To them, behavioural approaches seemed to ignore a student's perceptions, insight into, and cognition of the essential relationships between the elements of a situation (Gage and Berliner, 1984). They further questioned whether learning can be understood by considering only one factor.

In contrast to the psychologists of the behavioural school, cognitive learning theorists such as Jean Piaget, Jerome Bruner, the Gestalt psychologists, and the information processing theorists, focus almost exclusively on inner cognitive processes. They look at behaviour to the extent that it illustrates the underlying cognitive process. Jean Piaget, whose theories were discussed in the section on human development, joins other cognitive psychologists in classifying learning according to the different intellectual processing skills or cognitive operations that develop with age.

Together with the behavioural and cognitive theories, there is a humanistic view of learning. While psychologists who adopt a humanistic view of learning do not offer a theory per se, they do have definitive views about how schools and teachers can best facilitate learning, as the opening quote by Combs illustrates. The work of humanistic psychologists such as Combs, Carl Rogers, and Abraham Maslow are interspersed with such words as maintaining, sharing, enhancing, and experience. They promote a student-centred

school of curriculum founded squarely on students' interests and needs. The humanistic educator acts as a facilitator, concerned with creating an open climate of trust and acceptance in which children are free to experiment and learn. Children are given the freedom to choose what they wish to learn, instead of being directed by the expectations of teachers or department curriculum guides. Facilitators work cooperatively with the students to establish classroom guidelines and design activities which will facilitate maximal cognitive growth. They help students find answers to questions they are concerned about—and therefore eager to learn about—by making materials and resources available as needed.

There are different kinds of learning situations that require different types of concepts and strategies. Current scientists are working toward establishing principles of learning by bringing ideas from various lines of research to bear in shaping different instructional approaches. Additional typologies, if not comprehensive theories, have emerged that distinguish several types of learning according to differences in what is being learned; for example, Benjamin Bloom's classification of cognitive objectives (Bloom et al., 1956) and the classification of learning hierarchies of Gagné (1977) and Gagné and Briggs (1979).

While this section will clearly delineate the disparate views held by behavioural, cognitive, and humanistic psychologists in regard to learning, it is important to note that each school of thought offers a great deal of useful information to the classroom teacher. Scientific principles of learning can be translated into classroom use in order to make learning more productive and efficient. For this reason the fourth chapter of this section will delineate the instructional implications of these theories.

# BEHAVIOURAL THEORIES OF LEARNING

**Learning:**
a relatively permanent change in behaviour that is brought about by interactions with the environment.

## INTRODUCTION

**Learning** is a relatively permanent change in behaviour brought about by interactions with the environment. Psychologists concerned with behavioural theories of learning explain learning in terms of the associations that we make between our behaviour and what is going on around us. They see changes in behaviour as occurring as a function of the environmental events that precede or follow them.

Radical behaviourists confine their studies to external observable responses and events. Today, fewer behaviourists conform to this extreme position and most reject the position that internal mental processes such as thinking or feeling are irrelevant. However, most would still insist that such things as thinking and feeling do not lend themselves to scientific analysis because they cannot be directly observed and measured. Behaviourists believe that the only way to determine whether an individual has learned something is to observe that person's behaviour or performance. A relatively permanent change in behaviour that is repeated in different performances indicates that learning has taken place.

As psychological theory, behaviourism was born in the United States in the opening decades of the twentieth century. Much of the initial impetus for the work, however, came from the work of several Russian scientists, among them Ivan Petrovich Pavlov (1849-1936). Pavlov is remembered as a highly respected researcher. In 1904, he won a Nobel Prize for his work on the digestive activity in dogs. However, a large part of his enduring eminence rests on a discovery that eventually had a far greater impact on the fields of psychology and education than in his own field of physiology. Pavlov was one of the first to identify a particular phenomenon that is encompassed within the term "classical conditioning."

# CLASSICAL CONDITIONING

**Neutral stimulus:**
an environmental stimulus that does not automatically elicit a response from the organism.

**Unconditioned stimulus:**
an environmental stimulus that automatically elicits some type of unlearned response from the organism.

**Unconditioned response:**
an unlearned response emitted by the organism in response to a particular environmental stimulus.

**Conditioned stimulus:**
an environmental stimulus that acquires the ability to elicit some type of learned response from the organism.

**Conditioned response:**
a learned response emitted by an organism in response to a particular environmental stimulus.

**Response strength:**
the quantitative measure of a response.

Pavlov's work on classical conditioning began with a chance discovery when he was studying the salivation reflex in dogs. He was particularly interested in discovering how reflexes were influenced by the placement of substances in the digestive system. By placing food or food powder near the dog's mouth, Pavlov would stimulate the digestive system. He had surgically implanted tubes on the salivary glands and so was able to obtain very precise measures of salivation.

Pavlov had been used to dogs that salivated only when they were being fed. However, his experimental dogs soon began to salivate in what seemed to be an unpredictable fashion. They would salivate at the mere sight of food or even the sound of approaching footsteps associated with the trainer bringing food. Pavlov considered this to be important, as it indicated that the digestive process could be altered in the absence of direct physical stimulation (the consumption of the food). In other words, what the dogs had learned through experience influenced their reflexive behaviour, which in this case was salivation.

Pavlov abandoned his original course of research in order to investigate this puzzling phenomenon. In a typical experiment, he would begin by sounding a tone and recording the dogs' salivation response. Because the dogs had not previously been exposed to the tone, they did not respond by salivating to the sound. The tone was a **neutral stimulus** because it did not elicit the salivation response from the dogs. Then the dogs were fed, and they responded to the food by salivating. The food was an **unconditioned stimulus**, since it automatically elicited the **unconditioned response** of salivation. The salivation response was unconditioned because it had not been taught or "conditioned," but rather occurred naturally in response to food. This is the basis of classical conditioning; the key to learning is what happens before the response is made.

As the experiment continued, Pavlov repeatedly paired the tone with the presentation of food. Soon, the dogs began to salivate after they heard the tone, even before the food was delivered. Through conditioning, the tone had become a **conditioned stimulus** that could elicit the salivation response. The **conditioned response** that occurred as a result of the tone was very similar, albeit not identical, to that which occurred in response to the food. Pavlov (1927) found that the dog's salivation response to the conditioned stimulus alone was much stronger when the bell sound preceded the meat powder by approximately half a second during training than when there were longer or shorter intervals between conditioning stimulus and the unconditioned response of salivation. Pavlov concluded that **response strength**, the quantitative measure of a response, was affected by the time interval between the presentation of the conditioned stimulus and the unconditioned response.

In such experiments, Pavlov and his colleagues demonstrated that learning could affect reflexive behaviours, which had always been considered to be involuntary and unaffected by experience. Figure 8-1 presents a visual representation of Pavlov's experiment.

**Figure 8-1**
Classical conditioning

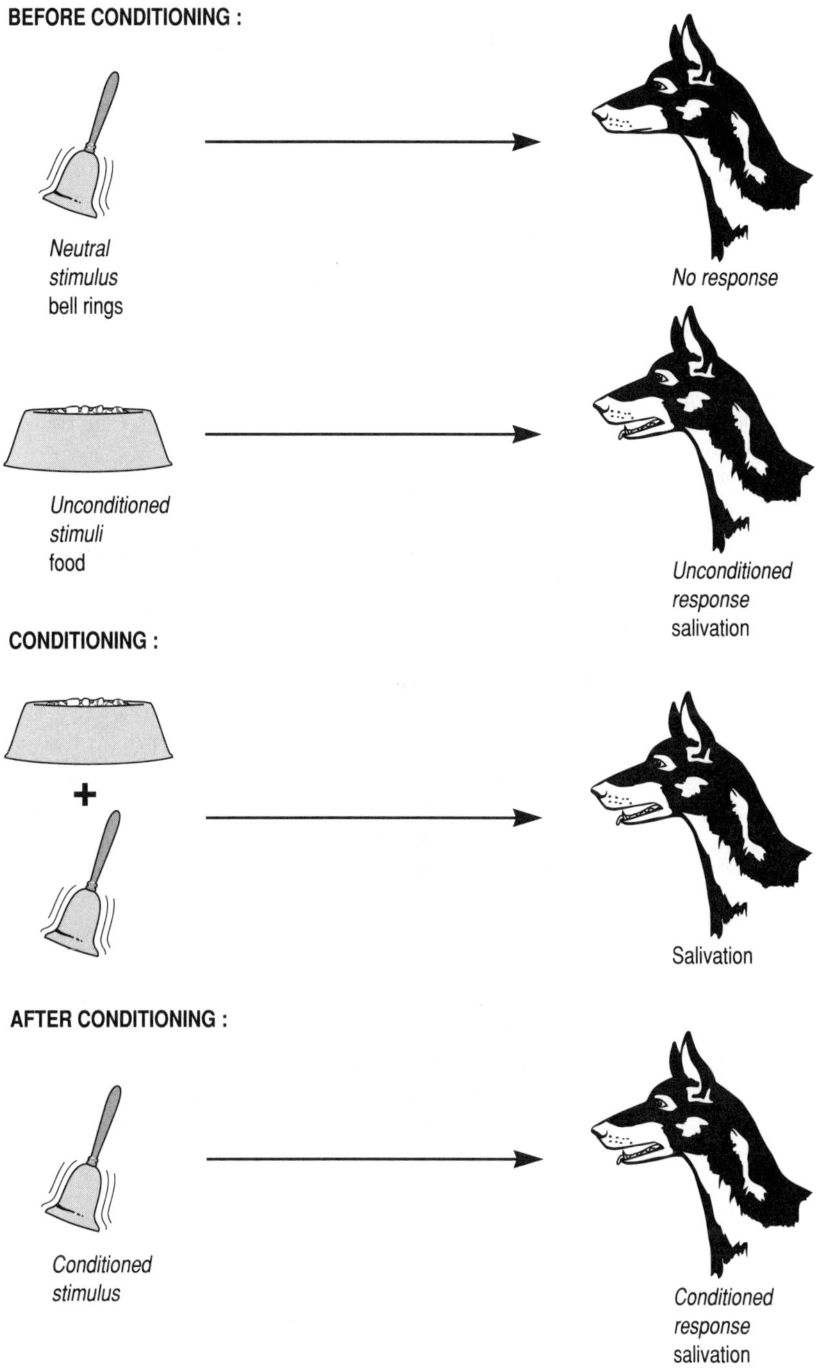

**BEFORE CONDITIONING :**

*Neutral
stimulus*
bell rings

*No response*

*Unconditioned
stimuli*
food

*Unconditioned
response*
salivation

**CONDITIONING :**

+

Salivation

**AFTER CONDITIONING :**

*Conditioned
stimulus*

*Conditioned
response*
salivation

**Classical conditioning:**
occurs when people or animals learn to respond automatically to an object or event (stimulus) that previously had no effect, or a very different effect, on them.

**Respondents:**
unlearned responses.

**Extinction:**
(classical conditioning) the disappearance of the conditioned response when the conditioned stimulus is repeatedly presented in the absence of the unconditioned stimulus.

**Generalization:**
(classical conditioning) the extension of the response to similar stimuli.

**Discrimination:**
(classical conditioning) the ability of the individual to respond differently to similar stimuli.

**Second-order conditioning:**
the chaining or connection of conditioned responses.

This kind of learning is referred to as classical conditioning. **Classical conditioning** occurs when people or animals learn to respond automatically to an object or event (stimulus) that previously had no effect, or a very different effect, on them. It is learning through stimuli that elicits or automatically produces a reflexive response. Such responses are referred to as **respondents**, or unlearned responses—they are not under voluntary control and they are not learned. For example, a puff of air in the eye will elicit a blink; a loud noise will elicit a startle response; a tap on the right part of the knee will elicit a kick. Therefore, a reflex must have an identifiable stimulus that automatically elicits the response, even though no learning has occurred.

As Pavlov's experiment illustrated, repeatedly pairing a neutral stimulus with an unconditioned stimulus will eventually give the neutral stimulus the power to elicit a conditioned response. For example, if a bell was repeatedly sounded at the same time as a puff of air was directed towards a person's eye, soon that individual would blink only in response to the bell.

## Principles of classical conditioning

Further experimentation by Pavlov and others led to the development of the following principles of classical conditioning. The first is the process of **extinction**. It was found that if the tone (conditioned stimulus) was repeatedly sounded, yet no food (unconditioned stimulus) produced, the dogs would eventually stop salivating. The conditioned response would be extinguished.

**Generalization** implies the extension of the response to similar stimuli. It occurs when an animal or human responds in the same way to similar stimuli or transfers a response to a new situation. The conditioned response is elicited by a variety of different stimuli that are similar, but not identical, to the original conditioned stimulus. For example, if dogs had been conditioned to respond to a particular tone, they would also salivate to other similarly pitched tones, even if those tones had never been used in training.

**Discrimination** is the opposite of generalization and refers to the ability of an individual to respond differently to similar stimuli. For example, the dogs would salivate to a 2000 cycle tone but not a 2700 cycle tone if only the former was repeatedly paired with food. The response to the 2700 cycle tone was extinguished while the response to the 2000 cycle continued to be reinforced.

**Second-order conditioning** involved the chaining, or connection, of conditioned responses. For example, again consider the dogs that were conditioned to salivate to the tone. If the conditioned stimulus, the tone, was repeatedly presented together with another neutral stimulus, such as a flash of light, soon the dogs would salivate even when the light was presented alone. In this case, the light became a new conditioned stimulus for the conditioned response of salivation.

Pavlov's work was influential as it outlined an entirely new method by which learning could occur. Attempts were made to extend the principles of classical conditioning to all types of human learning, including the acquisition of language and knowledge as well as the development of aberrant behaviours such as alcoholism. However, it became rapidly apparent that classical conditioning could not adequately explain learning in such areas (Kazdin, 1989). In addition, recent research on classical conditioning reveals that conditioning is not a simple or straightforward proposition.

However, Pavlov's careful and precise work provided a model for scientific study that inspired many other researchers in psychology and other disciplines. B.F. Skinner observed that he "learned from Pavlov a respect for controlled experimental conditions and for simple facts" (Skinner, 1983, p. 287). Pavlov's stress on carefully controlling experimental conditions, his meticulous recording of his procedures, and the resulting data made it possible for others to replicate his work. He helped greatly to advance a scientific approach to the study of behaviour (Kazdin, 1989).

## John Broadhus Watson

John B. Watson, the brilliant, provocative, and controversial American psychologist, was the first to build upon Pavlov's findings and develop a behavioural theory of learning. Watson is generally recognized as the founder of behaviourism; in fact, he coined the term (Watson, 1913). Details about Watson are found in Box 8-1.

**Box 8-1  Biographical note: John Broadhus Watson (1878-1958)**

Born in Greenville, South Carolina, Watson had an unpromising early career. His mother was a religious woman who wished for John to become a Baptist minister. His father was a violent man with a notorious reputation who abandoned the family when Watson was 13. In school, young Watson was considered lazy and insubordinate, more skilled with his fists than with his lessons. By the age of 16, however, he reached Furman University where he earned his way as a laboratory assistant in chemistry. He made only passing grades and found few close friends. After graduating, Watson taught in a one-room school and was very popular with the students. For his biology class, he taught rats to do tricks, one of his first experiences with the animals that were to lay the basis for his psychology.

Eventually Watson traveled to Chicago to obtain a higher degree. He received his Ph.D.

from the new department of psychology in Chicago. His doctoral program was based on the work of Thorndike respecting animal behaviour, with minors in philosophy and biology. He worked on his thesis for three years, day and night, graduating *cum laude* in 1903 with a thesis that correlated the behaviour of white rats with different stimuli (EAB, 1958). Watson was offered several academic positions but chose to remain in the department of psychology at Chicago. In his classes in experimental psychology, Watson used traditional psychological methods, teaching students to use introspection to analyze their own minds. However, he felt more comfortable with the rats and other animals used in research and veered sharply in that direction. In fact, even after he became a skilled and experienced experimenter, Watson frankly affirmed his stong dislike for any role as a participating subject or indeed for using human subjects at all (EAB, 1958).

Watson married in 1903 and then, after repeated offers, accepted a position at Johns Hopkins where he remained from 1908 to 1920, except for a few months' military service.

After many abortive attempts to find his niche in the army (one of which nearly led to court-martial [EAB, 1958]), Watson returned to Johns Hopkins, and worked out his ideas about behaviourism which he first aired in 1913. In 1919 he published his general text-book, *Psychology from the Standpoint of a Behaviorist*.

Regardless of his contributions to psychology and the emerging school of behaviourism, Watson's personal life became the focus of public interest and abruptly terminated his academic career. Watson became involved with a graduate assistant, Rosalie Raynor,

and wrote her compromising letters which were eventually obtained by his wife and found their way into print. His divorce was a sensation, played up particularly by the Hearst press, and was page-one copy all across the country. Watson married Raynor on the New Year's Eve following his divorce. He was also asked to resign his teaching position, not so much because he had become divorced but because he violated the unwritten code about faculty and student liaisons. Before 1920 ended, Watson was employed by the J. Walter Thompson company, became vice-president in 1924, and remained with them until 1936 when he joined the William Coty Company as vice-president. He continued until his retirement in 1945 (EAB, 1958).

**SOURCE:** Winzer 1990b.

As a behaviourist, Watson saw psychology as a "purely objective experimental branch of natural science" (Watson, 1913, p. 154) and he therefore studied only observable, measurable behaviours. While this may not seem like a revolutionary idea today, it was quite a change for a field that was characterized by introspection in the latter decades of the nineteenth century. Introspection had been the main focus of William Wundt at his Leipzig laboratory and he influenced a band of early American psychologists. Psychologists would study their own thought and images, a process that was necessarily subjective and unscientific (see Winzer, 1990b).

John Watson soundly rejected this methodology. He contended that psychologists had to abandon the study of the unobservable thoughts, intentions, images, or mental states, and focus on overt, measurable behaviours. Watson believed that it was not genetic heritage but learning through experience that was the primary determinant of human behaviour. Influenced by Pavlov, Watson saw classical conditioning as the process by which most behaviours are acquired. He urged his colleagues to study relationships between stimuli (S) and the responses (R) that were evoked. For this reason, Watson's brand of psychology was referred to as S-R psychology.

In one of the most often cited experiments in psychology, Watson and Rosalie Rayner (1920) attempted to demonstrate the importance of classical conditioning on the development of emotional responses. The subject of the investigation was an 11-month-old boy, Albert, who was observed to play quite freely with a white rat. It was further noted by Watson that sudden loud noises comprised an unconditioned stimulus (US) that naturally elicited an unconditioned response (UR) of fear from little Albert.

In order to show the conditioning of a fear response, Watson would smash a steel bar with a hammer each time Albert touched the rat (the neutral stimulus). After seven pairings of the rat with the loud and startling noise (US) (in two sessions, one week apart), Albert showed fear and avoidance, the conditioned response (CR), whenever the rat, now a conditioned stimulus (CS), was near. Some generalization of this fear response was seen (such as to other small animals and to a fur coat), although the responses were inconsistent and appeared to extinguish rapidly.

Watson's experiment with Little Albert has been often repeated and just as often embellished and exaggerated. Watson's experiment is most accurately described as a subjective case study rather than a convincing demonstration of the conditioning of human emotions. The source of some of the confusion arising from the Little Albert experiment lay with Watson himself who frequently added or deleted details in his many descriptions of the study. These inaccuracies have often been repeated and many new distortions created in subsequent reports of this research in textbooks and other sources. Certain ethical considerations also surround Watson's study. He deliberately produced a behaviour that would have a deleterious impact on the life of the subject and did not make any provisions for reversing the damage that he had created.

But regardless of the ethical concerns, it is important to note the impact of this study on the field of psychology. Despite the problems with the research design, it was accepted as a demonstration that aberrant behaviours, such as extreme fears or phobias, could be learned, contradicting the prevailing psychoanalytic viewpoint of the day. Further work by one of Watson's colleagues, Mary Cover, demonstrated that such fears could also be "unlearned." This novel view prompted many psychologists to pay closer attention to the delineation of behavioural principles, as well as their application to human problems.

Watson's experiment with Little Albert suggested that some abnormal behaviours—such as extreme fears—could be learned.

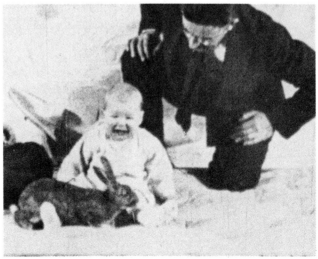

Photo courtesy of Prof. Benjamin Harris.

## Research applications of classical conditioning

While Watson, in particular, oversimplified the learning process, it appears that classical conditioning processes play a role in the development of generalized emotional responses (such as phobias or prejudices) that occur as the result of specific stimuli. Early applications of the principles of classical conditioning were described by Mowrer and Mowrer (1938) who used the principles to treat enuresis (bedwetting). This problem can be seen as a failure of the individual to respond (by waking) to the presence of the stimuli (pressure caused by the distension of the bladder). A liquid sensitive pad was placed in the child's bed and, when the child urinated, an alarm sounded. The alarm was the unconditioned stimulus that elicited waking behaviours. Eventually, after repeated pairings of the unconditioned stimulus and the feeling of bladder distension, the child would eventually wake up before urinating. Similar strategies have also been used to reduce smoking, deviant sexual behaviours, overeating, and so on (Kazdin, 1989).

Further evidence of the strength of the principles of classical conditioning was provided in a series of studies in which subjects were asked to learn two lists of words, consisting of names of nationalities and adjectives. One list was presented visually on a screen while, at the same time, a word was presented through headphones. Thus, each nationality would be repeatedly paired with either a positive or negative adjective. Although subjects were not aware of the associations, when they were later asked to rate the nationalities their ratings were influenced by the positive or negative nature of the adjectives with which the nationalities had been presented (Staats and Staats, 1958). It may be that children learn prejudices in the same way. While they may not be directly taught to dislike, fear, or avoid a particular ethnic group, the ethnic label may come to be associated with the reactions demonstrated by parents or teachers (Alcock, Carment, and Sadava, 1989). Uses of classical conditioning are further illustrated in Box 8-2.

### Box 8-2   Classical conditioning in therapy: Systematic desensitization

Phobias are intense fears that can have a devastating effect on a person's life. The suggestion of a trip to the mountains might be inviting for most, but a horrendous prospect for a person with a fear of snakes, spiders, or animals. Out of eggs? The quick trip down to the corner store may be an impossible achievement for a person with agorophobia, or a fear of open spaces. People who suffer from intense phobias often spend their lives taking elaborate precautions to avoid situations that most others take for granted.

One therapeutic technique that has been widely used and highly effective in the treatment of phobias or fears is systematic desensitization. Originally developed by Wolpe

(1958), it is based on the classical conditioning model and can even be described as a process of "counter-conditioning." That is, as the person has been conditioned to fear a particular object, person or event, behavioural therapists suggest that this response can be "unlearned," and a more appropriate response learned in its place. The goal of systematic desensitization therapy is to teach the client to substitute a positive response—relaxation—for the unwanted feelings of anxiety or fear. This approach, consistent with its behavioural roots, focuses only on the behaviour rather than causes such as past traumatic events, unconscious motives, or the childhood years as might be found in more conventional therapy.

An example of the use of systematic desensitization was described by McGrath et al. (1990), who treated a nine-year-old girl. Lucy had an intense fear of sudden loud noises, such as balloons popping, fireworks, car backfires, and so on, which interfered with her ability to function normally in daily life. For example, Lucy could not go to parties where it was likely that balloons or noisemakers would be used. This was Lucy's only significant fear; she was otherwise not a fearful child. After the therapists had determined that her phobia did not have a physical base, therapy was begun.

The first step in systematic desensitization is to teach the client to achieve a deep sense of relaxation. Lucy was taught to achieve deep muscle relaxation by breathing deeply while imagining herself at home, lying on her bed with her toys, a setting in which she was quite comfortable. Second, the client is asked to construct a hierarchy of anxiety-producing events, which range from least to most fear-producing situations. Lucy's hierarchy included doors banging, cap-guns popping, balloons bursting, and the unexpected explosion of party poppers. To help Lucy gauge her fear reaction, the therapists introduced the idea of a "fear thermometer," which

allowed Lucy to rate her level of fearfulness on a scale from one to 10.

In Lucy's first session, she was taken out into a long hallway, at the far end of which was a helper holding a balloon. Lucy was asked to signal the helper to pop a balloon. This strategy was intended to give her a sense of control over the situation, but even with that, she was unable to bring herself to give the command to pop the balloon. Finally, the therapist ordered the helper to pop the balloon, which severely upset Lucy. When this occurred, she was taken back into the therapy room and told to relax using the procedure outlined for her.

Over four more therapy sessions (during which time over 60 balloons were popped), Lucy was able to order the popping of the balloon at ever closer distances. At the end of the fourth session, the helper was standing at a distance of only ten metres. Lucy showed only mild anxiety and was very pleased with her progress. During the fifth session, a new strategy was tried in which Lucy herself first held an uninflated balloon and then a small inflated balloon. When she gave her usual signal, 20 balloons were rapidly popped, one after the other, in the therapy room. Lucy appeared to gain confidence with each pop, and by the end of the session, she popped eight balloons herself.

During the sixth to ninth sessions, Lucy blew up balloons and popped them herself. By this time, she began to enjoy the excitement of the noise—her playful behaviour was quite a contrast to her initial fears. At this stage, the next item from the fear hierarchy, party poppers, was introduced. As she found these even more frightening than balloons, Lucy again reacted with anxiety. A similar desensitization procedure was used in which the poppers were sounded at an ever-decreasing distance. By the end of two additional sessions, the therapists were able to bring the poppers back into the room with her. The next item from the hierarchy was introduced in a similar fashion, and again the speed with which the therapists could bring it into the room with Lucy was shorter than that before. By the end of the session, the therapists noted that Lucy was enjoying herself. The change in Lucy's fearfulness was also reflected in her scores on the fear thermometer; for example, the level of fearfulness in relation to balloons went from 7 to 3 (out of 10) from the beginning to end of therapy, while her score for party poppers went from 9 to 5 (out of 10). During her last session, the therapists were able to unexpectedly pop very large balloons without inducing a pronounced fear response from Lucy. Therapy was terminated at this point.

At a three month follow-up to the therapy, it was found that the gains obtained in therapy were maintained. Her parents reported that Lucy no longer became upset over unexpected noises, and that she was now confident enough to participate in class parties and field trips.

Although some of the first systematic and objective accounts of classical conditioning were performed by using animals as subjects, the principles hold relevance for classroom teachers. If conditioning is the learning that occurs through association, and classical conditioning the learning that occurs through the association of two stimuli, then educators must know about conditioning so it can be used to the advantage of children in schools.

In schools, we can see many positive and negative examples of classical conditioning. We can think of the many students who feel anxious or ill when confronted with a test. And yet as tests are originally neutral stimuli, what might cause tests to elicit a negative conditioned response? (Such conditioning can be the result of a series of negative or positive experiences, or from a single traumatic event). For example, a student might have linked tests with feelings of failure, parental disapproval, or peer ridicule. Thus, a test (or the mere mention of one) becomes a conditioned stimulus which elicits the conditioned response of anxiety or nausea. Many fears—of public speaking, mathematics, or physical education—can be learned in the same manner.

## OPERANT CONDITIONING

The earliest applications of the behavioural model focused upon instinctive, reflexive responses that occur naturally in response to particular stimuli. However, as behaviourists continued to explore animal and human behaviour, it was clear that classical conditioning could not explain the origin of purposeful, or deliberate, actions. The examination of these behaviours led to an expansion of the behavioural theory of learning and the delineation of another type of conditioning known as operant conditioning. If Pavlov and Watson are most closely associated with classical conditioning, then those most intimately connected with operant conditioning are Edward Thorndike and B.F. Skinner.

## Box 8-3 **In the classroom: Principles of classical conditioning**

Kofi was a bright and friendly young boy about to start grade one. Because Kofi neither had any older siblings to fill his head with tales of school, nor had attended any type of formal preschool program himself, he didn't know what to expect from the experience. He had no particular emotional or physical reaction when first confronting the school building or his new grade one teacher. In other words, they were neutral stimuli. However, Kofi soon discovered that his grade one teacher, Mr. Kennedy, was a warm, responsive, and affectionate man. Kofi had lots of trouble with his printing and other fine motor tasks but Mr. Kennedy always found some reason to give a congratulatory hug or a kind word. Kofi responded by being an attentive and eager student who begged to participate during the day and had to be shooed out of the classroom at the final bell.

In this example, the teacher's warmth, hugs, and positive comments were the unconditioned stimulus that elicited Kofi's feelings of pride and accomplishment, or the unconditioned response. With each passing day, the neutral stimuli (the school as well as the teacher) were repeatedly paired with the unconditioned stimulus. It did not take long for the school and the teacher to become a conditioned stimulus which had the power to elicit the same positive feelings from Kofi (conditioned response).

When Kofi moved on to grade two, how would you have expected him to respond to his new teacher? It would seem likely that he would behave in much the same way. He would show the same conditioned response (positive regard) to the new, but similar stimulus (the new teacher). As you will recall from the earlier discussion, this is an example of generalization. However, if Kofi was unfortunate enough to get a nasty, punitive grade two teacher, he might learn to fear that teacher, but would continue to respond positively to his previous teacher (discrimination). But if Kofi continued to be exposed to aversive situations (and nasty teachers) in school, his initial positive response to school would likely be extinguished.

**Connectionism:** learning is seen as a process of "stamping in" or forming connections between a stimulus and a response.

## Edward Lee Thorndike

In 1898, at the same time that Pavlov was conducting his pioneering work, E.L. Thorndike (1874-1949) published a paper titled "Animal intelligence" that immediately elevated him to a dominant position in North American psychology. Thorndike's early work, to some extent, paralleled Pavlov's. Thorndike viewed most behaviour as a response to stimuli in the environment and paid little attention to the possibility of concept formation on thinking (Thorndike, 1898). So even before this branch of psychology had a name, Thorndike adhered to behavioural principles, although he never classified himself as a behaviourist (Hilgard, 1987). He developed a theory of connectionism in which he proposed

**Instrumental conditioning:**
learned behaviours that allow the organism to reach a particular goal.

**Law of Effect:**
Thorndike's principle that any act that produces a satisfying effect will cause the connection between the stimulus and response to be strengthened.

**Law of Exercise:**
Thorndike's principle that the repetition of the stimulus-response strengthens the bond: if it is not practised, it weakens.

that learning was a process of "stamping in," or forming, connections between a stimulus and response.

One of Thorndike's most famous experiments illustrates the evidence on which this theory was based. A hungry cat would be placed in a cage or "puzzle box," held shut by a simple latch, and a piece of fish placed just outside the door to provide an incentive for the cat to escape from the box. The cat would try to reach the food by reaching through the bars. When that didn't work, it tried to escape in a trial and error fashion: clawing the floor, rubbing against the bars of the cage, or batting at a piece of looped string that hung from the roof of the cage. Eventually the cat would accidentally get its claw caught in the string (which was connected to the door latch) and, yanking on it to free its paw, would open the door. Out of the cage, the cat would gobble down the fish. Each time the experiment was repeated, the cat would escape from the cage sooner until eventually the cat would pull the string immediately upon being placed in the cage. By plotting the time that it took for the cat to escape over repeated trials, Thorndike described a learning curve.

In these types of experiments, Thorndike was studying deliberate actions that were instrumental in helping the animal reach its goal, as opposed to reflexes or emotional responses. The learning of these instrumental behaviours was referred to as **instrumental conditioning**; in other words, the animal learned behaviours that allowed it to reach a particular goal. This work differed from studies of classical conditioning because the cats were not demonstrating reflexive behaviours in response to some stimuli. Rather, they were demonstrating and refining new responses according to the demands of the situation.

With much data in hand, Thorndike (1913) formulated his most important and influential principle. The **Law of Effect** stated that any act that produces a satisfying effect will cause the connection between the stimulus and response to be strengthened. As a result, the act is more likely to be repeated in the future. The key factor is the reward, or "satisfying effect," which ensures that a bond or connection is strengthened between the stimulus and the response. Thus, unlike Pavlov's classical conditioning, learning was seen to occur as a consequence of behaviour, not simply because of contiguity. A second principle, the **Law of Exercise**, stated that the repetition of the stimulus-response strengthens the bond: if it is not practised, the bond is weakened. In his later writing, Thorndike modified this law to assert that repeated practice leads to improvement only if accompanied by positive feedback or rewards.

For most of the first part of this century, Thorndike was the preeminent authority in educational psychology and his work had a profound effect on school practice. The Law of Effect led to the use of rewards (gold stars, verbal praise and so on) to reinforce appropriate academic performance. The Law of Exercise led to much repetitious work and drill and practice in an attempt to strengthen stimulus-response bonds.

## Burrhus Frederick Skinner

Watson's principles and applications of classical conditioning made behaviourism a force in North American psychology. Still, it was not until the arrival of B.F.

**Operant behaviours:** responses that are not elicited by particular stimuli but are affected by the reinforcers or punishers that follow the behaviour.

**Operant conditioning:** the process through which an organism's behaviour is influenced by the particular consequence that follows the response.

Skinner (1904-1990), the most eloquent and persuasive of the behaviourists, that behaviourism achieved a dominant position. Nevertheless, the link between Skinner's line of reasoning, and that of Watson, Thorndike and other early associationalists, is clear and direct.

In his 1938 publication, *The behavior of organisms*, Skinner outlined two types of behaviours. First he spoke about the familiar reflexive behaviours that are elicited by preceding stimuli. However, because Skinner found that much of human behaviour could not be accounted for simply through an examination of respondent behaviours, he identified a second type of behaviour which he termed operant behaviours. To Skinner, operant behaviours are not elicited by particular stimuli; instead they are affected by the consequences that follow the behaviour, and these consequences are called either reinforcers or punishers. Skinner's idea of reinforcement was borrowed from Thorndike's Law of Effect which Skinner streamlined (Sprinthall and Sprinthall, 1988).

Skinner proposed that operant behaviours can be either strengthened or weakened by the consequences that follow them, and this process of learning is referred to as operant conditioning. Skinner's formulations were based on the careful and systematic study of the behaviour of laboratory animals under specified conditions. He is perhaps most famous for the development and use of a piece of mechanized laboratory equipment referred to as the "Skinner box." A Skinner box for rats was a carefully controlled environment which was soundproof and did not allow the rat to observe the experimenter located outside. It contained a bar for the rat to press and a food and water dispenser.

The "Skinner box" was used to show the effects of operant conditioning in laboratory animals.

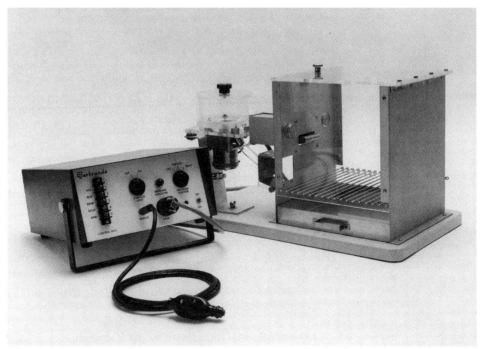

Photo courtesy of Gerbrands Corp., Arlington, Massachussetts.

**Antecedents:**
stimuli before the behaviour.

**Behaviour:**
response performed by the individual.

**Consequence:**
a change in the environment which occurs after the behaviour, the effect of which is to alter the probability that the behaviour will or will not occur in the future.

Skinner would systematically alter the rate and schedule at which "consequences" were delivered in order to measure their effect on the rat's behaviour. For example, the apparatus might first be set up so that a rat received a food pellet each time it accidently pressed the bar. This consequence would lead the rat to press the bar frequently and reduce the probability that it would demonstrate other behaviours, such as wandering around the box. At this point, the experimenter might alter the consequences, by withholding the food pellet or requiring the rat to press the bar several times before receiving food, or delivering food after some bar presses and not others. The rat's behaviour was automatically recorded in order to assess the impact of differing consequences on its behaviour. Skinner used his system to explain all animal and human learning. In education circles he is particularly known for his proposed use of teaching machines that provide immediate reinforcement to the learner.

### Principles of operant conditioning

As we pointed out, the principles of operant conditioning describe the relationship between behaviour and the environmental events which influence behaviour. This relationship is referred to as contingency and it encompasses three components: antecedent events, behaviours, and consequences. The relationship is often written as the following equation:

$$A \longrightarrow B \longrightarrow C$$

Given this equation, we can see that behaviourists view human behaviour as being predictable. They do not suppose behaviours to be arbitrary; they propose that behaviours occur in an orderly fashion dependent upon the events that precede and follow them. Therefore, antecedents refer to stimuli before the behaviour, such as instructions, gestures, school bells, red lights, and so on. Behaviours are the actions performed by the individual in response to the antecedents, and in anticipation of the consequences, the events which occur after the behaviour.

Unlike respondent behaviours, operant behaviours are not elicited by the preceding stimuli (Skinner, 1969). For example, food is seen to elicit the respondent or reflexive behaviour of salivation; a puff of air in the eye will elicit a blink; and a tap on the knee may elicit a kick. In contrast, in operant conditioning, antecedent stimuli do not force a response to occur; rather, antecedents acquire their control only because they have been associated with certain consequences in the past.

For example, the doorbell chimes, and Susan runs to open the door. She opens the door because her behaviour has been reinforced in the past by the presence of a desired visitor. The chime does not elicit her behaviour; it is her past experience that influences her behaviour. Thus, while antecedent stimuli signal the individual by telling him or her what to expect, the consequences have ultimate control over behaviour. If the doorbell were to chime repeatedly and no one was there when Susan answered the door, the change in consequences would mean that the antecedent stimuli would no longer signal the door-answering

**Discriminative stimulus:** an antecedent stimulus that cues the learner that certain consequences will follow a particular behaviour.

**Discrimination:** (operant conditioning) the learner responds differently under different antecedent conditions.

**Stimulus control:** when behaviours are under the control of antecedent stimuli.

behaviour. Figure 8-2 outlines the relationship or contingency between antecedents, behaviours, and consequences.

To elaborate, we can say that when Susan learns that a certain stimulus (the doorbell ringing) leads to a certain consequence (visitor outside), the antecedent stimulus is referred to as a discriminative stimulus (Sd). Susan is likely to answer the door when the bell sounds (Sd) because this Sd has been associated with the reinforcing event: receiving a visitor. However, in the absence of the Sd (ringing of the chime), she is not likely to open the door. Behaviourists would say that Susan has made a discrimination—she responds differently under different antecedent conditions. Behaviour that is under the control of antecedent stimuli is said to be under stimulus control

**Figure 8-2**
Antecedents, behaviours and consequences

**ANTECENDENT:**
Door bell rings

**BEHAVIOUR:**
Sally answers door

**CONSEQUENCE:**
Friend outside door

**ANTECENDENT:**
Seat work assigned in classroom

**BEHAVIOUR:**
Student works on worksheet

**CONSEQUENCE:**
Receives gold star

Stimulus control is seen in many aspects of daily life. In a classroom, for example, children's talking behaviour may be under stimulus control. Perhaps the students have learned that talking out in art class is acceptable, but talking without raising their hands in social studies class is not. The different Sds (art class versus social studies class) have set the stage for differing behaviours. Similarly, the behaviour of students may change when the teacher is out of the room. The teacher (Sd) may set the stage for quiet work, but when he or she is out of the room, the students may act in a very different fashion. Because different consequences are expected (or signaled by the Sd) students discriminate between the two differing antecedent conditions.

Of course, the antecedent stimuli in the preceding examples are relatively easy to identify. In real-life classrooms the connection between the antecedents, behaviours, and consequences may not be so readily recognizable. However, behaviourists would argue that even though behaviour may be influenced by a complex series of interrelated events, sufficient study can always lead to the indentification of antecedents to behaviour.

Behaviourists always define behaviours in observable, measurable terms—in other words, they feel that two people observing an individual should be able to agree that the behaviour did or did not occur. Thus, a behaviourist would focus on the child's action in writing "54" in response to the question $49 + 5 = ?$ rather than the unobservable, inferred mental process such as his or her "comprehension" of the addition operation. Similarly, a behaviourist would observe a child verbally describing the features of the parliamentary system without making reference to his or her "understanding" of the principles of democracy.

Many possible events can occur as the result of a behaviour and the consequences that occur after a behaviour will influence whether or not the behaviour will occur again in the future. Consequences can be precisely defined as a change in the environment that occurs contingent upon a behaviour, the effect of which is to alter the probability that the behaviour will or will not occur in the future (Skinner, 1953). There are two important components of this definition. First, the change in the environment must be be dependent upon, or contingent on, the behaviour. A consequence is contingent when it occurs immediately following the behaviour and is otherwise not available. If a consequence occurs independently of the behaviour, it is not contingent. For example, if a teacher attends to students each time they raise a hand, the attention is contingent upon the act of raising hands. However, if students find that the teacher will attend to them regardless of what they are doing—calling out answers, jumping out of their seats, or whispering an answer to a friend—the attention is noncontingent. Noncontingent delivery of consequences will not have an impact on the behaviour, because they fail to follow the behaviour consistently (Kazdin, 1989).

Second, the consequence can be said to influence a behaviour only if it alters the probability that the behaviour will or will not occur in the future. If a girl is praised or given a gold star for completing her mathematics homework, this act may have the effect of increasing the likelihood that the student will complete her work quickly in the future. Of course, if the student finds the attention embarrassing, it may lead her to avoid demonstrating the response again. In either case, the consequence has influenced the future occurrence of the behaviour.

**Positive reinforcement:** the contingent presentation of a consequence immediately after the occurrence of a behaviour, which has the effect of increasing the likelihood that the behaviour will occur again.

Consequences can be either added to or removed from the environment, and two effects are possible: the behaviour will be either more likely, or less likely to occur in the future. Broad categories of consequences can be defined, each dependent upon the effect that they have on behaviour (Skinner, 1953). These are summarized in Figure 8-3.

**Figure 8-3**
Effect of consequences

WHAT HAPPENS AFTER BEHAVIOR

| | Consequemces added to environment | Consequences taken away from environment |
|---|---|---|
| EFFECT ON BEHAVIOUR — Less likly to occur again in future | PRESENTATION OF PUNISHMENT | NEGATIVE REINFORCEMENT |
| EFFECT ON BEHAVIOUR — More likly to occur again in future | POSITIVE REINFORCEMENT | REMOVAL OF PUNISHMENT |

**Positive reinforcement**

**Positive reinforcement** is defined as the contingent presentation of a consequence immediately after the occurrence of a behaviour, which has the effect of increasing the likelihood that the behaviour will occur again. It doesn't matter what occurs after the behaviour; rather, it is only the effect on the behaviour that counts. For example, imagine the keen student teacher, Ms Harris. Eager to get her grade ten students to participate more in class discussions, Ms Harris decided to use praise as a reinforcer for this behaviour. During a social studies class, one of her most stubbornly quiet students, Emilio, finally volunteered an answer. With her determination to reinforce voluntary answers with praise, Ms Harris gushed "Great! Wonderful! What a good boy! I like it when you participate in class!" Not surprisingly, Emilio immediately flushed a deep red as his peers snickered. It is easy to predict that in future classes, Emilio would refuse to even look at Ms Harris, much less say anything. To return to our definition, the consequence—verbal praise—has failed to reinforce Emilio's behaviour, as it did not have the effect of increasing the probability that the behaviour will occur again. Even though such praise might be an effective reinforcer for some students, (for example, a younger child might respond well to such enthusiastic praise), it did not serve to reinforce Emilio's behaviour.

**Primary reinforcers:**
things that satisfy inborn biological needs, such as food, drink, warmth, sleep, or sex, and which act to strengthen the behaviour that they follow.

Unfortunately, positive reinforcement often serves to maintain many inappropriate behaviours that children demonstrate in classrooms. Often a teacher can positively reinforce a student who acts disruptively in class by reprimanding his or her behaviour and thereby giving attention to the child and the behaviour. While the teacher might not consider the reprimand to be "positive" in the common sense of the term, it can still serve to maintain or strengthen the undesired behaviour—or positively reinforce it (e.g., Madsen et al., 1970). In addition, by reprimanding the student, the teacher may cause the other students to positively reinforce the student's behaviour. Whether they make negative comments, some that are more admiring in nature, or even if they just guffaw appreciatively, the peer attention may serve to positively reinforce, or strengthen, the behaviour.

Kazdin (1989) has pointed out the importance of distinguishing between rewards and positive reinforcers. Rewards are widely used in our society and consist of positive events such as receiving certificates, gold stars, and salary increases. A reward, then, can be defined as something that is given or received in return for doing something. In contrast, positive reinforcers are defined only through their effect on behaviour. Rewards do not necessarily increase the likelihood that the behaviour will occur again and, because rewards are seen as pleasurable events, they may obscure the realization that many "unpleasant" events can positively reinforce behaviour. As we have seen, reprimands can often serve to reinforce student behaviour, yet these would hardly be considered to be a reward. Thus, a reward is not synonymous with a positive reinforcer.

However, positive reinforcement is one of the most powerful techniques used in the classroom. Research has shown that the appropriate use of reinforcement can increase the rate of occurrence of a wide range of academic and social behaviours related to school success. Reinforcement can also be used to shape or produce new behaviours, as well as to modify existing responses. The teacher can use any of the many different types of positive reinforcers that we discuss below. Further details of the use of reinforcement in the classroom are found in Chapters 11 and 15.

### Types of positive reinforcers

**Primary reinforcers**    Food, drink, warmth, sleep, and sex are examples of primary reinforcers, those things that satisfy inborn biological needs and act to strengthen the behaviour they follow. As they are necessary for the perpetuation of life, it is assumed that primary reinforcers are innately or naturally reinforcing. Thus, primary reinforcers are often referred to as natural, unconditioned, or unlearned reinforcers because their effect is automatic and they will reinforce behaviour in the absence of any specific training or learning. Of course, a person must be in a state of deprivation in relation to that reinforcer if it is to be effective. Sleepy university students will complete their work more rapidly if they get to rest after their task is done. Similarly, a hungry student may complete her mathematics homework more quickly if she gets supper when the work is finished.

In school settings, edible reinforcers are often used with younger students or students with handicaps who may not readily respond to the use of other reinforcers, such as teacher attention or praise. They can be very useful when teaching a new behaviour, because, when they are properly chosen, they are likely to have a rapid effect on the rate or quality of a behaviour. Because a primary reinforcer

**Secondary reinforcers:** things which are initially neutral or meaningless but acquire their reinforcing value by being associated with primary reinforcers or an already established secondary reinforcer.

will only be effective when the student is in a state of deprivation in relation to the reinforcer, the ethics of inducing a state of deprivation is a major consideration when using primary reinforcers (Alberto and Troutman, 1986; Kazdin, 1989).

Further, edible reinforcers cannot be overused since when satiation occurs, a reinforcer will no longer have the desired effect. A child may work rapidly for the first candy, but after several the reinforcer ceases to have an effect on behaviour. Typically, primary reinforcers are used with very young children or those who have severe or profound handicapping conditions.

**Secondary reinforcers** It is generally not necessary to use edible reinforcers in a regular classroom. Secondary (or unconditioned) reinforcers are those which are initially neutral or meaningless but acquire their reinforcing value by being associated with primary reinforcers or an already established secondary reinforcer. To understand how they acquire reinforcing value, consider one common example—currency. A dollar bill, by itself, is simply a piece of paper. However, we quickly learn to value that piece of paper because it can be exchanged for primary or other secondary reinforcers. In a similar fashion, praise, grades, or completing a project acquire reinforcing value through learning.

Of the three types of secondary reinforcers, the first category is social reinforcers, which include verbal or nonverbal actions which provide attention or communicate approval. Teachers indicate approval in many ways: they smile, wink, pat a shoulder, or say "Well done!" There exist numerous studies that demonstrate that verbal approval for academic work (often paired with nonverbal messages, such as positive physical contact, a wink or smile) can increase academic performance (e.g., Pffifner, Rosen, and O'Leary, 1985) and social interaction (Strain and Timm, 1974). Also, simply reinforcing academic performance can have the effect of increasing student attention to task (Kirby and Shields, 1972) and can decrease levels of disruptive behaviour (Ruggles and LeBlanc, 1982). Even nonverbal attention alone, such as a smile, nod, and positive physical contact, has been shown to increase appropriate classroom behaviours (Kazdin and Klock, 1973).

In fact, one study (Barringer and Gholson, 1979) showed that certain kinds of reinforcers seem more appropriate to the classroom and work better than others. Verbal and symbolic reinforcement produce better results for most children than do tangible reinforcers although, in general, the younger the child the more effective tangible reinforcers are. Moreover, Martinez (1985) argued that external reinforcements, if given too frequently, produce dependency.

While social reinforcers are used by teachers to change student behaviour, the effect can be reciprocal. In other words, while adults can change children's behaviour, children also influence the behaviour of adults in the environment (see Bell and Harper, 1977). Because of their behaviour, personality characteristics, physical attractiveness, academic performance, or some other hard-to-identify factor, some children seem to garner more praise and positive attention from teachers. The opposite can happen: some students, such as those who are disruptive or demonstrate other negative behaviours, are likely to encounter negative attention or disapproval. When this happens, a negative cycle of interaction is set in motion. Negative attention fails to teach children more appropriate behaviour, so that the behaviour will probably remain the same or worsen, leading the

**Token reinforcers:**
secondary reinforcers which are initially meaningless but can attain reinforcing value if they are exchangeable for other primary or secondary reinforcers.

**Premack principle:**
states that activities which occur at a high frequency (more preferred activities) can be used to reinforce the completion of lower-frequency (less preferred) activities.

teacher to continue providing negative attention and so on. However, changing a student's behaviour can influence a teacher's reaction to the student.

Sherman and Cormier (1974) examined the teacher's response to two disruptive children in her fifth grade classroom. When an outside experimenter used feedback and reinforcement to help the students demonstrate more appropriate classroom behaviours, such as raising their hands, following instructions, and paying attention, it was found that the teacher's attention to their more positive behaviour increased. The teacher also directed more praise towards the students and rated their classroom behaviour as more appropriate. Similar results were reported for a junior-high school student who was trained to socially reinforce (verbally and nonverbally) four teachers in different subject areas. The change in student behaviour led to increased verbal and nonverbal reinforcement of the student by three of the four teachers and a decrease in disapproval from all four teachers. So when the student ceased being negative towards her teachers, the teachers responded in kind. Indeed, the teachers commented on the student's "remarkable socialization" and "newfound maturity," while the student commented on how much nicer her teachers had become (Polirstok and Greer, 1977).

In another study, researchers taught seven- to ten-year-old children to be more responsive to their teachers by looking and smiling at them, talking enthusiastically with them, and by asking them for feedback after the completion of building and drawing tasks ("How does this look?"). Data showed that these students received more attention and assistance than did nonresponsive children and were rated more positively on personality characteristics such as likability, adeptness at tasks, naturalness of behaviour, and intelligence (Cantor and Gelfand, 1977).

The second category of secondary reinforcers consists of token reinforcers. In school, tokens can consist of buttons, poker chips, bottle caps, and so on. These initially meaningless items attain reinforcing value through the same method by which we come to value money: tokens will be reinforcing if they are associated with, or exchangeable for, other primary or secondary reinforcers. For example, a teacher may allow students to trade ten tokens for five minutes of free reading, a candy, or the opportunity to hand out textbooks in the next class.

The final category of secondary reinforcers consists of activities, but activities that are handled in a specific way. The Premack principle asserts that activities which occur at a high frequency (more preferred) can be used to reinforce the completion of lower frequency (less-preferred) activities (Premack, 1965). In other words, if access to a activity that is enjoyed by students (playing a game) is made contingent upon the completion of a less-preferred activity (completing mathematics seatwork), the students are likely to finish their seatwork more quickly. This simple yet powerful principle has also been referred to as "Grandma's Law," as in "Finish your turnips, then you can have dessert." By observing student behaviour, particularly during their free time, teachers can find school activities that students engage in at a higher frequency—such as working on the computer, playing games, or reading books. These high-frequency events can be used as reinforcers for behaviours that are demonstrated at a lower frequency (perhaps completing seatwork).

The important thing to remember is that the less-preferred activity must be finished before the preferred activity is given—"Finish reading this chapter, then go out with your friends." Do not make the mistake of reversing the order as in, "You can go out with your friends for a couple of hours—but then you will have to finish reading chapter eight!" This isn't likely to work any better than if Grandma had said, "Okay children, eat dessert, but then you must finish your turnips."

Allen and Iwata (1980) demonstrated the use of the Premack principle when attempting to increase the rate at which adults with mental handicaps completed their daily exercise. Game playing, a high-frequency activity, was used to reinforce exercising. Everyone in the group was required to complete a minimum number of exercises before games could be played. The lower-frequency behaviour (exercising) was increased when it was followed by the high-frequency activity.

On the other hand, Kazdin (1989) has noted several limitations associated with the use of activity reinforcers. While research in operant conditioning clearly demonstrates that reinforcement is most effective when it immediately follows the desired response, it is often difficult for teachers to ensure that the high-frequency activity immediately follows the student's behaviour. For example, if a student enjoys playing basketball, this might be used to reinforce his completion of mathematics seatwork. But if Joey finishes his math work by 10:30 who will supervise him when he's shooting baskets in the gymnasium and the teacher has to stay with the rest of the class?

A related problem is that using an activity reinforcer may cause an interruption in the desired behaviour—teachers would not want their students to jump up and run to the computer for five minutes every time they finished a math problem. However, if the low-frequency behaviour is well-established, students can usually tolerate a delay in reinforcement. Best results are obtained if the teacher gives feedback on the student's performance immediately and provides a token or some other item that indicates that the student has earned the activity. At an appropriate time in the future, students can "cash in" their tokens for the desired activity.

Activities tend to be "all or nothing" propositions which can pose a real conundrum for the teacher administering the reinforcement. One class in a school, for example, was working toward earning a trip from Calgary to Vancouver. Across the semester, students were required to earn points which were awarded for appropriate classroom behaviours as well as for completion of academic work. When the results were tallied, students were either allowed to go on the trip, or they were not. But what of the female student who had completed 60 percent of the desired work—should she be allowed to travel as far as Penticton? Similarly, what if Philip becomes aware three weeks before the departure that there is no way that he will be able to meet the set criterion? There exists no further incentive for Philip to comply with the expectations for, regardless of his effort, the activity reinforcer will not be forthcoming. In some cases, it may be possible to get around this problem by calibrating the level of performance to the time engaged in the activity.

### Applications and cautions

When using positive reinforcement in the classroom setting (or elsewhere), several factors should be carefully considered. Ensuring that reinforcement is delivered correctly is of critical importance as it will determine the degree to which the consequences will affect or alter behaviour. Major considerations include learning history, contigent application, amount of reinforcement, and contiguity.

**Learning history**   While some reinforcers, such as praise or positive attention, will be effective with most students, such predictions can never be made with complete confidence. Because each person's learning history is unique, no two individuals will respond in the same way to a particular reinforcer. Further, the same person will react in different ways to various reinforcers at different times and in different situations. Each person has a unique and ever-evolving list of reinforcers. Therefore teachers will need to ensure that the reinforcers selected actually function to increase student behaviour (Cooper, Heron, and Heward, 1987).

Different students may receive different reinforcers for performing the same or similar behaviours: one child may get a token or gold star for completing her worksheet, while another receives teacher attention and approval. Teachers are often reluctant to use differing contingencies in the classroom setting as they are afraid that giving a reinforcer to one student and not another will have an adverse effect. In practice, however, this is often not a serious problem and may actually have a positive "spill-over" effect on the other class members. For example, Christy (1975) used praise and edible treats to reinforce the in-seat behaviour of individual six-year-old children. Reinforcers were delivered when the children were working with small groups of peers on various activities. Not only did the reinforcer significantly increase the in-seat behaviour of children receiving reinforcement, but a moderate increase in the rate of in-seat behaviour was also seen in the children who simply observed the delivery of reinforcers. In addition, there was no increase in aggression or disruptive behaviour on the part of the observers. Verbal complaints (usually requests for the treat) were not excessive and, when ignored by the teacher, the rate of complaints decreased over time. Similar results were obtained when teacher attention was used to increase the attending behaviour of one child. When the contingency was in operation, it was found that the attending behaviour of the adjacent child also increased (Kazdin, 1973). However, such results are not consistent, as other researchers have reported little or no spill-over effect on the behaviour of other children (Ward and Baker, 1968).

**Contingent application**   It almost goes without saying that reinforcement must be contingent upon behaviour; that is, delivered only when the behaviour occurs. Otherwise, the behaviour is not likely to be affected (Kazdin, 1989). But it has been found that in natural classroom settings, reinforcement is applied in a haphazard, often counter-productive fashion. For example, in one study, it was found that a good proportion of positive feedback to students was misdirected or given contingently upon the occurrence of noncompliant behaviour (Strain et al., 1983).

**Amount of reinforcement**   There is no easy answer to the question of how much reinforcement should be given. Teachers should consider the effort that the student has to expend and calibrate the amount of reinforcement according-ly. However, the amount of reinforcement is related to performance; the greater the amount of reinforcement, the more frequent the response will be. Moreover,

**Continuous schedule of reinforcement:**
occurs when every single instance of a behaviour is reinforced.

**Intermittent schedule of reinforcement:**
occurs when only a certain fraction of all correct behaviours are reinforced.

reinforcement cannot be increased without limit as it will be curbed by the inevitable onset of satiation (Kazdin, 1989). Aspects of novelty are also important in the delivery of positive reinforcement; teachers should remember to vary the type of reinforcers used.

**Contiguity**    When the question of the optimal time for reinforcement is discussed it can be said that, for maximum effectiveness, the consequence should immediately follow the behaviour that it is intended to reinforce so as to clearly outline the connection between the behaviour and the consequence for the student. Delayed consequences may have little or no effect or may inadvertently reinforce the wrong behaviour.

Immediate delivery of reinforcement is particularly important when students are first learning a new behaviour as it will promote the fastest acquisition of the new response. After students demonstrate the behaviour consistently, the delay between the reinforcement and the behaviour can be increased. In every instance, however, reinforcement should be delivered on a planned basis, not as a random occurrence.

For example, when grade one children are first learning classroom rules (staying in-seat, raising their hands before speaking, taking turns, and so on), they will initially need immediate reinforcement each time they demonstrate a desired response. After the behaviours have reached an acceptable level and have been shown consistently over time, the teachers may praise or otherwise reinforce children at the end of the school day, then every few days, and so on, without causing the desired behaviours to diminish (Kazdin, 1989).

### Schedules of Reinforcement

While consistency of reinforcement is important, this does not imply that every single desired behaviour should be reinforced. In fact, research by Ferster and Skinner (1957) has demonstrated that even if it were practical to deliver reinforcement after every behaviour, in most cases it would not be an effective practice. The frequency and timing of reinforcement can be determined by following various schedules of reinforcement as outlined below.

**Continuous schedule**    When every single instance of a behaviour is reinforced, a **continuous schedule** is in effect. A continuous schedule is most appropriately used when students are learning a new behaviour or to increase the frequency of a known, but unused, behaviour. For example, a young student just learning to print capital letters might receive reinforcement for every correct "B" produced. Similarly, imagine a student who is able to arrive on time for class, but who is frequently tardy. Reinforcing punctual behaviour every time it occurs is likely to strengthen this learned, but unused, behaviour. While the continuous schedule of reinforcement will produce rapid changes in behaviour, it does not produce a durable behaviour. If reinforcement were discontinued, rapid extinction would occur.

**Intermittent schedule**    When only a certain fraction of all correct behaviours are reinforced, an **intermittent schedule** is achieved. There are many variations of intermittent schedules, but they all tend to produce behaviours that are durable or resistant to extinction. Once a behaviour is well established through a continuous schedule of reinforcement, an intermittent schedule

**Interval schedule of reinforcement:**

occurs when the delivery of reinforcement is determined by varying the time period between instances of reinforcement.

**Ratio schedule of reinforcement:**

occurs when the delivery of reinforcement is based on the amount of behaviour emitted; every nth response would be reinforced.

**Fixed schedule of reinforcement:**

occurs when the ratio or interval for reinforcement remains constant.

**Variable schedule of reinforcement:**

occurs when the ratio or interval for reinforcement will change after each reinforced response.

**Fixed interval schedule of reinforcement:**

occurs when reinforcement is given to the first correct response to occur after a constant period of time has passed.

should be used to ensure maintenance of the behaviour (Skinner, 1969). This can be accomplished in many ways.

First, the delivery of reinforcement can be determined by varying the time period between instances of reinforcement on an **interval schedule**. A teacher, for example, might reinforce on-task behaviour at the 15 minute mark of the class period, wait another 15 minutes, and then reinforce the next instance of on-task behaviour, wait another fifteen minutes, and so on. The second option is a **ratio schedule**, based on the amount of behaviour emitted; that is, every nth response would be reinforced. Further, interval and ratio schedules can be fixed or variable. A **fixed schedule** requires that the ratio (amount of behaviour) or interval (period of time) remains constant, while the **variable schedule** implies that the ratio or interval requirement will change after each reinforced response.

Each of the four possible combinations has a different effect on the pattern of responses, the rate of response, as well as the durability of the reinforced behaviour. A summary can be found in Table 8-1.

**Table 8-1** Effects of schedules of reinforcement

| NAME | DEFINITION | PATTERN OF PERFORMANCE | RATE OF RESPONSE |
|---|---|---|---|
| Fixed Interval | Based on predictable or set time intervals. | Repeated bursts of behaviour, with low rates at the beginning of the interval, gaining speed as the end of the interval approaches. A pause in behaviour after reinforcement. | Speed is slow to moderate, depending upon the size of the interval; the longer the interval, the lower the average rate of response. |
| Variable Interval | Based on unpredictable or variable time intervals. | The rate of behaviour is consistent and stable. Only a small pause in behaviour after reinforcement. | Speed is slow to moderate, depending upon the size of the interval; the longer the interval, the lower the average rate of response. |
| Fixed Ratio | Based on a predictable or set number of responses. | A pause in behaviour after reinforcement. The length of the pause will be related to the size of the ratio. | A high rate of response. |
| Variable Ratio | Based on an unpredictable or variable number of responses. | Constant and stable rate of behaviour. Little pause in behaviour after reinforcement. | A high rate of response. |

Within a **fixed interval** (FI), reinforcement is given to the first correct response to occur after a constant period of time (seconds, minutes, hours, or days) has passed. If a teacher reinforced the first correct math problem completed after the first five-minute mark, waited for five minutes and then reinforced the next correct response, waited another five minutes and so on, a five-minute fixed interval schedule (FI 5) would be in effect. For this to work, not only must the designated time interval pass, but the student must emit the target behaviour in order to receive reinforcement.

**Variable interval schedule of reinforcement:** occurs when reinforcement is given to the first correct response to occur after a variable (or unpredictable) interval of time has passed since the last reinforced response.

**Fixed ratio schedule of reinforcement:** occurs when the correct response is reinforced only after a fixed number of responses have occurred.

The fixed interval schedule can be used easily in the classroom—a simple kitchen timer can be used to remind the teacher to deliver reinforcement. However, the teacher must be alert to the possibility that students may engage in off-task behaviours during the post-reinforcement pause. We can see this in a teacher who is providing reinforcement on a ten-minute fixed interval schedule (FI 10) in order to enhance "creative writing behaviour." Once they adjust to the schedule, students would be aware that a certain period of time must pass before reinforcement is delivered. Thus, after reinforcement is given, they are likely to become idle, or do something else during the initial stages of the time interval. In other words, as reinforcement is not provided during that part of the interval, the desired behaviour has been extinguished. However, as the time for reinforcement draws nearer, students will begin to studiously write their creative passages in order to ensure that reinforcement is obtained. Following the delivery of reinforcement, another pause in behaviour will occur.

As this example illustrates, a fixed interval schedule will result in a pattern of response that is characterized by repeated bursts of behaviour which correspond with the time when reinforcement will be delivered. The overall rate of performance will be dependent upon the length of the time interval: the longer the interval, the longer the learner will pause following reinforcement, and thus the lower the average rate of performance.

In a **variable interval** (VI) schedule, reinforcement is given to the first correct response to occur after a variable, or unpredictable, interval of time has passed since the last reinforced response. First, the teacher would decide how often reinforcement would be given—for example, it might be determined that on-task behaviour should be reinforced every ten minutes on average (VI 10) so that students will have the opportunity to be reinforced four times during a 40-minute period. Using a variable schedule, the teacher could reinforce the "on-task" behaviour after four minutes have passed, after 16 minutes, after 25 minutes, and at the 38 minute mark. The amount of time elapsed between reinforcers varies from nine to 13 minutes but, on average, reinforcement is delivered every ten minutes.

The unpredictable nature of the variable interval schedule tends to produce a steady rate of behaviour. Unlike the fixed interval schedule, students continue working because they do not know when the next opportunity for reinforcement will occur. However, similar to the fixed interval schedule, the rate of responses will be influenced by the size of the interval; the less frequently reinforcement is given (the larger the interval) the lower the average rate of performance.

In a **fixed ratio** (FR) schedule, the correct response is reinforced only after a fixed number of responses have occurred. For example, students could be given five extra minutes of free time for every ten correctly completed science questions, regardless of how long it took them to complete the work. A common example of the use of a fixed ratio schedule is found when workers are paid for piece-work; that is, they will be paid for the amount of work completed (such as shirts sewn) rather than the time it took to finish the work.

As with the fixed interval schedules, students will typically demonstrate a pause in performance immediately following the delivery of reinforcement. The length of the pause is related to the size of the ratio: requiring a large number of responses prior to the delivery of reinforcement results in a long pause; a smaller

**Variable ratio schedule of reinforcement:** occurs when the correct response is reinforced only after a variable (or unpredictable) number of responses have occurred.

ratio produces a proportionately smaller pause. Because reinforcement is dependent upon the amount of behaviour produced, individuals will work rapidly in order to meet the ratio requirements. In general, the higher the ratio, the higher the rate of response. However, a teacher must handle the setting of the ratio schedule with caution: if the ratio is set unrealistically high, the rate of response will rapidly diminish. This can be avoided by ensuring that the ratio requirements are increased gradually, rather than in large leaps.

Finally, in **variable ratio** (VR) schedules, the target response is reinforced only after a variable, or unpredictable, number of responses have occurred since the last reinforced response. A common example of the variable ratio schedule is the slot machine: the player might win after the tenth pull, then after the fiftieth, and so on. Reinforcement, albeit sparse, is sufficient to maintain the gambling behaviour. In the classroom, the teacher will decide the average number of responses that will be reinforced: for example, like the teacher using the fixed ratio schedule, the teacher might wish to reinforce, on average, every tenth correct response. Using a VR 10 schedule, the teacher might reinforce the fourth correct math problem completed, the eighteenth, the thirty-fifth, and the fortieth problem. The range of responses required before reinforcement is delivered varies from five to 17, but averages ten.

The variable ratio schedule produces a more consistent, stable rate of behaviour, with little pause after reinforcement. The pause seen in the fixed ratio schedule is virtually eliminated, unless the average ratio is very high. The person does not pause because the reinforcement may be forthcoming after only a few more responses. It also produces high rates of behaviour but, as with the fixed ratio schedule, the rate of performance will be related to the size of the ratio.

In summary, as reinforcement is dependent upon the amount of behaviour produced, both variable and fixed ratio schedules produce faster response rates than interval schedules do. Their use is often particularly relevant to many skills taught in school where high rates of performance are desirable. If the teacher's goal is to produce a rapid and consistent pattern of behaviour in which few pauses are seen or a very durable behaviour that is most resistant to extinction, then variable schedules should be used. When the more predictable fixed schedules are used, learners are more likely to stop responding if the reinforcement does not arrive as expected. Because variable schedules are inherently unpredictable, learners are more likely to continue, even if reinforcement is not forthcoming, and the behaviour is therefore more likely to be maintained over time.

### Thinning reinforcement

One of the most important skills for a teacher to master is to effectively "thin" or reduce the amount of reinforcement given. Certainly, when teaching a new skill, the most effective strategy is to reinforce every correct response. However, once the skill is mastered, the behaviour will be most successfully maintained if the amount of reinforcement is systematically reduced. It is important not to move too quickly—imagine what might happen if a teacher suddenly shifted from continuous reinforcement to a fixed ratio schedule in which every fiftieth response was reinforced (FR 50). It is likely that a student, used to a continuous schedule, would give up long before the reinforcement was due to be delivered.

When teaching a new skill, the most effective strategy is to reinforce every correct response.

To avoid extinction of a behaviour, a teacher should gradually shift from continuous reinforcement to a rich intermittent schedule in which reinforcement is given relatively frequently, and then continue to thin, or reduce, the amount of reinforcement given. Unfortunately, there is no magic formula that can guide this thinning process. The effect that reinforcement has on behaviour is the only true measure of its effectiveness, so it is critical that a student's behaviour be carefully monitored. The systematic reduction of the amount of reinforcement given to the student will ensure the maintenance of the desired level of behaviour.

While it is not necessary to inform students that reinforcement is to be reduced, doing so may facilitate a smooth transition (Cooper, Heron, and Heward, 1987). For example, consider the student who is used to getting teacher approval and feedback after every mathematics problem solved. Once the teacher has determined that his behaviour is well-established, he might be told, "You have been doing a great job with your math problems. From now on, finish three problems before you show me your work." If the reinforcement schedule for an entire class is to be altered, the teacher can simply announce it to the group, or post a sign which outlines the reinforcing contingencies to be in effect, such as, "All students must now correctly complete four worksheets before earning free time at the computer."

### Who delivers reinforcement?

To this point in the discussion, it has generally been assumed that delivery of reinforcing contingencies remains an exclusive responsibility of the teacher. However, there is considerable research that indicates that even very young

**Shaping:**
teaching new skills or behaviours by reinforcing learners for approaching the desired final behaviour.

**Negative reinforcement:**
occurs when an unpleasant stimulus is immediately taken away or removed from the situation as a consequence for a behaviour, with the effect of increasing the probability that the behaviour will occur again.

children, or students with handicaps, can be trained to deliver reinforcement to each other (Strain, Shores, and Timm, 1977).

Training peers to act as behaviour-change agents holds some distinct advantages for teachers. Peer-mediated interventions can produce effects that are comparable to adult-mediated reinforcement programs (e.g., Carden-Smith and Fowler, 1984; Hendrickson et al., 1982). Children and adolescents can be taught to deliver praise and feedback, points, tokens, or other tangible reinforcers contingent upon a desired behaviour. This can be most effectively done in situations when it is difficult for teachers to provide consistent feedback and reinforcement. For example, a teacher on playground supervision may be unfamiliar with a particular child, unaware of some behaviour, and/or too far away to provide reinforcing contingencies.

## Shaping behaviour

While reinforcing appropriate behaviour and eliminating inappropriate behaviour should be a goal for all teachers, we do not want students to work solely for gold stars or pats on the back. The ultimate aim, or course, is for students to develop their own inner or intrinsic behaviour that propels them toward appropriate academic and behavioural performance. To accomplish this, teachers can shape behaviour and then move on to the process of extinction.

The term shaping is used in behaviour learning theories to refer to the teaching of new skills or behaviours by reinforcing learners for approaching the desired final behaviour (Slavin, 1988). The principle is that students are reinforced for behaviours that are within their current repertoires but which also stretch them towards new skills. Shaping is successful when students move rapidly from success to success. This requires breaking tasks down into small steps, analyzing them, and reinforcing students as they accomplish each step.

## Negative reinforcement

When an unpleasant stimulus is immediately taken away or removed from the situation as a consequence for a behaviour, with the effect of increasing the probability that the behaviour will occur again, negative reinforcement is said to occur (Skinner, 1953). There are many examples of negative reinforcement in our daily lives: a driver will fasten his seatbelt to terminate the unpleasant buzzer; a mother picks up her infant to stop the fussing and crying; students study to avoid parental nagging; a window is closed on a cold day; or a father may buy his child a candy bar to stop a temper tantrum in a grocery store. In each of these cases, the aversive situation is terminated by the response, which increases the likelihood that the behaviour will occur again in the future. Of course, all of the cautions cited for positive reinforcement also apply here—some events might be aversive to some people and not others. Or a person may find something aversive in one situation and not another, or at one time and not another. It is only possible to identify a negative reinforcer by examining its effect on behaviour.

In many of the examples cited above, both positive and negative reinforcement are in operation. For example, the infant's crying behaviour is positively reinforced by maternal attention and comforting (the consequence). At the same time, the mother's behaviour is negatively reinforced by the termination of the aversive noise. Similarly, the child who throws a temper tantrum to get a candy

**Punishment:**

the contingent presentation of a consequence immediately after the occurrence of a behaviour, which has the effect of decreasing the likelihood that the behaviour will occur again.

bar is more likely to demonstrate the same behaviour the next time he or she is in the grocery store, as the consequence (getting the candy bar) has positively reinforced the behaviour. In the same manner, the father's behaviour was negatively reinforced by the cessation of the embarrassing temper tantrum.

Similar interaction patterns can develop in classrooms: the teacher might be negatively reinforced for paying attention to a child who is whining, acting out, or behaving aggressively, as the teacher's action has led to the termination of the aversive situation. The child's behaviour is simultaneously positively reinforced, making it more likely that he or she will continue to behave this way in the future. Thus, a vicious cycle is set up—and unless the cycle is broken, the reinforcing contingencies will continue to foster the negative social interaction (Kazdin, 1989).

In the previous examples, the individuals escape from aversive situations by demonstrating particular behaviours. In addition to escaping an aversive situation, individuals can also experience negative reinforcement when their behaviour allows them to avoid an undesired consequence. People behave in a manner designed to allow them to avoid aversive situations every day; children do not cross against the light on a busy highway; students may never talk out loud in Mrs. Isaac's class; or teenagers may experiment with drugs. In each case, the behaviour has allowed them to avoid an aversive situation: being hit by a car, being yelled at by Mrs. Isaac, or being ridiculed by peers. Avoidance therefore occurs before the presentation of an aversive situation.

Like positive reinforcement, negative reinforcement is used to strengthen or increase the probability that many behaviours related to school success will occur with greater frequency. However, as pointed out by Cooper and his colleagues (1987), because the use of negative reinforcement requires that the teacher first create an aversive or unpleasant environment, two potential problems might arise. First, students may simply begin to avoid the classroom or other settings in which an aversive environment is frequently created. Second, students who are frequently exposed to a negative environment may direct anger, resentment, or other negative emotional responses toward the source of the aversive stimuli—in this case, the teacher. Because of this, negative reinforcement is less frequently used to alter student behaviour and, when it is, it should only be used in combination with a liberal amount of positive consequences which will minimize the undesirable side effects of the use of negative reinforcement.

## Punishment

Any discussion on behaviourism in the classroom must include a discussion of punishment. No matter how we define it, or how we regard its effects, we recognize that punishment for wrong-doing is an integral part of our society and of our school systems. Corporal punishment, so widely used until quite recently, is now mostly banned in Canadian schools. However, students are open to many other types of punishments and punishers, and teachers must be acutely aware of the effects of punitive interventions.

Negative reinforcement is not a synonym for punishment. **Punishment** is defined as the contingent presentation of a consequence immediately after the occurrence of a behaviour, which has the effect of decreasing the likelihood that the behaviour will occur again (Skinner, 1953). Like reinforcement, the actual

**Punishment I (presentation punishment):**

case in which an aversive stimulus is added to the environment or presented following a behaviour, which has the effect of decreasing the likelihood that the behaviour will occur again.

**Punishment II (removal punishment):**

the removal of a reinforcer following a behaviour, which has the effect of decreasing the likelihood that the behaviour will occur again.

**Primary punishers:**

forms of punishment which automatically or naturally act to reduce the probability that a behaviour will occur again. Also referred to as unconditioned punishers.

**Secondary punishers:**

stimuli that were initially neutral but which have become aversive through repeated pairings with a primary or already established secondary punisher. Also referred to as conditioned punishers.

characteristics of the consequence are immaterial. Even if an event seems unpleasant, it cannot be defined as punishment if it does not act to reduce the frequency of the behaviour.

Punishment is often used because it causes a rapid reduction in the response rate. While the response will not generally disappear immediately, if the punisher has been properly selected, the effects should be seen after relatively few sessions. For this reason, punishment is often appropriate for use with behaviours that are dangerous to the child or others, highly destructive to property, or significantly interfere with ongoing class activities. Punishment can also be used when it is difficult to reinforce an alternative behaviour (Kazdin, 1989).

### Types of punishers

Punishment can involve either the presentation or removal of stimuli from the environment contingent upon the occurrence of the behaviour. In the former case, often referred to as **Punishment I** (presentation punishment), an aversive stimulus is added to the environment or presented following an undesired behaviour. Examples include such things as giving a detention, having the student write lines, or reprimanding the student. **Punishment II** (removal punishment) implies the removal of a reinforcer and includes such actions as the loss of a privilege, removal of toys, or being excluded from a fun activity in class.

In addition, two categories of punishment can be identified. **Primary** (or unconditioned) **punishers** are those which automatically or naturally act to reduce the probability that a behaviour will occur. Unconditioned punishers result in physical pain or discomfort, and include such stimuli as slaps, pinches, electric shocks, extreme temperatures, loud noises, noxious smells, and so on. Responses to these stimuli have an effect on behaviour without the need for previous experience. Thus, they are often referred to as natural, unconditioned or unlearned punishers. **Secondary** (or conditioned) **punishers** consist of stimuli that were initially neutral but which have become aversive through repeated pairings with a primary, or already established, secondary punisher. For example, expressions such as "Bad boy!", "Naughty girl!" or "No!" are, of course, initially meaningless to children. But if Johnny is told "No!" and gets a swat on the rear-end often enough, "No" will eventually become a conditioned punisher. In other words, that word becomes aversive to Johnny because his experience tells him that "No" is associated with pain. However, pain need not be physical; if the teacher pairs a neutral stimulus, such as "Come to the front of the room," with psychological pain or discomfort, such as ridicule or humiliation, those words can become a conditioned punisher. They acquire their ability to punish behaviour through their association with other aversive stimuli.

### Applications and cautions

A number of basic concerns revolve around the use of punishment. Each of the following have some bearing on effectiveness of punishment and the ethical issues surrounding the use of punishment.

**Learning history** Conditioned punishers are learned as a result of a person's experiences with the environment. Thus, it is not possible to predict with any confidence which events or actions will function as a conditioned punisher for any child. However, because many children come to school with shared cultural and social experiences, many common conditioned punishers used in schools, such as verbal reprimands, are likely to influence their behaviour.

**Amount of punishment**   While teachers must select a punishing consequence that is effective in suppressing a target behaviour, they have an ethical responsibility to use the least aversive technique. While it is often assumed that the more aversive the punishment, the greater the resulting response suppression, this is not supported by the research. Rather, it has been found that a firm reprimand is as effective as screaming at a student and that a very brief period of time-out (15 to 90 seconds) can be as effective as prolonged periods. Mild punishers are often particularly effective when all positive reinforcement for a behaviour can be terminated.

But this rule does not imply that the teacher should begin with a mild punishment and gradually escalate the severity of the punishers. Punishment will be most effective if first delivered at its ultimate level, rather than gradually intensifying the use of the aversive over time. For example, a reprimand given repeatedly in a mild tone of voice is unlikely to be as effective as a firm reprimand given once. When punishers are repeatedly used, it is likely that students will simply "tune out," rather than respond as expected. Thus, even when the reprimand is finally delivered in full intensity, it will not have an effect on the student's behaviour (Kazdin, 1989).

Moreover, aversive consequences that fail to produce the expected response suppression in a relatively short period of time should not be continued. It is not ethical or good teaching practice to continue the use of an ineffective aversive stimuli. Therefore, teachers should carefully monitor the effectiveness of any punishing contingency through the collection of performance data. The punisher should be seen to produce a decrease in the overall rate of undesirable behaviour.

**Contiguity**   A punishing consequence will be most effective when it immediately follows the behaviour that it is intended to suppress. The longer the delay between the punisher and the behaviour, the less effective the punisher will be. Thus, the strategy used by many parents who say "Wait until your mother (or father) gets home!" is likely to have a minimal effect on the child's behaviour. Further, delaying the administration of punishment enhances the possibility that the parent or teacher may inadvertently punish an appropriate behaviour. If the child is quietly watching television, playing appropriately with his or her sibling, or completing homework when Mom or Dad gets home, the administration of punishment at that time might suppress these desired behaviours. Regardless of what happens during the intervening period, delayed punishment is not likely to be associated with the response that it is intended to suppress (Kazdin, 1989).

**Consistency**   To be most effective, punishment should be used each and every time the behaviour occurs; in other words, a continuous schedule of punishment. An intermittent schedule, or the occasional use of punishment, will not produce the desired suppression. Also, if warnings are used, they should only be given once. The teacher who gives a random number of warnings before finally administering the punishment will greatly diminish, if not entirely destroy, the power of the warning to suppress undesired behaviours. Who can blame the student who continues to engage in an undesired behaviour if the teacher gives three warnings one day, one warning the next, and four warnings the next? Because the warning is not consistently followed by the punishment, it loses its power to influence behaviour.

**Elimination of extraneous positive reinforcement**    If a student demonstrates a particular behaviour, it must be assumed that some type of reinforcement is maintaining the behaviour; otherwise, it would extinguish on its own. Unless all sources of positive reinforcement that serve to maintain the behaviour can be eliminated, the power of the punishment will be greatly diminished. For example, consider the junior high student who gains peer attention and approval for disruptive behaviour. Teacher punishment of this behaviour is unlikely to be effective unless this positive reinforcement can be terminated.

Imagine a classroom in which several students continually shout out answers in class rather than raising their hands as their teacher would prefer. None of the strategies tried by the teacher had succeeded in reducing this behaviour and so he decided to send the offending students to sit in the hall every time this occurred. While this action was intended to punish the students' behaviour, the teacher soon found that the frequency of the shouting-out behaviour increased dramatically. How would the behaviourist explain this situation? Observations of the students' behaviour would lead to the conclusion that the consequences—being sent out to the hall—has reinforced, not punished the behaviour. So, even though the teacher considered "sitting in the hall" to be an unpleasant event, it did not function as punishment.

**Punishment early in the response chain**    Punishing a behaviour early in its response chain (or as soon as it begins) is more effective than waiting until the chain has been completed. Consider the preschool child who is punished for stealing toys from his peers. The chain of behaviours leading to this response may consist of getting up from his assigned place, walking over to the classmate, demanding the toy and, finally, taking the toy. Punishing the boy as soon as he leaves his designated spot will suppress the toy stealing better than if the punishment is delayed until the toy is taken. This effect can be explained by examining the consequences that the child experiences by stealing the toy. If the chain of behaviours is successfully completed, the attainment of the toy positively reinforces the child's stealing behaviour. The positive reinforcement can therefore counteract the effectiveness of the punisher (Kazdin, 1989). However, if the sequence can be stopped, the positive reinforcer is not obtained and the punishment is more likely to have a suppressive effect.

However, there is a danger that using punishment early in the response chain will inadvertently suppress desired behaviours. For example, the child may leave his designated space intending to approach a peer and engage in an appropriate social interaction. Using punishment when the child first leaves his spot will, in this case, suppress the desired social behaviour (Kazdin, 1989).

**Variation**    It has been suggested that the effects of punishment can be enhanced by using a variety of punishers to consequate an undesired response, rather than repeatedly using the same technique (Charlop et al., 1988).

**Punishment in conjunction with a program of positive reinforcement**    Punishment should never be used alone. Instead, it should always be

**Fair-pair rule:**
states that for every behaviour suppressed, the child must be reinforced for one or more alternative positive behaviours.

accompanied by a program of positive reinforcement. Unfortunately, when teachers are angry, frustrated, or annoyed with a student's behaviour, they tend to focus only on the poor behaviour. But eliminating one behaviour does not guarantee that the student will demonstrate an appropriate alternative response. Punishment only tells the student what not to do; it does not teach alternative behaviours. Thus, when suppressing Johnny's out-of-seat behaviour, the teacher must also consider what Johnny should be taught to do instead. This has been referred to as the **fair-pair rule** (White and Haring, 1980) which states that for every behaviour suppressed, the child must be reinforced for one or more alternative positive behaviours.

Combining positive reinforcement for appropriate behaviour with the use of punishment has several advantages. First, it ensures that the teacher continues to have some positive interaction with the student, rather than contacting the student only when punishment is to be delivered. Second, use of positive reinforcement has been shown to enhance the effectiveness of punishment (Azrin and Holz, 1966). Even mild punishers, which on their own would be not be powerful enough to suppress the behaviour, have been shown to be effective when combined with positive reinforcement for appropriate behaviour. Using positive reinforcement appears to eliminate or reduce the many negative side-effects that are often associated with the exclusive use of punishment (Carey and Bucher, 1986). Finally, the long-term effectiveness of punishment appears to be enhanced when the student is taught to demonstrate a more appropriate behaviour. When the punisher is withdrawn, the chances of the undesired behaviour returning appear to be reduced.

Think, for example, of the child who is frequently out of her seat. Rather than using punishment for out-of-seat behaviour, the teacher may successfully use a program of reinforcement to strengthen in-seat behaviour. Naturally, when the student is sitting at her desk more often she cannot be wandering around the classroom. But what of the very active child who may not stay in her seat long enough for the teacher to deliver reinforcement? A mild punishment may be used to produce in-seat behaviour which can then be strengthened through the enthusiastic and consistent use of reinforcement.

It must be appreciated that just as punishment is likely to cause a rapid reduction in the level of a behaviour, withdrawal of punishment is likely to cause the behaviour to quickly re-emerge. This will be particularly evident if the teacher has failed to use reinforcement techniques to establish an alternative positive response (Kazdin, 1989). In other words, the teacher may have stopped David from hitting his friends during recess through the use of punishment. But has David learned a more appropriate method of interacting with his friends? If not, it is likely that his aggressive behaviour will re-emerge after the punishment is stopped. However, if he has learned more appropriate social behaviours, and these are reinforced (either by the teacher or through the positive interactions he has with his friends), the need to use punishment will be diminished. Indeed, it can be discontinued entirely and, as long as positive reinforcement for the desired behaviour is still available, it is unlikely that the undesired behaviour will reappear.

**Negative side effects**   Punishment not only affects the recipient but also has an effect on the teacher administering the punisher. Most often, the teacher's use of punishment is negatively reinforcing as it tends to terminate a student's disruptive, aggressive or otherwise annoying behaviours which tend to be highly aversive to the teacher. Because of the pleasing effect of the use of punishment, it likely that the teacher's punitive behaviour will be strengthened and the teacher is likely to use punishment again in the future. This increased rate may be maintained even though there is no long-term or enduring change seen in the student's behaviour.

As well, children's negative emotional responses to punishment are of great concern to teachers, for they will undoubtedly interfere with learning (Kazdin, 1989). It is not possible for the student who is upset, angry, or withdrawn to benefit from the instruction provided in the classroom. Further, it is often found that negative emotional responses are transferred to the environment or person administering the punishment. Thus, simply being in the school or in the presence of the teacher will produce the negative emotional response even when the punishment is not used.

Moreover, punishment often produces a common response—the student will avoid or escape the situation in which punishment is to occur. If successful, escape behaviour is negatively reinforced as it allows the person to avoid the aversive situation. Escape and avoidance are obviously problematic for teachers as they cannot help or teach a student who fails to turn up for class. Punishment does not have to be severe to result in escape or avoidance behaviour. In one study (Redd, Morris, and Martin, 1975) children were exposed to adults who delivered different consequences (praise only, reprimands only, or neutral responses) during play activities. When the children were asked to choose the adults with whom they wished to play, the adults who had used reprimands were chosen far less frequently than were those who had praised the children. Similarly, adolescents dislike it when adults describe only what they have done wrong (Willner et al., 1977). Thus, it appears that students will avoid adults who tend to overuse punishment during their interactions.

Further, whenever punishment is used, there is a possibility that the student will respond by becoming aggressive. Consider, for example, the preschool teacher who tries to remove a toy from Kenny, who has stolen it from another student. Kenny reacts wildly—kicking, scratching, and biting the teacher. Aggressive behaviour may be negatively reinforcing to the student as it may have the effect of terminating the punishing event.

Finally, teachers must be aware that whenever they punish a student, they model the use of aversive strategies. Because the teacher is a powerful model, students may imitate the teacher's model. Teachers and parents are very important models for children who learn how to interact with others by observing adult behaviour. That children imitate the aggressive behaviour of models has been repeatedly demonstrated (Bandura, 1965; Bandura, Ross, and Ross, 1963). Some studies have also shown that children imitate punishment procedures that they have experienced. For example, children who had been punished with a response cost procedure (fine) for wrong responses in a marble dropping game later imposed similar fines on peers when they played the game with them (Gelfand, 1974). Children who had been reprimanded and forced to wait before being allowed to play a game later used the same punishers with other children (Mischel and Grusec, 1966).

**Extinction:**
(operant conditioning) the suppression or weakening of a behaviour by withholding the reinforcers that have been maintaining it.

**Generality**   When teachers use punishment, they typically expect the behaviour they are punishing to be generally suppressed in other environments as well as when the teacher is not present. Unfortunately, this has generally not been found to be true. Punishing a student in one class does not mean he or she will behave in another class or when the teacher steps out into the hall. Generalization of treatment effects tend only to be seen when the behaviour is consistently punished in all settings, and/or punishment is delivered by multiple agents (Van Houten, 1983).

### Extinction

Extinction occurs when a behaviour is suppressed or weakened by withholding the consequences that have been maintaining it. It differs from the use of punishment in that a consequence is not added or removed from the environment: rather, the consequence(s) that usually reinforce the behaviour are withheld. For example, imagine the teacher who had a student who constantly made jokes in class. Depending upon her mood, each time Tina joked in class, the teacher would respond with a grin, an exasperated sigh, or a sharp reprimand. What would happen if the teacher decided to suppress Tina's joking by ignoring her comments? Tina's behaviour was maintained through the provision of positive reinforcement; her jokes were usually followed by some type of teacher attention which had the effect of increasing the probability that the behaviour would occur again in the future. Teacher attention maintained Tina's behaviour, so it would be expected that the withdrawal of attention would cause the behaviour to diminish over time. Thus, withholding the reinforcer (attention) placed Tina's behaviour on extinction.

Behaviours maintained by negative reinforcement will be extinguished when the response no longer terminates the aversive circumstance. Consider the case of Cecilia, the child who acts out whenever asked to work on mathematics seatwork. In the past, the teacher had been sending Cecilia out into the hall whenever she acted out. However, this procedure had the effect of negatively reinforcing behaviour, as being sent to the hall terminated the situation that Cecilia found aversive. To extinguish Cecilia's acting out behaviour, the teacher would stop sending the student out of the room whenever she became disruptive. By withholding the negative reinforcement, it would be expected that the rate of disruptive behaviour would eventually decline.

A number of factors influence the use of extinction. If the teachers had correctly identified the positive or negative reinforcers that were maintaining the students' behaviour in the cases cited above, and if reinforcers were withheld, it would be expected that the behaviour would diminish over time. However, the process of extinction is not a smooth or easy one to implement. For one thing, a behaviour may be reinforced by multiple sources and these sources may be difficult to identify and/or control. For example, consider the teacher who finds that, while she has studiously ignored Tina's behaviour, it still has the effect of eliciting whoops of laughter or other positive attention from her classmates? In that case, the behaviour is unlikely to be affected. In other words, even though the teacher's attention has been withdrawn, the peer attention will function to maintain the behaviour.

Secondly, before the behaviour begins its decline, the immediate effect of extinction is to increase the frequency or magnitude of the behaviour. In other words, teachers can expect things to get worse before they get better. Thus, when a teacher ignores students who are used to getting attention when they shout out answers, the students will likely respond by making comments more frequently, and in a louder tone of voice, in an attempt to attain the desired attention. Similarly, the student who is used to escaping work by acting out may become highly disruptive in order to attain the usual consequence. This increase in behaviour, referred to as the extinction burst, will precede any decline in the rate of the behaviour. The positive sign for the teachers who observe this phenomenon, however, would be that they had correctly identified the reinforcing contingency that had been maintaining the students' behaviour. Thus, continuing to withhold the reinforcer would eventually lead to the extinction of the behaviour. See Figure 8-4 for a visual representation of a typical pattern of behaviour seen when extinction is used.

**Figure 8-4**
Extinction burst

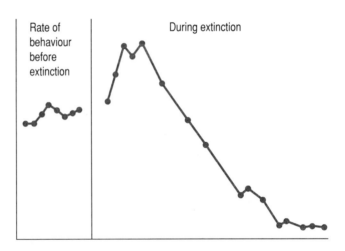

Unfortunately, this burst in behaviour is often very difficult for teachers, parents, or others in the student's environment to tolerate. Yet once the reinforcers to target behaviours have been identified, the complete and total withdrawal of reinforcement must be consistently implemented. Any "accidental" reinforcement provided by a teacher, peer, or even a visitor to the classroom, will cause the quick re-emergence of the behaviour (Kazdin, 1989). Or it may be that because of frustration, anger, or concern, people in the child's environment may "give in" and provide the reinforcer. When this happens, it is likely to reinforce the behaviour at its new higher rate. The warning is that withdrawing reinforcement for a while and then reintroducing it will likely cause the behaviour to be even worse than it was before. However, if the response is accidently reinforced, teachers should continue with the extinction program. After a brief time, the behaviour will resume its downward trend.

When all reinforcers have been withdrawn, after the initial burst of negative behaviour, extinction will result in a gradual decrease in the frequency and/or magnitude of the behaviour. The rate of decline will be related to a variety of factors, including the schedule of reinforcement that has been maintaining the behaviour. A behaviour that has been reinforced on a continuous schedule (each and every occurrence of the behaviour has been reinforced) will be much less resistant to extinction than behaviours that have been reinforced on an intermittent schedule. Because an intermittent schedule is used to maintain the behaviour, it is highly resistant to extinction. Further, a rich intermittent schedule will lead to quicker extinction than will a sparser schedule, and fixed schedules are less resistant to extinction than are variable schedules.

As well, resistance to extinction is related to the length of time that the student has been demonstrating a behaviour. For example, if a student had been talking out in class (and receiving teacher attention) for years, the behaviour will take longer to extinguish than if the behaviour is of relatively recent origin. The amount and quality of reinforcement typically received as a consequence of a behaviour will also influence the rate at which the behaviour is extinguished. If the student highly values the reinforcer, or receives a large amount of reinforcement as a consequence of a behaviour, the behaviour will decline at a much slower rate.

The amount of effort required from the individual to demonstrate a behaviour will also influence rate of decline: if it takes great effort to complete the behaviour, it is more likely to decline more rapidly than if the behaviour can be easily accomplished. Finally, when extinction is used, the teacher should be prepared for spontaneous recovery (Skinner, 1953). In other words, it is often found that after a behaviour has been extinguished for some time, it may briefly re-emerge. But as long as reinforcement continues to be withheld, it is likely that the behaviour will rapidly disappear. However, if a behaviour is inadvertently reinforced, that behaviour is likely to be strengthened and maintained. Box 8-4 provides some guidelines concerning the use of extinction in the classroom.

## Box 8-4  In the classroom: Using extinction

When children shout out answers in class, throw temper tantrums in grocery stores, or persistently pester their parents or teachers, perhaps some of the most common advice that the adult receives is, "The child is just trying to get your attention. Just ignore it!" Ignoring a behaviour, however, is likely to cause the behaviour to worsen both in frequency and intensity before any diminution is seen. And so this is not a strategy that should be chosen lightly; although when properly implemented under appropriate conditions, it can be highly effective. Before implementing an extinction program, the following procedures should be observed:

1. *Identify and control all sources of reinforcement.* For extinction to be successful, all reinforcers that maintain the behaviour must be entirely eliminated. If a teacher is unable to control all reinforcing contingencies, an alternative intervention should be used. If a student's behaviour is also reinforced by other events, such as peer attention, classmates can often be encouraged to

participate in the extinction program (e.g., Patterson, 1965; Salend and Meddaugh, 1985).

2. *Reinforce other appropriate behaviours that can replace the undesired behaviour.* The extinction of a behaviour will be hastened in a child who is reinforced for demonstrating another more appropriate behaviour as a replacement for the undesired behaviour. This also gives a student an opportunity to experience alternative reinforcing events instead of simply being ignored. Remember, the intention is to withhold attention from the behaviour, not to stop responding to the student entirely.

3. *Inform the student of the new consequences that are in operation.* While an extinction program can certainly be run without informing the student first, it has been shown that effects are hastened if the student is aware of the change in consequences.

4. *Be consistent.* Consistency is absolutely critical to the success of an extinction program. Any accidental or intentional delivery of reinforcement for the undesired behaviour will have the effect of strengthening the undesired behaviour. But if an accidental event occurs, don't despair. Simply continue with the extinction program for, after a brief increase, the behaviour will likely regain its downward trend.

5. *Be on guard for spontaneous recovery* (Skinner, 1953). It is often found that after a response has been extinguished for some time, it may briefly re-emerge in the future. This can be quickly terminated by continuing to withhold reinforcement. Resist the temptation to comment on the undesired behaviour as this will only serve to strengthen it.

## OBSERVATIONAL LEARNING

**Modeling:**
the imitation of the behaviours of others.

**Vicarious experiences:**
learning from the successes and failures of others.

**Social learning:**
builds upon operant conditioning principles, and concerns itself chiefly with the ways in which people acquire behaviour appropriate to their social context and to their immediate circumstances.

Recent work in conditioning is offering a strong challenge to the traditional behavioural position. Seligman (1975), for example, has shown that responses to some stimuli are much easier to condition than responses to other stimuli. Moreover, Skinner's emphasis on the effects of consequences of behaviour largely ignored **modeling** the (imitation of the behaviours of others) and **vicarious experiences** (learning from the successes and failures of others).

Other researchers, most notably Albert Bandura, a professor of psychology at Stanford University and a Canadian by birth, have expanded on behavioural principles while also acknowledging the importance of cognitive processes. Although Bandura recognizes that the environment plays a large role in the determination of an individual's behaviour, he does not believe that all learning occurs as a direct result of reinforcement or punishment of behaviours. Rather, he stresses the role of internal cognitive structures which allow people to learn through observation and imitation of others—learning which therefore occurs in the absence of direct reinforcement. To Bandura and others of the social learning persuasion, reinforcers and punishment are only part of the story. A major incentive to behaviour is identification and modeling.

Social learning theory is sometimes described as neobehaviourist because Bandura builds upon operant conditioning principles. It is called **social learning**

Children will often model the types of behaviour they see on television.

because it concerns itself chiefly with the ways in which people acquire behaviour appropriate to their social context and to their immediate circumstances (Owen, Blount, and Moscow, 1978). Social learning theories have already been mentioned in a number of contexts. We noted that social learning theory opposes Kohlberg's developmental-cognitive model in the area of the acquisition of morals, social values, and social conventions. We also stressed the role of imitation in children's development of gender identity and sex roles and in their play and general socialization.

## Elements of observational learning

According to Bandura's social (or observational) learning theory some responses are not directly reinforced; instead, the behaviour of a model is imitated. Social learning involves knowing what not to do, what to do, and where to do it. It comes about by observation instead of by direct instruction. For example, we may imitate the fellow next to us at the formal dinner and pick up the salad fork; or the young toddler may sing along with Sharon, Lois, and Bram; or the teenager may dye his hair to match his favourite rock star's. One of Bandura's most famous studies of the imitation of aggression is found in Box 8-5.

Bandura (1977, 1986) has outlined four processes that are associated with observational learning. First, attentional processes govern how a person explores and perceives modeled events. Next, an individual must remember what has been seen: retentional processes allow modeled behaviour to be stored in memory. These internal symbolic representations of the modeled behaviour will later guide an individual in the reproduction of the behaviour and will also serve as a standard against which the accuracy of such reproductions will be judged.

## Box 8-5  Classic study: Imitation of aggression

Some of the best known research on observational learning has occurred in the area of aggression. In a classic study (Bandura, Ross, and Ross, 1963), children were shown a television film of a boy playing with his toys. This child refused to share the toys with a second boy. The second boy then began to beat up the first and to throw darts at his toy cars. In one version of the film, the aggressor ended up with all the toys and left with them. The alternate version showed the aggressor being subjected to a punishing counterattack by the first boy. While most children reported that they disapproved of violence, those who saw the first version were subsequently observed to behave more aggressively in a play situation than those who had either seen the second version, or no film at all.

Bandura (1965) also noted that observing the reinforcement given a subject can affect probability of behaviour in another subject (vicarious reinforcement). Bandura's most famous study in this area concerns a Bobo doll.

Children saw an aggressive adult model who punched, kicked, hit with a mallet, and verbally abused an adult-sized Bobo doll. One group saw the model rewarded with praise and candy; the second saw the model punished, and the third saw the model neither rewarded nor punished. Later, in a play situation involving several toys, including a Bobo doll, those children who saw the model either rewarded or unrewarded were much more imitatively aggressive than those who saw the model punished. However when given a positive incentive to reproduce the modeled behaviour, all three groups were able to do so equally well.

Processes of motor reproduction allow the individual to organize subskills needed to successfully produce the new pattern of behaviour, while motivational processes will determine whether skills, attitudes, or behaviour will be actually used. Figure 8-5 presents a visual representation of the process.

**Figure 8-5**
Social learning
process

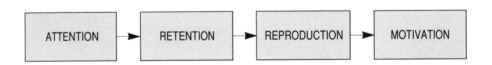

### Attention

In order to learn from a model, we must first attend to and accurately perceive the important elements of the model's behaviour. The question is how, among all the available models, do children select the ones to imitate? Attentional processes govern the choice of models to be selectively observed, as well as what aspects of the modeled behaviour are to be extracted from the stream of behaviour.

Many factors influence the attentional process, including various features of the model as well as learner characteristics. Research appears to demonstrate that people pay attention to models who are attractive, popular, interesting, and competent. People also attend to models who have high status, and/or models who are of the same race or gender as themselves. For most children, particularly those in the elementary grades, parents and teachers usually fit these qualifications. However, if the student comes from a racial or cultural background that differs from the teacher, or if a student has some type of handicapping condition, the lack of similarity between the student and the teacher diminishes the power of the teacher as model. Indeed, if the model does not hold any of the qualities cited, they may be ignored or actively rejected by the students.

Moreover, our environment can limit the types of behaviours that we repeatedly observe, and therefore those which will be best learned. People will be strongly influenced by the type of people with whom they regularly associate, as those associates provide regular models for various types of behaviour. The child growing up in the inner city, for example, who regularly observes people engaged in drug-dealing or violence has very different models than the child growing up in rural Newfoundland.

At the same time as they observe live models, children and adults are exposed to a great variety of symbolic models with different cultures or diverse lifestyles. In this regard, we cannot ignore the impact of television in the social learning process. Depending upon the programs selected, the child from a rural area may, in fact, be quite familiar with the behaviour seen on inner city streets. Not only does television provide diverse models, but these models are extremely powerful influences. It appears that television models are so effective in gaining our attention that the viewer learns much of what is seen, even without the benefit of any extra incentives (Bandura, Grusec, and Menlove, 1967).

The complexity and distinctiveness of and rate at which a behaviour is modeled will also influence the learning process. For example, if the model demonstrates a very complex behaviour, and/or the behaviour is completed very quickly, observational learning will necessarily be limited and fragmented. For example, no one learns how to serve a tennis ball like Boris Becker from simply watching him do it once. Rather, it will require repeated presentations of the model, as well as a great deal of practice, before the learner is ready in order to produce, complete, and precisely match the tennis serve. In contrast, simple acts that are clearly presented can be readily modeled by a student.

Moreover, learners cannot model a behaviour, or elements thereof that they have not noticed. Thus, social learning is affected by the salience of the model. Parents and teachers of younger children seem to instinctively know this—note how they will greatly exaggerate their actions in an attempt to increase the salience of the model in order to capture the child's attention. Regardless of the age of the learner, teachers regularly use strategies intended to increase the salience of the model and therefore elicit student attention. For example, the teacher who says: "Pay attention to this; it will be on the test" is providing an incentive for attending behaviour.

A modeled behaviour is much more likely to be learned if it is perceived to have functional value. In other words, if the behaviour is perceived to be a useful or successful method of coping with a particular situation, the observer is more likely to pay attention and learn the modeled behaviour better. Students will pay greater attention to events that provide pleasurable outcomes for the model. The student, for example, who observed another earning a reinforcer for a successful science fair project, will be likely to model that behaviour in order to achieve the same reinforcer. Similarly, observing another student being punished for a particular action is likely to inhibit observers from demonstrating similar behaviour. This does not mean that the observers have not learned the behaviour, but that even though they know how to break a window, the observed punishment will inhibit them from demonstrating their newly learned skill.

Students' characteristics, such as their cognitive capabilities, developmental level, and expectations, will also determine the extent to which they will attend to a model. First, a student's level of cognitive development will set limits on the amount of observational learning that can take place during one session. A very young child may not possess a well-developed coding system, and thus is unable to store what he or she has seen or heard. Indeed, in the very early years, imitative behaviours typically occur immediately after they have been modeled. In contrast, older children will show the ability to demonstrate imitative behaviours long after the model has been observed. This is related to the older child's ability to relate new models to existing knowledge and store the event for future recall; increased language ability and the developing cognitive structures enable the child to learn from models. Thus, models must always be calibrated to the level of cognitive development demonstrated by the student, for if the child cannot adequately process the information provided, learning will be incomplete. Repeated models may be needed before complete learning can occur.

Further, the greater the person's previous experience with the modeled event, the more complete the observations will be. More experiences means that children will be able to pick up on the subtle, yet important aspects of the modeled behaviour. For example, think of the controversy that often surrounds athletic competitions, such as gymnastics or figure skating. Even when the crowd is convinced that a certain competitor was the best, the judges, because of their knowledge and experience, are often able to notice fine differences and/or errors in performance that escaped the less knowledgeable audience.

"We see what we want (or expect) to see" is an old truism that seems to be borne out by research in observational learning. In other words, the perceptual set held by the observer (derived from past experience and the situational requirements) will influence the features of the model that are attended to, as well how the observer interprets what has been seen or heard. Thus, it is possible for two different observers to draw very different information and conclusions from the identical modeled event.

Since students must first pay attention to a modeled event before observation learning can occur, teachers often use various strategies to elicit attention. This can be done by physically accenting or exaggerating the essential features of the model, and/or providing verbal instructions about the importance of particular components of the event. Similarly, features of the model can be enhanced by comparing examples of "good" and "poor" performance. When very complex skills are to be modeled, observational learning can be enhanced by breaking the activity into natural segments. Students are presented with each segment in turn and, once they have learned each segment, the activity is then put back together.

Finally, students must not only observe—they need to practice the modeled activity repeatedly. The teacher should provide specific feedback about deficiencies or errors in performance, so the student can pay particular attention to those aspects of the performance the next time the model is presented.

## Retention

In order to reproduce a behaviour, students must remember what they have seen. Accurate memory codes which preserve pertinent information will guide correct re-enactment of the model as well as provide a standard against which the performance will be judged. Observers who code modeled events into verbal codes or visual images learn and retain information better than those who simply observe or are preoccupied with other matters when watching. Indeed, the human ability to remember vast amounts of information through symbolization enables us to learn behaviour through modeling. As we have pointed out, the ability to code and retain information is related to the cognitive development of the students.

Modeled events are generally represented as verbal steps or as visual images. When a student sees repeated models of events, an enduring visual image of the performance is created which will later guide performance when the model is absent. This is particularly important with younger children who have limited verbal skills, or when behaviour does not lend itself to verbal coding, such as hitting a slapshot or dancing a complex ballet sequence. Often, the mere mention of an activity that has been repeatedly observed will arouse its image: for example, it would be virtually impossible for an enthusiastic hockey fan to hear the word "slapshot" without conjuring a vivid image of Wayne Gretzky slamming a hockey puck. Similarly, when a name and face are repeatedly paired, one cannot hear the name without "seeing" the face. However, most cognitive processes will be verbally coded. Verbal steps may guide performance of activities such as putting together a complicated piece of machinery, baking a pie, or solving an algebraic equation.

While coding is important to retention of information, rehearsal can also be an important memory aid. Students are much less likely to forget modeled events when they either mentally rehearse the action or actually perform the activity. Visualizing oneself performing a skill, or mentally rehearsing it, becomes important when the actual performance of the skill is prohibited, or the student does not have the opportunity to perform the skill, and has been shown to lead to increased retention and proficiency. Indeed, the best observational learning has been obtained when students first organize and rehearse the activity symbolically and then act it out (Jeffery, 1974). Further, a person's ability to remember an event will be enhanced when the information is meaningful. In other words, when teachers help students relate new models to already well-known activities they will be more likely to retain the new information.

## Motor reproduction

The next step in the process is to physically act out the behaviour that was observed. Reproducing a behaviour consists of four distinct steps: cognitive organization of responses, initiation, monitoring, and refinement. Thus, a student will recall the internal representation of a behaviour, or what the behaviour

**Vicarious reinforcement:**
the tendency of humans to imitate a model in order to increase the probability that they will be reinforced.

looked like and the steps needed for completion. However, such internal representations are rarely accurate during the initial stages of observation learning and the student may not be able to perform the activity smoothly. The student will need a great deal of practice, feedback, and/or coaching before he or she can produce the desired behaviour. With each subsequent attempt, the student will refer to the internal representation of the behaviour, another viewing of the model, and/or the corrective feedback, in order to correct discrepancies in performance.

When students perform an activity in the absence of supervision, they will improve and perfect their performance by seeing, feeling, and hearing what they have done. However, this can be troublesome, for students often cannot fully observe their own actions. For example, when swimming, serving a tennis ball, or swinging a golf club, it is not possible to simultaneously view one's own performance. Thus, students may continue to practice a skill, assuming that they are correct, when in fact their reproduction is faulty. In some cases, observation of the outcome—the golf ball slices off to the left, or the basketball does not go through the hoop—tells the learner that some part of the performance is faulty. However, best performance is facilitated by observer feedback which precisely relates the changes in performance that are necessary to improve performance.

In order to reproduce an observed behaviour, students must have mastered the necessary component skills. Learners who possess component skills can easily organize them into the new pattern; if not, reproduction will be faulty. In other words, while many children may wish to imitate the goal-scoring behaviour of Wayne Gretzky or the graceful dance steps of Karen Kain, few will have the ability to accurately reproduce their performance. When students have deficits in component skills, they must be taught through modeling and guided practice.

### Motivation
Social learning theory makes a clear distinction between acquisition and performance—in other words, students will not always demonstrate everything that they have learned. This is particularly seen when learned behaviours are not perceived to be useful, or have functional value, or when they carry a high risk of punishment.

Performance will be influenced by three types of reinforcement: direct, vicarious, and self-produced. Of particular importance to the social learning view of learning is **vicarious reinforcement**, which refers to the tendency of humans to imitate a model in order to increase the probability that they will be similarly reinforced. In this case, learners have not experienced the reinforcement directly: they imitate the behaviour because they expect to be reinforced in the same way. Teenagers may imitate heavy metal rock stars because they see that these musicians are successful and popular and they hope to acquire some of this popularity for themselves. Indeed, they often do gain status in the eyes of their peers, which maintains the imitative behaviour.

In summary, Bandura's model cannot be seen as consisting of the simple imitation of behaviours: rather, we observe the person who is performing the act, the situation in which it is performed, and the reinforcement or punishment which occurs as a result of the behaviour. Thus, through observation, we may choose not to perform the modeled behaviour: if the model is unattractive to us in some way or the consequences of the behaviour are negative, we will be unlikely to imitate the behaviour.

Social learning differs from operant conditioning in two important ways. First, in operant conditioning, emphasis is placed upon the role of reinforcement in learning: a behaviour must be followed by a reinforcer in order to be repeated. Bandura would claim that students first learn when they observe a model. When the behaviour is demonstrated and reinforced, more learning occurs. The second difference is the attention paid to thinking—or the mental reproduction of what has been observed.

## SUMMARY

1. Almost all of our thoughts and behaviours have been learned, yet the process is so complex and diverse that very different theoretical positions on learning have emerged. No single theory can encompass all aspects of learning.

2. From about 1930 to 1960, behaviourism was the dominant force in North American psychology. Pavlov and Watson identified the principles of classical conditioning and B.F. Skinner detailed the principles of operant conditioning. To Skinner, the study of such behaviours represented quite a separate and important field of science.

3. Behavioural principles have been widely translated into classroom practices. Teaching according to behavioural principles involves systematic planning in order to ensure that the antecedent events set the stage for appropriate behaviour and learning and that the consequences strengthen and/or maintain the desired response.

4. The most direct application of behavioural theories is to classroom management and discipline. Teachers should be thoroughly conversant with principles such as positive and negative reinforcement, schedules of reinforcement, and extinction.

5. Behavioural learning theories are limited in scope. Although Skinner and other strict behaviourists continue to believe that behaviour can be explained without reference to cognitive processing, most behaviourists have incorporated at least some of these principles into their thinking.

6. Neobehaviourists, such as Albert Bandura, study human learning that occurs in social situations. Although Bandura recognizes the importance of the principles of behaviourism, he also incorporates modeling and vicarious experiences.

## Key Terms

antecedents
classical conditioning
conditioned stimulus

behaviours
conditioned response
connectionism

consequences

discrimination

extinction

fixed interval schedule of reinforcement

fixed schedule of reinforcement

instrumental conditioning

interval schedule of reinforcement

Law of Exercise

modeling

neutral stimulus

operant conditioning

Premack principle

primary reinforcers

Punishment I (presentation punishment)

ratio schedule of reinforcement

response strength

secondary punishers

shaping

social reinforcers

token reinforcers

unconditioned stimulus

variable ratio schedule of reinforcement

vicarious experiences

continuous schedule of reinforcement

discriminative stimulus

fair-pair rule

fixed ratio schedule of reinforcement

generalization

intermittent schedule of reinforcement

Law of Effect

learning

negative reinforcement

operant behaviours

positive reinforcement

primary punishers

punishment

Punishment II (removal punishment)

respondents

second-order conditioning

secondary reinforcers

social learning

stimulus control

unconditioned response

variable interval schedule of reinforcement

variable schedule of reinforcement

vicarious reinforcement

# COGNITIVE THEORIES OF LEARNING

**Cognitive psychology:**
a field of study that examines the whole range of mental activities–attention, perception, memory, reflective and creative thinking, the use of language, and problem-solving.

## INTRODUCTION

Behavioural theories of learning dominated North American psychology and education during the period from about 1930 to 1960. However, mounting dissatisfaction with the ability of these theoretical frameworks to accommodate issues such as problem-solving and language acquisition led many psychologists to return to the cognitive view of learning (Di Vesta, 1987). The change that took place in North American psychology in the 1950s and '60s was so profound that it came to be called the cognitive revolution. This so-called cognitive revolution was was led by psychologists such as Jerome Bruner and David Ausubel and linguists such as Noam Chomsky, and was fueled by the translation of Piaget's work into English.

In ordinary language, cognition means knowing. In psychological terms, it encompasses the processes of thinking and learning—how human beings organize, store, and use information. Hilgard (1987) observes that, by definition, cognitive psychology deals with the whole range of mental activities, including attention and perception, but extending beyond these to the so-called higher mental processes of remembering, reflective and creative thinking, the use of language, and problem-solving in various forms.

In some ways, this could be seen as a return to the roots of psychology, just a newer form of introspection. But today's cognitive theories are far more empirically based than those of Wundt; modern cognitive theorists analyze mental events in terms of their behavioural effects—effects that can be measured and observed readily. Their study of cognition is based on the following:

- only by studying mental processes can we fully understand what organisms do; and

- we can study mental processes in an objective fashion by focusing on specific behaviours, just as behaviourists do, but interpret them in terms of underlying mental processes (Atkinson et al., 1990).

**Problem-solving strategies:**

methods that lead to problem solutions in a step-by-step manner.

Information processing theorists also think in terms of models, such as short-term and long term memory and the feedback relations within each. This makes it possible for the new cognitive psychology to be reorganized as something quite different from a rediscovery of introspection.

As theoretical constructs, cognitive theories have expanded to include formulations of great diversity and complexity and there are many possible approaches to each aspect of cognition and many interpretations of the research data. Thus, while most of the behavioural theorists outlined in the preceding chapter hold a generally consistent view of the learning process, there is more variability among the theorists that we have grouped under the rubric of cognitive views of learning. However, they are presented together because of their basic assumptions about the manner in which humans acquire knowledge.

One general school of cognitive theories learning follows Jean Piaget's theories. The theorists of this school argue that human beings develop increasingly differentiated and integrated cognitive structures that represent and organize their knowledge. Like Piaget, cognitive theorists place considerable emphasis on the role of the individual in learning. In contrast to the behavioural view, which sees people in more passive roles, influenced by environmental events, cognitive psychologists see humans as critical participants in the learning process. Learning is seen to be the result of individuals' active attempts to make sense of the world by paying attention selectively to certain events, manipulating and processing information, and constructing their own individual meaning. Cognitive theories hold that humans will initiate experiences that lead to learning, seek out information to solve problems, practise skills, and reorganize what they already know to achieve new learning.

Cognitive theorists are also interested in what the individual brings to the learning situation, or the role of prior knowledge in learning. Learning is not seen to occur in isolation; instead what learners already know is thought to influence what they learn, remember, and forget. New information is best processed and stored when it can be related to existing cognitive structures or schemata. Learners seek to find the relationships between various facts, concepts, and principles, and their learning represents an elaboration and expansion of these cognitive structures.

Many cognitive psychologists are especially interested in the area of study known as information processing, which represents the newest view of the learning process. Information processing in the field of cognitive science focuses on how people learn to solve problems. The emphasis developed when scientists using computers to solve problems saw the need to clearly outline **problem-solving strategies**, those step-by-step methods that lead to problem solutions (Newell and Simon, 1972). It was the operation of computers that suggested to these theorists that a human being could be viewed as a symbol-manipulating system. The main features of this system are the memory stores, where information is held, and the processes that govern how information is coded, stored, retrieved, and manipulated. Therefore, using the computer as an analogy, and the vocabulary from computer science for terminology, theorists in this area address issues such as selective attention, perception, memory, and forgetting.

Information processing theorists have shown that the relationship between particular items of input and a learner's larger cognitive structures are surprisingly active and continuous (Good and Brophy, 1986). In doing so, information processing approaches revolutionized the study of memory by taking a fresh look at facts that had fallen into neglect during the period when behavioural theories dominated.

Information processing is not a unified theory but more a generally agreed upon psychological orientation. Theorists share some basic notions about learning and memory but do not agree upon a single model of learning. However, no matter how much they may diverge on other issues, many proponents of information processing accept a three-stage model of human information processing that comprises the sensory register, short-term memory, and long-term memory.

Cognitive theories are particularly important to classroom teachers. While behaviourism has not lost all of its influence in psychology or education, many see the cognitive approach as particularly applicable to the teaching and learning process. An understanding of how students process information and acquire new knowledge and skills is essential to the practice of instruction. Since the storage and later retrieval of information is so important to learning, teachers should develop ways to help students store information for easy and rapid recall later. Teachers, therefore, must take into account information processing capabilities and limitations.

Not only have cognitive theorists generated broad laws of learning, they have also paid attention to the instruction of specific subject matters, such as reading, mathematics, science, social studies, and so on. The theories of information processing have influenced the design of curricula and the manner in which instruction is presented in the classroom.

Nonetheless, not everyone agrees with the concepts inherent in the information processing theory. Some feel it downplays the affective components of the mind (Izard, Kagan, and Zajonc, 1983). Jerome Bruner, for example, is harshly critical of some of the formulations of the information processing theorists. He finds their theoretical formulations, which are based on computer models, to be incomplete as they emphasize the logical mode of thinking (Bruner, 1987).

In this chapter we shall discuss many different theorists, beginning with a brief review of Piaget's view of cognitive development together with a discussion of the educational implications of his work. We discuss the contribution of Jerome Bruner, a highly influential cognitive psychologist whose theoretical views have been widely used in contemporary classrooms. One of Bruner's major contributions to classroom instruction and learning has been his advancement of the principles of discovery learning. Of course, it must be acknowledged that this approach has been articulated by previous philosophers and educational psychologists. Bruner has had a great deal of impact in encouraging the use of discovery learning in contemporary North American classrooms. Because the concepts of information processing are so important for classroom teachers, much attention is directed to the ideas of this branch of cognitive thought.

## PIAGET REVISITED

Most cognitive theorists focus on human learning, especially the meaningful learning of information that is mediated through language and the intellectual skills that occur in school (Good and Brophy, 1986). Cognitive theorists concentrate on understanding the laws of learning and on how to facilitate these through instruction rather than attempting to formulate general laws of behaviour that apply across species.

The one exception here is Jean Piaget, at least as far as the application of cognitive theories to school instruction goes. As we pointed out in Chapter 3, Piaget did not delve into school learning; he left it to others to translate his work to the classroom. Nevertheless, his work reveals a great deal about how children learn.

Piaget was one of the first psychologists to recognize explicitly that humans are born as active, exploratory information processing organisms. His theory offered an alternative to behavioural notions of learning and cognitive development. Piaget's approach focuses on the organism; rather than the environment. According to Piaget, the motivation for learning is inherent, thus decreasing the need for external reinforcement. It is not so much that stimuli elicit our responses as that our own activity engenders a search for relevant stimuli. Thus, consequences are important, not because they motivate or reinforce, but because they provide feedback about the effects of our activity. Learning results from a balancing of new information with the child's growing concept of the world.

The emphasis of Piaget's theory, and those of most other cognitive psychologists (such as Bruner, Vygotsky, Werner, Kagan), is on a gradual progression through a fixed sequence of skills and discoveries. The major principles underlying Piaget's theory are:

1. the changes in the structure of behaviour and thought in the developing child are continual and progressive;
2. the order of stages is fixed;
3. accommodation and assimilation that operate in the child's continuous interactions with the environment are invariant functions;
4. thought is related to action; and
5. thought processes have logical properties (Hunt, 1961).

But what are the implications of Piaget's theories for the classroom teacher? Certainly, Piaget's views have significantly influenced educational practice; the first most important application of his views of child learning took hold in the schools in the 1960s when his principles were linked to the practice of open education. The idea that children learn best through interaction with materials, constructing their own conceptions of the world through individual experiences, underlay the commitment of open education to experiential learning. While the open education movement diminished during the "back to the basics" movement of the 1970s and '80s, a resurgence of these views is clearly evident in the schools of today. For example, the idea of continuous learning and the importance of learning through experience has been widely accepted in the elementary school curriculum in most Canadian provinces.

If teachers accept the view that children learn differently at different stages of cognitive development, this will certainly have implications for their educational practices, including the presentation of information, the teaching strategies used, the type of questioning techniques, the number of visual aids, and the number of manipulative materials.

According to Piaget, the motivation for learning is inherent, thus decreasing the need for external reinforcement.

## JEROME BRUNER

Jerome Bruner has been one of the most influential figures in the school of cognitive psychology. Bruner is a leading cognitive structural theorist and his ideas about how children develop and learn have much in common with Piaget's. Like Piaget, Bruner believes that children of different ages learn differently; that children of different ages view the world in unique ways, and that they pass through specific identifiable stages as they do so. Bruner's stages are, however, broader than Piaget's. These are shown in Table 9-1.

Table 9-1  Cognitive stages of Bruner and Piaget

| AGES | PIAGET | BRUNER |
|------|--------|--------|
| 0–2 | Sensorimotor | Enactive Iconic |
| 2–4 | Preoperational | Iconic symbolic |
| 4–7 | — | Icionic symbolic |
| 7–12 | Concrete operations | |
| 12+ | Formal operations | Abstract |

**NOTE:** The comparison is not easily made since Bruner's stages are not tied as closely as Piaget's to ages. Bruner further believes that instruction must be directed to their style of learning. He also emphasizes the role of experience.

Bruner proposes that toddlers and preschoolers perceive the world primarily through the actions that can be performed upon it. He calls this stage the enactive mode of representation. Even though Bruner sees language development as occurring primarily during the enactive stage, children of this age will understand best if instruction is framed in terms of actions, and when the teacher allows them to act upon their environment with less attention paid to verbal instructions. For example, children can demonstrate their understanding of balance by referring to their experiences on a seesaw or balance beam. They will also define objects in terms of the actions that are associated with them: a spoon is to eat with, a toy is to play with, or a chair is to sit on. Of course, sometimes even adults revert to an enactive mode of learning; for example, when teaching a new motor skill such as serving a tennis ball, the instructor is likely to show the student the appropriate grip rather than simply giving a verbal description of the hand placement.

Children later progress to the iconic or concrete mode of representation in which ideas are represented primarily in terms of images. It is now possible for children to think of an object without reference to the action. This has significant implications for teachers as they are now able to use pictures and diagrams to impart information, rather than having to have the children act upon the object itself. Iconic representation begins as small children hold mental images and can think of an object without reference to the actual thing. Soon, as they develop language, children add a symbolic component, using a linguistic marker to refer to the thing.

Finally, in late childhood and early adolescence, students begin to use abstract or symbolic representations. They are now able to translate their experiences into actions. As Bruner points out, "Powerful representations of the world of possible experience are constructed and used as search models in problem solving" (Bruner, 1966, p. 14). Now, for example, students can explain the principles of balance by talking about a seesaw or pendulum.

Unlike other learning theorists, Bruner has paid a great deal of attention to the actual instructional applications of his work. His interest in education stemmed from his doctoral work at Harvard in the areas of human perception and learning. Bruner calls his formulations a theory of instruction rather than a theory of learning. He believes that a theory of learning is descriptive in that it describes what has happened after the fact. In contrast, a theory of instruction is prescriptive, or prescribed in advance of how best to teach a given subject. Thus, rather than simply describing what a child can or cannot do at a particular age, Bruner directs attention to how best to facilitate the cognitive development of children, particularly through school curriculum.

Bruner has published a number of important books which outline his views of instruction. Box 9-1 presents biographical information on Bruner.

Box 9-1  **Biographical note: Jerome Bruner (b. 1915)**

Jerome Bruner was born into an upper middle class family. While his parents had expected him to become a lawyer, Bruner studied psychology at Duke University and Harvard, receiving his doctorate from the latter institution in 1941. Since that time, he has been a highly influential and productive thinker; he has made major contributions to many different fields of psychology and has been frequently represented in the professional literature. However, part of his enduring eminence and influence lies in the fact that he is not only read by his professional colleagues in psychology; his work has also been embraced by professional educators.

Bruner has had a diverse and rich career in psychology, with interests ranging from topics such as public opinion, perception, thought, education, to the development of cognitive skills and abilities in infancy and childhood. When Bruner first arrived at Harvard, he enrolled in the recently created (1933) department of psychology, chaired by the renowned E.G. Boring. The department was primarily geared towards research, particularly with animals and in the area of perception, and Bruner studied under the great physiological psychologist, Karl Lashley. However, the advent of World War II shifted Bruner's attention to social psychology,

addressing topics such as group attitudes, propaganda, and prejudice. His doctoral thesis addressed the propaganda techniques used by the Nazis.

After the war, Bruner's attention shifted back to the study of perception and with his colleagues he published many original and important studies in this field between 1946 and 1958. His work was important to the extent that it represented a "new view" of the process of perception. Bruner and his colleagues conceptualized perception not as an isolated process but rather one that interacted with experiences and motivational, personal, and social factors. This new look at perception provided a major impetus for the cognitive revolution of the late 1950s and 1960s.

The interest in the use of inference in the process of perception led Bruner to the study of the inferential processes inherent in other types of reasoning. A five year research program begun in 1951 culminated in the publication of *The process of thinking* (1956), in which he examined the process of concept attainment. However, Bruner did not deal exclusively with empirical research: he also published in 1962 a book called *On knowing: essays for the left hand*, which addressed the intuitive and creative aspects of human thinking. It reflected his view that humans should not only be thought of as logical, rational thinkers, but also as artists, poets, and humanists.

During the late 50s, The Woods Hole Conference on Education, which gathered experts under the direction of Bruner to discuss the the improvement of teaching, fueled the next phase of Bruner's work: education and representation in childhood. He became interested in developing a curriculum designed to meet the intellectual development of children. His work on the cognitive stages in childhood reflects the degree to which Bruner had been influenced by Jean Piaget. These beliefs naturally led to Bruner's notion of discovery learning, or involving the learner actively in the learning process.

Unlike many theorists, Bruner has attempted to apply his theoretical formulation to the practice of education. Volumes such as *The process of education* (1960), *Toward a theory of instruction* (1966), and *The relevance of educa-*

*tion* (1971) have been widely read and applied by professional educators. Through such volumes, Bruner put forward his ideas concerning the importance of teaching the "structure" of a discipline rather than the facts and figures; the importance of spiral curriculum, which proposes that any topic can be taught to any child if done so in an appropriate fashion; and the importance of allowing children to develop problem-solving techniques.

In addition to the acclaim received from educators, in 1963 Bruner was awarded the Distinguished Scientific Award from the American Psychological Association. He was elected president of this organization in 1965. His fundamental belief in the dignity of the human being, and in the importance of integrating human rationality with the creative, emotional aspects of thinking represents a unique and inspiring view of human potentiality.

## Bruner's theory

At its most basic level, Bruner's theory consists of four principles: motivation, structure, sequences, and reinforcement. In this case, motivation specifies the conditions that predispose an individual to learn. Bruner believes that any discipline (be it mathematics, biology, literature, or physics) can be organized into a coherent structure that can be understood by almost any student. "The curriculum of a subject," he said, "should be determined by the most fundamental understanding that can be achieved of the underlying principles that give structure to the subject" (1960, p. 31). Rather than memorizing isolated facts or concepts, students are led to see the principles on which a discipline is based. Once this has been accomplished, learners are able to explore new problems or questions from the perspective of those basic elements.

Bruner believes that if the structure of a discipline is properly developed "any idea or problem or body of knowledge can be presented in a form simple enough so that any particular learner can understand it in a recognizable form" (Bruner, 1966, p. 44). In turn, this concept is related to the idea of the spiral curriculum, as is the notion of sequence, the progression of learning tasks.

As for the notion of reinforcement, Bruner sees children as possessing a built-in or innate will to learn. He certainly does not abandon reinforcement, but believes that only through intrinsic motivation is the will to learn sustained.

## Spiral curriculum

Bruner proposes that children should never wait in order to learn. He states that "Any subject can be taught effectively in some intellectually honest form to any child at any stage of development" (1971, p. 52). Not surprisingly, this statement, often misinterpreted, has elicited lively debate. However, Bruner does not propose that teachers launch into a discussion of advanced physiology with grade one students; rather, he suggests that aspects of a subject matter can be understood by students if presented in a fashion that is related to the cognitive capabilities of the children.

In any teaching and learning situation, the instructional strategies used by a teacher will not only be directed towards the cognitive capabilities of the children, but will also take into account the subject matter itself. When teaching motor tasks to adults or older children, for example, it is likely that enactive representations will be used even if the students are capable of symbolic representation. Similarly, subjects such as geography are best suited to iconic representations, while problems in ethics or logic are best suited to symbolic representation. In some cases, such as mathematics, all three types will be used.

Since Bruner believes that *any* topic can be taught to any child, as long as the matter is presented in a manner that allows the student to grasp the ideas, he sees no need to wait to present certain concepts or topics to children. Rather, he proposes the idea of the spiral curriculum in which a topic is presented in a simple enactive form with younger children, returned to again in a more complex iconic form (through pictures and diagrams) as the child's thinking ability progresses, and finally moves on to symbolic representation as the students move through their school years. In this manner, pupils study the same topic again and again but each time at a level of complexity that can best be understood by the student at his or her stage of cognitive development.

## Discovery learning

When behavioural approaches to teaching and learning are employed, teachers are responsible for organizing the content to be learned in some logical fashion and then presenting this information to the students. Bruner believes that far too much school learning is accomplished in this manner and that, although students are able to reproduce information on examinations, they are unable to use it in their daily lives. His alternative is a process of discovery learning in which students are presented with problems and are allowed to seek their own solutions through independent work or group discussion. Bruner believes that when students come to their own understanding, these conceptions will be more meaningful to them than those presented by the teacher or others. Being more meaningful, material is more apt to be retained.

Bruner feels that discovery learning reduces the need for external reinforcers since he sees the intrinsic rewards of solving intriguing problems to be sufficiently motivating. This is not to say that he has entirely discarded the notion of extrinsic reinforcement; in some cases, he believes that rewards may be necessary to help students initiate certain actions or for making sure that actions are repeated. However, he holds that intrinsic reinforcement will last a lifetime

Human curiosity provides one of the clearest examples of the human desire to learn.

while extrinsic reinforcement will have, at best, a transitory effect. He firmly endorses the notion that all humans have an innate desire to learn and that only through a reliance on intrinsic motivation will this desire be maintained. Human curiosity provides one of the clearest examples of the human desire to learn; Bruner sees this trait an an innate characteristic that has biological relevance since curiosity is necessary for the survival of the species.

Bruner further claims that, with repeated opportunities, students will learn problem solving abilities and also gain confidence in their ability to confront problematic situations. They not only learn material; they also learn how to learn. This is a valuable life-skill that will serve the students well in their adult lives. The process of learning through discovery is also important in facilitating the development of creative thinking, which Bruner believes is crucial in a well-developed person. When individuals can think creatively, they are able to break away from standard rules of logic and concern themselves with beliefs, desires, expectations, emotions, and intentions.

While Bruner supports the idea of discovery learning, he does not go so far as to suggest that it is the only form of learning that can be used. Children could not discover for themselves the solutions to all problems that they confront: to expect them to do so would be absurd. Indeed, taken to the extreme, a sole reliance on discovery learning would mean that every new generation of learners would be responsible for "discovering" the ideas and formulations that undergird their culture. It is neither necessary for the student of geography to rediscover that the world is round nor for the student of chemistry to rediscover the elements. Some information is best presented to the students through a more conventional mode. However, this does not mean that the teacher must return to rote learning strategies; in many instances, students may be able to come to their own understanding of basic principles through questioning, discussion, and careful prompting.

How is discovery learning implemented in the classroom? At first glance it might seem to be an easy strategy to use since the students appear do all the work. In reality, teachers are very busy; they must be acutely aware of student activity and progress, and well prepared and highly knowledgeable about the subject matter. Teachers must also be patient and flexible: discovery learning takes time and it is not possible to strictly schedule lessons and timetables as is done in more traditional modes of instruction. It is also not possible to control the learning process; teachers must be flexible enough to accommodate the different strategies that may be applied by the students. Further, care must be taken to create a safe and secure classroom environment in which students feel free to take risks. Discovery learning means that students will often make errors or reach incorrect conclusions on their way to understanding. If they are afraid of appearing foolish or feel that the teacher is critical of their errors, students will not have the courage to pursue their studies. Box 9-2 contains a description of a curriculum developed by Bruner which illustrates the application of discovery learning to social studies.

## Box 9-2  In the classroom: Man: A Course of Study

Man: A Course of Study (MACOS) is a curriculum that was developed under the supervision of Jerome Bruner in order to illustrate the use of discovery learning in the classroom. Bruner describes the unit in the following manner: "The content of the course is man: his nature as a species, the forces that shaped and continue to shape his humanity. Three questions recur throughout: What is human about human beings? How did they get that way? How can they be made more so?" (1966, p. 74).

However, the important goal of the unit is not to "get across" or impart information; it is to help learners explore their own consciousness or learning processes, deepen their views of the world, and establish views of their own. To accomplish this, the unit addresses the above questions through five themes or subject areas, each of which is associated with the distinctiveness of humans and their evolution.

The five humanizing forces include tool-making, language, social organization, the management of people's prolonged childhood, and the human urge to explain the world.

Consistent with Bruner's ideas, students not only explore the role of language or tools in the evolution of humans but also are exposed to the fundamentals of linguistics or the theory of tools in the belief that they cannot understand the relevance of the topic to humankind unless they understand these fundamental concepts. For example, Bruner and his colleagues feel that it is more important for the children to *understand* mythology rather than simply memorize examples. But rather than directly discussing the "theory" of myths—which would be an inappropriate topic for fifth grade students—they expose the children to multiple examples. Through such readings, children develop an intuitive sense of the structures of narratives and grow to understand the human need to make sense of the world, regardless of culture.

Various instructional techniques are presented in the unit to facilitate the student's acquisition of concepts. These include contrast; for example, comparing animal and human social organizations, as well as differences in social organization between peoples or cultures, or even between adults and children within the same culture. Simulation is used to to help the students understand or become more sensitive to differences. For example, to illustrate the differences in social organization, hunting parties (patterned on the Bushmen of the Kalahari desert) are simulated. Children are encouraged to use informed guessing, hypothesis making, and conjectural procedures. For example, before watching a film of a group hunting seal by

watching breathing holes, children are asked to figure out the problem on their own. Bruner claims that it is more interesting for the children to learn the facts after they have tried to figure out problems for themselves. Children actively participate in learning. For example, so that they can get a sense of what tools are, they are asked to design a tool (an orange peeler). Finally, the unit is intended to stimulate self-consciousness about thinking and its ways, for it is believed that children should be at least as aware of their patterns of thought as they are about their attempts to commit facts to memory. This also includes the tools of thought such as language, causal explanation, and categorization. Children learn what it is like to use a theoretical model, and gain a sense of what it is like to test out a theory.

## THE INFORMATION PROCESSING MODEL OF LEARNING

The information processing model is one of the newest views of the learning process. Information processing theorists consider how the raw materials of memory are processed much as goods are sent down an assembly line or a computer processes information.

Many theorists have used the information processing framework to describe the process of learning (e.g., Atkinson and Shiffrin, 1971; Kintsch, 1977; Klatzky, 1980; Loftus and Loftus, 1976). While each formulation differs from the others in some significant ways, they do agree that learning can be conceptualized as a three-stage process involving the sensory register, short-term memory and long-term memory. Information processing theorists also share certain principles:

- humans are bombarded with incoming stimuli;

- humans are equipped in various ways to select the information that they require;

- they are also equipped to deal with the selected information in a variety of ways;

- when humans apply particular processes to information repeatedly, they develop lasting systems to deal with the information called cognitive structures of schemata;

• cognitive structures change and develop.

Information processing models can be particularly useful to teachers as they help address questions such as why students pay attention to and learn certain information and not other material, why students forget, and how forgetting can be minimized. Answers to these questions lead teachers to the use of teaching strategies that will best facilitate learning and improve memory and recall.

## Components of the model

Information constantly enters our minds through our senses. Some of this bombardment of stimuli we ignore; some we remember for a short time and forget; some we place in long-term memory. Memory is a crucial component, for without memory we could not learn. In fact, lacking memory, we could not qualify as intelligent animals, much less human beings. Lacking memory, people would have to relearn everything each time they encountered an object, event, person, or idea.

Figure 9-1 presents a simplified representation of the process as it is understood by information processing theorists. The three boxes represent the three stages of the information processing model: information is gathered and initially processed in the sensory register, then, as the arrow indicates, some information is passed on to short-term memory and, if not discarded, is then passed to long-term memory.

**Figure 9-1**
Information
processing model

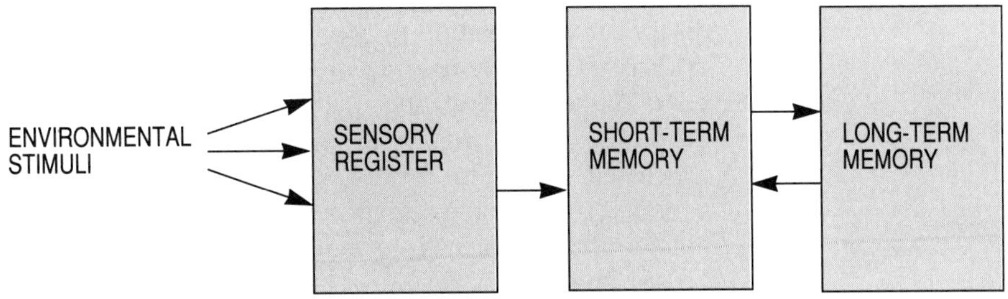

ENVIRONMENTAL STIMULI → SENSORY REGISTER → SHORT-TERM MEMORY ⇄ LONG-TERM MEMORY

Information processing theorists assume that all people have the same mechanisms, but acknowledge that there exist individual differences in the capacity of one or more of the parts and the manner in which each is used (Di Vesta, 1987). Further, each component—sensory register, short-term memory, and long-term memory—has its own inherent limitations, although these can be modified to some extent through the use of various strategies or control processes.

## Sensory register

Information processing begins when a person experiences input from the outside world: smells a flower, hears a telephone ringing, or sees words presented

**Receptors:**
the components of the sensory register for seeing, hearing, tasting, smelling, and feeling.

on the page. This information is detected by **receptors**, which are the components of the sensory register for seeing, hearing, tasting, smelling, and feeling. Most sensory information is monitored at a low level of attention. However, when brain function is examined, physical evidence that the receptors are in operation can be seen in the form of very brief patterns of neural activity that are produced when stimuli reach the receptors.

It has been proposed that there are developmental variations in the ability of human beings to take in information to the sensory register. However, while young children were once thought to be much less able to hold data in the sensory register, some more recent research has suggested that children do not differ significantly from adults in the amount of information that they perceive, nor in the time they hold it in the sensory register (see Lasky and Spiro, 1980).

The information received through the senses is held in a form resembling the sensation from the original stimulus. To illustrate this, Lindsay and Norman (1972) suggest trying the following activities:

- Tap four fingers against your arm. Feel the immediate sensations. Note that as they fade away you at first still retain the actual feeling of the tapping, but later on only the recollection that you were tapped lingers.

- Listen to some sounds, say the tapping of your fingers or a few whistled notes. Notice how the distinctness of the image in your mind fades away.

- Wave a pencil (or even your finger) back and forth in front of your eyes while you stare straight ahead. See the shadowy image that trails behind the moving object (pp. 287-288).

Information is held in the sensory register only very briefly before it begins to disappear. Information in the sensory register rapidly disappears through decay or displacement by new input. Retention time ranges from less than a second for visual sensations to about four seconds for auditory sensations (Good and Brophy, 1986). To retain any memory of events, the sensations must be further processed, or encoded in short-term memory. But this can only be done if we attended to the original experience in the first place and, of course, humans cannot attend to all of the information that they are exposed to at any given moment. To see how this happens, stop reading for a moment and pay attention to the other stimuli in the environment. Is a clock ticking, your ear itching, or is there an odor in the air? Unless you had directed your attention to these stimuli, you would not have been aware of the sensations reaching your sensory register. Like a volume control, you have "turned down" the intensity to an undetectable level.

When humans do not attend to some of the information coming in to the sensory register, it will not be further processed. This means that much of the information that we are exposed to will never be passed along to the short-term memory and therefore cannot be retrieved at a later time. It may be that many "memory lapses" are, in fact, related to the failure to attend (Atkinson et al., 1990). For example, if you were out with friends last night, try to recall the colour of their shoes or the type of watch that one of them wore. It was likely that you will not be able to recall this information because you failed to attend to it at the time. Similarly, the student who does not attend to the teacher's lecture cannot possibly remember the data or retrieve it at a later time—in essence, no information has been acquired.

**Sensation:**
the information received through the senses.

**Perception:**
the meaning attached to information received through the senses.

**Gestalt:**
a German word referring to an organized, integrated whole that has identity and meaning in its own right and is not merely the sum of its parts.

## Perception

In addition to selective attention, the processes of perception are critical to information processing. Early psychologists such as Wilhelm Wundt made a sharp distinction between sensation and perception. They believed that perceptions, feelings, sensations, intentions, and the like all had an independent existence. Today, sensations are thought to be experiences elicited by simple stimuli such as colours. Perceptions involve making meaning out of the stimuli in the environment and are still assumed to involve an integration of sensations. Sensory perceptions are those associated with the sense organs and peripheral levels of the nervous system; perceptual processes are associated with higher levels of the nervous system.

**Sensation** relates to the information we receive through our senses. **Perception** is more complex; it refers to the meaning attached to information received through our senses. When the sensory receptors are activated by stimuli, sensation occurs. But when the mind begins to process the information and attach some meaning to it, we have perception. Perception forms a link between sensation and cognition.

Perception and conceptualization are inseparable, although they are not synonymous. Perceptual abilities develop fairly early in life, and are critical for school learning because there is hardly any academic activity that does not require the student to engage in some type of perception.

The perception of the stimuli that were seen, heard, felt, or smelled will not be an exact "copy" of the objective reality because perception is influenced by beliefs, knowledge, mental state, expectations, and so on. The meaning attributed to a perception will be constructed partly from objective reality and partly from the way we organize the information. This helps explain why two different people experience the same event in very different ways; their perception of that event may differ radically. For example, it is fairly well established that if two separate observers view an event, say a terrible car accident, they have vastly different stories to tell when interviewed later by police. One may have seen the cars speeding, the other thought that they were barely moving; one saw the driver of the red car at fault while the other saw that driver as the innocent victim. Are one or both of these observers lying? Probably not. It is more likely that they are accurately describing their perceptions of the event but that they have perceived the same event in very different ways.

### Gestalt psychology

The modern understanding of how humans receive and process information has its roots in the the gestalt movement in psychology, which flourished in the early part of this century. It was developed in Germany by Max Wertheimer and his associates, Kurt Koffka and Wolgang Kohler. All of these researchers later came to the United States to escape the Nazi regime.

This view of learning takes its name from the German word "gestalt" which can be roughly translated into *form* or *configuration*. A **gestalt**, then, is an organized, integrated whole that has identity and meaning in its own right and is not merely the sum of its parts.

The gestalt theorists represented a departure from the prevailing behavioural view of the process of learning. While investigators such as Edward Thorndike

**Closure:**
a Gestalt principle referring to the human tendency to reorganize perceptions into simplified, logical wholes, filling in the missing information if necessary.

**Figure-ground:**
a Gestalt principle referring to the tendency of humans to focus their attention on the primary figure and its details while the remaining scene blends into the background.

and John Watson focused on overt behaviours and saw learning as a process of trial and error, the gestalt psychologists redirected attention to the study of the internal processes involved in learning. They suggested that people have a tendency to organize sensory information into coherent wholes in order to make sense of the world. Thus, rather than paying attention to bits and pieces of information, humans tend to perceive the gestalt, or the whole.

Take a quick look at the figures presented in Figure 9-2. What did you see? A triangle, square and circle? Did you even notice that parts of the figures were missing? Perhaps not—and even if you noticed the missing pieces, these absent pieces of information did not prevent you from recognizing the figures. This demonstration illustrates the Gestalt principle of **closure**, which refers to the human tendency to reorganize perceptions into simplified, logical wholes, filling in the missing information if necessary.

**Figure 9-2**
Gestalt principle of closure

Another important gestalt principle is known as **figure-ground**, the tendency of humans to focus their attention on the primary figure and its details while the remaining scene blends into background. The classic example of figure ground in illustrated in Figure 9-3. Look at the picture—do you see a vase or two faces directed towards each other? What you see is likely to be related to your expectations; for example, if you were told to look for a vase (the figure), you would not perceive the faces (which become "ground") and vice versa. Or we can draw an example from classroom life. Take the teacher who is having trouble with one particularly obstreperous child in the classroom. The tendency may be to focus on that student (figure) while all of the others blend unnoticed into the background. The teacher may be acutely aware of what that student is doing at all times but may not notice that others are demonstrating similar or even worse behaviour (Woolfolk, 1990).

**Figure 9-3**
Gestalt principle of figure-ground

The gestalt view of learning essentially reversed the process of instruction as proposed by the behaviourists. Rather than breaking material down into parts, and teaching in a step by step fashion, the gestalt approach started from the whole, and then proceeded back to a consideration of the parts (Mueller, 1974). Box 9-3 describes some research conducted by Wolfgang Kohler concerning the gestalt view of problem-solving which had a significant impact on the field of psychology.

## Box 9-3  Classic study: Kohler's study of insight in chimpanzees

Insight is an important principle in gestalt psychology, referring to the human ability to understand the relationships between elements in a problem situation. The learner gains insight when they understand the gestalt, the "wholeness" or entirety of the problem. The gestalt view of problem-solving was at odds with the "trial and error" view of the learning process, which was developed by theorists such as Thorndike through his work with cats in puzzle boxes. Wolfgang Kohler was one of the early psychologists working in this area. Kohler proposed that humans ponder problems and examine various aspects until they see the solution in a flash of insight. During the thinking phase, Kohler felt that the problem-solver mentally tries out a variety of solutions. When the correct answer is found, it appears completely and suddenly. He proposed that sometimes very complex learning can occur rapidly through insight.

Kohler studied chimpanzees and concentrated on two different problems for his chimpanzees to solve. In both, the chimpanzees were placed in a situation in which a desired item, a piece of fruit (usually a banana) was placed out of reach, either outside the cage or hung from the ceiling of the cage. Sometimes the chimps solved the problem immediately; at other times, after some unsuccessful attempts to gain the desired treat, the chimpanzee would sit back, apparently thinking about the problem, and then suddenly see the solution to the problem.

The manner in which the chimpanzees solved the problem suggested that they had gained insight into the situation. Their behaviour was not gradual, as seen in trial and error learning, nor was it systematically shaped through the use of reinforcement. Rather, once a chimpanzee had solved the problem by perceiving it in its entirety and relating the separate parts to the whole, it rapidly moved to solve the problem with few wasted motions. Further, it was found that the chimpanzees transferred their learning to new situations, indicating that the learning was maintained.

Kohler's experiments opened up an entirely new area of research in learning. The results were viewed as evidence that learning did not occur in "bits," as seen in trial and error learning, but rather was a process of understanding the entire situation in order to determine how the various parts fit together to achieve a solution (Mueller, 1974).

## Attention

For perceptions to be retained, they must be passed to the memory stores. Control processes govern the manner in which information is encoded and

**Selective attention**

the ability to focus on the relevant features of stimuli.

**Sustained attention:**

the ability to attend to stimuli over a period of time.

flows between the memory stores. Among control processes are recognition, attention, maintenance, and rehearsal.

Once stimuli are reorganized, they must be attended to. In a classroom, students must pay attention to information in order to retain it, for it takes time to bring all the information seen in a moment into consciousness. Attention span is the length of time an individual can remain actively involved in an activity before becoming bored and restless. There are two types of attention. Selective attention refers to the ability to focus on the relevant features of stimuli. Once students have located the relevant stimuli, they must develop sustained attention in order to attend to the stimuli over a period of time (Winzer, 1989).

Both types of attention are critical to the learning process; when we attend to certain stimuli and ignore others, we determine which bits of information will be passed along to the short-term memory. In some cases, attention will be consciously directed toward a particular environmental stimulus; sometimes a novel, surprising, or otherwise noticeable stimulus will capture our attention automatically.

Because attention is a finite resource, we must be selective in its allocation. Humans learn to allocate their limited attention so that we consciously attend to some items and not to others. The "cocktail party phenomenon" is an example of this: when you are at a loud and noisy party, you screen out all stimuli except the conversation you are having with a friend. Of course, the other stimuli are not blocked out entirely; they are simply "turned down." To illustrate this, consider what happens if your name is spoken, even very softly, in a conversation across the room. It is likely that your attention will immediately shift over to that conversation, demonstrating that other stimuli, while not actively attended to, have not been blocked out entirely.

Some interesting studies have shown how well human beings develop the ability to attend to information. In one study (Cherry, 1953), subjects were asked to wear headphones in which two different messages were transmitted, one through each ear. Most of the subjects who were told to attend to only one message had no difficulty in doing so. At the same time, the subjects were apparently unaware of what was being transmitted to the other ear.

Attention is a limited resource. When teachers call on students for attention, the students must forsake other stimuli and shift their priorities to the teacher. Moreover, there are individual differences in attention; some students have a greater ability than others to consciously direct their attention to relevant classroom activities.

The manner in which attention is allocated will also depend upon the task at hand. That is, when we are very proficient at a task, it will not require full attention. For example, remember when you first learned to drive a car? It was impossible to operate the car simultaneously with keeping a conversation going. As you gained competence and the parts of the driving process became automatic, you were able to direct some of your attention to a chat with a friend.

This process of automatization (Shiffrin and Schneider, 1977) is important to classroom teachers who want students to learn some processes so well that the students are able to direct their short-term memory capacity to more complex tasks. Students who are struggling with the correct formation of letters, for example, cannot direct their attention to a creative writing task; nor can

**Overlearning:**
learning material to the point beyond which it appears to be mastered.

students who are focusing on the decoding of individual words attend to the meaning of a sentence. Such fundamental academic tasks as these must be learned extremely well—in fact, overlearned—so that they become automatic for the students. Retention is longer and material is more easily retrieved when it is **overlearned**—learned to the point beyond where it appears to be mastered (Keppel, 1968).

As attention is critical to the processing of information, teachers must be able to capture and hold student attention in the classroom. Because attention is limited, students who are writing a note to a pal, scratching a persistent itch, gazing out the window, or even thinking about their hungry stomachs cannot devote full attention to what the teacher is saying. Lacking full attention to the task at hand, those students will be precluded from the efficient processing and retention of information. To assist students in attending to the important message, teacher can help them to learn to screen out or ignore other incoming stimuli. This becomes even more important with younger children who are less able to control their attentional processes, attend to relevant information, and ignore the irrelevant. There are many ways to accomplish this; Box 9-4 offers some suggestions for use in the classroom.

## Box 9-4 **In the classroom: Gaining student attention**

We have noted that students must pay attention to information if it is to be further processed; that is, learned and retained.

1. *Attention is limited: do not present too much information at one time.* If the teacher presents a great deal of material at one time, without highlighting the important bits, the students may not process any of the material at all (see Case, 1978a). Further, the instructional environment should be as free of distraction as possible, thus enhancing the probability that students will attend to the teacher, rather than other interesting and distracting elements in the classroom.

2. *Use cues.* Teachers often use their voices dramatically to catch student attention: raising or lowering their tones when giving important information; or repeating or emphasizing important information by writing on the blackboard or using an overhead. (Glynn and DiVesta, 1979). An example of the use of cues can be found in this book; note how different typefaces are used to help the reader attend to the most important information. If novel cues are used (but not over used) to guide attention they can improve learning (Hershberger and Terry, 1965).

3. *Tell students what is important.* This is another direct way to cue students that the forthcoming information is important to them; prefacing your remarks with comments such as "This is important..." or "Listen carefully..." is a good way to garner student attention. Perhaps the best way to gather rapt student attention is to use the phrase: "This will be on the test..."

4. *Arouse curiosity or interest.* This can be accomplished in many ways. For example,

if material is introduced in a manner that makes it personally meaningful. Open a class by asking questions such as: "What would happen to you if...," or use students' interests in favourite television shows, popular music, sports, and so on as a vehicle to present information. Similarly, use novel, unexpected, or unusual stimuli. The teacher who bursts in to the classroom dressed up as a mad scientist to open a biology class is likely to capture student attention—at least the first time it is done. Of course, novel ideas become old hat when overused. The teacher who dresses up in a different costume every day is likely to be greeted with a great yawn on the fourth or fifth occasion.

5. *Use emotionally arousing terms.* Our emotional responses to certain stimuli—be it anger, joy, surprise, or despair—will serve to direct our attention. Using emotionally arousing terms such as kill, gold, or burn helps students retain information better than do more neutral words (Olson and Pau, 1966).

**Encoding:**
the transformation of the sensations held in the sensory register into some type of interpretation of the event.

**Acoustic encoding:**
the retention and recall of sounds.

## Short-term memory

After its brief stay in the sensory register, some information passes to short-term memory. Again, the retention is brief. Short-term memory is limited by two things—the length of time unrehearsed information can be retained and the number of items that can be held at one time.

Once we have attended to information in the sensory register, we filter this input through a process called encoding which prepares the information for storage in short-term memory by selecting the essential features to form an image. **Encoding**, then, involves the transformation of the sensations held in the sensory register into some type of interpretation of the event (Lindsay and Norman, 1972). Research has indicated that there are different ways that information can be encoded. **Acoustic encoding** refers to the recall of sounds: for example, we recall a name or phone number by retaining the sounds of the words. To illustrate the use of acoustic coding in short-term memory, look at the following list of consonants for a few seconds:

R  L  B  K  S  J

Now cover the letters and write down the six letters in order. Did you get them all correct? If not, examine the errors that you made. In a study in which a similar procedure was used, it was found that when subjects made errors, they tended to list an incorrect letter that was similar in sound to the correct letter; for example, substituting "B" for "T" (Conrad, 1964). This would suggest that the subjects were encoding the letters acoustically and, although recall was imperfect, a similar sounding letter or word was substituted (Atkinson et al., 1990).

Acoustic coding is used primarily for verbal material. Nonverbal information, such as pictures that are not easily described, are visually encoded in short-term memory. Some individuals, most often children, seem to have the ability to hold almost perfect representations of visual material in their short-term memories.

**Rehearsal:**

a control process that affects the flow of information through the information-processing system; the process of maintaining an item in short-term memory by repetition so that it can be retrieved or sent to long-term memory.

After even a brief scanning of a picture, they will be able to hold a photographic-like image in mind. This eidetic image can be held for as long as a few minutes and, when subjects are asked questions about even the smallest detail in the picture, they respond as if reading the details directly from the image. Eidetic imagery, albeit fascinating, is rare: some degree of this ability is found among elementary-aged children but very few have this ability after the adolescent years (Ahsen, 1977a, b).

Regardless of the manner in which information is encoded, short-term memory has a very limited capacity. In general, research has shown that the short term memory of an adult can be expected to hold about seven items (+/-2). This limit also holds for non-Western cultures (Yu et al., 1985). With such a limited capacity in short-term memory, an adult can remember only five to nine separate and unrelated bits of information at a time; elementary-aged children will remember even less (Case, 1985a).

Short-term memory is sometimes called working memory because the information stored there can only be held briefly. Unless a person tries actively to retain the information, it will usually remain in short-term memory for about 15 to 20 seconds (Good and Brophy, 1986). Information will be lost either because items are displaced by newer information or because they decay over time. Displacement is related to the fixed capacity of the short-term memory. In other words, new information can be seen as "pushing out" old material.

To illustrate, consider this common situation. You have called directory assistance to get a new phone number and, lacking pen or paper, you start to repeat the number given by the operator so you can remember it long enough to make the call. But just as you are starting to ring the number, a person goes by and asks you a question. You respond, and when trying to resume dialing, find that you have forgotten the number. The new information has displaced the old (the telephone number), and there is no way that you will be able to bring back the forgotten numbers—unless you call the operator again. Alternatively, information in the short-term memory will decay over time, even if no new information follows it. That is, the information will simply fade away if no attempt is made to retain it.

While short-term memory is extremely limited in capacity and storage time, a variety of control processes can be used to help focus attention, manipulate information, and organize and assist in the retention of information. Control processes do not directly affect the capacity of short-term memory; instead, they help a learner use the capacity more effectively. Some control processes operate automatically; however, it is possible for humans to consciously manipulate the use of control processes in order to facilitate learning and recall. For example, return to the situation where you repeat and repeat a phone number in order to help yourself retain that information. In this case, you are using maintenance rehearsal, one of the most common control processes, in which information is repeated mentally or out loud until no longer needed. As long as you focus on and repeat the information in the short-term memory, it will remain available. That is, we retain information better when it is rehearsed over and over as this helps us organize the material better, which, in turn, aids later retrieval.

Rehearsal, therefore, is the process of maintaining an item in short-term memory by repetition so that it can be retrieved or sent to long-term memory.

**Chunking:**

grouping information into more meaningful units in order to increase the amount of information retained without exceeding the capacity of short-term memory.

Rehearsal may be viewed as a control process that affects the flow of information through the information processing system. Most children discover the use of rehearsal at about age ten and, as they grow older, they develop more organized uses of rehearsal strategies; they are able to pass more information along to long-term memory (Ornstein, Naus, and Liberty, 1975).

If short-term memory is capable of retaining only a certain amount of information, how do we hold larger amounts of data, such as a long distance telephone number? If we try to remember each number—4013278919—the capacity of the short-term memory will be exceeded. What do we do? A common and successful strategy is to group the numbers in some fashion; for example, 401—327—89—19. As result, we have only four pieces of information to remember. This strategy is referred to as chunking, a process which allows us to keep more than seven (+/-2) pieces of information in short term memory. The use of **chunking**, or grouping information into more meaningful units, can increase the amount of information retained without exceeding the capacity of short-term memory (Miller, 1956).

Chunking requires a person to draw on the resources of both long- and short-term memory. For example, look at the line below for a few seconds:

DOGAPERADIONATO

Can you remember all of the letters? Probably not, because the 15 separate letters exceed the capacity of your short-term memory. However, if you were to chunk the letters together, the result would be four meaningful units that can be more easily accommodated:

DOG APE RADIO NATO

These units are meaningful because you have drawn on your long-term memory in which word knowledge is stored, allowing you to recode the letters into units which are then stored in the short-term memory (Atkinson et al., 1990). Of course, if you were not an English speaker, the units would be meaningless and this chunking strategy not likely to be very helpful. Similarly, a phrase such as $(a + b)^2$ might be a single chunk to a math major, but will be six separate chunks of information to the beginning student of algebra (Di Vesta, 1987).

Chunking techniques depend upon an individual's ability to organize and form abstractions. Older learners, for example, are much more likely to remember chunks of information that are related in some fashion as opposed to random chunks of information. However, younger children, even when they are helped to form chunks of information, have problems memorizing such lists. Up to about grade three, children seem not to do any better on easily categorized items than they do on unrelated items.

Once information is in short-term memory, learners have considerable flexibility in what they will do with it. The information can be used as a cue to retrieve other information from long-term memory; it can be elaborated; it can be used to form images; it is used in thinking; it can be structured to be placed in long-term memory; or it can be discarded (Di Vesta, 1987). Of course, if information is discarded or forgotten while in short-term memory, there will be no possibility that the learner will be able to retrieve the information at a later date.

Even when retained, the manner in which it is organized will affect how the information is retained in long-term memory—as an isolated bit of information or as part of some logical, organized structure.

It is not always a disaster if information is discarded from short-term memory. In fact, this ability sometimes has a very useful function: it allows a person to use a piece of information without having to remember it permanently. What if we remembered every phone number that we ever dialed—or the name of every person that we have met? If we stored every piece of information we encountered in long-term memory, it would be very difficult, if not impossible, to retrieve a needed bit of information from the massive body of stored knowledge. Having a system that provides temporary storage of information is very useful to everyday human functioning.

In summary, short-term memory holds in the "consciousness" a small number of pieces of information. More information can be held if the pieces of data are chunked or related in some fashion. The information will be held for an extremely brief period of time and, without continued rehearsal, information will be lost in about 20 seconds. Short-term memory is extremely useful as it holds information in mind so that a person can manipulate, organize, or otherwise use the information in ongoing cognitive functioning.

## Long-term memory

Processed information is of little use unless it can be retrieved. Information is retained only briefly in short-term memory; information needed for future reference must be stored in long-term memory. People tend to think of long-term memory as a continuous, sequenced record of experiences that begins with the earliest memories and proceeds through to the present. In some senses, this may be true. On the basis of neurological, experimental, and clinical evidence, most cognitive psychologists believe that the storage capacity of long-term memory is limitless and that long-term memory contains a permanent record of everything an individual has learned.

Neurological evidence comes from memory traces found in people operated on for epileptic seizures. Perhaps some of the most interesting research in this area was conducted by Wilder Penfield (1969), the Canadian neurosurgeon. When conducting brain surgery on a conscious patient, Penfield used a weak electric current to stimulate various parts of the cerebral cortex. As each area was stimulated, the patient experienced extremely vivid memories of long-past events. So vivid, in fact, were the memories that the patient felt as though the experiences were being relived even though these memories represented experiences that the patient had long thought forgotten. As soon as the stimulation ceased, so did the memory, which led Penfield to argue that memories are organically intact for life.

Lists of words and the way they are remembered offers experimental evidence. In addition, clincial psychologists have reported cases of individuals who have been helped in recalling seemingly forgotten events through hypnosis and other techniques (Erdelyi and Goldberg, 1979).

**Episodic memory:**
the memory for personal experiences stored in the form of images that are organized on the basis of when and where events happened.

**Semantic memory:**
memory for facts, concepts, principles, rules and the knowledge of how to use them, problem-solving skills, and generalized information mentally organized into networks of connected ideas or relationships called schemata.

**Procedural memory:**
the ability to recall how to do something, especially a motor task.

Long-term memory, it seems, permanently stores all of the information that a person possesses. While information in short-term memory is active, or part of some ongoing, conscious cognitive process, information in long-term memory is in storage, waiting to be activated for use. Thus, memories of things that have just happened are direct and immediate; as they have not left the consciousness, they can be easily recalled. More time and effort is involved in recalling information from long-term memory. This can be illustrated in the following questions:

- What were the first few words of this sentence?

- What did you have for dinner last Sunday?

In the first question, the information was immediately accessible from short-term memory and thus relatively easy to recall. However, it probably took more time to retrieve the information required to answer the second question from long-term memory (Lindsay and Norman, 1972).

It is easy for information to enter short-term memory; more time and effort is required to encode and store it in long-term memory. Information in long-term memory must be organized and the nature of this organization is a crucial area in the study of memory. There are various interpretations about how information is represented and stored in the long-term memory that should be seen as complementary rather than conflicting.

### Encoding in memory

The organization of memory has been described in various ways which, are not mutually exclusive. Some theorists propose that information in long-term memory is coded into visual images or verbal representations, or both (Pavio, 1971). For example, try to recall your first elementary school and perhaps the faces of your first grade teacher and some of your classmates. Even though you may not have thought of these things for years, you may still be able to pull up visual images. Verbal representations also play an important role in long-term memory. In fact, some investigators suggest that language is so important to memory that a person is unable to recall memories of events that occurred before the acquisition of language.

Other cognitive theorists examine what seem to be three types of long-term memory—episodic, semantic, and procedural—which store and organize information in different ways. **Episodic memory** relates to personal experiences. It is stored in the form of images that are organized on the basis of when and where events happened. However, episodic memories are often difficult to retrieve because most episodes in our lives are repeated so often that later memories become mixed in with the earlier ones.

**Semantic memory** refers to facts and generalized information and is organized in the form of a network of ideas. It includes concepts, principles, rules and the knowledge of how to use them, and problem-solving skills. Semantic memory is mentally organized into networks of connected ideas or relationships called schemata.

Slavin (1988) describes the third type, procedural memory, as a complex of stimulus-response pairings. **Procedural memory** is the ability to recall how to do something, especially a motor task. Procedural memory may be described as

**Propositional network:**
an interconnected set of bits of information that consists of the smallest bits of information that can be judged true or false.

**Schemata:**
(information processing theory) mental data structures that allow for swift and economical processing of incoming stimuli.

"knowing how" rather than "knowing what" (Tulving, 1972). It includes motor and automatic activities such as typing a letter or driving a car.

Theorists have also suggested that humans use propositional networks (Anderson, 1985) as a means to store information in long-term memory. A **propositional network** is an interconnected set of bits of information and consists of the smallest bits of information that can be judged true or false. But even if propositional networks can adequately explain the representation of small units of meaning, they cannot explain the organization of larger sets of information that are needed to understand certain concepts (Anderson, 1985).

If memory is the storage of information then, in the view of many cognitive psychologists, cognitive structures form an essential component of memory as they interpret new information in light of what is already known and reinterpret what is already known in light of new information. Piaget used the term **"schemata"** to describe cognitive structures. In a similar fashion, information processing theorists see schemata as networks of mental structures that guide behaviour and allow us to understand and learn new information. Specifically, information processing theorists see schemata as larger abstract data structures that allow the learner to represent or organize vast amounts of information in memory (Rumelhart and Ortony, 1977).

A schema is like an outline with different concepts or ideas organized under larger categories. Various aspects of schemata may be related by series of propositions or relationships (Slavin, 1988). In the instructional process, schemata are seen as critical because they will be the primary determinant of what a person will learn from a verbal or written message. New information that fits into well-developed schemata will be retained more readily than information that does not fit into any schemata.

For example, as Anderson, Spiro, and Anderson (1978) point out, an adult who is reading a text passage about an unfamiliar nation is already equipped

Episdodic memories are often difficult to retrieve because most episodes in our lives are repeated so often that later memories become mixed with the earlier ones.

**Forgetting:**
inability to retrieve information from long-term memory.

with a well-developed "nation" schema which can be related to other sub-schemata containing knowledge about political systems, economics, geography, and climate. In contrast, younger children may not possess a nation schema that will allow them to assimilate the information presented in the text. Indeed, if the children do not possess a relevant schema, they will not be able to make any sense of the material or, if they possess a less elaborate schema, they will be able to make some sense of the text, but will not construct a mental representation of comparable breadth and depth as that of an adult. Teachers, therefore, must remember that information that can be related to an existing schema will be retained far better than isolated bits of information.

The relationship of long-term memory to intelligence is another important aspect. Many studies, for example, indicate that students who are mentally retarded do not encode information into short-term memory as well as do other students. However, once students with mental handicaps have information in long-term memory, they remember as well as any one else (see Winzer, 1990a). In a series of studies, first reported in 1959 by Klausmeier, Feldhausen, and Check, children with high, average, and low IQs were shown to retain about the same proportion of what they had learned (Klausmeir, Feldhausen, and Check, 1959). That is, although in absolute terms the high IQ children learned and retained the most, the percentage of what was retained over time was the same for all IQ groups. Thus, the proportion of information retained seems to be constant across a wide range of IQs.

### Forgetting

No discussion of memory and its various aspects would be complete without reference to its opposite, constant, and often frustrating companion—forgetting. According to information processing theorists, **forgetting** is defined as an inability to retrieve information from long-term memory.

Many people hold the view that we remember material used frequently and forget that which is not used. This explanation, termed the disuse theory is, at best, vulnerable. Some psychologists hold that we intentionally forget when we do not want to remember; we use intentional or motivated forgetting. The most pervasive explanation of forgetting, however, is that of interference. It is believed that new information places a roadblock to the retrieval of old information while old information can make us forget new material.

While failure to retrieve information will explain most forgetting, some information may actually be lost from storage (Loftus and Loftus, 1980). For example, think of what happens when patients with severe depression are given electro-convulsive shock therapy to relieve their symptoms. The shock—in which a mild electric current is applied to the brain, producing a seizure and brief period of unconsciousness—produces memory loss for events occurring months prior to the shock, but not for earlier events (Squire and Fox, 1980). Such memory losses are probably not due to retrieval problems. If that were the case, it would be expected that all memories would be affected, rather than only recent ones. It is likely that the shock disrupts the storage processes that consolidate memories over a few months or longer, and if consolidation does not take place, the memories are lost (Atkinson et al., 1990).

**Decay:**
the passive loss of memory trace due to inactivity or lack of rehearsal.

**Interference:**
situation in which recall of new information interferes with remembering old things or both old and new information become mixed up together in some fashion.

**Retroactive interference:**
occurs when new information interferes with the recall of previously learned information.

Such memory losses are clearly the exception and most forgetting can be explained by retrieval problems. While any amount of information can be stored in long-term memory, it is not always easily retrieved. It is unlikely that information is truly lost; rather, it is located somewhere in long-term memory, unamenable to access. It is like the long-lost file on a computer disk—while you know the file is there, you are unable to call it up.

## Decay

Decay occurs when information becomes weaker over time until it disappears. **Decay** may be defined as the passive loss of memory trace due to inactivity or lack or rehearsal (Sprinthall and Sprinthall, 1987). Decay is an important influence in forgetting, especially at the input stage of the processing sequence.

Decay is particularly important in relation to the sensory register and short-term memory. Information in the sensory register will decay or disappear in a matter of seconds while information in short term memory, if not rehearsed, will decay in less than a minute. In both cases, once information is lost, it is lost forever; there is no chance of retrieving the information. Psychologists are less sure of the role of decay in long-term memory although most believe that information brought into long-term memory is stored permanently. Others believe that decay is a factor in long-term memory, but that it takes place at a much slower rate (a matter of years) as contrasted with the quick decay seen in short-term memory.

### Interference

**Interference** refers to the situation in which the recall of new information will interfere with remembering old things or both old and new information become mixed up together in some fashion. Thus, while it seems that long-term memory may never actually lose information, interference can inhibit a person's ability to recall information.

Two different types of interference have been identified. **Retroactive interference** occurs when new information interferes with old material. Previously learned information is lost because it is mixed up with new and somewhat familiar information. If a teacher, for example, presents children with the letter "b" and then immediately presents "d," young children are likely to get the two letters mixed. Or think of the harried university student preparing for two examinations in foreign languages: French and Spanish. After studying French vocabulary for a few hours, the student then turns to the study of Spanish. During the French examination the next day, he may find that the French and Spanish vocabularies are confused. In other words, the newer information, Spanish vocabulary words, has worked backwards and prevented the recall of the older information, the French vocabulary. Of course, the learning of the material does not have to be so closely related in time. For example, take the person who traveled in France and learned some French language, then moved on to Spain, picking up some Spanish words on the way. On return to France (days or months later), the person may confuse French and Spanish words. Again, we can see that the new information has interfered with the old. A conceptualization of retroactive interference is shown in Table 9-2.

**Proactive interference:** occurs when old information interferes with recall of newly acquired information.

Table 9-2 Retroactive and proactive interference

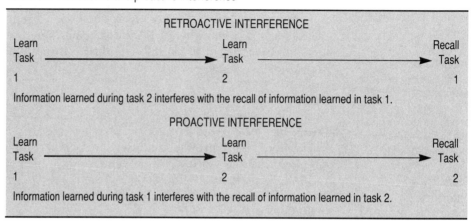

Slavin (1988) observes that, of all the reasons for forgetting, retroactive inhibition is probably the best. However, there is also **proactive interference** which occurs when old information interferes with learning later information. Again, return to our example of foreign language learning. The student who has studied French for a time may find a new course in Spanish very difficult to master: in this case, the old information is interfering with the new. Table 9-2 also shows proactive interference.

It should be pointed out that there are analogous learning strategies to retroactive and proactive interference. Looking again at the student learning French and Spanish, we can say that if learning a first language helped in learning the second, this would be an instance of proactive facilitation. If learning the second language helped with the first, this would be retroactive facilitation (Slavin, 1988).

Interference does not necessarily imply that information stored in long-term memory is lost—the problem is in the recall of information, not in the storage. So how can the teacher reduce the probability of interference? As interference is related to the degree of similarity between instructional tasks (see Dempter, 1985a, b), it is important not to present similar concepts or material too closely in time. To return to our example above, it was probably not a good idea for the student to take courses in two foreign languages in the same semester as it was likely that the material would become confused. Similarly, if the teacher is presenting material that is similar, such as the sound-symbol association or the letter formation of "b" and "d," one concept should be presented first and teaching continue until the material is well mastered. Only then should a similar concept be introduced.

Research has also shown that varying instructional methods and materials can also reduce retroactive interference. One study (Andre, 1973) had students study material about two African tribes. Those who were given the material organized and presented in the same fashion were more likely to get the two descriptions confused than were students who were given the information organized differently and presented on different colours of paper. Similarly, when students were asked to memorize two lists of information, those who used the

**Retrieval cue:**
a prompt that helps the learner recall information.

same memory strategy for both were more likely to confuse or forget the information than were those who used a different strategy for each list (Andre, Anderson, and Watts, 1976).

Teachers should also be aware of primary and recency effects. The tendency to learn the first things presented is the primacy effect; to learn the last, the recency effect. It seems that much more mental rehearsal is placed on the earlier items than the later items (Rundus and Atkinson, 1970) while recency effects are attributable to the fact that little or no information interposes between the final and last items (Greene, 1986).

## Enhancing retrieval

The most efficient way to intentionally store material in long-term memory is to consciously process the information at deeper levels. Such strategies may involve developing linkages between new and old material, rehearsal, mnemonic devices, examining the implications or applications of new material, answering questions about material, or previewing or reviewing the material. A number of strategies can be used to minimize retrieval failures and help students remember. The strategies outlined below can be used in classrooms, either singly or in combination.

### Retrieval cues

Sometimes the correct prompt or **retrieval cue** can help recall information. If you were asked, "Was Susan in class today?" the question itself gives a retrieval cue. In contrast, a question such as "Who was in class today?" requires you to produce a memorized list that has minimal retrieval cues (Atkinson et al., 1990). Retrieval cues help us recall information which explains why recognition tasks are much easier than recall tasks. This can be seen in the difference between recall and recognition tasks on school examinations. Reference to retrieval cues helps us see why multiple choice or true-false examination questions are easier than those questions that require unaided recall. Take, for example, the following items:

**1.** Who followed Lester Pearson as Prime Minister?

**2.** Pierre Trudeau was Prime Minister immediately after Lester Pearson. True or False?

Because question 2 provides more information, it should be easier to answer. To return to the analogy of the diskette, students will be able to search for the "files" on both Pierre Trudeau and Lester Pearson and, while they may not find the answer in one file, it may be available in the other. In the first question, only the cue "Lester Pearson" guides memory search; if enough information cannot be gleaned from that cue, there is nowhere else to search.

Providing retrieval cues or prompting is a useful strategy that can be used to help students retrieve information as it gives them cues about where the information is stored in long-term memory. Keep in mind, however, that the speed at which information can be recalled will vary with the ability levels of the students. Students with higher ability will retain more information and recall it faster than will students of lower ability.

## Hierarchical structures

In addition, the manner in which information is encoded in the first place will influence retrieval. First, the organization is critical: when information is organized in some logical fashion, it will be much easier to retrieve. This is particularly important when students are learning very complex information.

One method that has been used by students of all ages is to place information into hierarchical structures, in which specific facts or items are grouped under more general topics (Van Patten, Chao, and Reigeluth, 1986). For example, look at the top of Table 9-3 to the list of words presented in random order. Now compare that list with the hierarchical structure seen in the bottom of the table. Which would be easier to memorize? In a study conducted by Bower and his colleagues (1969), one group of research subjects were taught 112 words relating to minerals in random order. Another group were taught the words presented in a hierarchy as seen in Table 9-3. Not surprisingly, the researchers found that the subjects presented material in an organized fashion remembered far more than those subjects who were given the lists in random order.

**Table 9-3**  Hierarchical structures

RANDOM LIST OF ITEMS

| | | |
|---|---|---|
| platinum | silver | gold |
| aluminum | copper | lead |
| bronze | steel | brass |
| sapphire | emerald | ruby |
| limestone | granite | slate |

HIERARCHICAL ORGANIZATION OF ITEMS

Minerals

Metals — Stones

| Rare | Common | Alloys | Precious | Masonry |
|---|---|---|---|---|
| platinum | aluminum | bronze | sapphire | limestone |
| silver | copper | steel | emerald | granite |
| gold | lead | brass | ruby | slate |

**SOURCE:** Adapted from Bower, Clark, Winzenz, and Lensgold (1969).

Such research has direct classroom implications. It is clear that material should be presented in an organized form with more general concepts related to the more specific facts. By understanding the organization of material, student recall will be greatly facilitated and this may make the search for information easier. Hierarchical structures allow the learner to divide a large search into a sequence of smaller ones (Atkinson et al., 1990). For example, by beginning at the top of the hierarchy, learners can follow the pattern of the hierarchy to the next chunk or cluster, and so on. This can be contrasted with the groups that learn the large group of randomly ordered words; they have to search the entire set to find a specific bit of information.

For students to understand hierarchical structures, they must have appropriate concept development. Humans tend to think in concepts, not scattered bits of information and, in this sense, concepts reduce the complexities of life. A concept represents a set in one's mind; a category under which specific elements may be grouped. Generally, children learn concepts in two ways—by observation of the environment or by definition.

Every object, person, or event has certain attributes or characteristics. Attributes such as roundness, rollability, colourful, and plaything maybe ascribed to a ball, while an apple may be seen as having such characteristics as roundness and edibility. Concepts are formed on the basis of relevant attributes which are shared by two or more objects, persons, events, or ideas. Relevant attributes are referred to as defining attributes because they determine the definition of a category. In conjunctive concepts, all relevant attributes must be present and may not vary; with disjunctive concepts, one attribute or another will serve. Once a child has developed some concepts, then the relationships between concepts establish principles. The child may first learn, for example, the attributes that go to make up the category of "birds." Once the concept is attained, the child can move to the principle that "winged animals fly."

Ausubel (1960; Ausubel, Novak, and Hanesian, 1978) has proposed that individuals learn concepts that are generalized ideas or mental images of a class of objects. Those general concepts are then used as anchors onto which new details

Children learn concepts in two ways: by observation of the environment or by definition.

**Transfer:**
the processes that enable individuals to make previously learned responses to news

**Context cues:**
prompts that help someone retrieve information based on the context in which the information was learned.

**Context:**
the physical environment or the dominant emotional state in which information has been learned.

**State dependent learning:**
enhances recall if the dominant emotional state during retrieval matches that during encoding.

can be attached. Hence, as children develop the ability to classify information, they have a correspondingly greater ability to recall information.

Classification involves grouping items into logically related categories. For example, imagine that you had to recall the following lists of items:

pen   apple   pencil   cup   pancake   spoon   crayon   fork   cookie   plate   bread

Rather than trying to remember each of the 11 items on its own, it would be much easier to remember the items if you classified them into groups: writing instruments (pen, pencil, crayon); food (apple, pancake, cookie, bread) and eating utensils (cup, spoon, fork, plate). In a study of memorization strategies, researchers gave children from first to sixth grade sets of pictures related to four categories (animal, furniture, clothing, and transportation). The children were not told that the pictures belonged to any class, but were given three minutes to look at the randomly placed pictures and were able to arrange them in any way that would help them remember the items. Children in first to third grades (with the exception of a few third graders) did not classify the items, but older children showed a tendency to arrange pictures by classification. The better the children were in arranging the pictures in classifications, the more successful they were in recalling the items (Neimark, Slotnik, and Ulrich, 1971).

## Context cues

The process that enables individuals to make previously learned responses to new situations is called **transfer**. Transfer often, although not always, provides the ability to perform sensibly and adequately in a new task as a result of having performed other tasks previously. **Context cues** are related to this process.

It has been found that replicating the **context** in which information has been learned can assist in the retention of the information (Estes, 1972). For example, students who learned material in one type of room recalled the information better if the test was taken in a similar room rather than in a different type of room. Of course, it is not always possible to return to the original context in an attempt to enhance recall; however, it is possible to mentally recreate the context. In a study by Williams and Hollan (1978), subjects were asked to mentally recreate their high school milieu (classes, clubs, activities, and so on). These subjects were able to recall names of high school classmates that they had thought were long-forgotten.

The physical environment is not the only important context affecting recall. Recall will also be enhanced if the dominant emotional state during retrieval matches that experienced during encoding. Referred to as **state dependent learning**, evidence in this area suggests that memory is dependent, to some degree, on the internal state during learning. If you were happy, sad, angry, or joyous during the encoding of data, you will retrieve that data better when you are in a similar emotional state (Bower, 1981). Similarly, while research in this area is still controversial, there is some evidence that replicating the internal state that was present during encoding, such as being under the influence of drugs or alcohol, will facilitate later recall (Eich et al., 1975).

The emotions felt by the learner can either inhibit or enhance the ability to remember information. It is believed that anxiety interferes with recall because it is often accompanied by extraneous thoughts, which will interfere with the retrieval of relevant knowledge. In other words, if the anxious student is thinking

**Flashbulb memory:**
extremely vivid memory produced when the individual is in a highly charged emotional state.

**Elaborative rehearsal:**
relating new information to previously stored information to aid memorization.

about the career consequences of failure or parental reactions to bad marks, it will not be possible to fully concentrate on retrieval (Holmes, 1974).

Anxiety-inducing situations are more likely to occur when a learner is unsure about the material that is to be recalled. The better the learner knows the material, the less anxious he or she is likely to be. Of course, an exception to this are people who have well-developed phobias; such individuals are likely to respond with anxiety no matter how well the material is learned. Both nervous scholars and phobic individuals can often be helped to recall information better if they are given training in deep muscle relaxation. It is not possible to feel anxious and relaxed at the same time and thus it may be easier to recall information better.

We also may recall emotionally charged events better than more neutral happenings. It may be that we think more about positive or negative emotional events, thus rehearsing and organizing them better (Atkinson et al., 1990). As these factors are critical to enhanced retrieval, it is not surprising that research shows that we have improved memory for emotional as opposed to unemotional events (Neisser, 1982).

Most of us have some extremely vivid memories that were indelibly impressed upon our memory because we were in a highly charged emotional state at the time (Brown and Kulik, 1977). This has been referred to as a **flashbulb memory** and it has been proposed that a special memory mechanism is triggered, making a permanent record of everything being experienced at the moment. There appears to be a physiological basis for the flashbulb memory; strong emotional reactions apparently release a group of hormones that appear to influence this phenomenon (McGaugh, 1983). Thus, you may have extremely detailed memories about what you were doing, wearing, and saying at the time you learned of the death of a close friend or relative. Sometimes, an entire culture seems to share a flashbulb memory; for example, along with Americans, most Canadians of the appropriate age can remember precisely what they were doing when John F. Kennedy was assassinated. Memories seem to be most vivid and enduring when they involve death, accidents, and sex (Rubin and Kozin, 1984). However, some researchers dispute the ideas of a special memory mechanism, arguing that flashbulb memories can also become less retrievable over time. As with memory for other emotionally-charged events, such memories may remain vivid because we repeatedly talk, read, or hear about such events, thus facilitating organization and rehearsal (McCloskey, Wibble, and Cohen, 1988).

### Rehearsal
Rehearsal is one of the most common methods that we use to facilitate the processing of information. There are two types of rehearsal; maintenance rehearsal allows us to hold information for immediate use; for example, when we repeat a phone number. The second type of rehearsal is **elaborative rehearsal** in which the learner relates new information to previously stored information to aid memorization. By making associations with existing knowledge, the number of retrieval cues is increased, making it easier for the learner to recall the information at a later date.

### Advance organizers
Organization during encoding greatly facilitates recall and teachers should consider this factor during instruction. One method that has been shown to be

**Advance organizers:**
techniques that provide an outline for the facts that are to follow and show the relationship among concepts to be learned.

**Rote learning:**
mastery of material that is not inherently meaningful.

effective in classrooms is the use of **advance organizers**, a technique intended to help students organize information, thus facilitating learning and recall (Ausubel, 1978).

Essentially, advance organizers provide the context in which to anchor new material to make it meaningful. Advance organizers act as a sort of outline for the facts that are to follow and show the relationship among concepts to be learned. Used to preface instruction, oral or written advance organizers provide an introductory summary of the material that is to follow. By sketching the structure of the instruction that is to follow, advance organizers function as a framework or skeleton, on which students will hang the details that are provided. This allows students to prepare themselves by calling up related information or schemata that will help them understand the new information.

Ausubel and Youssef (1963) gave two groups of college students a passage on Buddhism to study. While one group did not receive any introductory material, the other was given an advance organizer which compared Buddhism to Christianity. The latter group were able to recall much more of the material than did the group without the advance organizer. The researchers proposed that the difference lay in the fact that those who experienced the advance organizer were able to use their current knowledge about Christianity as a framework in which to incorporate the new and unfamiliar information.

Research has shown that beginning a learning session with an advance organizer facilitates the learning and recall of information (Luiten, Ames, and Ackerson, 1980). However, while advance organizers work well with material that has a clear structure, they are less successful when the information is not readily or clearly organized or when it consists of a large number of separate topics (Ausubel, 1978; Barnes and Clawson, 1975).

### Meaningfulness

Rote learning refers to the memorization of facts or associations, such as multiplication tables, words in a foreign language, or the elements in chemistry. Rote learning is often associated with drill and practices and has as its aim automization. The task, even a high level one, can be performed without much attention.

In contrast to rote learning, meaningful learning relates to information or concepts learners already have. Good teachers know that one of the best methods for facilitating recall is to make curriculum material meaningful to the students. New information should be presented in such a way that it can be attached to existing anchors. This means linking new learning to information already in long-term memory: teaching poetry by using current pop tunes, or discussing the impact of the GST by relating it to the students' shopping. Considering the students' existing schemata, new concepts, facts, or terms should be clarified using familiar words and ideas or by giving examples and analogies.

While meaningfulness facilitates information processing, not all material can be made meaningful to students, particularly in the early stages of learning. Mathematics students must master their multiplication tables, immersion students large amounts of vocabulary, and psychology students large numbers of definitions. This is referred to as **rote learning**, which is used with material that is not meaningful.

**Serial position effect:**
tendency that when recalling a long list of items, learners are more likely to recall items at the end and beginning of the list and to forget the middle items.

**Distributed practice:**
working for short periods distributed over time.

**Mass practice:**
practice of material for an extended period of time.

**Mnemonic devices:**
memory tactics that help a learner transfer or organize information to enhance its retrievability.

It has been found that when learners attempt to recall a long list of items, they will be more successful in recalling items at the end and beginning of the list, and more likely to forget the middle items. If students have to recall a long list of material, memorization will be facilitated if they break the list down into parts. This will help them avoid the **serial position effect** or the initial and recency effects mentioned earlier.

Further, **distributed practice** is better than long period of study; in other words, the student who practises a long passage of music will learn it better if he or she practises every night for a short period of time, rather than practising for a long time on the night before a performance. This latter strategy, studying for a long period of time, is referred to as **mass practice** (Underwood, 1961).

Further, material must be overlearned. This was demonstrated in a study in which subjects were asked to learn a list of words until they could recite it with no errors. Some of the subjects were then asked to overlearn the material by continuing to study the list for the same amount of time taken to originally memorize it. Four days later, when all of the subjects were tested, the students who had overlearned the material recalled six times as many words as did the other subjects. Twenty-eight days later, the subjects who had not overlearned the material had forgotten all the words while the overlearning group could still recall some of the words.

Teachers should pay attention to overlearning when teaching facts that must be accurately recalled for long periods of time but which have relatively little meaning. Examples of items that have to be overlearned in the classroom might include things such as multiplication tables, spelling words, capital cities, and so on.

### Mnemonic devices

Many of us have been amazed by memory experts who seemingly effortlessly learn the names of an entire audience in a short period of time, memorize lengthy lists of objects, or recite pages from a phone book. Most of these experts employ complex mnemonic devices to assist them in these amazing and seemingly impossible feats of memory. A term drawn from Mnemosyne, the Greek goddess of memory, **mnemonic devices** are memory directed tactics that help a learner transfer or organize information to enhance its retrievability (Biehler and Snowman, 1990). Mnemonic devices, of which there are many variations, can be used in the classroom to help students transform or organize information in a manner that makes it easier to acquire and to retrieve.

One type is the rhyme mnemonic, which includes old saws such as "i before e except after c;" and "Thirty days has September, April, June, and November...." Another type of mnemonic is the *acronym* or first-letter mnemonic. Examples of acronyms that might be used in schools are "HOMES," which contains the first letters of the lakes in the Great Lakes system (Huron, Ontario, Michigan, Erie, and Superior); or "ROY G BIV," which contains the first letters, in order, of the colours of the rainbow (red, orange, yellow, green blue, indigo, and violet). When learners recall the acronym, each letter cues or helps them recall the word that is associated with it. Certainly, this is a widely used strategy, particularly useful when students have to recall short lists of items in serial order. As long as the acronym is not too complicated, it has been shown that these devices definitely aid recall (Nelson and Archer, 1972).

If it is not possible to form an acronym, another strategy which can be used is the *acrostic*, or sentence mnemonic. The acrostic requires the learner to form a sentence or phrase out of the first letters of each word or item in a list. Music students are likely to remember this one: "Every Good Boy Does Fine," in which the first letter of each word stands for the name of a line of the G clef. Similarly, by memorizing the sentence: "Men Very Easily Make Jugs Serve Useful New Purposes," students can recall the nine planets in order from the sun (Mercury, Venus, Earth, Mars, Jupiter, Saturn, Uranus, Neptune, and Pluto).

The *pegword* is a method that is commonly used to remember lists of items. It first requires that the learner memorize a series of rhyming "pegs":

| | |
|---|---|
| one-bun | six-sticks |
| two-shoe | seven-heaven |
| three-tree | eight-gate |
| four-door | nine-line |
| five-hive | ten-hen |

Once these have been mastered, the learner links up items to be remembered with a peg. For example, consider the student who has many different tasks to complete during a particular day. By linking up each item on the "To Do" list with a memory peg, it is possible to discard the list and still get everything done. For example, if the first thing to be done is to meet a friend at the library, the friend could be visualized eating a huge bun in a library desk. The second task, picking up a book from the library, could be remembered if the book is visualized as sitting in a giant shoe. Next, attend psychology class: visualize the professor up a tree. This process of linking items to be recalled with the memory pegs continues until all items are accounted for. Because the pegword strategy involves visual imagery, it works best when remembering lists of concrete items, and can work well with anything that can be arranged in a list. Another advantage of the pegword method is that the learner can access the list at any point, ("What was number five? Oh, yes, the librarian caught in a bee hive—I have to return my books") and work backwards and forwards from there.

The *loci method* is quite similar to the pegword, and involves using loci (which means places) as the memory pegs. For example, the person might use familiar places which are naturally related, numbered, and easily remembered, such as rooms in their house, stores on a well-known street, or campus buildings. Once a series of loci have been established, each item on the list to be remembered (events, ideas, objects) are mentally "placed" in each location as the learner "walks" from one place to another. It facilitates recall if there is some distinctive feature in each location by which the item can be placed; for example, a special chair or a distinctive architectural feature. To recall the list, the learner has only to mentally retrace his or her steps through the locations, retrieving each bit of information from its designated spot.

Ross and Lawrence (1968) used the loci method to have students recall lists of 40 nouns, placing each in a familiar place on their college campus. Each noun was studied once for 13 seconds. When asked to immediately recall the nouns, the average score was 30 out of 40 correct nouns, in serial order. The next day, the subjects were able to recall an average of 34 of the 40 nouns studied. Certainly, this was an amazing improvement over the results that might be expected from more traditional study methods if they were used for a comparably brief period of time.

The *keyword* method was developed as a means to facilitate foreign language learning (Atkinson, 1975; Atkinson and Raugh, 1975) but has been used in a variety of other areas. To illustrate this approach, consider the Spanish student who is learning the word "pato" (Atkinson, 1975). As this word is roughly pronounced as "pot-o," the English word "pot" becomes the keyword. Next, the learner forms a visual image that links the keyword with the English translation of the foreign word, which in this case is "duck." Thus the learner visualizes a duck with a pot on its head or a duck swimming in a pot of water. When recalling the visual image, the learner is given a cue both to the pronunciation and meaning of the word. Alternatively, the learner could make up a sentence that facilitates remembering the connection between the keyword and the translation as in, "The duck fell into the pot." The keyword method has been repeatedly demonstrated as successful in teaching foreign languages (e.g., Atkinson and Raugh, 1975; Pressley, Levin, and Delaney, 1982). It has also been used to recall names of capital cities and English vocabulary words (Miller, Levin, and

Physical activity combined with learning enhances the mastery and recall of information.

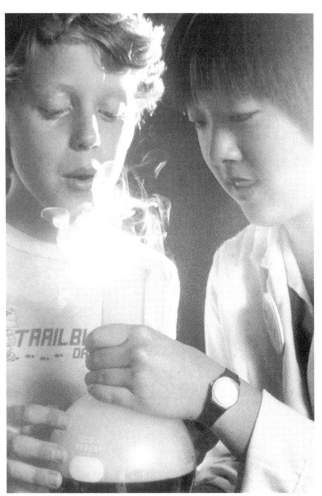

383

Pressley, 1980), as well as with children with learning problems (Peters and Levin, 1986).

With proper use, mnemonic devices can be extremely valuable in aiding student recall of important information and have been successfully used with students from preschool to college ages (McCormick and Levin, 1987). However, they must be taught carefully and the students must master the mnemonic accurately. Mnemonic devices that require visual imagery are more successful with students at the later elementary grades and above as younger students are often unable to form their own images (Rohwer, 1972). Levin (1976) found that for children below the age of seven, instructions to use imagery generally are not helpful. If teachers choose to use such strategies with younger students, it will be necessary to help the pupils find appropriate images or keywords (Pressley, Levin, and Delaney, 1982).

But once the mnemonics are in place, they serve as a well-organized filing system, allowing students to more easily recall information. Sometimes the results are astounding; for example, studies which have examined a Japanese method, Yodai mnemonics, have shown that students learn to manipulate fractions in a matter of hours. Contrast this with our traditional methods of teaching fractions which may require instruction over a period of two or three years. However, like any form of rote memory task, it is important for teachers to remember that being able to recite information does not necessarily imply that the student understand the concepts represented.

### Activity
Physical or verbal activity combined with learning seems to enhance the mastery and recall of materials. Recitation of material (saying it out loud) seems to enhance learning. Memorization tends to be better if the students engage in verbal or physical activity: for example, talk about material or act out sequences.

## METACOGNITION

As students develop, they learn skills such as assessing themselves to see if they are understanding, deciding how much time they will need to study material, organizing their materials and time, and finding effective and appropriate ways to learn. Pupils seem to spontaneously develop the use of various strategies that aid their retrieval of information stored in long-term memory. This is not only a reflection of better organized and complex cognitive structures, but also of children's ability to "think" about their own thinking. In other words, children are able to think about various retrieval strategies and use the technique that is most likely to help them retrieve the desired information.

Individuals become more aware of their own cognitive processes (or the strategies to be used to learn material) and how to control or regulate cognitive behaviour. In other words, learners know what to do as well as how to do it. This ability to monitor and direct one's own thinking processes is referred to as metacognition.

The notion of metacognition was proposed by John Flavell (1976), a developmental psychologist attempting to explain why children of different ages dealt

**Metacognition:**
knowledge concerning one's own cognitive processes, including the active monitoring and consequent regulation and orchestration of these processes.

with learning tasks in different ways. To Flavell (1976), metacognition refers to one's knowledge concerning one's own cognitive processes; it includes the active monitoring and consequent regulation and orchestration of these processes. Thus, metacognitive awareness involves becoming acquainted with oneself as a thinker. It plays an important role in attention, problem-solving, self-control, self-instruction, and behaviour modification. Palincsar (1986) explains the process to her students with a football metaphor. Every good team has a number of strategies and can select the one that best fits the play. The coach and players continually evaluate how effectively the strategies are working and select new ones as necessary.

Developmental trends can be seen in the study of metacognition. In general, children begin to develop metacognitive abilities about the age of five to seven and these abilities improve steadily with age. As with any other developmental skills, there is great variability within any age group; often, younger children are able to use metacognitive skills, although they must be reminded to do so (Brown, Campione, and Day, 1981).

The abilities to control and optimize conscious cognitive processes develop over time. Recent research indicates that metacognitive skills are important factors that affect pupil performance. Studies which have directly taught metacognitive strategies have produced encouraging results (e.g., Bereiter and Scardamalia, 1985).

As knowledge concerning metacognition grows, more attention has been paid to the instruction of cognitive strategies. Students must not only be given knowledge; they must also be taught how to use cognitive learning strategies. Unfortunately, providing pupils with appropriate learning strategies is not always done. In one study of elementary teachers, it was found that they gave students hints about how to use various memory and learning strategies only about three percent of the time (Moely et al., 1986).

Simply telling students about effective learning strategies is not enough. In addition to being taught how to use metacognitive strategies, students must be taught when strategies should be appropriately used and how to tell whether the strategy is working (Levin, 1986; Pressley, 1986). Students need training in using such things as context clues, subvocalization, and prediction, and they need feedback on their use of learning strategies.

Cognitive strategy training or metacognitive training is used to help students to organize their thought patterns, social behaviours, and learning behaviours through self-assessment, self-verbalization, self-instruction, self-guidance, self-monitoring, self-recording, and self-reinforcement. Various studies have shown that training can have dramatic effects on school performance when students generalize the strategies to natural environments (e.g., Ellis, 1983).

Metacognitive training teaches students first to consider the variables involved in solving a problem; second, to regulate the processes that they use to solve it; and third, to apply specific cognitive skills to the task effectively (Ellis, 1986). One important learning strategy is self-instruction. One of the leaders in the field of metacognition, Meichenbaum of the University of Waterloo (1981), suggests that teachers implementing self-instruction programs should first listen for the strategies that a student is presently using to determine whether or not they are appropriate and then make a careful analysis of the behaviours to be

**Metamemory:**
an aspect of metacognition referring to knowledge about one's own memory.

**Metacomprehension:**
an aspect of metacognition referring to the strategies that a reader uses in monitoring and evaluating the comprehension of written text while reading that text.

changed. Prior to training, the teacher can ensure that the student possesses the necessary skills to use self-instruction (such as memory and sequencing), and should collaborate with the student to devise a routine. Once training begins, the training task should reflect the target behaviour as closely as possible.

To initiate the procedures, an adult first performs the specified task while verbalizing aloud; addressing questions about the task, guiding herself through the several steps, and evaluating her own performance. The student then performs the task while the adult instructs him aloud. He then performs the task, first while verbalizing aloud; second, while self-instructing in a whisper; and, finally, while using subvocalizations. Throughout, the teacher should give the student feedback about the utility of his particular self-instructions for performance. To increase the efficacy of the procedures, teachers can point out situations in which self-instruction will be useful, and use a variety of trainers, settings, and tasks to encourage the student to use self-instruction successfully outside the training session. Students should be trained in the techniques until a reasonable criterion for performance has been reached, and then given occasional booster sessions to maintain the skills.

It is critical that training make use of relevant academic materials. Self-instruction should also be specific: students must be taught to use particular sets of instructions that apply to special situations, such as problem-solving in mathematics (Hallahan, Kneedler, and Lloyd, 1983; Hallahan et al., 1983). More examples of metacognitive strategies that can be used in a classroom environment will be found in Chapter 11.

## Metamemory

The aspect of metacognition that refers specifically to knowing something about our own memory is known as metamemory. This includes knowing about the memory system; knowing how good we are at memory tasks; knowing what kinds of information we remember best; and the techniques (such as the mnemonic strategies discussed earlier) that we can use to help aid retrieval. Metamemory will affect how well we recall information as well as the strategies that we use to store the information.

While metamemory is an important part of cognition, the development of this ability is not well understood by researchers. We do know that it grows as children develop. (Hagen, Jongeward, and Kail, 1975).

## Metacomprehension

Another aspect of metacognition is metacomprehension—the strategies that a reader uses in monitoring and evaluating the comprehension of written text while reading that text (Paris, Lipson, and Wixon, 1983). Metacomprehension processes are the strategies that we select to direct our learning such as planning, revising, and evaluating. There are many strategies; Wittrock (1983), for example, has identified no fewer than 32 that one might teach to enhance reading comprehension.

Students may be assisted with metacomprehension by strategies such as:

• generalizing and responding to questions about the material;

• making connections between the various parts;

• identifying relevant background knowledge;

• drawing inferences from the material; and

• summarizing and organizing the material (Pearson and Gallagher, 1983; Tierney and Cunningham, 1984).

## SUMMARY

1.  The cognitive revolution was in part a reaction to behaviourism and in part a return to the cognitive roots of psychology. Cognitive theory holds that meaningful learning involves the understanding of various facts and principles as well as the relationships between them. In this way, cognitive structures are built that allow information to be retained in an organized way.

2.  Jerome Bruner emerged as a leader of the cognitive school. Bruner's theory is prescriptive rather than descriptive. Bruner calls his theory a theory of instruction, not a learning theory, and constantly aims his message at the practising classroom teacher. Bruner stresses the importance in learning of forming global concepts, of building coherent generalizations, and of creating cognitive gestalts.

3.  Information processing theorists take a cognitive approach to learning. Taking the computer as the basic model, information processing is used as a means for studying cognitive processes.  There are several variations of the specifics of how the information processing model appears to work. The consensus view is that learning and remembering are based on the flow of information that passes within the organism. Sense organs respond to and pass along incoming information, some of which is then encoded into memory in a manner that allows it to be retrieved and acted upon.

4.  The modern study of how humans receive and process information from the environment largely began with the gestalt movement in Germany around World War I. Gestalt psychologists were interested in perception as well as learning and especially the fact that perception tends to be organized into meaningful patterns that include the relationships between elements as well as the elements themselves. Gestalt psychologists suggested that humans perceive whole units rather than pieces of sensation and that the whole of a sensation is more than its parts. The perception of stimuli is influenced by our mental state, past experiences, knowledge, motivation, and so on.

5.  The capacity of human memory is awe inspiring. There seem to be distinct storage systems—the sensory register, short-term memory, and long-term memory. Sensory information in the form of environmental stimuli bombards us and enters the sensory storage system. It remains there only briefly;

much of it decays while some moves to short-term storage. Short-term memory has limited storage capacity; it can hold only a few things at a time and then can hold them for only a few seconds. Unless information is transferred from short-term to long-term memory, it will not be permanently stored. Long-term memory has a far greater storage capacity. Knowledge is stored in an organized and meaningful fashion.

6. Many psychologists believe that our store of knowledge in long-term memory is organized in terms of schemata. Schemata can be likened to a hierarchical mental scaffolding, with general concepts being related to more specific pieces of information.

7. Long-term memory is a permanent store of knowledge with unlimited capacity, yet we have trouble remembering some information. Recalling information is not always easy. When we search for information, we depend upon cues, information that is available to guide that search.

8. There are many different explanations for the phenomenon of forgetting, including decay and interference. Interference occurs when information gets mixed up or pushed aside by other information.

9. Information processing theories have translated in varying and sometimes conflicting opinions about how to arrange learning activities in classrooms. However, many of the principles used by information processing theorists can be used to make comprehension and memorization more efficient and to help students apply what they have memorized.

10. Metacognition refers to one's own cognition and the regulation of one's cognition. Recently, educators have focused on the need to teach these students how to learn, by developing instructional programs that stress methods of processing and applying information, organizational and study skills, and strategies to work through problematic issues.

## Key Terms

| | | |
|---|---|---|
| acoustic encoding | advance organizers | chunking |
| closure | cognitive psychology | context |
| context cues | decay | distributed practice |
| elaborative rehearsal | encoding | episodic memory |
| figure-ground | flashbulb memory | forgetting |
| gestalt | interference | mass practice |
| metacognition | metacomprehension | metamemory |
| mnemonic devices | overlearning | perception |
| proactive interference | problem-solving strategies | procedural memory |
| propositional network | receptors | rehearsal |
| retrieval cue | retroactive interference | rote learning |
| schemata | selective attention | semantic memory |
| sensation | serial position effect | state dependent learning |
| sustained attention | transfer | |

# HUMANISM

## 10

## INTRODUCTION

Understanding students—their feelings, their moods, and their perceptions of the learning process—is critical to effective teaching. These are the concerns of humanistic psychologists. However, this group is somewhat different from those discussed in earlier chapters. As we saw, behavioural and cognitive theorists devote considerable attention to the description of principles that govern the acquisition of knowledge, skills, and other abilities. Those coming from the humanistic school of psychology assert that classroom learning and student behaviour are simply too complex to be understood from a single point of view. They acknowledge the importance of notions about reinforcement, shaping and memory to student learning in the classroom, but they stress that teachers must also be conscious of the affective side of learning. They must establish supportive milieu where students can build their self-concepts and self-esteem as they develop.

Many believe that the primary function of schools is to teach the learner to be intellectually competent; humanistic educators, however, argue that affect is of equal importance and, indeed, cannot be separated from cognition. The standard curriculum is no longer enough to prepare today's youths for the world they will enter; adherents of humanistic education believe in the healthy growth of the student as a person—with a clear understanding of the dynamics of human interaction and in possession of personal skills for living effectively with other people.

While school children have traditionally been rewarded for learning, humanistic educators see this as a limiting practice which denies the importance of the student as a thinking, feeling person (Brown, 1971). Thus, humanistic educators place as much, if not more, emphasis on the affective goals of education as they do upon the cognitive. These affective goals address the learner's emotions, attitudes, and values that are associated with experiences.

They include how people feel about wanting to learn, how they feel as they learn, and how they feel after the learning experience is concluded (Brown, 1971).

As you can easily see, humanistic educators view the roles of teachers and students and the goals and processes of education quite differently than the behaviourists and cognitive psychologists whom we have already discussed. Nevertheless, many of the ideas of these schools of thought can be seen as complementary rather than contradictory. Alternative educational approaches based on humanistic principles include open education, confluent education, affective education, and, the most recent strategy, cooperative learning. Humanistic psychologists also oppose many of the traditional practices in the schools. For example, they are opposed to typical grading practices. However, this does not imply that humanistic educators eliminate all traditional forms of evaluation. But rather than a method of simply passing judgment, they see evaluation as a means of providing feedback to a student, as well as diagnostic information to the teacher. Further, consistent with the view that students should be self-directed, humanistic educators see them as integrally involved in the evaluation process.

While each approach arising from humanistic views is unique, they are all similar in that they are all fundamentally based on the notion of student-centred education. All are intended to maximize growth of the whole student, including emotional, social, and cognitive growth. This latter aspect should not be forgotten, for while humanists pay attention to the affective growth of students as well as to the personal relationship between teachers and students, they do not ignore the importance of cognitive goals. As Combs (1982) has stated, "Humanistic education does not require the surrender of traditional goals and objectives. Quite the contrary. It is a way of making certain that students achieve them" (p. 135). Some humanistic educators take the study of affective goals even further, presenting curricular materials that are directed towards the expression, understanding, and analysis of emotions, values, and attitudes.

Humanistic psychologists, however, do not offer a theory of learning per se. They instead focus on the affective and interpersonal nature of the teaching and learning process. By the same token, it is not possible to define a single humanistic view of psychology. It is "not so much a content area as it is an attitude or outlook about how to think about psychology, how to use it, and how to apply our knowledge about it to solving human problems and enhancing human existence on a day-to-day basis" (Hamachek, 1987, p. 160).

A constellation of scientific, social, and political concerns fostered the emergence of a humanistic approach to education in the late 1950s. Prior to this, North American schools had been largely dominated by the behavioural approach to learning. At the beginning, educators and the public had great faith that this scientific or technological approach to learning would solve all of the ills of schooling. But partly because the behaviourist school of learning had not yet been fully developed and was often inappropriately implemented in schools, it was not possible for the behavioural approach to live up to such high expectations. Dissatisfaction grew and was accentuated when the Soviets made their exciting and surprising advances in space technology. North Americans were aghast at the evidence that other nations were further ahead of them, particularly in the areas of science and mathematics. When the schools were criticized for failing to educate their students adequately, governments and educational professionals alike began to focus on methods that could be used to improve the educational system.

The early 1960s were a time of great social upheaval, with traditional institutions such as schools undergoing greater scrutiny by the public than ever before. As the social attitudes of the time began to stress autonomy, independence, and "finding oneself," the regimentation of traditional schools appeared to be sorely out of place. Parallel to the demands for improvements in student learning came calls from a growing body of laypeople and professionals to pay greater attention to the affective needs of children—their emotional and social growth and the development of self-concept and values. Psychologists holding a humanistic view of psychology not only were concerned with issues of education but also disputed the dominant paradigms that dominated psychology at that time.

Some areas arising from a humanistic stance have already been explored in this text. In this chapter we examine some of the roots of humanistic education, look at some of the prevalent notions, and illustrate how these are applied in classrooms. Further applications from humanistic education are found in Chapter 11.

## DEVELOPMENT OF HUMANISTIC PSYCHOLOGY

The humanistic view of psychology emerged during the late 1950s as a response to the deeply held dissatisfaction with the ability of then prevailing views in psychology to address the totality of human problems or give direction towards assisting in the development of happy and healthy individuals. Humanism appeared as a new competitor to behaviourism, a critic of psychoanalytic approaches, and in tandem with the new cognitive psychology.

Hilgard (1987) points out that as humanistic psychology developed in America, it combined a study of human significance and values with a holistic interest in personality change and psychotherapy according to unconventional methods. Hilgard also observes that there was a certain zealousness about advocating lifestyles viewed as certain to enhance the fulfillment of individual potential and pertinent to solving social problems.

Carl Rogers, one of the doyens of humanistic psychology, wrote one of the first books on child psychology in the 1940s. Rogers had long advocated client-centred therapy in which the client was the master of his or her own fate. Additional information about this important and influential figure in humanistic psychology is found in Box 10-1. Another leader, Abraham Maslow (1908-1970) wrote *Motivation and personality* in 1954 in which he distinguished a hierarchy from the lowest survival motives to the highest motives of "being," including self-actualization. Arthur Combs, one of the foremost thinkers in the humanistic movement, stressed the recognition of the crucial importance of self-concept to every aspect of human growth and development. "A person's image of beliefs of self are a vital part of his or her every activity," he noted (1981). "People behave in terms of what they believe to be true about themselves. People who believe they can, do; people who believe they cannot, avoid confrontation" (p. 447).

**Box 10-1  Biographical note: Carl Rogers (1902-1987)**

Carl Rogers was born in a suburb of Chicago, and spent much of his young life trying to find direction for his future career. He began at the University of Wisconsin in 1919 as a student of scientific farming. However, he was an active member of his church, even attending a Christian youth conference in China. Upon his return, Rogers switched his major to history, which he felt fit better with his new ambition to become an evangelic minister. He received his undergraduate degree in 1924, with only one course in psychology to his credit.

He then went on to New York to study for the ministry, but again experienced a change in intent. He began to downplay the importance of formal religion, focusing instead on questions that addressed the nature of helping relationships between humans. As his interests changed, Rogers switched from the Union Theological Seminary to the Columbia Teachers college. He received his Ph.D. in 1931.

Rogers's interest in preventative mental health had its roots in his experiences during his doctoral training, when he did field work with Rochester, New York's child study department for the prevention of cruelty to children. Rogers felt that psychology must attempt to prevent emotional difficulties from occurring, rather than focusing on the identification and treatment after the fact. Thus, rather than focusing on pathology, Rogers began to explore methods that could be used to enhance positive growth in all individuals. Not surprisingly, he encountered much oppo-

sition from his traditionally trained, professional colleagues.

It was at the University of Chicago that Rogers founded his famous client-centred agency, where he not only demonstrated his approach but also conducted research on the effectiveness of this model. For example, he was the first therapist to tape his therapy sessions so that he would be more precise in the analysis of each session. This and other research began to show that successful therapy had three characteristics: unconditional positive regard, empathy, and congruence. These ingredients were also considered to be important for the process of education and Rogers became one of the foremost leaders in the application of humanistic principles to education. He emphasized the relationship between teachers and students and advocated student freedom. He also suggested methods that could be used to make content exciting and interesting to students. His ideas were promulgated to professional and laypeople alike in his popular books: *Freedom to Learn*, and later, *Freedom to Learn for the '80s*, which translated the principles of his client-centered therapy into classroom applications.

Carl Rogers died in 1987 at the age of 85 during an operation for a broken hip. His friends and foes alike mourned the loss of a great spokesman and social activist who had devoted his life to the cause of human rights, peace, and the development of happy and fulfilled human beings.

In 1961, the first issue of Journal of Humanistic Psychology appeared. In the next two years, a group of psychologists formed the American Association of Humanistic Psychology.

The objectives of humanistic psychology, as outlined by the Association for Humanistic Psychology, are:

- A focus on experience as the primary phenomenon in the study of humans. Both theoretical explanation and overt behaviour are considered secondary to experience itself and to its meaning to a person.

- An emphasis on such distinctly human qualities as choice, creativity, valuation, and self-realization, as opposed to thinking about human beings in mechanistic and reductionist terms.

- An allegiance to meaningfulness in the selection of problems for study and of research procedures, and an opposition to a primary emphasis on objectivity at the expense of significance.

- An ultimate concern with and valuing of the dignity and worth of humans and an interest in the development of the potential inherent in every person. Central to this view is the person discovering his or her own being and relating to other persons and to the social group (in Evans and Hearn, 1977).

With their own platform in place, those assuming a humanistic stance began to criticize existing psychology and to promote their views.

One target was behaviourism. Humanistic psychologists rejected the notion that human behaviour could be explained with reference to data drawn from studies with rats, pigeons, or chimpanzees. They viewed this approach to human nature as sterile and limiting and deplored the fact that behaviourists such as B.F. Skinner had entirely discarded the notion of free will or people's ability to make choices about their destiny. They set out, according to Carl Rogers (1965), "to resist the way in which man [was] treated as an object in ... behavioural science, to protest against the view of man as completely mechanical, and to disavow the view that the world is a clock already wound up and running its completely determined course" (pp. 125). Further, humanistic psychologists strongly rejected the view that human behaviour was determined solely by environmental factors, or what was referred to as "S-R" psychology (e.g., Rogers, 1965). Rather, they believed that explaining humanity could only be achieved by studying human beings, and studying not only their behaviour, but also their beliefs, thoughts, perceptions, and knowledge.

The second major force in psychology, psychoanalysis, evolved in Europe largely under the pioneering aegis of Sigmund Freud at about the same time that behaviourism was developing in the United States. Freud blended the cognitive concepts of consciousness, human perception, and memory with physiological views of biological impulses to formulate a new theory of personality or human behaviour (Atkinson et al., 1990).

While behaviourists saw the environment as the critical factor influencing behaviour, Freudians saw humans as products of their biological instincts (Hamachek, 1987). However, while behaviourists like Skinner called upon psychologists to use the principles of operant conditioning to improve human nature, the psychoanalytic view is essentially a pessimistic view. Freud saw the very structure of human personality as reflecting a constant and inevitable series of conflicts between innate instincts and the demands of the environments.

Humanism—the "third force" in psychology—emerged as a reaction to the perceived deficiencies of both of these views of human behaviour. Humanists

One of the objectives of
humanistic psychology is to
focus on experience as the
primary phenomenon in the
study of humans.

countered the notion that human behaviour could be reduced to simple S-R response or biological instincts. They argued that such views ignored the whole person, or the intangible features that made human beings "human" (Hamachek, 1987). Rather than being driven by innate drives or governed by the environment, humanists saw individuals as having the freedom to choose their own actions, thus emphasizing free choice instead of determinism (Bell and Schniedewind, 1989). The manner in which people view themselves and their world is critical to understanding their growth, development, and learning (Hamachek, 1987). People are central to the humanistic view of behaviour—which sees our "needs, wants, desires, values and unique ways of perceiving and understanding [as causing] us to behave the way we do" (Hamachek, 1987, p. 160).

Humanistic psychology was rapidly translated into educational endeavours. In one way, the humanistic movement in education can be seen as a belated successor to the Progressive education movement of John Dewey and others which had a strong impact on North American schools in the 1920s and 1930s (Winzer, 1990b). Progressive education was a reaction to the rote and drill learning widely used in the schools. Dewey stressed the importance of a child-centred curriculum, which promoted personal development in the physical, emotional, spiritual, cognitive, and aesthetic realms. The purpose of education was not to pass on static knowledge but to develop creative intelligence and divergent thinking in children (Bell and Schniedewind, 1989).

While the Progressive education movement sensitized educators to the importance of human relationships in schools and the affective aspects of learning, the movement was limited. Most educators continued to focus attention on the cognitive outcomes of learning, an emphasis that continued unabated throughout the 1950s. However, growing discontent with this approach began to be articulated by parents, educators, and psychologists who protested the lack of concern for students (Hamachek, 1987).

Some ideas of Progressive education were resurrected, although humanistic educators paid greater attention to self-actualization, as articulated by Abraham Maslow (1954), as well as the importance of integrating emotions into the learning process. It was believed that long-lasting learning would occur only when knowledge was connected to the affective state of the learner (Bell and Schniedewind, 1989).

The timing of the rise of humanistic views of education roughly paralleled the "cognitive revolution" in psychology and education. While they differed along many important dimensions, in others ways these two approaches can be seen to be complementary. Cognitive theorists such as Jerome Bruner, for example, also stress the importance of individual perception, or how individuals' reaction to events or information will be determined by their unique experiences, expectations, and mood. In other words, meaning is brought to an experience by the individual.

## Humanistic view of behaviour

It is difficult to summarize the complex and often diverse views of human development and learning held by humanistic psychologists. However, some general principles underlie this approach to psychology which focuses on the whole person. Humanistic psychologists believe in free will, stress the importance of subjective experience, understand self-actualization as the primary motivational force, and identify self-concept as crucial to developments.

**Free will**    Humanistic psychologists believe that individuals can be understood only when considering them as persons with free will. It is in the issue of free will versus determinism that we see the sharpest difference between humanism and other views of human nature. Humanists reject determinism and see people as agents of free will, able to control their own destiny. They do not believe that people are acted upon by other forces but that they construct their own lives by making choices and setting goals. Thus, in their view, people are ultimately responsible for the shape and focus of their lives because they are accountable for the choices that they make.

**Subjective experience:** the individual's personal view of the world.

**Subjective experience**   The humanistic movement recognizes the profundity of subjective experience, or the individual's personal view of the world. This view, in essence, determines what each person considers "reality" to be. While others can try to understand a person's perceptual world, they will never be able to fully know that reality.

However, humanists argue that a great deal of human behaviour can be better understood by the observer if they "walk a mile in the other's shoes," or try to understand how a particular individual experiences the world. What may seem to be strange, irrational, or otherwise inexplicable behaviour may become understandable when viewed from that person's perspective. Thus, when teachers puzzle over their student's "lack of motivation" or parents are shocked by their adolescent child's delinquent behaviour, humanistic psychologists would say that they could comprehend the reasons for the behaviour—although they may still consider it to be inappropriate—when they view the situation from the unique perspective of the child. As they see it, the only way to change a person's behaviour in any given situation is to change that person's perceptions or beliefs. So rather than focusing on the behaviour, humanists believe that helping a person to see a situation differently will make them behave differently (Combs et al., 1974).

**Communication**   Given the importance of understanding other's perceptions of the world, humanistic psychologists emphasize the need for open, honest communication, whether it be between parent and child, therapist and client, or teacher and student (e.g., Gordon, 1970, 1974; Rogers, 1983). For example, Thomas Gordon, a student of Carl Rogers, applied Rogerian principles to the parent-child relationship (1970) as well as to that of the teacher and student (1974). Gordon stressed the importance of communication, particularly when problems arise, such as disruptive behaviour, personal problems, or interpersonal difficulties. To improve the quality of student-teacher communication, Gordon recommends that teachers practise active listening which requires the teacher to paraphrase or summarize what students have said. The goal is that students will feel they have been understood, and will be thus encouraged to communicate more honestly and directly (Gordon, 1974).

A further communication strategy recommended by Gordon (1974) is the use of "I-messages," or statements which describe the student's behaviour and how it negatively affects the teacher. Effective I-messages contain three components:

1. A description of the student's behaviour, stated in a straightforward, nonjudgmental fashion.

2. A description of the effect that the behaviour has on the teacher.

3. A description of how the behaviour makes the teacher feel.

When talking to a student who disrupts a class discussion by making irrelevant sarcastic remarks, for example, the teacher might say "When you make sarcastic remarks, you are not contributing in a meaningful way to the discussion, and that makes me feel angry and frustrated." This I-message clearly communicates the behaviour (making sarcastic remarks); the effect on the teacher (it disrupts the class discussion); and how it makes the teacher feel (angry and frustrated).

**Self-actualization:**
the basic and inborn need for people to develop or actualize their talents and capacities to the limits of their heredity.

Gordon believes that I-messages are effective because they have a high probability of changing student behaviour; the I-message gives the student the responsibility to change his or her behaviour. The student will be motivated to do so because the teacher has described the negative effect that the behaviour has on the teacher or the class. Because the statements are only minimally negative, it is less likely that the statements will impair the student-teacher relationship.

Contrast the I-message to another potential response—a "you-message"—that might be made by a teacher when the student makes a sarcastic remark: "You stop that right now! Why don't you just grow up and stop that stupid behaviour?" Gordon believes that you-messages are usually interpreted by the student as an expression of how bad he or she is, and that such messages will have a negative effect on student self-esteem, making the student feel inferior.

**Self-actualization**     The basic and inborn need for people to develop or actualize their talents and capacities to the limits of their heredity is known as **self-actualization** (Maslow, 1954). According to humanistic psychologists, this need for self-actualization motivates or directs human behaviour. Given optimal conditions, human beings will tend to move in the direction of growth, maturity, and positive change. While individuals may not always be able to distinguish between progressive and regressive actions, they will choose to grow when the choice is clear (Rogers, 1983).

Of course, this implies that many individuals fail to actualize their potential. However, rather than placing the blame on the individual's early childhood experiences, or flawed personality, humanists point to the role of the environment. For example, Carl Rogers believes that people are often forced into socially determined roles, or made to "become" something by parents, teachers, churches, and other organs of social control. Unfortunately, such roles are often not consistent with the drive for self-actualization. But if individuals are accepted for what they are, they will live in ways that enhance themselves and the wider society.

It is not possible for teachers, parents, or others to direct or guide a student in the appropriate direction to self-actualization—instead, they can only try to provide a facilitative environment. This is perhaps best illustrated by examining "person-centred" therapy as pioneered by Carl Rogers. In this approach, the therapist does not "tell" clients what to do to achieve their potential, or even what that potential is. Rather, the Rogerian therapist believes that all persons will develop their potential—or self-actualize—under the right circumstances. The role of the therapist is to develop a climate of trust and acceptance which allows individuals to determine their own directions for growth since they are the people best qualified to decide what direction it should take. The therapist does not recommend, advise, or direct, but rather serves as a sounding board as individuals explore their problems. The therapist provides honest acceptance and understanding as clients work toward a greater understanding of their experiences.

Of course, people will actualize their potential in different ways. Some may seek to expand their talents and capacities by focusing on their families and will spend a great deal of time and effort working within this context. For others, the actualizing tendency may guide them towards professional growth and they will achieve their best within the work setting. Both of these very different methods of behaving reflect the actualizing tendency (Nye, 1981). The common characteristics of the actualized individual are flexibility, openness, and autonomy, or freedom from external controls. However, human beings never know their full potential—they are always in a state of "being and becoming." Humans can never reach, nor even know how to define full actualization.

**Self-concept**    The concept of self or self-concept is central to the humanistic view. Of course, the emphasis on self or self-concept is consistent with the view of subjective reality. This helps explain why two different students will respond in very different manners to the same situation: their perception of the event as well as their views of themselves will determine their responses to academic challenges or interpersonal relationships.

While humanistic psychologists have varying ways of defining and explaining the concept of self, they generally agree that the self consists of all the ideas, perceptions, and values that make up "I" or "me", and includes awareness of "what I am" and "what I can do." As we discussed in Chapter 4, self-awareness begins to develop in infancy and the early childhood years, as children interact with their environment and, most importantly, the people in it. Infants are initially not aware of themselves as unique entities, but as they develop, their growing awareness of "self" is reflected in their behaviour and speech—the young child begins to say things like "I want" or "It's mine" that indicate the development of the sense of self (Nye, 1981).

The sense of self is ever-changing, constructed through the person's interactions with the world. Of particular importance is the evaluative feedback received from others. Parents, teachers, and other significant people in a child's life can strongly influence the development of the self-concept by giving or withholding

Humans can never reach, nor even know how to define full actualization.

positive regard. Children who experience a warm and nurturing home environ-ment, who are accepted for themselves, and who are supported when they express their feelings, are likely to develop a positive sense of themselves. Of course, the reverse can be true; children who are consistently criticized, who are told (implicitly or explicitly) they are unable or incompetent, and who experience rejection and failure through their activities will develop a negative sense of self.

Even if the person is valued by a parent or teacher, this does not mean that all of his or her behaviours are equally accepted. The behaviour of a child who hits another child, throws food, or teases the dog may garner displeasure from oth-ers. At the same time, however, the child must be aware that the behaviour does not trigger a withdrawal of love or acceptance. Thus, the child should not have to deny his or her inner experiences, even though his or her behaviour may be changed.

The sense of self will, of course, directs or guides the person's behaviour across contexts. In other words, humans act in ways that are consistent with their views of themselves. The man who perceives himself as a gifted athlete is likely to jump at the chance to try a new sport while the one who views himself as hopelessly uncoordinated would shrink at the thought.

## PRINCIPLES OF HUMANISTIC EDUCATION

There exists no pat theory of humanistic education. It can be considered as a larger view of education that emphasizes the human being as central to the teaching and learning process. It is a matter of emphasis, rather than a rejection of principles from other theories. The cognitive view of learning can fit quite comfortably within the humanistic perspective and, while humanists have been sharply critical of the behavioural view, they do not reject the notion that oper-ant conditioning can occur under some circumstances. It would be possible to see techniques such as positive reinforcement and contingency contracts or rein-forcement schedules in operation in a humanistic classroom. While humanists do not believe that the behaviourist can adequately describe all human function-ing, the humanistic teacher is likely to use a variety of behavioural strategies if those strategies are useful in a particular context.

Choosing to teach as a humanist does not require the rejection of strategies and techniques drawn from other schools. However, instruction and class struc-ture, goals and objectives, and teacher and student behaviour will reflect a much different focus. Teachers operating from a behavioural perspective, for example, would rely primarily on the manipulation of external events, measuring the overt behaviours of the students in order to measure learning. In contrast, the humanistic educator would tend to focus on internal processes; the individual student's search for meaning, the student's self-concept, and the interpersonal relationships seen in the classroom.

### New role for the teacher

Humanistic psychologists point out that learning always has two sides; exposure to new information or experience, on the one side, and the personal discovery of meaning on the other. Most educators know very well how to deal with providing information. It is the second part that may cause teachers more difficulties. Humanistic theorists have defined new and unique roles for teachers which are very different from those found in traditional school structures.

Carl Rogers sees traditional teaching as based on the "mug and jug theory"—in other words, the teacher asks, "How can I make the mug hold still while I fill it from the jug with these facts which the curriculum planners and I regard as valuable?" (Rogers, 1983, p. 136). In contrast, the humanistic educator acts as a facilitator of learning, concerned with creating an open climate of trust and acceptance in which children are free to experiment and learn. Students are given the freedom to choose what they wish to learn rather than being directed by the expectations of teachers or department curriculum guides. Facilitators help students find answers to questions they are concerned about—and therefore eager to learn about—by making materials and resources available to the children as needed. The facilitator works cooperatively with the students to establish classroom guidelines and design activities which will facilitate maximal cognitive, emotional, and social growth. Children evaluate their own progress and set future learning goals based on their own self-evaluations.

Rogers (1983) reassures teachers that taking the role of facilitator does not increase their workload; rather, he believes that when children are eager to learn, they will initiate their own study, most of which is completed without teacher input or extensive supervision. Discipline problems are diminished, for when children are working on issues of real concern and interest at the appropriate level for their stage of development, they will be much less likely to act out or become disruptive. Further, the teacher's responsibility is reduced when students help each other learn. Thus, the facilitator spends most of his or her time making resources available to the children, for while they do not need to be taught, they will need exciting and interesting resources to spark their imaginations.

## Qualities of teachers

Rogers and other humanistic educators have pointed out that good facilitators possess certain attitudinal qualities that enhance their ability to work effectively with students. These characteristics allow the facilitator to form a positive personal relationship with the learner. "Good teachers," notes one educator, "are not those who are simply experts in subject matter, or experts in teaching methods, or curriculum experts, or who utilize the most resources, such as audiovisual aids. The best teacher is one who, through establishing a personal relationship, frees the student to learn" (Patterson, 1973, p. 98).

The first attitudinal quality that Rogers refers to is realness or genuineness. Effective teachers cannot present an artificial facade to their students; rather, they must be capable of accurately and openly communicating their feelings to their students; they are being themselves, rather than denying themselves. Realness does not mean that teachers pass judgment on others or project their own feelings on another. The teacher, observed Rogers (1983), "can be enthusiastic, can be bored, can be interested in students, can be angry, can be sensitive and sympathetic. Because she accepts these feelings as her own, she has no need to impose them on her students" (p. 122).

Realness, respectfulness, and empathetic understanding are characteristics of the ideal humanistic teacher.

Feelings must be shared in an honest way, even when the emotions are negative. If the child's behaviour makes the teacher angry, the child must understand that it is the behaviour, rather than the individual, who is the target of the anger. Of course, Rogers does not claim that being real is easy, or that realness can be achieved overnight. But being real is necessary for the person who wishes to become a true facilitator of learning (Rogers, 1983).

Patterson (1973) also stresses the importance of being a genuine or real person, or an authentic teacher. He believes that many teachers assume an artificial role when they begin their careers because their education has not prepared them to enter into a facilitative relationship with their students. New teachers are told by faculty supervisors, cooperating teachers, and/or administrators to "be tough" or to play a authoritarian role in order to avoid losing control of their classes. To be warm and open toward, or trusting of their students is to risk losing disciplinary control.

Humanists believe that the second most important characteristic of effective teachers is a profound and deeply felt respect for each student. Each is seen as an unique human being who has worth in his or her own right. This respect is unconditional—children are accepted for what they are. According to Rogers, the learner is prized "as an imperfect human being with many feelings, many potentialities. The facilitator's prizing or acceptance of the learner is an operational expression of her essential confidence and trust in the capacity of the human" (Rogers, 1983, p. 124). The teacher cares for students, and feels warmth towards them, but it is a nonpossessive caring, recognizing the basic integrity of each of them as persons. Children are trusted, for the teacher believes in the capacity of children to grow and to develop and to actualize their potential in an appropriate classroom environment (Patterson, 1973).

**Empathic understanding:** ability to understand student reactions from the inside as well as to be aware of how the process of learning is experienced by students.

When teachers respect their students, they value and accept their students' feelings and opinions, regardless of their content (Patterson, 1973; Rogers, 1983). Of course, this does not mean that the students will always agree with the teacher, nor that the students' behaviours, thoughts or opinions will always be what the teacher had hoped for. But the students' mistakes, errors, changing moods, and behaviours are seen simply as a reflection of the fallible human nature. The teacher may not like what a student has done or said, but this does not diminish the teacher's respect for the student as a person. This distinction must be clearly made for a student—"I don't like what you did, but I still like and accept you as a person" (Patterson, 1973).

The third quality demonstrated by a good facilitator is empathic understanding, or the ability to understand student reactions from the inside, as well as to be aware of how the process of learning is experienced by students (Paterson, 1973; Rogers, 1983). Indeed, as a reflection of the humanistic view, educators from this school place a great deal of emphasis on human subjectivity as they believe that a student's perception of reality will determines his or her behaviour. The teacher must be able to view the world through the students' eyes in order to understand their feelings and perceptions, without analyzing or judging (Rogers, 1983).

Realness or authenticity, respectfulness or the ability to prize, and empathic understanding are the characteristics that make up the humanistic teacher. But do these teacher characteristics actually lead to improved student development and learning? While there is still no definitive answer to this question, Rogers (1983) reviewed research conducted by the National Consortium for Humanizing Education (NCHE) which studied the relationship of Rogers's facilitative conditions to factors such as attitudes, discipline problems, physical health, attendance, IQ changes, and cognitive growth. In summarizing studies that took place over 17 years in 42 American states and seven other countries, David Aspy and Flora Roebuck stated "Students learn more and behave better when they receive high levels of understanding, caring and genuineness, than when they are given low levels of them" (cited in Rogers, 1983, p. 199).

In one large study of 600 teachers and 10 000 students (kindergarten to grade 12), the students whose teachers had been trained to provide high levels of empathy, congruence, and positive regard were compared to control students of teachers who did not offer such facilitating behaviours. The students of highly facilitating teachers missed fewer days of school, had increased self-concept, made greater academic gains, presented fewer discipline problems, committed less vandalism, increased their scores on IQ tests, made gains in creativity scores, were more spontaneous, and used higher levels of thinking. The more years that students had a facilitative teacher, the greater the gains shown.

Upon further examination of their data on teacher behaviour, Aspy and Roebuck found that teachers high in empathy were more likely to demonstrate other related behaviours than teachers rated as low in empathy were. Empathic teachers demonstrated:

- more response to student feeling;

- more use of student ideas in ongoing teacher interaction;

- more discussion with students (dialogue);

- more praise of students;

- more congruent speech (less ritualistic);

- more tailoring of contents to the individual student's frame of reference. (That is, explanations tend to be created to fit the immediate needs of the learners); and

- more smiling with students (in Rogers, 1983, p. 210).

Further, these teachers tended to implement classroom activities that reflected the same characteristics. In their classrooms:

- learning goals were derived from cooperative planning between teacher and students;

- classrooms were individualized for and by the present class to meet its needs. There were more projects and displays created by the students and the room looked "lived in";

- more freedom from time limits: there were fewer deadlines and more flexible sequences of order; and

- more emphasis on productivity and creativity than evaluation; there was less emphasis upon grades and tests (in Rogers, 1983, p. 210).

## The learner

The term "student-centred" is often applied to this approach to education because the learner is central to the process. This can be contrasted with the traditional notion of schooling which is "teacher-centred" or which places the teacher in the primary role of directing instruction.

One of the most important tenets of humanistic education is that students should have substantial choice in what they study, helping them to become self-directed learners. Humanistic educators deplore a teacher-centred approach to education, believing that placing learners in a passive role dampens their curiosity, minimizes true learning, destroys motivation, and makes learning a joyless and stultifying process. Traditional educators, who see their role as structuring knowledge for children as well as determining when and how children should study, garner responses such as the following from humanists:

> *Every time we show Tommy how his engine works we are stealing from that child the joy of life—the joy of discovery—the joy of overcoming an obstacle. Worse! We make that child come to believe that he is inferior, and must depend on help (Neill, 1960, p. 25).*

When teachers facilitate rather than direct learning activities, they help students attain one of the most important goals of humanistic education—becoming self-directed learners. When students direct their own learning, they have substantial input into what they study, as well as when and how they will study. When the curiosity of the students is unleashed, and they are allowed to pursue subjects of interest to them, classroom activities become meaningful and personally significant to them. Then teachers can take advantage of their natural or innate desire to learn.

When children are engaged in the study of a material that is of interest to them, the issue of motivation becomes moot.

Goodman (1964) believes that nothing is really learned unless it satisfies some need, want, curiosity, or fantasy and therefore self-directed learning will be retained much better, since it is relevant to the students' lives. It is further argued that when children are engaged in the study of material that is of interest to them, the issue of motivation becomes moot. Humanistic educators see motivation as inherent in the learning process when children are free to choose their own topics of interest. And, if motivation becomes part of learning, then discipline problems are also greatly diminished (Rogers, 1983).

The second major goal held for students by humanistic educators is that they will develop a positive attitude toward learning and value learning for its own sake. Thus, rather than focusing on the coverage of curriculum goals, humanistic educators help students take responsibility for their own education (Gardner, 1963). In our rapidly changing world, where "truths" and "certain knowledge" are rapidly supplanted by new information, students are best equipped for adult life when they possess a sense of inquiry, are helped to question and explore any topic or assumption, and are able to recognize that everything is in a process of constant change (Rogers, 1983). They recognize that new learning is always needed, that they must always be in a process of "self-renewal" (Gardner, 1963).

Humanistic educators are not the first, nor will they be the last, to stress the importance of "learning to learn" or "learning to think." Cognitive theorists also stress the importance of metacognitive skills, or the ability to understand one's own thinking processes, as well as knowing when and how to apply these abilities. However, cognitive theorists would point out that this humanistic emphasis on self-directed learning becomes somewhat problematic when considering the learning of fundamental skills, or the basic building blocks upon which more complex learning is based. While the overuse of drill and rote learning has been justifiably criticized (e.g., Holt, 1964), it is also clear that some skills must be mastered before more complex learning can be accomplished. And it may be that the fastest and more efficient way that such skills are learned is through teacher-directed instruction.

## Approaches to schooling

Humanistic educators have been associated with many approaches to education. However, it is clear that certain broad generalizations can be drawn concerning the humanistic approach to education that characterize all of the diverse approaches. To a certain extent, it will be seen that these characteristics, including opposition to grades and support for open education, have developed in protest against the perceived deficiencies of traditional approaches to education.

### Opposition to grades

In school, grades can be extremely motivating, especially for older students (Gold et al., 1971). Humanistic educators however are opposed to traditional forms of evaluation, whether they take the form of teacher-given letter grades, standardized testing, or diploma examinations. One of the reasons for their opposition is the belief that such evaluations make children feel inferior (Rogers, 1983). When students continually experience low or failing grades in school, self-concept is likely to suffer. Children feel anxious or unhappy, and those who do not do well become labeled by peers, teachers, and others as "dumb" or "under-achievers." Such labels can become self-fulfilling prophecies: children who see themselves as incompetent or otherwise unable do not try in school. If the goal of humanistic education is to instill positive self-concepts and love of learning in children, then many grading practices can certainly be seen to conflict with this goal. Many students simply work for a grade rather than for the personal satisfaction that comes with the mastering of understanding. But humanistic educators further believe that evaluation can destroy intrinsic motivation. People work harder towards goals they set for themselves than for goals set by others.

Grading is seen to have a negative impact on the interpersonal relationships of students in the classroom. With the common practice of grading on the curve, only a certain number of high marks will be awarded. When this system is in use, as each A is awarded, there is necessarily one less to go around. Therefore, the success of one student necessarily means the failure of others. Not surprisingly, students are motivated to see each other as competitors. While competition is often assumed to be a positive force in the classroom, more recent research has shown that students learn more, and also feel better about themselves, their peers and the process of schooling, when they function under more cooperative learning structures (See Chapter 11).

Humanistic educators further believe that standard grading practices encourage limited or inappropriate forms of learning. For example, Glasser (1969) criticized objective tests as misleading to students, for they imply that there is a single "right" answer to any question. In addition, most tests prompt students to memorize material by rote rather than coming to any true understanding of the information.

### Open education

Open education in North America had its roots in the British primary schools. Reports of its success were widely disseminated through documents such as the Plowden Report (1967) and open education soon spread like wildfire through Canadian schools of the 1970s. While the most visible manifestations of this movement remain in some of the schools built at this time (i.e., those without interior walls), we cannot assume that open education or instructional programs derived from humanistic principles were actually in operation within these structures. Many schools without walls were run in accordance with traditional educational models whereas many schools with self-contained classrooms implemented many of the features of open education.

Herein lies the problem of discussing or evaluating open education: many paid lip service to the implementation of the philosophy and methods of open education but, in practice, very few programs were true to the principles of the approach. Indeed, when researchers view much of the writing and research in this area, they have difficulty in clearly describing what open education truly is. Certainly, it draws many of its features from the cognitive theories of Jean Piaget

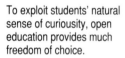

To exploit students' natural sense of curiousity, open education provides much freedom of choice.

as well as incorporating humanistic principles. For example, open education embraced the view that children learn best through interaction with their world, as such experiences formed the basis from which cognitive development grows and expands. To exploit the innate desire to make sense of the world, open education provided much freedom of choice for students. The form, content, and sequence of instructional activities were unique to each child and students were allowed to progress at their own rate and in their own way.

But while it is possible to delineate the general principles of open education, a more precise description of the specific dimensions that characterize an open program are more difficult to obtain. In an attempt to do so, Walberg and Thomas (1972) conducted an exhaustive review of the literature on open education and solicited the opinions of various experts associated with the field. They produced a list of eight general dimensions that seem to characterize open education. These are summarized in Table 10-1.

**Table 10-1** Open education themes

| OPEN EDUCATION CLASSROOMS DIFFER FROM TRADITIONAL CLASSROOMS MOST SPECIFICALLY ON THE FIRST FIVE CRITERIA. | |
| --- | --- |
| 1. Provisions for learning | Diverse manipulative materials; children move freely around the room; interaction among children is encouraged; children may be grouped by ability level, but are able to re-group themselves by choice. |
| 2. Respect, openness, warmth | Children read books written by peers; environment includes materials developed or supplied by students; teacher deals with conflicts or disruptive behaviour individually, without involving the group. |
| 3. Diagnosis of learning events | Teacher observes the work of children, asking immediate, experience-based questions. Children correct their own work. |
| 4. Instruction: guidance and extension of learning | Teacher bases instruction of individual child on his or her interaction with materials; diagnostic information gives direction to further extension of redirection of activities. |
| 5. Evaluation of diagnostic information | Teacher keeps individualized histories of each child's development. Few formal tests: evaluation guides instruction. |
| 6. Collaborative teaching | Teacher has assistance from others, including helpful colleagues with whom to discuss teaching. |
| 7. Good discipline | Teacher tries to keep all students in sight to monitor their activities. |
| 8. Assumptions about children and learning. | Classroom climate is warm and accepting; clear guidelines are made explicit. Children are deeply involved in what they are doing. |

**SOURCE:** Adapted from Walberg and Thomas, 1972, pp 200-201.

Despite the great fanfare and high expectations that surrounded the implementation of open education, much of the research on its effectiveness has been quite disappointing. Not surprisingly, theorists such as B.F. Skinner were highly critical of this approach; his views are outlined in Box 10-2.

## Box 10-2  **Skinner's view of open education**

It will not surprise the reader to learn that B.F. Skinner is one of the most severe critics of open education. While he recognizes the deficiencies of "traditional education," he disputes the idea that open education represents a better method of instruction. Instead, Skinner (1978) sees it as a throwback to the days of Jean Jacques Rousseau, who urged educators to allow children to learn in school in the same manner in which they learn outside school. That is, by unleashing children's natural love of learning and their innate sense of curiosity, they will experience the joy of discovery.

He admits that "The proposal is especially appealing in contrast with what goes on in the joyless punitive schools which have so long characterized education. It is also attractive because it seems to raise no problems .... The real world is conveniently at hand and it does not need to be made to work" (Skinner, 1978, p. 131). But Skinner goes on to argue that such strategies have been tried over and over again through history, and that few attempts have lasted longer than a few months or years.

He believes that such failures demonstrate that, without guidance, children will not learn much simply through their interaction with the natural environment. That the real world alone is not the best teacher can be seen when one looks at a feral child. "The feral child, the child said to have been raised by wolves, or one said to have matured alone in a benevolent environment, is about all we have to show for unaided natural curiosity or a love of learning" (p. 132).

Skinner argues that unguided learning from a natural environment is just as likely to result in awkward, dangerous, or superstitious behaviour as it is to produce positive effects; without feedback from others, the social environment can breed hostile as well as friendly behaviour. Further, children in open school environments, because they are not required to learn anything, often fail to acquire new knowledge and skills. Less and less is taught, by definition, as learning is left to the natural environment, but to that we must add that less and less is learned (Skinner, 1978, p. 132).

While Skinner and some others opposed to open education did not conduct research that directly compared open education to other educational techniques, there is a limited body of research which does address this issue. One of the difficulties in interpreting this research is the fact that while the term open education is often used, the actual implementation can vary significantly from program to program. And not only are researchers unclear about what they are looking at, there is also frequent disagreement about the traits, behaviours, or abilities that should be measured. Existing instruments are inefficient for measuring many of the goals of open education (such as self-direction in learners) or affective outcomes (such as the levels of self-actualization) that might have been obtained.

Because the implementation of open education differs so greatly from setting to setting, Marshall (1981) suggests that open education should be evaluated in

**Confluent education:**
a form of instruction that integrates the affective and cognitive elements of individual and group learning.

terms of its components (or combinations thereof), rather than as any single unified whole. This not only makes the data more amenable to interpretation, but also assists researchers in determining which aspects of open education seem to lead to the best outcomes. An example of an analysis of this type was conducted by Giacona and Hedges (1982), who conducted a meta-analysis of 153 studies of open education. It is possible to conclude from their complex and comprehensive analysis that open education yields no consistent effects on either academic or affective outcomes. Similar inconclusive results were obtained in several other reviews (e.g., Marshall, 1981).

## Affective education

There are many approaches to affective education, and although the division is somewhat arbitrary, they can be categorized as those which meld cognitive and affective goals together; or those which directly study emotions, values, or attitudes. Perhaps the most well-known application of the former approach was put forward by George Brown (1971), the founder of the Center for Humanistic Education at University of California, Santa Barbara. Brown uses the term **confluent education** to describe "the integration or flowing together of the affective and cognitive elements of individual and group learning" (p. 3). He believes that there can be no intellectual learning without the involvement of some type of feeling or, conversely, there are no feelings without involvement of the mind.

In his *Human teaching for human learning*, Brown (1971) outlines basic affective techniques as well as lessons and units that could be used in the classroom. For an example of how cognitive and affective domains are related, see Box 10-3 for an illustration of how Brown (1971) describes a unit of instruction for the classroom.

### Box 10-3 **In the classroom: Confluent education**

Brown (1971) describes an integrated conceptual unit in driver education developed for ninth graders. The three major topics of the unit included the concept of the machine; anger, frustration, and behaviour change in driving; and the concept of courtesy. When considering the first topic, the concept of the machine, students were exposed to both cognitive and affective issues. The cognitive context comprised the study of the internal-combustion engine and the other parts of the automobile. Affective exercises included "the

machine," which started with one student beginning an action as a machine part, along with an accompanying sound. Other students joined in, fitting into the machine with their own actions and sounds. This activity was intended to illustrate the structure and function of the parts making up the whole as well as how each part contributes to the whole. After completing the exercise, students discussed how they felt being parts of the machine—some liked it, while others reported frustration and feelings of anonymity resulting from being part of a mechanistic system or society.

When discussing the second topic—anger, frustration, and behaviour change—the cognitive context was concerned with the question, "What do the extreme emotions of anger and frustration do to your driving behaviour?" One affective exercise was an improvisational theatre game in which one student stands in the way of another who must get somewhere in a hurry. The game was structured in a manner that prevented the second student from getting around the first, and was sustained until the "victim" began to experience real feelings of anger and frustration. Through questioning, the student later explored these feelings and how they influenced his or her behaviour and judgment. The discussion then applied these reflections to the driving situation, allowing students to see how emotions affect performance. They further explored strategies that could be used to alleviate such inner tensions when operating a car. Thus, rather than just hearing a dry lecture urging them to "remain calm" when driving, the affective exercises helped the students truly experience the impact of these emotions.

Other humanistic educators have argued that affect should be studied directly, rather than in relation to other topics. One of the most common examples is the study of values, or the attitudes and beliefs held by the individual.

## SUMMARY

1. Humanistic education grew out of the general humanistic approach to psychology, which emerged in the late 1950s as a response to dissatisfaction with behaviourism and the psychoanalytic approach.

2. Humanistic psychology is essentially an optimistic view of human nature, which stresses attention to the whole person, endowed with free will and a unique perception of reality.

3. Self-actualization is seen as the primary motivating force. When it is not thwarted by parents, schools, or other outside forces, individuals are free to grow and reach the limits of their potential.

4. Humanistic educators hold a new vision of education, but do not present a theory per se. They rather try to redefine the role of the teacher and the students, as well as modify many traditional educational practices, such as grading.

5. A variety of instructional approaches have emerged from the humanistic perspective, including open education, confluent education, and affective or values education.

6. While many of the humanistic notions may not seem to be applicable in contemporary classrooms, it is equally clear that no teacher can ignore the impor-

tance of seeing their students as thinking and feeling human beings, each of whom will bring their own feelings, emotions and perceptions to the classroom environment.

7. The views from humanistic psychology will emerge again in later parts of this book, when we examine further the view of motivation put forward by Abraham Maslow in Chapter 12.

## Key Terms

confluent education          empathic understanding          self-actualization
subjective experience

11

# APPLICATIONS OF LEARNING
# THEORIES TO THE CLASSROOM

## INTRODUCTION

The teacher's primary task is to help students learn. Theories of learning describe the process of learning and therefore should guide and inform teaching practice. Since there is no single, definitive view of learning, teachers must be aware of, and knowledgeable about, all of the contributions made by the many different views of learning. Teachers require a range of alternative perspectives, approaches, and techniques; this is true whether we are discussing something as broad as learning or as restricted as ways to teach reading. With a range of alternatives, teachers can employ what is applicable in different situations and with different students.

In this chapter, we will focus on the application of major theories of learning to the classroom. The behavioural approach to learning emphasizes the importance of structuring knowledge and carefully manipulating the consequences of behaviour. In contrast, the cognitive view stresses the importance of unobservable processes or mental events that are involved in learning: thinking, perceptions, intentions, emotions, and so on. The current emphasis on teaching students thinking skills arises from the cognitive school. This emphasis encompasses reasoning as a major cognitive focus and stresses problem-solving skills as well as metacognitive abilities. Finally, humanistic educators present viewpoints rather than theories or models of learning. They concentrate on the affective domains. However, a strategy such as cooperative learning can be viewed as closely aligned with humanistic perspectives.

There is little question that education in the 1990s is dominated by the cognitive view of learning; nevertheless, behavioural principles are not without influence. Many instructional programs for children with special learning needs—particularly those with more severe intellectual, physical, or behavioural disabilities—emerge from the behavioural view. Do not think, however, that behavioural principles are today restricted to handicapped learners, for this is patently untrue. In regular classrooms, teachers can apply behavioural principles in many different ways and in many different teaching situations.

Behavioural strategies have been widely used in the management of student behaviour in the classroom. To demonstrate the application of behavioural principles, we present some strategies here; we return to a consideration of the application of behavioural principles in Chapter 15 when we consider classroom management. In addition, a number of systematic and structured instructional approaches have been squarely based on behavioural principles.

While we have stressed, in other chapters, that the cognitive and behavioural theories can be sharply separated from each other in terms of their theoretical views of learning, it is clear that when discussing classroom applications of these principles they tend to overlap to a great extent. Aside from the few remaining radical behaviourists, many applications of behavioural principles take a more balanced view of the human learning and include aspects of cognition—or thinking—when using behavioural strategies in the classroom. Similarly, many applications of cognitive principles can be seen to incorporate principles of reinforcement and punishment borrowed from the Skinnerian view of human behaviour.

## INSTRUCTIONAL APPROACHES

During the 1960s, a number of applications of operant conditioning emerged in the form of what is known as programed instruction. B.F. Skinner was in the forefront in advocating programed instruction and his interpretations, along with those of his contemporaries, were initially hailed as a revolution in teaching. It was predicted that programed instruction would make the teacher's life easier by removing some of the marking and supervision duties. On the other hand, critics feared that teaching machines would replace the human teacher altogether.

### Programed instruction

Skinner's initial involvement with teaching machines and programed instruction resulted from a visit to his daughter's fourth-grade math class where he saw students sitting at their desks doing seatwork while the teacher circulated. Some pupils waited in frustration for needed aid; others finished earlier and waited impatiently for the next task to be assigned. At the end of the class, papers were collected for later grading. To Skinner, "the teacher was violating two fundamental principles: the students were not being told at once whether their work was right or wrong (a corrected paper seen twenty-four hours later could not act as a reinforcer), and they were all moving at the same pace regardless of preparation and ability" (Skinner, 1983, p. 64).

Skinner pondered the problem of how a teacher could deliver reinforcement to 20 or 30 pupils at the right time while still providing them with learning materials that were appropriate to their needs and abilities. Harking back to his laboratory, Skinner compared early experiments where scientists had been forced to watch and record by hand the behaviour of each individual experimental animal with the later, more sophisticated use of mechanized laboratory equipment. Pursuing this notion, Skinner set out to design an instrument that would allow students to know immediately whether their answers were right or wrong (in the absence of teacher feedback) and which would provide material that was appropriate to their level.

Skinner's first primitive teaching machine used an arithmetic problem presented on a card. The student placed a card in the machine and composed a two-digit answer along one side by moving two levers. If the answer was correct, a light appeared in a hole in the card. In a later, more sophisticated model, problems were printed on a pleated tape and appeared one at a time in order. The student moved sliders bearing the numbers 0 to 9 so that the correct figure appeared in a hole in the card. When the holes were filled, a knob was turned. Immediate feedback was provided; if the student was correct, a new problem appeared. If the student was wrong, the knob would not turn and the student had to return the sliders to zero and start again.

Skinner's machine exploited operant conditioning principles, particularly those which demonstrated the importance of immediate contingent reinforcement. The content presented was programed so that the student was guided along in small steps. To further ensure success, behaviour was prompted and then reinforced. Prompts were faded as soon as possible (Skinner, 1983, 1989).

Skinner's work lead to an explosion of interest in programed instruction and the use of teaching machines throughout the 1960s. Although not as popular today, programed instruction remains in the arsenal of educators. Good programed instruction first breaks a complex skill or task down into its component parts, and then asks the student to proceed in small steps, mastering each step before moving on to the next. Steps are designed so that success is highly probable, and progress through the program may be sufficiently reinforcing to ensure a student's continuing work (Skinner, 1973). When errors are made, they are promptly corrected. Properly done, programed instruction should allow any student to master the material in an efficient manner.

### Keller's Personalized System of Instruction

This system of mastery learning was first developed in 1962 by Brazilian and North American psychologists who were establishing a department of psychology at the University of Brasília. Given almost total freedom and dissatisfied with traditional instructional approaches, they applied the principles of operant conditioning and knowledge of programed instruction to their task. Keller (1969) listed the features of the Personalized System of Instruction (PSI) that distinguish it from conventional instruction as follows:

1. Students were allowed to progress at their own pace, with speed being determined by the student's ability and other demands placed on his or her time.

2. Students were required to demonstrate mastery of material contained in each small unit before being allowed to progress to the next unit. This was accomplished by passing mastery tests or completing a relevant experiment. The number of times that students took the test was not held against them; as Keller pointed out in his course outline: "It is better that you get too much

testing than not enough, if your final success in the course is to be assured" (p. 81). Keller (1969) reported that some students were tested 40 or 50 times during a semester without registering a single complaint.

3. Lectures and demonstrations were used as motivational techniques, rather than to provide important information. Students were only allowed to attend lectures if they had demonstrated their readiness to appreciate them. No examinations were based on the lectures and attendance at them was not compulsory.

4. Stress was placed upon written rather than oral communication between the teacher and student.

5. Proctors were used extensively as they allowed for repeated testing, immediate scoring, and supplementary tutoring. When tests were scored, students were given the chance to defend an incorrect answer, or were asked to elaborate further upon correct answers. Finally, the tutors were considered important as they ensured that each student, regardless of the size of the class, received some individual attention, approval, and encouragement.

6. A final examination covering the content of the entire course was given to ensure review and integration of content. The examination consisted primarily of questions that had been previously addressed in the readiness quizzes. Twenty-five to 30 percent of the grade was determined by the final examination, with the remaining percentage based on the number of units completed successfully during the term.

Keller reported the repeated successful use of PSI at various universities, and many other researchers have investigated its use. When comparing the Keller method and traditional college instruction, most studies find that PSI students do better (Block and Burns, 1976), with the average effect size nine percent or one letter grade better for PSI students (Robin, 1976). Perhaps this is because students put in more effort. Born and colleagues (1972) found that students averaged 45.5 hours of study time on materials placed in the library for an introductory psychology course compared to 30.2 hours for students in a conventional course. Students report that they enjoy the features of PSI: self-pacing, individualized tutoring, and the guarantee of specific grades for specific amounts of work (Kulik, Kulik, and Carmichael, 1974; McKeachie and Kulik, 1975; Robin, 1976). However, these comparisons may be related to the often unsatisfactory use of traditional lecture-discussion courses. When PSI was compared to a well-designed lecture course, taught by excellent instructors, both were equally effective (Thompson, 1980).

While Keller's program is certainly one of the best known of the systems of programed instruction, it was rapidly followed by hundreds of different programs, used in kindergarten classes, high schools, colleges and universities, technical schools, and industrial training centres. While the predominance of this approach to education ended during the 1960s, such methods are still widely used in correspondence and business training programs. For classroom use, many of the materials used in programed instruction are self-correcting which is important in reducing failure, for providing practice and repetition, and in increasing attention to tasks. Programs may be linear, wherein a series of structured statements and questions require a response from a student, or branched, wherein an incorrect response means going to easier material or another place in the booklet.

## BEHAVIOURAL PRINCIPLES AND CLASSROOM MANAGEMENT

Ms Estevan, the teacher we meet in Box 11-1, was not having an enjoyable year; in fact, for this teacher, classroom management and behaviour control were so arduous and she met with such little success that she was thinking of leaving the profession of teaching.

### Box 11-1  In the classroom: One teacher's day

Ms Estevan was having another rotten day. Her colleagues tried to smile sympathetically as she dragged herself into the staffroom after the lunch bell, sank into the nearest comfortable chair, and buried her head in her hands. After a period of embarrassed silence, the school busybody just couldn't resist. "What's wrong dear?" asked Mrs. Morrow brightly, as if she hadn't heard the commotion spilling from Ms Estevan's classroom all morning. The rest of the staff averted their eyes—they all knew that this new teacher had been experiencing a great deal of difficulty with her class, but no one but Mrs. Morrow had the nerve to address the situation directly.

While Ms Estevan was terribly embarrassed—she knew that everyone must be aware of her problems with classroom management—frustration and anger prompted her to confess, "I'm just at my wits' end! That Pamela never sits still for longer than 2 seconds. She is always running around the room. And then Bobby gets the class going with his wisecracks—I don't see the humour, but he is always interrupting my lectures with little

jokes and comments that just break up the class. And Glenn—well you know him, and Emilio—and Simon—oh, I just don't know what to do!"

Now that the situation was out in the open, her colleagues were more than eager to help. From every side of the room came suggestions: "Just send them down to the office to see me," offered Ms Pearson, the principal, "I'll straighten them out p.d.q.!" "I know why you're having trouble," piped Mr. Jenson, "Ever since they disallowed the use of the strap, no one can control their classes! A good whack would cure those kids!" "Just take away their recess time," added another teacher. "Make them sit in the hallway," "Give them extra homework—that'll teach 'em!"

As Ms Estevan listened, the number of suggestions grew and grew. Finally, she broke in to the discussion saying, "But I've tried so hard to be nice to my students—I've forced myself to never punish them. Do you really think that I should try that?" "YES!" boomed the staff in chorus.

**Fair-pair rule:**
states that for every behaviour suppressed, the child must be reinforced for one or more alternative positive behaviours.

The scenario illustrates an all too common phenomenon: whenever humans confront inappropriate, annoying, or dangerous behaviours, the tendency is to immediately punish the perpetrator. It may be that the typical effect of punishment—the immediate cessation of the behaviour—negatively reinforces the teacher's or parent's behaviour. Social learning theorists would also suggest that because most adults have been punished in the past, they have learned that yelling, spanking, or assigning extra homework is the appropriate method of coping with undesired behaviors. But if punishment works so well, why do the behaviours return? And why does it make everyone feel so miserable?

Every teacher will encounter aggressive, defiant, disruptive, and other downright annoying behaviours in the classroom. But research on behavioural techniques would suggest that automatically resorting to the use of punishment to deal with these behaviours is not the best choice for teachers. Rather, a range of alternative strategies have been suggested. Strategies should begin with the least intrusive or most positive approaches—modifying the environment—and gradually extend to the use of aversive or unpleasant stimuli. While the use of punishment in the classroom is not ruled out, it should only be implemented after the use of less aversive strategies has failed. In many cases, the research indicates that less aversive strategies have the potential to accomplish the teacher's goal—the reduction or elimination of undesired responses.

We suggest that the best way to approach misbehaviour is not to focus on the act itself, but rather view the situation as the absence of positive behaviours. In other words, when Glenn is always out of his desk, the teacher should look at ways to teach appropriate in-seat behaviour. If Johnny always hits his peers, attention should be paid to teaching him appropriate methods of social interactions. This has been referred to as the **fair-pair rule** (White and Haring, 1980), which states that for every behaviour to be suppressed, the child must be reinforced for one or more alternative positive behaviours.

Every teacher will encounter aggressive, defiant, disruptive, and other downright annoying behaviours in the classroom.

**Applied behaviour analysis:**

the study of the use of behavioural principles in real-life situations.

# Applied behaviour analysis

The application of behavioural approaches specifically to real-life situations in classrooms is known as **applied behaviour analysis**. Behaviourists argue that teachers must take a systematic and scientific approach to student behaviour. This includes assessment or examination of the antecedents and consequences of students' behaviour, the precise definition of the target behaviour, and the careful measurement of the response to be changed. Measuring student behaviour before and after the implementation of a behavioural strategy, such as reinforcement or punishment, allows the effect of that technique to be objectively determined.

Operant conditioning principles describe the relationship between human behaviour and the environmental events that precede (antecedents) and follow (consequences) the behaviour. But in practice, it is often difficult for teachers to identify the relationship between these factors. Even the most experienced behaviour analyst must repeatedly observe a student's behaviour before he or she will be able to begin to see the patterns or relationships between certain events and particular actions.

Examination of this contingency relationships has been referred to as an ABC (antecedent-behaviour-consequence) analysis, and requires the observer to carefully record the social events (for example, teacher requests, task demands, peer comments, praise, and so on) that occur before and after the behaviour under study. In addition, other relevant environmental characteristics, such as the number of people present in the environment, noise level, time of day, and room temperature are also recorded, as they are likely to influence student behaviour. By repeating this process several times, it should be possible to form some hypotheses about the factors that appear to cue the occurrence of the target behaviour as well as those consequences which seem to maintain or reinforce the behaviour. For example, think of Johnny, a grade two student who frequently has temper tantrums in school. Through the ABC analysis, the teacher notices that temper tantrums usually occur when Johnny is asked to practise fine motor skills, such as printing or art work. She further notes that when Johnny has a temper tantrum, he is usually sent to the quiet corner to sit by himself. The teacher could hypothesize that Johnny acts out when he is asked to complete a task that he finds difficult and that his tantrums are reinforced when he is placed in the quiet corner (which terminates the task at hand).

It can be seen that the ABC analysis not only helped the teacher to determine the events that precipitate and maintain Johnny's behaviour but it also suggested an appropriate solution to this problem. That is, the teacher would likely be successful if she modified the antecedents to the temper tantrums (for example, by changing the task so that it better suits Johnny's ability level) as this may avert them. If the teacher instead focused on the consequences of the behaviour, the analysis would indicate that the use of a strategy such as time-out was not an appropriate punishment for Johnny's tantrums.

The ABC analysis helps the teacher make an educated guess about the relationships of a student's behaviour to the events that precede and follow it. Of course, ABC analyses should not only be used to examine negative behaviours but also can help teachers identify the factors that are associated with desirable responses. Describing antecedent conditions and/or effective reinforcers provides teachers with the data they can use to ensure that appropriate behaviour will occur more often.

The testing of hypotheses must be careful and systematic. It is not enough to hope that a strategy is working. Instead, practitioners should obtain measures of a student's behaviour before and after changes are made in the environment. They will then be able to see whether or not changes in the antecedents or consequences have actually influenced the student's behaviour. Most teachers do not have the time (nor is it necessary) to collect such extensive information about all of their students. Data collection is likely to be implemented when teachers use an unpleasant or aversive punisher. It is particularly important in this case, for an aversive intervention should not be continued unless it can be shown to have a positive effect on a student's behaviour.

## Manipulating the antecedents of behaviour

Antecedent events can be thought of as setting the stage for—or cuing—behaviour by informing the student about the consequences that are likely to follow. There are a number of ways in which behaviourists attempt to maintain positive behaviours or eliminate negative behaviours by using techniques which alter the antecedents.

### Prompting and cueing

In the classroom, teachers help students to respond in a particular fashion when certain antecedents are in place. Students learn, for example, to fill in their names on a worksheet in the space marked: NAME:_____ or to read "zebra" when confronted with a flashcard containing the letters z-e-b-r-a. But what of the student who is given the worksheet and does not put his name on it or the student who sees the flashcard, and says "zipper" instead of "zebra"? The teacher might point to the correct spot on the worksheet, or model as desired response: "No, say zebra." These behaviours are referred to as **prompts**, which are used to elicit student behaviour when the normal environmental conditions have failed to produce the desired response.

There are many different kinds of prompts and the use of each will be dependent upon the situation and/or the response to be elicited. Prompts and cues are actually fairly natural and we all use them everyday. The mother of a ten-month-old infant says "shoe" and points to the object; the grade five teacher use a pointer to stress words on the chalkboard; someone even holds up "laughter" and "applause" cards in television studios. When prompts are used in the classroom situation, however, the teacher's goal should be to fade the prompt gradually so that the student does not become dependent upon it.

**Verbal prompts** include the use of rules, instructions, and hints. They are easy to use with individuals or groups of students, but are dependent upon the students' ability to comprehend the message given. When using rules, the student is prompted to remember a specific rule that will guide behaviour. For example, the teacher might say, "Spell receive. Remember, i before e, except after c." If the student is learning a series of behaviours that follow the same rule, stating rules can be an effective prompt, but they must be brief, easily understood, and accurate.

**Physical prompts:**
cues to help students perform tasks that can be manually guided when the normal environmental conditions have failed to produce the desired response.

Instructions can be used to prompt students when they do not appear to know "what to do next." When the bell rings for recess, for example, teacher may prompt the students who do not get ready for departure by saying, "Put your books away and sit quietly." Similarly, a child who cannot solve a worksheet problem may be given detailed instructions concerning the steps to be followed. Prompts may take the form of hints or indirect statements which are less elaborate and directive than rules or instructions. If a child cannot read the word "hockey," for example, the teacher might say, "What game do you play on an ice-rink?" in an attempt to garner the correct response.

**Physical prompts** are often used to help students perform tasks that can be manually guided, such as handwriting, holding a hockey stick, or washing hands. As little pressure as possible should be used to assist the child and the amount of guidance should be faded as quickly as possible. Moreover, physical prompts should never be used with students unless their full cooperation can be obtained: using physical guidance to force a student to complete a given activity

Pictorial prompts help young children decode words.

**Visual prompts:**
cues presented in pictorial or written form to elicit student behaviour when the normal environmental conditions have failed to produce the desired response.

**Model prompts:**
demonstrations of behaviour that show the student what to do after the normal environmental conditions have failed to produce the desired response.

creates a very unpleasant situation for the teacher and student and is unlikely to produce much learning.

Visual prompts can be either presented in pictorial or written form. As with verbal prompts, they should be clear and easily understood by the students. Examples of *pictorial prompts* are often found in books for beginning readers, where the pictures are intended to help students decode words. Similarly, preschool teachers often help students find their coat-hooks by placing the child's picture nearby. *Written prompts* are seen when rules for student conduct are posted to remind students of behavioural expectations. Model prompts are used when someone shows the student what to do. Anyone can be used as a model—the teacher, a classmate, or a special visitor to the class.

## SOCIAL REINFORCERS

While it seems reasonable that teachers should reinforce appropriate behaviour, research suggests that positive attention is not often used. Unfortunately, it appears that teachers are much more apt to criticize or reprimand inappropriate actions while failing to acknowledge desirable behaviour.

Reinforcement is one of the most powerful tools in the teacher's repertoire but often is not used in a systematic or deliberate fashion. Teachers sometimes assume that the use of positive reinforcement will involve the introduction of something new or artificial into the classroom. However, a closer examination of the school environment reveals many natural reinforcers that strengthen or maintain the appropriate behaviour of many—but not all—students.

Social reinforcers are easy to use in the classroom for they can be given quickly and efficiently; unlike activities or food treats, praise or feedback do not unduly interrupt the student's ongoing behaviour (Kazdin, 1989). As long as the teacher varies the type and amount of social reinforcement given, the student is unlikely to become satiated. Naturally, the type of social reinforcer chosen must be carefully determined for each individual student.

Teacher approval is one type of reinforcer that has been repeatedly shown to have a powerful effect on student behaviour. Other techniques commonly used in school, such as appointing a "student of the day," handing out gold stars, or publicly posting student work are all intended to encourage future excellent work. Similarly, special privileges or activities are often used to reinforce behaviour; younger students will often work very hard to earn the right to clean the blackboard, hand out worksheets and so on, while older students are more likely to be reinforced by release from homework or the opportunity to play computer games.

Grades are another natural reinforcer used in most schools. However, the delay between the behaviour and the delivery of grades leads some to suggest that grades have a relatively weak or inconsistent effect on student behaviour. Aspects of the grading process, such as use and consequences are further discussed in Chapter 14.

But most teachers will find that the reinforcers traditionally used in schools have little or no effect on the behaviour of some students. So if teachers wish to encourage maximum learning and appropriate behaviour from all students, they must first identify the appropriate reinforcers for each. How does the teacher find out about the preferences of the 30 or so students in the classroom? While there are many ways that the teacher can accomplish this, perhaps the simplest is to ask the students. This can be accomplished through individual interviews or, more efficiently, by using a group-administered questionnaire such as that presented in Figure 11-1.

**Figure 11-1**
Reinforcement
questionnaire

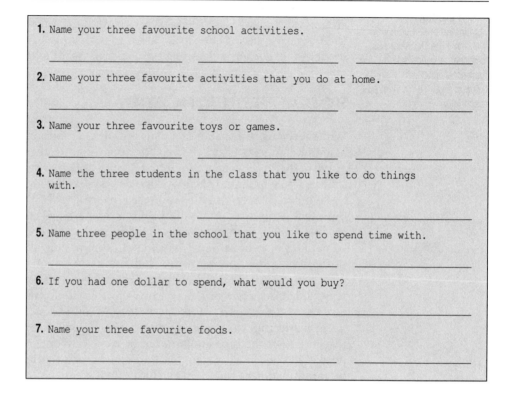

1. Name your three favourite school activities.

2. Name your three favourite activities that you do at home.

3. Name your three favourite toys or games.

4. Name the three students in the class that you like to do things with.

5. Name three people in the school that you like to spend time with.

6. If you had one dollar to spend, what would you buy?

7. Name your three favourite foods.

Some teachers will find it necessary to develop their own instrument that suits the ages, interests, and social backgrounds of their students. When choosing possible items for the questionnaire, as many items as possible should be natural reinforcers present in the classroom or school; these can be presented more readily and cheaply. Of course, teachers should include only those reinforcers which they are willing or able to deliver. If school regulations prohibit early dismissal or if the principal is highly critical of the use of edible reinforcers, such items would not be listed on the questionnaire.

Alternatively, the teacher could construct a list of available reinforcers and have the students rate the reinforcers in order of preference, and add some additional items that they might particularly prefer. Of course, whenever a student suggests an item, the teacher maintains ultimate decision-making power. The teacher might veto such possibilities as "kissing Cecilia," "having daily pizza parties," or "skipping school for a month."

**Premack principle:**
states that activities which occur at a high frequency (more preferred activities) can be used to reinforce the completion of lower-frequency (less preferred) activities.

**Praise:**
verbal expression of approval used to reinforce behaviour.

**Feedback:**
information about some aspect of a person's performance.

Teachers can also assess student preferences by observing their free-time activities and by remembering the **Premack principle**: that is, by watching for high-frequency or preferred activities which can be used to reinforce low-frequency or less preferred activities. If a student often plays basketball or computer games during her free time, such an activity could be used to reinforce low-frequency activities, such as completing mathematics seatwork or creative writing.

Everyone likes to receive positive verbal and nonverbal messages about himself or herself: teachers respond well when told that they are doing a good job; teenaged boys preen (unobtrusively) when girls notice them walk by; and little children beam when they're told that their art work is pretty. While we all recognize praise and positive feedback when we see (or hear) it, praise and feedback are not the same thing; praise implies a congratulatory message while feedback includes some commentary. Nor are they really easy to define. **Praise** is generally understood to be a verbal expression of approval, such as "Great!" "Good stuff!" "Fabulous!" **Feedback** provides information about some aspect of a person's performance (Kazdin, 1989).

The effectiveness of statements of praise are enhanced when coupled with feedback about the performance, and vice versa. In fact, although selective praise is useful, too much praise can actually interfere with student learning. In general, feedback is more effective and, if praise is used, the timing and quality of the praise is more important than its frequency (Brophy, 1981).

Teachers should not only approve of a student's performance but they should provide specific information about the aspect of the response that is being praised by saying, for example, not only, "What a beautiful picture!" but also, "I like the way you used so many different colours." In other situations, praise and feedback will be used to correct performance: "Good start, you got three of the problems right. Now go back and complete the others in the same way," or, "A nice try. You printed five letters correctly. Now try to make these ones look the same."

It would seem that praise and feedback are conducive to a warm, supportive classroom environment and that social reinforcers are very powerful tools for teachers. Yet some research suggests that such social reinforcement is not often used in regular classrooms. M.A. White (1975), for example, reported results from a series of studies which examined 104 teachers in grade levels from one to 12. While pupils in the first and second grades received relatively high rates of praise (1.3 messages of approval per minute), the rate declined sharply in subsequent grades. The decline stabilized in the high school grades, where teachers gave about one message of approval every five to ten minutes. When White compared rates of approval and disapproval, it was found that students in grades one and two received more approval than disapproval; in later grades, the rate of teacher disapproval was higher. Across all grades, teachers usually praised students for academic performance, while praise for classroom deportment was virtually nonexistent. Another study (Thomas et al., 1978) made similar findings. After studying rates of approval and disapproval for children's on-task and off-task behaviour, the researchers reported that teachers disapproved of student behaviour three times more often than they gave positive feedback about performance.

When Strain and his colleagues (1983) examined 19 kindergarten to grade two classrooms, they not only found that teachers used more negative than positive feedback with their students, but also that the general rate of feedback (both positive and negative) was relatively low. For example, when children obeyed a teacher request, there was only a ten percent chance that they would be recognized or rewarded. It appeared that students got relatively little positive attention when they performed appropriately in class. The authors also showed that a good proportion of the positive feedback was misdirected: some students were reinforced even though they were not behaving properly. This usually occurred when the teacher praised the group, not noticing that a particular child was still engaged in inappropriate behaviour. This was frequently noted for students who had been initially rated in the study as "not having made a good adjustment in school." Those children were much more likely to receive positive feedback after they had failed to comply with the teacher's request. Thus, the students who were most in need of accurate feedback from the teacher—those who had not yet learned to function effectively in the school environment—actually received consequences that were likely to increase their non-compliant behaviour.

Teachers who fail to use praise and feedback consistently and appropriately are losing a potentially powerful teaching tool. To use social reinforcers more effectively, the following guidelines should be considered:

1. Praise should be given as soon as possible after the student has behaved appropriately (O'Leary and O'Leary, 1977). To avoid the problem revealed by Strain et al. (1983), teachers should not give general reinforcement to the group unless all members have complied with the request or command.

2. Feedback is much better than praise alone, and comments should be specific; for example, "Great, Simon! You picked up all the books and put them back neatly in the shelf"—rather than, "Great work, Simon!" (O'Leary and O'Leary, 1977).

3. Feedback about performance is particularly important when students are striving to meet a goal. When students are trying to master a complex academic task, for example, feedback can be very useful to let them know how they're doing (Kazdin, 1989).

4. Comments should be sincere, spontaneous, and appropriate for the situation. As well, teachers should avoid the use of stock phrases. Expressions should be as imaginative and novel as possible in order to catch student attention. Further, the remarks used should be varied: after being told that they were doing "great work" for the fiftieth time, students are unlikely to even pay attention, much less change their behaviour (O'Leary and O'Leary, 1977).

5. Nonverbal reinforcers such as smiles, winks, and pats on the back can be effective on their own and have been shown to enhance the effectiveness of verbal messages (Kazdin and Klock, 1973).

Is it really possible for teachers to maintain appropriate classroom behaviour and/or academic productivity in their classrooms by using only social reinforcers? In a stringent test of the effectiveness of praise, one study (Pfiffner, Rosen, and O'Leary, 1985) investigated the use of an "all positive" approach to

**Shaping:**
teaching new skills or behaviours by reinforcing learners for approaching the desired final behaviour.

classroom management with students with behaviour disorders. When praise alone was delivered for appropriate on-task behaviour and academic work, the students' level of performance in both areas declined below the levels seen when both praise and negative consequences (reprimands, time-out, and withdrawal of privileges) were used. However, when a program of "enhanced positive consequences" (praise and more powerful secondary reinforcers such as special activities) was introduced, the students' performance equaled that seen when both positive and negative consequences were employed.

While such results are not definitive, they do point to the potential of using alternative secondary reinforcers to supplement the use of praise and feedback in the classroom setting. This would be particularly important if the teacher finds that the systematic use of social reinforcers alone does not produce acceptable levels of student behaviour. But rather than automatically resorting to the use of punishment, a program which provides more powerful secondary reinforcers could be implemented.

## DEVELOPING NEW POSITIVE BEHAVIOURS

When a student has already learned a behaviour, such as appropriate in-seat behaviour, writing a term paper, or solving a math problem, it is possible to use reinforcement or prompting procedures to strengthen or maintain the desired behaviour. But teachers are most often concerned with teaching new behaviours to their students, and certainly, if a skill or behaviour is new to the student, no amount of reinforcement or prompting is likely to produce the desired response. Researchers in behavioural learning thus have delineated a number of strategies that can be used to teach new behaviours to students.

### Shaping

Reinforcing small improvements in performance in order to lead eventually to the desired terminal behaviour is known as shaping. In other words, the student's current level of performance is used as a starting point and closer and closer approximations of the desired goal are reinforced. When a student is not capable of performing the desired behaviour, when the behaviour does not occur for a sufficient length of time, or when the required level of accuracy has not been obtained, shaping techniques can be used to guide the student.

Four main steps are involved in shaping a behaviour—choosing a goal, finding out where the students are in relation to the goal, devising a series of steps, and providing feedback (Slavin, 1988). The shaping method used will depend upon the type of behaviour to be modified. When teaching complex skills such as writing a term paper, solving an algebraic equation, or baking a cake, the target behaviour is broken down into its component parts, or sub-skills. The student is then systematically reinforced for mastery of each subsequent sub-skill. When skills such as solving math problems are taught, for example, the teacher may initially reinforce the student for completing certain steps in the sequence, then require additional steps to be completed, and so on, until the student is correctly solving the entire problem.

**Differential reinforcement of incompatible behaviour (DRI):** reinforcement of positive behaviours that are incompatible with the behaviour targeted for reduction.

As can be seen in Figure 11-2, shaping can be conceptualized as a staircase in which each ascending step requires behaviour that is an ever closer approximation to the desired terminal behaviour. Before implementing a shaping program, the teacher must have established the student's current level of performance and described the behavioural goal. Next is the more difficult process of delineating the steps that will lead the student to the goal. How are the "sizes" of the step determined? After all, if the steps are too small, student learning will be unnecessarily slow. Yet if the steps are too large, the student may find it impossible to reach the criterion and fail to receive reinforcement.

**Figure 11-2**
Shaping

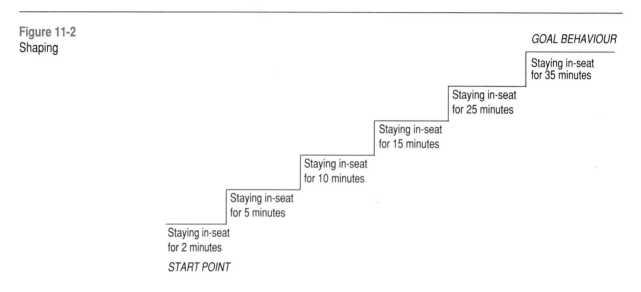

GOAL BEHAVIOUR

Staying in-seat for 35 minutes

Staying in-seat for 25 minutes

Staying in-seat for 15 minutes

Staying in-seat for 10 minutes

Staying in-seat for 5 minutes

Staying in-seat for 2 minutes

START POINT

There are no sure-fire guidelines which can guide a teacher's decision-making during a shaping program. The best decisions will be made when the teacher pays careful attention to the student's current level of performance and sets realistic goals. The goal should be a challenge but it should also be possible for the student to receive frequent reinforcement. Once the goal has been set and the program implemented, the teacher continues to monitor student progress in order to determine if the student is obtaining sufficient reinforcement. If reinforcement is routinely obtained by the student (indicating that the behaviour is well-established at that level), the performance standard should be increased (Bullock, 1982). Increasing standards is particularly important in learning skills in many subjects such as music, physical education, and typing (Gibson and Chandler, 1988). If the student appears to be having difficulty meeting the set criterion, the teacher may decide to ease back slightly.

## Differential reinforcement

One way to put an end to misbehaviour is to strengthen or reinforce other actions that interfere with the student's ability to perform the undesired response. **Differential reinforcement of incompatible behaviour (DRI)** occurs

**Differential reinforce-
ment of alternative
behaviour (DRA):**
reinforcement of alternative
positive behaviours to discourage a specific undesired
behaviour.

when behaviors that are incompatible with the behaviour targeted for reduction are reinforced (Dietz and Repp, 1983). Incompatible responses are those which effectively prevent the student from simultaneously engaging in the targeted response. For example, it is impossible for a student to be both in his desk and wandering around the room, or both reading a comic book and completing math problems. If the rate of the desired response is increased, it will prevent the appearance of the undesired behaviour and eventually replace it.

Differential reinforcement of alternative behaviour (DRA) is a very similar strategy except that the behaviour to be reinforced is an alternative behaviour; that is to say, it does not prevent the undesired behaviour from occurring (Dietz and Repp, 1983). For example, think of Jerry, who hits his friends on the arm when he wants their attention. He could be reinforced for saying "Hello, Sally," a more appropriate social behaviour. While this response does not stop him from hitting his friends, he has the opportunity to be reinforced for the use of a more appropriate behaviour.

The incompatible or alternative behaviour selected for reinforcement should be one that the student performs readily and often so the teacher does not have to spend time teaching the alternative response. As well, when selecting the alternative behaviours, the purpose or function of the original behaviour should be considered. Reinforcing sitting quietly as an alternative to calling-out behaviour, for example, does not teach the student an appropriate method of achieving teacher attention. But when alternative behaviours are useful to the student, they are more likely to be maintained by natural reinforcers in the environment once the program is withdrawn (Dietz and Repp, 1983).

## Token economies

The token economy is perhaps the most widely researched and successful method of maintaining control and producing enhanced performance. While their positive effects are well documented, token economy systems are relatively simple. Essentially, the teacher targets behaviours to be reinforced and tokens are awarded to students when they demonstrate a particular desired behaviour. Earned tokens can be traded in for a variety of primary or secondary reinforcers. When tokens are used to bring about appropriate behaviours, it has often been found that, as academic behaviour increases, students simultaneously reduce their levels of disruptive behaviour even though no specific consequences have been directed toward the inappropriate behaviours (Robinson, Newby, and Ganzell, 1981).

Research shows that tokens can be very powerful reinforcers, even more effective than other secondary reinforcers such as praise (Kazdin and Polster, 1973; O'Leary et al., 1969). While time and effort is required to implement a token economy, teachers generally find that using the system does not unduly interfere with ongoing class activities. Tokens can easily be administered immediately and usually can be delivered without interrupting the student's ongoing performance and/or disturbing other students. Because tokens can be exchanged for a variety of back-up reinforcers, a single reinforcer can be used while still accommodating individual reinforcer preferences. As well, a good variety of back-up reinforcers will reduce the possibility of satiation (Kazdin,

1989). Moreover, because the use of a token system is relatively convenient and therefore readily transferred to other settings and individuals, it is often possible to persuade parents and/or other teachers to adopt its use across settings (Cooper, Heron, and Heward, 1987).

To initiate a token economy, some general steps should be followed:

**Define the behaviours to be targeted, keeping the number at a minimum**   In the initial stages of a token program, it is best to target one or two behaviours that every student can accomplish at some level, such as completing work assignments. As the program continues and teachers and students gain familiarity with its use, additional target behaviours can be added.

**State the targets in positive terms**   "Students will complete their assigned work" is better than "No goofing off." Responses should also be described so that everyone in the classroom can agree whether or not the behaviour occurred. For example, it is often difficult to determine whether children are "on-task"; students gazing off into space may not be daydreaming, but rather thinking about their work. Failure to deliver a token is therefore likely to produce great protests. And, while targeting broad goals such as "responsibility," "cooperation," or "friendliness" are likely to create difficulties, this does not mean that such traits are not admirable targets for a token system. However, they should be described in observable terms; responsibility might be defined as "bringing completed homework to school every day," or "putting books away neatly"; cooperation as "helping classmates with their work," and friendliness as "saying only nice things to classmates."

**Establish the criterion used to judge the adequacy of performance**  For example, the time limit for performance, the level of accuracy required, and the number and types of errors acceptable can be used. In most cases, individualized goals for particular students will be established.

**Be aware that tokens can take many forms**   Objects such as poker chips, play money, and buttons; or symbols such as check marks, holes punched in a card and happy face stamps are common examples. Figure 11-3 contains some examples of cards that can be used to monitor token delivery; teachers can design their own or consult sources such as Kaplan, Kohfeldt, and Sturla (1974).

Sometimes tokens can serve a "double" purpose: when play money was used with younger students, for example, it was found that it helped students learn to add and subtract (Bacon, 1990). Similarly, older students could use a chequebook system in which earned points are stored in their accounts. When they wish to purchase reinforcers, they write a cheque for the correct amount (Carter, 1988 cited in Bacon, 1990).

Tokens should be inexpensive, portable, and durable. To prevent cheating, tokens can be marked in some fashion to ensure authenticity or, if checkmarks are used, the teacher may wish to use an unusual pen or vary the writing instrument used in some systematic fashion. Record cards can be securely taped to the students' desks or pinned to their shirts. In one study (Robinson, Newby, and Ganzell, 1981), disks of metal-edged cardboard were used as tokens and students strung them together on bracelets.

**Figure 11-3**
Token cards

Mark an "X" in each section when you _____.

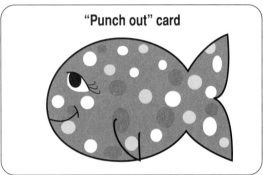

"Punch out" card

**Ensure that tokens have little or no inherent reinforcing value**
They should attain their value only through exchange for primary or secondary reinforcers. Depending upon the age and ability level of the students, the array of reinforcers will probably represent all or most of the following categories of reinforcers: edible reinforcers (juice, candy, raisins); tangibles (pencils, erasers, crayons, small toys); activities (going to the story corner, using the computer, free reading); and privileges (handing out textbooks, erasing the board). Selecting as many back-up reinforcers from the latter two categories as possible will facilitate the later withdrawal of the program as these activities are usually present in the natural classroom setting.

When the system is presented to the class, the teacher should be prepared to answer the following questions (Alberto and Troutman, 1986):

- "What do we have to do to earn the tokens?" Target behaviours should be described clearly to the students, along with the criteria for successful performance. If students are involved in establishing the program and/or identifying target behaviours, discussion should continue until very precise definitions have been established. It should be noted that the success of a token program can be enhanced by involving students in the development as well as the implementation of the program (Stahl and Leitenberg, 1976). It is best to post a written record of the target behaviours along with expected standards of performance so students can review them as needed. A brief daily review of the expected behaviours can increase the effectiveness of the token economy. Rosenshine (1986) found that the reduction in disruptive talking was greater when the rules were briefly reviewed each day.

- "What can we buy with our tokens?" Many teachers construct attractive displays of the selection of back-up reinforcers, including the items or pictures of what is available.

- "What does everything cost?" In the early stages of the token program, it is recommended that at least some items are priced relatively cheaply so that students have an early opportunity to experience success. Student effort should be proportionate to the reward.

- "When can we go shopping?" Token trading times should be regularly scheduled. In the initial stages of the program, particularly for young children or children with learning difficulties, frequent "shopping times" should be allowed so students will experience success. As time goes on, the number of exchange periods can be gradually reduced.

Rules that will govern exchanges should be clearly outlined to the students. To avoid unruly lineups, battles over items and/or mass confusion, students could be required to use order blanks to check off or write in items to be purchased. Those items are placed in a bag with the order form stapled to the top and returned to the buyer (Sulzer-Azaroff and Mayer, 1977). Teachers can also reduce their workload by assigning students to be "clerks," "baggers," or "accountants" during these exchange periods. These roles are often highly valued by students, so that they included as one of the duties which are purchased with tokens.

Token systems can be used with an entire class or a smaller group of students within the class.

Once the token economy has started, teachers must deliver tokens immediately following the occurrence of the appropriate behaviour. If tokens are not delivered in a timely and accurate fashion it is unlikely that the program will have the desired effect. Token presentation should not foster a highly competitive classroom environment; competitiveness can be reduced by keeping token amounts private (Bacon, 1990). Further, a student's failure to obtain a token should never be treated as a punishment. Failure to earn a token should be responded to with disappointment and a message of encouragement to try harder. Comments such as "I told you so" or "I warned you this would happen" negate the central purpose of using positive reinforcement to create a positive classroom climate free of aversive aspects (Bacon, 1990).

From the earliest descriptions of the use of token economies, researchers have reported cases in which some individuals do not respond to the system (Kazdin, 1982). However, further examination typically revealed that the problem lay with the implementation of the program, rather than with the individual. If a student's behaviour does not change as expected, the teacher should first examine the response requirements that have been established. If the student is not capable of meeting the standard, he or she may simply "give-up." If this problem can be ruled out, the range of back-up reinforcers should be re-examined. In most cases, it has been found that after changes in the back-up reinforcers, previously

The teacher's ultimate goal should be to maintain appropriate behaviour with naturally occurring reinforcers.

uncooperative or uninterested individuals have readily responded to the program (Kazdin, 1982).

After a time, the token program should be reviewed by the teacher. Criteria for behaviours may be modified, behaviours added or deleted, prices of items may be increased or reduced, and back-up reinforcers added or deleted from the selection. Better cooperation will be obtained if changes are explained to the students.

Token programs often work so well that teachers are tempted to keep them in place indefinitely. However, the teacher's ultimate goal should be to maintain appropriate student behaviour with naturally occurring reinforcers. This will not happen without careful planning—thus, even as the token program is begun, plans should be made for its eventual withdrawal.

A variety of strategies can be used to systematically withdraw a token program once desired levels of behaviour have been maintained (Cooper, Heron, and Heward, 1987; Kazdin, 1982). First, during all stages of the token program, delivery of the token should be paired with descriptive praise and feedback. The goal is that praise will eventually maintain the behaviour once the tokens have been withdrawn. Second, the stock of back-up items should be gradually modified to contain more and more activities and events that are found in the natural classroom environment so that student behaviour will be maintained by natural reinforcers which can be awarded after the token system has been fully withdrawn. Third, the performance standards should be made more stringent over time. For example, if the student initially received a token for completing ten math problems, the requirement could be raised to 20 problems, then 30 problems, and so on. Thinning the schedule of reinforcement systematically will eventually allow the removal of the reinforcer without negatively affecting the rate or level of behaviour. Similarly, the length of time that the program is in effect during the day can be systematically reduced: for example, tokens may first be delivered all day, then only during two thirds of the class periods, one third of the class periods, and so on. Students should be informed that the behavioural expectations are the same whether or not tokens are being administered. If fading is not accomplished too rapidly, the desired behaviour levels should be maintained across the day.

## Response cost

Token systems are often used in connection with response-cost programs in which earned tokens are forfeited as a consequence of inappropriate behaviours. Response-cost programs require the withdrawl of a reinforcer when the undesired behaviour occurs, with the intention of reducing the probability that the behaviour will recur in the future (Kazdin, 1972). Reinforcers are actually taken away, rather than simply withheld. Of course, the student must first have access to some type of reinforcer before they can be taken away. This can be accomplished by giving the student "free" tokens, or those which do not have to be earned. For example, a student may receive ten markers at the beginning of a class, and the teacher takes away one marker for each incident of inappropriate behaviour. The student is either praised for having tokens remaining at the end of class (Salend and Kovalich, 1981), or allowed to exchange the tokens for other back-up reinforcers (Kazdin, 1989). "Free token" response-cost programs have been used successfully to modify stuttering during speech therapy (Salend and Andress, 1984), reduce inappropriate behaviour in special education settings (Axelrod, 1973), and in regular class settings (Salend and Henry, 1981).

When properly administered, a response-cost program will produce a rapid to moderate decrease in the levels of performance (Cooper, Heron, and Heward, 1987), and are generally convenient and easy to implement in regular classroom settings. The strategy gives the teacher a low-key method that can be used to deal with inappropriate behaviour; once the program is established, it is not necessary to frequently reprimand or directly confront a misbehaving student. Instead, the simple removal of the token indicates the teacher's disapproval of the behaviour. Disputes or protests from students upon the removal of the token can be diminished if the rules of the program are clearly specified and the contingencies consistently applied. This method yields response cost gives fewer negative side effects such as aggression, avoidance, or escape than are typically seen with other punishment procedures (Kazdin, 1972). It is generally considered to be a socially acceptable form of punishment; indeed, response-cost programs are widely used in our society. Dangerous drivers, fore example, may have their licences suspended.

To implement a response-cost program, the following procedures are used:

1. As with any behaviour change program, the behaviours targeted must be carefully defined in order to minimize disagreements about the occurrence or lack of occurrence of the behaviour.

**Contingency contract:** a permanent record of the reinforcement, punishment and behavioural standards which are intended to guide a student's behaviour.

2. Regardless of the variation used, the pool of reinforcers possessed by the student must be related to the typical rate of the behaviours. If the baseline or pretreatment level of behaviour is high, the student must have access to a correspondingly large number of reinforcers. The initial rate of behaviour should be determined through repeated observations of the student's behaviour. If, for example, the student typically talks out of turn 30 times during an average class, he or she must have 35 or 40 reinforcers available (Walker, 1983) for removal.

3. The magnitude of the fines or number of reinforcers which are to be taken away immediately after the performance of the undesired behaviour must be carefully considered. The research in this area has been inconsistent: while some researchers use severe fines (Burchard and Barrera, 1972), others have obtained good results using smaller fines (Siegel, Lenske, and Broen, 1969). In general, fines should be proportional to the seriousness of the behaviour. Extracting very large fines can be counter-productive. For example, if a student finds that tokens attained through an entire day's work are lost as the result of a single incident, he or she is less likely to be motivated to earn tokens (Alberto and Troutman, 1986).

4. When a student demonstrates an inappropriate behaviour, the fines should be levied immediately. Also, if a student is likely to become aggressive or highly disruptive when tokens are withdrawn, the teacher should maintain control of the reinforcers. Rather than using objects that must be taken away from the student, teachers may keep in their possession a card on which points are accumulated and/or withdrawn. While students should be unobtrusively signaled when their behaviour has warranted the withdrawal of a token, this action should be taken without interrupting ongoing activities and/or providing potentially reinforcing attention.

Most research attention has been paid to teacher-managed response-cost programs. However, Salend and Allen (1985) report that externally managed and self-managed programs were equally successful in reducing inappropriate behaviour. In self-managed programs, students are usually given "free" tokens and monitor their own behaviour by removing a token after each occurrence of the undesired response. Salend, Tintle, and Balber (1988) used a self-managed response-cost system to increase on-task behaviour and academic performance in an fourth grade student with behavioural problems and a sixth grade student with learning disabilities in a mainstreamed setting. Academic behaviour showed a simultaneous improvement, even though it was not directly targeted. Teachers overwhelmingly preferred the self-managed program and indicated that they would continue to use it after the termination of the research project.

## Contingency contracts

A contingency contract provides a permanent, written record of the expectations for behaviour and the reinforcing and/or punishing contingencies that will be delivered. It may be consulted at any time by the parties involved (Alberto and Troutman, 1986). An "if...then" arrangement is specified: if the student demonstrates the desired behaviour (or fails to demonstrate the behaviour), then certain consequences will follow (Homme et al., 1970). By making all contingencies explicit, the student is given specific rules or instructions about how he or she is to behave. Although rules alone may not produce long-lasting changes in behaviour, they do seem to increase the effectiveness of reinforcement (Kazdin, 1989). As well, teachers will find that use of a contract allows them to individualize contingencies for specific students within the classroom (Kelley and Stokes, 1982).

Contingency contracts have been used for a variety of behaviours and academic problems. These include reducing levels of disruptive behaviours (White-Blackburn, Semb, and Semb, 1977); increasing academic productivity and accuracy (Kelley and Stokes, 1982; White-Blackburn, Semb, and Semb, 1977); school attendance (MacDonald, Gallimore, and MacDonald, 1970); appropriate social interactions (Arwood, Williams, and Long, 1974); and improving personal hygiene and grooming (Allen and Kramer, 1990).

Because of the work involved in their development and implementation, contracts are usually used with individuals or small groups of students. A teacher rarely uses a contingency contract unless that student is confronting significant academic or social difficulties in school. Because academic goals usually require the student to complete work independently, contracts are best used with problems of motivation rather than as a method of overcoming academic deficiencies (Cantrell et al., 1969). Parents must be told about the problem and the strategy that the teacher intends to use. When appropriate, the teacher may wish to encourage parents to become active partners in the contract so as to give parents the opportunity to become involved in a positive fashion with a child who is experiencing problems.

---

**Figure 11-4**
**Contingency contract**

| | |
|---|---|
| Student Name: | Liam | Start Date: Sept. 29 |

Review Date: Oct 15        Termination Date: Dec. 1

Behaviour Target: Liam will complete his math assignment accurately every night.

Criterion: (how well, how often): To receive a point each day, Liam must complete the homework assignment with no more than two errors and the assignment must be ready to be handed in at the beginning of class.

Recording system: Mr. Smith (math teacher) will check Liam's homework every day, and the completed sheets will be placed in a folder. A note listing points earned will be sent home each Friday to Liam's parents and they will be responsible for the delivery of the rewards.

Reward: If Liam completes his homework as specified each day, he will earn one point. Points can be traded in for the following privileges:

3 points: One extra hour of television on the weekend

5 points: Picking his favourite Sunday night dinner.

10 points: Using the family car for five hours on a week-end night.

15 points: Ordering his favourite pizza for a family dinner.

Penalties: If the homework is not completed as specified, Liam will be penalized 2 points.

Signed:

_____     _____     _____
Student                Teacher                Parent

---

**Dependent group-oriented contingency system:**

system in which all members of a group get a positive reinforcer only if the performance of one student or a small subset of the group reaches the desired criterion.

A contingency contract is not an opportunity for teachers or parents to arbitrarily impose their standards upon the student. Rather, contracts should be the result of fair negotiation between the adults and students (Homme et al., 1970). If everyone is to conform to the contract, it should be clear, complete and fair. When younger students, or students with learning problems are involved, they should be asked to restate the terms of the contract in his or her own words before signing. If any misunderstandings become apparent, the contract should be rewritten (Alberto and Troutman, 1986). Finally, contracts should be as short and simple as possible (Cantrell et al., 1969). See Figure 11-4 for an example of a completed contract.

## Group-oriented contingencies

In all of the reinforcement techniques discussed so far, the behaviour of the individual student determines what consequences are received. However, in group-oriented contingencies, the behaviour of one or more students in a group directly affects the consequences obtained by others in the group. A group-oriented contingency uses the influence of the peer group to foster appropriate behaviour and decrease misbehaviour among the members of the group. Group systems, of which there are many different variations (Litlow and Pumroy, 1975), have several advantages over more traditional methods of managing student behaviour. Not only are they much easier to manage within the regular classroom but they can be as effective as individual contingencies in changing student behaviour (Axelrod, 1973; Darch and Thorpe, 1977). Further, group-oriented strategies have the potential to foster group cohesiveness and cooperation among classmates, as well as teaching responsibility and enlisting the support of the entire class in solving classroom management problems (Salend, 1987). The social status of some students may be enhanced through the use of group-oriented contingencies and may foster cooperative peer interactions (McCarty et al., 1977).

In the dependent group-oriented contingency system, members of the group get a positive reinforcer only if the performance of one individual student or a smaller subset of the group reaches the desired criterion. To illustrate this method, consider the classroom in which the teacher, Ms Singh, finds that three students rarely finish their mathematics seatwork during class even though the students have the skills necessary to accomplish the task. Ms Singh could establish a dependent group-oriented contingency that states that if the students complete their mathematics seatwork correctly during the class period, the entire class will receive ten minutes of free time at the end of the day. This type of contingency generally works best when the behaviour of the larger group is better than that of the individual or small group targeted (Hayes, 1976).

This method can be also very useful if the teacher finds that an undesired behaviour is reinforced by peer approval or attention (Salend, 1987). For example, if Myra makes inappropriate comments in class which amuse her peers, the program might state that all students will get ten minutes of free time if Myra refrains from that behaviour for an entire class. Assuming that the students desire the free time, it will be in their best interest to ignore Myra's antics or even help her stay on task.

**Interdependent group-oriented contingency system:** system in which all members of the group must meet the desired criterion before any member can receive reinforcement.

**Time out from positive reinforcement (time-out):** the withdrawal of access to reinforcers for a specified period of time contingent on appropriate behaviour.

Before implementing a dependent group-oriented contingency, the teacher should first meet with the individual or small group to describe the behaviour to be targeted and the goals set. Students must understand that when they reach the goal, the entire class will get a reinforcer. The student(s) might even suggest the reinforcer to be delivered to the entire class. The whole class is then informed of the program, including the goals which have been set for the student and the reinforcers to be delivered. Classmates may also give suggestions about how they can help the smaller group or individual student meet the goal (Kerr and Nelson, 1989).

Whenever an individual or small group of students has the opportunity to earn reinforcers for their peers, there is the potential for positive social interaction. But this will not happen automatically, so the teacher must carefully structure the situation (Salend, 1987). In particular, the teacher must ensure that the student is able to meet the performance standard. If it is unreasonably high, the student isn't likely to earn the reinforcer and the anticipated peer support could turn into adverse pressure or outright bullying (Kerr and Nelson, 1989). However, the research is unclear on the occurrence of negative peer interactions; some studies report that students have been harassed or threatened by their peers (e.g., Axelrod, 1973), while others have noted the absence of any negative interactions (e.g., Fishbein and Wasik, 1981).

The interdependent group-oriented contingency system is most often used when a certain behaviour problem is common among several students in a class (Hayes, 1976). All members of the group must meet the criterion before any member of the group can earn reinforcement. For example, if the teacher has a difficult time settling her class down after recess, she might divide the classroom into groups and announce that all students in the group must be in their seats and ready to work when the bell rings. If all are ready, they will earn five minutes of free time. If any one member of the group did not meet this standard, none of the students in the group would be allowed the reinforcer.

A commonly used variation of the interdependent group-oriented contingency is the group response-cost system. The entire class is first given a number of "free tokens" and after the rules or behaviour standards have been carefully explained, the teacher simply removes a token each time a class member demonstrates one of the undesired behaviours. If any tokens remain at the end of the predetermined time period, the reinforcer (a class party, free time, game time) is given to the entire class (Salend and Kovalich, 1981). As the group becomes more successful, the number of free tokens should be gradually decreased. This system can be adapted to allow students within the group to remove the tokens (Salend and Lamb, 1986) or by making the tokens worth a predetermined amount. For example, each token might be worth one minute of free time and, at the end of the class, the group would be given free time equal to the number of tokens remaining (Salend, 1987).

## Time-out from positive reinforcement

Time-out from positive reinforcement or "time-out" as it is commonly called, is defined as the "period of time in a less reinforcing environment made contingent on behaviour" (Branter and Doherty, 1983, p. 93). Time-out procedures have

**Planned ignoring:**
removing attention from a student for a given period of time.

**Nonexclusionary time-out:**
restricting a child's access to reinforcement without removing the child from the classroom environment.

**Exclusionary time-out:**
physical removal of a child from the area of reinforcement although not from the classroom.

**Seclusionary time-out:**
removal of a student from the classroom situation.

been effective with a number of different populations and behaviours. Zabel (1986), for example, comments that 70 percent of teachers of students with behaviour disorders use some form of time-out in their classrooms.

Time-out is based on the premise that removing students from ongoing class activities will punish their behaviour. If the "time-in" environment is interesting and reinforcing, only a very brief period of time-out will be needed (Solnick, Rincover, and Peterson, 1977). To enhance the reinforcing nature of the time-in environment, the teacher should provide frequent opportunities for students to earn reinforcement for appropriate academic and social responses. Of course, time-out will not work if the student is able to escape unpleasant activities or if reinforcers are available during time-out.

When time-out is used appropriately, it should result in a rapid suppression of the undesired behaviour. There is also some evidence that the effects of time-out generalize across settings (Bishop and Stumphauzer, 1973), and spill over to other students (Wilson et al., 1979). However, since any type of time-out requires the student to change location, it should not be used in circumstances when the student is likely to be aggressive, highly disruptive or totally noncooperative. Physical force should never be used to place a child in time-out as the chances for injury (to student or teacher) are simply too great.

There are variations of time-out. These differ in the manner and degree to which access to reinforcement is denied (see Skiba and Raison, 1990). The variations are as follows:

- **Planned ignoring**, in which social attention is simply removed from the student for a given length of time.

- **Nonexclusionary time-out**, in which the child is not removed from the classroom environment but access to reinforcement is restricted by some means; for example, the child might be required to sit on the periphery of the room.

- **Exclusionary time-out** requires the individual to be physically removed from the area of reinforcement although not from the classroom. For example, the student may be required to sit behind a screen or bookcase located in a remote area of the room.

- **Seclusionary time-out** in which the student is entirely removed from the classroom situation, often to a special time-out room. In these last two variations, the student is not able to view class activities or model the appropriate behaviours demonstrated by other students.

There are many different ways to use nonexclusioary time-out. One research team (Porterfield, Herbert-Jackson, and Risley, 1976) used a technique referred to as contingent observation with children aged one to three. When a child exhibited disruptive behaviour, the infraction was explained and a more appropriate alternative was suggested. The teacher might say, for instance, "No, don't take toys from other children. Ask me for the toy you want." The child was then required to sit and watch class activities from the side of the room. After one minute, the child was asked if she or he had learned the more appropriate behaviour, "Do you know how to ask for a toy you want?" If the student said "Yes," he or she was allowed to return to the class activity. If the student did not respond, said "No," or was engaged in some inappropriate behaviour such as

**Self-management:** process by which students record, reinforce, punish, or guide their own performance.

crying or yelling, time-out was extended. After another minute or so, the adult would return and ask the child again. Once the child had rejoined the group, praise was given for appropriate behaviour. This combination of time-out and modeling of appropriate peer behaviour was shown to be an effective means of coping with disruptive behaviour.

For a variety of practical and ethical reasons, we recommend that teachers use planned ignoring or nonexclusionary time-out. Indeed, because the other variations have been so badly misused in the past, use has been severely restricted or banned in many school districts. Problems tended to arise when students were left in time-out for extended periods of time, injured themselves, or damaged the environment. Surveys indicate that nonexclusionary time-out techniques are more acceptable to teachers and laypeople than exclusionary or seclusionary time-out (Fee, Matson, and Manikam, 1990; Kazdin and Matson, 1981). Moreover, nonexclusionary time-out is preferable because it is easier for teachers to monitor student behaviour.

## APPLYING BEHAVIOURAL AND COGNITIVE PRINCIPLES

Cognitive psychology deals with the whole range of mental activities and processes, including attention and perception of stimuli and further extending to the higher mental processes of remembering, reflective and creative thinking, and problem-solving (Hilgard, 1987). Cognitive theorists devote considerable attention to the knowledge, skills, expectations, and beliefs that people bring to the learning situation, since knowledge will be better learned and maintained when it can be related to existing mental structures or schemata. Effective instruction helps learners to find the relationship between various facts, concepts, and principles. The goal of instruction is that learners will develop more sophisticated and elaborate mental structures.

Behavioural and cognitive theories of learning are often posed as competing models. While it is true that specific parts of these theories are contradictory, it may be more accurate today to see the these views of learning as complementary—they simply tackle different problems. In recent years, the line between behavioural and cognitive strategies has become blurred and some of the most exciting instructional strategies developed recently have borrowed freely from both schools of thought. Self-management, for example, demonstrates the melding of behavioural and cognitive approaches to learning.

### Self-management

Ultimately, many common behaviour problems that interfere with learning and/or classroom operations can be prevented through the use of self-management strategies (Strain and Sainato, 1987). Self-management allows control to pass from the teacher's hands to the students' and serves to enhance student independence as the students record, reinforce, punish, or guide their own performances.

For students, learning to monitor and evaluate their own actions, making correct judgments about the appropriateness of their behaviour, and changing their conduct on the basis of that information is not only important in school, but will serve them well in later life (Sainato et al., 1990). Also, the ability to monitor and evaluate their own behaviour helps students transfer and maintain newly learned skills to other situations and in the presence of other people (Holman and Baer, 1979; O'Leary and Dubey, 1979). In the classroom, students who can work independently and manage their own behaviour have diminished dependence on the presence of the teacher (Burgio, Whitman, and Johnson, 1980). The teachers are then freed from the need to continuously monitor student behaviour, and can invest that time in other academic pursuits (Burgio et al., 1980; O'Leary and Dubey, 1979).

### Self-monitoring

"Self-monitoring," "self-recording," and "self-assessment" are terms that are used interchangeably to describe a process in which students monitor their own behaviour and then record the event. The system was originally developed as a method of collecting information on behaviours that only the individual could accurately observe or record. When it was found that the simple act of recording had an effect on behaviour, self-recording became a therapeutic technique in its own right (Cooper, Heron, and Heward, 1987). The reactive effect of self-recording not only causes the behaviour to change but the change is often observed to occur in the desired direction. For example, when individuals monitor positively valued behaviours, such as completing work, being friendly toward others, or eating nutritious foods, the act of recording tends to cause the behaviour to increase. When monitoring negatively valued behaviours, such as smoking, aggression, or being off-task, the act of recording tends to cause the behaviour to decrease (Nelson, 1977).

There is no definitive explanation about why self-recording changes behaviour. However, it may be that the act of observation itself takes on reinforcing or punishing properties. In other words, when students evaluate themselves and are required to record that they have been "on-task" or "off-task," this action may be accompanied with either a self-reinforcer—"I'm good because I was working hard"—or self-punisher—"That's not good, I have to get back to work" (Kanfer, 1970). It also may be that self-recording provides an environmental cue that increases the student's awareness of potential consequences that will accrue as a result of a behaviour (Hayes and Nelson, 1983).

Keeping accurate records of student behaviour in order to monitor the effectiveness of any behaviour change program is important. However, it is not always necessary for the teacher to undertake the responsibility for recording the relevant information. When students are taught to record their own behaviour, they are taking an active role in the management of their own behaviour. The strategy has been used to increase on-task performance and therefore academic productivity (Hallahan, Kneedler, and Lloyd, 1983; Lloyd, et al., 1989) and increase independent work skills in preschool students with disabilities (Sainato et al., 1990).

Children must be specifically taught to use self-recording procedures. Self-recording is best used in situations in which the target behaviour has reached a criterion level—in other words, to maintain effects when other teacher-mediated intervention has been withdrawn. Behaviours that happen privately, such as

**Self-reinforcement:**
system in which students increase or maintain their own behaviour with reinforcers that they give themselves whenever a certain standard has been met.

homework or studying, are also good candidates for self-recording. The following general guidelines may be used in initiating instruction in this area:

• Define the behaviour explicitly;

• Keep the recording simple;

• Train students in the use of data collection methods;

• Set time limits; and

• Fade the self-recording system

### Self-reinforcement

Self-reinforcement is a process in which individuals increase or maintain their own behaviour with reinforcers that they give themselves whenever a certain standard has been met (Bandura, 1976). In many cases, teachers implement programs of self-reinforcement by transferring control of an existing reinforcement system (such as a token system) over to the students. Drabman, Spitalnik, and O'Leary, (1973) used the following sequence to transfer responsibility for a token system:

1. Students recorded points awarded by the teacher;

2. Students were given bonus points if their rating matched that of the teacher;

3. Matching was gradually faded out, with fewer and fewer students being required to match the teacher; and

4. Students judged their own behaviour and determined their own reinforcement.

In some research, students set their own standards for reinforcement, while in others, the standard was set by an external agent, such as the teacher. While the research is not clear on this point, some suggests that students tend to select more lenient standards (e.g., Felixbrod and O'Leary, 1974; Frederiksen and Frederiksen, 1975). If teachers find that their students repeatedly select lower standards, students can be prompted to select more stringent standards, and then reinforced for doing this on their own.

Ballard and Glynn (1975) used self-reinforcement to improve the story-writing abilities of grade three students. First, students self-recorded the number of sentences, descriptive words, and action words used in their stories on a record sheet provided by the teacher. Self-recording alone, however, did not cause a change in their story-writing behaviour. In the next phase, students were told that they would be able to give themselves one point for every sentence written. Points could be exchanged for a variety of reinforcers: books, art materials, games, and so on. In the self-reinforcement phase, the writing output of the students nearly doubled. When reinforcement was extended to other writing behaviours, such as the use of descriptive and action words, substantial increases were also seen. Not only did the quantity of work increase but the quality of the stories, as judged by two English professors who were unaware of the program, was rated as higher during the treatment phases when compared to stories written earlier.

**Self-punishment:**
process by which the student discriminates his or her own inappropriate behaviour and self-administers a negative consequence.

**Self-instruction:**
verbal statements to oneself which prompt, direct or maintain behaviour.

## Self-punishment

**Self-punishment** occurs when the student is taught to discriminate his or her own inappropriate behaviour, and self-administer a negative consequence. The most common method of self-punishment is response-cost, used in conjunction with a token system, in which students withdraw tokens contingent upon the occurrence of an undesired behaviour (Humphrey, Karoly, and Kirschenbaum, et al., 1978).

Results reported by Humphrey and colleagues (1978), from a grade two class which included a high proportion of students who demonstrated inappropriate behaviour, demonstrated the efficacy of self-punishment techniques. Using an answer key that also specified the number of tokens to be awarded for each answer, students evaluated their own performances on reading assignments. The students who self-administered punishment were provided with "free" tokens at the beginning of the day and simply removed tokens as warranted. Performance was randomly monitored by the teacher to minimize inaccuracy and cheating. The amount of work completed by the students significantly increased without any corresponding decreases in levels of accuracy.

## Self-instruction

**Self-instruction** comprises the "verbal statements to oneself which prompt, direct or maintain behaviour" (O'Leary and Dubey, 1979, p. 450). Many examples of self-instruction can be seen in our daily lives: think of how often adults and children "talk" themselves through unfamiliar tasks. In an earlier part of this chapter, the importance of prompts to set the stage for desired behaviours was stressed. The principles guiding the use of prompts remain the same here, the only difference being that the prompts come from within the students themselves.

When teaching self-instructional strategies to students, the focus is on the process to be used to complete the task, rather than on the academic content (Alberto and Troutman, 1986). Students are trained in the strategies used to solve a particular task or problem first, then given the opportunity to apply this strategy to the actual content. Most self-instruction procedures are taught in combination with self-recording and self-reinforcement. This requires students to prompt and record their own behaviour as well as deliver the consequences for performance.

Most studies of self-instruction have used some variation of the five-step training program developed by Meichenbaum and Goodman (1971), which was originally used to teach second graders to increase their on-task behaviour. Instruction takes place on a one-to-one basis, using the following steps:

1. The teacher performs the task while talking out loud (cognitive modeling).

2. The student performs the task while the teacher says the steps aloud (overt, external guidance).

3. The student performs the task while saying the steps aloud (overt self-guidance).

4. The student performs the task while whispering the steps to him/herself (faded overt self-guidance).

5. The student performs the task while thinking the steps to him/herself (covert self-instruction).

It is generally useful to provide concrete checklists to students which outline each step necessary to complete the task. These checklists help students to respond correctly and consistently (Kneedler and Hallahan, 1981).

When Dunlap and Dunlap (1989) used a self-instructional package to help learning disabled students master subtraction (with regrouping) problems, an analysis of the errors made by each of the three students studied allowed the development of individualized checklists which were then used to guide student completion of the subtraction problem. Checklists were written in the first person. Students referred to them and checked off each step as they completed the problem. One pupil's checklist consisted of the following steps:

1. I copied the problem correctly.

2. I regrouped when I needed to (top number is bigger than the bottom).

3. I borrowed correctly (number crossed out is one bigger).

4. I subtracted all numbers.

5. I subtracted correctly.

Students often have difficulty mastering problem-solving in mathematics—a task that requires students to learn a general strategy that can be applied to many different problems, regardless of the specific mathematical operation to be used. Enright and Beattie (1989) provide a five-step plan that can be used to help students become better problem-solvers. Given a copy of the five steps, the students first use the plan with the help of the teacher, then with peers and finally on their own. It is stressed that students must go through each of the five steps every time, rather than completing problems haphazardly. It is more important for students to complete a few problems well than to complete many in an unsystematic fashion. The five steps are:

1. *Study the problem.* Read the problem and find out what needs to be solved. Of course, this must be done before the student can tackle any aspect of the task.

2. *Organize the facts.* Students must be taught to distinguish between facts or information that is needed to solve the problem and that which is irrelevant.

3. *Line up a plan.* Students need to develop a plan that will be used to solve the problem.

4. *Verify the plan with computation.* Students should then select the proper math operation that will allow them to implement the plan.

5. *Examine the answer.* Once the students have followed their plans, they need to check the resulting answer to see whether it "makes sense." This goes beyond checking the accuracy of the calculation; it makes sure that the correct operation was selected.

Self-instruction may also be applicable to more creative academic pursuits. Baker and Winston (1986) described an interesting application of this technique to art and creative writing. The experimenter first modeled self-instruction for drawing for the student:

> *Now what is it I have to do? I have to draw a picture. What should I draw? (pause) I know. I'll draw a picture of a playground....That looks good. Now, what else can I put into this picture? (pause) I think I'll put in a slide and a teeter-totter....That's good! Now what else can I put in the picture? [continues to add elements]...This is a really good picture! (p. 118).*

The pupil was then asked to use the same procedure on his own picture, repeating the questions aloud and acting upon them. The second time, the experimenter modeled the questions, and the student suggested the answers. Note that the procedure did not tell the student what to draw, but rather how to think when drawing. The student is trained to use a general strategy rather than to demonstrate a particular response. Independent judges, (grade one teachers familiar with the level of creativity generally demonstrated by students of this age) were used to assess the pictures and stories. They judged these products to be higher in diversity (such as the number of different actions, people and objects represented) than normally seen in students of this age. In a second similar study, the novelty of the the pictures and stories were rated (the unusualness or creativity of the elements used and the novelty of the manner in which they were combined), and these were also judged to be higher than those typically produced by six-year-old students.

A follow-up of the students six weeks after the termination of the study indicated that training effects were maintained. However, generalization of the principles did not occur. When the experimenters looked at how the students went about writing stories, they found that the students did not transfer the use of the self-instructions to this context: the researchers found it necessary to directly teach students to use a similar procedure and directly teach the application to the writing task.

## METACOGNITIVE STRATEGIES

In addition to the self-instructional strategies, there exist a number of metacognitive strategies that can be used to facilitate student learning, studying, and problem solving. Learners must actively monitor their use of thinking processes and regulate them according to their cognitive objectives.

Metacognitive abilities enable learners to be aware of whether or not they are understanding new material, to decide how much time they will need to master a body of information, to know the strategies that should be used to organize information and the available time, and to find effective and appropriate ways to learn. While some pupils seem to spontaneously develop the use of metacognitive strategies, other do not.

One of the most salient characteristics of metacognition is that it involves growing consciousness. One becomes more aware of the thinking processes themselves and their specific procedures, as well as more conscious of oneself as a thinker and performer. As learners acquire an understanding of what the various thinking processes are, they can better understand and apply them. Some researchers suggest that is why, initially, thinking skills should be taught directly and in relatively context-free situations (Berger, 1983). See Figure 11-5 for a model of metacognitive thinking skills.

**Figure 11-5**
Metacognitive
thinking skills

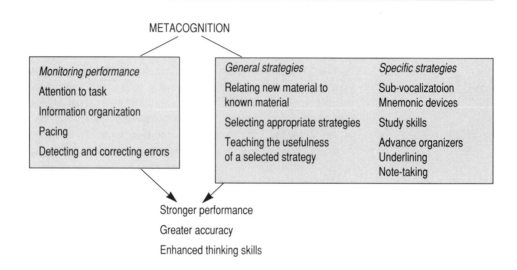

Learning strategies are systematic plans that help learners encode information (Weinstein, Goetz, and Alexander, 1988). Not only do strategies improve immediate performance and generalize beyond the learning context, but the belief that one can apply a strategy to improve learning may also instill a sense of efficacy for influencing achievement outcomes (Schunk, 1990).

Metacognitive thinking has two main dimensions. The first is task-oriented and relates to monitoring the actual performance of a skill. The second dimension is strategic: it involves using a skill in a particular circumstance and being aware of getting the most informative feedback from carrying out a particular strategy.

Despite the importance of metacognition, few teachers provide direct instruction in this area (Moely et al., 1986). It is clear that simply telling students about the various strategies is not enough; instead, they must be directly taught.

## Study skills

The most efficient way to intentionally store material in long-term memory is to consciously process it at deeper levels. Strategies (see Chapter 9) include developing linkages between new and old material, rehearsal, mnemonic devices, examining the implications of new material, and answering questions about the material. Each of these techniques is intended to facilitate the storage of new information and to minimize retrieval problems.

Studying is often the bane of student existence, an unpleasant, if necessary, task to facilitate acquisition and retention of new material. Like other metacognitive skills, research in this area demonstrates that most students are inefficient in their use of study skills. Some techniques, however, can make this process more efficient and effective.

### Underlining

Most of you are probably reading this text with a pencil or highlighter pen in hand and are dutifully noting the most important information. You might be surprised (and perhaps discouraged) to learn that research generally indicates that this strategy is not an effective means of studying (Anderson and Armbruster, 1984; Snowman, 1984). The problem seems to lie in the fact that most users of this strategy underline too much and therefore do not separate important from less important information. Snowman (1984) found that when students were asked to underline only one sentence in each paragraph, they tended to retain more information. This may arise from the fact that students were using a higher level of processing when deciding which line to underline.

### Note-taking

Students reading a book or listening to a lecture often take notes of what they have learned. The notes function as a sort of storage device which can be consulted when needed. When notes are carefully taken, they not only provide a permanent record of information but also help the learner process information more readily. That is, when the learner reorganizes material and connects the new information with already acquired knowledge, learning will be greatly enhanced. Thus, note-takers should not only record a verbatim transcript of what is seen or heard but should also process the information in some manner (Kiewra, 1985a). For example, summarizing information in their own words or taking notes that prepare them to teach others will help students activate the needed mental processes (Bretzing and Kulhavy, 1979).

Effective note-taking involves the processing, rather than reproduction, of materials.

Teachers can help students to be more effective note-takers by providing instruction in paraphrasing and summarizing (Kiewra, 1985a). Further, frequent pauses during lectures will help the students acquire complete and well-organized notes (Aiken, Thomas, and Shennum, 1975; Peper and Meyer, 1978). Providing brief notes that outline the structure of the lesson to follow can guide the students to take more comprehensive and complete notes. Such notes, when elaborated with student note-taking and review, have been shown to increase learning (Kiewra, 1985b).

Of course, notes are usually intended for use in a later review session and research shows that those students who actually do review their notes learn more (Fisher and Harris, 1973), particularly when they take the opportunity to reorganize the information into categories that are meaningful to them. This could be accomplished, for example, by reorganizing notes into an outline form (Kiewra, 1985a). But the effects of notetaking are by no means unanimously positive; in particular, it may be a less effective strategy for students of lower ability (Berliner, 1971).

### SQ4R

SQ4R stands for survey, question, read, reflect, recite, and review. This study strategy was suggested by Thomas and Robinson (1972) and is used to study text material as follows:

- Survey—scan the material quickly to get a feel for organization; for example, the headings, subheadings, and major and minor topics. This clarifies for the reader what he or she is going to read about.

- Question—begin to generate questions relevant to the material, such as Why? What? Who? and Where?

- Read—do not take notes, but attempt to answer the questions that have been formulated.

- Reflect—try to understand the material by relating it to existing knowledge. Relate subheadings to the main themes or principles, try to resolve contradictions within the text, and apply new knowledge to relevant problems.

- Recite—pose questions and provide the answers.

- Review—ask questions and re-read material only when the answers cannot be readily recalled.

### MURDER

Another study strategy uses the acronym MURDER to represent a method developed for the use of post-secondary students (Dansereau, 1985). The acronym represents the following steps:

- Mood—the learner must get in the mood to learn.

- Understand—the learner must understand the goal of the activity, or what is to be learned.

- Recall—the learner then tries to call up information relevant to the task, using appropriate recall strategies such as paraphrasing or imagery.

- Detect—the learner tries to detect omissions, and errors, and to find methods that can be used to organize the material.

- Elaborate—the learner elaborates upon the information by relating it to prior knowledge. Questions that might be asked include, "What would I ask the author if I had a chance?" or "How can this information be applied?"

- Review—the learner reviews the material, paying particular attention to material that had not been well-learned.

## Reciprocal teaching

Metacognitive strategies have also been developed for specific curriculum areas, such as reading and mathematics. One such application is **reciprocal teaching** (Palinscar and Brown, 1984), which was designed for use with students experiencing problems in reading comprehension. These students could read the words, but were unable to understand the meaning of a passage. Through reciprocal teaching, students are taught to:

**1.** Think of important questions that emerge from the passage and formulate an answer to each.

**2.** Summarize the most important information in their own words.

**3.** Predict what the author might discuss next.

**4.** Recognize anything in the text that does not make sense and then see if they can make it clearer.

As with self-instructional strategies, the teacher helps students master these skills by first modeling their use and then gradually transferring responsibility and control to the students. After initial sessions with the teacher, students assume the teaching role with other classmates, leading their peers through the use of the four skills. This method has greatly improved the reading comprehension in low-achieving junior high students (Palinscar and Brown).

## APPLYING COGNITIVE PRINCIPLES

Self-management strategies meld the cognitive and behavioural approaches to learning. We can also describe some teaching strategies that are solely attributed to the work conducted by cognitive learning theorists.

As we discussed, information processing began as an attempt to delineate human problem-solving strategies, the step-by-step process through which humans come to solutions to problems (Newell and Simon, 1972). The operation of computers suggested that human beings could be viewed as symbol-manipulation systems. The system comprises different memory stores in which

**Discovery learning:**
a process in which students are presented with problems and are allowed to seek their own solutions through independent work or group discussion.

**Meaningful receptive learning:**
learning through concepts, ideas and other information in a manner that is relevant to the students' own prior knowledge.

information is coded, stored, retrieved, and manipulated. Specific classroom applications of cognitive theories include approaches to teaching concepts, facilitating student problem-solving, transfer of learning, and studying behaviour.

## Discovery learning

In Chapter 9, we noted that Jerome Bruner places a great deal of emphasis on the importance of meaningful learning—or making learning tasks personally relevant to the individual learner. Bruner proposes that this is accomplished through discovery learning, a process in which students are presented with problems and are allowed to seek their own solutions through independent work or group discussion. Bruner sees discovery learning as a vehicle through which students learn problem-solving abilities and practise their use in a non-threatening environment. As they continue to practise, students gain confidence in their ability to confront and solve problems.

Bruner believes that when students come to their own understanding, these concepts will be more meaningful to them than those presented by the teacher. Being more meaningful to the learner, it is more likely that the knowledge will be retained.

## Ausubel's theory of learning

Achievement is maximized when teachers structure material by beginning with overviews, advance organizers, or objectives; outlining the content and signal transitions between parts; calling attention to main ideas and summarizing parts of the lesson when they are completed; and review the main ideas at the end. In general, classroom research supports the ideas of Ausubel (1968), Bruner (1966), and other cognitive structuralists on organizing and structuring content (Brophy, 1986).

Both Bruner and Ausubel are classified as cognitive psychologists; however, their views of learning and instruction are quite different. Bruner believes that students learn best by discovering ideas for themselves; in contrast, Ausubel suggests that students gain knowledge primarily through reception, which implies that learners gather or receive learning rather than seeking it out for themselves. The teacher's task is to structure information and then present it to students in an organized and clear manner.

Specifically, Ausubel maintains that the teacher should carefully structure knowledge in a sequential format ready for students to learn. He believes that people learn best by placing newly acquired information into hierarchical structures or coding systems. In other words, individuals learn more general concepts that are generalized ideas of mental images or a class of objects. These general concepts are then used as anchors onto which new details can be attached. The teacher presents the main theme (principle or rule), before discussing the specifics—a deductive process. The basic framework or structure is provided, and then further lessons fill in the details.

Like Bruner, Ausubel stresses the importance of linking new material to existing knowledge. The philosophy of meaningful receptive learning, as defined by Ausubel, states that students learn best when they are presented with concepts,

**448**

**Expository teaching:** an instructional model intended to encourage meaningful rather than rote learning.

**Advance organizers:** techniques that provide an outline for the facts that are to follow and show the relationship among concepts to be learned.

ideas and/or other information that was organized by the teacher in a manner that is relevant to their own prior knowledge. The instructional model he presents is known as expository teaching. It is a strategy intended to encourage meaningful rather than rote learning.

Ausubel tries to enhance this process by providing an advance organizer, or a broad statement that summarizes the information which will follow (see Chapter 9). Advance organizers are intended to facilitate learning by providing an organizing structure that helps students relate new information to old. Oral or written advance organizers orient the student to the material that is to follow and show the relationship among concepts to be learned. Advance organizers function as a skeleton upon which students will attach the details provided during the lesson and allows them to prepare themselves by calling up related information that will help in understanding the new material. Because it is not possible to know what knowledge each student possesses, Ausubel suggests that good advance organizers will be abstract and general so that all learners can relate to them.

## Robert Gagné

Gagné (1977) is another cognitive theorist who suggests that hierarchical structures are the most appropriate method with which to present academic content. Like Ausubel, Gagné promotes the use of structures in which specific ideas are subsumed under more general principles. Gagné has categorized the skills people can learn, or the outcomes of learning under five headings. These are attitudes, motor skills, verbal information, intellectual skills, and cognitive strategies (Gagné, 1974, 1977).

While Ausubel first presents the general rule and then the specifics, Gagné reverses the process. In other words, the student moves from lower level concepts in steps that lead toward the more complex and inclusive concepts. More detail concerning this approach are provided in Chapter 14.

## Promoting thinking skills

Of all the skills one learns during a lifetime, one of the most basic is the ability to think. Thinking subsumes all the other basic skills associated with learning and is inherent to human survival. Thinking is generally assumed to be a cognitive process, a mental act by which knowledge is acquired (Presseisen, 1984, 1986). Currently, there is a great deal of emphasis on improving students' thinking abilities. It may seem trite to say that school should teach thinking, basic as this skill is to all learning, and yet we have tended to ignore thinking per se, perhaps on the assumption that students somehow automatically develop the ability to think logically and solve problems. This appears to be anything but true. For example, Whimbey (1975) reported that a significant percentage of the students in an advanced education course at a major university were unable to solve the following problem:

*What day follows the day before yesterday if two days from now will be Sunday?*

Slowly, teachers and administrators across Canada and the United States are taking up the challenge of teaching students to think. Their aim is to teach academic content in a way that encourages students to develop their ability to think. They do not aim to replace content with thinking, but rather to teach students the intellectual skills they need to make use of the content (Porat, 1986).

The ability to proceed through a sequence of analytical steps is the foundation of all higher-order reasoning and comprehension. All complex abstractions, classifications, transformations, problem solutions, and applications of generalizations are products of accurate sequential thought (Whimbey, 1975). The question is not whether to teach students to think but to identify certain skills that can be practised in a variety of situations and environments to make people better thinkers. We must provide activities and experiences that give an opportunity for practice and development of those skills. Just as musicians, athletes, artists and others must develop and depend on fundamental skills in order to reach full potential, so must students be aware of the fundamental thinking skills in order to develop their potential as thinkers and problem solvers.

When we talk about the complex process of thinking, there seem to be four important subprocesses involved. Cohen (1971) and others suggest that these are problem solving, decision making, critical thinking, and creative thinking.

**Problem solving**    This entails the basic thinking processes to resolve a known or defined difficulty; to assemble facts about the difficulty and determine additional information needed; to infer or suggest alternate solutions and test them for appropriateness; to reduce potentially to simpler levels of explanation and eliminate discrepancies; to provide solutions; and to check for generalizable value.

**Decision making**    This involves the use of basic thinking processes to choose a best response from among several options; to assemble information needed in a topic area; to compare advantages and disadvantages of alternative approaches; to determine what additional information is required; and to judge the most effective response and be able to justify it.

**Critical thinking**    This process seeks a rational basis for beliefs and provides procedures for analyzing, testing, and evaluating them. It includes using basic thinking processes to analyze arguments and generate insight into particular meanings and interpretations; developing cohesive, logical reasoning patterns and understanding assumptions and biases underlying particular positions; attaining a credible, concise, and convincing style of presentation.

**Creative thinking**    This is the process that is responsible for the invention or development of novel, esthetic, or constructive ideas or products. It relates to percepts as well as to concepts, and stresses the intuitive aspects of thinking as much as the rational. Emphasis is on using known information or material to generate the possible, as well as to elaborate on the thinker's original perspective.

Thinking operations are dimensions of higher-order mental functioning that may serve as guides for developing classroom activities for exercising thinking (Wasserman, 1987). They include comparing, interpreting, observing, summarizing, classifying, making decisions, suggesting hypotheses, imagining and creating, criticizing and evaluating, designing projects and investigations, identifying assumptions, applying principles in new situations, coding for certain patterns of thinking and gathering and organizing data (Wasserman, 1987).

**Problem solving:**
the process of applying what is known to new and unfamiliar situations.

However, teaching thinking runs into a particular difficulty. Generally there are two phases to teaching any skill: the skill is explained and demonstrated to the student and the student practises the skill with guidance and feedback. But skilled reasoning is generally carried out inside one's head and this makes the skill difficult for the teacher to teach and for students to learn. There is no easy way for students to actually see how a teacher solves complex problems or analyzes complex ideas.

Elementary students can benefit from early exposure to varied thinking processes and to different media of presentation but probably can only approach more complex sequences as they gain experience and apply similar skills in multiple content areas. Beyer suggests that an effective thinking skills curriculum would introduce only a limited number of skills at a particular grade level, would teach these across all appropriate content areas, and would vary the media and contents of presentation. Subsequent grades should enlarge the thinking skills base and provide additional and more elaborate applications of skills already introduced.

Some complex thinking processes may be more relevant to certain subject areas than others. For example, problem-solving thinking skills seem ideal for mathematics or science instruction. Decision making may be useful for social studies and vocational studies, while critical thinking may be more relevant for the debate team, language arts class, and for discussing problems of democracy. Creative thinking might enhance all subjects, as well as being particularly meaningful to art, music, or literature programs.

One solution to teaching thinking skills is to have both students and teachers think aloud as they work through ideas. Students can vocalize their thoughts as they analyze relationships, sort concepts, and form generalizations (Whimbey, 1985). Another strategy is to use comparisons. Wasserman (1987) points out that children in the primary grades do not have to stray from the regular curriculum in order to compare two stories, two characters in a story, two words, two leaves, two illustrations, or two arithmetic problems. In asking pupils to make these comparisons, we are asking them to discriminate intelligently among similarities and differences, thereby exercising their mental processes and heightening their conceptual understandings. The data suggest that, as pupils engage in such operations, they increase both the depth and breadth of their knowledge. Basic skills are strengthened as well.

There are other ways to incorporate thinking operations into the curriculum. Students can summarize news reports, historical events, and films; they can classify spelling and vocabulary words, bridges, and musical instruments; they can analyze political speeches for generalizations, attributions, and extreme statements; or they can observe the weather, the way a musical instrument is played, or the behaviour of an animal (Wasserman, 1987).

## Problem solving

Although each may use his or her own terminology, sequence, and varying amounts of elaboration, most cognitive researchers would define problem solving as the process of applying what is known to new and unfamiliar situations. Since the goal of schooling is to help students become adept in solving various problems in real-life settings, researchers have begun to examine the specific manner in which this ability can be taught. This is of vital importance for, like any metacognitive skill, research has demonstrated that while some children seem to develop problem-solving strategies on their own, many need more specific guidance and instruction (Kontos, 1983).

One method of problem solving suggests that this task can be conceptualized as a five-stage process, represented by the acronym IDEAL (Bransford and Stein, 1984; Bransford et al., 1986). The steps are:

- Identification—if students are to solve a problem, they must first realize that a problem exists.

- Definition—once the problem has been identified, the student must define or classify the problem. The manner in which the problem is solved will naturally give rise to the type of solution.

- Exploration—students begin to seek out the appropriate solutions to the problem.

- Action—once potential solutions have been identified, students must act upon their ideas.

- Look—students examine the effects of the use of any problem-solving strategy so that errors or the application of inappropriate methods can be spotted. Effective problem-solvers will carefully monitor the process of problem-solving, revising their behaviour as needed. Less effective problem-solvers tend to persist in the application of inappropriate strategies.

## Transfer of learning

When teachers help their students acquire new knowledge, skills, and learning strategies, the underlying assumption is that the students will be able to transfer these abilities to other settings. It means nothing if students get an "A" in French if they are unable to negotiate their way through the Montreal subway or if students can complete mathematics worksheets and yet are unable to determine whether they have received the right amount of change in a store. School learning is therefore not best demonstrated on tests; instead, teachers must ensure that students are able to transfer knowledge to situations they encounter every day.

**Transfer of learning** refers to the student's ability to use knowledge or skills in situations other than that in which the skill was initially acquired. Transfer will depend on how well the knowledge or skills were learned as well as the degree of similarity between the situations in which the skill was learned and the environment in which it is to be applied (Slavin, 1988). While many teachers simply assume that students will be able to readily transfer skills from the classroom to a store, restaurant, or job site, this is by no means a certainty. In particular, students of lower ability will experience even greater disability in transfer or generalization of skills (Winzer, 1989).

Not surprisingly, research in metacognition indicates that the cognitive skills of students who are able to transfer skills across settings are different than those

**Participation structures:**
rules defining who can talk, what they can talk about, and when, to whom, and for how long they can talk.

**Goal structure:**
the degree to which students are in competition with each other.

**Individualistic goal structure:**
system in which students work by themselves to achieve goals that are independent of those held by their classmates.

demonstrated by students who fail to transfer. However, it is encouraging to note that transfer skills can be directly taught. While there is a great deal of research in this area, the strategy that is of most use to regular classroom teachers it to use models during instruction. For example, one study, (Wollman, 1983) taught science students about a model of a balance beam and then showed them how use of the model could be transferred to other similar problems.

Further, teachers can facilitate transfer by emphasizing similarity across settings. This can be accomplished, for example, by using a cash register when teaching money skills. Students who are taught in this manner are more likely to demonstrate money skills in a store than students who practise money skills on a worksheet.

## APPLYING HUMANISTIC PRINCIPLES

Educators and psychologists who assume a humanistic stance have not devised models or theories of learning, per se, but cooperative learning approaches and techniques are aligned with humanistic educational thought. Cooperative learning activities can be employed for all school subjects. They are most successful when students must manipulate concrete materials, as in mathematics or science fair projects. It is also possible to use the activities in less structured areas, such as games. Pairs of students may act out an event in pantomime, for example, increasing their level of cooperation as skills develop (Winzer, 1989).

Implementing cooperative learning strategies requires most teachers to significantly alter their usual instructional style to act as facilitators rather than leaders. However, cooperative learning does not absolve the teacher of instructional responsibility. On the contrary, the teacher must establish heterogeneous groups of appropriate size, determine instructional goals for them, and set evaluative criteria.

### Cooperative learning

Cooperative learning strategies have evolved out of the body of literature which examines various structural aspects of the classroom. Participation structures are the rules defining who can talk, when, to whom, what about, and for how long (Erickson and Schultz, 1977). There are also goal structures, which refer to the degree to which students are in competition with each other.

Under the individualistic goal structure, students work by themselves to achieve goals that are independent of those held by their classmates as in, for example, programed instruction. Individualized objectives are established on a regular basis, student effort is evaluated according to a predetermined standard, and rewards are given accordingly. Students have their own materials and work at their own pace, ignoring the work of their peers. Goal achievement is unrelated to that of others. Students seek outcomes that are beneficial to themselves and they ignore the progress or achievements of their classmates. This goal structure encourages students to isolate themselves, but in some cases, students may begin to compete with each other even though the structure does not require it (Johnson and Johnson, 1986).

**Competitive goal structure:**
system in which students work against each other to achieve a grade or other reward that is reserved only for a few.

**Cooperative goal structure:**
system in which students work together to achieve common goals.

When placed under competitive goal structures, on the other hand, students work against each other to achieve a grade or other reward that is reserved only for a few. Grades may be placed on a normal curve; thus, students must not only do their best, but must also must surpass their classmates. When students achieve the highest mark, it necessarily means that all or most others in the class will fail to achieve the same goal or reward. Students therefore may be motivated to seek outcomes that are of benefit to themselves but detrimental to their classmates for, under this competitive goal structure, students are often implicitly or explicitly discouraged from helping one another. Students will either work very hard to surpass their classmates or give up and refuse to try because they do not think they have a chance to win (Johnson and Johnson, 1986).

With a few exceptions, competitive goal structures have dominated educational practice for most of this century. It is a widely held sentiment that competition is motivating and satisfying, and that it prepares a child for life in the real world. Many students come to school with the pressure to "do better" than their peers.

However, recent research challenges the popular view that competition leads to superior performance—indeed, it seems that the opposite is true. For example, students who perceived their learning environment to be highly competitive had lower reading achievement gains than students who perceived their classroom to be less competitive (Talmage and Walberg, 1978). Other research suggests that high standards, competitive class environments, and a large percentage of lower grades are associated with increased absenteeism and increased drop-out rate (Moos and Moos, 1978; Tricket and Moos, 1974), particularly among disadvantaged students (Wessman, 1972). Further, there is a growing body of evidence that success in the workplace is also related to the development of cooperative skills, rather than success accruing to the most competitive worker.

Increasing attention is being directed toward cooperative goal structures, in which students work together to achieve common goals. Students are assigned to small groups and instructed to learn the material themselves as well as help others learn the material. In contrast to competitive and individualistic goal structures, students working cooperatively can reach their goal only if all others in their groups also reach their goal. Thus, students seek outcomes that are beneficial to everyone in the group.

Numerous reviews of cooperative learning strategies have been unanimous in their judgment that cooperative learning can improve students' achievement, thinking skills, problem-solving, and personal interactions (e.g., Davidson, 1985; Slavin, 1983; Slavin, Madden, and Stevens, 1989/90). However, for benefits to accrue, cooperative learning strategies must be implemented correctly. In particular, academic achievement benefits are dependent upon two critical elements, at least at the elementary and secondary levels. First, the strategy must include some type of group goal which facilitates positive interdependence among students by having them work together to obtain recognition. Of equal importance is individual accountability. That is, group success is dependent upon individual learning—totals of quiz scores, a report to which each student contributes a chapter, and so on (Slavin, Madden, and Stevens, 1989/90). Studies of methods in which students work together to prepare a single worksheet or project, without separating individual contributions rarely find achievement benefits. However, group goals and individual accountability may not be necessary when cooperative learning strategies are used at a college level, as some research has shown positive results in the absence of these factors (Dansereau, 1988; Davidson, 1985).

Gains in academic achievement as a result of cooperative learning are not limited to the simple acquisition of knowledge. For example, in five studies at the elementary and secondary levels, students generally demonstrated a higher level of academic achievement than their peers who were taught with the whole-class method, and they also did better on questions assessing high-level learning. On occasion, however, they did only as well as students from the traditional methods on questions evaluating acquisition of knowledge (Lazarowitz and Karsenty, 1989; Sharan et al., 1984a; Sharan et al., 1980; Sharan and Shachar, 1988; Sharan and Shaulov, 1989). Reviews by Sharan (1980) and Slavin (1983) reported that cooperative learning methods are superior to traditional classroom methods. However, Sharan (1980) reported that gains were not consistent for all groups on all measures. Slavin (1983) noted that achievement gains result only if the co-operative learning methods include group study and group reward for individual learning.

Similar positive results were obtained when cooperative learning strategies were used to enhance computer assisted instruction. When compared to competitive or individualistic learning conditions, cooperative instruction promoted greater quantity and quality of daily achievement and more successful problem-solving (Johnson, Johnson, and Stanne, 1986). While it is often feared that interaction with computers will decrease student interaction with teachers and peers, the cooperative learning groups actually lead to increased task-related student-student interaction. These results also show that successful computer-assisted instruction can take place even when a school does not provide a single computer for each student—in fact, learning is better when students work cooperatively in groups rather than individually. However, working in groups alone was not sufficient to produce the positive results; a clear cooperative goal structure was needed to facilitate greater achievement.

Of course, teachers who take a humanistic perspective are not only concerned with the academic outcomes of cooperative learning, but with affective outcomes as well. Cooperative learning strategies require students to interact constructively and use their interpersonal and collaborative skills (Lew et al., 1986). Several studies have shown that cooperative strategies promoted cooperation and mutual assistance among peers (Hertz-Lazarowitz, Sharan, and Steinberg, 1980; Sharan et al., 1984b; Sharan and Rich, 1984; Sharan, and Shachar, 1988). Kagan and Madsen (1971) found that students who had cooperative experiences allocated more rewards to peers than to themselves. Wheeler and Ryan (1973) found that cooperative classroom experiences positively influenced students' attitudes towards cooperation.

## Implementing cooperative learning

Some general guidelines should be considered by teachers prior to the implementation of cooperative learning since preparation is crucial (Johnson and

Johnson, 1986; 1989/90). The older the students, the longer they will have been exposed to the traditional competitive model in school and the less likely they are to possess the communicative or collaborative skills needed for successful cooperative work in groups. Implementation steps are to specify objectives, place students in groups, arrange the room in a manner supportive of group work, explain the goals of the activity, and finally, to evaluate learning.

Initially groups should be limited to two or three members. As children gain increasingly sophisticated collaborative skills, the size of the team can be increased, although groups should never grow to a size that precludes the meaningful participation of all members. Generally, teams will be heterogeneous in nature and include students from different sexes, ethnic backgrounds, ability levels, and social classes. Teams may last for weeks, months, or even an entire school year, but sooner or later, all students should have the opportunity to work together in at least one curriculum area (Johnson and Johnson, 1986).

The heterogeneous nature of groups is crucial to a cooperative learning strategy if the affective benefits are to be accomplished. For example, children from different cultural backgrounds often cluster together in traditional situations.

Cooperative learning groups structured around computer activities tend to increase the status of female students.

456

**Student Teams–Achievement Divisions (STAD):** a cooperative learning strategy consisting of a sequence of related activities: (1) a lesson is taught; (2) students engage in cooperative study in mixed groups; (3) a quiz is administered to individual students; and (4) rewards or recognition are given to the teams whose members most exceed their previous level of performance.

But when children from diverse backgrounds work cooperatively together, the status of group members tends to be equalized, with all members developing personal regard and respect for one another (Johnson, Johnson, and Maruyama, 1983; Slavin, 1985). Studies in Israel found that cooperative work promotes positive social interaction among students from different ethnic groups (Hertz-Lazarowitz, Sharan, and Steinberg, 1980; Sharan et al., 1984b; Sharan and Rich, 1984; Sharan and Shachar, 1988).

Similar social gains accrue to students with disabilities. When cooperative learning strategies are used, students with handicaps are placed in a situation in which interaction and positive relations can develop, positive social skills are taught and used, and students gain self-confidence in their abilities to interact with others (Lew et al., 1986). Moreover, the positive social relations developed in group situations have been shown to generalize to free play and other unstructured situations (Johnson et al., 1986) for learning disabled and emotionally disturbed students, and such positive effects were maintained after the discontinuation of the cooperative groups (Lew et al., 1986).

Cooperative learning strategies can also be used to change stereotyped attitudes and behaviours about sex roles. Lockheed and colleagues (1983) found that equal-status cross-sex interactions can be achieved in problem-solving groups, which lead both boys and girls to hold more positive perceptions of the competence and leadership abilities of girls. Similarly, cooperative learning groups structured around computer activities tended to increase the perceived status of the female students, who are often rejected as work partners in computer activities because males are considered to be more competent in the area (Johnson, Johnson, and Stanne, 1986).

## Examples of cooperative learning strategies

### STAD

Student Teams—Achievement Divisions (STAD) is a widely researched and effective cooperative learning strategy that can be used in many different subject areas (Slavin, 1978b, 1983) It consists of the following sequence of related activities: (1) a lesson is taught; (2) students engage in cooperative study in mixed groups; (3) a quiz is administered to individual students; and (4) rewards or recognition are given to the teams whose members most exceed their previous level of performance.

**Teaching the lesson** Using standard teaching strategies, the teacher presents the instructional unit or lesson to the class over one or two class periods. A worksheet for group study and a short quiz for the lesson or unit should also be prepared.

**Cooperative studying in teams** First, students are assigned to groups that typically contain four members. Students are ranked from highest to lowest in terms of their performance on some measure of academic proficiency related to the curriculum area at hand, such as scores on teacher-made unit tests, standardized test results, or previous report card grades. The ranked list is divided into equal quarters, with any extra students placed in the middle quarters. One student from each quarter is placed on each team; each team is further mixed in terms of the sex and ethnicity of the members. Any extra students from the middle quarters become the fifth members of teams.

After teaching the lesson, the teacher reads the team assignments. After students have taken their place with their group, they should be given a few minutes to pick a team name. Worksheets are then distributed which allow the teams to practise the skills or concepts introduced in the lesson. Answer sheets are also provided so that students can evaluate their performance. Students are informed that during team study (one or two class periods) each individual team member must learn the material presented in the lesson as well as help the others accomplish this goal. It must be stressed that students are not finished studying until every member of the group will make 100 percent on the quiz. Two copies of the worksheets and answer sheets are provided for each team, so that teammates are required to work cooperatively. However, if some students prefer to work alone or want their own copies, additional copies should be made available.

Within each team, students will generally work in pairs or threes. In a subject area such as mathematics, each student should complete a question and then check with his partner. If any member of the group makes an error, the teammates have a responsibility to explain the question rather than just giving the correct answer. Alternatively, if students are working on short-answer questions in language arts, they may quiz eachother, taking turns holding the answer sheet. Students must be aware that worksheets are not to be filled out and handed in: rather, they are used to guide study.

When any member of the team has a question, it should be directed to members of the group first. Research indicates that giving help to others is related to improvement in achievement (Peterson and Janicki, 1979; Peterson, Janicki, and Swing, 1981). Webb (1980) found that students who gave explanations learned more than students who did not give explanations, even when level of ability was held constant.

During team study, the teacher circulates around the room monitoring performance, praising teams that are working well together, and, if really necessary, providing help. Teachers must monitor group functioning carefully and intervene when necessary: without such intervention, negative group interaction patterns tend to become stable over time (Webb and Cullinan, 1983).

**Individual quizzes**    Students take individual quizzes without any collaboration between team members. Quizzes should be brief—ten items are usually sufficient to cover the small amount of material studied—and students should be given adequate time to finish the quiz. Upon completion, students will be either allowed to exchange quizzes with members of other teams for marking or the teacher might collect the quizzes to score after class.

**Team recognition**    Team scores are computed on the basis of students' improvement over their own past levels of performance—or according to their individualized learning expectations (ILE). The ILE is based on the assumption that students should be recognized for improving on their past performance rather than comparing them to a predetermined group standard. In this way, all students have an opportunity to earn recognition for academic work simply by doing their best.

The first step to establish ILE is to compute initial base scores for each student.

**Teams-Games-Tournaments (TGT):**

a cooperative learning strategy in which the teacher presents a lesson, student teams complete worksheets, study together, and quiz one another on the material to be covered. Matched by ability, students then represent their team at class tournaments.

Base scores represent the students' average percent correct on past quizzes in the curriculum area. So if the teacher is implementing STAD in a mathematics class, the teacher would compute average scores from students' past quizzes. If such information is not available, as would be the case at the beginning of the school year, base scores reflect the students' grades in the same subject the preceding school year. Improvement points are determined by comparing the students' current quiz scores (average percent correct) with their base scores, and giving students improvement points as follows:

| QUIZ SCORE | IMPROVEMENT POINTS |
|---|---|
| 5 or more points below base score. | 0 |
| 4 points below to 4 points above base score. | 1 |
| 5 - 9 points above base score, or a perfect score. | 2 |

Improvement points are given in relationship to past performance: for example, the student who has averaged 55 on previous quizzes and gets a 60 would get the same number of improvement points (2) as a student who has averaged 90 percent and gets 95 percent on the quiz. Even those students with very high base scores, such as 96 percent or higher, have the opportunity to earn maximum improvement points for students are awarded the maximum number of points (3) if they get a perfect score.

Every two weeks or so, base scores should be recalculated to reflect the student's current level of performance. This is done by adding the percentage of correct scores on each quiz given to the past base score. Consider the student who has a current base score of 75 percent. This figure is added to the scores obtained on the four quizzes given since the calculation of the base score. For example,

1. 75 (base score) + 65 + 85 + 90 + 87 (new quiz scores) = 402

2. $402 \div 5 = 80.4$

3. Round off the decimal: the new base score is 80 percent.

For each team, improvement points are calculated for each member and the team total calculated. Any teams that average two improvement points or more should receive recognition. The type or manner of recognition will be dependent upon the age and preferences of the students but could include recognition in a class newsletter, special certificates, or special announcements. Regardless of the form used, the teacher must be sincere and enthusiastic in her or his recognition of the team effort so that students learn to value team success. After five or six weeks of working with established STAD teams, students should be reassigned to new teams. This keeps the program fresh and gives students the opportunity to work with new peers.

### TGT

The strategy known as **Teams-Games-Tournaments** (TGT) (DeVries and Slavin, 1978) also involves four- or five-member teams that are assigned in a manner to

**Group Investigation:**
a cooperative learning strategy in which students take an active role in determining what they will study and how they will accomplish their study goals.

diversify variability in ability, sex, race, and ethnicity. After the teacher presents a lesson, teams complete worksheets, study together, and quiz one another on the material to be covered. Tournaments are held once a week and consist of students taking turns picking cards and answering questions on the material studied. Students represent their teams at "tournament tables," which comprise three students matched on the basis of their previous performance on quizzes in the relevant curriculum area. Because low achievers are competing with students of similar ability, they have as much opportunity to win points for their teams as do students of greater ability. Points are awarded on the basis of the tournament competition, and teams that have the highest point score(s) are recognized in some fashion, such as a newsletter or certificates. When continuing to use TGT, the teams stay the same but tournament tables assignments will change, reflecting students' weekly performance.

### Group Investigation

The cooperative learning strategy known as Group Investigation is different in that students take an active role in determining what they will study and how they will accomplish their study goals (Sharan and Sharan, 1976, 1989/90; Sharan and Hertz-Lazarowitz, 1980). The questions that students choose to answer will reflect their different interests, backgrounds, values, and abilities. Such differences positively contribute to the diversity within groups and, by working in teams based on a common interest in a topic, students can achieve more than they would as individuals studying the same topic (Sharan and Sharan, 1989/90).

Group Investigation consists of six stages which can be carried out over weeks or even months, depending upon the scope of the topic and the ability of the students.

**Identify the topic to be studied and form cooperative research groups**   The teacher begins the process by presenting a broad topic to the students that might have been derived from the curriculum, student interests, or issues of the day. The topic is presented in a form of a question that defines the scope of the investigation; for example, "What can we learn from the aboriginal cultures of Canada?" or "How do the aboriginal people of the North differ from those in the southern parts of Canada?" Motivating materials such as films, articles, or books can be used as can a field trip taken to a relevant location in order to acquaint the students with the area and help them identify the aspect of the topic that interests them most. Through such activities, the teacher encourages students to formulate questions that reflect what they want to know.

Writing the general topic on the board, the teacher asks students to list the questions that they wish to investigate. This could be accomplished through a large group discussion with the entire class or by first having small groups brainstorm topics and then present their suggestions to the larger group. Whenever possible, teachers should avoid directing the discussion or rejecting any expressed student interest.

The next step requires that a record of the suggested questions be made available to the class. Students then classify questions into logical categories which will form the subtopics for separate groups to investigate. Students decide which subtopic they wish to study, and join others with similar interests.

**460**

**Plan the investigation in groups**   Under the guidance of a student leader or coordinator, the members of the group form a plan which will guide their study by clarifying the questions to be asked, and breaking the topic into areas that will be taken on by single students or pairs of students. A recorder should be appointed to record the organizational plan to ensure that ideas are not lost and later to monitor progress and meeting of deadlines. Teachers should circulate around the class, giving assistance in the development of a workable plan that is of interest to the students. Once the final planning document has been established, a copy should be posted in the classroom. It not only reminds the group of what they should be doing, but shows that while each student contributes to the group, each group also contributes to the whole class's study of the larger topic.

**Carry out the investigation**   Each class period should begin with a brief review of the group's plan in order to guide their activities for the day. The recorder should note progress, and each member may present a brief summary of their work to date. As students become more experienced with this format, such session can become a problem-solving discussion where students not only share information but also compare their findings and search for ways to apply them to their overall research question. New problems or questions may emerge that will have to be integrated into the existing plan.

**Prepare a final report**   The students must not only organize their findings but must also engage in higher order intellectual activities such as abstracting the main idea of the project, gathering parts into an integrated whole, and planning an informative and interesting final report. Depending on the topic, final reports can take the form of written papers, exhibits, models, dramatic or audiovisual presentations, or learning centres. In planning their final reports, students take the role of the teacher; they must teach their peers in other groups about the information that they have discovered.

**Present the report**   Reports are presented to the entire class and students in the audience are encouraged to express their opinions about what they have seen and heard.

**Evaluate**   Throughout their studies, students will have received useful evaluative feedback from the teacher and their peers about their performance. However, at this point, the teacher will wish to evaluate the students' higher-level thinking and abilities to apply knowledge to new problems, use inferences, and draw conclusions.

It is possible to involve students in the evaluation process. For example, each group might be asked to submit two questions about the most important aspects of their topics. These questions form the test instrument and each student in the class completes the test (excluding the test items from his or her own group). After the exam, the teacher may ask the groups to correct everyone's answers to the questions that they submitted.

Second, the teacher evaluates the investigation process itself by having students examine the processes that they have used. Last, but not least, teachers should also assess the affective components of the process. Students should reflect on how they felt about the topic they studied as well as about how they

**Jigsaw Method:**
a cooperative learning strategy in which each member of a group works on one aspect of a group task, and then all members present what they have learned to the group.

performed during the investigation. This can be accomplished by having students write a brief report about their feelings or through small group discussions.

### The Jigsaw

The Jigsaw Method of teaching (Lucker et al., 1976), requires that students be assigned to small heterogeneous teams, which are referred to as their "home group." The following steps are followed:

1. The academic task at hand is divided into several parts or topics; the number of which will equal the number of team members.

2. Within each home group, each member is assigned a topic on which to become an "expert."

3. Students then leave their home group to form "expert groups," in which students with the same topic meet together to discuss topics, master them, and plan how they will teach them to the other members of their home group.

4. Once the work in the expert groups has been accomplished, members return to their home groups and teach their topic to all members.

5. All students are given individual quizzes to assess their mastery of the topic. Scores are recorded only as grades for individual students; there is no team score. However, in a variation, called Jigsaw II, quiz scores are combined to form team scores, and highest scoring teams are recognized in some rewarding fashion.

## SUMMARY

1. Behavioural and cognitive theories of learning approach learning in different ways. Both models have much to offer to classroom teachers as do techniques that arise from a melding of behavioural and cognitive approaches.

2. Behavioural theory has spawned a number of classroom instructional approaches, the best known of which is Skinner's programed instruction. Discovery learning and the hierarchical approaches of Ausubel, Gagné, and others arise from the cognitive school.

3. The major use of behavioural principles in the classroom is in the area of maintaining, modifying, or eliminating behaviour. A wide range of strategies appropriate for individuals or groups have demonstrated success.

4. Learning self-management and appropriate metacognitive strategies enhances student achievement and classroom management. These skills must often be directly taught.

5. Instruction in thinking skills and problem-solving strategies is currently emphasized. Without altering the regular curriculum, students can gain enhanced skills in these areas through instruction and practice.

6. Cooperative learning has emerged from research examining the effects of different goal structures in classroom. Many different variations of coopertive learning methods have been developed and research indicates that many positive academic and affective outcomes are associated with the use of this approach.

## Key Terms

advance organizer

competitive goal structure

cooperative goal structures

differential reinforcement of alternative
    behaviour (DRA)

discovery learning

expository teaching

feedback

Group Investigation

interdependent group-oriented contingency system

meaningful receptive learning

nonexclusionary time-out

physical prompts

praise

problem solving

reciprocal teaching

self-instruction

self-punishment

shaping

Teams-Games-Tournaments (TGT)

transfer of learning

visual prompts

applied behaviour analysis

contingency contract

dependent group-oriented contingency system

differential reinforcement of incompatible
    behaviour (DRI)

exclusionary time-out

fair-pair rule

goal structures

individualistic goal structure

Jigsaw Method

model prompts

participation structures

planned ignoring

Premack principle

prompts

seclusionary time-out

self-management

self-reinforcement

Student Teams—Achievement Divisions (STAD)

time-out from positive reinforcement

verbal prompts

# 5

**EFFECTIVE CLASSROOMS**

To keep the school room neat and clean, you must sweep the floor at least once daily, scrub the floor at least once a week with hot soapy water, clean the blackboards at least once a day, and start the fire at 7:00 a.m., so the room will be warm by 8:00 a.m. (c. 1890, in Clamp, 1990).

Teacher Wanted

Bilingual expert in special education with familiarity in computer literacy who has a sound basis in learning theory and knowledge of multicultural issues and who possesses guidance skills necessary to deal with the diverse and changing needs of society, such as the single-parent family and child abuse, and who can teach by precept and example the morals and values acceptable to the entire community. Candidates must be able to individualize the learning process for thirty or more students, identify learning problems, and have good entrepreneurial skills. As well, the successful candidate must be able to work well under wage restraints and with limited resources. Additional consideration will be given to the teacher who has skills in music, art, drama, and macramé and who can supervise three hundred children on a five-acre playground after a twenty-minute lunch break.

The individual must be in good physical and mental condition; be able to work eight periods each day, plan lessons and mark tests at night; and be willing to improve skills during after-school professional growth programs. Above all else, the person must display an inordinate amount of love, patience, and understanding for each child (Dunphy, 1989).

**M**
**A**
**J**  **This section is designed to:**
**O**
**R**     • present the principles of motivation as they apply to classroom instruction and student learning;

          • illustrate the effects that the expectations and attitudes held by teachers can have on student learning and achievement;

**O**     • demonstrate that the evaluation of student learning underlies effective instruction;
**B**
**J**     • discuss the various types of measurement used in classrooms and the uses of measurement;
**E**
**C**     • outline the principles, approaches, and techniques that underlie effective teaching;
**T**
**I**     • emphasize the importance of good classroom management and its components; and provide an overview of classroom discipline.
**V**
**E**
**S**

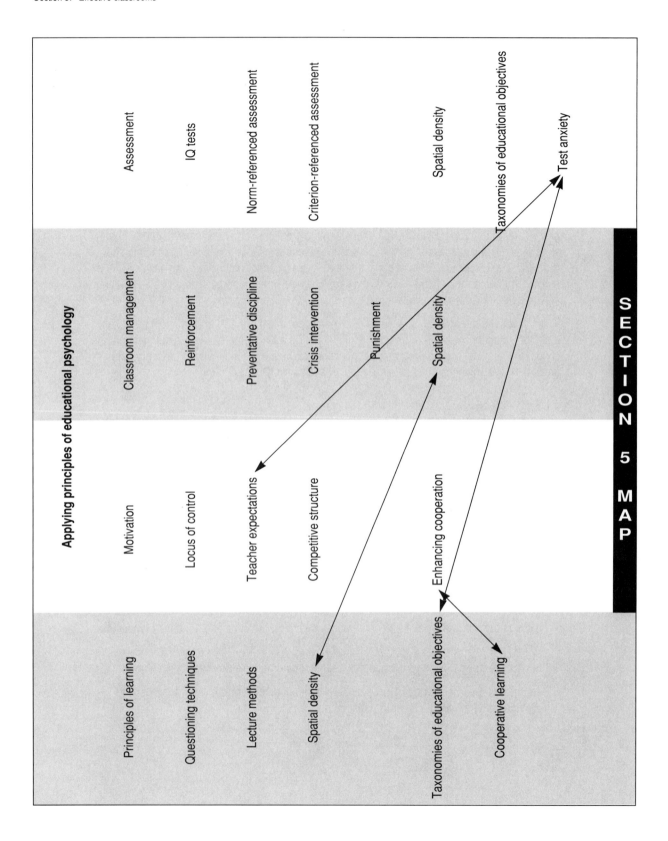

**Applying principles of educational psychology**

Assessment

IQ tests

Norm-referenced assessment

Criterion-referenced assessment

Spatial density

Taxonomies of educational objectives

Test anxiety

Classroom management

Reinforcement

Preventative discipline

Crisis intervention

Punishment

Spatial density

Motivation

Locus of control

Teacher expectations

Competitive structure

Enhancing cooperation

Principles of learning

Questioning techniques

Lecture methods

Spatial density

Taxonomies of educational objectives

Cooperative learning

SECTION 5 MAP

For about five and a half hours everyday for about 190 days a year, teachers are responsible for the education, training, and care of students in their classrooms. In order to create harmony, teachers must orchestrate a number of different jobs and activities. Today's teachers are responsible for an array of instructional activities. Teachers at the elementary level will lead 20 or 30 children of varying abilities and interests through diverse activities each day. At the secondary level, teachers will have a number of classes, often with students of widely varied abilities that may require different teaching methods and different materials. In addition, an implicit goal of contemporary schooling is to foster growth and development in many non-academic dimensions, such as personality, morality, and social skills.

As our opening quotes illustrate, teaching changes with the times. Cleaning the snow form the school steps is no longer within the job specifications of the average classroom teacher, and children no longer sit passively in long rows of benches under the charge of an authoritarian lecturer. Indeed, Dunphy's (1989) "Teacher wanted" advertisement is instructive about the increasing expectations placed on school systems and teachers. As Dunphy says, "Exaggeration, if any, is meant for effect only."

Today's teachers must assume responsibility for a range of activities. Effective teaching presupposes not only that teachers know what pupils are to learn, but that they can evaluate student learning and program success, understand the difficulties that some students will encounter in attempting to learn material, and motivate all students to achieve their full capacities. In the classroom, teachers must teach what provincial curricula charges them to teach, gear their instruction to the varied interests and abilities of their students, devise interesting teaching and practice materials, and workout systematic, consistent and fair ways to evaluate student learning. As well, teachers must be deeply concerned about the social and emotional development of their students and use appropriate means to enhance each student's self-concept and motivation. Not only that, but while they try to present varied curriculum activities they will deal with interruptions,

handle student misbehaviour, and juggle individual student schedules.

In the previous sections of this book we have discussed how children develop across various domains, how individual differences affect development and learning, and how the various theories of learning may be applied to classroom situations. Knowledge about child development is crucial to effective teaching. There are also other elements which, while firmly mounted on theory, are the basis of everyday instruction and interaction in classrooms. This section is concerned with the way in which students can be motivated to learn, the evaluation of the learning, the principles of teaching, and classroom management and discipline.

Motivation is a key factor in all learning and achievement. Motivation can serve as both an objective in itself and as a means of facilitating the achievement of other ends. As an objective, motivation becomes one of the purposes of teaching; as a means, motivation becomes one of the factors—like intelligence or previous learning—that determine whether students will achieve the knowledge, understanding, or skills they require (Gage and Berliner, 1986).

The ability to motivate students in an appropriate fashion is critical to effective teaching. But every day, teachers have to deal with students who do not do their assigned academic work, and who do not appear motivated to reach the goals the teacher has in mind. Yet how can schools expect higher productivity and achievement unless students somehow become more interested in and committed to their own educational improvement? This is the essential challenge of instructional motivation, and the challenge is one that confronts the overburdened classroom teacher daily.

Teachers who are systematic and consistent in their teaching tend to maintain better morale in their classrooms than disorganized teachers (Ryans, 1960). Effective classroom management also involves motivating students—increasing or sustaining their progress toward educational goals.

Classroom management is an inescapable part of teaching. It must be among the first consideration of teachers for, without a favourable classroom climate, very little teaching or learning will occur. The management style of teachers is an important variable in students' productivity. Classroom management controls student output—the quality and quantity of work—and it determines students' attitudes toward their peers, their learning, and school life in general. Teachers must keep class members organized and busy; production and morale high, rewards meaningful, motivation maintained, and adverse behaviours reduced to a minimum (Winzer, 1989).

The confusion of authority and authoritarianism is one of the most basic dilemmas facing teachers. A teacher who does not have a sound and defensible concept of discipline is unable to integrate its many facets cohesively and will be unable to readily produe a rationale for his or her approach to classroom management. Educational theory and research have provided teachers with a plethora of principles and practices that are appropriate in establishing good order and classroom discipline. These approaches require skill and discipline but have the potential for creating positive relationships, cooperation, and self-direction in students.

Strong classroom organization and management, consistent and fair discipline, and high motivation provide optimal conditions for student learning. The teacher's methods, approaches, and techniques determine how instruction will be presented. Clear goals and objectives, varied and interesting approaches, alternate instructional methods and individualization for unique students optimize learning in the classroom. Also, a consistent range of evaluative procedures gives teachers information regarding students' progress toward the attainment of objectives and knowledge about the success of programs.

# MOTIVATION IN THE CLASSROOM

**12**

## INTRODUCTION

The word "motivation" is apt to bring to mind a variety of ideas and concepts. The word is widely used in everyday language and we hear about all sorts of people who are motivated to do, or not to do, all sorts of things. Parents wonder why their children are motivated to act the way they do. Newspapers are filled with speculation about the motives—ulterior and otherwise—of politicians, crooks, and philanthropists. Teachers, too, make frequent use of the term, especially when they are frustrated over some student's lack of motivation to complete his or her studies. However, when a teacher says that a student is not motivated, that often means that the student is not doing what the teacher has in mind.

In our classrooms, there are certainly students who do not learn in the manner and at the pace of average students. Individual differences, such as mildly handicapping conditions or sensory impairments, account for some of the problems. Yet every teacher meets children who, no matter how exciting the program or how interesting the content, seem notably unwilling to participate and learn. Such students frustrate and bother teachers who must then search for methods to motivate these youngsters.

What makes a student move toward instructional goals and how to maximize that movement are questions that arise in every classroom, in every school, and are resolved—for good or ill—by individual teachers (McDaniel, 1984). What does a teacher need to do to motivate a student to learn? Fifty years ago the topic of motivation was virtually ignored in teacher education programs. Teachers of that day were told to "have a good lesson plan," "be enthusiastic," and use "grades and prizes" to stimulate interest (McDaniel, 1984). Today psychologists recognize the complexity of motivation as a crucial element in instructional success. Theories abound and form the bases for

**Motivation:**

the energy or force that directs human behaviour; the affect, or emotional response to a problem situation which then influences how the problem will be viewed and solved.

techniques and approaches designed to enhance students' motivation to participate and learn.

Psychologists vary in their definition of motivation but almost all definitions encompass the notion of energy and direction and the term is used to describe a general tendency to strive toward certain types of goals. Simply, motivation can be defined as the energy or force that directs human behaviour. It is "a combination of an internal predisposition to initiate, sustain and terminate behaviour in well-defined areas as well as external stimulating conditions which activate, sustain, or depress behaviour" (Feldhusen and Hoover, 1986, p. 140).

In the classroom, motivation refers to a student's affective—or emotional—response to a problem situation which then influences how the problem will be viewed and solved. Motivation arises from a number of sources: success, knowledge of results, interest, level of concern about and fear of failure, and various types of intrinsic and extrinsic forces. Further, motivation may vary in both intensity and direction. Motivation is best seen as a state that can be altered by the environment, rather than as a fixed or stable trait. "Motivation to learn," says Brophy (1986), "is a situationally activated scheme or script developed in part by socialization from the teacher." Simply stated, students are motivated to learn when they are interested. Atkinson (1980) observed that one of the most important conclusions drawn from motivational research is that the relationship of time spent on particular tasks and motivation for that kind of learning is almost linear. Motivation is an essential ingredient of efficient learning. In fact, a student lacking motivation is unlikely to learn anything very well at all.

Theories of learning are concerned with how people acquire knowledge and behaviours while theories of motivation are concerned with why individuals act the way they do. When studying motivation, psychologists generally address one or more of these three basic questions:

1. What causes a person to initiate a behaviour or action?

2. What prompts a person to choose one action over another?

3. What causes a person to either continue or cease behaving in a certain manner?

Like descriptions of the learning process, no single theory adequately encompasses all human behaviour and all human motivation. The major explanations for motivation tend to fall into three fairly clear categories—cognitive, behavioural, and humanistic. Each school provides a different answer to the question "Why do students act the way they do?"

Behaviourists eschew the need for a separate theory of motivation. To them, motivation may be explained by the "incentive function of consequences" (Catania, 1979, p. 147). Behaviourists believe that human behaviour is influenced by antecedents (events that cue behaviour) and consequences (events that reinforce or punish behaviour) and that any given behaviour can be explained with reference to that person's reinforcement history.

Cognitive theorists do not entirely discount the importance of reinforcers, but they place much greater emphasis on the thought processes that guide human decision-making and the resulting behaviours. Cognitive psychologists pay attention to individual perceptions, or the manner in which people perceive their

**Attribution theory of motivation:**
cognitive theory that deals with perceived causes of success and failure in classroom settings.

**Self-actualization:**
the basic and inborn need for people to develop or actualize their talents and capabilities to the limits of their heredity.

Students are motivated to learn what they are interested in.

capabilities, efforts, environmental conditions, and so on. Trying to view the world through students' eyes—or understanding the personal meaning that individuals bring to an event—is critical to the accurate interpretation of their performance. This is particularly the case with the **attribution theory of motivation**, a cognitive theory that deals with individual perceived causes of success and failure in classroom settings.

In concept with the cognitive theorists, humanistic psychologists pay great attention to the individual perceptions held by students. However, they differ in the emphasis that they place on the process of personal development—**self-actualization**—and how this need to explore and expand human potential guides or directs behaviour.

The theories presented here represent a way to interpret student behaviour in the classroom, as well as suggesting techniques that can help students behave more appropriately and achieve more. There is no single recipe for success, but the judicious application of various techniques will enhance the teacher's effectiveness. One area that influences students' achievement, and therefore must be

seen as complementary to motivation, is that of teacher expectations. A body of research demonstrates that the expectations teachers hold for students are contributing factors to student success.

## BEHAVIOURAL VIEW OF MOTIVATION

Those who subscribe to the views of B.F. Skinner see human behaviour as influenced by events that precede (antecedents) and follow (consequences) a response. The manner in which students have been treated in the past—or their reinforcement history—determines their future behaviour. If a student has received reinforcing consequences for completing academic tasks, it is likely that he or she will continue to work hard in class. In contrast, the student whose work has met with an unpleasant stimuli or has simply been ignored will appear to be "unmotivated" to complete class work. Of course, rather than referring to such an unobservable construct as "motivation," behaviourists would refer to the contingency between the student's work and its consequences to explain the student's failure to complete academic tasks. In other words, different reinforcement histories will account for the differences in performance viewed in a particular classroom.

From the behavioural perspective, enhancing student behaviour and achievement is a function of understanding and, if necessary, systematically manipulating the environment in order to produce, maintain, or suppress a response. This can be accomplished by using different types of reinforcers, schedules of reinforcement, and/or aversive consequences. Most contemporary behavioural psychologists have extended their formulations to include at least some aspects of cognitive functioning. The work of one such neobehaviourist, Albert Bandura, has generated some unique ideas concerning the issue of motivation. These are discussed in Box 12-1.

### Box 12-1 Bandura's view of motivation

Albert Bandura believes that human motivation can be explained with reference to two issues: expectations and the setting of goals. First, he feels that humans confront any situation—whether it is a geography lesson or a dive off a ten-metre board—in terms of expectations for success or failure. Of course, these expectations will be based on past experience (e.g., "The last time I dived off a board, I managed a belly-flop"); the consequences of the past behaviour (e.g., "That belly-flop hurt"); and observations of others, or vicarious learning. If a person had observed the previous diver completing a beautiful dive to thunderous applause, the tendency would be to strive harder to achieve the same reward (assuming that reward is valued by the learner).

The second source of motivation identified by Bandura is goal setting, or the setting of standards that will be used to judge the adequacy of a person's performance. Humans set goals for themselves in relation to any activity—and they will continue to strive to meet the standards that they have set. As people work toward their goals, they will reflect on the positive consequences that will occur if the goal is met, as well as the negative consequences of failure. Once the goal is reached, the person will be momentarily satisfied, but soon will launch into a new round of goal setting.

In addition, research and clinical data seem to indicate that the beliefs held by an individual about his or her ability to succeed will influence the amount of effort expended in a particular task, as well as how long that person will persist in the face of obstacles (Bandura, 1977). But a person's sense of self-efficacy may not be the same across all set-tings; for example, a person could have a positive sense of self in relation to diving, yet a negative sense in relation to geometry. Bandura believes that understanding the individual's sense of efficacy can illuminate his or her motivation.

In the classroom, teachers can use modeling, prompting and reinforcement to help facilitate improved goal setting. Students will benefit when they learn to set individualized and realistic goals that are characterized by standards which are precise, moderately difficult, and obtainable in a reasonable period of time. When precise standards are developed, students have unambiguous criteria against which to judge their performances. A goal of moderate difficulty provides a real challenge, but one that could reasonably be accomplished. Therefore, such goals are likely to motivate persistent behaviour and greater effort, and thus will enhance the person's sense of self-efficacy.

## Utility in the classroom

In the classroom, there are three major reinforcers—the peer group, the work itself, and the teacher. There exists a considerable body of research that demonstrates the effectiveness of behavioural principles in producing appropriate student behaviour and enhanced academic performance. However, reinforcement from any source will be of little value in increasing motivation for skill acquisition unless reinforcers are used properly.

Too often, extrinsic reinforcers are inappropriately applied in classroom settings or teachers overlook their value. Many believe, for example, that extrinsic rewards spoil children, or diminish their interest in activities that are otherwise intrinsically interesting. Some research indicates that if students receive external rewards for something they enjoy doing anyway, their motivation may actually diminish (Woolfolk, 1990). Other studies (Lepper and Greene, 1975; Lepper, Greene, and Nisbitt, 1973) found that external rewards can decrease both current performance and motivation to continue.

In a classic study that purported to demonstrate this effect, Lepper and colleagues (1973) gave preschoolers felt-tip markers to play with. Those who demonstrated interest in the markers were randomly divided into three separate groups. The first group was told that they would get a "Good Player Award" for

**Deficiency needs:**
a set of physical and psychological needs. When humans are deficient in relation to one of these needs, their behaviour will be directed towards the fulfillment of that need.

drawing a picture; the second group was given the award unexpectedly after drawing was completed; and the third group did not receive an award. Subjects were observed over a four-day period and their free play activity choices were recorded. Those children who had expected to receive a reward spent about half as much time drawing as did children from the other two groups. The researchers suggested that a promise of an extrinsic reward for an activity that was intrinsically interesting seemed to undermine interest.

Later investigations using older children completing more school-like tasks did not support the results of the Lepper study. Rather, these studies suggest that extrinsic rewards increase intrinsic motivation, especially when reinforcement is given for quality of performance rather than for simple participation (Bates, 1979; Lepper, 1983), or when the task itself was not very interesting (Morgan, 1984).

Therefore, while reinforcement should not be indiscriminately used, it does appear to have a crucial place in the school environment. While teachers might hope that every school activity would be intrinsically interesting to their students, it is true that students are often asked to engage in difficult, boring, or otherwise unpleasant tasks. In such cases, extrinsic reward will likely produce better student behaviour and achievement.

## Humanistic view of motivation

One of the most influential humanistic psychologists was Abraham Maslow (1943; 1954; 1970), who conceptualized motivation as stemming from the human's drive to satisfy basic needs. Box 12-2 describes Maslow's life and work in more detail. As shown in Figure 12-1, Maslow (1954, 1970) suggests that human needs fall into a hierarchy, which can be separated into two general need systems. The first system encompasses deficiency needs, which are so named because they motivate humans (or direct their behaviour) when they are deficient in relation to that need. Fulfilling these deficiency needs is necessary for physical and psychological well-being. The basic deficiency needs include:

1. Physiological needs: these are the basic biological needs that must be met to ensure the continuation of life, such as food, sleep, and water.

2. Safety needs: these needs reflect the human tendency to seek a nonthreatening, predictable, and socially satisfying environment, such as security and psychological safety.

3. Needs for belonging and love: these needs are involved with the establishment of human relationships and the need for affiliation, to belong to social groups, and include love, affection, and acceptance.

4. Need for self-esteem: humans have a need to develop and maintain a good feeling about themselves (their worth and competence) as well as to garner authentic and sincere respect and approval from others.

**Figure 12-1**
Maslow's hierarchy
of needs

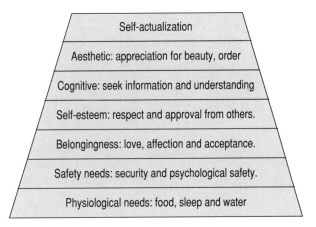

Self-actualization

Aesthetic: appreciation for beauty, order

Cognitive: seek information and understanding

Self-esteem: respect and approval from others.

Belongingness: love, affection and acceptance.

Safety needs: security and psychological safety.

Physiological needs: food, sleep and water

---

Box 12-2 **Biographical note: Abraham Maslow (1880–1961)**

Abraham Maslow was a talented experimental psychologist who, by the late 1940s, had begun to rebel against the traditional tenets of his discipline. Indeed, although his students enjoyed his teaching, his forays into unconventional subjects led to his ostracism from most of his professional peers. The climate improved somewhat by 1952, when Maslow was asked to chair the new department of psychology at Brandeis University; nevertheless, he felt out-of-step with the behavioural view taken by most psychologists of the day.

Since he was not interested in conducting research in the behavioural domain, he had a great deal of difficulty disseminating his ideas through the professional literature. He compensated by forming a mailing list of like-minded thinkers—termed the Eupsycian Network—who exchanged mimeographed copies of their writings. The group was so termed because its members were all interested in "helping the individual grow toward fuller humaneness, the society grow toward synergy and health, and all societies and all people move toward becoming one world and one species (Maslow, 1968, p. 237). This list grew over the years, and in 1960 it represented the first subscribers to the new Journal of Humanistic Psychology and members of the new formed American Association of Humanistic Psychology. By this time, the work of Maslow and his colleagues had emerged as a viable challenge to the practices of the day.

**Growth needs:**
human tendency towards psychological growth.

At the upper levels of Maslow's hierarchy are growth needs. These needs do not redress deficiencies; instead, they reflect the human tendency toward psychological growth. People will pay attention to growth needs only after their deficiency needs have been met. The growth needs include:

1. Cognitive needs: the human tendency to seek information and understanding, including how to do things and the meaning of things, events and symbols.

2. Esthetic needs: this includes a person's appreciation for beauty and the balance of order of life.

3. Self-actualization needs: humanistic psychologists believe that the process of self-actualization is central to the human condition. Maslow (1954) describes this as the need for humans to "become everything that one is capable of becoming" (p. 92).

Maslow placed these needs in a hierarchy to reflect his belief that needs occurring higher in the structure will be addressed by the individual only after lower-level needs have been met. In other words, the child who is not getting enough to eat will not be concerned with the higher needs for safety and love and belongingness; similarly, the child whose home is disrupted by death or divorce may lack a sense of security and belongingness and will therefore not be concerned with the higher needs for self-esteem. However, Maslow (1943) noted that some people may be satisfied by meeting needs at various levels simultaneously, but that satisfaction will decrease as the learner moves up the hierarchy without satisfying lower needs.

Maslow further believes that growth needs are never met in the same sense that deficiency needs can be fulfilled. Rather, the satisfaction that comes with fulfilling growth needs enhances the person's tendency to strive for further fulfilment. The process is endless; under appropriate conditions, humans will continue to seek greater and greater actualization of their potential.

## Utility in the classroom

Maslow's conception of the hierarchy of needs is still influential in school and clinical settings, even though it is generally acknowledged that it does not fully explain human behaviour. Most readers could easily generate historical and personal examples of persons who have neglected nutrition, affiliation, or even personal safety needs in their pursuit of knowledge (Woolfolk, 1990). It is not possible, for example, to explain the behaviour of Joan of Arc, Mother Teresa, or Soviet dissidents with reference to Maslow's formulations.

However, Maslow's hierarchy remains influential in the classroom, if only because it reminds teachers of the humanistic emphasis on the needs of the whole child. Humanistic educators have two general, simultaneous goals—to cultivate their students' interest in subject matter and to develop their students' self-regard.

When problems in motivation are encountered, instructors must consider the physical, emotional, and social needs of children, rather than simply their performance on academic tasks. While research may not entirely support Maslow's hierarchy of needs, it makes intuitive sense that children who are hungry, abused, neglected, or feeling frightened and unsure about their places in the world are unlikely to be motivated to learn fractions or the capitals of the ten provinces.

While we would like to believe that all children come from warm, safe, and nuturing home environments, the reality of the classroom starkly illustrates that many have not had their basic human needs met. In most classes such children are in the minority; however, it is possible that many motivatoinal problems in the classroom can be traced to these basic deficiencies. Recognizing this, many Canadian school systems have implemented breakfast or snack programs to feed hungry students, and warm clothing and footwear are distributed to children who lack such necessities.

Physiological needs can be met in a relatively straightforward fashion; it is more difficult to address the remaining deficiency needs—those for safety, love and belongingness, and self-esteem. Difficult, that is, but not impossible; the teacher can strive to make the classroom a safe, warm, and accepting environment. Chances of failure should be minimized whenever possible and those mistakes that do occur should be seen as opportunities for growth and understanding, rather than as occasions for ridicule or embarrssment. This effort may be particularly important for students whose parents have separated or divorced, for they often feel a lack of security that will negatively impinge upon their performance in school. If children do not find security in their own homes, school may be the only refuge in which they can seek a feeling of belongingness. When students feel safe and secure, they will turn toward the fulfillment of their affiliation needs. Friendships with peers, acceptance from the group, and love relationships become paramount. If these needs cannot be met, Maslow believes that maladjustment may result.

Consistent with his humanistic perspective, Maslow does not view schools simply as places where knowledge is learned and skills are acquired. Instead, he views

Teachers can help make the school a place where interpersonal relationships flourish.

schools as places where interpersonal relationships are allowed to flourish. Teachers can facilitate this goal through the careful monitoring of social interactions in order to identify those children who have difficulty in achieving acceptance and recognition from their groups. It may be necessary to intervene to ensure that every child has the opportunity for affiliation and acceptance from peers. The need for affiliation can be accomplished during instructional activities by using methods such as cooperative learning which allows students to work together in a structure that maximizes their appreciation of the contributions of others.

The need for esteem—receiving respect from others as well as feeling positive regard for oneself—forms the next level of the hierarchy. Children who regard themselves as worthy and who sense that they have the respect of others will be confident and seek independence. There are many ways that self-esteem can be enhanced in the classroom. These are discussed in Box 12.3.

---

### Box 12-3 In the classroom: Building self-esteem

While self-esteem is multifaceted and influenced by many factors other than school life, it has been shown that teachers play an important role in generating high esteem in their students in the classroom (Hoge, Smit, and Hanson, 1990). Some suggestions for helping students develop and maintain high self-esteem follow:

- Tailor work demands to the ability level of the students. Students who experience success in school are more likely to feel pride and a sense of accomplishment.

- Praise student work, but sincerely and only when such positive feedback is deserved. While kindly intended, overly effusive feedback or undeserved praise is likely to be aversive to students, rather than boosting their sense of esteem.

- Act with respect for students, showing how the unique abilities of each are valued. In Maslow's opinion, this type of modeling will help students see that everyone has something important to contribute.

- Create a school climate that encourages student choice and creative self-expression (for a review, see Purkey and Novak, 1984). In addition, a school climate that allows students autonomy and initiative—where they are not treated as pawns to be manipulated by the teacher—results in high self-esteem (Ryan, 1984).

- Ensure that students work under a firm but flexible set of rules. Order and organization are also associated with high self-esteem (Ryan, 1984).

---

The humanistic view of teaching and learning stresses the importance of the teacher's role in facilitating self-actualization. Humanistic educators would neither attempt to determine how a student should go about the process of self-actualization nor what the result from such a process should be. Instead, they recognize that individuals actualize their potential in their own way and that the teacher's task is to facilitate rather than guide this process. By understanding and accepting learning styles, interests, and aptitudes, the teacher can produce a safe, nonthreatening environment in which all students can reach their potential.

## Cognitive view of motivation

While cognitive psychologists will acknowledge the usefulness of extrinsic reinforcers in some circumstances, they believe that intrinsic motivation explains much of human behaviour. When applied to scholastic endeavours, this position implies that well-conceived learning activities will motivate students to seek knowledge on their own and enjoy learning for its own sake. Learners will be motivated by their curiosity as well as the satisfying sense of accomplishment that comes with the completion of a challenging task.

The importance of intrinsic motivation has been emphasized in a somewhat different way in Piaget's theory of cognitive development. According to Piaget's theory, cognitive development can be characterized by a sequence of mutually interrelated stages. Individuals advance through these stages as a result of their interactions with the environment, whether it is defined in physical, social, or cognitive terms. It is the individual's attempt to assimilate increasingly complex and abstract aspects of the environment that promotes developemnt. Although Piaget does not explicitly refer to motivation, it is implicit in his theory that cognitive development and learning are based on the individual's desire to understand and therefore master salient and significant aspects of their environment. Piaget would argue that the motivation to learn, or to seek a solution, comes from the sense of discomfort or disequilibrium that is experienced by an individual who confronts a new and thorny problem. It is not necessary to promise a reward to the person experiencing such disequilibrium; instead, that person will seek to solve the problem and in so doing, modify existing schemata in order to achieve understanding or a renewed sense of equilibrium.

Cognitive theorists such as Jean Piaget and Jerome Bruner believe that properly structured learning situations preclude the need for the extensive use of rewards, such as gold stars, grades, or other forms of recognition. Instead, they believe that, when properly challenged, students will be self-motivated. Students will work hard in the absence of any apparent external rewards in order to achieve a sense of understanding.

### Utility in the classroom

Theorists from the cognitive school obviously have a great deal of information relevant to classroom settings. The importance of intrinsic motivation cannot be minimized and teachers should always try to ensure that activities are intrinsically interesting. This is probably easier with some curriculum areas than others; it is easy to see the intrinsic interest of art while more imagination is needed to enhance the study of grammar. Of course, obtaining a match between the students' interests and ability levels and the curriculum is more easily accomplished within more open structures, such as the open education or discovery learning models advocated by some cognitive theorists. However, implementing such learning models is difficult, if not impossible, for the teacher restricted by the demands of curriculum guides and monitored by standardized examinations. Finally, it cannot be denied that despite the teachers' best attempts, some classroom activities simply will not be intrinsically interesting to every student.

## Attribution theory

There exist a number of other theories of motivation that can be seen to derive from the cognitive perspective. The first is attribution theory, as articulated by theorists such as Bernard Weiner (1972, 1979). Consistent with the cognitive perspective, attribution theory studies the individual's perception of events, or more specifically, the explanations people formulate regarding their successes or failures. We can see many examples of this in our daily lives; for example, when psychology students do poorly on a mid-term examination, they may try to explain the reason for this failure by attributing their performance to factors such as their own ability, effort, interest, or the clarity of the material presented by the instructor. We hear, "I'm just not smart enough," "I didn't study enough," "I couldn't care less," and "No one could answer those stupid questions."

By attributing success or failure to such factors, people are attempting to justify, explain, or determine the reasons for their performance. When applied to the classroom, Weiner believes that attributions can be classified in three different ways, and that each has important implications for instruction:

1. External or internal. These are attributions to factors that are either outside the person or inside (or characteristic) of them. For example, students who blame their poor performance on a poorly constructed test are attributing their failure to an external factor. But if those same individuals were to attribute their failure to a lack of intellectual ability, the reference is to an internal factor. This dimension appears to be closely related to the person's sense of self-esteem, personal confidence, pride, guilt, or shame (Weiner, 1980). If the cause of success is seen to be due to internal factors, such as intellectual ability, the person is likely to feel a sense of pride and accomplishemnt; failure to achieve is likely to lead to shame or guilt. If the cause is seen to be external, the student who feels that the examination was poorly constructed is likely to feel anger and frustration, while a student who feels that the examination was well-done and easy to complete would likely feel gratitude towards the instructor.

2. Stable or unstable. As well, the reasons used to explain performance can be considered as either stable or unstable. For example, most adults would consider their level of intellectual ability to be a relatively stable or unchanging factor while such factors as mood, luck, or time spent preparing for an examination are unstable (or amenable to change). This dimension is highly related to personal expectations for the future. For example, if psychology students doubt their inherent ability, they will likely hold the expectation that they will perform poorly on future psychology examinations. However, if students feel that their failure can be attributable to an unstable factor,

such as insufficient preparation, a bad mood, or simply bad luck, they are more likely to expect success in the future.

3. Controllable or uncontrollable. Some factors are perceived by the individual to be controllable, such as time spent in preparation, while others such as ability, luck, or mood are considered to be uncontrollable.

People will try to explain their performance with reference to some combination of internal or external, stable or unstable, and controllable or uncontrollable factors. The research on attributions reveals that only a small number of categories are regularly used by students to account for their successes and failures. The most frequently used include effort, ability, mood, task difficulty, and luck (Bar-Tel and Darom, 1979; Frieze and Snyder, 1980).

There appear to be clear patterns in the manner in which certain students will make attributions. In a review of many studies (Whitley and Frieze, 1985), it was noted that many adults and children hold to an egotistic attribution system, which leads them to attribute success to internal factors such as ability and effort and failure to external factors, such as luck or task difficulty. For example, if you ask such people why they did poorly on an examination, they would likely respond along these lines: "I guess I didn't study enough." And because such a factor is both internal as well as controllable, students will be able to generate strategies that would allow them to do better the next time. But even if they attribute their failure to an external cause, such as an unfair examination, this will not affect their expectations for future success.

However, some students do not use such ego-sustaining strategies. That is, students who generally perform poorly on school tasks are likely to attribute their failure to a lack of ability and therefore come to expect repeated failure in the future. Since they doubt their ability, they are likely to avoid achievement-oriented activities or to avoid working hard at achievement-oriented tasks (Gage and Berliner, 1986).

At the same time, these students are likely to attribute their success to an external, uncontrollable factor such as luck or an easy test. Because they are unable to change such factors, they have no reason to expect repeated success in the future and become resigned to failure (Weiner, Russell, and Lerman, 1978). Who could blame such students for being "unmotivated"? They feel that there is nothing that they can do to alter their performance at school and, unlike students who feel that they are able to control their successes, such students are unlikely to seek help since they feel nothing can change their situation (Ames and Lau, 1982). It has been demonstrated that attribution patterns are faily stable over time and settings, and that specific intervention is needed to change such self-defeating attribution patterns (Bar-Tel, Raviv, and Bar-Tel, 1982).

Do be aware, also, that attributional cues can be communicated by others, such as teachers. For example, it has been documented that such seemingly positive teacher behaviours as praise for success at easy tasks, the absence of blame for failure at such tasks, and affective displays of sympathy or compassion can communicate to the recipients of this feedback that they are low in ability (Barker and Graham, 1987; Graham, 1984; Weiner et al., 1983). Thus, indirect sources of negative feedback are to be found in prevalent teacher behaviours and in situations of success as well as imminent failure (Graham and Barker, 1990).

**Achievement motivation:**

the generalized tendency to strive for success and to choose goal-oriented success/failure activities.

## Achievement motivation

Work emerging from the study of attribution theory has resulted in another perspective on motivation. It was during the 1950s that McClelland and his colleagues (1953) identified four primary motives: the need for achievement, affiliation, power, and approval. The motive that is most relevant to the classroom situation is achievment motivation.

McClelland and Atkinson were among the first to concentrate on **achievement motivation** (McClelland et al., 1953), the generalized tendency to strive for success and to choose goal-oriented success/failure activities. People who strive for excellence in a field for the sake of achieving and not for some reward are considered to have high need for achievment (n-Ach).

The concept of achievement motivation tries to explain why some students appear to have a need or drive to achieve while others seem to fear or avoid success. Achievement-motivated students both want and expect to succeed and when they fail they redouble their efforts until they do succeed (Weiner, 1980). Most of us have observed students who persisently work toward the accomplishment of some goal, and whose work is usually successful. In contrast, others seem to lack such persistence, showing only half-hearted attempts to complete a task.

Many personality factors affect achievement motivation, often in complicated ways. This applies to all age groups (Howell, Ohlendorf, and McBroom, 1981). The origins of high achievement motivation are assumed to be the familial and cultural groups of the child. Research suggests that parenting practices are related to the degree to which children develp the need to achieve or to avoid failure. For example, in a classic study, Winterbottom (1953) observed parents of 30 middle-class boys, aged eight to ten. It was found that mothers of boys with high achievement motivation set higher standards for their children, expected more independence and mastery at an earlier age, and used affectionate rewards, such as hugs and kisses, more often than did the mothers of boys with low achievement motivation. Similarly, Rosen and D'Andrade (1959) studied parents interacting with their sons when the boys were attempting a task. Parents of boys with higher achievement motivation set higher standards for their sons, expected more improvement, and controlled behaviour more directly by expressions of warmth or rejection than did parents of boys with lower achievement motivation.

Peers certainly affect adolescent achievement motivation. While some educators and social scientists have argued that peer influence contributes to a lack of effort and interest in schoolwork (Bishop, 1989; Goodlad, 1984), most adolescents in a recent study said that their peers pressured them to work hard to get good grades more often than they discouraged schoolwork (Brown, Clasen and Eicher, 1986). Probably the effects of peer influence can be either negative or positive; its effects depend on the attitudes and values of peers with whom an adolescent spends most of his or her time (Epstein, 1983; Kandel, 1978). If these peers have little motivation to achieve in school, the adolescent's own motivation is likely to decrease over time; if they have a high level of achievement motivation, the adolescent's motivation is likely to increase (Berndt, Laychek, and Park, 1990).

Not surprisingly, achievement motivation is a difficult concept to measure. Most research has used the Thematic Apperception Test (TAT) (McClelland et al., 1953) in which a subject is shown a series of pictures depicting people engaged in some activity and is asked to write a story about what has happened in the past, what is happening now, and their predictions for the future. The TAT is a projective test. The underlying assumption is that individuals will project their own personal thoughts and feelings into their interpretation of the situation. Those who are judged to be high in achievement motivation tend to write about high standards of performance, and pursuit of long-range goals, reflecting achievement-related motives and themes.

Despite the problems with measurement, research has shown that measures of achievement motivation tend to be highly correlated with other standards of success, such as school achievement and economic success (Dweck and Elliott, 1973; Wendt, 1955). But while students high in achievement motivation tend to do well in school, the cause-effect relationship is difficult to unravel. Does high

Students with a high need to achieve commonly persist with complex problems.

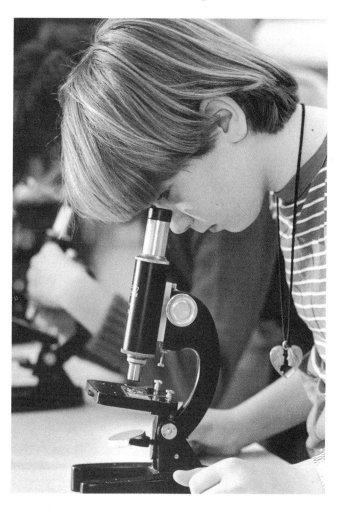

achievement motivation lead to success in school, or is the reverse true? In fact, it appears that each supports the other for when the student is successful, the experiences will enhance the desire for more success, and so on (Gottfried, 1985). Unfortunately, the opposite can also occur, for when a student experiences failure he or she will be more likely to expect failure in the future.

Other research has shown that students with a high need to achieve are more likely than other children to be challenged by the personal effort required in solving problems (Gibson, 1978). They will demonstrate more task persistence, staying with complex problems longer than those with lower levels of achievement motivation and are more likely to reach a solution to the problem (French and Thomas, 1958). Persistence was demonstrated in a study when subjects were asked to complete simple tasks, such as easy arithmetic problems and word unscrambling. Those with a high need to achieve completed more problems in the time allowed than did those with a low need to achieve (Lowell, 1952).

Wendt (1955) demonstrated that as the level of achievement motivation increased in a sample of high school students, so did both the number of arithemetic tasks attempted and the number completed correctly. This held true even when the subjects' rate of performance was measured in an unscheduled period in which students could determine their own rate of performance. It appeared that their achievement orientation prompted them to maintain a high level of performance even in the absence of supervision.

Those with high levels of achievement motivation will also persist in a task even when they are failing (Weiner and Kukla, 1970). This may be the result of the attributions made by the learners; it appears that those with a high need to achieve see their failure as a result of lack of effort (an internal orientation), rather than as a result of some external force. Thus, in order to succeed, they believe that if they maintain or increase their effort, success will eventually come (Gage and Berliner, 1986).

In addition, high achievement motivation is linked with students' tendencies to complete interrupted tasks. Such students seem to create a complex, long-lasting mental structure made up of main activities, side activities, and subactivities. This structure will guide them through a series of steps that lead to the end goal. Thus the process can be sustained for long periods of time, even when repeatedly interrupted (Heckhausen, 1967).

**Avoiding failure versus approaching success**     Atkinson and Raynor (1974) have suggested that achievement motivation consists of two opposing features: the tendency to approach success and the tendency to avoid failure. Some individuals will focus on the need to succeed, while the energy of others will be devoted to the avoidance of failure. Atkinson feels that a person's achievement motivation for any particular task is the strength of the tendency to approach the task minus the strength of the tendency to avoid failure.

In this sense, there seem to be three different types of students—those who are mastery-oriented, those who are failure-avoiding, and those who are failure-accepting (Covington, 1984; Covington and Beery, 1976). These characteristics are shown in Table 12-1.

**Table 12-1** Types of students

| MASTERY-ORIENTED | FAILURE AVOIDING | FAILURE ACCEPTING |
|---|---|---|
| • generally successful | • experience some success and a good bit of failure | • become convinced that problems are due to low ability and that there is little hope for change |
| • view themselves as capable | • have not formed a firm sense of their own competence and self-worth | |
| • high in achievement motivation | • may procrastinate to avoid failure | |
| • select moderately challenging problems | • may eventually become failure accepting | |
| • tend to take risks | | |
| • perform best in competitive situations | | |
| • learn fast and assume responsibilty | | |
| • readily demonstrate more self-confidence and energy | | |

SOURCE: Alderman, 1985; McClelland, 1985.

A classic study illustrates how individuals with a need to succeed differ from those who tend to avoid failure. Male subjects were asked to play a ring-toss game and were allowed to select the distance from which they were to toss the rings (Atkinson and Litwin, 1960). Men with high achievement motivation tended to stand at a intermediate distance from the peg, showing a high tendency to approach success with a corresponding low tendency to avoid failure. They did not shy away from the challenge but also did not set an impossible task for themselves. In contrast, men with low achievement motivation tended to either stand very far away from the peg or very close. In either case, they were able to avoid failure: by setting such an impossible goal that they could not be blamed for their failure or by structuring an easy task to assure their success. Their tendency to avoid failure was greater than their tendency to approach success.

In a similar study, subjects were given a choice between a task with a definite single correct answer (completing a puzzle) or one that had no one answer (judging a picture). Subjects who tended to seek success chose the puzzle while those who wished to avoid failure chose to judge the picture (Weiner and Rosenbaum, 1965). Smith (1964) noted that students with a high need to seek success will leave an examination more quickly than students with a need to avoid failure when they perceive the answers as easy, while the reverse is true when they perceive the questions as more difficult.

When looking at real-life experiences that might occur in the classroom, it was found that when students are free to choose a work partner, those with a high need for achievement will choose the more competent partner over the

**Locus of control:**

the source to which an individual attributes responsibility for the outcome of events or behaviours. The tendency of individuals to perceive reinforcements as deriving either from within themselves or from forces beyond their immediate control indicates an internal or external locus of control.

**Internal locus of control:**

a student's view of success or failure as a consequence of his or her own actions.

**External locus of control:**

a student's view that success or failure is due to circumstances beyond his or her control.

opportunity to work with a friendly partner. But a person with a high affiliation need and low achievement need will choose the friendly partner (French,1956). Adult learners in college who are seeking success will choose courses of moderate difficulty, while those trying to avoid failure choose either very easy or very difficult courses (Isaacson, 1964). Even when students with a high need to achieve fail when completing a task, they will react by increasing their effort to succeed. In contrast, when individuals who wish to avoid failure encounter an unsuccessful experience, their efforts will be diminished (Weiner, 1972).

In addition, those who tend to avoid failure are more likely to make unrealistic career choices than those who seek success (Mahone, 1960). Moreover, people who choose different professions differ from one another in the factors that motivate them to achieve. Erez and Sheorson (1980) found that most university professors are motivated by the opportunity to make scientific contributions, by autonomy, and by the status of their jobs. Professionals in industry tend to be highly motivated by the opportunity to exercise power.

It should be noted that most research in achievement motivation has been completed with male subjects. As recently as twenty years ago, females were seen as demonstrating different patterns of achievement motivation. However, as the society changes, there is also a corresponding change in achievement motivation in girls and women.

**Locus of control**

Locus of control, self-esteem and tolerance of ambiguity are three affective variables that have been shown to be highly related to achievement. Related to locus of control are the concepts of learned helplessness and emotional overlays. The construct of locus control was first suggested by Rotter (1954). **Locus of control** describes the degree to which individuals attribute their success or failure to their own efforts and abilities or to external factors. When students view success or failure as a consequence of their own actions, they have an **internal locus of control** ("I failed because I didn't study." "I succeeded because I'm smart"). In contrast, those who attribute success or failure to external events (luck, task difficulty, or actions of others) have an **external locus of control** ("I succeeded because I was very lucky." "I failed because the teacher hates me").

Like self-concept, locus of control emerges over time, and is primarily influenced by the child's experiences in school: it is a learned behaviour. Seligman (1975) marshalled impressive evidence to show that people (and animals) become passive—initiate little activity and lose motivation—when placed in situations where outcomes are unaffected by their behaviour. In students, the development of locus of control may be primarily influenced by the child's experiences in school. Kifer (1975) measured locus of control and self-concept in high- and low-achieveing second, fourth, sixth, and eighth graders (those who comprised the upper and lower 20 percent of the class). There were no differences between the measures of internality in successful and unsuccessful second grade students. However, by the fourth grade, differences could be seen between the high and low achievers, with the former group measuring higher in internality than the latter. The differences became even more pronounced as the students got older. In terms of self-concept, while all of the subjects in second grade had similar self-concepts, the scores of low-achieving students began to drop after grade four, an effect that accelerated as the students proceeded through school.

Thus, it is believed that most students begin school on a similar, if not equal footing. If some do not succeed, they will first place the blame on external events, such as luck or task difficulty. But after these students have been repeatedly told (implicitly or explicitly) that they are incompetent, they will begin to attribute their failure to internal causes (Buys and Winefield, 1982). After repeated failures, children do not expect to succeed in academic tasks, and not surprisingly, they stop trying. And of course, this starts a never-ending cycle of lack of effort, failure, even lower expectations for success, and thus less effort, and so on.

Students who are mentally retarded, for example, appear less motivated to succeed. They don't seem to take the pleasure that non-retarded children do in manipulating and mastering the environment. This lack of motivation seems to be accompanied with an expectation for failure. As several studies have shown, retarded children tend to experience failure more often than other children, and therefore learn to expect it (MacMillan, 1971; MacMillan and Keogh, 1971). As children picture themselves as underachieving or non-achieving, they try less and achieve even less.

In contrast, students whose locus of control is highly internal believe that their success or failure is due to their own efforts. If they desire success, such students will simply work harder to achieve their goal. In fact, the most successful students may overestimate the importance of their own efforts. Some studies have shown that in situations in which student success or failure is completely due to luck, students who have a strongly internal locus of control will still attribute their success or failure to their own efforts (Lefcourt, 1976).

There is a substantial consensus that young children define intelligence behaviourally. Until approximately the ages of seven or eight, children understand ingelligence to be a skill or performance, not an intellectual trait (see Goodman, 1989). They are apt to explain success or failure in terms of situational factors (a difficult problem, limited time, or personal effort) rather than ability (Goodman, 1989). Up to adolescence, children are likely to attribute their problems to external causes—environment, social pressures, family, or parents. Later in adolescence, youths are more likely to attribute problems to internal factors such as thier own thoughts and feelings (Kazdin, 1989).

While locus of control can change as a result of experience, it can also vary for the same individual in different circumstances. For example, a student who is a gifted athlete may have an internal locus of control when she participates in sports, but an external locus of control in language arts (which may reflect lower academic ability in this area).

Determining a student's locus of control can help to interpret that student's behaviour. It has been shown, for example, that students who have a low internal locus of control will usually have lower grades and test performances than students of the same level of intelligence who have a high internal locus of control (Lefcourt, 1976; Nowicki, Duke, and Crouch, 1978). Locus of control has been demonstrated to be one of the most important predictors of student achievement, surpassed only by student ability level (Brookover et al., 1979). Individuals with an internal locus of control will prefer and do better in situations in which skill determines the outcome, while persons with an external locus of control prefer and perform better in situations in which the outcome is determined by chance (Lefcourt, 1966).

A relationship between locus of control and school achievement does not mean that locus of control causes success or failure. Cunningham, Gerald, and Miller (1978) demonstrated this when they gave false information to learners about whether they had succeeded or failed in reaching a goal. They found that the information had far less effect on locus of control than real performance. The researchers concluded that increasing externality is the result, rather than the cause, of long-term experiences of failure. Kifer (1975) found that changes in locus of control and self-esteem both occur gradually and with repeated experiences of success or failure.

### Learned helplessness

Students who do not believe in themselves develop feelings of shame and self-doubt (Covington and Omelich, 1981), particularly in the face of successive failures. Students who retain an outward locus of control may revert to learned helplessness, a situation in which they attribute failure to external causes rather than to effort and tend to show decreases in performance following failure (Licht and Dweck, 1984). Students who have learned helplessness believe events in their lives have little or nothing to do with their efforts (Abramson, Seligman, and Teasdale, 1978). No matter what they do, they see themselves as doomed to failure. Learned helplessness can therefore be seen as an extreme form of the motive to avoid failure (Slavin, 1988). Because students do not have faith in their abilities, they often refuse to even try school tasks. By not attempting school tasks, their poor performance is attributed to lack of effort, which is less stigmatized in our society than lack of ability is (Covington and Omelich, 1981).

### Utility in the classroom

For many students, attending school represents a series of success and/or failure experiences. Attribution theory is therefore particularly relevant to classroom practice, for it explains the manner in which students interpret these events. Teacher behaviour is assigned a central role in this approach to motivation, as the feedback given by teachers will certainly influence the perceptions held by the students (Pintrich and Blumfield, 1985).

The old saying that success breeds success is as true for children as it is for anybody else. While motivation is a construct that is accessible only through its manifestations, success in academic tasks increases motivation (Atkinson and Feather, 1966; Bloom, 1971). When attempts are made to motivate children to do their school work, increasing the success rate for children with a high ratio of failure would be an important starting point (Dickenson and Butt, 1989).

Schunk (1985) has suggested that teachers need to give immediate positive feedback to students so that they see the connection between their effort and past accomplishments, as well as to highlight the progress that they have made. Children who get such information about their performance are more likely to learn more effectively than are those who do not get such feedback. Unfortunately, many classroom events or comments can implicitly or explicitly denigrate the level of ability demonstrated by some students. Of course, few teachers would make direct comments on a student's ability, but many common classroom practices can communicate this message just as effectively.

For example, in highly competitive classrooms, the grading system will create a hierarchy or pecking order in the class. Even though there may be little difference in the achievement between two students, the process of ranking may magnify the relative differences in performance (Slavin, 1988). But if competitive practices are minimized, the teacher will be better able to communicate to students that effort, rather than ability, counts highly. Since effort is an internal factor, and therefore under student control, pupils are given the impression that their efforts in the future will lead to success (Ames and Ames, 1984). Regardless of the range of ability levels seen in the classroom, rewarding effort rather than ability is likely to serve as a motivator for all students.

### Programs

In addition to general guidelines for teachers, there exist a series of specific educational programs which are intended to improve achievement motivation in the classroom. One program developed by DeCharms (1976) was intended to help minority students who were from low-income families and who demonstrated low achievement and a sense of learned helplessness. Among other techniques, DeCharms taught the students to become originators, or individuals that control their own fate rather than pawns who are pushed around by others. In other words, students were helped to replace their external locus of control with an internal locus of control. Students were trained to recognize their own strengths and weaknesses, to take responsibility for their actions, to choose realistic objectives, and to plan the concrete actions that they would take in order to meet their objectives. Compared to a control group, these students showed significantly higher levels of achievement in reading and arithmetic and improved achievement motivation. They also attended school more often. In a follow-up study (DeCharms, 1980), it was found that these subjects were more likely to graduate from high school.

Kolb (1965) reported on a six-week achievement training program that was intended to change the behaviour of underachieving high school boys. During the summer, Kolb lived with the boys, all the while providing counseling and modeling behaviour characteristic of those with a high need to achieve. High expectations were communicated to the boys and they were helped to use achievement concepts in planning to improve their future school performance. Simulations, games, and other strategies were used as a means of practising new ways of thinking and behaving. Such a stragety was successful with middle-class students; however, positive results were not seen with lower-class students.

Aronoff, Raymond, and Warmoth (1965) followed Kolb and attempted to formulate a program that would be successful with students from lower-income families. Two achievement motivation courses were conducted, which included the use of material such as case studies, programed text materials, games, and exercises. The subjects included 12 high school students chosen from a larger group of students judged to be potential drop-outs. The remaining students served as a control group. After a year, only one member of the experimental group had dropped out of school while eight of the 35 untrained students had left school (Auschuler, 1967). Trained students improved their average grades, even though they were taking more difficult courses than untrained students, and they reported more new interests and activities.

Other strategies have been developed to help students modify their attributions, or the reasons that they give to explain their successes and failures (see Fosterling, 1985). For example, Dweck (1975) worked with students who exhibited learned helplessness in an attempt to change their attribution tendencies. Through daily exercises over a period of 25 days, subjects learned to take more responsibility for their behaviour when solving mathematics problems, and they learned to attribute failure to a lack of effort. Dweck's positive results were replicated by Andrews and Debus (1978). Similarly, children with mental handicaps (who also frequently demonstrate learned helplessness) have been helped to change their attribution patterns, with resulting improvements in performance (Gold and Ryan, 1979). Students therefore can be helped to change their attributional patterns and can learn to make internal attributions when they observe teachers model and systematicaly reinforce such behaviour.

## TEACHER EXPECTATIONS

Although it does not represent a theory of motivation, no discussion of the topic of motivation would be complete without a discussion of teacher expectations. Teachers are human, and they bring stereotypes and preconceived notions to the classroom. Teachers often do not carefully examine the assumptions that they make about various students, and yet the research indicates that over time, "student behaviour may change to be more congruent with the teacher's implicit or explicit expectations" (Brophy and Good, 1986, pp. 486-487). Therefore, while teachers are often entirely unaware of the effects of their behaviour, they may, in fact, be inhibiting student progress. Teachers who expect students to succeed and treat them accordingly are likely to see them succeed, while teachers who expect children to fail and treat them accordingly are likely to see them fail (Good and Brophy, 1987). This applies to both conduct and learning. Teacher's attitudes determine the classroom atmosphere as well as teachers' expectations about the academic and social progress of their students.

Teacher's expectations may be defined as "inferences that teachers make about the present and future academic achievement and general classroom behaviour of students. Teacher expectations may concern either the entire class or specific individuals" (Good and Brophy, 1986, pp. 486-487).

Teachers' expectations and students' behaviour interact in complicated ways that influence both students' actual achievement and teacher's perceptions about their achievement and the type of assignments they need (Good and Weinstein, 1986). Teachers' expectations are influenced by many factors that include socioeconomic level (Myles and Ratslaff, 1988), race, (Rubovitz and Maehr, 1973), gender (Palardy, 1968), test scores, comments from other teachers, type of school, student appearance (Ross and Salvia, 1975), neatness, behaviour (Lavoie and Adams, 1974), generalizing from poor behaviour, generalizing from a weakness in one area, and standard or nonstandard English patterns.

Students who use standard English, for exmaple, with appropriate intonations and speech that is soft, and moderately pitched are more likely to receive

Until the age of seven or eight, children are apt to explain success or failure in terms of situational factors.

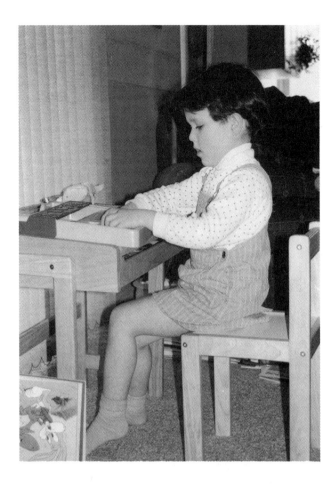

better grades from teachers (Seligman, Tucker, and Lamber, 1972). Further influences may include tracking and grouping patterns, and even seating positions. Teachers seem to hold lower expectations for students seated on the sides and in the back of the classroom (Good and Weinstein, 1986). Sibling performance is also a factor when a teacher holds a predisposition toward a student based upon what a brother or sister did (Seaver, 1973).

Although the literature on academic underachievement is voluminous, Ashbury (1974) points out that there is "a striking lack of clearcut comprehensive exploration" (p. 424). We do know that more boys than girls are underachievers (Pringle, 1970), that boys show more discipline problems than girls, and that boys are more likely to be chastised by teachers. Carrier (1983) points out that "docile, industrious, polite and conforming students.often get grades higher than their objective performance and aptitude merit" (p. 963). These students are more often female. It seems, then, that performance differences between the sexes are for the most part learned behaviours which are influenced by social expectations and the behaviour of adults (Good and Brophy, 1987).

Studies conducted in Canada have shown that Canadian educators are subject to the same influences in regard to students; this has been shown to be true when students are referred by teachers for possible special education. Support

**Sustaining expectation effect:**
effect that occurs when teachers hold unchanging expectations, regardless of student change.

**Self-fulfilling prophecy:**
case where the expectations of the teacher determine the ways in which students are treated, and this treatment will eventually shape the student's behaviour and achievement to become more congruent with these expectations.

was provided for concerns about the high proportion of referred students classified as exceptional on the basis of subjectively experienced characteristics in spite of objective test results which do not qualify them as exceptional. Herbert, Hemingway, and Hutchinson (1984), for example, found that preservice teachers were influenced by gender and race (Native, non-Native) as well as by referral information when required to make diagnostic, classification, and placement decisions for students with test results in the normal range. Similarly, experienced Canadian teachers were found to make decisions that students were exceptional on the basis of student characteristics (gender and race) and referral reports in spite of normal test scores in intelligence and achievement (Hutchinson and Hemingway, 1984).

Of particular concern is whether children from differing cultures have an equal opportunity to succeed within the school system. It has been suggested that teachers often assume that children from some ethnic groups can learn more and faster than children from other ethnic groups. Although we live in a culturally pluralistic society, many of us have difficulty in ceding validity to behaviours that differ from those that we were taught. In the school setting, teacher expectations and student behaviour may clash and the child from a different cultural background may be disadvantaged in the classroom. Teachers form impressions of their students' abilities very quickly and build their expectations for those students upon impressions. Students from visible ethnic minority groups may be discriminated against by school personnel as well as school policies (Myles and Ratslaff, 1988).

Myles and Ratslaff (1988) studied discrimination toward visible minority groups. In Vancouver, 591 public elementary school teachers were sent questionnaires describing fictitious grade five male students whith academic and behavioural problems. The students were identical except for a brief reference to ethnic background—either Native, Asian, East Indian, or Caucasian. The results provided evidence of teacher discrimination or teacher negative bias against the children described as Native, while they showed a positive bias toward Asian and Caucasian children. The Native child was described as not likely to graduate from high school and to have parents who would not be cooperative. In addition, Native children were most often described as appropriate candidates for placement in a class of behaviourally disordered children.

It seems that two kinds of expectation effects can occur in classrooms. First is the self-fulfilling prophecy effect where a teacher's beliefs about a student's abilities are actually incorrect but the student's behaviour comes to match the initially inaccurate expectations. Secondly, teachers can be fairly accurate in their initial reading of children's abilities and respond to children based on those abilities. When teachers hold unchanging expectations, regardless of student change, this is a **sustaining expectation effect**.

With a **self-fulfilling prophecy**, the expectations of the teacher determine the ways in which students are treated. Eventually, the differential treatment will shape the student's behaviour and achievement to become more congruent with these expectations. This effect of teacher expectations was first illustrated by one of the most well-known studies in educational psychology. Robert Rosenthal and Lenore Jacobson's *Pygmalion in the Classroom* (1968) prompted a great deal of interest and controversy; this study is fully explored in Box 12-4.

## Box 12-4 **Classic study: Self-fulfilling prophecy**

In 1968, Rosenthal and Jacobson published *Pygmalion in the Classroom*, a controversial book that caused more than a stir among educators, parents, and the media. To carry out their study, Rosenthal and Jacobson chose several students in grades one through six at random from elementary school classrooms in a single San Francisco public school (Biehler and Snowman, 1990). All the students had been given a test of mental ability at the beginning of the year, a little-known test of intelligence, named Flanagan's Test of General Ability. The teachers were not told the true name of nature of the test but were instead informed that the students had taken the "Harvard Test of Inflected Acquisition." Based on this, randomly selected students were described to their teachers as "late bloomers" who would probably make significant academic gains during that school year. No actual differences existed between the selected students and other pupils not selected for the study.

The selected students did, indeed, make larger gains than normal that year; the same test of general ability used at the outset was administered at the end of the year and showed great gains in the students. It must be noted, however, that the advances seen were mainly in grade one and two students. Children in grades three to six showed no differences.

Since the information given to the teachers about the students was not based on test performance and since, except for the effect of the teacher's expectations, there was no reason to predict increased performance, the researches suggested the existence of a self-fulfilling prophecy in the classroom. Rosenthal and Jacobson referred to this as the Pygmalion effect because they felt that teacher expectations had influenced the students.

When first published, *Pygmalion in the Classroom* created a minor sensation. As they are apt to do, secondary sources describing the Rosenthal and Jacobson study often made exaggerated claims. Educational writers proposed that the results provided the key to revolutionizing the education of disadvantaged students, saying that their low performance was due solely to low teacher expectations (Biehler and Snowman, 1990).

Rosenthal and Jacobson's original study was heavily criticized for the experimental and statistical methods used (Elashoff and Snow, 1971; Snow, 1969). Several researchers tried but could not replicate the findings (Claiborn, 1969; Wilkins and Glock, 1973). Others pointed out that just because positive expectations led to higher scores, it could not be assumed that negative expectations cause lower scores (Wineburg, 1987). But other research continues to demonstrate that teacher expectations can influence student performance (Cornbleth, Davis, and Button, 1974; Good, 1970). Cooper and Good (1983), for example, found the effect to be particularly evident with younger students and when teachers know less about their students' actual level of achievement (Raudenbush, 1984).

Good and Brophy (1978, 1984) propose that the effect of teachers' expectations can be conceptualized as occurring in the following five-step process:

1. The teacher begins by forming expectations about how individual students will behave or how each will do in class and then expects specific behaviour and achievement from particular students.

2. Because of these different expectations, the teacher behaves differently toward the different students.

3. The teacher's treatment tells each student what behaviour and achievement is expected from him or her and affects the student's self-concept, achievement motivation, and level of aspiration.

4. The teacher treats each student according to expectations and students then respond differently, often in ways that complement the teacher's expectations. If the teacher's treatment is consistent over time, and if the student does not actively resist or change it in some way, it will tend to shape his or her achievement and behaviour. Those students who meet with high expectations will be led to achieve at high levels, while the achievement of students who are expected to do poorly will decline.

5. With time, students' achievement and behaviour will conform more and more closely with that orginally expected (p. 12).

This five-step process outlines the manner in which teacher's expectations can indeed become self-fulfilling. As the teacher's behaviour changes as a result of his or her expectations, this change will, in turn, shape the student's behaviour. Of course, this implies that teachers hold definite expectations for students, that these expectations will influence teacher behaviour, and that the student will

Current research shows that teachers generally seat students whom they expect to be low achievers farthest away from themselves—along the back and up the sides of the room.

change to meet those expectations. If any of these conditions are absent, the expectations will not become self-fulfilling. For example, some teachers do not change their behaviour in accordance with their expectations, and some students may act in such a way that the teacher is required to revise his or her expectations. As well, some students appear to be more vulnerable to the effects of teacher expectations: this includes those who are more sensitive to subtle communication cues, more dependent or directed toward others, heavily dependent upon teachers for information, or more disruptive (Brophy, 1985).

Through what means does a teacher communicate his or her expectations? Much of the research on school effectiveness points to the importance of high expectations for students (McDaniel, 1984). The principle of high expectations addresses the importance of self-fulfilling prophecies and of teachers' behaviours that communicate high expectations. Unfortunately, negative expectations abound in classrooms, especially in those filled with low-achieving students.

Teachers' expectations about students can be manifested in a number of ways. For example, teachers tend to approve of girls' behaviour more frequently than they approve of boys' behaviour, while female teachers tend to perceive the behaviour of girls as closer to the behaviour of "ideal" students than do male teachers. As well, teachers appear to spend more time with and interact more frequently with high achievers than low achievers, and high-achieving pupils receive more praise than low-achieving ones (Brophy and Good, 1974).

Current research shows that teachers generally seat low-ability students farther away from themselves, call on them less often, pay less attention to them, give them less time and fewer clues for answering questions, and interrupt their performance more often (McDaniel, 1984). In general, students for whom teachers hold low expectations are given less time to answer questions, rewarded less frequently for inadequate answers, criticized more often and praised less often, and offered fewer opportunities to interact with the teacher (Good,1987). Such behaviours communicate lower expectations, less tolerance, and even less affection for low-ability students than for their high-ability classmates. Consequently, the students create negative self-fulfilling prophecies that lead them to become less confident, more passive or disruptive, and less motivated to work up to their capacity (McDaniel, 1984).

Biehler and Snowman (1990) stress that these factors usually act in concert to produce an expectancy. A teacher may be influenced not just by a single test score, but by a test score, plus appearance, plus grades assigned by other teachers, and so forth. In addition, it appears that teachers' expectations are more likely to maintain already existing tendencies than to drastically alter well-established behaviours. If a pupil has consistently earned low scores and grades, for example, teachers may reinforce these tendencies by treating the child as inept (Cooper, 1979).

Teachers' expectations about the ability of students can greatly influence grading practices. In one study, (Hills, 1976), elementary school teachers gave higher grades based on the attached names. Papers supposedly written by Michael or David gained higher grades than papers written by Elmer or Hubert. Adelle gained more points than Karen or Bertha.

# SUMMARY

1. Motivation is a term used to describe what energizes people and what directs their activity. It is a diffuse concept that is often tied to other factors that influence these aspects of behaviour, such as interests, needs, values, aspirations, and incentives.

2. Motivation is one of the most important prerequisites for learning. Ideally, we want children to be intrinsically motivated to learn new skills. However, intrinsic motivation is often insufficient—teachers often rely on external motivators such as rewards.

3. Children and youth will learn new academic and social skills if they are motivated to do so. Yet motivating children, especially those with already battered self-concepts and poor self-esteem, is a tremendous challenge for teachers. Children who have suffered years of school failure often develop emotional overlays—aversive reactions to learning problems—and outward loci of control—tendencies to attribute all events, whether good or bad, to outside forces or luck.

4. Students with high levels of motivation have high levels of aspiration. They have high achievement motivation which directs their views of success and failure and therefore their performance in the classroom.

5. Rosenthal and Jacobson provided one of the most controversial reports to appear in educational research. They isolated the Pygmalion effect which they argued essentially meant that the expectations that teachers hold about student's abilities and attributes can mold student achievement.

6. Much research supports the idea of teachers' expectations having at least some effect on student achievement. Teachers treat children of different ability levels differently. They interact with low-achieving students differently then with average or high-achieving students.

## Key Terms

| | | |
|---|---|---|
| achievement motivation | attribution theory of motivation | deficiency needs |
| external locus of control | growth needs | internal locus of control |
| locus of control | motivation | self-actualization |
| self-fulfilling prophecy | sustaining expectation effect | |

# PRINCIPLES OF INSTRUCTION

**13**

## INTRODUCTION

In the first chapter of this book, we briefly introduced the debate that exists between those who believe that teaching is an art and those who see it as a scientific endeavour. We noted that teaching is best viewed as a combination of science, technology, and art, firmly grounded on the theoretical principles and research that emerge from the study of educational psychology.

On a practical level, teaching consists of a number of elements. First, there is the curricula and the accompanying documentation which lay out goals and target behaviours. Second there is the methodology to be employed in the educational setting. Then there are the instructional meaterials. Hence, while teacher decision-making is informed by scientific principles, it must also incorporate emotions, values, flexibility, improvisation, ingenuity, spontaneity, humour, and style. All these things constitute the practice of teaching.

The art, the science, the technology, and the theories meld together when teachers try to transmit information or skills to a class of students. In a year, a typical elementary or secondary school teacher may teach 800 to 1000 class lessons (Slavin, 1988).

Organizing for instruction comes down to two broad issues—what to teach and how to teach it. What to teach involves the clear identification of instructional objectives, planning how to meet these objectives, preparing to evaluate student achievement of these objectives, and monitoring where change is needed. How to teach includes the teaching methods, questioning techniques, classroom climate, and activities provided for students. Teaching is a constant process of implementing techniques or methods, assessing their effectiveness, modifying where necessary, and implementing new techniques. Only when teachers continually and systematically examine their own teaching practice will teaching performance be improved.

Lesson organization and development is the heart of a teacher's work. Teachers engage in several levels of planning and, once a plan is established, most teachers really try to "get through" all the material (Denham and Lieberman, 1980; Doyle, 1983). There is no recipe for good planning, yet such preparation is a critical component of effective instruction. While provincial curricula may specify "what" is to be learned, the individual teacher is held responsible for deciding "how" the objectives are to be attained. Individual lesson plans, learning activities, and the pace at which information is to be introduced are all under the control of the teacher.

The first step in the construction of this framework is specifying the goals of instruction, or setting clear performance expectations for the students. At the end of a well-designed lesson, everyone in the class should be able to describe what skills were learned or what knowledge was acquired. But while it is necessary to detail the specifics of each lesson, effective planning also involves a consideration of how instruction will be implemented across the day, month, semester, and the entire school year (Bowd, 1982; Clark and Peterson, 1985).

To assist in long- and short-range planning, teachers can employ taxonomies of educational objectives which force them to specify their goals and the means of reaching them. In this way teachers can fit procedures and materials to instructional strategies.

Once planning is complete, certain procedures are essential to successful lesson development. For example, it is crucial that teachers focus on academic work and that they recognize and honour student ideas (Denham and Lieberman, 1980; Rosenshine, 1971). Whatever students encounter in class activities will determine to a large extent what they learn. Extensive research has identified some of the conditions of classroom learning. One important finding is that the amount that students are involved in learning is positively associated with measure of achievement (Denham and Lieberman, 1980).

In this chapter we will discuss many of the principles of instruction that are inherent in the process of instructional planning and address some of the steps that can be taken in the improvement and refinement of teaching.

## OBJECTIVES

Each province issues its own series of educational goals and objectives. Educational goals tend to be broad statements of the intended outcomes of schooling and they are often very general and rather vague. Goals, therefore, must be broken down into smaller units. It is the objectives that specify what is to be accomplished in each grade and/or curriculum area. One of the most important tasks for teachers is to translate these overriding goals and objectives into instructional objectives for a particular course, its units, and its individual lessons.

The research on teachers' planning suggests that most teachers do not pay nearly enough attention to instructional objectives when planning instruction (Clark and Peterson, 1985), yet many advantages accrue to their use. The use of instructional objectives helps to organize teacher planning, helps to guide instruction, and may improve student achievement (Mager, 1975). Instructional

**Entry-level skills:** knowledge that students possess prior to instruction.

objectives provide a clear and precise definition of the outcomes (skills, competencies, and/or knowledge) that are expected to result from a particular educational experience. That is, the teacher identifies the end point of instruction before determining what methods, materials, and strategies will be used to help students get to this point. Instructional objectives therefore guide instruction, for teachers must know where they are going before they can decide how they will get there. Gage and Berliner (1988) suggest that unless objectives focus on student outcomes, teachers will tend to focus on the content of instruction rather than what the students should do with the content.

Research suggests that students may perform better when provided with the objectives at the beginning of the instructional sequence. Students who receive explicit objectives, for example, are better able to attend to the relevant aspects of a lecture than those students who have not received such information (Long and Huck, 1972). Similarly, students who are given detailed descriptions of objectives require less training time than those who are instructed without objectives (Mager and McCann, 1961).

Students may perform better on tests if the instructional objectives clearly specify what is to be learned. Preparation for examinations is more relevant to the topic and time is more likely to be spent on appropriate content. Students can better judge their own performance and the amount and type of preparations needed for an examination (Deterline, 1968).

Different goals and methods will be used for different age levels. For example, those that are appropriate for grade one students will be sorely out of place for grade nine students. Moreover, strategies and objectives must often be modified to meet the wide range of abilities, motivations, styles of learning, aptitudes, and interests that will exist even within a single class. When writing objectives, the instructor must be cognizant of the skills and knowledge that the students currently possess, or their **entry-level skills**. In particular, teachers must identify the learner characteristics that are relevant to the objectives and then determine how to build on these strengths. Such clearly stated objectives can also help the teacher individualize instruction. Before instruction can be tailored for individual needs, the teacher must be aware of each student's abilities and progress. The more precise the goals of instruction are, the easier it will be to determine whether the student has reached them (TenBrink, 1986).

Ausubel (1968), one of the prominent cognitive psychologists discussed in Chapter 9, believes that assessing student entry-level skills and teaching accordingly is one of the most important components of effective instruction. This may seem axiomatic, yet often teachers concentrate too much on the content of instruction without considering the needs or abilities of the students. This often leads to inappropriate, irrelevant, or unecessary teaching (Giusti and Hogg, 1973). Teachers may waste time by teaching outcomes that have already been mastered by the students or, conversely, by specifying goals that are far beyond the level of the group. It is best to match the students' current level of performance with objectives for instruction that are challenging yet can be reasonably accomplished.

Clear and definitive instructional objectives enhance rather than limit teacher flexibility. They do not dominate the instructional sequence but help the teacher take advantage of the many powerful learning opportunities that spontaneously arise during the course of any lesson. Teachers who have clear objectives can seize these opportunities as alternative ways to reach their objectives. If the teacher is unsure of the terminal objective, spontaneous activities are more likely to get the class off-track, instead of leading them to the desired goal (TenBrink, 1986).

Evaluation is directly tied to the planned goals and objectives whether student performance is assessed through observation, written asignments, or through some type of test. However, evaluation is not limited to a consideration of student performance because this data again feeds into the teacher decision-making process. If the stated objective is met, determining the factors that lead to success can help the teacher repeat the outcome again. If the objective is not met by all or some of the students, the teacher should learn from this failure. Teachers should ask themselves whether the objectives match the abilities of these students, whether appropriate teaching methods were used, and whether any remedial actions should be taken. By asking and answering such questions, teachers are able to refine teaching methods and make plans that will better facilitate student learning in the future.

## Types of objectives

Students are expected to learn many different things in the classroom. While we most often think of the cognitive goals of schooling, teachers also focus on affective outcomes, such as values, emotions, and attitudes and the acquisition of psychomotor skills, such as handwriting, keyboarding, or running. The translation of these broad areas of educational goals into instructional activities can be accomplished in many ways and through the use of different types of objectives.

Teaching objectives include cognitive, affective, and psychomotor goals.

There are many different types of instructional objectives and many different ways they can be written. Mager (1975) recommends that objectives contain three components:

1. A precise description of *behaviour*, or what the student is to do.

2. The conditions under which the student is to perform, including those factors which are given and those which limit or restrict the student's performance.

3. The criterion that will be used to evaluate the students' performance which describes the minimum or lower limit of performance that is acceptable as an indication of mastery of the objective and how the students are to be evaluated.

The first component calls for the specification of a particular action that can be observed and measured. For example, "The student will solve...," or "The student will describe the principles of democracy in writing...," or "The student will recite a Shakespearean sonnet..." Specifying the behaviour so clearly would allow another teacher to determine whether the students had achieved the objective. However, this would not be true if more ambiguous terms were used. For example, objectives that merely require students to "know," "understand," or "comprehend" certain material can be interpreted in a number of ways since they lack clarity and precision.

By "conditions" (the second component), Mager is referring to how a task is presented to students. Students may perform, for example, when "Given a series of ten problems...," or when "Using a calculator...," or "Without reference to the text..." Finally criteria specify student performance, usually in terms of accuracy or speed, or both. Students may, for example, respond "with 90 percent accuracy," "with fewer than two errors," or "within thirty minutes."

Although Mager's approach to composing instructional objectives is widely accepted, some suggest that this procedure is best suited to situations in which students are to acquire specific material or master simple skills. As well, these objectives may be narrow for some situations. Objectives that are too specific may teach poor study habits by focusing the students' attention on specific facts and encouraging students to skip anything that is not mentioned in the objective (TenBrink, 1986). And, without doubt, behavioural objectives are more difficult to write for the higher grades because of the increased complexity of the subject matter and because teaching objectives more frequently involves understanding and appreciation.

## Gronlund's general objectives

As an alternative to Mager's (1962) objectives, Norman Gronlund (1985, 1988) proposes the use of general objectives which, he suggests, are more appropriate for more advanced or complex learning. Gronlund argues that Mager's specific objectives result in long and cumbersome lists that can inhibit teacher flexibility. The objectives as suggested by Mager may lead teachers to focus on less complex learning outcomes, such as recall of facts or mastery of simple skills. Gronlund promotes the use of general objectives because many learning activities are too complex to be described in terms of a specific objective for each and every learning outcome.

According to Gronlund (1985, 1988), the three components of instructional objectives in Mager's outline—behaviour, conditions, and criteria—are not required in many teaching situations. He specifically suggests that criteria should not be a component of the objective in order to enable the teacher to vary criteria without having to rewrite the objective. This is particularly important if the same skill is to be repeatedly assessed over time, with students being expected to demonstrate increasingly higher levels of performance.

Instead of centring on behaviour, condititions, and criteria, Gronlund proposes that teachers state the general objective of the lesson, along with a representative sample of up to five types of student leaning outcomes that would be accepted as mastery of the objective. Each learning outcome begins with an action verb and describes the specific observable response that is to be demonstrated by the students. Outcomes are a representative rather than exhaustive list of the different student actions that would demonstrate mastery of the general objective. The use of general objectives helps alert teachers to the fact that students can demonstrate mastery of an objective in many different ways.

For example, the specific learning outcomes that would accompany the general objective, "Understand the meaning of technical terms," would be: "students must be able to 1) define the terms in their own words, 2) identify the meaning of the term when used in context, and 3) distinguish between terms that are similar in meaning" (Gronlund, 1985, p. 5).

## Expressive objectives

Eisner (1969), another critic of behavioural objectives, outlined an alternative approach, termed *expressive objectives*. These objectives are based on the rationale that teachers cannot possibly specify all possible learning outcomes for all students, because each is likely to derive something different from each learning situation. Within Eisner's framework, students are invited to explore what could be learned rather than having the teacher dictate what is to be learned. The teacher does not describe the behaviours that the student should demonstrate. Instead, an expressive objective "identifies a situation in which children are to work, a problem in which they are to engage, but it does not specify what from that encounter, situation, problem, or task they are to learn" (Eisner, 1969, pp. 15-16). Teachers and students are given "an invitation to explore, defer, or focus on issues that are of particular interest or importance to the inquirer" (Eisner, 1969, pp. 15-16).

## Selecting objectives

Even though research on the use of objectives is unanimously positive, there is no definitive answer to the type of objectives that a teacher should use. Hamilton (1985) reviewed a series of studies and found that various types of objectives helped students better recall material that they had read. Retention of verbal information was enhanced regardles of the type of objective, providing that the objectives clearly specified the material to be learned. Klauer (1984) compared 23 studies and noted that when students were given objectives prior to reading instructional text, they learned more of the material related to the stated objectives. However, students tended to learn less of the information that was not related to the objective. Therefore, objectives may help students learn the targeted

**Taxonomy:**
a classification scheme of educational objectives with categories arranged in a hierarchical order from the simplest outcomes to the more complex outcomes of instruction.

material, but may minimize learning of other information. Since objectives seem to direct student attention, teachers who want students to learn more general material should use a more general objective rather than one which is highly specific.

Suchastel and Merrill (1973) reviewed over 50 studies and found no consistent results; an equal number of studies showed that objectives facilitated learning and showed that they had no effect. But while use of objectives may not guarantee success, the authors suggested that since the research did not indicate that objectives inhibited learning, they could be used with confidence by teachers. Duell (1974) further suggested that objectives may be most helpful when they highlight information that the students might otherwise not consider important.

However, some critics charge that specific objectives often focus on trivial outcomes, and that since many of the important outcomes of education cannot be easily expressed in behavioural terms, they may therefore be neglected (Gage and Berliner, 1984). Moreover, while some curriculum areas, particularly mathematics and science, seem to lend themselves to expression in behavioural terms, in other areas it is more difficult to formulate outcomes specifically. Art or music teachers, for example, often find it difficult to specifically define and quantify the outcomes of instruction.

Some believe that objectives are not an essential part of good teaching as many teachers are effective without specifying their goals in behavioural terms (Gage and Berliner, 1984). Research appears to support the contention that experienced teachers often do not use instructional objectives in their planning. Zahorik (1975) asked teachers to describe the decisions made before instruction and the order in which they were made. Teachers made decisions about numerous issues: the most frequently mentioned factors were student activities (81 percent) and content (51 percent). Only 28 percent of the experienced teachers made decisions about instructional objectives prior to teaching. Similar results have been obtained by other researchers (e.g., Peterson, Marx, and Clark, 1978).

Not surprisingly, humanistic educators such as Rogers (1983) and Combs (1979) believe that behavioural objectives are unnecessarily restrictive and inappropriate for use within a humanistic approach to schooling. As pointed out by Combs (1979), "human feelings and personal meaning of inforamtion do not lend themselves to measurement in behavioural terms" (p. 53).

Of course, this should not be seen as a suggestion that instructional objectives are not valuable. Even though some experienced teachers may be able to plan very adequately without written objectives, we strongly recommend that new teachers continue to use this approach.

## TAXONOMIES

A taxonomy is a classification system which attempts to categorize the various outcomes of instruction. Generally designed in a hierarchical fashion, a taxonomy begins with the simplest outcome and then progresses to the more complex outcomes of instruction. During the 1950s, a group of educational psychologists and measurement experts surveyed the learning taxonomies existing in the field of education. Somewhat dissatisfied with the results of this survey, this group of experts published their own taxonomies of educational goals.

The best known taxonomy was developed by Benjamin Bloom and his colleagues (1956). Bloom felt that one of the major difficulties confronting anyone interested in education was the definition of goals. Bloom's scheme stresses the cognitive goals and outcomes of instruction; it classifies educational objectives and relates each objective to specific classroom procedures.

## Bloom's taxonomy of cognitive goals

This taxonomy of educational objectives for the cognitive domains delineates six levels of cognitive complexity, ranging from the knowledge level (the least complex) to evaluation (the most complex) as illustrated in Table 13-1. However, while this progression seems to form a hierarchy of sorts, it is not necessary for the learner to have mastered the first levels before going on to the more complex. For example, while knowledge is at the lowest level of Bloom's taxonomy, this does not mean that students have to master all factual information before they analyze or evaluate this knowledge. Nor does this imply that this is the best sequence for instruction (Bergan, 1980). Indeed, it is often difficult during instruction to clearly separate one level of cognitive thinking or processing from another.

**Table 13-1**  Bloom's taxonomy

| LEVEL | DEFINITION | ACTION VERBS | EXAMPLES |
|---|---|---|---|
| Knowledge | To recall or recognize information previously presented. | define; describe; identify, list, match, name | The student will name the date of Confederation. |
| Comprehension | To make use of ideas or facts that have been learned. | defend, explain, rewrite, paraphrase, infer, give examples | The student will summarize the main theme of the story. |
| Application | To use previously learned concepts in new situations or to solve new problems. | predict, prepare, use, relate, solve, modify, operate, compute, discover | Given a set of materials, the student will demonstrate the principle of momentum. |
| Analysis | To break something down into its component parts. | differentiate, point out, discriminate, infer, relate | Given a series of statements, the student will distinguish between fact and opinion. |
| Synthesis | To create a meaningful new "whole" by combining different ideas. | combine, compose, design, devise, organize, plan, revise, summarize | Given the question, "What would happen to Canada if Quebec separated?" the student will compose compose a plausible description. |
| Evaluation | To make judgments about the value of materials or methods that have been learned. | appraise, compare, conclude, contrast, criticize, interpret, support, justify | The student will compare the democratic and communist forms of government. |

**SOURCE:** Taken from Borich, 1988.

504

## Mastery learning

The increasing use of taxonomies stimulated the development of mastery learning, the concept that students should be taught until they have mastered a subject or segment of a subject, no matter how long it takes. John B. Carroll (1963) proposed that the focus of instruction should be the time required for different students to learn a given amount of material. He suggested that teachers should allow more time and provide additional and better instruction for students who learn less esily and less rapidly than their peers.

Benjamin Bloom (1968) used the Carroll model as the basis for a statement in favour of mastery learning. The traditional approach, he argues, promotes the concept that if a normal distribution of students (with respect to aptitude for a subject) is exposed to a standard curriculum, achievement after instruction will be normally distributed. This approach, Bloom maintains, causes both teachers and students to expect that only a third of all students will adequately learn what is being taught, and this expectation leads to a disastrous self-fulfilling prophecy. Bloom (1968) argues that most students—perhaps over 90 percent—can master whatever it is that the educational system is charged with teaching them.

Gibson and Chandler (1988) stress three major theoretical implications associated with mastery learning. First, it should improve student achievement. Second, students' self-concepts should improve as they perceive their own success. Finally, the relationship between commonly accepted definitions of student ability and student achievement should approach zero.

Teachers who use mastery learning efficiently create a positive learning environment, model caring and trust, and assure students that they all can learn (Hamilton, 1983).

## Gagné's taxonomy

Robert Gagné's (1974, 1977, 1985) taxonomy also deals with different types of learning but makes finer distinction at the lower levels of learning and fewer distinctions at the upper levels of learning than are seen in Bloom's taxonomy of cognitive skills (Brophy and Good, 1986). Gagné's learning hierarchy consists of seven categories: signal learning, stimulus-response learning, chaining, verbal associations, discrimination learning, concept learning, and rule learning.

1. Signal learning occurs when the learner acquires a general response that is made in reaction to a specific signal, such as a knowing that he or she should become quiet and ready to listen to the teacher when the school bell rings.

2. Stimulus-response learning occurs when the learner makes a specific response when presented with a particular stimulus: for example, reading "cat" when presented with that word on a flashcard.

3. Chaining occurs when the learner develops the ability to connect a sequence of learned responses, such as combining a series of letters to spell a word, or performing the series of actions needed to sink a basketball through the net.

4. Verbal associations occur when the learner has linked stimuli including combinations of words with a particular response; for example, learning to recognize whole words on sight when reading English.

5. Discrimination learning occurs when learners are able to distinguish among members of a set of similar stimuli so that they can respond in a different fashion to each. For example, when reading a word that has several alternative meanings, the learner is able to use the context of the word to discriminate which meaning is appropriate.

6. Concept learning is the ability to classify items with similar characteristics as members of a single conceptual category; for example, being able to identify all the verbs in a sample of writing.

7. Rule learning implies mastering general principles or rules so that they can be applied in appropriate situations or in solving problems; for example, using the rules of English grammar when writing, or applying mathematical principles to solving different problems.

Later in his career, Gagné began to focus more on the higher classifications of learning, and how these categories can be used to describe the competencies that learners acquire. Gagné and Briggs (1979) identified five major types of learning, and outlined how each could be taught. These include:

1. Attitudes—internalized values that influence the behaviours and actions that an individual chooses to take;

2. Motor skills—organized patterns of movement that learners use to accomplish specific tasks;

3. Information—all of the facts and other bits of organized knowledge about the world that the learner stores in his or her memory;

4. Intellectual skills—the skills that allow the learner to carry out symbol-based procedures, including discriminations, concrete concepts, rules, and higher-order rules; and

5. Cognitive strategies—the strategies that learners use to control their own thinking or cognitive processes.

To a great extent, the Gagné and Briggs classification system overlaps the taxonomy proposed by Bloom and his colleagues; certainly these two systems can be seen to be complementary rather than oppositional. However, they do address some aspects of learning differently. For example, Gagné and Briggs distinguish between several different types of learning that might be included in Bloom's levels of comprehension and application, while Bloom's highest levels are not addressed by Gagné and Briggs. Thus, the teacher who uses both systems together to analyze the content of instruction would have completed a more exhaustive examination than the teacher who uses only one (Good and Brophy, 1986).

## Affective taxonomies

While teachers are most often concerned with the cognitive outcomes of schooling, this does not dominish the importance that should also be attached to the affective and psychomotor domain. As noted repeatedly throughout this book, only by considering the whole child will a teacher be able to function effectively in the classroom.

In an attempt to address the complex area of affective outcomes, Krathwohl, Bloom, and Masia (1964) developed a separate taxonomy for affective goals and objectives. As with the cognitive taxonomy, the goals range from the simple to the complex, or from the lest committed to the most committed. As students move up the hierarchy, they demonstrate more involvement, commitment, and independence, relying less and less upon the feelings, attitudes, or values dictated by others (Borich, 1988).

The affective taxonomy (Krathwohl, Bloom, and Maria, 1964) is in Table 13-2, which also includes a listing of some of the action verbs that might be used in the formulation of objectives at each level.

Table 13-2 Affective Taxonomy

| LEVEL | DEFINITION | ACTION VERBS | EXAMPLES |
|---|---|---|---|
| Receiving | Demonstrates an awareness of and sensitivity to different views. | listens, chooses, follows, identifies replies, uses, attends to, holds. | The student will listen to the opinions of others during group discussions. |
| Responding | Reacts in some way as a result of experience. | assists, complies, performs, helps, tells, reports. | The student will participate in class discussions. |
| Valuing | Holds a sustained belief in the worthiness of an idea, event, or group of people. | forms, initiates, invites, joins, proposes, reads, selects, shares, explains, completes. | The student will show concern for the welfare of others. |
| Organizing | Demonstrates possession of an integrated set of values. | adheres, compares, integrates, relates, synthesizes, alters, explains. | The student will formulate an occupational plan that is consistent with his or her talents, skills, values, and interests. |
| Characterizing by a value | Acts consistently according to a set of values over time and across situations. | acts, discriminates, performs, practices, qualifies, questions, uses, verifies. | The student will work well independently and in small and large group settings. |

SOURCE: Adapted from Gronlund (1985).

## Psychomotor taxonomies

Psychomotor goals were originally the province of physical education teachers. In more recent years, however, all instructors have been urged to take psychomotor goals into consideration. A science teacher might be concerned with the students' ability to manipulate equipment, a language arts teacher might be concerned with handwriting skills, or the computer teacher might be concerned with keyboarding abilities.

The first cognitive and affective taxonomies were developed in the 1950s; however, the first taxonomy of psychomotor skills did not emerge until the late 1960s (Moore, 1967). Today, we find many different variations in this area. A common theme in all is that the development of the psychomotor domain is characterized by the development of muscular skills and coordination. The learner must perceive input from the environment and then respond in a particular fashion in order to synchronize or match performance to the demands of the situation (Orlich et al., 1985). As well, in concert with the cognitive and affective domains that we have discussed, all psychomotor taxonomies arrange skills in a hierarchial fashion.

One of the earlier taxonomies was developed by Harrow (1972). As seen in Table 13-3, Harrow's taxonomy begins with reflexes (level one) and basic fundamental movements (level two), such as learning to grasp, walk, and crawl. These skills form the building blocks for the later, more complex skills seen in the higher levels of the taxonomy.

**Table 13-3** Harrow's taxonomy of psychomotor domain

| LEVEL | EXAMPLES OF BEHAVIOURS |
|---|---|
| Reflex movement | Innate, involuntary movements elicited in response to some stimuli, such as knee jerks. |
| Basic, fundamental movements | Occur in first year of life; include visual tracking, reaching, grasping creeping, crawling, and walking. |
| Perceptual abilities | Kinesthetic discriminations (body awareness, body image), visual discrimination; auditory discrimination, tactile discrimination, coordinated abilities (hand-eye; eye-foot). |
| Physical abilities | Endurance, strength, flexibility, agility. |
| Skilled movements | Complex movement tasks that require learning, from sawing wood to playing tennis. |
| Nondiscursive activities | Movement communication; developing a style of moving that communicates feelings. Include both innate and learned movements. |

**SOURCE**: Harrow, 1972.

A more recent and comprehensive psychomotor taxonomy was developed by Jewett and Mullan (1977). Ths taxonomy combines elements contained in the taxonomies of Moore and Harrow. However, Jewett and Mullan begin with fundamental movements and end up with creative movements. There are three levels of this taxonomy: generic, ordinative, and creative.

1. *Generic movement* includes those operations and processes that will facilitate later development of motor patterns. They usually take the form of exploratory movements which are adjusted by learners as they take in information from the environment. This includes perceiving, the awareness of total body relationships and self in motion, and patterning, the arrangement and use of

Generic movement facilitates later development of motor patterns.

body parts in successive and harmonious ways to achieve movement patterns or skills.

2. *Ordinative movement* refers to the processes of organizing, refining and performing skilful movement. These processes are directed toward the organization of perceptual-motor abilities in order to solve a particular movement task. This level includes adapting or modifying a patterned movement in order to meet the demands imposed by different situations when performing a task. It also includes refining, the acquisition of a smooth, efficient control when performing a movement pattern or skill.

3. *Creative movement* includes original motor performances that meet the needs of the learner. To accomplish this, the learner would use the processes of discovery, integration, abstraction, idealization, emotional objectification, and composition. This includes varying, the invention of personally unique options in motor performance; improvising, the extemporaneous originations of initiation of personally novel movements or combinations of movements; and composing, the combination of learned movement into personally unique motor designs or the invention of movement patterns new to the learner.

# TABLE OF SPECIFICATIONS

Once the teacher has delineated educational goals and objectives, the next step is to draw up a table of specifications which describes each objective and the type of learning that is required. This is accomplished by categorizing each objective in terms of the expected learning outcomes. Categorization of the objectives is achieved by using a taxonomical hierarchy, such as Bloom's. A partial table of specifications, developed for a unit in social studies and classified according to Bloom's taxonomy, is presented in Table 13-4. Of course, other taxonomies, such as that developed by Gagné, could be used as well (Seifert, 1990).

**Table 13-4** Table of specifications

Simplified table for social studied unit on the principles of parliamentary democracy

| Objectives: | KNOWLEDGE | COMPREHENSION | APPLICATION | ANALYSIS | SYNTHESIS | EVALUATION |
|---|---|---|---|---|---|---|
| • Define election procedures | √ | | | | | |
| • List defining features of Parliament | √ | | | | | |
| • Explain the function of the House of Commons | | √ | | | | |
| • Explain the function of the Senate | | √ | | | | |
| • Establish a student parliament | | | √ | | | |
| • Critique the parliamentary system as applied in Canada | | | | √ | | |
| • Compare and contrast the Soviet and Canadian forms of government | | | | √ | | |
| • For an imaginary new country, design a new democratic form of government | | | | | √ | |
| • Critique the government's speech from the throne | | | | | | √ |

A table of specifications is useful for three reasons. First, it focuses teachers' attention on the outcomes of learning—or what the students are to accomplish. Rather than getting wrapped up in a consideration of what is to be done (teacher methods and student activities), planning in this manner ensures that students' needs are not neglected. Second, the table of specifications will help the teacher ensure that the instructional units are balanced in terms of the types of learning that are expected. You can see, for example, that the table of specifications illustrated in Table 13-4 delineates the different types of cognitive outcomes required. Teachers can then ask themselves questions such as, "Have knowledge

**Unit plan:**
integrated package of instruction that consists of a related series of lesson plans addressing a particular theme or topic.

goals dominated at the expense of higher cognitive processes, such as analysis and synthesis?" An examination founded on a concrete table of specifications allows a teacher to assess the balance that has been attained in any instructional unit and to modify the objectives if necessary.

Finally, the table of specifications will guide test development and assignments. That is, if final grades are to accurately reflect the unit taught, test items and assignments should be in proportion to the goals. If the instructional unit places 20 percent emphasis on knowledge and 30 percent on analysis, for example, the evaluation procedures should reflect this balance (see Chapter 14).

## UNIT AND LESSON PLANNING

Once instructional goals and objectives are clearly delineated, the teacher is ready to construct lesson and unit plans. Plans are the actual consideration and writing out of the environmental events that are related to learning; they can be seen as an individual teacher's model of how to produce learning.

A unit plan includes a related series of lesson plans as well as a description of how the lessons fit into an integrated whole that addresses a particular theme or topic, usually over a period of one to four weeks. A lesson is a process by which information, skills, or concepts are communicated from the teacher to the student (Slavin, 1988) and lesson plans are some of the most important tools in the educational trade. Teachers of all ages and all degrees of experience devise and use lesson plans (Winzer, 1989). Lesson plans provide evidence that the teacher has thought about the lesson in terms of reivew, pre-testing, the progression of steps, aids and materials, seatwork, evaluation, and individualiztion (Winzer, 1989).

### Unit planning

There are many different ways of preparing unit plans and one is no more logical than another. However, good unit plans share some elements. A **unit plan** should begin with a statement of rationale which defines the content and assumptions underlying the unit of instruction. If the unit will be conducted in an unusual fashion, such as through learning centres, entirely through computer-assisted instruction, or with a stress on individualized problem-solving strategies, this should be outlined. The introductory statement of rationale should also include explanation about how this unit relates to other units and the curriculum as a whole; how the unit addresses the goals and aims listed for the curriculum area; and how cognitive, affective and psychomotor goals are to be addressed (Loewen, 1990).

The second component of the plan is the unit map, or a chart that shows the "unit at a glance." A unit map is similar to the table of specifications. The purpose is to provide an overview of the objectives to be addressed, the activities to be used, and the predicted time-line. Figure 13-1 demonstrates a common format that is used for unit maps.

**Figure 13-1**
Unit map

UNIT MAP

| OBJECTIVE | ACTIVITY | EVALUATION | EXTENSION | TIME | TEXT |
|---|---|---|---|---|---|
|  |  |  |  |  |  |
|  |  |  |  |  |  |
|  |  |  |  |  |  |
|  |  |  |  |  |  |
|  |  |  |  |  |  |
|  |  |  |  |  |  |
|  |  |  |  |  |  |
|  |  |  |  |  |  |

The unit map is further broken down into a detailed analysis of the unit content, which shows the unit map in greater detail. As shown in Figure 13-1, the major components are objectives, activities, materials, evaluation, and extension.

**Objectives**    This column lists all the objectives that will be covered in the unit. The objectives may be chosen because they cover a particular topic in the textbook used or because they all fall within one strand of curriculum. There may be a collection of objectives that need to be retaught.

The objectives can be sequenced by placing all core objectives together and placing the elective objectives after them, or the objectives can be ordered in the sequence in which they are to be taught. In the latter case, objectives should be designated as either core or elective. Objectives can be composed by the teacher or drawn from the curriculum guide.

**Activities**    This category specifies the range of activities that will be used to address each objective. It delineates the appropriate activities that meet the interests and abilities of the students. Common activities might include the use of games, manipulatives, lectures, discussions, debates, projects, overhead presentations, or brainstorming sessions. Great detail is not necessary here; the idea is to give a flavour for the various ways that an objective can be addressed. Detailed descriptions will be addressed in individual lesson plans.

**Materials**    A list of materials needed for the activities should be included.

**Evaluation**    The description of evaluation directly relates to the corresponding objective, rather than addressing the manner in which the entire unit is to be evaluated. Evaluation strategies may include games, quizzes, guided interviews, or self-reports.

**Extension**   An extension section is necessary in classrooms that include students with disabilities or with other special learning needs (including gifted students) who may not benefit from the activities planned for the entire class. The format used is identical to that used for the section described above.

The five components of the unit can be organized in a vertical fashion that lists each component in turn. That is, a listing of all objectives, followed by all activities, materials, and so on. The advantage of this approach is that the lists are simple and easy to construct. However, vertical organizations are often difficult to interpret, and it may be difficult to determine which activities are matched to which objectives, or which evaluation tools go with each activity (Loewen, 1990).

Alternatively, a horizontal organization may be chosen where each objective is grouped with relevant activities, materials, and evaluation listing as shown in Figure 13-2. The blocks may be sequenced in any order but are usually presented in the order in which they are to be taught. The advantage of this configuration is that it shows each of the objectives developed in full and enables the teacher to compare the different approaches used for each objective (Loewen, 1990).

**Figure 13-2**
**Horizontal organization**

- Objective:
- Status:       Core or Elective or Text
- Examples:
- Activities:
    (a)
                    Materials:
    (b)
                    Materials:
    (c)
                    Materials:
- Evaluation:    Optional
- Extension Activities:    Optional
    (a)
                    Materials:
    (b)
                    Materials:
- Problem Solving:    Optional

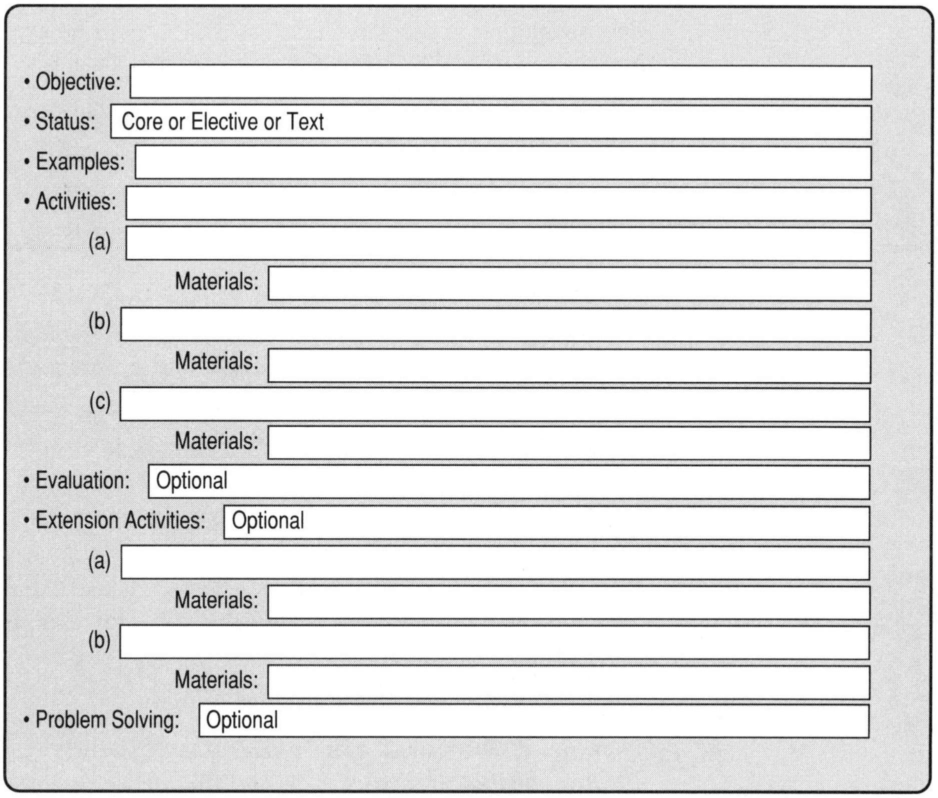

**Lesson plan:**
plan that describes the objectives, methods, content, and evaluation procedures that are to be used in each discrete instructional period.

Unit evaluation should specify how the teacher will evaluate or describe individual student achievement with respect to the objectives of the unit. Different techniques will be chosen, depending upon the skill or knowledge to be assessed, the age and ability of the students, the available materials, and time. Evaluation materials should assess all aspects of student growth—cognitive, affective, and psychomotor—as well as appropriate levels within each domain. The teacher may also wish to include a statement which defines how the effectiveness of instruction is to be evaluated.

For unit evaluation, many techniques can be used such as tests, quizzes, worksheets, interviews, anecdotal records, journals, checklists, games, projects, manipulative activities, and self-reports. Where heavy emphasis is placed on examinations, the teacher should include a table of specifications showing that the distribution of the test items corresponds with the objectives of the unit and the time spent on each topic.

The last component of the unit plan is the collection of the individual lesson plans that will be taught. The new teacher will need to develop these lessons more fully, while an experienced teacher will develop only skeletal lesson plans, relying more heavily on the unit plan to guide instruction.

## Lesson planning

A lesson plan describes the objectives, methods, content, and evaluation procedures that are to be used in each discrete instructional period. The lesson plan describes the specific day-to-day work that will be accomplished by the teacher and the students. Written lesson plans serve to:

- give direction to teacher and student efforts, permitting the teacher better preparation of lessons;

- bring the sequence and continuity of learning into clear focus;

- provide a reference point for teachers while instructing;

- provide a record for the teacher;

- set the foundation for future lessons (careful evaluation following the presentation of the lesson reveals strengths and problems); and

- provide a valuable resource for teachers. While plans must be reviewed and updated from year to year to meet the needs of different classes, they serve as valuable beginning points (Winzer, 1989).

Lesson plans must first include the specific instructional objectives that will be addressed in the lesson. There is no magic number of instructional objectives that can be targeted for a particular lesson; this will depend upon the time available and the characteristics of the students. However, it has been suggested that the average high school student can grasp, at most, four or five major ideas within a 50-minute class period; younger students usually have shorter class periods (ranging from five to 20 minutes) and therefore lessons should probably focus on the attainment of a single objective (Orlich et al., 1985).

Once the teacher knows what the students should be able to do at the completion of the lesson, it is possible to determine how this outcome is to be achieved.

**Task analysis:**
a procedure which breaks down an instructional goal into a series of sub-objectives or steps that will guide students to the attainment of the final objective.

The first step is to delineate the precise content that is to be taught as well as the most appropriate sequence to be used in its presentation to the students. One method that can be used to determine the sequence of instruction is task analysis, a procedure which breaks down an instructional goal into a series of sub-objectives or the steps that will guide students to the attainment of the final objective. Task analysis can be used on simple motor tasks such as throwing a football or on complex academic tasks such as writing a term paper (Reigeluth and Merril, 1984).

In completing a task analysis, the teacher must ask the following questions:

- What prerequisite skills or knowledge are required?

- What steps (performance of skills or application of knowledge) are needed to complete the task?

- What sequence must be followed in the completion of the steps? (Jonassen, Hannum, and Tessher, 1989).

By carefully examining the objective and acting out each step if possible, the teacher will end up with a series of steps that can be used to guide instruction. Alternatively, there are many prepared task analyses included in materials such as curriculum guides, textbooks, or the research literature.

To take a concrete example, consider the following steps that would be used to teach division, using 28 divided by 4 as an example. When given a division problem the students should:

1. Identify the divisor (4).

2. Count by the divisor and make a mark for each count. (For example, as the students count "4, 8, 12..." they make one mark for 4, add a second for 8, a third for 12, and so on.)

3. When the dividend (28) is reached, stop counting and making marks.

4. Count the number of marks made.

5. Write the numeral that represents the number of marks made (7) in the correct place on the worksheet (Hallahan et al., 1983).

This sequence of steps assumes that the students possess some prerequisite skills. They would have to know which number to count by, how to count by numbers, how to stop counting at different points in the counting sequence, number-numeral relationships (for counting marks), and how to write numbers.

Once the prerequisite skills and steps of the task analysis have been delineated, it is possible to pretest the students on each in order to determine what must be directly taught. One student may need to return to a consideration of the prerequisite skills, another may need instruction on all steps in the sequence, while others need only to master a few of the steps. This allows the teacher to individualize instruction, for students are only taught those skills which they do not possess.

Now that the teacher has determined what is to be taught and the sequence that is to be used, the lesson can be constructed. Research has demonstrated that student learning seems to be facilitated if the following elements are included in a lesson plan: an introduction, review, presentation of new content, formative checks or learning probes, independent practice, and evaluation.

**Introduction or focusing event**   Any good lesson begins with an interesting, attention-grabbing opening that orients the learner to the content of the information and motivates the student to pursue the topic that is to be presented. The learner is placed in a receptive state of mind that will facilitate the cognitive, affective, or psychomotor learning that is to follow. More specifically, the first purpose of the lesson introduction is to focus student attention on the learning (Shostak, 1986). A motivated learner will acquire knowledge and skills more rapidly than will a learner who is neither curious about nor interested in the lesson that is to follow (Orlich et al., 1985).

This means that the lesson will be introduced in a fashion that stimulates student interest and involvement in the lesson. For example, questions can be used to heighten student interest in the lesson, arouse curiosity and tie the new material to be learned to previously mastered content. Properly formulated opening questions do not have any single correct answer but are intended to amuse, stimulate interest, or sometimes bewilder students, so that they will be more receptive to the content that is to follow. Examples might include:

• Why do some scientists think that traveling in space might make the space traveler younger? (from a lesson in physics)

• Why do we have the word "its" and another word "it's"? (from a lesson in punctuation)

• Why do you think the Greek empire collapsed when it was at its strongest? (from a lesson in world history)

• Why is the dollar worth more today in Mexico than Switzerland? (from a lesson in economics)

• Why do you think some eloquently speaking lawyers become disliked by the juries they speak to? (from a lesson in public speaking) (Borich, 1988, p. 122).

Diagrams, pictures, illustrations, scale models, and films are other types of attention-getting aids which appeal to the students' sense of sight, while the oral presentation provides them with auditory input. Similarly, manipulative materials can be used to introduce lessons so that students can actually experience the materials or equipment that will be used during the course of the lesson.

But simply getting the student's attention is not enough. Rather, the second purpose of a good lesson introduction is to provide students with an organizational framework upon which the ideas, principles, or knowledge that follow are to be placed. We have previously discussed the importance of the use of use of advance organizers, or telling the learners what is to follow. Such information can help the students learn and perform better. Of course, the manner in which this information is to be communicated must be comprehensible and interesting to the students. For that reason, the language used by teachers in composing instructional objectives will rarely be the same used to communicate this information to the class. For example, consider the following objective that was developed for a third grade mathematics class and the manner in which this information was communicated to the class.

***Lesson plan objective:*** *Given ten problems, the student will demonstrate the ability to add two-digit numbers and will get nine out of ten correct.*

*Oral statement of objective:* Today we're going to learn to add two-digit numbers. Last week we worked on one-digit numbers. Adding two-digit numbers is a lot like what we did then (Orlich et al., 1985, p. 137).

In addition, the teacher may wish to provide specific examples of the behaviours or skills the students will be expected to demonstrate at the close of the lesson. For example, if the teacher was beginning a lesson on lower forms of animal life, one or more of the following examples of student behaviour might be listed on the blackboard:

*Give a definition of an ameba;*
*Draw the cellular structure of an ameba;*
*Explain the reproduction cycle of the ameba;*
*Using a microscope, properly identify an ameba from other single-celled animals (Borich, 1988, pp. 124).*

By telling the students which behaviour they will be expected to demonstrate, the teacher focuses their attention and helps them to direct their learning activities. It prepares the learners for the content that is to follow and gives them an indication of what they must do in order to demonstrate mastery of the content. Thus, if the students know that they are to master a certain mathematical

Attention-getting aids appeal to the students' sense of sight while the oral presentation provides auditory input.

**Methods:**
the formal aspects of teaching, such as the ways in which teachers interact with students, how they ask questions, how questions are addressed to students, and student activities.

operation, to define a particular concept, or to conduct a particular procedure, they are able to direct their cognitive processes toward that goal during the lesson (Borich, 1988). In other words, the learning process is activated so that the learners can focus their efforts in the most effective and efficient manner.

In addition to these general purposes of lesson introductions, experienced teachers use these situations as an opportunity to:

- focus the students' attention on the presentation that the teacher is to make by employing an activity, event, object, or person that relates directly to their interests or previous experience;

- provide a framework that enbales the students to visualize the content or activities of the presentation;

- clarify the goals of the lesson;

- provide a smooth transition from known material to new material by capitalizing on the use of examples, analogies, and student activities which the students have interest in or experience with (Shostak, 1986).

**Review**     Before the teacher moves on to new material or activities, students must demonstrate understanding of previously learned content (Shostak, 1986), so the second step in the lesson plan is to quickly review previously learned material. If the lesson is part of an ongoing unit, and the teacher is relatively sure of the students' level of understanding, this review can take the form of a quick review of the preceding lesson as well as asking a few brief questions to check for comprehension. In other situations, particularly at the beginning of a new instructional unit, the teacher may wish to directly assess students' prerequisites through more extensive question-and-answer sessions, a brief pretest, an examination of their worksheets, or other assignments. If an individual or a small group of students show deficits in prerequisite skills, supplementary instruction will be needed before the new lesson can be taught (Slavin, 1988).

**Presentation of new content**     Once the stage is set for learning, the teacher is ready to present the content of the lesson. Here a wide variety of teaching methods can be used. **Methods** are the formal aspects of teaching, such as the ways in which teachers interact with students, how they ask questions, how questions are addressed to students, how they plan student activities, and so on.

When deciding which teaching methods to use, teachers must consider many different varibles. First, the strategy to be used will be determined, at least in part, by the content to be learned. Not all learning tasks are the same, and therefore different strategies must be used (Gagné, 1985). For example, if a major objective of the lesson focuses on affective outcomes, the teaching methods used will be quite different from a lesson that focuses on cognitive or psychomotor skills. A small group discussion may be quite useful in helping students to clarify their own values and to take positions that are consistent with such values, but are of less use in teaching basketball or gymnastic skills (Orlich et al., 1985).

Second, teachers' decisions will be guided by their own personal teaching style, strengths, and experiences. They may use methods that they have used successfully before or they may choose a method that replicates the fashion in which they learned a particular concept or set of knowledge. But a third factor must also be considered: just as teachers bring their own preferences and experiences to the classroom setting, so students have their own unique combinations of likes, dislikes, values, attitudes, skills, and interests (Orlich et al., 1985). For example, some students may enjoy engaging in large group discussions, while others may recoil at the thought of speaking before more than three or four peers at a time. The sensitive teacher will try to balance the needs and preferences of the students when selecting instructional methods.

In addition, the physical environment in which instruction is to be conducted will influence the selection of teaching strategies. The teacher will be restricted by such variables as the availability of materials, audiovisual resources, or the time of year. While there are many interesting ways to present different concepts, the teacher's ability to take field trips, conduct certain demonstrations, or even have students practise particular athletic skills will be restricted by the practical demands of the setting.

Regardless of the teaching method that is to be used, the teacher should ensure that instructional content is presented in a logical and coherent fashion that highlights the most important concepts and/or skills. Research in cognitive learning and information processing underlines the importance of carefully structuring knowledge for students. The better organized a lesson is perceived to be, the more students are likely to learn. This includes the maintenance of a smooth flow of information throughout the lesson: teachers who make orderly and smooth transitions from topic to topic within a lesson are more effective instructors than those teachers who make choppy transitions or stray from the main intent of the lesson (Smith and Cotten, 1980).

Moreover, not all content presented through a lecture, film, demonstration, or discussion will be of equal importance. More effective teachers help students attend to and retain the most important aspects of the presentation (Maddox and Hoole, 1975). This can be accomplished through repetition, by verbally emphasizing important details, telling students what to attend to in a film, video, or filmstrip; underlining, circling or otherwise highlighting important information on the board or overhead projector; and using verbal cues, such as "This is important..." (Borich, 1988).

There is a high correlation between student attention and student learning (Bloom, 1976), so instructional strategies should be selected with an eye to enhancing variety and therefore maintaining student interest. Once student interest has been obtained through a novel or otherwise captivating opening, attention must be maintained throughout the course of the lesson. By varying the modality through which learning is done (visual, auditory, or tactile) or combining various instructional procedures (discussion, question-and-answer sessions, lectures or demonstrations) the teacher is more likely to hold students' interest. Presenting the same content through a variety of methods not only reinforces the material, it also helps the teacher address the different learning styles and preferences in the class.

**Formative checks or learning probes**   A lesson plan is a flexible document that must be modified "on the go" in reaction to the responses of the students. To help the teacher recognize when such modifications should be made, formative checks or learning probes should be frequently used to check students' comprehension (Hunter, 1984; Orlich et al., 1985). There is no point teaching for a

20 or 40 minute period, only to come to the end of the lesson and find that students have not understood any of the material that has been presented. Sometimes students' confusion will be evident through their questions or nonverbal indications of uncertainty; however, such hints may not be immediately apparent for all students. Formative checks therefore should be used continuously throughout the lesson to assess their understanding so that the teacher can address problems, modify lesson procedures, or even hasten instruction when students are mastering information more quickly than anticipated.

There are many ways to conduct formative checks, ranging from the most specific and formal to more general and informal means. Sometimes checks will be completed with individual students or small groups; some may require the completion of small quizzes, while others can be conducted through question-and-answer sessions or by asking students to summarize what has just been learned. Regardless of the format used, such checks should allow the students to demonstrate that they are able to use the content provided at the intended level of complexity.

Further, formative checks allow students to become actively involved in the learning process, rather than simply passively receiving information from the teacher. They prevent students from advancing on to new concepts before prerequisite knowledge has been mastered and/or alert the teach to the need to enrich instruction for students who are mastering the material more quickly than their peers. Whatever their format, formative checks should help teachers better individualize instruction to the needs and abilities of their classes and take best advantage of the available instructional time (Orlich et al., 1985).

**Independent practice** During most lessons, students are given the opportunity to practise the concepts or skills that are presented during some type of independent work. Seatwork is the most common context for individual practice. In fact, research shows that students may spend a majority of time doing independent seatwork. Students in grades one through seven spend approximately 50 to 75 percent of their time at seatwork, more time than at any other activity. (Fisher et al., 1980). Studies of elementary mathematics and reading also reveal that students spend 50 to 70 percent of their time doing seatwork (Fisher et al., 1980; Rosenshine, 1980).

However, while independent seatwork can be a useful instructional strategy, it is often misused and overused (Brophy, 1979; Good and Grouws, 1977). Basically, students will learn when they pay attention and when they practise (Doyle, 1983). But if students lack motivation, self-organizational skills, or reading ability, their ability to benefit from seatwork is limited. The time students spend receiving direct instruction from the teacher may be far more productive than time spent on seatwork (Good and Grouws, 1977).

To enhance the effectiveness of seatwork, the following guidelines should be used:

- Seatwork should only be used when students demonstrate the ability to complete the work independently with a high level of success (Brophy and Good, 1986).

- Instruction and learning from seatwork can be improved when more time is spent in lecture, discussion, and guided practice and the class is structured and guided through the first seatwork problems (Winzer, 1989).

- Seatwork assignments should last no longer than ten minutes, as students are more likely to benefit from short periods of practice in class supplemented by further practice in homework assignments (Slavin, 1988).

- Students' performance should be continuously monitored by the teacher to ensure that they are performing correctly (Slavin, 1988).

- During seatwork, teachers should circulate actively, providing feedback, asking questions, and providing short explanations. However, contacts should be short, averaging 30 seconds or less. Longer contacts suggest that the initial learning experience was not complete and more rehearsal is necessary.

- Brophy and Good (1986) suggest that seatwork should be checked, errors corrected, and the results counted toward the class grade.

- Learning is also enhanced when seatwork is broken into smaller segments. This is particularly effective for difficult materials and for slower students (Emmer et al., 1982).

**Closure**    The introduction to the lesson has told the students what they were to learn and the body of the lesson has used instructional methods that help them attain that information. Now we reach closure which synthesizes and summarizes all of the elements of the lesson, or tells students what they have learned (Orlich et al., 1985). Various actions or statements made by the teacher can help bring the lesson to an appropriate conclusion, allowing students to bring things together in their own minds, making sense of what they have just experienced (Shostak, 1986).

While lesson closures should accomplish such objectives, most lesson closures tend to look something like this:

*TEACHER A: Okay, that's the bell. Get going, you're going to be late for your next class.*
*TEACHER B: Enough of this! Let's close our books and get ready for recess.*
*TEACHER C: The bell? All right, we will stop here and pick up at the same point tomorrow.*
*TEACHER D: Any questions? No? Good. Let's move on to the next chapter (Shostak, 1986, p. 129).*

While these teachers have brought the lessons to an end, they have done so in a most unsatisfactory fashion. It is better if teachers keep a careful eye on the clock and initiate closure activities while there remains sufficient time to do a thorough and comprehensive job. An effective closure summarizes the lesson and singles out the most important aspects that have been learned (Orlich et al., 1985).

Closure can be achieved in a number of ways but should be as interesting and captivating as the lesson introduction. It should not consist of a dry recitation of the objectives of the lesson but rather provide an opportunity for students to become actively and directly involved in the process. For example, the teacher might pose a question such as "What have we learned today?" which forces students to think about their learning and to make meaningful connections between the new and previously learned information (Orlich et al., 1985).

While closure is, of course, used to end each lesson, other situations arise in which closure should be used to cap the activity:

- to end a long unit of work;
- to consolidate learning of a new concept or principle;
- to close a discussion;
- to end a skill-building activity;
- to follow a film, record, or tape;
- to close a question-and-answer session;
- to consolidate a learning experience on a field trip;
- to reinforce the presentation of a guest speaker;
- to follow-up a homework assignment reviewed in class; and
- to end a laboratory activity (Shostak, 1986).

Teachers are likely to assign homework to older students. Assigning homework seems to increase student achievement (Walberg, Pascal, and Weinstein, 1985), at least when it consists of brief (perhaps 15 minutes) assignments (Good and Grouws, 1977). The value of homework appears to lie in its provision of distributed practice of the skills being learned. This is especially true when the homework is checked and comments on it are given to the students (Elawar and Corno, 1985). However, more research is needed on what kinds of homework are effective and how much homework is ideal for different types of students (Brophy, 1986).

**Evaluation of the lesson**   Every lesson should include some type of evaluation component that allows the teacher to assess the degree to which the lesson objectives were accomplished. This assessment may be informal, such as questioning during the lesson closure, or more formal and structured, such as a brief quiz or submission of independent work. The results of such an assessment should be communicated to the students as soon as possible so that they can use the feedback to improve their performance (Barringer and Gholson, 1979). Further, as noted earlier in the discussion of the unit plan, at some point students should be tested on larger blocks of information in order to assess their ability to synthesize and integrate the information provided.

## Increasing students' learning

Most studies of the learning process have shown that the acquisition of new information or of a new skill proceeds in a predictable fashion. When confronting a new subject, we begin by learning slowly, and then increase the speed at which we learn rather dramatically. Our pace then slows and begins to level.

There are a number of crucial stages of learning that apply to all students in all teaching and learning situations. The first learning stage is initial acquisition. It is vital to present a new task in a logical, organized manner. Much hands-on activity is necessary in the initial acquisition stage.

**Engaged time:**
the amount of time actually spent learning.

**Allocated or instructional time:**
time that students actually have to learn.

Teachers have high rates of success when initial instruction proceeds in small steps that are not too difficult and when their pupils practise the new knowledge and skills until they are overlearned (Brophy, 1982). For younger children, successful learning requires a large amount of successful practice spaced over time.

Proficiency is achieved by building on the original task. In order to reach this stage, the pupils need to repeat the task over and over again. In mathematics and spelling, automaticity should be the terminal objective. Learning is enhanced when basic skills become automatic. Moreover, the overlearning of basic skills is necessary for higher cognitive processing (Beck, 1978). The same strategies are successful with older students.

When the students have reached the maintenance stage, the skill learned in an instructional situation can be performed even after instruction ceases. Children do not maintain those skills which they simply forget, those over which they have a lack of control, or those which they are not motivated to use.

Retention refers to what the students remember over a given period of time. Retention is aided when the material is meaningful. Teachers can make material more meaningful to students by organizing it carefully, by teaching it in chunks, and by helping students to understand the inherent concepts and the relevant language.

Generalization and transfer are ongoing through any teaching. Generalization is achieved by developing strategies with which to discriminate the relevant dimensions of similar stimuli rather than the same stimuli.

When the stage of generalization and transfer has been attained, learning in one situation influences learning in another context so that a behaviour learned in one situation can be performed in another. Children can use the skills they have learned in school outside the classroom in a variety of ways.

While the general processes of learning are important, teachers need to be aware of ways to increase the students' achievement. In the research literature, the most consistently replicated findings link students' achievement with their opportunity to learn the material and, in particular, to the degree to which teachers carry the content to them personally through active instruction at a brisk pace (Brophy, 1986).

It may seem a trite observation, but students achieve more in classes where they spend most of their time being taught or supervised by their teachers rather than working on their own or not working at all (Arehart, 1979; Brophy and Evertson, 1976; Good and Grouws, 1977; Stallings, 1975; Stallings et al., 1978). However, the time spent on academic tasks varies from classroom to classroom. Much time is lost through interruptions, disruptions, late starts, and rough transitions. Probably 25 percent of all instructional time disappears in this way (Woolfolk, 1990).

The more students pay attention, practise, and study, the more they learn. This is referred to as academic engagement or academic engaged time (Rosenshine and Berliner, 1978), academic learning time (Denham and Lieberman, 1980), time spent in direct instruction (Rosenshine, 1979), explicit teaching (Rosenshine, 1986), and on-task time.

**Engaged time** is the amount of time actually spent learning. **Allocated or instructional time** is the time that students actually have to learn. Across

**On-task time:**
the time that students are actively engaged in learning or in interacting with materials.

Canada, the school year is generally from about 180 to 195 days long and students are in class for about $5\frac{1}{2}$ hours a day. **On-task time** refers to the time that students are actively engaged in learning or in interacting with materials. As students work on task, they are learning information and practising operations (Doyle, 1983).

The amount of time that students devote to learning is consistently reported to be a necessary prerequisite to effective increases in school achievement (Frederick and Walberg, 1980; Gettingen, 1984). Student achievement is closely related to the opportunity to learn and the amount and type of content covered. The amount learned is related to the opportunity to learn, which is determined in part by the allocated time. The opportunity to learn may be measured either in pages of curriculum covered (Borg, 1979; Good, Grouws, and Beckerman, 1978) or percentage of test items taught through lectures or recitation activities (Arehart, 1979; Armento, 1977; Cooley and Leinhardt, 1980; Nuthall and Church, 1973; Smith, 1979).

High task-engagement rates attained through successful classroom management are among the most powerful correlates of student achievement (Brophy and Evertson, 1976; Coker, Medley, and Soar, 1980; Stallings, 1975; Stallings et al., 1978). Brophy (1986) tells us that engagement rates depend on the teacher's ability to organize the classroom as an efficient learning environment where activities run smoothly, transitions are brief and orderly, and little time is spent getting organized or dealing with misconduct. Teachers should keep to a minimum such activities as giving directions and organizing the class for instruction. Teachers can do this by writing daily schedules on the board, and ensuring that the pupils know where to go, what books to use, and so on. Also, teachers

The more students pay attention, practise, and study, the more they will learn—but students who appear to be paying attention may actually be thinking about nonacademic issues.

enhance student achievement when they see academic instruction as basic to their roles and expect their students to master the curriculum. Effective teachers allocate most of the instructional time to activities designed for curriculum mastery (Brophy and Evertson, 1976; Fisher et al., 1980; Stallings, 1975).

Although there is not an exact relationship between time on-task and learning outcomes, learning time is an important varible of effective teaching and considerable attention has been centred on student time devoted to learning as a predictor of academic gains. Recent studies have shown that the amount of on-task behaviour can vary as much as 40 percent from one classroom to the next (Good, 1983). One study also showed that students who appeared to be paying attention (engaged in academic learning time) were actually thinking about nonacademic issues (Peterson and Swing, 1982).

More time spent learning means more content coverage. The correlation between content covered and students' learning is usually larger than the correlation between specific teaching behaviours and students' learning (Rosenshine, 1979). Effective teachers maintain a brisk pace that sustains interest, increases engagement, and permits the teachers to cover plenty of content (Davis and Thomas, 1989). The pacing may change to accommodate different students—high groups may be paced as much as 15 times faster than lower groups (Shavelson, 1973).

If students are involved in tasks that are neither overwhelming nor unchallenging, achievement will be higher than in classes in which such involvement is absent (Denham and Lieberman, 1980). When students work independently, teachers should ensure that assignments are interesting and worthwhile and can be completed without undue teacher attention (Gage, 1978). In addition, achievement is enhanced when students have the opportunity to learn the material in an active and personal format.

Brophy (1986) observed that students learn more when their teachers' presentations are clear rather than vague and rambling (Smith and Land, 1981) and when they are delivered with enthusiasm (Armento, 1977; Bettencourt, et al., 1983). Students also learn more when the information is well-structured (Armento, 1977) and when it is sufficiently redundant and well-sequenced (Armento, 1977; Nuthall and Church, 1973; Smith and Sanders, 1981). Clear presentations come from an intimate knowledge of the subject matter. However, the relationships between the teacher's knowledge of the subject matter and students' learning is not clearly defined, but appears to be indirect. There are, however, indications that a teacher's knowledge of teaching methods is related to student learning (McDonald, 1976).

## Questioning techniques

One of the most important and yet underestimated teaching strategies is the posing of questions. Research shows that questioning is a critical part of instruction, if not the essential function of teaching (Borg et al., 1970). Questions can serve many functions: to diagnose students' progress, to determine their entry-level competence, and to find out whether they require additional study or enrichment in an area of study (Orlich et al., 1985). Moreover, if instructional objectives are intended to guide students to the acquisition of certain cognitive and affective outcomes, the questions posed during the lesson can either enhance or hinder this effort.

If appropriately used, questions posed by the teacher will stimulate students' thinking and help them reflect in a meaningful fashion on what they are learning. The research shows that teachers who ask more academically relevant questions are more instructionally effective than those who ask relatively few questions related to the lesson at hand. (e.g., Dunkin and Biddle, 1974).

Unfortunately, research shows that many teachers do not use questions effectively. This relates to the type of question asked, how they are asked, how students are called upon to respond, and how long teachers wait for an answer.

These findings are distressing given the fact that questioning takes up the bulk of instruction time. Early and recent studies examining classroom practices reveal that up to 80 percent of classroom time is taken up with question-and-answer sessions (Gall, 1970; Stevens, 1912). In 1971, a sample of high school teachers were found to ask an average of 395 questions a day (Clements, 1971). Similarly, Gall (1970) cited a number of studies that showed that elementary teachers asked a large number of questions, ranging from 64 to 180 questions in one class period to an average of 348 questions during an entire school day.

Teachers generally ask factual questions (Sitko, Bachor, and Slemon, 1980) and this is especially prevalent in classrooms for low-achieving pupils (Brady, 1977). Despite all of the possible alternatives that exist, over 70 to 80 percent of questions in elementary and secondary classrooms focus on simple recall of facts, while the remaining small percentage requires all higher level thought processes such as clarification, expanding, generalizing, or making inferences (Corey, 1940). More contemporary research demonstrates that teachers tend to focus primarily on memory questions (Clegg, 1971). Daines (1982) reported that data on elementary and secondary social studies teachers demonstrated that they posed literal types of questions at a rate of 1.5 per minute.

Asking rapid-fire questions calling for rote answers does not increase achievement. But why, with the many different types of questions that they can ask, do teachers focus on low-level knowledge questions? Many reasons have been proposed and one suggestion is that this practice exists because most teachers have not been systematically trained to use higher-level questions. A remedy does exist: when training methods such as films, modeling, self-feedback, and micro-teaching were used to encourage enhanced questioning skills, a significant increase in the teachers' proficiencies was noted. For example, it was found that teachers increased their use of redirection questions (those requiring multiple student responses) from 27 percent to 41 percent; increased thought-provoking questions from 37 percent to 52 percent; and increased probing or prompting questions from 8 percent to 14 percent. There was a corresponding decrease in the repetition of student answers (from 31 percent to 4 percent) and decreased repetition of teacher questions from 14 percent to 5 percent. The practice of teachers answering their own questions decreased from 5 percent to .6 percent (Borg et al., 1970).

It has been further suggested that teachers may ask low-level questions because they lack a quick and easy method to use to classify questions (Orlich et al., 1986). While many methods can be used to categorize such questions, Bloom's taxonomy is perhaps the most useful (Sadker and Sadker, 1986). As we noted earlier, teachers can use Bloom's taxonomy to ensure that instructional objectives promote thinking at different levels. Similarly, teachers should use questions that encourage students to engage in a variety of different cognitive processes. An if-then relationship exists; if the teacher wishes a student to respond at a particular level of the taxonomy, then an appropriate question must be posed that will elicit the proper response from the student (Orlich et al., 1985). Examples of questions that would tap the different levels of thinking are found in Table 13-5. While knowledge of the taxonomy alone may not improve the quality of questions, it should make the teacher more aware of the process (Riegle, 1976).

**Table 13-5** Asking questions using Bloom's taxonomy

| LEVEL OF BLOOM'S TAXONOMY | EXAMPLES OF QUESTIONS | OTHER WORDS THAT MIGHT BE USED IN QUESTIONS |
|---|---|---|
| Knowledge | What is the capital of British Columbia? Who wrote *Hamlet*? | define, recall, who, what, where, when, identify, remember |
| Comprehension | What is the main idea? Describe democracy in your own words. | compare, contrast, rephrase, put in your own words, explain the main idea |
| Application | In which case is the principle of operant conditioning used? | apply, classify, use, choose, write an example, solve |
| Analysis | What influenced the writing of Margaret Laurence? | identify the cause or motivation, why, draw conclusions, support, analyze |
| Synthesis | How can we raise money for our project? What would Canada be like if it joined the U.S.? | predict, produce, write, design, develop, synthesize, construct, how can we improve, what would happen if |
| Evaluation | Which movie do you prefer? Which Member of Parliament is most effective? | judge, argue, decide, evaluate, assess, give your opinion, do you agree, which is the best |

A high-level question is a query that requires the student to analyze and produce a reasoned response, rather than mimic the teacher's words. Studies of the use of high-level questions indicate that varying levels of questions seems to affect students' thinking. Hunkins (1969) conducted a study with 260 sixth graders in 11 social studies classrooms. It was concluded that use of high-level questions not only helped students use evaluation skills better but also improved their understanding of low-level facts. However, while the formulation of diverse questions is important, it does not necessarily mean that students will respond in an appropriate manner.

Mills et al. (1980) found, for example, that when teachers asked application, analysis, or synthesis questions, there was only a 50 percent chance that students would respond at the corresponding level. Similarly, Dillon (1982) observed that there was a 50 percent chance that a student would respond with a low-level response when asked a high-level question and vice versa. Thus, teachers must monitor student responses and ensure that they react to students in a way that enhances appropriate responding. However, other research (Dillan, 1982; Winne, 1979) found that teachers who ask relatively more questions at the higher, more complex levels also tend to elicit students' behaviour at relatively high levels. That is, there is a tendency for students' responses to be at the same level of cognitive complexity as the teacher's questions.

Findings on the level of difficulty of questions (the probability that the question will be answered incorrectly by the first respondent) are mixed. It seems clear that many questions (perhaps 75 percent) should elicit correct answers (Anderson, Evertson, and Brophy, 1979; Brophy and Evertson, 1976) and that most of the rest should elicit substantive responses (incorrect or incomplete answers) rather than failures to respond at all (Brophy and Evertson, 1976). For students of high ability, the successful pattern of questioning includes harder questions at both higher and lower levels of a cognitive taxonomy and more critical feedback (Ward and Tikunoff, 1976).

Questioning techniques involve more than just the appropriate framing of the questions. Teachers must also consider how to go about soliciting responses to questions. The research is unclear on this issue although it appears that most teachers tend to primarily call on volunteers for responses. However, using this practice means that some students can avoid participating in the lesson simply by failing to raise their hands (Brophy and Evertson, 1974). Studies have found that calling on volunteers correlated negatively with reading achievement (Anderson, Evertson, and Brophy, 1979; Brophy and Evertson, 1974). In the same studies, the frequency of call-outs also correlated negatively with average class achievement in reading.

Findings on the selection of respondants to questions vary with context. In the early grades, and especially in small group lessons, it is important for each student to respond overtly and often. In small-group reading lessons, this can be accomplished by allowing each student to take a turn in order, training students not to call out answers, and calling on non-volunteers as well as volunteers (Anderson, Evertson, and Brophy, 1979).

As an alternative, it has been suggested that when a single correct answer is required, teachers can request a choral response from all students (Becker and Carnine, 1980). Students could also be asked either to use hand signals (such as holding up the correct number of fingers to answer a computation problem) or to write their answers on a sheet of paper or small chalkboard and hold up their answers as a group. Such all-pupil responses have been shown to have a positive effect on learning (McKenzie, 1979).

Gage (1978) suggests that when teachers select pupils to respond to questions they should call on a child before asking the question as a means of ensuring that all students are given an equal opportunity to answer questions. Teachers should always give less academically oriented students the opportunity to respond to a question. Rephrasing, giving clues, or asking a new question can be helpful (Gage, 1978).

When working with small reading groups, Anderson and colleagues (1979) found that it was better to call on students in a predictable order (such as around the circle) rather than in an unpredictable fashion. One of the advantages of this approach is that it ensures that all students will be called upon. However, these authors suggested that such an approach may be inappropriate for large group

**Wait-time:**
the time intervening before
the student responds to a
teacher's question.

work, for when students are aware that they will not be required to answer for some time, they are likely to become inattentive.

Teachers are not the only ones to pose questions in the classroom; students must also be given the encouragement to pose questions and express ideas and opinions (Borg et al., 1970). While most research shows that teachers do most of the talking and questioning in classrooms, this situation can be altered. The advantages of doing so were underlined by a review conducted by Cornbleth (1975) who examined a series of studies and found evidence that supported the practice of teachers encouraging students' questions. Cornbleth (1975) concluded that students can be encouraged to ask more productive and higher-level questions and that the more questions they ask, the more likely they are to be at a higher level. He also found that praise will encourage and stimulate more productive thinking on the part of children of lower socioeconomic status and that students are more involved in classes in which they are encouraged to ask questions.

What the teacher does after the question will also influence the type of response received. Perhaps the most important factor is wait-time, the time that intervenes before the student responds to a teacher's question.

Many teachers expect rapid responses and seem to be embarrassed by a sea of lowered hands, even if topped by thoughtful faces (Winzer, 1989). Some teachers, in fact, report a sense of panic when their questions are not answered immediately (Gambrell, 1980). This may be why the average amount of time allowed by teachers for student responses is only one second (Rowe, 1974). Research indicates that if students do not immediately respond to a question, the teacher's typical response is generally to repeat, rephrase, ask a different question, or switch to another student (Sadker and Sadker, 1986).

Moreover, teachers generally give up more rapidly on students they perceive to be low-achievers, which communicates to the students that the teacher does not really expect a response (Rowe, 1974; Tobin and Capie, 1982).

However, teachers must be prepared to cope with silence. Some children may abandon their attempts to answer as they cannot construct a response in the time provided (Cacha, 1981). Teachers who wait approximately three seconds after asking a student a question obtain better learning results than those who give up more easily (Tobin, 1986). When teachers increase wait-time, students are more likely to give longer answers, ask more questions, demonstrate a decreased likelihood of failure to respond, be more involved in the lesson, and show increased reasoning abilities. Students are also more likely to participate, volunteer appropriate answers, and be more confident in their answers. As well, students' comments involving analysis, synthesis, inference, and speculation tend to increase (Sadker and Sadker, 1986).

Students of lesser ability are more likely to respond when the teacher increases wait-time; Rowe (1978) found that this led to a decrease in the amount of disciplinary action necessary. Other researchers have substantiated these results (e.g., Honea, 1982), indicating that it is indeed true that "silence is golden" (Orlich et al., 1985). It has been suggested that by waiting for students to respond, or by staying with them when they fail to respond immediately communicates positive expectations, which are in turn related to achievement (Brophy and Good, 1974).

Research also suggests that the pauses following questions should vary with their complexity or cognitive level. Students are more likely to respond with higher-level thinking when they are given time to think about their answer.

The feedback given to students after they answer a question will also influence the type of response they will give in the future. Unfortunately, research shows that after a student answers, the most common teacher response (50 percent of the time) is "Okay" or "Uh-huh" (Sadker and Sadker,1986). In previous chapters, we have directed a great deal of attention to the importance of providing praise and feedback for appropriate responding and these guidelines hold true for responses to questions. Feedback can be particularly important when teachers use students' ideas to build and develop their lessons. Applying, comparing, and building on the contributions of students are important in encouraging them to respond. As well, it has been shown that classrooms in which students are reinforced for contributions have higher achievement and students have more positive attitudes toward learning as compared to classes where student ideas are not incorporated into lessons (Sadker and Sadker, 1986).

Of course, repeatedly reinforcing students' performance with the same word or phrase is unlikely to encourage enhanced behaviour. Students would grow accustomed to the teacher's behaviour and simply tune it out. As well, there are times when reinforcement given too quickly or too frequently may interfere with the students' ability to fully develop their ideas; in fact, it might block their problem-solving altogether. When students are engaged in ongoing problem-solving, repeated reinforcers may interrupt their thought processes and cause them to cease their thinking processes altogether. Student-to-student interactions can also be inhibited when the teacher constantly interrupts with reinforcers or feedback (Sadker and Sadker, 1986).

Asking follow-up probing questions is another way to increase the quality and quantity of student participation. This is particularly important when a student has been asked a question and responds with an incomplete answer or fails to respond at all (Orlich et al., 1985). Prompting or asking probing questions following a student's response helps to stimulate students to think through their answers. Probes also develop the quality of responses and expand upon the initial answer. They require the students to provide more support for their answer, and provide the opportunity for greater clarity, accuracy, specificity, or orginality (Sadker and Sadker, 1986).

For an example, consider the following dialogue in which the teacher uses a series of probing questions at various levels of Bloom's taxonomy. Rather than accepting the student's initial response, the teacher probes for more specific details and moves the student to higher levels of thinking:

*TEACHER: How can we convince auto manufacturers to build smaller cars that burn less gasoline?*
*STUDENT: Pass a law.*
*TEACHER: Can you be more specific? [probe]*
*STUDENT: Sure. Put a limit on the size of the cars.*
*TEACHER: Why do you think that would work? [probe]*
*STUDENT: Well, smaller cars burn less gas. If you just ask them to make smaller cars, they wouldn't do it. So pass a law requiring it.*

*TEACHER: Wouldn't car manufacturers rebel at being forced to make smaller cars? [probe]*

*STUDENT: I guess, but they would do it.*

*TEACHER: What effect might such a law have on businessmen in other industries? How would they perceive such a law? [probe]*

Without probing, the teacher would have been left with a superficial answer and the student would not have had the chance to consider his or her response more carefully. Thus, the probing questions have enhanced the quality of the response as well as the level of cognitive thinking. Probing or prompting students must always be done in a positive fashion, which implies that the teacher must accept and acknowledge the student's response before going on to press for additional clarification or amplification. The student must always receive positive feedback from the teacher so he or she is more inclined to finish an incomplete response or revise an incorrect answer (Orlich et al., 1986).

But what happens when the student gives a response that is entirely incorrect? This is an inevitable occurrence, despite the teacher's attempts to frame the question properly, provide appropriate prerequisite information, and/or use adequate instructional methods. Prompting or probing can be used when an answer is partially correct or incomplete; in this manner, the teacher focuses on the appropriate section of the answer and ignores the negative or incomplete component. But when the answer is entirely incorrect, it is difficult to find much to reinforce. The most productive approach is to tell students why they are wrong so they can learn more appropriate strategies (Bloom and Bourdon, 1980).

But comments such as "You are way off," "No," or "That's wrong" should be avoided as they will only serve to punish student responding, and may discourage the student—and perhaps others who observe the interaction—from responding to questions in the future. And of course, sarcastic or otherwise embarrassing responses to student questions should never be used (Borich, 1988; Orlich et al., 1985).

One method that can be used to respond to an incorrect answer is to quickly examine the response for some correct component. This may be difficult, but often some portion of the answer can be acknowledged. For example, if the student gives an incorrect answer to a computation question in mathematics, the teacher might respond by saying "Your answer is in the right magnitude," "Can you tell us how you came to that answer?" or "Could you rethink your solution and take another try?" (Orlich et al., 1985). Another strategy is to rephrase the question; for example, by asking a question that requires a lower level of thinking.

## Lecture

Lectures have an undeservedly bad reputation among teachers and students alike. While poorly handled lectures can certainly be dull, boring, irrelevant, and/or redundant, the format itself is not to blame. However, the problem lies with the inappropriate use or overuse of the method and is not inherent in the method itself (McMann, 1979). Despite the constant criticism of this methodology, the lecture remains as an important and commonly used strategy in the teacher's arsenal of instructional methods. Some studies have found that lecturing takes up one-sixth to one-quarter of classroom time (Woolfolk, 1990). As we would expect, teachers in higher grades lecture more than teachers in lower grades (Duncan and Biddle, 1974).

When should the lecture method be used? Brophy and Good (1986) summarizd the research and suggested that lectures should be used in the following situations:

- when the objective is to present information;

- when the information is not available in a textbook or other readily available source;

- when the material should be organized or presented in a particular way;

- when it is necessary to arouse interest in a subject;

- when it is necessary to provide an introduction to a topic that students will then read about on their own or to provide instructions about learning a task;

- when information is original or must be integrated from a number of sources;

- when material needs to be summarized or synthesized;

- when text or curriculum materials should be updated or elaborated;

- when the teacher wants to present alternative points of view or interpretations, or to clarify issues in preparation for discussion or debate; or

- when the teacher wants to provide supplementary explanations of material that students are likely to have difficulty with on their own (Brophy and Good, 1986, p. 365).

Perhaps one of the most important considerations in the preparation of a good lecture is the organizational structure that is developed. The process used here is not unlike that used to develop a good lesson plan. That is, an effective lecture includes an attention-grabbing introduction which describes the objectives to be covered, well-sequenced presentation of new material, frequent probes or checks of student understanding, and an appropriate closure that summarizes and synthesizes the material that has been covered.

While the organization of the lecture is important, even the best organized lecture will lose the students' attention if delivered in a dry, humourless fashion. Teachers are more effective when they use such techniques as planned repetition of important points, marker expressions (such as "Note this" or "This is important"), and underlining, colours, or diagrams when using chalkboards, slides, or other displays (Pinney, 1969). Students learn more from lectures that are presented with enthusiasm and expressiveness (Coats and Smidchers, 1966; Corker and Brooker, 1986). Gestures and movements can enhance the effectiveness of a lecture, as long as they do not distract from the message to be delivered (Wyckoff, 1973). Of course, this cannot be overdone, as too much variation in the mode of presentation can actually hurt achievement by distracting students from the lesson (Wyckoff, 1973).

One consistent feature of effective lessons is clarity—the use of direct, simple, and well-organized language to present concepts (McCaleb and White, 1980; Smith and Land, 1981). The communication skills of the teachers are paramount: they must be able to introduce variety, activity, and humour into the lecture (Kaplan and Pascoe, 1977). Although the research on voice and body language is in its infancy, preliminary studies indicate that comprehension is aided by a maximum speaking rate of 150 words per minute. Studies also suggest that voice variations are preferred over other vocal qualities, such as volume, phrasing, and rate (Carver, 1973; Diehl and McDonald, 1956).

## Discussions

Group discussion methods can be used for a variety of purposes: to encourage critical thinking, to actively engage average and less able learners in the learning process, and to promote the students' ability to interact with others in a reasoned fashion (Gall and Gall, 1976). Discussions are rarely appropriate in situations when the teacher is addressing a topic in which little controversy or room for the formulation of personal opinions or judgments exist such as the process of photosynthesis. Discussions are instead best conducted when the questions raised by the content have no simple answers. Many topics in social studies, art, music, and literature lend themselves to discussions. The lack of consensus that is likely to exist in the classroom is likely to make a discussion rewarding and fruitful (Borich, 1988).

Discussing controversial issues has been found to increase student knowledge about the issues as well as enhance the understanding of the various sides of an argument (Johnson and Johnson, 1979). Similarly, a discussion is often an appropriate choice when the teacher focuses on affective outcomes of learning, such as the development of values or attitudes. Discussions, particularly when the students are required to publicly commit themselves, are far more effective in changing attitudes and behaviours than lectures are (Lewin, 1947).

The role of the teacher during discussion is to moderate the discussion, rather than to guide conclusions or to dominate the conversation. The teacher's role, therefore, includes orienting students to the objectives of the discussion; providing new or accurate information where required; and reviewing, summarizing, or putting comments together in a meaningful fashion. During discussions, teachers must also alter the flow of the conversation in a manner that is most productive to the goals of the lesson and combine ideas and promote compromise to end at a final consensus (Borich, 1988).

Discussion can take place in a large group format (involving the entire class) or in small groups of five to ten students. The former format is by far the most difficult to handle, for discipline and management problems are more likely to arise when large numbers of students are interacting in a situation characterized by minimal teacher control. Certainly, the use of the previously outlined moderating strategies can help the teacher maintain control of a large group discussion, keeping students on-task and minimizing management problems (Borich, 1988).

Small group discussions can increase student achievement more than traditional lessons.

Research on small group instruction shows that this activity can increase student achievement more than traditional lessons if the students are well-prepared for the discussion format and the task is well-organized (Sharan et al., 1980). Small group discussions are useful for accomplishing instructional goals, particularly when multiple topics must be discussed within a single lesson and time does not permit discussion of each by the entire gorup. Generally, it has been found that the smaller the number of students, the greater the consensus on the topic under discussion. In addition, the students' ability to grasp the concepts and abstractions to be learned is greater, and the teacher is more able to turn control over to the group (Slavin, 1983).

In small group discussions, students will be working without teacher supervision most of the time and a higher level of skill will be needed from the participants. Students below the fourth grade level or poorly organized students will need a great deal of preparation before they can benefit from the use of this format, if it is used at all (Slavin, 1988).

The teacher must form the small groups with care, distributing children of various abilities across groups and separating potential troublemakers. The teacher circulates among the groups as they continue their conversations, performing moderating functions as required. Stopping the groups occasionally, either to inform the entire group about the insights attained by various groups or to apply moderating functions across groups, will help keep students at the same pace and underline the teacher's authority (Borich, 1988).

Another method of implementing small group instruction is to use cooperative learning groups. This is a more complex and comprehensive strategy than forming small discussion groups, but it has been shown that this strategy can be a useful and highly effective method of promoting academic achievement and facilitating positive affective outcomes, such as positive relationships among students, better motivation to learn, and higher self-esteem. These benefits are seen across curriculum areas and age levels, from tasks as simple as the rote learning of multiplication tables to more complex problem solving. Given the burgeoning body of research that demonstrates the efficacy of such approaches, they are likely to be used more frequently in contemporary classrooms. We suggest that readers review the discussion of cooperative learning found in Chapter 11.

## SUMMARY

1. Instructional planning is one of the most important skills in effective instruction. Planning involves both the art and science of teaching, for while it is based on a consideration of the scientific principles of instruction, good instruction is sensitive and intuitive.

2. Many different types of objectives can be formulated by teachers, including behaviour objectives as outlined by Mager, general objectives described by Gronlund, or the expressive objectives described by Eisner. The research appears to indicate that while many experienced teachers do not explicitly use instructional objectives while planning, their use does facilitate the appropriate development of instructional plans. Clear objectives provide guidelines to teachers about what to teach and how to teach it.

3. There are many ways to classify the different outcomes of learning. One of the most common methods is the use of taxonomies, which may focus on cognitive, affective, or psychomotor objectives. Taxonomies tend to be constructed in a hierarchical fashion, beginning with the most simple skill, progressing to the more complex. A taxonomy for the cognitive domain was prepared in 1956 by Benjamin Bloom and his associates.

4. Tables of specifications are used to help teachers classify the instructional objectives that are to be used in a specific unit of instruction. Such tables focus teachers' attention on the outcomes of learning, help ensure that instructional units are balanced in terms of the different types of learning that are expected, and help guide the process of evaluation.

5. Unit plans are integrated packages of instruction that consist of a related series of lesson plans addressing a particular theme or topic. Individual lesson plans outline the specific instructional objectives to be addressed, the manner in which the lesson is to be introduced, the content to be presented, the instructional methods to be used, as well as procedures for evaluation.

6. There are many different types of instructional methods that can be used, and selection will be based on a consideration of the content to be presented, teachers' and students' preferences and skills, and the physical and practical limitations of the settings.

7. There is little research evidence on how to use seatwork or homework activities effectively.

8. The approprite use of questioning techniques is central to effective instruction, yet the research shows that many teachers do not use questions effectively. When framing questions, teachers must consider the level of cognitive thinking that is desired, and must respond to student answers in a constructive fashion.

9. Lecturing is a much maligned instructional technique, yet the research demonstrates that when properly designed and delivered, lectures can be a most efficient and effective means of delivering information to students.

10. Large and small group discussions can be used to encourage critical thinking, to actively engage students in learning, and to promote students' interaction skills. They are particularly appropriate for use in situations in which controversial topics are addressed, or to develop affective abilities such as values or attitudes.

## Key Terms

| | | |
|---|---|---|
| allocated or instructional time | engaged time | entry-level skills |
| lesson plan | mastery learning | methods |
| on-task time | task analysis | taxonomy |
| unit plan | wait-time | |

# TESTING AND ASSESSMENT

## 14

## INTRODUCTION

A teacher's job is made up of more than just interaction with students. Before actual classroom instruction even begins, teachers do a great deal of thinking and planning. They plan courses of study, strands and units, goals and objectives, and individual lessons. Teachers devise ways to organize and manage their classrooms, to handle misbehaviour, and to individualize instruction for students encountering problems. As well, teachers devote much time to evaluating the success of instruction. Teachers are particularly concerned about the level at which their students presently function, the effectiveness of the instructional program, and the rate at which students progress through the curriculum.

Measuring and evaluating students' performance is something that every teacher has to do, usually quite frequently. In contemporary schools, students spend substantial amounts of time taking quizzes and tests and completing projects and assignments for marking; teachers spend even more time preparing and marking these and otherwise measuring student performance.

Evaluation is not new to the teaching profession. In fact, ancient sources can trace evaluation procedures back to China in 3000 B.C. and to Classical Greece. European universities adopted measures of achievement as early as the thirteenth century (Winzer, 1990b). In Canadian classrooms, the assessment process has become formalized over the past 70 or 80 years through the use of standardized tests of intelligence and achievement. Recently, there has been seen an increased interest in the relationship between educational measurement and the classroom practices used in evaluating student achievement (Stiggins, 1988). Questions revolve around whether testing is a common classroom practice, what kinds of abilities or characteristics should be measured, what methods are used to collect this information, and what is the extent to which external sources of instrumentation or data are of interest to teachers (Anderson, 1989).

However, from its inception and right up to the present, the entire area of classroom measurement and evaluation has been fraught with controversy. Some educators, especially those who hold a humanistic orientation, see evaluation that leads specifically to grading as unnecessary. Others propose a greater adherence to measurement and evaluation in contemporary classrooms. There is a belief among the public and professionals that testing will monitor student performance, so calls for more and expanded testing reflect a theme of greater accountability (Rogers, 1990).

The traditional and current controversy surrounding evaluation seems to arise from a number of sources. First of all, testing has always been socially significant in that results have been and continue to be used for decisions of considerable importance to individuals and to society generally (Winzer, 1990b). Today as we question the legitimacy of science, one major issue in the interpretation of standardized test scores is the question of whether tests are biased against lower class or minority group children (Schueneman, 1984).

As we saw in the case of Larry P. in California (see Chapter 6), values about the use of tests are being weighed against the constitutional values and individual rights and protection of individuals (Adair, 1980). Then, as Snow (1986) observes, the use of standardized assessment measures to assess variability among students and guide their subsequent program placement is a double-edged sword: it has the potential to help students, but also to harm them (Snow, 1986). Inappropriate measures, inefficient administration of tests, or inadequate interpretation of results can place students in unsuitable streams or programs.

In our schools, students are often rigidly tracked into skill/ability groups (Burry et al. 1981). Schools track students in different ways but the sorting function begins early in children's educational careers. Elementary teachers, for example, assign children to reading or math groups. Tracking is more widespread at the junior high level and very common in secondary programs. Other students are tracked when they are assigned to special education, generally to resource rooms but sometimes to segregated classrooms. Underlying much, if not all, of the various forms of tracking is assessment of students' aptitudes and abilities.

Secondly, critics see problems with the measures themselves. Ever since their first appearance in 1905, IQ tests have been controversial. As well, the most widely accepted measures of achievement have been roundly criticized (Deno, 1985). Achievement tests have been attacked because they are biased regarding curriculum content (Jenkins and Pany, 1978) and because they are technically inadequate for making decisions about individual students (Salvia and Ysseldyke, 1985).

Generally, however, the misuse of data predominates and the attack is less against the tests themselves than against their use. There is no problem with evaluation per se, argues Ebel (1980) but with the inadequate or inappropriate use of evaluation data.

Teachers accept testing as an integral part of their professional lives and devote a considerable amount of time to it. In one study (Hiatt, 1979) it was found that 22 percent of a typical elementary teacher's morning was taken up with activities in this category. These activities ranged from listening to oral reading to administering written tests. In addition, tests, assignments, and projects are developed, administered, and marked by teachers at all levels in order to generate information about the achievement of groups and of individual students.

Teachers tend to hold ambivalent attitudes toward evaluation. In Gander, Newfoundland, Paul and MacLeave (1989) found that educators across all positions surveyed "appeared to be satisfied with the current testing practices" (p. 380). Yet despite this, and despite the amount of time spent measuring and evaluating students' performance, teachers do not cede a high priority to formal measurement and evaluation and it is a task that most teachers dislike.

One likely reason is that many teachers feel that measurement and evaluation are rather mechanical processes that they go through to determine how much of something has been learned. Teachers may also feel they do not understand the measurement process very well. Many teachers are unsure about the processes and procedures involved in classroom and diagnostic assessment. They have often had only one measurement course. Usually, the course was a component of their teaching education when they were more concerned with learning how to construct classroom tests, or assign grades, or make a good grade in the course, than they were in gaining a firm grasp of the finer points of measurement theory (Winzer, 1989). Indeed, the generally held opinion of teachers about courses on measurement and testing is that they are burdensome requirement that is irrelevant to teaching practice (Deno, 1985).

Another possibility is that the role of evaluator is seen as being inconsistent with the role of teacher or helper (Biehler and Snowman, 1990). Also, teachers' interests and needs may not necessarily match the issues and procedures of mainstream educational measurement research and literature. Gullickson (1986), in an American study of teachers perceived needs in measurement, noted that teachers would favour more emphasis on non-test methodologies in measurement and evaluation courses, including an emphasis on rating scales, anecdotal records, and observation.

Variations in assessment practices exist across subject areas and grades (Green and Stager, 1987 a, b) as do the ways that teachers view assessment practices. Elementary teachers favour observation; secondary teachers prefer testing (Stiggins and Bridgeford, 1985). Teachers, especially those at the elementary levels, tend to rely on informal observations of student performance to evaluate progress; they give low priority to concepts of measurement and evaluation. In a study conducted in Ontario (Wahlstrom and Donley, 1976), both elementary teachers and elementary principals considered teachers' observations of children's work to be of the utmost importance. At the secondary level, observation ranked a close second behind standardized testing. Secondary teachers, compared with elementary teachers, seem to support the increased use of test scores.

Research shows that teachers usually don't use the results of norm-referenced tests in their academic decision making (Salmon-Cox, 1981). Teachers view standardized tests as being of greater value to people outside the classroom—principals, parents, and school boards—than they are to practitioners (Salmon-Cox, 1981). Hence, teachers' reluctance to use some standardized measures, coupled with mounting attacks by researchers on them, has led to a search for additional or alternative evaluative measures (Winzer, 1989).

However, measurement and evaluation relate to individual differences, learning, motivation, and instruction. Tests of mental ability determine aptitude differences among pupils. In this regard, Paul and MacLeave (1989) found that IQ testing and the use made of the data were viewed more positively by educators who were more influenced by the theory of heredity and by educators who had pursued post-graduate education.

In special education, assessment data are required not only for prescribing programs but also for determining when pupils will enter and leave programs. When teachers refer students for special education, psychological testing is ranked higher than it usually is. Wilson and Humphries (1986), for example, provided a description, based on events in Ontario, of the demand for intellectual assessment as a major source of data in the designation and placement of students in special classes.

Traditionally, evaluation and the concomitant grades have been viewed as a major motivating force in the classroom. While grades actually may not motivate learning, they certainly assume elevated levels of importance for a great many students. Teachers likewise are apt to stress grades and, in the classroom, the issue of grades is always a serious one involving difficult decisions for teachers.

Assessment and evaluation are inseparable, fundamental tasks in teaching. Indeed, an instructional program that consists of only routine teaching skills is inefficient and may even be detrimental to students. A teacher must always teach, test, and reteach. Using assessment data to prescribe, implement, evaluate, and revise instructional programs is an integral part of contemporary education (Winzer, 1989).

Measurement has several roles in the classroom and teachers have a variety of ways to measure what students have learned. Effective teachers use a range of assessment procedures, depending upon the needs of individual children, the

Assessment and evaluation are inseparable, fundamental tasks in teaching.

540

**Educational measurement:**
a field of development and research that addresses issues and develops procedures for the evaluation of student achievement.

**Assessment:**
any process of gathering data on a student's skills and behaviour.

information required, and the purpose of the information. Specific measuring instruments are designed to perform certain functions, and the particular functions of a measure should always be kept in mind. Finally, evaluation is a prerequisite for grading, one of the most perplexing and controversial tasks facing teachers (Aiken, 1983).

This relatively brief chapter is founded on two major premises: First, that efficient assessment and evaluation underlies and directs efficient programing, and second, that classroom teachers should assume a central role in the assessment process. An overview of assessment processes and procedures is presented here. Details regarding methods and instruments for assessing students and for judging aptitude and progress in specific curriculum areas are beyond the scope of this chapter. Nearly all students aspiring to the teaching profession in Canadian universities are exposed to at least one course on evaluation where principles and practices are explicitly detailed so this chapter merely overviews some points and illustrates the principles of educational psychology in evaluative practices.

## MEASUREMENT IN THE CLASSROOM

**Educational measurement** is a field of development and research that addresses issues and develops procedures for the evaluation of student achievement. These issues include test reliability, validity, standard error of measurement, item bias, test equating, and models underlying response data (Anderson, 1989). The relationship between educational measurement and classroom practice should be one of utility: educational measurement should produce information and procedures that are useful in the evaluation of student achievement (Anderson, 1989).

Assessment and evaluation of students' progress in mastering the curriculum are basic tasks of teaching. Most teachers must collect some systematic achievement data to provide a basis for grading, but even teachers who are not required to assign formal grades still need to assess student achievement in order to gather feedback about the effectiveness of their own teaching, to identify topics that require and individual students who need additional instruction, and to provide guidance for planning new instruction.

Assessment is a general term encompassing all types of in- and out-of-classroom measurement. **Assessment** centers on the collection of information; it is a systematic process used to gather data that allows more effective instruction. Assessment functions on a number of levels and serves a variety of purposes. Assessment:

- is an essential component of teaching (Prior to planning and initiating instruction, teachers must devise comprehensive and effective evaluative procedures.);

- provides teachers with an awareness of the individual strengths and weaknesses of children across many domains;

- determines an effective instructional program for all children, allowing programing at a general level and also promoting individualization;

- provides students with feedback on their performances;

**Measurement:**
the assignment of numbers to certain attributes, objects, events, or people according to a rule-governed system.

**Evaluation:**
the use of a rule-governed system to make judgments about the value or worth of a set of measures.

- helps the teacher in the systematic collection of achievement data that will serve as the basis for grading;

- aids in assessing the effectiveness of instruction, and assists in identifying areas that require greater concentration;

- provides guidelines for future planning;

- can place students at different levels;

- is important for students functioning above or below the norm (Through assessment, teachers and diagnosticians attempt to discover whether a given child in fact exhibits a problem, what the problem is, the cause, the potential course and developmental consequences, and the best approaches to intervention.);

- determines eligibility for special education services for exceptional children; and

- is the first step in the development of individual education plans for exceptional students.

Within the broad parameters of assessment, we talk about measurement and evaluation. Essentially, measurement asks the question, "How much?" But measurement results are meaningless unless we have some basis for interpreting them. Evaluation thus asks, "What does it mean?"

Therefore, measurement may be viewed as a tool used to summarize the behaviour of a student in manageable terms (scores) so that evaluation can take place (Howell and Morehead, 1987). **Measurement** implies the assignment of numbers to certain attributes, objects, events, or people according to a rule-governed system. When we discuss the assignment of numbers to people, the rules that are used to do so will ordinarily create a ranking that reflects how much of the attribute different people possess (Hills, 1981). Thus, we can measure someone's level of typing proficiency by counting the number of words a person accurately types per minute, or a child's reading fluency by the number of miscues counted.

Evaluation is a thoughtful process that has been defined in a variety of ways. All the definitions have at their core the idea of comparison. While measurement is a rule-governed system to assign numbers, **evaluation** involves using a rule-governed system to make judgments about the value or worth of a set of measures (Hills, 1981).

To measure and evaluate learning, we often use tests. While many people employ the term "test" to encompass all forms of evaluation, Allison (1982) points out that the word "test" in the term "standardized test" is rather a misnomer. Strictly speaking, a test is something that you pass or fail. The more correct term in psychology and education is "measuring instrument" because such tools are designed to measure, among other things, achievement, aptitudes, personality, interests, behaviour, performance, opinions, and relationships. Only the first factor measured—achievement—can really be tested; you cannot pass or fail on such things as personality and interests (Allison, 1982). Yet even measurement texts talk about personality tests and interest tests so the term is coming into common usage, albeit somewhat incorrectly.

**Test:**

a procedure for measuring a sample of a person's behaviour to be evaluated against standards and norms.

A **test** may be seen as "a systematic procedure for measuring a sample of a person's behaviour in order to evaluate that behaviour against standards and norms" (Gage and Berliner, 1978, p. 654). Testing means collecting data and a test score is a numerical summation of behaviour. Tests are used to plan teaching, group students, decide grades, motivate pupils, and provide feedback for teachers and students about recent learning. [1]

Although teachers may prefer not to test and may not always agree with the results of standardized tests, Burry and colleagues (1981) found that elementary and secondary teachers share some common positive perceptions about tests. Among other things, teachers feel that:

- tests motivate students to work hard;

- the pressure of testing has a beneficial effect;

- commercial tests are high quality products;

- district-developed tests are very good;

- curriculum is more complex today than it was in the past;

- skills on required tests are similar to those taught in classrooms;

- basic skills instruction and assessment account for a much larger proportion of the time and effort than content skills;

- teachers now spend more time preparing students for tests than they did in the past;

- teachers should not be held accountable for students' scores on published achievement tests;

- minimal competency or functional literacy should be required for promotion at certain grade levels; and

- some students are unfairly treated by minimum competency tests.

Nevertheless, many educators remain unimpressed with standardized tests (Coffman, 1980; Harootunian and Yarger, 1981; Lazer-Morrison et al., 1980; Nemeth and Samiroden, 1990). Critics complain that:

- teachers may be pressured to teach to the test, therefore allowing the test to determine what is taught in the classroom, often at the expense of other equally valuable educational goals (Nemeth and Samiroden, 1990);

- the tests sample only a limited portion of the curriculum and are geared to measure only those aspects of knowledge that are most easily measured (Samiroden, 1987);

- tests may contribute to rote learning rather than to understanding;

- tests emphasize the end product of education, rather than the process;

- thinking skills are affected by the degree to which students are acquainted with the subject matter;

- performance is influenced by the mental and emotional states of the students at the time of the test;

**Formative evaluation:** a procedure designed to provide feedback during the learning process.

**Summative evaluation:** a procedure used as an end product after the learning process.

- performance is subject to external stimuli;

- scores do not yield diagnostic clues as to how students derived the answers (their metacognition), how students processed the data, and the emotions necessary to arrive at the best answer (cognitive mapping) (Costa, 1985);

- results are often available only several weeks or months after the tests were administered; and

- test results are not generally considered to be good predictors of future success.

## Assessment strategies

Classroom measurement and evaluation may be investigated in a number of closely related ways. First of all, there is the distinction between formative and summative evaluation. **Formative evaluation** is designed to provide feedback to learning; it answers the question, "How are we doing?" **Summative evaluation** is used as an end product; it answers the question, "How did we do?" We find formative evaluation in such things as weekly quizzes or marked projects and assignments. Summative evaluations are given at different points in students' educational careers such as in report cards and college finals.

Further, the procedures that make up the assessment process can be broadly categorized as informal and formal. When we consider how evidence of student achievement is collected, we most often think of testing as using some form of paper and pencil instrument to determine how many questions a student can answer correctly. Generally, teacher-developed tests and classroom observations are the most common methods of assessing students (Herman and Dorr-Bremme, 1983). Yet not all the evaluation decisions made by teachers involve educational measurement. Some decisions are based on information from parents, previous experience, case histories, past school records, and even intuition.

Sattler (1988) describes the four pillars of assessment—informal assessment, interviews, observation, and norm-referenced tests. The three former procedures may be generally classified as informal; the latter as formal, since standardized tests and standardized conditions are used and students are required to respond to the same set of questions or tasks, or to equivalent forms that measure the same items of knowledge and skills. Ideally, all students are measured under standardized conditions; they are instructed in the same ways and under the same conditions. In general, everything is arranged to ensure that each student's score accurately represents his or her level of mastery.

In many provinces, standardized common measures such as the Canadian Test of Basic Skills, the Canadian Cognitive Abilities Test, the Canadian Achievement Test, the Gates McGinitie Reading Tests, the Metropolitan Achievement Tests, and the Stanford Achievement Tests are used to make a variety of educational decisions ranging from placement of individual students to efficacy of programs.

Formal testing is not the only way that teachers can obtain information, and not always the best way. In addition to formal testing or rating, teachers can use informal measures—they can collect information by observations of students, by questioning, and by inspecting the way their students perform.

**Norm-referenced test:**
instrument that has been administered to a large group of people so that any one individual score can be compared to the average, or norm (e.g., an IQ test).

**Criterion-referenced tests:**
instruments that assess a student's progress against specific predetermined criteria set for the instructional objective, rather than against group norms.

**Psycho-educational diagnosis:**
testing children across a variety of domains relevant to social and educational performance.

Informal assessment is used to identify areas of strengths and weaknesses within individuals while formal assessment tends to be used to investigate the nature of students' aptitudes and achievements. Informal measures encourage teachers to look closely at what specific skills are involved in the learning of academic tasks. Informal measures provide ongoing assessment and encompass measures such as interviews, behavioural observations, case histories, work samples, and rating scales. Used in conjunction with more formal measures, these tools supply information for planning and revising programs, and for reporting pupils' progress to parents and others.

One of the most fundamental and important distinctions is between norm-referenced tests and criterion-referenced tests. A **norm-referenced test** is one that has been administered to a large group of people so that any one individual score can be compared to the average, or norm. IQ tests, as we have seen, are a good example of norm-referenced instruments. However, an IQ test or a standardized achievement test is not really useful in developing a program within a given curriculum.

**Criterion-referenced tests** assess a student's progress against criteria set for instructional objectives for that student, rather than against group norms. Criterion-referenced tests are useful to compare the performance or skill level of a particular pupil on the material to be mastered; a child's performance is measured against an absolute or a specific predetermined criterion (Wallace and Larsen, 1978). In other words, criterion-referenced instruments are concerned with assessing the extent to which a student has reached a number of specific objectives.

Norm-referenced instruments should be used for monitoring the pupil's or program's progress over the long run (Shephard, 1979). This type of assessment is more appropriate for estimating progress toward higher level, complex learning outcomes where continuous development is possible as is typically the case in higher level cognitive skills (Gronlund, 1988). On the other hand, criterion-referenced tests should be preferred for the day-to-day testing in the classroom (Shephard, 1979). Gronlund contends that criterion-referenced tests are especially helpful in measuring the minimum knowledge or skills to be obtained from an instructional program.

All tests can assay proficiency in domains of either basic skills or content knowledge, although tests usually emphasize one dimension over the other. Examples of basic skills include oral reading fluency and spelling with correct letter sequences; content knowledge includes verbal information in content areas and the rules for sequencing information. As well, there are two levels of data that may be collected: survey data in which test items are broadly sampled and many skills are represented, and specific data wherein test items are arranged narrowly around a few skills (Howell and Morehead, 1987).

Students may be evaluated by group or individually. They may experience classroom-based testing as well as what may be termed *pull-out testing*, which the students complete outside the classroom context under the guidance of professionals other than teachers. Pull-out testing is sometimes referred to as **psycho-educational diagnosis**, testing children across a variety of domains relevant to social and educational performance.

**Standardized test:**
a test that can be given to a large and representative sample of some population so that the scores on the test can be compared with those of persons in the sample.

**Norms:**
the average scores obtained by the students who took the tests when the norms were being established and the standard of comparison by which to measure later scores.

**Raw score:**
the actual number of correct answers that a student gets on a test.

Most classroom tests and many achievement tests are designed for group administration. The Canadian Test of Basic Skills, for example, is given to groups of children. However, a teacher may often wish to assess a student's functioning more closely. To do this, the teacher could devise an individual criterion-reference test based on the objectives set for that student. An individual achievement test, such as the Peabody Individual Achievement Test, could be used, or an individual test in different subject areas such as the Test of Early Reading Ability or the Test of Early Mathematical Ability, both used with young children, may be chosen. Diagnostic tests such as the KeyMath Diagnostic Arithmetic Test are used to closely examine exactly where a child is meeting difficulties.

Different forms of evaluation should be used at different grade levels. Young elementary children, with the instructional stress on basic skills, require different evaluation procedures from those used for secondary students, who can think more abstractly.

## STANDARDIZED TESTS

A **standardized test** is one that can be given to a large and representative sample of some population so that the scores on the test can be compared with those of persons in the sample (Gage and Berliner, 1978). Three types of standardized tests are commonly used in school settings—aptitude tests, norm-referenced achievement tests, and criterion-referenced achievement tests (Slavin, 1988). While norm-referenced achievement tests and many aptitude tests are strictly standardized, do remember that teachers may also construct aptitude and criterion-referenced tests.

Standardized tests are usually prepared for use on a national scale by experts using the techniques, statistics, and research knowledge of the testing field. Most standardized tests are norm-referenced which means that they supply norms or standards that enable us to interpret the results. The **norms** are the average scores obtained by the students who took the tests when the norms were being established, the standard of comparison by which to measure later scores. Therefore, norm-referenced standardized tests provide norms that make possible the comparison of any student's scores with those of many other students.

Professional test developers begin by analyzing carefully the goals of many programs, courses of study, sets of examinations, and opinions of experts in the field. They develop standardized instructions and test items in a series of pilot testings. The tests are administered to a large sample and then test makers revise items that measure a set of goals to ensure that items have validity and reliability. Scoring norms, the typical scores obtained by the standardization sample at a given age and grade level, are developed on the basis of responses by a large and presumably representative sample of students. These norms are then converted into standardized scores, grade level equivalent scores, IQ equivalent scores, or other scores that enable test users to compare data on their students with national norms.

For a test score to have any meaning, it has to be compared with some yardstick or measure of performance. Final scores on standardized tests are determined when students' **raw scores**—the actual number of correct answers they

**Standard score:**
a score based on the standard deviation describing test results according to a normal curve.

**Z score:**
a common standard score that tells how many standard deviations above or below the average the raw score is.

**Percentile:**
a point in a distribution at or below which a given percentage of scores fall. The percentile rank shows the percentage of students in the norming sample who scored at or below a particular raw score.

**Grade equivalents:**
relate scores to the average scores attained by students at a particular grade level.

**Reliability:**
the consistency of a test; its ability to produce the same results on different occasions under the same circumstances.

get on a test—are compared with the norms of the standardized sample. Raw scores can be converted and described in a number of ways:

- **Standard scores**, which are based on the standard deviation, describe test results according to a normal curve. Distribution puts the scores in order; it is an arrangement of any set of scores in order of magnitude. Scores can then be placed on a normal curve and the standard deviation—a distance from the mean—computed.

- A *z* score is a common standard score that tells how many standard deviations above or below the average a raw score is.

- A raw score can be described very precisely by converting it into a **percentile**, that point in a distribution at or below which a given percentage of scores fall. In percentile rankings, every students' raw score is compared with the raw scores obtained by the students in the norming sample. The percentile rank shows the percentage of students in the norming sample who scored at or below a particular raw score.

- **Grade equivalents** relate scores to the average scores attained by students at a particular grade level. Grade equivalent scores are generally obtained from separate norming samples for each grade level. For example, the average of all the scores of all third graders in the norming sample defines the third grade equivalent score.

Standardized tests are usually accompanied by manuals that provide detailed information concerning the test, including content, items, reliability, validity, and the sample. As well, the term "standardized" refers in part to the way the tests are given. Manuals also include clear instructions for administration and scoring. Standardized tests have a fixed set of questions, the same set of directions, timing constraints, and delineated and precise scoring procedures.

The functions of standardized instruments in education are multifaceted; however, we could sum up their use by stating that they should help in decision making. Many different factors should be considered in selecting a test. These include the purpose of the measure, the data to be gathered, the student population, specialized training needed for administration of the test, time, scoring, useability, cost, interpretation, reliability, and validity.

## Test construction

Those who administer tests are usually interested in obtaining scores but, if test scores are to be useful in making decisions, they should be repeatable and meaningful reflections of behaviour. Therefore, test specialists are particularly concerned with the technical adequacy of a measure. Technical adequacy deals chiefly with reliability (the consistency and repeatability of scores) and validity (the truthfulness of scores). Test specialists use a variety of statistical techniques to estimate reliability and validity.

**Reliability** refers to the consistency of a test, to its ability to produce the same results on different occasions under the same circumstances. The correlation coefficients expressing a test's reliability may be quite high (at least .70 and

**Validity:**
the degree to which a test measures what it claims to measure, how well it measures it, and what can be inferred from the measurement.

preferably .90) for a test to be reliable enough to be useful for confident measurement and decision making (Good and Brophy, 1986). Moreover, a highly reliable test is reliable even at the item level, not just for total scores.

Reliability is important because if there are any differences in the two sets of results obtained when students are tested on two different days, or given two different versions of the test, or retested after a period of time, these differences should reflect changes in the students, not in the test. Unreliable tests are not only imprecise but they are unfair to students.

Good and Brophy (1986) indicate that a number of factors affect test reliability. These include:

- test length—generally, a longer test is more reliable than a shorter one because it involves a larger sample of the knowledge or skills tested.

- heterogeneity of the testees—reliability tends to be higher when scores are spread out over a larger range. In other words, the more diverse the population, the higher the reliability is likely to be.

- item difficulty—reliability is higher when most items are of medium difficulty for the group tested because this spreads scores out over a greater range, in comparison to scores that would be obtained if most items were either too easy or too hard.

- objectivity of scoring—the reliability of tests that can be scored objectively tends to be higher. With subjective scoring, equivalent performances might be scored differently because of differences in scorers' judgments at various times, even if the scorer is the same person (Kubiszyn and Borich, 1984; Mehrens and Lehmann, 1978).

Reliability is only one of the attributes of a good test; an even more basic attribute is validity. Reliability is a precondition for validity in the sense that a test cannot be valid if it is not reliable (Good and Brophy, 1986). Test **validity** tells us whether a test measures what it claims to measure, how well it measures it, and what can be inferred from the measurement. Test validity cannot be determined in the abstract but only in the context of the relationship between the specific uses to which the test results will be put and the construct that is being measured. Thus, information and conclusions regarding the validity of a given test in one context may not be relevant and applicable in other contexts.

Specialists in test construction talk about many different kinds of validity but, for teachers, content validity and criterion validity are the most important. The most important criterion for the usefulness of a test is whether it assesses what the user wants it to assess (Popham, 1981). This criterion is called *content validity*—the degree of overlap between what is taught and what is tested (Slavin, 1988). Content validity refers to the extent to which a test adequately samples both the tasks and the content of the domain of measurement. A test of arithmetic skills should sample the students' ability to add, multiply, subtract, and so on. For this test, appreciation of poetry and music is irrelevant (Violato, 1980).

*Criterion validity* compares test performance (for example, on a reading test) against a standard that independently measures the trait (such as reading ability) that the test purports to measure. Criterion validity becomes important as attention shifts from mastery of specific knowledge and skills toward attempts to measure probable success in generalizing and applying these skills. Criterion validity takes two forms, concurrent and predictive. When tests are designed to predict current performance, they give concurrent validity. Predictive validity predicts performance that will take place in the future.

*Construct validity* examines how well a test actually correlates with the underlying theoretical characteristics of the trait that it purports to measure. Construct validity refers to an instrument's ability to measure a variable such as creativity, risk-taking, or intelligence. These variables are called constructs because, in a sense, we cannot measure them but only use them to explain observed differences. A test measures the construct by measuring the behaviour that the construct describes or predicts. Most psychological tests are designed to measure some construct and, to the degree that they are successful, they have construct validity.

The validity of a test is reduced by anything that reduces the degree to which the test measures what it is supposed to measure. Some tests are not valid for anything because they have poorly constructed items that are inappropriate for the student population being assessed. Other tests are valid for some purposes, but not for others. Other potential sources of invalidity include inappropriate administration of a test, inappropriate interpretation of a test, or inappropriate application of the assessment data. Further threats to validity concern the content of the test or types of items that compose it. Written tests are fine for assessing knowledge and comprehension, but behavioural skill objectives may require behavioural tests for valid assessment (Good and Brophy, 1986).

Usability, which encompasses many of the practical features of measuring instruments, is also important. Usability includes the method of administration and scoring of a test, as well as the economical use of time and money (test feasibility). Dick and Hagerty (1971) refer to the latter as cash validity, how well a test sells.

Other components which may be included in the usability category are whether the test has appropriate levels of difficulty in reading and vocabulary, whether it makes provisions for interpreting results with adequate norms and tables, and whether there is a general acceptance of the instrument. But regardless of the popularity or prestige of a test, it is a poor evaluative device if the items do not correspond well with the curriculum. Sometimes substantial differences in scores between classes and schools occur simply because the groups used different curriculum packages, and one of them included many more objectives assessed by the test than the other did (Pidgeon, 1970).

Some instruments require special training or equipment to administer and score and, if these are not readily available, the tests are not usable. Other tests cost too much or take too long to administer. Other instruments look very interesting, but if there is no basis for interpreting the results, local norms have to be developed (Winzer, 1989).

## Values of standardized tests

Standardized norm-referenced published tests offer a host of advantages about which there is little controversy (Thorndike and Hagen, 1978). They possess:

- carefully prepared items;

- items of known difficulty, since the number of students who answer the question correctly is known;

- scores of known reliability which help in interpreting student performance;

- national norms; and

- far more objectivity than teacher-made tests.

While many values accrue to standardized tests, there is also a downside. Standardized norm-referenced tests:

- do not tell the teacher whether a student is ready to move on to new material. Norm-referenced tests do better on this when curriculum content is relatively homogeneous (such as reading and math in the early grades) but are not as reliable when there is little universal content (such as social studies at any grade level and most subject at higher levels).

- do not provide information on which to build educational planning.

- are not effective for measuring affective and psychomotor behaviour. While most school learning tasks tend to be in the cognitive realm, other skills are crucial and need to be measured in some manner.

- may disadvantage some students in some schools because there exists no national curriculum. Certain students may be favoured because of differences in what they learned originally or in what they emphasized in preparing for the test.

- sample only limited items. The test itself is just a sample of the full range of material that students have been taught, so results indicate only a small sample of a child's performance and provide only a limited measure of achievement.

- do not take into account the variability in students' daily performances. Situational factors can affect performance on a test. Those who are well-prepared, well-rested, and able to concentrate are likely to do well; those who are tired or ill obviously will not.

- may include items selected because of their wide appeal or simply for their psychometric properties.

- may have limited technical adequacy. The statistical validity and reliability on a number of standardized tests has been seriously questioned.

- may foster competition rather than cooperation (Gibson and Chandler, 1988).

- may teach students, who effortlessly receive average grades on norm-referenced tests, not to learn more than what they need to get by (Gibson and Chandler, 1978).

- are generally normed on samples in the United States. Compared to the United States, Canada has a small school population and it is sometimes more economical to import tests. Only two achievement tests are standardized for use across English-speaking Canada—the Canadian Test of Basic Skills (CTBS) and the Canadian Achievement Test (CAT). Using American-normed tests, especially for achievement, can place Canadian students at a severe disadvantage.

## Aptitude tests

Aptitude tests are used to measure abilities developed over many years and to predict how well a student will do in learning unfamiliar material in the future. They assess intelligence or specific aptitudes such as mechanical or perceptual abilities. IQ tests are the most influential aptitude tests of all but also the most controversial standardized tests used in schools.

### IQ tests

Intelligence testing has been controversial since its inception (Winzer, 1990b). Lately it has come under attack from those who believe that it simply labels students without doing them any good, and by those who hold that intelligence tests are inherently biased in favour of white, middle-class students, and against students from lower class backgrounds and minority groups (Mercer, 1973).

Despite controversy and criticism, IQ tests remain the most reliable predictors of school achievement and, to a degree, of student potential, particularly in the elementary grades. Though intelligence tests do not measure any fixed general mental ability, they do measure important abilities such as understanding and following instructions, reasoning and drawing conclusions, solving problems, vocabulary acquisition and use, reading comprehension, arithmetic computation, and other skills taught in school. Most people recognize these abilities as general cognitive skills important for everyone, and not as specialized knowledge reflecting the cultural tradition or bias of middle-class whites or any other particular group (Ebel, 1975).

If used to measure students' potential and not as a tool to label or restrict them, IQ tests can enable teachers to make decisions that will optimize instruction. This is especially true of students who are deficient in reading, writing, and test-taking skills, because ordinary school tests underestimate the knowledge and capabilities of these students. IQ tests can also be reliable indicators of the capacity of students who are unfamiliar with the English language. These students may be tested with the so-called culture fair or nonverbal IQ tests that eliminate the need for verbal instructions and responses.

## Problems with IQ tests

Intelligence tests are merely one measure in the total assessment of a child, yet they have all too often been used as the definitive measure. In special education, for example, test scores have tended to dominate labeling and placement decisions (Smith and Knoff, 1981). Because in the past too much uncritical faith was placed in IQ scores, the validity and usefulness of intelligence tests has come under fire from psychologists and educators, and the misuse of IQ test scores has been well substantiated. Intelligence is not a single thing, as IQ scores seem to hint, but a composite of behaviours and skills. And, whatever intelligence is, the tests do not measure it perfectly. To some extent at least, an IQ (or any test) score only reflects how well a certain child does on a certain day with a certain tester. Many things—a bad mood, no breakfast, or fear or dislike of the tester—can influence scores. The age at which the test is taken also affects the score—the younger the child, the greater the possibility of achieving a higher score (Silverman, in Berdine and Meyer, 1987). (However, tests of infants under two years of age are not predictive of IQ at school age. In fact, the intelligence of the parents is a better predictor of the child's later intelligence [Hilgard, 1987].)

By about age six, IQ estimates tend to become relatively stable and most people's IQs remain about the same into adulthood (Hopkins and Bracht, 1975). Some people, however, will experience substantial changes in their estimated IQ, often because of schooling or other environmental changes (Petty and Field, 1980).

One early longitudinal study (Honzig, McFarlane, and Allen, 1948) found that change, rather than stability, characterized the IQ scores of middle-class children during middle childhood and adolescence. A majority of the children in this study had IQs that changed by at least 15 points, and one-third changed 20 points or more. In another more recent longitudinal study of children from two and a half to 17 years of age (McCall, Appelbaum, and Hogarty, 1973), the researchers found changes in the Stanford-Binet scores between those ages to average 28.5 points; one-seventh of the changes were of 40 points or more. Moreover, such IQ changes may not be random. Studies (McCall, Appelbaum, and Hogarty, 1973; Willerman, 1979) found that children from higher socioeconomic (SES) groups tended to maintain or gain IQ while lower SES children tended to drop.

Intelligence tests are merely one measure in the total assessment of a child—not the definitive measure. Creativity and non-academic talents cannot be qualified through testing.

IQ scores are highly predictive of school performance (De Myer, 1975), since they indicate a child's ability to comprehend the ideas of instruction, and to analyze problems and find solutions. Therefore, it may be said that the test requires children to know many things that are taught in school and that are general knowledge among their classmates. But, as Das (1988) observes, those who fail to do well in school or those who cannot go to good schools are the same children who usually fare poorly on IQ tests. Thus, some researchers suggest that intelligence tests test academic achievement rather than ability (Horn, 1978). It is interesting to note that IQ scores are not likely to predict who will be successful in the normal adult world of business, teaching, and other pursuits. There is little correlation between measures of intelligence and measures of life success (Baird, 1985).

The usefulness of IQ tests has also been called into question since it is known that they are not fully objective. They include words that are not in general use today or that are typically used in urban but not in rural areas, or vice versa. Some questions assume a cultural experience or perspective that is not shared by all children. When measures reflect a cultural bias, they may reinforce existing inequalities in the selection of children for special programs (Bailey and Harbin, 1980). The WISC-R, for example, asks, "What is the thing to do when you cut your finger?" The best response is "Put a bandage on it," although children receive partial credit for an answer such as "Go to the hospital," but no credit for "Cry," "Bleed," or "Suck on it." Children from minority groups usually perform poorly on this item. When children in Baltimore, for example, were asked to explain their answers, they said that they'd "Go to the hospital," for a "big cut," but would suck a small cut since they did not have bandages in their homes (*The culture fair*, 1981).

Nevertheless, Violato (1989) makes some interesting points about the cultural bias of the WISC-R. He points out that an item on the Information subtests that asks children to "Name two men who have been president of the United States since 1950" is obviously designed for American testees. Frequently, Canadian psychologists change the item to, "Name two men who have been prime ministers of Canada since 1950." In doing so, they may make the item more difficult for Canadian children than it was for their American counterparts simply because of the high media profile accorded to the leaders of a superpower such as the United States. It is also known that IQ tests are inappropriate for students who are learning English as a second language. Researchers have discovered that the elaborate, stylized English commonly used in standardized tests prevents such tests from accurately measuring the achievements, abilities, or skills of students who speak nonstandard dialects (Hoover, Politzer, and Taylor, 1987).

Finally, although the tests relate to one another and to performance in the classroom (Beihler and Snowman, 1990), IQ tests do not measure the same things. An examination of the WISC-R and the Stanford-Binet will show that the various subtests differ greatly from one another. In study after study, moderate to high correlations are found among all the different tests that are used to measure intellectual ability (McNemar, 1964), but the correlations between the subtests on IQ are not perfect.

**Cultue-fair measures:**
aspects of a test that are written from the perspective of a particular minority culture or subculture.

**Culture-free measures:**
instruments free from culturally loaded content.

## Culture-free and culture-fair measures

Some attempts have been made to devise measures that will reduce the misrepresentation of minority group children in special programs. There has been seen increased interest in a broad range of nondiscriminatory measures including measures of creativity, cognitive processing, and nonverbal assessment (Maker, Morris, and James, 1981).

While today the WISC-R is clearly the test of choice for the assessment of the intellectual functioning of individual Canadian students, problems do exist. The increased popularity of the WISC-R has been accompanied by increasing concerns about whether the use of an American-normed psychometric measure results in significant cultural bias against Canadian majority or ethnic and racial minority children (Mueller et al., 1986). In order to overcome possible test bias, a number of local norms have been obtained for the WISC-R (e.g., Holmes, 1981).

Culture-fair and culture-free tests have also emerged. **Culture-fair** (or culture specific) **measures** are those that are written from the perspective of a particular minority culture or subculture. Validation occurs in terms of the accuracy of the measures in predicting educational, vocational, and social competence within those specific cultures or subcultures. **Culture-free measures** purport to be free from culturally loaded content. These tests contain items that are common to all cultures so that children will not be disadvantaged by the nature of the measures (Winzer, 1990a).

The Kaufman Assessment Battery for Children (K-ABC) (Kaufman and Kaufman, 1983), for example, was partly aimed at reducing the "potential 'community gap' with preschool, minority group, and exceptional children" (Kaufman, 1983, p. 8). Mercer and Lewis (1977) devised the System of Multi-Pluralistic Assessment (SOMPA) that uses traditional measures of intelligence but weighs the results according to the social and family characteristics of the child. For example, according to Day (1985), a child with an IQ of 111 can, when compared with children of similar socio-cultural backgrounds, obtain an estimated learning potential score of 134. This would place that child in the top one percent of children in that socio-cultural group.

Certainly, the notion of culture-fair and culture-free tests sounds logical and reasonable, but results have been generally disappointing. Since knowledge and language are culture-bound, it is doubtful that a culture-free test can actually be constructed. There is no way to measure aptitudes such as memory, learning, perceiving, and problem-solving except through content, and content is always culturally related.

Keep in mind, too, that on culture-fair tests the gap in scores between minority and Anglo-American children is almost as great as it is on traditional IQ tests (Barton, 1973). On many of the so-called culture-fair tests, the performance of students from deprived backgrounds and minority groups has been the same or worse than their performance on the standard WISC-R or Stanford-Binet scales (Costello and Dickie, 1970; Sattler, 1982).

## Achievement tests

Whether part of the general classroom assessment of progress and learning or as a component of psycho-educational diagnosis, it is certain that students will face achievement tests. In fact, the most common standardized test given to students is the achievement test. Unlike IQ measures, which are designed to assess general intellectual functioning, achievement tests serve to discover what a child has learned in a particular area.

Most achievement tests are norm-referenced. Therefore, if a child takes a norm-referenced math achievement test, the number of items which are answered correctly will be compared with the scores for other children at the same age and grade level, and the child will be assigned a score reflecting the grade or age level of math functioning. If the number of items that a child gets right is equal to that of the average child, then the math score can be said to be average on that particular normed test.

Standardized achievement tests are most useful in the lower grades. Although they are highly correlated with IQ scores, standardized achievement tests for the early grades are relatively valid methods for assessing student progress in achieving basic skills such as letter identification and discrimination, spelling, and so on (Gage and Berliner, 1986). This is because content validity is less problematic. There is more agreement about the core curriculum for language arts and mathematics in the early grades and the same basic skills are taught using different curriculum packages and various methods.

Standardized test data must be interpreted carefully if they are to be used appropriately. As Gage and Berliner (1986) note, relatively few schools have student populations comparable to the students used to develop the norms for the test, so the test norms are inappropriate in many cases. Schools populated by students whose home backgrounds and IQ scores are clearly higher than average can and should exceed expectations based on standardized tests. Depending on the nature of the school, it might be realistic to expect high numbers of students to score above grade level even though theoretically many students should score at grade level and half of the rest should score above grade level and half below. Similarly, in a school populated primarily by students from disadvantaged backgrounds who have lower than average IQs, it might be appropriate to expect that not a great proportion would score at grade level (Gage and Berliner, 1986).

Comparisons across classes should be minimized. They are most meaningful if confined to the same grade in the same school (assuming that these classes are not grouped by ability or otherwise organized so that some would be expected to do better than others). Comparisons across years should also be made cautiously (Gage and Berliner, 1986).

Obviously, the values and disadvantages we noted that apply to standardized tests in general also apply to norm-referenced achievement tests. We should also mention that, because the tests are timed, some students may be discriminated against. The measures, for example, may not report accurately when the children taking the test are slow workers or poor readers. In addition, achievement tests measure only broad parameters of achievement; they are not sensitive enough to assess daily progress or program effectiveness and are therefore not useful for making instructional decisions.

We mentioned earlier that many teachers, especially those at the elementary levels, do not like standardized tests and tend not to base educational decisions upon their results (Salmon-Cox, 1981). One reason may be traced to the differences

**Diagnostic tests:**
instruments designed to identify specific problems in perceiving or responding; used to identify the precise nature of a student's difficulties.

found between standardized achievement tests and teachers' ratings. One study (Leiter and Brown, 1985) found that primary school children's math grades showed a slight correlation with their demonstrated mastery on standardized tests, but their reading grades showed no correlation with their reading achievement test scores. Many teachers argue that such discrepancies indicated problems with achievement tests, rather than with their grades. However, Schroder and Crawford (1970) concluded that, because teachers' ratings did not agree with scores from standardized achievement tests, the teachers' ratings should be seen as adjuncts to standardized tests.

Much centres on the objectivity of norm-referenced achievement tests and the subjectivity of teachers' ratings. The attributions a teacher makes about the causes of students' successes or failures can affect the grades that students receive (Woolfolk, 1990). Despite their best efforts and despite teachers' faith in their grading, many academically irrelevant factors can influence grades. These include the same factors that can influence teachers' expectations about students such as physical appearance, race, and socioeconomic status.

There is evidence to suggest that sex biases exist. For example, female teachers perceive male students more negatively than female students (Prawat and Jarvis, 1980). Teachers evaluate children who are compliant and who participate enthusiastically in classroom activities positively (Roedell, Jackson, and Robinson, 1980), and these traits seem to be more overt in girls than in boys. This may explain in part why teachers give higher grades to girls than their performances warrant (Stockard, Lang, and Wood, 1985). As well, teachers' attitudes toward students and the amount of instructional time spent in class can adversely affect boys' ratings (Brophy and Good, 1970; Leinhardt, Seevald, and Engel, 1979). In addition, teachers are more likely to give higher grades for effort than for ability. Teachers are more likely to assign lower grades on achievement tests when they attribute a student's failure to lack of effort rather than lack of ability (Weiner, 1979).

This does not mean that achievement tests are not widely used, since they certainly are. Teachers should not feel that the results of achievement tests should be discounted but rather that the tests must be placed in their proper perspective. Norm-referenced achievement tests must be realistically viewed as only one part of ongoing assessment and as only one of a range of measures used for the evaluation of progress and the program. In addition, achievement tests should be recognized as methods used to rapidly ascertain learning and to broadly suggest areas for program direction.

## Other test types

Norm-referenced achievement tests do not provide much diagnostic or prescriptive information. On the other hand, **diagnostic tests** are designed to identify the precise nature of a student's difficulties in perceiving or responding. Teachers who suspect a problem may use diagnostic tests to determine whether a problem actually exists and what its parameters may be. These tests provide a microscopic view of the components of performance in a relatively short time.

Diagnostic measures are characteristically administered on an individual basis. They allow teachers to analyze a child's functioning within a given subskill and

**Process-oriented measures:**

instruments that attempt to assess how a child integrates and uses stimuli–including auditory processing, visual processing, visual-motor functioning, and motor skill development.

to observe any of his or her faulty habits. Directions for remediation are offered through a precise delineation of problem areas.

The great majority of diagnostic tests are available for use in the core subject areas such as language arts, especially reading, and math. The subtests usually focus upon central areas. For example, on a diagnostic math test the questions may cluster around general areas such as basic operations, numeration, time, and money. A diagnostic reading test may cover areas such as word attack skills, word recognition, and reading comprehension.

**Process-oriented measures** attempt to assess how a child integrates and uses stimuli. Areas assessed include auditory processing, visual processing, visual-motor functioning, and motor skill development. The tester focuses on the areas that are assumed to comprise the underlying psychological causes of a child's learning problems.

## Criterion-referenced tests

Norm-referenced procedures depend on variability in performance. The tests are concerned primarily with discriminating students from one another which means that items are included on the basis of this power in addition to their content validity. Norm-referenced tools are losing much of their appeal among many educators. Parents and educators alike complain that norm-referenced tests offer too little information about students' strengths and weaknesses. Educators have also come to believe that clearly stated, specific objectives constitute performance standards or criteria that are best assessed with criterion-referenced measures.

Criterion-referenced tests are keyed to the learning objectives taught to the specific students who take the tests. The purpose is not to compare students to other students but to determine the degree to which they have mastered these objectives. Criterion-referenced tests are deliberately constructed to provide information that is directly interpretable in terms of an absolute criterion of performance (Glaser and Nitko, 1971). The absolute criterion is based on the teacher's experience with a student, particular curriculum area, and records of past performance.

The selection of items for criterion-referenced tests is straightforward: content is confined to material that is actually taught to students, and the tests include either all the objectives that students are supposed to have mastered or a sample of them. Samples typically stress the final or higher objectives toward which related lessons are built. Well-designed criterion-referenced tests are those that are based on task analysis; employ instructional objectives that precisely describe conditions, standards, and performance; and measure each skill in a valid and reliable manner. Good tests may be effectively used in the selection of suitable instructional objectives and serve to measure progress (Cypher et al., 1984).

Criterion-referenced tests are directly related to the classroom curriculum. They are more useful for identifying objectives that have been taught successfully or that need to be retaught than norm-referenced tests. This means that reliability has a different meaning for criterion-referenced tests. The precision of the score is less important than the dependability of the decision that is made about whether a student has or has not mastered a skill (Mehrans and Lehrmann, 1980).

Criterion-referenced measures serve as valuable assessment procedures at the mastery instructional level since basic skills are relatively sequential in nature and the skills to be learned are limited in scope. Criterion-referenced measures are more difficult to use after the developmental level of learning or beyond basic skill areas since scope and sequence charts do not lend themselves well to testing the higher thinking skills used to learn complex materials.

Whether commercially developed or constructed by the teacher, criterion-referenced tests have the following advantages:

- they provide teachers with useful information for planning future teaching;

- they are useful for the organization of teaching resources, teaching groups, and team teaching;

- they are flexible for individual needs and provide a basis for individualizing instruction and allowing pupils to progress at their own rates; and

- they evaluate a child's performance in terms of an absolute or a specific criterion that has been established for that student. This is the major advantage of criterion-referenced testing. If the child does not achieve, it must be presumed that the criterion was not appropriate, or that additional practice is needed.

Of course, there are some disadvantages. For example, criterion-referenced tests usually give little or no information about how local students compare with national norms. Moreover, they are not efficient in areas that cannot be broken down into specific objectives.

## TEACHER-MADE TESTS

Despite their problems, standardized norm-referenced tests provide objective measures of aptitude and achievement and are widely used, especially for summative ratings. However, the major component of classroom evaluation is carried out by teachers using informal methods and other measures of their own construction. It appears that most achievement testing is carried out by classroom teachers as part of the process of ongoing evaluation. Students in a measurement class in British Columbia, for example, estimated that they had taken between 500 and 600 achievement tests in their school years, and that the vast majority were not standardized but were developed by classroom teachers (Anderson, 1989).

Most tests made by teachers are criterion-referenced since many teachers prefer to construct their own criterion-referenced tests. There are three basic steps involved: choosing the specific skill, writing objectives describing the skill, and describing methods to evaluate acquisition of the skill (Howell, Kaplan, and O'Donnell, 1979).

These tests are not based on relative performance but on absolute performance. The focus is on what absolute fraction of the material covered in a test a student masters. A teacher makes up a test and scores it on the absolute percentage of a student's correct answers, rather than on the basis of what percentage of the class did worse or better than that student.

Criterion-referenced tests often must be individualized, especially if they are used in programs that allow students to proceed at their own paces. Criterion-referenced tests are often designed by the teacher to assess the progress of an individual child. Unlike standardized tests, they do not compare the child's results to an age, grade, or performance norm. Instead, criterion-referenced tests attempt to measure the child's specific degree of knowledge or skill attainment in a particular area of learning. For example, the long-term goal, or criterion, for six-year-old Betty is to say and write the letters of the alphabet in order. Betty would be assessed in light of her individual attainment of the skill rather than in light of the norm for any group, such as the rest of her class. First, the teacher would break the long-term goal into attainable short-range objectives written in behavioural form. The tasks would then be presented to Betty in small increments. Attainment would be judged against the individual criterion, learning the alphabet.

Teacher-developed tests are more versatile than standardized tests, since the teachers can match the curriculum being taught exactly; create multiple and interchangeable forms of their tests; create assessment devices that are sensitive to small changes in student performance; and use tests flexibly to conform to their current needs and schedules (Salvia and Hughes, 1990).

## Informal measures

Teachers know their students well and are in a good position to observe behaviours and performances in various types of situations and settings. The thousands of behavioural events that occur in the classroom every day can

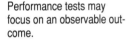
Performance tests may focus on an observable outcome.

**Performance test:**
instrument that requires an individual or group of individuals to make a decision, solve a problem, or perform some prescribed behaviour under more or less realistic conditions.

provide a wealth of information (Winzer, 1989). Teachers can do a great deal of assessment informally during the processes of observing students' attention to lessons and engagement in assignments, monitoring their answers to questions during class activities, and correcting their written assignments.

Informal assessment is very important but is subjective and open to the influence of teachers' expectations and other biasing sources. It is also unsystematic. Teachers monitor certain students much more closely than others (Marshall and Weinstein, 1984). Some students have learned to "look good" during class activities and to get help with their written assignments so that they appear to have mastered much more material than they really have. Some will make generally good progress but consistently make certain kinds of mistakes because they do not know a key concept or lack a skill (Slavin, 1988).

Many deficiencies in learning may not be obvious from casual daily observation. Therefore, it is important to supplement informal monitoring with assessment that measures student achievement through teacher-constructed measures and occasionally with norm-referenced, standardized tests.

## Performance tests

Measures of knowledge are often called written tests. However, performance tests measure how well someone does something. They are within the category of aptitude tests. Performance tests may either be standardized or teacher-devised.

A **performance test** demands that an individual, or sometimes a group of individuals, make a decision, solve a problem, or perform some prescribed behaviour. The test attempts to measure how well a person performs the particular task or set of skills under more or less realistic conditions. Brown (1976) lists the following examples of skills that could be measured directly: painting a water colour, typing forty words a minute, conducting an opinion poll, conducting a counseling, interview, programing a computer, making a soufflé, or assembling a carburetor.

Performance tests may focus on the process (the underlying skills that go into a performance) or the product (an observable outcome, such as a speech or a painting) or both. The measurement of process will often be emphasized for tasks that involve psychomotor skills. Product ratings tend to be summative ratings, as in the case of a concert recital.

Gronlund (1988) identified four types of performance tests:

1. *Paper and pencil performance tests* emphasize the application of knowledge or skills. Students might be asked to construct something, such as a map or a graph, or to describe the functions of something, such as a piece of equipment.

2. *Identification performance tests* ask students to identify or describe certain things, such as the function of the heart.

3. *Simulated performance tests* ask students to reproduce exactly, under controlled conditions, the response that should be made in real-life situations. An individual learning CPR from the St. John's Ambulance is an example.

4. *Work samples* are realistic representations of behaviour under realistic conditions. For example, the performance of a teacher-in-training presenting a lesson to a class in a school might be tested.

Teachers may use performance tests or oral presentations as part of their assessment programs. The general procedures that teachers follow is the same as that for construction of classroom tests: identify general instructional goals and objectives; plan instructional activities; assess student learning and the instructional program.

To obtain reliable scores on performance tests, students need to know precisely what they are to demonstrate and the criteria by which their performance will be judged. Teachers should prepare checklists and rating scales that adequately describe performance in order to make the evaluation realistic (Biehler and Snowman, 1990).

Checklists are actually very simple devices that merely contain a group of items which are checked off to describe the presence or absence of a behaviour. Items may focus on expected behaviour, characteristics of performance, or parts of a product. The advantage of checklists is the accumulation of a great deal of information very quickly (Winzer, 1989).

Checklists indicate the presence or absence of a behaviour; rating scales force the observer to judge the quality of the performance. Most rating scales contain a selection of items that cover behaviours readily observed by anyone involved with the child. As such, they are a successful method for quantifying and documenting behaviour and performance and for recording and communicating information (Winzer, 1989).

## Test construction

There are a number of factors that should be considered when constructing tests. These include whether the test is objective or subjective; the domains of the cognitive, psychomotor, or affective realms to be assessed; the adequacy of the test items to indicate performance; the focus of content; and how the test must be presented and scored. Teachers must also consider the length of the test, the difficulty of the items, the recording of grades, and the explanation of the grades to the students.

Test items may be thought of as opportunities for students to respond. Two types of responses are possible—selection or production (Hopkins and Antes, 1978). A question that invites a selection response includes all information for answering the question within itself, such as multiple-choice tests, where students select correct answers but do not produce them. A question that invites a production response requires students to produce the answer which is not embedded within the question itself. Short-answer and essay questions are examples of items that require production responses.

Scoring may be either subjective or objective. Selection responses are frequently scored objectively and production responses are often more subjective. However, it is possible to create test items requiring selection responses that are scored subjectively or production responses that are scored objectively. Therefore whether scoring is objective or subjective is actually independent of the response format (Good and Brophy, 1986).

Earlier in this chapter we discussed validity, or how well a test measures what it purports to measure. Obviously, teacher-constructed tests will not approach the validity of commercial measures, but there are certain cautions that teachers can observe to ensure better validity. These concern the students' test-taking skills and the focus of the test.

**Power test:**
an instrument that probes students' mastery (their power) over material.

Students' test-taking skills pose a large category of threats to the validity of a given test. These include writing skills, the ability to work efficiently under time constraints, the amount of test anxiety, and related individual differences. Slavin (1988) notes that while these skills are not specific to the subject matter, they do affect test scores. For example, except when speed is one criterion for success, tests should either have no time limits at all or generous limits that will minimize the effects of ability to work under time pressure (versus degree of mastery of the material). The result will be what is called a power test, a test that solely probes students' mastery (their power) over the material (Slavin, 1988). Tests must also focus specifically on the content being assessed. For example, unless language skills such as punctuation and capitalization are considered part of the criterion for successful performance on a test of history or science, these tests should be scored completely for correct responses with no extra credit for good writing or deduction for poor writing. (Slavin, 1988).

When we discussed educational objectives in Chapter 13, we mentioned a number of types of objectives and how these can be written so that the procedures of evaluation are also specified. We stressed that clear objectives provide guidance about what to teach and how to teach it, and about learning outcomes and how to evaluate them. Objectives should contain clear specifications of the target behaviour, specifications of the conditions under which the behaviour will be demonstrated, and the criteria for acceptable performance.

As we also pointed out, psychologists interested in testing took the lead in describing specific instructional objectives. They reasoned that group tests used to measure school achievement could be made more effective and relevant if they were based on a school curriculum derived from a systematic listing of objectives. Benjamin Bloom (1956) and others offered taxonomies of educational objectives that cover three domains of objectives—cognitive, affective, and psychomotor.

Bloom's taxonomy of educational objectives contains six levels—knowledge, comprehension, application, analysis, synthesis, and evaluation. The importance of systematically planning for these various levels of cognitive processing is underlined by research that shows that many instructional programs and teaching materials focus on a very limited range of cognitive skills.

Trachtenberg (1974) found that most items used in classroom tests and in books used by teachers and students—95 percent in one study—actually measure only the knowledge and comprehension levels of Bloom's taxonomy. Bloom himself (1964) said that, although more than a million copies of the *Taxonomy of educational objectives—Cognitive domain* (Bloom et al., 1956) were sold, and although the taxonomy was used extensively in pre-service and in-service teacher training, the objectives still were not being used effectively. He felt that "Over 90% of test questions that U.S. public school students [were] expected to answer [dealt] with little more than information," and that the U.S. "instructional material, our classroom teaching methods, and our testing methods rarely [rose] above the lowest category of the Taxonomy—knowledge" (p. 13). Obviously, if classroom measurement is to become more efficient, teachers need training in testing and assessment of higher-order thinking skills (Haertel, 1986; Stiggins, 1988).

One reason for the common stress on knowledge and comprehension questions may be because it is easier by far to write these than to compose those that ask the student to analyze or synthesize. As well, the notion of cognitive level as reflected in taxonomies such as Bloom's is sometimes confused with the notion of the difficulty level of a task or question when, in fact, these concepts are independent. A low-level knowledge item (e.g., "What is the capital of Canada?") is extremely difficult to a person who does not know the answer, but that same individual may be able to respond to high-level synthesis or evaluation tasks (e.g., "Evaluate the theory that all wars ultimately result from accidental causes.") (Good and Brophy, 1986).

To overcome the narrow focus on knowledge and comprehension, Gronlund (1985, 1988) and Bloom and colleagues (1971) suggest that teachers make up a table of specifications. These list the various objectives taught and the different levels of understanding to be assessed.

If the teacher is to ensure that students are actually performing a particular task at each different level of cognitive processing, assessment strategies must allow them to demonstrate their performances (Gronlund, 1988). On a table of specifications teachers list the important topics that have been covered in a unit and compare these to a taxonomy of objectives such as Bloom's. This assists teachers in measuring objectives and evaluating students' knowledge in a systematic, comprehensive manner. It also makes teachers think about the relative importance of objectives and helps them devise test questions that move through a taxonomy from knowing to evaluating. Teachers can also adapt the type of evaluation used to the domains to be assessed. For example, while multiple choice items are an appropriate and efficient method to assess student knowledge and comprehension, multiple choice questions would not enable the teacher to assess students' ability to analyze or synthesize information.

The various levels within the taxonomies must be assessed in different ways. The six within Bloom's hierarchy, for example, can be assessed using the following various techniques:

- Knowledge—testing is intended here to sample the students' ability to recall or recognize material that has been previously presented, not to assess higher levels of thinking, such as analysis or the ability to make judgments (Sprinthall and Sprinthall, 1990). Student performance at the knowledge level could be assessed through question types such as multiple choice, true-false, or fill-in-the-blank.

- Comprehension—a wider variety of strategies can be used to assess students' performances at the comprehension level. Students can demonstrate comprehension by stating information in their own words, predicting, or extrapolating ideas. Test items similar to those used at the knowledge level can be used, such as multiple choice items. However, they must be constructed in a manner that taps a higher level of cognitive processing (Sprinthall and Sprinthall, 1990).

- Application—by its nature, application requires different evaluative procedures. Certainly, some evaluation can be in a written form but the teacher might also observe the students' performance in more real-life situations using some of the ideas we mentioned under performance tests earlier.

- Analysis—the final three domains on Bloom's taxonomy require more varied and innovative evaluative procedures. To assess analysis, for example, Sprinthall and Sprinthall (1990) suggest such things as having the students use their critical-thinking skills to analyze political debates or other arguments; for example, they may be asked to identify the assumptions upon which the argument is based. Through separating fact from opinion and comparing theoretical strands in arguments, the students are able to take a stand based on logic.

- Synthesis—assessment in this area must allow the students to demonstrate a new idea or method such as composing a story or writing a poem. The teacher's judgments determine whether students have, in fact, presented novel ways to solve the problem.

- Evaluation—while evaluating evaluation sounds difficult, it involves the development of critical evaluative skills in the students. When students write a term paper, for example, the teacher must judge the degree to which they have used a logical and comprehensive framework in which to develop their arguments. This conclusion cannot be intuitive or spontaneous; it must rather follow from a logical train of thought developed in the paper (Sprinthall and Sprinthall, 1990).

### Objective tests
Objective tests can be roughly categorized as multiple choice, matching, simple recall, true-false, and completion.

When using these everyday, relatively simple measures, there are still some procedures to follow that will make the testing more accurate and objective. Teachers should:

- vary the form of the tests given to the class;

- teach students how to do the test (Children are at a great disadvantage if they do not understand the format or the instructions of a test.);

- analyze test errors carefully (Ensure that it was the material, rather than the test, that caused problems.);

- note consistent patterns of errors for reteaching or remediation;

- record all results carefully, including the date and the type of test format (This is essential because of the high amount of guessing in formats such as true-false.); and

- allow special students to use different strategies in test taking. (For example, a physically handicapped youngster may respond more easily if allowed to tape record test answers).

**Multiple-choice tests**   Some educators consider the multiple-choice format to be the most versatile and useful form of objective test item (Gronlund, 1988; Linderman and Merenda, 1979). Good multiple-choice questions measure the ability of students to make important distinctions and perform subtle reasoning. The answers are objective, designed to minimize guessing, and rapidly scored. Items may be written to measure recall, inference, discrimination or judgment, as well as recognition.

Multiple-choice questions have two parts—the stem, which represents the problem, and a series of answers, one of which is correct and the others which are distractors. The stem may be a question, a complete or incomplete statement, or even a single word. The distractors are plausible alternatives for students who do not know the answer.

A number of guidelines should be observed in writing multiple-choice items:

- Present the problem in the stem.

- Include most of the item in the stem and keep options as short as possible.

- Keep the stem as short as possible.

- Use negatives sparingly; underline negatives when they are used.

- Use new material in stem problems and attempt to measure application.

- Include only one correct or best answer.

- Try to make all the options plausible; distractors should distract, not confuse.

- Do not cue the answer by making it longer or shorter, or by using predictable patterns of responses.

- Vary the position of the correct responses.

- Avoid familiar textbook phrases.

- Take care that singulars and plurals are consistent and do not provide clues to the correct answer (Garrett, 1965; Thorndike and Hagen, 1978).

Owen (1985), Hoffman (1985), and many others argue that multiple-choice tests discriminate against the creative person. This is a very common but mistaken belief about multiple-choice tests; research clearly shows that those who do well on this type of format are also those who do well on other types of measures, such as laboratory work, essays, speeches, and problem solving (Violato, 1985).

**True-false questions**  In general, true-false questions can be constructed more quickly than multiple-choice items. Brown (1976) notes that true-false questions can be used to good advantage with young children, especially when only a general estimate of performance is required. True-false questions provide a sampling of much subject matter in a very short time.

Nevertheless, the disadvantages of true-false formats may well outweigh the advantages: many items do not lend themselves to the true-false format, and items are difficult to prepare if they are to measure anything but the most factual information. Also, the diagnostic power of the true-false format is lower because students have an even chance of guessing the correct answer. These disadvantages make the true-false format relatively undesirable. It tends to be further misused when the teacher picks sentences out of the textbook and uses them exactly as they are. When this happens, the items measure verbatim knowledge, not understanding. Moreover, true-false questions have been found to elicit a response set of answers—people tend to answer true when in doubt.

If teachers wish to use a true-false format, they should do the following:

- Avoid giving clues.

- Keep away from grammatical confusions such as using double negatives.

- Try to avoid statements that are ambiguous or neither completely true nor completely false.

**Short-answer and completion items**    These items require the students to finish a statement from recall rather than recognition. They also demand thought and the ability to perceive overall relationships. Short-answer questions enable the teacher to pinpoint the particular fact, concept, or principle on which he or she wants to test the students. These types of questions are particularly useful in math and science courses where equations can be tested, or for testing areas where specific pieces of information are demanded.

In preparing short-answer and completion items:

- Ensure that the response is short.

- Allow sufficient space for answers.

- Do not copy sentences straight from the text since this places too much stress on rote learning.

- Do not have too many blanks, and delete words rather than phrases in order to keep the scoring objective.

**Matching exercises**    These require students to link items in one column to the corresponding items in another column. Matching exercises have limited usefulness; however, they can be useful for testing memory of specific facts such as definitions, terms, and dates. Matching items are rarely given orally, but they are a popular device in written examinations to determine whether pupils are acquainted with facts, concepts, and generalizations.

In preparing matching exercises:

- Have more items in the reference list (answer column) than in the entry list (first column).

- Do not include more than one type of information in a single matching exercise and do not include too many items. Twelve matching items is the maximum.

- Clearly explain the basis of the matching to the students taking the test.

### Essay tests

Considerable controversy exists regarding the merits of objective versus essay tests. But both types, in fact, should be used to measure student achievement (Fox, 1985). Essay questions are useful when the teacher wants to evaluate a student's ability to organize and carry out an attack on a fairly complex problem.

Essay questions are often fairly simple to construct but more difficult to mark because teachers' biases and expectations come into play. Although no essay question can be totally objective, teachers can improve their ability to measure school performance by knowing the mental processes they want students to use before starting to write the test questions. Essay questions should be written so that students have clear tasks with specific demands and expectations. In preparing essay questions, teachers will want to ensure that the answers require analysis and synthesis. Questions that ask students to predict or to write their own examples are better than questions that require students to merely present facts.

On essay tests, teachers should ensure that the questions are neither too numerous nor too lengthy, and should include questions that vary in difficulty. Some teachers, perhaps because they feel uncomfortable asking so few questions that neglect so much content, ask too many essay questions and undermine the unique role that an essay examination can play. It is possible to ask a few essay questions (four or five) in fifty minutes and it is useful to vary the difficulty of these questions. If the questions are all simple, students with average mastery will not be differentiated from students with excellent mastery. Similarly, if all the essay questions are very difficult, the test will not differentiate students with minimal mastery from students with average mastery (Slavin, 1988). It is generally desirable to arrange test items in order of expected difficulty to prevent some students from giving up on initially reading the most difficult or detailed questions (Slavin, 1988).

Teachers should provide clear directions for older students, as well as allowing some choice. Students must be told precisely what type of response is required. Too often, essay questions merely tell students to discuss an issue and they force students to guess that the teacher really wants.

Essay questions can be rendered more objective when they are recast into short-answer forms and restricted in coverage. Furthermore, essay questions may be made more controlled and more specific by using recall questions or problem situations (Garrett, 1965).

Recall items are essay questions reduced to the simplest terms. Problem situations are extensions of the multiple-choice type of questions that incorporate essay answers. In problem situations, a problem is stated, and a number of specific questions are asked, each focusing on some important aspect of the situation. Additionally, the student is asked to present a paragraph about the situation (see Table 14-1).

---

**Table 14-1** Examples of objective tests

RECALL QUESTIONS

1. Name three scientists who

   (a) contributed to atomic theory and

   (b) list the major contributions of each.

   (a) 1. _____  2. _____  3. _____

   (b) 1. _____  2. _____  3. _____

or

1. The sun and its nine planets are called the _____.

2. North, south, east and west are called the four _____.

3. Canada and France are both in the _____ hemisphere.

EXTENDING MULTIPLE CHOICE QUESTIONS

1. A skilful teacher has been characterized as one who

   (a) maintains a permissive atmosphere.

   (b) avoids negative discipline.

   (c) conforms to the wishes of the parents.

   (d) does not use repetitive drill and practice.

Write one paragraph each for (a), (b), (c), and (d) defending or attacking each of these propositions.

---

Green (1975) lays out two methods for grading essay questions: the sorting method and the point-score method. The latter is stronger in terms of objectivity. In the sorting method, the teacher quickly reads all the papers, and then sorts them into piles according to rough grades. The papers are then reread with special attention paid to borderline cases. A grade is then assigned to each paper. To use the point-score procedure, the teacher should prepare a grading key that notes all the salient points to be included for full credit. Then all the responses to the same question are read consecutively and points assigned to each question. When all questions are read, the scores are totalled and grades assigned.

## GRADING

There is probably no aspect of schooling that teachers and students dislike more than testing and grading, but there is also probably no aspect of schooling that is more durable (Slavin, 1988). Wherever teaching and learning go on, grades are a grim reality for most people.

In the touchy area of grading, the spectrum of opinion ranges from those who advocate the outright abolition of grades to those who favour more frequent and more strict grading. As with assessment in general, teachers of different age levels seem to see the purposes of grading differently (Burton, 1983). In one study, 52 percent of primary teachers reported that the main reason for grading was that the school district required it. They saw evaluation and grades as unimportant. However, junior high and high school teachers felt that informing students about grades was very important and that they owed this to students as part of the students' education.

The notion of grading by letters or percentages began in the early twentieth century in an attempt to rate education more effectively. The idea persists because of the need to match teachers' expectations and students' performance. The teacher evaluates in order to determine the value of a product, an attitude, or a problem-solving strategy and to decide whether it is desirable or undesirable (Kinnison, Hayes, and Acord, 1981). The end product of teacher evaluation in this sense is the grade.

Grades reflect task performance and measure the degree to which students meet certain norms. They represent evaluation, feedback, and incentive (Slavin, 1978a). Grades, however, are not inherently meaningful. They are generally low in reliability because they are assigned by different teachers who may mark papers inconsistently and who may stress different aspects of a given curriculum. Teachers may also assign higher grades than are merited to the work of students who "try hard." (Blumenfeld et al. 1977).

Grades have commonly been used to motivate students. In fact, they represent one of the most common motivating devices used in schools. Teachers believe that tests motivate students to work hard (Burry et al., 1981), but evidence remains somewhat contradictory. There is little evidence either way on the effects of grading in elementary or secondary schools and equally little research comparing written evaluations to letter grades (Slavin, 1988).

For older students, substantially higher performance is found in graded classes. Research on graded versus ungraded (pass-fail) courses indicates that the use

There is probably no aspect of schooling as durable—and disliked—as grading.

of some sort of grading increases student achievement at the college level (e.g., Gold et al., 1971). Students at this level learn more in courses that use tests than in those that do not (Bangert-Drowns, Kukic, and Kukic, 1986).

In elementary and secondary schools, some research indicates that evaluating students according to their improvement over their own performance was found to increase their achievement (Slavin, 1988). For some students at least, success in the form of marks and grades leads to a realistic level of aspiration and fosters the development of a need for achievement (Beihler and Snowman, 1990). For children who generally get high grades, grades tend to be a positive reinforcer, but students who consistently get low grades may see them as punishment. There is some evidence that high standards, a competitive classroom atmosphere, and a large percentage of lower grades are associated with increased absenteeism and increased dropout rates (Moos and Moos, 1978; Tricket and Moos, 1974). This seems especially the case for disadvantaged students (Wessman, 1972).

A strong motivating factor associated with grades is the home. Grades serve as one consistent form of communication between school and home and most parents naturally reinforce their children for bringing home good grades, thereby making grades more important as incentives (Natriello and Dornbusch, 1984).

Grades tend to lose their motivating power when they are given too infrequently, are too removed from the time of the evaluation, or are poorly tied to specific behaviours. Frequency and timeliness (how soon evaluation should be made after the student performance) of evaluations are critical when evaluations are used to increase incentive and to provide feedback to students (Slavin, 1988).

There is evidence that the more frequently students are evaluated, the more they generally achieve (Bloom et al., 1971; Peckham and Roe, 1977). Correcting students' work immediately after it is completed increases work output far more than correction a day later does (Leach and Graves, 1973). Frequent, brief quizzes are better than infrequent, long tests because they require students to pay attention all the time instead of cramming for the occasional exam (Slavin, 1988). They also provide better feedback to students and give reinforcement for hard work closer to the time that the work was done (Slavin, 1988). Further, Cross and Cross (1980-81) found that students who received written feedback in addition to letter grades were more likely than other students to feel that their efforts, rather than luck or any other external factors, determined their success in school.

There are perhaps as many sets of grading criteria as there are teachers who assign grades. Grading on the curve—the bell shaped curve of the statisticians—simply applies to norm-referenced measurements. It rests on the assumption that abilities and achievement are normally distributed and that classroom achievement will naturally vary among a group of heterogeneous students because of differences in such characteristics as prior knowledge, learning skills, motivation, and aptitude (Beihler and Snowman, 1990). Grades are determined by comparing each student's level of performance to the normal or average level of other similar students. Grading on the curve has the advantage of placing each score in relation to all the others without regard to the difficulty of the particular test.

Norm-referenced evaluation compares the student's performance to that of comparable students, who usually are referred to as the standardization, or normative sample. Criterion-referenced evaluation uses an absolute criteria to ascertain outcomes on a specific set of skills. Frequently, the evaluator uses performance to divide students into two groups: those who are at and above or those who are below a certain minimal performance level, which can be established using different sources.

While norm-referenced and criterion-referenced grading systems both spring from a normative data base (that is, comparisons among students) the former system uses these comparisons to directly determine grades, whereas the latter uses the same comparisons to establish criteria: how well the student masters the criteria determines the grade (Beihler and Snowman, 1990). Criterion-referenced tests focus attention on the degree to which students have mastered specific objectives. Under a criterion-referenced system, grades are determined by comparing how far each student has progressed toward attaining a defined standard (or criterion) of achievement or performance.

A common version of criterion grading assigns letter grades on the basis of the percentage of test items answered correctly. For example, the teacher may decide to award an A to anyone who answers at least 85 percent of a test's questions and a B to anyone who answers 75 percent (Beihler and Snowman, 1990). To use this type of grading system fairly, which means specifying realistic criterion levels, the teacher will need to have some prior knowledge of the levels at which students typically perform. This then involves using normative information to establish absolute or fixed standards of performance.

Multiple grades for the evaluation of the progress have been used successfully, especially for low-achieving and low-functioning students. One type of multiple grade system involves the three areas of ability, effort, and achievement. Ability in this sense reflects the student's growth in the content area being studied, based on expectations of the child's ability to grasp the material. Effort is determined by how hard the student tried, and achievement compares the student's achievement with others in the group. An average of ability, effort, and achievement provides the final grade (Kinnison, Hayes, and Acord, 1981). In a point system, the student accumulates points for specified activities over a semester. Equal weight is given to activities beside tests in order to accommodate students who may have difficulty with reading, writing, or working under time constraints (Kinnison, Hayes, and Acord, 1981).

Teachers will need to explain the meaning of grades to students (Burton, 1983). Also, if teachers hope to assign grades fairly, objectively, and in a manner that they can explain and defend to parents and students, they need to be well-organized. Records of pupil performance in various areas should be kept and meticulously maintained.

Each classroom, each testing situation, and each grading procedure is unique. However, there are some general guidelines that can be followed that are shown in Box 14-1.

## Box 14-1 **In the classroom: Guidelines for testing and grading**

- Test frequently, using criterion-referenced tests where possible.

- Use the test data for reteaching and individualized instruction as necessary.

- Be clear about learning objectives.

- Allow students ample time to finish a test unless time is a relevant factor.

- Ensure that tests sample equally from different parts of the course when testing the entire course's content.

- Tell the students when certain content areas will be stressed on a test so that they can adjust their preparation plans accordingly.

- Provide students with a number of potential test questions and inform them that the test will be composed of a subset of these questions. This will ensure that the students will study the material that you consider important.

- Try to maintain a balance between essay tests and objective tests because some students may do better on one type than the other.

- Vary the question types in objective tests but use such items as true-false sparingly.

- Assess all levels of a taxonomy using varied techniques.

- Decide when and how often to give tests and other marked assignments as early as possible.

- Consider distributing a course outline on the first day of class when teaching older students.

- Announce tests and assignments well in advance.

- Prepare a content outline or table of specifications of the objectives to be covered on each exam or otherwise take care to obtain a systematic sample.

# TEST ANXIETY

Teachers believe that the pressure of testing has a beneficial effect (Burry et al. 1981). However, the greatest anxiety-arousing situation in schools at every level is the test (Woolfolk, 1990). The negative relationship between test anxiety and academic performance of university undergraduates, for example, has been well-documented (e.g., Culler and Holahan, 1980).

Test anxiety is one of the biggest threats to obtaining accurate information about students' performances. Some students experience debilitating anxiety during testing or evaluation and they underperform; children who experience an unpleasant emotional state in test situations perform more poorly on tests than those who do not experience such feelings. Hill and Eaton (1977) discovered that anxious fifth and sixth graders worked as quickly and accurately as their less anxious classmates when there was no time limit to a test. But when there was a time limit, very anxious students made three times as many errors as their classmates, spent about twice as much time on each problem, and cheated twice as often as the less anxious group.

Although test anxiety and learned helplessness may not be strongly related to children's performances initially, this relationship apparently changes with age (Fencham, Hokada, and Sanders, 1989). It also seems that rather than poor performance causing the anxiety, high anxiety can cause poor performance (Woolfolk, 1990). Anxiety appears to improve performance on simple tasks and on skills that have been practised at length but to interfere with the accomplishment of more complex tasks or skills that are not thoroughly practised (Ball, 1977).

Some students may lack test-taking skills. Coaching on how to take a test can improve performance. A correlation of over .70 exists between the time spent on coaching students and improvement on the Scholastic Aptitude Test (Messik, 1982), with a great deal of that improvement coming from just small amounts of coaching time. Improvements can sometimes be dramatic for minority and low-income students (Anastasi, 1981; Messik, 1982). Students should be taught to focus on the types of questions that are likely to arise, to answer the easy questions first, to allot time properly during a test, to answer all the questions, and to check their work.

# SUMMARY

1. Student evaluation comprises all the means used in school to evaluate students' performances. Without evaluation, students would not receive the feedback they need for learning and teachers would not know whether classroom objectives had been reached.

2. Evaluations may be made on a group or individual basis. They may be given in order to assess ongoing learning or to measure what has been accomplished.

3. Formal assessment implies the use of standardized tests, instruments commercially prepared by measurement experts that provide uniform methods of

obtaining samples of behaviour. Recently, there has been a growing disenchantment with formal tests and a trend toward the use of informal measures. Informal measures include such things as case histories, observations, checklists, inventories, and rating scales.

4. While the evaluation of student achievement is a characteristic element of formal classroom education, the area remains fraught with considerable controversy. Assessment and testing is under attack from both within and without the educational profession.

5. Performance may be interpreted through methods of evaluation that are either norm- or criterion-referenced. Each approach utilizes a different comparative standard for interpreting performance and providing meaning to test scores. Norm-referenced evaluation compares a student's performance against the norm of other students taking the test. Evaluation that is used to determine whether students have mastered specific learning objectives is called criterion-referenced evaluation.

6. Assessment and testing occur in three distinct stages: construction, in which instruments for measuring student performance are created; analysis, in which these instruments are scrutinized for possible flaws; and interpretation, in which performance outcomes are summarized and interpreted.

7. Grading involves evaluation which by its very nature is subjective and dependent on comparisons. Teachers' expectations affect grading, student achievement, and other student behaviour.

## Key Terms

| | | |
|---|---|---|
| assessment | criterion-referenced test | culture-fair measures |
| culture-free measures | diagnostic tests | educational measurement |
| evaluation | formative evaluation | grade equivalents |
| measurement | norm-referenced test | norms |
| percentile | performance tests | power test |
| process-oriented measures | psycho-educational diagnosis | raw scores |
| reliability | standard scores | standardized test |
| summative evaluation | test | validity |
| z scores | | |

15

# CLASSROOM MANAGEMENT

## INTRODUCTION

**Classroom management:**
the way in which the classroom environment is manipulated so that all children have the optimum opportunity to reach academic and social goals.

Lacking good management, a classroom will slide toward apathy or chaos; with it, a classroom runs efficiently. Motivation and learning are enhanced, the instructional program proceeds smoothly, and poor behaviour is kept to a minimum. As manager of the instructional team the teacher is the primary designer, developer, and evaluator of the instructional program. As classroom leader, the teacher is responsible for efficient and effective organization and management.

The terms *classroom management* and *behaviour management* are often used synonymously, but they are not the same thing. Classroom management refers to the ways in which the classroom environment is manipulated so that all children have the otpimum opportunity to reach academic and social goals. Emmer (1987) defines classroom management "as a set of teacher behaviours and activities directed at engaging students in appropriate behaviour and minimizing disruptions" (p. 13). Behaviour management includes all the ways in which students are taught to control their own behaviour (e.g., preventative discipline, reinforcement, crisis intervention, and punishment).

The importance of classroom management cannot be overemphasized—indeed, management is an integral part of good instruction (Jones and Jones, 1986; Sanford, Emmer, and Clements, 1983), and may even be seen as a prerequisite for instruction (Doyle, 1985). Classrooms can be organized or chaotic, supportive or authoritarian, pleasant learning environments or difficult places to exist (Winzer, 1989).

Good classroom managers provide a bright and stimulating classroom. They assume an active role in creating a positive, expectant, and orderly classroom environment in which positive learning experiences take place. Good classroom managers also possess the personal qualities of patience, commitment, and understanding which further ensure a warm and supportive environment (Winzer, 1989). Strong correlations exist between good management and student achievement and positive attitudes toward school. Correlations also exist between good management and the levels of teachers' stress and job satisfaction (Davis and Thomas, 1989).

Many components combine to make up classroom management. The most important elements are the physical environment, the instructional approaches, the materials, and the methods of discipline and control employed. Within the broad concept of classroom management, then, behaviour control and discipline are only components, albeit crucial ones. In fact, to many teachers, to the public, and to the media, discipline is the essential problem in contemporary schools. The media is full of tales of problem behaviour in schools, leading parents and other concerned members of the public to question whether or not the schools are functioning well. While there is no research that directly compares the incidence of behavioural problems from the past with those of present day, surveys of teachers (e.g., Check, 1979) indicate that experienced teachers believe the problems to be more serious today.

When the Canadian Education Association (CEA) undertook a poll in 1984, similar to the annual Gallup Poll taken in the United States about schools (MacLeod, 1985), results from the two countries were similar. Yet in each Gallup survey conducted in the U.S. during the past ten years, approximately one-quarter of the respondents mentioned lack of discipline as a major school problem. By contrast, only 16.5 percent of the Canadians surveyed by the CEA in 1984 cited lack of discipline as a major problem for their schools. The problems most frequently mentioned in Canada were drugs, smoking, and alcohol (cited by 17.2 percent of the respondents). Lack of discipline was second, and lack of interest/truancy/bad attitudes represented the third most serious problem (cited by 13.4 percent). The full results of the CEA Poll are shown in Table 15-1.

**Table 15-1** CEA Poll

THE BIGGEST PROBLEMS WITH WHICH THE SCHOOLS IN CANADA MUST DEAL

| | %* | | %* |
|---|---|---|---|
| Drugs, smoking, alcohol | 17.2 | Domestic problems | 5.8 |
| Lack of discipline | 16.5 | Aspects of multiculturalism | 2.8 |
| Pupil's lack of interest/truancy/attitudes | 13.4 | Problems with school boards/organization of school | 2.6 |
| | | There are no problems | 2.6 |
| Curriculum problems | 10.6 | Declining enrolment | 2.1 |
| Teachers' lack of interest/quality of performance | 8.0 | Distance to school/busing | 2.0 |
| | | Vandalism | 2.0 |
| Inadequate financial support | 7.0 | Too much free time/distractions | 1.5 |
| Pupil/teacher ratio | 6.3 | Communication between teacher and pupil | 1.2 |
| Miscellaneous | 6.1 | Don't know/no answer | 19.1 |

Figures add to more than 100% because of multiple answers. *National Totals

**SOURCE:** MacLeod, 1985.

There is little question that teachers view discipline as a major problem. Managing students of any age, any grade, and any functional level can be a challenging and often frustrating task. Yet all teachers have to devote some time to classroom control: typically, teachers spend about ten percent of their time engaged in this activity (Crealock, 1983).

Behaviour control is of paramount importance. In fact, the success achieved by teachers in educating children is often directly proportional to their ability to use appropriate management strategies to direct individuals, and small and large groups. The way they perceive their roles and activities as teachers affects the way teachers behave (Ames, 1983; Clark and Paterson, 1985). Moreover, the ways in which teachers perceive students and interpret misbehaviour influence the way that they respond to behaviour problems.

New teachers are particularly concerned with discpline—indeed, most report that their greatest fear is that they will "lose control." When using discipline, inexperienced teachers had to rely on restrictive disciplinary strategies such as verbal reprimands and denying privileges (Moore and Cooper, 1984). These teachers are often operating on a survival level—they worry chiefly about making it through the day and tend to be preoccupied with who they are and how they will respond in the classroom. They misinterpret student misbehaviour as a threat to their authority (Lasley, 1989). More than one promising teacher has been driven out of a teaching career because of an inability to manage student behaviour.

Experienced teachers who are good classroom managers appear to be happier and to suffer less stress; they are also perceived by their colleagues to be good teachers, especially if their management of children's behaviour is above average (Winzer, 1989). These teachers are task-oriented—they focus on management and organization and are deeply concerned with whether and how students learn (Lasley, 1989).

No matter how well teachers manage their classrooms, there will inevitably be some students who fail to respond as positively as others. Individual differences, the age of the students, the location of the school, and a host of other factors come into play when discipline is discussed. In the younger grades, behavioural problems usually take the form of attention-seeking and acting-out behaviour, but are more likely to involve peers, peer presure, and interpersonal relationships as children reach adolescence. The opening years of adolescence are highlighted by the conflicting attractions of independence, especially in relation to parents and teachers, and of the security promised by more childish activities. Check (1979) found that junior high teachers reported nearly twice as many discipline problems as high school teachers.

A teacher functions as the leader of the classroom group. The teacher's authority depends upon the children's perceptions of their instructor as an efficient director of teaching and discipline. But when children do not comply, teachers have no control. Without control, teachers cannot establish an environment where teaching can take place. And where teaching cannot take place, students cannot learn.

Students expect teachers to manage their classrooms effectively; they expect teachers to act as figures of authority and they desire a predictable structure in their classrooms. Nash (1976) discovered six major themes in the attitudes and expectations of elementary students concerning their teachers: They expect teachers to keep order, teach, explain, be interesting, treat everyone fairly, and act in a friendly manner. Metz (1978) found similar attitudes among high school students. It has also been found that when students define their classroom situations as orderly, they are more likely to comply with the rules (Pestello, 1973).

Ideally, a warm climate and good academic atmosphere would maintain good attitudes and high academic engagement and prevent inattentive, off-task, and disruptive behaviour. In reality, this rarely occurs. Teachers face both minor behavioural problems every day as well as others that are actually or potentially far more serious. Sometimes there is too little behaviour: students fail to pay attention and show little interest in their work or little joy in interacting properly with other students. They may fail to even attend school or, when they do, be consistently tardy. Other students demonstrate too much of various types of behaviour. They may be aggressive, move around the room inappropriately, make too much noise, challenge authority, or be physically or verbally destructive.

Many classroom problems are essentially trivial and can be quite readily handled. As far as the more serious problems go, there has been much debate but little research and certainly no definitive findings about how to handle them (Good and Brophy, 1986). There remain significant differences of opinion regarding the choice of management strategies (Braaten et al., 1988).

Teachers have been found to be chiefly concerned with behaviour that disrupts and hampers achievement and management in their classrooms. "Socially defiant" behaviour most upsets teachers (Algozzine, 1977a). Also, the behavioural characteristics of boys are more bothersome to teachers than those of girls (Schlosser and Algozzine, 1979). When teachers encounter children who manage to move the process of behaviour management from a task to a preoccupation, they look to special education. In fact, classroom management problems constitute the most common reason that children are referred to special education (Ysseldyke and Algozzine, 1984). One study (Phipps, 1982) found that 82 percent of boys referred to special education were referred primarily because of behavioural problems.

Nearly all teachers develop their own personal methods of behaviour control that serve to enhance learning and promote classroom stability. Teachers acquire discipline and management startegies in techniques in various ways; some teachers hark back to the manner in which they were disciplined in school and adopt those principles. Some discuss the problems with other teachers and adapt their methods; others glean ideas about behaviour control from reading or from courses, and quite a few simply use intuition (Winzer, 1989). Although no definitive answers exist, much research directs teachers' classroom management and discipline. In one study (Cantrell, Stenner, and Katzenmeyer, 1977) teachers who scored high on a test of the behavioural principles of classroom management and who held positive attitudes toward students were more successful than teachers who had less knowledge of these methods.

Classroom management, classroom discipline, and individual behaviour control interweave and influence each other. Effective teaching and learning demands a controlled, regulated, and rewarding milieu where individual rights are respected (Winzer, 1989). However, numerous factors must be considered in planning a functional, attractive work environment for teachers and students that will maximize appropriate behaviours and facilitate the best learning. Before the students even enter the door, the teacher must first:

- ready the physical classroom environment;

- make plans to develop a positive classroom climate;

- develop rules and procedures to guide classroom operations;

- plan the consequences that will follow appropriate and inappropriate behaviour in the classroom; and

- organize instruction.

Teachers need both knowledge and practice to develp their own techniques of management. As they plan instruction and maintain classroom organization, they should become aware of those techniques that affect students' behaviour and reinforce a stable learning environment. Teachers need to be flexible enough to adopt or adapt various techniques to deal with behaviours that range from inattentiveness to aggression. People are so complex that no method will work every time with a particular student, nor indeed suit every teacher. Interventions must match the teacher's personality, teaching style, and pedagogical philosophy. If a teacher does not feel secure with a particular intervention, it will not be successful (Winzer, 1989).

In this chapter, we examine many of the elements of classroom management, with a focus on the components so crucial to teachers—discipline and behaviour control. The strategies presented represent a melding of the behavioural, cognitive, and humanistic views of human learning and development. Certainly, the approach taken by teachers will be influenced by their own personal views and teaching style; they may select more heavily from one school of thought than the others. There is no single good way to manage a classroom—what is important is careful planning, good communication with students, and consistent follow-through.

## ESTABLISHING THE CLASSROOM ENVIRONMENT

At the beginning of the school year, teachers—particularly new teachers—are very busy people. They are concerned with lesson planning, scheduling, gathering materials, and all of the other administrative tasks that seem to inevitably make their way to a teacher's desk. As a result, teachers may not pay enough attention to the physical environment of the classroom. But unless they consider the physical environment in which they and their students will work, teachers may actually be precipitating management problems and hindering students from reaching their full potential. Of the many factors that can facilitate or inhibit children's responses, the learning environment itself is vital, for the environment has great impact on the energy that children expend in reaching educational goals.

The classroom is an environment for learning and classrooms are organized for different purposes. The physical features of a classroom can be arranged so

Classrooms should be set up with as much open space and as little clutter as possible.

as to increase, maintain, or reduce certain types of student involvement and communication. This involves arranging seating, designing certain task areas, establishing small group instructional areas, and reducing open spaces. Settings should be arranged so that active interaction with the students is possible. Space can be structured so as to increase the teacher's control of the children and to head off possible disciplinary problems. Much misbehaviour can be prevented if the workspace is well-organized so that it utilizes space efficiently, permits orderly movement, and minimizes distractions.

First, classrooms should be set up with as much open space and as little clutter as possible. In order to facilitate movement around the room, the teacher must ensure that any arrangement of classroom furniture and equipment allows for large unobstructed traffic lanes. Traffic patterns should be efficient and non-disruptive. It is also important to structure the classroom so that children will create the smallest disturbance possible when they move into small groups, walk to cupboards for supplies, or go to their lockers for materials. It should not disrupt the entire class each time someone uses the pencil sharpener nor should the teacher have any difficulty when moving toward a student who is beginning to misbehave.

The first step is to carefully examine the likely traffic patterns around the classroom. Where are the main entrance and exit routes? Routes in and out of the classroom must be wide enough and free of obstacles. Permanent features of the classroom must also be examined. Since it is usually not possible to change the location of storage shelves, bookshelves, coat closets, or even pencil sharpeners, the traffic patterns to and from these frequently used areas must also be considered. Probably the single most effective management technique for behaviour control is visual scanning of the classroom. The arrangements should then facilitate the teacher's ability to scan the class with maximum efficiency. Visual scanning is necessary for safety and maintaining on-task behaviour and classroom discipline (Winzer, 1989). The teacher must decide whether students will routinely sit in rows or be seated in small group arrangements. Most regular classrooms assign a child a place at a seat or a table which is a kind of home base where tasks are done. Straight rows of desks are more conducive to quiet individual tasks; conversely, less formal seating arrangements usually signal collaborative activities or group discussions (Winzer, 1989). Seating arrangements in the classroom will be influenced by the teacher's style of instruction. Those who frequently use cooperative learning strategies would opt for group seating, while teachers who typically use large group lectures would probably seat students in rows.

Seating patterns should not be chosen lightly for they have been shown to influence the patterns of interaction seen in a classroom. Raviv, Raviv, and Reisel (1990) found that students in classes in which group seating was used perceived themselves as having better friendships with their peers (getting to know each other better, helping each other, and enjoying working together) than students sitting in rows. They also perceived their classes as being more innovative (students contributed to planning class activities; the teacher used new techniques and encouraged creative thinking). This is consistent with other studies which have found more interaction among children in open settings as opposed to traditional classroom environments (Minuchin and Shapiro, 1983). Moreover, the teachers in group classes perceived themselves as being more supportive of children (helpful, friendly, and interested) and more innovative. Teachers in row classes perceived themselves as more task-oriented, placing more emphasis on getting planned activities completed and staying on the subject matter than did teachers in group classes (Raviv, Raviv, and Reisel, 1990).

Seating arrangements also have a good deal of effect on the ability of children to maintain visual contact, to communicate, and to learn. Axelrod and colleagues (1979) showed how seating arrangements could affect the amount of time it took children to finish assignments. In a small group learning session, first graders were placed facing each other across a table. These youngsters were able to work more effectively and to complete their assignments more quickly than when they were seated facing the same direction and without the opportunity to make visual contact.

When arranging the desks, the teacher should detemine where he or she will stand when addressing the entire class. This area is usually near the chalkboard and audiovisual screen and should include a desk, table, or other workspace on which to place needed materials. Desks are arranged around these central areas, and sightlines from each should be checked. Students must be able to directly face the teacher at times when attention is needed (Emmer, 1987). Students should not have to strain to see the teacher, chalkboard, screen, or any other instructional display that will be used frequently. In addition, student seating should be arranged in a way that maximizes attention and minimizes distractions and disruptions. Avoid having students face distracting sights: windows, doorway, small group work area, or eye-catching displays (Emmer, 1987).

Of course, even when desks are in rows, students will not always be taught in a large group format and so provisions for small group instruction should be made. Whenever possible, small group tables or learning centres should be located in a place that will not distract other students. If several such centres are planned, they should be as widely dispersed as possible to minimize the possibility of disruptions and distractions. Careful monitoring of students is a key to classroom management: clear lines of sight must be maintained between the areas of the room the teacher frequents and the students' work areas (Emmer, 1987). Because screens, bookshelves, or other dividers are often used to separate learning centres or quiet areas, such as reading corners, teachers must ensure that they can see what is happening behind the screens. Otherwise, students may take the opportunity to nap or to settle an argument by beating up on a pal.

Frequently used teaching materials and student supplies should be placed in readily accessible locations. Decisions about placement of materials can be made by estimating their frequency of use: materials used daily or weekly should be readily available while less frequently used materials can be stored in less accessible places if necessary. Students should be able to easily get to supply shelves, wastebaskets, pencil sharpeners, the teacher's desk, and so on, without distracting others, tripping over desks, or stomping on someone's lunch (Emmer, 1987). Easy access to, and efficient storage of, materials and supplies will aid management by allowing activities to begin and end promptly and by minimizing time spent getting ready and cleaning up.

## Classroom density

Anyone who has sat on a overloaded subway, shopped on Christmas Eve, or attended a Grey Cup game or similar public event will realize that forced crowding can have negative effects on people's behaviour. Not surprisingly, research suggests that overcrowding in classrooms can have equally negative effects on student behaviour: one study revealed that overcrowding is associated with distractability, inattention, off-task behaviour, dissatisfaction, aggression, and a reduction in positive social interaction (Shapiro, 1975).

To investigate this phenomenon further, Krantz and Risley experimented with two different seating arrangements for a group of young children during story time. In the crowded condition, the students sat cross-legged on a blanket in front of the teacher; in the uncrowded condition, they were dispersed over a wider area. Children paid less attention to the teacher in the crowded condition, possibly because they were more likely to poke, shove, and exhibit other aggressive behaviour. Similarly, Hutt and Vaizey found that children behaved more aggressively when crowded, and McGrew (1970) noted increased fighting among children on smaller, more crowded playgrounds.

However, other studies have shown the opposite results—that increased spatial density does not necessarily result in more aggression. Loo (1972) found that four and five year olds were less aggressive under more crowded conditions although they tended to isolate themselves more. Freedman (1975) examined three levels of spatial density on the behaviour of nine high school students and found that there was no difference in task performance although boys tended to become more competitive under crowded conditions. Further, the positive or negative aspects of an activity tended to be enhanced in the crowded condition; in other words, enjoyable activities were more enjoyable under crowded conditions while unpleasant activities became even more aversive.

**Classroom climate:**
a composite of the prevailing conditions in a classroom.

It may be that teachers learn to adapt to the more crowded conditions and modify their instructional style accordingly. Other factors in operation may be the teacher's consistent use of rules, the seating arrangements, the attractiveness of the activity, and the nature of the students (whether they tend to be aggressive or not). Further, the relationship between aggression and spatial density is not linear: there may be more aggression in extremely crowded conditions, but too much space may not be desirable either (McAfee, 1987). This is consistent with research that shows that when students and teachers are in close proximity, the frequency of positive teacher-student interactions increases (Orme and Purnell, 1970). When teachers are close to students it may allow them to intervene more quickly to stop misbehaviour, but proximity control may be diminished in very large rooms. The ages of the students may also be an important factor: studies which did not find that crowdedness led to more aggresive acts were conducted with preschoolers (Fagot, 1977), while some of those studies that did show increases in aggression were done with older children (McAfee, 1987; McGrew, 1970).

## Classroom climate

Teachers are necessarily concerned with creating a learning environment that facilitates appropriate student behaviour and increased learning. They are interested in maintaining a warm and supportive **classroom climate**, a composite of the prevailing conditions in a classroom. Charles (1983) suggests that the psychosocial climate of the classroom is more important to achievement, self-concept, and school attitudes than the physical environment. Further, Hoge, Smit, and Hanson, (1990), in a two-year study of the sixth and seventh grades, found that the school climate and evaluation practices used by teachers had an impact on the students' self-esteem, while grading practices did not.

While the teacher initially creates the classroom climate, the prevailing milieu necessarily includes students' perceptions of general school factors, such as attitudes, policies, and motivations (Beane and Lipska, 1984). So important is this that students' perceptions of the classroom climate can be used to predict student achievement and school satisfaction (Galluzi, Kirby, and Zuchner, 1980; Wright and Cowen, 1982).

Classroom climate needs to be viewed from three perspectives—the features of a supportive clasroom climate, creating this climate, and maintaining the climate. In terms of the salient features, research is difficult to conduct and most studies have asked junior high or high school students to reveal their perceptions of the clasroom. Data reveals that a well-organized class that provides supportive relationships and student participation promotes student morale, interest in subject matter, and academic self-efficacy. In addition, students in task-oriented classes that set specific academic goals in the context of supportive relationships and clear structure show greater gains on sandard achievement tests (Moos, 1987).

Less research has been conducted in the elementary grades; however, it appears that cohesiveness, task orientation, and structure facilitate greater student achievement, as reflected in improved reading and mathematics scores (Moos, 1987). In the elementary grades, both teachers and students prefer the class to function in an orderly fashion, with more student cooperation and opportunity for student initiative (Raviv, Raviv, and Reisel, 1990). Fourth and fifth grade students exhibited greater self-control in classes perceived as having a clearly defined organizational structure and as encouraging active and independent engagement in tasks (Humphrey, 1984).

When they are asked to describe their ideal classroom environment, there is a great deal of similarity between how students and teachers respond (Fraser, 1986; Raviv, Raviv, and Reisel, 1990). In the ideal classroom, both teachers and students would like to have students become more involved and take greater initiative in class activities, have teachers introduce new ideas and techniques, and have the class function in a calm and orderly fashion. Teachers would not only be supportive but also responsible for clarifying the rules of the class. Both students and teachers prefer less competition, teacher control, and task orientation. An Australian study of elementary school teachers and students reported that both groups would prefer more cohesiveness, more satisfaction, less friction, and less competitiveness in the classroom environment. It appears that elementary students probably require orderliness in the classroom and rule clarification as a means of attaining a satisfying environment devoid of friction (Raviv, Raviv, and Reisel, 1990).

But while teachers and students know what they want their classes to be, they generally agree that the existing classroom environment does not approach their ideal (Fraser, 1986; Raviv, Raviv, and Reisel, 1990). Further, while teachers and students tend to be in agreement when asked to describe their ideal classroom environment, they differ when asked to describe the actual environment

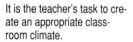

It is the teacher's task to create an appropriate classroom climate.

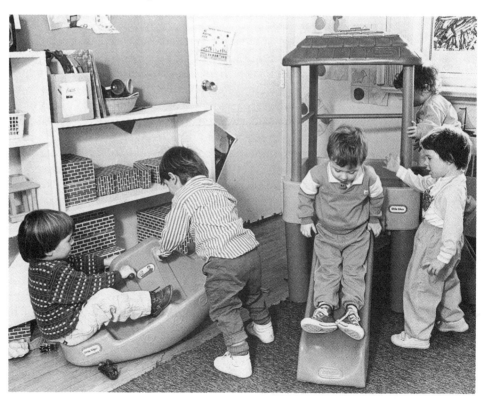

**Rules:**
general expectations or standards for student behaviour.

in which they function. Teachers tend to view the classroom environment more favourably than their students do (Humphrey, 1984; Moos, 1979). Raviv, Raviv, and Reisel (1990) found that teachers tend to perceive their classroom environments as being more supportive and as facilitating greater student involvement. They also perceived a greater amount of order and organization, rule clarity, and innovation. It may be that teachers' authoritarian roles and desire to function optimally influenced their perceptions. However, this research would suggest that teachers may have to be more systematic in their assessment of the students' perceptions of the classroom environment.

Essentially, it is the teachers' task to create an appropriate classroom climate. The beginning of the school year is of critical importance; in those first few days and weeks, the teacher sets that tone that will influence his or her effectiveness for the remainder of the school year. This includes setting clear expectations for student learning and behaviour, planning well, and maintaining control.

Many novice teachers are often told, "Don't smile until Christmas—show those kids who is boss!" But is it really necessary for the teacher to assume the role of the harsh authoritarian? It seems not; in fact, the research argues that such a stance creates a situation where students may view the teacher as the enemy and establishes a year-long climate of alienation, mistrust, and hostility. On the other hand, an overly friendly attitude is not appropriate; the teacher must command respect and be seen by students as the leader of the classroom. Good and Brophy, (1986) recommend that teachers be likable, credible, and trustworthy. When teachers display these traits, they are more likely to advance good student-teacher relationships and positive student-teacher interactions, which in turn promote positive student attitudes (Brophy, 1979; Purkey and Novak, 1984).

Studies of effective teachers have revealed some of the things they do in the opening weeks of school year to create an effective classroom climate. In a study of third-grade teachers, the more effective teachers in the early weeks set up a more workable system of rules than the ineffective teachers did. Effective teachers demonstrated a greater degree of being in touch with the students' needs and problems and showed a tendency to give clear direction and instructions (Emmer, Evertson, and Anderson, 1980). Similar practices characterized more effective junior high school teachers observed during the first three weeks of the school year (Evertson and Emmer, 1982). At the secondary level, effective managers establish rules, procedures, and expectations on the first day of class. Standards pertaining to academic work and classroom behaviour are clearly communicated to the students and consistently enforced during the opening weeks of the school year.

## Planning rules and procedures

Any group must live by rules if it is to be orderly and all classes that are well-managed specify those rules that will guide student behaviour and academic work (Emmer, Evertson, and Anderson, 1980; Emmer et al., 1982; Evertson et al., 1983; Sanford and Evertson, 1981). Rules identify general expectations or standards for behaviour; they tell students what they should do and describe forbidden actions in the class (Evertson et al., 1984).

The list of rules should be kept to a minimum—the more rules, the more difficulty will the teacher have enforcing compliance adequately. It is better to have a few general rules than many specific ones, and rules are best written in positive rather than negative terms.

No specific or infallible set of classroom rules exists; teachers must decide reasonable rules and reasonable limits for themselves. Evertson and colleagues (1984) have provided a sample of rules appropriate for elementary grades:

1. Be polite and helpful.

2. Take care of your school.

3. Behave in the cafeteria.

4. Do not hit, shove, or hurt others.

5. Keep the bathroom clean.

In secondary schools, different rules will be needed. Five possible rules are:

1. Bring all needed material to class.

2. Be in your seat and ready for work when the bell rings.

3. Obtain permission before speaking or leaving your seat.

4. Respect and be polite to everybody.

5. Respect other people's property (Emmer et al., 1984).

In some circumstances, a separate set of rules that govern behaviour during various instructional activities or in different areas of the school must be specified. That is, the students will be expected to behave differently in the library or in the gymnasium from how they behave during lectures or in reading groups. Thus, brief lists of rules that will govern behaviour in these areas should be specified.

By the time rules have been established, students must understand the reason why they should conform to these expectations (Brophy, 1987). Children often do not understand the rules or know how to obey them, even when the rules are clearly stated (Smith, 1985). The way classroom rules are set and sustained in children's memories differs according to the developmental level of the students. Young children in the first few years of school are still being socialized into the roles of the school child; they need direct instruction and consistent repetition of rules (Canter and Canter, 1976; Emmer, Evertson, and Anderson, 1980). Behaviours that conform and do not conform to the rules need to be directly discussed and/or taught. For example, what does it mean to "Take care of your school"? Students must be given the chance to practise the behaviours, and to have their efforts reinforced. In very young classes, the teacher can introduce rules by modeling. As well, pictures to accompany the written rules are effective devices (Winzer, 1989).

Children at the middle elementary levels are quite accustomed to their roles and many classroom and school rules and procedures have become automatic. They still, however, need to have the old rules reviewed for them and to have the new ones taught directly to them. Occasionally, students should be reminded of the rules, especially if they have been breaking them with any frequency. Specifying the rules and reviewing them occasionally may also prompt students to rehearse them to themselves, and perhaps remind others of them (O'Leary and O'Leary, 1977).

Junior high school students may be perfectly aware of the rules but at this stage the teacher's influence has declined and students may be more interested in the peer group. The uncertainty and unpredictability of early adolescence make discipline challenging for junior high school teachers. Rules must be consistently and systematically enforced. By late high school, the focus returns to academics and classroom management is more concerned with managing the curriculum and fitting academic material to the students' interests and abilities (see Brophy and Evertson, 1978; Winzer, 1989, Woolfolk, 1990).

When teachers use an informational rather than a controlling style, stressing the reasons for limits and procedures, and implying that there are useful rules for students to follow in order to meet their own goals, then the students are more likely to use these guidelines in new situations (Koestner et al., 1971). Whenever possible, students should be involved in the setting of rules in the classroom. However, Baumrind (1971) argues that the important issue is not whether students participate in establishing rules but whether they perceive the rules set by the teacher as useful and reasonable.

In addition to rules, the teacher will wish to specify the procedures that will operate in the classroom. Procedures specify how routine class matters are to be accomplished. They describe how to accomplish activities such as material distribution, homework, and group arrangements.

## Organizing instruction

Giving children meaningful and challenging work is a key to preventing management problems (Evertson and Smylie, 1987). The good teacher not only plans for individual needs, readiness, and interests but incorporates variety and challenge into the school day. On the other hand, it is not surprising that students become inattentive or indulge in inappropriate behaviour when they are bored with work that is too easy, frustrated with work that is too difficult, or tired from working on one activity for too long. Failing to accommodate individual differences in ability, or becoming insensitive to the effects of too much repetition, or too much of a good thing, will lead to management problems.

The prevalence of lecture, recitation, and seatwork in classrooms is well documented. Doyle (1986) has suggested that the enduring prevalence of these formats is realted to classroom management. That is, the routinization of classroom procedures is a reasonable strategy for maintaining order. This does not imply that classroom activities should be so easy that students can accomplish them with little effort or that routines are so structured that no flexibility exists. However, tasks that are too easy can be unchallenging and boring, just as tasks that are too hard breed failure and frustration. Students are refreshed and challenged when the teacher plans for lots of variety in their school day. Kounin (1970) observed that "to reduce satiation by learning-related variety is a significant dimension of classroom management" (p. 43). Variety in activity, content, level of thinking, props, and group configuration is most inmportant for children

Variety in activity, content, level of thinking, and group configuration is most important for children in the lower elementary grades.

in the lower elementary grades. For older elementary students, feelings of accomplishment can do much to reduce boredom and satiation (Kounin, 1970).

One study of 58 elementary classrooms (Stodolsky, Ferguson, and Wimpelberg, 1981) found 17 different types of classroom activities including:

| | |
|---|---|
| Seatwork | Recitation |
| Individualized seatwork | Lecture |
| Diverse seatwork | Discussion |
| Demonstration | Checking work |
| Tests | Group Work |
| Films and other audiovisual aids | Contests |
| Student reports | Tutoring |
| Preparation | Other activities |

Effective teachers allow students to play an important role in determing what, when, and how they study. This shared responsibility gives students a needed sense of control. Involving students in determining what they are to learn increases motivation; if students want to find the answer, they will be motivated to investigate a question.

Of course, given the demands to cover a certain amount of curriculum, student initiative in contemporary classrooms must be limited to some extent. But such mandated material can be made meaningful for students and this will facilitate learning and later recall. Meaning can be established by building a bridge between content and the learner's background (Hunter, 1982). When teaching about money, for example, the teacher can relate it to shopping for groceries or toys.

While many classroom activities often take place in a large group format, variations in group size and configuration as well in the activities that take place in each variation can provide a selection of alternatives for the students. Teachers can introduce variety by having students work at learning centres, in science labs, or other classrooms, such as the music or art rooms or the gymnasium. It is common knowledge that a field trip outside the school can be a highly motivating and refreshing change of pace.

The teacher's enthusiasm is important in stimulating the students' enthusiasm. It is manifested by movements, gestures, variations in voice, eye contact, and overall energy level. The ability to move a class along at a good pace is affected by the teacher's movement in the classroom (Apter and Conoley, 1984). In other words, the physical presence, stance, and movement of the teacher is a component of the learning process (Winzer, 1989).

For example, teachers who always stand or sit behind a desk may be sending a message about the barrier or distance between them and the class. Since much learning depends on the emotional bond between teachers and students, the very act of distancing may produce negative effects on learning. Even generally active teachers may avoid one part of the room because of discomfort with a particular student. Ultimately this is self-defeating because it serves to decrease the teacher's influence on the student (Apter and Conoley, 1984.)

## Seatwork

Instruction does not always mean that the teacher talks and the students listen. Rather, students will often be engaged in independent and cooperative work. This is not, however, an opportunity for the teacher to catch up on marking or grab a cup of coffee. Instead, teachers need to supervise student work; research has shown that as teacher supervision increases, students' engaged time also increases (Emmer and Evertson, 1981), and there exists a positive relationship between this attention to task and achievement (Bloom, 1976; Rosenshine, 1978). Supervised students are off-task only about five percent of the time, while students working alone and pacing themselves (without supervision) are off-task about 15 percent of the time (Rosenshine, 1979).

Of course, the teacher cannot always be everywhere and students will sometimes have to work with relative independence. Since it is important for students to learn how to manage their own behaviour, effective teachers will always devise systems that allow students to manage their own work (Emmer et al., 1984; Evertson et al., 1984). This can be facilitated by careful design of instruction materials as well as effective introduction of the task. Students should always be clear about what they are to do. Student involvement will be greater if cues are provided on how to complete the task, as well as the necessary materials to do so (Kounin and Gump, 1974; Kounin and Doyle, 1975). Written prompts can be employed to help remind students; for example, a sample book report could be posted in the classroom to help students complete their work without having to consult the teacher repeatedly.

Before students start on independent work, it is important to determine that all understand the task at hand. Teachers often check for understanding through ineffective means: they ask "Does anyone have a question?" or wait for students to come forward on their own. But many students will not ask for help and will struggle on without constructive results. After every student has started the

**Ripple effect:**
the way the teacher's method of handling the misbehaviour of one child influences other children in the classroom who are not the targets of the teacher's action.

**Desist:**
any teacher action intended to stop misbehaviour.

work properly, progress should be checked periodically and reinforcement and corrective feedback provided. Unless this is done, some students will struggle. Others will merrily complete their work incorrectly unless the teacher intervenes swiftly; some may simply decide to "take a break" and won't do any work at all.

The teacher should also plan for frequent academic feedback and evaluation. Reinforcement for completed work is not likely to be effective when received long after the work has been completed. This is particulary important for younger elementary students who should receive feedback as soon as possible. Teachers can speed up the process of evaluation as well as reduce the marking load by arranging for peer tutors, using answer keys, and employing other strategies that allow for immediate feedback. Student help may be enlisted to record grades, maintain work folders, and so on, which not only reduces teacher workload, but has also been shown to be highly reinforcing for many students. Older students tend to be assigned projects that will be weeks or even months in the works. It is generally a good idea to break the projects up into logical units so that students are submitting part of their work more frequently, thereby giving the teacher the opportunity to provide feedback.

## TEACHER BEHAVIOURS DURING INSTRUCTION

Jacob Kounin kindled interest in the significance of classroom management with his *Discipline and group management in the classroom* (1970). Kounin's work began accidently. In one of his university classes, he reprimanded a student for reading a newspaper during his lecture and noticed that the behaviour of the other students immediately changed. Their side glances to each other stopped, they stopped whispering, and their eyes went from the instructor to their notebooks or their desks. Silence reigned in the classroom. Kounin found this response quite pzuzling: why had the students reacted in this way? They had not been reading newspapers and were not the target of the reprimand. Why were they affected by an instructor's action that was not directed toward them (Kounin, 1970)?

### Ripple effect

Kounin's interest in classroom management led to a series of observational and experimental studies of student reactions to techniques of teacher control at the university, kindergarten, and high school levels. Kounin focused on the **ripple effect**, how the teacher's method of handling the misbehaviour of one child influences other children in the classroom who are not the targets of the teacher's action. Kounin used the term **desist** to refer to anything a teacher did to stop misbehaviour; thus, he was examining the effects of desists on the other members (nontargets) of the classroom.

In the kindergarten study, Kounin found that the quality of characteristics of the desist influenced the student's conforming behaviour. These included:

1. *Clarity*—a simple "stop that" lacks clarity while a clear desist includes information about the misbehaviour—e.g., "Billy, stop pushing"; "Sally, turn around and look at the group"; or "We ask for things in this room. Don't

Withitness:
a teacher's ability to communicate to students that he or
she knows what is going on
in the classroom.

grab." Clear desists were more effective in producing conformity among other children.

2. *Firmness*—holding eye contact until the student stops the misbehaviour, walking towards the student, using a firm tone of voice, or touching or guiding the student toward appropriate behaviour communictes "I mean it—now!" Firmness also influenced the ripple effect, although clarity had a greater impact.

3. *Roughness*—expressions anger or exasperation, such as angry looks or threatened or actual punishment; and physical pressure beyond firmness do not have a greater effect on children's misbehaviour or conforming behaviour than firmness or calirty. A student who observed a rough desist was no more likely to conform more or misbehave less than when witnessing a desist without roughness.

The time spent in the setting was also related to the ripple effect. For example, on the first day of kindergarten, children witnessing a desist were less likely to misbehave and more likely to conform or become upset. However, this effect diminished over time.

As we observed earlier, the ages of the students influence the type of behaviour control that is appropraite as well as the students' responses to the disciplinary method. In his study of high school students, Kounin found that the type of desist chosen had no effect on the degree to which students conformed. However, very angry desists (roughness) were likely to make students feel emotional discomfort. The presence of punishment in the classroom increased student on-task behaviour only in classes where the students had a high motivation to learn the subject; when motivation was low, punishment did not influence behaviour. Similarly, teacher firmness incresed the students' inclination to behave appropriately only when they had a high motivation to learn the subject. When students liked the teacher and had a high motivation to learn (these varibles were highly correlated), they were more likely to be involved in their work and less likely to misbehave. Overall, it appears that the ripple effect is most pronounced in the earlier grades, and desists have less effect on students in the upper grades.

## Withitness

Kounin continued his research on disciplinary techniques by videotaping over 80 classrooms and analyzing the teacher behaviours that seem to promote student involvement and reduce the amount of misbehaviour. One factor that he identified was withitness, a teacher's ability to communicate to students that the teacher knows what is going on in the classroom. Actually, withitness should be viewed as a combination of two teaching skills—close monitoring of the class and prompt handling of inappropriate behaviour (Emmer, 1987). "Withit" teachers know what is happening at all times and usually have fewer disciplinary problems than teachers who appear to be unaware of incipient disruptions. An expert in classroom management will nip trouble in the bud by commenting on a potentially disruptive behaviour before it gains momentum (Beihler and Snowman, 1990).

**Overlapping:**
the ability to handle two or more class activities simultaneously.

In Kounin's study, teachers who targeted the wrong student (such as asking the wrong student to stop a behaviour) or who timed their requests incorrectly were given low scores on withitness. Imagine, for example, the following scenario. Luc and Anna were chatting when they were supposed to be doing their seatwork. John joins in, then Marielle giggles and says something to Luc. Danielle and Sally begin to whisper and, as the situation escalates, the teacher finally speaks out: "Sally and Danielle, stop that talking right now!" In this example, the teacher has not only targeted the wrong students, but she has left her warning too late (poor timing). The students are sent the message that the teacher is not aware of what is happening in the classroom. In contrast, a teacher high in withitness would intervene quickly, targeting Luc and Anna early on and thus stopping the behaviour before it is picked up by the other students.

Mistakes in targeting may also include addressing a minor problem rather than focusing on a serious one. For example, if Luc is chatting in the corner while Danielle is dismantling the science lab in the other, the teacher who focuses on Luc and ignores Danielle is targeting the wrong (or less serious) offence.

Timing mistakes mean being late in asking students to desist from a behaviour, thus allowing a problem to spread or become more serious. It is much better to intervene when students are quarreling about the use of materials rather than waiting until they are beating up on each other. Kounin found that if students perceive that teachers are "withit," they are less likely to misbehave, especially in teacher-directed lessons. Targeting the correct student on time was more important to classroom control than the firmness or clarity of the desist.

Effective classroom managers do not appear to treat inappropriate behaviours any differently from ineffective managers—they just do it sooner (Emmer, Evertson, and Anderson, 1980). Teachers who are "withit" will be alert to early signs that a student is straying from the behavioural expectations of the class, will promptly stop the misbehaviour, and will redirect the student to a more appropriate activity. Thus, the teacher should scan the class repeatedly to see what students are up to, keep track of individual progress, and be sure that students are engaged in approprite learning activities.

## Overlapping

Another important teacher behaviour noted in Kounin's videotape studies was **overlapping**, or the ability to handle two or more class activities simultaneously. This includes the ability to deal with misbehaviour without stopping or significantly interfering with an ongoing lesson. For example, consider the teacher who is working with one reading group when she notices that Luc and Danielle are squabbling in another group. To stop the reading group—"Stop here, and wait until I get back"—in order to go over to the squabbling pair is an example of nonoverlapping. Can you imagine what the reading group might do while the teacher is over coping with the squabblers? A more appropriate alternative would be for the teacher to ask one student to continue reading while she deals with the situation.

Similarly, the teacher is often required to conduct more than one instructional activity simultaneously. Again, in the reading group, the teacher may be interrupted by another student asking for assistance with a vocabulary word. The

**Group focus:**
the ability to keep as many students as possible involved in appropriate class activities.

**Group format:**
the steps that the teacher takes to ensure that all students are involved in the activity so that maximum participation is encouraged.

**Accountability:**
the responsibility each student in the group has for learning the concepts taught in the lesson.

overlapping teacher deals with the individual student—"Marcy, continue reading"—while he quietly helps the individual. Overlapping thus helps prevent misbehaviour or interruptions from interfering with ongoing activities.

Not surprisingly, Kounin found that teachers who were able to overlap activities tended to be aware of what was going on in all areas of their classrooms—were withit—and that both were related to successful classroom management. For example, he obtained scores for deviancy rates and task involvement in 49 first- and second-grade classrooms. Teachers high in overlapping and withitness produced higher task involvement and lower deviancy rates in recitation and seatwork activities. It is possible to keep many groups of students working simultaneously because they perceive the teacher as being aware of what they are doing.

## Group focus

When teachers are working with their students, they must be able to keep the entire class on-task. **Group focus** is the ability to keep as many students as possible involved in appropriate class activities, avoiding a focus on one or two students. Kounin found that the ability to maintin a concerted group focus is essential to a productive, efficient classroom environment. Teachers can help maintain group focus by taking into account the group format, the degree of accountability demanded of each student and by effectively focusing the group's attention.

**Group format** refers to the seating of students so that maximum participation is encouraged. The size of the group is not important; rather, Kounin focuses on the steps that the teacher takes to ensure that all students are involved in the activity. For example, the teacher may ask the group to respond in unison or one student to do a problem on the board while the other students complete the same problem at their desks. Having everyone involved eliminates the need for students to wait while one of their peers performs.

**Accountability** means that each student in the group is responsible for learning the concepts taught in the lesson. Teachers can enhance accountability by being aware of how each student is progressing in his or her academic work. In addition, teachers must communicate that they are aware of what the students are doing. One of the most common methods to obtain information about student learning is having them produce or demonstrate their knowledge.

Group accountability is similar to overlapping, in that the teacher is dealing with the entire group, yet asking individual students to be accountable for their learning. Kounin (1970) recommends several techniques for holding all members of a group accountable:

1. All students hold up their worksheets or other products so that the results can be readily seen by the teacher.

2. All students recite in unison.

3. When one student is performing, such as solving an equation on the board, the other students can be asked to watch the student and report what is done right or wrong.

4. After asking a question, the teacher asks all students to write down the answer, and then randomly asks one or more to respond.

5. When one child is performing, the teacher can circulate and check the work of nonparticipants.

6. The teacher requires a child to demonstrate and checks his/her performance.

**Group alerting** refers to the degree to which teachers maintain students' attention to task at all times, even when an individual or small group is performing. Kounin found that some well-meaning teachers had fallen into a pattern of calling on students in a predictable order and in such a way that the rest of the class served as a passive audience. As a means to maintaining group focus, Kounin advocates:

1. Creating suspense, by pausing, looking around the class, and saying, "Let's see, how can..." before calling on an individual to perform.

2. Avoiding a predictable pattern by picking participants randomly so that no child knows when he or she will be called upon to perform. Alternatively, the teacher can ask for a show of hands before selecting a student.

3. Interspersing individual performances with unison responses.

4. Alerting nonresponders that they might be called on in connection with what the reciter is doing: they might be asked to correct an error, or be asked questions about what the student has said. "Listen to what Phong is reading, and see if you can figure out who stole the basket."

5. Using novel or alluring materials during the lesson to gain the students' attention.

While each of these strategies can bring student attention to bear on a task, Kounin also warns that the following errors are common:

1. The teacher becomes completely immersed in the performance of an individual student, ignoring the group, or directs a new question and subsequent attention only toward one student.

2. The teacher prepicks a responder before asking the question. For example, the teacher says, "Stephanie, please tell me who stole the basket," rather than saying "Everyone, remember who stole the basket. (pause) Stephanie?" In the former case, all members of the group can relax and stop listening, because they know that they will not be called on. In the latter case, all students think about the answer and then Stephanie is given the chance to answer.

3. The teacher calls upon the students to respond in a predictable fashion, by going up and down rows or in a clockwise fashion. Students only need to pay attention when their turn grows near.

Readers should note that some research has disputed the importance of these latter two points: in some cases, student achievement is higher when they are called upon in a predictable sequence. For example, Evertson and Weade (1989) found that effective teachers established consistent routines for distributing

**Fragmentations:**
the unnecessary breaking up of any activity into subparts when the activity should be performed as a single unit.

turns, and expected students to participate when called on. In contrast, less effective teachers were inconsistent and students called out without being designated as the next speaker.

Of the three factors, group format, accountability, and group alerting, the last variable seems to be related most highly to effective classroom management. When group alerting is used, students are more involved in their work and are less likely to engage in misbehaviour. Accountability is also important: indeed, it appears that teachers who engage in behaviours that relate to group alerting are also more likely to maintain accountability. Both indicate that the teacher is maintaining a focus on the group, and is not becoming immersed in individuals to the point of neglecting other students.

## Momentum

During the school day, teachers and students engage in many different activities. According to Doyle (1985), Burns (1984), and Gump (1982), teachers oversee some 31 major transitions every day, spending about 15 percent of the class day in transitions. As well as between-lesson transitions, this also includes housekeeping tasks such as handing papers or sharpening pencils. Some transitions require students to physically move; for example, from their desks to the learning centres. Other changes are psychological, or involve some change of props, as when students switch from social studies to mathematics. These transitions can be minor, as between speaking turns, or major, as when changing activities, lessons, or classes (Kounin, 1970).

Regardless of the type of transition, the manner in which it is made is critical. It can be awkward and time-wasting, setting the stage for inattention, disruptive behaviour or other inappropriate responses—or it can be smooth and efficient. For every moment spent in inefficient transitions, learning time is lost.

Kounin (1970) refers to momentum as the ability to keep the class moving smoothly within and between lessons. Teachers who maintain instructional momentum have fewer disruptions than teachers who allow the momentum to drag or die, as in a clumsy transition to a new activity (Kounin, 1970). There are a number of ways in which teachers impede or destroy momentum. Momentum can be inhibited by slowdowns, which are behaviours initiated by the teacher which decrease the rate of movement or progress of ongoing class activities. Two different types of slowdowns were identified: fragmentations and overdwelling.

**Fragmentations**  A teacher can fragment directions or activities and thereby try the patience of students. **Fragmentations** involve the unnecessary breaking up of any activity into subparts—or jerky steps—when the activity should be performed as a single unit. Group fragmentation occurs when students do something singly and separately instead of as a unit and at one time, meaning that some children have to wait, slowing down the activity. For example, if after social studies the teacher wants to send a group of students to a reading centre, he or she might first send Mary, then Jane, them Tom, and so on, rather than having them move as a group. Even though the goal was to have all the students move to the reading centre, by breaking the target into three (or more) separate targets, the teacher required some students to wait, and slowed the transition from social studies to reading.

**Overdwelling:**
staying on an issue much longer than necessary for the children to understand.

**Smoothness:**
the absence of teacher behaviours that disrupt transitions between activities or break up the continuity of an ongoing lesson.

**Flip-flops:**
occur at transitions when the teacher terminates one activity, begins a second activity, but then goes back to the first activity.

**Dangles:**
occur when a teacher starts the students on one activity and then suddenly reacts to a different matter, leaving the class in mid-air.

Prop fragmentation involves breaking up into unecessary subparts a meaningful unit of behaviour that could be performed as a single uninterrupted sequence. That is, rather than having students put away their art materials, take out their mathematics books and turn to page 24, the teacher might say: "All right, everyone close your art folders. (pause) Put away your crayons. (pause) Put your mathematics scribblers on your desk. (pause) Now, put your mathematics textbooks on your desk. Keep everything off your desk except your mathematics work. (pause) Open your textbooks to page 24. (pause) Let's all sit up straight. (pause) Now, lets get to work."

**Overdwelling**    A teacher can disrupt an ongoing activity by overdwelling, or staying on an issue far beyond that necessary for the children to understand. This is likely to elicit a response from students like, "All right, all right, that's enough already!" (Kounin, 1970, p. 102). The teacher can nag, preach, or otherwise overdwell on student behaviour. For example, Kounin cites the teacher who looked at one sutdent and said, "Richard, stop that talking." But rather than leaving it at that, she changed her focus to the entire class, and says, "Some of you are cooperating and some of you aren't. Mary is cooperating and doing her work and so is Jimmy. Mabel is not listening. Now you all know this is not a playground. This is a classroom and we're supposed to be learning. Good citizens don't bother other children who are trying to learn, do they? So let's all cooperate and be good citizens and not disturb other children. You know its hard to learn when there's a lot of noise." (Kounin, 1970, p. 102-103). Because the students already knew what the teacher was saying, and because the speech interrupted ongoing class activities, the teacher was not clarifying issues for the students but was simply nagging. Similarly, the teacher can overdwell on a task by overemphasizing explanations or directions unnecessarily.

**Smoothness**    Related to the concept of momentum is the idea of smoothness, or the ability of teachers to facilitate transitions between activities or enhance the continuity of an ongoing lesson. These can be short, momentary jerks or relatively long episodes. Of course, smoothness and momentum can be interrupted by many uncontrollable factors, such as announcements over the P.A. system, a sick student, fire-engines screaming by, and so on. While these are not under the control of the teacher, the smoothness of lessons can be otherwise enhanced by avoiding the behaviours or activities identified by Kounin as flip-flops, dangles, truncations, stimulus-boundedness, and thrusts.

Flip-flops occur at transitions as the teacher terminates one activity, (mathematics class) and then begins a second activity (social studies). However, rather than continuing with social studies, the teacher flops back to the first activity, by asking, for example, "How many of you finished your math worksheets?"

Dangles occur when the teacher starts the students on one activity and then suddenly reacts to a different matter entirely, leaving the class in mid-air, or dangling. For example, the teacher might ask Sally to come to the front of the room to solve an equation on the board, and then suddenly ask, "Where is Tom? Is he ill? Does anyone know where he is?" Sally and the rest of the class are left dangling. Dangles can also occur at transition points—for example, as the students finish their work at a learning centre, the teacher gets up, walks towards the blackboard and says, "Let's now look at this arithmetic problem." But

**Truncation:**
a long-lasting dangle in which the teacher does not resume the initiated, then dropped, activity.

**Stimulus-boundedness:**
situation in which teachers are unable to maintain focus on the goal of the activity, reacting to irrelevant events that grab their attention.

**Thrusts:**
a teacher's sudden interruption of a student's activity with an order, statement or question without any awareness or sensitivity to the student's readiness to receive the message.

halfway to the blackboard, the teacher detours to his desk, and spends some time looking at his day book. After a few seconds at his desk, he returns to the problem on the blackboard. A truncation is similar to a dangle, except that the teacher does not resume the initiated then dropped activity. This can be considered a long-lasting dangle.

**Stimulus-boundedness** refers to teachers who cannot resist reacting to any unimportant or irrelevant event that grabs their attention and are unable to maintain focus on the goal of the activity. Kounin (1970) gives an example of a teacher conducting a recitation activity with a group of students. As she walks towards a reciting student, she notices the class fishbowl. "Heavens, I forgot to feed the fish!" Running to get the fish food, she feeds the fish, commenting "My, poor thing, look how hungry it is." She then turns to a nearby student, "Margaret, you forgot to feed the fish. Look how hungry it is!"

**Thrusts** consist of a teacher's sudden interruption of a student's activity with an order, statement, or question without any awareness of or sensitivity to the student's readiness to receive the message. Kounin (1970) draws an analogy between the teacher who thrusts and the person who "butts-into" an ongoing conversation without waiting to be noticed or attempting to find out what is being discussed. In the classroom, thrusts can occur at transition points; for example, when working with one reading group, the teacher might suddenly just close her book, and without pausing or looking up, ask another group to come to the table. They can also occur during an ongoing activity, as illustrated in the following example: the children in a reading group are discussing shopping experiences, when the teacher turns abruptly to the board, ignoring students who still wish to participate in the discussion, saying, "These are the new vocabulary words. Harry, please read the first one." The teacher's behaviour may be seen as a thrust since the timing was not keyed to the students' readiness but only to the teacher's desired goal.

Obviously, smoothness and momentum are significant contributors to successful classroom managment. Both are more successful in preventing deviant behaviour than specific techniques to deal with deviant behaviour, and both have the added advantage of promoting work involvement (Kounin, 1970). However, it is more important to maintain momentum by avoiding actions that slow down activities than it is to maintain smoothness by avoiding sudden stops and starts.

## CLASSROOM DISCIPLINE

*Discipline* is not to be confused with punishment. It is a form of behaviour management, or a type of habit training. It is a process whereby certain relationships are established and encompass those methods used to maintain an environment conducive for learning and for managing students' behaviour (Cartwright, Cartwright, and Ward, 1984).

Discipline must be taught, learned, and internalized. The goal is to help students to become better able to manage themselves. Many factors contribute to effective discipline, one being consistency. Students need consistency: they need to know what to expect of the teacher, what is expected of them, and what to expect when they succeed or fail. Most authorities agree that whatever system of classroom management teachers use, it can be successful only if they implement it in a systematic and consistent fashion (Winzer, 1989).

Most discussions of school discipline consist of what to do after an event that calls for some intervention. Although it is likely that, whatever they do, teachers will encounter instances of negative behaviour in the classroom, this should not become a preoccupation. Not only is the time spent disciplining students negatively related to student achievement (Evertson, Emmer, and Brophy, 1980; Crocker and Brooker, 1986), but aversive techniques disrupt the classroom climate and cause stress for teachers and students.

Preventative discipline is an integral component of classroom discipline. The challenge is to convert the vast and exhausting task of mopping up after incidents to forward-looking strategies that are far more productive for both pupils and teachers. Preventative discipline consists of techniques designed to prevent poor behaviour from happening by organizing the classroom, setting up consistent rules and routines, and providing approprite rewards for correct behaviour. The teaching behaviours prescribed by Kounin contribute to preventative discipline. In addition, we shall discuss how classroom meetings, classroom rules, and positive reinforcement, are all extremely useful for the day-to-day management of the classroom.

## Rewarding appropriate behaviours

Students must be taught to demonstrate appropriate social and academic behaviours in the classroom, and this is best accomplished when the teacher consistently provides reinforcement for appropriate behaviour. Again and again in this text, we have stressed the importance of teachers making sure that students are reinforced for appropriate social and academic behaviours. Teachers must direct as much attention to appropriate responses as they do to disruptive and other undesired behaviours, for lack of reinforcement is likely to extinguish the behaviour. Many mild problems can be averted if teachers ensure that appropriate behaviours do not disappear because of lack of teacher attention or approval.

Teachers should also remember that reinforcement is not only useful in strengthening desired responses; it can also be used to diminish undesired behaviours as well. This is known as differential reinforcement, which involves the systematic scheduling of reinforcement in order to produce a desired response. Reinforcement can be used to strengthen an alternative response which would prevent the student from demonstrating the undesired behaviour (see Chapter 11).

Other forms of differential reinforcement can be used in other circumstances. Consider the situation in which a student demonstrates an appropriate behaviour but performs it at such a high rate that it is unacceptable. For example, participating in a class discussion is a desirable behaviour, but monopolizing the discussion to the exclusion of all others is not (Alberto and Troutman, 1986). Differential reinforcement of low rates of behaviour (DRL) is the application of reinforcement in order to decrease the rate of a behaviour. It is most commonly used by reinforcing the student if the number of times he or she perorms the behaviour does not exceed a designated limit (Dietz and Repp,1973). In the case of the student who monopolizes class discussions, the teacher might decide that it is appropriate for the child to volunteer a response no more than three times during a 30-minute discussion. After informing the student of the limit and the reinforcer to be given, the program is started. The teacher or student will take responsibility for monitoring the behaviour and reinforcement given whenever the target is achieved.

Differential reinforcement of other behaviours (DRO) is accomplished by reinforcing any behaviour other than the one targeted for reduction that occurs during a specified period of time in order to decrease the undesired behaviour. Consider the child who frequently speaks without raising his hand. The teacher would break the class into smaller time intervals and reinforce the student for sitting quietly in his desk without calling out during these intervals. Of course, if another inappropriate behaviour occurs during the time interval (such as spitting on the floor) reinforcement will not be delivered.

## Class meetings

A method for facilitating good communication between students and teachers has been suggested by Glasser (1969). He believes that when children feel connected with what is going on in the classroom, they are more likely to engage in appropriate behaviour and develop feelings of importance and self-worth. One method to make children feel involved is to conduct regular classroom meetings in which "the teacher leads the whole class in a nonjudgmental discussion about what is important and relevant to them" (Glasser, 1969, p. 121). As a result of such meetings, they are more likely to become involved with their peers, teacher, and school. They also gain a sense of self-confidence as they prove to themselves that they can express their ideas and opinions in front of others.

There are three different types of meetings, each of which serves a different purpose.

1. *The social problem-solving meeting* is intended to help students solve individual and group problems that arise when people live and work together in a classroom and school.

2. *The open-ended meeting* is concerned with helping students discuss questions related to their own lives or to the classroom curriculum.

3. *The educational-diagnostic meeting* is designed to help the teacher evaluate the effectiveness of his or her teaching and/or the students' understanding of the curriculum.

Meetings are always conducted with teachers and students seated in a circle, and may last ten to 30 minutes for primary children and longer for older students. It is important that meetings be conducted regularly—every day, or at a minimum, every other day. When the teacher is first starting to use class meetings, Glasser (1969) recommends beginning with the open-ended meting as these are the easiest to conduct and participate in, thus helping the students understand what is expected of them.

To begin, the teacher identifies a problem or topic or asks the students to identify a topic of interest to them. Students must be aware that there are no right or wrong answers and they should feel free to express their opinions and feelings. This can only be accomplished in a nonthreatening environment in which the teacher is nonjudgmental about the students' contributions. The role of the teacher is simply to guide the discussion, keeping everyone on topic and encouraging all to participate.

Any topic that is of importance to the students is an appropriate topic for discussion—but the goal must always be to solve the problem in a constructive fashion. Blaming must never enter into the discussion, nor should students be allowed to dwell on past history. It is what is happening now in the classroom that is important. To facilitate understanding between participants, the teacher may wish to paraphrase or restate the student's comments—this also makes the students feel that they are being listened to. While some issues may be satisfactorily resolved in a single meeting, others will take much longer to resolve. In addition, it may be necessary to rediscuss an issue if the solution fails to work.

## INTERVENTION FOR MISBEHAVIOUR

Teachers are expected to manage most of the behavioural problems that arise in their classrooms. And most do. An interested teacher with a flexible curriculum, organized plans, and a realistic marking system is well-equipped to provide the structure, motivation, and control essential to learning.

Even the best classroom managers will sometimes encounter defiant, disruptive, or other inappropriate behaviours in their classrooms. Not all problem behaviour will be eliminated; there is no way to program out all social misadventures in growing youngsters. There will be times that crises will arise even when a good preventative program is planned.

No behaviour occurs in a vacuum, and children misbehave for many reasons. They may have problems with self-esteem and then feel inadequate or insignificant. If children are unable to reach their goals through appropriate behaviour, they seek out other less acceptable means. Acting out brings attention from teachers and peers and enhances a child's feeling of sigificance. Sometimes academic inadequacies may be masked by poor behaviour. Visibly deficient skills in math, reading, and the content areas may be covered up by students who present themselves inappropriately, who skip classes, and who just avoid developing responsibility toward classroom interactions and tasks. Hence, laziness, arrogance, and refusal to accept responsibility may be hiding poor academic, communication, social, or adaptive skills.

There are few behaviours that affect only the individual student, only the teacher, or only others in the environment. If children are misbehaving they are probably engaging in off-task behaviour. Hence, as well as disrupting the classroom to some extent, they are not learning effectively. Indeed, behaviour problems are clearly associated with lower achievement and ability (Oliver, 1974).

One important factor in dealing successfully with these situations is being prepared: teachers must have clear ideas about what they will do when misbehaviour occurs. In a classroom in which rules and behavioural expectations have been clearly established, students should have a clear understanding of the consequences of their behaviour. Consequences should never be capriciously applied: the student should always be aware of what will happen.

Spettel (1983) has argued that no punishment, or the threat of punishment, will be effective in classrooms unless students know that it will be carried out consistently. In some cases misbehaviour will be minor and will not significantly interfere with classroom functioning. When such minor misbehaviours are promptly handled, there is less chance that they will spread to other students and/or become much more serious. It is always easier to deal with minor problems that involve only a few students than it is to deal with an entire class, or large group of students who have gone out of control. However, despite the teacher's best efforts, some misbehaviours will be more serious and will significantly interfere with the class operation and/or the individual student's learning.

All infractions will not be treated equally. Instead, the teacher should always differentiate between major and minor infractions, and deal with them accordingly. Brophy (1987) points out that although the teacher must maintain authority, his or her teaching style is crucial. Any poor behaviour should be handled calmly and objectively. Research indicates that angry and punitive expressions of disapproval tend to provoke students to respond with further disruptions (Kounin, 1970).

## Minor behaviour problems

In Mr. Hunt's classroom, like any other, minor behaviour infractions are common. During the course of one morning, for example, he notices that Jerry is not attending to his lecture, that Monique is passing notes, and that Donald, rather than contributing to the learning at his cooperative group table, is flirting with the girl sitting next to him.

Mr. Hunt, as classroom manager, fulfills half of his responsibility; that is, through the careful monitoring of his students' performances, he notices that Donald, Monique, and Jerry starting to stray off-task. But the intervention is not as easy. Certainly Mr. Hunt should not respond in the same way to all instances of misbehaviour; as Emmer (1987) points out, overreacting is as bad as underreacting. He may simply make eye contact with Jerry to let the student know he is aware of his behaviour and prompt greater attention. Proximity control, or moving closer to Monique may stimulate her to work, and moving Donald to another seat will separate him from the distracting element.

Behaviours that are likely to interfere with other students' work, those that disrupt class activities, those that involve straying from correct procedures or rules, or those that become aggressive (even if they are playful at first), must be dealt with promptly as they are likely to become more intense or spread to other students. However, minor violations that can be safely ignored include those behaviours that do not interfere with class operations or other students, those that are very short in duration, or those that appear to be inadvertent—for example, the student who gets so excited during a class discussion that he shouts out an answer is likely to correct himself and not repeat the action.

Emmer (1987) recommended that misbehaviour should be dealt with unobtrusively—without interrupting an ongoing lesson, disrupting other students or calling unnecessary attention to the misbehaviour. When requesting students to desist from an activity, such as inattention or talking out of turn, the teacher should be as low-key and matter-of-fact as possible without unnecessarily slowing down the ongoing lesson.

Various strategies have been suggested to help teachers deal with minor disruptions:

1. Make eye contact with the student and hold it until the misbehaviour stops (the infamous "teacher stare").

2. Move closer to the student.

3. Use a nonverbal signal, such as placing a finger over the lips, to quiet down a student.

4. State the student's name, along with an assertive request to stop the misbehaviour.

In addition, the teacher will often want to redirect a student from an inappropriate to a more desired activity. In other words, the teacher does not simply tell the students what not to do; he or she indicates what they should be doing instead. This can take many forms, such as telling the students what they should be doing, asking the students if they know what they should be doing at time, or asking the students to state the rule or procedure that they are violating.

When a large group or the entire class seems to be heading toward misbehaviour, they can be redirected by an instruction that requires them to engage in an appropriate behaviour (replacing the inappropriate response) or that supplies a model for appropriate behaviour. Emmer (1987) recommends that the teacher use a variety of statements such as the following, rather than overusing any one:

- Let me see everyone's eyes please.

- Everyone look at the chart on page 24.

- Please write the material on the overhead in your notebooks.

- Everyone look at the chalkboard. What is the next step?

- I see two tables where the students have done a good job of cleaning up.

- Most of you are doing a good job of listening.

- I count ten people who are quiet and have their workbooks out... Now I see five more... Good.

- Let's wait until everyone is listening.

- I like the way that most of you are listening and working together quietly.

## Ignoring behaviour

Not every instance of misbehaviour needs an involved response. Many simple techniques exist that may be employed without even stopping the lesson or activity: planned ignoring, signal interference, proximity control, restructuring the activity, and direct appeals (Winzer, 1989). Signal interferences include such non-verbal cues as making eye-contact, raising an eyebrow, and so on. Proximity control simply involves standing near a student to help him or her maintain or regain composure. Both of these methods act as effective checks on minor disturbances. An alternative method of intervention is to restructure the activity. Teachers should be flexible enough to vary the lesson in response to the tone of the class. Finally, the teacher may also make a direct appeal to students to behave appropriately, invoking class rules, peer reactions, or personal relationships. Just mentioning to some students "Your behaviour today makes me feel uncomfortable (unhappy, angry, disappointed)" can induce more appropriate behaviour (Winzer, 1989).

If minor behavioural problems are really only a bid for attention then they are best ignored. This advice is based on behavioural principles (Skinner, 1953), and assumes that the withdrawal of reinforcement (teacher attention) will result in the cessation of the behaviour.

However, it is not quite as simple as that. First, the teacher must remember that if his or her attention is actually maintaining the student's inappropriate behaviour, withholding attention will cause the behaviour to get worse—often much worse—before it gets better. That is, the behaviour can be expected to increase in magnitude and frequency—a pattern of response referred to as the extinction burst—before any diminution in response rate is seen. In cases where the student's behaviour appears to be maintained by the peer approval or attention, classmates can often be encouraged to participate in the extinction program. For example, Patterson and colleagues (1965) implemented an extinction program by reinforcing peers to withhold attention when the target student was out-of-seat, talking, or hitting others. For extinction to be successful, all reinforces that maintain the behaviour must be entirely eliminated. If the teacher is unable to control all reinforcing contingencies, an alternative intervention should be used.

Before ignoring behaviour as a method of extinction, the teacher must first carefully assess the negative effects that will be derived initially from the implementation of the program. In other words, can the extinction burst be tolerated or will it create an untenable or even dangerous situation in the classroom? Since we can predict the extinction burst with a great deal of certainty, this method should never be used with behaviours that are dangerous, destructive, and/or very disruptive. The safety of the student and his or her peers, the security of the environment, and the effect of the behaviour on class operations must be considered.

This important decision cannot be delayed because it is equally unwise to give up on an extinction program once it has begun. The research suggests that when a behaviour is placed on extinction for some time and then reinforcement is reintroduced, the response will likely to be maintained at the new higher rate. However, if the teacher manages to stay with the program it will be found that, after the burst of the behaviour, a gradual decrease in the response level over time will be seen. The rate at which an undesired behaviour extinguishes can be hurried by simultaneously reinforcing alternative or incompatible behaviours. Not only does the pairing of extinction with a reinforcement program seem to

**Active listening:**

paraphrasing or summarizing what the speaker has said.

speed the rate at which undesired behaviour declines, but it gives the student an opportunity to experience alternative reinforcing events, instead of simply being ignored. Remember, the intention is to withhold attention from the behaviour, not to stop responding to the student entirely.

While it is certainly possible to implement an extinction program without directly informing a student, it has been found that behaviour will decrease more rapidly if the student is informed of the contingencies in operation. For example, the teacher might say, "Homer, I'm not going to pay attention to you unless you raise your hand first." Also, if the behaviour is to be extinguished, all reinforcers that might be maintaining the behaviour should be withheld. Behavioural psychologists have also developed some specific strategies that can be used in classroom settings when problems exist which have not been remediated through the use of positive rule-setting and the use of social reinforcers such as teacher attention and approval. These include such things as token economies, contingency contracts, and group contingencies that were fully discussed in Chapter 10.

## Communication with students

Communication is not a simple matter of sending a verbal message—the perceptions of the receiver are also important. Miscommunication of noncummunication is a dilemma that confronts students and teachers in the classroom.

To improve the quality of student-teacher communication, Thomas Gordon (1974) developed a method of interaction that is intended to enhance the student-teacher relationship through the development of better communication skills. Teacher Effectiveness Training (TET) provides a model for establishing open communication in the classroom, and to deal with conflict resolution in a way that is beneficial to both the student and the teacher.

First of all, Gordon recommends that teachers practise active listening. **Active listening** requires the teacher to paraphrase or summarize what the student has said. This helps students feel that they have been understood and encourages them to communicate more honestly and directly. Active listening helps students to express feelings, solve problems, and develop trust in the teacher (Gordon, 1974). Gordon provides the following examples of active listening:

> STUDENT: *Richard always cheats. I'm not going to play with him anymore.*
> TEACHER: *You hate the way Richard treats you so much that you're gong to quit playing with him.*
> STUDENT: *Yes, I'll play with Tommy and David instead.*
>
> STUDENT: *This school isn't as good as my last one. The kids there were friendly.*
> TEACHER: *You feel pretty left-out here.*
> STUDENT: *I sure do. (Gordon, 1974, p. 90).*

In each of these examples, the teacher has simply paraphrased what the student has said or reflected back the meaning of the student's message. This is done in a clear and objective fashion; the teacher does not pass judgment, interpret, or give advice. The student's feelings are focused upon, so that he or she feels the teacher understands what the student is experiencing.

**603**

Gordon's (1974) strategy of active listening has been demonstrated as a means of reducing classroom problems and minimizing the potential for conflict between students and teachers. According to Gordon, problem solving can only be accomplished once the issue of *ownership* has been addressed. Gordon believes that problems are either "owned" by the teacher or the student. When it is determined that the student owns the problem, the solution is to use active listening, and when the teacher owns the problem, "I-messages" or conflict resolution will be used.

Gordon describes the difference between student-owned and teacher-owned problems in terms of their effects. In other words, if the problem has a direct and undesirable effect on the teacher, it is the teacher's problem; if the problem has a direct and undesirable effect on the student, it is the student's problem. Some problems are more difficult to diagnose in that they are really shared problems that do not directly affect the teacher but have a general impact on the classroom operation (Brophy and Rohrkemper, 1981). For example, the student who is highly active might not directly affect the teacher and/or interfere with the fulfillment of the teacher's role but will still influence ongoing activities.

When students own the problem, a number of strategies can be employed (Gordon, 1974). The first may go against the grain, for teachers often feel that they must say or do something when a student comes to them with a problem. But Gordon recommends that the teacher simply listen to the student's problem. It is not necessary to say anything, since "Silence—'passive listening'—is a powerful nonverbal message that can make a student feel genuinely accepted and encourage him to share more and more with you" (1974, p. 61). While passively listening, Gordon also recommends that the teacher use acknowledgement responses, nonverbal and verbal cues that tell the student that the teacher is really listening and understands what the student is trying to say. Smiling, nodding, saying "Uh-huh," or "I see" are responses that we commonly use to tell listeners that we are attentive to what they are saying.

But what of the shy or withdrawn student, or the one who is simply reluctant to express a problem? Gordon suggests using door openers or reopeners which are messages that take the form of nonevaluative questions and statements that encourage students to talk more openly and honestly about their feelings and concerns. Phrases such as "Tell me more," or "That sounds like a serious problem, I'd like to hear more about it" can help to encourage students to communicate more fully.

When the problem belongs to the teacher, such as Sally's spitballs disrupting the class, Gordon (1974) endorses I-messages, those statements made by the teacher which clearly describe the student's behaviour, the effect it has on the teacher, and how it makes the teacher feel.

Gordon believes that I-messages are effective because they have a high probability of changing student behaviour, are only minimally negative, and therefore will not impair the student-teacher relationship. I-messages give students the responsibility to change their behaviour and motivate them to do so because they realize that they are creating a genuine problem for the teacher.

When the I-message is used, the student is less likely to respond negatively, either with anger or aggression, for the teacher has only described his or her own feelings. In contrast, you-messages, such as "You stop that right now Sally!"

or "Why don't you just grow up and stop that stupid behaviour?" are usually interpreted negatively by the students and have a negative effect on their self-esteem, making them feel inferior. Students fear that they carry a hidden message like "There's something wrong with you—or you wouldn't be causing this problem!" I-messages, because they are noncritical statements about the effects of the behaviour rather than any statement about the student herself, are more likely to cause the student to be motivated to be more considerate and helpful. The student is free to change voluntarily and often does so.

Not all problems can be solved by the use of an I-message or active listening. Situations often arise when teachers and students interfere with the fulfillment of each other's needs—both the own the problem. Gordon suggests a no-lose strategy in which both the teacher and student work cooperatively to find a solution to the problem. The sequence is as follows:

1. *Define the problem*—what exactly are the behaviours involved? What does each person want? The teacher will use I-messages and active listening to ensure that the feelings of both the teacher and student are brought forward.

2. *Generate possible solutions*—the teacher and student brainstorm ideas but do not evaluate them at this point.

3. *Evaluate the solutions*—any participant can veto a solution, and this brainstorming/evaluation continues until they decide which solution is best.

4. *Choose one solution by consensus*—at this point both parties should be satisfied with the solution.

5. *Determine how to implement the decision*—what materials will be needed? Who will be responsible for what? When is the solution to be implemented?

6. *Assess how well the solution solved the problem*—after trying the solution for a while, the teacher and student should meet again to be sure that each is satisfied with the solution. If necessary, changes will be made, again using the steps listed above.

## Punishment

Many people see punishment and discipline as synonymous, but this is not strictly true. Discipline should spring from internal controls, not from fear of punishment. Successful approaches to discipline respect the rights of individuals, enhance students' self-esteem, and encourage cooperation.

Punishment is defined as the contingent presentation of a consequence immediately after the occurrence of a behaviour which has the effect of decreasing the likelihood that the behaviour will occur again. Punishment has been widely used by parents and teachers to extinguish undesirable behaviours (Winzer, 1989). Punishing strategies are used frequently in schools to deal with inappropriate, annoying, or dangerous behaviours that interfere with students' learning or the operation of the classroom. It may be that the effect of the typical effect of punishment—the immediate cessation of the behaviour—negatively reinforces the teacher or parent's behaviour. Social learning theorists would also suggest that, because most adults have been punished in the past, they have learned that yelling, spanking, or assigning extra homework can be the appropriate methods of coping with undesired behaviours. Unfortunately, it has been noted that punishment is often used too frequently, and/or in an ineffective fashion. Winzer (1989) points out that punishment may produce undesirable side effects and can be a poor deterrent to unwanted behaviour for several reasons. First, the fear of punishment generates anger and may produce greater conflict. Often, too, students will associate the punishment with the punisher. Second, punishment does not answer two crucial questions: do students know that they are breaking the rules and are they interpreting social cues correctly? Third, punishment in the classroom may suppress the problem but reinforce other unwanted behaviours and even teach aggressive behaviour through modeling (Polsgrove and Reith, 1983). It neither indicates correct behaviour nor stops poor behaviour from returning.

Nevertheless, although the term has acquired many negative connotations, punishment is still used in classrooms. Teachers cannot tolerate all situations, and rewards will not work all the time. Punishment notifies the student that the behaviour or set of behaviours is unacceptable, usually by removing possible pleasant events (Winzer, 1989). Sometimes punishment is used to eliminate a behaviour more quickly. At other times, a student may be punished for a behaviour that is simply too disruptive or extreme to be ignored. Some children respond to punishment if they are accustomed to it at home and may react poorly when teachers use positive reinforcement alone (Gardner, 1974).

When using punishment, a few cautions should be kept in mind. First, ethical considerations would dictate that a teacher never use a more aversive strategy than necessary to deal with an inappropriate behaviour. It should also be recalled that in many cases, the research indicates that less aversive strategies have the potential to accomplish the teacher's goal—the reduction or elimination of undesired responses. The rare exceptions to this rule are those behaviours that are dangerous to the child or his or her peers or that are highly destructive to the environment. Such behaviours are not dealt with by use of techniques such as reinforcement of alternative behaviours or extinction which take a longer time to work. The child who routinely runs out of the playground onto the nearby freeway cannot be ignored in an attempt to withdraw reinforcement for his or her behaviour. Similarly, aggressive behaviour that has the potential to harm another child and destructive behaviour that may result in severe damage to the classroom or home environment typically call for interventions that have a more rapid effect.

Whenever punishment is used, it must be used consistently, indeed, the inconsistent application of punishment has been shown to have little or no effect on the behaviour it is intended to decrease (Kazdin, 1989). Because the use of aversive strategies can have many potential negative side-effects, they should not be entered into lightly. Careful consideration must be taken to develop an intervention plan that is both effective and respectful of the student's rights. Finally, the teacher must always keep the "fair-pair" rule in mind, teaching the child a more appropriate behaviour to replace the response that is being reduced.

Whenever punishment is used, teachers must be careful to administer it with an air of disappointment, rather than a sense of vengeance or righteous indignation

(Brophy, 1987). The teacher must send the message, "I don't want to punish you, but your behaviour makes it necessary." This attitude is important for it stresses the students' responsibility for their behaviour. If they had wished to, they could have behaved in a more disciplined and appropriate fashion; however, since they chose to act in this particular way, they will be punished.

As we observed earlier, it will be much easier for teachers to manage behaviour if they are prepared to deal with the inappropriate behaviours when they arise.

Decisions about punishment made "on the spot" are often overly harsh or punitive and the teacher is likely later to regret the action. Or it may be that the punishment is too mild and the behaviour will be unaffected. In either case, the teacher is left with an even bigger problem. Indeed, whenever teachers confront a very serious or dangerous behaviour in the classroom, they are strongly urged to seek consultative help from a psychologist or counselor who is proficient in the management of behaviour so that the correct program can be established.

There are many different methods which can be used to guide the teacher's use of punishment. As with reinforcement, any system of dealing with inappropriate behaviour must be communicated clearly to students, so that they know what the consequences of their behaviour will be, and any method must be consistently enforced.

### Assertive discipline

Lee and Marlene Canter have been the primary proponents of a system of classroom management called assertive discipline, an alternative system which has been developed to assist the teacher to use punishing contingencies appropriately and fairly. Assertive discipline (Canter and Canter, 1976) consists of an entire disciplinary package that can be used to reinforce appropriate and discourage negative behaviours in the classroom.

Many teachers often demonstrate nonassertive or hostile response patterns with their students, rather than being assertive. Canter and Canter (1976) believe that teachers must eliminate these first two patterns of interactions if they wish to be effective with their students. They must become assertive teachers, those who clearly and firmly communicate needs and requirements to students, follow these statements with firm and appropriate actions, and respond to students in ways that maximize compliance without violating the best interests of the students (Canter and Canter, 1976).

Teachers who take a passive or nonassertive approach to students have often given in to their students or feel that it is wrong to place strong demands on student behaviour. For example, consider the situation where Pamela and Rick are giggling, and otherwise interfering with the lesson. Ms Jones, the teacher, may look up and say, "Look, I've told you ten times. Please stop that behaviour." She continues with her lesson and, not surprisingly, Pamela and Rick are soon back up to their tricks.

Teachers using a nonassertive style are passive, and either do not establish strong standards or fail to back up their rules with consistent consequences. They hope that being nice to students will lead them to comply with teacher requests; thus, they often ask students to "please try" or "think about" good behaviour, rather than simply telling students to do something. Passive teachers often wait too long before dealing with a behaviour, or ignore behaviour that should be responded to. When they do act, they are not firm or insistent. Often a teacher who is passive will become hostile when the students persist in misbehaviour.

Teachers who feel they are losing control of a class will also often use a hostile response style. They rule with an iron fist, fearing that otherwise they will be overwhelmed by chaos. They rely heavily on aversive techniques such as sarcasm or ridicule and often shout at students with many "you-messages." Because they often threaten students angrily and overstate the consequences, they often do not follow through on their threats. Not surprisingly, students who do not respond well to hostile teachers. Their feelings are often hurt or the comments may elicit disrespect and a desire to get even. Hostile teachers fail to meet their students' need for security and warmth. Because of their inconsistency, students are often not sure what the consequences for their behaviour will be.

Assertive teachers are quite different in labelling behaviour and demanding compliance. Let's use an example to demonstrate the teacher who uses an assertive style:

> *Ms O'Reilly is conducting her lesson on genetics. Rick and Pamela are talking and giggling so Ms O'Reilly looks directly at the students, writes their names on the board, and says, "It is against class rules to speak without permission during the lesson." The offenders know which rule has been broken and know that having their names placed on the board is a warning. As the lesson resumes, the misbehaviour recurs. Ms O'Reilly looks at them again and, without saying anything, places a checkmark beside their names. This communicates to the students that they will be required to spend 15 minutes in detention after class—and they know that nothing will stop Ms O'Reilly from following through.*

Teachers are assertive when they make their expectations clear and follow through with established consequences (Canter and Canter, 1976). In this example, Ms O'Reilly, an assertive teacher, had made the rules of the classroom as well as the consequences for breaking the rules well known to the students. The consequences are reasonable—in other words, the punishment was made to fit the crime and the students have a clear choice: follow the rules or accept consequences. Thus, when Ms O'Reilly confronted the situation with Pamela and Rick she was able to deal with the problem in an assertive and businesslike manner. She has insisted that the students comply with the rules, and has backed up her expectation with action. One warning was given, and when this was not heeded, the expected consequences followed. It was not necessary to disrupt the ongoing class activities yet the consequence was firmly delivered.

Canter and Canter (1976) clearly state that "[n]o matter what the activity is, in order to be assertive, you need to be aware of what behaviours you want and need from the students" (p. 65). Teachers should identify the specific behaviours they want from students, such as taking turns, or starting work on time, and then instruct their students very clearly on the expectations. This often takes the form of a succinct list of dos and don'ts as well as specific directions and reminders which are posted in the classroom.

The next step is to decide how compliance and noncompliance with the rules are to be treated. Usually, when students comply with the rules, a simple verbal acknowledgement is sufficient or special reinforcers or privileges may be given.

When children do not comply with the rules, the teacher must be sure of how they are to deal with the situation.

When setting verbal limits on student behaviour, certain techniques can be used. First the teacher can request appropriate behaviour by using any of the following methods:

1. Hints—remind students about what they should be doing ("It's time for everyone to be working on their workbooks").

2. I-messages—tell the students what they are doing and how it affects the teacher.

3. Questions—use hints put into the interrogative form (e.g., "Would you get back to your seatwork please?").

4. Demands—use statements that direct students on what to do (e.g., "Get back to your seatwork now"). Canter warns that demands can have negative effects and issues his only command of assertive discipline: "Thou shalt not make a demand thou art not preparest to follow through on."

The teacher must be prepared to deliver the verbal message properly. The tone of voice should be firm and businesslike and the teacher should gain and hold eye contact with the students. Appropriate facial expressions and gestures can enhance meaning, while using the student's name can add impact to the message, particularly if it is delivered from a distance. When the teacher is next to the student, light physical contact (touch, not grabbing the student) can communicate forcefulness as well as sincerity. However, touches should be carefully used as some students may pull away or even respond aggressively. Further, they may later claim that the teacher has hurt them.

Canter also recommends the broken record technique which involves the insistent repetition of the original message. This is particularly effective when students try to divert the teacher from the intended message. By repeating himself or herself, the teacher can maintain firm, positive insistence that certain behaviours are not allowed in the classroom. This technique is different from the overdwelling as discussed by Kounin (1970). However, it should be employed sparingly, only used when the student(s) refuse to listen, persist in responding inappropriately, or refuse to take responsibility for their actions. Repetitions should be prefaced with phrases such as "That's not the point..." or "I understand, but...." Repetitions should only be used a maximum of three times and, after the third, the teacher should follow through with the appropraite consequence (Canter and Canter, 1976).

It is essential that teachers follow through on limits. Limits are the positive demands that the teacher has made on students, and following through means that appropriate action will be taken when the students comply or when they fail to comply. When students have been informed of the positive and negative consequences early on, they know what the consequences of their actions will be. Canter (1976) provides the following guidelines for following through appropriately:

1. Make promises, not threats. A promise is a vow to take appropriate action when necessary; a threat is a statement that shows intent to harm or punish. When promises are made to students, they know what is expected of them

and can choose to either comply or not comply with the rules. In either case, they are fully aware of what the consequences of their behaviour will be.

2. Select appropriate consequences in advance. Teachers should select both positive and negative consequences that will be used in the classroom. The severity of the negative consequences should be consistent with the severity of the rule infraction. Negative consequences could include loss of privileges, detentions, visits to the principal, and so on. All consequences should indicate that teachers care for their students and their behaviour and should help influence students' behaviour in the positive direction.

3. The system of consequences should be easily enforced. Canter suggests the following system, but urges teachers to develop their own system, one with which they feel most comfortable. Canter's system is designed to deal with individual student behaviour and is started fresh each day. The sequence is:

| MISBEHAVIOUR | CONSEQUENCE |
| --- | --- |
| First | Name on board (warning) |
| Second | Check by name (15-minute detention) |
| Third | Second check (30-minute detention) |
| Fourth | Third check (30-minute detention; student phones parents and explains) |
| Fifth | Fourth check (30-minute detention; student phones parents, explains and meets with principal) |
| Sixth | Student suspended, taken home by principal or counselor |

While Canter and Canter (1976) have included the use of suspension in their list on consequences, readers should be aware that this practice may not be allowed in their school district or, even when it is, there are strong reservations about its use. For example, Pare (1983) argues that school suspension does not increase discipline because it keeps students away from the learning environment.

4. Practice verbal confrontations that call for follow-through. Teachers must be comfortable with using assertions and follow-throughs and the best way to acquire this level of comfort is practice, practice, and more practice. Teachers can practice describing the system to the class and verbally rehearse what they would do when confronting a defiant student.

Assertive discipline as a model need not be restricted to conflict or inappropriate behaviour. The system of assertive discipline will only be effective if used in its entirety, and that includes using positive consequences for appropriate behaviours as well. Positive consequences strengthen appropriate student conduct, decrease negative behaviour, and make the classroom a more positive place to be. Canter and Canter (1976) have recommended many different positive consequences which are very similar to many of the reinforcers we discussed earlier. They include personal attention from the teacher, positive notes to parents, special awards, special privileges, material awards, awards delivered at home, and group rewards.

Although a program of assertive discipline is best started on the first day of school, it can be implemented at any time. Charles (1983, p. 114-115) suggests the following procedures:

1. Teachers should decide on the behaviours they want from students together with positive and negative consequences.

2. Take the list to the principal for approval and support.

3. At the first meeting with new students, discuss the behaviours, consequences, and methods of follow-through to be used. Behaviours (rules) should be kept to no more than six.

4. Teachers should stress that no student will be allowed to break the rules. Students are told exactly what will happen each time a rule is broken (first, second, third offence, etc.).

5. Students write the behaviours and consequences on a sheet of paper, take the plan home, have their parents read and sign it, and return it the next day.

6. It is emphasized repeatedly that these rules will help the class become responsible for learning and behaving acceptably.

7. Students repeat orally what is expected and what will happen for compliance and for violations.

8. The teacher prepares a short letter concerning the plan to go home to parents, indicating the need for their support and the teacher's pleasure in collaborating with the parents for the benefit of their child.

9. The assertive discipline plan is implemented immediately (pp. 136-139).

Implementing an assertive discipline plan requires the cooperation of both the school administration and the parents. Indeed, it may have to be tailored to meet the needs of particular classes and/or school systems; for example, the use of student suspension may not be an acceptable consequence in some circumstances. While assertive discipline has been shown to be an effective and widely used stragegy, it will only work when it is implemented consistently and fairly.

## Involving parents in behaviour change programs

Most educators agree that working cooperatively with parents increases the probability that students will be successful in school. School systems typically use a variety of means to communicate with parents, such as report cards and Parent Days. However, these techniques are usually criticized as being too infrequent and generally ineffective. Indeed, they are certainly insufficient to meet the needs of a child who is experiencing considerable difficulty in meeting the behavioural expectations of the classroom. In such cases, the parents need to be told of the difficulty that their child is experiencing, to be regularly informed of their child's progress and, ideally, to be actively involved in attempts to change the child's behaviour. When children are given the opportunity to change their behaviour, the parents are given the opportunity to hear good news from the school for a change since, in most cases, families of children with behavioural

Involving parents in a child's education usually produces positive results.

problems only hear bad reports from the school. Further, by involving parents in a program that emphasizes reinforcement rather than punishment, the teacher might help break down the negative criticism-punishment cycle that is often found to be prevalent in homes with problem children.

### Contingency contracts

One stragety that can help the school and home work together to change student behaviour is the contingency contract. These are written documents that provide a record of the expectations for behaviour and the reinforcing and/or punishing contingencies that will be delivered. Contingency contracts can be used to deal with classroom behaviour and/or academic goals, and have been shown to be highly successful. This strategy was described in detail in Chapter 10.

Involving parents in the development of the contract is advantageous because their involvement greatly increases the potential array of natural reinforcers that would otherwise not be available in the classroom setting: special meals, television programs, using the family car, and so on (Cantrell, et al., 1969). This is particularly important when the reinforcers available at school have not been successful in producing the desired behaviour change (Cooper, Heron, and Heward, 1987). However, teachers should only attempt to involve the family when they are definitely willing and able to commit the time and effort needed since contingencies must be delivered consistently to have the desired effect. While parents are usually eager to cooperate, compliance with a special program may not be possible within a busy family day.

### Daily report cards

Contingency contracts provide teachers with the opportunity to involve parents in a constructive means of dealing with their child's inappropriate behaviour. A key factor is that negotiating and implementing the contract requires the teacher and parents to be in frequent communication with each other about the student's behaviour, future goals, and daily progress. Another method used to accomplish this goal is the daily report card. Daily report cards require that teachers send home daily and weekly reports about the student's performance in specified social or academic domains.

Studies of the use of report cards have focused either on improving academic behaviours (Martin and McLaughlin, 1981), reducing disruptive behaviours (Lahey et al., 1977), or both simultaneously (Dolliver, Lewis, and McLaughlin, 1985). It has been suggested that academic goals are a more appropriate target: they are easier to implement because data is easier to gather and parents are able to help students attain their goals. When academic goals are targeted, there is usually a concurrent reduction in disruptive behaviours, even though they are not directly targeted (De Witt et al., 1983).

Drew and colleagues (1982) found that elementary students with histories of behavioural problems and difficulties with completing their in-class assignments were helped to change their behaviour when the teacher sent report cards home daily. Parents cooperated by working with their children at home and provided reinforcers when good reports were received. Ayllon, Gerber, and Pisor (1975) sent a good behaviour letter home with third grade students who met the criterion for good conduct. Parents were instructed to give appropriate contingencies when the child either brought a letter home or came home empty-handed. Disruptive behaviour, which had not been appreciably affected by a school-based behaviour change program, decreased significantly when the good behaviour letters were used. Davies and McLaughlin (1989) found that daily report cards reduced disruptive behaviour and increased task completion with three primary school boys. Report cards have also been used successfully with older students at the junior high level (Martin and McLaughlin, 1981).

When teachers set up report cards, they must tell parents:

- what to expect, or what information they will receive about their child's performance;

- when to expect it, or whether reports will be sent on a daily or weekly basis; and

- how they are to respond, or what reinforcers or negative consequences are to be delivered (Kerr and Nelson, 1989).

Figure 15-1 provides examples of daily report cards that can be used with students of various ages. The first report card would be appropriate for kindergarten or primary grade students, and the second for junior high or high school students. Note that the first report card contains a three-point scale rather than simply indicating that the student has met or not met the criterion. This allows the teacher to reward early success, while still indicating that further improvement is needed.

Figure 15-1
Daily report cards

Figure 15-1
Daily report cards

ELEMENTARY

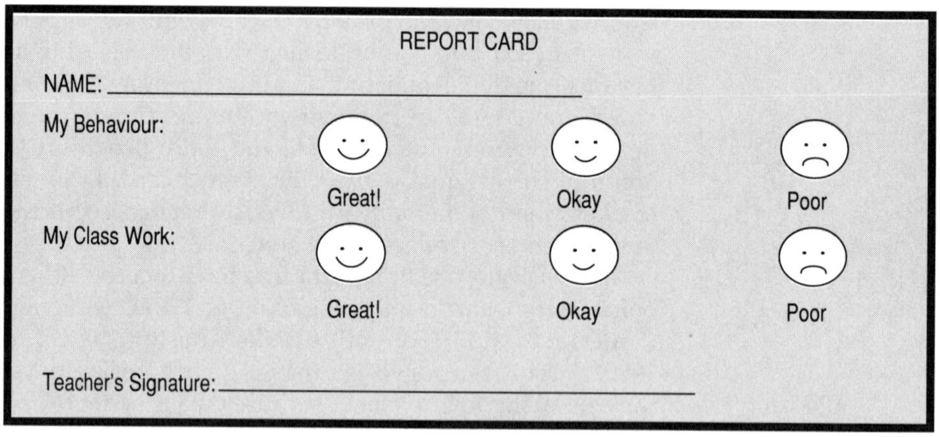

REPORT CARD

NAME: _____

My Behaviour:

Great!          Okay          Poor

My Class Work:

Great!          Okay          Poor

Teacher's Signature: _____

JUNIOR/SENIOR HIGH SCHOOL

| Name: | | | | | Date: |
|---|---|---|---|---|---|
| Class | Social Behaviour | Academic Work | Homework to be done: | | Teacher Initials |
| English | | | | | |
| Social St. | | | | | |
| Art | | | | | |
| Science | | | | | |
| Math | | | | | |
| Rating Scale: 1=Acceptable    2=Unacceptable | | | | | |

Of course, the teacher will need to make plans to make sure these report cards actually make it home. In some cases, advising parents to respond to a missing report card as if it were a poor card (not meeting the established criterion), causing the student to miss the reinforcer and/or lose privileges, will often motivate students to ensure delivery. When the teacher is concerned that parents do not read the cards, he or she may ask the parents to sign the cards and return them to school the next day (Kerr and Nelson, 1989).

A variation of the report card is the Passport (Runge, Walker, and Shea, 1975), a notebook that the student takes to all classes and home each day. All teachers—as well as any other adults that the student interacts with during the day, such as the librarian, teacher's aide, principal, or even the janitor—have the chance to write notes about the student's behaviour, reminders of assignments and so on. Parents respond in the same notebook, either commenting on performance or by asking specific questions as required. As with the daily report card, parents and teachers should be sure to balance negative reports with positive comments: no child should be required to take home a litany or overly harsh or critical string of comments about his or her behaviour.

## Helping students gain self-control

Brophy (1987) points out that a main goal of classroom management is to help students learn to discipline themselves, or to grow beyond the need for the teacher to provide external control. To help students attain this sense of control, the teacher may wish to use strategies that provide individualized support and counseling for the students so that they are able to solve their own problems.

According to Heuchert (1989), teachers have two interactive functions in the classroom: the teacher-director role, and the teacher-facilitator role. He differentiates them as follows:

> In the teacher-director role, students depend on the teacher to make decisions, provide the classroom structure, order the learning activities and materials, critique their productions, direct the classroom activities, and administer rewards and consequences. In the teacher-facilitator role, the teacher structures the behaviour management strategy in a way that provides students the opportunity to learn responsible behaviour, make their own choices, assess and clarify their value systems, and develop internal control (Heuchert, 1989, p. 295).

Teachers who use an informational rather than controlling teaching style—those who stress the reason for rules and limitations, showing students that they are useful in helping them to meet their goals—will be more likely to have students that will use these guidelines in new situations (Koestner et al., 1987). It is critical to set rules and to give the students an explanation for why the rules are necessary. When students are allowed to be responsible decision-makers, they will not need teachers to control their behaviour. This is important, because teachers cannot be with their students all of the time; instead, students must develop the ability to make socially appropriate and responsible choices that are in agrement with the rules of the school and the wider society (Heuchert, 1989).

### Reality therapy

When teachers first confront the term *Reality therapy*, they often recoil, saying that only psychologists and psychiatrists are capable of conducting therapy. However, Heuchert (1989) urges teachers to think of therapy rather as "doing and saying the right thing at the right time" (p. 296). Therapy in this sense involves providing students with a supportive and encouraging environment in which limits for appropriate behaviour are well-defined, where they are reminded of the consequences of inappropriate behaviour, and where they are helped to choose more effective behaviour. All teachers do this to some extent; some are simply better at it than others (Heuchert, 1989).

Reality therapy is based on the assumption that student behaviour is a reflection of five basic innate needs. Glasser (1984) identified these as the needs for physiological survival, love and belonging, power, freedom, and fun. Behaviour is not entirely motivated by external events, but students will only act when they believe that their behaviour will satisfy an innate need. Problems will arise when a student's needs are unfulfilled; the resulting inappropriate behaviour further alienates the person from the reality of the world around him or her. The primary goal of Reality therapy is to help students meet their needs in the context of the real world in ways that are sensitive to the needs of others (Glasser, 1965).

## TEACHING SOCIAL SKILLS

A crucial goal of psycho-affective learning and an integral part of the self-exploratory process appears to be fostering an awareness of alternative courses of action in social conflicts. Both social skills and adaptive behaviour fall under the broader construct of social competence and constitute crucial areas of development for all school-age children (Reschly and Gresham, 1981). Recently social skills training for children has emerged as a primary prevention technique (Cartledge and Milburn, 1978; Rotherman, 1982).

Social skills are the thoughts, feelings, and behaviours that help a child achieve his or her goals and maintain approval of others in the environment (O'Malley, 1977).

Social skills constitute a crucial area of development for all school-age children.

Interpersonal competence with peers and teachers has been related to IQ, academic achievement, deportment and, in general, to healthy adjustment (McKinney et al., 1975).

Social skills instruction begins by recognizing the specific problems. It identifies solutions by determining realistic and appropriate social skills, and helps children evaluate and monitor their own behaviour. Coaching works best as a sequential process involving modeling, rehearsal, feedback, and generalization (Cartledge and Milburn, 1980). Quite a few commercial programs are available, most offering a variety of skills in communication and courtesy suitable for any setting. Programs are available for all age groups and usually provide guidelines, activities, and materials.

Social skills have been defined as "those responses which, within a given situation, prove effective; or in other words, maximize the probability of producing, maintaining, or enhancing the positive effects for the interactor" (Foster and Ritchey, 1979, p. 626). Social competence is the ability to understand and to use the culturally accepted and contextually specific behaviour patterns of an environment (Hymes, 1974).

Self-management skills enable children to select appropriate choices based on probable consequences. They include:

- Values involving loyalty, honesty, truthfulness, and dependability.

- Sharing and having a conversation.

- Positive methods of gaining teacher attention; for example, when asking about a work assignment.

- Academic success.

- Positive ways of dealing with social conventions.

- Ways to deal with personal feelings and the feelings of others.

- Methods to deal with stressful situations.

- Ways to handle teasing.

- Positive listening skills.

- Proper ways to ask questions.

- Greeting behaviours.

- Ways to extend and receive invitations.

- Giving verbal and nonverbal compliments and positive feedback.

- Conversational skills, such as asking about other people's interests, responding to others' questions, and maintaining an extended conversation by taking turns to comment on a topic.

- Understanding the rules and routines of the regular classroom (Cartledge and Milburn, 1980; LaGreca and Mesibov, 1979).

Despite growing concerns about their validity, instructional programs designed to teach children to verbalize appropriate solutions to hypothetical interpersonal problems continue to be recommended as a remediation strategy for socially incompetent children (Michelson and Mannarino, 1986; Pellgrini and Urbain, 1985).

Le Capitaine (1985) used the *Toward affective development* program (Dupont, Gardner, and Brody, 1974) with 111 sixth grade pupils and found that the selected students showed, after 18 lessons, significant positive gains in their ability to generate alternatives in social situations.

It has been repeatedly demonstrated that programs for improving the skills of antisocial youth have not achieved reduction in other antisocial symptoms (Wilson and Herrnstein, 1985). Similar findings have also been obtained for social skills training (Kazdin, 1987).

## Aggressive behaviour

One of the worst nightmares for teachers is the prospect of being physically attacked—or having other students assaulted—by an out-of-control student. How this can happen is described in the incident in Box 15-1.

### Box 15-1  In the classroom: Student conflict

Gerry is ten years old, and is enrolled in Ms Jenson's grade five class. Ms Jenson had not really looked forward to having Gerry in her class—since grade one, he has been labeled as "over-active." While he is a bright, capable boy, most of his school work is below average. This is not surprising, as he rarely pays attention to the teacher's lesson, nor does he concentrate on his seatwork for longer than three to five minutes at a time. However, in one-to-one instructional or testing situations, Gerry easily performs at or well above grade level.

Ms Jenson has tried to be patient with him, gently reminding him to follow the class rules: e.g., "Raise your hand before you speak" or "Do not leave your desk without permission." However, lately she has noticed that Gerry has become more defiant and even aggressive in response to her reminders. The worst confrontation happened last week during a science lesson. Gerry appeared to really enjoy the lesson, and was repeatedly and enthusiastically yelling out answers to all of Ms Jenson's questions. Each time, Ms Jenson asked him to raise his hand before speaking. When he did so, she would call on him and his answer was usually correct. About the sixth time this happened, Gerry reacted quite violently to the teacher's request, and to her horror, started throwing books, pens—anything at hand—in her direction, all the while yelling obscenities at the top of his lungs. While the teacher desperately tried to get to him (dodging books all the while), Gerry roared around the classrom, knocking over desks, and running into one student.

After what seemed to her like a lifetime, the teacher finally managed to corner Gerry in the back of the room, and grab his arm. Doing her best to avoid his other pounding fist, she began to drag him bodily from the classroom. He managed to whack a few more students on the way out of the room, and as they progressed down the hall, he continued to scream obscenities. Battered and bruised, Ms Jenson pulled Gerry towards the school office, crying, "Help me! Please get out here and help me!" Even with the principal's help, it took several minutes to quieten Gerry.

Even a brief conversation with teachers who actually work in schools—both urban and rural—indicate that violence and aggression are on the upswing. Statistics will confirm this—reports of violence in classrooms have shown a sharp upswing in recent years. But what should a teacher do when confronted with a violent student? Of course, the best strategy is to prevent the occurrence of the aggressive behaviour. In addition to the preventative strategies mentioned so far, teachers should remember that some children are more distractible when seated near certain classmates. Some pay more attention when seated near the front of the room and other children may need a desk rather than a table, or vice versa. A child prone to conduct disorders may perform better if seated among peers who continually provide models of appropriate classroom behaviour. Disruptive students who are grouped with well-behaved students display fewer disruptive behaviours and the group as a while tends to remain well behaved (Stainback, et al., 1986).

As well, Kerr and Nelson (1989) provide some suggestions for teachers who wish to avert aggressive episodes:

1. Remember that adolescence is a time for students to express their growing independence by challenging authority, and this might be manifested through aggressive and rude verbal confrontations. Keeping this knowledge in mind might help teachers avoid getting trapped into an unnecessary battle with the student. Many confrontations can be avoided simply by the teacher refusing to participate.

2. Stay in control of your own emotions. Teachers should not deal with a student when their own emotions are out of control. Take some cool-down time and then return to the issue later.

3. Suggest a later conference to discuss the confrontation; both the teacher and the student will have had time to "cool down."

4. Give students choices rather than orders. When this is done, teachers must be willing to accept either option selected by the student.

5. Listen to students, avoid sarcasm, and try to keep your sense of humour.

While such preventative strategies can do a great deal to prevent aggression from occurring in the first place, they are little help when the teacher is in the middle of a crisis situation. Some immediate action is required. The imperative at this time is to physically manage the student to prevent self-injury, injury to others, or injury to the teacher (Kerr and Nelson, 1989). If the teacher is aware that a physically aggressive student will be present in the class, he or she should seek out training in physical management strategies. It is only with such training that the teacher will be able to appropriately handle this type of student.

If teachers do not have training in physical restraint and management, Kerr and Nelson (1989) recommend that they not try to intervene in a physical confrontation unless they are attacked without warning. When an episode occurs, teachers should remove themselves and students from the immediate vicinity and immediately send for help from others (sending a dependable student to get help if needed).

# SUMMARY

1. If classrooms are to be effective learning environments, it is essential that teachers develop adequate management strategies. Good management and organization spills over to affect the classroom climate, the teaching and learning, peer interactions, and student-teacher relationships.

2. Punishment should only be used when consistent reinforcement of behaviour has been tried and failed. Punishment can be seen as two primary forms—aversive stimuli such as writing lines or a detention and removal of reinforcers, such as losing recess.

3. Classroom management is a broad concept, emcompassing an academic climate and effective teaching practices, both of which promote high task engagement and good attitudes that prevent misbehaviour.

4. Seating should be arranged to maximize students' attention, minimize distractions and disruptions, and enable the teacher to monitor the class visually at all times.

5. Maintaining classroom discipline is one of the most feared duties of teachers, especially beginning teachers. Research clearly indicates ways of treating students that prevent disorder and create a well-managed classroom. The type of management strategy a teacher uses depends on that teacher's disposition and skills. As well, individual teachers are disposed to react in certain ways to misbehaviours.

6. Behavioural control is of paramount importance. In fact, instructional success is often directly proportional to a teacher's ability to use appropriate management strategies. A punitive classroom environment is not conducive to learning, but neither is a chaotic one. Even the most interesting and well-prepared lesson will fail if students are misbehaving.

7. Classroom management involves the manipulation of the classroom environment to facilitate the active engagement of students toward the achievement of academic and social goals. The ultimate aim of good management is to ensure that all students will be able to manage their own behaviour and be able to act cooperatively with others. Some procedures for classroom management and organization are unusually effective in basic skills achievement. Decisions about the use of time and space, the pace of instruction, the way the curriculum is structured, and the way that students are grouped for instruction can directly affect basic skills outcomes.

8. There are two major categories of behaviour control—preventative discipline and crisis intervention. Preventative discipline is the most appropriate and includes such things as reinforcement, curriculum methods, motivation and interest, as well as specific techniques such as rules and class meetings.

## Key Terms

accountability

classroom management

discipline

group alerting

overdwelling

rules

thrusts

active listening

dangles

flip-flops

group focus

overlapping

smoothness

truncation

classroom climate

desist

fragmentations

group format

ripple effect

stimulus-boundedness

withitness

# GLOSSARY

**Accommodation:** transformation of cognitive structures in response to external stimuli that do not fit into any available schema and therefore cannot be assimilated.

**Accountability:** the responsibility each student in the group has for learning the concepts taught in the lesson.

**Achievement motivation:** the generalized tendency to strive for success and to choose goal-oriented success/failure activities.

**Acoustic encoding:** the retention and recall of sounds.

**Active listening:** paraphrasing or summarizing what the speaker has said.

**Adaptation:** the function or tendency of all organisms to change in response to their environment.

**Adaptive behaviour:** the degree and efficiency with which an individual meets the standards of personal independence and social responsibility of his or her age or cultural group.

**Adolescence:** period from the onset of puberty to the beginning of adulthood.

**Advance organizers:** techniques that provide an outline for the facts that are to follow and show the relationship among concepts to be learned.

**Affectivity:** mental state pertaining to emotion–how one feels, how one manifests those feelings–and all other motivating conditions such as drive states and intentions.

**Affective variables:** feelings that, along with cognition, govern all behaviour.

**Age scale tests:** tests arranged into age levels according to their difficulty and without regard for content.

**Aggression:** any form of behaviour designed to harm or injure another living being who is motivated to avoid such treatment.

**Aggressive behaviour:** behaviour intended to hurt another, either physically or verbally, or intended to injure property.

**Allocated or instructional time:** time that students actually have to learn.

**Antecedents:** stimuli before the behaviour.

**Antisocial behaviour:** repeated infractions of socially prescribed patterns that violate social norms and the rights of others.

**Anxiety:** a strong feeling of uneasiness or apprehension that occurs in anticipation of something unpleasant.

**Apgar score:** score assigned to every newborn which provides general information about whether the infant's life-sustaining systems appear normal and what kinds of potential problems may be present.

**Applied behaviour analysis:** the study of the use of behavioural principles in real-life situations.

**Articulation:** the generation of speech sounds by modifications of the vocal tract, the mouth, and nasal and pharyngeal cavities.

**Articulation problems:** communication disorders characterized by omissions, substitutions, distortions, and additions of speech sounds.

**Assessment:** any process of gathering data on a student's skills and behaviour.

**Assimilation:** the use of existing schemata or cognitive structures to incorporate external stimuli.

**Attachment:** the bonding between the infant and the caretaker that is necessary for survival and successful growth.

**Attribution theory of motivation:** cognitive theory that deals with individual perceived causes of success and failure in classroom settings.

**Autosomal:** identical; refers to the first 22 pairs of chromosomes.

**Behaviour:** response performed by the individual.

**Behavioural genetics:** the study of the genetic factors involved in characteristics such as intelligence, musical ability, or temperament.

**Behavioural schemes:** the cognitive structures of the sensorimotor period, such as grasping.

**Bilingual education:** schooling provided fully or partly in the second language with the object of making students proficient in the second language while at the same time maintaining and developing their proficiency in the first language and fully guaranteeing their educational development.

**Bound morphemes:** sound units that are not words by themselves but are units of

meaning when combined with words.

**Category:** an extension of a concept which implies a class or partition of objects, sets of objects, events, people, etc.

**Categorization:** treating two or more distinct entities as if, in some way, they are equivalent.

**Centration:** the tendency to centre attention on a single feature of an object or situation.

**Cephalocaudal principle:** the tendency for development to reach from the head downward.

**Child development:** the scientific study of the way children change over time.

**Chunking:** grouping information into more meaningful units in order to increase the amount of information retained without exceeding the capacity of short-term memory.

**Classical conditioning:** occurs when people or animals learn to respond automatically to an object or event (stimulus) that previously had no effect, or a very different effect, on them.

**Classroom climate:** a composite of the prevailing conditions in a classroom.

**Classroom management:** the way in which the classroom environment is manipulated so that all children have the optimum opportunity to reach academic and social goals.

**Closure:** a Gestalt principle referring to the human tendency to reorganize perceptions into simplified, logical wholes, fill-

ing in the missing information if necessary.

**Cognitive development:** the thinking processes and how children understand and learn about the world in which they live.

**Cognitive psychology:** a field of study that examines the whole range of mental activities–attention, perception, memory, reflective and creative thinking, the use of language, and problem-solving.

**Cognitive scheme:** concepts, images, thinking, reasoning ability, and the ability to solve problems.

**Cognitive styles:** tendencies to respond to a variety of intellectual tasks and problems in a particular fashion.

**Communication:** the process of exchanging information and ideas between participants.

**Communicative competence:** the degree to which someone is successful in communicating, as measured by the appropriateness and effectiveness of the message.

**Competitive goal structure:** system in which students work against each other to achieve a grade or other reward that is reserved only for a few.

**Concept:** a mental structure of representation that defines how a set or class of entities, events, or abstractions are related.

**Conditioned reinforcers:** things which are initially neutral or meaningless but acquire their reinforcing value by being associated with primary reinforcers or an already established conditioned reinforcer. Also referred to as secondary reinforcers.

**Conditioned response:** a learned response emitted by an organism in response to a particular environmental stimulus.

**Conditioned stimulus:** an environmental stimulus that acquires the ability to elicit some type of learned response from the organism.

**Confluent education:** a form of instruction that integrates the affective and cognitive elements of individual and group learning.

**Connectionism:** learning is seen as a process of "stamping in" or forming connections between a stimulus and a response.

**Consequence:** a change in the environment which occurs after the behaviour, the effect of which is to alter the probability that the behaviour will or will not occur in the future.

**Conservation:** the ability to understand that the same amount remains, regardless of shape or the way an object or substance looks.

**Constructive play:** using materials to build, play, or model.

**Content scales:** tests organized in a hierarchical fashion that contain a number of subtests, each of which deals with the assessment of a single type of content or ability.

**Context:** the physical environment or the dominant emotional state in which information has been learned.

**Context cues:** prompts that help someone retrieve information based on the context in which the information was learned.

**Contingency contract:** a permanent record of the reinforcement, punishment and behavioural standards which are intended to guide a student's behaviour.

**Continuous schedule of reinforcement:** occurs when every single instance of a behaviour is reinforced.

**Control group:** the group in an experimental study that is not given treatment.

**Convergent thinking:** a type of thinking that focuses on one right answer, or toward a uniquely determined answer.

**Cooperative goal structure:** system in which students work together to achieve common goals.

**Correlation co-efficient:** expresses the degree of relationship between variables as a numerical index ranging from -1.00 (a perfect negative correlation–individuals high on one measure are likely to be low on the other) to +1.00 (a perfect positive correlation–individuals high on one measure are likely to be high on the other).

**Creativity:** capacity to restructure the world in unusual or useful conceptual terms; results in new, unusual, original, independent or innovative ways of thinking about and dealing with problems and leads in directions not predicted prior to the thinking.

**Criterion-referenced tests:** instruments that assess a student's progress against specific predetermined criteria set for the instructional objective, rather than against group norms.

**Critical period:** time at which a body part or organ system is growing most rapidly in both cell number and size.

**Culture:** denotes works of art, philosophy, music, and literature as well as the ways that different groups of people organize their daily lives within national and ethnic groups, urban neighbourhoods, companies and professions, and other settings. It includes the rules, expectations, attitudes, beliefs and values that guide behaviour in a particular group of people.

**Culture-fair measures:** aspects of a test that are written from the perspective of a particular minority culture or subculture.

**Culture-free measures:** instruments free from culturally loaded content.

**Dangles:** occur when a teacher starts the students on one activity and then suddenly reacts to a different matter, leaving the class in mid-air.

**Decay:** the passive loss of memory trace due to inactivity or lack of rehearsal.

**Decentration:** the ability to consider several aspects of a physical problem at once instead of focussing on only one attribute.

**Deduction:** reasoning from general rules to particular instances.

**Deficiency needs:** a set of physical and psychological needs. When humans are deficient in relation to one of these needs, their behaviour will be directed towards the fulfillment of that need.

**Dependent group-oriented contingency system:** system in which all members of a group get a positive reinforcer only if the performance of one student or a small subset of the group reaches the desired criterion.

**Dependent variables:** variables that are hypothesized to change as a result of the manipulation of independent variables.

**Depression:** characterized in children as a disorder of mood.

**Desist:** any teacher action intended to stop misbehaviour.

**Development:** changes in the mind and body that occur in humans between conception and death.

**Developmental delay or maturational lag:** failure to develop according to normal patterns.

**Developmental milestones:** the various critical behaviours, such as sitting, walking, and using the first words, that children learn to perform at roughly the same age.

**Developmental period:** the time between conception and the eighteenth birthday.

**Developmental psychology:** the study of the changes that take place in people as they age; views

the process of growing up as a sequence of stages characterized by specific types of behaviour that increase in complexity.

**Developmental stage:** a description of age-related behaviour and changes that are predictable with increasing age.

**Deviation IQ score:** a number that tells exactly how much above or below the average an individual scored on the test.

**Diagnostic tests:** instruments designed to identify specific problems in perceiving or responding; used to identify the precise nature of a student's difficulties.

**Dialect:** a language variation that is systematic and associated with a specific geographic, cultural, or socioeconomic group.

**Differential reinforcement of alternative behaviour (DRA):** reinforcement of positive alternative behaviours to discourage a specific undesired behaviour.

**Differential reinforcement of incompatible behaviour (DRI):** reinforcement of positive behaviours that are incompatible with the behaviour targeted for reduction.

**Differentiation:** pattern of general development in which physical responses move from global reactions to more controlled, specific reactions.

**Discovery learning:** a process in which students are presented with problems and are allowed to seek their own solutions through independent work or group discussion.

**Discrimination:** (classical conditioning) the ability of the individual to respond differently to similar stimuli.

**Discrimination:** (operant conditioning) the learner responds differently under different antecedent conditions.

**Discriminative stimulus:** an antecedent stimulus that cues the learner that certain consequences will follow a particular behaviour.

**Distributed practice:** working for short periods distributed over time.

**Divergent thinking:** a type of thinking in which many possible answers for a given problem are imagined.

**Dramatic play:** using materials in a make-believe manner.

**Dysfluency:** a speaking disorder (also known as stuttering) characterized by blocking, repetitions, or prolongations of sounds, words, phrases, or syllables.

**Educational measurement:** a field of development and research that addresses issues and develops procedures for the evaluation of student achievement.

**Educational psychology:** discipline which combines the paradigms, methods, and skills of psychology with the functioning of teachers, students, and schools.

**Egocentrism:** seeing only one's own point of view.

**Elaborative rehearsal:** relating new information to previously stored information to aid memorization.

**Empathic understanding:** ability to understand student reactions from the inside as well as to be aware of how the process of learning is experienced by students.

**Encoding:** the transformation of the sensations held in the sensory register into some type of interpretation of the event.

**Engaged time:** the amount of time actually spent learning.

**Entry-level skills:** knowledge that students possess prior to instruction.

**Episodic memory:** the memory for personal experiences stored in the form of images that are organized on the basis of when and where events happened.

**Equilibration:** maintaining a balance between present understanding and new experiences.

**Evaluation:** the use of a rule-governed system to make judgments about the value or worth of a set of measures.

**Exclusionary time-out:** physical removal of a child from the area of reinforcement although not from the classroom.

**Experiments:** procedures completed in order to investigate the cause-and-effect relationships between independent and dependent variables.

**Expository teaching:** an instructional model intended to encourage meaningful rather than rote learning.

**Expressive language disorders:** problems which affect the formulation of grammatic utterances.

**External locus of control:** a student's view that success or failure is due to circumstances beyond his or her control.

**Extinction:** (classical conditioning) the disappearance of the conditioned response when the conditioned stimulus is repeatedly presented in the absence of the unconditioned stimulus.

**Extinction:** (operant conditioning) the suppression or weakening of a behaviour by withholding the reinforcers that have been maintaining it.

**Fair-pair rule:** states that for every behaviour suppressed, the child must be reinforced for one or more alternative positive behaviours.

**Feedback:** information about some aspect of a person's performance.

**Field dependence:** a global perceptual style; field dependent people tend to perceive a pattern as a whole and have difficulty focussing on one aspect of a situation or analyzing a pattern with different parts.

**Field independence:** an analytic perceptual style; field independent people are more likely to perceive separate parts as a total pattern and be able to analyze a pattern according to its components.

**Figure-ground:** a Gestalt principle referring to the tendency of humans to focus their attention on the primary figure and its details while the remaining scene blends into the background.

**Fixation:** a Freudian term for the arresting of development and progress caused by frustration of basic needs.

**Fixed schedule of reinforcement:** occurs when the ratio or interval for reinforcement remains constant.

**Fixed interval schedule of reinforcement:** occurs when reinforcement is given to the first correct response to occur after a constant period of time has passed.

**Fixed ratio schedule of reinforcement:** occurs when the correct response is reinforced only after a fixed number of responses have occurred.

**Flashbulb memory:** extremely vivid memory produced when the individual is in a highly charged emotional state.

**Flip-flops:** occur at transitions when the teacher terminates one activity, begins a second activity, but then goes back to the first activity.

**Fluency:** the smoothness with which sounds, syllables, words, and phrases flow together.

**Forgetting:** inability to retrieve information from long-term memory.

**Formative evaluation:** a procedure designed to provide feedback during the learning process.

**Fragmentations:** the unnecessary breaking up of any activity into subparts when the activity should be performed as a single unit.

**Functional play:** first stage of play; using objects as they are without building or dramatic intent.

**Gender identity:** perception of oneself as male or female and the acceptance of one's identity as male or female.

**Generalization:** (classical conditioning) the extension of the response to similar stimuli.

**Genetic epistemology:** how children develop knowledge related to an innate tendency to develop cognitive structures.

**Gestalt:** a German word referring to an organized, integrated whole that has identity and meaning in its own right and is not merely the sum of its parts.

**Goal structure:** the degree to which students are in competition with each other.

**Grade equivalents:** relate scores to the average scores attained by students at a particular grade level.

**Grammar:** the conventions that govern the communication of meaning of a particular language and the procedures employed by a speaker to build up a functionally satisfying symbol sequence.

**Group alerting:** the degree to which the teacher maintains student attention to task at all times.

**Group focus:** the ability to keep as many students as possible involved in appropriate class activities.

**Group format:** the steps that the teacher takes to ensure that all students are involved in the activity so that maximum participation is encouraged.

**Group Investigation:** a cooperative learning strategy in which students take an active role in determining what they will study and how they will accomplish their study goals.

**Group-oriented contingencies:** behavioural procedures in which the behaviour of one or more students in a group will directly affect the consequences obtained by others in the group.

**Growth:** changes in height, weight, and other aspects of physical size.

**Growth needs:** human tendency towards psychological growth.

**Habituate:** to become familiar with a stimulus and show a decreasing reaction to it.

**Hereditability:** a statistic that describes the proportion of observed variance for the behaviours that can be ascribed to genetic differences among individuals in a particular population.

**Hereditability ratio:** the proportion of a characteristic's variability attributable to genetic causes.

**Holophrasic speech:** the use of single utterances to express a more complex idea.

**Hostile aggression:** aggressive behaviour that seems to occur for its own sake and is its own goal.

**Hyperactive children:** children who display rates of motor behaviour that are too high for their age groups and engage in excessive, non-purposeful movement.

**Immersion program:** program in which students learn a second language not as a subject but through being exposed to it as the language of instruction and interaction.

**Independent variables:** variables that are manipulated or changed by the researcher and are the hypothetical cause of the relationship being studied.

**Individualistic goal structure:** system in which students work by themselves to achieve goals that are independent of those held by their classmates.

**Induction:** reasoning in which we start with particular facts and use them to formulate general rules.

**Instrumental aggression:** aggressive behaviour that is directed toward achievement of a nonaggressive goal.

**Instrumental conditioning:** learned behaviours that allow the organism to reach a particular goal.

**Intelligence quotient (IQ):** the relationship between the child's mental age (MA) and chronological age (CA); it reflects the difference between a child's performance on the tests and the normative performance for that child's age level.

**Interdependent group-oriented contingency system:** system in which all members of the group must meet the desired criterion before any member can receive reinforcement.

**Interference:** situation in which recall of new information interferes with remembering old things or both old and new information become mixed up together in some fashion.

**Inter-individual differences:** variations among members of an age group or grade level.

**Intermittent schedule of reinforcement:** occurs when only a certain fraction of all correct behaviours are reinforced.

**Internal locus of control:** a student's view of success or failure as a consequence of his or her own actions.

**Interval schedule of reinforcement:** occurs when the delivery of reinforcement is determined by varying the time period between instances of reinforcement.

**Intra-individual differences:** the variations of performance that are observed as an individual performs several tasks.

**Jigsaw Method:** a cooperative learning strategy in which each member of a group works on one aspect of a group task, and then all members present what they have learned to the group.

**Judgment:** incorporating assimilation.

**Kinesics:** the study of communication codes that use body movements to construct meanings.

**Labeling:** categorizing children on the basis of their primary disability.

**Language:** a system of symbols organized into conventional patterns to communicate meaning.

**Language Acquisition Device (LAD):** term used by Chomsky to denote the innate genetic factor in humans that gives them the unique ability to acquire language.

**Language disorders:** problems in the recognition and understanding of spoken language or in the ability to formulate well-organized grammatical sentences.

**Language maturity:** the ability to use the phonological, morphological, syntactical, and semantic elements of language.

**Law of Effect:** Thorndike's principle that any act that produces a satisfying effect will cause the connection between the stimulus and response to be strengthened.

**Law of Exercise:** Thorndike's principle that the repetition of the stimulus-response strengthens the bond: if it is not practised, it weakens.

**Learning:** a relatively permanent change in behaviour that is brought about by interactions with the environment.

**Learning style:** the way individuals respond to the world around them.

**Lesson plan:** plan that describes the objectives, methods, content, and evaluation procedures that are to be used in each discrete instructional period.

**Locus of control:** the source to which an individual attributes responsibility for the outcome of events or behaviours. The tendency of individuals to perceive reinforcements as deriving either from within themselves or from forces beyond their immediate control indicates an internal or external locus of control.

**Mainstreaming:** the physical, intellectual, social and emotional integration of exceptional children and youth into the regular educational milieu.

**Mass practice:** practice of material for an extended period of time.

**Mastery learning:** the belief that students should be taught until they have mastered a subject or segment of a subject, no matter how long it takes.

**Maturation:** biologically controlled development that is independent of outside learning experiences.

**Meaningful receptive learning:** learning through concepts, ideas and other information in a manner that is relevant to the students' own prior knowledge.

**Measurement:** the assignment of numbers to certain attributes, objects, events, or people according to a rule-governed system.

**Mental retardation:** significantly sub-average intellectual functioning resulting in, or associated with, impairments in adaptive behaviour, and manifested during the developmental period.

**Metacognition:** knowledge concerning one's own cognitive processes, including the active monitoring and consequent regulation and orchestration of these processes.

**Metacomprehension:** an aspect of metacognition referring to the strategies that a reader uses in monitoring and evaluating the comprehension of written text while reading that text.

**Metalinguistic skills:** the abilities to talk about language, analyze it, think about it as an entity separate from its content, and judge it.

**Metamemory:** an aspect of metacognition referring to knowledge about one's own memory.

**Methods:** the formal aspects of teaching, such as the ways in which teachers interact with students, how they ask questions, how questions are addressed to students, and student activities.

**Mnemonic devices:** memory tactics that help a learner transfer or organize information to enhance its retrievability.

**Model prompts:** demonstrations of behaviour that show the student what to do after the normal environmental conditions have failed to produce the desired response.

**Modeling:** the imitation of the behaviours of others.

**Modulation:** ability to control the loudness of the sounds produced.

**Morphology:** system of word-building in the language. Morphemes may be words or significant elements, such as prefixes and suffixes.

**Motherese:** child-adult communicative interaction characterized by unique alterations in speech, meaning, form, and even language usage.

**Motivation:** the energy or force that directs human behaviour; the affect, or emotional response to a problem situation which then influences how the problem will be viewed and solved.

**Motor skill:** a smoothly integrated series of movements undertaken for a specific purpose.

**Negation:** the ability to see that a process can be reversed.

**Negative reinforcement:** occurs when an unpleasant stimulus is immediately taken away or removed from the situation as a consequence for a behaviour, with the effect of increasing the probability that the behaviour will occur again.

**Neutral stimulus:** an environmental stimulus that does not automatically elicit a response from the organism.

**Nonexclusionary time-out:** restricting a child's access to reinforcement without removing the child from the classroom environment.

**Nonlinguistic clues:** gestures, body language, facial expressions, hand and body move-

ments, and physical distance which complement and supplement language and account for a great deal of communicative competence.

**Normal distribution:** a continuum of scores that vary from the average score by predictable amounts.

**Normalization:** the philosophical belief that all exceptional individuals, no matter what their level and type of handicap, should be provided with an education and living environment as close to normal as possible.

**Norm-referenced test:** instrument that has been administered to a large group of people so that any one individual score can be compared to the average, or norm (e.g., an IQ test).

**Norms:** the average scores obtained by the students who took the tests when the norms were being established and the standard of comparison by which to measure later scores.

**Object permanence:** ability to mentally represent an object or person when that object or person is no longer in sight.

**Obsession:** a persistent preoccupation or idea someone can't get out of his or her head.

**On-task time:** the time that students are actively engaged in learning or in interacting with materials.

**Operant behaviours:** responses that are not elicited by particular stimuli but are affected by the reinforcers or punishers that follow the behaviour.

**Operant conditioning:** the process through which an organism's behaviour is influenced by the particular consequence that follows the response.

**Operation:** a mental routine for transposing information; an action in which an experience can be mentally transformed back to its original shape.

**Organization:** the way humans arrange, develop, and use their cognitive structures.

**Otitis media:** a condition in which the mucosal lining of the middle ear becomes inflamed and the cavity filled with fluid, hindering the air conduction of sound.

**Overdwelling:** staying on an issue much longer than necessary for the children to understand.

**Overlapping:** the ability to handle two or more class activities simultaneously.

**Overlearning:** learning material to the point beyond which it appears to be mastered.

**Paralanguage:** aspects of communication that may enhance or change the linguistic code.

**Participation structures:** rules defining who can talk, what they can talk about, and when, to whom, and for how long they can talk.

**Pedagogy:** the link between what a teacher wants students to learn and students' actual learning.

**Percentile:** a point in a distribution at or below which a given percentage of scores fall. The percentile rank shows the percentage of students in the norming sample who scored at or below a particular raw score.

**Perception:** the meaning attached to information received through the senses.

**Performance test:** instrument that requires an individual or group of individuals to make a decision, solve a problem, or perform some prescribed behaviour under more or less realistic conditions.

**Personality:** pattern of behaviours and thoughts that characterize individuals and distinguish them from others.

**Phobia:** a severe and excessive fear aroused by a particular object or situation and characterized by an extreme desire to avoid that object.

**Phonemes:** the smallest sound units in the sound system of language.

**Phonetics:** the description of the speech sounds of a language.

**Phonology:** the sound system of language.

**Physical development:** physical growth and motor control.

**Physical prompts:** cues to help students perform tasks that can be manually guided when the normal environmental conditions have failed to produce the desired response.

**Planned ignoring:** removing attention from a student for a given period of time.

**Positive reinforcement:** the contingent presentation of a consequence immediately after the occurrence of a behaviour, which has the effect of increasing the likelihood that the behaviour will occur again.

**Power test:** an instrument that probes students' mastery (their power) over material.

**Praise:** verbal expression of approval used to reinforce behaviour.

**Pragmatics:** an individual's ability to use language appropriately in social situations.

**Predict:** given a value for one variable, to foretell the value of another.

**Prehension:** the ability to reach for and grasp objects.

**Premack principle:** states that activities which occur at a high frequency (more preferred activities) can be used to reinforce the completion of lower-frequency (less preferred) activities.

**Primary punishers:** forms of punishment which automatically or naturally act to reduce the probability that a behaviour will occur again. Also referred to as unconditioned punishers.

**Primary reinforcers:** things that satisfy inborn biological needs, such as food, drink, warmth, sleep, or sex, and which act to strengthen the behaviour that they follow.

**Proactive interference:** occurs when old information interferes with recall of newly aquired information.

**Problem behaviour:** behaviour that makes it difficult for children to interact with peers, parents, teachers, and others.

**Problem solving:** the process of applying what is known to new and unfamiliar situations.

**Problem-solving strategies:** methods that lead to problem solutions in a step-by-step manner.

**Procedural memory:** the ability to recall how to do something, especially a motor task.

**Process-oriented measures:** instruments that attempt to assess how a child integrates and uses stimuli–including auditory processing, visual processing, visual-motor functioning, and motor skill development.

**Prompts:** cues to elicit student behaviour when the normal environmental conditions have failed to produce the desired response.

**Propositional network:** an interconnected set of bits of information that consists of the smallest bits of information that can be judged true or false.

**Prosody:** system in which the phonemes of a particular language are arranged in patterns of stress, rhythm and pitch, and also includes volume, tone of speech, duration, and juncture.

**Proxemics:** the study of how people use spaces between them and the characteristics of the territory used for communication.

**Proximodistal principle:** the tendency for development to occur from the torso out.

**Psycho-educational diagnosis:** testing children across a variety of domains relevant to social and educational performance.

**Psychoses:** serious mental disorders in which behavioural and thought processes become so disturbed that the person is out of touch with reality.

**Puberty:** period when an individual reaches sexual maturity.

**Punishment:** the contingent presentation of a consequence immediately after the occurrence of a behaviour, which has the effect of decreasing the likelihood that the behaviour will occur again.

**Punishment I (presentation punishment):** case in which an aversive stimulus is added to the environment or presented following a behaviour, which has the effect of decreasing the likelihood that the behaviour will occur again.

**Punishment II (removal punishment):** the removal of a reinforcer following a behaviour, which has the effect of decreasing the likelihood that the behaviour will occur again.

**Ratio schedule of reinforcement:** occurs when the delivery of reinforcement is based on the amount of behaviour emitted; every nth response would be reinforced.

**Raw score:** the actual number of correct answers that a student gets on a test.

**Receptive language disorders:** problems which interfere with the comprehension of spoken language.

**Receptors:** the components of the sensory register for seeing, hearing, tasting, smelling, and feeling.

**Recidivist:** one convicted of an offence within one year of release from incarceration.

**Reciprocal teaching:** a metacognitive strategy designed for use with students experiencing problems in reading comprehension.

**Reflexes:** natural responses with which children are born.

**Rehearsal:** a control process that affects the flow of information through the information-processing system; the process of maintaining an item in short-term memory by repetition so that it can be retrieved or sent to long-term memory.

**Reinforcer:** an event or stimulus that strengthens behaviour.

**Related services:** services such as transportation, physical and occupational therapy, and diagnostic medical services that permit an exceptional student to benefit from special education.

**Reliability:** the consistency of a test; its ability to produce the same results on different occasions under the same circumstances.

**Respondents:** unlearned responses.

**Response strength:** the quantitative measure of a response.

**Retrieval cue:** a prompt that helps the learner recall information.

**Retroactive interference:** occurs when new information interferes with the recall of previously learned information.

**Reversible mental operations:** these enable children to recognize that changes can be undone or reversed.

**Rhyme mnemonic:** mnemonic device which uses rhyme to enhance the retrievability of information.

**Ripple effect:** the way the teacher's method of handling the misbehaviour of one child influences other children in the classroom who are not the targets of the teacher's action.

**Rote learning:** mastery of material that is not inherently meaningful.

**Rules:** general expectations or standards for student behaviour.

**Sample:** a portion of the population that accurately represents the entire group.

**Schema:** (Piaget) a set of ideas that helps an individual organize information; mental representations of classes of people, objects, events, and so on.

**Schemata:** (information processing theory) mental data structures that allow for swift and economical processing of incoming stimuli.

**Seclusionary time-out:** removal of a student from the classroom situation.

**Second-order conditioning:** the chaining or connection of conditioned responses.

**Secondary punishers:** stimuli that were initially neutral but which have become aversive through repeated pairings with a primary, or already established, secondary punisher. Also referred to as conditioned punishers.

**Secondary reinforcers:** things which are initially neutral or meaningless but acquire their reinforcing value by being associated with primary reinforcers or an already established secondary reinforcer.

**Selective attention:** the ability to focus on the relevant features of stimuli.

**Self-actualization:** the basic and inborn need for people to develop or actualize their talents and capacities to the limits of their heredity.

**Self-awareness:** an attempt to explain ourselves to ourselves and to organize our impressions, feelings, and attitudes about ourselves in some way. Self-awareness leads children to compare themselves with others.

**Self-concept:** the composite of ideas, feelings, and attitudes people have about themselves.

**Self-esteem:** the degree of satisfaction with the self.

**Self-fulfilling prophecy:** case where the expectations of the teacher determine the ways in which students are treated, and this treatment will eventually shape the student's behaviour and achievement to become more congruent with these expectations.

**Self-instruction:** verbal statements to oneself which prompt, direct or maintain behaviour.

**Self-management:** process by which students record, reinforce, punish, or guide their own performance.

**Self-punishment:** process by which the student discriminates his or her own inappropriate behaviour and self-administers a negative consequence.

**Self-reinforcement:** system in which students increase or maintain their own behaviour with reinforcers that they give themselves whenever a certain standard has been met.

**Semantic memory:** memory for facts, concepts, principles, rules and the knowledge of how to use them, problem-solving skills, and generalized information mentally organized into networks of connected ideas or relationships called schemata.

**Sensation:** the information received through the senses.

**Sensorimotor scheme:** behavioural knowledge or skills in the sensorimotor area.

**Serial position effect:** tendency that when recalling a long list of items, learners are more likely to recall items at the end and beginning of the list and to forget the middle items.

**Seriation:** the ability to place a group of objects in order from least to most in length, width, weight, or some other common property.

**Sex role:** the way in which individuals internalize the roles considered appropriate for their own sex.

**Sex-role adoption:** the actual performance of sex-typed behaviour.

**Sex-role preferences:** the desire or preference for sex-typed activities.

**Sex-role stereotype:** the belief that an individual should act in certain ways because of sex.

**Sex typing:** the acquisition of characteristics and behaviour that a culture considers appropriate for each of the sexes.

**Shaping:** teaching new skills or behaviours by reinforcing learners for approaching the desired final behaviour.

**Smoothness:** the absence of teacher behaviours that disrupt transitions between activities or break up the continuity of an ongoing lesson.

**Social anomie:** absence of a sense of right and wrong.

**Social class:** class distinction defined in a personal way that expresses local prestige and respectability.

**Social cognition:** the knowledge of social relationships which includes an awareness and understanding of how people think, feel, and see things from a different point of view and what they mean or intend.

**Social learning:** builds upon operant conditioning principles,

and concerns itself chiefly with the ways in which people acquire behaviour appropriate to their social context and to their immediate circumstances.

**Social reinforcers:** a type of secondary reinforcer, which includes verbal or nonverbal actions that provide attention or communicate approval.

**Social transmission:** learning from others.

**Socialization:** a process by which children learn the behaviours, ideas, attitudes, and values accepted by their culture.

**Socio-economic status (SES):** a statistic compiled from indices such as type of occupation, years of education, size of income, quality of housing, and desirability of neighbourhood.

**Socio-emotional development:** the development of personality, the ability to interact socially, the ability to make value judgements, and the ability to understand cultural mores.

**Spatial visualization:** the ability to see, manipulate, and compute the position of an abstract or real figure in the mind's eye.

**Special education:** instruction specially designed to meet the needs of exceptional children.

**Speech disorders:** speech patterns which interfere with communication.

**Standard score:** a score based on the standard deviation describing test results according to a normal curve.

**Standardized test:** a test that can be given to a large and representative sample of some population so that the scores on the test can be compared with those of persons in the sample.

**State dependent learning:** enhances recall if the dominant emotional state during retrieval matches that during encoding.

**Stimulus-boundedness:** situation in which teachers are unable to maintain focus on the goal of the activity, reacting to irrelevant events that grab their attention.

**Stimulus control:** when behaviours are under the control of antecedent stimuli.

**Student Teams–Achievement Divisions (STAD):** a cooperative learning strategy consisting of a sequence of related activities: (1) a lesson is taught; (2) students engage in cooperative study in mixed groups; (3) a quiz is administered to individual students; and (4) rewards or recognition are given to the teams whose members most exceed their previous level of performance.

**Students with exceptionalities:** those whose intellectual, emotional, physical, or social performance falls below or rises above that of other children, and thus, have difficulty in realizing their full human potential.

**Sub-average intellectual functioning:** a tested potential of 70 IQ or below, two standard deviations below the mean.

**Subjective experience:** the individual's personal view of the world.

**Summative evaluation:** a procedure used as an end product after the learning process.

**Sustained attention:** the ability to attend to stimuli over a period of time.

**Sustaining expectation effect:** effect that occurs when teachers hold unchanging expectations, regardless of student change.

**Symbol:** an image, word or activity that represents something else.

**Syntax:** the network of organizational principles underlying linguistic expression which govern the grammar of language.

**Task analysis:** a procedure which breaks down an instructional goal into a series of sub-objectives or steps that will guide students to the attainment of the final objective.

**Taxonomy:** a classification scheme of educational objectives with categories arranged in a hierarchical order from the simplest outcomes to the more complex outcomes of instruction.

**T-Chart:** a strategy used in cooperative learning to help show students what collaborative skills are and when they should be used.

**Teams-Games-Tournaments (TGT):** a cooperative learning strategy in which the teacher presents a lesson, student teams complete worksheets, study together, and quiz one another on the material to be covered. Matched by ability, students then represent their team at class tournaments.

**Telegraphic speech:** a stripped-down form of language containing only the elements that are essential to the meaning of the message.

**Temperament:** the behavioural style of an individual.

**Test:** a procedure for measuring a sample of a person's behaviour to be evaluated against standards and norms.

**Theory:** a set of assumptions or a system of beliefs that tries to explain events that have happened in the past as well as predict events that will happen in the future.

**Thrusts:** a teacher's sudden interruption of a student's activity with an order, statement or question without any awareness or sensitivity to the student's readiness to receive the message.

**Time out from positive reinforcement (time-out):** the withdrawal of access to reinforcers for a specified period of time contingent on appropriate behaviour.

**Token reinforcers:** secondary reinforcers which are initially meaningless but can attain reinforcing value if they are exchangeable for other primary or secondary reinforcers.

**Transduction:** reasoning that two events are connected because they occur together.

**Transfer:** the processes that enable individuals to make previously learned responses to new situations.

**Transfer of learning:** the student's ability to use knowledge or skills in situations other than that in which the skill was initially acquired.

**Truncation:** a long-lasting dangle in which the teacher does not resume the initiated, then dropped, activity.

**Unconditioned response:** an unlearned response emitted by the organism in response to a particular environmental stimulus.

**Unconditioned stimulus:** an environmental stimulus that automatically elicits some type of unlearned response from the organism.

**Unit plan:** integrated package of instruction that consists of a related series of lesson plans addressing a particular theme or topic.

**Validity:** the degree to which a test measures what it claims to measure, how well it measures it, and what can be inferred from the measurement.

**Variable:** anything that can take on one or more values, such as sex, age, or academic level.

**Variable schedule of reinforcement:** occurs when the ratio or interval for reinforcement will change after each reinforced response.

**Variable interval schedule of reinforcement:** occurs when reinforcement is given to the first correct response to occur after a variable (or unpredictable) interval of time has passed since the last reinforced response.

**Variable ratio schedule of reinforcement:** occurs when the correct response is reinforced only after a variable (or unpredictable) number of responses have occurred.

**Verbal schemes:** word meanings or communication skills.

**Verbal prompts:** rules, instructions and hints used to elicit student behaviour when the normal environmental conditions have failed to produce the desired response.

**Vicarious experiences:** learning from the successes and failures of others.

**Vicarious reinforcement:** the tendency of humans to imitate a model in order to increase the probability that they will be reinforced.

**Visual acuity:** the measure of the smallest image distinguishable by the eye.

**Visual functioning:** what the impaired person is doing with his or her residual vision.

**Visual prompts:** cues presented in pictorial or written form to elicit student behaviour when the normal environmental conditions have failed to produce the desired response.

**Vocalization:** the ability to produce sound; produced when air expelled from the lungs passes between the vocal folds.

**Voice disorders:** vocal problems including voices that are too high, too low, too loud, too soft, or too nasal. In children, most voice disorders are functional, and are related to poor learning of voice control.

**Wait-time:** the time intervening before the student responds to a teacher's question.

**Withitness:** a teacher's ability to communicate to students that he or she knows what is going on in the classroom.

**Z score:** a common standard score that tells how many standard deviations above or below the average the raw score is.

# BIBLIOGRAPHY

A

Abel, R.R. and Burke, J.P. (1985) Perceptions of school psychological services from a staff perspective. *Journal of School Psychology, 23,* 121-131.

Abramson, L., Seligman, M. and Teasdale, J. (1978) Learned helplessness in humans: Critique and reformulation. *Journal of Abnormal Psychology, 87,* 49-74.

Achenbach, T.M. and Edelbrock, C.S. (1981) Behavior problems and competencies reported by parents of normal and disturbed children aged four through sixteen. *Monographs of the Society for Research in Child Development, 46.*

Adair, J.G. (1980) Psychology at the turn of a century: Crisis, challenges, promises. *Canadian Psychologist, 21,* 165-178.

Ahsen, A. (1977a) *Psych eye: Self-analytic consciousness.* New York: Brandon House.

Ahsen, A. (1977b) Eidetics: An overview. *Journal of Mental Imagery, 1,* 5-38.

Aiken, E.G., Thomas, G.S. and Shennum, W.A. (1975) Memory for a lecture: Effects of notes, lecture rate and information density. *Journal of Educational Psychology, 67,* 439-444.

Aiken, L.R. (1983) Determining grade boundaries on classroom tests. *Journal of Educational and Psychological Measurement, 43,* 759-762.

Ainsworth, M.D. (1979) Infant-mother attachment. *American Psychologist, 34,* 932-937.

Akerly, M.S. (1975) Parents speak. *Journal of Autism and Childhood Schizophrenia, 5,* 373-380.

Alberto, P.A. and Troutman, A.C. (1986) *Applied behavior analysis for teachers* (2nd ed.) Columbus, OH: Merrill.

Alcock, J.E., Carment, D.W. and Sadava, S.W. (1988) *A textbook of social psychology.* Toronto: Prentice-Hall.

Alderman, M.K. (1985) Achievement motivation and the preservice teacher. In M.

Alderman and M. Cohen (Eds.) *Motivational theory and practice for preservice teachers* (pp.37-49). Washington, DC: ERIC Clearing House on Teacher Education.

Algozzine, B. (1977a) The emotionally disturbed child: Disturbed or disturbing? *Journal of Abnormal Child Psychology, 5,* 205-211.

Algozzine, R.F. (1977b) Perceived attractiveness and classroom interactions. *Journal of Experimental Education, 46,* 63-66.

Algozzine, B. (1980) The disturbing child. A matter of opinion. *Behavior Disorders, 5,* 112-115.

Algozzine, B., Morsink, C.V. and Algozzine, K.K. (1988) What's happening in self-contained special education classrooms? *Exceptional Children, 55,* 259-265.

Allen, L.D. and Iwata, B.A. (1980) Reinforcing exercise maintenance: Using existing high rate activities. *Behavior Modification, 4,* 337-354.

Allen, S.J. and Kramer, J.J. (1990) Modification of personal hygiene and grooming behaviors with contingency contracting: A brief review and case study. *Psychology in the Schools, 27,* 244-251.

Alleyne, M. (1976) Dimensions and varieties of West Indian English and the implications for teaching. In V. D'Oyley and H. Silverman (Eds.) Black students in urban Canada. *Special Issues, TEST, 7,* 35-60.

Allison, D. E. (1982) Some of the things you always wanted to know about measurement and evaluation but were afraid to ask. *B. C. Journal of Special Education, 6,* 111-120.

Allport, F.H. (1924) *Social psychology.* Boston, MA: Houghton Mifflin.

Alter, M.M. and Goldstein, M.T. (1985) The 'G.S.' paradigm: A tool for IEP preparation. *Teaching Exceptional Children, 18,* 135-138.

Alwin, D. and Thornton, A. (1984) Family origins and schooling processes: Early versus

late influence of parental characteristics. *American Sociological Review, 49,* 784-802.

American Psychiatric Association (1987) *Diagnostic and statistical manual of mental disorders.* (3rd ed.). Washington, DC: American Psychiatric Association.

Ames, C. and Ames, R. (1984) Systems of student and teacher motivation: Toward a qualitative definition. *Journal of Educational Psychology, 76,* 535-556.

Ames, R. (1983) Teachers' attributions of responsibility: Some unexpected nondefensive effects. *Journal of Educational Psychology, 67,* 668-676.

Ames, R. and Lau, S. (1982) An attributional analysis of student help-seeking in academic settings. *Journal of Educational Psychology, 74,* 414-423.

Amman, J. (1700/1873) *Dissertatio de loquela, a dissertation on speech in which not only the Human Voice and the Art of Speaking are traced from their origin, but the Means are also described by which those who have been Deaf and Dumb from their birth may acquire Speech, and those who speak imperfectly may learn how to correct their impediments.* London: Sampson, Low, Marston, Low and Searle.

Anastasi, A. (1958) Heredity, environment, and the question "How"? *Psychological Review, 65,* 197-208.

Anastasi, A. (1981) Coaching, test sophistication and developed abilities. *American Psychologist, 36,* 1086-1093.

Anderson, J.O. (1989) Evaluation of student achievement: Teacher practices and educational measurement. *Alberta Journal of Educational Research, 35,* 123-133.

Anderson, J.R. (1985) *Cognitive psychology and its implications* (2nd. ed.) San Francisco, CA: Freeman.

Anderson, L.M., Evertson, C.M. and Brophy, J.E. (1979) An experimental study of effective teaching in first-grade reading groups. *Elementary School Journal, 79,* 193-233.

Anderson, R.C., Spiro, R.J. and Anderson, M.C. (1978) Schemata a scaffolding for the representation of information in connected discourse. *American Educational Research Journal, 15,* 433-440.

Anderson, R.J. and Sisco, F.H. (1977) *Standardization of the WISC-R Performance Scale for deaf children.* Washington, DC: Gallaudet College, Office of Demographic Studies.

Anderson, T.H. and Armbruster, B.B. (1984) Studying. In P.D. Pearson (Ed.) *Handbook of reading research.* New York: Longman.

Andre, T. (1973) Retroactive inhibition of prose and change in physical or organizational context. *Psychological Reports, 32,* 781-782.

Andre, T., Anderson, R.C. and Watts, G.H. (1976) Item-specific interference and list discrimination in free recall. *Journal of General Psychology, 72,* 533-543.

Andrews, G.R. and Debus R.L. (1978) Persistence and the causal perceptions if failure: Modifying cognitive attributions. *Journal of Educational Psychology, 70,* 154-166.

Apgar, V. and Beck, J. (1974) *Is my baby all right?* New York: Pocket Books.

Apter, S. J. and Conoley, J. C. (1984) *Childhood behavior disorders and emotional disturbance.* Englewood Cliffs, NJ: Prentice-Hall.

Archer, S. (1982) The lower age boundaries of identity development. *Child Development, 53,* 1551-1556.

Arehart, J. (1979) Student opportunity to learn related to student achievement of objectives in a probability unit. *Journal of Educational Research, 72,* 253-269.

Aries, P. (1962) *Centuries of childhood: A social history of family life.* (trans. R. Baldick) New York: Vintage Books.

Arlin, P. (1975) Cognitive development to adulthood: A fifth stage. *Developmental Psychology, 11,* 602-606.

Armento, B. (1977) Teacher behaviors related to student achievement on a social science concept test. *Journal of Teacher Education, 28,* 46-52.

Aronfreed, J. (1971) The cognitive and the affective in moral action. In C. Beck, B. Crittenden, and E. Sullivan (Eds.) *Moral education: Interdisciplinary approaches.* Toronto: University of Toronto Press.

Aronoff, J., Raymond, N. and Warmoth, A. (1965) The Kennedy-Jefferson school district: A report of neighborhood study in progress. Unpublished ms, Harvard Univeristy. In N. L. Gage Gage and D.C. Berliner (1984)

*Educational psychology* (3rd. ed.) Boston: Houghton Mifflin.

Arwood, B., Williams, R.L. and Long, J.D. (1974) The effects of behavior contracts and behavior proclamations on social conduct and academic achievement in a ninth grade English class. *Adolescence, 9,* 425-436.

Ashbury, C.A. (1974) Selected factors influencing over- and under-achievement in young school-age children. *Review of Educational Research, 44,* 409-427.

Asher, S.R. and Markell, R. (1974) Sex differences in comprehension of high- and low-interest reading material. *Journal of Educational Psychology, 66,* 680-687.

Asher, S.R. and Hymel, S. (1981) Children's social competence in peer relations: Sociometric and behavioral assessment. In J.D. Wine and M.D. Syme (Eds.) *Social competence.* New York: Guilford Press.

Ashworth, M. (1975) *Immigrant children and Canadian schools.* Toronto: McClelland and Stewart.

Atkins, D. (1980) Gifted high school students: A study of personality characteristics. *Delta Kappa Gamma Bulletin, 46,* 35-38.

Atkinson, J.W. and Raynor, J.O. (1974) *Motivation and achievement.* New York: Halstead Press.

Atkinson, J.W. (1980) Motivational effects of so-called tests of ability and educational achievement. In L.J. Fyans (Ed.) *Achievement motivation.* New York: Plenum.

Atkinson, J.W. and Feather, N.T. (Eds.) (1966) *A theory of achievement motivation.* New York: Wiley.

Atkinson, J.W. and Litwin, G.H. (1960) Achievement motive and test anxiety conceived as motive to approach success and motive to avoid failure. *Journal of Abnormal and Social Psychology, 60,* 52-63.

Atkinson, R.C. (1975) Mnemotechnics in second-language learning. *American Psychologist, 30,* 821-828.

Atkinson, R.C. and Raugh, M.R. (1975) An application of the mnemonic keyword method to the acquisition of Russian vocabulary. *Journal of Experimental Psychology: Human Learning and Memory, 104,* 126-133.

Atkinson, R.C. and Shiffrin, R.M. (1971) The control of short-term memory. *Scientific American, 224,* 82-90.

Atkinson, R.L., Atkinson, R.C., Smith, E.E., and Bem, D.J. (1990) *Introduction to psychology* (10th. ed.) New York: Harcourt Brace Javonovich.

Ault, R., Crawford, D. and Jeffrey, W.E. (1972) Visual scanning strategies of reflective, impulsive, post-accurate, and slow-inaccurate chil-

dren in the Matching Familiar Figures Test. *Child Development, 43,* 1412-1417.

Auschuler, A.S. (1967) *The achievement motivation development project: A summary and review.* Cambridge, MA: Center for Research and Development on Educational Differences.

Ausubel, D.P. (1953) The nature of educational research. *Educational Theory, 3,* 314-320.

Ausubel, D.P. (1960) The use of advanced organizers in learning and retention of meaningful verbal material. *Journal of Educational Psychology, 51,* 267-272.

Ausubel, D.P. (1968) *Educational psychology: A cognitive view.* New York: Holt, Rinehart and Winston.

Ausubel, D.P. (1969) Is there a discipline of educational psychology? *Psychology in the Schools, 6,* 232-244.

Ausubel, D.P. (1978) In defense of advance organizers: A reply to critics. *Review of Educational Research, 48,* 251-257.

Ausubel, D.P. and Youssef, M. (1963) Role of discriminability in meaningful parallel learning. *Journal of Educational Psychology, 54,* 331-336

Ausubel, D.P., Novak, J.D. and Hanesian, H. (1978) *Educational psychology: A cognitive view* (2nd. ed.) New York: Holt, Rinehart and Winston.

Axelrod, S. (1973) Comparison of individual and group contingencies in two special classes. *Behavior Therapy, 4,* 83-93.

Axelrod, S., Hall, R. and Tooms, A. (1979) Comparison of two common classroom seating arrangements. *Academic Therapy, 15,* 29-36.

Ayllon, T., Gerber, S. and Pisor, K. (1975) The elimination of discipline problems through a combined school-home motivation system. *Behavior Therapy, 6,* 616-626.

Azrin, N.H. and Holz, W.C. (1966) Punishment. In W.K. Honig (Ed.) *Operant behavior: Areas of research and application* (pp. 380-447). New York: Appleton-Century-Crofts.

**B**

Bachor, D.G. and Crealock, C. (1986) *Instructional strategies for students with special needs.* Toronto: Prentice-Hall.

Bacon, E.H. (1990) Guidelines for implimenting a classroom reward system. *Academic Therapy, 25,* 183-193.

Bain, B. and Yu, A. (1980) Cognitive consequences of raising children bilingually: "One parent, one language." Canadian *Journal of Psychology/ Review of Canadian Psychology, 34,* 304-313.

Baird, L.L. (1985) Do grades and tests predict adult accomplishment? *Research in Higher Education, 23,* 3-85.

Baker, L. and Cantwell, D.P. (1982) Psychiatric disorders in children with different types of communication disorders. *Journal of Communication Disorders, 15,* 113-126.

Baker, L., Cantwell, D.P., and Mathison, R.E. (1980) Behavior problems in children with pure speech disorders and in children with combined speech and language disorders. *Journal of Abnormal Child Psychology, 8,* 245-256.

Baker, H. and Leland, B. (1967) *Detroit Tests of Learning Aptitude.* Indianapolis, IN: Bobbs Merrill.

Baker, J.D. and Gottlieb, J. M. (1980) Attitudes of teachers toward mainstreaming retarded children. In J.M. Gottlieb (Ed.) *Educating mentally retarded persons in the mainstream.* Baltimore, MD: University Park Press.

Baker, J.E. and Winston, A.S. (1986) Modifying children's creative drawing: Experimental analysis and social validation of a self-instructional procedure. *Education and Treatment of Children, 8,* 115-132.

Ball, S. (1977) A postscript: Thoughts toward an integrated approach to motivation. In S. Ball (Ed.) *Motivation in education.* New York: Academic Press.

Ballard, K.D. and Glynn, T. (1975) Behavioral self-management in story writing with elementary school children. *Journal of Applied Behavior Analysis, 8,* 387-398.

Balow, B. (1979) Definitional and prevalence problems in behavior disorders of children. *School Psychology Digest, 8,* 348-354.

Bandura, A. (1965) Influence of a model's reinforcement contingencies on the acquisition of imitative responses. *Journal of Personality and Social Psychology, 1,* 589-595.

Bandura, A. (1976) Self-reinforcement: Theoretical and methodological considerations. *Behaviorism, 4,* 135-155.

Bandura, A. (1977) *Social learning theory.* Morristown, NJ: General Learning Press.

Bandura, A. (1986) *Social foundations of thought and action.* Englewood Cliffs, NJ: Prentice-Hall.

Bandura, A., Grusec, J.E. and Menlove, F. (1967) Vicarious extinction of avoidance behavior. *Journal of Personality and Social Psychology, 5,* 16-23.

Bandura, A., Ross, D. and Ross, S.A. (1963) Imitation of film-mediated aggressive models. Journal of Abnormal and Social Psychology, 66, 3-11.

Bangert-Drowns, R.L. Kukic, J.A. and Kukic, C.L. (1986, April) Effects of frequent classroom testing. Paper presented at American

Educational Research Association, San Francisco.

Banks, J.A. (1981) *Multiethnic education: Theory and practice.* Boston, MA: Allyn and Bacon.

Barker, G. and Graham, S. (1987) Developmental study of praise and blame as attributional cues. *Journal of Educational Psychology, 79,* 62-66.

Barnes, B. and Clawson, E. (1975) Do advance organizers facilitate learning? *Review of Educational Research, 45,* 637-659.

Barnes, H.V. (1975) Physical growth and development during puberty. *Medical Clinics of North America, 59,* 1305-1317.

Barnette, W.L. (1957) Advanced credit for the superior high school student. *Journal of Higher Education, 28,* 15-20.

Baron, R.A. and Byrne, D. (1981) *Social psychology: Understanding human interaction.* Boston, MA: Allyn and Bacon.

Barr, M.W. (1913) *Mental defectives: Their history, treatment and training.* Philadelphia, PA: Blakiston's.

Barringer, C. and Gholson, B. (1979) Effects of type and combination of feedback upon conceptual learning by children. *Review of Educational Research, 49,* 459-478.

Barron, A.P. and Earls, F. (1984) The relation of temperament and social factors to behavior problems in three-year-old children. *Journal of Child Psychology and Psychiatry, 25,* 23-33.

Bar-Tel, D. and Darom, E. (1979) Pupils' attributions of success and failure. *Child Development, 50,* 264-267.

Bar-Tel, D., Raviv, A., and Bar-Tel, Y. (1982) Consistency of pupils' attributions regarding success and failure. *Journal of Educational Psychology, 74,* 104-110.

Barth, R. (1979) Home-based reinforcement of school behavior: A review and analysis. *Review of Educational Research, 49,* 436-458.

Barton, K. (1973) Recent data on the culture-fair scales. In *Information Bulletin.* Champaign, IL: Institute for Personality and Ability Testing.

Bates, J.A. (1979) Extrinsic reward and intrinsic motivation: A review with implications for classrooms. *Review of Educational Research, 49,* 557-576.

Baumrind, D. (1971) Current patterns of parental authority. *Developmental Psychology Monographs, 1,* 1-103.

Baumrind, D. (1973) The development of instrumental competence through socialization. In A.D. Pick (Ed.) *Minnesota Symposium on Child Psychology* (vol. 7). Minneapolis, MI: University of Minnesota Press.

Baumrind, D. (1986) Sex differences in moral reasoning: Responses to Walker's (1984) con-

clusion that there are none. *Child Development, 57,* 511-521.

Beach, F.A. (1975) Behavioral endicronology: An emerging discipline. *American Scientist, 63,* 178-187.

Bear, G. and Richards, H. (1981) Moral reasoning and conduct problems in the classroom. *Journal of Educational Psychology, 73,* 644-670.

Beare, P. L. (1985) Difficulties and alternatives in emotional/behavioral disorders. *B.C. Journal of Special Education, 9,* 1-10.

Bechtold, A., Naccarato, M.E. and Zanna, M.P. (1986, June) Need for structure and the prejudice-discrimination link. Paper presented at the Annual Meeting of the Canadian Psychological Association, Toronto.

Beck, C. (1971) Moral education in Ontario schools. *Orbit, 2,* 6-7.

Beck, I. L. (1978) *Instructional ingredients for the development of beginning reading competence.* Learning Research and Development Center, University of Pittsburgh: University of Pittsburgh.

Becker, W.C. and Carnine, D. (1980) Direct instruction: An effective approach for educational intervention with the disadvantaged and low performers. In B. Lahey and A. Kazdin (Eds.) *Advances in child clinical psychology.* New York: Plenum.

Bee, H. L. (1978) *The developing child* (2nd. ed.) New York: Harper and Row.

Beisser, A., Glasser, N. and Grant, M. (1969) Psychological adjustment in children of schizophrenic mothers. *Journal of Nervous and Mental Disease, 145,* 429-440.

Bell, L. and Schniedewind, N. (1989) Realizing the promise of humanistic education. *Journal of Humanistic Psychology, 29,* 200-223.

Bell, L.V. (1980) *Treating the mentally ill: From Colonial times to the present.* New York: Praeger.

Bell, R.Q. and Harper, L.V. (1977) *Child effects on adults.* Lincoln, NB: University of Nebraska Press.

Belmont, L., Stein, Z.A. and Wittes, J.T. (1976) Birth order, family size and school failure. *Developmental Medicine and Child Neurology, 18,* 421-430.

Benbow, C.P. and Stanley, J.C. (1980) Sex differences in mathematics ability: Fact or artifact. *Science, 210,* 1262-1264.

Benbow, C.P. and Stanley, J.C. (1982) Consequences in high school and college of sex differences in mathematical reasoning ability: A longitudinal perspective. *American Educational Research Journal, 19,* 598-622.

Benbow, C.P. and Stanley, J.C. (1983) Sex differences in mathematical reasoning ability: More facts. *Science, 222,* 1029-1031.

Benedict, H. (1979) Early lexical development: Comprehension and production. *Journal of Child Language, 6,* 183-200.

Berdine, W.H. and Meyer, S.A. (1987) *Assessment in special education.* Boston, MA: Little, Brown.

Bereiter, C. and Scardamalia, M. (1985) Cognitive coping strategies and the problems of 'inert' knowledge. In S. Chipman, J.W. Segal, and R. Glasser (Eds.) *Thinking and learning skills: Current research and open questions* (vol. 2) (pp. 65-80) Hillsdale, NJ. Erlbaum.

Bergan, J. (1980) The structural analysis of behavior: An alternative to the learning-hierarchy model. *Review of Educational Research, 50,* 625-646.

Berger, K.S. (1983) *The developing person through the life span.* New York: Worth.

Berko, J. (1958) The child's learning of English morphology. *Word, 14,* 150-177.

Berlin, C.M. Jr. (1983) Biological causes of exceptionality. In R.M. Smith, J.T. Neisworth and F.M. Hunt (Eds.) *The exceptional child: A functional approach.* New York: McGraw-Hill

Berliner, D.C. (1971) Aptitude-treatment interactions in two studies of learning from lecture instruction. Paper presented at the American Educational Research Association, New York. ERIC Document No. ED 046 249.

Bernard, H. (1973) *Child development and learning.* Boston: Allyn and Bacon.

Berndt, T.J., Laychak, A.E.and Park, K. (1990) Friends' influence on adolescents' academic achievement motivation: An experimental study. *Journal of Educational Psychology, 82,* 664-670.

Berscheid, E. and Walster, E. (1972) Beauty and the beast. *Psychology Today, 5,* 42-46.

Bersoff, D.N. (1981) Testing and the law. *American Psychologist, 36,* 1046-1056.

Bettencourt, E., Gillett, M. Gall, M., and Hull, R. (1983) Effects of teacher enthuisism training on student on-task behavior and achievement. *American Educational Research Journal, 20,* 435-450.

Biehler, R.F. and Snowman, J. (1990) *Psychology applied to teaching* (6th ed.) Boston, MA: Houghton Mifflin.

Binet, A. and Simon, T. (1916) *The development of intelligence in children.* Baltimore, MD: Williams and Wilkins.

Birch, J. W. (1976) Definitions, development, and characteristics. In J. B. Jordan (Ed.) *Teachers, please don't close the door.* Reston, VA.: Council for Exceptional Children.

Birns, B., Blank, N. and Bridges, W.H. (1966) The effectiveness of various soothing techniques in human neonates. *Psychomatic Medicine, 26,* 316-327.

Bishop, J.H. (1989) Why the apathy in American high schools? *Educational Researcher, 18,* 6-10.

Bishop, B.R. and Stumphauzer, J.S. (1973) Behavior therapy of thumbsucking in children. *Psychological Reports, 33,* 939-944.

Blacher-Dixon J. and Turnbull, A.P. (1979) Preschool mainstreaming: Definitions, rationale and implimentation. *Education Unlimited, 1,* 16-22.

Blackman, S. and Goldstein, K. (1982) Cognitive styles and learning disabilities. *Journal of Learning Disabilities, 15,* 106-115.

Block, J. and Block, J.H. (1980) *The California Child Q-set.* Palo Alto, CA: Consulting Psychologists Press.

Block, J. Block, J.H and Keyes, S. (1988) Longitudinally foretelling drug usage in adolescents: Early childhood personality and environmental precursors. *Child Development, 59,* 336-355.

Block, J. and Shedler, J. (1990) Adolescent drug use and psychological health: A longitudinal enquiry. *American Psychologist, 45,* 612-630.

Block, J.H. (1983) Differential premises arising from differential socialization of the sexes: Some conjectures. *Child Development, 54,* 1335-1354.

Block, J.H. (1984) *Sex role, identity and ego development.* San Francisco, CA: Jossey-Bass.

Block, J.M. and Burns, R.R. (1976) Mastery learning. In L.S Schulman (Ed.) *Review of research in education.* Itiska, IL: F.E. Peacock.

Bloom, B. S. (1964) *Stability and change in human characteristics.* New York: Wiley.

Bloom, B.S. (1968) *Learning for mastery: Evaluation comment.* Los Angeles, CA: Center for the Study of Evaluation and Instructional Planning, University of California.

Bloom, B.S. (1971) Mastery learning. In J. Block (Ed.) *Mastery learning theory and practice.* New York: Holt, Rinehart and Winston.

Bloom, B.S. (1976) *Human characteristics and school learning.* New York: McGraw Hill.

Bloom, B.S. (1982) The role of gifts and markers in the development of talent. *Exceptional Children, 48,* 510-522.

Bloom, B.S. (1985) *Developing talent in young people.* New York: Ballantine Books.

Bloom, B. S., Englehart, M., Furst, E., Hill, W., and Krathwohl, D. (1956) *Taxonomy of educational objectives: The classification of educational goals. Handbook I: Cognitive domain.* New York: Longmans Green.

Bloom, B.S., Hastings, J.T. and Madaus, G.F. (1971) *Handbook of formative and summative evaluation in student learning.* New York: MacGraw Hill.

Bloom, L. (1970) *Language development: Form and function of emerging grammars.* Cambridge, MA: MIT Press.

Bloom, L. (1973) *One word at a time: The use of single-word utterances before syntax.* The Hague: Mouton.

Bloom, R. and Bourdon, L. (1980) Types and frequencies of teachers' written instructional feedback. *Journal of Educational Research, 74,* 13-15.

Blumenfeld, P. Hamilton, V. Bossert, S. Wessels, K., and Meece, J. (1977) Teacher talk and student thought: Socialization into the student role. In J. Levine and M.Wang (Eds.) *Teacher and student perceptions: Implications for learning.* Hillsdale, NJ: Erlbaum.

Blumstein, A., Cohen J. and Farrington, D.P. (1988) Criminal career research: Its value for criminology. *Criminology, 26,* 1-35.

Boocock, S.S. (1980) *Sociology of education* (2nd. ed.) Boston, MA: Houghton Mifflin.

Borg, W. (1979) Teacher coverage of academic content and pupil achievement. *Journal of Educational Psychology, 71,* 653-645.

Borg, W., Kelley, M.L. , Langer, P., and Gall, M. D. (1970) *The Minicourse: A micro-teaching approach to teacher education.* Beverly Hills, CA: MacMillan Educational Services.

Borich, G.D. (1988) *Effective teaching methods.* Columbus, OH: Merrill.

Boring, E.G. (1923, June 6) Intelligence as the tests test it. *New Republic, 36,* pp. 35-36.

Borkowski, J.G., Peck, V.A. and Reid, M. (1983) Impulsivity and strategy transfer: Metamemory as mediation. *Child Development, 54,* 459-473.

Born, D., Davis, M., Whelan, D., and Jackson, D. (1972) College students' study behavior in a personalized instruction course and in a lecture course. Paper presented at the Kansas Conference on Behavior Analysis in Education, Lawrence. In T.L. Good and J.E. Brophy, (1986) *Educational psychology* (3rd. ed.) New York: Longman.

Bornstein, M. (1985) How infant and mother jointly contribute to developing cognitive competence in the child. *Proceedings of the National Academy of Science, 82,* 7470-7473.

Boshier, R. and Thom, E. (1973) Do conservative parents nurture conservative children? *Social Behavior and Personality, 1,* 108-110.

Borthwick, B., Dow, I., Levesque, D., and Banks, R. (1980) *The gifted and talented students in Canada: Results of a CEA study.* Toronto: Canadian Education Association.

Bouchard, T.R. Jr. (1981) A study of mental ability using twin and adoption designs. *Progress in Clinical Biology Research, Pt. B.,* pp. 21-23.

Bouchard, T.J. Jr. and McGue, M. (1981) Familial studies of intelligence: A review. *Science, 212,* 1055-1059.

Bowd, A. (1982) *Quiet please: A practical guide to classroom discipline.* Toronto: Gage.

Bower, G.H. (1981) Mood and memory. *American Psychologist, 36,* 129-148.

Bower, G.H., Clark, M., Winzenz, S. and Lesgold, A. (1969) Hierarchical retrieval schemes in recall of categorized word lists. *Journal of Verbal Learning and Verbal Behavior, 8,* 323-343.

Bowey, J. (1986) Syntactic awareness and verbal performance from preschool to fifth grade. *Journal of Psycholinguistic Research, 11,* 417-436.

Bowles, S.S. and McGintis, J. (1976) *Schooling in capitalist America*: Educational reform and the contradictions of economic life. New York: Basic Books.

Brabeck, M. (1983) Moral judgment: Theory and research on differences between males and females. *Developmental Review, 3,* 274-291.

Bracey, G.W. (1984) Now then, Mr. Kohlberg, about moral development in women. *Phi Delta Kappan, 66,* 69.

Bracey, G.W. (1988) Selective retention. *Phi Delta Kappan, 69,* 379-380.

Bradbard, M. and Endsley, R. (1983) The effects of sex-typed labeling on preschool children's information-seeeking and retention. *Sex Roles, 9,* 247-260.

Brady, M. E. (1977) A comparison of CATTS and audio feedback in developing teacher prompting skills in reading. Paper presented to the American Educational Research Association, New York City.

Braine, M.D.S. (1963) On learning the grammatical order of words. *Psychological Review, 70,* 323-348.

Braken, B.A. (1980) Comparison of self-attitudes of gifted children in a non-gifted normative group. *Psychological Reports, 47,* 715-718.

Bransford, J.D., Sherwood, R., Vye, N., and Rieser, J. (1986 ) Teaching thinking and problem solving. *American Psychologist, 41,* 1078-1089.

Bransford, J.D. and Stein, B.S. (1984) *The IDEAL program solver.* New York: W.H. Freeman.

Branter, J.P and Doherty, M.A. (1983) A review of timeout: A conceptual and methodological analysis. In S. Axelrod and J. Apsche (eds.) *The effects of punishment on human behavior* (pp. 87-132) New York: Academic Press.

Brazelton, T.B. (1962) A child-oriented approach to toilet training. *Pediatrics, 29,* 121-128.

Bretherton, I. (1985) Attachment theory: Retrospect and prospect. In I. Bretherton and I. Walters (Eds.) Growing points of attachment theory and research. *Monographs of the Society for Research in Child Development, 50* (1-2, Serial no. 209).

Bretzing, B.B. and Kulhavy, R.W. (1979) Note taking and depth of processing. *Contemporary Educational Psychology, 4,* 145-153.

Bronfenbrenner, U. (1979) Contexts of child rearing: Problems and prospects. *American Psychologist, 34,* 844-850.

Brookover, W., Beady, C., Flood, P., Schweiter, J., and Wisenbaker, J. (1979) *School social systems and school achievement.* New York: Praeger.

Brooks-Gunn, J. and Furstenberg, F.F. (1989) Adolescent sexual behavior. *American Psychologist, 44,* 249-257.

Brooks-Gunn, J. and Matthews, W. (1979) *He and she: How children develop their sex-role identity.* Englewood Cliffs, NJ: Prentice-Hall.

Brooks-Gunn, J. and Warren, M.P. (1989) Biological and social contributions to negative affect in young adolescent girls. *Child Development, 60,* 40-55.

Brophy, J.E. (1970) Mothers as teachers of their own preschool children: The influence of socioeconomic status and task structure on teaching specificity. *Child Development, 41,* 79-94.

Brophy, J.E. (1979) Teacher behavior and its effects. *Journal of Educational Psychology, 71,* 733-750.

Brophy, J. (1981) Teacher praise: A functional analysis. *Review of Educational Research, 51,* 5-32.

Brophy, J. E. (1982) How teachers influence what is taught and learned in classrooms. *Elementary School Journal, 83,* 1-13.

Brophy, J.E. (1985) Teacher—student interaction. In J. Dusek (Ed.) *Teacher expectancies.* Hillsdale, NJ: Erlbaum.

Brophy, J.E. (1986) Teacher influences on student achievement. *American Psychologist, 41,* 1069-1077.

Brophy, J.E. (1987) Classroom management as instruction: Socializing self-guidance in students. In H. Clarizio, R. Craig and M. Mehrans (Eds.) *Contemporary issues in educational psychology* (pp. 328-336) New York: Random House.

Brophy, J.E. and Evertson, C.M. (1974) *Process-product correlations in the Texas teacher effectiveness study: Final report.* Austin, TX: Research and Development Center for Teacher Education, University of Texas.

Brophy, J. and Evertson, C. (1976) *Learning from teaching: A developmental perspective.* Boston, MA: Allyn and Bacon.

Brophy, J. and Evertson, C. (1978) Context variables in teaching. *Educational Psychologist, 12,* 310-316.

Brophy, J.E. and Good, T.L. (1970) Teachers' communication of differential expectations for children's classroom performance: Some behavioral data. *Journal of Educational Psychology, 61,* 365-374.

Brophy, J.E. and Good, T.L. (1974) *Teacher-student relationships.* New York: Holt, Rinehart and Winston.

Brophy, J.E. and Good, T.L. (1986) Teacher behavior and student achievement. In M. Wittrock (Ed.) *Handbook of research on teaching* (3rd. ed.) (pp. 328-375). New York: MacMillan.

Brophy, J.E. and Rohrkemper, M.M. (1981) The influence of problem ownership on teachers' perceptions of and strategies for coping with problem students. *Journal of Educational Psychology, 73,* 295-311.

Brown, A.L., Campione, J.C. and Day, J.D. (1981) Learning to learn: On training students to learn from tests. *Educational Researcher, 9,* 14-21.

Brown, B.B., Clasen, D.R. and Eicher, S.A. (1986) Perceptions of peer pressure, peer conformity dispositions, and self-reported behavior among adolescents. *Developmental Psychology, 22,* 521-530.

Brown, F. (1976) *Principles of educational and psychological testing* (2nd. ed.) New York: Holt, Rinehart and Winston.

Brown, G.I. (1971) *Human teaching for human learning: An introduction to confluent education.* New York: Viking Press.

Brown, L.L., Sherbenou, R.J. and Dollar, S.J. (1982) *Test of Nonverbal Intelligence.* Austin, TX: Pro-Ed.

Brown, R. (1973) *A first language: The early stages.* Cambridge: Harvard University Press.

Brown, R. (1986) *Social psychology, the second edition.* London: Collier MacMillan.

Brown, R. and Kulik, J. (1977) Flashbulb memories. *Cognition, 5,* 73-99.

Bruce, M.G. (1988) Making the grade or marking time. *Phi Delta Kappan, 69,* 383-384.

Bruch, H. (1973) *Eating disorders.* New York: Basic Books.

Bruck, M. (1978) The suitability of early French immersion programs for the language disabled child. *Canadian Journal of Education, 3,* 51-72

Bruck, M. (1982) Language impaired children's performance in an additive bilingual education program. *Applied Psycholinguistics, 3,* 45-60.

Bruck, M., Lambert. W.E. and Tucker, G.R. (1976) Cognitive consequences of bilingual schooling: The St. Lambert project through grade six. *International Journal of Psychology, 6,* 13-33.

Brumbeck, R.A., Staton, R.D. and Wilson, H. (1980) Neuropsychological study of children during and after remission of endogeneous depressive episodes. *Perceptual and Motor Skills, 50,* 1163-1167.

Bruner, J.S. (1956) *The study of thinking.* New York: Wiley.

Bruner J.S. (1960) *The process of education.* Cambridge, MA: Harvard University Press.

Bruner, J.S. (1962) *On knowing: Essays for the left hand.* Cambridge, MA: Belknap Press of Harvard University Press.

Bruner, J.S. (1966) *Toward a theory of instruction.* Cambridge, MA: Harvard University Press.

Bruner, J.S. (1969) Cognitive consequences of early sensory deprivation. In R.C. Sprinthall and N.C. Sprinthall (Eds.) *Educational psychology: Selected readings* (pp. 34-36) New York: Van Nostrand-Reinhold.

Bruner, J.S. (1971) *The relevance of education.* New York: Norton.

Bruner, J.S. (1987) *Actual minds, possible worlds.* Cambridge, MA: Harvard University Press.

Bryan, T. (1974) Peer popularity of learning disabled children. *Journal of Learning Disabilities, 7,* 121-125.

Bryan, T. (1978) Social relationships and verbal interactions of learning disabled children. *Journal of Learning Disabilities, 11,* 107-115.

Bryan, T. and Bryan, J. (1978) *Understanding learning disabilities* (2nd. ed.) Sherman Oaks, CA: Alfred Publishing.

Bullock, D. (1982) Behaviorism and NSPI: The erratically applied discipline. *NSPI Journal: Performance and Instruction, 21,* 4-8.

Bullock, L.M. and Brown, R.K. (1972) Behavioural dimensions of emotionally disturbed children. *Exceptional Children, 38,* 740-742.

Burchard, J.D. and Barrera, F. (1972) An ananlysis of time-out and response cost in a programmed environment. *Journal of Applied Behavior Analysis, 5,* 271-282.

Burgemeister, B.B., Bluma, L.H. and Lorge, I. (1972) *Columbia Mental Maturity Scale* (3rd. ed.) New York: Psychological Corporation.

Burgio, L.D., Whitman, L. and Johnson, M.R. (1980) A self-instructional package for increasing attending behavior in educable mentally retarded children. *Journal of Applied Behavior Analysis, 13,* 443-454.

Burnett, S.A. (1986) Sex-related differences in spatial ability: Are they trivial? *American Psychologist, 41,* 1012-1014.

Burns, R.B. (1982) *Self-concept development and education.* London: Holt, Rinehart and Winston.

Burns, R.B. (1984) How time is used in elementary schools. The activity structure of classrooms. In L.W. Anderson (Ed.) *Time and school learning: Theory, research and practice.* London: Crook Helm.

Burry, J. et al. (1981, April) Teaching and testing: Allies or adversaries. Paper presented at the Annual Meeting of the National Council on Measurement in Education, Los Angeles. ERIC Document, ED. No 218 337.

Burton, F. (1983) A study of the letter grade system and its effects on the curriculum. ERIC Document, No. ED 238 143.

Buss, R. and Plomin, R. (1975) *A temperament theory of personality development.* New York: Wiley.

Butt, R., Raymond, D. and Yamagashi, L. (1988, April) Paper presented at the American Educational Research Association, New Orleans.

Buys, N. and Winefield, A. (1982) Learned helplessness in high school students following experience of noncontingent rewards. *Journal of Research in Personality, 16,* 118-127.

Byrd, M. (1974) *Visits to Bedlam: Madness and literature in the eighteenth century.* Columbia, SC: University of South Carolina Press.

Byrne, B.M. (1984) The general-academic nomoligical network: A review of construct validation research. *Review of Educational Research, 54,* 427-456.

Byrne, B.M. (1986) Self-concept/academic achievement relations: An investigation of dimensionality, stability, and causality. *Canadian Journal of Behavioural Science, 18,* 173-186.

Byrne, M. E. and Shervanian, C.C. (1977) *Introduction to communication disorders.* New York: Harper and Row.

Byrnes, D. and Yamamato, K. (1984) Grade retention: Views of parents, teachers and principals. Utah State University paper.

C

Cacha, F.B. (1981) Managing questions for student participation. *The Clearing House, 54,* 263-264.

Calfee, R.C. (1977) Assessment of independent reading skills: Basic research and practical applications. In A.S. Reber and D.L. Scarborough (Eds.) *Toward a psychology of reading.* Hillside, NJ: Erlbaum.

Callahan, C.M. (1981) Superior abilities. In J.M. Kauffman and D.P. Hallahan (Eds.) *Handbook of special education.* Englewood Cliffs, NJ: Prentice-Hall.

Caldera, Y.M., Huston, E. and O'Brien, (1989) Social interactions and play patterns of parents of toddlers with feminine, masculine and neutral toys. *Child Development, 60,* 70-76.

Callen, M. (1978) Feeling, reasoning and acting: An integrated approach to moral education. In P. Scharf (Ed.) *Readings in moral education.* Minneapolis, MN: Winston Press.

Campos, J.J. and Keating, R. (1988) The Carpenteria language-minority student experience: From theory, to practice, to success. In T. Skutnabb-Kargas and J. Cummins (Eds.) *Minority education: Shame to struggle* (pp. 299-307) Clevedon, England: Multilingual Matters.

Campos, J.J., Barrett, K.C., Lamb, M.E., Goldsmith, H.H., and Sternberg, C. (1983) Socioemotional development. In P. Mussen (Ed.) *Handbook of child psychology* (vol. 2) New York: Wiley.

Canada, Health and Welfare (1984) *Childhood hearing impairment: Report of a Task Force convened by the Health Service Directorate, Health Services and Prevention Branch.* Ottawa: Department of Health and Welfare.

Canadian Consultative Council on Multiculturalism (1978) *Notes on multiculturalism.* Ottawa: Ministry of Supply and Services.

Canadian National Institute for the Blind (1980) Brochure. Toronto: CNIB.

Canter, L. and Canter, M. (1976) *Assertive discipline: A take-charge approach for today's educator.* Los Angeles, CA: Lee Canter and Associates.

Cantor, N.L. and Gelfand, D.M. (1977) Effects of responsiveness and sex of children on adults' behaviour. *Child Development, 48,* 232-238.

Cantrell, R.P., Cantrell, M.L., Huddleston, C.M., and Wooldridge, R.L. (1969) Contingency contracting with school problems. *Journal of Applied Behavior Analysis, 2,* 215-220.

Cantrell, R.P., Stenner, A.J. and Katzenmeyer, W.G. (1977) Teacher knowledge, attitudes, and classroom teaching correlates of student achievement. *Journal of Educational Psychology, 69,* 180-190.

Cantwell, D.P. and Baker, L. (1977) Psychiatric disorders in children with speech and language retardation: A critical review. *Archives of General Psychiatry, 34,* 583-591.

Caparulo, B. and Zigler, E. (1983) The effects of mainstreaming on success expectancy and imitation in mentally retarded students. *Peabody Journal of Education, 60,* 85-98.

Carden-Smith, L.K. and Fowler, S.A. (1984) Positive peer pressure: The effects of peer monitoring on children's disruptive behavior. *Journal of Applied Behavior Analysis, 17,* 213-227.

Carew, J. (1980) Experience and the development of intelligence in young children at home and in day care. *Monographs of the Society for Research in Child Development, 45* (6-7, Serial No. 187).

Carey, R.G. and Bucher, B.B. (1986) Positive practice overcorrection: Effects of reinforcing correct performance. *Behavior Modification, 14*, 71-80.

Carey, S. T. (1978) The child as word learner. In M. Halle, J. Bresnan and G. Miller (Eds.) *Linguistic theory and psychological reality.* Cambridge, MA: MIT Press.

Carey, S.T. (1987) Reading comprehension in first and second languages of immersion and Francophone students. *Canadian Journal for Exceptional Children, 3,* 103-108.

Carey, S.T. and Cummins, J. (1983) Achievement, behavioral correlates and teachers' perceptions of francophone and anglophone inmmersion students. *Alberta Journal of Educational Research, 29*, 159-167.

Carey, W.B. (1983) The validity of temperament assessments. In T. Brazelton and H. Als (Eds.) *Behavior assessment of newborn and young infants* (pp. 97-99) Boston, MA: Erlbaum.

Carlson, E.T. and Dain, N. (1962) The meaning of moral insanity. *Bulletin of the History of Medicine, 36*, 130-140.

Carpenter, C.J. (1983) Activity structure and play: Implications for socialization. In M. B. Liss (Ed.) *Social and cognitive skills: Sex roles and children's play* (pp. 117-145) New York: Academic Press.

Carr, J. (1975) *Young children with Down's syndrome.* London: Butterworths.

Carrier, J.G. (1983) Masking the social in educational knowledge: The case of learning disability theory. *American Journal of Sociology, 88*, 948-974.

Carroll, J.B. (1963) A model of school learning. *Teachers College Record, 64*, 723-733.

Carrow, E. (1973) *Test for Auditory Comprehension of Language.* Austin, TX: Learning Concepts.

Carter, D.B. (1987) The role of peers in sex role socialization. In D.B. Carter (Ed.) *Current conceptions of sex roles and sex typing.* New York: Praeger.

Cartledge, G. and Milburn, J.F. (1978) The case for teaching social skills in the classroom: A review. *Review of Educational Research, 1*, 133-156.

Cartledge, G. and Milburn, J.F. (1980) *Teaching social skills to children.* New York: Pergamon Press.

Cartwright, G. P., Cartwright, C. A. and Ward, M. E. (1984) *Educating special learners* (2nd. ed.) California: Wadsworth Publishing.

Caruso, D. (1986, April) Longitudinal study of individual differences in infant's exploratory behavior: Relationships to problem-solving ability. Presented at American Educational Research Association meeting.

Carver, R.P. (1973) Effect of increasing the rate of speech presentation on comprehension. *Journal of Educational Psychology, 65*, 118-126.

Case R. (1978a) A developmentally-based theory and technology of instruction. *Review of Educational Research, 48*, 439-463.

Case, R. (1978b) Intellectual development from birth to adulthood: A neo-Piagetian interpretation. In R. Siegler (Ed.) *Children's thinking: What develops?* Hillsdale, NJ: Erlbaum.

Case, R. (1985) A developmentally-based approach to the problem of instructional design. In R. Glaser, S. Chipman and J. Segal (Eds.) *Teaching thinking skills* (vol. 2) (pp. 545-562) Hillsdale, NJ: Erlbaum.

Casper, R.C. et al., (1980) Bulimia: Its incidence and clinical significance in patients with anorexia nervosa. *Archives of General Psychiatry, 37*, 1030-1035.

Casserly, P.L. (1979) Helping young women take math and science seriously in school. In N. Colangelo and R.T. Zaffran (Eds.) *New voices in counseling the gifted* (pp. 346-369).

Cassidy, J. (1988) Child-mother attachment and the self in six-year-olds. *Child Development, 59*, 121-134.

Catania, A.C. (1979) *Learning.* Englewood Cliffs, NJ: Prentice-Hall.

Cattell, R.B. (1963) Theory of fluid and crystallized intelligence: A critical experiment. *Journal of Educational Psychology, 54*, 1-22.

Cazden, C. (1974) Play and metalinguistic awareness: One dimension of language experience. *The Urban Review, 7*, 28-39.

Chan, K.S. (1978) Locus of control and achievement motivation— Critical factors in educational psychology. *Psychology in the Schools, 15*, 104-110.

Chapman, P.D. (1981) Schools as sorters: Testing and tracking in California, 1910-1925. *Journal of Social History, 14*, 701-707.

Chapman, J.W. (1988) Learning disabled children's self-concepts. *Review of Educational Research, 58*, 347-371.

Charles, C.M. (1983) *Elementary classroom management.* New York: Longman.

Charlop, M.H., Burgio, L.D., Iwata, B.A., and Ivancic, M.T. (1988) Stimulus variation as a means of enhancing punishment effects. *Journal of Applied Behavior Analysis, 21*, 89-95.

Chase, A. (1977) *The legacy of Malthus: The social costs of the new scientific racism.* New York: Alfred Knopf

Check, J.F. (1979) Classroom discipline: Where are we now? *Education, 100*, 134-137.

Cherry, E.C. (1953) Some experiments on the recognition of speech, with one and with two ears. *Journal of the Acoustical Society of America, 25*, 975-979.

Chess, S. and Rosenberg, M. (1974) Clinical differentiation among children with initial language complaints. *Journal of Autism and Childhood Schizophrenia, 2*, 99-109.

Chess, S. and Thomas, A. (1984) *Origins and evolution of behavior disorders.* New York: Brunner/Mazel.

Chilman, C.S. (1980) *Adolescent sexuality in a changing American society: Social and psychological perspectives.* Bethesda, MD: Department of Health, Education and Welfare, Public Health Service, National Institute for Health, Publication No. 80-1426.

Chinn, P.C. and Hughes, S. (1987) Representation of minority students in special education classes. *Remedial and Special Education, 8*, 41-46.

Chomsky, N. (1957) *Syntactic structures.* The Hague: Mouton.

Chomsky, N. (1959) Review of Verbal behavior by B.F. Skinner. *Language, 35*, 26-58.

Chomsky, N. (1965) *Aspects of the theory of syntax.* Cambridge, MA: MIT Press.

Christy, P.R. (1975) Does use of tangible rewards with individual children affect peer observers? Journal of *Applied Behavior Analysis, 8*, 187-196.

Clairborn, W (1969) Expectancy effects in the classroom: A failure to replicate. *Journal of Educational Psychogy, 60*, 377-383.

Clamp, P. (1990) Just a teacher. *ATA Magazine, 71*, 6-10.

Clark, C.M. and Peterson, P. (1985) Teachers' thought processes. In M. Wittrock (Ed.) *Handbook of research on teaching* (3rd. ed.) New York: MacMillan.

Clegg, A.A. Jr. (1971) Classroom questions. In *The encyclopedia of education* (pp. 183-190) New York: MacMillan.

Clements, D. (1984) Training effects on the development and generalization of Piagetian logical operations and knowledge of number. *Journal of Educational Psychology, 76*, 766-776.

Clifford, M.M. and Walster, E. (1973) Effect of physical attractiveness on teacher expectations. *Sociology of Education, 46*, 248-258.

Coats, C.D. and Smidchers, U. (1966) Audience recall as a function of speaker dynamism. *Journal of Educational Psychology, 57*, 189-191.

Coffman, W.E. (1980) Those achievement tests— how useful? *Executive Review, 1*, 2-5.

Coggins, T.E. and Morrison, J.A. (1981) Spontaneous imitations in Down's syndrome children: A lexical analysis. *Journal of Speech and Hearing Research, 24*, 303-308.

Cohen, D. (1971) Piaget and his critics, pt. 1. *Times* (London) Educational Supplement, p. 2937.

Coker, H., Medley, D. and Soar, R. (1980) How valid are expert opinions about effective teaching? *Phi Delta Kappan, 62,* 131-134, 149.

Cole, H. and Sarnoff, D. (1980, June) Interactive creativity: Explorations of basic meanings and their implications for teaching and counselling. Paper presented at the Twenty-Sixth Annual Creative Problem Solving Institute, Buffalo.

Coleman, H.M. (1968) Visual perception and reading dysfunction. Journal of Learning Disabilities, 1, 116-123.

Colenbrander, A. (1976) Low vision: Definition and classification. In E. Faye (Ed.) *Clincial low vision.* New York: Little, Brown.

Collard, R.R. (1971) Exploratory and play behaviors of infants reared in an institution and in lower- and middle-class homes. *Child Development, 42,* 1003-1015.

Combs, A.W. (1962) Perceiving and becoming. In *Perceiving, behaving and becoming* (pp 65-82). Association for Supervision and Curriculum Development Yearbook, Washington, DC: National Education Association.

Combs, A.W. (1979) *Myths in education.* Boston, MA: Allyn and Bacon.

Combs, A.W. (1981, February) Humanistic education: Too tender for a tough world? *Phi Delta Kappan,* pp. 446-449.

Combs, A.W. (1982) *A personal approach to teaching: Beliefs that make a difference.* Boston, MA: Allyn and Bacon.

Combs, A.W., Blume, R., Newman, A., and Wass, H. (1974) *The professional education of teachers* (2nd ed.) Boston, MA: Allyn and Bacon.

Commons, M., Richards, F. and Kuhn, D. (1982) Systematic and metasystematic reasoning: A case for levels of reasoning beyond Piaget's stage of formal operations. *Child Development, 53,* 1058-1069.

Condry, J. and Condry, S. (1976) Sex differences: A study in the eye of the beholder. *Child Development, 47,* 812-819.

Cone, J.D., Delawyer, D.D. and Wolfe, V. V. (1985) Assessing parent participation: The parent/family involvement index. *Exceptional Children, 51,* 417-424.

Conference of Executives of American Schools for the Deaf (1974) *Report of the Ad Hoc Committee to define deaf and hard-of-hearing.* Washington, DC: Author.

Conger, J.C. and Keane, S.P. (1981) Social skills intervention in the treatment of isolated or withdrawn children. *Psychological Bulletin, 90,* 478-495.

Conger, J.J. (1975) Sexual attitudes and behavior of contemporary adolescents. In J.J. Conger (Ed.) *Contemporary issues in adolescent development.* New York: Harper and Row.

Conrad, R. (1964) Acoustic confusions in immediate memory. *British Journal of Psychology, 55,* 75-84.

Cooley, W.W. and Leinhardt, G. (1980) The instructional dimensions study. *Educational Evaluation and Policy Analysis, 2,* 7-26.

Coop, R.H. and Seigel, I.E. (1974) Cognitive style: Implications for learning and instruction. In R.J. Jones and D.K. MacMillan (Eds.) *Special education in transition.* Boston, MA: Allyn and Bacon.

Cooper, H. (1979) Statistically combining independent studies: A meta-analysis of sex differences in conformity research. *Journal of Personality and Social Psychology, 37,* 131-146.

Cooper, H.M. and Good, T.L. (1983) *Pygmalion grows up: Studies in the expectation communication process.* New York: Longman.

Cooper, J.O., Heron, T.E. and Heward, W.L. (1987) *Applied behavior analysis.* Columbus, OH: Merrill

Corballis, M.C. (1983) *Human laterality.* New York: Academic Press.

Cordes, C. (1984, October) 'Feminine' morality ignored by theorists. *Monitor,* p.23.

Corey, S. (1940) The teachers out-talk the students. *School Review, 48,* 745-752.

Cornbleth, C. (1975) Student questioning strategies. *Social Studies Journal, 4,* 39-41.

Cornbleth, C. Davis, O.L. Jr. and Button, C. (1974) Expectations for pupil achievement and teacher-pupil interaction. *Social Education, 38,* 4-58.

Cortes, J.B. and Gatti, F.M. (1965) Physique and self-description of temperament. *Journal of Consulting Psychology, 20,* 432-439,

Cosand, B.J., Bourque, L.B and Kraus, J.F. (1982) Suicide among adolescents in Sacremento County, California 1950-1979. *Adolescence, 17,* 917-930.

Costa, A.L. (1985) How can we recognize improved student thinking. In A.L. Costa, (Ed.) *Developing minds: A resource book for teaching thinking.* Alexandria, VA: ASCD.

Costello, J. and Dickie, J. (1970) Leiter and Stanford-Binet IQs of preschool disadvantaged children. *Psychological Reports, 28,* 755-760.

Cote, J. and Levine, C. (1983) Marcia and Erikson: The relationships among ego identity status, neuroticism, dogmatism, and purpose in life. *Journal of Youth and Adolescence, 12,* 43-53.

Council of Ministers of Education (1983) *Survey of special education in Canada, 1982-83.* Winnipeg: Candid Research and Council of Ministers of Education, Canada.

Covin, T. (1976) Comparability of WISC and WISC-R Full Scale IQs in elementary school children with learning difficulties. *Psychological Reports, 39,* 2869B.

Covington, M. V. (1984) Strategic thinking and the fear of failure. In J. Segal. S. Chipman and R. Glaser (Eds.) *Thinking and learning skills: Relating instruction to basic research.* Hillsdale, NJ: Erlbaum.

Covington, M. V. and Beery, R. (1976) *Self-worth and schooling.* New York: Holt, Rinehart and Winston.

Covington, M.V. and Olemich, C.L. (1981) As fortunes mount: Affective and cognitive consequences of ability demotion in class. *Journal of Educational Psychology, 73,* 796-808.

Crealock, C. (1983) Teacher and student behaviors in regular and special education settings. *B.C. Journal of Special Education, 7,* 321-330.

Crocker, R.K. and Brooker, G.M. (1986) Classroom control and student outcomes in grades 2 and 5. *American Educational Research Journal, 23,* 1-11.

Cross, L.H. and Cross, G.M. (1980-81) Teachers' evaluative comments and pupil perception of control. *Journal of Experimental Education, 49,* 68-71.

Csapo, M. (1981) *Children with behaviour and social disorders: A Canadian focus.* Vancouver: Centre for Human Development and Research.

Culler, R.E. and Holahan, C.J. (1980) Test anxiety and academic performance: The effects of study related behavior. *Journal of Educational Psychology, 72,* 16-20.

The 'Culture Fair' WISC-R IQ test (1981, spring) *The Testing Digest,* p. 21.

Cummings, E.M., Ianotti, R.J. and Zahn-Waxler, C. (1989) Aggression between peers in early childhood: Individual continuity and developmental change. *Child Development, 60,* 887-895.

Cummings, S.T. and Finger, D.C. (1980) Emotional disorders. In H.E. Rie and E.D. Rie (Eds.) *Handbook of minimal brain dysfunction.* New York: Wiley.

Cummins, J. (1981) The role of primary language development in promoting educational success for language minority students. In *Schooling and language minority students: A theoretical framework* (pp. 3-49) Los Angeles, CA: Evaluation, Dissemination and Assessment Center.

Cummins, J. (1984) *Bilingualism and special education: Issues in assessment and pedagogy.* Clevedon, England: Multilingual Matters.

Cummins, J. (1985) *Disabling minority students: Power, programs, and pedagogy.* Ontario: OISE Press.

Cummins, J. (1987) Psychoeducational assessments of study related behavior. *Journal of Educational Psychology, 72,* 16-20.

Cummins, J. (1989) A theoretical framework for bilingual special education. *Exceptional Children, 56,* 111-119.

Cummins, J. and Mulcahy, R. (1978) Orientation to language in Ukranian bilingual children. *Child Development, 49,* 1239-1242.

Cunningham, J., Gerald, H. and Miller, N. (1978) Effects of success and failure on children's perceptions of internal-external locus of control. *Social Behavior and Personality, 6,* 1-9.

Curci, R.A. and Gottlieb, J. (1990) Teachers' instruction of noncategorically grouped handicapped children. *Exceptionality, 1,* 239-248.

Cypher, R., Hinves, D., Baine, D., and Sobsey, D. (1984) Contemporary considerations in educating students with severe and multiple handicaps. *B. C. Journal of Special Education, 8,* 137-148.

Cytryn, L., McKiew, D.H., Zahn-Waxler, C., Radke-Yarrow, M., Gaensbauer, T.J., Harmon, R.J., and Lamour, M. (1984) A developmental view of affective disturbance in the children of affectively ill parents. *American Journal of Psychiatry, 141,* 219-222.


D

Daines, D. (1982) Teachers' oral questions and subsequent verbal behavior of teachers and students. Provo, UT: Brigham Young University. ERIC document ED 223 979.

Daly, E.M., Abromovitch, R. and Pliner, P. (1980) The relationship between mothers' encoding and their children's decoding of facial expressions of emotion. *Merrill-Palmer Quarterly, 26,* 25-33.

Damon, W. (1977) *The social world of the child.* San Francisco, CA: Jossey Bass.

Damon, W. and Killen, M. (1982) Peer interaction and the process of change in children's moral reasoning. *Merrill-Palmer Quarterly, 28,* 347-367.

Dansereau, D.F. (1985) Learning strategy research. In J. Segal, S. Chipman, and R. Glaser (Eds.) *Thinking and learning skills: Relating instruction to basic research* (vol. I) Hillsdale, NJ: Erlbaum

Dansereau, D.F. (1988) Cooperative learning strategies. In E.E. Weinstein, E.T. Goetz, and P.A. Alexander (Eds.) *Learning and study strategies: Issues in assessment, instruction and evaluation.* New York: Academic Press.

Daraul, A. (1961) *Secret societies.* London: Muller.

Darch, C.B. and Thorpe, H.W. (1977) The principal game: A group consequence procedure to increase classroom on-task behavior. *Psychology in the Schools, 14,* 341-347.

Darley, J.M. and Gross P. (1983) A hypothesis-confirming bias in labeling effects. *Journal of Personality and Social Psychology, 44,* 2-33.

Darou, W. (1982) Canadian native people and psychological testing. *The School Guidance Worker, 37,* 37-41.

Darwin, C. (1859) *On the origin of the species.* London: Murray.

Darwin, C.A. (1877) A biographical sketch of an infant. *Mind, 2,* 285-294.

Das, J. P. (1988) Intelligence: A view from neuropsychology. *Alberta Journal of Educational Research, 34,* 76-82.

Davenport, C. (1915a) *The feebly inhibited: Inheritance of temperament.* Washington, D.C.: Carnegie Institution.

Davenport, C. B. (1915b) *The feebly inhibited: Nomadism, or the wandering impulse, with special reference to heredity.* Washington, D.C.: Carnegie Institution.

Davidson, N. (1985) Small-group learning and teaching in mathematics: A selective review of the research. In R.E. Slavin, S. Sharan, S. Kagan, R. Hertz-Lazarowitz, C. Webb, and R. Schmuck (Eds.) *Learning to cooperate, cooperating to learn.* New York: Plenum.

Davies, D.E., and McLaughlin, T.F. (1989) Effects of a daily report card on disruptive behaviour in primary students. *B.C. Journal of Special Education, 13,* 173-181.

Davis, G.A and Thomas, M.A. (1989) *Effective schools and effective teachers.* Boston, MA: Allyn and Bacon.

Day, C. with S.A. Kirk and J.J. Gallagher (1985) *Educating exceptional children* (Canadian edition) Toronto: Nelson.

Day, E.M. and Shapson, S. (1988) A comparison study of early and late French immersion programs in British Columbia. *Canadian Journal of Education, 13,* 290-305.

Deaux, K. (1984) From individual differences to social categories: Analysis of a decade's research on gender. *American Psychologist, 39,* 105-116.

De Blassie, R.R. and Franco, J.N. (1983) Psychological and educational assessment of bilingual children. In D.R. Omark and J.G. Erickson (Eds.) *The bilingual exceptional child.* San Diego, CA: College Hill.

DeCharms, R. (1976) *Enhancing motivation.* New York: Irvington Press.

DeCharms, R. (1980) The origins of competence and achievement motivation in personal causation. In L.J. Fyons, Jr. (Ed.) *Achievement motivation.* New York: Plenum

De l'Epee, M. C. (1784/1860) *The true method of educating the deaf and dumb, confirmed by long experience. American Annals of the Deaf and Dumb, 12,* 1-131.

DeLisi, R. and Staudt, J. (1980) Individual differences in college studetns' performance on

formal operations tasks. *Journal of Applied Developmental Psychology, 1,* 201-208.

Delisle, J.R. (1986) Death with honors: Suicide among gifted adolescents. *Journal of Counseling and Development, 64,* 558-560.

De Mause, L. (1974) *The history of childhood.* New York: Psychohistory Press.

Dempter, F.N. (1985a) Memory span: Sources of individual and developmental differences. *Psychological Bulletin, 89,* 63-100.

Dempter, F.N. (1985b) Short term memory development in childhood. In C.J. Brainerd and M. Pressley (Eds.) *Basic processes in memory development: Progress in cognitive development research.* New York: Springer/Verlag.

Denham, C. and Lieberman, A. (1980) *Time to learn.* Washington, DC: National Institute of Education.

Den Houler, K.V. (1981) To silence one's self: A brief analysis of the literature on adolescent suicide. *Child Welfare, 60,* 2-10.

Dennis, A.B. (1978) The relationship between ethnicity and educational aspirations in post-secondary students in Toronto and Montreal. In M.L. kovacs (Ed.) *Ethnic Canadians.* Regina: Plains Reseach Centre, University of Regina.

Deno, S. L. (1985) Curriculum-based assessment: The emerging alternative. *Exceptional Children, 52,* 219-232.

Deterline, W.A. (1968) The secrets we keep from students. *Educational Technology, 8,* 7-10.

de Villiers, J.G. and de Villiers, P.A. (1978) *Language acquisition.* Cambridge, MA: Harvard University Press.

de Villiers, J.G. and De Villiers, P.A. (n.d.) Out of the mouths of babes. Nova videotape.

DeVries, D.L., and Slavin, R.E. (1978) Teams-games-tournments (TGT): Review of ten classroom experiments. *Journal of Research and Development in Education, 12,* 28-38.

de Vries, J. and Vallee, F. (1980) *Language use in Canada.* Ottawa: Statistics Canada.

Dick, W. and Hagerty, N. (1971) *Topics in measurement: Reliability and validity.* New York: McGraw Hill.

Dickinson D.J. and Butt, J.A. (1989) The effects of success and failure on the on-task behavior of high achieving students. *Education and Treatment of Children, 12,* 243-252.

Diehl, C.F. and McDonald, E.T. (1956) Effects of voice quality on communication. *Journal of Speech and Hearing Disorders, 21,* 233-237.

Dietz, D.E.D. and Repp, A.C. (1973) Decreasing classroom misbehavior through the use of DRL scedules of reinforcement. *Journal of Applied Behavior Analysis, 6,* 457-464.

Dillon J.T. (1982) Cognitive correspondence between question/statement and response.

*American Educational Research Journal, 19,* 540-551.

Dishart, M. (1981) Special education and personal needs of gifted and talented childfren. *Association of Educators of Gifted, Talented and Creative Children in B.C., 3,* 6-12.

Di Vesta, F.J. (1987) The cognitive movement and education. In J.A. Glover and R.R. Ronning (Eds.) *Historical foundations of educational psychology* (pp. 203-233). New York: Plenum.

Dixon, C. (1977) Matching reading instruction to cognitive style for Mexican-American children. Paper presented at the California Reading Association, Anaheim.

Dodge, K.A. and Frame, C.L.(1982) Social cognitive biases and deficits in aggressive boys. *Child Development, 53,* 620-635.

Dolliver, P., Lewis, A.F. and McLaughlin, T.F. (1985) Effects of a daily report card: A simplified and flexible package for classroom behaviour management. *Psychology in the Schools, 14,* 191-195.

Domino, G. (1979) Creativity and the home environment. *Gifted Child Quarterly, 23,* 818-827.

Dore, J. (1986) The development of conversational competence. In R. Schiefelbusch (Ed.) *Language competence: Assessment and intervention.* San Diego, CA: College Hill Press.

Down, J.L. (1866) Observations on ethnic classifications. *London Hospital Report, 3,* 229-262.

Doyle, W. (1983) Academic work. *Review of Educational Research, 53,* 287-312.

Doyle. W. (1985) Classroom organization and management. In M.E. Wittrock (Ed.) *Improving teaching: 1988 ASCD yearbook.* Alexandria, VA: Association for Supervision and Curriculum Development.

Doyle, W. (1986) Classroom organization and management. In M.C. Wittrock (Ed.) *Handbook of research on teaching* (3rd. ed.) (pp 392-431) New York: MacMillan.

D'Oyley, V. (1976) Entering urban education: The case of the black student. In V. D'Oyley and M. Silverman (Eds.) *Black students in urban Canada.* Toronto: Ministry of Culture and Recreation.

Drabman, R.A., Spitalnik, R, and O'Leary, K.D. (1973) Teaching self-control to disruptive children. *Journal of Abnormal Psychology, 82,* 10-16.

Drabman, R. S. and Patterson, J. (1981) Disruptive behavior and the social standing of exceptional children. *Exceptional Education Quarterly, 1,* 45-55.

Drew, B., Evans, J., Bostow, D., Geiger, G., and Drash, P. (1982) Increasing assignment accuracy using a daily report card procedure. *Psychology in the Schools, 19,* 540-547.

Drews, E.M. (1972) *Learning together.* Englewood Cliffs, NJ: Prentice-Hall.

Duell, O.K. (1974) Effect of type of objective, level of test questions, and the judged importance of tested materials on posttest performance. *Journal of Educational Psychology, 66,* 225-232.

Dumont, F. (1987) School psychology in Canada: An evolving profession. *McGill Journal of Education, 22,* 101-116.

Duncan, O.D., Featherman, D.L. and Duncan, B. (1972) *Sociometric background and achievement.* New York: Seminar Press.

Dunkin, M.J. and Biddle, B.J. (1974) *A study of teaching.* New York: Holt, Rinehart and Winston.

Dunlap, L.K. and Dunlap, G. (1989) A self-monitoring package for teaching subtraction with regrouping to students with learning disabilities. *Journal of Applied Behavior Analysis, 22,* 309-314.

Dunn, R. (1981) Teaching in a purple fog: What we don't know about learning style. *NASSP Bulletin, 65,* 33-36.

Dunphy, B. (1989) Workload, expectations and stress. *ATA Magazine, 69,* 51.

Dupont, H. Gardner, O.S. and Brody, D.S. (1974) *Toward Affective Development.* Circle Pines. MN: American Guidance Services.

Durkin, D. (1966) *Children who read early.* New York: Teachers College.

Dusek, J.B. (1987) *Adolescent development and behavior.* Englewood Cliffs, NJ: Prentice-Hall.

Dweck, C. S. (1975) The role of expectations and attributions in the alleviation of learned helplessness. *Journal of Personality and Social Psychology, 4,* 474-485.

Dweck, C.S. and Bempechat, J. (1983) Theories of intelligence and achievement motivation. In S.G. Paris, G.M. Olsen and H.W. Stevenson (Eds.) *Learning and motivation in the classroom* (pp. 239-256) Hillsdale, NJ: Erlbaum.

Dweck, C.S. and Elliott, E.S. (1973) Achievement motivation. In E.M. Hetherington (Ed.) *Socialization, personality, and social development.* New York: Wiley.

Dwyer, C. (1974) Sex differences in reading: An evaluation and a critique of current theories. *Review of Educational Research, 43,* 455-468.

E

EAB (1958) John Broadhus Watson, 1878-1958. *Canadian Psychologist, 7,* 4-8.

Eagly, A.H. (1987) *Sex differences in social behavior: A social role interpretation.* Hillsdale, NJ: Erlbaum.

Ebel, R. L. (1975) Educational tests: Valid? Biased? Useful? *Phi Delta Kappan, 58,* 83-88.

Ebel, R.L. (1980) Evaluation of students: Implications for effective teaching. *Educational Evaluation and Policy Analysis, 2,* 47-51.

Eccles, J.S. and Jacobs, J.E. (1986) Social forces shape math attitudes and performance. *Signs, 11,* 367-389.

Eccles, J., Adler, T.F. and Kaczala, C.M. (1982) Socialization of achievement attitudes and beliefs: Parental influences. *Child Development, 53,* 310-321.

Eccles, J., Adler, T.F. Futterman, R., Goff, S.B., Kaczala, C.M. Meece, J.C., and Midgley, C. (1983) Expectation, values and academic behavior. In J.T. Spence (Ed.) *Achievement and achievement motivation* (pp. 75-146). San Francisco, CA: Freeman.

Eccles, J., Kaczala, C.M. and Meece, J.L. (1982) Socialization of achievement attitudes and beliefs: Classroom influences. *Child Development, 53,* 322-339.

Edward, T.K. (1988) Providing reasons for wanting to live. *Phi Delta Kappan, 70,* 296-298.

Eich, J., Weingartner, H., Stillman, R.C., and Gillian, J.C. (1975) State-dependent accessibility of retrieval cues in the retention of a categorized list. *Journal of Verbal Learning and Verbal Behavior, 14,* 408-417.

Eisenberg, N., Lennon, R. and Roth, K. (1983) Prosocial development in childhood: A longitudinal study. *Developmental Psychology, 19,* 846-855.

Eisner, E.W. (1969) Instructional and expressive educational objectives: Their formulation and use in curriculum. In W.J. Popham, E.W. Eisner, H.J. Sullivan and I.L. Tyler (Eds.) *Instructional objectives* (pp. 1-31) AERA Monograph Series on Curriculum Evaluation, no. 3 Chicago: Rand McNally.

Elashoff, J.D. and Snow, R.E. (1971) *Pygmalion reconsidered.* Worthington OH: Charles A Jones.

Elawar, M.C. and Corno, L. (1985) A factorial experiment in teachers' written feedback on student homework: Changing teacher behavior a little rather than a lot. *Journal of Educational Psychology, 77,* 162-173.

Elkin, W.F. (1982) Rethinking Bill 82. *Ottawa Law Review, 14,* 317-336.

Elliott, A.J. (1981) *Child language.* Cambridge: Cambridge University Press.

Elliott, D.S., Huizinga, D. and Ageton, S.S. (1985) *Explaining delinquency and drug use.* Beverly Hills, CA: Sage.

Ellis, E.S. (1983) The effects of teaching learning disabled adolescents an executive strategy to facilitate self-generation of task-specific strategies. Doctoral dissertation, Lawrence, KA: University of Kansas.

Ellis, E.S. (1986) The role of motivation and pedagogy on the generalization of cognitive strategy training. *Journal of Learning Disabilities, 19,* 66-70.

Emmer, E.T. (1987) Classroom mangement and discipline. In V. Richardson-Koehler (Ed.) *Educators' handbook: A research perspective.* New York: Longman.

Emmer, E.T. and Evertson, C.M (1981) Synthesis of research on classroom mangement. *Educational Leadership, 38,* 342-347.

Emmer, E.T., Evertson, C.M. and Anderson, L. (1980) Effective classroom management at the beginning of the school year. *Elementary School Journal, 80,* 219-231.

Emmer, E. T., Evertson, C., Sanford, J., and Clements, B. S. (1982) *Improving classroom management: An experimental study in junior high classrooms.* Austin, TX: Research and Development Center for Teacher Education, University of Texas, Austin.

Emmer, E.T., Evertson, C.M., Sanford, J.P., Clements, B., and Worsham, M. (1984) *Classroom management for secondary teachers.* Englewood Cliffs, NJ: Prentice-Hall.

Emmerich, W. (1966) Continuity and stability in early social development: 11-Teachers' ratings. *Child Development, 37,* 17-27.

Enright, R. and Beattie, J. (1989) Problem solving step by step in math. *Teaching Exceptional Children, 22,* 58-59.

Enright, R. Lapsley, D. Harris, D., and Shaver, D. (1983) Moral development interventions in early adolescence. *Theory into Practice, 22,* 134-144.

Entwistle, D.R. and Hayduk, L.A. (1978) *Too great expectations: The academic outlook of young children.* Baltimore, MD: Johns Hopkins University Press.

Epstein, J.L. (1983) The influence of friends on achievement and affective outcomes. In J.L. Epstein and N.L. Karweit (Eds.) *Friends in school* (pp. 177-200). New York: Academic Press.

Epstein, J.L. (1987) Parent involvement: What research says to administrators. *Education and Urban Society, 19,* 119-136.

Erdelyi, M.H. and Goldberg, B. (1979) Let's now sweep respression under the rug: Toward a cognitive psychology of repression. In J. Kihlstrom and F. Evans (Eds.) *Functional disorders of memory.* Hillsdale, NJ: Erlbaum.

Erez, M. and Scheorson, Z. (1980) Personality type and motivational characteristics of academics versus professionals in industry in the same occupational discipline. *Journal of Vocational Behavior, 17,* 95-98.

Erickson, F. and Schultz, J. (1977) When is context? Some issues and methods in the analysis of social competence. *Quarterly Newsletter of the Institute for Comparative Human Development, 1,* 50-10.

Erickson, M. (1982) Learning to read educational research. *Phi Delta Kappan, 64,* 276-277.

Erikson, E.H. (1950/1963) *Childhood and society.* New York: Norton.

Erikson, E.H. (1958) *Young man Luther: A study in psychoanalysis and history.* New York: Norton.

Erikson, E.H. (1968) *Identity: Youth and crisis.* New York: Norton.

Erikson, E.H. (1969) *Gandhi's truth.* New York: Norton.

Eriñ, J.E. (1986) Frequencies and types of questions in the language of visually impaired children. *Journal of Visual Impairment and Blindness, 80,* 670-674.

Erlenmeyer-Kimling, L. and Jarvik, L.F. (1963) Genetics and intelligence: A review. *Science, 142,* 1479.

Eron, L.D. and Huesmann, R.L. (1987) Television as a source of maltreatment of children. *School Psychology Review, 16,* 195-202.

Eshel, Y. and Klein, Z. (1981) Development of academic self-concept in lower-class primary school children. *Journal of Educational Psychology, 73,* 287-293.

Estes, W.K. (1972) An associative basis for coding and organization in memory. In A.W. Melton and E. Martin (Eds.) *Coding processes in human memory.* Washington, DC: Winston.

Evans, D.R. and Hearn, M.T. (1977) The growth of humanistic psychology: A review essay. *Journal of Educational Thought, 11,* 64-76.

Eveleth, P.B. (1986) Timing of menarche: Secular trends and population differences. In J.B. Lancaster and B.A. Hanking (Eds.) *School-age pregnancy and parenthood: Biosocial dimensions* (pp. 39-52) Hawthorne, NY: Aldise de Gruyter.

Evertson, C.M. and Emmer, E.T. (1982) Effective management at the beginning of the school year in junior high classes. *Journal of Educational Psychology, 74,* 485-498.

Evertson, C.M. and Smylie, M.A. (1987) Research on classroom processes: Views from two perspectives. In J.A. Glover and R.R. Ronning (Eds.) *Historical foundations of educational psychology.* New York: Plenum.

Evertson, C.M. and Weade, R. (1989) Classroom management and teaching style: Instructional stability and variability in two junior high English classrooms. *The Elementary School Journal, 89,* 379-393.

Evertson, C.M., Emmer, E.T. and Brophy, J.E. (1980) Predictors of effective teaching in junior high mathematics classrooms. *Journal for Research in Mathematics Education, 11,* 167-178.

Evertson, C.M., Emmer, E.T., Clements, B., Sanford, J.P., and Worsham, M. E. (1984)

*Classroom management for elementary teachers.* Englewood Cliffs, NJ: Prentice-Hall.

Evertson, C.M., Emmer, E.T., Sanford, J.P., and Clements, B. (1983). Improving classroom management: An experiment in elementary school classrooms. *Elementary School Journal, 84,* 173-188.

Eysenck, J.J. and Cookson, D. (1970) Personality in primary school children, 3, Family background. *British Journal of Educational Psychology, 40,* 117-131.


F

Fagot, B.I. (1977) Consequences of moderate cross-gender behavior in pre-school children. *Child Development, 48,* 902-907.

Falbo, T. (1977) The only child: A review. *Journal of Individual Psychology, 33,* 47-61.

Falbo, T. (1981) Relationship between birth category, achievement, and interpersonal orientation. *Journal of Personality and Social Psychology, 4,* 121-131.

Fancher, E. (1985) *The intelligence men: Makers of the IQ controversy.* New York: Norton.

Farebow, N.L. and Reynolds, D.K. (1981) Sources of suicide and schizophrenia within the family. *Psychiatria Fennica,* 41-51.

Farrington, D.P. (1987) Early precursors of frequent offending. In J.Q. Wilson and G.C. Loury (Eds.) From children to citizens (vol. 3) *Families, schools, and delinquency prevention* (pp. 27-51) New York: Springer/ Verlag.

Faust, M. (1977) Somatic developments of adolescent girls. *Monographs of the Society for Research in Child Development, 42* (1) (Serial no. 169).

Fee, V.E., Matson, J.L., and Manikam, R. (1990) A control group outcome study of a nonexclusionary time-out package to improve social skills with preschoolers. *Exceptionality, 1,* 107-101.

Feitler, F. and Tokar, E. (1982) Getting a handle on teacher stress: How bad is the problem? *Educational Leadership, 39,* 456-458.

Feldhusen, J. (1979) Student behavior problems in secondary schools. In D. L. Duke (Ed.) *Classroom management: The 78th. Yearbook of the National Society for the Study of Education.* Chicago: University of Chicago Press.

Feldhusen, J.F. and Hoover, S.M. (1986) A conception of giftedness: Intelligence, self concept and motivation. *Roeper Review, 8,* 140-143.

Felixbrod, J.J. and O'Leary, K.D. (1974) Self-determination of academic standards by children: Toward freedom from external control. *Journal of Educational Psychology, 66,* 854-850.

Felker, D. (1974) *Building positive self-concepts.* Minneapolis, MI: Burgess.

Fencham, F.D., Hokada, A. and Sanders, R. Jr. (1989) Learned helplessness, test anxiety, and academic achievement: A longitudinal analysis. *Child Development, 60*, 138-145.

Fennema, E. (1973) Mathematics learning and the sexes: A review. Paper presented at the American Educational Research Association, New Orleans.

Fennema, E. (1981) Women and mathematics: Does research matter? *Journal for Research in Mathematics Education, 12*, 380-385.

Fennema, E. and Sherman, J. (1978) Sex related differences in mathematics achievement and related factors. *Journal for Research in Mathematics Education, 9*, 189 203.

Fernald, W.E. (1924) Feeblemindedness. *Mental Hygiene, 8*, 964-971.

Ferster, C.B. and Skinner, B.F. (1957) *Schedules of reinforcement*. New York: Appleton-Century-Crofts.

Feshbach, S. (1970) Aggression. In P. Mussen (Ed.) *Carmicheal's manual of child psychology* (3rd. ed) New York: Wiley.

Finklestein, B. (1985) Schooling and the discovery of latency in nineteenth-century America. *Journal of Psycho-History, 13*, 3-12.

Finkelsten, B. (1988, August) Teachers as symbolic mediators in nineteenth century United States. Paper presented at the Standing committee for the History of Early Childhood Education, Joensuu, Finland.

Fisch, R.O., Bilek, M.K., Horribin, J.M., and Chang, P.N. (1976) Children with superior intelligence at 7 years of age. *American Journal of Diseases in Children, 130*, 481-487.

Fischer, K.W. (1980) A theory of cognitive development: The control and construction of hierarchies of skills. *Psychological Review, 87*, 477-531.

Fishbein, J.E. and Wasik, B.H. (1981) Effect of good behavior game on disruptive library behavior. *Journal of Applied Behavior Analysis, 14*, 89-93.

Fisher, C., Berliner, D., Filby, N., Marliave, R., Cahen, L. and Dishaw, M. (1980) Teaching behaviors, academic learning time, and student achievement: An overview. In C. Denham and A. Lieberman (Eds.) *Time to learn*. Washington, DC: National Institute of Education.

Fisher, J. and Harris, M. (1973) Effects of note-taking and review on recall. *Educational Psychology, 65*, 321-325.

Flavell, J. H. (1963) *The developmental psychology of Jean Piaget*. New York: Van Nostrand.

Flavell, J.H. (1976) Metacognitive aspects of problem solving. In L. Resnick, (Ed.) *The nature of intelligence*. Hillsdale, NJ: Erlbaum.

Flynn, P.T. and Byrne, M.C. (1970) Relationship between reading and selected auditory abilities of third grade children. *Journal of Speech and Hearing Research, 13*, 731-740.

Ford, C. and Beach, F. A. (1951) *Patterns of sexual development*. New York: Harper and Row.

Foster, S.L. and Ritchey, W.L. (1979) Issues in the assessment of social competence in children. *Journal of Applied Behavior Analysis, 12*, 625-638.

Foster, G.G., Ysseldyke, J.E. and Reese, J.H. (1975) "I wouldn't have seen it if I hadn't believed it." *Exceptional Children, 41*, 469-473.

Fosterling, F. (1985) Attributional retraining: A review. *Psychological Bulletin, 48*, 495-512.

Fouts, R. (1972) Use of guidance in teaching sign language to a chimpanzee. *Journal of Comparative and Physiological Psychology, 80*, 515-522.

Fox, L. (1977) Sex differences: Implications for program planning for the academically gifted. In J.C. Stanley, W.C. George and C.H. Solarno (Eds.) *The gifted and the creative: A fifty year perspective*. Baltimore, MD; Johns Hopkins University Press.

Fox, L. and Denham, S. (1974) Values and career interests of mathematically and scientifically precocious youth. In J.C. Stanley, D.P. Keating and L.H. Fox (Eds.) *Mathematical talent: Discovery, description and development* (pp. 140-175) Baltimore, MD: Johns Hopkins University Press.

Fox, R.A. (1985) How to control and evaluate an essay examination: A practical approach. *Performance and Instructional Journal, 24*, 7-8, 15.

Fraenkel, J.R. (1976, April) The Kohlberg bandwagon: Some reservations. *Social Education*, pp. 216-222.

Fraenkel, J.R. (1978) The Kohlberg bandwagon: Some reservations. In P. Scharf (Ed.) *Readings in moral education*. Minneapolis, MI: Winston Press.

Fraser, B.J. (1986) *Classroom environment*. London: Croom Helm.

Frederick, C.J. (1985) An introduction and overview of youth suicide, In M.L. Peck, N.L. Farbrow and R.E. Litman (Eds.) *Youth suicide* (pp. 1-16) New York: Springer/Verlag.

Frederick, W.C. and Walberg, H.J. (1980) Learning as a function of time. *Journal of Educational Research, 73*, 183-194.

Fredericksen, L.W. and Fredericksen, C.B. (1975) Teacher-determined and self-determined token reinforcement in the special education classroom. *Behavior Therapy, 6*, 310-314.

Freeberg, N. and Payne, D. (1967) Parental influences on cognitive development in early childhood: A review. *Child Development, 38*, 65-87.

Freedman, J.L. (1975) *Crowding and behavior*. New York: Viking Press.

Freeman, F.N. (1926) *Mental tests: Their history, principles and applications*. Boston, MA: Houghton Mifflin.

French, E.G. (1956) Motivation as a variable in work partner selection. *Journal of Abnormal and Social Psychology, 56*, 96-99.

French, E.G. and Thomas, F. (1958) The relation of achievement motivation to problem-solving effectiveness. *Journal of Abnormal and Social Psychology, 56*, 45-48.

Freud, A. (1958) Adolescence. In *Psychoanalytic study of the child* (vol 13) New York: International Universities Press.

Frieze, I.H. and Snyder, H.N. (1980) Children's beliefs about the causes of success and failure in school settings. *Journal of Educational Psychology, 72*, 186-196.

Frymmer, J. (1989) Understanding and preventing teen suicide: An interview with Barry Garfinkel. *Phi Delta Kappan, 70*, 290-293.

Fuchs, I., Eisenberg, N., Hertz-Lazarowitz, R., and Sharabony, R. (1986) Kibbutz, Isreali City, and American children's moral reasoning about prosocial moral conflicts *Merrill-Palmer Quarterly, 32*, 37-50.

Furstenberg, F.F. Jr., Brooks-Gunn, J. and Chase-Lansdale, L. (1989) Teenage pregnancy and childbearing. *American Psychologist, 44*, 313-320.

Fuson, K., Secada, W. and Hall, J. (1983) Matching, counting, and conservation of numerical equivalence. *Child Development, 54*, 91-97.

## G

Gadow, K.D. (1979) *Children on medication: A primer for school personnel*. Reston, VA: Council for Exceptional Children.

Gage, N.L. (1978) The yield of research on teaching. *Phi Delta Kappan, 60*, 229-235.

Gage, N.L. and Berliner, D.C. (1984/1986/1988) Educational psychology (3rd., 4th. 5th. ed.s) Boston, MA: Houghton Mifflin.

Gagné, R.M. (1974) *Essentials of learning for instruction*. Hillsdale, NJ: Dryden Press.

Gagné, R. (1977/1985) The conditions of learning (3rd, 4th. eds.). New York: Holt, Rinehart and Winston.

Gagné, R.M. and Briggs, L. (1979) *Principles of instructional design* (2nd ed.) New York: Holt, Rinehart and Winston.

Gall, M.D. (1970) The use of questions in teaching. *Review of Educational Research, 40*, 707-721.

Gall, M.D. and Gall, J.P (1976) The discussion method. In N.L. Gage (Ed.) *The psychology of* teaching methods: Seventy-fifth yearbook of the National Society for the Study of Education (Pt. 1, pp 166-216). Chicago, IL: University of Chicago Press.

Gallagher, J.J. (1966) Research summary of gifted education. Illinois: State of Illinois, Office of Superintendent of Public Instruction.

Gallagher, J.J. (1975) The gifted child in the elementary school. Washington, DC: American Educational Research Foundation.

Gallagher, J.J. (1985) Teaching the gifted child (3rd. ed.) Boston, MA: Allyn and Bacon.

Gallup, A.M. (1984) Gallup Poll of teachers' attitudes toward the public schools. Phi Delta Kappan, 66, 97-107.

Galluzi, E., Kirby, E. and Zuchner, K. (1980) Students' and teachers' perceetions of classroom and self and other concepts. Psychological Reports, 46, 747-753.

Gambrell, L.M. (1980) Extending think-time for better reading instruction. Reading Teacher, 34, 143-146.

Garber, M. and Ware, W.B. (1970) Relationship between measures of home environment and intelligence scores. American Psychological Association Proceedings, 5, 647-648.

Gardner, H. (1983) Frames of mind: The theory of multiple intelligences. New York: Basic Books.

Gardner, J.W. (1963) Self-renewal. New York: Harper and Row.

Gardner, R.A. and Gardner, B.T. (1969) Teaching sign language to a chimpanzee. Science, 165, 664-672.

Gardner, R.A. and Gardner, B.T. (1975) Early signs of language in child and chimpanzee. Science, 187, 752-753.

Gardner, W.I. (1974) Children with learning and behavior problems: A behavior management approach. Boston, MA: Allyn and Bacon.

Garfinkel, B.D. and Golumbek, H. (1974) Suicide and depression in children and adolescents. Canadian Medical Association Journal, 110, 1278-1281.

Garfinkel, P.E. and Gardner, D.M. (1982) Anorexia nervosa: A multi-disciplianary perspective. New York: Brunner/Mazel.

Garfinkel, P.E., Gardner, D.M. and Moldofsky, H. (1977) The role of behavior modification in the treatment of anorexia nervosa. Journal of Pediatric Psychology, 2, 113-121.

Garmezy, N. (1974) The study of competence in children at risk for severe psychopathology. In E. Anthony and C. Koupernik (Eds.) The child in his family (vol. 3) (pp. 77-97) New York: Wiley.

Garrard, S.D. and Richmond, J.B. (1975) Mental retardation: Nature and manifestations. In M.F. Reiser and S. Arieti (Eds.)

American handbook of psychiatry (vol. 4) (2nd. ed.) New York: Basic books.

Garrett, H. E. (1965) Testing for teachers (2nd. ed.) New York: American Book Company.

Geiger, K. and Turiel, E. (1983) Disruptive school behavior and concepts of social convention in early adolescence. Journal of Educational Psychology, 75, 677-685.

Gelb, S.A. and Mikokawa, D.T. (1986) Special education and social structure: The commonality of 'exceptionality'. American Educational Research Journal, 23, 543-557.

Gelfand, D.(1974) The effects of adult models and described alternatives on children's choice of behavior management teachniques. Child Development, 45, 585-593.

Gelman, R. (1979) Preschool thought. American Psychologist, 34, 900-905.

Gelman, R. and Baillargeon, E.E. (1983) A review of some Piagetian concepts. In J.H. Flavell and E.M. Markman (Eds.) Handbook of child development (4th ed.) Vol 3: Cognitive development. New York: Wiley.

Genesee, F. (1978) Is there an optimal age for starting second language instruction? McGill Journal of Education, 13, 145-154.

Gentner, D. (1982) Why nouns are learned before verbs: Linguistic relativity versus natural partitioning. In S. Kuczaj (Ed.) Language development (vol. 2). Language, thought, and culture. Hillsdale, NJ: Erlbaum.

Gentner, D. (1983) Nouns and verbs. Symposium at the meeting of the New England Child Language Association, Tufts Univeristy.

Gersten, J.C., Langer, T.S., Eisenberg, J.B., and Simcha-Fasgen, O., (1976) Stability and change in types of behavioral disturbances of children and adolescents. Journal of Abnormal Child Psychology, 4, 111-127.

Gesell, A. (1925/1929) The mental growth of the preschool child. New York: MacMillan.

Gesell, A. (1934) An atlas of infant behavior (vols. 1 and 2) New Haven, CT: Yale University Press.

Gesell, A. (1954) The ontogenesis of infant behavior. In L. Carmichael (Ed.) Manual of child psychology. New York: Wiley.

Gesell, A. and Amatruda, C.S. (1947) Developmental diagnosis (2nd ed.). New York: Paul B. Hoeber.

Gesell, A. and Ilg, F.L. (1946) The child from five to ten. New York: Harper and Row.

Gesell, A. Ilg, F.L., Ames, L., and Rodell, J. (1974) Infant and child in the culture of today (revised ed.). New York: Harper and Row.

Gettingen, M. (1984) Achievement as a function of time spent in learning and time needed for learning. American Educational Research Journal, 21, 617-628.

Giacona, R.M. and Hedges, L.C. (1982) Identifying features of effective open education. Review of Educational Research, 52, 579-602.

Gibboney, R.A. (1989) The unscientific character of educational research. Phi Delta Kappan, 71, 225-227.

Gibson, J.T. (1978) Growing up: A study of children. Reading, MA: Addison Wesley.

Gibson, J.T. and Chandler, L.A. (1988) Educational psychology: Mastering principles and applications. Boston, MA: Allyn and Bacon.

Gibson, M.A. (1976) Approaches to multicultural education in the United States: Some concepts and assumptions. Anthropology and Education Quarterly, 7, 4.

Gibson, R. (1986) Critical theory and education. London: Hodder and Stoughton.

Gilligan, C. (1977) In a different voice: Women's conception of self and morality. Harvard Educational Review, 47, 481-517.

Gilligan, C. (1982) In a different voice: Psychological theories and women's development. Cambridge, MA: Harvard University Press.

Gilligan, C., Langdale, S., Lyons, N. and Murphy, J. (1982) Contribution of women's thought to developmental theory. In M.W. Pratt, G. Goldberg and W.J. Hunter (1985) Does morality have a gender? Sex, sex role, and moral judgment relationships across the adult lifespan. Merrill-Palmer Quarterly, 31, 321-340

Ginsburg, H. and Opper, S. (1979) Piaget's theory of intellectual development (2nd. ed.) Englewood Cliffs, NJ: Prentice-Hall.

Giusti, J. and Hogg, S. (1973) Management in instruction. Journal of Teacher Education, 24, 41-43.

Glaser, R. and Nitko, A.J. (1971) Measurement in learning and instruction. In R.L. Thorndike (Ed.) Educational measurement (2nd. ed.) Washington, DC: American Council of Education.

Glasser, W. G. (1965) Reality therapy: A new approach to psychiatry. New York: Harper and Row.

Glasser, W.G. (1969) Schools without failure. New York: Harper and Row.

Glasser, W.G. (1984) Control theory. New York: Norton.

Gleason, J.B. (1985) The development of language. Columbus, OH: Merrill.

Gleitman, H. (1986) Psychology (2nd. ed.) New York: Norton.

Gleitman, H. and Glietman, L.R. (1978) Language and language judgment. In C.J. Fillmore, D. Kepler and W.S. Y. Wang (Eds.) Individual differences in language ability. New York: Academic Press.

Glynn, S.M. and Di Vesta, F.J. (1979) Control of prose processing via instructional and typographical cues. *Journal of Educational Psychology, 71*, 595-603.

Goddard, H. (1911) Two thousand normal children measured by the Binet measuring scale of intelligence. *The Pegagogical Seminary, 18*, 232-259.

Gold, M. (1970) *Delinquent behavior in an American city.* Belmont, CA: Brooks/Cole.

Gold, M.W. and Ryan, V.M. (1979) Vocational training for the mentally retarded. In I.H. Frieze, D. Bar-Tel and J.S. Carroll (Eds.) *New approaches to social problems: Applications of attribution theory.* San Francisco, CA: Jossey Bass.

Gold, R.M., Reilly, A. Silberman, R., and Lehr, R. (1971) Academic achievement decline under pass-fail grading. *Journal of Experimental Education, 39*, 17-21.

Goldberg, J.P. and Bordman, M.B. (1975) The ESL approach to teaching English to hearing impaired students. *American Annals of the Deaf, 120*, 22-27.

Goldberg, S. and Lewis, M. (1972) Play behavior in the year old infant: In J. Bardwick (Ed.) *Readings in the psychology of women* (pp. 30-34) New York: Harper and Row.

Golden, N.E. and Steiner, S.R. (1969) Auditory and visual functions in good and poor readers. *Journal of Learning Disabilities, 2*, 476-481.

Goldstein, M.J. (1981) Family factors associated with schizophrenia and anorexia nervosa. *Journal of Youth and Adolescence, 10*, 385-405.

Good., T.L. (1970) Which teachers do teachers call on? *Elementary School Journal, 70*, 190-198.

Good, T.L. (1983) Classroom research: A decade of progress. *Educational Psychology, 18*, 127-144.

Good. T.L. (1987) Teacher expectations. In D.C. Berliner and B.Y. Rosenshine (Eds.) *Talks to teachers* (pp. 159-200) New York: Random House.

Good, T.L. and Brophy, J.E. (1978/1984/1987) Looking at classrooms (2nd., 3rd. 4th. ed.). New York: Harper and Row.

Good, T.L. and Brophy, J.E. (1986) *Educational psychology* (3rd. ed.) New York: Longman.

Good, T.L. and Grouws, D. (1977) Teaching effects: A process-product study in fourth grade mathematics classrooms. *Journal of Teacher Education, 28*, 49-54.

Good, T., Grouws, D. and Beckerman, T. (1978) Curriculum pacing: Some empirical data in mathematics. *Journal of Curriculum Studies, 10*, 75-81.

Good, T.L. and Weinstein, R.S. (1986) Teacher expectations: A framework for exploring classrooms. In K.W. Zumwalt (Ed.) *Improving teaching: 1986 ASCD yearbook.* Alexandria, VA: Association for Supervision and Curriculum Development.

Goodenough, F. (1949) *Mental testing: Its history, principles and applications.* New York: Rinehart and Co.

Goodland, J.I. (1984) *A place called school.* New York: MacGraw Hill.

Goodland, J.I. (1954) Some effects of non-promotion on the achievement of groups matched from retained first-graders and promoted second-graders. *Journal of Educational Research, 60*, 472-475.

Goodman, J.F. (1989) Does retardation mean dumb? Children's perception of the nature, cause and course of mental retardation. *The Journal of Special Education, 23*, 313-323.

Goodman, P. (1964) *Compulsory miseducation.* New York: Horizon Press.

Goodstadt, M.S. and Willett, M.M. (1989) Opportunities for school-based drug education: Implications from the Ontario school drug surveys, 1977-1985. *Canadian Journal of Education/ Revue canadienne de l'education, 14*, 338-351.

Gordon, T. (1970) *Parent effectiveness training.* New York: Peter H. Wyden.

Gordon, T. (1974) *Teacher effectiveness training.* New York: Peter H. Wyden.

Gottesman, I.I. (1974) Developmental genetics and ontogenetic psychology. *Minnesota Symposia on Child Psychology, 8*, 54-78.

Gottfried, A.E. (1985) Academic intrinsic motivation in elementary and junior high school students. *Journal of Educational Psychology, 77*, 631-645.

Gottlieb, J., Campbell, D. H. and Budoff, M. (1975) Classroom behavior of retarded children before and after integration into regular classes. *Journal of Special Education, 9*, 307-315.

Gottlieb, J. Leyser, Y. and Michaels, C. (1990) Parental attitudes toward mainstreaming:. A new look at an old question. In R.A. Curci and J. Gottlieb (1990) Teachers' instruction of non-categorically grouped handicapped children. *Exceptionality, 1*, 239-248.

Gowan, J.C. (1980) The use of developmental stage theory in helping gifted children become creative. *Gifted Child Quarterly, 24*, 22-28.

Gowan, J.C. and Bruch, C.B. (1971) *The academically talented student and guidance.* Boston, MA: Houghton Mifflin.

Graden, J., Kaufman, N., Christenson, S. Ysseldyke, J., and Meyers, J. (1984) A national survey of students' and practitioners' perceptions of training. *School Psychology Review, 13.* 297-405.

Graham, S. (1984) Communicating sympathy and anger to black and white children: The cognitive (attributional) consequences of affective clues. *Journal of Personality and Social Psychology, 47*, 40-54.

Graham, S. and Barker, G.P. (1990) The down side of help: An attributional-development analysis of helping behavior as a low-ability cue. *Journal of Educational Psychology, 82*, 7-14.

Granowsky, S. and Davis, L.T. (1974) Three alternative roles for the school psychologist. *Psychology in the Schools, 11*, 415-421.

Grant, L. (1984) Black females 'place' in desegregated classrooms. *Sociology of Education, 57*, 98-111.

Green, J. (1975) *Teacher-made tests* (2nd. ed.) New York: Harper and Row.

Green, K.E. and Stager, S.F. (1987a) Differences in teacher test and item use with subject, grade level taught, and measurement coursework. *Teacher Education and Practice, 4*, 55-61.

Green, K.E. and Stager, S.F. (1987b) Testing: Coursework, attitudes, and practices. *Educational Research Quarterly, 11*, 48-55.

Greenberg, J.W. and Davidson, H.H. (1972) Home background and school achievement in black urban ghetto children. *American Journal of Orthopsychiatry, 42*, 803-810.

Greene, R.L. (1986) Sources of recency effects in free recall. *Psychological Bulletin, 99*, 221-228.

Grinder, R.E. (1967) *A history of genetic psychology: The first science of human development.* New York: Wiley.

Gronlund, H. (1959) *Sociometry in the classroom.* New York: Harper and Row.

Gronlund, N.E. (1985) *Stating behavioral objectives for classroom instruction* (3rd. ed.) New York: MacMillan.

Gronlund, N.E. (1988) *How to construct achievement tests* (4th. ed.) Englewood Cliffs, NJ: Prentice-Hall.

Grosjean F. (1982) *Life with two languages.* Cambridge, MA: Harvard University Press.

Grossman, H. (Ed.) (1977/1983) *Manual on terminology and classification in mental retardation.* Washington, D.C: American Association on Mental Deficiency.

Gualtieri, T. and Hicks, R.E. (1985) An immunoreactive theory of selective male affliction. *The Behavioral and Brain Sciences, 8*, 427-441.

Guetzloe, E. (1988) Suicide and depression: Special education's responsibility. *Teaching Exceptional Children, 20*, 25-28.

Guilford, J.P. (1967) *Way beyond the IQ.* Buffalo, NY: Creative Educational Foundation.

Gullickson, A.R. (1986) Teacher education and teacher-perceived needs in educational measurement and evaluation. *Journal of Educational Measurement, 23,* 347-354.

Gump, P.V. (1982) School settings and their keeping. In D.L. Duke (Ed.) *Helping teachers manage classrooms.* Alexandria, VA: Association for Supervision and Curriculum Development.

Guralnick, M.J. (1986) The peer relations of young handicapped and nonhandicapped children. In P.S. Stein, M.J. Guralnich and H.M. Walter (Eds.) *Children's social behavior: Development, assessment, and modification* (pp. 95-140) New York: Academic Press.

H

Haertel, E. (1985) Construct validity and criterion-referenced testing. *Review of Educational Research, 55,* 23-46.

Hafez, E. (1973) Reproductive life cycle. In E. Hafez and T. Evans (Eds.) *Human reproduction: Conception and contraception* (pp. 100-150). New York: Harper and Row.

Hagen, J.W., Jongeward, R. H. Jr., and Kail, R.B., Jr. (1975) Cognitive perspectives on the development of memory. In H.W. Reese (Ed.) *Advances in child development and behavior* (vol. 10) New York: Academic Press.

Hains, A. and Miller, D. (1980) Moral and cognitive development in delinquent and non-delinquent children and adolescents. *Journal of Genetic Psychology, 137,* 21-35.

Hakuta, K. and Garcia, E.E. (1989) Bilingualism and education. *American Psychologist, 44,* 374-379.

Hall, E.T. (1959) *The silent language.* Garden City, NY: Doubleday.

Hall, G.S. (1891) The content of children's minds on entering school. *Pedagogical Seminary, 1,* 139-173.

Hall, G.S. (1905) *Adolescence: Its psychology and relationship to physiology, anthropology, sociology, sex, crime, religion and education.* New York: D. Appleton.

Hallahan, D.P. (1975) Comparative research studies on the psychological characteristics of learning disabled children. In W. Cruickshank and D.P. Hallahan (Eds.) *Perceptual and learning disabilities in children: Psychoeducational practices* (vol. 1) Syracuse, NY: Syracuse University Press.

Hallahan, D.P. and Kauffman, J.M. (1986) *Exceptional children: Introduction to special education* (3rd. ed.) Englewood Cliffs, NJ: Prentice-Hall.

Hallahan, D.P. and Reeve, R.E. (1980) Selective attention and distractibility. In B.K. Keogh (Ed.) *Advances in special education* (vol. 1) (pp. 141-181) Greenwich, CT: JAI Press.

Hallahan, D.P., Kneedler, R.D. and Lloyd, J.W. (1983) Cognitive behavior modification for learning disabled children: Self-instruction and self-monitoring. In J.D. McKinney and L. Feagans (Eds.) *Current topics in learning disabilities* (vol. 1) New York: Ablex Publishing

Hallahan, D.P., Lloyd, J.W., Kauffman, J.M., and Loper, A.B. (1983) Academic problems. In R.J. Morris and T.R. Kratochwill (Eds.) *Practice of child therapy: A textbook of methods* (pp. 113-141) New York: Pergamon Press.

Hamachek, D.E. (1987) Humanistic psychology: Theory, postulates, and implications for educational processes. In J.A. Glover and R.R. Ronning (Eds.) *Historical foundations of educational psychology* (pp. 159-182) New York: Plenum.

Hamburg, D.A. and Takanishi, R. (1989) Preparing for life: The critical transition of adolescence. *American Psychologist, 44,* 825-827.

Hamilton, R.J. (1985) A framework for the evaluation of the effectiveness of adjunct questions and objectives. *Review of Educational Research, 55,* 47-85.

Hamilton, S.F. (1983) The social side of schooling: Ecological studies of classrooms and schools. *Elementary School Journal, 83,* 313-334.

Hammermeister, F. and Timms, M. (1989) Nonverbal communication: Perspectives from teachers of hearing-impaired students. *Volta Review, 79,* 133-141.

Hammill, D.D. (1984) *Detroit Tests of Learning Aptitude* (2nd. ed.) Austin, TX: Pro-Ed.

Handel, R.D. (1983) Teachers of gifted girls: Are there differences in classroom management? *Journal for the Education of the Gifted, 6,* 86-97.

Hanid, T.K. (1976) Hypothryoidism in congenital rubella. *Lancet, 76,* 854.

Harbin, G.L. and Bailey, D.B. (1980) Nondiscriminatory evaluation. *Exceptional Children, 46,* 590-596.

Hardy, W.G. and Bordley, J.E. (1973) Problems in diagnosis and management of multiply handicapped deaf children. *Archives of Otolaryngology, 73,* 269-274.

Harley, R.K. and Lawrence, G.A. (1977) *Visual impairments in the schools.* Springfield, IL: Thomas.

Harootunian, B. and Yarger, D. (1981) Teachers conceptions of their own success. ERIC Clearing House on Teacher Education; ERIC Document No. SP 017 372.

Harris, A. and Sipay, E. (1980) *How to increase reading ability: A guide to developmental and remedial methods* (7th. ed.) New York: Longman.

Harris, A.C. (1986) *Child development.* St. Paul, MN: West.

Harris, D.B. (1963) *Goodenough-Harris Drawing Test Manual.* New York: Harcourt, Brace and World.

Harris, F.C. and Ammerman, R.T. (1986) Depression and suicide in children and adolescents. *Education and Treatment of Children, 9,* 334-343.

Harrow, A.J. (1972) *A taxonomy of the psychomotor domain: A guide for developing behavioral objectives.* New York: David McKay.

Hartshorne, H. and May, M. (1928-1930) *Studies in the nature of character* (vol. 1,2,3) New York: MacMillan.

Hartup, W.W.(1974) Aggression in childhood: Developmental perspectives. *American Psychologist, 29,* 336-341.

Hartup, W.W. (1979) The social world of children. *American Psychologist, 34,* 944-950.

Hartup, W. W. and Zook, E. (1960) Sex role preferences in three- and four-year-old children. *Journal of Consulting Psychology, 24,* 420-426.

Hasenstab, M.S. (1983) Child language studies: Impact on habituation of hearing impaired infants and preschool children. *Child Language Studies, 85,* 88-100.

Havinghurst, R. (1972) *Developmental tasks and education.* New York: David McKay.

Hawton, K. (1986) *Suicide and attempted suicide among children and adolescents.* Beverly Hills, CA: Sage.

Hayes, L.A. (1976) The use of group contingencies for behavioral control: A review. *Psychological Bulletin, 83,* 628-648.

Hayes, S.C. and Nelson, R.O. (1983) Similar reactivity produced by external cues and self-monitoring. *Behavior Modification, 7,* 183-196.

Hayes, M.L. and Sloat, R.S. (1988) Preventing suicide in learning disabled children and adolescents. *Academic Therapy, 24,* 221-230.

Haywood, H.C., Meyers, C.E. and Switzky, S.N. (1982) Mental retardation. *American Review of Psychology, 33,* 309-342.

Hazen, N.L. and Black, B. (1989) Preschool peer communication skills: The role of social status and interactive context. *Child Development, 60,* 867-876.

Hebb, D.O. (1942) The effect of early and late brain injury upon test scores and the nature of normal adult intelligence. *Proceedings of the American Philosophical Society, 85,* 275-302.

Hebb, D.O. (1949) *The organization of behavior.* New York: Wiley.

Heckhausen, H. (1967) *The anatomy of achievement motivation.* New York: Academic Press.

Hendrickson, J.M., Strain, P.S., Tremblay, A., and Shores, R.E. (1982) Interactions of behaviorally handicapped children: Functional effects of peer social initiations. *Behavior Modification, 6,* 323-353.

Henker, B. and Whalen, C.K. (1989) Hyperactivity and attention deficits. *American Psychologist, 44,* 216-223.

Herbert, W. Hemingway, P. and Hutchinson, N. (1984) Classification and placement decisions of Canadian teachers-in-training as a function of referral information. *Canadian Journal for Exceptional Children, 1,* 56-60.

Herbst, D.S. and Baird, P.A. (1983) Non-specific mental retardation in British Columbia as ascertained through a registry. *American Journal of Mental Deficiency, 87,* 506-513.

Herman, J. and Dorr-Bremme, D.W. (1983) *Testing and assessment in American public schools: Current practices and directions for improvement.* Los Angeles, CA: University of California, Center for the Study of Evaluation.

Hershberger, W.A. and Terry, D.F. (1965) Typographical cuing in conventional and programmed texts. *Journal of Applied Psychology, 49,* 55-60.

Hertz-Lazarowitz, R., Sharan, S. and Steinberg, R. (1980) Classroom learning style and cooperative behavior of elementary school children. *Journal of Educational Psychology, 73,* 97-104.

Hess, R. D. (1970) Class and ethnic influences upon socialization. In P. Mussen (Ed.) *Carmichael's manual of child psychology* (3rd. ed.) New York: Wiley

Hess, R.D. and McDevitt, T. (1984) Some cognitive consequences of maternal intervention techniques: A longitudinal study. *Child Development, 55,* 2017-2030.

Hess, R.D. and Shipman, V.C. (1970) Early experiences and the socialization of cognitive modes in children. In M.W. Miles and W.W. Charters Jr. (Eds.) *Learning in social settings.* Boston, MA: Allyn and Bacon.

Hessler, G. and Kitchen, D. (1980) Language characteristics of a purposive sample of early elementary learning disabled students. *Learning Disability Quarterly, 3,* 36-41.

Hetherington, E.M. and Parke, R.D. (1979) *Child psychology: A contemporary viewpoint* (2nd. ed.) New York: MacGraw Hill.

Heuchert, C.M. (1989) Enhancing self-directed behavior in the classroom. *Academic Therapy, 24,* 295-303.

Heyns, B. (1978) *Summer learning and the effect of schooling.* New York: Academic Press.

Hiatt, D.B. (1979) Time allocation in the classroom: Is instruction being short changed? *Phi Delta Kappan, 61,* 289-290.

Hiebert, B., Wong, B. and Hunter, M. (1982) Affective influences on learning disabled adolescents. *Learning Disability Quarterly, 5,* 334-342.

Hilgard, E.R. (1987) *Psychology in America: A historical survey.* New York: Harcourt Brace Javonovich

Hilgard, E.R., Atkinson, R.L. and Atkinson, R.C. (1979) *Introduction to psychology* (7th. ed). New York: Harcourt Brace Jovanovich.

Hill, J.P. (1987) Research on adolescents and their families. Past and prospect. In C.E. Irwin (Ed.) *Adolescent social behavior and health* (pp. 13-31) San Francisco, CA: Jossey Bass.

Hill, K.T. and Eaton, W.O. (1977) The interaction of test anxiety and success-failure experiences in determining children's arithmetic performance. *Developmental Psychology, 13,* 205-211.

Hills, J.R. (1976/1881) *Measurement and evaluation in the classroom.* Columbus, OH: Merrill.

Hirsch, J. (1971) Race, intelligence and IQ: A debate. In N. Chalmer, R. Crawley and P.D. R. rose (Eds.) *The biological bases of behavior* (pp. 244-245) London: Open University Press, Harper and Row.

Hiskey, M.S. (1966) *Hiskey-Nebraska Test of Learning Aptitude.* Lincoln, NA: Union College Press.

Hodapp, A.F. and Hodapp, J.B. (1986) Correlations of the PPVT and WISC-R: A function of diagnostic category. *Psychology in the Schools, 17,* 33-36.

Hodgson, K. (1973) *The deaf and their problems: A study in special education.* London: Watts, 1952 (Fasc. ed.) Ann Arbor: University Microfilms.

Hoffman, L.W. (1977) Changes in family roles, socialization and sex differences. *American Psychologist, 32,* 644-657.

Hoffman, L.W. (1989) Effects of maternal employment in the two-parent family. *American Psychologist, 44,* 283-292.

Hoge, R.D. (1988) Issues in the definition and measurement of the giftedness construct. *Educational Researcher, 17,* 12-16, 22.

Hoge, D.R., Smit, E.K. and Hanson, S.L. (1990) School experiences predicting changes in self-esteem of sixth and seventh grade students. *Journal of Educational Psychology, 82,* 117-127.

Hollinger, C.L. and Fleming, E.S. (1984) Internal barriers to the realization of potential: Correlates and interrelationships among gifted and talented female adolescents. *Gifted Child Quarterly, 28,* 135-139.

Holman, J. and Baer, D.M. (1979) Facilitating generalization of on-task behavior through self-monitoring of academic tasks. *Journal of Autism and Developmental Disorders, 9,* 429-446.

Holmes, B. J. (1981) Individually administered intelligence tests: An application of anchor test norming and equating procedures in British Columbia. Ed. D. thesis, University of British Columbia.

Holmes, C.T. and Matthews, K.M. (1984) The effects of non-promotion on elementary and junior high school pupils: A meta-analysis. *Review of Educational Research, 54,* 225-236.

Holmes, D.S. (1974) Investigations of repression: Differential recall of material experimentally or naturally associated with ego threat. *Psychological Bulletin, 81,* 632-653.

Holt, J. (1964) *How children fail.* New York: Pitman.

Holtzman, W.H. and Polyzoi, E. (1987) Assessment of speech and language disordered limited English proficient Hispanic students: The use of pragmatics for distinguishing a 'true' handicapping condition from a language difference. Paper presented at Texas Council for Exceptional Children, Austin.

Homme, L., Csanyi, A.P., Gonzales, M.A., and Rechs, J.R. (1970) *How to use contingency contracting in the classroom.* Champaign, IL: Research Press.

Honea, J.M. Jr. (1982) Wait-time as an instructional variable: An influence on teacher and student. *The Clearing House, 56,* 167-170.

Honzig, M.P., McFarlane, J.W. and Allen, L. (1948) The stability of mental test performance between two and eighteen years. In R. C. Kuhler (Ed.) *Studies in educational psychology.* Waltham, MA: Blaisdell.

Hoover, M.R., Politzer, R.L. and Taylor, O. (1987, April-July) Bias in reading test for black language speakers: A sociolinguistic perspective. *Negro Educational Review,* pp. 81-98.

Hopkins, C.O. and Antes, R.L. (1979) *Classroom testing: Administration, scoring and some interpretation.* Itasca, Il: F.E. Peacock.

Hopkins, K.D. and Bracht, G.H. (1975) Ten-year stability of verbal and nonverbal IQ scores. *American Educational Research Journal, 12,* 469-477.

Horn, J.L. (1978) The nature and development of intellectual abilities. In R.T. Osborn, C.E. Noble and N. Weizl (Eds.) *Human variation: The biopsychology of age, race, and sex.* New York: Academic Press.

Horn, J.L. and Donaldson, G. (1980) Cognitive development in adulthood. In O. Brim and J. Kagan (Eds.) *Constancy and change in human development.* Cambridge, MA: Harvard University Press.

Hothersall, D. (1984) *History of psychology.* Philadelphia, PA: Temple University Press.

Howell, F., Ohlendorf, G. and McBroom, L. (1981) The 'ambition-achievement' complex: Values as organizing determinants. *Rural Sociology, 46,* 465-482.

Howell, K. W., Caplan, J. S. and O'Donnell, C. Y. (1979) *Evaluating exceptional students.* Columbus, OH: Merrill.

Howell, K.W. and Morehead, M.K. (1987) *Curricula-based evaluation for special and remedial education.* Columbus, OH: Merrill.

Howley, C. (1982) Relationship between structural class background and intelligence. Masters thesis, West Virginia College of Graduate Students.

Hsu, L., Crusp, A. and Harding, B. (1979, January 13) Outcome of anorexia nervosa. *Lancet*, pp. 61-65.

Huessman, L. R. and Eron, L. D. (1983) Factors influencing the effect of television violence on children. In I.M. Howe (Ed.) *Learning from television: Psychological and edcuational research* (pp. 153-178). New York: Academic Press.

Huessman, L.R., Eron, L.D. and Yarmel, P.W. (1987) Intellectual functioning and aggression. *Journal of Personality and Social Psychology, 52,* 232-240.

Huessman, L.R., Eron, L.D., Lefkowitz, M. and Walder, L. (1984) Stability of aggression over time and generations. *Developmental Psychology, 20,* 1120-1134.

Humphrey, L.L. (1984) Children' self-control in relation to perceived social environment. *Journal of Personality and Social Psychology, 46,* 178-188.

Humphrey, L.L., Karoly, P. and Kirschenbaum, D.S. (1978) Self-management in the classroom: Self-imposed response cost versus self-reward. *Behavior Therapy, 9,* 592-601

Hunkins, F.P. (1969) Effects of analyses and evaluation questions on various levels of achievement. *Journal of Experimental Education, 38,* 45-58.

Hunt, J. McV. (1961) *Intelligence and experience.* New York: Ronald Press.

Hunter, M. (1984) Knowing, teaching and supervising. In P.L. Hosford (Ed.) *Using what we know about teaching.* Alexandria, VA: Association of Supervision and Curriculum Development.

Hurt, H.T., Scott, M.D. and McCrokey, J.C. (1978) *Communication in the classroom.* Reading, England: Addison-Wesley.

Huston, A.C. (1985) The development of sex-typing: Themes from recent research. *Developmental Review, 5,* 1-17.

Huston, A.C., Carpenter, C.J. Atwater, J.B, and Johnson, L.M. (1986) Gender, adult structuring of activities, and social behavior in middle childhood. *Child Development, 57,* 1200-1209.

Huston-Stein, A. and Higgins-Trenk, A., (1978) Development of females from childhood through adulthood: Career and feminine role orientations. In P.B. Bates (Ed.) *Life-span development and behavior* (vol. 1) New York: Academic Press.

Hutchinson, N. and Hemingway, P. (1984) Educational decision-making of experienced teachers exposed to biasing information. *B.C. Journal of Special Education, 8,* 325-332.

Hutt, R. B. (1923) The school psychologist. *Psychological Clinic, 15,* 48-51.

Hyams, N. (1986, October) Core and peripheral grammar and the acquisition of inflection. Paper presented at the Boston University Conference on Language Development, Boston. ERIC Document, ED No. 291 237.

Hyde, J. (1981) How large are cognitive gender differences? *American Psychologist, 36,* 292-301.

Hyde, J.S. and Linn, M.C. (1988a) Are there sex differences in verbal abilities? *Psychological Bulletin, 104,* 53-69.

Hyde, J.S. and Linn, M.C. (1988b) Gender differences in verbal ability: A meta-analysis. *Psychological Bulletin, 104,* 53-69.

Hymes, D. (1972) On communicative competence. In J.B. Pride and J. Holmes (Eds.) *Sociolinguistics* (pp. 269-285). Harmondsworth, Middlesex, Eng.: Penguin.

I

Ianni, F.A. (1989) Providing a structure for adolescent development. *Phi Delta Kappan, 70,* 673-682.

Irwin, C.E. and Millstein, S.G. (1986) Biopsychosocial correlates of risk-taking behaviors during adolescence. *Journal of Adolescent Health Care, 7,* 82-93.

Isaacson, R.L. (1964) Relation between achievement, test anxiety, and curricular choices. *Journal of Abnormal and Social Psychology, 64,* 447-452.

Izard, C.E., Kagan, J. and Zajonc, R. (Eds.) (1983) *Emotion, cognition, and behavior.* New York: Cambridge University Press.

J

Jacklin, C.N. (1989) Female and male: Issues of gender. *American Psychologist, 44,* 127-133.

Jacklin, C.N. and Maccoby, E.E. (1978) Social behavior at thirty-three months in same-sex and mixed-sex dyads. *Child Development, 49,* 557-569.

Jacklin, C.N. and Maccoby, E.E. (1982) Length of labor and sex of offspring. *Journal of Pediatric Psychology, 7,* 355-360.

Jackson, A.W. and Hombeck, D.W. (1989) Educating young adolescents: Why we must restructure middle grade schools. *American Psychologist, 44,* 831-836.

Jackson, G.B. (1975) The research evidence on the effects of grade retention. *Review of Educational Research, 45,* 613-635.

James, W. (1890) *The principles of psychology.* New York: Holt.

James, W. (1899) *Talks to teachers on psychology: And to students on some of life's ideals.* New York: Holt.

Jeffery, R.W. (1974) Influence of symbolic and motor rehearsal on observational learning. *Journal of Research in Personality, 10,* 116-127.

Jenkins, J. R. and Pany, D. (1978) Standardized achievement tests: How useful for special education? *Exceptional Children, 44,* 448-453.

Jennings, K.D., Harmon, R.J., Morgan, G.A., Gaiter, J.L., and Yarrow, L.S. (1979) Exploratory play as an index of mastery motivation: Relationships to persistence, cognitive functioning, and environmental measures. *Developmental Psychology, 15,* 389-394.

Jensema, C.J., Karchmer, M.A. and Trybus, R.J. (1978) *The rated speech intelligibility of hearing impaired children: Basic relationships and a detailed analysis.* Series R, No. 6. Washington, DC: Gallaudet College, Office of Demographic Studies.

Jensen, A.R. (1968) Social class, race and genetics: Implications for education. *American Educational Research Journal, 5,* 1-42.

Jensen, A.R. (1969) How much can we boost IQ and scholastic achievement? *Harvard Educational Review, 39,* 1-123.

Jessor, R. and Jessor, S.L. (1977) *Problem behaviors and psychosocial development.* New York: Academic Press.

Jewett, A.E. and Mullan , M.R. (1977) Movement process categories in physical education in teaching learning. In *Curriculum design: Purposes and processes in physical education teaching-learning.* Washington, DC: American Alliance for Health.

Joffe, R.T. and Offord, D.R. (1983) Suicidal behavior in childhood. *Canadian Journal of Psychiatry, 28,* 57-63.

Johnson, C. (1982) Anorexia nervosa and bulimia. In T.J. Coates and C. Perry (Eds.) *Adolescent health: Crossings and barriers.* New York: Academic Press.

Johnson, D.D. (1972) *An investigation of sex differences in reading in four English-speaking nations* (Technical report no. 209). Washington, DC: Office of Education.

Johnson, D.D. (1976) Cross cultural perspectives on sex differences in reading. *Reading Teacher, 29,* 747-752.

Johnson, D.W. and Johnson, R.T. (1979) Conflict in the classroom: Controversy and learning. *Review of Educational Research, 49,* 51-70.

Johnson, D.W. and Johnson, R.T. (1986) Mainstreaming and cooperative learning strategies. *Exceptional Children, 52,* 553-561.

Johnson, D.W. and Johnson, R.T. (1989/90) Social skills for effective group work. *Educational Leadership, 47,* 29-33.

Johnson, D.W., Johnson, R.T. and Maruyama, G. (1983) Interdependence and interpersonal attraction among heterogeneous and homogeneous individuals: A theoretical formulation and a meta-analysis of the research, Review of Educational Research, 53, 5-54.

Johnson, D.W., Johnson, R.T., Warring, D., and Maruyama, G. (1986) Different cooperative learning procedures and cross-handicap relations. Exceptional Children, 53, 247-252.

Johnson, J.E. and Roopnarine, J.L. (1983) The preschool classroom and sex differences in children's play. In M. Liss (Ed.) Social and cognitive skills (pp. 193-218) New York: Academic Press.

Johnson, J.O., and Boyd, H.F. (1981) Nonverbal Test of Cognitive Skills. Columbus, OH: Merrill.

Johnson, R.T., Johnson, D.W. and Stanne, M.B. (1986) Comparison of computer-assisted, cooperative, competitive and individualistic learning. American Educational Research Journal, 23, 382-392.

Jonassen, D., Hannum, W. and Tessner, M. (1989) Handbook of task analysis procedures. New York: Praeger.

Jones, C. and Jones, L. (1986) Comprehensive classroom management. Newton, MA: Allyn and Bacon.

Jones, J.C. and Mussen, P.H. (1958) Self-conceptions, motivations and interpersonal attitudes of early and late maturing girls. Child Development, 29, 491-501.

Jones, M. (1957) The labor careers of boys who were early or late maturing. Child Development, 28, 113-128.

K

Kacerguis, M. and Adams, G. (1980) Erickson stage resolutions: The relationship between identity and intimacy. Journal of Youth and Adolescence, 9, 117-126.

Kagan, J. (1964) Developmental studies of reflection and analysis. Cambridge, MA: Harvard University Press.

Kagan, J. (1965) Impulsive and reflective children: Significance of conceptual tempo. In J.D. Krumboltz (Ed.) Learning and the educational process. Chicago, Il: Rand McNally.

Kagan, J. (1971) Change and continuity in infancy. New York: Wiley.

Kagan, J. (1979) Overview: Perspectives on human infancy. In J.D. Osofsky (Ed.) Handbook of infant development. New York: Wiley.

Kagan J. (1980) Jean Piaget's contributions. Phi Delta Kappan, 62, 245-246.

Kagan J. (1989) Temperamental contributions to social behavior. American Psychologist, 44, 668-674.

Kagan, J. and Kagan, N. (1970) Individual variations in cognitive processes. In P. Mussen (Ed.) Carmichael's manual of child psychology (3rd. ed.) New York: Wiley.

Kagan, J., Rosman, B., Day D., Albert, J. and Phillips, W. (1964) Information processing and the child: Significance of analytic and reflective attitudes. Psychological Monographs, 78 (1) (Whole number 578)

Kagan, J. and Moss, H.A. (1962) Birth of maturity. New York: Wiley.

Kagan, S. (1983) Social orientation among Mexican-American children: A challenge to traditional classroom structures. I. E. Garcia (Ed.) The Mexican-American child: Language, cognition and social development. Tempe, AZ: Centre for Bilingual Education.

Kagan, S. and Madsen, M. (1971) Cooperation and competitition of Mexican, Mexican-American, and Anglo-American children of two ages under four instructional sets. Developmental Psychology, 5, 32-39.

Kaluger, G. and Kolson, C.J. (1978) Reading and learning disabilities (2nd. ed.) Columbus, OH: Merrill.

Kamii, C. (1984) Autonomy: The aim of education envisoned by Piaget. Phi Delta Kappan, 65, 410-415.

Kandel, D.B. (1978) Homophily, selection, and socialization in adolescent friendships. American Journal of Sociology, 84, 427-436.

Kandel, D.B., Kessler, R.C., and Margulies, R.Z. (1978) Antecedents of adolescent initiation into stages of drug use. In D.B. Kandal (Ed.) Longitudinal research and drug use: Empirical findings and methodological issues (pp. 73-98). Washington, DC: Hemisphere.

Kanfer, F.H. (1970) Self-monitoring: Methodological limitations and clinical applications. Journal of Consulting and Clinical Psychology, 35, 148-152.

Kanter, J.F. and Zelnik, M. (1972) Sexual experiences of young unmarried women in the US. Family Planning Perspectives, 4, 9-17.

Kaplan, P., Kohfeldt, J. and Sturla, K. (1974) It's positively fun: Techniques for managing learning environments. Denver, CO: Love Publishing.

Kaplan, R.M. and Pascoe, G.C. (1977) Humourous lectures and humorous examples: Some effects upon comprehension and retention. Journal of Educational Psychology, 69, 61-65.

Karnes, F.A. and Brown, K. (1979) Comparison of the SIT with the WISC-R for gifted students. Psychology in the Schools, 16, 478-482.

Karpoe, K. and Olney, R. (1983) The effect of boys' or girls' toys on sex-typed play in preadolescents. Sex Roles, 9, 507-518.

Kauffman, J.M. (1985) Characteristics of children's behavior disorders (3rd ed.) Columbus, OH: Merrill.

Kaufman, A.S. and Hagen, J. (1977) Investigation of the WISC-R for use with

retarded children: Correlation with the 1972 Stanford-Binet and comparison of WISC and WISC-R profiles. Psychology in the Schools, 14, 10-14.

Kaufman, A. S. and Kaufman, N. L. (1983) Kaufman Assessment Battery for Children (K-ABC) Circle Pines, MN: American Guidance Services.

Kazdin, A.E. (1972) Response cost: The removal of conditioned reinforcers for therapeutic change. Behavior Therapy, 3, 533-546.

Kazdin, A.E. (1973) The effects of vicarious reinforcement on attentive behavior in the classroom. Journal of Applied Behavior Analysis, 6, 71-78.

Kazdin, A.E. (1982) The token economy: A decade later. Journal of Applied Behavior Analysis, 15, 432-445.

Kazdin, A.E. (1989) Behavior modification in applied settings (4th. ed.) Pacific Grove, CA: Brooks/Cole.

Kazdin, A.E. and Klock, J. (1973) The effect of nonverbal teacher approval on student attentive behavior. Journal of Applied Behavior Analysis, 6, 643-654.

Kazdin, A.E. and Matson, J.L. (1981) Social validation with the mentally retarded. Applied Research in Mental Retardation, 2, 39-59.

Kazdin, A.E. and Polster, R. (1973) Intermittent token reinforcement and response maintenance in extinction. Behavior Therapy, 4, 386-391.

Kazdin, A.E., French A.S., Unis, A.S., Esvaldt-Dawson, K. and Sherick, R.B. (1983) Hopelessness, depression, and suicidal intent among psychiatrically disturbed inpatient children. Journal of Counseling and Clincal Psychology, 51, 504-510.

Keating, D.P. (1975) Precocious cognitive develoment at the level of formal operations. Child Development, 46, 276-280.

Keating D.P. and Schaefer, R.A. (1975) Ability and sex differences in the acquisition of formal operations. Developmental Psychology, 11, 531-532.

Keith, L. and Hughey, M.J. (1979) Twin gestation: Gyneocology and obsterics (2nd. ed.) Hegerstown, MD: Harper and Row.

Kellam, S.G., Branch, J.D. Agraival, K. and Ensminger, M.E. (1975) Mental health and going to school: The Woodlawn program of assessment, early intervention, and evaluation. Chicago, IL: University of Chicago Press.

Kellam, S.G., Brown, C.H. Rubin, B.R. and Ensminger, M.E. (1983) Paths leading to teenage psychiatric symptoms and substance use: Developmental epidemiological studies in Woodlawn. In S.B. Guze, F.J. Earls, and J.E. Barrett (Eds.) Childhood psychopathology and development (pp. 17-47) New York: Raven.

Keller, F.S. (1969) Good-bye teacher! *Journal of Applied Behavior Analysis*, 1, 79-84.

Kelley, M.L. and Stokes, T.F. (1982) Contingency contracting with disadvantaged youth: Improving school performance. *Journal of Applied Behavior Analysis*, 15, 447-454.

Kemper, R. (1985) Metalinguistic correlates of reading ability in second grade children. Doctoral dissertation, Kent State University.

Keogh, B. K. and Levitt, M. C. (1976) Special education in the mainstream: A confrontation of limitations. Focus on *Exceptional Children*, 8, 1-11.

Keogh, B.K. and Margolis, J. (1976) Learn to labor and to wait: Attentional problems of children with learning disabilities. *Journal of Learning Disabilities*, 9, 276-286.

Keppel, G. (1968) Retroactive and proactive inhibition. In T.R. Dixon and D.L. Norton (Eds.) *Verbal behavior and general behavioral theory* (pp. 172-213) Englewood Cliffs, NJ: Prentice-Hall.

Kerr, M.M. and Nelson, C.M. (1989) *Strategies for managing behavior problems in the classroom* (2nd ed.) Columbus, OH: Merrill.

Kessen, W. (1965) *The child.* New York: Wiley.

Key, E. (1909) *The century of the child.* New York: S.P. Putnam.

Kiewra, K.A. (1985a) Investigating notetaking and review: A depth of processing alternative. *Educational Psychologist*, 20, 23-32.

Kiewra, K.A. (1985b) Providing the instructor's notes: An effective addition to student notetaking. *Educational Psychologist*, 20, 33-39

Kifer, E. (1975) Relationship between academic achievement and personality characteristics: A quasi-longitudinal study. *American Educational Research Journal*, 12, 191-210.

Kinnison, L.R., Hayes, C. and Acord, J. (1981) Evaluating student progress in mainstream classes. *Teaching Exceptional Children*, 13, 97-99.

Kintsch, W. (1977) On comprehending stories. In M. Just and P. Carpenter (Eds.) *Cognitive processes in comprehension.* Hillsdale, NJ: Erlbaum.

Kirschenbaum, R. (1980) Combatting sexism in the preschool environment. *Roeper Review*, 2, 31-33.

Klatzky, R.L. (1980) *Human memory. Structures and processes* (2nd ed.) San Francisco, CA: Freeman

Klauer, K.L. (1984) Intentional and incidental learning with instructional texts: A meta-analysis for 1970-1980. *American Educational Research Journal*, 21, 323-339.

Klausmeier, H.J., Feldhausen, J.F. and Check, J. (1959) *An analysis of learning efficiency in arithmetic of mentally retarded children in comparison with children of average intelligence.* US Office of Education, Research project no. 153. Madison: WI: University of Wisconsin.

Klausmeier, K., Shitala, P.M. and Maker, J.C. (1987) Identification of gifted learners: A national survey of assessment practices and training needs of school psychologists. *Gifted Child Quarterly*, 31, 135-137.

Kloss, H. and McConnell, G. (1978) *Linguistic composition of the nations of the world, volume 2, North America.* Quebec: Les Presses de l'Universite Laval.

Kneedler, R., with D.P. Hallahan and J.M. Kauffman (1984) *Special education for today.* Englewood Cliffs, NJ: Prentice-Hall.

Kneedler, R.D. and Hallahan, D.P. (1981) Self-monitoring of on-task behavior with learning disabled children: Current studies and directions. *Exceptional Education Quarterly*, 1, 73-82.

Knowles, D.W. and Boersma, F.J. (1971) A comparison of optimal shift performance and language skills in middle-class and Canadian Indian children. *Canadian Journal of Behavioral Science*, 3, 246-258.

Knowlson, J. (1965) The idea of gesture as a universal language in the seventeenth and eighteenth centuries. *Journal of the History of Ideas*, 26, 495-508.

Koestner, R., Ryan, R., Bernieri, F., and Holt, K. (1971) Setting limits on children's behavior: The differential effects of controlling versus informational styles on instrinsic motivation and creativity. *Journal of Personality*, 100-103.

Kohlberg, L. (1964) Development of moral character and moral ideology. In M.L. Hoffman and L.W. Hoffman (Eds.) *Review of child research development* (vol. 1) (pp. 383-432) New York: Russell Sage.

Kohlberg, L. (1967) Moral and religious education and the public schools. In T.R. Sizer (Ed.) *Religious and public education.* Boston: Houghton Mifflin.

Kohlberg, L. (1969a) *Stages in the development of moral thought and action.* New York: Holt, Rinehart and Winston.

Kohlberg, L. (1969b) Stage and sequence: The cognitive-developmental approach to socialization. In D.A Goslin (Ed.) *Handbook of socialization theory and research.* Chicago: Rand McNally.

Kohlberg, L. (1973) Implications of developmental psychology for education: Examples from moral development. *Educational Psychologist*, 10, 2-14.

Kohlberg, L. (1975) The cognitive-developmental approach to moral development. *Phi Delta Kappan*, 56, 171.

Kohlberg, L. (1976) Moral stages and moralization. The cognitive developmental approach. In T. Lickona (Ed.) *Moral development and behavior* (pp.12-41) New York: Holt, Rinehart and Winston.

Kohlberg, L. (1978) Revisions in the theory and practice of moral development. In W. Damon (Ed.) *Moral development.* San Francisco: Jossey Bass.

Kohlberg, L. (1981) *Essays on moral development, (vol.1): The philosophy of moral development.* San Francisco, CA: Harper and Row.

Kohlberg, L. (1982) Reply to Owen Flanagan and some comments on the Puka-Goodpaster exchange. *Ethics*, 92, 513-528.

Kohlberg, L. and Turiel, E. (1971a) Developmental methods in moral education. In G. Lesser (Ed.) *Psychological approaches to teaching.* Chicago: Scott, Foresman.

Kohlberg, L. and Turiel, E. (1971b) Moral development and moral education. In G. Lesser, (Ed.) *Psychology and educational practice.* Chicago: Scott, Foresman.

Kohlberg, L. Levine, C. and Hewer, A. (1983) *Moral stages: A current formulation and a response to critics.* New York: Karger.

Kolb, B. and Whishaw, I. (1980) *Fundamentals of human neurophysiology.* San Francisco: CA: W.H. Freeman.

Kolb, D.A. (1965) Achievement motivation training program for under-achieving high-school boys. *Journal of Personality and Social Psychology*, 2, 783-792.

Kontos, S. (1983) Adult-child interaction and the origins of metacognition. *Journal of Educational Research*, 77, 43-54.

Kounin, J.S. (1970) *Discipline and group management in classrooms.* Melbourne, FL: Robert E. Krieger.

Kounin, J.S. and Doyle, P.H. (1975) Degree of continuity of a lesson's signal system and task involvement of children. *Journal of Educational Psychology*, 67, 159-164.

Kounin, J.S., and Gump, P.V. (1974) Signal systems of lesson settings and the task related behavior of preschool children. *Journal of Educational Psychology*, 66, 554-562.

Kozens, J. (1990, March/April) A closer look at continuous learning. *ATA Magazine*, pp. 9-11.

Kozoil, S. (1973) The development of noun plural rules during the primary grades. *Research in the Teaching of English*, 7, 30-50.

Krantz, P. and Risley, T. (1977) Behavioral ecology in the classroom. In K. O'Leary and S. O'Leary (Eds.) *Classroom management: The successful use of behavior modification* (2nd. ed.) New York: Pergamon Press.

Krashen, S. (1981) Bilingual education and second language acquisition theory. In *Schooling and language minority students: A theoretical framework* (pp. 51-79). Los Angeles, CA: Evaluation, Dissemination and Assessment Center.

Kratchowill, T.R. and Van Someren, K.R. (1985) Barriers to treatment success in behavioral consultation: Current limitations and future directions. *Journal of School Psychology, 23*, 225-239.

Krathwohl, D.R. Bloom, B.S., and Masia, B.B. (1956) *A taxonomy of educational objectives: Handbook II: Affective domain*. New York: David MacKay.

Kubiszyn, T. and Borich, G.D. (1984) *Educational testing and measurement*. Glenview, IL: Scott, Foresman.

Kuhn, D. (1979) The application of Piaget's theory of cognitive development to adolescence. *Harvard Educational Review, 49*, 340-360.

Kulic, J. Kulic, C. and Carmicheal, K. (1974) The Keller plan in science teaching. *Science*, 379-384.

Kyle, J. (1980-81) Signs of speech: Cooperating in deaf education. *Special Education: Forward Trends, 7*, 21-29.


L

Lachapelle, R. (1990, fall) The position of French improves: The proportion declines. *Language and Society*, pp. 9-11.

La Greca, A.M. and Mesibov, G.B. (1979) Social skills intervention with learning disabled children: Selecting skills and implimenting training. *Journal of Clinical Child Psychology, 8*, 234-241.

Lahaderne, H. and Jackson, P. (1970) Withdrawal in the classroom: A note on some educational correlates of social disability among school children. *Journal of Educational Psychology, 61*, 97-101.

Lahey, B.B., Genrich, J.G., Genrich, S.I., Schnelle, J.F., Gant, D.S., and McNees, M.P. (1977) An evaluation of daily report cards with minimal teacher and parent contracts as an effective method of classroom intervention. *Behavior Modification, 1*, 381-394.

Lahey, B.B., Hammer, D. Crumrine, P.L. and Forehand, R.L. (1980) Birth order x sex interactions in child development problems. *Developmental Psychology, 16*, 608-615.

Lamb, M. E.(1974) Interaction between two-year-olds and their mothers and fathers. J.T. Gibson (1978) *Growing up: A study of children*. Reading, MA: Addison Wesley.

Lamb, M. E. (1975, Spring) The sociability of two-year-olds with their mothers and fathers. *Child Psychiatry and Human Development*, pp. 182-188.

Lamb, M.E. (1978) The father's role in the infant's social world. In J.H. Stevens and M. Mathews (Eds.) *Mother/child/father/child relationships*. Washington, DC: National Association for the Education of Young Children.

Lamb, M.E. (1979) Parental influences and the father's role: A personal perspective. *American Psychologist, 34*, 938-943.

Lamb, M.E. and Baumrind, D. (1978) Socialization and personality development in the preschool years. In M.E. Lamb (Ed.) *Social and personality development*. New York: Holt, Rinehart and Winston.

Lambert, W. (1974) A Canadian experiment in the development of bilingual competence. *Canadian Modern Languages Review, 31*, 108-116.

Lambert, W. (1977) The effects of bilingualism on the individual: Cognitive and sociocultural consequences. In P. Hornby (Ed.) *Bilingualism: Psychological, social, and educational implications*. New York: Academic Press.

Lambert, W.E. and Tucker, G.R. (1977) A home/school language switch program. In In W.F. Mackay, and T. Andersen (Eds.) Bilingualism in early childhood (pp. 327-333) Rowley, MA: Newbury House.

Lane, H. and Pillard, R. (1978) *The wild boy of Burindii*. New York: Random House.

Langdon, H.W. (1983) Assessment and intervention strategies for the bilingual language-disordered child. *Exceptional Children, 50*, 34-76.

Langer, E.J. and Abelson, R.P. (1974) A patient by any other name ... Clinician group differences in labeling bias. *Journal of Consulting and Clinical Psychology, 42*, 4-9.

Langlois, J.H. and Downs, A.C. (1980) Mothers, fathers and peers as socialization agents of sex-typed play behaviors in young children. *Child Development, 51*, 1237-1247.

Langlois, J.H., Roggman, L.A., Casey, R.J., Ritter, J.M., Rieser-Danner, L.A., and Jenkins, V.Y. (1987) Infant preferences for atttractive faces: Rudiments of a stereotype? *Developmental Psychology, 25*, 363-369.

Laosa, L. (1982) School, occupation, culture, and family: The impact of parental schooling on the parent-child relationship. *Journal of Educational Psychology, 74*, 791-827.

Larry P. vs Wilson Riles, 1975 495F Supp. 926 (ND Cal. 1979).

Lasky, R.E. and Spiro, D. (1980) The processing of teachers' tachospically presented visual stimuli by five-month-old infants. *Child Development, 51*, 214-225.

Lasley, T.J. (1989) A teacher developed model for classroom management. *Phi Delta Kappan*, 71, 36-38.

Lavach, J.F. and Lanier, H.B. (1975) The motive to avoid success in 7th., 8th., 9th. and 10th. grade high-achieving girls. *Journal of Educational Research, 68*, 216-218.

LaVoie, J. and Adams, G. (1974) Teacher expectancy and its relation to physival and interpersonal characteristics of the child. *Alberta Journal of Educational Research, 20*, 122-132.

Lawson, A. (1975) Developing formal thought through biology teaching. *American Biology Teacher, 37*, 411-429.

Lawson, G., Paterson, J. and Lawson, A. (1983) *Alcoholism and the family*. Rockville, MD: Aspen Systems.

Laycock, F. (1979) *Gifted children*. Glenview, IL: Scott, Foresman.

Lazarowitz, R. and Karsenty, G. (1989) Cooperative learning and students' academic achievement, process skills, learning environment and self-esteem in tenth grade biology classrooms. In S. Sharan, (Ed.) *Cooperative learning: Theory and practice*. New York: Praeger.

Lazar-Morrison, C., Polin, L., May, R., and Burry, L. (1980) *A review of the literature on test use*. Los Angeles, CA: Center for the Study of Evaluation.

Leach, D.M. and Graves, M. (1973) The effects of immediate correction on improving seventh grade language arts performance. In A. Enger (Ed.) *Individualizing junior and senior high instruction to provide special education within regular classrooms*. Burlington, VT: University of Vermont.

Le Capitaine, J. (1985) The effectiveness of the Toward Affective Development program in creating an awareness of alternatives to psycho-social situations in children. *Psychology in the Schools, 22*, 444-448.

Lee, V. (1981) Terminology and conceptual revision of the experimental analysis of language development: Why? *Behaviorism, 9*, 25-55.

Lee, S. and Stevens, E. (1981) *The rise of literacy and the common school in the United States: Socioeconomic analysis to 1870*. Chicago: University of Chicago Press.

Lefcourt, H. (1966) Internal versus external control of reinforcement: A review. *Psychological Bulletin, 65*, 206-220.

Lefcourt, H. (1976) *Locus of control: Current trends in research and theory*. Hillsdale, NJ: Erlbaum.

Leinhardt, G., Seevald, A.M. and Engel, M. (1979) Learning what's taught: Sex differences in instruction. Journal of *Educational Psychology, 71*, 432-439.

Leiter, J. and Brown, J.S. (1985) Determination of elementary school grading. *Sociology of Education, 58*, 166-180.

Leiter, R. (1948) *The Leiter International Performance Scale*. New York: Wiley.

Lempers, J., Block, L. Scott, M. Draper, D. (1987) The relationship between psychometric brightness and cognitive-developmental precocity in gifted preschoolers. *Merrill-Palmer Quarterly, 33*, 489-503.

Leonard, L.B. (1982) Early language development and language disorders. In G. Shames and E. Wiig (Eds.) *Human communication disorders*. Columbus, OH: Merrill.

Lepper, M.R. (1983) Extrinsic reward and intrinsic motivation: Implications for the classroom. In J.M. Levine and M.C. Wang (Eds.) *Teacher and student perceptions: Implications for learning* (pp. 281-317). Hillsdale, NJ: Erlbaum.

Lepper, M.R. and Greene, D. (1975) Turning play into work: Effects of adult surveillance and extrinsic reward on children's motivation. *Journal of Personality and Social Psychology, 31*, 479-486.

Lepper, M.R., Greene, D. and Nisbitt, R.E. (1973) Undermining children's intrinsic interest with extrinsic rewards: A test of the overjustification hypothesis. *Journal of Personality and Social Psychology, 28*, 129-137.

Lerner, R.M. and Lerner, J.R. (1983) Temperament-intelligence reciprocities in early childhood. In M. Lewis (Ed.) *Origins of intelligence* (2nd. ed.) New York: Plenum.

Lerner, R.M., Palmero, M., Spiro, A. and Nesselroade, J.R. (1982) Assessing the dimensions of temperamental individuality across the life span: The Dimensions of Temperament Survey (DOTS). *Child Development, 53*, 149-159.

Leroux, J.A. (1986) Suicidal behavior and gifted adolescents. *Roeper Review, 9*, 77-79.

Levenson, M. and Neuringer, C. (1971) Problem-solving behavior in suicidal adolescents. *Journal of Consulting and Clinical Psychology, 37*, 433-436,

Levin, J.R. (1976) What have we learned about maximizing what children learn. In J.R. Levin and V.L. Allen (Eds.), *Cognitive learning in children*. New York: Academic Press.

Levin, J.R. (1986) Four cognitive principles of learning-strategy instruction. *Educational Psychologist, 21*, 3-17.

Levine, E. (1981) *The ecology of early deafness: Guides to fashioning environments and psychological assessments*. New York: Columbia University Press.

Levinson, D.J., Darrow, C. Klein, E.B., Levinson, M.H., and McKee, B. (1978) *The seasons of a man's life*. New York: Knopf.

Lew, M., Mesch, D., Johnson, D.W., and Johnson, R.T. (1986) Positive interdependence, academic and collaborative skills, group contingencies and isolated students. *American Educational Research Journal, 23*, 476-488.

Lewin, K. (1947) Group discussion and social change. In T. M. Newcomb and E.L. Hartly (Eds.) *Readings in social psychology*. New York: Holt, Rinehart and Winston.

Lewontin, R., Rose, S. and Kamin, L. (1984) *Not in our genes*. New York: Pantheon Books.

Licht, B. and Dweck, C.S. (1984) Determinants of academic achievement: The interaction of children's achievement orientations with skill area. *Developmental Psychology, 20*, 628-632.

Lichenstein, R. (1982) New instruments, old problems for early identification. *Exceptional Children, 49*, 170-172.

Liden, G. and Renvall, U. (1977) Impedence audiometry for identification of conductive component in school children. In E.R. Hartford, F.H. Bess, L.D. Bluestone and J.O. Klein (Eds.) *Impedence screening for middle ear disease in children*. New York: Grune and Stratton.

Lieberman, L.M. (1980) Decision making model for in-grade retention (nonpromotion). *Journal of Learning Disabilities, 13*, 40-44.

Limber, J. (1977) Language in child and chimp. *American Psycholigist, 32*, 285.

Linden, K. and Linden, J. (1968) *Modern measurement: A historical perspective*. Boston, MA: Houghton Mifflin.

Linderman, R.H. and Merenda, P.F. (1979) *Educational measurement*. Glenview, IL: Scott Foresman.

Lindfors, J. (1987) *Children's language and learning* (2nd. ed.) Englewood cliffs, NJ: Prentice-Hall.

Lindsay, P.H. and Norman, D.A. (1972) *Human information processing: An introduction to psychology*. New York: Academic Press.

Lindsey, J.D. and Kerlin, M.A. (1979) Learning disabilities and reading disorders: A brief review of the secondary level literature. *Journal of Learning Disabilities, 12*, 412-414.

Linn, M.C. and Hyde, J.S. (1989, February) Gender, mathematics, and science. Paper presented at the Annual Meeting of the American Association for the Advancement of Science, San Francisco.

Lippmann, W. (1923) Mr. Burt and the intelligence tests, etc. *New Republic, 34*, 263-264, 295-296, 322-323.

Lipsitt, L.P. (1966) Learning processes of human newborns. *Merrill-Palmer Quarterly, 12*, 45-71.

Lipsitt, L.P. (1990) Learning and memory in infants. *Merrill-Palmer Quarterly, 36*, 53-66.

Litlow, L. and Pumroy, D.K. (1975) A brief review of classroom group-oriented contingencies. *Journal of Applied Behavior Analysis, 8*, 341-347.

Lloyd, J.W., Bateman, D.F., Landrum, T.J., and Hallahan, D.P. (1989) Self-recording of attention versus productivity. *Journal of Applied Behavior Analysis, 22*, 315-323.

Locke, J. (1690) An essay concerning human understanding. In I. Berlin (Ed.) *The age of Enlightenment*. New York: Mentor Books.

Lockheed, M.E., Harris, A.M., and Nemceff, W.P (1983). Sex and social influence: Does sex function as a status characteristic in mixed-sex groups of children? *Journal of Educational Psychology, 75*, 877-888.

Lockwood. A. (1978) The effects of values clarification and moral developmental curricula on school-age children: A critical evaluation of recent research. *Review of Educational Research, 48*, 325-364.

Loeber, R. (1985) Patterns and development of antisocial child behavior. *Annals of Child Development, 2*, 77-116.

Loewen, A.C. (1990) Primary mathematics instruction. Unpublished paper, University of Lethbridge.

Loftus, G. and Loftus, E. (1976) *Human memory: The processing of information*. Hillsdale, NJ: Erlbaum.

Long, J.D. and Huck, S.W. (1972) The effect of behavioral objectives on student achievement. Paper presented at the annual meeting of the American Educational Research Association, Chicago.

Loo, C.M. (1972) The effects of spatial density on the social behavior of children. *Journal of Applied Social Psychology, 2*, 372-381.

Looker, D.E. and McNutt, K.L. (1989) The effect of occupational expectations on the educational attainments of males and females. *Canadian Journal of Education, 14*, 352-367.

Loper, A. and Hallahan, D.P. (1980) A comparison of the reliability and validity of the standard MFF and the MFF20 with learning-disabled children. *Journal of Abnormal Child Psychology, 8*, 377-384.

Lowell, E.L. (1952) The effect of need for achievement on learning and speed of performance. *Journal of Psychology, 33*, 31-40.

Luce, L.F. and Smith, E.C. (Eds.) (1986) *Toward internationalism: Readings in cross-cultural communication*. (2nd. ed) Cambridge, MA: Newbury House.

Lucker, G., Rosenfield, D., Sikes, J., and Aronson, E. (1976) Performance in the interdependent classroom: A field study. *American Educational Research Journal, 13*, 115-123.

Luftig, R.L. (1989) *Assessment of learners with special needs*. Boston, MA: Allyn and Bacon.

Luiten, J., Ames, W. and Ackerson, G. (1980) A meta-analysis on the effects of advance organizers on learning and retention. *American Educational Research Journal, 17*, 211-218.

Luria, A. (1976) *Cognitive development: Its cultural and social foundations*. Cambridge, MA: Harvard University Press.

Lynch, E.W. and Stein, R. (1982) Perspectives on parent participation in special education. *Exceptional Education Quarterly, 3*, 56-63.

Lyons, N. (1983) Two perspectives: In self, relationships, and morality. *Harvard Educational Review, 53*, 125-145.

**M**

Maccoby, E.E. (1966) Sex differences in intellectual functioning. In E.E. Maccoby (Ed.) *The development of sex differences.* Stanford, CA: Stanford Univeristy Press.

Maccoby, E.E. (1980) *Social development: Psychological growth and the parent-child relationships.* New York: Harcourt Brace Javonovoch.

Maccoby, E.E. (1990) Gender and relationships: A developmental account. *American Psychologist, 45,* 513-520

Maccoby, E.E. and Jacklin, C.N. (1974) *The psychology of sex differences.* Stanford, CA: Stanford University Press.

Maccoby, E.E. and Jacklin, C.N. (1980) Sex differences in aggression: A rejoinder and reprise. *Child Development, 51,* 964-980.

Maccoby, E.E. and Martin, J. (1983) Socialization and the context of the family: Parent-child interaction. In P. Mussen (Ed.) *Handbook of child psychology* (4th. ed.) (vol. 4) New York: Wiley.

MacDonald, W.S., Gallimore, R. and MacDonald, G. (1970) Contingency counselling by school personnel: A economical model of intervention. *Journal of Applied Behavior Analysis, 3,* 175-182.

MacGregor, K., Rosenbaum, S. and Skoutajan, K. (1982) *Putting the pieces together: A parent's guide to special education in Ontario.* Toronto: Association for Children with Learning Disabilities.

MacLeod, G.E. (1985) Voices from the attic: Canadian public opinion on education. *Phi Delta Kappan, 66,* 344-348.

MacMillan, D.L. (1971) The problem of motivation in the education of the mentally retarded. *Exceptional Children, 37,* 579-586.

MacMillan, D.L. and Keogh, B. (1971) Normal and retarded children's expectancy for failure. *Developmental Psychology, 4,* 343-348.

Macnamara, J. (1977) Cognitive strategies of language learning. In W.F. Mackay, and T. Anderssen (Eds.) *Bilingualism in early childhood* (pp. 19-27) Rowley, MA: Newbury House.

Macy, D. J. and Carter, J. L. (1978) Comparison of a mainstreamed and self-contained special education program. *Journal of Special Education, 12,* 303-313.

Maddox, H. and Hoole, E. (1975) Performance decrement in the lecture. *Educational Review, 28,* 17-30.

Madsen, C.H., Becker, W.C., Thomas, D.R., Koser, L., and Plager, E. (1970) An analysis of the reinforcing function of "sit-down" commands. In R.K. Parker (Ed.) *Readings in educational psychology.* Boston, MA: Allyn and Bacon.

Maehr, M.L. (1974) *Sociocultural origins of achievement.* Monterey, CA: Brooks/Cole.

Mager, R.F. (1975) *Preparing instructional objectives.* Belmont, CA: Fearon.

Mager, R.F. and McCann, J. (1961) *Learner-controlled instruction.* Palo Alto, CA: Fearson.

Mahone, C.H. (1960) Fear of failure and unrealistic vocational aspiration. *Journal of Abnormal and Social Psychology, 60,* 253-261.

Maker, C.J., Morris, E. and James, J. (1981) The Eugene Field Project: A program for potentially gifted young people. In *Balancing the scale for the disadvantaged gifted.* Los Angeles, CA: National Stage Leadership Training Institute for the Gifted and Talented.

Malina, R.M. (1982) Motor development in the early years. In S.G. Moore and C.R. Cooper (Eds.) *The young child: Reviews of research* (vol.3) (pp. 211-230) Washington, DC: National Association for the Education of Young Children.

Malmquist, C. (1978) Development from thirteen to sixteen years. In J. Nishpitz (Ed.) *Basic handbook of child psychiatry* (vol. 1) New York: Basic Books.

Malone, G, (1975) Implimenting a differentiated school program for the gifted. *Gifted Child Quarterly, 19,* 316-327.

Mangold, S.S. (1982) Teaching reading in Braille. In S.S. Mangold (Ed.) *A teacher's guide to the special educational needs of blind and visually handicapped children.* New York: American Foundation for the Blind.

Maracek, J. (1979) *Economic, social and psychological consequences of adolescent childbearing: An analysis of data from the Philadelphia Collaborative Perinatal Project.* Final Report to the National Institute for Child Health and Human Development. Swarthmore, PA: Swarthmore College.

Maracek, J. (1985) The effects of adolescent childbearing on children's cognitive and psychosocial development. Cited in F.F. Furstenberg, J. Brooks-Gunn, and L. Chase-Lansdale (1989) Teenage pregnancy and childbearing. *American Psychologist, 44,* 313-320.

Marcia, J. (1980) Identity in adolescence. In J. Adelson (Ed.) *Handbook of educational psychology.* New York: Wiley Interescience.

Marge, M. (1972) The general problem of language disabilities in children. In J.V. Irwin and M. Marge (Eds.) *Principles of childhood language disabilities.* Englewood Cliffs, NJ: Prentice Hall.

Maris, R. (1985) The adolescent suicide problem. *Suicide and Life-Threatening Behavior, 15,* 91-109.

Marsden, L. and Harvey, E.B. (1971) Equality of educational access reconsidered: The post-secondary case in Ontario. *Interchange, 2,* 11-26.

Marsh, H.W. and Shavelson, R. (1985) Self-concept: Its multifaceted, hierarchial structure. *Educational Psychologist, 20,* 107-123.

Marshall, H. (1981) Open classrooms: Has the term outlived its usefullness? *Review of Educational Research, 51,* 181-192.

Marshall, M.H. and Weinstein, R.S. (1984) Classroom factors affecting students' self-evaluations: An interactional model. *Review of Educational Research, 54,* 301-325.

Marston, D. (1987) Does categorical teacher certification benefit the mildly handicapped child? *Exceptional Children, 53,* 423-431.

Martin, R., and McLaughlin, T.F. (1981) A comparison of the effects of free time and daily report card on the academic behavior of junior high students. *B.C. Journal of Special Education, 5,* 303-313.

Martinez, R. (1985) Reinforcing to failure. *Academic Therapy, 20,* 353-356.

Martinson, R.A. (1975) *The identification of the gifted and talented.* Reston, VA: Council for Exceptional Children.

Maslow, A. (1943) A theory of human motivation. *Psychology Review, 50,* 370-396.

Maslow, A.H. (1954) *Motivation and personality.* New York: Harper and Row.

Maslow, A.H. (1968) *Toward a psychology of being.* New York: Van Nostrand Reinhold.

Maslow, A.H. (1970) *Motivation and personality* (2nd. ed.) New York: Harper and Row.

Matas, L. Arend, R.A. and Sroufe, L.A. (1978) Continuity of adaptation in the second year: The relationship between quality of attachment and later competence. *Child Development, 49,* 547-556.

Mattes, L.J. and Omark, D.R. (1984) *Speech and language assessment for the bilingual handicapped.* San Diego, CA: College Hill.

Mayo, C. and Henley, N.M. (1981) *Gender and nonverbal behavior.* New York: Springer-Verlag.

Mayr, E. (1982) *The growth of biological thought.* Cambridge, MA: Belknap Press.

Mazurek, K. (1981, winter) The price of ethnicity. *Education Canada,* pp. 310-333.

Mazurek, K. (1987) Multiculturalism, education and the ideology of the meritocracy. In T. Wotherspoon (Ed.) *The political economy of Canadian schooling* (pp. 141-163) Toronto: Methuen.

Mazurek, K. (1991) Unpublished paper, University of Lethbridge.

McAfee, J.K. (1987) Classroom density and the aggressive behavior of handicapped children. *Education and Treatment of Children, 10,* 134-145.

McCabe, A.E. and Siegel, L.S. (1987) The stability of training effects in young children's class inclusion reasoning. *Merrill-Palmer Quarterly, 33,* 187-194.

McCaleb, J. and White, J. (1980) Critical dimensions in evaluating teacher clarity. *Journal of Classroom Interaction, 15,* 27-30.

McCall, R.B., Appelbaum, M. and Hogarty, P. (1973) Developmental changes in mental performance. *Monographs of the Society for Research in Child Development,* 38(3) (Serial no. 150).

McCall, R.B., Eichorn, D. and Haggarty, P. (1977) Transition in early mental development. *Monographs of the Society for Research in Child Development,* 42 (3, Serial No. 17)

McCall, R.J. (1983) *Effects of learning style and learning environment on achievement by levels of learning.* Norman, OK: University of Oklahoma.

McCarthy, D. (1972) *Manual for the McCarthy Scales of Children's Abilities.* New York: Psychological Corporation.

McCarty, T., Griffin, S., Apolloni, T., and Shores, R.E. (1977) Increased peer teaching with group-oriented contingencies for arithmetic performance in behavior disordered adolescents. *Journal of Applied Behavior Analysis, 10,* 313.

McClelland, D.C. (1973) Testing for competence rather than for intelligence. *American Psychologist, 28,* 1-14.

McClelland, D. (1985) *Human motivation.* Glenview, IL: Scott, Foresman.

McClelland, D.C. Atkinson, J.W., Clark, R.T., and Lowell, E.L. (1953) *The achievement motive.* New York: Appleton-Century-Crofts.

McCloskey, M., Wibble, C.G. and Cohen, N.J. (1988) Is there a flashbulb memory system? *Journal of Experimental Psychology, 117,* 171-181.

McCormick, C.B. and Levin, J.R. (1987) Mnemonic prose-learning strategies. In M. Pressley and M. McDaniel (Eds.), *Imagery and related mnemonic processes.* New York: Springer/Verlag.

McCullers, J.C.G. (1969) Stanley Hall's conception of mental development and some implications of its influence on developmental psychology. *American Psychologist, 24,* 1109-1114.

McDaniel, T.R. (1984) A primer on motivation: Principles old and new. *Phi Delta Kappan, 66,* 46-49.

McDonald, F. (1976) *Teachers do make a difference.* Princeton, NJ: Educational Testing Service.

McEachern, W. (1982) Parental decision for French immersion: A look at some influencing factors. *Canadian Modern Language Review, 36,* 239-249.

McGaugh, J.L. (1983) Hormonal influence on memory. *Annual Review of Psychology, 34,* 297-324.

McGrath, T., Tsui, E., Humphries, S., and Yule, W. (1990) Successful treatment of a noise phobia in a nine-year-old girl with systematic desensitization in vivo. *Educational Psychology, 10,* 79-83.

McGrew, P. (1970) Social and spacing density effects on aggressive behavior in preschool children. *Journal for Child Psychology and Psychiatry, 11,* 197-205.

McKeachie, W. and Kulik, J. (1975) Effective college teaching. In F. Kerlinger (Ed.) *Review of research in education* (vol. 3) Washington, DC: American Education Research Association.

McKenzie, G (1979) Effects of questions and tasklike events on achievement and on on-task behavior in a concept learning presentation. *Journal of Educational Research, 72,* 348-350.

McKinney, J. D. (1975) Teacher perceptions of the classroom behavior of reflective and impulsive children. *Psychology in the Schools, 12,* 348-352.

McKinney, J.D., Mason, J., Peterson, K., and Clifford, M. (1975) Relationship between classroom behavior and academic achievement. *Journal of Educational Psychology, 67,* 198-203.

McLaren C. (1988, December 30) Teaching immigrant children. *Toronto Globe and Mail.*

McLaughlin, B. (1978) *Second language acquisition in childhood.* Hillsdale, NJ: Erlbaum.

McLeod, K. W. (1975) A short history of immigrant students as New Canadians. In A. Wolfgang (Ed.) *Education of immigrant students.* Toronto: McClelland and Stewart.

McMann, F. (1979) In defence of lecture. *Social Studies, 70,* 270-274.

McMilen, M.M. (1979) Differential mortality by sex in fetal and neonatal deaths. *Science, 204,* 89-91.

McNeill, D. (1970) *The acquisition of language.* New York: Harper and Row.

McNemar, Q. (1964) Lost: Our intelligence? Why? *American Psychologist, 19,* 871-882.

McShane, E. and Cox, C. (1989, April) A case study of an effective teacher in a rural mainstream classroom. Paper presented at American Educational Research Association, San Francisco.

Mednick, B.R, Baker, R.L. and Hocevan, D. (1985) Family size and birth order correlates of intellectual, psychosocial and physical growth. *Merrill-Palmer Quarterly, 31,* 67-84.

Meece, J.L., Parsons, J.E., Kaczala, C.M., Goff, S.B., and Futterman, R. (1982) Sex differences in math achievement: Toward a model of academic choice. *Psychological Bulletin, 91,* 324-348.

Meehan, A. (1984) A meta-analysis of sex differences in formal operational thought. *Child Development, 55,* 1110-1124.

Mehrens, W.A. and Lehmann, I. J. (1978) *Measurement and evaluation in education and psychology* (2nd. ed.) New York: Holt, Rinehart and Winston.

Mehrens, W.A. and Lehmann, I. J. (1980) *Standardized tests in education* (3rd. ed.) New York: Holt, Rinehart and Winston.

Meichenbaum, D. (1981, April) Teaching thinking: A cognitive behavior approach. Presented at the meeting of the Society for Learning Disabilities and Remedial Education, New York.

Meichenbaum, D.H. and Goodman, J. (1971) Training impulsive children to talk to themselves: A means of developing self-control. *Journal of Abnormal Psychology, 77,* 115-126.

Melton, G.B. and Limber, S. (1989) Psychologists' involvement in care of child maltreatment. *American Psychologist, 44,* 1125-1133

Menser, M.A., Forrest, J.M. and Bransky, R.D. (1978) Rubella infection and diabetes mellitus. *Lancet, 78,* 57-60.

Menyuk, P. (1964) Styntactic rules used by children from preschool through first grade. *Child Development, 35,* 533-546.

Menyuk, P. (1984) Language development and reading. In J. Flood (Ed.) *Understanding reading comprehension* (pp. 101-122) Newark, DE: International Reading Association.

Mercer, J.R. (1973) *Labelling the mentally retarded.* Berkely, CA: University of California Press.

Mercer, C.D. and Mercer, A.R. (1981) *Teaching students with learning problems.* Columbus, OH: Merrill.

Mercer, J.R. and Lewis, J.F. (1977) *System of Multi-Cultural Pluralistic Assessment.* New York: Psychological Corporation.

Messer, S. (1970) Reflection-impulsivity: Stability and school failure. *Journal of Educational Psychology, 61,* 487-490.

Messer, S. (1976) Reflection-impulsivity: A review. *Psychological Bulletin, 83,* 1026-1052.

Messik, S. (1982) Issues of effectiveness and equity in the coaching controversy: Implications for edcuational and testing practice. *Educational Psychologist, 17,* 67-91.

Metcalfe, B.M. (1981) Self concept and attitude to school. *British Journal of Educational Psychology, 51,* 66-76.

Metz, M. (1978) *Classrooms amd corridors: The crisis of authority in desegrated secondary schools.* Berkely, CA: Univeristy of California Press.

Meyen, E. L. and Lehar, D. H. (1980) Least restrictive environments: Instructional implications. *Focus on Exceptional Children, 12,* 1-8.

Meyer, L.M. and Kishi, G.S. (1985) School integration strategies. In C. Lakin and R. Bruininks (Eds.) *Strategies for achieving community integration of developmentally disabled citizens* (pp. 231-252) Baltimore, MD: Paul H. Brooks.

Michelson, L. and Mannarino, A. (1986) Social skills training with children: Research and implications. In P.S. Strain and M.J. Guralanich (Eds.) *Children's social behavior: Development, asessment, and modification* (pp. 373-408) New York: Academic Press.

Michelsson, K. and WaszHockert, O. (1980) The value of cry analysis in neonatology and early infancy. In T. Murray and J. Murray (Eds.) *Infant communication: Cry and early speech.* Houston, TX: College Hill Press.

Milburn, G., Goodson, I.F. and Clark, R.J. (1989) *Re-interpreting current research: Images and arguments.* London, Ont: Althouse Press.

Milisen, R. (1971) The incidence of speech disorders. In L. Travis (Ed.) *Handbook of speech pathology and audiology.* New York: Appleton-Century-Crofts.

Miller, G.E., Levin, J.R. and Pressley, M. (1980) An adaptation of the keyword method to children's learning of verbs. *Journal of Mental Imagery, 4,* 57-61.

Miller, S., Bronwell, C. and Zukier, H. (1977) Cognitive certainly in children: Effects of concepts, developmental level, and method of assessment. *Developmental Psychology, 13,* 236-245.

Mills, S.R., Rice, C.T., Berliner, D.C., and Rousseau, E.W. (1980) The correspondance between teacher questions and student answers in classroom discourse. *Journal of Experimental Education, 48,* 194-209.

Millstein, S.G. (1989) Adolescent health: Challenges for behavioral scientists. *American Psychologist, 44,* 837-842.

Minuchin, P.P., and Shapiro, E.K. (1983). The school as a context for social development. In P.H. Mussen (Ed.), *Handbook of school psychology* (vol. 4). New York: Wiley.

Miranda, S.B. and Franz, R.L. (1973) Visual preference of Down's Syndrome and normal infants. *Child Development, 44,* 555-561.

Mischel, W. (1968) *Personality and assessment.* New York: Wiley.

Mischel, W. and Grusec, J. (1966) Determinants of the rehearsal and transmission of neutral and aversive behaviors. *Journal of Personality and Social Psychology, 3,* 197-205.

Mischel, W. and Mischel, H. (1976) A cognitive and social learning approach to morality and self-regulation. In T. Lickona (Ed.) *Moral development and behavior.* New York: Holt, Rinehart and Winston.

Mitchell, C. and Ault, R. (1979) Reflection-impulsivity and evaluation process. *Child Development, 50,* 1043-1049.

Moely, B.E., Hart, S.S., Santulli, K. Leal, L., Johnson, T., Rao, N., and Burney, L. (1986). How do teachers teach memory skills? *Educational Psychologist, 21,* 55-72.

Montagu, A. (1977) *Life before birth.* New York: Signet Books.

Moore, M.R. (1967) *A proposed taxonomy of the perceptual domain and some suggested activities.* Princeton, NJ: Educational Testing Service.

Moore, P. (1986) Voice disorders. In G. Shames and E. Wiig (Eds.) *Human communication disorders* (2nd. ed.) (pp. 183-229) Columbus, OH: Merrill.

Moore, W. and Cooper, H. (1984) Correlations between teacher and student background and teacher perceptions of descriptive problems and disciplinary techniques. *Psychology in the Schools, 21,* 386-392.

Moores, D.F. (1982) *Educating the deaf: Psychology, principles and practices* (2nd ed.) Boston, MA: Houghton Mifflin.

Moos, R.H. (1979) *Evaluating educational environments.* San Francisco: Jossey-Bass.

Moos, R.H. (1987) Learning environments in context: Links between school, work, and family settings. In B.J. Fraser, (Ed.) *The study of leraning environments* (vol. 2) (pp. 1-16) Perth, Western Australia: Curtin University of Technology.

Moos, R.H., and Moos, B.S. (1978) Classroom social climate and student absences and grades. *Journal of Educational Psychology, 70,* 263-269.

More, A. T. (1984) *Okanagan-Nikola Indian Quality of Education Study.* Penticton, BC: Okanagan Indian Learning Institute.

Morgan, M. (1984) Reward-induced decrements and increments in intrinsic motivation. *Review of Educational Research, 54,* 5-30.

Morse, W.C., Cutler, R.L. and Fink, A. (1964) *Public school classes for the emotionally handicapped: A research analysis.* Washington, D.C.: Council for Exceptional Children.

Mosher, R. (Ed.) (1980) *Moral education: A first generation of research and development.* New York: Praeger.

Mowrer, O.H. and Mowrer, W.M. (1938) Enuresis: A method for its study and treatment. *American Journal of Orthopsychiatry, 8,* 436-459.

Mueller, H.H., Mulcahy, R.F., Wilgosh, L. Watters, B., and Mancini, G.J. (1986) An analysis of the WISC-R with Canadian Inuit children. *Alberta Journal of Educational Research, 32,* 12-36.

Muma, J. (1978) *Language handbook.* Englewood Cliffs, NJ: Prentice-Hall.

Mussen, P. and Eisenberg-Berg, N. (1977) *Roots of caring, sharing, and helping.* San Francisco, CA: Freeman.

Myles, D.W. and Ratslaff, H. C. (1988) Teachers' bias towards visible ethnic minority groups in special education referrals. *B.C. Journal of Special Education, 12.*

Mylnek, S., Hannah, M.E. and Hamloin, M.A. (1983) Mainstreaming: Parental perceptions. *Psychology in the Schools, 19,* 354-359.

N

Nagy, P. and Klaiman, R. (1988) Attitudes to and impact of French immersion. *Canadian Journal of Education, 13,* 263-276.

Nash, R. (1976) Pupils' expectations of their teachers. In M. Stubbs and S. Delamont (Eds.) *Explorations in classroom observation.* New York: Wiley.

Natriello, G. and Dornbusch, S.M. (1984) *Teacher evaluation standards and student effort.* New York: Longman

Neill, A.S. (1960) *Summerhill: A radical approach to child rearing.* New York: Hart.

Neimark, E., Slotnik, N., and Ulrich, T. (1971) Development of memorization strategies. *Developmental Psychology, 5,* 427-432.

Neisser, U. (1982) *Memory observed: Remembering in natural contexts.* San Francisco, CA: Freeman.

Neisser, V. (1979) The concept of intelligence. *Intelligence, 3,* 217-227.

Nelson, D.L., and Archer, C.S. (1972). The first letter mnemonic. *Journal of Educational Psychology, 63,* 482-486.

Nelson, K. (1977) The syntagmatic-paradigmatic shift revisited: A review of research theory. *Psychological Bulletin, 84,* 93-116.

Nelson, R.O. (1977) Assessment of theurepatic functions of self-monitoring. In M. Hersen, R.M. Eister and P.M. Miller (Eds.) *Progress in behavior modification* (vol. 5) (pp. 345-367). New York: Academic Press.

Nemeth, J. and Samiroden, W. (1990) Diploma exams: A political approach to evaluation. *ATA Magazine, 70,* 28-31.

Newcomb, M.D. and Bentler, P.M. (1989) Substance use and abuse among children and teenagers. *American Psychologist, 44,* 242-248.

Newcombe, N., Dubos, J.S., and Baenninger, M.A. (1989) Associations of timing of puberty, spatial ability, and lateralization in adult women. *Child Development, 60,* 246-254.

Newell, A. and Simon, H. (1972) *Human problem-solving.* Englewood Cliffs, NJ: Prentice-Hall.

Newman, H.H., Freeman, F.N. and Holtzinger, K.J. (1937) *Twins: A study of heredi-*

ty and environment. Chicago: University of Chicago Press.

Newman, R. and Simpson, R. (1983) Modifying the least restrictive environment to facilitate the integration of severely emotionally disturbed children and youth. Behavior Disorders, 8, 103-112.

News Notes, (1979) Phi Delta Kappan, 61, p. 295.

Nicholls, J. (1979) Quality and equality in intellectual development: The role of motivation in education. American Psychologist, 34, 1071-1083.

Nicholls, J. and Miller, A. (1984) The differentiation of the concepts of difficulty and ability. Child Development, 54, 951-959.

Nikelson, L.B. (1984) Nonpromotion, a pseudo-scientific solution. Psychology in the Schools, 211, 485-495.

Nixon, M. (1989) An old problem: Will new approaches come? ATA Magazine, 69, 41-43.

Nowacek, E.J. and Saunders, S. (1989, April) A case study of an effective teacher in a suburban mainstream class. Paper presented at American Educational Research Association, San Francisco.

Nowicki, S., Duke, M.P., and Crouch, M.P.D. (1978) Sex differences in locus of control and performance under competitive and cooperative conditions. Journal of Educational Psychology, 70, 482-486.

Nuthall, G. and Church, J. (1973) Experimental studies of teaching behavior. In G. Chanan (Ed.) Towards a science of teaching (pp. 9-25) London: National Foundation for Educational Research.

Nye, R.D. (1981) Three psychologies: Perspectives from Freud, Skinner and Rogers. Monterey, CA: Brooks/Cole.

Nyiti, R.M. (1982) The validity of 'cultural differences explanations' for cross-cultural variation in the rate of Piagetian cognitive development. In D.A. Wagner and H.W. Stevenson, (Eds.) Cultural perspectives on child development. San Francisco, CA: Freeman.

O

Oakes, J. (1985) Keeping track: How schools structure inequality. New Haven, CT: Yale University Press.

O'Leary, S.G., and Dubey, D.R. (1979) Applications of self-control procedures by children: A review. Journal of Applied Behavior Analysis, 12, 449-465.

O'Leary, K.D. and O'Leary, S.G. (Eds.) (1977) Classroom management: The successful use of behavior modification (2nd ed.) New York: Pergamon Press.

O'Leary, K.D., Becker, W.S., Evans, M.B., and Saudargas, R.A. (1969) A token reinforcement

program in public school: A replication and systematic analysis. Journal of Applied Behavior Analysis, 2, 3-13.

Oliver, L.I. (1974) Behavior patterns in school of youths 12-17 years. Washington, DC: Department of Health, Education and Welfare.

Olson, D.R. and Pau, A. S. (1966) Emotionally loaded word and the acquisition of sight vocabulary. Journal of Educational Psychology, 57, 174-178.

Olson, S.L., Bates, J.E. and Bayles, K. (1984) Mother-infant interaction and the development of individual differences in children's cognitive development. Developmental Psychology, 20, 166-179.

Olweus, D. (1972) Personality and aggression. In Nebraska Symposium on Motivation, 1976 (p. 261-323) Lincoln, NB: Univerisity of Nebraska Press.

Olweus, D.(1979) Stability of aggressive reaction patterns in males: A review. Psychological Bulletin, 86, 852-875.

O'Malley, M. (1977) Research perspectives on social competence. Merrill-Palmer Quarterly, 23, 29-44.

Omark, D.R. and Watson, D.L. (1983) Psychological testing and bilingual education: The need for reconceptualization. In D.R. Omark and J.G. Erickson (Eds.) The bilingual exceptional child. San Diego, CA: College Hill.

Orlich, D.C., Harder, R.J., Callahan, R.C., Kravas, C. H., Kauchak, D.P, Pendergrass, R.A., and Keogh, A.J. (1985) Teaching strategies. A guide to better instruction (2nd ed.) Lexington, MA: D.C. Heath.

Orlofsky, J. (1976) Intimacy status: Relationships to interpersonal perception. Journal of Youth and Adolescence, 5, 73-83.

Orlofsky, J. and Ginsburg, S. (1981) Intimacy status: Relationship to affect cognition. Adolescence, 16, 91-100.

Orlofsky, J., Marcia, J. and Lesser, I. (1973) Ego identity states and the intimacy vs isolation crisis of young adulthood. Journal of Youth and Adolescence, 2, 211-219.

Orme, M. E. J. and Purnell, R.F. (1970) Behavior modification and transfer in an out of control classroom. In G.A. Fargo, D. Behrns, and P. Nolen (Eds.) Behavior modification in the classroom (pp. 116-138) Belmont, CA: Wordsworth.

Ornstein, P.A. and Naus, M.J. (1985) Effects of the knowledge base on children's memory strategies. In H.W. Reese (Ed.) Advances in child development and behavior. (vol. 19) New York: Academic Press.

Ornstein, P.A., Naus, M.J. and Liberty, C. (1975) Rehearsal and organization processes in children's memory. Child Development, 45, 818-830.

Ortiz, A.A. and Yates, J.R. (1983) Incidence of exceptionality among Hispanics: Implications for manpower planning. NABE Journal, 7, 41-53.

Orvaschel, H., Weissman, M.M. and Kidd, K.K. (1980) Children and depression: The children of depressed parents; the childhood of depressed parents; depression in children. Journal of Affective Disorders, 2, 1-16.

Otto, W. and Smith, R. (1980) Corrective and remedial reading (3rd. ed.) Boston, MA: Houghton Mifflin.

Ovanso, C.J. and Collier, V.P. (1985) Bilingual and ESL classrooms. Teaching in multicultural contexts. New York: MacGraw Hill.

Owen, D. (1985) None of the above: Behind the myth of scholastic aptitude. Boston, MA: Houghton Mifflin.

Owen, S.L., Blount, H.P. and Moscow, H. (1978) Educational psychology: An introduction. Boston, MA: Little, Brown.

Owens, R. E. Jr. (1988) Language development (2nd. ed.) Columbus, OH: Merrill.

P

Padilla, A. and Liebman, E. (1975) Language acquisition in the bilingual child. The Bilingual Review, 2, 34-55.

Padilla, A. and Lindholm, K. (1976) Acquisition of bilingualism: A descriptive analysis of the linguistic structures of Spanish-English speaking children. In G. Keller (Ed.) Bilingualism in the bicentennial and beyond. New York: Bilingual Review Press.

Palardy, J. (1968) What teachers believe—what children achieve. Elementary School Journal, 69, 370-374.

Palermo, D.S. and Molfese, D.L. (1973) Language acquisition from age five onward. In F. Rebelsky and L. Dorman (Eds.) Child development and behavior (2nd. ed.) New York: Kapel.

Palincsar, A.S. (1986) Metacognitive strategy instruction. Exceptional Children, 53, 118-124.

Palincsar, A.S. (1987, April) Reciprocal teaching: Field evaluation in remedial and content area reading. Paper presented at the annual meeting of the American Education Research Association, Washington, D.C.

Palincsar, A.S. and Brown, A.L (1984) Reciprocal teaching of comprehension fostering and comprehension monitoring activities. Cognition and Instruction, 2, 117-175.

Pallas, A.M. and Alexander, K. (1983) Sex differences in quantatative SAT performance: New evidence on the differential coursework hypothesis. American Educational Research Journal, 20, 165-182.

Pare, J. (1983) Alternative learning centers: Another option for discipline problems. NASSP Bulletin, 67, 61-67.

Parker, J.G. and Asher, S.R. (1987) Peer relations and later personal adjustment: Are low-accepted children at risk? *Psychological Bulletin, 102,* 357-389.

Paris, S. Lipson, M and Wixon, K. (1983) Becoming a strategic reader. *Contemporary Educational Psychology, 8,* 293-316.

Passow, A.H. (1981) The nature of giftedness and talent. *Gifted Child Quarterly, 25,* 5-10.

Patterson, C. (1973) *Humanistic education.* Englewood Cliffs, NJ: Prentice-Hall.

Patterson, G.R. (1976) The aggressive child: Victim and architect of a coercive system. In L.A. Hamerlynck, L.C. Hardy and E.J. Mash (Eds.) *Behavior modification and families—1: Theory and research.* New York: Brunner/Mazel.

Patterson, G.R. and Stouthamer-Loeber, M. (1984) The correlation of family management practices and delinquency. *Child Development, 55,* 1299-1307.

Patterson, G.R., De Baryshe, B.D. and Ramsey, E. (1989) A developmental perspective on antisocial behavior. *American Psychologist, 44,* 322-335.

Patterson, G.R., Jones. R., Whittier, J., and Wright, M.A. (1965) A behavior modification technique for a hyperactive child. *Behavior Research and Therapy, 2,* 217-226.

Patterson, M.L. (1982) A sequential functional model of nonverbal exchange. *Psychological Review, 89,* 231-249.

Patterson, M.L. (1983) *Nonverbal behavior: A functional perspective.* New York: Springer.

Pattison, P. and Grieve, N. (1984) Do spatial skills contribute to sex differences in different types of mathematical problems? *Journal of Educational Psychology, 76,* 678-689.

Paulson, M.J., Stone, D. and Sposto, R. (1978) Suicide potential and behavior in children ages 4 to 12. *Suicide and Life Threatening Behavior, 8,* 225-242.

Paulston, C. (1980) *Bilingual education: Theories and issues.* Rowley, MA: Newbury house.

Pavio, A. (1971) *Imagery and verbal processes.* New York: Holt, Rinehart, and Winston.

Pavlidis, G.T. and Miles, T.R. (1981) *Dyslexia research and its application to education.* New York: Wiley.

Pavlov, I. (1927) *Conditioned reflexes.* London: Oxford University Press.

Pearson, P. and Gallagher, M. (1983) The instruction of reading comprehension. *Contemporary Educational Psychology, 8,* 317-344.

Peck, C.A. and Cooke, T.P. (1983) Benefits of mainstreaming at the early childhood level: How much can we expect? *Analysis and Intervention in Developmental Disabilities, 3,* 1-22.

Peck, M.L. (1985) Crisis intervention treatment with chronically and acutely suicidal adolescents. In M.L. Peck, N.L. Farebow and R.E. Litman (Eds.) *Youth suicide* (pp. 112-122) New York: Springer.

Peckham, P.D. and Roe, M.D. (1977) The effects of frequent testing. *Journal of Research and Development in Education, 10,* 40-50.

Pelham, W.E. (1981) Attention deficits in hyperactive and learning-disabled children. *Exceptional Education Quarterly, 2,* 13-23.

Pellegrini, A.D. (1982) Development of preschoolers' social-cognitive bahavior. *Perceptual and Motor Skills, 55,* 1109-1110.

Pellegrini, D.S. and Urbain, E.S. (1985) An evaluation of inpterpersonal cognitive problem solving training with children. *Journal of Child Psychology and Psychiatry, 26,* 17-41.

Penfield, W. (1969) Consciousness, memory, and man's conditioned reflexes. In K.H. Pribram (Ed.) *On the biology of learning.* New York: Harcourt Brace Jovanovich.

Peper, R.J., and Meyer, R.E. (1978, March) Notetaking as a mathematic activity. Paper presented at the annual meeting of the American Psychological Association, San Francisco.

Perkins, W.H. (1978) *Human perspectives in speech and language disorders.* St. Louis, MO: Mosby.

Perks, B. (1984) Identification of gifted children. Ed.D. Thesis, University of British Columbia.

Perl, E. and Lambert, W.E. (1986) The relation of bilingualism to intelligence. *Psychological Monographs, 76,* 1-23.

Peskin, H. (1967) Pubertal onset and ego functioning. *Journal of Abnormal Psychology, 72,* 1-15.

Pestello, F.G. (1983) Fear and misbehavior in a high school. *Sociological Quarterly, 24,* 561-575.

Peter, D., Allan, J. and Horvath, A. (1983) Hyperactive children's perceptions of teachers' classroom behavior. *Psychology in the Schools, 20,* 234-240.

Peters, E.E. and Levin, J.R. (1986) Effects of a mnemonic imagery strategy on good and poor readers' prose recall. *Reading Research Quarterly, 21,* 179-192.

Petersen, A.C. and Boxer, A. (1982) Adolescent sexuality. In T. Coates, A. Petersen and C. Perry (Eds.) *Adolescent health: Crossing the barriers.* New York: Academic Press.

Peterson, P.L. and Janicki, T.C. (1979) Individual characteristics and children's learning in large-group and small-group approaches. *Journal of Educational Psychology, 71,* 677-687.

Peterson, P. L. and Swing, S. (1982) Beyond time on task: Students' reports of their thought processes during classroom instruction. *Elementary School Journal, 82,* 481-491.

Peterson, P.L., Janicki, T.C. and Swing, S.R. (1981) Individual characteristics and children's learning in large-group and small-group approaches: Study II. *American Educational Research Journal, 18,* 453-473.

Peterson, P., Marx, R., and Clark, C. (1978) Teacher planning, teacher behavior, and student achievement. *American Educational Research Journal, 15,* 417-432.

Pettergill, B.D. (1872). The instruction of the deaf and dumb. *American Annals of the Deaf, 17,* 21-33.

Pettifor, J., Perry, D., Plowman, B., and Pitcher, S. (1983) Risk factors predicting childhood and adolescent suicides. *Journal of Child Care, 1,* 17-49.

Petty, M.F. and Field, C.J. (1980) Fluctuations in mental test scores. *Educational Research, 22,* 198-202.

Pfeffer, C.R. (1986) *The suicidal child.* New York: Guilford.

Pfiffner, L.J., Rosen, L.A., and O'Leary, S.G. (1985). The efficacy of an all-positive approach to classroom management. *Journal of Applied Behavior Analysis, 18,* 257-261.

Phi Delta Kappa Task Force on Adolescence: Suicide (1988) *Responding to adolescent suicide.* Bloomington, IN: Phi Delta Kappa Educational Foundation.

Phillips, K. (1990) Why can't a man be more like a woman— and vice versa. *Omni,* 42-48, 68.

Phipps, (1982) The learning disabled learner is often a boy— Why? *Academic Therapy, 17,* 425-430.

Piaget, J. (1926) *Language and thought of the child.* London: Routlege, Kagan Paul.

Piaget, J. (1932) *The moral judgment of the child.* New York: Free Press.

Piaget, J. (1948) *The moral judgment of the child.* (M.Cabain, trans.) Glencoe, IL: Free Press (originally published 1932).

Piaget, J. (1950) *The psychology of intelligence.* London: Routledge and Kegan Paul.

Piaget, J. (1952) *The language and thought of the child.* London: Routledge and Kegan Paul.

Piaget, J. (1964) *The moral judgment of the child.* New York: Free Press.

Piaget, J. (1967) *Six psychological studies.* New York: Random House.

Piaget, J. (1970) Piaget's theory. In P. Mussen (Ed.) *Carmicheal's manual of child psychology* (vol. 1) New York: Wiley.

Piaget, J. (1971) *Genetic epistemology.* New York: Norton.

Piaget, J. (1973) *The child and reality*. New York: Grossman.

Piaget, J. (1974) *Understanding causality*. New York: Norton.

Piaget, J. (1977) Problems of equilibration. In M.H. Appel and L.S. goldberg (Eds.) *Topics in cognitive development* (vol. 1) New York: Plenum.

Piaget, J. and Inhelder, B. (1969) *The psychology of the child*. New York: Basic Books.

Piaget, J. and Inhelder, B. (1973) *Memory and intelligence*. New York: Basic Books.

Pidgeon, D. (1970) *Expectation and pupil performance*. Slough, England: National Foundation for Educational Research.

Pinney, R.H. (1969) Presentational behavior related to success in teaching. Doctoral dissertation, Stanford University.

Pintrich, P.R. and Blumfield, P. (1985) Classroom experience and children's self-perceptions of ability, effort, and conduct. *Journal of Educational Psychology, 77*, 646-657.

Plomin, R. (1989) Environment and genes: Determinants of behavior. *American Psychologist, 44*, 105-111.

Plowden Report (1967) *Children and their primary schools*. London, Eng.: Her Majesty's Stationary Office.

Plumb, J.H. (1974) The great change in children. In S. Coopersmith and l. Feldman (Eds.) *The formative years: Principles of early childhood education* (pp. 28-37) San Francisco, CA: Albion Publishing.

Polirstok, S.R. and Greer, R.D. (1977) Remediation of mutually aversive interactions between a problem student and four teachers by training the student in reinforcement techniques. *Journal of Applied Behavior Analysis, 10*, 707-714.

Polit, D.E., Nuttall, R.L. and Nuttall, E.V. (1980) The only child grows up: A look at some characteristics of adult only children. *Family Relations, 29*, 99-106.

Polloway, E. A. (1984) The integration of mildly handicapped students into the schools: A historical review. *Remedial and Special Education, 5*, 18-28.

Polloway, E.A. and Smith, J.E. (1982) *Teaching language skills to exceptional children*. Denver, CO: Love Publishing.

Polsgrove, L. and Reith, A.J. (1983) Procedures for reducing childrens' inappropriate behavior in special education settings. *Exceptional Education Quarterly, 3*, 20-33.

Poole, A. and Kuhn, A. (1973) Family size and ordinal positions: Correlates of academic success. *Journal of Biosocial Science, 5*, 51-59.

Popham, W.J. (1981) *Modern educational measurement*. Englewood Cliffs, NJ: Prentice-Hall.

Porat, K. (1986) Teaching students to think: The challenge facing educators. *ATA Magazine, 66*, 16-18.

Porat, K. (1989) Celebrate the difference. *ATA Magazine, 69*, 36-39.

Porterfield, J.K., Herbert-Jackson, E. and Risley, T.R. (1976) Contingent observation: An effective and acceptable procedure for reducing disruptive behavior of young children in a group setting. *Journal of Applied Behavior Analysis, 9*, 55-64.

Powers, S.L. Hauser, S.T and Kilmer, L.A. (1989) Adolescent mental health. *American Psychologist, 44*, 200-208.

Pratt, E.J. (1920) The social significance of mental defect. *Social Welfare, 2*, 263-264.

Prawat, R.S. and Jarvis, R. (1980) Gender differences as a factor in teachers' perceptions of students. *Journal of Educational Psychology, 72*, 743-749.

Preece, M.A., Kearney, P.J. and Marshall, W.C. (1977) Growth-hormone deficiency in congenital rubella. *Lancet, 77*, 842-844.

Premack, D. (1965) Reinforcement theory. In D. Levine (Ed.) *Nebraska symposium on motivation* (vol. 13) Lincoln, NE: University of Nebraska Press.

President's message (1988, Jan. 3) *Newsletter of the Newfoundland and Labrador Association for Multicultural Education*, p. 1.

Presse, D.P. and Reschly, D.J. (1986) Larry P.: A case of segregation, testing, or program efficacy? *Exceptional Children, 52*, 333-346.

Presseisen, B. (1984) Thinking skills: Meanings. models, and materials. ERIC Document, ED No. 257 858.

Presseisen, B. (1986) Critical thinking and thinking skills: State of the art definitions and practice in public schools. Paper presented at the American Education Research Association, San Francisco. ERIC Document, ED No. 268 536.

Presser, H.B. (1978) Childrearing, work, and welfare: Research issues. *Journal of Population, 1*, 167-180.

Pressley, M. (1986) The relevance of the good strategy user model to the teaching of mathematics. *Educational Psychologist, 21*, 139-161.

Pressley, M., Levin, J. and Delaney, H.D. (1982) The mnemonic keyword method. *Review of Research in Education, 52*, 61-91.

Preston, R. (1962) Reading achivement of German and American children. *School and Society, 90*, 350-354.

Prince, G.H. (1967) The operational mechanism of Synectics. *Journal of Creative Behavior, 1*, 1-13.

Pringle, M.L. (1970) *Able misfits*. London: Longman Group.

Pugash, M.C. (1985) The limitations of special education policy: The role of the classroom teacher in determining who is handicapped. *Journal of Special Education, 19*, 123-137.

Purkey, W., and Novak, J. (1984) *Inviting school success: A self-concept approach to teaching and learning* (2nd ed.). Belmont, CA: Wadsworth.

Q

Quay, H.C. and Werry, J. (1986) *Psychopathological disorders of children* (3rd. ed.) New York: Wiley.

Quinn, P.C. and Eines, P.D. (1986) On categorization in early infancy. *Merrill-Palmer Quarterly, 32*, 331-363.

R

Rabinowitz, F.M. (1987) An analysis of the motivation/learning controversy. *Canadian Psychologist,/Psychologique canadienne, 28*, 322-337.

Rae, L. (1848) The great peril of Sicard. *American Annals of the Deaf and Dumb, 1*, 16.

Ramirez, A.G. and Stromquist, N.P. (1978) ESL methodology and student language learning in bilingual elementary schools. ERIC Document, ED No. 150 879.

Raths, L. E. (1972) *Meeting the needs of children*. Columbus, OH: Merrill

Raudenbush, S.W. (1984) Magnitiude of teacher expectancy effects on pupil IQ as a function of the credibility of expectancy induction: A synthesis of findings from 18 experiments. *Journal of Educational Psychology, 76*, 85-97.

Raven, J.C. (1948) *Progressive matrices*. New York: Psychological Corporation.

Raven, J. C. (1962) *Progressive Colored Matrices*. New York: Psychological Corporation.

Raviv, A., Raviv, A. and Reisel, E. (1990) Teachers and students: Two different perspectives?! Measuring social climate in the classroom. *American Educational Research Journal, 27*, 141-157.

Ray, D. (1989) Human rights: Is Canadian schooling a privelege, a right, or an obligation? *McGill Journal of Education, 24*, 143-158.

Redd, W.H., Morris, E.K. and Martin, J.A. (1975) Effects of positive and negative adult-child interactions on children's social preferences. *Journal of Experimental Child Psychology, 19*, 153-164.

Reed, S. and Rich, S. (1982) Parent-offspring correlations and regressions for IQ. *Behavioral Genetics, 12*, 535-542.

Reed, S. and Saulter, R.C. (1990) Children of poverty: The status of 12 million young Americams. *Phi Delta Kappan, 71*, K1-K11.

Reich, C., Hambleton, D. and Houldin, B. K. (1977) The integration of hearing impaired children into regular classrooms. *American Annals of the Deaf, 122,* 534-543.

Reich, P.A. (1986) *Language development.* Englewood Cliffs, NJ: Prentice-Hall.

Reigeluth, C.M. and Merril, M. (1984) *Extended task analysis procedure: User's manual.* Landam, MD: University Press of America.

Reilly, T.P. Drudge, O.W. Rosen, J.C. Loew, D.E. and Fischer, M. (1985) Concurrent and predictive validity of the WISC-R, McCarthy Scales, Woodcock-Johnson, and academic achievement. *Psychology in the Schools, 22,* 380-382.

Reimer, J. (1981) Moral education: The just community approach. *Phi Delta Kappan, 64,* 485-493.

Reinert, H. (1976) *Children in conflict.* St. Louis: Mosley Co.

Renzulli, J.S. (1978) What makes giftedness? Reexamining a definition. *Phi Delta Kappan, 60,* 180-184, 261.

Renzulli, J.S. (1979) *What makes giftedness?* Los Angeles: National/State Leadership Training Institute on the Gifted and Talented, Brief no. 6.Report, (1981)

*Report of the Northlands School Division* (1981) Edmonton: Alberta Education.

Reschly, D.J. (1988) Minority EMR overrepresentation and special education reform. *Exceptional Children, 88,* 316-323.

Reschly, D.J. and Gresham, F.M. (1981) *Use of social competence measures to facilitate parent and teacher involvement and unbiased assessment.* Iowa: Iowa State University.

Rest, J.R. (1973) The hierarchial nature of moral judgment. *Journal of Personality, 41,* 86-109.

Rest, J.R. (1974) Developmental psychology as a guide to value education: A review of Kohlberg's programs. *Review of Educational Research, 44,* 241-259.

Reynolds, M.C. and Birch, J.W. (1982) *Teaching exceptional children in all America's schools.* Reston, VA: Council for Exceptional Children.

Reynolds, W.M. (1980) Self-esteem and classroom behavior in elementary school children. *Psychology in the Schools, 17,* 273-277.

Rheingold, H. and Cook, K. (1975) The content of boys' and girls rooms as an index of parents' behavior. *Child Development, 46,* 459-463.

Rice, M.L. (1989) Children's language acquisition. *American Psychologist, 44,* 149-156.

Rich, L.H. (1982) *Disturbed students: Characteristics and educational strategies.* Baltimore, MD.: University Park Press.

Richmond, B.O. and Weiner, G.P. (1973) Cooperation and competition among young children as a function of ethnic grouping, grade, sex, and reward condition. *Journal of Educational Psychology, 64,* 329-334.

Riegel, K. (1973) Dialectic operations: The final period of cognitive development. *Human Development, 16,* 346-370.

Riegle, R.P. (1976) Classifying classroom questions. *Journal of Teacher Education, 27,* 156-161.

Riese, M.L. (1987) Temperament stability between the neonatal period and 24 months. *Developmental Psychology, 23,* 216-222.

Risko, V. (1981) Oral langage. In D.D. Smith (Ed.) *Teaching the learning disabled.* Englewood Cliffs, NJ: Prentice-Hall.

Ritter, D. R. (1978) Surviving in the regular classroom: A follow-up of mainstreamed children with learning disabilities. *Journal of School Psychology, 16,* 253-256.

Ritter, D.R. (1989) Teachers' perceptions of problem behavior in general and special education. *Exceptional Children, 55,* 559-564.

Robin, A. (1976) Behavioral instruction in the college classroom. *Review of Educational Research, 46,* 313-354.

Robins, D.R. and Alessi, N.E. (1985) Depressive symptoms and suicidal behavior in adolescents. *American Journal of Psychiatry, 142,* 588-592.

Robins, L.N. (1979) Follow-up studies. In H.C. Quay and J.S. Werry (Eds.) *Psychopathological disorders of childhood* (2nd ed.) New York: Wiley.

Robins, L.N. and Earls, F. (1985) A program for preventing antisocial behavior for high-risk infants and presechoolers: A research prospectus. In R.L. Hugh, P.A. Gongla, V.B. Brown, and S.E. Goldston (Eds.) *Psychiatric epidemiology and prevention: The possibilities* (pp. 73-84) Los Angeles, CA: Neoropsychiatric Institute.

Robinson, P.W., Newby, T.J. and Ganzell, S.L. (1981) A token system for a class of under-achieving hyperactive children. *Journal of Applied Behavior Analysis, 14,* 307-315.

Roedell, W.C., Jackson, N.E. and Robinson, H.B. (1980) *Gifted young children.* New York: Teachers College Press.

Rogers, C. (1965) Some questions and challenges facing a humanistic psychology. *Journal of Humanistic Psychology, 5,*

Rogers, C. (1969) *Freedom to learn.* Columbus, OH: Merrill.

Rogers, C. (1983) *Freedom to learn for the '80s.* Columbus, OH: Bell and Howell.

Rogers, D. (1985) *Adolescents and youth* (5th. ed.) Englewood Cliffs, NJ: Prentice-Hall.

Rogers, J.A. (1972) Darwinism and Social Darwinism. *Journal of the History of Ideas, 33,* 265-280.

Rogers, W.T. (1990) Current educational climate in relation to testing. *Alberta Journal of Educational Research, 36,* 52-64.

Rogow, S. (1987a) Children with communication disorders. In M. Winzer, S. Rogow and C. David, *Exceptional children in Canada.* Toronto: Prentice-Hall.

Rogow, S. (1987b) Children with visual impairments. In M. Winzer, S. Rogow and C. David, *Exceptional children in Canada.* Toronto: Prentice-Hall.

Rohner, R. and Nielson, C. (1978) *Parental acceptance and rejection: A review and annotated bibliography of research and theory.* New Haven, CT: HRAP Press.

Rohwer, W.D., Jr. (1972) Decisive research: A means of answering fundamental questions about instruction. *Educational Researcher, 1,* 5-11.

Rose, J.S., Medway, F.J. Cantell, V.L., and Marus, S.H. (1983) A fresh look at the retention-promotion controversy. *Journal of School Psychology, 21,* 201-211.

Rosen, B. and D'Andrade, R. (1959) The psychosocial origins of achievement motivation. *Sociometry, 8,* 361-401.

Rosenblith, J.F. and Sims-Knight, J.E. (1985) *In the beginnning: Development in the first two years.* Monterey, CA: Brooks\Cole.

Rosenholtz, S.J. and Simpson, C. (1984) The formation of ability conceptions: Developmental trend or social construction? *Review of Educational Research, 54,* 31-63.

Rosenshine, B. V. (1971) *Teaching behaviors and student achievement.* London: National Foundation for Educational Research.

Rosenshine, B. V. (1978) Review of teaching styles and pupil progress. *American Educational Research Journal, 15,* 163-169.

Rosenshine. B. V. (1979) The third cycle of research in teacher effects: Content covered, academic engaged time, and direct instruction. In P.L. Peterson and H.J. Walberg (Eds.) *Research in teaching: Concepts, findings, and implications.* Berkley, CA: McCutcheon.

Rosenshine, B.V. (1980) How time is spent in elementary classrooms. In C. Denham and A. Lieberman (Eds.) *Time to learn.* Washington, DC: National Institute of Education.

Rosenshine, B.V. (1986) Synthesis of research on explicit teaching. *Educational Leadership, 43,* 60-69.

Rosenshine, B. V. and Berliner, D. (1978) Academic engaged time. *British Journal of Teacher Education, 4,* 3-16.

Rosenthal, R. and Jacobson, L. (1968) *Pygmalion in the classroom.* New York: Holt, Rinehart and Winston.

**663**

Ross, J. and Lawrence, K.A. (1968) Some observations of memory artifice. *Psychonomic Science, 13*, 107-108.

Ross, M. and Salvia, J. (1975) Attractiveness as a biasing factor in teacher jugdments. *American Journal of Mental Deficiency, 80*, 96-98.

Rotherman, M.J. (1982) Social skills training with underachievers, disruptive and exceptional children. *Psychology in the Schools, 19*, 532-539.

Rotter, J. B. (1954) *Social learning and clinical psychology*. Englewood Cliffs, NJ: Prentice-Hall.

Rotter, J. B. (1980) Interpersonal trust, trustworthiness and gullibility. *American Psychologist, 35*, 1-7.

Rouland, T. and McGuire, C. (1969) The development of intelligent behavior, V: Central process theorists. *Psychology in the Schools, 6*, 24-37.

Rowe, M.B. (1974) Wait time and rewards as instructional variables, their influence on language, logic, and fate control I: Wait time. *Journal of Research in Science Teaching, 11*, 81-94.

Rowe, M.B. (1978) *Teaching science as continuous enquiry*. New York: McGraw Hill.

Royce, J. (1891) Is there a science of education? *Educational Review, 1*, 32.

Rozin, P., Fallon, A. and Mandell, R. (1984) Family resemblance in attitudes to foods. *Developmental Psychology, 20*, 309-314.

Rubin, D.C., and Kozin, M. (1984) Vivid memories. *Cognition, 16*, 81-95.

Rubin, K.H., Maioni, T.L. and Hornung, M. (1976) Free play behaviors in middle- and lower-class preschoolers: Palen and Piaget revisited. *Child Development, 47*, 414-419.

Rubin, K.H., Watson, K.S. and Jambon, T.W. (1978) Free-play behavior in pre-school and kindergarten children. *Child Development, 49*, 534-536.

Rubovitz, P.C. and Maehr, M. L. (1973) Pygmalion black and white. *Journal of Personality and Social Psychology, 25*, 210-218.

Rudowski, V.A. (1974) The theory of signs in the eighteenth century. *Journal of the History of Ideas, 35*, 683-690.

Ruggles, T.R. and LeBlanc, J.M. (1982) Behavior analysis procedures in classroom teaching. In A.S. Bellack, M. Hersen, and A.E. Kazdin (Eds.) *International handbook of behavior modification and therapy* (pp 959-996). New York: Plenum.

Rumbaugh, D. (1980) An explanation of the language of a chimpanzee. *Science, 208*, 313-314.

Rumelhart, D. and Ortony, A. (1977) The representation of knowledge in memory. In R. Anderson, S. Spiro, and W. Montague, (Eds.)

*Schooling and the acquisition of knowledge* Hillsdale, NJ: Erlbaum.

Rundus, D. and Atkinson, R.C. (1970) Rehearsal processes in free recall: A procedure for direct observation. *Journal of Verbal Learning and Verbal Behavior, 9*, 99-105.

Runge, A., Walker, J. and Shea, T. (1975) A passport to positive parent-teacher communication. *Exceptional Children, 7*, 91-92.

Rutter, M. (1975) *Helping troubled children*. Harmondsworth, England: Penguin.

Rutter, M. (1981) Stress, coping and development: Some issues and some questions. *Journal of Child Psychology and Psychiatry, 22*, 323-356.

Rutter, M. (1982) Temperament: Concepts, issues and problems. In *Temperament differences in infants and young children*. CIBA Foundation Symposium 89 (pp. 1-16) London: Pitman.

Rutter, M., Graham, P., Chadwick, O. and Verle, W. (1976) Adolescent turmoil: Fact or fiction? *Journal of Child Psychology and Psychiatry, 17*, 35-56.

Ryan, E.B. and Ledger, G.W. (1984) Learning to attend to sentence structure: Links between metalinguistic development and reading. In J. Downing and R. Valtin (Eds.) *Language awareness and learning to read* (pp. 149-172) New York: Springer/Verlag.

Ryans, D.G. (1960) *Characteristics of effective teachers: Their descriptions, comparisons and appraisal: A research study*. Washington, DC: American Council on Education.

**S**

Sadker, M. and Sadker, D. (1986) Questioning skills. In J.M. Cooper (Ed.) *Classroom teaching skills* (3rd. ed.) (pp. 139-180). Lexington, MA: D.C. Heath.

Safran, S.P. and Safran, J.S. (1985) Classroom context and teachers' perceptions of problem behaviors. *Journal of Educational Psychology, 77*, 20-28.

Safty, A. (1988) French immersion and the making of a bilingual society: A critical review and discussion. *Canadian Journal of Education/Review canadienne de l'education, 13*, 243-262.

Sainato, D.M., Strain, P.S., Lefebvre, D., and Rapp, N. (1990) Effects of self-evaluation on the independent work skills of preschool children with disabilities. *Exceptional Children, 56*, 540-549.

Salend, S.J. (1984) Factors contributing to the development of successful mainstreaming programs. *Exceptional Children, 50*, 409-416

Salend, S.J. (1987) Group-oriented behavior management strategies. *Teaching Exceptional Children, 20*, 53-55.

Salend, S.J., and Allen, E.M. (1985) A comparison of the effects of externally managed and self-managed response-cost systems on inappropriate classroom behavior. *Journal of School Psychology, 23*, 59-67.

Salend, S.J., and Andress, M. (1984) Decreasing stuttering in an elementary level student. *Journal of Language, Speech and Hearing Services in the Schools, 15*, 133-140.

Salend, S.J. and Henry, K. (1981) Response cost in mainstreamed settings. *Journal of School Psychology, 19*, 242-249.

Salend, S.J. and Kovalich, B. (1981) A group response-cost system mediated by free tokens: An alternative to token reinforcement in the classroom. *American Journal of Mental Deficiency, 86*, 184-187.

Salend, S.J. and Lamb, E.M. (1986) The effectiveness of a group-managed interdependent contingency system. *Learning Disability Quarterly, 9*, 268-274.

Salend, S.J. and Meddaugh, D. (1985) Using a peer-mediated extinction procedure to decrease obscene language. *The Pointer, 30*, 8-11.

Salend, S.J., Tintle, L. and Balber, H. (1988) Effects of a student-managed response-cost system on the behavior of two mainstreamed students. *Elementary School Journal, 89*, 89-97.

Salkind, N. (1990) *Child Development* (6th ed.) Fort Worth, TX: Holt, Reinhart and Winston.

Salmon-Cox, L. (1981 Teachers and standardized achievement tests. *Phi Delta Kappan, 63*, 631-634.

Salvia, J. and Hughes, C. (1990) *Curricula-based assessment: Testing what is taught*. New York: MacMillan.

Salvia, J. and Ysseldyke J.E. (1985) *Assessment in special education* (3rd. ed.) Boston, MA: Houghton Mifflin.

Salvia, J., Sheare, J. and Algozzine, B. (1975) Facial attractiveness and personal-social development. *Journal of Abnormal Child Psychology, 3*, 171-178.

Samiroden, W. (1987) Diploma exams: Limiting what is taught. *ATA Magazine, 67*, 5-7.

Sampson, E.E. (1962) Birth order, need achievement, and conformity. *Journal of Abnormal and Social Psychology, 64*, 155-159.

Samuda, R.J. and Crawford, D.H. (1980) *Testing, assessment, counseling and placement of ethnic minority students*. Toronto: Ontario Ministry of Education.

Sanborn, S. (1971) Means and ends: Moral development and moral education. Harvard Graduate School of Education Bulletin. Cited in J.T. Gibson and L.A. Chandler (1988) *Educational psychology: Mastering principles and applications*. Boston, MA: Allyn and Bacon.

Sanford, J.P. and Evertson, C.M. (1981) Classroom management in a low SES junior high: Three case studies. *Journal of Teacher Education, 38,* 34-38.

Sanford, J., Emmer, E.T. and Clements, B. (1983) Improving classroom management. *Educational Leadership, 41,* 56-60.

Sattler, J.M. (1982) *Assessment of children's intelligence and special abilities* (2nd. ed.) Boston, MA: Allyn and Bacon.

Sattler, J.M. (1988) *Assessment of children* (3rd. ed.) San Diego, CA: Author.

Sattler, J.M., Bohanan A.L. and Moore, M. (1980) Relationship between PPVT and WISC-R in children with reading disabilities. *Psychology in the Schools, 17,* 331-334.

Saunders, G. (1982) *Bilingual children: Guidance for the family.* Clevedon, Avon, UK: Multilingual Matters.

Saywitz, K. and Cherry-Wilkinson, L. (1982) Age-related differences in metalinguistic awareness. In S. Kaczaj (Ed.) *Language development* (vol. 2) Hillsdale, NJ: Erlbaum.

Scandura, J.M. and Scandura, A.B. (1980) *Structural learning and concrete operations.* New York: Praeger.

Scarr, S. (1981) *Race, social class, and intellectual differences in IQ.* Hillsdale, NJ: Erlbaum.

Scarr, S. and Weinberg, R.A. (1976) IQ test performance of black children adopted by white parents. *American Psychologist, 31,* 726-739.

Scarr, S. and Weinberg, R. (1978) Attitudes, interests and IQ. *Human Nature, 1,* 33.

Scarr, S. and Weinberg, W. (1983) The Minnesota adoption studies: Genetic differences and malleability. *Child Development, 54,* 260-267.

Scarr-Salapatek, S. (1975) Genetics and the development of intelligence. In F.D. Horowitz (Ed.) *Review of child development research* (vol. 4) Chicago, IL: University of Chicago Press.

Schlaefli, A., Rest, J.R. and Thomas, S.J. (1985) Does moral education improve moral judgment? A meta-analysis of intervention studies using the Defining Issues Test. *Review of Educational Research, 55,* 319-352.

Scheuneman, J.D. (1984) A theoretical framework for the exploration of causes and effects of bias in testing. *Educational Psychologist, 19,* 219-225.

Schiedel, D. and Marcia, J. (1985) Ego, identity, intimacy, sex role orientation, and gender. *Developmental Psychology, 21,* 149-160.

Schiff, M., Duyne, M., Dumaret, A., and Tornkiewicz, S. (1982) How much could we boost scholastic achievement and IQ scores: A direct answer from a French adoption agency. *Cognition, 12,* 165-192.

Schlesier-Stropp, B. (1984) Bulimia: A review of the literature. *Psychological Bulletin, 95,* 247-257.

Schlosser, L. and Algozzine, B. (1979) The disturbing child: He or she? *Alberta Journal of Educational Research, 25,* 30-36.

Schlossman, S. (1981) Philanthrophy and the gospel of child development. *History of Education Quarterly, 21,* 275-299.

Schrader, W.R. and Leventhal, T. (1979) Birth order of children and parental report of problems. *Child Development, 38,* 1165-1175.

Schroder, C. and Crawford, P. (1970) *School achievement as measured by teacher ratings and standardized achievement tests.* Ontario: Toronto Board of Education, Research Department.

Schunk, D.H. (1990) Introduction to the special section on motivation and efficacy. *Journal of Educational Psychology, 82,* 3-6.

Schwartz, J.C. (1979) Young children's fears: Modeling or cognition? Paper presented at the Society for Research in Child Development, San Francisco.

Schwartz, L.L. (1980) Advocacy for the neglected gifted: Females. *Gifted Child Quarterly, 24,* 113-117.

Seaver, B. (1973) Effects of naturally induced teacher expectancies. *Journal of Personality and Social Psychology, 28,* 333-342.

Seifert, K.L. (1990) *Educational psychology* (2nd. ed.) Boston, MA: Houghton Mifflin.

Seigel, J.P. (1969) The Enlightenment and the evolution of the language of signs in France and England. *Journal of the History of Ideas, 30,* 96-115.

Seliger, H. (1978) Implications of a multiple critical periods hypothesis for second language learning. In W. Ritchie (Ed.) *Second language acquisition research.* New York: Holsted Press.

Seligman, C., Tucker, G. and Lambert, W. (1972) The effects of speech style and other attributes on teachers' attitudes toward pupils. *Language in Society, 1,* 131-142.

Seligman, M.E. P. (1975) *Helplessness.* San Francisco, CA: Freeman.

Seller, W. (1989) Institutionalizing field-based research grounded in the practical. *McGill Journal of Education, 24,* 5-13.

Selman, R.L. (1971) The relation of role-taking to the development of moral judgment in children. *Child Development, 42,* 79-92.

Selman, R.L. (1976a) Social-cognitive understanding: A guide to educational and clinical practice. In T. Lickona (Ed.) *Moral development and behaviour: Theory, research, and social issues.* New York: Holt, Rinehart and Winston.

Selman, R.L. (1976b) Toward a structural analysis of developing personal relations concepts.

In A. Pick (Ed.) *Minnesota symposia on child psychology.* Minneapolis, MN: Univeristy of Minnesota.

Selman, R.L. (1980) *The growth of interpersonal understanding.* New York: Academic Press.

Shaie, K.W. and Willis, S.L. (1986) Can decline in intellectual functioning in the elderly be reversed? *Developmental Psychology, 22,* 223-232.

Shames, G. and Florance, C. (1982) Disorders of fluency. In G. Shames and E. Wiig (Eds.) *Human communication disorders.* Columbus, OH: Merrill.

Shannon, D.C. (1957) What research says about acceleration. *Phi Delta Kappan, 39,* 70-73.

Shapiro, S. (1975) Preschool ecology: A study of three environmental variables. *Reading Improvement, 12,* 236-241.

Sharan, S. (1980) Cooperative learning in small groups: Recent methods and effects on achievement, attitudes, and ethnic relations. *Review of Educational Research, 50,* 241-272.

Sharan, S. and Hertz-Lazarowitz, R. (1980) The group investigation method of cooperative learning in the classroom. In S. Sharan, P. Hare, C. Webb, and R. Hertz-Lazarowitz (Eds.) *Cooperation in education* (pp. 14-46). Provo, UT: Brigham Young Press.

Sharan, S. and Rich, Y. (1984) Field experiments on ethnic integration in Israeli schools. In Y. Amir and S. Sharan, (Eds.) *School desegregation* (pp. 189-217). Hillsdale, NJ: Erlbaum.

Sharan, S. and Shachar, H. (1988) *Language and learning in the cooperative classroom.* New York: Springer.

Sharan, S. and Sharan, Y. (1976) *Small group teaching.* Englewoods Cliff, NJ: Educational Technology Publications.

Sharan, S. and Shaulov, A. (1989) Cooperative learning, motivation to learn and academic achievement. In S. Sharan (Ed.) *Cooperative learning: Theory and research.* New York: Praeger.

Sharan, S., Bejarano, Y., Russell, P., and Peleg, R. (1984a) Achievement in English language and literature. In S. Sharan (Ed.) *Cooperative learning in the classroom: Research in desegregated schools* (pp. 46-72). Hillsdale, NJ: Erlbaum.

Sharan, S., Raviv, S., Kussell, P., and Hertz-Lazarowitz, R. (1984b) Cooperative and competitive behavior. In S. Sharan (Ed.) *Cooperative learning in the classroom: Research in desegregated schools* (pp. 46-72). Hillsdale, NJ: Lawrence Erlbaum.

Sharan, S., Russel, P., Hertz-Lazarowitz, R., Bejorano, Y., Raviv, S. and Sharan, Y. (1980) *Cooperative learning in the classroom: Research in desegregated schools.* Hillsdale, NJ: Erlbaum.

Sharan, Y. and Sharan, S. (1989/90). Group investigation expands cooperative learning. *Educational Leadership, 47,* 17-21.

Sharav, T. and Schlomo, L. (1986) Stimulation of infants with Down syndrome: Long-term effects. *Mental Retardation, 24,* 81-86.

Shavelson, R.J. (1973) What is the basic teaching skill? *Journal of Teacher Education, 14,* 144-151.

Shavelson, R.L. and Bolus, R. (1982) Self-concept: The interplay of theory and methods. *Psychology, 74,* 3-17.

Sheehy, G. (1976) *Passages.* New York: Dutton.

Sheldon, W.H. (1954) *Atlas of men; A guide for somotyping the adult male at all ages.* New York: Harper and Row.

Shepard, L.A. and Smith, M.L. (1987) Effects of kindergarten retention at the end of first grade. *Psychology in the Schools, 24,* 346-359.

Shephard, L. (1979) Norm-referenced versus criterion-referenced tests. *Educational Horizons, 68,* 26-35.

Sheras, P.L. (1983) Suicide in adolescents. In G.E. Walker and M. C. Roberts (Eds.) *Handbook of clinical child psychology.* New York: Wiley.

Sherman, J. (1978) *Sex-related cognitive differences.* Springfield, IL: Thomas.

Sherman, J. (1980) Mathematics, visual spatialization, and related factors: Changes in boys and girls, grades 8-11. *Journal of Educational Psychology, 72,* 476-482.

Sherman, T.M., and Cormier, W.H. (1974) An investigation of the influence of student behavior on teacher behavior. *Journal of Applied Behavior Analysis, 9,* 41-54.

Shiffrin, R.M. and Schneider, W. (1977) Controlled and automatic human information processing. Perceptual learning, automatic attending, and a general theory. *Psychological Review, 84,* 127-190.

Shostak, R. (1986) Lesson presentation skills. In J.M. Cooper (Ed.) *Classroom teaching skills* (3rd. ed.) (pp. 111-138) Lexington, MA: Heath.

Shuell, T.J. (1981a) Dimensions of individual differences. In F.H. Farley and N.J. Gordon (Eds.) *Psychology and education: The state of the union.* Berkeley, CA: McCutchan.

Shuell, T.J. (1981b, April) Toward a model of learning from instruction., Paper presented at American Education Research Association, Los Angeles.

Siegel, M. (1980) Kohlberg vs Piaget: To what extent has one theory eclipsed the other? *Merrill-Palmer Quarterly, 26,* 285-297.

Siegel, G.M., Lenske, J. and Broen, P. (1969) Suppression of normal speech dysfluencies through response cost. *Journal of Applied Behavior Analysis, 2,* 265-276.

Sigel, I.E. (1981) Child development research in learning and cognition in the 1980s: Continuities and discontinuities from the 1970s. *Merrill-Palmer Quarterly, 27,* 347-371.

Sigel, I. (1985) (Ed.) *Parental belief systems: The psychological consequences for children.* Hillsdale, NJ: Erlbaum.

Signorella, M.L. and Jamison, W. (1986) Masculinity, femininity, androgny, and cognitive performance: A meta-analysis. *Psychological Bulletin, 100,* 207-228.

Silva, P.A. (1980) The prevalence, stability and significance of developmental language delays in preschool children. *Developmental Medicine and Child Neurology, 22,* 768-777.

Simon, S., Howe, L., and Kirschenbuam, H. (1972) *Values clarification: A handbook of practical strategies for teachers and students.* New York: Hart.

Simonton, D. (1983) Intergenerational transfer of individual differenes in hereditary monarchs: Genetic, role modeling, cohort, or sociocultural effects? *Journal of Personality and Social Psychology, 44,* 354-364.

Simpson, R.L. and Myles, B.S. (1989) Parents' mainstreaming preferencers for children with educable mental handicap, behavior disorders, and learning disabilities. *Psychology in the Schools, 26,* 292-301.

Sitko, M.A., Bachor, D. and Slemon, A. (1980) Teacher questioning techniques: The state of the art. Paper presented at the Annual Meeting of the Canadian Society for Studies in Education, Montreal.

Skiba, R.J. and Raison, J. (1990) The relationship between use of timeout and academic achievement. *Exceptional Children, 57,* 36-46.

Skinner, B.F. (1938) *The behavior of organisms: An experimental analysis.* New York: Appleton-Century.

Skinner, B.F. (1953) *Science and human behavior.* New York: Macmillan.

Skinner, B.F. (1957) *Verbal behavior.* New York: Appleton.

Skinner, B.F. (1969) *Contingencies of reinforcement: A theoretical analysis.* New York: Appleton-Century-Crofts.

Skinner, B.F. (1973) Some implications of making education more efficient. In C.E. Thoresen (Ed.) *Seventy second yearbook of the National Society for the Study of Education, part 1.* Chicago: Univeristy of Chicago Press.

Skinner, B.F. (1973) The free and happy student. *Phi Delta Kappan, 55,* 13-16.

Skinner, B.F. (1978) Some implications of making education more efficient. In B.F. Skinner (Ed.) *Reflections on behaviorism and society* (pp. 129-139). Englewood Cliffs, NJ: Prentice-Hall. (Original work published 1973).

Skinner, B.F. (1983) *A matter of consequences. Part three of an autobiography.* New York: Alfred A. Knopf.

Skinner, B.F. (1986) Program instruction revisited. *Phi Delta Kappan, 68,* 103-110.

Skinner, B.F. (1989) The origin of cognitive thought. *American Psychologist, 44,* 13-18.

Slavin, R.E. (1978a) Separating incentives, feedback and evaluation: Toward a more effective classroom system. *Educational Psychologist, 13,* 97-100.

Slavin, R.E. (1978b) Student teams and achievement divisions. *Journal of Research and Development in Education, 12,* 38-49.

Slavin, R.E. (1983) Does cooperative learning increase student achievement? *Psychological Bulletin, 94,* 429-445.

Slavin, R.E. (1985) Team assisted individualization: Combining cooperative learning and individualized instruction in mathematics. In R.E. Slavin, S. Sharan, S. Kagan, R. Hertz-Lazarowitz, C. Webb, and R. Schmuck (Eds.) *Learning to cooperate, cooperating to learn.* New York: Plenum.

Slavin, R.E. (1988) *Educational psychology: Theory into practice.* (2nd. ed.) Englewood Cliffs, NJ: Prentice-Hall.

Slavin, R.E., Madden, N.A. and Stevens, R.J. (1989/90) Cooperative learning models of the 3R's. *Educational Leadership, 47,* 22-28.

Sleeter, C.E. (1986) Learning disabilities: The social construction of a special education category. *Exceptional Children, 53,* 46-54.

Slosson, R.L. (1981) *Slosson Intelligence Test.* East Aurora, NY: Slosson Educational Publications.

Smith, A., Hays, J. and Solway, K. (1977) Comparison of the WISC-R and Culture Fair Tests of Intelligence in a juvenile delinquent population. *Journal of Psychology, 97,* 179-182.

Smith, B.O. (1985) Research bases for teacher education. *Phi Delta Kappan, 66,* 184-185,

Smith, C.P. (1964) Relationships between achievement-related motives and intelligence, performance level, and persistence. *Journal of Abnormal and Social Psychology, 68,* 523-532.

Smith, C.R. and Knoff, H.M. (1981) School psychology and special education students' placement decisions: IQ still tips the scale. *Journal for Special Educators, 15,* 55-64.

Smith, L. and Land, M. (1981) Low-inference verbal behaviors related to teacher clarity. *Journal of Classroom Interaction, 17,* 37-42.

Smith, L. and Sanders, K. (1981) The effects of student achievement and student perception of varying structures in social studies content. *Journal of Educational Research, 74,* 333-336.

Smith, L.R. and Cotten, M.L. (1980) Effect of lesson vagueness and discontinuity on student achievement and attitudes. *Journal of Edcuational Psychology, 72,* 670-675.

Smith, M.L. and Shepard, L.A. (1987) What doesn't work: Explaining policies of retention in the early grades. *Phi Delta Kappan,* 129-134.

Snarey, J. (1985) Cross-cultural universality of social-moral developmemnt. *Psychological Bulletin, 97*, 202-232.

Snow, C. (1987) Relevance of the notion of a critical period of language acquisition. In M.H. Bornstein (Ed.) *Sensitive periods in development: Interdisciplary perspectives.* Hillsdale, NJ: Erlbaum.

Snow, C. and Hoefnagel-Holle, M. (1978) The critical period for language acquisition: Evidence from second language learning. *Child Development, 49*, 1114-1128.

Snow, M.E., Jacklin, C.N. and Maccoby, E.E. (1983) Sex-of-child differences in father-child interactions at one year of age. *Child Development, 54*, 227-232.

Snow, R.E. (1969) Unfinished Pygmalion. *Contemporary Psychology, 14*, 1970-199.

Snow, R.E. (1986) Individual differences and the design of educational programs. *American Psychologist, 41*, 1029-1039.

Snowman, J. (1984) Learning tactics and strategies. In G. Phye and T. Andre (Eds.) *Cognitive instructional psychology.* New York: Academic Press.

Snyderman, M. and Rothman, S. (1987) Survey of expert opinion on intelligence and aptitude testing. *American Psychologist, 42*, 137-144.

Solnick, J.V., Rincover, A. and Peterson, C.R. (1977) Some determinants of the reinforcing and punishing effects of timeout. *Journal of Applied Behavior Analysis, 10*, 415-424.

Spearman, C.E. (1904) General intelligence objectively determined and measured. *American Journal of Psychology, 15*, 201-293.

Spettel, G. (1983). Classroom discipline—Now? *The Clearing House, 56*, 266-268.

Spettigue, C.O. (1955) *An historical review of Ontario legislation on child welfare.* Toronto: Ontario Department of Public Welfare.

Sprinthall, N.A. and Sprinthall, R.C. (1987) *Educational psychology: A developmental approach* (4th. ed) New York: Random House.

Squire, L.R. and Fox, M.M. (1980) Assessment of remote memory: Validation of the television test by repeated testing during a seven day period. *Behavioral Research Methods and Instrumentation, 12*, 583-586.

Sroufe, L.A. and Fleeson, J. (1986) Attachment and the construction of relationship. In W.W. Hartup and Z. Rubin (Eds.) *Relationships and development* (pp. 51-72) Hillsdale, NJ: Erlbaum.

Sroufe, L. A., Fox, N. and Pancake, V. (1983) Attachment and dependency in developmental perspective. *Child Development, 54*, 1615-1627.

Staats, A.W. (1968) *Language, learning and cognition.* New York: Holt, Rinehart and Winston.

Staats, A.W., and Staats, C.K. (1958) Attitudes established by classical conditioning. *Journal of Applied Social Psychology, 57*, 37-40.

Stainback, W., Stainback, S., Etscheidt, S., and Daud, J. (1986) A nonintrusive intervention for acting out behavior. *Teaching Exceptional Children, 19*, 38-41.

Stallings, J. (1975) Implimentation and child effects of teaching practices in Follow-through classrooms. *Monographs of the Society for Research in Child Development, 40*, (Nos. 708, Serial No. 163).

Stallings, J., Cory R., Fairweather, J., and Needels, M. (1977) *Early childhood education classroom evaluation.* Menlo Park, CA: SRI International.

Stallings, J., Cory, R., Fairweather, J., and Needels, M. (1978) *A study of basic reading skills taught in secondary schools.* Menlo Park, CA: SRI International.

Stanchfield, J. (1973) *Sex differences in learning to read.* Bloomington, IL: Phi Delta Kappan Educational Foundation.

Staub, E. (1979) *Positive social behavior and morality: Socialization and development.* New York: Academic Press.

Steinberg, L. (1981) Transformations in family relations at puberty. *Developmental Psychology, 17*, 833-840.

Stellern, J., Marlowe, M. and Croissard, A. (1984) Cognitive mode and classroom behavior. *Psychology in the Schools, 21*, 103-111.

Stern, W. (1914) *The psychological methods of testing intelligence.* Baltimore, MD: Warwick and York.

Stern, D. (1977) *The first relationship: Infant and mother.* Cambridge, MA: Cambridge University Press.

Sternberg, R. (1985) *Beyond IQ.* Cambridge: Cambridge University Press.

Sternberg, R.J., Conway, B.E., Ketron, J.L., and Berndeen, M. (1981) People's conceptions of intelligence. *Journal of Social Psychology, 41*, 37-55.

Stevens, R. (1912) The question as a measure of efficiency in instruction: A critical study of classroom practice. *Teachers College Contributions to Education, No. 48.*

Stevenson, H. and Bitterman, M. (1955) The distance effects in the transportation of immediate size by children. *American Journal of Psychology, 68*, 274-279.

Stevenson, H., Parker, T., Wilkinson, A., Bonevaux, B. and Gonzalez, M. (1978) Schooling, environment, and cognitive development: A cross-cultural study. *Monographs of the Society for Research in Child Development, 43*, (Serial no. 175).

Stiggins. R.J. (1988) Revitalizing classroom assessment: The highest instructional priority. *Phi Delta Kappan, 65*, 363-368.

Stiggins, R.J. and Bridgeford, N.J. (1985) The ecology of classroom assessment. *Journal of Educational Measurement, 22*, 271-286.

Stipek, D. (1984) The development of achievement motivation. In R. Ames and C. Ames (Eds.) *Research on motivation in education* (vol. 1). Orlando, FL: Academic Press.

Stockard, J., Lang, S.D. and Wood, J.W. (1985) Academic merit, status variables, and students' grades. *Journal of Research and Development in Education, 18*, 12-20.

Stoddard, G.D. (Chr.) (1940) *Intelligence: Its nature and nurture. 39th Yearnook of the National Society for the Study of Education, pts. 1 and 2.* Bloomington IL: Public School Publishing Company.

Stodolsky, S.S., Ferguson, T.L., and Wimpelberg, K. (1981). The recitation persists, but what does it look like? *Journal of Curriculum Studies, 13*, 121-130.

Stolz, H. and Stolz, L. (1951) *Somatic development in adolescent boys.* New York: MacMillan.

Stone, L. and Church, J. (1973) *Childhood and adolescence.* New York: Random House.

Stott, L. (1985) Moral education and mystery. *McGill Journal of Education, 20*, 197-205.

Strain, P.S. and Sainato, D.M. (1987) Preventative discipline in early childhood/special education. *Teaching Exceptional Children, 19*, 26-30.

Strain, P.S. and Timm, M.A. (1974) An experimental analysis of social interaction between a behaviorally disordered preschool child and her classmates. *Journal of Applied Behavior Analysis, 7*, 583-590.

Strain, P.S., Lambert, D.L., Kerr, M.M., Stagg, V., and Lenkner, D.A. (1983) Naturalistic assessment of children's compliance to teachers requests and consequences for compliance. *Journal of Applied Behavior Analysis, 16*, 243-249.

Strain, P.S., Shores, R.E. and Timm, M.A. (1977) Effects of peer social initiations on the behavior of withdrawn preschool children. *Journal of Applied Behavior Analysis, 10*, 289-298

Strother, D.B. (1986) Practical applications of research: Suicide among the young. *Phi Delta Kappan, 67*, 756-759.

Sullivan, E., McCullough, G. and Stager, M. (1970) A developmental study of the relationship between conceptual, ego, and moral development. *Child Development, 41*, 399-411.

Sullivan, P. and Vernon, M. (1979) Psychological assessment of hearing-impaired children. *School Psychology Digest, 8*, 271-290.

Sulzer-Azaroff, B. and Mayer, G. (1977) *Applying behavior analysis procedures with chil-*

dren and youth. New York: Holt, Rinehart and Winston.

Swain, M. (1978) French immersion, early, late or partial? Canadian Modern Languages Review, 33, 180-187.

Swain, M. and Barik, H. (1978) Bilingual education in Canada. In B. Spoklsky, B. Cooper and R. Cooper (Eds.) Case studies in bilingual education (pp. 22-71) Rowley, MA: Newbury House.

Swain, M. and Lapkin, S. (1982) Evaluating bilingual education: A Canadian case study. Avon, England: Multilingual Matters.

Swan, R. and Stavros, H. (1973) Child-rearing practices associated with the development of cognitive skills of children in low socio-economic areas. Early Child Development and Care, 2, 23-38.


T

Talmage, H., and Walberg, H.J. (1978) Naturalistic decision-oriented evaluation of a district reading program. Journal of Reading Behavior, 10, 185-195.

Tanner, J.M. (1962) Growth at adolescence (2nd. ed.) Oxford: Blackwell Scientific Publications.

Tanner, J.M. (1970) Physical growth. In P. Mussen (Ed.) Carmicheal's manual of child psychology (vol. 1) (3rd. ed.) New York: Wiley.

Tan-Willman, C. and Gutteridge, D. (1981) Creative thinking and moral reasoning of academically gifted secondary school adolescents. Gifted Child Quarterly, 25, 149-153.

Taylor, R.L. (1990) The Larry P. decision a decade later: Problems and future directions. Mental Retardation, 28, iii-v.

TenBrink, T.D. (1986) Writing instructional objectives. In J.M. Cooper (Ed.) Classroom teaching skills (3rd. ed.) (pp. 67-110) Lexington, MA: D.C. Heath.

Terhune, K.W. (1974) A review of the actual and expected consequences of family size. Washington, DC: National Institute of Health (Pub. no 76-779).

Terman, L. (1920) The use of intelligence tests in the grading of school children. Journal of Educational Research, 1, 20-21.

Terman, L. (1922, Dec. 27) The great conspiracy. New Republic, p. 117.

Terman, L.M. (1926) Genetic studies of genius: Mental and physical traits of a thousand gifted children (2nd. ed.) Stanford, CA: Stanford University Press.

Terman, L.M. and Childs H.G. (1912) A tentative revision and extension of the Binet-Simon measuring scale of intelligence. Journal of Educational Psychology, 3, 61-74, 133-143, 198-208, 277-289.

Terman, L.M. and Merrill, M.A. (1973) Stanford-Binet Intelligence Test (3rd. ed.) Boston, MA: Houghton Mifflin.

Terman, L.M. and Oden, M.H. (1951) The Stanford studies of the gifted. In P. Witty (Ed.) The gifted child. Lexington, MA: D.C. Heath.

Terman, L. and Oden, M.H. (1959) Genetic studies of genius: The gifted population at mid-life (vol. 5). California: Stanford University Press.

Terrance, H., Pettito, L., Sanders, R., and Bever, T. (1979) Can an ape create a sentence? Science, 206, 189-206.

Terrasi, S. and Airosian, P.W. (1989) The relationship between adaptive behavior and intelligence for special needs students. Psychology in the Schools, 26, 202-208.

Tetenbaum, T. and Houtz, J. (1978) The role of affective traits in the creative and problem-solving performance of gifted urban children. Psychology in the Schools, 15, 27-32.

Thomas, A., Chess, S. and Birch, H. (1968) The origin of personality. Scientific American, 233, 102.

Thomas, A. and Chess, S. (1977) Temperament and development. New York: Brunner Mazel.

Thomas, J.D., Presland, I.E., Grant, M.D., and Glynn, T.L (1978) Natural rates of teacher approval and disapproval in grade 7 classrooms. Journal of Applied Behavior Analysis, 11, 91-94.

Thomas, E.J. and Robinson, H.A. (1972) Improving reading in every class: A source book for teachers. Boston, MA: Allyn and Bacon.

Thompson, S.B. (1980) Do individualized mastery and traditional instructional systems yield different course effects in college calculus? American Educational Research Journal, 17, 361-375.

Thompson, R.J., Cappleman, M.W. and Zeitschel, K.A. (1979) Neonatal behavior of infants of adolescent mothers. Developmental Medicine and Child Neurology, 21, 47-48.

Thorndike, E.L. (1898) Animal intelligence. Psychological Review, Monograph Supplement 2, no. 8.

Thorndike, E.L. (1913) Educational psychology. New York: Columbia University, Teachers College Press.

Thorndike, R. and Hagen, E. (1978) Measurement and evaluation in psychology and education. New York: Wiley.

Thurstone, L.L. (1938) Primary mental abilities. Psychometric Monographs (no. 1). Chicago: University of Chicago Press.

Tieger, T. (1980) On the biological basis of sex and developmental differences in aggression. Child Development, 51, 943-963.

Tierney, R. and Cunningham, J. (1984) Research on teaching reading comprehension.

In P. Pearson, M. Camil, R. Barr, and P. Mosenthal (Eds.) Handbook of reading research. New York: Longman.

Tobin, K. (1986) Effects of teacher wait time on discourse characteristics in mathematics and language arts classes. American Educational Research Journal, 23, 191-200.

Tobin, K. and Capie, W. (1982) Relationships between classroom process variables and middle-school science achievement. Journal of Educational Psychology, 74, 441-454.

Tomlinson, J.R., Acker, N. and Chan, K.S. (1977) Minority status and school psychological services. Psychology in the Schools, 14, 456-460.

Toolan, J.M. (1962) Depression in children and adolescents. American Journal of Orthopsychiatry, 32, 404-415.

Torrance, E.P. (1961) Factors affecting creative thinking in children: An interim research report. Merrill-Palmer Quarterly 7, 171-180.

Torrance, E.P. (1962) Guiding creative talent. Englewood Cliffs, NJ: Prentice-Hall.

Trachtenberg, D. (1974) Student tasks in text material: What cognitive skills do they tap? Peabody Journal of Education, 2, 54-57.

Trachtenberg, S.J. (1990) Multiculturalism can be taught only by multicultural people. Phi Delta Kappan, 71, 610-611.

Traupman, J. and Hatfield, E. (1981) Love and its effects on mental and physical health. In R.W. Fogel, E. Hatfield, S.B. Kiesler, and E. Shanas (Eds.) Aging: Stability and change in the family. New York: Academic Press.

Tricket, E. and Moos, R. (1974) Personal correlates of contrasting environments: Student satisfaction with high schoool classrooms. American Journal of Community Psychology, 2, 1-12.

Trites, R.L. and Price, M.A. (1978) Specific learning disability in a primary French immersion. Interchange on Educational Policy, 9, 73-85.

Tulving, E. (1972) Episodic and semantic memory. In E. Tulving and W. Donaldson (Eds.) Organization of memory. New York: Academic Press.

Turiel, E. (1976) A comparative analysis of moral knowledge and moral judgment in males and females. Journal of Personality, 44, 195-208.

Tyler, L.E. (1974) Individual differences: Abilities and motivational directions. New York: Appleton-Century-Crofts.


U

Underwood, B.J. (1961) Ten years of massed practice on distributed practice. Psychological Review, 68, 229-247.

**V**

Vaidya, S. and Chansky, N. (1980) Cognitive development and cognitive style as factors in mathematics achievement. *Journal of Educational Psychology, 72,* 326-330.

Vaillant, G.E. (1977) *Adaptation to life.* Boston, MA: Little Brown.

Valliant, G.E. and Valliant, C.O. (1981) Natural history of male psychological health. X: Work as a predictor of positive mental health. *American Journal of Psychiatry, 138,* 1433-1440.

Van Dijk, J. (1982) *Rubella handicapped children: The effects of bilateral cataract and/or hearing impairment on behavior and learning.* The Netherlands: Swets and Zeitlinger.

Van Houten, R. (1983) Punishment: From the animal laboratory to the applied setting. In S. Axelrod and J. Apsche (Eds.) *The effects of punishment on human behavior* (pp. 13-44) New York: Academic Press.

Van Kleek, A. (1982) The emergence of linguistic awareness: A cognitive framework. *Merrill-Palmer Quarterly, 28,* 237-263.

Van Patten, J., Chao, C.I., and Reigeluth, C.M. (1986) A review of strategies for sequencing and synthesizing instruction. *Review of Educational Research, 56,* 437-471.

Van Riper, C. (1978) *Speech correction: Principles and methods* (6th. ed.) Englewood Cliffs, NJ: Prentice-Hall.

Van Stolk, M. (1978) *The battered child in Canada.* Toronto: McClelland and Stewart.

Vasdudev, J. and Hummel, R.C. (1987) Oral stage sequence and principles reasoning in an Indian sample. *Human Development, 30,* 105-118.

Vernon, P.E. (1969) *Intelligence and cultural environment.* London: Methuen.

Vikan, A. (1983) Piagetian inconsistencies: A note on the formal operational interpretation of adolescent psychological development. *Scandanavian Journal of Psychology, 24,* 339-342.

Vineland, (1894) *Annual Report of the New Jersey Training School for Feeble-Minded Boys and Girls at Vineland.*

Violato, C. (1986) Canadian versions of the information subtests of the Wechsler Tests of Intelligence. *Canadian Psychology, 27,* 69-74.

Violato, C. (1988) Interactionalism in psychology and eduation: A new paradigm or a source of confusion? Journal of Educational Thought, 22, 4-20.

Violato, C. (1989) Some prescriptions for the future. *Education Canada, 29,* 41-47.

Vliestra, A.G. (1978) Exploration and play in pre-school children and young adults. *Child Development,* 235-238.

Voeltz, L. (1982) Effects of structured interactions with severely handicapped peers on children's attitudes. *American Journal of Mental Deficiency, 86,* 38-39.

Volterra, V. and Taeschner, T. (1978) The acquisition and development of language in bilingual children. *Journal of Child Language, 5,* 311-326.

Voyat, G. (1982) *Piaget systemized.* Hillsdale, NJ: Erlbaum.

Vygotsky, L.S. (1962) *Thought and language.* Cambridge, MA: MIT Press.

**W**

Wade, T.C. and Baker, T.B. (1977) Opinions and use of psychological tests. *American Psychologist, 32,* 874-882.

Wahlstrom, M.W. and Donley, R.D. (1976) *Assessment of student achievement: A survey of the assessment of student achievement in Ontario.* Toronto: Ontario Ministry of Education.

Walberg, H. and Thomas, S. (1972) Open education: An operational definition and validation in Great Britain and the U.S. *American Educational Research Journal, 9,* 197-208.

Walberg, H., Pascal, R.A and Weinstein, T. (1985) Homework's powerful effects on learning. *Educational Leadership, 42,* 76-79.

Walker, H.M. (1983) Applications of response cost in school settings: Outcomes, issues, and recommendations. Exceptional *Education Quarterly, 3,* 47-55.

Walker, H.M. and Rankin, R. (1983) Assessing the behavior expectations and demands of less restrictive settings. *School Psychology Review, 12,* 274-284.

Walker, H.M., Shinn, M.R., O'Neill R.E., and Ramsey, E. (1987) Longitudinal assessment and long-term follow-up of antisocial behavior in fourth-grade boys: Rationale, methodology, measures, and results. *Remedial and Special Education, 8,* 7-16.

Walker, L. (1990, June) Language use in a multicultural society. Paper presented at the Language Arts Researchers of Canada Symposium, Victoria.

Walker, L. J. (1983) Sources of cognitive conflict for stage transition in moral development. *Developmental Psychology, 19,* 103-110.

Walker, L. J. (1984) Sex differences in the development of moral reasoning: A critical review. *Child Development, 55,* 677-691.

Walker, L.J. (1986) Sex differences in the development of moral reasoning: A rejoinder to Baumrind. *Child Development, 57,* 522-526.

Walker, R.N. (1962) Body build and behavior in young children. 1: Body and nursery school teachers' ratings. *Monographs of the Society for Research in Child Development. 27,* (Whole no. 84).

Wallace, G. and Larsen, S.C. (1978) *Educational assessment of learning problems: Testing for teaching.* Boston, MA: Allyn and Bacon.

Walton, J.K. (1979) Lunacy in the Industrial Revolution: A study of asylum admissions in Lancashire, 1848-50. *Journal of Social History, 13,* 1-22.

Wancyzki, W. (1983) The Kindergarten Early Identification component of Bill 82. *Special Education in Canada, 57,* 25-32.

Ward, M.H., and Baker, B.L. (1968) Reinforcement therapy in the classroom. *Journal of Applied Behavior Analysis, 1,* 323-328.

Ward, B. and Tikunoff, W. (1976) The effective teacher educational program: Applications of selected research results and methodology to teaching. *Journal of Teacher Education, 27,* 48-52.

Warren, D. (1984) *Blindness and early child development.* New York: American Foundation for the Blind.

Wassermann, S. (1987) Teaching for thinking: Louis E. Raths revisited. *Phi Delta Kappan, 69,* 460-466.

Waterman, A.S. (1982) Identity development from adolescence to adulthood. *Developmental Psychology, 18,* 341-358.

Watson, J.B. (1913) Psychology as the behaviorist views it. *Psychological Review, 20,* 154-177.

Watson, J.B. (1927) The behaviorist looks at instincts. *Harper's Magazine,* July, p. 233.

Watson J.B. and Rayner, R. (1920) Conditioned emotional reactions. *Journal of Experimental Psychology, 3(1),* 1-14.

Watson, J.S. and Ramey, C. (1972) Reactions to response-contingent stimulation in infancy. *Merrill-Palmer Quarterly, 18,* 219-227.

Webb, N.M. (1980c) A process-outcome analysis of learning in group and individual settings. *Educational Psychologist, 15,* 69-83.

Webb, N.M. and Cullinan, L.K. (1983) Group interaction and achievement in small groups: Stability over time. *American Educational Research Journal, 20,* 411-423.

Wechsler, D. (1958) *The measurement and appraisal of adult intelligence.* Baltimore: Williams.

Wechsler, D. (1967) *Wechsler Preschool and Primary Scale of Intelligence.* New York: Psychological Corporation.

Wechsler, D. (1974) *Wechsler Intelligence Scale for Children—Revised.* New York: Psychological Corporation.

Wechsler, D. (1981) *Wechsler Adult Intelligence Scale—Revised.* New York: Psychological Corporation.

Weinberg, R.A. (1989) Intelligence and IQ: Landmark issues and great debates. *American Psychologist, 44,* 98-104.

Weiner, B. (1972) *Theories of motivation: From mechanism to cognition*. Chicago: Markham.

Weiner, B. (1979) A theory of motivation for some classroom experiences. *Journal of Educational Psychology, 71*, 3-25.

Weiner, B. (1980) The role of affect in rational (attributional) approaches to human motivation. *Educational Researcher, 9*, 4-11.

Weiner, B. and Kukla, A. (1970) An attributional analysis of achievement motivation. *Journal of Personality and Social Psychology, 15*, 1-20.

Weiner, B. and Rosenbaum, R.M. (1965) Determinants of choice between achievement and nonachievement-related activities. *Journal of Exprerimental Research of Personality, 1*, 114-121.

Weiner, B., Graham, S., Taylor, S., and Meyer, W. (1983) Social cognition in the classroom. *Educational Psychologist, 18*, 109-124.

Weiner, B., Russell, D. and Lerman, D. (1978) Affective consequences of casual acriptions. In J. H. Harvey, W. Ickes and R.F. Kidd (Eds.) *New directions in attribution research* (vol. 2) Hillsdale, NJ: Erlbaum.

Weinstein, C.E. Geotz, E.T and Alexander, P.A. (1988) *Learning and study strategies: Issues in assessment, instruction, and evaluation*. San Diego, CA: Academic Press.

Weinstein, L. (1965) Social schemata of emotionally disturbed boys. *Journal of Abnormal Psychology, 70*, 457-461.

Weintraub, S., Neale, J.M. and Liebert, D.E. (1975) Teacher ratings of children vulnerable to psychpathology. *American Journal of Orthopsychiatry, 45*, 839-845.

Wells, G. (1981) *Learning through interaction: The study of child language development*. Cambridge, MA: Cambridge University Press.

Wendt, H.W. (1955) Motivation, effort, and performance. In D.C. McClelland (Ed.) *Studies in motivation* (pp. 448-459). New York: Appleton-Century-Crofts.

Werner, J.S. and Lipsitt, L.P. (1981) The infancy of human sensory systems. In E. Gollin (Ed.) *Developmental plasticity* (pp. 35-69) New York: Academic Press.

Wessman, A. (1972) Scholastic and psychological effects of a compensatory education program for disadvantaged high school students: Project A B C. *American Education Research Journal, 9*, 361-372.

Wheeler, R. and Ryan. F. (1973) Effects of cooperative and competitive classroom environments on the attitudes and achievement of elementary school students engaged in social studies inquiry activities. *Journal of Educational Psychology, 65*, 402-407.

Whimbey, A. (1975) *Intelligence can be taught*. New York: Dutton.

Whipple, C.I. and Kodman, F.A. (1969) A study of discrimination and perceptual learning with retarded readers. *Journal of Educational Psychology, 60*, 1-5.

White, B. (1975) *The first three years of life*. Englewood Cliffs, NJ: Prentice-Hall.

White, M.A. (1975) Natural rates of teacher approval and disapproval in the classroom. *Journal of Applied Behavior Analysis, 8*, 367-372.

White, O.R. and Haring, N.G. (1980) *Exceptional teaching* (2nd ed.). Columbus, OH: Merrill.

White, O.R., Edgar, E., Haring, N.G., Affleck, J., Hayden, A. and Bendersky, M. (1981) Uniform Performance Assessment System. Columbus, OH: Merrill.

White, T.H. (1979) Correlations among the WISC-R, PIAT, and DAM. *Psychology in the Schools, 16*, 497-501.

White-Blackburn, G., Semb, S., and Semb, G. (1977) The effects of a good behavior contract on the classroom behaviors of sixth grade students. *Journal of Applied Behavior Analysis, 10*, 312.

Whitehurst, G. (1977) Comprehension, imitation, and the CIP hypothesis. *Journal of Experimental Child Psychology, 23*, 23-38.

Whiting, B.B. and Whiting, J.T.M. (1975) *Children of six cultures*. Cambridge, MA: Harvard University Press.

Whiting, J.W.M., Burbank, V.K. and Ratner, M.S. (1986) The duration of maidenhood across cultures. In J.B. Lancaster and B.A. Hamburg (Eds.) *School-age pregnancy and parenthood: Biosocial dimensions* (pp. 39-52). Hawthorne, NY: Aldine de Gruytes.

Whitley, B.E. and Frieze, I.H. (1985) Children's causal attributions for success and failure in achievement settings: A meta-analysis. *Journal of Educational Psychology, 77*, 608-616.

Whitmore, J.R. (1980) *Giftedness, conflict and underachievement*. Boston, MA: Allyn and Bacon.

Whorf, B. (1956) *Language, thought and reality*. Cambridge, MA: MIT Press.

Wickman, E. (1928) *Children's behavior and teachers' attitudes*. New York: Commonwealth Fund.

Wiig, E. and Semmel, E. (1984) *Language assessment and intervention for the learning dissabled* (2nd. ed.) Columbus, OH: Merrill.

Wilkins, W.E. and Glock, M.D. (1973) *Teacher expectations and student achievement: A replication and extension*. Ithica, NY: Cornell University Press.

Willerman, L. (1979) Effects of families on intellectual development. *American Psychologist, 34*, 923-929.

Willerman, L. and Fiedler, M.R. (1974) Infant performance and intellectual precocity. *Child Development, 45*, 483-486.

Williams, M.D. and Hollan, J.D. (1978) The process of retrieval from very long-term memory. *Cognitive Science, 5*, 87-119.

Willings, D. and Arseneault, M. (1986) Attempted suicide and creative promise. *Gifted Education International, 4*, 10-13.

Willner, A.G., Braukman, C.T., Kirigin, K.A., Fixsen, D.L., Phillips, E., and Wolf, M.M. (1977). The training and validation of youth preferred social behaviors of child-care personnel. *Journal of Applied Behavior Analysis, 10*, 219-230.

Wills, J., Self, P. and Dalan, N. (1976) Maternal behavior and perceived sex of infant. *American Journal of Orthopsychiatry, 46*, 135-139.

Wilson, C.C., Robertson, S.J., Herlong, L.H., and Haynes, S.N. (1979) Vicarious effects of time-out in the modification of aggression in the classroom. *Behavior Modification, 3*, 97-111.

Wilson, J.Q. and Herrnstein, R.J. (1985) *Crime and human nature*. New York: Simon and Schuster.

Wilson, R.J. and Humphries, T. (1986) The impact of recent legislation on the role of Canadian school psychologists. *Canadian Journal of School Psychology, 2*, 1-6.

Windmiller, M. (1980) Introduction. In M. Windmilller, N. Lambert and E. Turiel (Eds.) *Moral development and socialization*. Boston, MA: Allyn and Bacon.

Wineburg, S.S. (1987) The self-fulfillment of the self-fulfilling prophecy. *Educational Researcher, 16*, 28-37.

Winer, G.A. (1980) Class-inclusion reasoning in children: A review of the empirical literature. *Child Development, 51*, 309-328.

Winter, J., Faiman, C. and Reyes, F. (1978) Normal and abnormal prenatal development. *Clinical Obstetrics and Gynecology, 21*, 67-86.

Winterbottom, M.R. (1953) The relation of childhood training in independecne to achievement motivation. Doctoral dissertation, University of Michigan, Ann Arbor.

Winzer, M.A. (1989) *Closing the gap: Special learners in regular classrooms*. Toronto: Copp Clark Pitman.

Winzer, M.A. (1990a) *Children with exceptionalities: A Canadian perspective*. Toronto: Prentice-Hall

Winzer, M.A. (1990b) From isolation to integration: A descriptive history of special education, Washington, DC: Gallaudet University Press (in press).

Winzer, M.A. (1990c, December) Taming the unruly: The development of special classes. Paper presented at the Australian and New

Zealand History of Education Conference, Auckland, NZ.

Winzer, M.A. and Lafleur, N. (1991, January) Otitis media: Educational implications. Paper presented at Closing the Circle Conference, Lethbridge.

Winzer, M.A., Harper, G. and Clarke, K. (1990, August) Using nomination scales to identify gifted elementary children. Paper presented at the International Conference of Special Education, Wales.

Wiss, C. (1987) Issues in the assessment of learning problems in children from French immersion programs: A case study illustration in support of Cummins. *Canadian Modern Language Review, 43*, 302-313.

Wittig, M.A. and Peterson, (1979) Sex-related differences in cognitive functioning. *Educational Psychologist, 13*, 15-29.

Wittrock, M.C. (1978) Education and the cognitive processes of the brain. In J. Chall and A. Mirsky (Eds.) *Education and the brain: The seventy seventh yearbook of the Society for the Study of Education, Part 2.* Chicago: University of Chicago Press.

Wittrock, M.C. (1983, April) Generative reading comprehension. Paper presented at American Educational Research Association Conference, Montreal.

Wolf, J.S. and Stephens, T.M. (1982) Gifted and talented. In N. Haring (Ed.) *Exceptional children and youth: An introduction to special education.* Columbus, OH: Merrill.

Wolfensberger, W. (1981) The primacy of values and ideologies in human services evaluation. *New directions for Program Evaluation, 10*, 1-7.

Wollman, W., (1983) Models and procedures: A classroom study of teaching and transfer. *School Science and Mathematics, 83*, 122-132.

Wolpe, J. (1958) *Psychotherapy by reciprocal inhibition.* Stanford, CA: Stanford University Press.

Wood, D. (1986) Multicultural education: Questions for the late 1980s. *Multicultural Education Journal, 4*, 10-23.

Wood, F.H. (1982) Living with the emotionally distrubed: Burden or opportunity? *B.C.*

*Journal of Special Education, 6*, 1-10.

Woodcock, R.W. and Johnson, M.B. (1977) *Woodcock-Johnson Psycho-Educational Battery.* Boston, MA: Teaching Associates.

Woolfolk, A.E. (1990) *Educational psychology* (3rd. ed.) Englewood Cliffs. NJ: Prentice-Hall.

Worthman, C.M. (1986) Developmental dysnchrony as normative experience: Kikuya adolescents. In J.B. Lancaster and B.A. Hamburg (Eds.) *School-age pregnancy and parenthood: Biosocial domains* (pp. 95-109). Hawthorne, NY: Aldine de Gruytes.

Wright, J. and Vliestra, A. (1977) Reflection impulsivity and information processing from three to nine years of age. In M. Fine (Ed.) *Intervention with hyperactivity.* Springfield, IL: Thomas.

Wright, S., and Cowen, E.L. (1982) Student perception of school environment and its relationship to mood, achievement, popularity and adjustment. *American Journal of Community Psychology, 10*, 687-703.

Wyckoff, W. (1973) The effects of stimulus variation in learning from lecture. *Journal of Experimental Edecation, 41*, 85-90.

Wynn, R.L. and Fletcher, C. (1987) Sex role development and early educational experiences. In D.B. Carter (Ed.) *Current conceptions of sex roles and sex typing.* New York: Praeger.

### Y

Yalden, M.F. (1981) The bilingual experience in Canada. In M. Ridge (Ed.) *The new bilingualism: An American dilemma* (pp 71-87) California: USC Press.

Yando, R. Seitz, V. and Zigler, E. (1979) *Intellectual and personality characteristics of children: Social-class and ethnic-group differences.* Hillsdale, NJ: Erlbaum

Yarrow, L.J., Rubenstein, J.L., Pedersen, F.A., and Jankowski, J.J. (1972) Dimensions of early stimulation and their differential effects on infant development. *Merrill-Palmer Quarterly, 18*, 205-218.

Young, J. (1979) Multiculturalism and its implications for youth. In K. McLeod (Ed.) *Multiculturalism, bilingualism and Canadian*

*institutions.* Toronto: Guidance Centre, University of Toronto.

Ysseldyke, J.E. and Algozzine, R. (1984) *Introduction to special education.* Boston, MA: Houghton Mifflin.

Yu, B., Zhang, W., Jing, Q., Peng, R., Zhang, G., and Simon, H.A. (1985). STM capacity for Chinese and English language materials. *Memory and Cogniton, 13*, 202-207.

Yu, M. (1988, June) Ethnicity and education: Perspectives on Chinese youth. Paper presented at the Canadian Asian Studies conference, University of Windsor.

Yussen, S.R. (1977) Characteristics of moral dilemmas written by adolescents. *Developmental Psychology, 13*, 162-163.

### Z

Zabel, M. (1986) Timeout use with behaviorally disordered students. *Behavior Disorders, 12*, 15-21.

Zagan, R. and Bowers, N. (1983) The effect of time of day on problem solving and classroom behavior. *Psychology in the Schools, 20*, 337-345.

Zahorik, J.A. (1975) Teachers' planning models. *Educational Leadership, 33*, 134-139.

Zelazo, P.R., Zelazo, N.A. and Kolb, S. (1972) Walking: In the newborn. *Science, 176*, 314-315.

Zelnik, M. and Kanter, J.E. (1977) Sexual and contraceptive experiences of young unmarried women in the United States, 1971 to 1976. *Family Planning Perspectives, 9*, 55-71.

Zelnik, M. and Kanter, J.E. (1978) First pregnancies to women aged 15-19, 1971 to 1976. *Family Planning Perspectives, 10*, 11-29.

Zelniker, T. and Jeffrey, W.E. (1976) Reflective and impulsive children: Strategies of information processing underlying difficulties in probem solving. *Monographs of the Society for Research in Child Develoment, 41*, (5, Serial No. 168).

Zivin, G. (1986) Processes of expressive behavior development. *Merrill Palmer Quarterly, 32*, 103-140.

# AUTHOR INDEX

# SUBJECT INDEX

# PHOTO CREDITS